Encyclopedia of
Educational
Leadership and
Administration

Encyclopedia of
Educational
Leadership and
Administration

Volume 2
L-Z

Fenwick W. English Editor

The University of North Carolina at Chapel Hill

A SAGE Reference Publication

SAGE Publications
Thousand Oaks ▪ London ▪ New Delhi

For information:

Sage Publications, Inc.
2455 Teller Road
Thousand Oaks, California 91320
E-mail: order@sagepub.com

Sage Publications Ltd.
1 Oliver's Yard
55 City Road
London EC1Y 1SP
United Kingdom

Sage Publications India Pvt. Ltd.
B-42, Panchsheel Enclave
Post Box 4109
New Delhi 110 017 India

Printed in the United States of America

Library of Congress Cataloging-in-Publication Data

Encyclopedia of educational leadership and administration / Fenwick W. English, [editor].
 p. cm.
Includes bibliographical references and index.
ISBN 0-7619-3087-6 (cloth : set)
 1. School management and organization—United States—Encyclopedias.
2. Educational leadership—United States—Encyclopedias.
3. Public schools—United States—Encyclopedias. I. English, Fenwick W.
LB2805.E527 2006
371.2′003—dc22   2005023061

This book is printed on acid-free paper.

06 07 08 09 10 9 8 7 6 5 4 3 2 1

Publisher:	Rolf A. Janke
Developmental Editor:	Paul Reis
Production Editor:	Laureen A. Shea
Typesetter:	C&M Digitals (P) Ltd.

Contents

List of Entries

Reader's Guide

ADMINISTRATION

Administration, theories of
American Association of School
  Administrators
Democracy, democratic education
  and administration
National Council of Professors of
  Educational Administration
Recruitment, of school administrators
Risk takers, in educational
  administration
Stress, in school administration
Theory movement, in educational
  administration
University Council for Educational
  Administration

BIOGRAPHIES

Adams, Charles Francis
Addams, Jane
Aristotle
Baer, Donald
Barnard, Chester I.
Bell, Ted
Bethune, Mary McLeod
Binet, Alfred
Bobbitt, John Franklin
Bryant, William Cullen
Burns, James MacGregor
Burroughs, Nannie
Burt, Cyril
Butler, Nicholas Murray
Carlyle, Thomas
Cattell, Raymond
Chavez, Cesar Estrada

Clark, Septima
Cocking, Walter
Coleman, James
Cooper, Anna Julia
Coppin, Fanny Jackson
Covey, Stephen
Csikszentmihalyi, Mihaly
Cubberley, Ellwood
Culbertson, Jack
Darwin, Charles
de Bono, Edward
Deming, W. Edwards
Dewey, John
Dorsey, Susan Miller
Du Bois, W. E. B.
Dyson, Michael Eric
Follett, Mary Parker
Freud, Sigmund
Friedman, Milton
Fullan, Michael
Gardner, Howard
Graves, Claire
Greenfield, Thomas Barr
Haley, Margaret
Hall, R. Vance
Halpin, Andrew
Harris, William Torrey
Havighurst, Robert
Hay, Henry (Harry)
Howe, Harold
Jefferson, Thomas
Jung, Carl
King, Martin Luther Jr.
Kuhn, Thomas
Lawrence-Lightfoot, Sara
Lindsley, Ogden R.
Loyola, Ignatius

Machiavelli, Niccolò
Malcolm X
Mann, Horace
Marshall, Thurgood
Marx, Karl
Maslow, Abraham
Maxwell, William H.
McGregor, Douglas
Meier, Deborah
Mendez, Felicitas
Montessori, Maria
Ossorio, Peter G.
Parker, Francis W.
Patri, Angelo
Peirce, Cyrus
Piaget, Jean
Picott, J. Rupert
Plato
Plutarch
Popper, Karl
Rice, Joseph Mayer
Risley, Todd R.
Rogers, Carl
Russell, Bertrand
Sanchez, George
Simon, Herbert
Sizemore, Barbara A.
Skinner, B. F.
Spearman, Charles
Spencer, Herbert
Strayer, George D.
Taylor, Frederick
Thorndike, Edward
Trenholm, Harper Councill
Tyler, Ralph Winifred
Washington, Booker T.
Weber, Max

LEADERSHIP

ORGANIZATIONS

Curriculum audit
Curriculum guides
Curriculum mapping
Expectations, teacher and student
  cultures
Faculty, educational leadership
  programs
Leadership, teacher
Licensure and certification
National Council for the
  Accreditation of Teacher Education
National Council of Professors of
  Educational Administration
Parent Teacher Association
Parental involvement
Student teaching
Teacher recruitment and selection
Team teaching
Unions, of teachers
Web-based teaching and learning
Writing, teaching of

TESTING

Achievement gap, of students
Achievement tests
Educational Testing Service
Effect size
Evaluation
Individual differences, in children
Item response theory
Measurement, theories of
No Child Left Behind
Performance assessment
Psychometrics
Scholastic Aptitude Test
Standardized testing
Testing and test theory development
Underachievers, in schools
Validity and reliability

THEORIES AND MODELS

Administration, theories of
Afrocentric theories

Axiomatic theory
Chaos theory
Child development theories
Cognition, theories of
Cognitive dissonance
Collaboration theory
Communications, theories in
  organizations
Compliance theory
Conceptual systems theory and
  leadership
Conditioning theory
Constructivism
Constructivism, social
Contingency theories
Creationism
Creativity, theories of
Critical race theory
Critical theory
Curriculum, theories of
Determinism, sociocultural
Disequilibrium, theories of
Economics, theories of
Efficacy theory
Egocentrism, theories of
Existentialism
Fascism and schools
Feminism and theories of leadership
Field theory
Flow theory
Frame theory
Functionalist theory
Gestalt theory and therapy
Great man theory
Hierarchical developmental models
Idealism, as philosophy in education
Item response theory
J-curve theory
Language theories and processes
Leadership, complex theory of
Leadership, theories of
Learning, theories of
Liberalism
Literacy, theories of
Management theories

Market theory of schooling
Measurement, theories of
Moral education
Motivation, theories of
Networking and network theory
Open systems theory
Organizational theories
Path-goal leadership theory
Perceptual control theory
Philosophies of education
Planning models
Positivism, postpositivism
Postmodernism
Pragmatism and progressivism
Principal-agent theory
Psychology, types of
Qualitative research, history, theories,
  issues
Queer theory
Rational organizational theory
Recognition theory/identity politics
Role theory
S-curve theory
Satisficing theory
Sexuality, theories of
Subjectivism, in theory
Systems theory/thinking
Testing and test theory development
Theories, use of
Theory movement, in educational
  administration
Theory X, Theory Y
Three-factor-model, five-factor-
  model
Trait theory
Vulnerability thesis, of
  superintendents

List of Figures and Tables

L

🏛 LANGUAGE THEORIES AND PROCESSES

All linguistic theories describe language as a learned system of sounds having an arbitrary value that meets a social need to communicate. This system is comprised of units, or subsystems, that are embedded into each other. Sounds are combined to produce words, words are combined to produce utterances, and utterances are combined to produce discourse.

More precisely, these subsystems can be classified as follows: *phonology*—the sounds of a language; *orthography*—the ways in which language is organized in a written text, including systems of punctuation, capitalization, and paragraphing; *graphophonics*—the relationship between the sound systems of language and the written systems of language; *syntax or grammar*—the study of the systematic ways in which words are organized and related to one another for meaning to occur; *semantics*—the study of vocabulary and how words and phrases relate to objects and ideas; *pragmatics*—the study of the ways in which language use changes depending on context, time, place, and the social relationships between speakers and listeners, readers and writers.

Knowledge of a language is knowledge of a set of subsystems that allows us to comprehend and produce an infinite number of utterances. People use language as a way of establishing contact, maintaining relationships, and sharing and categorizing experiences and ideas. But what causes acquisition of this knowledge?

LANGUAGE ACQUISITION

Most children complete the basic language acquisition process by the age of 5 without any direct instruction. Current theories of language acquisition posit that humans have a unique ability to test various hypotheses about the structure of language, to develop rules of a particular language and remember them, and to use these rules to generate appropriate language in various circumstances. As a child develops, these hypotheses about how language is structured are modified by particular language input. In other words, the set of rules available to the child changes as the child develops and recognizes what are and are not permissible structures in his or her particular language. Furthermore, the evidence of developmental change is clear in the types of utterances and discourse understood and produced at various ages.

This capacity for language acquisition follows a predictable pattern through different stages of acquisition. While the rate of acquisition may be different, the order is the same for all children and for languages other than English. Constance Weaver outlined the following stages in 1998:

1. *Babbling* is more a result of developing fine motor skills than an attempt to communicate. These sounds seem to be required in order for infants to develop the musculature needed to produce coherent speech later on.

2. *Single-word utterances* are usually nouns for common objects and people in the child's life. These utterances are the beginnings of the child's purposeful attempt to communicate. At this stage, overgeneralization, when a child formulates a rule and applies it too broadly, is common. For example, when a child learns that the four-legged friend in the house is a dog, or that the dog's name is Baxter, the child then generalizes

and refers to all four-legged animals (cats, cows, horses, etc.) as dogs or as Baxters. Near the end of this stage, children begin to apply words to the behavior of others and not just their own.

3. *Word combining and syntax* emerge when the child begins to combine first two or three, then many words together. The ability to combine words signifies the ability to convey deeper meaning and use more complex grammar.

Noam Chomsky, the originator of transformational-generative linguistics, suggested that what a grammar should do is account for native speakers' unconscious but functional knowledge of grammar (i.e., "deep structure"), which enables comprehension and production of language. This internalized knowledge is one meaning of the word *grammar.* In this sense, grammar refers to a capacity for language, a native ability to create and comprehend utterances. His work represented a marked shift from the structuralist theorists who based their grammars on an analysis of the structures of a language. They focused on the surface structure of sentences and analyzed them into increasingly smaller components. Grammar may also refer to these formal systems that theorists have developed and studied to explain and analyze language. It is important to point out that this type of study has not produced a single body of knowledge on which all linguists agree. Rather, it has produced different grammars that are each dependent on different underlying assumptions and different methods of analysis and, accordingly, have different results. We now turn to the primary distinctions between *prescriptive grammar* and *descriptive grammar.*

PRESCRIPTIVISM VERSUS DESCRIPTIVISM

As the term suggests, someone who subscribes to a *prescriptive* approach to grammar believes that there is a prescribed list of rules to which all speakers of a language must conform. Those who do not comply are said to be speaking "incorrectly." This is the approach taken in most language instruction and is still widely used in many language arts classrooms. A prescriptive approach reflects a transmission model of education that considers learning to be best fostered through continued practice of the rules.

However, in their 1989 article "Explaining Grammatical Concepts," Muriel Harris and Katherine E. Rowan found that continued practice, in most instances, does not promote adequate understanding. Being able to identify sentence fragments in an exercise written specifically for that purpose does not guarantee that the student knows the critical features of fragments in contrast to grammatically complete sentences, much less that the student can reliably distinguish between the two. Nor, as another example, does memorizing the rule that it is ungrammatical to end a sentence with a preposition ensure that the speaker who has memorized this rule will no longer construct such sentences. Furthermore, the problem for prescriptivists is that most sentences that are not grammatically correct sound perfectly acceptable to nearly all speakers, and nearly all speakers regularly use ungrammatical sentences.

Rather than prescribing how people should speak, contemporary linguistics and language theories and theorists are interested in observing and describing how people actually do speak. *Descriptive* grammar does not judge language production as correct or incorrect. A descriptivist works from the assumption that whenever native language speakers of a language speak, they are following a set of grammar rules. However, not all native speakers are following the exact same set of rules. Consider the following two sentences:

1. If I were you, I would choose a different teacher.
2. If I was you, I would choose a different teacher.

To some extent, there is certain to be disagreement among native speakers regarding which of these statements is grammatically correct and which is ungrammatical. For some, sentence (1) is grammatical and sentence (2) is ungrammatical; for others, the opposite is true. However, because sentences like (1) and (2) are spoken regularly by native speakers of English, they are both grammatical for the people who speak them. However, it is difficult to imagine any native speaker of English disagreeing that a sentence such as "Wish they for a teacher new" is ungrammatical. Descriptivists use examples such as these to highlight that while all native English speakers share certain rules, we do not share all rules. In fact, there is a tremendous amount of linguistic diversity among the speakers of English, as well as among the speakers of any language.

This is not to suggest that descriptivists do not acknowledge grammar rules; they do. For prescriptivists, however, rules are constructed (rather than prescribed) from observations of real language data—from language in use. Furthermore, the *correct versus incorrect* distinction gives way to the *appropriate versus inappropriate* distinction. That is, when speaking with people who prefer sentence (1) to (2), it would be appropriate to use (1), and when speaking with people who prefer (2), it would be appropriate to use (2).

In the language arts classroom, this concept becomes extremely important when considering instruction. For people to be successful in American society, knowing how to speak standard English (i.e., the variety of English accepted in formal contexts) is critical. Descriptive linguists, while being careful not to judge nonstandard English as incorrect, work to teach students the differences between the two and how to produce standard English in the appropriate contexts. The focus of descriptive linguists on actual utterances led quite naturally to the study of dialect.

LANGUAGE VARIATIONS AND DIALECTS

Working within the traditions of structural or prescriptive linguists, dialecticians have shown that most differences in usage among speakers cannot be considered aberrations from standard preferred speech. Rather, most variations in usage derive from different language communities that develop their own varying norms.

For example, William Labov showed in 1972 that Black Vernacular English (BVE) is a distinct subsystem within the larger grammar of English with its own regular conventions and rules. One such rule allows for what Labov calls a remote present perfect in the use of *been,* such as "I been know your name," in which *been know* means "have known for a long time and still know."

Shirley Heath described in 1983 instances when teachers who do not know BVE usage often interpret it as incorrect standard English. Ethnographic studies such as Heath's abundantly demonstrate how the different language conventions of people living and working in the same community can cause conflict and misunderstandings on the parts of teachers and students. As a result, these often lead to inappropriate judgments of students and failure to learn.

In an effort to address this and related issues, in 1972 the National Council of Teachers of English (NCTE) adopted a resolution on language and students' dialects titled "Resolution on the Students' Rights to Their Own Language." For 30 years, this position statement has served as a guidepost for NCTE's continued focus on the issue of dialects and language usage in the classroom and has been the basis for other professional and governmental organizations. Viewing language from this perspective positions language acquisition and usage as more than acquiring autonomous, cognitive skills. Rather, it situates language within social contexts and immerses it within human relationships. Theories of language, as we move through the twenty-first century, construe language as social practices.

SOCIAL AND POLITICAL APPROACHES TO LANGUAGE

Sociolinguistics, a part of the *new literacies,* perceives the function of language as more than to communicate information. Language is, in addition, also a device to think and feel with, as well as a device with which to signal and negotiate social identity. In other words, the new literacies of this century focus on language as *social practices.* Through the work of Lev Vygotsky, theorists, researchers, and teachers came to realize that what students can accomplish on their own was only a small part of what they could do with the help of others. Vygotsky's "zone of proximal development" referred to the spectrum of language activities that individuals could accomplish with the assistance of more able individuals in their social realm.

Understanding that language is shaped by social and cultural contexts contributed toward our enhanced understanding of the role of language in a democracy and its political implications. From such a perspective, issues of race, class, and gender are explicit aspects of understanding language processes. Much current language theory centers on the social and political implications of language.

Language theories, in large measure, constitute and are constituted by shifts in culture. Movements within the field are blended and complex, suggesting the fluidity of language as a living cultural, social, and political entity. In a democratic society such as that in the United States, understanding language theories and processes as dynamic and open systems provides a stronger sense of the purpose and consequences of the role of language for students, for communities, and for the nation.

—Gina DeBlase

See also affective education; at-risk students; Black education; cognition, theories of; computers, use and impact of; constructivism, social; critical race theory; critical theory; cross-cultural studies; curriculum, theories of; differentiation of stimuli; early childhood education; elementary education;

high schools; individual differences, in children; instructional technology; Latinos; learning environments; literacy, theories of; measurement, theories of; metacognition; minorities, in schools; multiculturalism; National Assessment of Educational Progress; reading, history of, use in schools; underachievers, in schools; writing, teaching of

Further Readings and References

Chomsky, N. (1957). *Syntactic structures.* The Hague, Netherlands: Mouton.

Chomsky, N. (1968). *Language and mind.* New York: Harcourt Brace Jovanovich.

Harris, M., & Rowan, K. E. (1989). Explaining grammatical concepts. *Journal of Basic writing, 8*(2), 21–41.

Heath, S. B. (1983). *Ways with words: Language, life, and work in communities and classrooms.* New York: Cambridge University Press.

Joshi, R., & Aaron, P. (2005). *Handbook of orthography and literacy.* Mahwah, NJ: Erlbaum.

Kist, W. (2005). *New literacies in action.* New York: Teachers College Press.

Kucer, S., & Silva, C. (2005). *Teaching the dimensions of literacy.* Mahwah, NJ: Erlbaum.

Labov, W. (1972). *Language in the inner city: Studies in the black English vernacular.* Philadelphia: University of Pennsylvania Press.

Marsh, J., & Millard, E. (2005). *Popular literacies, childhood and schooling.* New York: Routledge.

National Council of Teachers of English. (1974). *Resolution on the students' right to their own language.* Urbana, IL: Author.

Soler, J., & Openshaw, R. (2005). *Literacy crises and reading policies: Why our children still can't read.* New York: Routledge.

Vygotsky, L. (1962). *Thought and language.* Cambridge, MA: Harvard University Press.

Weaver, C. (1996). *Teaching grammar in context.* Portsmouth, NH: Boynton/Cook.

LATINOS

The term *Latinos* is often used interchangeably with the term *Hispanic* or with the various national origin terms (e.g. Mexican, Puerto Rican, Cuban) found in formal educational sources. Indeed, the choice of terms to describe this population has been the subject of considerable scholarly and political debate. The impact of these debates on education is ongoing, given that available data on the educational status and representation of Latinos in the United States can be misleading if one is not careful to identify such factors as national origin, economic class, native language, ethnic identity, and so forth to more accurately depict

the tremendous within-group diversity. Moreover, each of the groups that together comprise U.S. Latinos has its own particular history, often rooted in the regional or generational issues that likewise influence their particular educational experiences. Such within-group diversity notwithstanding, the available data on Latinos in U.S. schools do indicate that several significant issues exist and persist for this population.

LATINO DEMOGRAPHICS

Distribution of Latinos Across the United States

Latinos can be found all throughout the United States. In total, Latinos comprised 12.5% (35.3 million) of the country's total population in 2000, and this figure represents an increase of 58% since the 1990 census. The 2000 census indicates that this population is concentrated in the largest numbers in seven states: California, Texas, New York, Florida, Illinois, Arizona, and New Jersey, with half of all U.S. Latinos concentrated in California and Texas alone. Latinos were the highest proportion of the population in East Los Angeles (California) and Puerto Rico, with 96.8% and 98.9% of the total population in these areas, respectively. Throughout the United States, 58.5% of all Latinos identified themselves as Mexican (origin) and 9.6% as Puerto Rican, thereby representing the two largest Latino groups. Approximately 28% of all Latinos identified themselves as "Other Hispanic" in the 2000 census, including those who identified themselves as Central American (4.8% of all Latinos), South American (3.8%), and Cuban (3.5%).

Based on data derived from the Pew Hispanic Center in Washington, D.C., Latino workers made up 40% of the 2.5 million jobs created in 2004, even though they made up only 15% of the U.S. workforce. Of these, 88% of the 1 million new jobs were filled by Latinos from Mexico. According to Joel Millman in 2005, the Pew study bolsters the belief that immigrants do not take jobs from American workers but instead supplement the U.S. workforce.

Latinos in U.S. Public Schools

The significance of the Latino population figures is particularly apparent in the U.S. public schools. Among K–12 public schools, Latinos made up 17% of the total student population in 2000, according to the U.S. Department of Education. The concentration of Latino students in public schools varied by region, with most Latinos concentrated in the South and West. Latinos at least doubled their presence as a percentage of total regional K–12 enrollments in all four regions of the United States between 1975 and 2000. For example, Latinos comprised 31.6% of total public school enrollments in the West in 2000, showing an increase of 16.8 percentage points since 1975, or nearly a 114% increase.

The distribution of Latino students among school levels reflects the relative youth of this population. As noted by Richard Valencia in the book *Chicano School Failure and Success* (2nd ed.), although in 2000 Latinos represented 17% of total K–12 enrollments, they comprised 20% of the kindergarten enrollments versus 15% of the total enrollments in high school. Indeed, in California, Latinos, who made up about 45% of the state's total enrollments in 2003–2004, comprised 51% of the total kindergarten population versus 37% of all 12th graders. In Texas, Latinos, who made up 44% of the state's total enrollment in 2003–2004, comprised 48% of the total kindergarten population versus 43% of all 9th graders and 35% of all 12th graders. Part of this distribution pattern is attributable to significant dropout rates among Latinos (discussed below). Nevertheless, an optimistic view of these data indicates that the enrollments of Latinos will continue to grow and maintain a significant presence overall, particularly in states such as California and Texas, but also in states such as Illinois, Iowa, Georgia, and New York. (See Figure 1.)

Growing Presence of English Language Learners

It is important to note that among the K–12 Latino student population is quite a large and growing proportion of English language learners (ELL). The U.S. Department of Education reports that in 2001–2002,

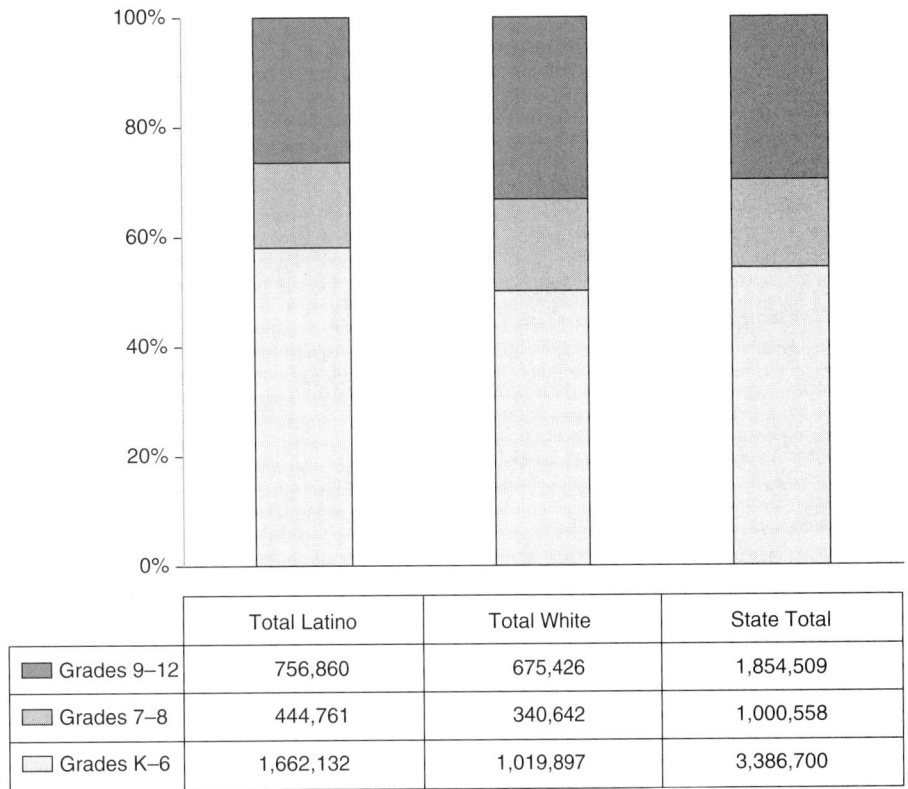

	Total Latino	Total White	State Total
Grades 9–12	756,860	675,426	1,854,509
Grades 7–8	444,761	340,642	1,000,558
Grades K–6	1,662,132	1,019,897	3,386,700

Figure 1   Total Latino, White, and Statewide Public School Enrollments by Grade Level, California 2003–2004

SOURCE: Adapted from California Department of Education, Educational Demographics Unit. (2004). *California public schools, statewide report: Enrollment by gender, grade, and ethnic designation, 2003–04* [Datafile].

ELL students numbered one in four students in California and one in seven students in Texas, where the vast majority of ELL students are Latinos and Spanish speakers. In California, for example, the state's department of education indicates that 85% of all ELL students were Spanish speakers and numbered over 1.3 million in 2003–2004. Unfortunately for many of the ELL students, only 30% of public school teachers instructing these students have received pertinent training, and a mere 3% have degrees in English as a Second Language (ESL) or bilingual education, as noted by the U.S. Department of Education in 1993–1994. Indeed, 2003–2004 data from the California Department of Education indicates that only 38% of ELL students had met the state board of education criterion for English proficiency.

Two scholars who have documented the complexities of serving Latino ELL students are Guadalupe Valdés and Eugene E. García. Valdés's work attends to the role of school-parental/family interactions and relationships in supporting Latino immigrant students' participation in schools. It also illuminates the interconnectedness of race, class, national origin, cultural heritage, and educational status in understanding how immigrant students and their families navigate the educational system in their own behalf. In a similar vein, García argues for the incorporation of an understanding of individual and shared cultural identity formation and maintenance into discussions of bilingual education policy. In doing so, he contends that bilingual education policy can be better aimed at producing learning environments for Latino ELL students that are more responsive to both their needs and their talents.

Despite such remarkable changes in the student demographics at the K–12 levels, Latinos in postsecondary institutions have not increased very rapidly over the past several decades. Affirmative action policies had enabled some states to make inroads in the recruitment of Latinos and other students of color into higher education institutions. However, recent changes in policy, including the elimination of affirmative action in some states, have likewise had an impact on the degree to which Latinos participate in college and graduate school. Over the past two and one half decades, Latinos have only increased their presence among students enrolled in graduate/first-professional programs by 3 percentage points, moving from 2% in 1976 to just 5% in 2000, according to the U.S. Department of Education. Translated into numbers, this means that of the 2.2 million students enrolled in graduate/first-professional programs across the country, only 110,000 were Latinos in 2000. Among 2 million individuals holding doctorates in the United States in 2001, only 71,000 were Latinos.

PERSISTENT CHALLENGES: HISTORICAL PATTERNS AND RECENT TRENDS IN LATINO EDUCATIONAL ATTAINMENT

Latinos have and continue to face tremendous challenges to their success in schools. The lack of educational success among Latinos has been attributed to what many researchers have deemed to be deficiencies in their genetics, home cultures and experiences, parental education, and socioeconomic class origins. Rather than rely on such "cultural deficit" explanatory models, other contemporary researchers instead explain the relative lack of educational success among Latinos as being tied to institutional and systemic barriers that perpetuate the unequal status of this

group relative to their White, middle-class counterparts. While more recent research on Latino educational experiences has focused on best practices for ensuring Latino success (as discussed in more detail below), the data indicate that challenges in educational access and attainment still persist.

Dropouts

Perhaps one of the most persistent challenges for Latino students in the United States is the high rate of dropping out of school. Although it is clear that there have been improvements in dropouts when one follows more recent cohorts of students through their high school years, scholars have pointed to the persistence of the gap that results in dropout rates among Latinos that are up to four times the rate of White students in similar age groups (using U.S. census data). Even if one only examines the dropout data in comparisons of U.S.-born Latinos and White students, the gap is still 2:1 in terms of dropout rates, and the gap has persisted for the nearly three decades of data available through the census. Nevertheless, the presence of immigrant students among the total Latino population, some of whom have had very little or no formal schooling prior to their arrival in the United States, at times contributes to overstated dropout rates relative to White students. In a recent report sponsored by the Pew Hispanic Center in Washington, D.C., among U.S.-born and immigrant Latinos, ages 16 to 19, the dropout rates varied widely across Latino subgroups in 2000. For 16- to 19-year-old Mexican-origin immigrants, the dropout rate was 39% versus 15% for their U.S.-born Mexican-origin counterparts. Among Puerto Rican students, the immigrant to U.S.-born difference was 22% versus 12%. Regionally speaking, among 16- to 19-year-olds, California's immigrant Latinos experienced a 34% dropout rate compared to U.S.-born Latinos with a 10% dropout rate. Likewise, in Florida, the dropout rate among immigrant Latinos was 26% for 16- to 19-year-olds, double the rate for U.S.-born Latinos in that state.

High School Completion

Simply examining dropout rates will not provide a sufficient picture of Latino graduation or completion rates, particularly given that Latinos may take significantly longer to graduate with a high school diploma than other students. According to the National Center for Education Statistics, Latino high school completion rates have fluctuated over the past two and one half decades. Nevertheless, in 2001, 58% of Latino 18- to 24-year-olds had completed high school. This percentage is markedly lower than their White counterparts, of whom 83% had completed high school. While high school completion, in and of itself, does not always translate into substantial returns to the students, for Latinos it can lead to higher education and thereby better employment opportunities.

College Eligibility Rates

Even for those Latino students who are able to persist in school in order to graduate, there remains an important hurdle to further educational and employment opportunities. College eligibility among Latino high school graduates has been the focus of the work of many scholars. In California, for example, only 21.5% of all Latino 12th-grade graduates completed all of the courses required for admission to the University of California and/or the California State University systems in 2002–2003. While 2002–2003 Texas data indicate that Latinos completed the "Recommended High School Program" at rates comparable to White students in that state (about 57% versus 56%, respectively), it appears that Latinos are disproportionately underrepresented among students completing their high school programs with the Distinguished Achievement Program designation. While Latinos comprised 34% of the total graduate population, they comprised 29% of those graduates completing the college-level coursework associated with the Distinguished Achievement Program. Comparable figures for White Texas graduates, however, show a disproportionate overrepresentation with their being 49% of the total graduate population and 60% of those accomplishing the Distinguished Achievement Program designation.

Representation Among Teachers and Administrators

Researchers have argued for the importance of representation of Latinos at all levels of K–12 and postsecondary education, particularly in light of scholarship on the role of Latino culture in their educational success. Table 1 presents data that reflect the disproportionate representation of Latino teachers and

administrators relative to students in U.S. public schools. For example, nationwide figures indicate that of all school principals and teachers, only 5% and 6%, respectively, are Latinos. Similarly, in the states of California and Texas, where Latinos are found in such high concentrations among students, Latino representation among teaching and administrative ranks is quite low. In both states, Latinos comprise well over 40% of the total student enrollments, yet they comprise much less than 20% of the teachers and administrators. Given the data on Latino participation in higher education, these figures are not necessarily surprising, but they do illuminate the challenge that schools face in becoming responsive learning environments, as recommended in the research of Patricia Gándara, García, Valdés, Valencia, and others. (See Table 1.)

Newly Emerging Educational Issues: Resegregation, High-Stakes Testing, and Zero-Tolerance Policies

There are several policy issues affecting the growing numbers of Latino students in the United States, particularly in urban settings: resegregation, high-stakes testing, and zero-tolerance policies. These issues potentially thwart educational efforts aimed at increasing Latino attainment and success in public schools. Data from 2003 on the distribution of Latino fourth graders, for example, show that 40% attend schools with concentrations of children of color of 90% or more. Latinos are more likely now than before desegregation efforts in the 1960s to attend segregated schools. Latinos face a variety of forms of segregation, such as that based on language and academic ability. Indeed, the movement toward high-stakes testing to determine the placement and progress of Latinos in schools has become a serious concern for many researchers. They argue that Latino students' learning, academic growth, and academic giftedness are not only inadequately captured by many of the standardized tests designed to "hold schools accountable" for their educational success, but the tests discriminate against students by testing them on material that they may not have been taught in the first place. This situation is particularly acute, according to these scholars, in the case of English-language-learning Latinos whose schools may not provide assessments that are appropriate measures of their progress. Moreover, given the relatively high concentration of Latinos in urban communities, with the added attention on

Table 1 Distribution of Latino, White, and Total U.S. Public School Teachers, Administrators/Principals, and
Students (in thousands)

	Teachers			Administrators[a]			Students		
	Latino	White	Total	Latino	White	Total	Latino	White	Total
US	169.0 (6%)	2,531.6 (84%)	3,002.3	4.3 (5%)	68.9 (82%)	83.8	8,103.3 (17%)	28,612.4 (60%)	47,440.5
CA	41.5 (14%)	227.7 (74%)	306.9	3.5 (13%)	19.3 (73%)	26.4	2,717.6 (45%)	2,138.1 (35%)	6,108.1
TX	50.4 (18%)	204.3 (73%)	279.8	2.9 (17%)	12.2 (72%)	17.1	1,735.0 (42%)	1,701.2 (41%)	4,163.4

SOURCE: Adapted from U.S. Department of Education, National Center for Education Statistics (NCES), The *Digest of Education Statistics, 2002*; NCES, "Public School Student, Staff, and Graduate Counts by State: School Year 2001-02," April 2004; California Department of Education, Educational Demographics Unit, 2001-2002, http://data1.cde.ca.gov; Texas Education Agency, *Snapshot 2002*, http://www.tea.state.tx.us.

a. NCES data source only reported ethnic demographics for school principals in the United States. California and Texas data include principals and all other administrators.

identifying violent behavior among urban youth (males, especially), Latino students face additional isolation as targets for zero-tolerance policies. Increasing numbers of Latinos in Texas, for example, are removed from school for a variety of disciplinary issues, resulting in the overrepresentation of Latino (and African American) males in suspensions, expulsions, and assignments to alternative educational settings.

Documenting Latino High Achievement

Latino high achievers are largely invisible in urban high schools and in educational research. Over the last three decades, numerous scholars have written about the connections between the academic *underachievement* of Latino students schooled in the United States and socioeconomic/academic barriers. Sonia Nieto, John Ogbu, Signithia Fordham, and William Vélez have variously discussed the impact of internal and direct colonialism, single-parent households, poverty, culturally irrelevant curricula, and nonacademic tracking on Latino students within traditional public urban schools. Other scholars contend that Latino academic underachievement has been exacerbated by the disproportionate representation of Puerto Rican- and Mexican-origin students in special education programs that academically miscategorize them and employ watered-down curricula.

While this scholarly work is important and theoretically rich, recent scholarship is turning the page from an exclusive overemphasis on academic underachievement to stories that describe the conditions that make it possible for working-class Latino students to become high academic achievers. Thus, to counteract the overabundance of scholarly literature that discusses why Puerto Rican- and Mexican-origin students drop out of school and/or academically underachieve, scholars on Latino issues have recently produced research that focuses on the institutional, familial, and community-based factors that have the potential to enable these students to become high academic achievers. In turn, this research has resulted in major implications for students, families/communities, policymakers, and school reformers.

Research With Puerto Rican Students

Scholars have focused on the high achieving schooling experiences of Puerto Rican students. With this line of inquiry, they have countered traditional perceptions of the overall lack of support and caring that working-class families and communities of color provide their children. What is especially interesting to note is that all of these researchers situate the multiple ways in which families, and especially mothers, serve as support systems to these students' academic success. Thus, the research directly challenges cultural deficit theories regarding the lack of academic success among Latinos by employing new theoretical frameworks that situate the experiences of Puerto Rican students within the context of their families and communities as a base (versus lack) of support.

For example, Pedro Antrop-González found that the families of Puerto Rican high achievers held their children to high academic expectations and expected their children's teachers to do the same. In addition, mothers took it upon themselves to help their children with homework. In the event that the mother, or any other family member, could not help with homework, outside help was found so that their child would not fall behind in their schoolwork. Other forms of familial support included children being encouraged to develop their bilingual language skills and bicultural frames of reference in order to navigate life inside and outside their homes and communities. Moreover, the families of these high achievers taught their children that many people, especially many of their teachers and peers, would hold them to low standards and expectations by virtue of being Puerto Rican; hence it was crucial that their high academic performance serve as a tool with which to dismantle these erroneous assumptions.

Other scholars have also located the high academic achievement of Puerto Rican students in relation to their access (or lack thereof) to community-based and school-based resources. These students' acquisition of social capital and their participation in social networks, including churches and extracurricular activities with institutional agents, greatly contributes to high academic achievement. These social networks serve multiple purposes, such as allowing for the establishment of trust-laden relationships between youth and adults and the consequent exchange of valuable information like the college entry process, the scholarship application process, and providing general mentoring/advice. This mentoring especially contributes to the development of a "school kid identity," which places emphasis on proschool behaviors like going to school every day, remaining on top of schoolwork/homework, seeking placement in safe social niches with other high achievers, participation in extracurricular activities, and conforming to institutionally sanctioned rules and norms. On the contrary, "street kids" found it very difficult to situate themselves in school-oriented peer networks, and often adopted negative means of resistance to schooling through membership in gangs and/or not going to school altogether. Finally, all these scholars ultimately contend that large, comprehensive high schools often do a poor job at equitably encouraging all students to access social networks that foment a school kid reality.

Research with Mexican-Origin Students

Scholars have contributed to the literature on the schooling experiences of high achieving Mexican-origin students. Like much of the aforementioned work regarding Puerto Rican high achievers, Mexican-origin students and their families have informed these scholars of similar institutional and familial/community conditions that have supported their high academic achievement. One thorough analysis of familial support among Mexican origin students, for example, can be found in *Latino High School Graduation: Defying the Odds* by Harriett D. Romo and Toni Falbo.

Families play a very active role in the academic success of their children because they go the extra mile to mentor them at home and seek positive support structures outside the home by way of larger outside communities. Institutions work to either help or hinder Mexican-origin students' academic success. While student membership in "cosmopolitan networks" and their access to positive support structures and resources are very helpful for students, Romo and Falbo also discuss the myriad ways in which institutions diligently work to inequitably offer them to all students.

While it is known that some teachers try very hard to construct additive curricula by weaving their students' linguistic and sociopolitical realities within their classrooms, it is also known that most teachers do not. Rather, as documented in a Texas high school, many school-related forces strive hard to maintain the status quo through subtractive schooling that demonizes the bilingualism and biculturalism that students and their families already bring to their classrooms. Furthermore, this subtractive schooling is reinforced through structures of large, comprehensive schools and overcrowded classrooms where students, their teachers, and other school staff members often find it impossible to authentically know each other and maintain mutually caring relationships.

Academic resiliency among Latino students is most evident in those high-achieving students who complete school and successfully complete college. These students are the ones who are high achieving throughout their school life. The research on high-achieving Latino students identifies their coping strategies. Gándara identifies protective factors that may assist a child in avoiding undesirable developmental and academic outcomes. Protective factors can generally be categorized under the role of parents, the students' behavioral and cognitive attributes, and school/institutional factors. Richard Duran identifies factors of resourcefulness in Latino students' ability to overcome incompatibilities between the student and the educational institution. Henry Trueba's work on the academic success of immigrant children shows that if children are able to manage to retain a strong and affirming self-identity and remain as part of the sociocultural community, they can achieve.

Future Directions for Documenting Latino Educational Success

Students have taught educational scholars that their academic success is often not attributable to school-related factors like teachers and other institutional agents. Rather, their success is more clearly linked to home and community-related factors like the influence and advocacy of their mothers, the importance of their ethnic identity, and their acquisition of social capital through community-based social networks like churches and extracurricular activities. The difficulties experienced by high-achieving Puerto Rican- and Mexican-origin students lead researchers, such as Festus Obiakor, to believe that even "good" large comprehensive urban high schools still inequitably structure opportunities for high achievement. That is, even for high-achieving Latino students, many schools do not tap into the funds of knowledge that these students bring to school.

Thus it is important that schools be encouraged to continually examine the ways in which their students' lives are reflected both inside and outside schools. Broader partnerships with community-based agencies, families, and area universities are also some of the recommendations emanating from the research on high-achieving Latinos. Through these types of school-community partnerships, high schools can further reinforce the social and cultural capital these students are already receiving in their homes and communities, which Latinos can employ to graduate from high school, enter college, and access opportunities that will improve their life chances.

—Gloria M. Rodriguez,
Rene Antrop-Gonzalez, and Augustina Reyes

See also accountability; achievement gap, of students; achievement tests; affirmative action; Chavez, Cesar

Estrada; cross-cultural studies; desegregation, of schools; discipline in schools; diversity; dropouts; equality, in schools; ethnicity; ethnocentrism; expectations, teacher and student cultures; high schools; immigration, history and impact in education; League of United Latin American Citizens; Mendez, Felicitas; minorities, in schools; multi-culturalism; underachievers

Further Readings and References

Antrop-González, R. (2003). "This school is my sanctuary": The Dr. Pedro Albizu Campos alternative high school. *Journal of the Center for Puerto Rican Studies, 15*(2), 232–255.

California Department of Education, Educational Demographics Unit. (2004). *California public schools, statewide report: Enrollment by gender, grade, and ethnic designation, 2003–04* [Data file]. Retrieved from http://data1.cde.ca.gov/dataquest.

Gándara, P. (1995). *Over the ivy walls: The educational mobility of low-income Chicanos.* New York: State University of New York Press.

García, E. (2001). *Hispanic education in the United States: Raíces y alas.* Lanham, MD: Rowman & Littlefield.

McCarthy, C., Crichlow, W., Dimitriadis, G., & Dolby, N. (Eds.). (2005). *Race, identity, and representation in education.* New York: Routledge.

Millman, J. (2005, May 2). Low-wage U.S. jobs get "Mexicanized," but there's a price. *Wall Street Journal,* p. A2.

Nieto, S. (2000). Puerto Rican students in U.S. schools: A brief history. In S. Nieto (Ed.), *Puerto Rican students in U.S. schools* (pp. 5–38). Mahwah, NJ: Erlbaum.

Obiakor, F. E. (2001). *It even happens in "good" schools: Responding to cultural diversity in today's classrooms.* Thousand Oaks, CA: Corwin Press.

Pedraza, P., & Rivera, M. (2005). *Latino education.* Mahwah, NJ: Erlbaum.

Reyes, A. (2001). Alternative education: The criminalization of student behavior. *Fordham Urban Law Journal, 29*(2), 539–559.

Valdés, G. (2001). *Learning and not learning English: Latino students in American schools.* New York: Teachers College Press.

Valencia, R. R. (Ed.). (2002). *Chicano school failure and success: Past, present, and future* (2nd ed.). London: RoutledgeFalmer.

🏛 LAW

The U.S. Supreme Court's 1954 decision in *Brown v. Board of Education* was the most important education-related case in U.S. history, perhaps its most significant judgment ever. With *Brown* providing a major impetus in the ensuing years, the United States has undergone a myriad of educational, legal, and social transformations. *Brown* not only ushered in an era of equal educational opportunities in striking down racial segregation in public schools but also signaled the birth of the field known as education law or school law.

Prior to *Brown,* the Court addressed only a handful of education-related cases. Yet, now almost every year the Court resolves at least one school-related case. In fact, since the Court first addressed a dispute under the Establishment Clause in 1947, upholding a state's providing transportation for children who attend non-public schools in *Everson v. Board of Education* (1947), it addressed more than 30 cases in both school desegregation and religion.

In light of the significance that education law has assumed in the daily activities of educational leaders, this entry reflects on the centrality of education law in educational leadership preparation programs. The centrality of education law is reflected in a study conducted on behalf of the University Council for Educational Administration (UCEA). The survey revealed that with 87.5% of UCEA's members offering courses in education law, it is the second most commonly taught subject in leadership programs. Furthermore, since many universities offer a variety of graduate and undergraduate classes in education law, it is likely to remain a crucial element in curricula, demonstrating that as an applied rather than a purely theoretical discipline, it is essential for educators at all levels.

The UCEA study and other indicators support the proposition that specialists in education law must help clarify the law so that it remains a valuable tool. Faculty members who specialize in education law can help to preserve the importance of education law by teaching students to focus on such basic concepts as due process and equal protection, essential elements in the development of sound policies and practices. In other words, as important as abstract legal principles or theories are, faculty members who teach education law must concentrate on ways to help practitioners apply these concepts rather than having them memorize case holdings apart from their applications in real-life situations.

Education law presents a unique intellectual challenge to prepare educational practitioners, whether board members, superintendents, principals, or teachers, to be proactive. Working in a discipline that tends to be reactive, faculty members teaching education law need to present their subject matter as a tool that should be applied in advance to help ensure that the school officials meet the needs of all of their constituents, ranging from students and parents to faculty, staff, and the local community. Yet, the goal of making the law proactive becomes complicated, because most changes generated by education law are reactive, and modifications come only after a decision has been reached via litigation. To this end, *Brown* is a typical example of how the law can be seen as reactive insofar as there would not have been a need for *Brown* if the schools in Topeka and elsewhere had met the needs of African American students.

Along with balancing the tension present between the proactive and reactive dimensions of education law, law classes in educational leadership programs should not become Law School 101. Rather than trying to turn educators into lawyers equipped to deal with such technical and procedural matters as jurisdiction, statutes of limitation, and the service of process, courses in education law should provide a broad understanding of the law that will allow them to accomplish two important goals.

First, classes in education law should provide educators with enough awareness of the legal dimensions of a situation so they can better frame questions for their attorneys to answer, performing a kind of triage to limit problems, when a legal controversy arises. To this end, educators must be taught to recognize the value in making their attorneys equal partners not only in problem solving after the fact but also in developing responsive, proactive policies. Such a proactive approach is consistent with the notion of preventative law wherein knowledgeable educators can identify potential problems in advance and in concert with their attorneys can work to ensure they do not develop into crises. Moreover, when educational leaders select attorneys for their boards, for example, they would be well advised to hire individuals with specialized practices in education law, thereby avoiding potential lapses in critical knowledge and ensuring their advice has the most up-to-date perspectives on legal matters. Second, classes in education law must teach educators how to rely upon their substantive knowledge of the law and where to look to update their sources of information through professional organizations such as the Education Law Association so they can develop sound policies to enhance the day-to-day operations of schools.

Education law is a dynamic, intellectually stimulating discipline that is constantly evolving to meet the needs of educational leaders as they direct the daily activities in schools. The merits of its decisions aside, and the impact that they are likely to have on educational leaders aside, one has only to read recent Supreme Court opinions in such areas as sexual harassment, religion, and special education, among others, to recognize the importance of keeping abreast of legal changes. In light of these cases, educators are charged with the task of developing and implementing policies to enhance school environments for all constituents.

Perhaps the only constant in education law is that as it evolves to meet the demands of a constantly changing educational world, it is likely to remain of utmost importance for all who are interested in schooling. In fact, the seemingly endless supply of new statutes, regulations, and cases speak of the need to be ever vigilant of how legal developments impact on education.

—*Charles J. Russo*

See also accountability; affirmative action; Black education; boards of education; civil rights movement; collective bargaining; critical race theory; critical theory; desegregation, of schools; Latinos; League of Latin American Citizens; Marshall, Thurgood; Mendez, Felicitas; *A Nation at Risk*; National Association for the Advancement of Colored People; No Child Left Behind; special education; state departments of education; unions, of teachers

Further Readings and References

Brown v. Board of Education, I, 347 U.S. 483 (1954).
Everson v. Board of Education, 330 U.S. 1 (1947).
Individuals With Disabilities Education Act, 20 U.S.C. §§ 1400 *et seq.*
Pohland, P. A., & Carlson, L. T. (1993). Program reform in educational administration, *UCEA Review, 34*(3), 4–9.
Russo, C. (2005). The role of law in leadership preparation programs. In F. English (Ed.), *The SAGE handbook of educational leadership* (pp. 168–186). Thousand Oaks, CA: Sage.
Russo, C., & Osborne, A. (2003). *Special education and the law.* Thousand Oaks, CA: Corwin Press.

LAW, TRENDS IN

The typical publication in school law, whether an article or a book, examines one or more topics for a relatively contemporaneous period or without a comprehensive and systematic trends analysis. The purpose of this entry is to help fill the gap by providing a compact longitudinal overview of the trends in school law. Inasmuch as the expansive school law literature provides the microlevel textual details, the focus of this overview will be on two key dimensions, or variables—volume and outcomes—of the education litigation.

The overall trend for these two dimensions, which is different from a prevailing perception among many educators and other segments of the public, is that court decisions in the context of K–12 education are on a gradual downswing rather than an explosive upswing and that the school defendants have won the majority of the published, final decisions, even in the turbulent 1970s and continuing to the present time.

Volume refers here to the frequency of published case law, which is the only available database for such overall purposes. Contrary to a common perception of a continuing "explosion" in education litigation, various empirical analyses have reached the opposite conclusion—the overall volume of published case law reached a high point in the 1970s and has gradually but rather steadily decreased since then. The major exception within this total downward trend is the special education segment, which has risen relatively dramatically since the end of the 1970s in terms of both published hearing/review officer and published court decisions. Yet, contrary to Richard Arum's 2003 characterization of the courts' hostility toward school authority, his own data show a steady and steep decline in the frequency of student discipline cases in regular education since the 1970s.

Outcomes refers here to who won these published decisions—the plaintiff or suing party or the defendant school authority. Again contrary to the common conception, the school authorities won the majority of the decisions overall in both the 1970s and the more modern era. Although the proverbial pendulum from the earlier to the later period did not swing for the overall published case law, it did do so for student cases. More specifically, there was a statistically significant shift in the outcomes of student-initiated court decisions from the mid-1970s to the mid-1990s. Within the student-initiated category, however, the outcomes of the special education decisions, both at the hearing/review officer as well as the court level, remained relatively stable, modestly favoring school districts, at least for the time period 1989 to 2000.

—*Perry Zirkel*

See also accountability; affirmative action; Black education; boards of education; civil rights movement; collective bargaining; critical race theory; critical theory; desegregation, of schools; Latinos; League of Latin American Citizens; Marshall, Thurgood; Mendez, Felicitas; *A Nation at Risk*;

National Association for the Advancement of Colored People; No Child Left Behind; school safety; special education; state departments of education; unions, of teachers; violence in schools

Further Readings and References

Arum, R. (2003). *Judging school discipline: The crisis of moral authority*. Cambridge, MA: Harvard University Press.

D'Angelo, A., Lutz, J. G., & Zirkel, P. A. (2004). Are published IDEA hearing officer decisions representative? *Journal of Disability Policy Studies, 14,* 241–252.

Joint Center & Common Good. (2003). *The effects of law on public schools.* Retrieved June 8, 2004, from http://cgood.org.

Lupini, W. H., & Zirkel, P. A. (2003). An outcomes analysis of education litigation. *Educational Policy, 17,* 257–279.

Zirkel, P. A., & D'Angelo, A. (2002). Special education case law: An empirical trends analysis. *West's Education Law Reporter, 161,* 731–753.

🏛 LAWRENCE-LIGHTFOOT, SARA

Sociologist Sara Lawrence-Lightfoot (1944–) built her research agenda describing interactions between families and schools. Throughout eight books and innumerable articles, Professor Lawrence-Lightfoot provided insightful analyses of the social conditions of school and family relations. She also expanded on qualitative research approaches adopting the reporting style called *portraiture.* Much of her work drew on personal perspectives formed during her life as a female African American professor at Harvard.

The daughter of a professor of sociology and a psychoanalyst, young Lawrence-Lightfoot shared her parents' educated view of the dynamics of race, gender, and culture in the intersection of home and school. Her Mississippi-born parents attended White institutions of higher education. Lawrence-Lightfoot attended rural New York schools. She noted her parents' remarkable vigilance negotiating her siblings' and her experiences in predominantly White schools. She earned her bachelor's degree from Swarthmore College, where she holds an endowed professorship, and a doctorate from Harvard University, where she holds the Emily Hargroves Fisher Professorship, a chair that will become the Lawrence-Lightfoot Endowed Chair upon her retirement. The Lawrence-Lightfoot Endowed Chair is Harvard's first to be named for an African American female.

Lawrence-Lightfoot also serves as the chair of the MacArthur Foundation, an organization that recognizes the betterment of the human condition. Among her many honors, Lawrence-Lightfoot received a MacArthur Fellowship in 1984.

Lawrence-Lightfoot's analysis of the tensions between families and schools, especially the divisions between mothers and teachers, began with *Worlds Apart* in 1978. Her subsequent descriptions of the interlocking networks among schools, communities, and families in *The Good High School* provided intimate depictions of high schools with healthy relationships. During this period of the mid-1980s, Lawrence-Lightfoot joined with another noted sociologist, James Coleman, to provide direction for high school reform and explain how schools and communities could exploit social capital in schooling. Their work exposed differences between public and nonpublic schools as less about students' socioeconomic status and more about the social networks ignored or severed by public high schools but nurtured and woven more tightly in nonpublic schools.

In addition to contributions illuminating the social complexity of school, parent, and community relationships, Lawrence-Lightfoot's approach to publishing her findings offered a more fluent presentation of the results of qualitative research. In the late 1990s, she published an explanation and a defense of her method, portraiture. With coauthor Jessica Hoffman Davis, Lawrence-Lightfoot extended ethnographers' debates over the role and place of *voice* as a means of relating research results. Lawrence-Lightfoot positioned portraiture as a phenomenological procedure. Portraiture provides a means of data reduction that has been criticized for its unspoken reification of a singular perspective on phenomena of interest.

Despite such critiques, Lawrence-Lightfoot's nuanced rendering of the emotional dimensions of racial and gendered relations in schools and their communities strikes a sustained resonance. Her parables and portraits of mothers and teachers engaged in contests over students' education and futures continue to provide an authentic description of highly charged social situations surrounding schooling.

—*Jane Clark Lindle*

See also Black education; Catholic education; children and families in America; communities, types, building of; cultural capital; cultural politics, wars; expectations, teacher and student cultures; feminism and theories of leadership; gender studies, in education; high schools; human capital; parental involvement; qualitative research, history, theories, issues; resiliency; social capital; stratification, in organizations

Further Readings and References

English, F. (2000). A critical appraisal of Sara Lawrence-Lightfoot's portraiture as a method of educational research. *Educational Researcher, 29*(7), 21–26.

Lawrence-Lightfoot, S. (1983). *The good high school: Portraits of character and culture.* New York: Basic Books.

Lawrence-Lightfoot, S. (2000). *Respect: An exploration.* Cambridge, MA: Perseus Books.

Lawrence-Lightfoot, S., & Hoffman Davis, J. (1997). *The art and science of portraiture.* San Francisco: Jossey-Bass.

LEADERSHIP, COMPLEX THEORY OF

Complex leadership theory is the study of the role of leadership in the emergence of ideas among neural-like networks of interactive, interdependent agents. It is premised on complexity theory, a science of emergent dynamics in interactive, adaptive networks.

Complexity theory itself derives from chaos theory, a science of nonlinear behavior in interactive, dynamically active systems (nonlinearity is defined as producing outcomes that are disproportional to inputs). Chaotic systems exhibit complicated, dynamic, deterministically derived order (thus they are distinguished from simple random systems that exhibit no order). Mathematically generated plots of the motion of such systems reveal convoluted—and hauntingly beautiful—patterns, the most famous of which looks like butterfly wings drawn with nonoverlapping, never-ending lines (the well-known Lorenz attractor). Chaotic systems are nonlinear and consequently unpredictable; they are so highly changeable that they carry little information about their past or future behaviors. A number of turbulent or potentially turbulent activities, such as weather patterns or fluid flows, are described by the science of chaos.

Before chaos theory, it was assumed that dynamic behavior was either random (hence of little interest) or stable. Stable systems, such as a clock pendulum, repeat themselves eventually; thus their past and their future are predictable. Neither chaos nor stability describes what happens in human systems, however.

One can see a bit of chaos and a bit of stability in social dynamics, but one can also identify characteristics (such as adaptability) that are not observed in either chaos or stability. Instead, social systems lie between chaos and stability but exhibit unique characteristics as well. This boundary is the realm of complexity theory.

Like chaotic systems, complex systems are nonlinear, but this nonlinearity manifests predominately as small change events rather than as the dramatic events characteristic of chaos. Like stable systems, complex systems are sufficiently unchanging to carry information about their past and their future; that is, they are predictable. However, information in complex systems is also dynamic (from its chaotic side), so memories and predictability are prone to dissipation. Unlike stable or chaotic systems, complex systems are adaptive, capable of solving problems (computer simulations of complex systems can solve difficult puzzles, for example), and are able to respond quickly and flexibly to satisfy their needs. Perhaps most important for leadership and organization, complex systems are also capable of reinventing themselves in surprising and creative ways.

Complex systems are networks of agents (individuals or groups) who are interactive, interdependent (the actions of one agent affects the fitness of other agents), and moderately coupled (directly affecting a limited number of other agents). The dynamics of complex systems are enhanced by the presence of catalysts, and indeed the system can generate its own catalysts. One important catalytic agent is the leader. Complex systems produce new structures or creativity with bottom-up rather than top-down activities; that is, their strength lies in the dynamics of their followers rather than the control of their leaders. Complex systems are typically coordinated by simple, local, minimally restrictive rules that govern the actions of agents. Because complex systems are adaptive and capable of rapidly producing creative surprises, they are ideally suited for knowledge-producing organizations in hypercompetitive environments such as the computer software industry, research and development systems, and, more topically, higher education institutions that value and promote research or public schools struggling to adapt rapidly and creatively to environmental demands.

Leadership plays an important role in enabling the emergence of complex systems. The study of such leadership is called complex leadership (to suggest leadership of complex systems rather than a description of the leader). Complex leadership differs dramatically from traditional models of leadership. Traditional models can be categorized either as management of influence or management of meaning models. Management of influence refers to leadership that directly influences follower behavior to accomplish organizational goals; these perspectives include command and control models, contingency theories, and bureaucracy theory. Management of meaning refers to leadership that seeks to align workers' sense of propriety, their worldviews, or their definitions of life goals with organizational goals; this category includes transformational leadership and culture leadership. Both influence and meaning models of leadership deal primarily with human relations and tend to depend heavily on social-psychological strategies.

Complex leadership moves away from (although it does not abandon) relational approaches and focuses instead on enabling conditions (i.e., network dynamics) that foster the creativity and flexibility available through complex systems. Because of its significant departure from traditional approaches, it is appropriately labeled with its own model categorization, which can be termed *management of emergence*. This terminology emphasizes the bottom-up, spontaneous nature of productivity in complex systems and underscores leadership's unique role in that process.

Complex leadership enables complex behavior within an organization. Its role can be defined in terms of several overlapping functions. First, complex leadership enables *interaction*. Agents in complex organizations need unfettered access to each other and to ideas, for it is the interaction of ideas that generates surprise and creativity. Interaction can be accomplished both passively and actively. Passive enabling involves the way space is structured. Educational facilities can be organized to either encourage or discourage interaction. Traditional school structures with classes staggered on both sides of long hallways (called the egg crate layout) are poorly suited for interaction. Leaders can ameliorate passive structures with effective organization, but there are more appropriate structures such as pod structures (a small number of classrooms open onto a common area) or even structures in which two or more classrooms share a glassed teacher workroom.

Active enabling of interaction refers to direct actions by leaders to build patterns of interaction, and usually is accomplished by the way school activities are scheduled and organized. Leaders can schedule teachers with common interests to common preparation time, they can foster interaction with judicious use of committees, they can encourage interdisciplinary units, and they can find creative ways to use inservice to foster interaction (sponsor a "teacher's" fair along the lines of student science fairs, for example).

A second function of complex leadership is fostering *interdependencies*. In interdependent networks, the actions of one agent directly or indirectly affect the actions of other agents. A decision by the English department to focus on grammar in the ninth grade, for example, might inhibit students' capacity to deal with word problems in algebra (such conflicts are called conflicting constraints). The manner in which a math department leads students to envision calculation of unknowns may make it difficult for them to solve quantity equations in chemistry. The complex leader finds ways to enhance such interdependencies in order to achieve three outcomes: (1) conflicting constraints (or task-related conflicts) that naturally occur in interdependent networks stimulate agents to find ever fitter solutions to their problems, (2) interdependence imposes a measure of accountability that fosters coordination, and (3) interdependent relationships provide pathways for the dissemination and coordination of innovations—without such linkages, a change agent must, in the extreme, introduce change to one person or department at a time.

Complex leadership seeks to foster moderate levels, as opposed to tight or loose levels, of *coupling* among agents. Coupling refers to the number of interdependencies any given agent experiences or the degree of effect that interdependent agents have on one another. In tightly coupled systems, conflicting constraints are difficult or impossible to resolve because many different agents must coordinate and participate in seeking mutually fit solutions. Consequently, such systems either freeze into inaction, or if they do change, that change is likely to perturb the entire system—which may be catastrophic. Leaders create tight coupling with, among other things, excess coordination or authoritarian behavior. Loosely coupled systems do not experience the tension of conflicting constraints and do not have channels for coordination or dissemination; thus there is little incentive to work together or to change. Loose coupling emerges when organizational patterns and leadership activities fail to foster interdependency; different disciplines in higher education tend to be loosely coupled because of organizational patterns and regulations, for example. Moderately coupled complex systems, in contrast, are sufficiently tight to experience motivating tension and channel innovation but sufficiently loose to change stably.

Complex leaders motivate action with *adaptive tension*. Adaptive tension is any pressure that pushes a system to perform. When Jack Welch, former CEO of General Electric, told employees that their product must be number 1 or number 2 in their field or be canceled, he was creating adaptive tension. Adaptive tension moves a system away from a steady state toward an unstable, unspecified, but urgent future; such conditions are conducive to nonlinear change and creative surprise.

Complex systems are focused on *indeterminate vision*. *Determinate* vision—the usual form of visioning—utilizes current states of understanding to define a specific desired future and focuses the organization on achieving that future. In such conditions, creativity is limited by the capacity of vision makers and by the state of current understanding. That is, determinate vision enables the unfolding of current knowledge but does not enable creative surprise. Indeterminate vision envisions generalized future states and behaviors and does not otherwise limit those futures. Welch envisioned number 1 or number 2; he did not envision what number 1 or 2 would look like. A principal whose vision is for the school to be the most creative school in the district does not specify what creativity is to look like; rather he or she envisions a behavior that can be realized in a variety of ways.

In addition to building indeterminate organization-wide vision, complex leadership fosters *heterogeneous agents* and *heterogeneous visions*. As implied in the preceding paragraph, traditional models of leadership have the effect, either by direction or indirection, of coordinating activity around a central determinate vision or set of visions to homogenize follower behaviors to a common perspective. Chester I. Barnard, for example, argued that the leader's role is to align worker preference with organizational goals. Transformational leadership seeks to define worker meaning relative to organizational vision. Complex leadership, on the other hand, seeks to foster multiple, decentralized visions. An important strength of the complex leadership approach is its ability to bring together a rich diversity of skills and visions in an interactive, interdependent network. Interaction of heterogeneous ideas enables potent surprise and creativity. Ideas combine, recombine, and aggregate in complex and surprising ways to produce a diversity of unanticipated meta-ideas, products, and environmental adaptations.

Complex systems are coordinated in part by simple, local *rules*. Rules for complex systems enable rather than limit behavior. Complex rules serve six primary roles: they stimulate action, enable interaction, foster interdependency, interject tension, enable bottom-up decision making, and focus conflict on task (rather than personal) behaviors. A good example is provided by Microsoft's "synch and stabilize" rule. Microsoft divides its programming staff into small teams—agents, in complexity terminology. These teams are responsible for particular elements of a given program. Programs such as XP or MS Word are extremely complex and require millions of lines of code. Top-down control of the programming function would be inefficient, produce programs with limited capability, and it would be difficult to respond rapidly to changing technological landscapes. Semiautonomous work groups and bottom-up decision making—complex structuring—overcomes these limitations. To coordinate programming workgroups, Microsoft has implemented local rules structures such as synch and stabilize. At the end of each week, groups are required to compile their code and combine it with the codes of other groups. If the different code sets fail to run together, the programmers are required to fix the problems before they leave for the day. One can readily see that this rule accomplishes all six of the primary roles described above.

Transformation is an important characteristic of complex leadership, but the traditional definition of transformation must be modified to be consistent with assumptions underlying complex leadership theory. In the traditional approach, transformation strategies tend to be constructed around two premises (although there are exceptions): the transformation of individuals into self-motivated, engaged follower/leaders, and the alignment of follower meaning with organizational goals. This definitional set works for complex leadership theory if we define organizational goals in terms of indeterminate rather than determinate vision, and if we further recognize the value of heterogeneous vision embedded within the more general, indeterminate vision focus. Efforts to align worker motivation to determinate goals stifle bottom-up behaviors and its advantage for creative behavior. Organizational vision is important, but complex leadership achieves transforming benefits with indeterminate vision that enable creativity.

Complexity leaders allocate *resources* in ways that support and foster network dynamics. For example, public schools traditionally allocate money on a per-pupil basis, or they make distributions based on the resource intensiveness of a given discipline (thus sciences get more money than do English classes). The complexity leader might make allocations to meet foundational needs, but remaining funds would be distributed in support of creative ideas—money follows creativity. Another important resource is information, and complex leadership finds strategies to maximize distribution of that commodity.

Finally, complexity leaders work to build *external networks* with clients, other educational organizations, resource providers, community agencies, and others. Primary attention is devoted to building network relationships with agencies that have a vested interest in education, but fit networks extend to a wide spectrum of outside agencies as well. At least two complexity-related functions are served by this. First, the construction of external networks serves the same purpose as internal, system-based networks: it fosters creativity and innovation in the educational (and broader) system. Second, fitness is derived from broad bases of support, and support can come from unexpected sources. For example, a recreation department may seem a somewhat unlikely ally for an elementary school, but it may be willing to share costs of a school-site recreation facility for mutual benefit. A farm bureau may seem an even more unlikely ally, but it may have influence with local school boards.

—Russ Marion and Phil McGee

See also adaptiveness of organizations; administration, theories of; boundaries of systems; bureaucracy; capacity building, of organizations; creativity, in management; frame theory; hierarchy, in organizations; infrastructure, of organizations; line and staff concept; management information systems; management theories; matrix organization (the "adhocracy"); motivation, theories of; networking and network theory; organizational theories; organizations, types of, typologies; planning models; rational organizational theory; role conflict; role theory; satisfaction, in organizations and roles; scalar principle; school improvement models; stratification, in organizations; table of organization; Theory X, Theory Y; total quality management; transformational leadership

Further Readings and References

Argyris, C. (1972). *The applicability of organizational sociology.* London: Cambridge University Press.

Barnard, C. (1938). *The functions of the executive.* Cambridge, MA: Harvard University Press.

Bass, B., & Avolio, B. (1994). *Improving organizational effectiveness through transformational leadership.* Thousand Oaks, CA: Sage.

Cusumano, M. (2001). Focusing creativity: Microsoft's "Synch and Stabilize" approach to software product development. In I. Nonaka & T. Nishiguchi (Eds.), *Knowledge emergence: Social, technical, and evolutionary dimensions of knowledge creation.* Oxford: Oxford University Press.

Lorenz, E. (1993). *Chaos theory.* Seattle: University of Washington Press.

Ogawa, R. (2005). *Leadership as social construct: The expression of human agency within organizational constraint.* In F. English (Ed.), *The SAGE handbook of educational leadership* (pp. 89–108). Thousand Oaks, CA: Sage.

Marion, R., & Uhi-Bien, M. (2001). Leadership in complex organizations. *Leadership Quarterly, 12,* 389–418.

McKelvey, B. (2003). Toward a 0th law of thermodynamics: Order creation complexity dynamics from physics & biology to bioeconomics. *Journal of Bioeconomics, 6,* 1–31.

🏛 LEADERSHIP, DISCRETIONARY (AND POWER)

A discretionary leader uses power—generally authority to achieve desired outcomes effectively and efficiently. Within classical hierarchical or linear organizational paradigms, discretionary leadership evokes great man/great woman theories. Because participatory leadership styles often are viewed as more enlightened, beneficial, and productive, leadership without attention to situations, needs of followers, and the like are less favored. Nevertheless, situational realities often require that leaders use power discreetly, according to the nature of decisions required, leadership demanded, and needs of the occasion. Discretionary leadership, then, emphasizes the nature of values, situational factors, organizational characteristics, participant behaviors or needs, ends sought, and demands for types of leadership. Cognizance of such factors enables leaders to act on existing contingencies toward positive organizational outcomes.

The need for discretionary leadership is driven by recent reliance on data-based decision making and accelerated by growing concerns for accountability. As organizational performance bows to environmental factors and aligns with contemporary forms of early emphases on scientific management, specialized professional roles become critical to organizational survival and success. Thus, administrative leaders often find themselves constrained by the system with little flexibility in decision making. Information-driven decisions or centralized systems too often leave little room for managers to use their own judgment. To overcome the constraints of such mechanistic systems, leaders necessarily use *discretion* when countermanding hard data or information so that decisions account for soft, hard-to-measure factors, factors that easily can nullify the best laid bureaucratic plans.

Discretionary leadership and the judicious exercise of power are synonymous. In the context of neo-great man/great woman theories and Frederick Taylor's time-and-motion job specifications, discretionary leaders must employ values, ethics, and sound judgment when considering issues of right and wrong, fairness, or the greater "good" of the organization. Furthermore, discretionary leaders must recognize changing organizational needs: increasing diversity, multiple constituencies at all levels, and the utility of distributed leadership. As a result, leadership roles are multifaceted with broad responsibilities and must deal with evolving cultural norms and values, pervasive technology, and external demands for effectiveness—and efficiency. These multiple complexities necessitate leaders who are flexible decision makers, who are contextual in orientation, and who balance organizational ends with those of both internal and external constituencies.

Various organizational and environmental variables also can determine the latitude a leader can assume. For example, an environment with a highly mechanistic organizational structure, a centralized managerial system, and rigid operational policies has little flexibility, and discretionary leadership is less possible. However, the way that a leader construes and reacts to a given situation determines leadership actions. Obviously, the position that leaders hold in a hierarchy affects their credibility and ability to act, and interpersonal dynamics have much to do with the amount of power that discretionary leaders have as well as their successful use of it.

Discretionary leaders usually have a wide repertoire of leadership attributes and styles that they can use. They vary their leadership depending upon the situation in which they operate. Hierarchical, environmental, and technological complexity and organizational structure all constrain leadership behavior. Macrovariables, including factors such as the general and specific environments, context (size and technology), structure, and cultural diversity, also add to the complexity with which leaders must grapple. Given these problems, leaders must still strive for successful organizational outcomes. Flexibility—and sufficient discretionary leadership—can be key to organizational success.

—Zav Dadabhoy and Rodney Muth

See also leadership, complex theory of; leadership, distributed; leadership, situational; leadership, task-oriented; leadership, theories of; path-goal leadership theory; scientific management; Taylor, Frederick

Further Readings and References

Clement, D. (2004). The veil of discretion: A new look at how much freedom the Fed should have in setting monetary policy. *Region*, June, 10–13, 42–47.

Dimmock, C., & Walker, A. (2005). *Educational leadership: Culture and diversity.* Thousand Oaks, CA: Sage.

Kochan, F., & Reed, C. (2005). Collaborative leadership, community building, and democracy in public education. In F. English (Ed.), *The SAGE handbook of educational leadership* (pp. 68–84). Thousand Oaks, CA: Sage.

Northouse, P. G. (2004). *Leadership: Theory and practice* (3rd ed.). Thousand Oaks, CA: Sage.

Taylor, F. W. (1911). *The principles of scientific management.* New York: Harper.

Tomlinson, H. (2004). *Educational management.* New York: Routledge.

LEADERSHIP, DISTRIBUTED

Educational researchers have long examined the link between the importance of principal leadership and student achievement, concluding that successful educational leaders have a powerful influence on the effectiveness of the school and student learning. In fact, school leadership has been found to have a significant impact on student learning, second only to the effects of the quality of curriculum and teachers' instruction.

Until recently, most research assumed that leadership must come from the school principal. For decades, studies on leadership have documented specific leader traits and behaviors, focusing on the top of the hierarchical organization—the principal. There is now much greater emphasis placed on the idea of *distributed leadership,* shared by multiple individuals at different levels of the school organization.

The idea that a single "hero" leader can lead and transform a school alone has become obsolete. The task of leading today's schools has become so multifaceted and complex that a single person cannot be expected to accomplish this alone. More than two decades of school reform has continually added to the workload and responsibility of the principal.

The multitude of demands placed on principals' time draws resources away from a focus on curriculum and instruction, as numerous tasks from the school, district, state, and federal government require the attention and consideration of school leaders. Because of this, many educational researchers and policymakers believe that school leadership today should be distributed throughout the organization, rather than focused on a single individual.

Distributed leadership is currently a buzzword in educational circles, and in the past few years has been used increasingly in discussions about school leadership. As attention to this perspective grows, so does its research base and empirical support. However, there seems to be little agreement as to the meaning of the term, and it lacks a widely accepted definition.

Some may define distributed leadership as simply the redistribution of the principal's responsibilities to other staff members. Other views move beyond this simplistic analysis and call for a fundamental change in organizational thinking, redefining school leadership as the responsibility of all in a school.

A fruitful way of considering distributed leadership is that it is a way of thinking about leadership, rather than a new technique of practice. Distributed leadership seeks expertise throughout an organization, rather than focusing it upon a single individual or individuals in a formal position or role. So the idea is that school leadership should be viewed as the cumulative activities of a broad set of leaders, both formal and informal, within a school, rather than as the work of one individual—such as the principal.

Distributed leadership is characterized as a form of shared or collective leadership in which expertise is developed by working collaboratively. The rationale is that in a knowledge-intensive situation found in schools, there is no way to perform tasks of great complexity without widely dispersing the responsibility for performance among various roles. Distributed leadership becomes the focal point that provides a common frame of values for performance.

This does not, however, suggest that there is no one responsible for the overall performance of the school. The job of the principal in a distributed environment is to hold the pieces together and maintain a productive relationship between the actors.

The National Association of Secondary School Principals (NASSP) insists that the principal should provide leadership by building and maintaining a vision, direction, and focus for student learning, but also argues that the principal of a school should never act alone. NASSP recommends that all schools establish a governing council for key decisions to promote student learning and an atmosphere of participation, responsibility, and ownership.

The central tenet behind distributed leadership is that the complex nature of instructional practice requires individuals to function in networks of shared and complementary expertise rather than in a structure with a hierarchical division of labor. With distributed leadership, knowledge and practice are extended across positions and individuals rather than being focused on a single role.

James Spillane, principal investigator for the Distributed Leadership Study, noted in 2005 that distributed leadership is primarily about leadership practice rather than leaders or their roles, functions, routines, and structures. A distributed perspective on leadership argues that school leadership practice is distributed in the interactions of school leaders, followers, and their situations. The critical issue is not that leadership *is* distributed but *how* it is distributed. The practice of leadership is not the same as the actions of the principal or other school leaders, nor is it a function of what a leader knows or does.

Effective principals do not just string together a series of individual actions, but systematically distribute leadership by building it into the fabric of school life. Leadership is distributed not by delegating it or giving it away but by weaving together people, materials, and organizational structures in a common cause.

Because this concept is relatively new, there is little empirical knowledge about how, or to what extent, distributed leadership is utilized by school leaders. Additional empirical studies examining the relationship between distributed leadership, school improvement, and student achievement are warranted and needed. Although these links have yet to be made, educational researchers, policymakers, and practitioners are all in agreement that school leadership, the principalship in particular, needs fundamental change—and that the distributed perspective on educational leadership is a potential prospect for the future of educational leadership.

—J. Patrick Grenda

See also administration, theories of; authority; bureaucracy; capacity building, of organizations; chain of command; chief academic officer; creativity, in management; differentiated staffing; governance; group dynamics; human resource development; infrastructure, of organizations; involvement, in organizations; leadership, task-oriented; leadership, theories of; networking and network theory; power; principal-agent theory; principalship; theories, use of; transformational leadership; women in educational leadership

Further Readings and References

Harris, A. (2004). Distributed leadership and school improvement: Leading or misleading? *Educational Management Administration & Leadership, 32*(1), 11–24.

Huber, S. (2004). *Preparing school leaders for the 21st century.* New York: Routledge.

Kochan, F., & Reed, C. (2005). Collaborative leadership, community building, and democracy in public education. In F. English (Ed.), *The SAGE handbook of educational leadership* (pp. 68–84). Thousand Oaks, CA: Sage.

National Association of Secondary School Principals. (2004). *Breaking ranks II: Strategies for leading high school reform.* Reston, VA: Author.

Spillane, J. (2004). *Distributed leadership: What's all the hoopla?* Evanston, IL: Institute for Policy Research, Northwestern University.

Spillane, J. (2005). Distributed leadership. *Educational Forum, 69*(2), 143–150.

LEADERSHIP, NATIONAL STANDARDS

Professional standards in educational leadership are established to seek consensus among scholars and practicing administrators about a common body of knowledge, set of competencies, skills, dispositions, and language to ensure quality in the professional preparation and development of school leaders. University scholars in educational administration and leaders in professional school administrator associations apply standards to direct their members to master a common knowledge base to ensure competent professionals. In addition, professional standards serve as benchmarks to add value to the accreditation of graduate programs and licensure of principals and system administrators. Licensure and entry into the profession are granted based on candidates' successful completion of the program and on their passing an examination closely aligned to standards of content and best practice. Stronger links among standards, accreditation, and licensure help ensure greater academic rigor and the quality of program graduates.

National standards in educational leadership are a relatively new development. Minimal curriculum guidelines for the preparation of school administrators

emerged in the early 1950s from the National Council for the Accreditation of Teacher Education (NCATE), but a quarter century passed before the American Association of School Administrators (AASA) and its Committee on the Advancement of School Administration (CASA) in 1982 produced a generic document on guidelines/standards for the preparation of school administrators. Drafts of the guidelines/standards were distributed for reactions to selected scholars, practicing school administrators, principal associations, and open forums at the National Conference for Professors of Educational Administration (NCPEA) and the American Educational Research Association (AERA). In 1983 the document *Guidelines for the Preparation of School Administrators* became the first widely recognized national effort to bring some consensus to the knowledge base and a common set of competencies, skills, and dispositions needed to become a competent school administrator at the building or system level. Thus, beginning in 1982, the following seven AASA competency and skill areas became benchmarks for standards later developed by several state departments of education, university preparation programs, and professional administrator associations and societies.

1. Designing, implementing, and evaluating a school climate/culture improvement program that utilizes mutual staff and student efforts to formulate and attain school goals (eight related mastery indicators)

2. Understanding political theory and applying political skills in building local, state, and national support for education (seven related mastery indicators)

3. Designing a systematic school curriculum that ensures both extensive cultural enrichment activities and mastery of fundamental as well as progressively more complex skills required in advanced problem solving, creative and technological activities (six related mastery indicators)

4. Planning and implementing an instructional management system that includes learning objectives, curriculum design, and instructional strategies and techniques that facilitate high levels of achievement (seven related mastery indicators)

5. Designing staff development and evaluation systems to enhance effectiveness of education personnel (five related mastery indicators)

6. Allocating human, material, and financial resources to efficiently and accountably ensure successful student learning (six related mastery indicators)

7. Conducting research and utilizing research findings in decisions to improve long-range planning, school operations, and student learning (four related mastery indicators)

After each of the seven AASA competencies/ standards, lists of specific skills to validate mastery of each standard are included. Additional standards, skills, and dispositions in the area of leadership ethics were added in the 1993 AASA standards and in the 1996 ISLLC Standards. In addition, emphases were placed on the technical core of teaching and learning and social justice for all students

Numerous studies of the competencies and skills in the guidelines were conducted to determine the validity and relevance of the seven competencies and related skills in the preparation and professional development of principals and central office administrators. The 1985 AASA book *Skills for Successful School Leaders,* by John Hoyle, Fenwick English, and Betty Steffy, compiled a knowledge/theory base for each of the seven guidelines/standards. The book—and subsequent editions in 1990, 1994, and 1998—explored the historical and theoretical foundations of educational administration, the standards, related competencies and skills for goal accomplishment, research and theoretical rationale for each standard and competency, the management system strategies, content domains, and a mastery check for each standard and related skill after each chapter to assist the student and professor engage in professional development and renewal activities.

Subsequent efforts to create professional standards by other administrator and professor associations and chief state school officers (CSSO) rest on the research base of the AASA *Guidelines for the Preparation of School Administrators: Performance-Based Preparation of Principals* was created by the National Association of Secondary School Principals (NASSP) after the AASA guidelines in 1985; *Principals for the Twenty-First Century* by the National Association of Elementary School Principals (NAESP) in 1990; *School Leadership: A Preface for Action* by the American Association of Colleges for Teacher Education (AACTE) in 1988; *Principals for Our Changing Schools* by the National Policy Board for Educational Administration (NPBEA) in 1993; *Professional Standards for the Superintendency* by AASA in 1993; the *Interstate School Leaders Licensure Consortium Standards for School Leaders* (ISLLC) by

the Council for Chief State School Officers (CCSSO) in 1996; and *Standards for Advanced Programs in Educational Leadership* by the National Council for the Accreditation of Colleges of Education (NCATE) in 2002. These NCATE standards are based on a combination of earlier *Curriculum Guidelines for School Administrators,* ISLLC Standards for building principals, and the *AASA Professional Standards for the Superintendency.* The ISLLC Standards are widely recognized and controversial. Martha McCarthy found that 40 states have adopted the ISLLC Standards and require individuals to pay a substantial fee to take the Educational Testing System (ETS) school leaders exam as a prerequisite to reward or deny initial administrative licensure. In addition, a National Policy Board advisory group advising the Educational Leadership Constituent Council (ELCC) responsible for preparing the 2002 *Standards for Advanced Programs in Educational Leadership* for NCATE concluded that the ISLLC Standards were limited in their scope, their skill, and the knowledge base for system administrators. Thus, components of the AASA and the earlier NCATE standards were included. Areas strengthened were school and district governance, policy development, political strategies, strategic visioning and long-range planning, school finance and financial management, district personnel processes and legalities, education law at state and national levels, and school facilities.

Researchers John Hoyle, Lars Bjork, Virginia Collier, and Tom Glass analyzed the limited research and theory base absent in the ISLLC/NCATE Standards for school administration. These and other writers claim that since the early AASA guidelines/ standards, minimal research has appeared to verify later iterations. Fenwick English has asserted that standards need to be more than popular; they need to be independently validated as true. Thus far, few validation studies have occurred other than those of the AASA guidelines listed above except more recent research to validate the AASA Professional Standards for the Superintendency by Linda Horler and Robert Wells and the ISLLC Standards by Cheryl McFadden, Darlene Mobley, James Burnham, Randy Joyner, and Henry Peel. Efforts are under way, moreover, to seek predictive evidence that NCATE preparation programs using national standards are superior to alternative and/ or unaccredited programs in preparing superior practicing school leaders.

Disagreements continue among scholars about the value of standards and their link to NCATE accreditation.

While professional administrator associations and state departments of education find standards useful in guarding licensure for principals and superintendents, members of the University Council for Educational Administration and the National Council of Professors of Educational Administration find the accreditation and program approval by the Educational Leadership Constituency Council (ELCC/NCATE) problematic. The strong emphases toward on-the-job performance and assessment and less emphasis on evidence of rigorous scholarship, theory development, and course content is viewed as quasivocational training by many university researchers. Scholars find this bias of ELCC/NCATE toward outcomes/success on the job at the expense of input measures and intellectual reflection valued in the scholarly community as troubling. According to Art Wise, executive director of NCATE, the institution under review must provide data related to the following leadership/outcome questions.

- Have candidates mastered the necessary knowledge for the job they will perform?
- Do candidates meet the state licensure requirement?
- Do candidates understand teaching and learning, and can they fulfill their responsibilities?
- Can candidates apply their knowledge in schools/ districts?
- Can candidates promote student learning in their schools/ districts?

While these questions are central to successful practice at the building and central office levels, they also assume that if graduates fail in any of these performance areas after 1 or 10 years in the field, then the graduate's advanced programs could be labeled inadequate and the institution given low marks for preparation. The ELCC has assumed the role of watchdog by serving as the program review body for NCATE institutions and for listing names of programs denied accreditation on their Web site as a warning to others. Because NCATE regulates only the certification arm of graduate programs, the 188 doctoral programs in NCATE institutions are not the focus of the program review process. Herein lies the dilemma: since some doctoral degree programs in colleges of education are in counseling, human development, higher education, and educational psychology and not subject to the NCATE process, a college can lose its accreditation due to program reviews linked to K–12 educator preparation and thus mar the image of the other programs in colleges of education. This issue and the time

commitment required by faculty and staff to prepare an NCATE report are listed as reasons that many colleges of education located in both prestigious and lesser known universities avoid the NCATE accreditation ordeal. This avoidance, according to James Cibulka, is harmful to the education profession. He speculates that the same avoidance strategy characterizes a high percentage of educational administration programs operating outside accreditation. While these include some online programs and deregulated alternative certification programs offered by state departments of education or other quasieducation agencies, there are also some top-rated educational leadership programs that are not NCATE accredited. At the same time, in spite of their generic limitations to apply to both campus and central office administrators, ISLLC and the new NCATE Standards have generated greater efforts to align curriculum with the standards central to the licensure examination—School Leaders Licensure Exam. This is similar to the reforms that occurred after the AASA guidelines in the 1980s. The current state of finding consensus about which standards to use and how to teach and measure them remains an unsolved puzzle that will not soon become a clear unified picture.

As difficult as assessing administrative performance is, it must be done if standards-based performance is to have any relevance in preparing and assessing daily performance of principals and central office administrators. Limited research points to the benefits of preparing and assessing school leaders by using the standards set forth by AASA, ISSLC, NCATE, and ELCC. These standards are grounded in 20 years of research and best practice about the roles of building and system administrators and the critical academic preparation for their roles. Professional associations and NCATE are calling for more measures of program outcome effectiveness to help ensure the success of school administrators once they are on the job. Greater links between national standards for the preparation and licensure of school and their actual job performance is an unending quest. Research is under way by scholars in UCEA and NCPEA to investigate relationships between the NCATE standards for campus and central office administrators and their on-the-job performance. In addition, research is needed to investigate relationships between the ISSLC Standards and successful practice in school leadership positions. Will researchers find positive relationships between scores on required ISSLC exams and NCATE accreditation ratings and successful practice? Standards are only as useful as those who apply and improve their relevance to quality performance. Also, there is a tendency in any profession to hold on to standards when they become overinstitutionalized. That is, when research and best practice reveal that standards are no longer guiding school administrator preparation to higher performance, standards need to be changed.

At this time, there is little clear evidence that the NCATE/ELCC or the AASA Professional Standards for the Superintendency will result in outstanding success by school administrators. It is striking, however, that iterations of the seven guidelines/standards created by AASA in 1983 are found in all graduate programs in educational administration. If a student masters all of the NCATE/ELCC/ISLLC/AASA Standards, will the student be guaranteed success? This belief is not realistic for the following reasons:

- It is possible to acquire an adequate level of performance in almost every standard and related skills, though few administrative roles require the same level of expertise in all of them.
- Educational administration/leadership is not static, but interactive and dynamic. Simply mastering each standard and skill ignores the reality of the entire job.
- The knowledge base is constantly being expanded, challenged, and refined.

Thus, national standards in educational leadership serve as a compass to lead university preparation programs to greater scholarship to produce the best and brightest for administrative positions in America's schools. Professionalism depends on the creativity and capacity of individuals and institutions to capitalize on new insights in the scholarship and practice to insure that all children succeed in school. Since uniform standards rigidly applied may impair the flexibility that administrator preparation programs need to meet local or regional needs, standards should be flexible, subject to change and not be used as a threat by national agencies to limit program development or the expertise of faculty or practicing school leaders. Professional standards in educational leadership have become avenues toward consensus among university scholars, professional school administrator associations and practicing building and system administrators to assure quality in the professional preparation and development of school leaders.

—John R. Hoyle

See also American Association of School Administrators; Council of Chief State School Officers; Education Commission of the States; expert power; Interstate School Leaders Licensure Consortium; National Association of Elementary School Principals; National Association of Secondary School Principals; National Council for the Accreditation of Teacher Education; politics, of education; principalship; school improvement models; schools of education; standard setting; universities, preparation of educational leaders in

Further Readings and References

Cibulka, J. (2004). The case for academic standards in educational administration: Toward a mature profession. *UCEA Review, 46*(2), 1–5.

English, F. (2003). Tsar khorosh, boyary polkhi: The ISLLC Standards and the enshrinement of mystical authoritarianism as anti-change doctrine in educational leadership preparation programs. In F. Lunenburg & C. Carr (Eds.), *Shaping the future: Policy, partnerships, and emerging practices* (pp. 112–133). Lanham, MD: Scarecrow Education.

English, F. (2004). Undoing the "done deal": Reductionism, ahistoricity, and pseudo-science in the knowledge base and standards for educational administration. *UCEA Review, 46,* 5–7.

Hoyle, J. (2001). I've got standards, you got standards, all God's children got standards. *AASA Professor, 24*(2), 27–32.

Hoyle, J. (2002). *Superintendents for Texas school districts: Solving the crisis in executive leadership.* Fort Worth, TX: Sid W. Richardson Foundation.

Hoyle, J., Bjork, L., Collier, V., & Glass, T. (2005). *The superintendent as CEO: Standards-based performance.* Thousand Oaks, CA: Corwin Press.

McFadden, C., Mobley, D., Burnham, J., Joyner, R., & Peel, H. (2003). Are national ISLLC Standards important to job performance? An eastern North Carolina perspective. In R. Lunenburg & C. Carr (Eds.), *Shaping the future: Policy, partnerships and emerging perspectives* (pp. 389–400). Lanham, MA: Scarecrow Press.

Murphy, J. (2005). Unpacking the foundations of ISLLC Standards and addressing the concerns in the academic community. *Educational Administration Quarterly, 41*(1), 154–191.

National Council for the Accreditation of Colleges of Teacher Education. (1996). *Curriculum guidelines.* Washington, DC: Author.

National Council for the Accreditation of Teacher Education. (2002). *Standards for advanced programs in educational leadership.* Washington, DC: Author.

Wells, R. (2004). *Perceptions of first-year superintendents in Texas of the importance of the professional standards for superintendents.* Unpublished doctoral dissertation, Texas A&M University, College Station.

Young, M., & Lopez, G. (2005). The nature of inquiry in educational leadership. In F. English (Ed.), *The SAGE handbook of educational leadership* (pp. 337–361). Thousand Oaks, CA: Sage.

🏛 LEADERSHIP, PARTICIPATORY

Participatory leadership is defined in terms of the degree of subordinate participation in the decision-making process. Rather than make arbitrary decisions, the participative leader seeks to involve other people in the process. The amount of subordinate participation varies depending on the manager's preferences and beliefs.

Participatory leaders provide direction, information, resources, and group facilitation. Proponents of this leadership style place emphasis on concern for people (relationship) over structuring the organizations. Collaborative leaders seek input from those affected by the decision while working actively with individuals and groups in making the decisions. They keep an open mind and are willing to adjust predetermined positions.

Participative leadership is about empowerment and power sharing. Gary Yukl pointed out that it is most often linked with the decision-making process that takes four main forms: (1) autocratic decisions in which managers make the decision on their own, (2) consultation of others for opinions and ideas with the manager making the final decision, (3) joint decisions where the manager and subordinates make the decision together, and (4) delegation in which the manager gives authority and responsibility for the decision to an individual or group.

For followers, participation is both mental and emotional involvement that leads to commitment and shared responsibility for group goals. R. G. Owens emphasizes that democratic consent, decision making by voting that creates winners and losers, is different than collaboration. Decision making by voting does not provide either incentives or opportunities to fully engage in addressing complex problems. However, participatory decision making does not mean everyone is involved in all decisions. Edwin Bridges suggested two rules to determine when teachers participate in decision-making. The first rule is the test of relevance. Relevance is when teachers have a personal stake in the decision. It involves issues such as discipline, curriculum, and teaching methods. The second rule is the test of expertise. Teachers need to be able to contribute effectively to the decision-making process. An example of not having the expertise would be involving science teachers in developing the English curriculum.

School leaders work in a dynamic environment that invites quick decision making. However, leadership is working with and through others to achieve organizational goals. Participatory leadership is a collaborative effort to achieve shared goals. Participatory leaders understand the importance of involving those affected by the decisions and when to involve others in the decision-making process. Effective involvement includes having those who are expected to implement the changes fully participate in the decision-making process.

Models of collaborative group decision making can be helpful. They are a starting point for potential improvement. An important decision for all groups to make is how it will make decisions. It is necessary for organizations to develop and make known the decision-making process to be used and to decide if it is acceptable to the participants. Equal and collaborative partnerships working toward a shared vision attain performance goals.

V. H. Vroom and P. W. Yetton's normative decision model demonstrates the importance of using the right model for the right situation. Leaders look at decision quality, decision acceptance by the followers, and time needed to make decisions. This model helps determine the amount of input followers should have based on a given situation through a set of sequential rules. The leader then behaves in the most proficient manner. Yukl states that the effectiveness of this model depends on several factors: the relevant information that the leader and subordinates have, how likely the followers will accept an autocratic decision, if the subordinates will participate if given an opportunity, the extent of conflict among followers regarding alternative solutions, and if the problem is unstructured and requires creative problem solving.

Peter Drucker provides an example of a rational decision-making model that assists in systematically solving problems: (a) classify the problem, (b) define the problem, (c) specify the conditions for the problem solution, (d) decide on the best action, (e) compromise, (f) implement the decision, and (g) review the effectiveness of the decision. Implicit in rational decision-making models are the assumptions of full disclosure of information and that there is one best possible solution.

Shared decision making (SDM) is a process of making educational decisions in a collaborative manner at the school level and provides the opportunity for school professionals, parents, community members, and students to collaborate in setting goals and promoting increased student achievement and teacher effectiveness. However, there is little evidence that SDM improves either teacher performance or student achievement.

T. J. Kowalski cited several presumed advantages of shared decision making: (a) participation increases subordinates' motivation, productivity and commitment, (b) subordinates are less competitive when working on shared goals, (c) the range of knowledge and skills increases with more people involved and better decisions are the result, and (d) increased communication and knowledge within and among the organization's members.

Some disadvantages of participative decision making are (a) it requires more time of leader and subordinates, (b) the group might make a mediocre decision in favor of group unity, (c) the group may be dominated by one or two members, and (d) the groups are not exempt from making the same errors in decision making as an individual might make. Another disadvantage is the lack of training for both teachers and administrators in group process skills.

The literature is clear: principals are critical to the development of school priorities, culture, and resources. Principals are currently trained to function as results-oriented leaders in hierarchical school systems. In 1999, Janet Chrispeels and colleagues called attention to the paradox between principal training and the school restructuring initiatives requiring collaborative or participatory leadership. The decision-making practices of organizations are reflections of the beliefs of those in authority. The increasing complexity and demands on school principals makes participatory leadership a good strategy for both individuals and the organizations.

—*Darlene Y. Bruner*

See also accountability; administration, theories of; boundaries of systems; capacity building, of organizations; collaboration theory; conceptual systems theory and leadership; conflict management; governance; involvement, in organizations; management theories; morale; motivation, theories of; personnel management; power; professional learning communities; role ambiguity; role conflict; Theory X, Theory Y; values of organizations and leadership; working conditions, in schools

Further Readings and References

Bridges, E. (1967). A model for shared decision making in the school principalship. *Educational Administration Quarterly, 3*(1).
Chrispeels, J., Strait, C., & Brown, J. (1999). The paradox of collaboration. *Thrust for Educational Leadership, 29*(2), 16–19.
Drucker, P. (2002). *The effective executive.* New York: HarperCollins.
Kowalski, T. J. (2003). *Contemporary school administration: An introduction.* Boston: Allyn & Bacon.
Owens, R. G. (2004). *Organizational behavior in education: Adaptive leadership and school reform.* Boston: Allyn & Bacon.
Vroom, V. H., & Yetton, P. W. (1973). *Leadership in decision-making.* Pittsburgh, PA: University of Pittsburgh Press.
Yukl, G. (2002). *Leadership in organizations* (5th ed., pp. 122–148). Upper Saddle River, NJ: Prentice Hall.

LEADERSHIP, SITUATIONAL

Situational leadership has its roots in the Ohio State Leadership Studies that were based on surveys of leaders and subordinates that focused on two elements of leadership: (1) *consideration* or relationship behavior of leaders toward their subordinates, and (2) *initiating structure* or task behavior of leaders and how their roles are defined and structured.

Situational leadership suggests that leaders demonstrate flexibility in determining and using an appropriate leadership style to fit their followers' needs and their work situations. This is done by making conscious choices between directive and supportive behaviors to achieve desired outcomes. The style a leader uses with individuals or groups depends on the readiness or maturity level of the people they are attempting to influence. The maturity level is determined by the person's motivation to set and reach high attainable goals and their willingness to be responsible for the success of group goals and performance. Maturity is decided on in relation to specific tasks and may vary from task to task.

Paul Hersey and Kenneth Blanchard's situational leadership model is based on a relationship between (a) the extent of guidance and direction (task behavior) a leader gives in one-way communication when explaining what each follower is to do and when, where, and how tasks are to be accomplished, (b) the amount of guidance and emotional support (relationship behavior) a leader provides in two-way communication in providing emotional support and facilitating behaviors, and (c) the readiness or maturity level that followers exhibit in performing a specific task, function, or objective.

When people need to be told specifically what and how to do a task and need constant feedback about their assigned tasks, the situational leader functions in the first stage as *directing* with high-task, low-relationship leadership behaviors. At the second level, people need to be sold on an idea, and then they are able to complete the tasks required without close direction. This stage needs *coaching* with high-task, high-support leadership behaviors with two-way communications and emotional support. The third stage, in Hersey and Blanchard's model, is *supporting* and has low-task, high-relationship leadership behaviors. People at this stage have the motivation, ability, and knowledge to complete the task and share in the decision-making process with the leader. The fourth stage involves low-task, low-relationship leadership behaviors. At the *delegating* level, people need only to be given a sense of the leader expectations, since they are willing, able, and motivated to take responsibility for completing the task successfully.

Yukl's criticisms of situational leadership theory stem from the lack of consistently defined leadership behaviors and an unclear description of the relationship between leader behavior and follower performance. Another shortcoming is the narrow focus on the subordinate's maturity level as the situational variable. Notwithstanding the criticisms, situational leadership has made positive contributions. The emphasis on flexible leader behaviors and the different treatment of individuals in varying situations helps in our understanding of effective leadership and provides opportunities for leaders to assist followers to grow in maturity.

—*Darlene Y. Bruner*

See also accountability; bureaucracy; contingency theories; creativity, in management; goals, goal setting; management theories; organizations, types of, typologies; path-goal leadership theory; transactional analysis

Further Readings and References

Hersey, P. (1985). *The situational leader.* New York: Warner Books.

Hersey, P., Blanchard, K., & Johnson, D. E. (2001). *Management of organizational behavior: Leading human resources* (8th ed.). Upper Saddle River, NJ: Prentice Hall.

Sheilds, C., & Sayani, A. (2005). Leading in the midst of diversity: The challenge of our times. In F. English (Ed.), *The SAGE handbook of educational leadership* (pp. 380–402). Thousand Oaks, CA: Sage.

Yukl, G. (2002). *Leadership in organizations* (5th ed., pp. 270–272). Upper Saddle River, NJ: Prentice Hall.

🏛 LEADERSHIP, SOCIAL DIMENSIONS OF

This entry constitutes a fairly macroscopic inquiry into the supporting phenomena that continue to make leadership one of the most compelling topics of more than two millennia of Western history, from our Greek origins to today. At least since then, we in the West have continued a passionate love/hate affair with leadership that dominates, constructs, and fashions our thinking and actions.

Undeniably, the behavior of leaders takes place in a social context. This focuses upon the dimensions of this social context. We first deal with the structure of organizations, including positions, roles and role expectations, the conflict generated by conflicting role expectations, and hierarchy and authority as components of structure. Next, we deal with social systems, the norms and subcultures generated by the organization and its social systems, and the concept of climate. The impact of such factors as race, gender, ethnicity, age, and social class stratification is analyzed, as will compelling images or metaphors of organizations upon our thinking.

Next, we look at cyclical organizational behavior and the style of leadership generated by each phase of the cycle, followed by various perceptions of leadership as social process, as social function, and as a behavior system. Next is a brief pass at divergent leadership theories, including new movements, such as transformative and constructivist leadership, followed by the role of authority, power, influence, and empowerment. Last are a summary and some conclusions.

ORGANIZATIONS ARE SOCIALLY CONSTRUCTED REALITIES, WHICH CREATE STRUCTURE: POSITIONS AND ROLES—THE BUILDING BLOCKS

The process of forming an organization—any organization—generates positions, which sociologists also call statuses. Positions comprise the structure of organizations. When a Wal-Mart store opens, it has managers, clerks, custodians, and customers. When a school opens, it starts with a principal, perhaps an assistant principal or two (depending upon size), an office manager, clerks, teachers, often department heads if a secondary school, students, cafeteria personnel, and a head custodian. We develop different expectations for the

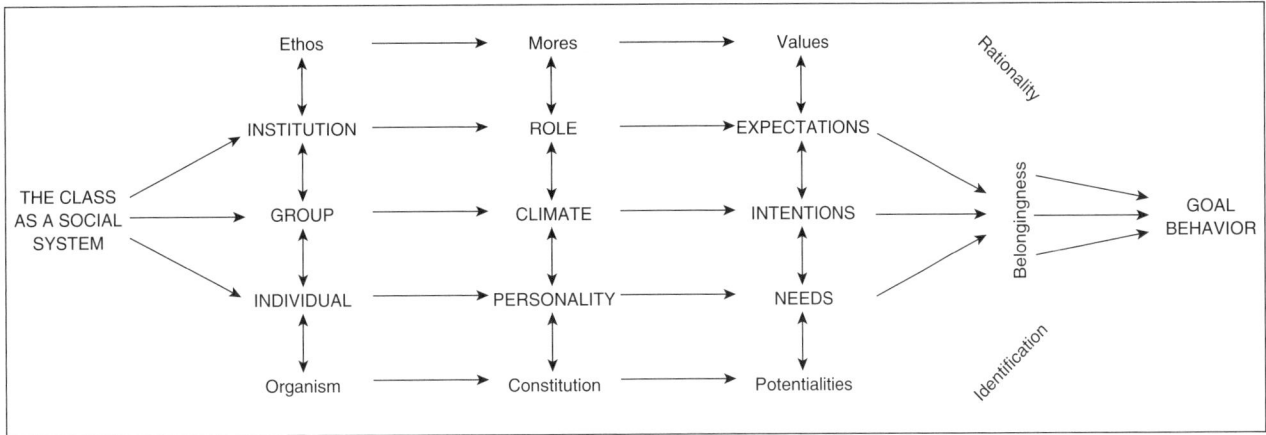

Figure 1   The Class as a Social System

SOURCE: Getzels, J. W., & Thelen, H. A. (1960). The classroom group as a social system. In N. B. Henry (Ed.). *The dynamics of instructional groups: Sociopsychological aspects of teaching and learning.* N.S.S.E. Yearbook (vol. 59, pt. 2, p. 80). Chicago: National Society for the Study of Education. Reprinted with permission.

people occupying each position, constituting their roles, which consist of clusters of expectations for any position. Obviously, expectations may differ, so that one can be a passive, laissez faire principal, an aggressive change agent, or a bureaucrat, among various interpretations of one's role.

How a person acts out a position becomes his or her role, depending upon the actor's interpretation of the bundles of expectations surrounding the role. Thus, a role is a dynamic enactment, one's interpretation of the expectations surrounding one's position. Often, clusters of expectations can be divergent for a role, which can cause conflict both for the person occupying the role and for those who may have different expectations for the role occupant. Indeed, each group (groups may also be considered social systems) may have a range of expectations for a role, some of which may be in conflict, thus causing role conflict within the group. And different social systems may develop conflicting expectations for a role.

Benne and Sheats approached roles by breaking them into role functions based on three levels of behavior: the first focused on achieving tasks, the second on maintaining the group or organization, the third termed idiosyncratic, need-meeting behavior. Illustrations of the first include initiating activity, summarizing, evaluating. The second includes encouraging, gate keeping, and consensus testing, and the last covers blocking behavior, aggressive actions, recognition seeking, and the like.

PEOPLE IN ORGANIZATIONS DEVELOP GROUPS (SOCIAL SYSTEMS)—THE BASIC STRUCTURE OF ALL ORGANIZATIONS

As people interact in organizations, inevitably they develop social systems or subgroups. A social system can be defined as two or more people interacting meaningfully. To diagnose social systems is to watch who relates to whom and who works with whom; in families, who allies with whom. The number of social systems in our organizations is immense. A group of 5 people totals 22. A faculty of 20 or 25 literally generates hundreds.

The model developed by E. G. Guba and J. W. Getzels, and later modified, clarifies expectations, sometimes divergent, both within and among social systems. Getzels and Guba pointed to two dimensions, the nomothetic and the idiographic, in understanding organizations and social systems. The nomothetic consists of the institution's developing certain roles, which in turn have clusters of expectations attached to them that are intended to achieve the goals of the organization. The idiographic consists of the individual's personality need dispositions. The authors noted that knowing role expectations and need dispositions is essential in understanding the behavior of role incumbents in an institution and that social behavior is a result of an individual attempting to cope with behavioral expectations consistent with his or her needs (see Figure 1).

Next, the model predicts several sources for conflict. The first is conflict within roles; the second focuses on conflict among roles a person may face. The model helps explain and predict the potential for conflict caused by facing differing expectations both within a social system and among several relevant social systems.

HIERARCHY, AUTHORITY

As people in organizations develop different positions, they place them in hierarchical order, one being more highly valued than another, as can readily be seen in virtually all organizations. In schools, principals are granted more prestige and authority than clerks, teachers more than students. Recently, organizational designers have flattened out the hierarchy with such devices as schools-within-schools.

PEOPLE IN ORGANIZATIONS SLOWLY DEVELOP NORMS (CUSTOMS, BELIEFS) THAT BECOME A CULTURE

Norms comprise customs, practices that all people and social systems develop as they interact. And as they interact, they develop shared expectations, feelings, attitudes, beliefs, and customs. In short, they develop a culture of shared patterns of expectations for behaving that everyone in a culture learns. Americans drive on the right, the English drive on the left, which confuses Americans in London. Culture can be defined as commonly accepted and expected shared ideas, attitudes, values, customs, and habits concerning social living that everyone in the culture learns.

Traveling to a different country informs us of our adherence to norms taken for granted, such as the English serving tomatoes with half-cooked bacon at breakfast contrasting with American models. Rural Mexicans do not have different breakfast food, morning meals being the same as other meals.

In organizations, we develop our own subcultures and our own norms. Those of the U.S. Marine Corps differ from those of a kindergarten (no cookies and milk at 10 AM and no afternoon naps for Marines). School-based people often consider their central office out of touch with their realities. Therefore, supervisors who make sure to be based in a school and attend faculty meetings regularly tend to be accepted, while those based centrally often are treated as visitors, as the Other. Those in leadership positions who fail to spend time grasping norms and subcultures of organizations into which they enter often create

considerable hardship for themselves, as well as for the other denizens. Sometimes ignoring such a basic norm has resulted in spectacular career flameouts.

ORGANIZATIONAL CULTURE AND CLIMATE

Culture and climate are different. Culture, which develops over time, is revealed, much like the iceberg, by customs and norms and by artifacts such as buildings, art, technology, and by values, attitudes, assumptions, and beliefs expressed in patterns of behavior, speech, and language. Climate focuses on determining perceptions of teachers in schools. Studies of climate provide tools to diagnose and to analyze perceptions regarding how the organization is functioning, developing a considerably more detailed insight into a host of phenomena. These include perceptions of such factors as leadership and group behavior, many of which impact people's satisfaction. Subsequently, other instruments have been developed to assess climate, such as the Organizational Climate Index (OCI).

In considering the social dimensions of leadership, such factors as race, gender, ethnicity, age, and social class stratification comprise major factors for those in leadership positions to be aware of in most areas in the West. In debating over whom to ask to serve on a committee, perceptions of the above factors must be taken into account, unless one wants the project to fail.

IMAGES/METAPHORS OF ORGANIZATIONS

Metaphors and images are so common in everyday use that we become unaware of their impact on our thinking and behavior. Treating the organization as a machine is readily displayed in Wal-Mart's and the fast-food industry's use of Frederick Taylor's principles that workers should be cheap, easy to train and supervise, easy to replace and to standardize. This makes workers (read, teachers) readily replaceable.

Other metaphors include the organization as

- An organism
- A culture
- A political system
- A self-learning system—a learning organization
- A family
- Involved in change
- An instrument of domination or a psychic prison
- A social sorting mechanism
- A refuge

Manifestly, utilizing each of these metaphors produces distinctly different behaviors as one operates within and outside the organization.

Henry Mintzberg's logo provides intriguing insights into the functioning of organizations (see Figure 2).

The strategic apex comprises those running the organization, with middle management considered the middle line. The operating core are the workers (read, teachers), while the technostructure consists of computer experts and other analysts. The support staff includes office workers and custodians. Calling these "pulls," Mintzberg's analysis explains a great deal of the dynamics of the pulling and hauling in many organizations, as each component tries to maximize its control and influence.

Clearly, the strategic apex wants to control decision making, pulling to *centralize.* The middle line wants to control their destinies to maximize their autonomy in decision making, driving to *Balkanize.* The operating core wants to control its destiny, pulling to *professionalize.* For decades, nurses and teachers have emphasized their professional roles.

The technostructure's goal is to *standardize* work processes, thus exercising some control. To gain influence, support staff push to *collaborate.* With this model of organization pulls, we can predict these social systems' behavior.

IMPACT OF THE SOCIAL FUNCTIONS OF SCHOOLS ON LEADERSHIP

Hidden by their diffuseness, the social functions of schooling impact leadership behavior usually without our being aware of their influence. For example, schools function as social sorting mechanisms, classifying kids according to their socioeconomic status. Thus, assistant principals dealing with discipline generally handle more minorities and tend to expel them in higher percentages than higher socioeconomic levels. Schools tend to display a warehousing function, keeping youth off the streets, by filling time. Study halls illustrate this function.

Schools also socialize kids and adults by inculcating people into the myriad symbols of the culture, its norms, expectations, myths, and practices. School is where kids learn to be kindergartners and later, adolescents. Recently, politicians have climbed aboard the train of the value of failure to enhance the worth of the diploma by eschewing social promotion, thereby increasing dropout proportions. Principals often buy into these functions without becoming fully aware of their impact.

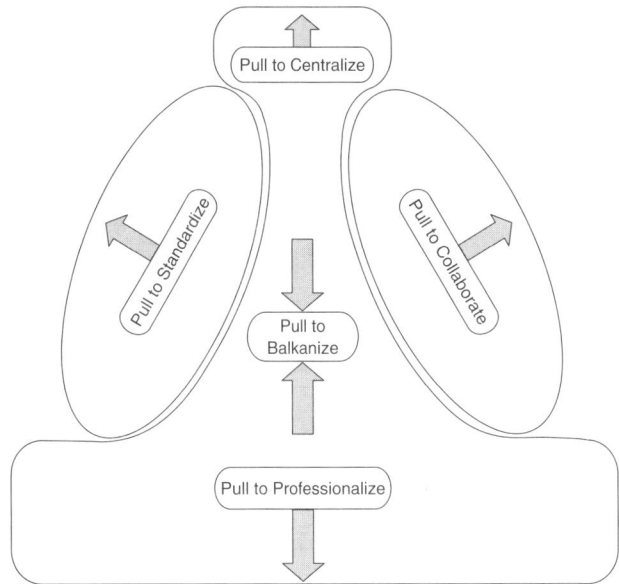

Figure 2   Five Pulls on the Organization

SOURCE: Mintzberg, H. (1979). *The structuring of organizations*, 1st edition (p. 20). Reprinted with the permission of Pearson Education, Inc., Saddle River, NJ.

CYCLICAL ORGANIZATIONAL BEHAVIOR

Do organizations display cycles in their careers? The tri-partite theory of organizational succession and change asserts that cycles occur and, in the process, impact leadership selection fundamentally, but generally over relatively long periods of time, thus escaping attention. (See Figure 3.)

The Charismatic Leader: The Person-Oriented Phase of the Organization's Career

The cycle becomes manifest when an organization, which seems to be living in the past, may become so out of sync with its purpose and environment that the strategic apex, or the board of the strategic apex (if it is that body that becomes so dysfunctional) decides something must be done to prevent disaster. Almost invariably, they select a dynamic person, a charismatic leader, to break the organization out of its doldrums. Such a charismatic leader energizes people, attracts followers, becoming the most creative, dynamic phase. In this person-oriented phase, many initiatives become developed and implemented, often uncoordinated, that excite people. The future is wide open.

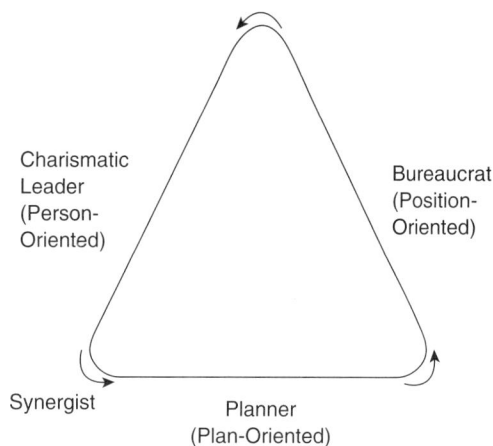

Figure 3   Phases of Organizational Change: Tri-Partite Theory

SOURCE: Shapiro, A. (2000). *Leadership for constructivist schools* (p. 79). Lanham, MD: Scarecrow Press. Reprinted with permission.

Examples include John F. Kennedy, Mahatma Gandhi, Indira Gandhi, John Dewey, Bill Clinton, Martin Luther King Jr., and Al Shanker.

The Planner and Plan-Orientation: The Planning Phase

After some time, usually short, the leader may become attracted to another position, or may be blown out. The leader's supporters, anxious to retain some initiatives, try to incorporate these into a plan, and look to recruit a planner to lead into the next phase, Planning. Planners can focus on a simple plan (block scheduling, uniforms, two teachers teaming) to complex, synergistic, multiyear plans (a middle school, continuous progress, a constructivist school with learning communities). Some planners often operate below the radar and so are more difficult to identify. Gen. Omar Bradley, Donald Trump, Sen. Hillary Rodham Clinton, Lee Iacocca, and Dale Parnell (the founder of the Tech-Prep movement) come to mind.

The plan guides thinking and resources, leading many to become loyal to it. However, the planning phase follows an inevitable, fixed, and fateful template. As time goes on, the bit-by-bit, day-to-day incremental nature of decision making by administrators focused on the immediate and crises tends to drift slowly away from holding the plan aloft as the decision-making prism. The cogency and force of the plan fades, and as new people enter, their loyalty is less than that of the pioneers. After 2 or 3 years, the plan becomes more honored in the breach. To achieve the plan, people develop red tape, rules, and regulations, which begin to rule the organization's life. After 5 years, the plan has slid out of consciousness, except by old-timers reminiscing about the good old days. Slowly priorities change, the planner often leaves to more hospitable shores, and the organization begins to drift. It has moved into the next phase.

The Bureaucrat: The Position-Oriented Phase

By this time the planner has been succeeded by the bureaucrat, whose main purpose is to stabilize and usually to increase his or her power and control in an organization dominated by red tape, routine, rules, and regulations. Hope, long stifled, has disappeared; the organization is backward looking, pointing to past glories, rather than looking proactively toward the future. The bureaucrat often is a tinkerer, at worst a stabilizer, often a high Theory X controller. Creative lines of action, even if suggested, are squelched, since with little or no charisma, the loyalty of personnel focuses on the *position* of the leader, not to the leader himself or herself. Examples of bureaucrats include Gerald Ford, George H. W. Bush, and other managers serving as functionaries.

Unfortunately, this phase usually lasts the longest, since the organization can drift for a long time until the people at the top realize again that disaster looms and a charismatic leader is needed.

The Synergist

Once in a blue moon, an organization finds a person who combines charisma and planning, a *synergist*. Gen. Douglas MacArthur, Robert E. Lee, John Dewey, Al Shanker, Robert Maynard Hutchins (the chancellor of the University of Chicago), Franklin Delano Roosevelt, Martin Luther King Jr., and Dale Parnell come to mind. The combination of charisma and planning skill gives an organization considerable power and direction, breaking it out of position orientation more readily. Since synergists are rare, combining a charismatic leader and a planner could be considered as a synergist staffing plan.

Recruiters armed with the tri-partite theory possess an invaluable tool in their armamentarium of theories, models, frames of reference, and concepts by which to improve their and their organization's career.

SOCIAL ASPECTS OF LEADERSHIP: AS SOCIAL PROCESS, SOCIAL FUNCTION, AND AS A BEHAVIOR SYSTEM

Leadership is obviously a social process, inasmuch as leaders function in social systems and in social settings. Leadership must take place in social systems and in social settings. Interactions among people comprise social processes, such as influence, acceptance and rejection, trust, conflict, competition, and cooperation, among others. Thus, as leaders interact with individuals and with social systems, they are engaging in social processes.

The very act of leadership is a social function in a social setting. It comprises a key role in any social system, particularly in formal systems, and often in informal systems, such as families and friendship groups. In virtually all formal social systems, the function of leadership is expected and usually respected. For schools, all states have legislated responsibilities to guide the roles of principals and superintendents. For example, a superintendent must recommend a candidate for a principalship, which the board of education can or cannot approve. In most states, the board cannot act without the superintendent's recommendation. Thus, leadership comprises a social function in the organization.

As for leadership as a system of behavior, we have huge numbers of books peering at the behavior of leaders, recommending various approaches to implement the efficacy of those in leadership roles. Many formulations have entered into pop culture, such as Stephen Covey's *The 7 Habits of Highly Effective People*, a non-research-based text. Clearly, attempts to modify or to improve the behavior of those in leadership positions comprises treating leadership as a behavior system.

DIVERGENT LEADERSHIP THEORIES

Numerous leadership theories have been proposed, often some being fads. The context of this entry prevents dealing with all, other than suggesting that the developing social contexts of our changing society and culture have led to theories reflecting the norms and beliefs of those cultures. It is no accident that Frederick Taylor's scientific management emerged in the early part and the human relations movement

developed in the middle part of the last century. Two theories developing in the last part of the twentieth century and in this century are transformative and constructivist leadership, reflecting contemporary thinking about the purposes of leadership as facilitative and empowering.

AUTHORITY, INFLUENCE, POWER, EMPOWERMENT

Chester I. Barnard contributed to understanding power by noting that it exists only when subordinates *accept* the leader's authority. The subordinate has to perceive the communication as authoritative subjectively, and accepts it. Next, objectively, authority is the characteristic of a communication that causes it to be accepted. Four conditions have to occur for a communication to be authoritative. First, it must be understood by the subordinate. Next, it cannot be inconsistent with the subordinate's perception of the organization's purposes. Third, the communication cannot be inconsistent with the subordinate's purposes. Last, the subordinate has to be able to carry out the communication both mentally and physically.

To this, we can add Max Weber's formulation (see Figure 4), which focused on influence over others' behavior, involuntary and voluntary compliance of others. Involuntary compliance he perceived as being based on power, forced compliance of others. Weber perceived authority and influence as based on voluntary compliance. Authority is willingly obeyed because people recognize that it comes from a legitimate source, and so suspend critical thinking to choose other alternatives. Persuasion was based on influence, thus useful to be charismatic or a referential person.

The last person to cite is Robert W. Bierstedt, a sociologist who dealt with social power. For Bierstedt, organizations are social entities, creating positions and roles, some of which have more and less power. For Bierstedt,

- Power is institutionalized authority.
- Authority rests on the capacity to apply sanctions.
- Sanctions are stored force.

Thus, social power rests on one's capacity to employ force. Power, thus, is a predisposition or a prior capacity to employ force. Power, therefore, is potential; it is stored force. If it fails in its use, you do not have it, the reason why the military is so hesitant to use force.

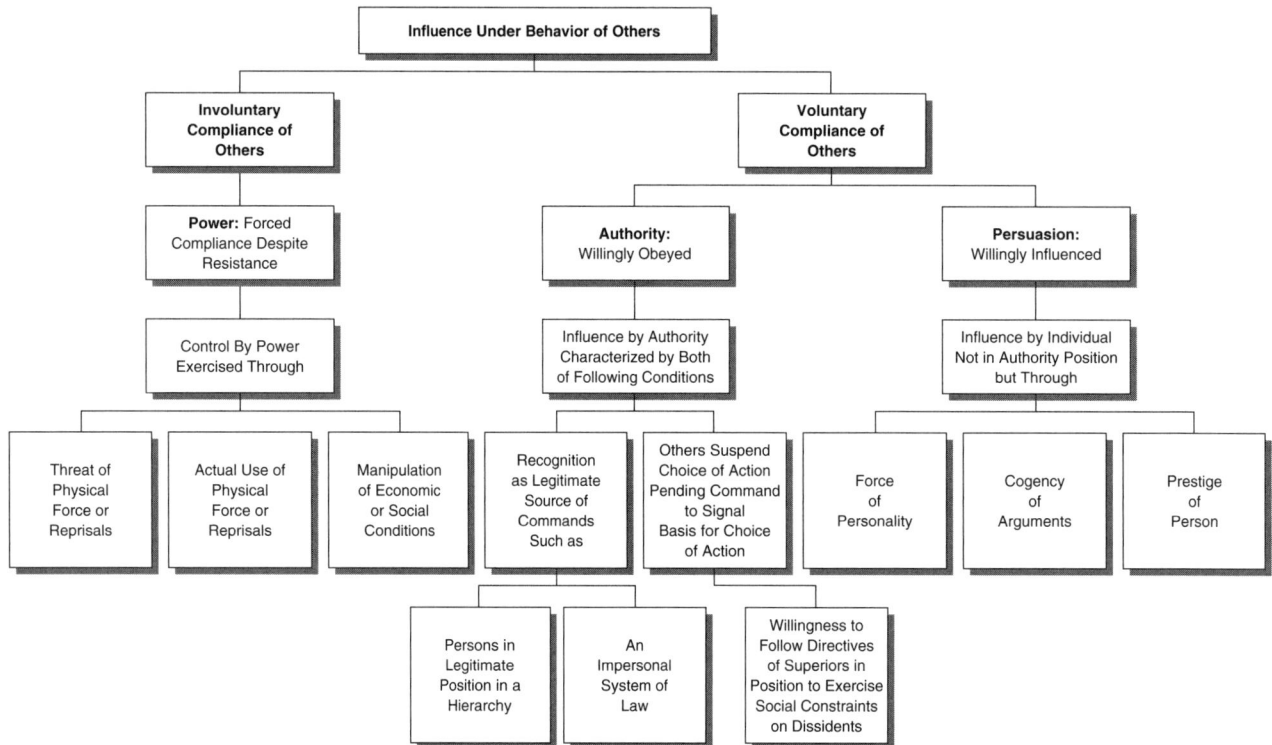

Figure 4   Relations and Difference

SOURCE: Blau, P.M., & Scott, W. R. (1962). *Formal organizations* (pp. 27–32). San Francisco: Chandler Publishing Co. Reprinted with permission.

Empowerment presently is considered a social good, since it enables people to control their own destinies. Many modern leadership theories point to empowerment as essential for the health of organizations and people.

—*Arthur Shapiro*

See also accountability; administration, theories of; axiomatic theory; behaviorism; bureaucracy; compliance theory; conceptual systems theory and leadership; contingency theories; critical theory; decision making; Dewey, John; empowerment; group dynamics; human resource development; King, Martin Luther Jr.; leadership, theories of; leadership effectiveness; management theories; nomothetic/idiographic dimensions; organizational theories; organizations, types of, typologies; rational organizational theory; role theory; social relations, dimensions of; Taylor, Frederick; Theory X, Theory Y; Weber, Max

Further Readings and References

Barnard, C. I. (1938). *The functions of the executive.* Cambridge, MA: Harvard University Press.

Bierstedt, R. W. (1950). An analysis of social power. *American Sociological Review, 15,* 730–738.

Dantley, M. (2005). Moral leadership: Shifting the management paradigm. In F. English (Ed.), *The SAGE handbook of educational leadership* (pp. 34–46). Thousand Oaks, CA: Sage.

English, F. W. (2002). Caveat emptor: A de-constructive reading of the stealth metaphysics of Stephen R. Covey. *Educational Leadership Review, 3*(3), 13–22.

English, F. W. (2003). *The postmodern challenge to the theory and practice of educational administration.* Springfield, IL: Charles C Thomas.

Getzels, J. W., & Guba, E. G. (1957). Social behavior and the administrative process. *School Review, 65,* 423–441.

Getzels, J. W., & Thelen, H. A. (1960). The classroom group as a social system. In N. B. Henry (Ed.), *The dynamics of instructional groups: Sociopsychological aspects of teaching and learning. NSSE Yearbook* (vol. 59, pt. 2, p. 80). Chicago: National Society for the Study of Education.

Gronn, P. (2003). *The new work of educational leaders.* London: Paul Chapman.

Mintzberg, H. (1979). *The structuring of organizations.* Englewood Cliffs, NJ: Prentice Hall.

Ogawa, R. (2005). Leadership as social construct: The expression of human agency within organizational constraint.

In F. English (Ed.), *The SAGE handbook of educational leadership* (pp. 89–106). Thousand Oaks, CA: Sage.
Owens, R. G. (2004). *Organizational behavior in education.* Boston: Pearson.
Shapiro, A. (2000). *Leadership for constructivist schools.* Lanham, MD: Scarecrow Press.

LEADERSHIP, SPIRITUAL

Spiritual leadership actually includes three elements. The first is connectivity and relationship building. The spiritual self motivates human beings to connect with one another and explains the synchronous ways in which people's lives intermingle and have a significant impact on each other. School leadership grounded in spirituality is one that clearly celebrates participatory practices in decision making and welcomes the articulation of the multiple voices that make up any learning community in completing the work of schools. This is the case because spirit-directed leadership clearly understands the interconnectivity of all the persons in any learning community and relishes the thought that the polyphonic nature of schools adds to their vibrancy and effectiveness.

The second element is both ontological and teleological, as the human spirit craves meaning-making and purpose to be consistent parts of the human experience. Spiritual leadership sees the work of educational leaders in a broad social and cultural context and perceives school leaders as those whose purpose, mission, or calling is to serve learning communities in a leadership capacity. Critical spirituality extends the notions of mission and calling by locating educational leadership responsibilities in the arena of helping to transform society from racism, classism, sexism, homophobia, and other marginalizing societal practices. Through critical self-reflection, recognizing the work of school leaders as being in a broader social, cultural, and political space, creatively strategizing to involve school practices in ameliorating the undemocratic and inequitable routines and traditions in mainstream society and finally taking action to bring about societal change, schools, through spiritual leadership, become arenas where social transformation is generated and nurtured.

Finally, spiritual leadership involves the ethical and moral dimensions of school administration. Educational leadership that is grounded in spirituality consistently asks the critical questions of whose interests are being served through administrative practices and who is being included as well as excluded through administrative decisions. Spiritual leadership compels school communities to embrace the ethics and morality of a social justice agenda along with the academic responsibilities of schools.

Some of the scholars and concepts that have nurtured the growth of spiritual leadership include Cornel West's notions of prophetic pragmatism, the idea of conscientization as developed by Paulo Freire's liberation theology and concepts of the psychology of ultimate concerns. Others include work on linking spirituality with democratic education, Carlyle Fielding Stewart's treatise on Black spirituality and consciousness, and David Purpel's pronouncements on the moral and spiritual crisis in education. Spiritual leadership has also become a part of the organizational theory discourse. Finally, the research by Michael Dantley, Khaula Murtadha, and others has moved the spiritual vernacular more deeply into the educational leadership and higher education discourse.

—*Michael Dantley*

See also cross-cultural studies; democracy, democratic education and administration; diversity; empowerment; esteem needs; expert power; involvement, in organizations; leadership, theories of; leadership effectiveness; morality, moral leadership; transformational leadership

Further Readings and References

Dantley, M. (2005). Moral leadership: Shifting the management paradigm. In F. English (Ed.), *The SAGE handbook of educational leadership* (pp. 34–46). Thousand Oaks, CA: Sage.
Freire, P. (1998). *Pedagogy of freedom: Ethics, democracy, and civic courage.* Lanham, MD: Rowman & Littlefield.
Murtadha, K. (1999). Spirited sisters: Spirituality and the activism of African American women in educational leadership. In L. Fenwick (Ed.), *School leadership: Expanding horizons of the mind and spirit: Proceedings of the National Council of Professors of Educational Administration.* Lancaster, PA: Technomic.
Purpel, D. (1989). *The moral and spiritual crisis in education: A curriculum for justice and compassion in education.* New York: Bergin & Garvey.
West, C. (1982). *Prophesy deliverance: An Afro-American revolutionary Christianity.* Philadelphia: Westminster Press.

LEADERSHIP, SYSTEM-ORIENTED

System-oriented leadership (SOL) is a goal-oriented approach to organizational leadership where the functioning of an organization is seen as a whole (i.e., cultural symbols and values, formal structures, environment) and allows organizational members to focus on factors that align key processes and resources to improve performance. SOL is not the purview of administrators, and may include students to school board members. In sports or medicine, SOL is analogous to including a person's state of mind and conditions of use or recovery in the treatment, in addition to the body.

As state governments have established learning standards to address accountability issues in public schools, student and stakeholder needs have become increasingly important. Meeting the challenge of accountability means a systemwide change in educational organizations from a product-focused, industrial model to a learner-focused, continuous quality-improvement model. SOL is a key component of a learner-focused, continuous quality-improvement model.

SOL was well described as a systems perspective in 1966 by Daniel Katz and Robert Kahn in *The Social Psychology of Organizations,* as well as in 1969 in *Systems Thinking,* a collection of essays on the topic edited by F. E. Emery. There are five basic characteristics of SOL that continue to reverberate through school reform literature. School leaders that are system oriented

1. Look for demands, opportunities, trends and patterns, and change in the external environment (e.g., stakeholder needs and requirements, funding sources, legislation).

2. Identify important internal organizational factors based on the needs, requirements, cultural symbols and values, and relationships between organizational subsystems (e.g., students, teachers, grade levels, classrooms, departments) and the organization as a whole.

3. Recognize that an organization is intertwined, influenced, and interactive (open) with its environment.

4. Filter environmental information for external factors that are related to important internal organizational factors to focus planning and action.

5. Provide freedom to diverge from the existing organizational structure and commingle organizational elements (e.g.. time, space, grade levels, content areas, departments, personnel, stakeholders) to achieve organizational goals.

The first two characteristics set the expectation that educational leaders seek information externally from stakeholders and internally from staff and students, as well as have knowledge of educational research and societal trends. Educational leaders must know how to identify local, state, and national resources that might be leveraged to improve educational performance.

There is interplay between characteristics 2, 3, and 4; needs, requirements, and cultural symbols and values identified externally from students and stakeholders, as well as internally from faculty and staff, should be reflected in the school's or district's goals and improvement planning. The interplay between internal and external factors through goal setting and planning should result in shared norms and alignment of learning standards, curriculum, instruction, performance standards, and feedback/reporting.

Finally, SOL sets the expectation that educational leaders will be able to look beyond the formal organizational structures of schools to accept, support, and capitalize on innovation to improve organizational performance. Important developments often surface on the boundaries of seemingly unconnected elements of a system.

—*George R. Stanhope*

See also administration, theories of; bureaucracy; communications, theories in organizations; conceptual systems theory and leadership; creativity, in management; ethos, of organizations; group dynamics; human resource development; leadership, discretionary (and power); leadership, distributed; leadership, participatory; leadership, theories of; management theories; organizational theories; organizations, types of, typologies; planning models; rational organizational theory; restructuring, of schools; role theory; strategic planning; systemic reform; systems theory/thinking; total quality management; values of organizations and leadership

Further Readings and References

Emery, F. E. (Ed.). (1969). *Systems thinking.* Middlesex, UK: Penguin.

Fullan, M. (2004). *Leadership & sustainability: System thinkers in action.* Thousand Oaks, CA: Corwin Press.

Hoyle, J., Bjork, L., Collier, V., & Glass, T. (2004). *The superintendent as CEO.* Thousand Oaks, CA: Corwin Press.

Katz, D., & Kahn, R. T. (1966). *The social psychology of organizations.* New York: John Wiley & Sons.

LEADERSHIP, TASK-ORIENTED

Task-oriented leadership is focused on achieving goals. Leaders who are task oriented are attentive to production and achievement. They are also more likely to keep their distance and be aloof. The assumptions they make about their roles, purposes, and behaviors reflect their commitment to completing the work requested of them. Successful task-oriented leaders are key in contributing to their organization's effectiveness by setting goals, allocating labor, and enforcing sanctions. They often accomplish this by working hard, being persistent with solving problems, and overcoming barriers. Descriptors for task-oriented leaders include "production emphasizing," "goal achieving," and "work facilitative and goal emphasizing."

TASK-ORIENTED VERSUS RELATIONS-ORIENTED LEADERSHIP

Task-oriented leadership is often discussed in connection with relations-oriented leadership. The distinction lies in the titles: *task-oriented* implies concentration on the task to be accomplished, while *relations-oriented* implies a concentration on the quality of relationships with others. Most effective are leaders who use both. Research on the effectiveness of task-oriented versus relations-oriented has not supported the superiority of either orientation.

TYPES OF LEADERS

Task-oriented leadership can be identified in selected types of leaders. For instance, with Hersey and Blanchard's situational leadership model, a task-oriented leader would define the role of others, explain what to do and why, establish well-defined patterns of organization and channels of communication, and determine the ways to accomplish assignments.

Task-oriented leadership behavior has also been associated with performance leadership in connection with behavior that prompts and motivates the group's achievement of goals. The focus on task to strategic thinking means projecting patterns of collective behavior to the whole situation. It is also evident in the leader's interest in issues and methods and the system that can connect people and things to achieve objectives. Immediate supervision, combined with management as a whole, can foster a "culture of productivity"—a shared image of a highly productive work setting—in which supervisors, managers, and workers alike focus on the work being done and how to maintain successful operations.

—*Jean M. Haar*

See also accountability; administration, theories of; leadership effectiveness; leadership styles; management theories

Further Readings and References

Bass, B. (1990). *Bass and Stogdill's handbook of leadership: Theory, research, and managerial applications* (3rd ed.). New York: Free Press.

Crow, G., & Grogan, M. (2005). The development of leadership thought and practice in the United States. In F. English (Ed.), *The SAGE handbook of educational leadership* (pp. 362–379). Thousand Oaks, CA: Sage.

Gronn, P. (2003). *The new work of educational leaders.* London: Paul Chapman.

Kowalski, T. (2003). *Contemporary school administration: An introduction* (2nd ed.). Boston: Pearson Education.

Tomlinson, H. (Ed.). (2004). *Educational management.* New York: Routledge.

🏛 LEADERSHIP, TEACHER

Definitions of *teacher leadership* abound, but most hold in common an expanded view of teachers' contribution to schooling through leadership activities and efforts beyond the boundaries of the classroom. Teacher leadership is generally considered to be the ability and energy to make a contribution to the school beyond one's classroom duties. Teacher leaders are those who work with colleagues to influence schoolwide educational and instructional practices. Underlying this practice is a philosophical perspective that by working in an extended capacity, it is possible to shape a better world.

Teacher leaders, then, are those who strongly value their contribution as teachers and take particular responsibility for decision making and activities outside their classrooms. They might help implement particular reforms within school sites or work in tandem with building principals to tackle obstacles, build rapport with the community, and support the improvement of the overall educational culture of schools. They might experiment with and examine particular innovative forms of instruction with students, analyze these, and invite or encourage colleagues to engage in similar activities. In general, teacher leaders are those who use inquiry, work collaboratively, understand the nature of adult learning, and regard the complexities of the school as an organization. In one study, teacher leaders were those identified by their peers as risk takers and people who seek challenge and growth for personal and professional development as teachers. These teachers were skilled collaborators and viewed as very supportive of their peers. Other researchers have identified an incidence of strong caring relationships as significant among teacher leaders. This, along with a high incidence of collaboration, teacher-led initiatives, and high levels of trust among faculty were factors that distinguished teachers as leaders. This also holds true for other researchers' work with groups of teacher leaders. Teacher leaders know how to build trust and rapport. They examine problems within the context of the organization. They deal with change processes well and work consistently to build skill and confidence in others through collaborative efforts.

It remains difficult to exactly define teacher leadership. In part, this is due to the fact that teachers are far from homogeneous in the variety of roles they take up as teacher leaders and in the multiple ways they define themselves as teacher leaders. In fact, teachers who are leaders take on a variety of roles that can be categorized as both formal and informal in their work as teacher leaders. Formal teacher leadership roles include positions such as lead teachers, master teachers, department heads, team leaders, grade-level leaders, union representatives, and members of the school governing boards, mentors, teacher coaches, and school facilitators. Such teachers might represent their colleagues in district-level or site-based decision making, act as sources of professional growth for peers, or advocate for their colleagues or students in a wider arena.

Informal roles taken by teacher leaders are those that also extend beyond classrooms but are concerned less with the overall organizational dimensions or management of schools. Teacher leaders in such roles might take the lead in shaping the curriculum of a school, setting standards for student behavior, deciding on student placement, designing staff development, setting specific school policies, evaluating teacher performance, selecting new teachers or administrators, deciding on school budgets, establishing community partnerships for resource allocation or other support, creating new program initiatives, promoting and advocating for their school, developing accountability processes for monitoring and evaluating student learning, and mentoring new or more inexperienced teachers.

The roles of teacher leaders in the conception of teacher leadership through the past decades of accelerated reform may be viewed as occurring in three distinct waves. In the first wave, teacher leaders were more formally assigned in roles that stressed management,

the effectiveness and efficiency of the school system. Such work is most typified in the work of teacher work in formal roles of leadership. The second wave emerged in recognition of teachers' instructional abilities and the capacity of this expertise to inform instructional improvement and curriculum development. In this wave, curriculum developer and staff development, teacher mentorship, and other roles were created to capitalize on teachers' pedagogical knowledge. Such work is most exemplified in the informal leadership roles taken up by teachers in particular school sites.

Finally, the third wave stemmed from the need for schools to be recultured for collegiality and systemic change as fundamental cultural changes in schools as organizations. In this current wave, teacher leaders are those who assisted in designing schools, mentoring colleagues, engaging in problem solving, and initiating professional development activities for other teachers. In this wave of teacher leadership work, teachers in both formal and informal roles of leadership in their schools are concerned overall with their abilities to effect significant change in school culture and improve the quality of school life.

THE SIGNIFICANCE OF LEADERSHIP IN TEACHER LEADERSHIP

Increasingly, teacher leadership has become significant in the process of school reform and school change. Leadership has always been a critical factor in the reform and improvement of schools today. Yet, ambiguity and uncertainty surround our understanding and conceptualization of leadership in schools. Is leadership a specialized role held by a designated figure, or is it a set of processes shared among a range of individuals entrusted with the educational fates of our youth? Many in educational administration and teacher education are challenging the pervasive notion that leadership resides in the figure of the school principal or another appointed administrator. Scholars have questioned the exalted responsibility given to one individual. Leadership, they argue, would be better understood as sets of processes that individuals engage in for the pursuit of various goals and objectives.

Moreover, given the increasing demands on schools today, it seems foolhardy to put such high expectations and demands on so few leadership figures. Traditional models of school leadership that rely too heavily on the leadership abilities of the school administrator have not explored the capacity of teachers to make a difference in their schools. School-based reform movements and the teacher professionalism movement or "re-professionaliation" that began in the United States, Canada, and Great Britain in the late 1980s have alerted us of the crisis in teaching as manifested in the recruitment and retention issues of the profession today. These movements have urged us to reconsider top-down initiatives of reform, reconsider notions of school leadership, develop wider models of distribution of leadership roles and practices across schools, and develop the capacity of teachers to make a significant impact on professional practice, quality, and the improvement of the school itself. Just as the teachers' movement advocated for changes in the roles, image, and general work of teachers, mainly through the enhancement and expansion of their roles within the school site, organizational school reforms have called for new site-based school management frameworks and a wider reliance on the leadership capacity of teachers within the site. These two reforms have garnered support for and attention to research and development in teacher leadership. Moreover, these reforms have fostered a timely reconsideration of teachers' work to include more enhanced roles, complex new responsibilities, and enhanced skills.

Recent notions of teacher leadership have called for theoretical orientations that acknowledge a "reconception" of what leadership means. Teacher leadership has been related to other concepts such as distributive leadership and professional learning communities. The distributive leadership view acknowledges the idea that leadership is fluid, emergent, and can be exhibited by anyone in the organization. Furthermore, this perspective elucidates leadership as an interactive and personal process of sense making and the creation of meaning that is continuously a part of organizational membership. It implies that leadership is socially constructed and culturally sensitive. Teacher leadership is also aligned with the goals of professional learning communities. These communities integrate three themes into the school: professionalism, organizational learning, and personal connection.

RESEARCH NEEDS IN TEACHER LEADERSHIP

The knowledge base of research on teacher leadership reflects a dearth of research in this area. Some research has indicated that teacher leadership results in increased perceptions of professional growth, more professional development opportunities for teachers, more instructional innovation, greater communication among faculty, and increased cooperation among teachers and administrators. Yet, little research reflects the ways that teachers engage alongside other leaders and how this might impact organizational culture. Likewise, there is little empirical research that examines the ways that principals and teachers understand this sharing of leadership and its contribution to school reform efforts. Researchers have only begun to examine the ways that teachers contribute in the leadership of schools and the ways that these efforts impact school improvement and reform. Given the high levels of accountability and the increased focus on student achievement of late, it seems pertinent to more seriously examine the perspectives and actual work of teachers and school administrators who share leadership roles and tasks and the relationship of this work to the overall improvement of school programs.

In summary, teacher leadership shows much promise in the reform of educational administration and may quite possibly facilitate the reform efforts aimed toward increased student achievement and quality school programming. As a concept, however, it remains vaguely defined to scholars and practitioners. Thus, teacher leadership is a concept of practical promise that would stand to benefit from theoretical expansion and research-based inquiry.

—*Audrey M. Dentith, Floyd D. Beachum, and Elise M. Frattura*

See also American Federation of Teachers; Bethune, Mary McLeod; capacity building, of organizations; career development; career stages; critical theory; Dewey, John; empowerment; Haley, Margaret; innovation, in education; involvement, in organizations; leadership, task-oriented; leadership, theories of; Picott, J. Rupert; professional development; professional development schools; professional learning communities; role ambiguity; role conflict; role theory; satisfaction, in organizations and roles; supervision; systemic reform; tutoring; universities, preparation of educational leaders in; women in educational leadership; Young, Ella Flagg

Further Readings and References

Beachum, F. D., & Dentith, A. (2004). Teacher leaders: Creating cultures of school renewal and transformation. *Educational Forum, 68*(3), 276–286.

Chrispeels, J. (2004). *Learning to lead together.* Thousand Oaks, CA: Sage.

Crowther, F. (1996). Teacher leadership: Exploration in theory and practice. *Leading and Managing, 2*(4), 304–321.

Crowther, F., Kaagan, S. S., Ferguson, M., & Hann, L. (2002). *Developing teacher leaders: How teacher leadership enhances school success.* Thousand Oaks, CA: Corwin Press.

Crowther, F., & Olsen, P. (1996). *Teachers as leaders: An exploration of success stories in socioeconomic disadvantaged communities.* Kingroy, Queensland, Australia: Queensland Department of Education.

Harris, A. (2003). Teacher leadership as distributed leadership: Heresy, fantasy, or possibility? *School Leadership & Management, 23*(3), 313–324.

Henning, J. E., Trent, V., Engelbrecht, D., Robinson, V., & Reed, G. A. (2004). *Cultivating teacher leadership through a school and university partnership.* Unpublished paper.

Murphy, J. (2005). *Connecting teacher leadership and school improvement.* Thousand Oaks, CA: Sage

LEADERSHIP, THEORIES OF

Leadership theories represent systematic organized knowledge to explain the nature and effectiveness of leadership. Theories provide a foundation for analyzing and predicting the complex nature of leadership behavior. Practitioners use theories as illustrations or as guiding principles to interpret leadership actions.

The amount of research on leadership theories is significant to the field, since understanding theories helps researchers and practitioners assess personal and organizational behaviors. Theories give insights about leader effectiveness and influence expectations and assessments of leaders as they relate to organizational goals.

The earliest theoretical studies were based on the assumption that effective leaders possess certain intellectual abilities, physical characteristics, and personality traits. Later studies centered on leadership behaviors, styles, and situations. Current theories involve characteristics of leaders who serve as change agents and visionaries able to deal with the complexity and uncertainty of today's organizations.

HISTORY OF LEADERSHIP THEORIES

Theory emerged during the late nineteenth century and early twentieth century as a means to define and explain the nature of leadership. Early focus was to examine and explain the emergence of great leaders based on their innate ability. Studying small group leadership emerged by 1920. Many researchers have attempted to identify universal traits common to leaders; others embraced psychoanalytic or political perspectives and attribution theories. Later, scholars conceptualized effective leadership based on specific behaviors, identifying behavior theories and leadership styles. As a result of the difficulty in isolating key behavioral patterns, researchers focused on contingency and situational theories, attempting to identify leadership behaviors that would succeed in specific situations.

More recent theories attempt to describe leadership effectiveness in terms of exchanges between leaders and followers. Researchers continue to offer models, approaches, and perspectives that build on previous studies and advocate for additional inquiry. Recent theories examine leadership and organizational change and the importance of vision shared by leaders and followers.

Theories, models, approaches, styles, and perspectives are all terms used in the literature. While most theories focus on one variable as being significant, the research includes varying assumptions and understandings about leadership effectiveness. Studies of theories have been prolific and encompass a variety of views, with early theories still resurfacing in both current literature and practice.

DISTINGUISHING THEORY FROM STYLE

While some leadership theories provide explanations based on traits, behaviors, situations, and processes, leadership styles refer to the patterns of behavior demonstrated by leaders as they influence others, with leadership styles representing one of four broad strands of leadership research. Other strands include leadership traits, behaviors, and situational contingencies. The styles approach provides a framework for assessing leadership behavior, and many studies on style attempt to measure preferred leadership behaviors so leaders can assess their behaviors and determine how to change or improve their styles. Leadership styles address a continuum from leaders being directive to facilitating delegation. Directive behaviors assist followers in accomplishing goals as leaders direct, clarify, and define direction. Delegation behaviors involve leaders helping followers feel comfortable about themselves and the situation related to the task.

CLASSIFYING THEORIES

Researchers often use concepts of leadership definitions to classify theories. Both definitions and classification methods vary widely. Common methods to classify theories include trait theories, behavior theories, attribution theories, contingency theories, situational theories, and transformational theories. Another approach relates to variables that influence leadership effectiveness, including categories about leader, follower, and situational characteristics. Other approaches focus on leader-centered or follower-centered behaviors, use universal or contingent descriptors, and conceptualize behaviors as descriptive or prescriptive.

Great Man and Trait Theories

Earliest theories focused exclusively on leader characteristics and neglected behaviors, interactions of leaders with followers, and situational variables. Although a century old, concepts from these theories still appear in current educational and corporate settings, as seen in job selection processes and professional development settings. These theories are generally described as great man and trait theories.

The notion of being a born leader captures the essence of great man theories. Leaders were seen as elitists, rising to power because of superior characteristics that appealed to those waiting to be led. Leader traits are not viewed as learned or developed but are viewed as being present primarily at birth. Because of innate abilities, individuals are destined to exert themselves as leaders when the need arises. Great leaders, like great politicians or military leaders, rise to the occasion whenever opportunity exists.

Heredity, natural endowment, and survival of the fittest were key concepts. Subsequent theories largely have dispelled the notion of leadership being innate and inherited, although great man theories still impact current views of leadership. The impact is most apparent during heroic acts of leadership when organizations honor those who step forward in extreme crises (i.e., faltering corporations or underachieving schools) and succeed in moving organizations from highly dysfunctional to highly functional in short periods of time. Great man theories provided a basis for the emergence of trait theory.

Trait Theories

Trait theories explain leadership in terms of leader characteristics and personality, identifying certain physical, social, and personal attributes in leaders. Hundreds of studies between 1930 and 1950 helped identify characteristics to differentiate leaders from followers. Relevance was on leader selection, and emphasis was on characteristics like gender, height, energy, appearance, integrity, self-confidence, intelligence, desire to lead, and charisma. Subsequent researchers maintained that personal characteristics could not accurately predict leadership, and that situational variables are important to explain effectiveness, causing researchers to reject trait theory and focus emerging theories on behaviors and situations.

Behavior Theories and Approaches

The next generation of theories focused on leader behaviors and differed dramatically from the trait approach—moving leadership conceptualization from what a leader *is* to what a leader *does*. Studies began to address how leaders behave with subordinates in varied contexts. Humanistic or personal behavioral theories are based on the development of the individual in an effective organization. Leaders by nature are motivated, while organizations by nature are structured and controlled. Leadership is seen as observable actions of the leader.

Psychodynamic and Psychoanalytic Theories

These theories explain leader behaviors related to associations, interpretations, and analyses from early childhood and family developments, and are grounded primarily in work from Sigmund Freud and Carl Jung. Popular interpretations perceive leaders as father figures, noting that the father of the family defined the leader's psychological world. Mother figures were also seen as playing a key role, with either strong mothers or absent fathers impacting the leadership role.

Psychohistorians were influenced by psychoanalysts in attempts to explain the behavior of historical political leaders, who were studied in terms of childhood deprivations, cultural environments, parental relationships, and psychodynamic needs of followers. Psychoanalytical theory was also used to explain the interaction of leader personalities and how situations are dramatized in times of crises.

Two-Factor Leadership Theorists

These theorists maintain that leadership is a combination of two kinds of behaviors and that a leader's effectiveness depends on using the best blend of behaviors appropriate for the situation. The two dimensions of behaviors addressed leaders being (1) task focused, by initiating structure towards goal attainment, or (2) relationship focused, by showing consideration for people. Leaders were believed to favor one particular dimension, although they did not function in one dimension exclusively.

Early work from Ohio State in the 1940s stressed leader behaviors over traits and identified two-driver dimensions of leadership behavior: initiating structure and consideration. Concurrently, researchers at the University of Michigan studied leader behavior on group performance, grounding the dimensions to production orientation and employee orientation. The second generation of Michigan studies identified the two dimensions as being independent, in that leaders could behave along both dimensions at the same time. The most widespread application of the two-factor theory became identified with the managerial or leadership grid, used widely in training and development settings. The two dimensions address how leaders align behaviors with concern for production and concern for people to achieve organizational goals. There are limitations to this approach, notably a failure to connect leadership behaviors to subordinate performance outcomes. Other critics say that this approach is not a refined theory, since it doesn't provide a well-organized prescription for leader behaviors.

Douglas McGregor suggested Theory X and Theory Y as types of leader behaviors, with Theory X based on the assumption that people are passive and resistant to organizational needs, thereby calling for the leader to direct and motivate people. Theory Y is based on the assumption that people are highly motivated and desire responsibility, with the leader offering organizational conditions so followers can fulfill needs while achieving organizational goals.

Chris Argyris proposed a maturity-immaturity theory identifying a fundamental conflict between organizations and individuals, because the nature of the organization is to achieve goals by structuring members' roles and controlling their performances. On the other hand, individuals tend to be self-directive and seek fulfillment by exercising initiative and responsibility. Argyris proposed that organizations are effective when leaders create situations for followers to make creative contributions as a result of their own internal needs.

Paul Hersey and Kenneth Blanchard presented a life cycle of leadership theory, where leader behaviors are related to the experiential and motivational maturity of subordinates. In this theory, leaders gradually decrease emphasis on task structures as subordinates mature.

SITUATIONAL LEADERSHIP THEORY

Situational theorists studied environmental contexts that promote leader emergence—noting that circumstances, time, and location largely determine when, how, and who will emerge as a leader. The theory directly contrasts trait theories that exclude leaders from the situational contexts.

Personal situational theorists proposed that it is an interaction of personal traits and situational factors that explain leader emergence, maintaining that neither traits nor situations alone account for leadership. Various theorists stressed the construct of fitting leader talents to the demands brought by particular situations and the importance of followers to the leader emergence, noting that theories must address the interplay of situations and the individuals. The theories have widespread application in predicting leadership potential and in matching individuals' background experiences, traits, and skills to job requirements.

Led by Fred E. Fiedler, *contingency theory* was a primary theory for over 40 years, stressing that the situation imposes demands on leaders who operate from two primary constructs—that of being task oriented or being relations oriented. These constructs were determined by how leaders judge their least preferred coworker. The concept of situational favorableness related to a leader's ability to be held in esteem by followers have legitimacy and power and lead a task that was structured, clear, and easily solved. Theorists maintained that task-oriented leaders succeed in situations with either high or low favorableness, and relations-oriented leaders succeed most in situations between the favorableness extremes.

Interaction theories grounded in social learning explain leadership through the lens of the leader-subordinate relationships. Theories are characterized by leader emergence resulting from interactions between demands of the individual and the situation. Leaders demonstrate behaviors based on how they perceive that others see them as leaders.

Attainment theories focus on explaining who emerges as a leader and why. One theory describes how leaders emerge in situations where tasks of the group are interdependent and are related to the solution of shared problems. The concept of structured interaction or predictable interaction is essential. The role structure of the group and the leader's role are defined by organizational expectations. Leadership effectiveness becomes a function of group members' perceptions of their freedom to accept or reject the interaction structure.

Ralph Stogdill developed an expectancy-reinforcement theory to explain the emergence and persistence of leadership in unstructured groups. He defined leadership emergence as the extent to which a leader initiates and maintains structure in interactions and expectations with the group. In another valence model, an emergent leader is one who emerges and is able to perform roles and functions that encourage participation of members and enable the group to achieve its goals.

The *managerial leadership approach* is based on an authority relationship between the leader and subordinate, with the model including role definitions, hierarchical structures, and patterns of interaction. Leadership and management are used interchangeably, with the leader seen as impersonal, formal, and task centered. The model suggests a structural approach to change, with unilateral decision making, and subordinate compliance leading to effective results. Several different leadership styles can be identified within management techniques, with each technique using leadership in a different way. Distinctions between management and leadership have been the focus of researchers over the years, despite the caution that stereotypical labeling of people as managers or leaders is too simplistic. Researchers usually attempt to make the distinction in terms of the person instead of the process.

Political theorists attempt to explain leadership in terms of influence and power. Political leadership is the ability to impress the will of the leader on those being led and to induce obedience, respect, loyalty, and cooperation. Leadership is expressed in terms of the power to command or the ability to dominate.

Reward and implicit coercion are the bases of power. Power is exercised in an institutional environment based on either authority, prestige, or both, including referent and expert power as two elements that comprise prestige power in organizations. The power to influence, which can be exerted downward, laterally, or upward, stems from three sources: position, personal, and political means.

Reinforced change theory rests on the notion that through their efforts, leaders change the motivation, understanding, and behavior of other group members to bring about successful organizational change. In this theory, congruence is a key dimension for leader success, and incongruence is viewed as bringing conflict and failure. Leaders are successful based on the degree to which followers' expectations for rewards and punishment are met. The theory lays groundwork for the path-goal theory.

Path-goal theory explains how leaders motivate followers to achieve work-related goals. Theorists applied the central theme of expectancy theory to understand how leaders clarify goals and incentives for followers and identify work behaviors needed to reach desired goals. Leaders motivate followers psychologically by enhancing their desire to work for rewards, with rewards resting under the control of the leader. Subordinates become satisfied by gaining rewards for performance along the desired "path" of behaviors identified by the leader. Leader behaviors are determined by variables including role clarity, environmental factors, and individual differences. Although path-goal theory has not been widely applied in practice to leadership development activities, the theory provides recommendations about how leaders should act in various situations. The theory gives leaders the opportunity to assess situational work needs and to adjust leadership approaches based on needs—relying on the assumption that a primary goal is for leaders to move subordinates towards work goal attainment.

Leader-member exchange (LMX) theory, also known as vertical dyad linkage theory, examines the role-making processes between leaders and each subordinate. Emphasis is on how leaders develop different exchange relationships over time with subordinates. The premise is that most leaders establish a special relationship with a small number of trusted subordinates. These relationships are usually formed on the basis of personal compatibility and subordinate competence and dependability.

Studies have varied as a result of the theory's definition. LMX is sometimes defined to include mutual trust, respect, affection, support, and loyalty. The theory is considered as a universal theory with little focus on situational variables that impact the leader-member exchange process. Gary Yukl advocates that more longitudinal research is needed to discover how exchange relationship evolves over time.

As one of two theoretical models in LMX, the leader's attribution about subordinates model describes the cognitive processes used by leaders to determine the reasons for subordinate performance. The leader assesses performance based on interpretation of the subordinate's behavior and performance. Whereas the subordinate's attributions about the leader model focuses on subordinates' interpretations of the leader's actions and behaviors.

Democratic and participative leadership theory involves leaders using various decision procedures that include follower input. Leaders usually consult with subordinates and integrate their suggestions into decisions, accommodating multidirectional communication with subordinates. With these theories, the organization is viewed as a democratic network, sharing power among followers and leaders.

Victor H. Vroom and P.W. Yetton's model is closely aligned to participative leadership and supports the notion that a major objective of the leader is to empower others. Supportive leadership is viewed as essential for participative leadership. The research on participative leadership accentuates the leader's role and perspective in sharing power. Group members may be involved in decision making or consultation. The notion of participative leadership has become increasingly popular in recent literature, and is sometimes described as cooperative or distributed leadership.

Team leadership theory relates to working with organizational teams and has become an important research focus in the past decade, fueled mostly by the shifting structure of the American workplace and the emphasis on teams in achieving goals. Earliest research in the 1940s dealt with understanding groups from a social science perspective, but research was not conducted on long-term groups, did not take into account leadership interplay, and did not inform real-life application for work groups. Working with teams is viewed as a way to distribute leadership functions beyond the shoulders of the formal leader. As a result, the function of group leadership becomes complex. Recent research focuses on the role of the leader in helping the team accomplish its task, maintain itself, and function effectively. Team leadership has not been researched fully or tested in practical settings.

Critical theorists maintain that oppressed groups in society, who often believe that systems are in their own best interests, sometimes support institutionalized oppression by those in power. In this theory, leaders sometimes manipulate beliefs and values of followers to maintain influence. Although this behavior may seem contrary to what would be expected regarding leadership theory, theorists maintain it is important to understand the manipulation of meaning by leaders and leaders' abilities to convince subordinates

that actions are in their best interests as a way to keep subordinate perceptions aligned with leader desires towards goal accomplishment.

Transactional leadership theorists, led by James MacGregor Burns, maintain that leaders engage in relationships with subordinates for the purpose of exchanging valued things. The theory describes two types of leader behavior to include contingent reward and passive management by exception. Contingent reward behavior uses rewards to influence motivation and clarification of the work required to obtain the rewards. Passive management by exception uses contingent punishments and other corrective action in response to deviations from acceptable performance by followers. Active management by exception was added later as a type of transactional leadership behavior, and is described as looking for mistakes and enforcing rules to avoid mistakes. Transactional leadership relies on an exchange process concerning leader influence and creates follower compliance. The compliance may or may not include high enthusiasm and motivation from the followers.

EMERGENCE OF RECENT THEORIES

Differing from earlier theories, current theories emphasize the leader's behaviors related to leading vision, the emotional appeal of vision to followers, and the influence of high-level leaders on organizational change and performance.

Charismatic leadership theory identifies charisma as a personality characteristic that gives leaders exceptional influence over others. Leader behaviors include achievement orientation, high energy levels, confidence, consideration for followers, and a high need for social influence. Theorists stressed the importance of leaders being moral, balancing their use of power, and influencing values, behaviors, and overall performance of followers by gaining loyalty and admiration. From an emotional perspective, followers see that leader behaviors inspire completion of organizational mission. The intense loyalty to leaders can be misguided by charismatic leaders who could use their influence for immoral or evil purposes. Charismatic leaders may generate integrations of institutions and loyalties or may engender opposition movements. Some scholars believe that support and loyalty from followers is at the base of intense love for charismatic leaders—since followers view charismatic leaders as superhumans.

Recent theorists contend that charismatic leadership needs alignment with situational variables. The theory suggests a return to principles of trait theory, noting that leadership behaviors result from innate characteristics. It has been noted that charismatic leaders emerge most often in weak rather than in strong situations and that charismatic leadership can alter self-concepts of followers and attempts to link followers to the organizational identity.

While further research on charismatic leadership is needed, the theory does provide an explanation of the marked emotional impact that some leaders have on followers. The concept of charisma has been embedded in a component of transformational leadership identified as idealized influence.

Symbolic leadership theory involves the signals to others of what is important in the organization. These leaders create and communicate a vision for followers, making clear to subordinates the connections between what they do and how it fits toward the achievement of excellence in the organization.

Transformation leadership theory is based on ideas of James MacGregor Burns and later supported by empirical research by Bernard M. Bass. In this approach, leaders attempt to change and transform individuals—moving both themselves and others to a higher level of motivation and performance. As a change-oriented theory, transformational leadership is broad in perspective and is one of the current approaches to leadership that has been researched and applied extensively across numerous organizational structures. Transformational leadership involves followers becoming motivated as a result of feeling trust, admiration, loyalty, and respect toward the leader. The leader transforms and motivates followers by inducing them to transcend their own self-interests to achieve organizational visions and goals. Followers become more aware of the importance of task outcomes and become more productive.

Many researchers have developed numerous surveys to assess aspects of transformational leadership, focusing primarily on leader behavior and linking motivation of followers to performance. While the theory provides new insights, some contend that it is necessary to examine group and organizational-level processes in order to determine a leader's long-term effectiveness. Strengths include the extensive nature of the research, the theory's alignment with common beliefs held about the role of visionary leadership, and the notion that leadership can emerge from others outside the formal leader.

Feminist leadership theories focus on leader behavior based on the demographic characteristic of gender dynamics. Some researchers have found that women use a more participative and a less autocratic or directive leadership style. Females may emphasize relational communication goals in their interactions with subordinates. Researchers tend to examine ways women respond as leaders, the differences in leadership behaviors and effectiveness of men and women, and questions regarding why women leaders exist in small numbers.

Carol Shakeshaft has contended that research findings that show no distinctions between males and females in leadership roles are flawed because a White male model has served as a conceptual framework. Shakeshaft offers that the work of female leaders has five major elements: (1) relationships with others, (2) teaching and learning, (3) building community, (4) awareness of their status, and (5) the line that separates their public and private lives.

The cultural leadership approach is viewed by Edgar Schein as a way to identify basic assumptions and patterns invented, discovered, or developed by groups and taught to new members as the correct way to behave in the organization. Organizations are viewed as cultural entities, where meaning from behavior is more important than the behaviors. Thomas J. Sergiovanni and John E. Corbally argue that no one theory can define or predict the best leadership situations, arguing that a total reconceptualization of leadership should occur. The next conception of leadership should focus on building identity, increasing understanding, and making the work of others more meaningful.

A decade of research about theories along with popular publications provide avenues for ongoing discussion and study of leadership. Theories have been explained and critiqued in numerous ways, and various frameworks have been created to classify and draw linkages and contrasts among the theories—ranging from such theories as great man to transformational leadership theories. Research literature includes explanations of leadership traits, behaviors, situations, and modern concepts about the role of the leader involved in complex organizational change. Serving as tributaries to the body of knowledge about leadership, historical and modern-day theoretical concepts about leadership are being applied in current organizations. The primary intent is to apply theory to connect leadership effectiveness to results and goal attainment.

—*Frankie K. Williams, Diane Ricciardi,*
and Richard Blackbourn

See also Barnard, Chester I.; Burns, James MacGregor; charisma, of leaders; Clark, Septima; contingency theories; creativity, in management; critical theory; Cubberley, Ellwood; DeBono, Edward; DuBois, W. E. B.; feminism and theories of leadership; gender studies, in educational leadership; governance; great man theory; Halpin, Andrew William; leadership, complex theory of; leadership, distributed; leadership effectiveness; leadership styles; Machiavelli, Niccolò; management theories; Mann, Horace; McGregor, Douglas; Montessori, Maria; organizational theories; path-goal leadership theory; Plato; Plutarch; power; resources management; theory movement, in educational administration; Theory X, Theory Y; trait theory; transformational leadership; Washington, Booker T.; women in educational leadership; Woodson, Carter G.; Young, Ella Flagg

Further Readings and References

Argyris, C. (1973). Personality and organization theory revisited. *Administrative Science Quarterly, 18,* 141–167.

Bass, B. (1997). Does the transactional-transformational paradigm transcend organizational and national boundaries? *American Psychologist, 52,* 130–139.

Bogotch, I. (2005). A history of public school leadership: The first century, 1837–1942. In F. English (Ed.), *The SAGE handbook of educational leadership* (pp. 7–33). Thousand Oaks, CA: Sage.

Brower, R., & Balch, B. (2005). *Transformational leadership & decision-making schools.* Thousand Oaks, CA: Sage.

Crow, G., & Grogan, M. (2005). The development of leadership thought and practice in the United States. In F. English (Ed.), *The SAGE handbook of educational leadership* (pp. 362–379). Thousand Oaks, CA: Sage.

Fiedler, F., Chemers, M., & Mahar, L. (1976). *Improving leadership effectiveness: The LEADER MATCH concept.* New York: Wiley.

Hersey, P., & Blanchard, K. (1972). The management of change: Change and the use of power. *Training & Development Journal, 26*(1), 6–10.

Shakeshaft, C. (1987). *Women in educational administration.* Newbury Park, CA: Sage.

Wheatly, M. (1992). *Leadership and the new science: Learning about organization from an orderly universe.* San Francisco: Berrett-Koehler.

Yukl, G. (2002). *Leadership in organizations* (5th ed.). Englewood Cliffs, NJ: Prentice Hall.

🏛 LEADERSHIP EFFECTIVENESS

Effective leaders carry the dreams of others to the finish line. The history of effective leadership is laden with inspiring tales of prophets, explorers, military heroes, athletes, scientists, and educators. Effective leaders have shaped nations, corporations, education systems, and the lives of millions of people. From ancient times to the present, observers remain perplexed about the actual essence of effective leadership and how to teach it. While researchers report multiple studies about leadership effectiveness, they find that myth and historical accounts of historical figures influence the definitions and characteristics of effective leaders. Warren Bennis and Burt Nanus found 350 definitions of leadership in the literature, and others challenge the lingering belief that personal physical, gender, and personality traits determine successful leadership. Physical size is a factor in athletics and other endeavors that require strength and agility, but weight, height, race, gender, and personality traits are not dominant factors in determining effective leadership.

Mother Teresa and Mohandas Gandhi were not tall, imposing persons, but their spiritual and intellectual gifts made them effective, caring leaders in the eyes of the world. These and others have modeled and helped transform the archaic view of top-down rule by stoic leaders toward bottom-up team builders in empowered organizations stressing relationships. The traditional top-down controlling bureaucratic model is being replaced by organizations with effective leaders with vision and selflessness. Most Fortune 500 companies, top 10 universities, and exceptional school districts have moved away from well-oiled, predictable, clockwork systems with rigid line-and-organizational charts with isolated executives making decisions in secret.

Larry Hirschorn's 1997 postmodern premise is that there is no single best way to organize schools for success. He and other transformers realize that centralization of authority is no longer the best structure in contemporary school organizations. To model shared leadership, the superintendent of schools, central office staff, and principals empower teacher leaders to guide colleagues to make site-based decisions about new personnel, curriculum, and selected budget items. Effective school leaders stress professional development for all staff members in the areas of servant leadership, delegation, communication, and the sharing of data for district, campus, and student performance.

The origins of transforming school organizations toward relationships and team building are found in the early works by Hemphill and Coons, who, in 1950, distinguished the difference between leading and administering. Later, Gordon Donaldson believed that contemporary school administrators must take people beyond outdated administrative practices to mobilize staff practices and beliefs so that the school fulfills its vision and mission for all children. James MacGregor Burns calls these changes toward more human organizations transformational leadership that helps employees find fulfillment in the workplace. Leadership studies have been divided into five themes: (1) leadership as personal quality, (2) leadership as a type of behavior, (3) leadership depending on the situation, (4) leadership as relational, and (5) leadership as a moral quality for systemic improvement. John Hoyle recently added a sixth theme—leadership as a force of love and spirituality.

Leadership as a personal quality is a remnant of the great man theories of the 1950s, when personality traits and other human capabilities that gave individuals advantage over others dominated the literature on leadership. In 1981, Ralph Stogdill classified these personal qualities or traits as capacities in intelligence, scholarship, or athletic abilities for achievement, initiative to meet responsibilities, sociability for participation, and socioeconomic position and popularity for status. Superintendents and principals using this personal quality theme tend to hire only those people who look like and act like the boss, which can be discriminatory against women and minorities.

Leadership as a type of behavior or activity is an attempt to move beyond the great man habit. This theme dominated research in educational administration in the 1960s and 1970s. John Hemphill and Alvin Coons were pioneers in discovering the two factor dimensions of *initiating structure* and *consideration* in 1950. *Initiating structure* identified the leader's skills in developing goals, assignment of tasks, explaining details, and communicating responsibilities of team members. *Consideration* identified the leader's human side, that is, interpersonal relationships, trust, respect, support, and sense of caring about team members. These and related studies helped establish the use of employee perceptions about leader behavior and verified two major factors of task and people orientation that remain central to current leadership models. Wayne Hoy and his students conducted numerous studies linking leadership behavior to school reform, health, decision making, and other factors.

Leadership depending on the situation has been influenced by Fred Fiedler, Paul Hersey and Ken Blanchard, Victor Vroom and R. J. House, among others. This research focused on emerging leadership in the context of group norms, tasks, position power, and leader-member relations. Since situations are fluid, leadership strategies must be adaptive to successfully complete a team project on time and with high quality. Hersey and Blanchard added maturity level of the worker to the two dimensions of concern for task completion and the worker. They reasoned that if people lacked the skills or knowledge to complete a task, they must be taught to do the task, inspired with a reason to build quality into task activities, participate as a team member, and finally delegate the task when an employee has fully matured on the job.

Leadership as relational stresses that leadership and followership are inextricably linked. Rosabeth Kanter and Amitai Etzioni and others provide keys into the understanding of the use of power and influence in organizations, and how power relationships are displayed in corporate and school life. School superintendents are often viewed as the king on the hill who have lost touch with the peasants doing the real work of teaching, and the personality of schools varies widely according to interpersonal relationships and the people skills of the principal.

Leadership as a moral quality for systemic improvement has taken center stage in leadership research and professional development. The ideas of Thomas Sergiovanni, Lee Bolman, Terry Deal, and others have nurtured ideas on servant and transformational leadership and the importance of a moral compass for more caring and community-centered workplaces. Effective moral leaders help create shared visions and respect for the values of others in the organization. A growing area of inquiry on social justice as a moral quality focuses on supporting the theories of leadership that will guide leaders to shape schools and communities toward greater equity and justice through educational programs.

Leadership and the force of love and spirituality goes a step beyond moral quality and servant leadership. In today's schools, effective leaders are finding that unconditional love for staff, parents, and students is the quality needed to find solutions for human frailties and system failures. Unselfish, loyal, and benevolent concern for the good of others—even the unlovable—is key to effective leadership in today's schools. John Hoyle and Michael Fullan suggest that school administrators apply love as the key to high performance and problem solutions. The concept of spiritual leadership in educational administration is new. Effective leaders have a sense of spiritual awareness beyond mere religious doctrine to help gain a sense of profound connection to human issues and problems beyond themselves. Spiritual leaders sense a power greater than mere human knowledge and experience. Margaret Wheatley observed that those who speak about a vocation or calling are spiritual thinkers.

Effective leadership has been transformed in many ways since the behavioral/theory movement in the mid-1950s. Effective leaders understand that cooperation cannot be forced on others, but leading others to destinations beyond their imaginations and gaining their commitment to shared goals can capture cooperation to seek higher goals for themselves and for children.

—John R. Hoyle

See also accountability; administration, theories of; authority; bureaucracy; capacity building, of organizations; charisma, of leaders; Chavez, Cesar Estrada; civil rights movement; communication, theories in organizations; contingency theories; empowerment; ethos, of organizations; feminism and theories of leadership; great man theory; human resource development; leadership, task-oriented; leadership, theories of; leadership styles; line and staff concept; locus of control; management by objectives; management theories; morality, moral leadership; personality; role model; stewardship; superintendency; transformational leadership; values of organizations and leadership; vulnerability thesis, of superintendents

Further Readings and References

Bennis, W., & Nanus, B. (1985). *Leaders: The strategy for taking charge.* New York: Harper & Row.

Bolman, L., & Deal, T. (1997). *Reframing organizations: Artistry, choice, and leadership* (2nd ed.). San Francisco: Jossey-Bass.

Hersey, P., & Blanchard, K. (1988). *Management of organizational behavior: Utilizing human resources* (5th ed.). Englewood Cliffs, NJ: Prentice Hall.

Hirschorn, L. (1997). *Reworking authority: Leading and following in a post-modern organization.* Cambridge, MA: MIT Press.

House, R. (1996). Path-goal theory of leadership: Lessons, legacy, and a reformulated theory. *Leadership Quarterly, 3*(2), 323–352.

Hoy, W., & Miskel, C. (2004). *Educational administration: Theory, research, and practice* (7th ed.). Boston: McGraw-Hill.

Hoyle, J. (2002). *Leadership and the force of love: Six keys to motivating with love.* Thousand Oaks, CA: Corwin Press.

Sergiovanni, T. (1992). *Moral leadership: Getting to the heart of school improvement.* San Francisco: Jossey-Bass.

Stogdill, R. (1981). Traits of leadership: A follow-up to 1970. In B. Bass (Ed.), *Stogdill's handbook of leadership* (pp. 73–97). New York: Free Press.

Wheatley, M. (2002). Spirituality in turbulent times. *School Administrator, 8*(59), 42–48.

🏛 LEADERSHIP STYLES

The mystery of why one leader's style is more effective than another's is unsolved. Leadership style consists of a leader's general personality, demeanor, and communication patterns in guiding others toward reaching organizational or personal goals. Leadership style research has been dominated by self-report perceptions of subordinates about their leader's behavior patterns in decision making, interpersonal relations, planning, instructional leadership, and management efficiency. Among widely used instruments to assess leadership style are the organizational climate description questionnaire (OCDQ), leadership behavior description questionnaire (LBDQ), and the organizational health inventory (OHI). These instruments gather faculty and staff perceptions of the leadership style of the principal and other organizational dynamics in a school organization. The results of these perceptions have been helpful to principals who may see themselves as democratic, inclusive leaders, while the data reveal an authoritarian, aloof bureaucrat. A principal may organize for and believe in site-based decision making, but subordinates' perceptions may reveal that the principal "owns" the site and makes all decisions. The literature reveals little empirical research about why some leadership styles in certain situations are triumphant successes and others are dismal failures. Observers have pondered why some successful leaders use a consistent style in all situations and others use a more situational style. Research is silent in analyzing leadership styles across schools, school leaders, and situations, but there is general consensus that some leaders are better than others in reading the environment and adjusting their style to address issues.

Categories of leadership styles have increased in the postmodern literature. Among the more recent categories are charismatic leadership, social justice leadership, gender and race leadership, moral leadership, and spiritual leadership. The four rather global categories of leadership styles chosen for this entry, however, are authoritarian, participative, transactional, or transformational.

Authoritarian leaders employ coercive tactics to enforce rules, use Machiavellian cunning to manipulate people and decision making, and reward loyalty over merit. Control is the primary management strategy employed by authoritarian leaders. This form of leadership emphasizes objectivity in the workplace, tends to be impervious to human problems, is insensitive to race and gender, and displays little emotion or affection toward employees. Douglas McGregor's Theory X becomes the authoritarian's motif, believing that people must be forced to work, closely supervised, and rewarded or punished based on individual productivity. They believe in a top-down, line-and-staff organizational chart with clear levels of authority and reporting processes. Fred Fiedler found that authoritarian leaders can be viewed as successful in certain task situations—allowing for the extremes of consideration and ruthlessness, depending on the situation.

School boards looking for a "take charge" superintendent encourage authoritarian leadership types. When the focus is primarily on high stakes test scores and a board of education's mandate to "right the ship," authoritarian leadership will rule and will be rewarded throughout the entire school district. Research is silent in analyzing leadership styles across school leaders and situations, but there is a general consensus that some leaders are better than others in reading the environment and adjusting their style to address issues. Regardless of more recent democratic leadership styles, scientific management and the ghost of Frederick Taylor continue to prevail in many schools across America. Excessive accountability demands by legislators, school boards, and communities can lead to top-down authoritarian environments.

Participative leaders strive to move away from the authoritarian boss-led mode of leadership to the human side of the enterprise espoused in the 1930s by Mary Parker Follett, Elton Mayo, Frederick Roethlisberger, and others. They found that productivity and human relationships were closely linked, and opened inquiry into informal structures and social systems. Follett's vision guided her to challenge the grip of scientific management on early twentieth-century industry. She believed managers should treat workers with dignity and change the workplace from strict authoritarian control over workers to a more collegial team concept. Chester I. Barnard in 1938 viewed successful organizations as humans working together to reach goals rather than impersonal structures to force productivity. These and other pioneers espousing participative leadership viewed organizations as social systems in which people's social needs were the most important factors in motivating workers to higher productivity. Later, Douglas McGregor, Rosabeth Kanter, Tom Sergiovanni, Terry Deal, and many others stressed shared decision making and group participation in building productive organizations centered on people and their needs. These

writers greatly influenced the creation of site-based decision making in public education. Without a site-based approach to problem solving, organizations become tightly controlled by rules and policies that are not conducive to effective teamwork. When the communication pattern is top to bottom and ruled by the chain of command, teams become guided missiles for management. These missiles are told when to fire, how to fly, and where to strike. If the team missiles hit the wrong target, management blames the teams for the failures. Participative leadership, however, leads to delegation and communication about goals, processes of goal accomplishment, respect for diversity in team members, and a collective effort to seek quality in each task and final product. This collaborative process brings a family atmosphere to the workplace and creates respect for the contributions by each member. The X generation believes in the participative leadership style, provided they have the support and opportunities from upper management to contribute to and influence team outcomes.

Transactional leaders attempt to balance initiating structure in order to get things done with meeting the needs of the people while things are getting done. This type of leadership requires the integration of organizational goals and expectations with the needs of the people doing the work. This style of leadership is based in the dual organization where the bureaucratic side conflicts with the professional one. The Gezels-Guba social systems model is widely known but abandoned in some recent textbooks. The model presents the two dimensions: idiographic (the needs of individuals) and nomothetic (the goals of the organization) and transactions between the two. This model depicts the dynamics of balancing the needs and productivity of the organization with the needs, personality, and dispositions of people doing the work. The workers may feel that the production goals of management are beyond the ability and energy of the workers. This dynamic is found in organizations of all kinds and is important for management to understand for morale and production reasons. Transactional leaders play the tit-for-tat game of rewarding employees as long as they are producing what management needs. James MacGregor Burns explains that transactional leaders motivate workers by offering rewards for what the leaders need done. According to Robert Owens, this popular form of leadership is an example of quid pro quo; leaders offer the lure of employment and security in return for collaboration and assistance, for example.

Transactional leadership reflects the reality of the workplace and continues to be the predominant model in most organizations, including public schools.

Transformational leaders demonstrate the elixir of human understanding. If applied with integrity, transformational leadership can reform organizations in magic ways. Leaders using this style create an environment where every person is empowered to fulfill his or her highest needs and becomes a member of a productive learning community. Transformational leaders are servants to others and guide them in creating and embracing a vision for the organization that inspires and brings forth top performance and creates a belief system of integrity, a cause beyond oneself, diversity of thought, and inclusiveness for all races and gender. Subsumed in this style is moral leadership, leading with love, and spiritual leadership. Moral leadership is based on dignity and respect for the rights of others to self-determination within moral bounds of the organization. Rather than an arbitrary set of rules to follow, moral leadership is a covenant to do the right things for others and live that covenant in all human interactions. Schools living moral leadership focus on the generic child and ensure that all staff members share in the belief that the school family must constantly work to inspire new and higher levels of trust and commitment to every child and each other in the school community.

Also linked to transformational leadership is leading with love. This leadership style reaches beyond leading with heart, soul, and morality and moves on to the concept of love in an attempt to reteach the lesson of history's great leaders. The most powerful leaders in history are remembered not for their positions, wealth, and number of publications or position but for their unconditional love for others. Leading with love revisits ideas that guide human kindness, social justice, and servant leadership and rediscovers ways to replace anger, mistrust, and hatred with love. This type of love is unselfish, loyal, and benevolent concern for the good of another. The Greeks used the work *agape* as the highest form of love. *Agape* is unselfish love, love of unlovable people, and love that overwhelms animosity in schools and other organizations.

Another important and emerging movement linked to transformational leadership is leadership for social justice. This postmodern position has heightened the urgency for research in educational administration to continue to reexamine its theories to ensure that no voices have been excluded and to direct efforts to guide superintendents, principals, and teachers in their efforts to guide schools toward greater inclusiveness, equity, and justice.

Perhaps the capstone of transformational leadership is spirituality. Deepak Chopra believes that leaders are the symbolic soul of the organizations they lead, that great leaders respond from the higher levels of spirit, and that leaders grow from the inside out. Others writers support the proposition that spiritual leadership calls for a power greater than mere human knowledge and experience. The spiritual and administrative sides are of equal importance when guiding a school or a school system dedicated to helping each student become a successful, ethical individual. Spiritual leaders assert that without a spiritual side, a leader lacks depth in understanding human motives and can destroy organizations and innocent lives. In addition, school administrators can be spiritual leaders and take charge of a given problem. Sometimes assertive and forceful leadership is the *only* strategy for school leaders. When students are not learning, teachers are not teaching, administrators are not administering, and support staff are not supporting, the superintendent and other administrators must take charge and create change in attitude, performance, and, if needed, personnel. Scholars write that spiritual leaders cannot allow children and youth to fail, nor can they stand idly by and ignore incompetence. To ignore children's failure and injustice and blame it on the child's background or family is spiritless leadership. Spiritual leadership is encouraging others to seek the highest vision, reaching for the highest human endeavors, and serving before being served. Writers concur that this is the most sought after form of the transformational leadership style.

A gradual shift from top-down authoritarian to transformational leadership is occurring in America's schools, but the need remains to conduct research that centers on research about leadership styles, staff morale, and student performance. Until definitive research can provide evidence that transformational leadership promoting equity, empowerment, morality, and love is the superior style for all schools and school districts, schools will continue to be a patchwork of authoritarian, participative, transactional, and transformational leadership styles.

—John R. Hoyle

See also authority; Barnard, Chester I.; bureaucracy; Burns, James MacGregor; capacity building, of organizations; charisma, of leaders; cognitive styles; consideration, caring;

creativity, in management; Follett, Mary Parker; human resource development; involvement, in organizations; leadership, system oriented; leadership, theories of; management theories; McGregor, Douglas; role model; Taylor, Frederick; Theory X, Theory Y; transformational leadership; women in educational leadership

Further Readings and References

Creighton, T. (2004). *Leading from below the surface.* Thousand Oaks, CA: Corwin Press.

Dimmock, C., & Walker, A. (2005). *Educational leadership: Culture and diversity.* Thousand Oaks, CA: Sage.

Fiedler, F. (1973). Recent developments in research on the contingency model. In E. Fleishman & J. Hunt (Eds.), *Current developments in the study of leadership.* Carbondale: Southern Illinois University Press.

Hoyle, J. (2002). *Leadership and the force of love.* Thousand Oaks, CA: Corwin Press.

Marshall, C., Tillman, L., Lopez, G., Larson, C., Capper, C., & Scheurich, J. (2003). Leadership for social justice: Identifying the terrain. Crafting a mission, and purpose. In F. Lunnenburg & C. Carr (Eds.), *Shaping the future: Policy, partnerships, and emerging perspectives. The 11th Yearbook of the National Council of Professors of Educational Administration* (pp. 85–98). Lanham, MD: Scarecrow Press.

McGregor, D. (1964). *The human side of enterprise.* New York: McGraw-Hill.

Ogawa, R. (2005). Leadership as social construct: The expression of human agency within organizational constraint. In F. English (Ed.), *The SAGE handbook of educational leadership* (pp. 89–108). Thousand Oaks, CA: Sage.

Sergiovanni, T. (1999). *Rethinking leadership.* Arlington Heights, IL: Skylight Professional Development.

Snowden, P., & Gorton, R. (2002). *School leadership and administration* (6th ed.). Boston: McGraw-Hill.

🏛 LEAGUE OF UNITED LATIN AMERICAN CITIZENS

The League of United Latin American Citizens (LULAC) was founded in 1929 in Corpus Christi, Texas. LULAC was actually the consolidation of three previous Mexican American organizations in existence at the time. LULAC is concerned with the economic condition, educational attainment, political influence, health, and civil rights of Hispanic Americans through advocacy and community-centered programs that exist in a nationwide network of 600 local councils. LULAC develops and works toward implementing a national platform of activities and programs via its national assembly and conventions.

The most recent LULAC national legislative platform endorsed (a) supporting affirmative action, (b) the use of adjusted census figures for redistricting purposes as well as for the distribution of federal funds for the states, (c) voter registration, encouraging all eligible immigrants to become U.S. citizens, (d) reform of the criminal justice system to reduce the numbers of Latinos who are incarcerated and eliminate the death penalty, (e) ending child labor, (f) legislation that enables Latinos to obtain driver's licenses, (g) diversity in the workplace, (h) expanding federal support to stimulate Latino businesses, job growth, and training, (i) expanding the number of enterprise zones along the border, (j) the renegotiation of trade agreements that will raise the standard of living for labor and protect the environment, (k) legislation that will decrease Latino dropout rates in schools, (l) the improvement of public schools and the admission of undocumented immigrant children with good records and moral character to be admitted to colleges and universities and obtain citizenship, (m) a national holiday in honor of Cesar Chavez, (n) stronger measures and prosecution of those committing hate crimes, (o) universal health care, (p) expansion of insurance coverage for children in poverty, (q) an increase in the number of representative Latinos in federal employment, (r) expansion of affordable housing, (s) an increase in Latino-oriented programming in all facets of the media, (t) legislation that provides for a congressionally recognized framework for the 4 million U.S. citizens living in Puerto Rico, (u) a guarantee to protect the quality of life for Latino seniors, and (v) pay equity for women and worker's rights.

Concurrently, LULAC opposes efforts (a) to prevent the collection of data based on race and ethnicity, (b) the exploitation of children working anywhere for low wages and under dangerous conditions, (c) the incarceration of youth in adult prisons, (d) the growing federal deficit, (e) national origin discrimination, (f) vouchers for schools, (g) college entrance exams as the sole or primary determinant in the admissions process, (h) all legislation that designates English as the official language of the United States, (i) the location of dump sites in or near Latino communities, (j) the expansion of the agricultural guest worker program that does not provide adequate labor rights protections, health benefits and housing, (k) any effort to require hospital emergency room personnel to check on the immigration status of patients, (l) the militarization of the border, including the use of vigilante patrolling groups, (m) drilling for oil on federal lands, and (n) the privatization of Social Security.

LULAC's emphasis on education is embodied in LULAC's National Education Service Centers (LNESCs) established in 1973, an effort to educate and prepare America's future workforce by providing over 1,000 scholarships through the National Scholarship Fund and helping nearly 400,000 students enroll in college. The core of the programs within LNESC includes Educational Talent Search, Gear Up, Upward Bound, the LULAC National Scholarship Fund, the Hispanic Leadership Opportunity Program, Science Corps, the Washington Youth Leadership Seminar, and Young Readers. Additional information on LULAC may be secured online at www.lulac.org. Over the years, LULAC has provided funds for the legal defense of Latinos and Latino interests and agendas in the nation. It was a LULAC-supported attorney who helped overthrow school segregation in Southern California in 1945 in *Mendez v. Westminster*, an action that predated *Brown v. Board of Education* by 8 years. Newer Latino political organizations include the Mexican American Legal Defense Fund (MALDEF) and the Mexican American Youth Organization (MAYO). The newer political awareness, militancy, and pride of the Mexican American heritage is referred to as *chicanismo*.

—*Fenwick W. English*

See also accountability; adult education; affirmative action; Chavez, Cesar Estrada; civil rights movement; compensatory education; critical race theory; cross-cultural studies; cultural capital; cultural politics, wars; desegregation, of schools; discipline in schools; discrimination; diversity; elementary education; ethnicity; ethnocentrism; immigration, history and impact in education; individual differences, in children; Latinos; Mendez, Felicitas; National Assessment of Educational Progress; Office of Economic Opportunity; performance assessment; politics, of education; power; school districts, history and development; social context; standardized testing; tracking, of students; underachievers, in schools

Further Readings and References

Chapa, J., & de la Rosa, B. (2004). Latino population growth, socioeconomic and demographic characteristics, and implications for educational attainment. *Education and Urban Society, 36*(2), 130–249.

Contreras, A. (2004). Latinos at the portal of the 21st century. *Education and Urban Society, 36*(2), 223–234.

Cortina, R., & Gendreau, M. (2003). *Immigrants and schooling: Mexicans in New York*. New York: Center for Migration Studies.

Garcia, E. (2005). *Teaching and learning in two languages*. New York: Teachers College Press.

LEARN, OPPORTUNITY TO

Opportunity to learn refers to the degree to which education is freely available and accessible to students in the United States. Although it may seem self-evident that our public institutions should provide a free and adequate education for all children and should adjust their curriculum and teaching/learning methods to ensure that every child has the *opportunity to learn,* this concept has always been and will probably continue to be a controversial one. The term has evolved over the years based on changing political and economic circumstances in the country and on the extent to which the society in general views education as a fundamental right of all its citizens.

HISTORICAL ROOTS

When state constitutions in the United States were created, most included the principle of free schools and citizen education funded through taxation. Public education in the United States was founded on the belief that in a democracy, the citizenry must have the *opportunity to learn.* However, this concept was not universally accepted without controversy, and there were many arguments about whether tax dollars should support education for all and about the extent to which the opportunity to learn should or should not be connected to promoting Christian religious beliefs. This issue persists today in the battle for separation of church and state in the school curriculum and continues to impact the degree to which citizens do or do not provide financial support for public institutions. In recent years, it has manifested itself with calls for using tax dollars to support private religious schools, expanding student opportunities to learn in contexts that explicitly foster religion in educational environments.

In most states, public education had an uneven beginning, with communities making individual decisions about whether schools would be formed and who would attend them. Horace Mann, the first secretary of the State Board of Education in Massachusetts, is generally considered the first educator to initiate the creation of a state system of public education. His goal was to provide common schools in which most children, including immigrant children, would have the opportunity to learn. Controversy about this inclusion and about making public schooling mandatory was loud and constant, with even those in the immigrant community sometimes voicing their opposition. Arguments regarding the inclusion of children whose parents are illegal immigrants in public education today are extensions of this disagreement about who should be educated using public dollars.

Eventually, public schooling was established in all states. It was mandatory for most, but not all students. Most students with disabilities were not required to attend these schools. In the South, political and social realities created the policies of separate but equal schools for Black and White children. Even though the schools were not in fact equal, the concept of providing children an equal opportunity to learn was a theoretical notion underlying this practice.

EXPANDING THE PARAMETERS OF OPPORTUNITY TO LEARN

In 1954, the *Brown v. Board of Education* Supreme Court ruling that separate schools are inherently unequal opened up a whole new framework of thinking in which equity became more comprehensively incorporated within the concept of opportunity to learn. Issues of adequate funding, quality of facilities, considering cultural differences, and meeting student needs became part of the conversation about how our society should provide opportunities for all children to learn. Though serving needy children was not a new conversation (ensuring opportunities for needy children was discussed by Mann, Maxwell, and others in the early 1900s), the responsibility of the states and the nation to provide equal opportunities for all students brought the issue out into a much more public arena.

In 1975, another issue entered the national dialogue when considering opportunities to learn when the Education for All Handicapped Children Act, commonly called 94–142, was passed. Among other things, this law held states and the nation accountable for ensuring that children with disabilities had the opportunity to learn, stressing that appropriate accommodations must be made to ensure this goal. These children had often been excluded from the notion and realities of educating "all" students. Many were kept at home or shunned in schools. This law forced a reexamination of these exclusive practices. Today, the move toward inclusion of children with disabilities in classes with children not so classified is another part of the movement toward ensuring all children have the opportunity to learn. This topic is filled with controversy as parents, teachers, students, and administrators strive to find an appropriate balance to ensure that learning opportunities are maximized for all.

Moving to a National Agenda

With the advent of the accountability movement in the United States, states have begun to demand that all children demonstrate competence at some level. The passage of the No Child Left Behind legislation expanded accountability to include national regulations. This law holds schools responsible for ensuring that all children achieve a minimum level of competency as measured by standardized tests. Under this legislation, gaps between minority and majority race children, between children of high and low socioeconomic levels, and between children with disabilities and those who are not so classified are to be narrowed. Thus, theoretically, all children are not only to be given the opportunity to learn, but they must achieve at a minimum level, or serious consequences will fall upon schools they attend. Students will be permitted to leave those schools to attend others that appear to be more successful in fostering student achievement.

Arguments are being made that since all students are being held to the same standards, they all must have equal access to high-quality instruction in order to ensure that they all have an equal opportunity to learn. Some writers have suggested that mandating that students pass tests, without ensuring that they have had the opportunity to learn what is being tested, is immoral and creates an accountability system that victimizes students.

Closely related to the imposition of national standards, based on standardized testing, is the notion that examining the opportunity to learn must include dealing with how students should demonstrate learning. The narrow system of standardized testing is being questioned as not adequately measuring student ability or performance. Those opposing this approach to measuring student performance suggest that discussing the opportunity to learn in the present accountability environment, without dealing with giving students varied opportunities to demonstrate learning, is doing a disservice to students, teachers, and learning and ignores the realities of student differences that must be a part of the conceptualization of learning opportunities.

EXAMINING FACTORS THAT IMPACT OPPORTUNITY TO LEARN ON AN INDIVIDUAL BASIS

Researchers are also expanding the concept of opportunity to learn by examining factors that inhibit or facilitate learning for students of differing backgrounds and abilities. They have begun to uncover structural processes within schools that appear to enhance or limit students' opportunity to learn based on the types of courses students take, particularly in high schools. Their research examines how learning opportunities are distributed among students based upon whether they are considered slow, low, or high learners. Such issues center on whether there are differences in how these students are taught, in the quality of the teachers they have, and in the kinds of knowledge they have access to. This research is tied to equity issues as researchers suggest that denying similar learning opportunities to students in lower-level classes hinders their employment capacities and stifles the development of their higher order thinking skills. They suggest that all students should be given similar learning opportunities in order to facilitate their potential for learning and eventually their status in life.

Other factors being studied in terms of opportunity to learn deal with the teaching and environmental strategies that maximize student learning. Examining learning styles, creating alternative teaching methods, constructing facilities and classroom spaces around teaching and learning, and establishing varied classroom environments are the types of topics that are dealt with when investigating what to consider when dealing with providing the opportunity to learn to all.

Another research area related to opportunity to learn examines the extent to which students' past experiences and the experiences they have in their classrooms relate to their ability to learn a specific subject such as science or mathematics or to succeed in specific learning environments such as preschool or college. Researchers have examined this issue in terms of such things as gender differences and motivational levels and have related them to specific subject areas such as science, geography, and computer science to aid educators in devising teaching/learning models that will compensate for lack of experience and build upon strong experiential foundations.

When schools were established in this country, providing an opportunity to learn seemed like a simple concept of providing free public education for all. However, differences in beliefs about the purposes of schools and the extent to which schools must adapt in order to meet student needs make this a complex and difficult issue to address. While there appears to be agreement that all children should succeed in school,

the degree to which the society and educational leaders are willing to (a) invest resources, (b) conduct research to determine how best to teach and measure student performance to meet individual needs, and (c) change teaching/learning strategies and environments to meet diverse needs is unknown. There is a growing body of knowledge that suggests we must make major changes in the teaching/learning environment and in the way in which learning is judged if all students are to receive an opportunity to learn. Whether this will occur is yet to be determined.

—Frances K. Kochan

See also accountability; achievement gap, of students; achievement tests; affective domain; at-risk students; Black education; class size; classroom management; climate, school; cognition, theories of; compensatory education; critical race theory; critical thinking; cross-cultural studies; cultural capital; cultural politics, wars; curriculum, theories of; diversity; dropouts; early childhood education; equality, in schools; equity and adequacy of funding schools; human capital; individual differences, in children; intelligence; learning environments; Mann, Horace; mastery learning; Maxwell, William H.; minorities, in schools; motivation, theories of; No Child Left Behind; performance assessment; psychology, types of; reading, history of, use in schools; rural education; special education; standardized testing; systemic reform; time-on-task; tracking, of students; underachievers, in schools

Further Readings and References

Alexander, B., Anderson, G., & Gallegos, B. (2005). *Performance theories in education.* Mahwah, NJ: Erlbaum.

Ansalone, G., & Biafora, F. (2004). Elementary school teachers' perceptions and attitudes to the educational structure of tracking. *Education, 125*(2), 249–259.

Bogotch, I. (2005). A history of public school leadership: The first century, 1837–1942. In F. English (Ed.), *The SAGE handbook of educational leadership* (pp. 7–33). Thousand Oaks, CA: Sage.

Clements, D., Sarama, J., & DiBiase, A. (Eds.). (2004). *Engaging young children in mathematics.* Mahwah, NJ: Erlbaum.

DeStefano, A., Rudestam, K., & Silverman, R. (2004). *Encyclopedia of distributed learning.* Thousand Oaks, CA: Sage.

Levstik, L., & Barton, K. (2005). *Doing history.* Mahwah, NJ: Erlbaum.

Smutny, J., & von Fremd, S. (2004). *Differentiating for the young child.* Thousand Oaks, CA: Corwin Press.

Stone, R. (2004). *Best teaching practices for reaching all learners.* Thousand Oaks, CA: Corwin Press.

🏛 LEARNING, ONLINE

Online learning is delivered via the Internet. Courses or learning experiences are designed to take advantage of being online and having a range of tools and options not available in the same ways within a traditional classroom. It offers a rich potential to students, and this potential is beginning to be tapped by school leaders.

Before online learning became widely available and affordable, students in small high schools frequently were unable to take advanced placement courses. They were restricted to a single foreign language option. Often physics or other higher-level science classes were not taught, and even years 3 and 4 of foreign languages were taught together, denying students opportunities to engage in programs that would enable them to be prepared for college and career. Online learning has increased the options and opportunities for students.

In the academic year 2002–2003, approximately 8,200 public K–12 schools had students engaged in distance learning. These figures are from a National Center for Education Statistics report, based on survey data, released in March 2005. Over three quarters of the schools offering distance courses were high schools. At the high school level, a large percentage of the distance courses were advanced placement, foreign language, or college-credit opportunities for students. Smaller schools and rural schools reported higher numbers of distance courses. Recent samplings suggest that the numbers of online courses are increasing, with more schools providing them to students.

Online courses may be taught through synchronous (at the same time) or asynchronous (time period set in general terms, not specific hours) methods. Often the online courses are a combination, providing lectures and discussion at a particular time, and further discussions and activities are provided asynchronously. Some online courses include an opportunity to be synchronous and have visual and sound connectivity. Many utilize a chat-type setting. There are increasing numbers of conference opportunities employed within courses, depending on resources, equipment, and other considerations. As more K–12 schools are connected to Internet2 or other powerful connections, these options will become common. Hybrid courses involve multiple ways of disseminating material and engaging students. These may include DVD-based lectures, live chat sessions, asynchronous discussions and activities, learning objects (including simulations), video conference sessions, print materials, and even occasional face-to-face conferences or meetings.

Some schools establish a time within the school day when students are engaged in online learning at the school site, eliminating the issue of attendance accounting. The context is a regular time and a regular place with a teacher or paraprofessional as a support. Students may be taking one or more courses, and the adult present often is not expert in any of the fields, yet he or she is there for technology support, examinations, and general supervision. Students may or may not have access to the course outside the context of this daily session. Often the school, which may have the best Internet connectivity in the area, provides priority access for students taking online courses before and after school in addition to within the school day.

Many online courses are offered as if they were an additional period before or after school but without the place and time being designated. Students select their own time and place to be engaged in the course. Frequent reports may be provided by the course instructor to satisfy attendance requirements in the local districts, since seat time remains the major means of determining attendance for districts.

There are many reasons for schools and regional coalitions to utilize online courses. Scheduling conflicts, small and scattered populations of learners or potential learners for a particular subject, the need to target specific groups with specialized instruction, requirements to offer advanced placement courses without adequate numbers of students and/or qualified faculty, a desire to offer college-credit-attaining courses without numbers or faculty, or infusing richness into the curriculum that is not possible due to isolation cause school leaders to consider this opportunity. There are some schools that are using the online courses to mitigate the limited space on the campuses due to growth and lack of immediate funding. Others use online courses to allow students to retake a course for a higher grade. A few districts see online courses as a way to offer a rich program while saving money.

Homeschooling utilizing online courses, both through programs connected to the public schools and through private enterprises, increasingly is a medium of choice for families. Sometimes this choice is based on convenience, as in the case of families distant from the closest schools, traveling families, or children employed in the entertainment business, and other times the choice is based on concern about the local schools. Instead of being used as an addition or enhancement to the school curriculum, these students are educated primarily through online sources, never visiting a school building. There is precedent for the virtual school, such as the distance programs, largely radio based, utilized in remote areas of Canada and Australia for dozens of years.

Students whose school experience is largely an online one are a different population from those whose classroom experience is supplemented by online courses. Socialization, attending to social cues, development of empathy, and similar social skills learned in the classroom environment are not as much a part of the online setting. Teaching cooperation and sharing, a part of the face-to-face elementary school experience, is not part of the online course. Collaboration and cooperative teaching and learning is expected in well-crafted online courses, but it is based on participants having had experience with such collaborations in a face-to-face environment. These are activities that should supplement any online or virtual schooling program that is the primary means of providing students their education.

Other difficulties with online teaching and learning include authenticating who is being tested and who actually is doing the assignments, providing active learning, meeting the needs of individual students and their learning styles, and maintaining a highly engaged learning situation. Teaching online is different from teaching in a face-to-face setting. Teachers frequently know what is happening with students in their classes from the expressions and physical cues. Online, there are few cues and clues to changes in attitudes unless the work is not being done. Reaching out and encouraging is different and, often, difficult. Even when there are sessions using video conferencing systems, the nuances of behaviors are much more subtle than in face-to-face settings. The key to success in the virtual school is having engaged adults at both ends of the teaching and learning so students know they are cared about and that their learning is monitored.

High-quality online teaching is not modeled after face-to-face teaching. because the modalities for delivering the instruction are significantly different. The increasing multimedia capabilities of computers help make the online classroom more engaging and responsive, but teaching within the online setting requires different pedagogical acumen. Educational organizations, whether at the school, regional, or state level, must invest in preparing teachers to be effective online instructors. They also must prepare students to

be effective online learners. In addition, the educational organizations must provide support for the online course venture. They must consider what effective teaching online is and how to prepare teachers for the task. In addition, they must establish ways to assess online teaching and online courses.

Teaching effectively online requires

- Responding frequently to posts and emails
- Extensive searching for Web-based resources
- Flexibility
- Hardware, software, and Internet competency
- Experience with course management systems as learner in addition to instructor
- Background in information literacy, law, and ethics
- Understanding of special needs and disability issues vis-à-vis the Web
- Ability to develop and implement student-centered activities
- Willingness and skill to be a facilitator and guide, not a lecturer
- Orientation toward collaboration, problem-based learning
- Encouraging and supportive
- Understanding of Bloom's taxonomy and how to encourage students to move from knowledge into higher-level thinking skills
- Recognition that online necessitates more feedback and engagement with students than face-to-face

To this end, a well-crafted, effectively conducted online professional development and, even better, certification course for those who will be teaching online courses should include modules on

- Effective facilitation of learning online
- Creating discussions that afford an entire class an opportunity to present and consider the topic
- How to encourage discussion, deal with "discussion busters," and support individual student learning through discussions
- Ways to ensure high-level involvement and quality participation
- Developing WebQuests and other learning objects that encourage targeted searching of the Web for high-quality materials
- Information literacy
- Matching learning activities to course objectives
- Comparing traditional methods with online pedagogies
- Assessment tools, including rubrics, quizzes, and more
- Copyright law as it applies to online teaching and learning
- Special needs, access, and online courses

- Feedback and how to use it to engage students
- Designing collaborative and/or problem-based projects for online learning
- Means for assessing one's own success
- Tools within the course management system and how to employ them effectively

An online venture includes students. They need to be prepared for the changes in how they will access the course and other aspects of learning online. Online students should be

- Able to work without constant supervision
- Good readers and writers
- Technology competent
- Good typists
- Self-motivated and self-starting
- Understanding and accepting of other ideas and opinions
- Curious
- Honest, honorable

Research on online learning and teaching has produced examples of best practice. Hallmarks of successful online courses and programs include

- Use of highly engaging activities
- Clear expectations with scaffolding to assist students in meeting the standards
- High touch environment and a sense of place despite the virtual nature of online courses
- Engaged adults at each end—teacher and parents or others near the students
- Media rich classes
- Timely, supportive, and encouraging feedback
- Flexible, yet well planned, classes
- Challenging activities that produce quality work and minimize violations of honesty
- Frequent assessment of students, instructor, course, and the experience
- Reliable technology with support provided
- Routine review of courses, matching activities and expectations with the standards for face-to-face instruction
- Accreditation
- Support for the online teaching and learning process from administration, governing board, parents, and other stakeholders

Online courses may be cost effective, since they enable a school or region to serve small and scattered populations with highly qualified teachers. The fact that they may not require school site space also may offer a savings. Online courses must, however, have a limited enrollment to enable the teacher to maintain quality contact with each student. These contacts are more time intense than those in face-to-face courses. Research-based estimates of time suggest 1.5 times as many hours go into teaching an effective online course as a similar face-to-face course.

The potential for online courses is great. Over 70% of the schools and districts currently involved in online courses plan to increase their offerings. Those not making such plans cited infrastructure weaknesses, attendance funding, and course quality. Legislatures in several states are grappling with ways to deal with attendance formulas to include online courses to remove this barrier. Accrediting bodies have developed guidelines for assessing quality in online courses. Teacher education institutions and other agencies are developing courses to prepare teachers for online instructing. As more university students receive a portion of their education online, teaching online will become a more understood option. Course and class Web pages are commonplace; increased instructional options are moving to online. More fully online courses for K–12 students are coming.

Online learning offers professional development opportunities to teachers, administrators, counselors, and other school staff members. Districts, counties, regions, and states are taking advantage of this option to conduct trainings that both save travel and reach targeted groups. Frequently, districts contract with nonprofit or private groups to offer a wide variety of courses online to support teachers. The growth in online learning at K–12 schools is reaching students and adults working in those schools.

—*Penelope Walters Swenson*

See also adult education; brain research and practice; communications, theories in organizations; computers, use and impact of; curriculum, theories of; digital divide; discourse theory; instructional interventions; instructional technology; language theories and processes; learning, theories of; life span development; literacy, theories of; management information systems; market theory of schooling; mentoring; motivation, theories of; schooling effects; time management

Further Readings and References

Berge, Z., & Clark, T. (Eds.). (2005). *Virtual schools: Planning for success.* New York: Teachers College Press.
Carr-Chellman, A. (2005). *Global perspectives on e-learning.* Thousand Oaks, CA: Sage.

Hiltz, S., & Goldman, R. (Eds.). (2005). *Learning together online.* Mahwah, NJ: Erlbaum.

North Central Regional Educational Laboratory. (2002). *Virtual schools and e-learning in K–12 environments.* Retrieved March 18, 2005, from http://www.ncrel.org/policy/pubs/html/piv0111/apr2002a.htm.

Seiter, E. (2005). *The internet playground: Children's access, entertainment, and mis-education.* New York: Peter Lang.

Setzer, J., & Lewis, L. (2005). *Distance education courses for public elementary and secondary school students: 2002–03.* Washington, DC: National Center for Education Statistics. Retrieved March 17, 2005,from http://nces.ed.gov/pubs2005/2005010.pdf.

Wenglinsky, H. (2005). *Using technology wisely.* New York: Teachers College Press.

LEARNING, THEORIES OF

Learning theory is characterized by two different conceptions of learning: (1) learning as a permanent change in behavior—the behaviorist perspective, and (2) learning as a permanent change in mental associations—the cognitivist perspective.

BEHAVIORISM

Behaviorists believe that learning is the result of environmental stimuli that "condition" behavior responses. Behaviorists assume that human beings and animals learn in the same way, so principles derived from research with animals are applied to human learning. Learning is studied by observing and measuring an organism's responses to environmental stimuli.

From his studies of cats trying to get out of a puzzle box, Edward Thorndike posited that learning generally involves trial-and-error behavior. When responses are followed by satisfying consequences, those responses are strengthened, but when responses are followed by discomfort, those responses are weakened. Practice facilitates the learning of responses.

Ivan Pavlov, a Russian physiologist, developed the theory of classical conditioning as he was studying salivation in dogs. Pavlov concluded that organisms could be conditioned to demonstrate an involuntary response (e.g., salivation) through the pairing of two stimuli (e.g., meat powder and a bell ringing).

B. F. Skinner proposed the principles of operant conditioning. Skinner believed we learn behaviors that are followed by certain consequences. He developed the Skinner box to study responses (e.g., a rat pressing a metal bar) and effects of reinforcers (e.g., getting a food pellet as a reinforcer for pressing a metal bar) in a controlled environment. Skinner observed that responses are strengthened by reinforcers or consequences that increase the frequency of a behavior. He also observed that a reinforcer must follow a response immediately and must be presented only if the desired response occurs.

Clark Hull suggested that the presence of intervening variables unique to each organism influenced a response to a stimulus. Hull posited that intervening variables (e.g., habit strength, drive, stimulus intensity, incentive) work together to increase the likelihood and relative strength of a particular response. Inhibitory factors (e.g., fatigue) decreased the likelihood and strength of a response.

Behaviorist learning theory has affected classroom practices in several ways. Teachers have been taught the importance of reinforcement and the fact that learning is more likely to occur in environments that provide positive consequences for learning. Reinforcers may be material objects, signs of positive regard, opportunity to engage in favorite activities, good feelings, or positive feedback on learning performance. It is important for students to be active respondents. Repetition and reinforcement strengthen desired stimulus-response habits.

SOCIAL AND HIERARCHICAL LEARNING THEORY

Social learning theory focuses on how people learn from one another in a social context. Albert Bandura at Stanford University was integral to the development of social learning theory. Bandura believed that people learn through observing and modeling what others do. He identified three types of models: (1) live (a person is demonstrating a behavior), (2) symbolic (a person or character in a film, television show, book, etc., is demonstrating a behavior), and (3) verbal instruction (a description is given about how one is supposed to behave). Bandura proposed that four conditions are necessary for someone to learn through modeling: (1) the individual must pay attention to the model and to essential components of the modeled behavior, (2) the individual must remember the behavior by developing verbal and visual memory codes as guides for performing the observed behavior, (3) the individual must want to demonstrate the behavior, and (4) the individual must replicate the behavior.

Bandura proposed that self-efficacy plays an important role in learning. When individuals believe they are capable of performing learned behaviors successfully, they are more likely to engage in those behaviors. Feelings of self-efficacy affect choice of activities, effort, and persistence. Individuals tend to choose activities where they believe they will be successful and avoid activities where they believe they may fail. Individuals with high self-efficacy tend to exert more effort and persist longer when encountering barriers or obstacles in working at a task.

Bandura also emphasized the role of self-regulation of behavior. Self-regulation involves setting standards for one's own behavior, observing oneself in action and identifying what aspects of one's performance are working well and which are not, judging and evaluating one's own behaviors based on the standards one has set, and self-praising when goals are accomplished or self-criticizing when standards are not met.

Robert Gagné proposed a hierarchy of eight types of learning behaviors. The behaviors transition from behaviorist to cognitivist learning principles and represent a cumulative learning process. Gagné's eight learning behaviors are as follows:

1. Signed learning, where a response is made to a given signal

2. Stimulus response, where a response is made to a given stimulus

3. Motor chains, where two or more stimulus-response connections are linked together to form a complex skill

4. Verbal association, where two or more words or ideas are linked together

5. Multiple discriminations, where different responses are made to different components of a particular set

6. Concepts, where abstract reactions are made to stimuli

7. Rules, where two or more stimulus situations or concepts are chained

8. Problem solving, where known rules or principles are combined in new ways to solve a problem

Gagné also identified five learning outcomes that he believed are observable and measurable and constitute for him the domains of learning: (1) intellectual skills—categorizing and using verbal and mathematical symbols, forming concepts through rules, problem solving, (2) information—knowing facts, names, dates, places, (3) cognitive strategies for processing and organizing information, (4) motor skills, and (5) attitudes.

Social and hierarchical learning theories have had several implications for classroom practice. Students learn what behaviors are and are not acceptable by seeing the consequences of behaviors in which others engage. Adults must be conscious of their behaviors and model appropriate behaviors. Appropriate behaviors can be increased by clearly describing consequences of behaviors. Students' self-efficacy affects their learning. Self-efficacy can be enhanced through confidence-building messages from others, watching others be successful, and experiencing success oneself. Teachers can help students set realistic standards for performance based on their current skills and ability levels, and they can help students develop self-instruction, self-monitoring, and self-reinforcement skills. Curriculum should be organized so that concepts, skills, and learning tasks are hierarchically sequenced to develop complex cognition.

COGNITIVISM

Cognitivism has dominated learning research and theory development since the 1960s but appeared in earlier decades in the work of Edward Tolman, the Gestalt psychologists, Jean Piaget, and Lev Vygotsky.

Like his behaviorist contemporaries, Edward Tolman conducted research on animals. He emphasized global or molar behaviors rather than isolated stimulus-response connections. He believed learning can occur without reinforcement and without change in behavior. Tolman also believed that individual intervening variables play important roles in learning. He stressed that behavior is goal directed and that organisms develop expectations about the outcomes of their behaviors. Tolman proposed that knowledge is organized and that organisms make inferences about situations and environments based on this organized knowledge.

German Gestalt psychologists Max Wertheimer, Wolfgang Köhler, and Kurt Koffka further stressed the importance of organizational processes in perception, learning, and problem solving. Max Wertheimer observed that perception is often different from reality. Köhler illustrated that experiences cannot be well understood by looking only at isolated parts; one may learn more from the whole in combination rather than from the individual parts. Organisms structure and organize experiences and are predisposed to organize experiences in particular ways.

Jean Piaget studied how children think and learn. Piaget proposed that people are not passive respondents to environments but are active processors of information. Knowledge is structured in schemes or mental units that are modified as individuals interact with others and their environments. People interact with their environments through assimilation (consistency with existing cognitive schemes) or accommodation (modification of existing schemes or formation of new schemes). He believed that people were intrinsically motivated to make sense of the world around them.

Piaget identified four distinct stages of cognitive development. In the sensorimotor stage (birth to 2 years), cognition is characterized by behavior- and perception-based schemes. In the preoperational stage (2 to 6 or 7 years), language skills develop and new mental schemes develop around words. In concrete operations (7 to 11 or 12 years), logical thinking emerges and is applied to concrete, observable objects and events. Formal operations develop after 11 to 12 years of age. Children develop the ability to reason with abstract, hypothetical, and contrary-to-fact information. Piaget also posited that children's progression through the four stages of cognitive development is limited by maturation (genetically controlled physiological changes).

Russian psychologist Lev Vygotsky also studied children's thinking in the 1920s and early 1930s, but his major writings were not translated into English until much later. Vygotsky believed that mental processes develop through social interactions and that thought and language processes develop independently, merging when children are about 2 years old. Vygotsky suggested that children have two kinds of abilities, an actual developmental level where the child can perform tasks independently without assistance and a level of potential development where the child can perform tasks with assistance from a more competent individual. Vygotsky proposed that children learn best in the zone of proximal development, that cognitive level where a child's problem-solving abilities are beginning to develop and where the child can be challenged to attempt tasks with the assistance of a more competent individual.

Cognitive theories share several important ideas:

- People and animals may not learn in the same ways. People possess abilities unique to the species.
- Mental events are central to studying learning.
- The study of learning should be objective, and learning theories should be based on evidence. However, inferences can be drawn about the nature of internal mental events that produce observed responses.
- Individuals are actively involved in the learning process and control their own learning.
- Learning involves the formation of mental associations not necessarily reflected in overt behavior changes.
- Knowledge, beliefs, attitudes, and emotions are all associated and connected, that is, organized.
- Learning involves relating new information to previously learned information.

INFORMATION PROCESSING THEORY

Information processing theory has been central to contemporary cognitivism. In information processing theory, learners are viewed as active seekers and processors of information. Computer processing is a common metaphor for information processing theory. The underlying assumption is that information must be moved through several different sequential stages in order for it to be remembered. Information comes in from the environment and is attended to. It must be encoded so that it can be stored in memory. Encoding involves the creation of memory traces that are then stored in internal memory, which is like a computer's disk drive storage system. Retrieval is the process of finding previously stored information so that it can be used again. Retrieval is somewhat like accessing a computer's database. Increasing students' ability to recall and use information is important for increased learning. Retention of information is longer and retrieval is easier if information is overlearned, if understanding concepts is stressed over repetition of facts, when new information is linked to and builds on existing information, and when students are helped to develop cue associations to enhance active searching for information.

CONSTRUCTIVISM

Constructivism is a perspective that has emerged over the last 20 years. In constructivism the learner is the active agent, internalizing, reshaping, or transforming information and constructing meaning or understanding. In constructing meaning, the learner connects new learning with existing knowledge and prior experiences. The learners conjecture, question, project, and form interpretations of the world reflective of their perceptions, experiences, and interactions with the world. Constructivism views knowledge as interpretive rather than objective.

An important component of constructivism is the learner's awareness of the mental processes being used to construct meaning and the regulation of those processes to enhance learning and memory. This metacognitive knowledge and skills include (a) being aware of one's own learning and memory capabilities and limitations, (b) knowing what one can realistically accomplish in a learning task, (c) knowing which learning strategies are effective for particular outcomes and which are not, (d) planning an approach to a learning task, (e) using effective learning strategies, (f) monitoring whether one has successfully learned information or not, and (g) knowing effective strategies for retrieving information from memory.

Cognitive learning theories have several implications for classroom practices. Cognitivism focuses on the active agency of learners. Learning is enhanced when students ask questions, are not fearful of being wrong, take thinking risks, and play with knowledge and ideas. What students learn is not the only important focus for classroom learning; how students are trying to process information and create meaning is also important. Instructional topics, strategies, and activities must take students' current level of cognitive processing into account. Helping students learn to take notes, identify important information, organize information, relate new information to existing information, make connections among different areas of information, and use prior knowledge to interpret or expand on new information can facilitate understanding. Students need to be aware of their own comprehension and engage in summarizing and self-questioning to monitor what they have and have not learned successfully. Cognizance of mental processes builds the learner's abilities to regulate and use those processes to construct knowledge and understanding.

—*Judith A. Ponticell*

See also adult education; affective domain; Baer, Donald; behaviorism; Binet, Alfred; Cattell, Raymond; cognition, theories of; conditioning theory; constructivism; Dewey, John; early childhood education; emotional disturbance; feedback; giftedness, gifted education; Havighurst, Robert; individual differences, in children; intelligence; Jung, Carl; language theories and processes; measurement, theories of; metacognition; Piaget, Jean; problem solving; professional learning communities; psychology, types of; psychometrics; Skinner, B. F.; Spearman, Charles; special education; standardized testing; Thorndike, Edward; Wolf, Montrose

Further Readings and References

Bandura, A. (1986). *Social foundations of thought and action: A social cognitive theory.* Englewood Cliffs, NJ: Prentice Hall.

Gagné, R. M., Briggs, L. J., & Wager, W. W. (1988). *Principles of instructional design* (3rd ed.). New York: Holt, Rinehart & Winston.

Koffka, K. (1935). *Principles of Gestalt psychology.* New York: Harcourt Brace.

Köhler, W. (1929). *Gestalt psychology.* New York: Liveright.

Pavlov, I. P. (1927). *Conditioned reflexes* (G. V. Anrep, Trans.). London: Oxford University Press.

Piaget, J. (1952). *The origins of intelligence in children* (M. Cook, Trans.). New York: W. W. Norton.

Skinner, B. F. (1938). *The behavior of organisms: An experimental analysis.* Englewood Cliffs, NJ: Prentice Hall.

Thorndike, E. L. (1898). Animal intelligence: An experimental study of the associative processes in animals. *Psychological Review Monograph Supplement, 2*(8).

Tolman, E. C. (1932). *Purposive behavior in animals and men.* New York: Century.

Vygotsky, L. S. (1978). *Mind in society: The development of higher psychological processes.* Cambridge, MA: Harvard University Press.

Wertheimer, M. (1945). *Productive thinking.* New York: Harper.

LEARNING ENVIRONMENTS

Every organization, whether educational, political, cultural, industrial, or business related, has a learning environment with its unique culture and climate. Together these create the personality or ethos of the organization. Research on 20 schools found a significant difference in student achievement between schools with a positive or negative climate. Thus, a positive learning environment promotes learning whereas a negative environment is known to deter optimal knowledge obtainment.

Climate can be defined as the social atmosphere of a setting; thus the learning environment in which participants have different experiences, depending upon the protocols wherein they are operating. These learning environments can be divided into three categories:

1. Relationships, including involvement, support, and affiliation with others

2. Personal growth or goal orientation, including personal development and self-enhancement of all members of the organization

3. System maintenance and system change, including the orderliness of the environment, clarity of the rules, and the strictness of the person enforcing them

A learning environment includes, but is not limited to, physical facilities and settings, types of students, school and community characteristics, resource availability, climate, and degrees of support. Research on which issues correlate to learning and student achievement has determined that schools must have a safe and orderly environment, a climate of high expectations for success, strong instructional leadership, a clear and focused mission, an opportunity to learn and have appropriate time on task, frequent monitoring of student progress, and strong home-school relations.

Organizational climate is often used interchangeably with organizational culture. They are closely intertwined and dependent, yet distinct. Culture is the psychological attributes that give an organization its personality, whereas climate is the institutional features that can be seen. An example would be a metaphor of an iceberg itself, whereas climate is the tip of the iceberg itself. Yet it is supported by the underlying value and belief systems and traditions that form the organizational culture. There appear to be six climate variables that are similar to Larry Lezotte's effective schools' correlates. These are instructional leadership, classroom instruction, high expectations, parent and community involvement, a sense of mission, and time on task. In the earlier Lezotte research, a safe and orderly environment is clearly one of the contributing factors to a positive school or organizational climate. The first generation correlate of a safe and orderly environment was defined in terms of the absence of undesirable or negative circumstances. However, in the second generation, the emphasis is on the presence of desirable circumstances. Thus, the emphasis has changed from the presence of positive versus negative factors.

The physical, emotional, and social components of an organization play a large role in the total well-being of the learners. This is particularly important within the educational society where more is expected from today's schools than within the last hundred years. Careful consideration must be given to an environment that fosters careful attention to the knowledge, skills, attitudes, and beliefs that learners bring to the educational setting. This includes the instructor possessing sensitivity to the cultural orientation of students and the effect of those perspectives and beliefs on classroom learning. Effective teachers help learners see the reason or purpose for learning by respecting and understanding their former experiences, understandings and assuming that these can serve as a foundation on which to build bridges to new learning.

—*Elaine L. Wilmore*

See also achievement gap, of students; arts education; behaviorism; capacity building, of organizations; class size; classroom management; climate, school; cross-cultural studies; coeducation; constructivism; differentiated instruction; discipline in schools; diversity; ethos, of organizations; expectations, teacher and student cultures; governance; Head Start; individual differences, in children; language theories and processes; middle schools; Montessori, Maria; morale; motivation, theories of; neuroscience; resiliency; schooling effects; social capital; social context; social psychology; social relations, dimensions of; special education; standardized testing; underachievers, in schools

Further Readings and References

Lezotte, L. (n.d.). *Correlates of effective schools: The first and second generation.* Retrieved February 22, 2004, from .

Wilmore, E. L. (2003). *Principal leadership.* Thousand Oaks, CA: Corwin Press.

🏛 *LEMON* TEST

In *Lemon v. Kurtzman,* 403 U.S. 602 (1971), the U.S. Supreme Court created a three-part test to determine when public aid to private religious schools violates the constitutional separation of church and state. To be permissible, public aid to a private religious school must meet the following criteria: (a) it must have a secular purpose, (b) its primary effect must neither advance nor prohibit religion, and (c) it must not foster excessive governmental entanglement with religion. As a general rule, private religious schools can receive government aid when the aid benefits students directly, is available equally to public school students, and is free of explicit religious content.

Initially, the Supreme Court rigidly applied the *Lemon* test and outlawed many government aid programs to private religious schools. Impermissible programs included those that subsidized teacher salaries and field trips, loaned maps and audiovisual equipment, and defrayed administrative and maintenance costs. Most often, the Court considered the public aid impermissible because significant resources would be needed to ensure that the public aid was not being used for religious purposes. Then the Court considered the government to be excessively entangled in the religious nature of the school.

During this same period, the Supreme Court also upheld a number of public aid programs that benefited private religious schools. Permissible programs included those that supplied state-prepared standardized tests, loaned textbooks, provided state employees to assist special needs students, and allowed students to participate in Title I programs. Textbooks were distinguished from maps and audiovisual equipment because their use was easily determined by inspecting their content. No excessive entanglements were necessary to monitor textbook compliance. In these initial cases, the Court presumed that any aid to private religious schools would benefit their religious mission.

Over time, the Court began to interpret the entanglement prong of the *Lemon* test less strictly, eventually making it part of the primary effect prong. Using this new interpretation, the Court began to permit programs requiring only that they be neutral on their face. For example, the Court permitted income tax deductions for expenses at private religious schools when comparable tax deductions were available for expenses at public schools. The income tax deduction did not excessively entangle the government in religion because it was a general benefit open to the parents of all students. Using similar reasoning, the Court eventually permitted tuition vouchers for private schools, even when they were used predominantly at religious schools.

In *Mitchell v. Helms,* 530 U.S. 1973 (2000), the Supreme Court reversed its presumption that aid to private religious schools would benefit their religious missions. The Court stated that it would permit the government to provide aid that could be used for either secular or religious purposes unless there was proof that the school used the aid to advance or inhibit religion. The aid at issue in this case was a government program that lent computers and other instructional materials to both public and private schools.

The *Lemon* test continues to be the standard for determining permissible government aid to private religious schools; however, religious neutrality rather than excessive government entanglement is the guiding principle.

—*Eric Haas*

See also Catholic education; charter schools; fundamentalism; prayer in school; religion, in schools; right-wing politics, advocates, impact on education; special education; standardized testing; Supreme Court, United States, key cases in education law; technology and the law; testing and test theory development; textbooks; voucher plans

Further Readings and References

Mueller v. Allen, 463 U.S. 388 (1983).
Russo, C. (2005). The role of education law in leadership preparation programs. In F. English (Ed.), *The SAGE handbook of educational leadership* (pp. 168–185). Thousand Oaks, CA: Sage.
Zelman v. Simmons-Harris, 536 U.S. 639 (2002).

LESBIAN/GAY/BISEXUAL/ TRANSGENDER ISSUES IN EDUCATION

Issues concerning same-sex desire and nonconforming gender identity have become among the most common and contentious ones facing education leaders today. Although persons who identify as lesbian, gay, bisexual, transgender (LGBT), or queer long have worked or studied in schools, critical public attention has focused on them in recent decades. Activists in the LGBT rights movement have drawn attention to persistent employment discrimination experienced by school workers who defy sexuality and gender norms. Student organizers of gay/straight alliances in high schools have compelled school communities to confront the harassment, violence, and discrimination often directed toward LGBT and questioning students. Conversely, organized conservative religious and political groups have fought against the employment of school workers they claim corrupt the nascent gender and sexuality identities of students, the inclusion of curricular materials depicting LGBT persons in a positive light, or the founding of school-based groups that support the unique concerns of LGBT and allied persons. While open clashes between these groups began to flare during the 1970s in high-profile events such as Anita Bryant's Save Our Children campaign or John Briggs's Proposition 6 referendum that would have enabled, if not required, California schools to terminate the employment of LGBT school workers and their allies, today such conflicts occur in every community and school. All students and school workers are affected by decisions such as those concerning (a) gender-bound dress codes, (b) what kinds of couples may dance together at school events, (c) if or when students may participate in activities traditionally reserved for one sex, (d) the boundaries between acceptable social interchange and that which harasses or intimidates on account of gender or sexual identity, and (e) who is chosen to work with students. In short, LGBT issues are pervasive in schools and affect everyone.

Gender and sexual orientation are distinct concepts. Gender is a set of stories that people tell themselves and each other about what it means to be men and women. These stories vary by culture and historical era. As is the case with any socially created quality, gender is quite complex. One's gender is negotiated throughout a lifetime in interaction with unique social contexts. Sexual orientation concerns sexual desire—who experiences it and for whom. Gender and sexuality are linked in that gender assists individuals in navigating sexual choices within a given culture, helping them find others with whom sexual activity may be a possibility. Like gender, sexual orientation contains important socially constructed components.

Despite distinctions between these concepts, they typically have been conflated. For example, during much of the twentieth century it has been popularly assumed that persons manifesting conventional gender qualities must be heterosexual. Conversely, those with cross-gender behaviors or characteristics have been thought to be homosexual. Essentially, in popular thought, gender connotes sexuality and vice versa. Fearing the spread of homosexuality, communities long have pressed schools to serve on the front lines in ensuring that youth develop conforming gender identities—and thus supposedly conventional heterosexuality. Schools have done so by encouraging gender-associated activities, supporting heterosexual courtship rituals, and hiring persons deemed to be models of acceptable sexuality and gender. This popular conception of a direct link between gender and sexuality overlooks the fact that many persons who desire those of the same sex present conventional gender; likewise, many persons whose gender presentation/identity crosses conventional bounds identify as heterosexual. Nonetheless, this misconception has

compelled strong school policies and practices aimed at ensuring gender conformity as a means of regulating sexuality. Not surprisingly, issues concerning sexual orientation in schools, then, tend to be linked with those about gender.

HISTORICAL CONTEXTS

One of the defining events of schooling during the 1800s was the gender transformation of schoolwork. Early in the century, men typically taught during their youth before establishing themselves fully in their communities. By the end of the century, women performed the staggering bulk of schoolwork, but a new office had emerged where male educators segregated themselves: school administration. The women who taught tended to remain unmarried because, by tradition, married women were thought to have untenable conflicts in their primary allegiances between their husbands and employers. By the 1930s, this practice of hiring single, rather than married, women had become so deeply entrenched that most school districts in the country had passed policies banning married women from the classroom. Meanwhile, the men who led schools and districts were expected to be married or engaged in serious heterosexual courtship. Men who remained single or wished to teach young children were viewed with suspicion. Those who crossed gender bounds risked being thought homosexual. In his 1932 classic work *The Sociology of Teaching,* the eminent sociologist Willard Waller suggested that school administrators could screen potential male teachers for homosexuality by watching for signs of effeminacy or listening for excessive enthusiasm for working with male students.

Through the 1930s, the practice of hiring large numbers of unmarried women teachers was endorsed widely as a cost-saving measure that also allowed "surplus women" to support themselves. To accommodate the hundreds of thousands of such women, a variety of new housing arrangements were needed such as apartments and boarding houses in cities and teacherages in rural districts. Unmarried women teachers typically lived near or with other single women, often establishing small communities that shared domestic, social, educational, and political activities. Some unmarried women teachers also formed romantic and/or sexual relationships with each other. Although such companionships generally were accepted at the time if women were discreet, in time, however, questions arose about the nature of these relationships.

A heightened general public awareness of lesbian relationships during the 1930s, fueled by popular novels, plays, movies, and high-profile national studies, gave way to increased scrutiny of the private lives of unmarried women teachers. Eventually, such women came to be suspected of having lesbian tendencies.

By the mid-1940s, districts dropped their restrictions on hiring married women teachers—and simultaneously they dramatically, though quietly, scaled back recruitment of unmarried women. Between 1940 and 1960, the proportion of the teaching force comprised of unmarred women dropped by half, while the proportion of married women doubled, greatly exceeding the rate for women in the general workforce.

While the displacement of unmarried women in the teaching force occurred with little fanfare, soon the sexuality of the nation's teachers would become an explicitly discussed focus of policy. In particular, the decades following World War II brought intense public awareness of homosexuality. This awareness was stimulated in part by Alfred Kinsey's 1948 and 1953 reports on human sexuality, which indicated, among other things, much higher rates of homosexual behavior among men and women than previously believed. Also, as the military downsized, it searched for and purged individuals thought to be homosexual. Finally, the rapid growth of lesbian and gay enclaves around urban military complexes during World War II quickly became sustained communities after the war. These new communities attracted media attention and frequent harassment by police.

As the visibility of homosexuality increased, a generalized public fear of it led to public panic that homosexuals would prey on children. One popular magazine in 1950 carried a sensational story about an adolescent boy who learned to engage in same-sex sexual activity after a teacher had taught him. Newspaper reports of supposedly intense homosexual activity around Florida led state legislators to establish a commission that eventually took as its charge the elimination of all homosexuals from teaching positions in the state. A change in California laws required police to report any teachers they ensnared in stakeouts at public bathrooms. School officials then routinely revoked teaching credentials, regardless of the truth or relevance of such charges. Around the country, teachers learned that betraying any nonconforming gender qualities might lead to suspicion of homosexuality, which meant expulsion from the profession.

Communities typically pressed school administrators to screen the teaching force carefully to eliminate any taint of homosexuality. School board members also chose school superintendents very carefully, looking specifically for married men with histories of engagement in athletics. Essentially, the persons called on to monitor the sexuality and gender of students and school workers needed to conform to very narrow definitions of masculine heterosexuality themselves. To this day, the proportion of male superintendents who are married is 95%, vastly higher than the 58% in the general population of adult men.

Following the Stonewall Rebellion in 1969, a grassroots gay liberation movement emerged in urban areas around the country. Lesbians and gay men began claiming their identities openly and challenging harassment and discrimination previously endured in relative silence. Several teachers who lost their jobs because of their lesbian or gay identities brought lawsuits that resulted in state or Supreme Court action. Lesbian and gay teachers in New York, San Francisco, Los Angeles, Boston, Chicago, Denver, and other cities organized groups to agitate for sexual orientation nondiscrimination policies, to provide social support for the challenges faced by lesbian and gay school workers, and to educate school communities about sexual orientation.

This increased visibility of gay and lesbian teachers, however, stirred the anxieties of persons such as Anita Bryant, who, in 1977, successfully led a campaign against Miami/Dade's fledgling nondiscrimination ordinance that included sexual orientation. Bryant garnered massive financial support from around the country as she raised the specter of gay men in skirts seducing children into homosexual lifestyles. John Briggs, a California legislator, followed suit a year later by introducing a referendum to pressure school districts to dismiss lesbian and gay teachers or persons who publicly supported gay rights. After a nationally reported campaign, the referendum went down in defeat because of effective grassroots organizing by lesbian and gay activists. Also, the referendum was worded so broadly that large numbers of persons stood to lose civil rights. Undaunted, though, politicians in Oklahoma and other states launched initiatives similar to Briggs's, although these too faced defeat—in court rather than by vote.

Attention gradually shifted away from LGBT school workers and toward LGBT students during the 1980s and 1990s. The rising threat of AIDS and the visibility of increasing numbers of students who claimed LGBT identities changed the tenor and focus of clashes around sexuality and gender in schools. A federally funded study released in the early 1990s detailed a severe risk of suicide among LGBT youth. Though conservative political and religious figures at first sought to bury the report, then to undercut its veracity, concern about the much-discussed suicide rates among LGBT youth compelled the establishment of a variety of new services around the country. The National Education Association endorsed the creation of programs and resources to meet the needs of LGBT youth. Chief among these was Virginia Uribe's Project 10, which assisted students in working out their sexual and gender identities and finding safety in school. The Gay, Lesbian and Straight Education Network (GLSEN) provided educational resources for teachers and students. It placed a particular emphasis on supporting the establishment of gay/lesbian/straight alliances at schools, often initiated by students themselves. Within the first decade that gay/lesbian/straight alliances existed, their numbers grew to nearly 1,000 across the country and have continued flourishing since. Largely because of student activism, in the early 1990s Massachusetts passed the first law in the country providing resources to support the unique needs of LGBT youth in schools. Individual students who have brought their concerns to court have claimed important victories as well. In 1996, Jamie Nabozny won a $1 million settlement against school administrators in his Wisconsin district who tolerated the violence, harassment, and discrimination directed against him throughout his years as a student. This precedent-setting judgment alerted school officials around the country to examine the extent to which such behaviors are tolerated in their own schools.

CURRENT CONTEXTS

Despite these accomplishments over the past decade, students who defy conventional sexuality and/or gender norms continue to experience intense mistreatment in schools inflicted not only by students but also by school workers. Some students have responded by asserting their nonconforming sexual/gender identities through the creation of spaces, traditions, styles, and alliances that affirm who they are. School workers who claim LGBT identities also remain vulnerable to discrimination and harassment. In 2004, only 14 states had passed laws barring discrimination because of sexual orientation, and of these, only four states include gender identity. Even though in 2003 the Supreme

Court struck down state sodomy laws, which had been used to legally justify discriminatory practices against LGBT persons, employment discrimination continues. Many school officials still maintain informal practices of screening job candidates for possible sexuality or gender nonconformity. LGBT persons who are hired sometimes fear that their identities will be discovered, that they will be dismissed from their chosen profession, and that their lives will be made miserable through rumor, harassment, and social ostracism. Students in turn are hurt by the lack of diversity among teachers, by a lack of LGBT role models or friends, and by the larger system that enforces sexuality and gender conformity among workers and students alike.

Educational leaders, who in the past have been summoned to regulate a narrow range of acceptable sexualities and genders among students and school workers, now stand at the forefront of these contemporary issues. Such leaders must listen to students, community members, and school workers to craft policies regarding appropriate dress, school-supported courtship rituals such as dances, permissible displays of affection on school grounds, and gender restrictions on some school activities. School officials must articulate and enforce policies regarding harassment because of sexuality and gender. They must consider broadening the curriculum to include LGBT persons in meaningful ways. Moreover, they must look carefully at long-entrenched but little-questioned personnel practices that have systematically denied schools of the services of some of their most talented professionals. At the same time, school leaders enjoy little protection of their own against discrimination based on sexuality or gender nonconformity. They serve at the pleasure of their school boards. Few of their professional associations have gone on record in support of LGBT members. Educational leaders, then, play a highly risky though centrally important role in contemporary debates on LGBT issues in schools.

—*Jackie M. Blount*

See also homophobia; queer theory; sexuality, theories of

Further Readings and References

Blount, J. (2005). *Fit to teach: Same-sex desire, gender, and school work in the twentieth century*. Albany: State University of New York Press.

Harbeck, K. (1997). *Gay and lesbian educators: Personal freedoms, public constraints*. Malden, MA: Amethyst Press.

Lipkin, A. (1999). *Understanding homosexuality, changing schools: A text for teachers, counselors, and administrators.* Boulder, CO: Westview Press.

Rofes, E. (2005). *A radical rethinking of sexuality and schooling: Status quo or status queer.* New York: Rowman & Littlefield.

🏛 LIBERALISM

This is a political philosophy, tradition, or movement aiming toward development of freedom of groups or individuals, originally founded on the Enlightenment tradition, that tries to circumscribe the limits of political power and to define and support individual rights. It can be perceived as political tradition or philosophy, or a general philosophical theory that encompasses the conception of persons, their value, and morality. The concept is itself a political current embracing several historical and present-day ideologies that claim defense of individual liberty as the purpose of government. It typically favors the right to dissent from orthodox tenets and established authorities in political or religious matters. In this respect, it is held in contrast to conservatism. Classically, liberals have tended to favor a free market economy, rejected government influence in society, insisted against mercantilism and what they identify as socialism or Marxism, and any form of collectivism.

Historically, liberalism is rooted in the Renaissance tradition of humanism but was first seen in coherent action in the Glorious Revolution in Great Britain. Later, primarily but not exclusively in France, ideas from the Enlightenment, which focused on the rule of law, the importance of rational governance, and the individual rights to contract and of ownership, were incorporated into a growing body of thought that asserted that a well-ordered society did not need to be constrained by ancient laws regulating everything from dress code to the price of a loaf of bread. By preaching liberty and tolerance, these movements began to oppose absolute monarchy, mercantilism, and various kinds of religious orthodoxy and clericalism.

The first conceptions of liberalism began in the United Kingdom. John Locke (1632–1704) defended religious freedom and so was the first philosopher identified as liberal (*free* in Latin). Enlightenment-era liberalism contrasted its then current philosophy to feudalism and mercantilism. As more radical philosophies were articulated in the course of the French Revolution and American Revolution and throughout the nineteenth century, liberal notions moved from being proposals for reform of existing governments to demands for changes. This notion added democracy to the list of values that liberal thought promoted, and based political sovereignty on the rights of man. This idea, that the people were sovereign, and capable of making all necessary laws and enforcing them, went beyond the Enlightenment's conception of rationality. Liberalism redefined and contrasted itself to the restrictiveness of socialism and communism. In the latter part of the nineteenth century, what is believed to be the classical liberalism and liberal thought was organized into a coherent set of economic and political doctrines that focused on the primary importance of the individual being unencumbered by the power of the state.

From the end of the nineteenth century through the onset of the twentieth century, a growing body of opinion appeared that asserted that to be free, individuals need to have access to all things required for fulfillment. So individual liberty requires that society is responsible for the provision of a basic level of opportunity, protection, and education in order to free the individual from economic and social coercion.

John Stuart Mill (1806–1873) was influential in developing the modern concepts of liberalism. He opposed collectivist tendencies while placing an emphasis on quality of life for the individual. He also had sympathy for female suffrage and (later in life) cooperatives. Mill became one of the key figures in the development of this strand of liberalism. His philosophy of utilitarianism grounded liberal ideas in the instrumental and pragmatic, allowing the unification of subjective ideas of liberty gained from the French thinkers in the tradition of Jean-Jacques Rousseau and the more rights-based philosophies of John Locke and the British tradition. After similar developments in continental Europe, John Dewey and other pragmatic philosophers become the first to be associated with this idea in the United States. Dewey summarized the roots of the trend in liberal thought, which rejected what was seen as the degradation of the individual by traditional social arrangements and industrialization, and argued that genuinely free markets would systematically refrain from the exploitation of human beings.

Proponents of liberalism see themselves as affiliates of freedom, particularly the freedom from the fetters of tradition. They favor constitutional government, representative democracy, and the rule of law. They have at various times embraced both constitutional monarchy and republican government, generally oppose all but the mildest forms of nationalism, stand in contrast to conservatives by their broader tolerance, and more readily embracing multiculturalism. Proponents believe in neutral government to the extent that it is not for the state to determine how individuals can pursue happiness. This self-determination gives way to an open mind in ethical questions. Most liberal parties support the pro-choice movement and advocate the emancipation of women and sexual preference. Equality under the law is crucial in liberal policies, and thus racism is incompatible with liberalism.

Even so, as a political tradition, liberalism has varied in different countries. For example, in England—in many ways the birthplace of liberalism—the liberal tradition in politics has centered on religious toleration, government by consent, and personal, and especially, economic freedom. In France, liberalism has been more closely associated with secularism and democracy. In the United States, liberals often combine a devotion to personal liberty with an antipathy to capitalism, while the liberalism of Australia tends to be much more sympathetic to capitalism but often less enthusiastic about civil liberties.

In Great Britain and the United States, the classic liberal program, including the principles of representative government, the protection of civil liberties, and laissez-faire economics, had been more or less introduced by the mid-nineteenth century. The growth of industrial society, however, soon produced great inequalities in wealth and power, which led many persons, especially workers, to question the liberal creed. It was in reaction to the failure of liberalism to provide a good life for everyone that workers' movements and Marxism arose. Because liberalism is concerned with liberating the individual, however, its doctrines shifted with the change in historical realities.

Because the concepts of liberty have changed in different historical periods, so have specific programs of liberalism changed. The ultimate aim and characteristic belief, however, remains rooted not only in essential human goodness but also in human rationality. Liberalism assumes that people are cogent, are able to recognize problems and solve them, and can achieve systematic improvement in the human condition. Liberalism, which seeks what it considers to be the improvement of progress, necessarily desires to change the existing order. The degree of any intervention in liberalism is often hotly debated, but there are greater extremes in the rhetoric than in practice.

—*Eunyoung Kim*

See also bureaucracy; civil rights movement; cultural politics, wars; democracy, democratic education and administration; Dewey, John; pragmatism and progressivism; recognition theory/identity politics

Further Readings and References

Dagger, R. (1997). *Civic virtue: Rights, citizenship and republican liberalism*. Oxford: Oxford University Press.
Gaus, G. F. (1994). Property, rights and freedom. *Social Philosophy and Policy, 11,* 209–240.
Rawls, J. (1993). *Political liberalism*. New York: Columbia University Press.
Skinner, Q. (1998). *Liberty before liberalism*. Cambridge, UK: Cambridge University Press.
Spector, H. (1992). *Autonomy and rights: The moral foundations of liberalism*. Oxford, UK: Clarendon.

LICENSURE AND CERTIFICATION

Although frequently used interchangeably, the terms *licensure* and *certification* do not, in reality, have the same meanings. Even many state departments of public instruction responsible for regulating school leader licensure often use *certificate* when they mean *license*. Confusion reigns. *Licensure* should be identified as permission granted by an official regulatory agency to practice a specific profession; for example, state departments of education or standards boards issue a license to be a principal or superintendent. *Certification* is the recognition by a professional association or other peer-oriented groups that one is exemplary in one's practice of a profession, for example, the National Board for Professional Teaching Standards (NBPTS).

A license is an official credential while a certificate is recognition for performance that far exceeds expectations. Striving for a certificate is voluntary and holds one to a higher level of excellence. It is recognition of a school leader whose performance is judged to be exceeding a commonly accepted set of standards. A license, on the other hand, is required in order to practice as a school leader. Policy-making groups such as state boards of education and state legislatures generally control licensure regulations. The professional associations generally control certification.

A licensure policy framework began to emerge with the development of complex licensure policies following World War II. These policies, having the impact of state law, actually control the entry requirements for initial and renewed licensing. By the mid-1950s,

41 states required at least a master's degree in order to be granted an administrator's license. Nearly 40 years later, in 1993, 45 states had this requirement. With an expansion of criteria, at the present time all states except Michigan require a license for principals.

There has been no realistic movement toward a certificate program for school leaders. Discussions were held in the late 1990s among the American Association for School Administrators (AASA), the National Association of Elementary School Principals (NAESP), and the National Association of Secondary School Principals (NASSP) concerning possible development of a certificate program for outstanding school leaders, but it was quickly determined that to make it a truly meaningful process would be cost prohibitive, and the effort was abandoned.

Licensure, however, has had major impacts on the profession of school leadership. There are approximately 500 institutions of higher education that offer preparation programs for educational administration, and the focus of these programs is on licensure requirements from the state. Clear trends have emerged for licensure criteria.

Most states require a master's degree, and teaching experience of from 3 to 5 years is usually expected. Since the release of the Interstate School Leaders Licensure Consortium's (ISLLC) Standards for School Leaders, more than 40 states have established licensure criteria linked to these standards. Fifteen states are also requiring passing the School Leaders Licensure Assessment (linked to the ISLLC Standards) in order to be licensed as a principal.

There is no coherent, organized, or standardized format for licensure policies across state lines. Gathering accurate information regarding criteria for licensure is difficult due to uneven reporting from each state. However, it is clear that states' use of licensure policies to ensure a do-no-harm entrance level to the profession of school administration has had a major effect on preparation programs in higher education, a standards-based approach to curriculum development, and implementation of assessments for initial licensing of beginning school administrators.

—*Neil J. Shipman*

See also American Association of School Administrators; Educational Testing Service; Interstate School Leaders Licensure Consortium; National Association of Elementary School Principals; National Association of Secondary School Principals; National Council for the Accreditation of Teacher Education

Further Readings and References

Hart, A., & Pounder, D. (1999). Reinventing preparation programs: A decade of activity. In J. Murphy & P. B. Forsyth (Eds.), *Educational administration: A decade of reform* (pp. 115–151). Thousand Oaks, CA: Corwin Press.
McCarthy, M. (1999). The evolution of educational leadership programs. In J. Murphy & P. B. Forsyth (Eds.), *Handbook of research on educational administration* (pp. 119–139). Thousand Oaks, CA: Corwin Press.
Sykes, G. (1999). The new professionalism in education: An appraisal. In J. Murphy & K. Louis (Eds.), *Handbook of research on educational administration* (2nd ed., pp. 227–249). San Francisco: Jossey-Bass.
Wilmore, E. (2002). *Principal leadership.* Thousand Oaks, CA: Corwin Press.

LIFE SPAN DEVELOPMENT

Life span development refers to the particular stages that are passed through during the course of a life span. This definition commonly refers to three elements: change, permanent or lasting impact, and growth through a progression of certain stages. Development involves movement from one state to another. A second aspect of development leads one to a lasting or permanent impact. The third aspect involves a model of human development moving through stages.

The human life cycle as argued by Daniel J. Levinson consists of four periods, each consisting of 25 years. The four periods are childhood and adolescence, early adulthood, middle adulthood, and late adulthood. According to Levinson, each period is unique and has a transition period to the next era. During the transition period, which may take from 3 to 6 years to complete, humans undergo a basic change in the character of their lives.

Mark Tennant and Philip Pogson provided another model for human development. They argue that the developmental process is not necessarily linear. Three elements were recognized as influencing development. First, the normative age-graded component included variables that were highly correlated with age such as physical maturation, commencement of education, and parents' death. The second influence included normative-history graded. This includes events such as wars, technological changes, and environmental influences that influence most members of a culture at the same time. The last influence refers to events that were significant to the particular individual but not part of an overall pattern tied to the life cycle, like traffic accidents, lottery winnings, and/or religious conversion.

The importance of life span development to education is that it allows for the creation and delivery of instructional and other educational services that are developmentally appropriate to students. Acquisition of knowledge and skills in many K–12 school settings is based on assumptions about life span development as are state accountability and testing processes. Similar parallels can be drawn to the adult education field.

Although many theories exist that define the periods of human development, there are many debates about the nature and extent of stages. Educators must avoid relying on predictable development stages, recognizing that human development is complex. With this knowledge, one will avoid the idea that stages of development are predictable.

—Larry McNeal, Talana Vogel,
and Edwinta E. Merriweather

See also adult education; career stages; child development theories; cognition, theories of; continuing education; diversity; flow theory; gender studies, in educational leadership; human resource development; personality; psychology, types of; self-actualization; women in educational leadership

Further Readings and References

Crowther, J., & Sutherland, P. (2005). *Lifelong learning.* New York: Routledge.

Jarvis, P. (2004). *Adult education and lifelong learning.* New York: Routledge.

Leicester, M., & Field, J. (2003). *Lifelong learning: Education across the lifespan.* New York: Routledge.

Levinson, D. (1978). *The seasons of a man's life.* New York: Knopf.

Tennant, M. (1988). *Psychology and adult learning.* London: Routledge.

🏛 LINDSLEY, OGDEN R.

Ogden R. Lindsley (1922–2004) was a pioneer in the area of behavioral psychology. He was the first individual to employ behavioral principles in the treatment of human subjects. His work directly affected the field of education through establishing the foundations of applied behavior analysis and behavioral interventions with individuals who possess disabilities.

Lindsley studied under B. F. Skinner at Harvard and received his PhD in psychology in 1957. During his time as director of the Behavioral Research Center of Harvard University, he applied the principles of behaviorism in the treatment of persons with mental retardation, emotional disorders, and developmental disabilities. The center was the first human operant laboratory, and Lindsley coined the term *behavior therapy* during this period.

Lindsley joined the growing number of behaviorally oriented faculty at the University of Kansas in 1965, where he served as a research associate in the Bureau of Child Research and as the director of Educational Research. While initially interested in special education, Lindsley eventually joined the Department of Administration, Foundations, and Higher Education to work with school administrators. It was his feeling that educational leaders had the greatest influence in reforming and restructuring the education system and that behavioral principles offered one of the most effective means of ensuring school improvement.

While much of his work involved curriculum and curriculum development, his work with direct instruction, precision teaching (a method he devised and developed), and the personalized system of instruction had a positive and ongoing influence on schools and schooling. Curriculum-based assessments were a direct outgrowth of Lindsley's work in the area of instruction and measurement. Lindsley often warned teachers of the danger in using high-takes consequences to enhance student performance and compliance (a technique with which he was familiar from his time as a POW during World War II) with a dull, irrelevant curriculum. For Lindsley, teacher-controlled consequences were the basis of initiating and maintaining student response. The pairing of these consequences with those that naturally occurred in the school setting would lead to high rates of academic response and low rates of problem behaviors. Eventually, the artificial, teacher-constructed consequences could be faded out and those inherent in positive learning activities and a relevant curriculum would control and maintain student behavior.

Lindsley was an outspoken critic of the public education system. He felt that much of the failure of the schools was due to their abandonment of effective, empirically validated instruction and assessment methods. His work is important for educational leaders because of his emphasis on consistent, regular measurement of student learning and the application of effective, research-validated practices as the foundation of school improvement.

—J. M. Blackbourn

See also behaviorism; conditioning theory; learning, theories of; psychology, types of; Skinner, B. F.

Further Readings and References

Lee, S. (2005). *Encyclopedia of school psychology.* Thousand Oaks, CA: Sage.
Lerner, R., Jacobs, F., & Wertlieb, D. (2005). *Applied developmental science: An advanced textbook.* Thousand Oaks, CA: Sage.
Lindsley, O. R. (1992). Precision teaching: Discoveries and effects. *Journal of Applied Behavior Analysis, 25,* 51–57.
Tennant, M. (2005). *Psychology and adult learning.* New York: Routledge.

LINE AND STAFF CONCEPT

The line and staff concept is related to how organizations are structured and how power and authority flow within them. Individuals who hold "line" positions are administrators who have supervisory authority over professional staff. Individuals who hold "staff" positions primarily serve a support function for the organization and report, directly or indirectly, to a line administrator.

Administrative positions vary in levels of responsibility and accountability from one school district to another. Although the titles used for administrative personnel serving in line positions can differ among districts, the most common titles used for line administrators are superintendent, assistant or associate superintendent, and principal. Individuals holding the position of coordinator are usually considered staff administrators, as are curriculum directors and specialists.

One objective of using the line and staff concept in organizations is to improve coordination and control through the design of task functions and authority relationships. A structural recognition of the distinctiveness between line and staff positions is also important because the role of the administrator is determined by these organizational patterns. The activities of line administrators are directly concerned with achieving organizational goals. Staff specialists provide technical expertise to support the appropriate line units in this pursuit.

The line and staff concept has its roots in the administrative management theory that emerged as part of the classical organizational theory in the early years of the twentieth century. While scientific management focused on the efficiency of individual jobs, administrative management theory focused on the overall administration of an organization. Henri Fayol and Max Weber were two notable contributors to the administrative management perspective. Fayol, a French steel and coal mining executive, defined basic functions of management and developed management principles that emphasized chain of command, allocation of authority, order, stability, equity, and efficiency. Weber, a German intellectual who studied the growth of large organizations, formalized organizational procedures for administrators and used a name already in circulation by Vincent DeGournay, "bureaucracy."

—Jane McDonald

See also administration, theories of; bureaucracy; governance; hierarchy, in organizations; infrastructure, of organizations; job descriptions; leadership, task-oriented; leadership, teacher; leadership effectiveness; locus of control; management theories; organizational theories; organizations, types of, typologies; personnel management; power; principalship; rational organizational theory; resource management; scalar principle; span of control; staffing, concepts of; table of organization; Weber, Max

Further Readings and References

Borgatti, S. P. *Bureaucracy.* Retrieved March 10, 2005, from http://www.analytictech.com/mb021/bureau.htm.
Bush, T. (2004). *Theories of educational leadership and management.* Thousand Oaks, CA: Sage.
Jones, J. (2004). *Management skills in schools.* Thousand Oaks, CA: Corwin Press.
Tomlinson, H. (Ed.). (2004). *Educational management.* New York: Routledge.

LITERACY, THEORIES OF

Multiple theories of literacy and schooling explain ways students gain competency in content fields such as language arts, science, mathematics, the arts, and computer technology. Literacy is inherently complex, and definitions range from describing skills, abilities, and knowledge at the individual level to examining social practices and competencies at the functional level to explaining it in terms of political goals and ideological values. Here, literacy means essential knowledge, skills, and abilities in receptive and expressive language processes that include reading, writing, oral language, listening, and thinking. Writing refers both to composition and mechanics (grammar, spelling, punctuation, letter formation). A brief review follows of basic theories explaining the nature of development and learning, representative theories/approaches regarding literacy acquisition, and references to several broader interpretations that include other current literacies.

Theories of literacy and schooling rest on assumptions about the nature of development and learning, and many come from the field of psychology. Most traditional print literacy acquisition theories derive, at least in part, from either a *developmental* or an *environmental* theoretical orientation. Resultant long-standing "nature versus nurture" controversy fuels current educational and literacy debates.

John Locke, seventeenth-century father of environmentalism and learning theory (followed by scientists such as Ivan Pavlov and B. F. Skinner), viewed a child's mind as a tabula rasa, or blank slate, shaped almost entirely by experience and learning. In the environmental view, the teacher is of imminent importance in shaping the learner and is seen to "pour out" information and learning into passively receptive students who are perceived as "empty vessels" waiting to be filled. This perspective may be seen today in behaviorist theory and in medical models of instruction currently being applied to the field of literacy (e.g., the scientifically based reading research methodology and language used in the No Child Left Behind [NCLB] Act of 2001). In this skills-based view, teachers disseminate instruction that is segmented into a series of sequential tasks that children master in order to be able to perform complex operations such as reading, mathematics, and so on. Materials are of prime importance and are often scripted so teachers follow models exactly as prescribed by experts.

A theoretical perspective almost opposite of Locke's is developmentalism. Jean-Jacques Rousseau, eighteenth-century father of developmentalism, was followed by theorists such as Arnold Gessell, Maria Montessori, Heinz Werner, and Jean Piaget. Rousseau's developmentalist/naturalistic perspective held that adults should not rush to teach children in "correct" ways but rather allow them to develop as nature had intended (i.e., to develop their own powers of thinking and judgment and to learn in their own ways). Maturationist theories that advocated giving

children time to "ripen" before beginning instruction were developmental in nature. "Readiness" prereading instruction of earlier decades came from the maturationist theoretical perspective. Today naturalistic theory is evident in preschools, kindergartens, and first grades that use developmentally appropriate practice (DAP). Constructivism is also a developmental theory. Here the teacher acts as facilitator and guide, and students are active constructors of knowledge.

From his sociocultural historical perspective, L. S. Vygotsky developed a dialogical theory of learning that described the zone of proximal development. He said children begin learning long before they attend school and that learning and development are interrelated from the child's very first day of life. He described the zone of proximal development as the distance between the actual developmental level as determined by independent problem solving and the level of potential development as determined through problem solving under adult guidance or in collaboration with more capable peers. In this theory, teachers are important in supporting and challenging student learning. Vygotskian Constructivism underlies many of the newer interpretations of literacy.

Until very recent years, rather than speaking of the teaching of *literacy,* educators referred to the teaching of *reading* and *writing,* treating them as discrete subjects and teaching them as separate skills. Historically, educators first taught students to read, and then they taught them to write. Reading was more important in the elementary years, while writing gained prominence in the secondary years.

Literacy expectations have changed drastically over the years. For example, early in U.S. schooling, individuals who could sign their names were considered literate, while now literacy is seen as a complex set of structures that allows individuals and communities to process meaning and communicate at high levels of competence within social and cultural frames. Reading and writing are often seen as so interrelated that one cannot be understood without the other, with students moving seamlessly between them so that they draw on their skills in one to develop the other as they build proficiency in both. Nonetheless, it is learning to read that remains so critical that entire elementary schools are judged as successful or not based on students' reading proficiency. And reading is at the core of NCLB legislation that mandates to educators what will be taught in the area of reading (and how) to students in the most struggling schools.

Looking historically at prevalent literacy theories used in schools reveals that no one set of practices works for every child and that U.S. educators have tried, discarded, and resurrected multiple approaches in search of a silver bullet (quick fix instructional method). Pendulum swings from one theory to another demonstrate that literacy complexity requires ample time and multiple approaches to meet individual needs of students. It is impossible to list here and adequately explain the numerous literacy theories used in the United States. Examples follow of a few that have figured prominently in American schooling and remain in use today.

BEHAVIORIST THEORY IN SKILLS EMPHASIZES INSTRUCTION

Behavioristic theory was the established literacy theory throughout much of the nineteenth and twentieth centuries. It was evidenced by the alphabetic (letters-to-words) approach used in the nineteenth century that continued to dominate U.S. instruction through World War I. In that classic synthetic phonics approach, students learned the parts before the whole (letter names, then letter sounds, then syllable blending in a strict drill and practice format). A modern version of synthetic phonics (involving "explicit, systematic, sequential" phonics instruction) is in effect in many U.S. schools today, particularly in NCLB-funded Reading First schools.

Another early twentieth-century approach, the words-to-letters approach, is the flip side of the alphabetic (letters-to-words) approach. Words are introduced early in the learning experience and then broken down into the component letters. This method, called analytic (or whole-to-part) phonics today, is used in many U.S. schools. Children learn sound correspondences for each letter in both synthetic and analytic phonics. Both approaches view teaching as the transmission of facts to students, who receive a fixed body of knowledge and reading as being made up of component skills studied in a set sequence, the order of which varies by expert.

DEVELOPMENTAL THEORY IN MEANING EMPHASIZES INSTRUCTION

At various times in U.S. educational history, developmental theory has been set in sharp contrast to behaviorist theory. A case in point is the meaning emphasis instruction of another early twentieth-century reform, the *whole word* or *look-say* method of teaching reading, in which students learned a substantial body of words before attempting to analyze words into letter-sounds. Behaviorists contended that the reason for low reading performance in the 1940s and 1950s was the failure of teachers to teach phonics, due primarily to predominance of the look-say method in schools and reading textbooks. Look-say instruction was usually combined with analytic phonics after students had learned about 100 or so sight words, though it did not break each word into its component letters but rather used a more focused analysis of specific patterns in words and groups of words. This combination was used from 1930 to 1970.

Another meaning-emphasis instructional approach, the language experience approach, described 50 years ago by Nila Banton Smith and other reading experts, is one in which reading, writing, listening, and speaking are intertwined. The experience chart was introduced as early as 1900, but the modern language experience approach, which gathered momentum after World War II, is much broader than that early predecessor. In explaining the language experience approach in the 1960s, Roach Van Allen said that what children could think about, they could talk about; what they could say, they could write (or have someone write for them); what they could write, they could read; and what others wrote for them to read, they could read. This approach builds language through interactions with reading, writing, speaking, listening, and thinking.

TESTING AND CURRICULUM CHANGES IMPACT LITERACY THEORY

In the first third of the twentieth century, systematic testing gained prominence. An important contribution of respected reading scholar William S. Gray was his 1914 creation of the first oral reading assessment, an individually administered instrument. Other assessments developed in the 1920s called for the newer silent reading method, paving the way for group-administered assessments in use today. Theory traditionally dictates assessment forms and practices, which often drive instruction.

During the first half of the twentieth century, attention turned to text difficulty, readability, readiness, reading skills, and reading comprehension as an expanded curricular phenomenon, and the emergence of child-centered reading pedagogy (the art and science of teaching). Nila Banton Smith explains these changes in American reading education. The theoretical pendulum swings that controlled both assessment and new emphases in reading actively shaped practice.

MID-CENTURY RESEARCH IMPACTS LITERACY THEORY

Two pieces of seminal research conducted in the middle of the twentieth century had an important impact on literacy theory and instruction. The First Grade Studies was an elaborate grouping of empirical studies that tried to settle once and for all the best way to teach reading. All that it settled was that the various methods tested were equal to or superior to the basal and that there were other significant issues that impacted reading, such as the importance of the teacher regardless of the method. The second piece of seminal research was Jeanne Chall's book *Learning to Read: The Great Debate,* which described a crisis in beginning reading. Chall cited arguments about the basic issues of reading instruction and categorized reading instruction as either *code emphasis instruction* or *meaning emphasis instruction,* recommending an early emphasis on the code (i.e., phonics of some sort) as a needed change from the look-say basals in use at the time. She also recommended a reexamination of basal content and grade level recommendations, testing, and research. Following publication of her book, basal readers reemphasized analytic phonics and changed content, featuring adaptations of children's literature rather than only selections with controlled vocabulary or based on a strict readability formula.

READING THEORY FEELS THE IMPACT OF OTHER FIELDS OF INQUIRY

In the 1950s and 1960s, reading was considered a relatively basic process in which readers translated graphic symbols (letters) into an oral code (letter sounds) that they then produced as speech (either in the mind or aloud) in order to comprehend. Changes from this basic premise came as scholars from many fields began to give attention to reading, causing several significant changes in the field.

Linguists of the 1950s and 1960s gave attention to reading by considering it part of the language processing family, akin to writing, listening, and speaking. Noam Chomsky, a leader in linguistics, developed his theory of language development, which made a significant impact on the way psychologists

thought about and studied language acquisition and language comprehension processes. In his theory, children are born with an innate system of language in which they generalize internal rules so that they convey and understand intended messages in grammatical transformations of language.

A new field of inquiry, psycholinguistics, emerged in the 1960s as scholars began to build on Chomsky's work and investigate rule-governed language acquisition. Leaders such as Kenneth Goodman and Frank Smith persuaded many that reading was a natural process, similar to the process of learning oral language. Psycholinguistic theory focused on meaning making as the prime purpose of reading. Smith identified four sources of cues for readers—orthographic (spelling), syntactic (grammatical), semantic (meaning), and visual (print)—and said readers who used prior knowledge in the first three areas could reduce dependence on visual aspects and focus more easily on meaning. Miscues (deviations from printed text) were seen as windows into a learner's mind.

Following psycholinguistic work with language, cognitive psychologists began studying the inner workings of the mind. This was a departure from traditional behaviorism that had studied observable phenomena for the first half of the twentieth century. Some cognitive psychologists began to study reading by looking at narrative text comprehension from a theory of story grammar (structural accounts of the nature of narratives), and others developed a theory of structural analysis of expository texts. Although both theories of text structure did account for text comprehension, neither took into account the relationship of a reader's prior knowledge of the world with the information in the text. Building on that work, the schema theory of the 1970s explained ways the structure of human knowledge is represented in memory. Simply put, in schema theory, schemata are "slots" in which people store experiences. Every experience one has ultimately must be stored in schemata that are constantly altered and rearranged to accept the new information. In this constructivist theory, prior experience plays a central role. Applied to literacy, this theory calls into question where meaning lies—in the text, in the reader, or in some alternative combination. This brought a renewed interest in Louise Rosenblatt's 1938 *Transactional Theory of the Literary Work,* in which she rejected the idea that a text carries a single determinate meaning. Her theory posits that socially generated language is always internalized by individuals in transactions (two-way interactions) with the environment at specific times and in specific cultural and social circumstances. She theorized that readers, writers, speakers, and listeners bring to transactions their personal experiences and linguistics that are part of their past transactions.

Sociolinguistics developed as a discipline along with psycholinguistics. In the early 1970s, Labov called attention to the importance of issues of dialect and reading, and Michael Halliday drew comparisons between oral and written language. Halliday cited seven functions of oral language and suggested that written language was similarly social. Shirley Brice Heath's early 1980s work comparing forms of literacy in two Appalachian communities and ways they did and did not prepare children for the literacy of schooling helped heighten awareness of social and cultural aspects of literacy. Critical theorists (e.g., Paulo Freire) heightened attention to power structures inherent in literacy instruction.

CONSTRUCTIVIST SOCIOPSYCHOLINGUISTIC THEORY

From these beginnings, a 1970s and 1980s grassroots movement of teachers and other educators fashioned a philosophy that eventually became known as *whole language.* This philosophy was based on constructivist sociopsycholinguistic theory in which children learned about reading and writing as they engaged in both in dynamic contexts. Learners made sense of reading and writing based on the social and cultural classroom contexts surrounding them and through their own evolving understandings of written language. In this top-down model of literacy, learners sought meaning (or understanding of the "whole") before they broke literacy elements into smaller segments. This was opposed to more traditional bottom-up theories in which learners were taught bits and pieces that were put together to form ever-larger chunks of meaning.

During the decades of the 1980s and 1990s, whole language held sway; connections between reading and writing were expanded. Experts such as Donald Graves and Lucy Calkins went into schools to conduct in-depth qualitative research about writing. From that work came the writing process as it is known today, in which writers work through a recursive process that generally follows these phases: prewriting (brainstorming/planning), drafting (capturing thoughts on paper), revising (making the content stronger), proofreading/editing (making the mechanics conventionally correct), and publishing (bringing the piece to a final, polished form for sharing in some way with an audience.) Portfolios of student work evidenced specific literacy progress over time. Toward the end of the 1990s, there was a growing resistance to whole language from some quarters, because not all children were successful using its techniques. At that point, a new set of practices, *balanced literacy,* came into being to try to use the best of both constructivist meaning-emphasis approaches (literature based with more implicit instruction) and behaviorist code-emphasis approaches (skills based with more explicit instruction). Because different factions meant different things by the term *balanced,* its use declined over time in favor of the earlier, more explicit code-emphasis and meaning-emphasis terminology.

LITERACY THEORY AND THE POLITICS OF THE TWENTY-FIRST CENTURY

In yet another pendulum swing, behaviorist theory regained supporters due to the influence of (a) Marilyn Adams's 1990 text in which she explained language acquisition from a bottom-up perspective and (b) brain research. In the late 1990s and early twenty-first century, the medical community asserted that reading was essentially a physiological response to sound and print stimuli and used brain imaging to demonstrate that various areas of the brain respond differently as children learn to read. This work was the impetus for the formation of the National Reading Panel, whose report was the basis of a law that was passed to ensure that the most struggling learners benefited from the experimental and quasiexperimental studies of reading. Effects of this law and the prescriptive medical model underlying it have been far reaching. The main objection to this type of reading instruction from certain reading educators and scholars lies in the fact that this one-size-fits-all model leaves teachers little room to adjust instruction to the needs of individual learners. The scripted programs and mandated materials may be effective with particular children; however, in many cases, they restrict the effective teacher's autonomy in the classroom so that other areas of literacy, such as oral language, writing, metacognition (thinking about one's thinking), the reading-writing connection, and integrated instruction, may not be given needed attention due to time constraints and curricular directives associated with mandated programs.

NEW THEORIES AND BROADER DEFINITIONS

Many changes in the definition of literacy have given rise to an upsurge in theorizing about it from many fields. One might speak narrowly of the *cultural literacy* of E. D. Hirsch that refers to knowledge of a specific set of cultural facts found in books that had a profound impact on Western culture. Or one may refer broadly to the *critical literacy* of Henry Giroux, Allan Luke, Colin Lankshear, and Norman Fairclough, or the *social literacy* of Michael Halliday, Paulo Freire, and others. Readers are encouraged to explore new literacies, such as media literacies and others, through texts such as *The New Literacy: Moving Beyond the 3Rs* and *Literacy and Schooling.* Use of Internet metasearch engines helped readers locate current information on the rapidly changing meanings of literacy.

—*Margaret T. Stewart*

See also behaviorism; brain research and practice; child development theories; cognition, theories of; constructivism; critical theory; curriculum, theories of; Dewey, John; early childhood education; elementary education; language theories and processes; learning, theories of; Montessori, Maria; philosophies of education; Piaget, Jean; politics, of education; portfolios; positivism, postpositivism; postmodernism; power; pragmatism and progressivism; reading, history of, use in schools; semiotics; writing, teaching of

Further Readings and References

Adams, M. J. (1990). *Beginning to read: Thinking and learning about print.* Cambridge: Massachusetts Institute of Technology Press.

Chall, J. S. (1967). *Learning to read: The great debate.* New York: McGraw-Hill.

Chomsky, N. (1965). *Aspects of a theory of syntax.* Cambridge: Massachusetts Institute of Technology Press.

Gessell, A. (1945). *The embryology of behavior.* New York: Harper & Row.

Graves, D. L. (1983). *Writing: Teachers & children at work.* Portsmouth, NH: Heinemann.

Heath, S. B. (1983). *Ways with words: Language, life, and work in communities and classrooms.* New York: Cambridge University Press.

Montessori, M. (1917). *The advanced Montessori method: Vol. 1. Spontaneous activity in education* (F. Simmonds, Trans.). Cambridge, MA: Robert Bentley.

National Association for the Education of Young Children. (1996). *Statement of the position: Developmentally appropriate practice in early childhood programs serving children from birth through age 8.* Retrieved August 1, 2004, from http://www.naeyc.org/resources/position_statements/dap2.htm.

Smith, N., & Robinson, H. A. (1980). *Reading instruction for today's children* (2nd ed.). Englewood Cliffs, NJ: Prentice Hall. (Original work published 1963)

Stewart, M. (2003). Early literacy instruction in the climate of No Child Left Behind. *Reading Teacher, 57,* 732–743.

Vygotsky, L. (1978). *Mind in society: The development of higher psychological processes.* (M. Cole, V. John-Steiner, S. Scribner, & E. Souberman, Eds.). Cambridge, MA: Harvard University Press.

🏛 LOCUS OF CONTROL

Locus of control is a personality construct describing an individual's perceived source of control over his or her behavior. Those with an *internal* locus of control believe that what happens to them results primarily from their own actions and behavior. They believe that they control their own destiny. Those with an *external* locus of control believe that sources outside themselves—fate, chance, luck or others in authority over them—determine what happens to them. Internal persons accept responsibility for their own behavior and see themselves as deserving praise for their successes and blame for their failures. Externals see circumstances beyond their control or the decisions and actions of others as responsible for their behavior.

The locus of control construct was formulated by Julian Rotter in the 1960s. Rotter developed the internal-external locus of control scale (I-E), an inventory of forced-choice items that, among a variety of other themes, focused primarily on belief in luck. The following are typical items:

1. a. Many of the unhappy things in people's lives are partly due to bad luck.
    b. People's misfortunes result from the mistakes they make.

2. a. In my case getting what I want has little to do with luck.
    b. Many times we might just as well decide what to do by flipping a coin.

3. a. What happens to me is my own doing.
    b. Sometimes I feel that I don't have enough control over the direction of my life.

Item-to-total correlations of Rotter's scale showed that the average correlation of a belief in luck item was 0.300 compared with 0.214 for the average of the other themes' items.

Research studies on locus of control indicate that both adult and children internals assume responsibility for their decisions, are not easily swayed by the perspectives of others, and tend to perform better at tasks when they can work at their own speed. Externals, on the other hand, are easily influenced by the views of others and are more likely to attend to the position of the opinion holder. Elementary- and middle-grade internals find it easier to delay gratification, and elementary-grade internals earn higher grades. As children mature, individual development tends to proceed toward an internal locus of control. Some evidence exists that a greater sense of internality can be developed.

—*James W. Keefe*

See also at-risk students; behaviorism; child development theories; cognition, theories of; conceptual systems theory and leadership; critical thinking; esteem needs; instructional interventions; intelligence; learning, theories of; learning environments; metacognition; motivation, theories of; personality; problem solving; psychology, types of; psychometrics; research methods; self-actualization; testing and test theory development; trait theory; underachievers, in schools; validity and reliability; variables

Further Readings and References

Gale Encyclopedia of Childhood and Adolescence. (1998). *Locus of control.* Retrieved from http://www.findarticles.com/cf_dls/g2602/0003/2602000356/p1/article.jhtml.

Lee, S. (Ed.). (2005). *Encyclopedia of school psychology.* Thousand Oaks, CA: Sage.

Rotter, J. B. (1966). Generalized expectancies for internal versus external control of reinforcement. *Psychological Monographs: General and Applied, 80*(1), No. 609.

🏛 LOGIC, HISTORY AND USE OF IN EDUCATIONAL LEADERSHIP

Before the 1920s, many people viewed educational administrators as leaders primarily concerned with promoting traditional spiritual values and developing and maintaining strong social connections within a school community. The community function of educational administrators mainly dealt with enlisting the cooperation of faculty in finding solutions to institutional problems and accurately sensing the social problems of the student body. Upon sensing social problems, the administrator was then to accurately correct them. School leaders of this era relied mainly on intuition and ideology to guide their decisions. The 1920s was a decade of radical change in the history of the use of logic in educational administration.

During the 1920s, the scientific management principles of Frederick Taylor gained currency among educators, and administrators were required to adhere to technical and organizational principles as they sought to create and manage efficient and productive schools and school systems. This orientation toward rational systems, principles, and processes led leaders in many fields, including educational administration, to develop a managerial science specific to the needs of their organizations. Broadly speaking, this movement represented a trend away from anecdotal and intuitive decision making as a logical framework and toward a leadership grounded in logical positivism and structural functionalism. During this era, the dominant orientation of educational administration was toward systematic, scientific practice that resulted in school efficiency and achievement of human potential. Optimism about the new science of educational administration dominated writing about educational administration in the 1920s. While managing schools that transmitted solid values and academic skills, principals were expected to be social leaders as well, remaining actively engaged in community activities and facilitating the development of relationships with community members. Systematic evaluation of individual principals was not required as long as the principal's efforts were founded on efficient organization, scientific facts, methodological values, and religious values.

The conception of the educational administrator as scientific manager continued to dominate the writings of the 1930s. The spiritual element of the administrator became less important, and the conception of schools as businesses, with the principal as an executive, became more popular. Business values such as cost-effectiveness and student-as-client came to dominate the individual and systemic logics of day-to-day decision making in school systems. Educational administrators were, metaphorically, business managers responsible for devising standardized methods of pupil accounting and introducing sound business administration practices in budgeting, planning, maintenance, and finance. While the prevailing metaphor shifted from administrator-as-scientific-manager to administrator-as-CEO, the zeitgeist of logical positivism and structural functionalism continued.

During the 1930s, school organization and supervision of employees were seen as critical components of educational administration. School leaders concerned themselves with designing rational and ordered school systems where expertise and efficiency governed the organization. As schools and school systems increased in size and population, educational administrators promoted hierarchical-linear and compartmentalized models of governance that positioned a single manager at the apex of an organizational pyramid. Middle managers reported on their differentiated charges to superiors, who in turn guided the organization from above with informed policy. During this era, university-based educators further contributed to the development of educational administration as a professional occupation by creating degree programs and special courses of study to prepare educational leaders.

World War II had an important effect on the logical orientation of educational administration. Society expected principals to be leaders of the war effort on the home front. With this new idea came a different social purpose for schooling and for educational administrators, who were expected to provide democratic leadership, thereby enabling students and teachers to engage in a productive way of life. As curriculum developers, group leaders, coordinators, and supervisors, principals increasingly became concerned with personnel development. During the post–World War II era, involvement of various stakeholders in decision-making processes and promoting a positive image for schools and systems became increasingly important.

Proponents of the administrative theory movement, which began in the late 1940s and continued through the 1950s, advocated that educational administrators develop and test theories like researchers in other scientific disciplines, which would in turn lead to the establishment of a stable knowledge base that could inform research and practice. In addition, a multiplicity of external issues influenced educational administration during this time: universities began offering administrator training courses on a larger scale, society became more centralized, the United States began to play an increasing role in international affairs, technology advanced rapidly, and schools became more crowded and more complex. As a result of these factors, educational administrators were expected to draw insights from educational, psychological, sociological, and business research to inform their actions and decisions. When schooling practices

were challenged, principals were expected to defend those practices with empirical and theoretical findings from behavioral science disciplines. Many theorists continued to concentrate on administrators' effective and efficient use of time and resources by focusing on details of school operations, including methods for handling daily attendance slips, change of classroom procedures, and effective ways of introducing new staff members to the school environment.

Partially as a result of social and political unrest of the 1960s, principals and academicians made efforts to maintain stability and a sense of normalcy in schools. Institutional equilibrium was the goal. Theorists and administrators upheld conceptions of schools as rational, goal-driven systems and relied heavily upon Max Weber's concept of organizations as rational bureaucracies. As a result, educational administrators came to believe that this type of governance structure was appropriate for schools, and began to stress bureaucratic processes as viable decision-making processes. With the proliferation of this belief in rationality, principals were expected to support the educational bureaucracy by protecting their own authority, respecting the position of superiors, and guarding against appropriation of power by teachers. In addition, school administrators became on-site researchers as categorical, quantitative, and empirical terms dominated discussions of the principal's work. Educational administrators were asked to use increasingly sophisticated, scientific strategies for planning and measuring. The belief that proper techniques and modern technology would produce expected outcomes resulted in principals being held accountable for their decisions and school activities. Because of this pressure and related political demands, many principals felt vulnerable and confused about role expectations.

External factors again exerted a heavy influence on administrators' use of logic in the 1970s. Increased federal involvement in local schools and a growing number of special interest groups altered many tasks of educational administrators. As a result of a renewed emphasis on community, administrators were expected to build alliances to ensure that schools and the community connected in meaningful ways. Most important, the professional success of principals hinged on the support of stakeholders outside the school organization. In the 1970s, principals were also expected to see that meaningful educational experiences were offered to students, teachers, staff, and community members. This emphasis on the human resource development side of schooling also led to the expectation that principals would engage in and encourage positive, supportive interpersonal relationships. Theorists called for principals to adopt a human resource model of administration.

The 1980s and 1990s saw an upsurge in the plurality of perspectives on the use of logic to solve various problems associated with educational inequity and poor student achievement. As a result of these expectations that educational administrators could help ameliorate these circumstances, leaders balanced many roles, including interpersonal facilitator, information manager, and decision maker. As interpersonal facilitators, principals acted as figurehead, leader, and liaison. As information managers, they were monitors, disseminators, and spokespersons. And finally, as decision makers, principals became entrepreneurs, disturbance handlers, resource allocators, and negotiators.

During these decades, powerful logical critiques of the extant knowledge base meant to inform educational administration came from several angles. Specifically, the emergence of various forms of critical theory, postmodernism, and pluralism became an important and sustained "metadiscourse" among researchers and practitioners. By the turn of the century, educational administrators were questioning whether there really was a *field* at all and were rather suggesting that there were actually *fields* of educational administration that were only loosely connected. At the turn of the twenty-first century, educational administration has made a "postmodern turn" and continues to explore ways that logic, and logics, inform the decisions of school leaders.

—*Jeffrey S. Brooks and Mark T. Miles*

See also administration, theories of; behaviorism; capacity building, of organizations; climate, school; collaboration theory; conflict management; creativity, in management; critical theory; decision making; dialectical inquiry; efficiency theories; empowerment; field theory; frame theory; governance; human resource development; innovation, in education; leadership, teachers; leadership, theories of; management theories; networking and network theory; rational organizational theory; resource management; satisfaction, in organizations and roles; satisficing theory; stewardship; transformational leadership; women in educational leadership

Further Readings and References

Bush, T., & Middlewood, D. (2005). *Leading and managing people in education.* Thousand Oaks, CA: Sage.

English, F. (2003). *The postmodern challenge to the theory and practice of educational administration.* Springfield, IL: Charles C Thomas.
Northouse, P. (2003). *Leadership: Theory and practice.* Thousand Oaks, CA: Sage.
Stanford-Blair, N., & Dickmann, M. (2005). *Leading coherently.* Thousand Oaks, CA: Sage.
Taylor, F. (1911). *The principles of scientific management.* New York: Harper & Row.
Tyack, D., & Cuban, L. (1995). *Tinkering toward utopia: A century of public school reform.* Cambridge, MA: Harvard University Press.
Willower, D., & Forsyth, P. (1999). A brief history of scholarship on educational administration. In J. Murphy & K. S. Louis (Eds.), *Handbook of research on educational administration* (pp. 1–24). San Francisco: Jossey-Bass.

LOSS OF POSITION (SCHOOL PRINCIPAL)

The principal's job has become significantly more demanding. State accountability mandates, changing student demographics, and conflicting political pressures combine to make the principal's role more complex and precarious. Sometimes principals are not able to navigate this environment and find themselves fired. Understanding why some principals are terminated is important for both practitioners and preparation programs.

Two recent studies have examined principal termination. One study compared the perceptions of public school principals and superintendents in California about the reasons principals lose their jobs. Both groups agreed that the primary causes for involuntary departure were related to personal characteristics and quality of interpersonal relationships rather than to technical or management skills. They differed in the ranking assigned to these factors. Principals more often attributed termination to external political forces, while superintendents were more likely to cite poor interpersonal skills and poor relationships as primary causes. The two groups also differed in what they perceived to be indicators of a principal at risk. Principals cited poor staff morale, while superintendents considered a high number of teacher and parent complaints early warning signs. Neither superintendents nor principals gave high rankings to factors such as failure to promote student achievement, inability to maintain a safe and orderly campus, inability to manage cultural diversity, and inability to manage time and administrative tasks as important contributors to principal termination, despite the prominence of these factors in the literature on effective leadership.

A similar study in Missouri examined the perceptions of superintendents and principals about the factors leading to principal terminations. Important factors identified in this research included ineffective communication skills, disregard for effective teaching and learning, inability to manage the school improvement process, inability to sustain an inclusive culture, unethical behavior, and an inability to work within the social and cultural context of the community.

While these studies differ methodologically, their results strongly suggest that personal characteristics and inability to build strong interpersonal relationships with significant stakeholders are the critical factors in a principal's involuntary departure from a school district.

Principals faced with the loss of an administrative position through termination may find limited legal protection. A few states provide administrators with tenure, including due process procedures. But many states limit tenure protection to the administrator's status as a *teacher* only. Principals are normally shielded from arbitrary removal from position during the life of a contract, but reappointment as an administrator is at the discretion of the local school board. The only legal safeguard afforded principals from adverse action during the life of a contract is the requirement that the employer establish "good (or just) cause" for dismissal.

—*Mike Boone*

See also accountability; boards of education; bureaucracy; consideration, caring; governance; human resource development; job descriptions; just cause; leadership, complex theory of; leadership, theories of; leadership effectiveness; line and staff concept; management theories; performance assessment; principalship; role conflict; school improvement models; stewardship; systemic reform; working conditions, in schools; workplace trends

Further Readings and References

Brown, K. (2005). Pivotal points: History, development, and promise of the principalship. In F. English (Ed.), *The SAGE handbook of educational leadership* (pp. 109–141). Thousand Oaks, CA: Sage.

Grady, M. (2004). *20 biggest mistakes principals make and how to avoid them.* Thousand Oaks, CA: Corwin Press.

Nelson, B., & Sassi, A. (2005). *The effective principal.* New York: Teachers College Press.

Young, P. (2004). *You have to go to school—You're the principal.* Thousand Oaks, CA: Corwin Press.

LOTTERY SYSTEMS

Lotteries are common sources of financial support for education. Their use for this purpose is politically popular; however, their effectiveness as a source of revenue is limited, at best. Moreover, several persons have raised moral objections and pointed to negative economic consequences of lotteries. In spite of those objections, lotteries (and other gambling activities) are a multi-billion-dollar industry in the United States and will most likely remain a part of public education for the foreseeable future.

WHAT IS A LOTTERY?

A lottery has three elements under the law: "consideration" (or an entry fee, which may but need not be money), a prize (cash or otherwise), and chance. If skill is involved (such as by solving a puzzle or making a hole-in-one), then the transaction, while it may still be gambling, is not considered a lottery. Varieties of lotteries include preprinted scratch-off tickets and pull-tab tickets, and drawings of numbers, such as Pick Three and Lotto games. A recent and wildly popular innovation in lotteries is the multijurisdictional lottery, such as the multistate Powerball game.

A BRIEF HISTORY OF LOTTERIES

Lotteries to finance public projects have been traced to many cities in ancient Europe and Asia. The first recorded instance where lottery patrons purchased tickets containing numbers occurred in Florence in 1530.

Lotteries and other forms of gambling were important to finance public works before and after the American Revolution. Schools and other public works were often financed by lotteries, as banking systems and municipal bond systems were insufficient or nonexistent. Early American colleges and universities were built using lottery proceeds, and lottery proceeds supported the Continental army during the revolution. American lotteries were wildly popular but horribly corrupt. Changing mores, in addition to disgust with corruption, sent lotteries into a steep decline. By the end of Reconstruction, nearly all lotteries were illegal.

In 1963, New Hampshire became the first state in decades to operate a state-sanctioned lottery. By the 1970s, poor economic conditions and taxpayer revolts (such as California's Proposition 13) led many states to turn to lotteries. Lotteries are now widespread, and ballot measures authorizing lotteries rarely fail.

LOTTERIES TO SUPPORT EDUCATION: WHAT DOES THE RESEARCH SHOW?

Many lotteries were promoted to support highly visible and popular social programs, such as education and environmental protection. Lottery advertising campaigns push these ties to politically popular programs, the effect of which is to "sanitize" an activity that many would otherwise find objectionable. The great weight of empirical research, however, shows no net financial gain for public schools receiving lottery proceeds. After finding no statistically significant relationship between lottery proceeds and education funding, Thomas Jones and John Amalfitano in 1994 recommended, as a matter of policy, that states no longer use lotteries as a means of supporting public education.

Several factors contribute to this conclusion. First, lottery proceeds represent a very small portion of financial support provided to public education. In most states, lottery proceeds account for less than 2% of education spending. Second, school leaders who request additional public funding are often rejected, as many policymakers either (a) wrongly assume lottery proceeds cover a large share of education costs or (b) use a school's receipt of lottery proceeds as political cover to deny additional funding. Also, lottery proceeds are unstable sources of income.

Perhaps the most important reason lottery proceeds do not increase education funding is that lottery proceeds tend to supplant, rather than supplement, other public financial support for public education. In other words, lottery proceeds are fungible. Lottery revenues are substituted for other public support, with minimal gain (if any) for education funding. In their study of lottery revenues and education funding in all 50 states of the United States in 2002, O. Homer Erekson and colleagues found that increased lottery revenues were fungible and were offset by decreases in other education funding sources in all states.

In 2003, Noel Campbell was one of very few researchers to find a positive and statistically significant relationship between lottery funding and education spending. In his study of the Georgia lottery, he noted that this relationship, while statistically significant, was so small that it had no practical significance.

Following the view that any money is welcome, especially during tight economic times, as a practical matter many school leaders do not object to lottery financing.

OTHER ISSUES ASSOCIATED WITH STATE-SUPPORTED LOTTERIES

Aside from seeing lotteries as an inefficient source of funding, many educators are uncomfortable with lotteries to support schools. Many education professionals object to being inadvertent promoters of gambling when their institutions receive lottery monies. Many people continue to view gambling as immoral. Many individuals object to profiting from addictive behaviors.

In addition, many persons object to lotteries as socially regressive. In a study of Georgia's lottery in 2002, Ross Rubenstein and Benjamin Scafadi found that the lottery's costs were more likely to be borne by persons with low incomes and members of minority communities, while its benefits were disproportionately distributed to school districts with higher average incomes and higher levels of educational attainment.

Finally, many persons note the harm to local economies caused by gambling. For example, spending on gambling is often diverted from other important sectors of the local economy. Even in the face of the great weight of empirical research and morality-based arguments against lotteries to support public education, they remain very popular. Although ineffective at best, lotteries as a source of education funding appear here to stay.

—Thomas A. Mayes

See also accountability; capital outlay; cost-benefit analyses; economics, theories of; elastic tax; fringe benefits; market theory of schooling; politics, of education; taxes, to support education

Further Readings and References

Campbell, N. D. (2003). Do lottery funds increase educational expenditure? Evidence from Georgia's lottery for education. *Journal of Education Finance, 28,* 383–402.

Erekson, O. H., et al. (2002). Fungibility of lottery revenues and support of public education. *Journal of Education Finance, 28,* 301–312.

Jones, T. H., & Amalfitano, J. H. (1994). *America's gamble: Public school finance and state lotteries.* Lancaster, PA: Technomic.

Reith, G. (Ed.). (2003). *Gambling: Who wins? Who loses?* Amherst, NY: Prometheus.

Rubenstein, R., & Scafadi, B. (2002). Who pays and who benefits? Examining the distributional consequences of the Georgia lottery for education. *National Tax Journal, 55,* 223–238.

Thompson, W. N. (2001). *Gambling in America: An encyclopedia of history, issues, and society.* Santa Barbara, CA: ABC-CLIO.

🏛 LOYOLA, IGNATIUS

Ignatius Loyola (1491–1556) established a religious order in the Catholic Church—the Society of Jesus, that is, the Jesuits. Loyola initiated, and members of his order continued, the development of a network of colleges and schools to deliver Jesuit education. Jesuit education was founded on the ideal of education as training of both mind and spirit and that certain core studies were essential for all students.

Loyola was born in Spain. He was the youngest of 13 children in a family of low-level nobility. No records of his early years exist, though it is known that he was neither studious nor pious. He joined the military where his major activities were gambling, dueling, and casual romances. In 1521, Loyola was wounded, and during his recuperation, his religious conversion occurred.

Following his conversion, Loyola realized the importance of education and so returned to school, attending with much younger students. He went on to earn a degree at the University of Paris. When Loyola and his companions were unable to travel to the Holy Land to convert what they would consider infidels, they remained in Rome. During this time, the group decided to stay together and form a new congregation in the church devoted to obedience. Loyola summarized the group's discussions and asked a cardinal to submit them to the pope. Pope Paul III approved the group immediately, and in 1539, the Society of Jesus was formally initiated. Jesuits went wherever church officials indicated a need, successfully carrying God's word from city to city. As their influence increased, they founded colleges to provide training for youth of the church. In 1551, Loyola established the Roman College, which was used as the model for Jesuit colleges throughout the world. Loyola died in 1556. He was beatified by Pope Paul V on July 27, 1609, and canonized by Pope Gregory XV on March 12, 1622.

The Jesuits introduced reform to the Italian electives system by establishing "required credits." This reform was introduced by Loyola and systematized some years later via the Ratio Studiorum. Jesuit education proposes to educate the whole person in the tradition of Christian humanism. A basic principle is that mind, will, and spirit must be trained as one. To accomplish this, schools operated by a variety of rules that governed the behavior of students, teachers, administrators of the school, and executives of the schools. According to T. Maynard, the Ratio is not the entirety of the curriculum but rather the foundation. The Jesuits insisted that every attempt be made to promote reasoning, intelligence, imagination, and observation instead of mastery of facts. They were the first to engage in systematic teacher training.

By 1773, the Jesuits had about 750 colleges. Currently, the Jesuit Secondary Education Association reports 46 member schools in the United States, serving over 40,000 students annually; the Association of Jesuit Colleges and Universities report 28 U.S. members.

—Anita Pankake

See also Catholic education; high schools; humanistic education; normal schools; philosophies of education; schools of education

Further Readings and References

Maynard, T. (1956). *Saint Ignatius and the Jesuits.* New York: P. J. Kenedy & Sons.

Smith, L., & Smith, J. (1994). *Lives in education: A narrative of people and ideas.* New York: St. Martin's Press.

Van Dyke, P. (1968). *Ignatius Loyola: The founder of the Jesuits.* Port Washington, NY: Kennikat Press.

M

⌂ MACHIAVELLI, NICCOLÒ

One of the outstanding figures of the Renaissance, Niccolò Machiavelli (1469–1527), civil servant, statesman, playwright, historian, and political philosopher, is most famous for his treatise *The Prince,* which has become a cornerstone of modern political philosophy. Machiavelli began his political career in the Florentine republic as a clerk to the second chancellor at the age of 25 when the ruling Medicis were overthrown. Once he became second chancellor and secretary, a position comparable to secretary of state and defense secretary, he traveled on diplomatic missions to various Italian city-states, France, and Spain; he met many of the important politicians of the day, including Cesare Borgia. In 1506 he helped the Florentine ruler Soderini with a plan to reorganize the military; subsequently, when the Medici family regained power in 1512, Machiavelli was dismissed from office, briefly imprisoned, tortured, and permanently removed from public life. He was exiled from Florence, retired, and spent the rest of his life writing on his country estate outside the city limits. He wrote numerous essays on the military and politics as well as comedy and drama. His chief works include *The Prince, La Mandragola* (a comedy), *Discourses, The Art of War,* and a *History of Florence.* In 1527 Machiavelli, the first great political philosopher of the Renaissance and of the modern era, died, disappointed and embittered at his inability to regain political appointment.

Themes echoed in Machiavelli's work offer insight into sixteenth-century Florentine values. *La Mandragola,* for example, is about the characters' use of fraud to accomplish their objectives. Machiavelli makes it clear that fraud is acceptable, so long as it furthers a worthwhile cause. In *The Art of War,* Machiavelli combines Roman military theories with the innovative concept that war and politics form a kind of functional unity, with war serving as an instrument of politics. In 1519, when the Medicis consulted Machiavelli on a new constitution for Florence, he responded with *Discourses.* Concerned with republics (states controlled by a politically active citizenry), he emphasizes that for a republic to survive, it needs to foster a spirit of patriotism and civic virtue among its citizens. Machiavelli argues in *Discourses* that a republic would be strengthened by conflicts generated through open political participation and debate. He stresses the importance of an uncorrupted political culture and a vigorous political morality. More vast and complex than *The Prince, Discourses* shows clearly Machiavelli's republican principles, also reflected in his *History of Florence.*

It is *The Prince,* however, that has become Machiavelli's most read (often misunderstood) and quoted (often misrepresented) work. Written during a historical period of blackmail, violence, political conflicts, instability, fear, and intrigue, when Italy was repeatedly won and controlled by foreigners, *The Prince* was Machiavelli's practical guide for Lorenzo de' Medici's as well as Machiavelli's attempt to regain influence with the ruling Medicis in Florence. *The Prince* stands apart from other political writings of the period because of its focus on the practical problems a monarch faces gaining and staying in power, rather than on more speculative, idealistic explanations of the foundation of political authority. Machiavelli suggests that the best way to maintain power is to rule well, but if this is not possible, then he presents a variety of practical strategies for remaining in power. His political philosophy was highly influenced by observations of Cesare Borgia, a cunning, cruel man, very much like the "ideal prince." While Machiavelli did not like his policies, he thought that with a ruler like Borgia, the Florentines could unite Italy—Machiavelli's goal throughout his life. To liberate Italy from the influence of foreign governments, Machiavelli explains that strong indigenous governments are important, even if they are absolutist.

Machiavelli recommended policies in *The Prince* that would discourage mass political activism and channel subjects' energies into private pursuits. He held that the monarch could preserve power by the prudent use of violence, understanding the art of war, avoiding being hated, respecting private property and the traditions of his subjects, promoting material prosperity, and comporting himself with dignity. Allowing for the unpredictable influence of fortune, Machiavelli argues that it is primarily the character or skill of the individual leader, as well as the appearance of having certain qualities, that determine the success of any state. He recommends approaches to acquire, assemble, maintain, and rule the principality and evaluates each suggestion by the likelihood of princely glory and practical success while serving the public interest.

Machiavelli held that political life cannot be governed by a single set of moral or religious absolutes. Moreover, the monarch may sometimes be excused for performing acts of violence and deception that would be ethically indefensible in private life. It is this focus on practical success by any means, even at the expense of traditional moral values, that earned Machiavelli's approach a reputation for ruthlessness, deception, and cruelty. His conception of the proper application of morality to practical political life is one that judges the skill of all participants in terms of the efficacy with which they achieve noble ends. He is enjoying a resurgence of interest as some authors claim that his ideas hold the key to the mystery of modern executive power.

—*JoAnn Danelo Barbour*

See also administration, theories of; charisma, of leaders; conflict management; democracy, democratic education and administration; ethics; ethos, of organizations; governance; great man theory; leadership, theories of; leadership effectiveness; leadership styles; power

Further Readings and References

De Grazia, S. (1989). *Machiavelli in hell.* Princeton, NJ: Princeton University Press.
Machiavelli, N. (1992). *The prince* (W. K. Marriott, Trans.). New York: Alfred A. Knopf. (Original work published 1513)
Machiavelli, N. (1985). *Discourses* (L. J. Walker & B. Crick, Trans.). New York: Viking. (Original work published 1531)
Mansfield, H. (1989). *Taming the prince: The ambivalence of modern executive power.* New York: Free Press.
Mansfield, H. (1996). *Machiavelli's virtue.* Chicago: University of Chicago Press.
Viroli, M. (2000). *Niccolo's smile: A biography of Machiavelli.* New York: Hill & Wang.

MAINSTREAMING AND INCLUSION

The term *mainstreaming* has come to be associated with the principle of educating children with and without disabilities in the same classroom and providing special education based on learning needs rather than categories of handicaps. In the decades before 1970, the most common treatment of children with mild to severe disabilities was to provide education in self-contained classrooms. The situation changed in the United States as a result of the civil rights and educational reform movements of the late 1960s and early 1970s and as an outcome of two court cases in 1972, the *Pennsylvanian Association for Retarded Children v. Commonwealth of Pennsylvania,* and *Mills v. Board of Education of the District of Columbia.* The rulings in these cases directed at state education systems established the expectation of the placement of students with disabilities in general education settings because of fair and equal treatment as guaranteed by the 14th Amendment of the U.S. Constitution.

The U.S. Congress responded to these cases with legislation guaranteeing all children a free and appropriate public education. Section 504 of the Rehabilitation Act of 1973 and the Education for All Handicapped Children Act (Public Law 94-142) approved in 1975 extended free and appropriate schooling to children with disabilities and required that children with special educational needs be educated in the least restrictive environment. Congress revisited the act in 1990, and the resultant Individuals With Disabilities Education Act (IDEA) confirmed the principle of including disabled children in regular classroom settings in public education. In 1997, an amendment to IDEA further defined the principle that special education should be a service for children rather than a place where they are sent. None of the aforementioned legislation uses the term *mainstreaming,* which has been superseded in general educational usage by *inclusion,* referring to the philosophy and practice of providing a common educational experience for all children in a common setting.

Current court cases now follow IDEA requirements, finding that an inclusive placement with supplemental aids and support as necessary are appropriate to a wide range of students. A school district's decision to place a student in anything other than a general classroom setting will only be upheld if school officials can show that their efforts at inclusion have failed or have strong evidence to support the need for a separate educational setting for the child.

THEORETICAL PERSPECTIVES

Underlying the move to an inclusive model of education for students with and without disabilities is the belief in the equal right of all students to access education and to achieve equitable and quality educational outcomes. In practice, this has implications for curriculum, finance, governance, and school personnel. Implicit in the development of an inclusive school is a single curriculum model based on (a) curriculum frameworks or guidelines that are sufficiently comprehensive to support the differentiated learning of all students, (b) a variety of assessments linked to this curriculum to accommodate different learning styles and disabilities, (c) a unified funding system that supports the varied learning needs and abilities of all students, (d) student representation under a single administrative structure rather than a dual system for regular and special education, and (e) teachers, administrators, and staff capable of working with students with a wide range of needs and cooperatively with disability specialists.

CONDITIONS FOR SUCCESSFUL INCLUSION

Studies of inclusive education in the United States suggest conditions that favor successful outcomes for all students. These include (a) a leadership that actively involves and shares responsibility with the entire school staff, (b) an acceptance by teachers and school staff of the need to change roles and responsibilities and work collaboratively, (c) flexible learning environments that emphasize participation but may still provide opportunities for children to receive separate instruction if needed, (d) curricular and instructional approaches that are participatory in that they emphasize the social construction of knowledge, encourage diverse approaches to problem solving, and allow for adaptations to accommodate individual needs and multilevel learning, and (e) collaboration between educators and parents. Practices associated with successful inclusion of students with disabilities are also promoted by the advocates of whole-school reform, who see the processes of inclusion and reform as closely linked.

DEBATE

Whether or not mainstreaming/inclusion is the best ideology from the perspective of the student with special needs remains the topic of much heated debate. Opponents of inclusion argue for a continuum of educational placement, noting that the least restrictive environment does not require full inclusion in a general classroom for all special needs students, some of whom may benefit form a separate classroom and the focused attention of a specialist teacher. Opponents also argue that the most important equity issue is the quality and not the place of instruction. The identification and funding issues have also figured significantly in the mainstreaming/inclusion debate—students who need special education, as well as the corresponding funds and personnel that are required, must be clearly identified to ensure they receive appropriate services. Special services will be compromised or lost unless both funding and students are specifically targeted.

Advocates of inclusion argue that the labeling of students and physically separate education is inherently discriminatory and unequal, that special education has become a convenient way for general educators to avoid their responsibility to teach all students and so reduce the quality of instruction for all students, and that the special targeting of funds for certain students is inequitable and would be better used to provide a high-quality education for every student.

INTERNATIONAL OVERVIEW

The debate surrounding mainstreaming/inclusion is no less fierce in national systems around the world. Ireland maintains a policy that integrates children with special needs where possible, and retains the right to segregate where necessary. Australia has a state-by-state approach—the state of Queensland, for example, has adopted a policy of inclusive schools and curricula within a framework of social justice.

Norway reversed its policy of segregated schooling for children with disabilities in 1975 and required that every child be given equitable and suitable education in the local school, and now has less than 1% of the school population in special units. New Zealand passed legislation in 1989 giving every child the right to attend a state school and age-appropriate mainstream classes; however, noncompliance by schools led to new special education policy guidelines in 1995 requiring schools to accept and value all learners. In the Netherlands, Germany, and Belgium—which share a high rate of students in special schools—attempts by policymakers to reduce exclusion are seen as arising from a mixture of changing views about segregation and a wish to reduce the expenditure on special schools, but these policies have achieved little success to date. A United Nations conference in Jomtien, Thailand, in 1990 and a UNESCO conference in Salamanca, Spain, in 1994 promoted the development of schools with an inclusive orientation as part of national school reform worldwide.

—Jill Sperandino

See also accountability; affective education; at-risk students; bureaucracy; consideration, caring; deaf education; Department of Education; early childhood education; Federal Privacy Act; giftedness, gifted education; Head Start; individual differences, in children; intelligence; parental involvement; psychometrics; Rehabilitation Act of 1973; resiliency; special education; state departments of education

Further Readings and References

Beveridge, S. (2004). *Children, families and schools: Developing partnerships for inclusive education.* New York: Routledge.

Bowe, R. (2005). *Making inclusion work.* Columbus, OH: Merrill.

Kluth, P., Straut, D., & Biklen, D. (2003). *Access to academics for all students.* Mahwah, NJ: Erlbaum.

Odom, S. (Ed.). (2002). *Widening the circle: Including children with disabilities in preschool programs.* New York: Teachers College Press.

Rotatori, A., Obiakor, F., & Utley, C. (2003). *Effective education for learners with exceptionalities.* St. Louis, MO: Elsevier.

Salend, S. (2005). *Creating inclusive classrooms: Effective and reflective practices for all students.* Columbus, OH: Merrill.

🏛 MALCOLM X

Born Malcolm Little on May 19, 1925, in Omaha, Nebraska, Malcolm X (1925–1965) was also known as El Hajj Malik El-Shabazz, convert to the Nation of Islam, and fighter for equality for all people. Malcolm X's early life was marked by the violent death of his father, separation from his mother and siblings, prison, and his conversion to Islam.

Malcolm X was the first minister (spiritual leader) of the Nation of Islam, Temple No.11, in Boston, Massachusetts. He quickly gained a reputation for his oratorical skills, his dedication to the Nation of Islam, and his ability to draw others to Islam. He also became known as a defender of human and civil rights and an outspoken critic of the condition of Blacks in the United States and abroad. He moved to New York and later married Betty (Sanders) X. He and Betty (also known as Betty Shabazz) were parents to six daughters.

During his short life, Malcolm X was a frequent speaker not only in Islamic mosques but also at schools and universities, rallies, and marches. He had a charismatic personality and often gave scathing critiques of a system that consistently oppressed Blacks. He was a frequent guest on panels, forums, and television and radio programs where he spoke about and debated the condition of Blacks in America and the best ways to achieve Black self-empowerment. In one of his early appearances, he debated the then president of the National Association for the Advancement of Colored People (NAACP), Walter Carrington, in a forum titled "The American Negro: Problems and Solutions." The forum as well as other appearances and debates with Black leaders were often heated and contentious and revealed the division in the Black community about Malcolm's X's influence. One of Malcolm X's most famous television appearances was a week-long special with reporter Mike Wallace in 1959. The program, titled "The Hate That Hate Produced," was an in-depth examination of the ideologies and philosophies of the Nation of Islam. More important, Wallace sought to reveal to the American public a complete picture of Malcolm X. Viewed as anti-White and a controversial figure in U.S. culture, the program traced Malcolm's rise as a leader in the Nation of Islam and the human rights movement and his eventual designation as the Nation of Islam's national spokesperson.

As spokesperson for the Nation of Islam, Malcolm X frequently spoke about the social, racial, economic, and political injustices that negatively affected Blacks and women and about the hegemonic practices in the United States that disenfranchised voters and led to destructive racial tensions in many parts of the United States. He was an influential leader not only in the

Nation of Islam but also for a significant number of Blacks of varying religions and socioeconomic classes.

A pilgrimage to Mecca represented a turning point in the spiritual and political life of Malcolm X. On April 4, 1964, he made his pilgrimage to Mecca and thus began a change in his philosophy toward Whites and his approach to Black self-empowerment. During his pilgrimage, he met with Whites who showed a spirit of unity and brotherhood, and that provided him with a new, positive insight into race relations. Malcolm now believed that Islam could be a catalyst to the power to overcome racial antagonism and to erase it from a dominant White America.

Malcolm X left school when he was a teenager, but he realized the value of a formal education. Shortly before his death, he revealed that one of his greatest regrets was not having a formal education. His belief in the power of education led him to speak frequently to teachers and educational leaders about instilling a thirst for academic excellence in students. He believed that education could change the lives of African American and other poor and minority students, and he encouraged students to view education as a way to develop academically, socially, and politically. His teaching and beliefs are instructive today, as there continue to be gaps in the educational achievement of Black students and their White peers.

Alex Haley collaborated in 1964 with Malcolm X to write the most widely read work about him, *The Autobiography of Malcolm X.* Haley wrote that Malcolm X appealed to the two most disparate elements in the Negro community: the depressed mass and the galaxy of Negro writers and artists who were devoted to his ideals and cause.

The year 1964 marked the beginning of a series of attempts on Malcolm X's life. He was killed on February 21, 1965, at the age of 39 while delivering a speech in Manhattan at the Audubon Ballroom. The legacy of Malcolm X has been documented in numerous documentaries, books, and movies. A renewed interest in his life and work occurred in 1992, when director Spike Lee released the movie *Malcolm X.* On February, 21, 2005, the 40th anniversary of his death, a celebration of his life was held at the Audubon Ballroom, renamed the Malcolm X and Dr. Betty Shabazz Memorial and Education Center.

—*Linda C. Tillman*

See also affirmative action; Afrocentric theories; Bethune, Mary McLeod; Black education; charisma, of leaders; civil rights movement; Coppin, Fanny Jackson; critical race theory; critical theory; cross-cultural studies; cultural capital; cultural politics, wars; desegregation, of schools; discrimination; DuBois, W. E. B.; ethnocentrism; literacy, theories of; minorities, in schools; multiculturalism; resiliency

Further Readings and References

Haley, A. (1964). *The autobiography of Malcolm X.* New York: Ballantine Books.
Shabazz, I. (2002). *Growing up X.* New York: Ballantine Books.
West, C. (1999). The making of an American radical democrat of African descent. In C. West (Ed.), *The Cornel West reader* (pp. 3–18). New York: Basic Civitas Books.

MANAGEMENT BY OBJECTIVES

Management by objectives (MBO) is a management system that includes cooperative goal setting throughout the organization, cooperative process identification for goal achievement, and appraisal of performance based on achievement of goals set. When implemented correctly, MBO can positively influence unit and organizational productivity, employee and managerial morale, employee attendance, and other organizational dimensions. Research on MBO has not shown positive results; generally, the causes for these disappointing results relate to poor or incomplete implementation of the system rather than any problem with the idea itself. Schools and districts were participants in the early popularity of MBO; while few reference MBO at this time, school improvement planning and program implementation and evaluation incorporate the major elements of the MBO process.

MBO was developed in the early 1950s and generally became a fad in the 1960s and early 1970s. The concept fell into disrepute in the 1980s and 1990s, with the research on MBO indicating that the negative reputation came about more as a consequence of how it was implemented than as an idea.

The term *management by objectives* was first used by Peter Drucker in his 1954 book *Practice of Management.* At that time, Drucker suggested that managers in the future would be held accountable for results rather than for the pattern of human relations within their plants and offices. As a consequence of this results-focused accountability, new roles, responsibilities, and needed knowledge and skills would be created for managers that differed greatly from those required in the past. This new manager was to (a) be judged by what his or her followers do, (b) have no definable "executive personality," (c) make things happen, (d) be more of a generalist than in the past, (e) be an organizer, and (f) be oriented toward results and responsibility.

A quality MBO program provides a synthesis of three processes that relate directly to the new results orientation expectations for managers: goal setting, participative decision making, and objective feedback.

Several conditions contribute to the success of an MBO program. First is the support of the top executives in the organization. Second is the extent to which this is a mutual process. Among the problems with implementation that have caused MBO to fall out of favor is that the involvement of others was not pursued; in fact, it became more a practice in which people are told they will be involved, but are not involved in any significant way. In many instances, individuals were forced to accept the boss's goals rather than actually be involved in the goal-setting process. When this occurred, people felt pressured to pursue goals to which they were not committed and might even have found undesirable. This development created mistrust, lowered commitment, and even precipitated withdrawal from the process A third important factor is continuous feedback. Once goals and objectives are set and processes for achievement are identified, monitoring of implementation must occur throughout the year or budget cycle. Open and frequent two-way communication between supervisors and subordinates aids in making adjustments as necessary in objectives, processe, and/or resource allocations.

When implementation of the process has these and other characteristics and key factors, the system is more likely to succeed, and productivity within the organization favorably influenced.

Unfortunately, however, the "typical MBO" process as implemented has little top management support or involvement, generally influences only a small percentage of employees, is more mandated than cooperative in nature, and is loosely (and poorly) linked to an appraisal system.

The general sequence of the MBO process has two major components: first, the process begins with the establishment of overall objectives for the total organization for the target period; second, once these objectives have been approved, they must be translated into action steps to be taken by each manager. Management by objectives is made up of many of the

things that are already a part of many organizations rather than an additional program.

—*Anita Pankake*

See also accountability; administration, theories of; decision making; economics, theories of; goals, goal setting; management theories; organizational theories; outputs, of systems; productivity

Further Readings and References

Bowditch, J. L., & Buono, A. F. (2001). *A primer on organizational behavior* (5th ed.). New York: John Wiley & Sons.
Drucker, P. (1954). *The practice of management.* New York: Harper & Row.
Drucker, P. (1974). Management by objectives and self-control. In *Management: Tasks, responsibilities, practices* (pp. 430–442). New York: Harper & Row.
Odiorne, G. S. (1965). *Management by objectives: A system of managerial leadership.* New York: Pitman.

MANAGEMENT INFORMATION SYSTEMS

Management information systems (MIS) are designed to arrange and interpret information stored in a digital format. These systems automate sorting and inquiry using computers and provide reports that are the bases for decision making by staff and officials. Schools, districts, and state education agencies are increasingly required to collect and manage large quantities of information about students, especially to meet legal reporting requirements such as those under the No Child Left Behind Act of 2001.

These computerized databases carry a load far greater than paper systems and allow the blending of separate data files. Advanced technology and digital communications require broad-based planning, interoperable components, training, and staffing. Ideally, the additional cost of implementation is offset by increased ability to collect and analyze data. Information management systems generally integrate data input and collection, data storage, computer-coded instructions to combine and separate data for analysis, reports to stakeholders, and security measures to protect, restore, and ensure privacy of the data.

The implementation of computer-assisted school information systems began in the mid-1980s. By 2001, No Child Left Behind called on school districts to test every K–12 student, collect these test scores, and sort the information on various student subgroups. Nowadays, schools must show that they examine and scrutinize the achievements of all students in order to isolate the most successful practices. Data are commonly collected using unique student identifiers, and include information on enrollment, state test scores, course completion, college entrance and proficiency exams and graduation, diploma and dropout rates.

At the school, district, and state level, educational agencies continue to build the capacity to collect and manage sizeable quantities of data and sort individual records in myriad ways. Computer equipment and software may vary, but good information management systems contain certain characteristics:

- Data are collected at the most elemental level possible.
- Data are included on students, teachers, principals, and other staff.
- Data are stored in relational databases that facilitate sorting in ways that may be unanticipated.
- Key elements are collected frequently, providing nearly real-time availability.
- Certain standard analyses are programmed into the system.
- Findings are reported to parents and the community using friendly access, such as Web sites.
- Systems ensure the privacy and security of individual records.
- Systems are automated to alert school officials if data are reported outside of acceptable range.
- To the extent possible, data are observable, reliable, and valid.
- Inferred data are as stable, reliable, and valid as possible.
- Systems allow maximum integration with existing equipment and software applications to lower cost.

Computer-based systems have become an integral part of school information management, but technology is the tool, not the goal. The data are essentially quantitative measures collected and stored electronically. Computers make information available to more people with less effort, time, and cost. When placed in context, interpreted, and disseminated to others, the data provide information that engages discussion and reflection for decision making about teaching, curriculum, and other education functions. In school environments, the goal of information management systems is ultimately to increase student success.

—*Tara Shepperson*

See also accountability; administration, theories of; bureaucracy; capacity building, of organizations; computers, use and impact of; decision making; forecasting; human resource development; instrumentation; leadership, task-oriented; management theories; measurement, theories of; needs assessment; operational definitions; organizations, types of, typologies; performance assessment; planning models; politics, of education; power; productivity; professional development; quantitative research methods; rational organizational theory; reductionism/parsimony; resource management; school improvement models; site-based management; standard setting; standardized testing; state departments of education; strategic planning; systems theory/thinking; technology and the law; time management; variables; work task measurement

Further Readings and References

Hardy, L. (2003). Information please: Managing all the data required under NCLB is a task made for technology. *American School Board Journal, 190*(7), 20–22.

Jonassen, D. (Ed.). (2004). *Handbook of research on educational communications and technology.* Mahwah, NJ: Erlbaum.

Rosenberg, R. (2004). *The social impact of computers.* St. Louis, MO: Elsevier.

Wenglinsky, H. (2005). *Using technology wisely: The keys to success in schools.* New York: Teachers College Press.

🏛 MANAGEMENT THEORIES

Professional management positions in schools evolved after other approaches failed to administer effectively the growing, complex, urban systems of public education. There have been four major theoretical shifts in management thinking, the roots of educational administration.

Frederick Taylor was credited with founding the "scientific management" or "efficiency" movement; this was the first movement considered to have professionalized school superintendency. In his 1917 text, *Scientific Management*, Taylor stated that that the waste and inefficiency prevalent in most industries was rife in the educational system as well. He emphasized organization—including scientific analysis of all aspects of work, the necessity of job descriptions, and clarification regarding recruitment, training, appraisal, and employee rewards—as the solution for making operations leaner and more effective. Time study, price rate, separation of planning from performance, and scientific methods of work were Taylor's chief principles of management. When those principles were applied to education, organization and efficiency would increase, but Taylor's critics claimed that education was becoming a production process, with schools as factories and students as raw materials en route to becoming products—all under the guidance of teachers being closely monitored by managerial staff who specified production goals and controlled all methods of achieving those goals.

Influenced by Taylor's attitudes toward management and workers, Ellwood Cubberley concluded that the duties of the superintendent were to organize and direct the work of the schools, lead the school board and staff, arbitrate between the board and staff, and supervise instruction. In 1949, Henry Fayol described a set of common processes and principles adopted by educators as descriptive of the functions of administrators. The processes included planning, organization, commanding, coordination, and control. Thus Taylor and Fayol addressed the same efficiency and productivity concerns using the scientific method—Taylor for the bottom of the organization pyramid up and Fayol for the top of the organization down.

In the 1930s and 1940s, the human relations movement in management developed as a reaction to Taylor's heavy emphasis on production and the apparent lack of respect for workers. Mary Parker Follett, the most influential contributor to the philosophy of the period, held in 1924 that the fundamental problem of any organization was the building and maintenance of dynamic, yet harmonious, human relationships. Among the first to speak out on the value and dignity of satisfied workers, she helped lay the groundwork for organizational behavior as an interdisciplinary science. Perhaps her best known contribution is her four principles of organization. Follett maintained that adherence to the principles should contribute to dynamic, harmonious human relationships; there should be direct contact with workers in the early stages of their work; coordination of work activities is a reciprocal and a continuing process; and, in dealing with conflict, which Follett considered a normal process in management, she urged the creative solution or problem-solving approach, "integration," rather than domination or compromise.

Follett's theories were bolstered by the writings of John Dewey and Kurt Lewin, but perhaps most significantly by the studies of Elton Mayo and colleagues at Western Electric Company's Hawthorne (Illinois) plant. From 1924 to 1932, Mayo and his colleagues dismissed the assumption that wages and physical working conditions did not drive employee motivation and productivity above all others. Mayo and colleagues also found that the amount of work completed was determined in part by workers' social capacities and their self-perceived importance to management; they also found that social codes, conventions, traditions, and routine or customary ways of responding to situations influenced effective work relations. Their studies prompted further research of behavior as the human relations approach to management escalated in profile between 1930 and 1950.

Chester I. Barnard, former president of the Rockefeller Foundation and the New Jersey Bell Telephone Company, influenced a third theoretical perspective of management—the management behavior theory within a social science framework. In 1938, Barnard amalgamated scientific management and humanistic concepts, resulting in a new view of effectiveness and efficiency. Barnard emphasized the importance of management's leadership role and organizational cooperation, but he recognized the influence of the individual, social groupings, and surrounding conditions on organizational leadership.

Thus, he considered authority delegated from the bottom of the organization rather than from the top. Using a functionalist's argument (that systems function in order to satisfy certain human needs), Barnard considered organizational effectiveness as having to do with achievement of goals, which are of two kinds, physical (environmental) and social. He suggests that the organizational systems of effectiveness and efficiency are linked together through an identifiable, stable system of communications, maintained by the executive. He considered executives of complex organizations to have three chief functions:

1. The executive preserves organizational communication through an organizational division of labor and the control or supervision of the organizational whole, which includes effective selection, promotion, demotion, and dismissal of personnel. The executive also maintains an informal communication system involving the compatibility of personnel.

2. The executive encourages recruiting and maintaining key personnel into cooperative relationships with the organization. This is accomplished mainly by maintaining morale, inducements and deterrents, supervision and control, inspection, education, and training.

3. The executive devises and characterizes the goals and objectives of the organization.

Barnard's sociological analysis of these two dimensions of organization (effectiveness and efficiency) is a precursor to other theories of management.

Included among the social scientists extending Barnard's social systems theory of management are Chris Argyris, Bernard Bass, Jacob Getzels, Daniel Griffiths, Andrew Halpin, Barbara Hemphill, James March, Michael Cohen, and Philip Selznick. Of these scholars, the work of Getzels has been most influential to the theory of educational management. With colleagues and students in the Midwest Administration Center at the University of Chicago, Getzels (and later, Getzels and Egon Guba) formulated a theoretical model that viewed administration as a social process, where the social system influenced operations. This model gave theoretical assistance to numerous empirical studies based upon the combination of the informal and the formal aspects of administration. These social scientists considered the educational organization as a unique social system where management functions within a network of interpersonal or social relationships. The network of interactions is a crucial factor in the administrative process. Within this social system, behavior is shaped by both psychological and sociological factors. In the two-component system of the Getzels-Guba model, the observed behavior is a function of the institutional role as defined by the expectations attached to it and the personality component of the role incumbent as defined by the person's needs. While social scientists made great strides in management theory in a relatively short period of time, a criticism of both efficiency and human relation theories is their closed system emphasis. By focusing almost exclusively on individual and group issues, the larger economic, social, political, and legal contexts of educational administration are underemphasized and often ignored.

A fourth theoretical perspective of management is a hybrid approach from critical theory and postmodern theory. From the Frankfurt School of Philosophy, critical theorists include Theodor Adorno, Herbert Marcuse, and Jürgen Habermas. These philosophers and anthropologist Pierre Bourdieu are opposed to closed philosophical systems and pretensions to absolute truth. To address the legitimacy of and potential for changing existing power structures, critical theorists generally hold the view that humans create their history and society, which, they believe, should be a society of free actors that go beyond the tension between, and abolish the opposition to, one's purposefulness, spontaneity, rationality, and the results of one's labor. While offering

a critique of other social theories, critical theorists provide tools for seeing anew ideas or processes taken for granted. Oppositional thinking is one of the keys for gaining such insight.

Postmodern management theory has as its focus the constructing or resurrecting of stories and voices of excluded, marginalized, and exploited members in modern organizations. Among the theories subsumed under postmodernism are structuralism, semiotics, poststructuralism, and deconstruction. Key theorists, including Jean Baudrillard and Jean-François Lyotard, posit the notion that culture is composed of fragments of experiences and images bombarding individuals. The speed and ease of reproduction of these images suggest that they can exist only as images, devoid of depth, coherence, or originality; there is no consideration for the unity of the whole. The postmodern manager, thus, should operate with an understanding that a more enlightened and empowering manager who has a great understanding of the whole as well as its parts can counter exploitation within the organization. Conversely, there is skeptical postmodernism, where any procedure for fairness and justice has the potential to be exploited into a routine of higher performance expectations and render any postmodern prescription into a modernist command and control tool.

In open systems theory, a bridge between social and critical theory, organizations are capable of self-maintenance based on environmental input or interaction, essential for open system functioning. Within the open systems perspective are several schools of thought of which contingency or situational theory has been influential in management theory development. Contingency theory sees organizational and management processes and choices as contingent upon the particular character or nature of the organization itself, the environment of the organization at that particular moment, and the specific task or tasks the organization seeks to accomplish at a particular time. Basically, when managers make a decision, they must take into account all aspects of the current situation and act on those aspects that are key to the situation at hand. Key scholars in this theoretical field include Henry Fielder, Henry Mintzberg, and Victor Vroom.

An emerging management theory within the critical postmodern perspective is chaos theory, the notion that while events are rarely controlled, within those existing events lie patterns of behavior. From the work of physicists James Gleick in 1987 and Edward Lorenz in 1993, chaos theory grounds a postmodern science of management that is ambiguous, at best unpredictable, and hence unknowable to the degree of precision demanded by modern science. Chaos theory is about how very simple things can generate very complex outcomes that could not be guessed by just looking solely at the parts. While the theory predicts that complex nonlinear systems are inherently unpredictable, concurrently, chaos theory ensures that often, the way to express such an unpredictable system lies not in exact equations but in representations of the behavior of a system, that is, to watch a system over time to find the patterns of behavior not immediately seen in the organization. Thus, chaos theory, which many think is about unpredictability, is at the same time about predictability in even the most unstable systems.

Chaos theorists suggest that systems naturally go to more complexity, and as they do so, these systems become more volatile (or susceptible to cataclysmic events) and must expend more energy to maintain that complexity. As they expend more energy, they seek more structure to maintain stability. This trend continues until the system splits, combines with another complex system, or falls apart entirely. According to the theory, life is caught in the tension between order and chaos. Too much order, everything becomes the same and there is no room for creativity or anything new. Too much chaos, and nothing can last long enough to create anything useful; the chaos is a jumble that destroys the lot before it can get started. Between order and chaos is found the "edge of chaos," the point at which there is enough chaos for creativity but enough order for appropriate patterns to endure. Complexity, also called the "edge of chaos," is the name given to the emerging field of research that explores systems in which a great many independent agents are interacting with each other in a great many ways. Complexity can occur in natural and human-made systems, and in social structures. There are several principles in complexity theory, but one key principle is the understanding that different parts of complex systems are linked and affect one another in a synergistic manner.

In management science, chaos theorist Margaret Wheatley and complexity theorists Peter Senge and Richard Pascale suggest that systems naturally go to more complexity, and as they do, become more volatile and must expend more energy to maintain that complexity. As systems expend more energy, they seek more structure to maintain stability. This trend continues until the system splits, combines with another complex system, or falls apart entirely. The focus of the manager or leader in a chaotic environment becomes one of managing change and the volatility brought by the change. A postmodern organization would include a network of diverse, self-managed, self-controlled teams with many centers of coordination that fold and unfold according to the requirements of the tasks. The teams are organized in a flat design, employees are highly empowered and involved in the job, information is fluid, and continuous improvement is emphasized throughout the organization.

Other trends continue the critical postmodern movement in management theory. One area of study, as noted by Michael Fullan in 2001, includes the management of change and the change process. Critical theory can make valuable contributions, for example, to the management of change in work organizations by revealing otherwise hidden agendas, power, and managerial assumptions embedded within organizations. Managers, within this perspective, are taught to look at the dynamic of systems, the fragmentation of contexts, and the emergence of new cyberspace, a new narrative understanding of management, one not trapped in linearity but based in complexity. Broader institutional questions are raised regarding how particular systems can be seen as "colonizing mechanisms" for those in power. Hugh Willmott suggested in 1992 that critical management learning should go beyond identifying power differences to address the legitimacy of and potential for changing the existing power structure, and promotes the notion of management for critical action. Research in management, from a critical postmodern perspective, might include political influence on decision making, diverse interests in organizations, uses and/or abuses of power, economics, managerial assumptions underlying decision making, organizational factors preventing change, critical action research, manipulation or social engineering masked as staff development, and the influence of women and diverse cultural groups on management.

There are many varied approaches to the management of any organization. As noted, the approaches to the management of schools and school districts seem to be concentrated in four major areas, over a historical period of about 100 years. The scientific management or "efficiency" period of Frederick Taylor at the turn of the nineteenth century led to the human relations movement of the 1930s and 1940s with Mary Parker Follett leading the way. Chester I. Barnard provided the grounding for the third shift in management theory promulgated by social scientists who provided a variety of theoretical frameworks for research and discussion about managing organizations. The conceptualization of management has begun to shift from the social sciences to critical and postmodern theory as scholars pursue research in chaos, complexity, and dialectical approaches to further understanding of organizational management.

—*JoAnn Danelo Barbour*

See also administration, theories of; Barnard, Chester I.; bureaucracy; chaos theory; constructivism; contingency theories; critical theory; Cubberley, Ellwood; Dewey, John; division of labor; empowerment; feminism and theories of leadership; Follett, Mary Parker; functionalist theory; Halpin, Andrew William; Hawthorne Studies, the; leadership, theories of; management by objectives; McGregor, Douglas; motivation, theories of; nomothetic/idiographic dimensions; organizational theories; path-goal leadership theory; postmodernism; rational organizational theory; scientific management; systems theory/thinking; Taylor, Frederick; Theory X, Theory Y; women in educational leadership

Further Readings and References

Alvesson, M., & Willmott, H. (Eds.). (1992). *Critical management studies.* London: Sage.

Barnard, C. I. (1966). *The functions of the executive.* Cambridge, MA: Harvard University Press. (Original work published 1938).

Cubberley, E. P. (1915). Superintendent of schools. *Elementary School Journal, 16,* 149.

English, F. (2003). *The postmodern challenge to the theory and practice of educational administration.* Springfield, IL: Charles C Thomas.

Fayol, H. (1949). *General and industrial management.* London: Sir Isaac Pitman & Sons.

Follett, M. P. (1924). *Creative experience.* New York: Longmans, Green.

Getzels, J. W. (1952). A psycho-sociological framework for the study of educational administration. *Harvard Educational Review, 22,* 235–246.

Jones, J. (2004). *Management skills in schools.* Thousand Oaks, CA: Corwin Press.

Marcuse, H. (1964). *One-dimensional man.* Boston: Beacon Press.

Pascale, R., Millemann, M., and Gioja, L. (2000). *Surfing the edge of chaos: The laws of nature and the new laws of business.* New York: Crown Business.

Starratt, R. (2003). *Centering educational administration.* Mahwah, NJ: Erlbaum.

Taylor, F. W. (1917). *Scientific management.* New York: Harper & Row.

Wheatley, M. (1999). *Leadership and the new science: Discovering order in a chaotic world* (2nd ed.). San Francisco: Berrett-Koehler.

MANN, HORACE

Horace Mann (1796–1859) is widely known as the Father of the Common Schools. Throughout his long and distinguished career, he viewed common knowledge as the sine qua non of a civilized society. As such, only a system of public education, specifically common schools attached to normal teacher training schools, could ensure social and economic progress as well as sustain democracy. To Mann, education and democracy were correlatives; neither could exist without the other. However, what separated Mann from other educational leaders, before and at least since John Dewey, was his ability to be both philosopher and the political activist on behalf of public education.

Like many educated men of his day, Mann turned to teaching as a way to support his own studies. He attended Brown University and enrolled in one of the most prestigious law schools of his day, Litchfield, in Connecticut. A year after he earned his law degree, he was elected to the Dedham, Massachusetts, School Committee. He would serve in both the Massachusetts state house and its senate as well as in the U.S. House of Representatives. In 1837, he was appointed by the governor to a newly constituted board of education and was selected as its first secretary. Mann held this position for 11 years, from 1837 to 1848. It was during his tenure that the first system of public education was developed in Massachusetts.

In his first lecture to the Massachusetts Common School Convention, in 1838, Mann described the current state of public schools as directionless. His plan was to create an organization that would disseminate the best practices of each local community school to all schools. Along with his colleague Cyrus Peirce, he built the state's first normal school in Lexington to train teachers in both pedagogy and subject matter.

Among his many progressive ideas, one rule stood above all others in teaching children, that is, that learning and pleasure are inseparable. Mann opposed corporal punishment and one-dimensional pedagogies that turned teaching into telling and school subjects into mere words on a page. He decried the deplorable conditions in which children learned, arguing that schoolhouses should be neat, attractive, and fittingly comfortable for children to learn. He chided textbook publishers for seeking profits and not publishing quality books appropriate to children. He was an ardent supporter of both public and school libraries, seeking to build collections of secular books for adults and children consistent with his advocacy of the separation of church and state. As for school improvement, Mann believed in standards of excellence that extended beyond individual schools and communities.

To Mann, the moral and social issues always turned on the necessity for a system of public education. He held up education as the most important of all subjects. He could not compromise causes in which he believed, whether the issues be education, temperance, or antislavery. He opened his house in West Newton to Chloe Lee, the first Negro applicant to that normal school. Later in his career, his antislavery views put him in opposition to the great Massachusetts statesman Daniel Webster. Mann, the system builder, understood that slavery itself undermined the potential of public education for all citizens.

As secretary of education, Mann wrote 12 *Annual Reports* (1837–1848), 10 volumes of the *Common School Journal* (1839–1848), and *Official Lectures* (1838–1842). After he left the position, he succeeded John Quincy Adams in the House of Representatives. During one of the most significant congressional debates in the history of the U.S. House of Representatives, on June 30, 1848, Mann argued that enslaving a man destroys ambition and ingenuity. Paradoxically, Mann would become the target of attacks by the abolitionist William Lloyd Garrison, who thought Mann lukewarm in his opposition to slavery. Mann did not seek reelection to the House but did allow himself to become a candidate for governor to promote the Free Soil Party. His resignation from Congress along with his defeat for governor left Mann with no electoral political future.

Although he continued to work throughout the states on behalf of common schools, he took on another great educational challenge, the first presidency of Antioch College in Yellow Springs, Ohio (1853–1859). From the beginning, this coeducational and nonsectarian school faced financial hardships. As with all of his past endeavors, he worked with a sense of urgency to see tasks accomplished.

—*Ira Bogotch*

See also administration, theories of; Black education; boards of education; capacity building, of organizations; character education; curriculum, theories of; discrimination; early childhood education; ethics; ethos, of organizations; finance, of public schools; governance; great man theory; individual differences, in children; infrastructure, of organizations; instructional interventions; knowledge base, of the field; learning, theories of; literacy, theories of; management

theories; motivation, theories of; normal schools; Peirce, Cyrus; philosophies of education; politics, of education; power; rational organizational theory; resource management; schools of education

Further Readings and References

Bogotch, I. (2005). A history of public school leadership: The first century, 1837–1942. In F. English (Ed.), *The SAGE handbook of educational leadership* (pp. 7–33). Thousand Oaks, CA: Sage.

Mann, H. (1969). *Lectures on education.* New York: Arno Press. (Original work published 1855)

Messerli, J. (1972). *Horace Mann: A biography.* New York: Alfred A. Knopf.

Tharp, L. (1953). *Until victory: Horace Mann and Mary Peabody.* Boston: Little, Brown.

Williams, E. (1937). *Horace Mann: Educational statesman.* New York: Macmillan.

MARKET THEORY OF SCHOOLING

Under certain well-defined conditions, markets in which buyers and sellers meet to exchange goods and services are able to produce efficient results. However, most national governments all over the world exercised great care not to rely on markets to produce and distribute educational services, particularly at the K–12 level. The logic behind this mistrust of market forces is grounded on the assumption that markets experience imperfections in producing and distributing some goods and services. These goods and services are called public goods in the field of public administration. Governments must intervene in such markets to produce socially efficient results.

Public goods theory uses five criteria for the evaluation of market efficiency for education and justification of government intervention. These five conditions must be met for a private sector of the economy—the market—to function efficiently. Indeed, these conditions are essential if the private sector is to perform in the public interest. These conditions are (1) *perfect information* about what is available, at what price throughout the economy, (2) all goods and services produced, as well as productive inputs, must be *perfectly mobile,* (3) there should be *no market domination* by either producers, consumers, or third parties of any sort, (4) there should be no *jointness in supply,* and finally (5) there should be *no externalities.*

Evaluation of education markets indicates that it is possible for them to operate, but at the same time it may lead systematically to socially inefficient results, particularly for basic education. For instance, mobility can be a serious problem in educational markets. A parent might be knowledgeable about a program well suited for his or her child but be stymied by the distance between the school and the home. Mobility problems occur in many other markets only once, at the time of purchase. On the other hand, in education markets, there is a recurring problem, and it can seriously undermine the efficiency of market solutions. To some degree, education is a jointly supplied service. When two students sit in a lecture hall, the fact that one student listens to the instructor does not preclude the other students from listening simultaneously. However, this interpretation may be oversimplistic, and at the price level, to which education is jointly supplied, it remains ambiguous. Jointness at least poses significant resource allocation issues because it becomes difficult to measure the flow of resources to individuals when it is unclear what conditions educational resources are in joint supply.

There has been a widespread agreement that the external effects of education are the main reason for both the justification of education as a public service and a failure of the market. In addition to private benefits to students, education benefits parents and society in general. External benefits are important for two reasons. First, from an equity point of view, if costs of private or public services are to be borne by those who benefit from them, then those who receive external benefits should contribute to the financing of education. Second, an optimal level of educational expenditure will result only if omitted; too little education will be consumed from an economic efficiency perspective. Despite these arguments, private production and distribution of education always found strong supporters in theory as well as in practice. For instance, 11% of K–12 students are educated in private schools. The supporters of private delivery of education claim that efficiency and choice, two of the three main principles of American education, are sacrificed to achieve equality. Supporters of private delivery of educational services argue that government monopoly in K–12 produces inefficiencies, while a competitive education market place would produce much greater upward pressures on quality and downward pressures on price. Similarly, satisfaction and choice by parents and the efficiency of schools have increased in competitive markets. The goals of competitive efficiency and educational freedom are inseparable.

There are clear indications that private delivery of basic education will carry the current momentum into the future. The Supreme Court's landmark 2002 decision in *Zelman v. Simmons-Harris* decisively approved choice plans, and thus public funds may flow to private schools. Another indication is the dramatic increase in charter schools and educational management organizations in response to these new conditions. There were about 700,000 students in 3,000 charter schools in 2004. Over the last decade, more and more school district boards of education have looked to private companies to manage poorly performing schools and school districts. The No Child Left Behind Act of 2001 (NCLB) has further increased the chances of private companies' involvement in public education. Schools that continuously fail to make adequate progress toward meeting state goals are eventually subjected to fundamental restructuring by the state, which includes turning the operation of the school over to a private company. Success stories of privatization of basic education in some other developed nations, such as the Netherlands, have exemplified the possible future look of our understanding of the market theory of schooling.

—Ibrahim Duyar

See also accountability; charter schools; choice, of schools; competition, forms of, in schools; cost benefit analyses; economics, theories of; equality, in schools; equity and adequacy of funding schools; finance, of public schools; global cultural politics; globalism; hierarchical developmental models; learning environments; management theories; parental involvement; planning models; productivity; resource management; voucher plans

Further Readings and References

Anderson, G., & Pini, M. (2005). Educational leadership and the new economy: Keeping the "public" in public schools. In F. English (Ed.), *The SAGE handbook of educational leadership* (pp. 216–236). Thousand Oaks, CA: Sage.

Andre-Bechely, L. (2005). *Could it be otherwise? Parents and the inequities of public school choice*. London: Routledge.

Belfield, C., & Levin, H. (2005). *Privatizing America's schools: How parents choose, how schools perform*. Boulder, CO: Paradigm.

Duyar, I. (1996). Market imperfections in education. *Journal of Educational Administration, 2*(1), 53–67.

Emery, K., & Ohanian, S. (2004). *Why is corporate America bashing our public schools?* Portsmouth, NH: Heinemann.

Green, C. (2005). *The privatization of state education*. London: Routledge.

Saltman, K. (2005). *The Edison Schools: Corporate schooling and the assault on public education*. New York: Routledge.

🏛 MARSHALL, THURGOOD

Thurgood Marshall (1908–1993) successfully led the legal team in *Brown v. Board of Education* for Black plaintiffs before the U.S. Supreme Court where the Court in 1954 declared racial segregation of public education unconstitutional. Marshall was born July 2, 1908, in Baltimore, Maryland, and died January 24, 1993 in Bethesda, Maryland, at age 84. He grew up in Baltimore in a middle-class home and attended Black schools and universities: Lincoln University in Pennsylvania, where he earned a bachelor's degree in American Literature and Philosophy in 1930, and law school at Howard University in Washington, D.C. In 1933, Marshall graduated from law school first in his class and passed the Maryland bar that same year. He was mentored in law school by the dean and chief counsel for the National Association for the Advancement of Colored People (NAACP), Charles Hamilton Houston, a distinguished Black attorney. Houston had finished first in his class at Amherst College and was a member of the *Law Review* at Harvard Law School.

Thurgood Marshall is most famous for successfully directing and arguing the 1954 *Brown v. Board of Education* case before the Supreme Court, but there were other accomplishments after *Brown*. In 1965, he became the first Black attorney to be appointed U.S. solicitor general, the nation's highest ranking lawyer. As solicitor general, Marshall won 14 of 19 cases argued during his 2-year tenure in that position. In 1967, he was the first Black to become a member of the U.S. Supreme Court, where he authored many majority and minority opinions for the Court.

In 1935, Marshall began the road to *Brown* by joining his law school mentor Houston at the NAACP as assistant legal counsel. His major cases in the early 1930s involved teacher salary equalization cases in states with segregated school systems, voting rights cases, and equal funding for Black schools. Marshall won several cases in the southern and border states outlawing segregation in graduate and professional programs in White universities. His first legal brief occurred in law school when he assisted with a 1932 case against the University of North Carolina. This and other cases against segregated higher education set the stage for his legal strategy to eliminate racially segregated schools. In 1938, Marshall replaced his mentor Charles Houston as chief counsel for the NAACP, and in 1939, he established a separate organization for the NAACP to handle legal issues, the Legal Defense and Education Fund, and became its director.

In 1929, upon graduation from Lincoln University, Marshall applied for admission to the University of Maryland Law School but was refused admission because of his race. He later successful litigated a case that integrated the Maryland law school. Marshall directed the Legal Defense and Education Fund for 21 years, argued 32 cases before the U.S. Supreme Court, and assisted with 11 other cases. He developed the strategy to end racial segregation under the law. He often declined cases involving legal segregation in other areas to focus exclusively on segregation in education.

No single individual has had a more profound and positive impact on American juris prudence in the Supreme Court's history than Thurgood Marshall. Marshall, almost single-handedly, improved democracy in America by his long and determined battle to rid the country of legally enforced racially segregated public education. The *Brown* decision led to elimination of racial segregation in other areas of America's life such as public transportation, movie theaters, restaurants, and parks. But Marshall saw education as the centerpiece of his strategy for improving the life chances for African Americans and at the same time provided the world with a more positive image of America.

—*Frank Brown*

See also affirmative action; Afrocentric theories; Black education; desegregation, of schools; DuBois, W. E. B.; equality, in schools; equity and adequacy of funding schools; ethnicity; governance; Mendez, Felicitas; minorities, in schools; multiculturalism; National Association for the Advancement of Colored People; politics, of education; resiliency; Washington, Booker T.; Woodson, Carter G.

Further Readings and References

Davis, M. D., & Clark, H. R. (1994). *Thurgood Marshall: Warrior at the bar, rebel on the bench.* New York: Carol.
Kluger, R. (1975). *Simple justice.* New York: Random House.

🏛 MARX, KARL

Karl Marx (1818–1883), a philosopher, journalist, economist, and revolutionary, was born on May 5, 1818, in Trier, Germany. Marx's father, Heinrich, was a respected attorney, owned several vineyards, and was a moderately prosperous member of the middle class. Marx's parents were Jewish, but in 1824, Heinrich converted the family to Protestantism to avoid the social and economic losses that would have followed from Prussian laws that banned Jews from holding public office or practicing in the professions. Supported economically by his father, Marx spent a year at Bonn University as a law student, studying sporadically, drinking heavily, and engaging in various acts of brawling and hell-raising. Heinrich Marx, dismayed at his son's behavior, arranged for Marx's transfer to the more rigorous University of Berlin, where Marx, though reading voraciously, continued his rabble-rousing ways, rarely attending lectures, and incurring many debts.

When Heinrich Marx died in 1838, Marx's mother, with whom Marx did not get along, essentially disowned him by cutting off his allowance and withholding his part of the family estate. From this time on, Marx had little to do with his mother and his seven siblings. Now experiencing economic hardship (a hardship that would last without interruption for the next three decades), Marx also experienced an intellectual crucible through a profound engagement with Hegel's work. Turning from the study of law (and an assured economic future in the profession his father had chosen for him) to the study of philosophy (which held little promise of an economically stable professional future), Marx read all of G. W. F. Hegel's work and became deeply involved with the Young Hegelians, a group that embraced Hegel's dialectical method while radically critiquing Hegel's idealism. Marx eventually finished his dissertation in 1841, but because of an anti-Hegelian purge at the University of Berlin, Marx submitted his dissertation to the University of Jena, receiving his doctorate in absentia.

In 1842, Marx moved to Cologne and became editor of the influential progressive newspaper *Rheinische Zeitung,* which the Prussian (i.e., monarchist, oppressive, militaristic) government shut down because of Marx's incisive critiques of the monarchy and its bureaucracy. In 1843, Marx married Jenny von Westphalen, the daughter of Baron von Westphalen, a prominent member of Trier society. Marx moved to Paris in the fall of 1843 and worked for *Vorwarts!,* a biweekly communist journal. Jenny gave birth to a daughter in May 1844, and it was at this time that Marx and Friedrich Engels (1820–1895) became friends. Engels's father was a prosperous German industrialist who owned cotton mills, one of which was in Manchester, which Engels managed. Engels was shocked by the poverty in Manchester and published *Condition of the Working Classes in England,* which deeply impressed Marx, who learned much from the book. Marx and Engels's friendship and collaboration

lasted for the rest of Marx's life. In the summer of 1844, Marx produced a series of writings that comprise the *Economic and Philosophical Manuscripts,* which were not discovered until 1930 and published in 1932. In this work, Marx began to formulate his ideas on class struggle, proletarian revolution, and the abolition of private productive property. Marx was expelled from Paris in 1844 for subversive journalism, and he and Jenny next moved to Brussels, where Engels also moved at this time.

During the next 3 years, Marx and Engels collaborated on one of their major achievements, *The German Ideology* (also published posthumously), which explains their materialist conception of history to a degree unparalleled in their subsequent writings. Marx and Engels joined the Communist League, which had its center in London, and they quickly became the organization's major theoreticians, publishing *The Communist Manifesto,* perhaps the most widely read political pamphlet in history. The *Manifesto* appeared just as a series of revolutionary uprisings were sweeping Europe (France, Prussia, Austria, England). In 1848, Marx moved first to Paris and then on to Cologne, where he founded the newspaper *Neue Rheinische Zeitung,* which was eventually suppressed by the government. In May of 1849, Marx sought refuge in London, where he and Jenny lived for the rest of their lives.

When Marx and Jenny arrived in London, they had four children and two more were soon born. During the first half of the 1850s, the Marx family lived in a small flat in the Soho district of London where they continued to experience economic hardship, mainly getting by through the economic support that Engels provided, along with the payment Marx received from his weekly articles for the *New York Daily Tribune,* a popular radical newspaper in America. Between 1850 and 1852, Marx wrote *The Class Struggles in France* and *The Eighteenth Brumaire of Louis Bonaparte,* lengthy pamphlets marked by a pessimistic tone that contrasts with Marx and Engels's earlier revolutionary hopefulness. During this time, Marx was also spending long hours in the British Museum engaged in an intense economic study, writing a huge manuscript (published posthumously) called the *Grundrisse* ("Outline"), which contained the outline of the six volumes of *Capital* that Marx had intended to write. In 1856, and because of a modest yet invaluable inheritance from Jenny's uncle, the Marx family moved into a house in a middle-class neighborhood. Marx continued to work on what would become the three volumes of *Capital.* In 1864, he was among the founders of the International Workingman's Association, and for the next 8 years he was the central figure of the organization's General Council in London. In 1867, Marx finally published Volume 1 of *Capital,* his classic analysis of the capitalist processes of production. Marx worked on Volumes 2 and 3 of the *Capital* trilogy for the rest of his life, and Engels published them posthumously. In 1870, Marx finally achieved lasting economic stability when Engels, having sold his partnership in the family business, provided Marx with a comfortable yearly pension for the rest of his life. Jenny Marx died on December 2, 1881, of bronchitis. Marx died on March 14, 1883, in London and was buried alongside Jenny in Highgate Cemetery.

—*James Trier*

See also critical race theory; critical theory; dialectical inquiry; economics, theories of

Further Readings and References

Antonio, R. (2003). Introduction: Marx and Modernity. In R. Antonio (Ed.), *Marx and Modernity: Key readings and commentary* (pp. 1–50). Malden, MA: Blackwell.
Callinicos, A. (Ed.). (1989). *Marxist theory.* New York: Oxford University Press.
Marx, K. (1970). *Das kapital: A critique of political economy.* Chicago: Henry Regnery.
Marx, K. (1969). *The communist manifesto.* Chicago: Henry Regnery.
McLellan, D. (Ed.). (1979). *Marxism after Marx.* Boston: Houghton Mifflin.
Wheen, F. (1999). *Karl Marx.* London: Fourth Estate.

MASLOW, ABRAHAM

Abraham Maslow's influence on the field of education involved a movement away from the scientific emphasis and method and toward a person-oriented approach to leadership and instruction. Maslow's focus on the needs common to all persons and each individual's struggle to fulfill specific needs changed both thought and practice in administration and instruction.

Maslow (1908–1970) was born in Brooklyn, New York, on April 1, 1908. He received his BA in 1930, MA in 1931, and PhD in 1934 from the University of Wisconsin. He became a Fellow at Columbia University from 1935 to 1937. He was on the Brooklyn College faculty from 1937 to 1951, and was

professor and chair of the department of psychology at Brandeis University from 1951 to 1961.

Maslow's theory concerns itself primarily with growth motivation that can lead to self-actualization. Human beings, according to Maslow, are essentially and innately good. The evil in human behavior is due to environmental factors rather than an inherent evil nature.

Maslow emphasized growth motivation rather than deficiency motivation. He stated that happier people are oriented to growth motivation (higher-degree needs), while more neurotic people are oriented toward deficiency motivation (lower-degree needs).

Maslow's theory is a unified organismic theory. His theory attempts to synthesize the three approaches to human personality: holistic, dynamic (or motivational), and cultural. In every personality there is a hierarchy of needs. These are degrees of psychological health in which one must successfully meet the needs at one degree in order to go on to the next degree. This hierarchy ranges from the instinctual level to the need for aesthetic reality.

Maslow proposed five degrees of need priority that lead to psychological health: (1) physiological needs, (2) safety needs, (3) love and belongingness needs, (4) self-esteem needs, and (5) self-actualization needs. The first and second are of the lower order. If they are not met, the following three cannot be met. Thus, love and belongingness, self-esteem, and self-actualization are considered to be needs of a higher nature. He proposed that self-actualization needs are different from the others. They involve the needs for cognition and for aesthetic reality. Humans have a strong desire and need to know and understand not only themselves but the world around them.

Maslow described the characteristics of psychologically healthy, self-actualized people. Among these are (1) being realistically oriented, (2) accepting self, others, and situations "as they are," (3) having a high degree of spontaneity and unaffected behavior, (4) being problem-centered rather than self-centered, (5) having a need for occasional privacy, (6) being autonomous and self-dependent, (7) having a unique view of people and the world, (8) being somewhat mystical with profound inner experiences, (9) having a strong identity with all of humanity, (10) having close, deep, and intimate relationships with a select few, (11) having strong democratically oriented values, (12) being highly ethical and moral, (13) being philosophical with a whimsical, inner-motivated sense of humor, (14) having a tremendous capacity for creativity and novel approaches to operating, and (15) being resistant to conformity and open to new experiences.

Maslow is significant to educators for his emphasis on the affective side of education and development. He also provided insight into the psychological features of leadership and the personal attributes of different types of leaders. His constructs can be applied equally to students, teachers, and administrators as strategies for growth and development.

—*J. M. Blackbourn*

See also coeducation; cognition, theories of; consideration, caring; constructivism; creativity, theories of; curriculum, theories of; esteem needs; Freud, Sigmund; humanistic education; imagination; Jung, Carl; learning, theories of; McGregor, Douglas; perceptual psychology; personality; philosophies of education; psychology, types of; qualitative research, history, theories, issues; resiliency; role theory; self-actualization; Theory X, Theory Y; transformational leadership

Further Readings and References

Maslow, A. (1954). *Motivation and personality.* New York: Harper & Row.

Maslow, A. (1999). *Maslow on management.* New York: John Wiley & Sons.

Milton, J. (2002). *The road to malpsychia: Humanistic psychology and our discontents.* San Francisco: Encounter Books.

MASTERY LEARNING

Mastery learning is a method of learning and teaching that involves the student reaching a level of predetermined mastery on units of instruction before being allowed to progress to the next unit. Proponents of mastery learning affirm that all students can learn and achieve the same level of content mastery when provided with the appropriate learning conditions in the classroom but within individual or personal time frames.

Introduced into American education in the first quarter of the twentieth century, mastery learning has its genesis in the work of Henry Morrison and Carleton Washburne. While Morrison developed scales to study instructional time and student attention, which led to the mastery system of teaching and learning now associated with Benjamin Bloom, Washburne developed the Winnetka Plan, a movement away from the

classic model of learning based on theories of intelligence in which all students are given the same amount of time to learn and the focus is on differences in ability. Washburne urged a departure from recitation as the primary form of classroom instruction. Students worked individually on assignments with a focus toward specific skill attainment and promotion based on individual subject achievement rather than grade placement. Interest in the mastery system waned in the 1940s due, most likely, to the lack of technology to sustain program development and implementation. Then, in the late 1950s, partly derived from B. F. Skinner's emphasis on individualized learning and the importance of feedback and reinforcement, a revival of mastery learning began with programmed instruction, an attempt to provide students with instructional materials that would allow them to move at their own pace and receive constant feedback on mastery level.

Although the work of others preceded them, John Carroll and Benjamin Bloom are generally acknowledged as the architects of mastery learning. Carroll posited that aptitude is the amount of time it takes someone to learn any given material, rather than the capability to master it, the traditional focus. His new theory was based on the idea that all students have the potential to learn material, but take different amounts of time to learn. Two factors identify the learning rate of a student: perseverance or motivation, the amount of time a student is willing to spend on learning (controlled by the student) and the opportunity to learn (controlled by other persons or factors). A student's aptitude determines how much time is needed to master a unit, not the likelihood that one will ever be able to master it. Carroll's theoretical shift in focus places more responsibility on the teacher, so the blame for a student's failure becomes instructional, a notion also embraced by Bloom. In a mastery learning environment, the challenge becomes providing enough time and appropriate instructional strategies so all students can achieve similar levels of learning.

Bloom closely followed Carroll, and is considered the creator of mastery learning. With attention toward "learning for mastery," Bloom believed that given sufficient time and quality instruction, nearly all students could learn. His mastery approach is based on three fundamental conditions: (1) the teacher provides initial instruction; it is group-based, whole-class, more or less conventional classroom teaching, (2) instruction is to be mastery-oriented, and students do not go on to new material until they demonstrate mastery, (3) help is to be available when needed; in order to help students achieve mastery, aid is provided, for example, in the form of test feedback, tutoring, supplemental materials, or small group instruction.

The instructional cycle of mastery teaching includes several components. A teacher or faculty develops a curriculum with major objectives representing the purposes of a course or unit and defines mastery of the subject. Subject matter is divided into units that have predetermined, clearly specified objectives of what is to be learned or expected (a sequence of learning units with a set of facts, concepts, principles, and skills), mastery performance standards, and evaluation processes, including short, highly valid assessment procedures and tests for criterion mastery. Learning materials and instructional strategies are identified that include a cycle of teaching. (Madeline Hunter's model is sometimes utilized.) Teachers use both group and individual instructional methods as students work through each unit in an organized manner, learning at their own pace. Because students must demonstrate mastery on unit exams before moving on to new material, teachers provide consistent and specific assessment, feedback, remediation, and extensions, as needed.

The research literature seems to indicate positive effects of mastery learning on students, especially in the areas of achievement, attitudes toward learning, and the retention of content. Mastery learning seems to work best with the traditional curriculum, one based on well-defined learning objectives organized into smaller, sequentially organized units, where prior knowledge is essential to progress, such as chemistry, mathematics, physics, and foreign languages. Proponents hold that the approach is most useful with basic skills in the elementary grades. They argue that this method of learning should break the cycle of failure, especially with low-achieving populations of students and that students have prerequisite skills to move to the next unit. In addition, teachers are required to perform task analyses and to state objectives before designating activities, thereby becoming better prepared to teach the unit.

Conversely, critics point to some theoretical and practical weaknesses in mastery learning. They note that people do differ in ability and tend to reach different levels of achievement. Not all students will progress at the same pace; this requires students who have demonstrated mastery to wait for those who have not, thus holding back fast learners. Opponents add

that mastery learning will not reduce the learning time that slow learners need (relative to the time needed by fast learners). When faster learners are given enrichment activities, those activities may be less value added and more time fillers to allow others to catch up. Some critics contend that mastery learning takes independent learning away from students, while others suggest that it may be more appropriate for teachers to concentrate on maximizing each student's achievement progress, even if this means maintaining or even increasing the range of individual differences in achievement levels in a class. Furthermore, mastery learning programs tend to require considerable amounts of time and effort to implement, committing major resource allocation to slower learners. Others challenge the assumptions of mastery learning that all subject matter can be hierarchically criterion-delineated and that all objectives in an instructional unit must be learned equally well by all. Also, teachers must have a variety of materials for remediation and have several tests for each unit. If only objective tests are used, critics note this can lead to memorizing and learning specifics rather than higher levels of learning. Finally, teachers' time and focus switch to evaluation rather than to explaining, discussing, and demonstrating.

Mastery learning as an instructional method is not new; it is based on the concept that all students can learn when provided with conditions appropriate to their situation. While traditionalists would preserve time as a constant and allow mastery to vary, proponents of mastery learning hold mastery constant and allow time to vary. The student must reach a predetermined level of mastery on one unit before being allowed to progress to the next. In a mastery learning setting, students are given specific feedback about their learning progress at regular intervals throughout the instructional period. This feedback helps students identify what they have or have not learned well. Principles of mastery learning have become part of directed instruction, computer-assisted instruction, and have provided the rationale for reform movements such as school accountability and outcomes-based education.

—*JoAnn Danelo Barbour*

See also at-risk students; behaviorism; Black education; brain research and practice; child development theories; cognition, theories of; cognitive dissonance; cognitive styles; conditioning theory; constructivism; differentiation of stimuli; early childhood education; grades, of students; Head

Start; intelligence; learning environments; learn, opportunity to; mainstreaming and inclusion; measurement, theories of; metacognition; motivation, theories of; performance assessment; psychology, types of; psychometrics; Skinner, B. F.; tutoring; underachievers, in schools

Further Readings and References

Bloom, B. (1968). Learning for mastery. *Evaluation Comment, 1*(2), 1–12.

Bloom, B. (1971). Mastery learning. In J. H. Block (Ed.), *Mastery learning: Theory and practice.* New York: Holt, Rinehart, & Winston.

Carroll, J. (1963). A model of school learning. *Teachers College Record, 64,* 723–733.

Guskey, T. (1985). *Implementing mastery learning.* Belmont, CA: Wadsworth.

Hunter, M. (1982). *Mastery teaching.* El Segundo, CA: TIP.

Morrison, H. C. (1926). *The practice of teaching in secondary school.* Chicago: University of Chicago Press.

Washburne, C. (1922). Educational measurements as a key to individualizing instruction and promotions. *Journal of Educational Research, 5,* 195–206.

🏛 MATH EDUCATION

The field of math education, both the teaching of mathematics and the preparation of math teachers, remained constant during much of the twentieth century. Yet, since the 1960s, reforms in math education have raised questions and caused debate about best practices in the teaching of mathematics and the preparation of math educators. These questions and debates have sparked a series of changes in the nature of the public school and college curricula and the focus of research on the teaching and learning of mathematics. The rise of technology for instruction, the standards and accountability movement, and new national and international measures of comparative assessment have further fueled the debates and continue to shape the evolution of the field of math education.

Prior to the twentieth century, math educators were primarily viewed as drillmasters charged with the utilitarian responsibility of teaching for the memorization of basic arithmetic skills, computation, and problem solving in mathematics. During the early part of the twentieth century, most math teachers were prepared with 1 or 2 additional years of schooling at a specialized high school called a "normal school." After 1900, when the concept of a universal high school curriculum took hold, math educators majored in mathematics in a teacher's college and were prepared to serve as secondary content specialists. Inherent in this program design was the assumption that math teachers for the elementary and primary grades learned all the mathematics they needed during their postsecondary schooling, and because of such thinking, most elementary and middle grade math teachers received only mathematics required of an elementary education major. After World War II, however, the curriculum emphasis shifted to more modern, sophisticated levels in public schools and colleges, including the inclusion of elements of geometry and algebra in elementary curriculum, greater emphasis on functions and less emphasis on trigonometry in high school, and the introduction of calculus into the curriculum of the first year of college. This shift caused subsequent rethinking of the math curriculum in colleges and schools of education for the preparation of math educators.

Today, the downplaying of basic memorization and computational skills during the twentieth century has surfaced as a serious problem in the P–16 curriculum evidenced by international comparisons of student performance on standardized tests. Students in the United States consistently perform below that of their counterparts in highly developed countries. Since the mid-1980s, international comparison studies, such as the Third International Mathematics and Sciences Study (TIMSS), show that mathematics instruction in many developed nations, particularly Eastern Asia, is definitely richer in comparison to math instruction in American classrooms. The TIMSS study, the largest cross-national, multiyear research study conducted in the history of math education, included 41 countries across five continents and compared over 500,000 students' scores in mathematics and science.

Other comparative assessments, such as the National Assessment of Educational Progress (NAEP), show equally alarming data. Positive press that was provided early during the release of main NAEP data occurred primarily because of the fact that fourth graders and eight graders increased overall from 1999 to 2003 by a range of 15 to 22 scale points respectively. However, a closer look at the comparisons of student performance over time as revealed on the specialized long-term-trend NAEP show that the gains portrayed by the main NAEP are 10 times larger than on the trend NAEP. In fact, in 1999 only 56% of 17-year-olds scored correctly on basic computation skills. Trend analysts blame hidden differences such as this one on differing curriculum frameworks. Test items for the main NAEP tests are developed from the National Assessment Governing Board (NAGB) and closely approximate changes within math instruction in the field, while the trend NAEP utilizes the same testing instruments in order to be able to make comparisons over time. Regardless of the reason, the dismal performance of American students on national measures of standardized assessment and in comparison to other developed nations has called the math curriculum and the preparation of math teachers into question. As the United States neared the end of the twentieth century, it was apparent that we would not achieve the federally legislated goal of *Academics 2000* for American students to place first in math and science achievement in the world.

Comparisons between textbook and curriculum guide content performed by researchers in the TIMMS study show a similar magnitude of difference across various countries in the TIMMS study. Textbooks produced for math instruction in the United States are on the average 25% larger and outweigh the average international length. For example, a fourth-grade mathematics textbook contains an average of 530 pages, while the international length for a fourth-grade math textbook is 170 pages. The reason for the difference in length is the breadth of coverage. U.S. textbooks contain a far greater number of topics than most other countries participating in the TIMSS. This broad coverage is typically presented at the expense of thorough in-depth treatment of the content.

These findings of this and other TIMMS studies show that the math curriculum in America is highly repetitive, revolving around a definition of basics that are largely repeated from the fourth grade and upward, while the view of what constitutes a focused curriculum in other countries involves a tightly regimented introduction of new content throughout the upper grades. For example, in the U.S. math curriculum, American textbooks introduce most of the core content by fourth grade, with only one topic introduced in depth in each grade between fourth and eighth grades. Yet, in most TIMMS countries, textbooks and curriculum guides between fourth and eighth grade introduce roughly 75% of new material each year from fourth grade and beyond, approximately 15 new topics in depth per year. As identified in the TIMMS study, the lack of focus and coherence in the American curriculum and other factors contributing to the mediocre performance of American

schoolchildren in mathematics suggest that the schooling itself—in other words, inadequate preparation of math teachers—may be responsible.

Following the initial release of the TIMMS data in the 1980s, heightened interest and intense debate about strengthening math curriculum and instruction began among the various math societies and professional associations, and in response, the National Council of Teachers of Mathematics (NCTM) published the first academic standards for subject matter instruction in mathematics, the Curriculum and Evaluation Standards. First released in 1989 and updated in 2000, the standards address issues of making math more engaging and demanding to meet the needs of a changing America in a global economy. However, the lack of guidance in the implementation of the standards and competition from state standards with accompanying subject matter test frameworks have diffused the results that were anticipated initially.

Some of the criticism of the NCTM standards and state standards stem from issues of racial equality as the achievement gap that persists among White, Black, and Hispanic subgroups on standardized tests widened in mathematics computation during the 1990s. Numerous research studies attest to the importance of arithmetic, in particular that computation skills are necessary for advancement in careers in math and science. Research studies also show that computation skills are a valuable predictor of adult earnings. Yet, reducing inequity in mathematics instruction by enforcing high standards for all, by raising teacher expectations, and by appropriating resources does not appear to be a priority of local school systems within the United States. Poor teacher preparation, the extensive reliance on calculators in early- and middle-level instruction in mathematics, and the reformist standards of the 1990s are recognized as contemporary issues in math education in the twenty-first century. Changing expectations for math knowledge, coupled with increased uses of technology applications for school mathematics instruction, has directed the rethinking of the current curriculum and preparation that is needed in the math education of prospective teachers.

In response to the criticism and in order to undertake such a massive curriculum reworking, the American Mathematical Society and the Mathematical Association of America joined and formed the Conference Board of the Mathematical Sciences. During the latter part of the 1990s, the board designed a series of federally funded research and development projects commonly called the Mathematics Education of Teachers Project (METP). Stemming from the ongoing debate over student performance, curriculum, and teacher education, METP was designed to examine two general themes: (1) the intellectual substance in school mathematics and (2) the special nature of the mathematical knowledge needed for teaching. The final report of the METP was published in 2000 as a resource for math faculty, administrators in schools and colleges, and others involved in the education of math teachers. While the report itself was not aligned with any particular mathematics curriculum for schools, its findings are consistent with the NCTM's *Principles and Standards for School Mathematics* and other recent national reports on school mathematics. Recognized as a synthesis of contemporary thinking on policy and issues affecting math educators, the METP report is being explored widely by the mathematical sciences community and educational sector to design new preparation programs for prospective math teachers, such as fostering math specialists for middle-level math instruction, and to redesign new professional development opportunities to implement national initiatives in public schools.

The METP report provides the 11 general recommendations to mathematics departments and the larger educational community to guide contemporary discourse and the direction of practice for math education stated below.

1. Prospective teachers need mathematics courses that develop a deep understanding of the mathematics they will teach.

2. Although the quality of mathematical preparation is more important than the quantity, the following amount of mathematics coursework for prospective teachers is recommended:
   a. Prospective elementary teachers should be required to take at least nine semester hours on fundamental ideas of elementary school mathematics.
   b. Prospective middle grades math teachers should be required to take at least 21 semester hours of mathematics, which include at least 12 hours of fundamental ideas of school mathematics appropriate for middle grades teachers.
   c. Prospective high school teachers of mathematics should be required to complete the equivalent of an undergraduate major in mathematics, which includes a 6-hour capstone course connecting their college mathematics courses with high school mathematics.

3. Courses on fundamental ideas of school mathematics should focus on a thorough development of basic mathematical ideas. All courses are designed for prospective teachers, who should develop careful reasoning and mathematical common sense in analyzing relationships and in solving problems.

4. Along with building mathematical knowledge, mathematics courses for prospective teachers should develop the habits of mind of a mathematical thinker and demonstrate flexible, interactive styles of teaching.

5. Teacher education must be recognized as an important part of mathematics department missions at institutions that educate teachers. More mathematicians should consider becoming deeply involved in K–12 mathematics education.

6. The mathematical education of teachers should be seen as a partnership between mathematics faculty and mathematics education faculty.

7. There needs to be greater cooperation between 2-year and 4-year colleges in the mathematical education of teachers.

8. There needs to be more collaboration between mathematics faculty and school mathematics teachers.

9. Efforts to improve standards for school mathematics instruction, as well as for teacher preparation accreditation and teacher certification, will be strengthened by the full-fledged participation of the academic mathematics community.

10. Teachers need the opportunity to develop their understanding of mathematics and its teaching throughout their careers, through both self-directed and collegial study, and through formal coursework.

11. Mathematics in the middle grades (five through eight) should be taught by mathematics specialists.

SOURCE: Conference Board of the Mathematical Sciences. (2001). *The Mathematical Education of Teachers*. Providence, RI, and Washington, DC: American Mathematical Society and Mathematical Association of America. Reprinted with permission.

The recommendations of the METP report are highly specific and differ widely from earlier recommendations found in reports such as Mathematics Association of America's 1983 *Recommendations on the Mathematical Preparation of Teachers*. The METP recommendations are organized around three common grade clusters—elementary, middle, and high school—and address the need for teachers to study within one of these three specialized clusters. The recommendations further contend that teachers need a deeper and broader understanding of the curriculum, in particular where their grade-level content is situated within the larger context of mathematical knowledge in the total curriculum. A number of statements in the recommendations express the need for prospective teachers to acquire a "deep understanding" of mathematics with the emphasis on nurturing the teacher's ability to be able to assess student work, to understand the nature of student errors in relation to student understanding, and to be able to foster high levels of engagement among students, thereby promoting interest in the study of mathematics.

The METP report acknowledges that the P–12 mathematics content is qualitatively different across the curriculum, and thus teachers need to be prepared to make connections that exist among math concepts as they are sequenced along the curriculum. One assumption of the METP report is that with this deeper understanding, math teachers across the various grade levels and clusters will be able to build on students' earlier mathematics knowledge. While the recommendations seem lofty for prospective teachers, the METP report allows that preservice teacher education is essential to a true understanding of school mathematics.

The expectations for high school math teachers in the METP report calls for teacher preparation programs to enable prospective teachers to develop awareness of the mathematics their students are likely to face after high school, either in college, technical studies, or employment, and to foster a mature attitude that will encourage continued growth in the teaching and learning of mathematics. In order to support the METP recommendations, mathematics departments are charged with redesigning their core courses to help secondary teachers make connections across the curriculum content and to offer a capstone course collaboratively taught by faculty in math education and secondary pedagogy for advanced exploration of conceptually challenging points in the teaching and learning of high school mathematics.

As the study of math education evolves to meet the needs of a diverse and changing student population in the United States, the direction of research in the twenty-first century continues to expand to address the complex issues of advancing the study of mathematics in our public schools and society. Instructional leadership for advanced mathematics, the role of technology in math instruction, and the inclusion of special needs students in mathematics programs are pressing topics being explored through research and development in math education. Together with the NCTM, the Mathematical Society of America, and other professional associations of math educators, the mathematical sciences community seeks ways to improve the preparation and professional development through national research and international comparative studies with other countries whose mathematics programs offer insight into best practices for understanding and improving the field of mathematics education in the United States.

—Karen Embry Jenlink

See also accountability; achievement tests; Black education; brain research and practice; cognition, theories of; constructivism; curriculum, theories of; gender studies, in educational leadership; learning, theories of; learning environments; literacy, theories of; measurement, theories of; National Assessment of Educational Progress; Trends International Mathematics and Science Study; underachievers, in schools

Further Readings and References

Clements, D., Sarama, J., & DiBlase, A. (Eds.). (2004). *Engaging young children in mathematics*. Mahwah, NJ: Erlbaum.

Conference Board of the Mathematical Sciences. (2001). *The mathematical education of teachers*. Providence, RI, & Washington, DC: American Mathematical Society and Mathematical Association of America.

English, L. (2002). *Handbook of international research in mathematics education*. Mahwah, NJ: Erlbaum.

English, L. (Ed.). (2004). *Mathematical and analogical reasoning of young learners*. Mahwah, NJ: Erlbaum.

Fernandez, C., & Yoshida, M. (2004). *Lesson study: A Japanese approach to improving mathematics teaching and learning*. Mahwah, NJ: Erlbaum.

Lamon, S. (2005). *Teaching fractions and ratios for understanding*. Mahwah, NJ: Erlbaum.

Loveless, T., & Coughlan, J. (2004). The arithmetic gap. *Educational Leadership, 61*(5), 55–59.

Martin, D. (2000). *Mathematics success and failure among African-American youth*. Mahwah, NJ: Erlbaum.

National Assessment Governing Board. (n.d.). Overview of recommendations. In *NAEP 2005 mathematics assessment framework* (ch. 1). Retrieved August 10, 2004, from http://www.nagb.org.

National Council of Teachers of Mathematics. (2003). *The use of technology in the learning and teaching of mathematics*. Retrieved August 10, 2004, from http://www.nctm.org/about/position_statements/position_statement_13.htm.

Rodriguez, A., & Kitchen, R. (2005). *Preparing mathematics and science teachers for diverse classrooms*. Mahwah, NJ: Erlbaum.

Romberg, T. (2004). *Standards-based mathematics assessment in middle school.* New York: Teachers College Press.

Senk, S., & Thompson, D. (2003). *Standards-based school mathematics curricula.* Mahwah, NJ: Erlbaum.

Sherman, H., Richardson, L., & Yard, G. (2005). *Teaching children who struggle with mathematics: A systematic approach to analysis and correction.* Columbus, OH: Merrill.

Watson, A., & Mason, J. (2005). *Mathematics as a constructive activity.* Mahwah, NJ: Erlbaum.

Wright, R., Martland, J., Stafford, A., & Stanger, G. (2002). *Teaching number: Advancing children's skills and strategies.* Thousand Oaks, CA: Corwin Press.

MATRIX ORGANIZATION (THE "ADHOCRACY")

Often called the "throwaway organizational pattern" or the "adhocracy" by futurist Alvin Toffler, matrix organizational structure involves the creation of a temporary structure within or apart from a traditionally organized structure when the following conditions pertain:

- There is an immediate challenge or crisis faced by the organization that involves multilevels and/or multifunctions of the organization as a rational response.
- The conditions of the organization's environment become highly unstable, ambiguous, and fluid, leaving much uncertainty as to how the organization should respond and casting doubt that any permanent or stable organizational pattern would last very long.
- The nature of a required organizational response would overload the existing chain of command.
- A situation requires a highly unusual and innovative response previously not faced by the organization.
- The political balance of power within an organization is constantly shifting because the organization's objectives and its technology cannot be fixed upon a stable set of objectives or tasks.
- The nature of the problem of issues to be addressed is highly complex and requires a long lead time to pursue, meaning that there will a long chunk of time in which no tangible results will be forthcoming.

The term *matrix* is often affixed to the U.S. aerospace industry, especially NASA. One set of managerial experts indicates that the most distinguishing feature of a matrix organization versus the traditional bureaucratic, pyramidal structure is that the former is characterized by a multiple command system in which persons may have multiple bosses. Along with this development is the creation of a "matrix culture," which is quite different from cultures that are connected with permanent bureaucracies. And matrix structures present a whole new array of personnel problems that traditional bureaucratic structures work hard to eliminate, notably a subordinate being caught between two bosses who cannot agree on what the subordinate should be doing. Job and role ambiguity present additional problems for employees who may not be assured of work after a project is completed.

Matrix structures have been described as "high tension" systems, where the potential for conflict is intensified by the demands for interdependent work among the members, the need to process huge amounts of information quickly, and the difficulty of finding a "boss" to arbitrate differences among and between the members. Matrix structures require a high degree of trust and collaboration to become productive and remain productive.

The leadership skills required to manage a matrix structure involve the ability of a boss who is secure professionally, remains objective about various functions and subfunctions and sees the big picture, works collaboratively and easily with people, involves others in decision making when appropriate but is not afraid to make decisions when required, can work in situations with high levels of ambiguity and uncertainty without becoming disoriented or affixed on single solutions, and knows how to work through problems in groups.

In the larger society, examples of matrix structures are the Manhattan Project (building the atomic bomb) and putting a person on the moon. Political campaigns are also examples of matrix organizations in action. The 1993 Academy Award film nominee *The War Room* showing the organization and operation of President Clinton's campaign managers, James Carville and George Stephanopoulos, is an excellent example.

Educational organizations have used matrix structures for passing bond referendums or tax overrides. However, the potential to attack other kinds of problems such as the achievement gap remain as possible situations to use a matrix structure as it meets many of the conditions requiring a matrix structure.

—*Fenwick W. English*

See also administration, theories of; boards of education; bureaucracy; capacity building, of organizations; chain of command; decentralization/centralization controversy; governance; line and staff concept; management theories; organizational theories; role ambiguity; role conflict; scalar principle; strategic planning

Further Readings and References

English, F. (1977). Matrix management in education: Breaking down school bureaucracy. *Educational Technology, 17*(1), 19–26.

Hill, C. W., & Jones, G. R. (1989). *Strategic management.* Boston: Houghton Mifflin.

Nadler, D., & Tushman, M. (1988). *Strategic organization design.* Glenview, IL: Scott, Foresman.

Toffler, A. (1970). *Future shock.* New York: Bantam Books.

🏛 MAXWELL, WILLIAM H.

William H. Maxwell (1852–1920), an Irish immigrant, rose to become city superintendent of schools, greater New York, in 1898. He arrived in the United States at the age of 22 and found work as a journalist with various New York City newspapers. As a reporter and later as managing editor of the *Brooklyn Times,* he developed an interest and concern for public education. Maxwell then taught briefly in evening high schools and in 1882 was elected associate superintendent of Brooklyn schools.

For the next quarter of a century, Maxwell served as a big-city superintendent in Brooklyn and New York City. He was of a generation of educators who combined leadership with both scholarship and public service. In his annual reports and presentations to the National Educational Association, he wrote about all aspects of school and district leadership. Among the many reforms he helped introduce to New York City's schools were the need for kindergartens; summer schools; physical education; elective courses, including music, singing, and cooking; teaching reforms in reading and writing; responsibilities of principals; pupil progression; teacher and administrative certification; remedial education; special education; school lunch program; the efficient use of school facilities; and a professional code of ethics.

Maxwell fought against the lack of adequate funding and corruption that permitted political bosses to hire teachers. He sought to hire better trained teachers, selected for their qualifications. He argued vigorously against scientific management (i.e., the cult of efficiency) and its excessive demands for data-driven decisions that turned teachers into bookkeepers. He opposed teaching that was dull, mechanical, routine, and where the child was burdened with a load of matter to be memorized at home—long lists of names without meanings or words without connections. He feared that principals were turning teachers into machines by demanding that they do everything exactly as prescribed.

Maxwell called on superintendents to step in and secure to the classroom teacher that reasonable liberty of thought and action. According to the historian Raymond Callahan, few educational leaders of this time dared to speak out as vociferously as Maxwell did against big business and local politicians and the direction being taken by school leadership.

Maxwell attributed weaknesses in curriculum and instruction to two factors: (1) teachers were not as well educated or trained in pedagogy as they should be and (2) in the absence of interesting subject matter, teachers required students to memorize dry and useless details in order to fill up the prescribed school day. In contrast, Maxwell proposed curricula based on children having a progressive knowledge of the outside world. His emphases were on real-life experiences, solving problems, and invention. He also pushed for subject matter to be taught thematically. As for principals, they should use their entire time during school hours to inspect and supervise teaching and do all of their record keeping outside of the regular school day.

Although Maxwell did not succeed in every aspect of his reform agenda, he was successful not only in changing the physical structures of schools to include fine architecture and roof playgrounds but also in addressing what he perceived to be the evils of poverty in which so many of the immigrant children lived.

—*Ira Bogotch*

See also architecture of schools; bureaucracy; chief executive officer; decentralization/centralization controversy; elementary education; high schools; innovation, in education; leadership effectiveness; normal schools; principalship; reform, of schools; superintendency; vulnerability thesis, of superintendents

Further Readings and References

Bogotch, I. (2005). A history of public school leadership: The first century, 1837–1942. In F. English (Ed.), *The SAGE handbook of educational leadership* (pp. 7–33). Thousand Oaks, CA: Sage.

Maxwell, W. H. (1912). *A quarter century of public school development.* New York: American Book.

🏛 McGREGOR, DOUGLAS

Douglas McGregor (1906–1964), a forefather of management theory, is considered to be one of the top business thinkers of all times. His greatest recognition came from his proposal that management must not treat employees as cogs in machines. McGregor believed that management's greatest responsibility was to unleash the vast creative potential of human beings.

With his management theories, McGregor debunked Frederick Taylor's scientific management styles and became one of the first persons to apply findings from the behavioral sciences to the world of business. His popular 1960s book, *The Human Side of Enterprise,* examines authoritarian management (Theory X) and participative management (Theory Y). McGregor proposed that under Theory X management, employees would not work if left to their own devices and that these employees would be inherently lazy and would need to be coerced to work. Under Theory Y management, however, McGregor proposed that employees would find work as natural as play. McGregor's contention was that all employees, if properly managed, are in actuality Theory Y employees. This assumption that employees can be motivated to be Theory Y employees places the responsibility for employee problems at the management level. McGregor contended that when management creates conditions whereby members of the organization can achieve personal goals, the employees will direct their efforts toward the success of the enterprise.

McGregor also had tremendous impact on what became known as total quality management (TQM). He promoted stress-distributed leadership, open-minded appraisal techniques, and employee/customer commitment

McGregor's upbringing greatly shaped his management vision. At a young age, he worked at the McGregor Institute, established in 1895 by his grandfather, housing and feeding 1,000 Great Lakes sailors and other transient workers a year. It was at his grandfather's institute that McGregor gained insight into problems of labor. During his college years, McGregor took a position as a gas station attendant and rose through the ranks to become a district manager for a retail gasoline company. It was during these experiences that McGregor credits himself with learning the concerns of management.

McGregor attended Oberlin College and Wayne State University, and in 1935 earned a PhD from Harvard in experimental psychology. He taught at Harvard for 2 years and then at M.I.T., where he was the first full-time psychologist on faculty. Several years later, he took the position of president of

Antioch College, where he served for 6 years. Then he returned to M.I.T. and served as a professor of psychology and as the executive director of the Industrial Relations Section. At this same time, he served as a consultant to the Dewy Alma Company of Cambridge, Massachusetts, where it was his job to explore and conduct experiments in industrial relations. The general manager of Dewy Alma has stated that the boldness of McGregor's experiments was disconcerting, but as McGregor's hypotheses were always right, the company gave him carte blanche to establish the company's industrial relations policy.

—*Brenda Kallio*

See also human resource development; management theories; Taylor, Frederick; Theory X, Theory Y; total quality management

Further Readings and References

Drucker, P. (1974). *Management: Tasks, responsibilities, practices.* New York: Harper & Row.
McGregor, D. (1960). *The human side of enterprise.* New York: McGraw-Hill.
McGregor, D. (1967). *The professional manager* (W. Bennis & C. McGregor, Eds.). New York: McGraw-Hill.

MEASUREMENT, THEORIES OF

Measurement is the process of estimating psychometric properties of variables or constructs. There are a number of measurement theories that represent different assumptions about and approaches to the estimation process, including the classical test theory (CTT), the generalizability theory (G-theory), the congeneric theory, and the item response theory (IRT).

CLASSICAL TEST THEORY

The most influential theory in psychometric measurement is the CTT. The theory relies on the test score to measure a person's ability or other psychometric properties. Central to the theory is the concept of reliability, first used by Charles Spearman in 1904. According to Spearman, the observed score of a variable or construct consists of two separate components: the true score and the error of measurement. The true score represents the perfect measurement of a construct, for instance, the true ability of a person to accomplish a task. In theory, if a person takes the same test an infinite number of times, the average of the scores will equal the true score. The measurement error, which accounts for the difference between an observed score and the true score, can be divided into systematic error and random error. The former is related to either the examinee or the measure, although not to the construct being measured; the latter results from chance happenings such as guessing and distractions in test administration. The presence of measurement errors makes a measure unreliable. Mathematically, the coefficient of reliability is the ratio of variance of the true score to that of the observed score. The estimation of reliability coefficient is based on the scores of a group of examinees. There are three methods for estimating reliability: (1) the test-retest method is based on repeated administrations of a measure to the same group of examinees and correlates the results from the different administrations, (2) the alternate form approach uses equivalent forms of the same test to be administered to a group of examinees and examines the correlation between the results, and (3) the most frequently used method for reliability estimation is the internal consistency approach that looks at the homogeneity of items within the same instrument. Related to this approach is the split half method of estimating reliability that divides an instrument into two halves and correlates the results from the halves. Estimation of internal consistency for dichotomous items is based on the Kuder-Richardson formulas, while the estimation for polytomous items is based on the Cronbach's coefficient alpha.

Another important index of reliability, the standard error of measurement, is based on individual examinee's scores. It is the standard deviation of the differences between observed scores and the true score for an individual. Standard error of measurement can be used to determine the score band for an individual examinee, the range of scores where the person's true score is most likely located. The standard error of measurement is equal to the standard deviation times the square root of 1 minus the reliability of the measurement.

The second important CTT concept is validity, which is defined as the extent to which an instrument measures what it is supposed to measure. This concept, however, is not considered a feature unique to CTT. Traditionally, there are three types of validity. Content validity concerns whether the sample of test items adequately represents the content of a subject tested.

Criterion-related validity uses an external measure as a criterion to validate the results of an instrument. A subcategory of criterion-related validity is concurrent validity, which can be established if high correlation is found between results of the test and results of a concurrent measure of the same variable. When the criterion is a measure available in the future rather than concurrent, the correlation between results of the test and results of the criterion can be used as evidence for predictive validity of the test, the other subcategory of criterion-related validity. Construct validity concerns whether a construct functions in a way consistent with a relevant theory. It can be established through convergent analysis or discriminant analysis. Evidence for convergent validity is established if high correlation is found between the construct in question and a theoretically related variable. Evidence for discriminant validity is established when a low correlation is found between the construct and a theoretically unrelated variable. Construct validity can also be established if the internal structure of a construct is confirmed through a statistical procedure called factor analysis.

GENERALIZABILITY THEORY

Originally developed by L. J. Cronbach and his colleagues, the G-theory uses the analysis of variance to estimate reliability and errors of measurement. The goal of the G-theory is to examine the degree to which the results of a set of measurements may be generalized to a more extensive set of measurements. All the conditions of the more extensive set of measurements are called the universe of generalization, which determines the universe score variance. The design used for collecting a set of measurements determines the observed score variance. The ratio of the latter to the former is the generalization coefficient. In G-theory, measurement conditions are referred to as facets, which may be fixed or random, and can be crossed with or nested within each other or with the examinees. A distinction is made between a generalizability study and a decision study. The former is concerned with the generalizability of a measurement procedure, while the latter is concerned with the use of data for making decisions about an examinee.

The G-theory is similar to CTT in that both make use of the concept of true score. In CTT, the true score is considered the average of all parallel measurements. In the G-theory, the true score is defined as the average of the universe of observable scores. One difference is that CTT assumes the same error variance across all examinees, while the G-theory allows the examinee error to vary. Another difference is that in CTT, the three types of reliability that represent different aspects of reliability are not estimated simultaneously. In G-theory, all sources of error may be estimated at the same time. This feature enables a researcher to decide which types of errors should be given sufficient attention during a study.

CONGENERIC THEORY

The congeneric or factor analytic theory is a statistical model in analyzing the structure of a construct. Often used in structural equation modeling, the model checks the relationships between items or indicators of an underlying construct or factor. Evidence for the existence of a construct is established if there is high correlation or factor loading between the items and the factor. The model can be broken down into exploratory and confirmatory factor analysis. The former is used when there is no theory available to guide the grouping of items or indicators as to what construct they measure. The latter is used to confirm a theoretically established relationship between a set of items and their corresponding latent variable or construct. It is an important tool in structural equating modeling and studies of construct validity.

According to the congeneric theory, each item score is a weighted function of the measured construct plus an error term that is attributed to unmeasured constructs. Because the weighting varies across items, each item can have a different true score as well as a different error. By allowing both the true score and the error to vary, the congeneric theory represents a less stringent assumption than CTT or the G-theory. Another major difference between the congeneric theory and the CTT is that the former is based on item scores rather than the total test score. Since the item true score and error may vary, item reliabilities may also vary across items. In CTT and G-theory, the item reliability is assumed to be the same.

Although the congeneric theory shifts its attention from a test to the item, it is still based on the response of a sample of examinees, just like the CTT and the G-theory. In other words, all three theories use a measurement model that is sample dependent. A major problem with this is that a different sample may yield a different estimate of the person or item parameter.

ITEM RESPONSE THEORY

The problem with sample dependency in parameter estimation is solved by another measurement model, item response theory (IRT). As a relatively new yet rapidly growing area in the field of measurement, IRT, sometimes called latent trait theory, is based on a probability model to link a person's level of a measured trait to item characteristics. Given the specific response patterns of an examinee to a set of items, IRT uses the maximum likelihood estimation to calibrate the person's trait level (theta) as well as item difficulty and item discrimination on a logit scale. The one-parameter logistic model or the Rasch model assumes that a person's response to a test item is determined by the person's level of trait in relation to the difficulty of the item. The two-parameter logistic model assumes that a particular response is determined by an interaction of the trait level, item difficulty, and item discrimination. The three-parameter model adds guessing into the factors that affect the probability of a correct response. The relationship between the probability of a correct response as a joint result of the person and item parameters can be represented as an S-shaped item characteristic curve (ICC).

IRT is widely used in large-scale test development, differential item functioning (DIF) analysis for potential bias, and equating of tests. One advantage of IRT is that the estimation of item parameter is not dependent on a particular sample. In other words, the use of two different samples of examinees will result in the same result in terms of item calibration. At the same time, the estimation of person parameter is not dependent on a particular set of test items. In fact, there is no need for a fixed number of items in the estimation of a person's trait level. IRT may be used to identify items that maximally match the trait level of a particular person. Such items are supposed to provide maximum information, hence increasing the efficiency of a test. For this reason, it is possible to customize items to different test takers, as in the case of computer adaptive testing, thus greatly reducing the number of items needed to test a person. Another advantage of IRT over CTT is that the former is based on an equal interval scale, while the latter uses an ordinal scale. This makes IRT the favored choice in studies of educational progress and in comparison and linking of different tests.

A drawback of IRT is the need for a large sample of examinees in order to obtain stable parameter estimates.

SUMMARY

The four measurement theories presented above represent different approaches to the measurement of psychological constructs. At the same time, they complement each other. For instance, the G-theory is built on CTT and yet represents a significant revision in its approach to the study of reliability and measurement errors. The congeneric theory, on the other hand, provides a powerful tool in analyzing the underlying structure of a construct. As a result, it can be used in the study of internal consistency as well as construct validity. The IRT, as a serious competitor of CTT, is a favorite tool in large-scale test development. The estimation results using IRT have been found to be more accurate than those from CTT, even though not always significantly different. However, the CTT is easy to comprehend and use, thus an indispensable tool to the classroom teacher. Its basic concepts of validity and reliability constitute the cornerstones in the measurement field.

—*Yuankun Yao*

See also attitudes; Spearman, Charles; testing and test theory development; validity and reliability

Further Readings and References

Anastasi, A., & Urbina, S. (1997). *Psychological testing.* Upper Saddle River, NJ: Prentice Hall.

Masters, G., & Keeves, J. (1999). *Advances in measurement in educational research and assessment.* St. Louis, MO: Elsevier.

Measurement Excellence and Training Resource Information Center. (n.d.). Retrieved June 1, 2004, from theories.asp.

Messick, S. (1995). Validity of psychological assessment: Validation of inferences from persons' responses and performance as scientific inquiry into scoring meaning. *American Psychologist, 9,* 741–749.

Schultz, K., & Whitney, D. (2005). *Measurement theory in action.* Thousand Oaks, CA: Sage.

Spearman, C. E. (1904). General intelligence objectively determined and measured. *American Journal of Psychology, 2,* 201–293.

Wilson, M. (2005). *Constructing measures: An item response modeling approach.* Mahwah, NJ: Erlbaum.

🏛 MEIER, DEBORAH

Throughout her life, Deborah Meier (1931–) has striven to improve the quality of inner-city schools. She has been a teacher, writer, school principal, and advocate for educational reform for over 30 years. Meier was born in New York City in 1931 to Joseph and Pearl Willen. She has had an extensive education, attending precollege at the Ethical Culture School in New York, Antioch College in Ohio, and later pursuing a doctoral degree in history at the University of Chicago. While attending graduate school, she married Fred Meier. They had three children and later divorced. At first, Meier had no plans to teach, but after working part time as a substitute kindergarten teacher, she developed a passion for the profession and quickly became a vocal advocate for educational reform.

Meier's achievements are many. She has been an adviser to New York City's Annenberg Challenge, and she was a senior fellow at the Annenberg Institute at Brown University from 1995 to 1997. She was on the editorial board for *Dissent* magazine, the *Harvard Education Letter,* and the *Nation.* She was the founding member of the National Board of Professional Teaching Standards, and in 1987 she became the first educator to receive the MacArthur Grant, sometimes called the "genius grant." In 1992, in partnership with Theodore Sizer, she raised $3 million and used the money to launch 10 new, small high schools in New York City. Through the course of her life, Meier has founded three elementary schools, started a high school, and influenced many school systems through her methods and practices.

Meier's career was launched by working as a teacher in several different cities. In 1972, Superintendent Tony Alvarado asked Meier to test her small-school theories in Harlem's District 4, the district with the lowest test scores in New York. Meier responded to this request by founding Central Park Elementary (CPE) and encouraging active learning. Meier offered teachers greater autonomy and created a democratic, interactive learning community. She encouraged strong parent involvement and provided adult role models and mentors for her students. Soon after the success of CPE, Meier opened two more Central Park Elementary Schools. In 1985, she opened Central Park East Secondary School (CPESS) and incorporated the same small-school methods and theories of active learning. Today, 18 buildings in Harlem's District 4 house 51 small elementary and junior high schools.

Meier argues that her schools worked because the teachers and the support staff had high expectations and goals for their students. Building strong relationships between children and adults outside the family, and going beyond test scores to assess student learning, are essential elements of this success. Meier has long been opposed to the use of high-stakes testing as the sole measurement of student success. At CPE/CPESS, rather than incorporating standardized testing, the students' success rate was measured by the graduation rate, how many students went on to college, and what they accomplished after they completed school. Meier has developed seven concepts to help guide educational systems as they adapt to the small-school design: (1) governance, (2) respect, (3) simplicity, (4) safety, (5) parent involvement, (6) accountability, and (7) belonging.

—Jane Dettmer and Margaret Grogan

See also accountability; achievement gap, of students; adaptiveness of organizations; at-risk students; capacity building, of organizations; class size; equality, in schools; governance; high schools; leadership, distributed; leadership, teacher; middle schools; No Child Left Behind; parental involvement; reform, of schools; school improvement models; school safety; school size; standardized testing; women in educational leadership

Further Readings and References

Bensman, D. (2000). *Central park east and its graduates.* New York: Teachers College Press.

Meier, D. (1995). *The power of their ideas.* Boston: Beacon Press.

Seller, M. S. (1994). *Women educators in the United States.* Westport, CT: Greenwood Press.

MENDEZ, FELICITAS

Born in Juncos, Puerto Rico, Felicitas Mendez (1916–1998) married Gonzalo Mendez and moved to Westminster, California, in 1943. They became tenant farmers on land owned by an interned Japanese family. When they attempted to enroll their three children in the nearest elementary school, they were informed that they had to attend an all-Mexican school. A meeting with the school superintendent was not productive in ending this form of racial segregation. The Mendezes worked with other parents to try and pass a bond issue for an integrated elementary school. When it failed, the Mendez family joined with the Guzman, Palomino, Estrada, and Ramirez families, and with the help of the League of United Latin American Citizens (LULAC), appointed attorney David Marcus and brought suit against four school districts (Westminster, Garden Grove, Santa Ana, and El Modena) to end the practice of racially segregating Mexican students.

In the 1945 trial before Judge Paul J. McCormick, the school systems' defense hinged on three arguments. The first was that community pressure was against schooling the children together. The second was that segregated schooling benefited Mexicans who were unable to keep up with white students. The third was that psychological testing (I.Q. tests) revealed that Mexican students were not as capable as White students. The Garden Grove superintendent personally declared that Mexicans were unkempt and inferior in their economic outlook, thus justifying racial segregation.

Amicus briefs were filed by the American Civil Liberties Union, American Jewish Congress, National Association for the Advancement of Colored People, National Lawyer's Guild, and the Japanese American Citizens League. The NAACP's brief was written by Thurgood Marshall. Judge McCormick took a year to reach a decision. However, he ruled that the segregation of Mexican students could not be supported in California law and that this practice was a clear violation of the equal protection clause of the U.S. Constitution's Fourteenth Amendment. The school district appealed the case, but again lost in 1947 when the Ninth Circuit Court of Appeals ruled in favor of the plaintiffs.

Felicitas Mendez ran the family farm while her husband, Gonzalo, worked with the attorneys. She also supplied vivid testimony during the trial. The success of the *Mendez v. Westminster* case was instrumental in ending racial segregation of Mexicans in California schools. It was the first case to persuade a federal court that the concept of "separate but equal" was unconstitutional. It was also influential in shaping the better known *Brown v. Board of Education.* For example, the Mendez case used arguments against segregation from educational research and the social sciences. Both of these lines of evidence were later adopted in the strategy of the NAACP in *Brown* eight years later.

—Fenwick W. English

See also accountability; achievement tests; at-risk students; child development theories; cognition, theories of; critical race theory; critical theory; cross-cultural studies; cultural capital; cultural politics, wars; desegregation, of schools; discrimination; diversity; dropouts; early childhood education; equality, in schools; equity and adequacy of funding schools; eugenics; expectations, teacher and student cultures; high schools; immigration, history and impact in education;

individual differences, in children; Latinos; minorities, in schools; multiculturalism; National Assessment of Educational Progress; psychometrics

Further Readings and References

Brisk, M. (2005). *Bilingual education.* Mahwah, NJ: Erlbaum.

Cortina, R., & Gendreau, M. (Eds.). (2003). *Immigrants and schooling: Mexicans in New York.* New York: Center for Migration Studies.

Mendez v. Westminster, A look at our Latino heritage. (n.d.). Retrieved on April 17, 2005, from http: www.mendezvwest minster.com/.

Mendez v. Westminster School District of Orange County, 64 F.Supp. (D.C. CAL. 1946).

McWilliams, C. (1948). *North from Mexico.* New York: Greenwood Press.

🏛 MENSA

Mensa is an international, not-for-profit organization for people who score at or above the 98th percentile on a standard test of intelligence. This is the only requirement for membership. Mensa's message for and example to educational leaders is simple: intelligence can flourish in social settings that promote its use and usefulness.

The goal of Mensa is to form a nonpolitical society free from any forms of discrimination. Founded in 1946 by Roland Berrill, a lawyer, and Dr. Lance Ware, a scientist and lawyer, Mensa is a society with the purposes of identifying and fostering intelligence, encouraging research, and promoting members' intellectual and social opportunities.

Mensans come from all walks of society. Some live in poverty. Others are multimillionaires. Age limits are nonexistent as preschoolers, high school dropouts, and octogenarians belong. In the United States, at least 5 million Americans are eligible for membership. To be a member in good standing, members must agree to abide by the Mensa constitution, pay the annual dues, and permit their names and addresses to be published in Mensa listings.

The organization believes that intelligence should be used for the benefit of humanity. As a result, the free expression of ideas and multiple points of view are encouraged. How do Mensans accomplish that? They get together and discuss ideas plus attend a variety of social functions sponsored by the organization. For example, in the United States, over 150 special interest groups (SIGs) exist. Some national events include the Colloquium, which offers members an opportunity to debate, evaluate, and study issues of importance to society. The Culture Quest is a 90-minute test of cultural knowledge that takes place at the same time on the same day in both Canada and the United States. Every spring, national games competitions are held. Members select winners based on originality, game play, play value, aesthetics, and clarity of instructions.

As a forum for the exploration of opinions, Mensa rests on the idea that humans are social animals and that intelligence works better in stimulating social circles. Mensa also believes that intelligence can be measured. Intelligence, however, is not the same as goodwill, and Mensa has had its share of malcontents and mischief makers.

Mensa makes no attempt to define intelligence. However, it does encourage members to contribute to the field of intelligence and conduct research into the characteristics and uses of intelligence. The Mensa Education and Research Foundation (MERF) gives out five different awards for outstanding research, creative achievement, teaching, and writing. MERF also awards college scholarships. The Mensa lifetime achievement award recognizes those members who have contributed to the fields of giftedness, brain function, human intelligence, creativity, or intelligence testing over a period of 15 years or more. Other competitions are also available. The American chapter annually challenges Americans to find out how smart they are by taking a test administered at more than 100 locations.

The hierarchical structure of Mensa consists of an international general council, which includes the CEO of each national Mensa and the international chairman. This council meets annually. The international board of directors formulates policy and conducts Mensa's international growth and internal affairs. As of 2003, Mensa had active organizations in 40 countries.

—*JoAnn Franklin Klinker*

See also achievement tests; Burt, Cyril; giftedness, gifted education; intelligence; psychometrics; Spearman, Charles; Thorndike, Edward

Further Readings and References

Borland, J. (Ed.). (2003). *Rethinking gifted education.* New York: Teachers College Press.

Coleman, L. (2005). *Nurturing talent in high school.* New York: Teachers College Press.

Mensa International. (2000). Retrieved January 29, 2004, from http://www.mensa.org.

🏛 MENTAL ILLNESS, IN ADULTS AND CHILDREN

Mental illness is any disease of the brain or mind that seriously affects an individual's emotions or mood, thoughts, behavior, or personality. Mental illness can significantly interfere with such everyday functions as learning, thinking, and communicating. Other terms used synonymously with mental illness include *mental, psychological,* and *psychiatric disorder or disease.*

Symptoms of mental illness may include extreme moods such as excessive sadness/depression or anxiety, a decreased ability to think clearly, memory impairment, or delusions and hallucinations. The type, intensity, and duration of symptoms vary from person to person. The symptoms of mental illness often can be controlled effectively through medication and/or psychotherapy. For some individuals, however, the illness continues to cause periodic episodes requiring treatment. Consequently, some people with mental illness will need little if any support, others may need only occasional support, and still others may require more substantial, ongoing support.

Diagnosis is the act of identifying and naming a disorder or disease by using an agreed-upon system. In the United States, mental illnesses are currently diagnosed according to the *Diagnostic and Statistical Manual of Mental Disorders,* Fourth Edition. The *DSM-IV-TR* is the standard handbook for psychodiagnosis employed by clinicians and researchers in the United States.

The terms *neurosis* and *psychosis* are sometimes used to describe the severity of various mental illnesses. A neurosis is a mild disorder that causes distress but may not interfere greatly with a person's everyday activities. A psychosis is a severe mental disorder that prevents an individual from functioning effectively and is a major mental illness with severe symptoms such as delusions and hallucinations as seen in schizophrenia and bipolar disorders. Neuroses are much less severe and include such illnesses as mood disorders, anxiety disorders, and posttraumatic stress disorders.

Mental illness has many forms, and it affects people of all ages, ethnic/racial backgrounds, and economic levels. Determining just how many people have mental illness is one of the many purposes of the field of epidemiology. According to current epidemiological estimates, at least one in five people has a diagnosable mental disorder during the course of a year. That is, about 20% of the U.S. population are affected by mental disorders during a given year. This estimate comes from two epidemiological surveys: the Epidemiologic Catchment Area (ECA) study of the early 1980s and the National Comorbidity Survey (NCS) of the early 1990s. Those surveys defined mental illness according to the prevailing editions of the *DSM-IV-TR.*

The most common types of mental illness are anxiety disorders (e.g., panic disorder, phobias), mood disorders (e.g., major depression, bipolar disorder), and schizophrenia. Some mental disorders, such as Alzheimer's disease, are caused by disease of the brain, but the causes of most others are not clearly known. Schizophrenia appears to be partly caused by genetic factors. Some mood disorders, such as mania and depression, may be caused by imbalances of certain chemicals in the brain. Neuroses seem to be caused by environmental factors such as emotional deprivation or abuse during childhood. Today, there is a growing consensus toward a biopsychosocial view of abnormal behavior—that the abnormal behavior of mental illness arises from an interaction of biological (genetic and physiological) factors and psychosocial influences (past and present experiences).

Mental health professionals have made important advances in the treatment of mental illness. Treatment methods used today usually help people recover from their symptoms more quickly than in the past. Although milder mental illness may not require any treatment, severe cases of mental illness may require extensive professional treatment, including psychopharmacology and therapy.

Neuroses are less severe and more treatable. Some mood disorders, such as mania and depression, are often treated by drugs that act to correct chemical imbalances. However, counseling and psychotherapy are typically the treatment of choice for the majority of individuals with neurotic conditions. Psychosis requires an intensive treatment protocol that usually includes strong prescriptions and, for some individuals, hospitalization.

CHILDREN AND ADOLESCENTS

The annual prevalence of mental disorders in children and adolescents is not as well documented as that for adults. The *2000 Surgeon General's Report* gave prevalence estimates from 17.6% to 22% in one study and 16% in another. Furthermore, child mental disorders often persist in adulthood. Regarding education, federal regulations define a subpopulation of children and adolescents with severe functional limitations known as "emotional disturbance." Under the federal Individuals With Disabilities Education Act (IDEA), this term means a condition exhibiting one or more of the following characteristics over a long period of time and to a marked degree that adversely affects a child's educational performance: an inability to learn that cannot be explained by intellectual, sensory, or health factors; an inability to build or maintain satisfactory interpersonal relationships with peers and teachers; inappropriate types of behavior or feelings under normal circumstances; a general pervasive mood of unhappiness or depression; or a tendency to develop physical symptoms or fears associated with personal or school problems. This definition also includes schizophrenia. This term does not apply to children who are socially maladjusted, unless it is determined that they have an emotional disturbance. Under IDEA, such children should be formally evaluated and, if found eligible, either placed in a special classroom or provided assistance in their regular classroom.

Children with mental health needs are usually identified by the schools only after their emotional or behavioral problems cannot be managed by their regular classroom teacher. For this reason, and the stringent functional limitations legislated by IDEA for the category "emotional disturbance," few children are found eligible in the school category of "emotional disturbance." Although the percentage of children who need intensive and consistent special education programming as a result of their emotional problems is small, the same behavioral and emotional symptoms at a lesser level of intensity are present in much larger numbers of youngsters.

—*Michael Mann*

See also affective domain; at-risk students; child development theories; counseling; emotional disturbance; psychology, types of; psychometric

Further Readings and References

American Psychiatric Association. (2000). *Diagnostic and statistical manual of mental disorders* (4th ed., text rev.). Washington, DC: American Psychiatric Association.

Brown, R. (Ed.). (2004). *Handbook of pediatric psychology in school settings.* Mahwah, NJ: Erlbaum.

Merrell, K. (2003). *Behavioral, social, and emotional assessment of children and adolescents.* Mahwah, NJ: Erlbaum.

U.S. Department of Education. (2002). *Twenty-fourth annual report to Congress on the implementation of the Individuals With Disabilities Act.* Washington, DC: Author.

U.S. Department of Health and Human Services. (2000). *Report of the Surgeon General's Conference on Children's Mental Health: A national action agenda.* Washington, DC: Author.

Valasquez. R. A., & McNeill, B. (Eds.). (2004). *The handbook of Chicana/o psychology and mental health.* Mahwah, NJ: Erlbaum.

🏛 MENTORING

Mentoring is often used interchangeably with assisting, guiding, teaching, learning, readiness, compensation, support, and socialization. Studies have focused on the mentoring of preservice and inservice teacher populations with attention gradually accommodating prospective and practicing administrators. This disequilibrium in mentoring is reflected in public school culture, as beginning and prospective administrators from among staff have been largely overlooked.

TRADITIONAL AND ALTERNATIVE CONCEPTIONS OF MENTORING

Traditionally, mentorship involves training in skills building and knowledge acquisition, both inside and outside education, and of youth or adults. This kind of relationship—typically needs based and short term—is guided by experienced persons in schools, universities, businesses, or other professional domains who transfer understanding and knowledge to apprentices. Within this framework, mentoring is a unidirectional process wherein the more experienced person teaches and the neophyte learns. This transmission model focuses on objectives in an advising or other situation, not the deeper, more sustaining processes of professional development, lifelong learning, or relationship building. Characteristically, traditional mentoring implies conditions for noncritical reflection and feedback whereby "authoritative knowledge" is mediated and satisfaction and recognition derived from the protégé's accomplishments.

The idea of a mentor as somehow separate from or above the group that follows one's charge is considered outdated. More contemporary conceptions of mentorship in the literature include co-mentoring, a proactive force that unites the mentor and mentee or a group of individuals in a reciprocal, mutual exchange that creates a context for the learning relationship. This structure can function as a catalyst for changing traditional practices, hierarchical systems, and homogeneous cultures. Specifically, co-mentoring is a relational or feminist value that seeks to transcend status and power differences and promote diversity by bringing women and minorities into the network. Similarly, collaborative mentoring offers a countercultural approach to entrenched exclusivity: when practiced effectively, this kind of mentoring mobilizes social equality among individuals of various statuses and ability levels, enabling productive synergy.

MENTORSHIP AS A CONTINUUM

Other forms of mentoring include autonomous or self-mentoring through such means as vicarious learning from seasoned professionals. The educational literature taken as a whole suggests that mentorship theory and practice reflect a continuum from self-mentoring to traditional mentoring, to co-mentoring or collaborative mentoring, to systemic or organizational mentoring. Traditional and alternative mentoring encompasses mentor-protégé relationships at the individual or group level, and they occur consciously or unconsciously and formally or informally.

Faculty-led mentoring programs produce benefits for participants. Mentoring cohorts that function powerfully as a compensatory network can increase student success, including for organizationally disadvantaged groups. At the extreme end of this continuum, support groups have been experimenting with more empowering approaches, operating, for instance, not only as a diverse entity but also as a collective critically studying itself. One such group in higher education implemented a "mentoring mosaic," making available to any one member multiple mentors and opportunities for growth. A significant strategy for schools therefore highlights how mentoring should be performed not just one-on-one but rather as a whole-school culture engaged in "re-culturing" itself.

Another variation, formal mentorship includes (1) a one-on-one mentor-protégé arrangement predicated upon assignment to the relationship and (2) a cohort that has been institutionalized and is led by a qualified mentor(s). In contrast, informal mentorship is spontaneous and supported through the mentor; consequently, these relationships are not managed, structured, or

officially recognized, and they involve risk, as the assistance may or may not occur. Interestingly, corporate management studies have found that informal mentoring can actually yield greater benefits for protégés than formal mentoring. Few descriptive studies of informal cohort mentoring in education have been published, but newly emerging research suggests that such contexts offer particular advantages and disadvantages, not unlike formal contexts.

SOME OBSTACLES AND SOLUTIONS

Mentoring, previously labeled as a compensatory support for the once excluded, is now identified as an essential element of graduate education, as well as a critical socializing force for beginning teachers and administrators. While many doctoral students consider their advising and mentoring relationship as the single most important element in graduate education, many have also appraised it as the most disappointing relationship.

Regarding the socialization of prospective school leaders, this population has primarily viewed administrative staff and principals as the critical influence in their own preparation, not graduate programs. Although such administrator programs teach examples of leadership behaviors, they are unlikely to transmit the practical knowledge that characterizes exemplary leadership. Many practitioners and scholars alike argue for adequate training opportunities for aspiring principals through longer, more rigorous internships, mentoring and shadowing practical experiences, and instruction by model practitioners.

—*Carol Mullen*

See also accountability; adaptiveness of organizations; adult education; attitudes toward work; capacity building, of organizations; career stages; democracy, democratic education and administration; instructional interventions; leadership, distributed; leadership, participatory; leadership, system oriented; leadership, theories of; professional development schools; reform, of schools; role model; school improvement models; tutoring

Further Readings and References

Blake-Beard, S. D. (2001). Taking a hard look at formal mentoring programs: A consideration of potential challenges facing women. *Journal of Management Development* 20(4), 331–345.

Bloom, G., & Krovetz, M. (2001). A step into the principalship. *Leadership, 30*(3), 12–13.

Gross, R. A. (2002). From "old boys" to mentors. *Chronicle of Higher Education*. Retrieved from http://chronicle.com/jobs/2002/02/ 2002022801c.

Lucas, K. F. (2001). The social construction of mentoring roles. *Mentoring & Tutoring, 9*(1), 23–47.

Malone, J. (2001). Principal mentoring, *Research Roundup, 17*(2), 1–8. Retrieved from http://eric.uoregon.edu/publications/roundup/Winter_2001.

Mullen, C. A. (2000). Constructing co-mentoring partnerships: Walkways we must travel. *Theory Into Practice, 39*(1), 4–11.

Mullen, C. A. (2003). The WIT cohort: A case study of informal doctoral mentoring. *Journal of Further and Higher Education, 27*(4), 411–426.

Wellington, S. (2001). *Be your own mentor: Strategies from top women on the secrets of success.* New York: Random House.

🏛 MERIT PAY

Merit pay is the simple notion that teachers should be paid in whole or in part on their performance in the classroom. Although there are records that teachers' salaries were determined in part on their students' examination scores in England in 1710, the first recorded attempt to install a merit pay plan in a school system in the United States was in 1908 in Newton, Massachusetts. Since then, about 183 school systems have tried and abandoned the idea. The latest attempt at merit pay was the Denver, Colorado, performance pay pilot. Early evidence has been that it did not work. The major drawbacks with merit pay are administrative problems, personnel problems, collective bargaining restrictions, financial problems, and adverse publicity.

Salary is not one of the reasons persons typically enter teaching. Therefore, persons entering teaching are not primarily motivated by money. Furthermore, the bulk of the teaching force is female. A female-oriented profession has been highly sensitive to forms of socialization and to matters of rank and differentiation. Females prefer to be in an egalitarian workforce. Working relations with others is a very important factor in such a workforce. Salary differentiations based on subjective factors other than seniority have not been widely accepted.

Alternative forms of pay that have a higher rate of acceptance are job enlargement (where increased pay is related to increased workload) and/or an extended contract year (where increased pay is related to spending more time on the job). Both of these approaches are more acceptable to teachers as forms of increasing their base pay than separation based on measures of performance. Another approach has been the creation of a career ladder related to differentiated staffing, that is, teachers are paid for different roles instead of on measures of pure classroom performance.

Other approaches to pay differentials involve such areas as market-sensitive pay. From this perspective, a science teacher might be paid more than a physical education teacher because fully qualified and certified science teachers are much scarcer than physical education teachers. Salary becomes a measure of scarcity, a factor that is already utilized extensively in higher education hiring and compensation practices. Some forms of market-sensitive pay are already utilized in some school districts where ESL teachers are paid a bonus or teachers who represent areas that require training beyond those otherwise employed, for example, in special education. However, market-sensitive pay is not a form of merit pay.

The major problems with merit pay have been identified as (1) the nonavailability of state funds to use in salary incentives, (2) the nonavailability of local funds for similar purposes, and (3) the potential threat of lowered teacher morale. From a teacher acceptance perspective, most merit pay plans are based on an assumption that only a few teachers can ever qualify for merit and that the amounts will not be very large. From this vantage point, the appeal of merit pay to the largest segment of the teaching force does not have enough critical mass to be an important leverage point to install a merit pay plan.

Other difficulties with installing merit pay cluster around finding acceptable indices to determine superior teaching, ensuring the technical competence of those doing the evaluations so that it is reliable and valid, and clarifying the reasons for the plan in the first place. Most traditional evaluation plans for teachers are inadequate for purposes of installing a merit pay approach. In considering implementing a merit pay plan, some districts have developed two teacher evaluation systems. The first is the traditional system centered on promoting growth. The second system is installed for the purpose of gathering data to make the finer distinctions required for determining merit increases. The traditional evaluation system is centered on creating minimal responses to uniform standards or expectations. A merit pay evaluation system assumes a common base and is aimed at providing the finer-honed criteria to determine exceptions to the common standards.

Merit pay continues to be much discussed in public education. The popularity of the topic waxes and wanes with the political tides. Since salaries of teachers are the largest single monetary item in school system budgets, when money becomes tight, talk of merit or performance pay escalates at these times. No one doubts that salary is an important tool to recruit and maintain competent personnel. But compensation does not occur in a vacuum. It takes place within a culture and a climate that often determine the success or failure of the salary mechanism beyond simply the methods and means of payment.

—*Fenwick W. English*

See also accountability; attitudes toward work; authority; boards of education; career stages; clinical supervision; contracts, with teacher unions; expectations, teachers and student cultures; fringe benefits; gender studies, in educational leadership; involvement, in organizations; performance evaluation systems; power; role conflict; salary and salary models; satisfaction, in organizations and roles; sexism (glass ceiling); staffing, concepts of; unions, of teachers

Further Readings and References

Chamberlin, R., Haynes, G., Wragg, E., & Wragg, C. (2004). *Performance pay for teachers.* London: Routledge.

English, F. (1984). Merit pay: Reflections on education's lemon tree. *Educational Leadership, 41*(4), 72–79.

English, F. (1992). History and critical issues of educational compensation systems. In L. Frase (Ed.), *Teacher compensation and motivation* (pp. 3–24). Lancaster, PA: Technomic.

Gratz, D. (2005). Lessons from Denver: The pay for performance pilot. *Phi Delta Kappan, 86*(8), 569–581.

Wolfe, M., McIntosh, P. I., & Steffy, B. (Eds.). (2004). *Life cycle of the career teacher in practice: Applications and outcomes for individual and school renewal.* Indianapolis, IN: Kappa Delta Pi.

METACOGNITION

Metacognition is the executive function of the human intellect. It is a mediating process that includes the ability to predict performance, monitor activity, and understand content. It also allows individuals to organize information to know when, what, and how to remember. Metacognition further involves the act of "thinking about how one thinks," or knowledge and cognition about cognitive phenomena. In essence, metacognition allows individuals to not only acquire content knowledge but also learn about themselves within the context of that content. Metacognition has been defined as "the deliberate conscious control of one's cognitive actions." However, metacognition was and remains a fuzzy concept in that it has no consistent, standard definition. It has become an even fuzzier concept as research on metacognition has proliferated and expanded into a variety of disciplines and directions. Metacognition-based instructional strategies include, but are not limited to (a) the strategic instruction model, (b) content enhancement, and (c) self-evaluation.

Initial research on metacognition began in the 1950s, and the development and application of metacognition-based instructional strategies began in the late 1960s and early 1970s. Metacognitive approaches are designed to foster an understanding of content and flexibility/adaptability in applied settings. Usable, functional knowledge, which is easily retrievable, is an observable outcome of the effective use of metacognition. Once individuals become proficient in the use of metacognitive approaches and employ them on a regular basis, those persons tend to become more effective at attacking and understanding content. In essence, the more these approaches are used by an individual, the greater the degree of the person's mastery of both the method and content.

Significant differences exist in the problem-solving approaches of those three groups of high school students who (a) are academically successful, (b) are academically at risk, and (c) possess specific learning disabilities. In essence, academically successful students spontaneously generate strategic methods for attacking, encoding, storing, and retrieving academic content. Students who are academically at risk or who possess specific learning disabilities do not systematically attack or process academic content. The latter two groups are almost identical in their low level of metacognitive skills. In addition, students in the former group possess an ability to distinguish vital information from irrelevant information, while this ability is absent in the latter groups. Overall, those students who are proficient at developing and applying strategies to process information (a) notice meaningful features of content and information that are not apparent to others, (b) can easily and flexibly retrieve various aspects of content with little difficulty, and (c) understand contextual applications of content instead of an isolated set of facts.

Beyond the differentiation of salient from irrelevant content features, metacognition also involves the generation and evaluation of alternative uses of content and the generalization of that content to novel situations. As only about 25% of all students spontaneously generate and apply metacognitive approaches in instructional settings, activities in such settings must support and encourage the development of metacognition in students.

Research has indicated that metacognitive strategies can be taught and can have a positive impact on student performance. However, the effectiveness of training and application of metacognitive strategies is influenced by a variety of factors. These factors include (a) the receptive and expressive language of an average 9-year-old, (b) intellectual capacity within or above the normal range, and (c) a long-term commitment to an intensive metacognitive training regime. This is not to mean that persons with cognitive disabilities or younger children cannot be taught to use metacognitive strategies to improve academic or social functioning. Simple strategies can be acquired, applied, and generalized by these persons. However, those metacognitive strategies that are more complex in nature may be more difficult (if not impossible) for such persons to acquire, due to the role that internal language or "self-talk" plays in strategy mediation by the individual. Furthermore, the more complex academic metacognitive approaches often require long-term instructional intervention and support before students become proficient in their use or can spontaneously generalize application to new settings and content.

The use of metacognitive strategies to improve student performance is not limited solely to the area of academic performance. A variety of metacognitive approaches to enhance the interpersonal, social, and organizational skills of students have been identified. These strategies include approaches to improve the perceptions and interactions between students and between students and their teachers in order to facilitate successful student movement between classes (i.e., arrive on time with all materials).

Metacognition as the basis for intervention and instruction holds promise for educational institutions. The approaches developed from research in metacognition are more consistent with how the human brain operates than more traditional approaches to instruction. "Brain-friendly" instruction allows for more effective processing of content information and, by definition, more rapid and extensive intellectual growth. As traditional and metacognitive instructional practices become aligned more closely, as new metacognitive instructional materials are developed,

as assessment focuses more on understanding as opposed to memory, as state and national achievement standards better reflect how students process and acquire information, and as the professional development of teachers incorporates metacognitive research to a greater extent, a new model for instruction and learning will emerge that better reflects the role of contextual understanding and cognitive diversity in the education process.

—*J. M. Blackbourn*

See also brain research and practice; cognition, theories of; cognitive dissonance; cognitive styles; intelligence; neuroscience; perceptual psychology; psychology, types of

Further Readings and References

Alley, G. R., & Blackbourn, J. M. (1980). *Acquisition and generalization of learning strategies in preschool handicapped children: A review of research* (Document 150). Lawrence: Kansas University Early Childhood Research Institute.

Blackbourn, J. M. (1989). Acquisition and generalization of social skills in elementary-age students with learning disabilities. *Journal of Learning Disabilities, 22,* 28–34.

Bransford, J. S., Brown, A. L., & Cocking, R. R. (Eds.). (2000). *How people learn: Brain, mind, experience, and school.* Washington, DC: National Academy Press.

Efland, D. (2002). *Art and cognition.* New York: Teachers College Press.

Taylor, L. (2004). *Introducing cognitive development.* New York: Routledge.

🏛 MIDDLE SCHOOLS

Middle schools grew out of the idea that the secondary schools at the time—1910 to 1925—should be separated into junior and senior divisions. Designed around the thought that the seventh grade was the natural turning point in an adolescent's life, junior high schools for Grades 7 to 9 gained in popularity through the 1950s. However, the demand for a rigorous ninth-grade curriculum at that time drove junior highs into becoming preparatory secondary schools. These mini–high schools were characterized by a departmentalized organization of subjects, a six-period schedule of 50-minute blocks, and instructional methods dominated by the lecture style of delivery. By 1960, educators began to reorganize schools for 10- to 15-year-old adolescents into what is known as the middle school concept of schooling.

In its seminal report *Turning Points: Preparing American Youth for the 21st Century,* the Carnegie Council on Adolescent Development provided a framework for middle-level education, the components of which would work collectively to ensure the success of all students: (a) create small communities for learning, (b) teach a core of common knowledge to all students, (c) empower teachers and principals with the responsibility to transform middle grade schools, (d) staff middle grades with teachers specifically prepared to teach young adolescents, (e) link the education and health of young adolescents, and (f) establish family-school-community partnerships. Ten years later, *Turning Points 2000* by Anthony Jackson and Gayle Davis provided guidelines on how to implement the middle school model. Core values outlined by Jackson and Davis, and an important change from the original *Turning Points,* include expectations of success for every student and a curriculum grounded in academic standards.

The mission of the middle school is to facilitate learning among young students at a critical time in their adolescent development—i.e., intellectual, physical, psychological, social, and moral development. The dominant grade structure of middle schools today is a Grades 5 to 8 pattern, but middle schools may also be comprised of Grades 5 to 7, 7 to 8, or 6 to 9.

This We Believe, the 2003 position paper of the National Middle School Association, outlines 14 characteristics for successful schools for young adolescents. The first eight present facets of the school culture: prepared, engaged educators; brave and collaborative leadership; decisions guided by a single vision; safe and supportive environment; raised expectations; active learning; adult advocates; and family-community partnerships.

The remaining six characteristics address the programmatic components of a developmentally responsive middle school: relevant and challenging curriculum; approaches to learning and teaching based on diversity; supportive assessment/evaluation programs; organizations supporting meaningful relationships and learning; policies and efforts toward health, wellness, and safety; and multifaceted guidance and support services.

Some emerging research has, however, indicated that students do better with grades and discipline if they remain in a K–8 setting. Some large school systems have dropped their middle school programs and are reverting to a K–8 pattern.

—*Kathleen Roney*

See also adolescence; affective domain; curriculum, theories of; discipline in schools; dropouts; elementary education; grades, of students; junior high schools; learning, theories of; literacy, theories of; philosophies of education; politics, of education; school districts, history and development; school improvement models; site-based management

Further Readings and References

Brown, E., & Saltman, K. (2005). *The critical middle school reader.* London: Routledge.
Carnegie Council on Adolescent Development. (1989). *Turning points: Preparing youth for the 21st century.* New York: Carnegie Corporation.
Jackson, A., & Davis, G. (2000). *Turning points 2000: Educating adolescents in the 21st century.* New York: Teachers College Press.
National Middle School Association. (2003). *This we believe: Successful schools for young adolescents.* Westerville, OH: Author.

MIGRANT STUDENTS

Migrants are defined in the U.S. Department of Education guidelines as migratory workers or the children of migratory workers who move for the purposes of obtaining seasonal or temporary work in agriculture or fishing. Each year approximately 3 million to 5 million farm workers and their families leave their homes to follow the crops. Their lives revolve around working and moving on, and these families travel from one harvest to another hoping to improve their finances.

Migrants in the United States are extremely diverse; approximately 92% of all migrants are culturally and linguistically diverse, of whom 85% are Hispanic. Of the Hispanic migrant population, 60% are Mexican American and are the largest subgroup, followed by Puerto Ricans, Cubans, and Central and South Americans.

Migrants primarily harvest fruits and vegetables. In the summers, they may harvest tomatoes or broccoli in Texas or possibly apricots, peaches, or grapes in California. They tend to migrate up and down along three known geographic routes: the East Coast stream, the midcontinent stream, and the West Coast stream following seasonal crops.

Over 80% of migrants and seasonal farm workers are U.S. citizens or are legally in the United States. The average annual income for these families is less than $7,500 per year, far below the federal poverty level.

The work of migrant farmworkers tends to be seasonal and often very inconsistent. The number of farmworkers needing housing exceeds the number of available substandard housing units. Therefore, farmworkers, particularly migrants, confront obstacles or barriers to obtain housing. Agricultural employers recognize that the lack of adequate housing is a serious challenge. They resort to temporary housing such as labor camps; however, construction and maintenance of these labor camps can be expensive, especially since labor camps are only occupied during harvest season. The housing that is readily available for most migrant families may not meet the minimum inspection standards, consequently posing a national health problem. Migrant families tend to live without adequate restroom facilities and clean drinking water in substandard housing, which are usually barrack-like structures, run-down farmhouses, trailer homes, or small shacks. Some migrants may be forced to sleep in tents, cars, or even ditches when housing is not available.

The census indicates that among Hispanic migrant children, 38.4% lived in poverty in 1990 as compared to 18.3% of non-Hispanic children. Some commonly reported health problems among migrant children include lower height and weight, respiratory diseases, parasitic conditions, chronic diarrhea, and congenital and developmental problems, to name a few. Poverty, hunger, fear, and uncertainty fill the lives of migrant children.

EDUCATIONAL EXPERIENCES OF MIGRANT STUDENTS

Children of migrant farmworkers have not been academically successful in public schools. Poverty and migration make it difficult for migrant children to create a different life and future than that of their parents. Their schooling may be interrupted several times throughout one school year; this high mobility puts an enormous stress on migrant children and on the schools. The challenges they confront as they progress through the grades eventually can become obstacles. These challenges must be removed so these students can realize their intellectual potentials. For example, their educational needs vary considerably; some lack the literary skills in Spanish, while English language abilities are limited for others. The quality of instruction for migrant students could be hampered if the curriculum does not adequately address their needs or provide supplemental instructional services to

overcome academic difficulties that result from frequent educational disruptions. Most school personnel have not prepared to adequately serve the academic needs of Hispanic students, but in particular, migrant students.

Migrant students have the lowest graduation rate of any population group in the U.S. public schools. The dropout rate among children of migrant farm workers is almost twice that of children from nonmigrant families. Their dropout rate is conservatively estimated at 45%, well above the national average of 25%. In two other studies, the dropout rates for migrant students ranged from 45% to 65%. These longitudinal studies focused on Hispanic students identified while they were in sixth grade; however, these students were not tracked for long because of a high disappearance rate. They moved, disappeared, dropped out, or no longer qualified for services. Some migrant students choose to drop out of school; research indicates that several factors influence the students to leave school before graduating. For example, approximately 50% of migrant students are one or more years below grade level. Thus, half of all migrants could be at risk of leaving school early. Poverty is another factor that leads to dropping out; the addition of another family member contributing to the family income is welcomed. Students also tend to drop out of school if they are not proficient in English; yet, learning English for all migrants is an economic asset. These students generally have suffered academically, dislike school, participate little in school activities, have no home base, are economically disadvantaged, and have low motivation and low persistence. Some teachers become uninterested in migrant students due to their diverse academic, social, and economic needs; consequently, the students leave school.

Migrant children must be assisted in adjusting to new environments. These children transfer to several schools during the span of their education. Some migrant children transfer to different schools as many as three times a year. These experiences are not pleasant and at times can be uncomfortable, because the children never feel grounded or feel like they truly belong. When some students do feel a sense of belonging or have made friends, they are uprooted to go to the next harvest site. What may compound the situation more is that these children may not be proficient in English; therefore, they may not be accepted by some of their classmates. These children tend to withdraw, are not noticed, and thus overlooked. They experience isolation for not being accepted for who they are, thus contributing to having low self-esteem. Thus, schools must provide an environment for migrant students to adjust as quickly as possible at each site.

Principals and teachers must be committed to high expectations and make every effort to ensure high student achievement for migrant students. They must be committed to improve the multiple changes that contribute to student achievement. When available, teachers can use bilingual education approaches with students who enter with limited English skills. Administrators should emphasizes regular attendance and recognize classrooms with all children present; good citizenship can be recognized and rewarded.

—Velma D. Menchaca

See also Chavez, Cesar Estrada; critical race theory; cross-cultural studies; desegregation, of schools; diversity; dropouts; immigration, history and impact in education; intelligence; Latinos; League of United Latin American Citizens; Mendez, Felicitas; underachievers, in schools

Further Readings and References

Chapa, J., & de la Rosa, B. (2004). Latino population growth, socioeconomic and demographic characteristics, and implications for educational attainment. *Education and Urban Society, 36*(2), 130–249.

Contreras, A. (2004). Latinos at the portal of the 21st century. *Education and Urban Society, 36*(2), 223–234.

Garcia, E. (2005). *Teaching and learning in two languages.* New York: Teachers College Press.

Gonzales, G. (2003). Segregation and the education of Mexican children, 1900–1940. In J. Moreno (Ed.), *The elusive quest for equality: 150 years of Chicano/Chicana education.* Cambridge, MA: Harvard Educational Review.

Lee, S. (2005). *Up against whiteness: Race, school, and immigrant youth.* New York: Teachers College Press.

Ritchie, W., & Bhatia, T. (Eds.). (2003). *Handbook of second language acquisition.* St. Louis, MO: Elsevier.

MINORITIES, IN SCHOOLS

Small or different groups of students have posed a problem and a threat to majoritarian school practices ever since Irish immigration brought huge numbers of Catholics into the public, largely Protestant schools on the East Coast. The humiliation of Catholics exposed to Protestant Bible readings and other pejorative practices helped create a separate school system.

In the Southwest, missions and presidios were the institutions providing informal education for the Indian population. The purpose of schooling this population was to replace the Indian identity with a Spanish identity and to inform them of their subordinate place in society. The intent was to smother or destroy their "indigenous religious and social beliefs" by teaching the Catholic ideals, Spanish customs, music, and literacy. Some Indian groups resisted the rule of the Spanish by engaging in significant battles over who controlled the Southwest. Others rejected the Spanish by leaving the missions or killing missionaries. Others were willing to learn the ways of the Spanish and accept their religion, rules, and customs. This provided them the opportunity to learn to read and write in Spanish, which brought forth the knowledge needed to inform other Indians of the Spanish culture.

With the decline of the missions and presidios in the early nineteenth century, the importance of educating the Indian population shifted to educating the Spanish settlers. Education became important in settlements that had large numbers of Spanish-speaking settlers such as Los Angeles, Santa Fe, and San Antonio. The purpose for educating them was to transmit the "social and cultural status" of the Anglo population by teaching literacy, religious ideals, and social order.

Between 1836 and the early 1850s, the United States annexed Texas, Arizona, California, and Colorado, and the Mexicans became subordinate to the Anglos. Catholic churches began to establish formal schooling for Mexican children. These schools had been established to maintain the Catholic ideals and beliefs, to learn about the Anglo traditions, and to acquire a place in the social order in American society. Later, Anglo officials began to establish public schools for Mexican American children. These schools were established to assimilate the growing numbers of racial minorities into the Anglo culture.

Between 1825 and 1870, the states began funding public education with trained staff and managed by a central organization. It was during this time that the organization, scope, and role of schooling became transformed and solidified. Schools became age graded, often compensatory, taught by trained teachers and led by full-time experts. Yet, minority students were excluded from these formal educational environments for Anglo children. In the South, most Blacks were denied schooling, while the North had a few pockets of Blacks attending public schools in segregated classrooms or informal settings. Laws were passed to prevent racial minorities from attending public schools

A similar dilemma faced Asians who came to America, particularly in the West. The discovery of gold in California brought Chinese adventurers like so many others. Later, Chinese were sought to help lay railroad beds and track. The image of Chinese "coolies" was established in textbooks and the public mind; the Chinese later became the subject of virulent attack by Samuel Gompers of the American Federation of Labor. Asiatics were considered inferior to Whites, which led to the passage of the Chinese Exclusion Acts of 1882. In San Francisco, Chinese children were prohibited from attending the public schools. Later, when the California Supreme Court ruled that Chinese students could not be barred from attending school, a separate school for them was constructed. Racial segregation lasted until 1946, following the *Mendez v. Westminster* school case in which it was prohibited.

Similarly, Japanese on the West Coast were maligned, their children excluded from attending public schools, fanned by newspaper stories warning Whites about the "yellow peril."

By 1868, laws prohibiting racial minorities were often considered illegal, yet states were prohibiting school boards from using state funds to school racial minorities. At the end of the nineteenth century, it became apparent that the federal government did not value education for racial minority students. In fact, the Supreme Court's 1896 decision in *Plessy v. Ferguson* validated this ideology. *Plessy v. Ferguson* gave states the right to segregate racial minorities from their Anglo counterparts. This court decision supported the segregation of racial minorities in all aspects of American society by also prohibiting them access to White establishments.

During the early twentieth century, most schools had begun to provide some form of education to Blacks, Mexican Americans, Asians, and Native Americans. While Native Americans were schooled in reservations, Blacks, Asians, and Mexican Americans were kept in separate facilities from their White counterparts. These all-Black, Asian, and Mexican schools were without adequate or appropriate resources and were usually rundown, dilapidated schools. They were usually located away from the schools for Anglo children. The *Mendez v. Westminster* case in California heralded the end of segregation for Mexican students in 1946. Eight years later, the U.S. Supreme Court passed *Brown v.*

Board of Education to desegregate American public schools and assigned the lower courts to implement the changes to come. However, more than a decade later, lower state courts were not forcing public schools to desegregate; consequently, schools in the South were making assignments according to race, and many Blacks were still attending all-Black schools.

The middle of the twentieth century was very challenging for racial minorities. Migrants or migratory workers uprooted their families several times a year for the purposes of obtaining seasonal or temporary work in agriculture or fishing. These families became an important thread of America's agricultural economy. Their lives revolved around working and moving from one harvest to another hoping to improve their lives. The schooling of migrant children was interrupted several times each year, and the challenges they confronted eventually became obstacles. This high mobility put an enormous stress on migrant children and on the schools, since most school personnel were not prepared to adequately serve the academic needs of migrant students.

During the 1960s, the civil rights movement brought dramatic reforms to American public schools and society. School reformers were trying to provide more equitable opportunities for Blacks and Mexican American children. As schools became desegregated, Blacks and Mexican American children were placed in segregated classrooms. Most racial minority students were moved into noncollege or vocational tracks. Tracking of Mexican American students was also based on linguistic differences. Blacks and Mexican American students were also more likely to be segregated into special education classrooms. While racial minority students were in lower-level classes, their White counterparts were in the higher-level, college-bound classrooms.

Throughout the rest of the twentieth century, research studies differed on the successes and failures of Blacks, Native American, and Latino children and the achievement gap that exists between Anglo and some racial minorities. Most recently, however, the Civil Rights Project at Harvard found that a dangerously high percentage of poor and minority students are not graduating from American high schools. Approximately 50% of Blacks, Native Americans, and Latino students drop out of schools. Graduation rates are even lower for minority males. These dropout students are more likely to be unemployed, in prison, and/or living in poverty.

In 1998, Latinos/Latinas comprised a larger percentage of the national school-age population than African Americans. While it is anticipated that within the next 40 years Whites will become a statistical minority, with Latinos making up a quarter of the entire population, traditional "minorities" are expected to continue to have difficulties in school systems dominated by White norms and White school culture.

—*Velma D. Menchaca*

See also accountability; achievement gap, of students; achievement tests; Asian Pacific Americans; Black education; boards of education; bureaucracy; Catholic education; civil rights movement; critical race theory; cross-cultural studies; cultural capital; cultural politics, wars; desegregation, of schools; determinism, sociocultural; discipline in schools; discrimination; diversity; dropouts; early childhood education; elementary education; ethnicity; ethnocentrism; eugenics; finance, of public schools; high schools; immigration, history and impact in education; Indian education; individual differences, in children; intelligence; Latinos; migrant students; multiculturalism; National Assessment of Educational Progress; politics, of education; resiliency; schooling effects; social capital; social context; special education; standardized testing; tracking, of students; underachievers, in schools

Further Readings and References

Contreras, A. (2004). Latinos at the portal of the 21st century. *Education and Urban Society, 36*(2), 223–234.

Fine, M., Weis, L., Pruitt, L., & Burns, A. (Eds.). (2004). *Off white: Readings on power, privilege and resistance.* New York: Routledge.

Gaiten, C. (2004). *Involving Latino families in schools.* Thousand Oaks, CA: Corwin Press.

Kivisto, P. (Ed.). (2004). *Incorporating diversity: Rethinking assimilation in a multicultural age.* Boulder, CO: Paradigm.

McCarthy, C., Crichlow, W., Dimitriadis, G., & Dolby, N. (2005). *Race, identity, and representation in education.* New York: Routledge.

Mendez v. Westminster School District of Orange County, 64 F. Supp. 544 (D.C. CAL. 1946).

Orfield, G., Losen, D., Wald, J., & Swanson, C. B. (2004). *Losing our future: How minority youth are being left behind by the graduation rate crisis.* Cambridge, MA: Civil Rights Project at Harvard University.

Plessy v. Ferguson, 163 U.S., 537–564 (1896).

🏛 MIXED METHODS, IN RESEARCH

Mixed methods or integrated methods (MMs) have gained popularity following a long history of debates over the legitimacy and preeminence of either the qualitative or the quantitative approaches to research. Traditionally, quantitatively oriented researchers (QUANs) have worked within the positivist (or postpositivist) paradigm and are principally interested in numerical data and statistical analyses, while qualitatively oriented researchers (QUALs) followed a constructivist paradigm and are interested in narrative data and analysis. In contrast, researchers who identify themselves as mixed, or integrative, work primarily within the pragmatist paradigm and utilize both narrative and numeric data and analyses for answering research questions.

Labeled as a "third methodological movement" in social and behavioral research, MMs have emerged as an alternative to the QUAN and QUAL traditions. This main tenet of the MM approach is that the research question (not the paradigm or the purpose) dictates the method of inquiry. Therefore, the MM approach encourages researchers to utilize the best combination of QUAN and QUAL methodological tools to provide the optimal and most comprehensive information for answering the research questions under study.

Although researchers across the social, behavioral, and health sciences have frequently employed MM in their studies throughout the twentieth century and into the twenty-first century, MM designs and procedures are still evolving. Also, despite the fact that combining QUAL and QUAN methods is largely widespread in applied research, there is still debate over the definition and the feasibility of MM.

Critiques of MM have advocated an incompatibility thesis, stating that it is inappropriate to mix QUAL and QUAN methods due to fundamental differences in the paradigms underlying those methods. Using pragmatism as their paradigmatic foundation, MM proponents advocated a compatibility thesis, which stressed the primacy of the research question and focusing on "what works" as the truth regarding the research questions under investigation. Pragmatism rejects the either/or choices associated with the paradigms debate, advocates for the use of MM in research, and acknowledges that the values of the researcher play a large role in interpretation of results.

Debate over MM has also focused on the definition and typology. It has been argued that studies should not be called mixed if they are simple collections of QUAL and QUAN data and their analyses, without serious attempts at integrating the conclusions. A strong appeal of MM is that it provides an opportunity for the investigator to integrate the understanding gleaned from QUAL and QUAN components into what has been labeled meta-inferences.

As a possible strategy for clarification of these issues, in 2003 Charles Teddlie and Abbas Tashakkori proposed a differentiation between mixed method and mixed model designs. Mixed method designs utilize both QUAN and QUAN data and analysis to answer research questions. Mixed model designs utilize QUAL and QUAN approaches in formulating research questions, in their research design, and in making final inferences. MM questions are queries that include both the known (explanatory/confirmatory) and unknown (exploratory) aspects of a phenomenon (e.g., do certain differences exist between schools? What kind of differences? Why do these differences exist?). These questions have both inductive and deductive components, and are answered with information that is typically presented in both narrative and numerical forms.

Mixed methodologists have proposed typologies of designs on the basis of four different dimensions: number of strands (component studies), priority/dominance of QUAL or QUAN approach, their sequence of implementation, and the purpose for mixing. MM studies might be monostrand, in which one type of data (QUAL or QUAN) is collected and analyzed, then transformed to the other format (i.e., QUAL data are quantitized, QUAN data are qualitized) and analyzed again. The inferences gleaned from the two sets of results are combined for a fuller understanding of the phenomenon under study. In comparison, they might be multistrand, in which two sets of data are collected and analyzed and the results integrated.

MM designs have also been differentiated based on priority/dominance of QUAL or QUAN approaches. Several authors have provided detailed typologies based on this as well as the sequence dimension.

Sequence of implementation is by far the most widely used dimension for classification. Strands (or phases) of an MM study might be concurrent or sequential. In concurrent designs, both QUAL and QUAN data are collected and analyzed in a parallel manner to answer different aspects of a research question, and the results are integrated. In sequential MM designs, a new set of QUAL or QUAN data are collected to clarify, expand, or test the findings of a previous strand.

Finally, purpose of mixing has been used for classification of designs that focus on either expansion of the findings of a previous phase, explanation of unclear or controversial findings, or testing of emergent

hypotheses. The purposes for conducting MM research can be personal, practical, or intellectual. Currently, the most commonly cited typology simultaneously focuses on sequence and purpose, and distinguishes between triangulation, exploratory, and explanatory designs. In triangulation design, the investigator collects and analyzes QUAL and QUAN data concurrently. In exploratory design, QUAN data are collected and analyzed in order to test or expand the findings of a QUAL study. Explanatory designs use a QUAL strand to gain an in-depth understanding of the findings of a QUAN study.

Mixed methodologists have discussed the importance of developing validity criteria and audits that incorporate and expand the QUAL and QUAN concepts. For example, they have proposed using the term *inference quality* as a term to incorporate the QUAN term internal validity and the QUAL terms of trustworthiness and credibility. Inference quality has a twofold definition: (1) the degree to which the interpretations and conclusions made on the basis of the results meet the professional standards of rigor, trustworthiness, and acceptability and (2) the degree to which alternative plausible explanations for the obtained results can be ruled out. Inference quality consists of design quality and interpretive rigor.

Another newly proposed MM term is *inference transferability,* which incorporates the QUAN concepts of generalizability and external validity with the QUAL term *transferability.* It is defined as the degree of generalizability or applicability of inferences obtained in a study to other individuals or entities (population transferability), other settings or situations (ecological transferability), other time periods (temporal transferability), or other methods of observation/measurement (operational transferability).

—Abbas Tashakkori and Charles Teddlie

See also pragmatism and progressivism; qualitative research, history, theories, issues; quantitative research methods; validity and reliability; variables

Further Readings and References

Chatterji, M. (2004). Evidence on "what works": An argument for extended-term mixed-method (ETMM) evaluation design. *Educational Researcher, 33*(9), 3–13.

Creswell, J. (2005). *Educational research: Planning, conducting, and evaluating quantitative and qualitative research* (2nd ed.). Upper Saddle River, NJ: Merrill.

Johnson, B., and Christensen, L. (2004). *Educational research: Quantitative and qualitative approaches* (2nd ed.). Boston: Allyn & Bacon.

Johnson, B., & Onwuegbuzie, A. (2004). Mixed methods research: A research paradigm whose time has come. *Educational Researcher, 33*(7), 14–26.

Niglas, K. (2004). *The combined use of qualitative and quantitative methods in educational research.* Tallinn, Estonia: Tallinn Pedagogical University.

Tashakkori, A., & Teddlie, C. (1998). *Mixed methodology: Combining qualitative and quantitative approaches.* Thousand Oaks, CA: Sage.

Tashakkori, A., & Teddlie, C. (2003). The past and future of mixed methods research: From data triangulation to mixed model designs. In A. Tashakkori & C. Teddlie (Eds.), *Handbook of mixed methods in social and behavioral research.* Thousand Oaks, CA: Sage.

Teddlie, C., & Tashakkori, A. (2003). Major issues and controversies in the use of mixed methods in the social and behavioral sciences. In A. Tashakkori & C. Teddlie (Eds.), *Handbook of mixed methods in social and behavioral research.* Thousand Oaks, CA: Sage.

MONTESSORI, MARIA

Maria Montessori's unique methods and practices sparked a classroom revolution, and hundreds of Montessori schools are thriving throughout the world today. Montessori (1870–1952) was born August 31, 1870, to Alessandro Montessori and Renilde Stoppani in Chiaravalle, Italy. In 1875, her family moved to Rome, where at the age of 6 she enrolled in public school. In 1883, at the age of 13, Montessori enrolled in technical college.

Montessori graduated from the technical college in 1886 and went to another technical institute, where she graduated in 1890. Afterward, she decided to pursue a career in medicine. At the time, there had never before been an Italian female doctor. Montessori attended the University of Rome in 1890 as a student of mathematics and natural science, and in 1892 she graduated with honors.

In medical school at the University of Rome, Montessori's male colleagues treated her with contempt. It was so unthinkable that a female student would be enrolled in the field of medicine that Montessori was forced to dissect her cadavers alone at night. Despite difficulties, she won the academic admiration of many. In 1896, she graduated as doctor of medicine, with honors. In 1904, she earned her PhD in anthropology from the University of Rome. In 1896, a month after her graduation, she was offered a position as a surgical assistant at the University of Rome's psychiatric ward. In the psychiatric ward, Montessori worked with children who had been named mentally "deficient," but who were most likely autistic or mentally handicapped. She experimented with these children and after several years found that some of them were able to read and write and pass public standardized tests.

In 1907, she began working with the children of impoverished families in the slums of Rome. With these children she started what would become known as the Casa dei Bambini, or Children's House. Her idea was to implement the methods she used at the psychiatric ward. Montessori was the first educator to incorporate child-sized furniture, toys, and other objects to manipulate in the classroom. She gave the children various tasks to do, such as making lunch, cleaning up, gardening, and caring for pets. Eventually, Montessori found that the children actually preferred work to play. Slowly and successfully, Montessori began to teach the children to read and write by using sensory objects.

Soon she was demonstrating to educators and others her techniques, which became known as the Montessori Method. A very charismatic figure, Montessori continued to travel and lecture, and by 1935, hundreds of Montessori schools opened throughout Europe and the United States. In 1929, she created the Association Montessori International. During World War II, she was forced to leave Italy, to live and work in India. In India, she was twice nominated for the Nobel Peace Prize. Montessori died in 1952 at the age of 81, but her teachings live on throughout the world today. Teachers incorporate the Montessori Method into their classrooms by encouraging children to work at their own pace and by using sensory materials.

—*Jane Dettmer and Margaret Grogan*

See also charisma, of leaders; child development theories; classroom management; consideration, caring; constructivism; creativity, theories of; curriculum, theories of; discipline in schools; early childhood education; elementary education; expectations, teacher and student cultures; individual differences, in children; innovation, in education; international education; learning, theories of; learning environments; special education

Further Readings and References

Kramer, R. (1988). *Maria Montessori: A biography.* Reading, MA: Addison-Wesley.

Montessori, M. (1965). *Dr. Montessori's own handbook.* New York: Schocken Books. (Original work published 1914)

Montessori, M. (1965). *Spontaneous activity in education.* New York: Schocken Books. (Original work published 1917)

Standing, E. (1962). *Maria Montessori: Her life and work.* New York: Mentor-Omega.

🏛 MORAL EDUCATION

There has been a growing interest in moral education in the last decade, leading to lengthy discussions on the approaches to teaching moral education in schools. Moral education has experienced a renaissance of sorts by calling attention to teaching and learning values and standards that everyone should have about what it takes to teach our children to be good citizens. While there is a vast amount of research available on moral education, there is a consensus that a specific curriculum involving moral education does not fit every situation. Instead, the majority of research suggests that moral education be integrated into the school community and reinforced in the home environment.

Moral education is a broad term used to describe many aspects of teaching and learning for personal development. It is what the schools do to help students become ethically mature adults, capable of moral thought and action. The Association for Supervision and Curriculum Development (ASCD) Panel of Moral Education's definition of moral education states that moral education is whatever schools do to influence how students think, feel, and act regarding issues of right or wrong. This definition leaves room for many different approaches and pedagogies related to moral education. Overall, moral education addresses the ethical dimensions of the individual and society and examines how standards of right and wrong are developed.

The inclusion of moral education in schools is often a point of contention for schools. Questions arise about "whose values" are to be taught. Others cite a national diversity in beliefs and values that make such education a family, rather than an institutional, imperative. Traditionally, three basic approaches were taken in moral education. First, there is the indoctrinative approach, which suggests a justified content (i.e., code of behavior) and proposes to teach that content by a variety of methods. The second approach is the romanticist approach in which the individual is assumed to have an innate tendency to develop into the role of a moral agent. The role of education is to provide the nurturing context in which this nature "flowering" can occur. The third approach is the cognitive-structural approach that focuses on the construction of moral reasoning capacities, which are understood to be a product of the interaction of one's genetic, developmental, and biological endowments with one's experience with the physical and social worlds. Proposed curricula do not endorse specific content; rather, they provide opportunity to apply one's reasoning to a variety of content. Kohlberg's Just Community Schools are examples of this approach. All three approaches have met criticism. However, the critical issue in evaluating the relativism of a moral education approach is not whether or not it relies on a specific content; rather, it hinges on how that content is justified.

There is extensive research on the core values/virtues that embody a moral person, regardless of religion or culture, that can be taught in schools. Suggested desirable traits are honesty, civility, courage, perseverance, loyalty, self-restraint, compassion, tolerance, fairness, respect for the worth and dignity of the individual, and responsibility for the common good.

While research has suggested a number of approaches to moral education, educators can help children differentiate between the norms and conventions of their culture and the universal concerns for justice (fairness) and human welfare. Larry Nucci identified five educational practices that enable teachers to engage in moral education that is neither indoctrinative nor relativistic: (1) moral education should focus on issues of justice, fairness, and human welfare, (2) effective moral education programs are integrated within the curriculum, rather than treated separately as a special program or unit, (3) moral discussion promotes moral development when students use "transactive" discussion patterns, are at somewhat different moral levels, and are free to disagree about the best solution to a moral dilemma, (4) cooperative goal structures promote moral and academic growth, and (5) firm, fair, and flexible classroom management practices and rules contribute to students' moral growth. Teachers should respond to the harmful or unjust consequences of moral transgressions rather than to broken rules or unfulfilled social expectations.

—*Carolyn Stevenson*

See also affective domain; attitudes toward work; character education; cognition, theories of; dogmatism and scales of Rokeach; esteem needs; ethics; learning environments; morality, moral leadership; values education

Further Readings and References

Kohlberg, L., & Mayer, R. (1972). Development as the aim of education. *Harvard Educational Review, 42,* 449–496.

Lakoff, G. (2002). *Moral politics.* Chicago: University of Chicago Press.

Nucci, L. (1982). Conceptual development in the moral and conventional domains: Implications for values education. *Review of Educational Research, 49,* 93–122.

Power, F. C., Higgins, A., & Kohlberg, L. (1989). *Lawrence Kohlberg's approach to moral education.* New York: Columbia University Press.

Simon, K. (2001). *Moral questions in the classroom.* New Haven, CT: Yale University Press.

Walker, V., & Snarey, J. (2004). *Race-ing moral formation: African American perspectives on care and justice.* New York: Teachers College Press.

MORALE

The concept of *morale* refers to broad feelings of well-being, satisfaction, and value for being part of a workplace. Morale is manifested in many ways, including enthusiasm, commitment or loyalty to an organization, willingness to work, and dedication to common goals.

Industrial-organizational psychologists consider morale and job satisfaction in studies of worker-management relations. Morale is viewed as an attitudinal response to one's work or work conditions. "High" morale is manifested when individuals feel satisfaction in work and the workplace and show determination to do their best under any circumstance. "Low" morale implies that individuals see themselves as those who are powerless or socially unimportant.

Formal organizational structures are often seen as having a negative influence on morale. However, formal structures can enhance morale if that structure helps employees get their work done. Formal structure has a negative impact on morale if it gets in employees' way, inundates them with red tape, and increases management control over their work. Formal structures that enable people to do their best can increase morale, and morale can be high even in bureaucratic organizations.

The morale of teachers and staff is often used to characterize the quality of a school or district as a workplace. Research on developing strong school communities suggests that increased professional community increases a sense of satisfaction with the personal dignity of work and a sense of belonging to and being part of the school organization—both of which contribute to teachers' sense of well-being or morale. Increased feelings of satisfaction and higher morale may help to ameliorate teachers' feelings of discouragement when they perceive that peers, supervisors, or the public do not respect or value their work.

—*Judith A. Ponticell*

See also attitudes toward work; bureaucracy; capacity building, of organizations; consideration, caring; decision making; empowerment; esprit (school climate); esteem needs; ethos, of organizations; fringe benefits; group dynamics; human resource development; job security; just cause; management theories; motivation, theories of; persuasion; productivity; professional development; reduction in force; satisfaction, in organizations and roles; satisficing theory; self-actualization; working conditions, in schools

Further Readings and References

Adler, P. S., & Borys, B. (1996). Two types of bureaucracy: Enabling and coercive. *Administrative Science Quarterly, 41,* 61–89.

Johnsrud, L. K. (1996). *Maintaining morale: A guide to assessing the morale of midlevel administrators and faculty.* Washington, DC: College and University Personnel Association.

Louis, K. S., Marks, H., & Kruse, S. D. (1996). Teachers' community in restructuring schools. *American Educational Research Journal, 33*(4), 757–798.

MORALITY, MORAL LEADERSHIP

Morality, ethics, and *values* are all terms used to indicate what is right or good. Some scholars distinguish moral from ethical by using moral to describe the rightness or wrongness of particular conduct or character, and ethical to refer to a more universal understanding of standards and principles. It is common to discuss personal morality in contrast to professional ethics, for instance. The term *values* is sometimes used interchangeably with principles, but some researchers and scholars define values as nonmoral preferences, opinions, beliefs, and attitudes that people hold in a relative sense. For educators, the notion of moral agency is a powerful one. Hugh Sockett defines moral agency in terms of an individual's capacity to consider the interests of others while being grounded in a clear set of virtues or principles that guide action. Elizabeth Campbell discusses moral agency both in the context of how educators treat students and in reference to what educators teach students.

These concepts have been applied variously to leadership. Two classical leadership theories stand out as ones incorporating a moral or ethical standpoint. They are James MacGregor Burns's theory of transactional leadership and transformational leadership and Christopher Hodgkinson's values typology. Burns differentiated between transactional leadership and transformational leadership based on which values were at work in each instance. In transactional leadership, modal values such as honesty, responsibility, fairness, and the honoring of commitments form the basis of the relationship between leader and follower. Such interactions can contribute to human purpose in the realization of individual goals within an organization. Transactional leadership involves an exchange of goods or services between leader and follower that results in the mutual satisfaction of independent objectives. On a higher level, transformational leadership deals with such end values as liberty, justice, equality, and equity. Transformational leaders are concerned with collective purpose and the common good. Both kinds of leadership include a moral dimension with attention paid to the role of the leader in helping to encourage followers through the stages of moral development. Burns argues that as leaders and followers both progress through the individual stages of needs, values, and morality, a broad base is formed for collective responsibility and common goals. Seeking success in this common enterprise encourages in leaders and followers the development of more principled judgment and better citizenry.

Hodgkinson posited that there are four motivational bases informing individual values, beliefs, attitudes, and actions. These are personal preference, consensus, consequences, and principles. He divides these into three categories of subrational, rational, and transrational. Personal preferences, including the concept of what is good, are grounded in self-interest and thus are subrational; consensus guided by expert opinion or peer pressure is rational, as are consequences, which include intentional action to bring about a desired outcome; and principles, at the top of Hodgkinson's hierarchy, informed by ethical codes or religious beliefs, are transrational, not scientifically verifiable. Since leaders operate primarily in the context of organizations, Hodgkinson argues that they are unlikely to be aware of their own consciousness, individuality, or will. All is subsumed by the interests of

the organization. Nevertheless, as a human actor, the leader has the capacity to make conscious and free choices to advance the human potential within organizational limitations. To achieve this, leaders must engage in reflection, introspection, and self-observation to increase their moral awareness.

Other scholars ground their notions of moral leadership in questions of purpose. For instance, as a public good, public education provides a clear context for moral leadership. Guided by the question of leadership for what, principals and superintendents of public school districts must keep the goal of educating all students in the forefront of their administrative activities. Principles of equity and equality compel the drive to eliminate the gaps in learning and achievement across race, ethnicity, class, gender, ability, and other markers of exclusion. Jerry Starratt introduced the multiethical lens of care, critique, and justice to guide educational leaders in examining the policies and practices in their own contexts that privilege some students at the expense of others. Moral leadership includes the ability to be mindful of the unequal distribution of wealth and happiness that is associated with students' educational attainment. A firm grasp of purpose assists leaders in making choices and decisions that help move them beyond focusing only on the instrumental ends of education to include the ideals of educating a democratic citizenry. Decisions of what to include in a curriculum as well as how to teach content ultimately determine students' capacity to be informed and critical thinkers prepared to accept the responsibilities of citizenship in a democracy.

An emphasis on the leader's behaviors and understanding is also found in the literature. Feminist scholars write of the importance of appreciating the local and the particular context within which decision making takes place. Informed by an ethic of care, leaders are encouraged to pay attention to the individual child or teacher to understand his or her specific needs, wants, and attitudes. This approach is person centered rather than rule oriented. It is founded on the establishment and maintenance of healthy relationships between leaders and those in their care. The knowledge to act on others' behalf in their best interest comes from deep knowledge of the other. Nel Noddings makes the important point that one arrives at knowledge and understanding of the other by attending to the other as he or she expresses himself or herself, not as a representative of a generalized category of student, teacher, parent, and so on. Feminist morality also includes a valuing of empathy as a reliable source of moral action. As a corollary to a reliance on reason, a leader's capacity to enter into another's situation empathetically improves the likelihood of morally appropriate decision making. Finally, feminist morality highlights the desirability of communication between leaders and those in their care as a means to improve and enrich the capacity for moral reasoning. In contrast to the more traditional notion of leaders arriving at appropriate moral action through contemplation and individual introspection, feminist approaches encourage dialogue with others in a common search for satisfactory ways of addressing competing claims.

—*Margaret Grogan*

See also Burns, James MacGregor; civics, civic education; consideration, caring; democracy, democratic education and administration; discrimination; equality, in schools; equity and adequacy of funding schools; ethics; feminism and theories of leadership; homophobia; leadership, theories of; moral education; sexism (glass ceiling); transformational leadership; values, of organizations and leadership

Further Readings and References

Burns, J. M. (1978). *Leadership*. New York: Harper & Row.
Campbell, E. (2003). *The ethical teacher*. Philadelphia: Open University Press.
Henz, R., Norte, E., Sather, S., Walker, E., & Katz, A. (2002). *Leading for diversity*. Thousand Oaks, CA: Corwin Press.
Hodgkinson, C. (1999). The will to power. In P. Begley (Ed.), *Values and educational leadership* (pp. 139–150). Albany: State University of New York Press.
Noddings, N. (2002). *Educating moral people*. New York: Teachers College Press.
Sockett, H. (1993). *The moral base for teacher professionalism*. New York: Teachers College Press.
Starratt, R. J. (1994). *Building an ethical school*. London: Falmer Press.

MOTIVATION, THEORIES OF

A general assumption of motivational theory is that individuals avoid tasks or activities that exceed their abilities and competencies. The literature reports conflicts and shortfalls associated with different perspectives theories that attempt to describe the assumption. Debates exist about the extent to which mastery goals versus performance goals motivate individuals and the use of rewards to reinforce behaviors. The differences have led to the promotion of self-choice, self-determination, and instructional applications aimed to increase motivation.

One perspective of motivation aligned with early behaviorist traditions suggested that motivation could not exist. They positioned behaviors as sole results of past experiences and conflicted with a present-future paradigm of motivation. A second perspective includes the theory of planned behavior that links motivation with intentions. A third perspective relates to the selective goal hypothesis, which proposed that individuals enhance their motivation when they choose goals relevant to their present situations. A fourth perspective, organismic worldview, asserts that the onset of motivation occurs when individuals' sensory organs respond to stimuli that require reactions. A fifth perspective, sociocultural engagement, suggests that individuals must alter their motivation in accord with social practices.

Research reported in the literature cannot be used to rule in or rule out certain perspectives of motivation. Gaps exist and result from faults associated with research designs and subject selections. Critics of motivational research doubted uses of particular perspectives theories that may have overlooked essential variables. They questioned whether researchers imposed goals that required subjects' motivation or observed subjects' self-initiated goals and related motivation. Furthermore, they questioned researchers' control for variance among subjects and accounted for experiences outside the research setting that may have influenced subjects' motivation (e.g., teacher-student interactions). The accumulated lack of universal acceptance of research designs fueled arguments about published motivational studies in the 1990s for which the educational research community debated the acceptance of meta-analyses results. At present, greater research attention focuses on subjects' broader contexts that may influence motivational behaviors. Specifically, it addresses individuals' orientations toward performance goals, mastery goals, or a combination of both goal types.

Individuals in pursuit of performance goals attempt to outperform their peers (e.g., "My goal is to sell more houses than any other real estate agent in the firm"). An individual's motivation is dependent on feedback from others. Common characteristics include (a) dependence on public recognition, (b) negative effects post failure, (c) overuse of short-term strategies (e.g., memorization), and (d) avoidance of challenging tasks. In contrast, individuals in pursuit of mastery goals attempt to acquire knowledge and skills for their personal betterment (e.g., "My goal in working at this firm is to learn as much as possible about successful real estate sales"). An individual's motivation is devoid of dependence on others and is self-regulated. Extensive positive characteristics include (a) increased task engagement, (b) adaptive patterns of achievement, (c) global perceptions of the self, (d) pursuit of and persistence with challenging tasks, (e) universal strategies, (f) pride and satisfaction, and (g) self-monitoring. Individuals' simultaneous pursuit of both performance and mastery goals suggest that motivation for certain tasks requires both goals, referred to as a multiple goal perspective.

Options to make personal choices must be present for individuals to formulate performance, mastery, or combined goals relative to their required (e.g., job performance) or desired (e.g., skills acquisition) performances. Research links autonomy with increased intrinsic motivation and the ability to infuse cultural practices with goal decisions. The combination of choice options with volition (the degree to which choices can be made versus imposed) and internal locus of control (the degree to which choices can be self-regulated) equate with the theory of self-determination.

Teachers' expectations and beliefs are variables that influence students' choices of goals. Furthermore, teachers may employ instructional and interaction strategies that increase a particular type of goal. Teachers' recognitions of students' performances give implicit and explicit notions of valued performances and are most evident in evaluations. For example, teachers' use of frequent grades, public evaluations, and social comparisons result in students' choices of performance goals. Teachers' uses of rewards influence students' intrinsic and extrinsic motivations and thus elicit either performance or mastery goals. The literature details arguments for and against rewards.

Proponents of rewards acknowledge that educators need to follow up with explanations for reward distributions, especially verbal rewards that include positive feedback. They posit that doing so increases students' performances. Antagonists argue that rewards undermine internal motivation, especially for individuals who do not need them in order to engage in tasks. They assert that rewards (a) control, not empower motivation, (b) require submission to imposed standards, and (c) limit goals' capabilities.

Implications for teachers' use of instructional strategies and rewards to improve students' motivation appear in the literature. Overall, academic tasks impact motivation the most and should differ among students and empower personal choices relative to mastery goals. Teachers should help students establish attainable mastery goals and point out how effort toward the goals results in fruition. Throughout the tasks, teachers should avoid and replace physical rewards with ongoing feedback and opportunities to improve performances. Evaluations should occur in private to avoid students' total focus on performance goals. Teachers should also help students establish positive performance goals and structure social interactions (e.g., cooperative learning) that allow students to give and receive constructive feedback throughout the groups' performances.

—*John Palladino*

See also attitudes toward work; Csikszentmihalyi, Mihaly; curriculum, theories of; esteem needs; flow theory; learning environments; locus of control; Maslow, Abraham; self-actualization; teacher recruitment and retention

Further Readings and References

Hickey, D. (2003). Engaged participation versus marginal nonparticipation: A stridently sociocultural approach to achievement motivation. *Elementary School Journal, 103*(4), 401–429

Reeve, J., Nix, G., & Hamm, D. (2003). Testing models of the experience of self-determination in intrinsic motivation and the conundrum of choice. *Journal of Educational Psychology, 95*(2), 375–392.

Thorkildsen, T. (2003). *Motivation and the struggle to learn: Responding to fractured experiences.* Boston: Allyn & Bacon.

Valle, A., Cabanach, R., Núñez, J., González-Pienda, J., Rodríguez, S., & Piñeiro, I. (2003). Cognitive, motivational, and volitional dimensions of learning: An empirical test of a hypothetical model. *Research in Higher Education, 44*(5), 557–580.

Wizel, B., & Mercer, C. (2003). Using rewards to teach students with disabilities: Implications for motivation. *Remedial and Special Education, 24*(2), 88–96.

MULTICULTURALISM

Multiculturalism is a philosophical stance that advocates for equal opportunity for individuals from diverse cultural backgrounds. As such, multiculturalism affirms the rights of individuals to the pursuit of personal meaning, equality, social justice, and democratic participation, regardless of cultural background or composite cultural makeup. Based upon the great foundational documents of U.S. democratic government, the Declaration of Independence, the Constitution of the United States, and the Bill of Rights, multiculturalism strives to extend the rights portrayed in these documents to all cultural groups in the United States. Multiculturalism is sometimes viewed as an approach to studying culture in an effort to analyze the effects of various microcultural characteristics upon access to the normalized rights of middle-class individuals in the United States.

As such, multiculturalism has implications for leadership, policy, curriculum, and instruction in the formal educational settings of prekindergarten, elementary, secondary schools, and of colleges and universities. While diversity-related scholarship has traditionally focused upon the cultural characteristics of class, race, and ethnicity, present-day scholarship includes the additional microcultures of gender, sexual orientation, age, ability and exceptionality, religion, language, and geography, among others. The preponderance of current research, however, involves the microcultures of race, ethnicity, gender, language, and class, or some combination of these factors in support of multiculturalism as a foundational element in multicultural education as a field of study.

MULTICULTURALISM AND MULTICULTURAL EDUCATION AS A FIELD OF STUDY

Scholarly writing on the subject of multiculturalism falls primarily within the purview of multicultural education as a field of study. Scholarship in the field of multicultural education, while integrating tenets of each, differs from global education and international education, both of which support their own fields of study. Most scholarly findings outlined from here forward refer to multicultural education as a field of study.

James A. Banks offers a definition of multicultural education that promotes a focus on increased equity in education for all students. As a field of study, multicultural education focuses upon students who are marginalized because of their specific microcultural makeup and upon solutions to issues of inequality in educational settings. Various aspects of this definition follow.

FUNDAMENTAL ASSUMPTIONS OF MULTICULTURAL EDUCATION

Current scholarship identifies fundamental assumptions of multicultural education: (a) cultural differences have strength and value, (b) expressions of human rights are valued, (c) social justice and equality are central to curriculum design and instruction, (d) a function of schooling is to promote the attitudes and values associated with the continuance of a democratic society, (e) a function of educational institutions is to promote the redistribution of power among diverse groups through its instruction and policies, (f) educators in their work with families and communities promote supportive environments for multiculturalism, and (g) there is a focus upon reducing prejudice and stereotypes and supporting individuals and groups in developing positive images of themselves.

Christine Sleeter and Carl Grant argue for five approaches to multicultural education with implications primarily for race, class, and gender: (1) teaching the exceptional and culturally different, (2) promoting human relations, (3) incorporating single-group studies, (4) instituting multicultural education in all aspects of schoolwork, and (5) promoting education that is multicultural and social reconstructionist. Sleeter and Grant promote education that is multicultural and social reconstructionist as having the most potential for sustained positive change because of its use of the following practices: replicating democracy, analyzing the circumstances of one's own life, developing social action skills, and forming coalitions for combating oppression.

MEASURE OF INSTITUTIONAL COMMITMENT TO MULTICULTURAL EDUCATION

Scholarship supports the measurement of an institution's commitment to multicultural education by its adherence to the following characteristics: (a) supporting a mission and policy statement affirming diversity, (b) accurately replicating the cultural pluralism of the country in its administration, faculty, and staff, (c) supporting the disappearance of differences in achievement levels among students from various class, gender, and dominant and oppressed microcultures, (d) incorporating a variety of contributions and perspectives from many cultural groups into the school curriculum and teaching methodologies, (e) celebrating cultural differences rather than relegating them to categories of deficiency, (f) encouraging students to incorporate their own cultures and voices in a critique of school curriculum, culture, and policy, (g) supporting faculty as members of a community of practice and believing that knowledge is socially constructed, (h) valuing parent participation as a context for and a valid link to student personal and cultural knowledge, and (i) committing to selection of administration, faculty, and staff who deal with the hard issues of multicultural education and intergroup relations with professionalism and fairness.

THE HISTORY OF MULTICULTURAL EDUCATION

The roots of multicultural education lie in the civil rights movement of the 1960s and 1970s and in two antecedent movements, the ethnic studies movement of the late nineteenth century and after and the intergroup education movement of the 1930s, 1940s, and 1950s.

The Ethnic Studies Movement

The early African American ethnic studies movement dates back to the nineteenth century with the writing and publication of such works as George Washington Williams's 1882 *History of the Negro Race in America* and W. E. B. Du Bois's 1896 *The Suppression of the African Slave Trade to the United States of America, 1638–1870.* These works and others were integrated with a high degree of success into the curriculum of segregated schools and institutions of higher education for African Americans. Support for this movement came from Carter G. Woodson, who founded the Association for the Study of Negro Life and History, now known as the Association for the Study of Afro-American Life and History, and who also founded the Associated Publishers, responsible for publishing many early works by African American scholars. The influence of the ethnic studies movement continued during the civil rights era, when African Americans fought with success to integrate ethnic content into the curriculum of all educational institutions at all grade levels.

The Intergroup Education Movement

The intercultural or intergroup education movement, hereafter referred to as the intergroup education movement, is another important antecedent to the multicultural education movement. Almost defunct by the time of the civil rights movement, the intergroup education movement left a lasting legacy of promising policy and procedural initiatives for public schools.

The intergroup education movement's roots lie in conflicts that occurred between ethnic and White groups during and immediately after World War II as these groups moved from rural settings to industrial communities of the North and West for employment. This movement recognized the multifaceted nature of ethnic group conflicts and supported social change both through community and school efforts. A number of significant human rights groups particularly concerned about immigrants and others on the margins of society offered support.

Major Initiatives of the Intergroup Education Movement

Having roots in intellectual communities and not with disenfranchised groups, the intergroup education movement supported three initiates of historical importance: the Service Bureau for Education in Human Relations, the Springfield Plan, and the University of Chicago's Center for Intergroup Education. The Service Bureau for Education in Human Relations, with roots in the intellectual community of Teachers College, Columbia University, established intercultural education programs for public schools, including curriculum materials for the study of ethnic groups, reading lists on intercultural education, and professional development opportunities for teachers.

The Springfield Plan, of Springfield, Massachusetts, in 1939, was created to ease intergroup tensions, and supported the belief that all citizens needed fully to participate in the democratic society or risk limiting everyone's freedom. Founded by Professor Clyde R. Miller of Teachers College, Columbia, and supported by Edward L. Thorndike and John Granrud, superintendent of schools, the plan included several components: a single-salary schedule for teachers, adult education promoting strong school ties to community, and a teacher selections board composed of administrators and members of the area's three major religious groups. Eventually failing, two legacies remained: a joint community and school staff selection policy and the single-salary schedule.

The University of Chicago's Center for Intergroup Education, founded by Hilda Taba in 1948 and operating until 1951, aided teachers in determining the human relations needs of their students and touched a wide network of teachers and school systems through a series of leadership training workshops.

Linking schools to communities with the purpose of promoting intergroup understanding, tolerance, and realizing democratic ideals is a legacy of the intergroup education movement.

The Civil Rights Movement

The civil rights movement, a direct precursor to the multicultural education movement, was initiated by African Americans and heavily supported by individuals from other ethnic and racial groups. The civil rights movement made pointed demands upon schools, colleges, and universities. One of the first responses to the movement was the inclusion of Black studies as an add-on to the established curriculum. The Black studies movement was followed by other ethnic studies courses and programs.

Since neither Black studies nor ethnic studies influenced the organizational, policy, and procedural changes advocated by members of the civil rights movement, the multiethnic education movement was initiated. This movement called for systemic and structural reform of all aspects of educational institutions so that equal educational opportunities could exist for all students. Reforms called for paradigm change in policy, teaching strategies, and styles, the content of the curriculum and the course of study, the method of assessment, the languages and dialects sanctioned, and required teaching materials.

This movement gave impetus to other marginalized groups, primarily persons with disabilities and women. Capturing the spirit of the 1954 *Brown v. Board of Education* and the civil rights movement, people with disabilities won a significant victory with the passage of the 1972 PL 94-142, Education for All Handicapped Children Act, giving a free public education to all students with disabilities, providing for objective evaluation, an individualized education program, and education in the least restrictive environment.

Women, prompted by the spirit and wording of the civil rights movement, renewed their quest for equal rights. A victory for this group was the Title IX educational amendment prohibiting sexual discrimination in all educational programs receiving federal support. Women's programs now exist as a norm on campuses of institutions of higher education, and feminist scholarship continues to challenge past scholarship in the areas of literature, history, philosophy, social and

behavioral science, natural and physical sciences, teacher education, and the general studies canon.

As a result, the civil rights movement provided impetus for new paradigms and epistemological assumptions in nearly every area of scholarship. Many disciplines continue to reconceptualize their traditionally based frameworks, concepts, and assumptions.

SCHOLARSHIP AND MULTICULTURAL EDUCATION AS A FIELD OF STUDIES

James Banks organizes research in the conceptualization of multicultural education as a field of study into five dimensions: (1) content integration, (2) knowledge construction process, (3) prejudice reduction, (4) equity pedagogy, and (5) an empowering school culture and social structure.

Content Integration

The first dimension, content integration, focuses upon the inclusion of content from a variety of cultures into the major concepts and theories of a discipline. This dimension also deals with the identification of components that should be a part of the standard curriculum of a discipline. Content integration research also includes scholarship about appropriate instructional methodology and arguments outlining where particular informational aspects of a discipline should be taught. Research for this dimension has its foundations in two historic movements: the ethnic studies movement of the early twentieth century that continued on into the civil rights movement and the intergroup education movement, each outlined above.

Knowledge Construction Process

The knowledge construction process is a second dimension of multicultural education and focuses upon the degree to which teachers, in schools, colleges, and universities, assist students in analyzing how the underlying cultural assumptions, frameworks, and perspectives of a particular discipline contain biases that dictate how knowledge is constructed. This dimension challenges the tenets of empirical research and promotes analyzing the predominant assumptions of all disciplines through lenses of accepted social, cultural, and power positions. Promoting the stance that all writers are influenced by cultural assumptions that must be identified, this dimension teaches that all students should identify the biases of researchers and scholars of a field and make their own meaning out of the presentation of knowledge. Telling stories about personal experience is one means of making meaning.

Scholars in this area generally advocate for two approaches to curriculum reform, transformational and social action. Transforming curriculum encourages students to view curriculum content from the point of view of various ethnic and cultural groups. Social action encourages student understanding of how to engage in action for just solutions.

Prejudice Reduction

The prejudice reduction dimension focuses on students' racial attitudes and how racial characteristics can be modified through teaching methods and materials so students are prepared for interactions that are equal status in quality. The true goal of prejudice reduction scholarship in multicultural education is to establish how students can best develop values that support democratic attitudes and behaviors. Showing that young children are aware of racial differences by the age of 3 and that they have internalized attitudes about race from the greater society, research indicates also that African American children both express high self-esteem and White bias at the same time. Cooperative learning is a teaching method noted for its ability to promote positive racial attitudes, cross-racial friendships, and increased academic achievement among students of color.

Equity Pedagogy

The dimension of equity pedagogy exists when teachers modify their instruction in ways that facilitate the academic achievement of students from diverse racial, cultural, and social class groups. This includes using a variety of teaching styles that are consistent with the wide range of learning styles of various cultural and ethnic groups. Researchers caution against offering only one explanation for multifaceted issues such as poverty, presenting differences as deficits.

Empowering School Culture and Social Structure

The dimension of empowering school culture and social structure involves an analysis of grouping and labeling practices, sports participation, inconsistency in achievement by group, and the interaction of staff and students across ethnic and racial lines. In addition, a school's implementation of basic skills programs coupled with strong expectations for high achievement in rigorous course work for all students is a factor. There are arguments for the supportive work of assertive principals who promote high academic achievement, positive discipline, and evaluation of success of basic skills and advanced academic programs. In addition, there is advocacy for staff acceptance of accountability and promotion of high parent involvement.

CURRENT INFLUENCES, ISSUES, AND TRENDS

Multiculturalism and multicultural education as conceptualized during the mid-twentieth-century civil rights movement face significant challenges during the twenty-first century as various societal issues and increased research on cultural groups provide potentially unexpected challenges to the movement's initial agendas. The U.S. social structures promise to become more complex with increased immigration, changing demographics, and globalization. Increased immigration means increased racial, cultural, ethnic, and language challenges for the society and schools. Gloria Ladson-Billings points out that considerations of individual versus group rights could become more complex when viewed from allegiances formed for reasons reaching beyond the purview of one nation and into multinational alliances based, for example, on shared languages.

Increasingly, scholarly studies in the areas of cultural studies and culturally centered teaching methodologies can prove to provide significant information for multiculturalism and multicultural education. Complex cultural identifications, while providing valid content for research, could also serve to obscure the focus of all cultural groups on the larger issues of oppression and disenfranchisement.

Of specific concern is the issue of assessment and the current national emphasis on standards. Whether research focused upon assessment initiatives will continue to conclude that assessment systems are based on racist frameworks or, instead, conclude that true accountability for learning is the focus remains to be seen. Measures of achievement and accountability remain important in a world that is increasingly global in nature and schools that have the potential of becoming more and more national in their curricular emphases.

Previous research and areas of borrowed research from other disciplines promise to provide informative heuristics and methodologies for further research. Such methodologies as autobiography, historical ethnographies, narrative inquiry, counter-stories, reframing, democratizing, naming, and language usage, among others, should prove to ferret out greater understandings.

Originally used in legal studies analysis to critique racist social structures, critical race theory (CRT) holds promise as a heuristic that can uncover a variety of types of oppression. Sleeter and Dolores Delgado Bernal promote CRT's use (a) as a promising reflexive tool, (b) as an analytical heuristic of class, corporate power, and globalization, (c) as an analytical tool for looking at empowering pedagogical practices, and (d) as a tool for a deeper critique of language and literacy.

While changing social landscapes and additive promises of research provide increased understanding of multiculturalism and multicultural education, scholars perceive that the key to continuing progress in fighting oppression will be in how effective the movement retains its focus on the ideals of liberation and social justice.

—*Roma B. Angel*

See also Afrocentric theory; Asian Pacific Americans; Bethune, Mary McLeod; Black education; critical race theory; desegregation, of schools; discrimination; diversity; DuBois, W. E. B.; equality, in schools; equity and adequacy of funding schools; ethnicity; ethnocentrism; gender studies, in educational leadership; immigration, history and impact in education; Latinos; Mendez, Felicitas; minorities, in schools; Sizemore, Barbara A.; staffing, concepts of; Woodson, Carter G.

Further Readings and References

Banks, J. A., & Banks, C. A. M. (Eds.). (2004). *Multicultural education: Issues and perspectives* (5th ed.). New York: Wiley.

Gay, G. (2004). Curriculum theory and multicultural education. In J. A. Banks & C. A. M. Banks (Eds.), *Handbook of research on multicultural education* (2nd ed., pp. 30–49). San Francisco: Jossey-Bass.

Gibson, M., Gandara, P., & Koyama, J. (Eds.). (2004). *School connections: U.S. Mexican youth, peers, and school achievement.* New York: Teachers College Press.

Ginwright, S. (2004). *Black in school: Afrocentric reform, urban youth, and the promise of hip-hop culture.* New York: Teachers College Press.

Grant, C. A., & Sleeter, C. E. (1986). Race, class, and gender in education research: An argument for integrative analysis. *Review of Educational Research, 56,* 195–211.

King, J. (2005). *Black education.* Mahwah, NJ: Erlbaum.

Kornhaber, M. L. (2004). Assessment, standards, and equity. In J. A. Banks & C. A. M. Banks (Eds.), *Handbook of research on multicultural education* (2nd ed., pp. 91–109). San Francisco: Jossey-Bass.

Ladson-Billings, G. (2004). New directions in multicultural education: Complexities, boundaries, and critical race theory. In J. A. Banks & C. A. M. Banks (Eds.), *Handbook of research on multicultural education* (2nd ed., pp. 50–65). San Francisco: Jossey-Bass.

Pedraza, P., & Rivera, M. (2005). *Latino education.* Mahwah, NJ: Erlbaum.

Peters-Davis, N., & Shultz, J. (2005). *Challenges of multicultural education.* Boulder, CO: Paradigm.

Phillion, J., Fang He, M., & Connelly, F. (2005). *Narrative and experience in multicultural education.* Thousand Oaks, CA: Sage.

Shields, C., & Sayani, A. (2005). Leading in the midst of diversity: The challenge of our times. In F. English (Ed.), *The SAGE handbook of educational leadership* (pp. 380–402). Thousand Oaks, CA: Sage.

Sleeter, C. D., & Grant, C. A. (2003). *Making choices for multicultural education: Five approaches to race, class, and gender* (4th ed.). New York: Wiley.

Sleeter, C. E., & Bernal, D. D. (2004). Critical pedagogy, critical race theory, and antiracist education: Implications for multicultural education. In J. A. Banks & C. A. M. Banks (Eds.), *Handbook of research on multicultural education* (2nd ed., pp. 240–258). San Francisco: Jossey-Bass.

Taba, H. (1962). *Curriculum development: Theory and practice.* New York: Harcourt, Brace & World.

🏛 MUSEUM EDUCATION

Museum education falls within the context of informal learning that is characterized by its position outside the walls of formal learning typical of schools. Originally, the primary role of a museum was to serve as a repository for the display, housing, and preservation of valued objects and artifacts. Since the 1970s, museums have redefined their role to incorporate visitor learning into their mission and support the view that learning is a lifelong process. Among the proliferation of museums are those with a focus on art, historical representations, natural history, science and technology, aeronautics, and botany, and some of these have children as the intended audience. Educational programs led by tour guides and the presence of interactive and interpretive displays have become commonplace.

However, rather than having a curriculum with subject mastery as the goal, museums offer opportunities that provide for variability and choices resulting in unique learning experiences for visitors.

A recent innovation is the virtual museum that allows the visitor to access electronic representations of physical museum exhibits. Virtual museums provide opportunities for individuals who may not be able to travel to the site where the physical museum is located. The audience for a virtual museum is geographically dispersed and more diverse than the audience at the typical physical museum. School-based Internet connections allow teachers and students to access virtual museums originating from sites located around the world. Examples of virtual museums include those sponsored by the National Gallery of Art, the Art Institute of Chicago, Colonial Williamsburg, the Buffalo Bill Historical Center, and the Lawrence Hall of Science at Berkeley. A virtual exhibit is comprised of a collection of digital images organized by a designer. Considerable variability in content, structure, navigation, design, and complexity is represented, ranging from a simple collection of images to complex interactive multimedia presentations.

Museums are forming partnerships with formal educational institutions in part to broaden their audiences and to compete for funding. These collaborations have resulted in the offering of pedagogical expertise from universities and schools to help develop learning modules, design interactive displays, and conduct research related to learning outcomes. The research on museum education is sparse and only has emerged in recent years. An important consideration for researchers interested in museum education is that each museum represents a unique social culture. Given this precept, naturalistic inquiry approaches are useful in establishing commonalities and variations in the learning experiences that occur among museums.

A framework for guiding research on learning in museums includes three integrating themes: how the design of the learning environment mediates learning, how social interactions are shaped by the exhibits, and how museum experiences may impact the identity of visitors. Research related to the first two themes has provided some insights to learning in museums. Orientation devices that focus visitors' attention using video, oral messages, or signals tend to support learning. Interactive displays that engage the visitor were found to be most effective when designed with structures that support relevant input. The social milieu of the museum, which includes beliefs of the tour guides, conversations that occur, and the nature of the museum space, was found to impact learning as well. Museums offer considerable opportunities for learning, and the partnerships between museums and formal institutions of learning are strengthening the depth of those opportunities.

—*S. Kim MacGregor*

See also affective domain; affective education; brain research and practice; child development theories; creativity, theories of; cross-cultural studies; history, in curriculum; learning environments; motivation, theories of; philosophies of education; problem solving; social studies

Further Readings and References

Cox-Petersen, A., Marsh, D., Kisiel, J., & Melber, L. (2003). Investigation of guided school tours, student learning, and science reform recommendations at a museum of natural history. *Journal of Research in Science Teaching, 40*(2), 200–218.

Crowley, K., & Jacobs, M. (2002). In G. Leinhardt, K. Crowley, & K. Knutson (Eds.), *Learning conversations in museums.* Mahwah, NJ: Erlbaum.

Dietz, S., Besser, H. Borda, A., & Geber, K. (2004). *Virtual museum: The next generation.* Retrieved from http://www.nyu.edu/tisch/preservation/program/readings/vm_tng.htm.

Mulligan, M., & Brayfield, A. (2004). Museums and childhood: Negotiating organizational lessons. *Childhood, 11*(3), 275–282.

N

🏛 A NATION AT RISK

A blue-ribbon commission was appointed by President Ronald Reagan in 1981 to study the status of K–12 and higher education in the United States. The commission, formally known as the National Commission on Excellence in Education, issued its results on April 26, 1983, in a document titled *A Nation at Risk*. This report became an impetus for a national school reform movement.

The purpose of the commission was to advise and make recommendations to the president, secretary of education, educational policymakers, and state boards of education. The work of the commission focused on teenage youth in K–12 education and youth who entered postsecondary education immediately after graduation from high school. The duties of the commission included reviewing and synthesizing data and education literature on teaching and learning in K–12 and higher education; examining, comparing, and contrasting curricula and the expectations of educational institutions of several advanced countries with those of the United States; studying university and college admissions standards and their impact on high school curricula and student achievement; reviewing educational programs that were recognized for preparing students with higher-than-average college entrance examination scores and who had met success in postsecondary education; reviewing major changes in American education and society that had significantly affected educational achievement; and making recommendations for future practice. Hearings about the findings were held, and testimony was given by educational scholars and policymakers.

A Nation at Risk began with a recognition and a warning that the "once unchallenged preeminence in commerce, industry, science, and technological innovation is being overtaken by competitors throughout the world." The report further stated, "Our nation is at risk. The educational foundations of our society are presently being eroded by a rising tide of mediocrity that threatens our very future as a Nation and a people. What was unimaginable a generation ago has begun to occur—others are matching and surpassing our educational attainments."

The commission noted that student test scores were falling, schools were requiring less rigor (fewer required courses in math, science, and advanced placement classes), and the United States fared poorly with other countries in producing a literate and educated society. Underlying the premise of the commission's report was an implication that the education of U.S. children could no longer be left solely to state and local governments. Rather, based on the commission's findings, it was clear that the federal government would need to take a more prominent role in educating America's youth and retaining America's prominence as a world leader in education. President Reagan called for a more vigorous approach to education that would include school vouchers, school prayer, and the elimination of the Department of Education. Reagan's philosophy would lead to a number of school reform initiatives, increased spending for education, an increased emphasis on excellence in math and science, and an increased emphasis on standardized testing in K–12 education.

The *risk,* as noted by the Commission, was that not only were the Japanese, South Koreans, and Germans receiving government subsidies for development and export and that these developments signified a redistribution of trained capability; more important, the commission's findings noted that the *risk* included the intellectual, moral, and spiritual strengths of the American people and American society. The commission went on to state "Part of what is at risk is the promise first made on this continent: All, regardless of race or class or economic status, are entitled to a fair chance and to the tools for developing their individual powers of mind and spirit to the utmost."

The findings of the commission focused on four areas of the educational process: content, expectations, time, and teaching. *Content* addressed the curriculum, which was found to be homogenized, diluted, and diffused to the point that it no longer had a central purpose. In addition, it was found that 25% of credits earned by students in a high school general track were in subjects such as physical and health education, work experience subjects, and remedial English and math. *Expectations* addressed the level of knowledge and abilities and readiness for postsecondary education for graduating seniors. Findings suggested many students took the maximum number of electives required, scored below average on college admission tests, and college admissions policies that accepted every high school graduate contributed to risk in this area. *Time* addressed the number of hours U.S. students spent in school and on homework and the amount of time spent developing study skills. Findings indicated that the U.S. school calendar year was 40 days shorter and 2 hours shorter per day than in England. In addition, a study of the school week revealed that many students were provided as little as 17 hours of academic instruction per week. *Teaching* addressed the shortage of teachers generally as well as the teacher shortage in key subject matter areas. Findings indicated that too many teachers were being hired from the lower quarter of graduating college students; teacher preparation programs lacked rigor, with an overemphasis on methods courses at the expense of subject matter expertise; and there were severe shortages of teachers in math, science, foreign language and special education.

A key purpose of the National Commission on Excellence in Education was "To report and to make practical recommendations for action to be taken by educators, public officials, governing boards, parents, and others having a virtual interest in American education and a capacity to influence it for the better." At

the conclusion of its work, the commission issued a set of recommendations, which constituted the "New Basics" as a foundation for success in postsecondary education and employment and should be considered the core of the modern curriculum:

- English should be taught to equip graduates to comprehend, interpret, evaluate, and use what they read.
- Mathematics in high school should prepare graduates to understand algebra, geometry, and statistics and to apply concepts in everyday situations.
- Science in high school should be taught to provide graduates with an introduction to concepts, laws, and processes of physical and biological sciences, and science courses should be updated as needed.
- Social studies in high school should be designed to understand the fundamentals of ancient and contemporary issues that have shaped the world and to understand the fundamentals of economic systems and how the U.S. economic and political systems function.
- Computer science in high school should be taught to prepare students to understand computer information, use the computer in the study of other "Basics," and understand other related technologies.

—*Linda C. Tillman*

See also accountability; achievement tests; at-risk students; cultural politics, war; decentralization/centralization controversy; democracy, democratic education and administration; Department of Education; economics, theories of; elementary education; globalism; literacy, theories of; management theories; minorities, in schools; multiculturalism; politics, of education; principalship; productivity; rational organizational theory; restructuring, of schools; school improvement models; site-based management; state departments of education; standardized testing; systemic reform; underachievers, in schools

Further Readings and References

Bell, T. H. (1988). *The thirteenth man: A Reagan cabinet memoir.* New York: Free Press.

Bell, T. H. (1993). Reflections on one decade after "A Nation at Risk." *Phi Delta Kappan, 74,* 592–597.

Brown, K. (2005). Pivotal points: History, development, and promise of the principalship. In F. English (Ed.), *The SAGE handbook of educational leadership* (pp. 68–84). Thousand Oaks, CA: Sage.

A Nation at Risk. (1983). Retrieved September 6, 2005, from http:// ed/gov/pubs/NatARisk/index.html

Sizer, T. (2003). Two reports. *Educational Week, 22*(32), 24–36.

⛪ NATIONAL ASSESSMENT OF EDUCATIONAL PROGRESS

The National Assessment of Educational Progress (NAEP), also known as the "Nation's Report Card," is a federally mandated program for assessing student achievement and progress in American education. The NAEP assessments cover areas such as reading, mathematics, science, writing, U.S. history, civics, geography, and the arts. The assessments are usually administered to randomly selected samples of students in such a way that different students in a sample typically receive different portions of a test. The sampling of students, administration, scoring, and reporting are done through a number of NAEP contractors, including the Educational Testing Service (ETS) and Westat. The Commissioner of Education Statistics, as head of the National Center for Educational Statistics (NCES), is charged with the carrying out of the NAEP project. The National Assessment Governing Board (NAGB), an independent bipartisan organization, develops the policy, content frameworks, and test specifications for the NAEP.

There are three basic components of the NAEP program. The long-term trend NAEP is designed to assess changes in student achievement in mathematics, reading, and science at ages 9, 13, and 17. The assessment is based on fixed content standards and administration procedures that were established from the beginning. A second component is the national NAEP, some times called the "main NAEP." Unlike the trend assessment, the national assessment is grade based, targeting students at Grades 4, 8, and 12. It also covers more subject areas, such as U.S. history, civics, and geography, which are tested in different years. More important, the national NAEP is based on the latest content frameworks and assessment innovations. The third component, the state NAEP, is designed to assess reading, mathematics, and science in the same year as the national assessment. It uses the same assessment content and item types as the national assessment. It is available for students only in Grades 4 and 8. In addition to these assessments, NAEP also conducts several special studies, including the ongoing high school transcript study and the technology-based assessment.

The original development of the NAEP took place in the 1960s. It was a single assessment when it became operational in 1969. With the release of the *A Nation at Risk* report in 1983, there was a strong sense in the nation to improve the international competitiveness of the nation's education system. In 1986, an unexpected decline in the nation's reading achievement, the so-called NAEP reading anomaly, further prompted NAEP to redesign its program. One major result was the separation of the national NAEP from the trend NAEP, with the former measuring the achievement of the latest innovations in curriculum and instruction and the latter yielding results comparable to previous ones. To meet the special needs of the main assessment, NAEP developed content frameworks as outlines for what students should be able to achieve in each subject area. The second major redesign took place in the 1990s with the addition of the state NAEP, partly as a result of the enhanced accountability at the state level. The new assessment, originally called the "trial state assessment" (TSA), was first field tested in 1990 in a number of participating states and became an official component of the NAEP in 1996. During that time, NAEP also updated its frameworks for the major subjects and incorporated more performance-based assessment items. There was also a major change in score reporting, from the original percentage of items answered correctly to the report of scale scores for a whole subject and major content areas, and scores by achievement levels. More recent changes include the sampling of students with disabilities and students with limited English proficiency and the use of accommodations and modifications during test administration. NAEP has also made most of its information available online through its Web site. The No Child Left Behind (NCLB) Act of 2001 provided the federal mandate for the continuation of all three components of the NAEP. The act required reading and mathematics to be continued in all three components of the NAEP program. The inclusion of additional subject areas in the main NAEP is conditional upon available resources. Participation in state NAEP reading and mathematics is required of schools that receive Title I funding. The act also authorized NAEP to conduct the feasibility of a trial urban district assessment. The first assessment was given in 2002 for five urban districts.

Over the decades, NAEP has become a barometer of the nation's educational progress by providing important educational data for the public and policymakers. The success NAEP has enjoyed has also brought high expectations for the program. Many people expect NAEP results to be utilized in evaluating the effectiveness of various federal programs and at the state level in validating state assessment programs. Some feel that past NAEP reports have not been user-friendly enough and that NAEP reports need to be customized to different state holders. To meet such expectations, however, would entail much more effort from the NAEP staff and its contractors, who have to meet the new requirements by the NCLB Act to conduct test administration and score reporting at a much faster pace than previously. A second issue is the efficiency and cost-effectiveness of the program. Some people question the wisdom of having both the long-trend and national assessments in separate operations. Others doubt the need for NAEP to expand into its state assessment. Nevertheless, there seems to be a consensus that the different components of the program serve distinct yet important purposes. Some people suggest merging the trend NAEP with the national assessment. The differences in content frameworks and administration procedures seem to make the merge a challenging task. Attempts at merging the national assessment with the state component were first made in 2002, when the same sampling procedure and test administration procedure were adopted for the two assessments. Although the new federal mandate sanctioned the continuation of all three NAEP components, efforts at streamlining and possibly merging its operations will most likely continue.

—*Yuankun Yao*

See also accountability; achievement tests; determinism, sociocultural; Education Commission of the States; literacy, theories of, measurement, theories of; performance assessment; politics, of education; psychometrics; quantitative research methods; standardized testing; testing and test theory development; validity and reliability

Further Readings and References

Jones, L. V., & Olkin, I. (2004). *The nation's report card: Evolution and perspectives.* Bloomington, IN: Phi Delta Kappa Education Foundation.

National Center for Educational Statistics. (2004). *The nation's report card* [Data file]. Retrieved from the National Center for Educational Statistics Web site, http://nces.ed.gov/nationsreportcard/

Pellegrino, J. W., Jones, L. R., & Mitchell, K. J. (Eds.). (1999). *Grading the nation's report card: Evaluating NAEP and transforming the assessment of educational progress.* Washington, DC: National Academy Press.

Raju, N. S., Pellegrino, J. W., Bertenthal, M. W., & others. (Eds.). (2000). *Grading the nation's report card: Research from the evaluation of NAEP.* Washington, DC: National Academy Press.

Robinson, G., & Brandon, D. (1994). *NAEP test scores: Should they be used to compare and rank state educational quality?* Reston, VA: Educational Research Service.

Sacks, P. (1999). *Standardized minds: The high price of America's testing culture and what we can do to change it.* Cambridge, MA: Perseus Books.

NATIONAL ASSOCIATION FOR THE ADVANCEMENT OF COLORED PEOPLE

The National Association for the Advancement of Colored People (NAACP) is America's most visible civil rights organization. Founded in 1909 by an interracial group of social activists, intellectuals, and descendants of abolitionists, the organization has consistently worked to socially and legally transform America from an exclusive to an inclusive democracy. Many of the NAACP founders were twentieth-century social luminaries, including distinguished scholar W. E. B. Du Bois, activist and journalist Ida Wells-Barnett, social reformers Jane Addams and Mary White Ovington, noted education professor John Dewey, and publisher and philanthropist Oswald Garrison Villard.

The impetus for the organization's founding has been traced to two events: the establishment of the Niagara Movement in 1905 and the race riot and lynching that occurred in the birthplace of Abraham Lincoln in August of 1908. The Niagara Movement, led by Du Bois, was an exclusively Black organization determined to secure the full rights of African Americans. Viewed by some as too militant, the Niagara Movement did not have the mass appeal necessary to attract a wide membership.

The Springfield, Illinois, riots illuminated the national hypocrisy and deep-seated racial hatred for African Americans. Though neither the first nor the last racist-inspired community murder, many felt the incident marred the legacy of Abraham Lincoln. In the spirit of freedom, the call for the founding of an organization committed to eradicating racism was issued on February 12, 1909, the date of the former president's birthday. Niagara Movement members responded to the call and formed, along with those present, the National Negro Conference, which eventually became the NAACP.

The NAACP has consistently challenged social mandates through legal challenges, grassroots activism, and the collection and dissemination of empirical evidence of state-sponsored and socially sanctioned racism and race-based violence. Its antilynching campaign is representative of the NAACP's strategy to simultaneously illuminate racial hatred while asserting African American humanity. The courageous and meticulous documentation of the lynching of African Americans through its organ, *The Crisis,* and its 1919 publication *Thirty Years of Lynching in the United States (1889–1918)* forced the nation to confront the physical, social, and psychological violence regularly inflicted upon African Americans.

Although considered radical at the beginning of the twentieth century, the perception of the NAACP has vacillated throughout its 90-year history. Descriptors such as *moderate, balanced,* and *progressive* have been used to compare the agenda of the NAACP with other civil rights organizations. From the early part of the twentieth century through the civil rights movement and the Black Power movement, the NAACP's diverse leadership, its embrace of middle-class values, and its structured advocacy seemed in contrast to more aggressive civil rights organizations, such as the Universal Negro Improvement Association (UNIA), the Southern Christian Leadership Conference (SCLC), the Student Nonviolent Coordinating Committee (SNCC), and the Black Panther Party (BPP).

The leadership of the NAACP has strongly influenced external perceptions and internal strategies. At the time of its founding, the Executive Committee included only one African American male. Du Bois also served as the association's director of publicity and research. Its first presidents were White men, and while progressive for their time, they were more likely to adopt a gradualist approach to social change. Even when the leadership mantle shifted to Black men, specifically Walter White in 1931, some contemporaneous African American organizations and leaders criticized the NAACP and its leaders as elitist and out of touch with the Black masses. Nonetheless, the organization continued to pursue its ultimate goal of racial equality for minorities. During most of its history, the NAACP has been the most well-known civil rights organization. However, a number of prominent African American leaders such as Marcus Garvey, Martin Luther King Jr., Malcolm X, and others were affiliated with groups that were viewed as more progressive.

It can be argued that educational access and equity has, since the NAACP's founding, been one of the United State's most pressing civil rights issues. As early as 1909, the NAACP's interest in education was evident when it conducted two investigations of the educational conditions of African Americans. However, the impact of the organization's work to dismantle legally mandated school segregation cannot be overstated. Led by attorneys Charles Houston and Thurgood Marshall, the NAACP challenged the constitutionality of a series of state laws that blocked African American access to public schools and colleges and universities. The NAACP's steady erosion of the fictive separate-but-equal standard that protected racial segregation began in 1936 when the NAACP prevailed in *University v. Murray* and culminated with the landmark Supreme Court decision in *Brown v. Board of Education, Topeka, Kansas* (1954). The carefully constructed strategy to dismantle the underpinnings of Jim Crow laws through legal challenges eventually led to the reversal of the *Plessy v. Ferguson* (1896) doctrine and the collapse of de jure segregation in schools and in all other public facilities.

In 1957, the legal branch of the NAACP became a distinct organization known as the Legal Defense Fund (LDF). The NAACP continues to be an advocate for educational access and equity; however, the judicial branch no longer serves as its primary site for educational advocacy. Instead, the NAACP sponsors hearings, conducts research, and encourages its members to work toward solving local and national educational, social, political, and economic challenges.

On the national level, the NAACP is governed by a 64-member board of directors and led by an executive director. The organization has 2,000 adult branches and 1,700 youth and college chapters in seven regions throughout the United States. Through its various initiatives, the national office and the branches are involved in building legal capacity, policy development, civil rights monitoring, economic and political empowerment, and health advocacy.

In 2004, President George W. Bush became the first president since Herbert Hoover to decline an invitation to speak at the NAACP's annual convention. The NAACP Chairman Julian Bond and President and CEO Kweisi Mfume expressed their deep dismay over the president's decision and soundly criticized President Bush and Republican Party policies. In response to the political lashing hurled by Bond and others during the convention, the White House called upon the Internal Revenue Service (IRS), to investigate the NAACP's status as a nonprofit organization. NAACP officials refused to comply with a request for documents from the IRS, citing their criticism of President Bush did not violate the nonpartisan political posture required of tax-exempt organizations.

Kweisi Mfume, a former United States congressman, resigned as the NAACP President and CEO in February 2005 and announced his intention to run for the United States Senate in 2006.

—Melanie Carter

See also affirmative action*;* Afrocentric theories; Bethune, Mary McLeod; Black education; Coppin, Fanny Jackson; critical race theory; Department of Education; desegregation, of schools; diversity; dropouts; Du Bois, W. E. B.; ethnicity; law, trends in; Marshall, Thurgood; minorities, in schools; multiculturalism; Washington, Booker. T; Woodson, Carter G.

Further Readings and References

Finch, M. (1981). *The NAACP: Its fight for justice.* Scarecrow Press.
Janken, K. R (2002). *White: The biography of Walter White, Mr. NAACP.* New York: New Press.
Kellog, C., F. (1973). *NAACP: A history of the National Association of the Advancement of Colored People.* Baltimore: John Hopkins University Press.
Kluger, R. (1977). *Simple justice.* New York: Random House.
Tushnet, Mark V. (1987) *The NAACP's legal strategy against segregated education, 1925–1950.* Chapel Hill: University of North Carolina Press.

🏛 NATIONAL ASSOCIATION OF ELEMENTARY SCHOOL PRINCIPALS

Founded in 1921 by a group of principals who sought to promote their profession and to provide a national forum for their ideas, the National Association of Elementary School Principals (NAESP) has grown to become the most powerful voice of pre-K–8 principals across the United States and around the world.

Since its beginning, NAESP has been dedicated to ensuring that all children get the best education possible. The association serves the professional interest of elementary and middle school principals and promotes the highest professional standards. Today, NAESP provides a peer network of more than 30,000 principals worldwide.

The mission of NAESP is to lead in the advocacy and support for elementary and middle-level principals and other education leaders in their commitment to all children.

To complete the mission of NAESP, the association has developed several key services and programs for its members.

PROFESSIONAL DEVELOPMENT

The professional development arm of NAESP is the NAESP Leadership Academy (NLA). NLA provides workshops, seminars, and e-learning opportunities for leadership training. Programs address a wide range of leadership and management issues. All NLA courses offer one continuing education or professional development unit (PDU/CEU) for each hour of engaged learning to be presented to state or school districts for certification or credit.

NAESP Advocacy Efforts

NAESP provides a strong unified voice for pre-K–8 principals across the United States and around the world, with the following programs:

- *NAESP's key contacts.* Members volunteer to develop relationships and maintain open communication with legislators on Capitol Hill. Key contacts partake in conference calls and have a newsletter to help them with their efforts.
- *Federal relations coordinators.* Each NAESP state affiliate has a federal relations coordinator to voice concerns on behalf of principals to legislators.
- *Federal legislative action center.* Members can visit this part of the NAESP Web site to receive alerts and legislative updates and find information on how to contact their elected officials.
- *Government relations training and information.* Two conferences during the year provide training and opportunities to visit Congress. Newsletters and columns in NAESP publications keep members informed on a more regular basis.

PROGRAMS AND SERVICES

NAESP has several other member benefits, including:

- *Legal Benefits Program.* The Legal Benefits Program safeguards members against unexpected expenses due to legal action that may be directed against them. NAESP members are entitled to $1 million worth of individual professional liability per individual of damage/settlement costs for eligible civil suit claims, with additional reasonable defense outside the limits of the policy. An individual also receives reimbursement up to $10,000 based on continuous years of membership (following a $500 deductible, accruing at $1,000 for each year of continuous membership) for eligible job-protection-related legal claims.

- *Annual convention and exposition.* NAESP's premier professional development and networking opportunity, the convention is attended by more than 5,000 education leaders to learn about best practices and the latest products and services.
- *Principals Advisory Leadership Services (PALS) Corps.* A training and certification program to develop experienced principals into mentors for principals in training.
- *National Distinguished Principals Program.* This awards program recognizes outstanding elementary and middle school principals from all 50 states and the District of Columbia. Private schools, Department of Defense Dependents' Schools, and the U.S. Department of State Overseas Schools are also recognized.
- *Community and student services.* Helps principals with resources to develop better connections with their community and recognize and foster student leaders.
- *The NAESP Web site.* Members create their own profiles on the NAESP Web site, where they can search the publications' archives, look for new jobs, download sample forms and letters from fellow principals, post a question on the Principals' Help Line, order books or renew membership, and interact with their colleagues in the forums.

—Candice Johnson

See also accountability; authority; bureaucracy; career development; chain of command; division of labor; elementary education; leadership, theories of; leadership effectiveness; leadership styles; management theories; morality, moral leadership; open-door policy; parental involvement; principal, assistant; principalship; productivity; school improvement models; site-based management; span of control; staffing, concepts of; total quality management; underachievers, in schools; women in educational leadership

Further Readings and References

Brown, K. (2005). Pivotal points: History, development, and promise of the principalship. In F. English (Ed.), *The Sage handbook of educational leadership* (pp. 109–141). Thousand Oaks, CA: Sage.

National Association of Elementary School Principals. (2004). *Leading learning communities: Standards for what principals should know and be able to do.* Alexandria, VA: Author.

Protheroe, N., Turner, J., & Vincent, P. (2003). *Essentials for principals: Developing and maintaining high staff morale.* Alexandria, VA: National Association of Elementary School Principals and Educational Research Service.

Quaglia, R. J., & Quay, S. E. (2003). *Changing lives through the principalship: A reflective guide for school leaders.* Alexandria, VA: National Association of Elementary School Principals.

Shellard, E. (2003). *Urban principals respond: Building and maintaining a high-achieving school.* Alexandria, VA: National Association of Elementary School Principals and Educational Research Service.

NATIONAL ASSOCIATION OF SECONDARY SCHOOL PRINCIPALS

The National Association of Secondary School Principals (NASSP), a professional organization of middle school and high school principals, assistant principals, and aspiring school leaders, was founded in 1916. NASSP seeks to promote excellence in school leadership through professional development opportunities, producing relevant research publications, and advocating on behalf of school leaders. The organization strives to advance middle and high school education by promoting high professional standards, focusing attention on school leaders' challenges, providing a "national voice" for school leaders, building public confidence in education, strengthening the role of the principal as instructional leader, and publicizing the issues and interests of NASSP, which is governed by an executive director and a board of directors.

A prime goal of the association is advocacy: bringing the issues of the principalship to federal and state legislatures and to the news media. NASSP's Office of Advocacy and Strategic Alliances monitors legislation "affecting education, communicates with Congressional offices, the U.S. Department of Education, and actively participates in coalition-building activities. Other advocacy activities include affecting public policy by changing attitudes, shaping public debate and informing public thought through editorials, policy briefings, and regular interaction with the nation's news media. The Office of Advocacy and Strategic Alliances translates complex education issues into compelling and persuasive arguments that inform the media, policymakers, and the public.

The association has three National Task Forces: the middle school task force, the high school task force, and the principal preparation task force. The task forces address pertinent issues and topics impacting leaders of middle level and senior high schools and the various principal preparation programs. In addition to the task forces, NASSP seeks to make a larger impact through its Speakers' Bureau, which, upon request, provides presentations by NASSP staff members. The goal of the Speakers' Bureau is to promote and advance the secondary school principalship and student leadership programs and activities.

NASSP also works to promote student academic achievement, character, and leadership development, through student leadership programs such as the National Honor Society, the National Junior Honor Society, and the National Association of Student Councils. Furthermore, NASSP sponsors a variety of scholarship and award programs and publishes an annual list of approved contests and activities (the National Advisory List of Student Contests and Activities). The list provides information to assist principals, teachers, parents, and students in making decisions regarding participation in a wide variety of extracurricular program opportunities: http://www.nhs .us/scaa/scaa_search.cfm.

The charitable arm of NASSP is called Together Reaching Education Excellence (TREE). Its goal is to increase students' access to leadership opportunities and principals' access to professional development opportunities. TREE provides grants and scholarship opportunities to high-poverty schools and the students they serve.

—*Bonnie C. Fusarelli*

See also accountability; athletics in schools; discipline in schools; expulsion, of students; extracurricular activities; high schools; junior high schools; leadership, complex theory of; leadership, distributed; leadership, teacher; middle schools; principal, assistant; principal succession; principalship; school plant management; stewardship; tracking, of students; vandalism in schools; violence in schools; women in educational leadership

Further Readings and References

Bogotch, I. (2005). A history of public school leadership: The first century, 1837–1942. In F. English (Ed.), *The SAGE handbook of educational leadership* (pp. 7–32). Thousand Oaks, CA: Sage.

Sergiovanni, T. (2001). *The principalship: A reflective practice perspective.* Boston: Allyn & Bacon.

National Association of Secondary School Principals. (n.d.). Available at http://www.nassp.org

NATIONAL COUNCIL FOR THE ACCREDITATION OF TEACHER EDUCATION

Founded in 1954, the National Council for the Accreditation of Teacher Education (NCATE) is the professional accrediting organization for colleges and universities that prepare teachers and other professional personnel for work in elementary and secondary schools in the United States. NCATE is a nonprofit, nongovernmental organization, comprised of more than 30 national education-related associations. The associations appoint representatives to NCATE's policy boards, which develop NCATE standards, policies, and procedures. Policy board membership typically includes representatives from teacher educators, teachers, state and local policymakers, and professional specialists in P–12 schools.

NCATE is the education profession's mechanism to help establish high quality teacher, educational specialist, and school administrator preparation. The organization has developed standards for teacher and administrator education and utilizes a performance-based system of accreditation to conduct reviews of educational institutions to determine which schools of education meet those standards. The work of the organization is conducted by the 2,000+ educational professionals who volunteer as policy board members, program reviewers, and onsite team members. NCATE revises its unit accreditation standards every 5 years to reflect current research and state-of-the-art practice in the teaching profession. Therefore, once accredited, institutions must go through the continuing accreditation process every 5 years. As of 2004, 575 colleges of education were accredited by NCATE—a recognition that indicates that the college of education has met national professional standards for the preparation of teachers and other educators and has provided evidence of competent teacher candidate performance. Reflecting the national trend of increased demand for accountability from state governments and the public, the number of institutions seeking accreditation and the number of accredited institutions has risen steadily since the late 1990s. Despite the fact that a number of top ranked schools of education decline to be NCATE accredited and the NCATE process has come in for criticism while a rival national accrediting organization has been established and recently recognized by the federal government (TEAC), NCATE standards remain dominant in teacher and administrator preparation, influencing teacher preparation in 48 states, the District of Columbia, and Puerto Rico. One indicator of the nationalization of the NCATE standards is that numerous states have reciprocity agreements for educator licensure based on graduation from NCATE-accredited schools. A further indicator is that as of 2004, 48 state/NCATE partnerships had been established in which the states and NCATE conduct joint or concurrent reviews of higher education programs in an attempt to save institutions and states time and money.

—Bonnie C. Fusarelli

See also accountability; accreditation; behaviorism; culture, school; expectations, teacher and student cultures; licensure and certification; normal schools; professional learning communities; schools of education; state departments of education; University Council for Educational Administration

Further Readings and References

English, F. (2003, March). Cookie-cutter leaders for cookie-cutter schools: The teleology of standardization and the de-legitimization of the university in educational leadership preparation. *Leadership and Policy in Schools, 2*(1), 27–46.
English, F. (2003). Tsar khorosh, boyary polkhi—The ISLLC standards and the enshrinement of mystical authoritarianism as anti-change doctrine in educational leadership preparation programs. In F. Lunenburg & C. Carr (Eds.), *Shaping the future: Policy, partnerships, and emerging perspectives* (pp. 112–133). Lanham, MD: Scarecrow Press..
National Council for the Accreditation of Teacher Education. (n.d.), Home page. Available at http://www.ncate.org/

NATIONAL COUNCIL OF PROFESSORS OF EDUCATIONAL ADMINISTRATION

The National Council of Professors of Educational Administration (NCPEA) is the preeminent organization of individual professors dedicated to the effective preparation and renewal of educational leaders. NCPEA is committed to the improvement of the practice and study of educational administration. Established in 1947, the council continues its commitment to serve the interests and needs of professors of educational administration. Members enjoy exceptional opportunities for professional growth and development in a welcoming, supportive, and collegial environment.

NCPEA is governed by a 10-member executive board and an executive director, with the executive office presently housed at Sam Houston State University.

The organization sponsors three annual meetings: (a) a summer conference held in different sections of the United States and Canada, (b) a midwinter conference in conjunction with the American Association of School Administrators, and (c) an October strategic planning meeting for the executive board. Members enjoy both the summer and midwinter conferences as opportunities to share their research and teaching.

NCPEA focuses on the following goals and objectives:

- Ensure the high-quality professional development of professors of educational administration.
- Refine the knowledge bases for preparing practicing school administrators and professors of educational administration.
- Promote the application of theory and research in the field to the practice of educational administration.
- Establish and promote a code of ethics for professors of educational administration.
- Ensure access and inclusion of underrepresented groups into the professorate and administration.
- Serve as an advocate for professors of educational administration and as an authority on critical issues.
- Develop the administrative application of technology in the preparation and renewal of educational leaders.
- Establish standards by which educational administration programs become certified, accredited, or approved.

PUBLICATIONS

NCPEA publishes annually a Tier I peer-refereed yearbook designed around the theme of the annual summer conference. Contributing authors represent professors and practitioners from the nation's universities and public schools. In addition, NCPEA publishes the *Education Leadership Review,* a nationally peer-reviewed journal focusing on the preparation of school leaders, and it edits and publishes the *Educational Administration Directory.* The purpose of the directory is to provide a service to the profession of educational administration and leadership by providing information that will improve communications among the universities and faculties of the educational administration departments throughout the United States and Canada.

STATE AFFILIATES

NCPEA state affiliates are separate organizations that work collaboratively as part of the NCPEA organization to foster the common values and goals of NCPEA. State affiliates influence educational policy and provide a forum for the improvement of the practice and study of educational administration in their states. Activities of NCPEA include, but are not limited to, providing information and leadership, improving the preparation of school administrators, encouraging research and service, promoting high professional standards, focusing attention on educational problems and opportunities, promoting NCPEA membership, cooperating with other professional organizations interested in excellence in education, and promoting participation in all activities deemed by the membership to be in the best interest of NCPEA.

The primary purposes of collaborating with state affiliate organizations include (a) to positively impact school leadership policy and practice through the collective influence of over 400 university preparation programs and over 3,500 professors of educational administration, (b) to network and share ideas and provide professional development opportunities, and (c) to keep professors and practitioners informed on national issues related to the work of the National Policy Board for Educational Administration (NPBEA) and the Educational Leadership Constituent Council (ELCC).

CREATING THE FUTURE

NCPEA has recently entered into a contractual agreement with Rice University and its Connexions Project to refine and assemble the knowledge base in educational administration. In combination with powerful software tools, Connexions fosters the development, manipulation, and continuous refinement of educational material by diverse communities of authors and practitioners. It represents a new paradigm for the electronic development and delivery of knowledge content by archiving existing knowledge and continually refining and updating knowledge. Modules of information with supporting links are developed by a community of authors from around the world under an open-content license, translated into several languages, and freely accessible to all in the world.

A critical aspect of this project is the evaluation of the quality and usefulness of the materials in improving the preservice preparation of principals in university and alternative certification programs as well as inservice preparation for practitioners already in the field.

—Theodore B. Creighton

See also accreditation; Interstate Leaders Licensure Consortium; knowledge base, of the field; professional development; professional learning communities; schools of education; standard setting; superintendency; universities, preparation of educational leaders in; University Council for Educational Administration

Further Readings and References

Alford, B. (2005). *The National Council of Professors of Educational Administration: The last thirty years.* Houston, TX: Sam Houston University Press.

Creighton, T., Busch, S., MacNeil, A., & Waxman, H. (2005). Narrowing the disconnect between the knowledge base in educational administration and the practice of school leadership. *NCPEA Education Leadership Review, 6*(1), 1–8.

NATIONAL EDUCATION ASSOCIATION

The nation's largest professional employee organization, the National Education Association (NEA) represents 2.7 million teachers, administrators, support personnel, student teachers, and retired educators in elementary, secondary, and higher education. The National Teachers Association was the starting point for the NEA. Forty-three educators, representing 12 state associations and the District of Columbia, met on August 26, 1857, in Philadelphia at the suggestion of Daniel B. Hagar of the Massachusetts Teachers Association to form a National Brotherhood of Teachers. Among the charter members was Robert Campbell, an African American from Jamaica. The original call aimed at the improvement of schools; advancement of teachers professionally, socially, and pedagogically; and the promotion of public interest in education.

The American Normal School Association and the National Association of School Superintendents joined their ranks in 1870.The history of the organization falls into several periods. During the Convention Period (1857 to 1892), the NEA had neither national staff nor permanent headquarters and focused primarily on pedagogy. Teacher welfare issues were left to local and state affiliates. The well-attended Madison

Convention in 1884 raised the NEA's profile among educators who were developing a professional identity. While the NEA's endorsement of public education reflected its interest in education for all, the NEA's attention to minority groups was limited during the late nineteenth century. Renowned African American educators, such as Booker T. Washington, spoke at several NEA conventions, and the NEA created a short-lived Department of Indian Education in 1899. During the nineteenth century, esteemed educators as William Torrey Harris and Nicholas Murray Butler made frequent appearances at NEA conventions. The Committee Period (1892–1917) marked the selection of the NEA's first full-time executive secretary, Dr. Irwin Shepherd. In 1918, the association's reputation expanded with the issuance of the highly influential Cardinal Principles of Secondary Education, crafted by the NEA Commission on the Reorganization of Secondary Education. The Cardinal Principles contained the major objectives of education that were enunciated for decades thereafter and were complemented by the emerging field of educational administration. In 1917, when Dr. James Crabtree became executive secretary, the NEA headquarters moved from Ann Arbor, Michigan, to Washington, D.C., and the NEA set its course on becoming an important player at the national political level.

Although women and classroom teachers expanded their participation in the NEA (Ella Flagg Young became the first female NEA president in 1910, and Margaret Haley of Chicago proposed the Department of Classroom Teachers), college presidents or professors and secondary school administrators dominated the NEA during the early twentieth century. Major restructuring, an increase in the number of associations affiliated with the NEA, and enrollment drives raised membership from 8,466 in 1917 to 170,053 in 1926. This increase marked the start of the "modern" NEA. In 1920, the democratization of the NEA resulted in the establishment of the Representative Assembly composed of delegates from state and local affiliates who formulated NEA policies. Expanding teacher membership was a way to enlarge and strengthen the organization in the face of competition from the American Federation of Teachers (AFT) after World War I.

The power held by the major units of the NEA (the board of directors, the executive committee, the board of trustees, and the representative assembly) changed over time as the control of the organization shifted to members at the classroom level. Constitutional provisions and by laws as well as the formal and informal alliances of groups within the organization determined the relationship between these main units. The executive secretary, elected by the board of trustees until its dissolution in 1968, was the glue that held these organizational units together until restructuring begun in the 1960s culminated in a new constitution in 1973. The Department of Classroom Teachers had increased its influence, and a succession of strong NEA presidents indicated significant changes in the NEA as it redefined its image as a professional association. Teacher welfare was defined in professional terms as the NEA challenged its rival, the AFT, for aggressiveness in collective bargaining, a labor union objective.

The NEA evolved as a federation of educational units at the national, state, and local levels. Unification of these three levels did not receive serious consideration until the mid 1940s and was realized in the 1970s after considerable acrimony. The NEA has been a canopy for commissions, departments, and committees such as the Department of Superintendence, the National Association of Secondary School Principals, and the Department of Classroom Teachers, all associated with education, but with different perspectives. Some, such as the National Commission on Teacher Education and Professional Standards, have been intimately associated with NEA policies, but others have been consultative units. The data collected and reports issued by the NEA's Research Division, set up in 1922, on topics such as teacher demographics, school facilities, and salaries were widely used even by competing organizations such as the American Federation of Teachers (AFT). While the NEA's core principles of individualism, professionalism, democracy, and universal education showed consistency of purpose, they were often subject to topical concerns and shifting interpretation. such as the NEA's support of ethnic and racial minorities, which accelerated after the NEA's merger with the American Teachers Association (ATA) in 1966. The creation of a Department of Education in 1979 by President Jimmy Carter was a long desired NEA goal.

While a possible merger of the AFT and NEA has surfaced periodically, the NEA and AFT have clashed on curricular issues, bilingual education, and affirmative action, although there have been successful mergers of NEA and AFT affiliates at the local level. While the antiunion orientation of the NEA has softened in recent years at the national level, regional differences among state and local NEA affiliates remain. In addition, the conduct of NEA and AFT affairs (voting, leadership, term limits, etc.) is markedly different. The "new unionism" promulgated by former NEA President Robert Chase in the 1990s merged traditional unionism with educational reform. An outgrowth of the "new unionism" has been a lessening of the antagonistic relationship between teachers and administrators and an increase in NEA efforts at collaboration in the transformation and improvement of public schools.

—*Carol F. Karpinski*

See also American Federation of Teachers; Butler, Nicholas Murray; career development; career stages; collective bargaining; conflict management; Department of Education; gender studies, in educational leadership; Haley, Margaret; Harris, William Torrey; Picott, J. Rupert; power; Trenholm, Harper Councill; unions, of teachers; Young, Ella Flagg

Further Readings and References

Blount, J. M. (2005). *Fit to teach: Same-sex desire, gender, and school work in the twentieth century.* Albany: SUNY Press.

Fenner, M. S. (1945). *NEA history: The National Educational Association: Its development and program.* Washington, DC: National Education Association.

Urban, W. J. (2000). *Gender, race, and the National Education Association: Professionalism and its limitations.* New York: RoutledgeFalmer.

Wesley, E. B. (1957). *NEA: The first hundred years.* New York: Harper.

West, A. M. (1980). *The National Education Association: The power base for education.* New York: Free Press.

🏛 NEEDS ASSESSMENT

Needs assessment is a term that covers several different types of analyses. It sometimes refers to a process of discovery, for example, going out and sampling some facet of public or professional opinion. This is essentially a perception check of sorts. Some questions might be:

- Survey teachers and determine what materials they think they need for teaching reading next year
- Ask parents what electives they would like to see in the school's curriculum
- Survey principals to determine how they rate the three different kinds of computers that might be purchased for the school district

The responses to these questions represent feelings and perceptions of a designated group of respondents. Needs assessment was an activity of discovering the state of such feelings and perceptions.

There is another use of the term needs assessment, which is quite different. In this approach, the process is more formal and is based on a *discrepancy* as opposed to a *discovery* model. The idea of a discrepancy requires beginning with some known facts, such as current achievement test scores, or frequency list of some kind, such as number of library books checked out over a given time period. This is the current situation, or the "what is" benchmark. A second benchmark is required to be developed. This second indicator is the "what should be." The creation of the "what should be" often involves the process of visioning or imagining a changed situation. Once the "what should be" is established, then the analyst proceeds to calculate the difference or the *gap* between the two. The discrepancy or gap is the *need.* A need is met when the gap is closed or erased.

Roger Kaufman's 1992 work, *Mapping Educational Success,* is seminal in the field. He posits that a gap-based needs assessment approach works on several different levels. The widest arc or level of thinking is called the *megalevel,* and it involves thinking about social goals, social problems, and issues and determining how these matters could be resolved globally. The gaps are between indicators of social problems (crime rate, poverty, etc.) and their amelioration. It is necessary to think about this wider arc because schools are part of the social fabric. They are either solutions to such problems or they perpetuate them by not addressing them. The *macrolevel* of needs assessment represents the place where a school system's graduates enter the larger society. A comparison of the skills, knowledge, and attitudes required of the graduates in order to live well and resolve societal issues is the locus of a macrolevel needs assessment. A third level is the *microlevel.* This is the juncture where internal to the school system, an analysis might occur. A comparison of test scores as students move from elementary to middle school might yield a microlevel gap analysis.

These three levels of needs assessment activities occur within a rational planning framework; that is, planning is based on assumptions regarding the stability, efficacy, and logic of the organization itself. As social service organizations, schools and school systems are expected to be rational, that is, be able to connect their resources to student learning. Even if the process is not well understood as to how such connections actually work within schools, the expectation is still dominant in nearly all approaches to thinking about how schools work or should work.

A third use of the concept of needs assessment is that it is connected to vague statements regarding psychological needs. Here, the phrase "based on student needs" may not refer to specific learning objectives, but to more global notions of needs for psychological security, esteem, recognition, or self-awareness, as in Abraham Maslow's 1954 idea of a "hierarchy of needs." This concept of need represents an archetypical psychosocial condition most often found in statements of philosophy regarding the need for nurturing and constancy within schools and classrooms. As such, they are much more difficult to measure and to use than in a needs assessment centered on specific learning outcomes.

—Fenwick W. English

See also accountability; achievement tests; behavior, student; feedback; field theory; forecasting; Gallup Polls, on public education; global cultural politics; hierarchical developmental models; individual differences, in children; innovation, in education; management theories; objectivity; path-goal leadership theory; performance assessment; planning models; productivity; quantitative research methods; rational organizational theory; resource management; standard setting; standardized testing; systemic reform; systems theory/thinking; total quality management; value-added indicators; values of organizations and leadership

Further Readings and References

Kaufman, R. (1992). *Mapping educational success.* Newbury Park, CA: Corwin Press.

Kaufman, R., & English, F. (1979). *Needs assessment: Concept and application.* Englewood Cliffs, NJ: Educational Technology.

Kaufman, R., Herman, J., & Watters, K. (1996). *Educational planning: Strategic, tactical, operational.* Lancaster, PA: Technomic.

Kaufman, R., Rojas, A., & Mayer, H. (1993). *Needs assessment: A user's guide.* Englewood Cliffs, NJ: Educational Technology.

Maslow, A. (1987). *Motivation and personality.* New York: Longman. (Original work published in 1954)

NEGLIGENCE

Perhaps the greatest daily challenge facing educators is how to avoid liability for accidental injuries that children suffer in schools. For a school system to be liable for negligence, an injured party must satisfy the four elements of negligence: duty and the related principle of foreseeability, breach, injury, and causation.

Absent a legal relationship with another, there is no legal duty to help a stranger. It is thus important to recognize that an educator who acts within the scope of his or her duties, whether in school or at a school-related activity, has a duty to assist all children in a group even if a teacher does not know a student personally. This duty, which is based on an educator's legal relationship with a school board, may not be limited to children (or others) from the building where the teacher works.

Once a legal relationship is present, an educator has the duty to anticipate reasonably foreseeable risks and take steps to try to prevent them from occurring. A flexible concept that varies based on the age and physical condition of students as well as the degree of danger in a situation, duty does not expect educators to foresee all harm that might befall children. Rather, educators are responsible only for events that can reasonably be anticipated or of which they are actually aware.

Two important questions arise when considering whether an educator has breached a duty. The first relates to how an educator has performed his or her duty. An educator can breach his or her duty in one of two ways: either by nonfeasance, or not acting when there is a duty to do so (such as not breaking up a fight), or by misfeasance, acting incorrectly under the circumstances (such as using too much force in breaking up a fight).

The second consideration under breach is the standard of care. In evaluating whether an individual applied the correct degree of care, the courts have adopted a reasonableness standard, typically instructing juries to consider educators' behavior in light of the legal fiction known as the "reasonable person," also known as the "reasonably prudent person." Although the courts have stopped short of creating a clear hierarchy, based on education and years of experience working with children, a reasonable teacher is likely to be held to a higher standard of care than a reasonable person, but not to the same level as a "reasonable parent." As such, courts have sought to create a standard to hold educators accountable to perform at the same level of care as reasonably prudent professionals of similar education and background.

For an injured party to prevail, the harm must be one for which compensation can be awarded. If, for example, a student slips and falls on water that accumulated moments earlier at a drinking fountain and the child's only "injury" was a wet pair of pants, then it is highly unlikely that a claim would proceed. However, if the child broke his leg by falling on water that accumulated over several hours, then there is a greater likelihood that this may be an injury for which compensation can be awarded.

The final element in establishing liability for negligence is that school personnel must be the legal, or proximate cause, of the injury resulting from the breach. In other words, the last person or persons in a chain of events who could have taken steps to prevent an injury is typically considered the legal cause.

Even if an injured party has established that the elements of negligence are present, educators have three primary defenses available to limit or eliminate liability. The defenses recognize that even though educators must care for children, they cannot be accountable for every conceivable harm that befalls students.

Perhaps the most common defense is governmental or statutory immunity, which is based on the principle that the state cannot be liable for the acts of its employees. A growing number of states have greatly reduced or eliminated the scope of governmental and charitable immunity.

Contributory and comparative negligence are premised on a person's having played a part in causing his or her injury. These defenses, which apply in an almost equal number of states, produce very different results. Under contributory negligence, a party whose actions led to the cause of his or her injury cannot recover for the harm. However, as this led to inequitable results, a growing number of states have adopted comparative negligence, wherein courts direct juries to apportion fault between the parties. As such, an injured party's award may be reduced by the degree to which he or she played a part in causing the injury.

Assumption of risk is also based on comparative fault. This defense can reduce an injured party's recovery in proportion to the degree to which his or her culpable conduct contributed to an accident if the individual voluntarily exposed himself or herself to a known and appreciated risk of harm.

—*Charles J. Russo*

See also accountability; law; personnel management; violence in schools; working conditions, in schools

Further Readings and References

Russo, C. J. (2004). Student supervision and risk management. *School Business Affairs, 70*(6), 39–41.
Streshly, W. A., & Frase, L. E. (1992). *Avoiding legal hassles.* Newbury Park, CA: Corwin Press.

NEO-NAZISM

Nazism and neo-Nazism can be traced to the regime of Adolph Hitler, who led the revolution in Europe and incited World War II. This xenophobic regime was distinguished by racial intolerance, tracing back to the radical chiliasts of late medieval Europe. These Christian fanatics believed that they were the chosen people of God to be saved from an impending catastrophe that would soon end the world. These sects also believed that a Golden Age on earth would soon begin, without the outsiders who were perceived as degraded and unworthy to survive in the new kingdom. These apocalyptic views continued into the early twentieth century, when two new factions were identified as Nazis and fascists, typified by dictatorship, suppression, and racism. As these new parties in Germany and Italy regenerated in World War II, they continued to follow their ancestral roots by anticipating the world's demise, which would destroy the infidels, leaving only the fascists and Nazis to rule the new Teutonic civilization. Representatives of the Aryan Elect then began a new era of contemporary traditional socialism that deviated from the norms of all other nations and cultures. This new order included effective practices and policies that divided other national cultures through the use of psychological estrangement, extremism, pluralism, mobilization, and status displacement, leaving the cultic milieu world strangely unified in only one respect: The total cultural system was fully separated from the dominant orthodoxies of the surrounding society.

Today, schools around the world have become dangerous places for students. In most nations of the world, teenagers and children have experienced violence in their schools, including harassment, injury, trauma, and death, and educational sites have become frequent locations for violent events. Many school-aged children have been harassed in the past three decades. These harassers are often neo-Nazi extremists who select their victims on the basis of the race, religion, color, disability, national origin, or ancestry of the students. These neo-Nazi groups include skinheads, White supremacists, and the White Aryan Resistance, a virulent hate group founded by William L. Pierce, who founded the neo-Nazi National Alliance in the United States. Members of these militant groups also use school grounds to intentionally recruit school-aged youths, who are easily persuaded to join these groups because of social deprivation and lack of family interpersonal bonds.

Neo-Nazism continues to flourish in the new millennium because of overlaps with social class, causing racially bifurcated societies, inequalities between class and/or race, technological divides, and global competition, which divide the haves and have-nots of the world. With the death of Pierce, their leader, neo-Nazi sects have splintered into underground groups but will surely reemerge and reconstruct their ranks and continue their neo-Nazi mission to follow Hitler and the socialist doctrine as long as inequities exist in the nations of the world.

—Carole Funk

See also adolescence; at-risk students; authority; critical race theory; dropouts; eugenics; fascism and schools; Holocaust education; homophobia; immigration, history and impact in education; minorities, in schools; peer interaction/friendships; personality; queer theory; right-wing politics, advocates, impact on education; school safety; terrorism; three-factor model, five-factor model; vandalism in schools; violence in schools

Further Readings and Resources

Addington, L. A. (2002). *The Columbine effect: The impact of violent school crime on students' fear of victimization at school.* Unpublished doctoral dissertation, University at Albany, SUNY.

Ezekiel, R. S. (1995). *The racist mine: Portraits of American neo-Nazis and Klansmen.* New York: Penguin Books.

Mann, M. (2004). *Fascists.* Cambridge, UK: Cambridge University Press.

🏛 NETWORKING AND NETWORK THEORY

Networking is a process by which individuals and/or organizations connect with one another for ideas or resources toward the achievement of a specific goal. Networking most commonly begins when a person with a need connects with another who has a resource. A *network* is defined as an interpersonal relationship that links together people, places, objects, or events. Since networks do not have a boundary, they can add or subtract members with ease and fluidity. The use of technology as a medium for communication, such as the Internet, has greatly expanded opportunities for network analysts.

Networks consist of informal sources (comprised of one's personal network) as well as formal sources (organizations and sources where one would expect to receive information). Both formal and informal sources of support have a structure and hierarchy to them. While the structure and hierarchy of one's informal network can be viewed as a spider web that overlaps and interacts with other spider webs, a formal network can be easily envisioned as "who talks to who to get what" in organizational flow charts. One should envision how computer networks talk to each other as a way of seeing networking in action. Network analysts differentiate between primary sources, also identified as the "first-order zone," consisting of all people connected directly to a particular individual; and secondary sources, those who "know someone who knows someone"; and into the third, fourth, and zones beyond. Networks are very complex. Typical informal networks consist of several hundred to thousands of people. An informal network includes one's relatives, colleagues, friends, neighbors, coworkers, and acquaintances.

On an organizational level, networking provides a structure that maintains the autonomy of individual organizations yet still makes it possible to have partnerships that provide resources through collaborative sharing. Networking furnishes a way to accomplish tasks through informal means. Network analysis provides a way to examine the dynamics of the relationship between an individual and the school organization. Networking provides a way to informally share information or communicate throughout an organization, such as a school system. It is believed that the informal, open nature of networking may enhance greater creativity and productivity.

The hallmarks of networking, such as "It's not *what* you know, but *who* you know" and "It's a small world," can be seen in films and in many popular games such as "six degrees of separation"—the idea that anyone can be reached through fewer than six people. On a practical level, there are many advantages to networking. Networking allows people and organizations the ability to maintain a balance between their independence and their reliance on one another. The boundaries that separate them are open.

Members of networks are usually peers of one sort or another. They are not conferring through a complicated hierarchy as a subordinate, but rather talking to one friend who knows another friend. The tone of the interaction is much more comfortable and relaxed.

Networking promotes horizontal, open communication. This allows for ideas and conversations to traverse across cultural and organizational barriers. This model of communication provides a means to communicate with people that had previously been separate. Often, networks have been formed on the basis of shared interest and vision, making it ideal for social service and educational programming.

Network theory, grounded in mathematics, is a way of abstracting and explaining interactions in social networks. It provides concepts for the systematic analysis of interactional and organizational linkages between persons, objects, and/or events. Such analysis allows for mapping interactions in ways that demonstrate they are not random and that uncover patterns and meanings. Network analysts believe the examination of how an individual is connected into the larger web of social connections can be used to determine one's failure or success.

Social network theory stems from network theory and is part of the social sciences. It is used to analyze the interactions among people who comprise a network. Social network theory is often used to identify how information is transmitted throughout the network, paying particular attention to how it is transmitted through cliques and social groups.

Computer networks were originally designed to support the exchange of information and ideas for people that were geographically dispersed, but interested in common areas. The online community created by the Internet through the use of e-mail and chat rooms has resulted in networking opportunities beyond the scope anyone could possibly have imagined. For network theory analysts, the Internet allows them to study networking on a very large scale, including all types of nuances, such as through professional Web sites or a chat room established for parents of a particular school.

Effective school leaders understand the power behind their network. This network consisting of peers, professional colleagues, employees, parents, and students is far-reaching. The ability to transform a school cannot be accomplished alone. A wise school leader will use networking to communicate with his or her constituency toward achievement of the goals of the school. Good networking enables the school leader to interact with many populations quickly.

—Iris M. Saltiel

See also capacity building, of organizations; communications, theories in organizations; community relations; conceptual systems theory and leadership; hierarchical developmental models; leadership, distributed; qualitative research, history, theories, issues; quantitative research methods; role theory

Further Readings and References

Kadushin, C. (2000, May 21–26). *A short introduction to social networks: A non-technical elementary primer.* Working background paper for the CERPE Workshop. Retrieved September 6, 2005, from http://www.ccs.neu.edu/home/perrolle/soc528/classnotes/kadushin.html

Kilduff, M., & Tsai, W. (2003). *Social networks and organizations.* London: Sage.

Lipnack, J., & Stamps, J. (1982). *The first report and directory of networking.* New York: Doubleday.

Sidele, C. C., & Warzynski, C. C. (2003, September/October). A new mission for business schools: The development of actor-network leaders. *Journal of Education for Business,* pp. 40–45.

🏛 NEUROSCIENCE

Neuroscience is the study of the human nervous system, the brain, and the biological basis of consciousness, perception, memory, and learning (understanding). The brain is a biological structure with 10 to 15 billion differentiated yet functionally connected cells. Brain scientists have learned much about the brain's hardware but remain as puzzled as ever about how the programs work that activate it. Basic research in neuroscience is typically done at the molecular, genetic, or cellular levels. What happens in education takes place at the macrolevel. The connections between the two are just beginning to emerge.

Much of the early brain-related research was conducted using brain-damaged individuals. Roger Sperry, Torsten Wiesel, and David Hubel, for example, won the Nobel Prize in 1981 for their research on the two cerebral hemispheres. They demonstrated, using "split-brain" subjects whose corpus callosi had been surgically severed, that each hemisphere of the brain has specialized functions (the left, for language and the right, for nonverbal functions). Jeanne Chall and Rita Peterson have argued that a new conception of the brain emerged in the 1960s and that four conceptual models explain a great deal of the current research in neuroscience:

1. Fixed circuitry: A set of fixed pathways are present in the brain before birth that carry messages from one part of the brain to another.

2. Critical periods: Specific periods of time exist in the development of organisms, including humans, when they are most receptive to specific kinds of stimuli, when both biological factors and environmental stimulation play a major role in brain development.

3. Plasticity: The brain changes with age and can recover from injuries, especially with proper stimulation from the environment. Nutrition is an early determinant of human intellectual development.

4. Modularity: Observations of how memory is lost through injury, alcoholism, or therapy have shown that there are two kinds of memory, declarative knowledge (content and rules) and procedural knowledge (how to perform).

There are four areas of brain research that have implications for classroom practice. First, the physiology of the brain changes as a result of experience. Educators need to know this basic physiology to reflect its applications in school scheduling and instructional strategy. Second, IQ is not fixed at birth; intelligence is multifaceted, and every brain is different. Learning opportunities need to be broadly based to meet individual differences. Third, windows of opportunity exist both in early childhood and adolescence, when abilities are acquired more easily. Adolescents are still ready to learn and need the support of their principals and teachers. Fourth, emotions strongly influence learning. Schools need to provide appropriate and enriched environments, high in challenge and low in threat.

Many neuroscientists and educators caution against exaggerating the implications of brain-based research for educational practice. Michael Gazzaniga deplores the overinterpretation of hemispheric differences by people who have no firsthand knowledge of neuroscientific research. Some experts posit that neuroscientific research has little to offer formal education. Others are very skeptical of the growing mythology of brain-based education. Too little of that research is actually concerned with the real tasks of teachers and the realities of schools and classrooms.

—*James W. Keefe*

See also brain research and practice; child development theories; cognition, theories of, cognitive styles; conceptual systems theory and leadership; critical thinking; diversity; instructional interventions; intelligence; learning, theories of; learning environments; metacognition; motivation, theories of; personality; problem solving; psychology, types of; psychometrics; research methods; testing and test theory development; trait theory; variables

Further Readings and References

Bruer, J. T. (1988). Brain science, brain fiction. *Educational Leadership, 56*(3), 14–18.

Chall J. S., & Peterson, R. W. (1986). The influence of neuroscience upon educational practice. In S. L. Friedman, K. A. Klivington, & R. W. Peterson (Eds.), *The brain, cognition and education* (pp. 305–314). Orlando, FL: Academic Press.

Wolfe, P., & Brandt, R. (1998). What do we know from brain research? *Educational Leadership, 56*(3), 8–13.

NO CHILD LEFT BEHIND

The No Child Left Behind Act of 2001 (Public Law 107-110), or NCLB, builds upon the 1965 Elementary and Secondary Education Act by adding additional specificity and requirements, particularly in the areas of the standards for accountability systems, including the definitions of annual yearly progress (ATP), expectations for all teachers and paraprofessionals to be highly qualified by 2005 to 2006, and unsafe school choice option.

According to the U.S. Department of Education (USDE), the overall purpose of NCLB is to ensure that all children have the opportunity to obtain a high-quality education and reach proficiency on challenging state academic standards and assessments. The specific goals of the law, as delineated by the Federal Register issued on December 2, 2002, are as follows:

- By 2013–2014, all students will reach high standards, at a minimum attaining proficiency or better in reading/language arts and mathematics.
- All limited-English-proficient students will become proficient in English and reach high academic standards, at a minimum attaining proficiency or better in reading/language arts and mathematics.
- By 2005–2006, all students will be taught by highly qualified teachers.
- All students will be educated in learning environments that are safe, drug free, and conducive to learning.
- All students will graduate from high school.
- States will identify and submit these performance targets to the USDE.

KEY ELEMENTS OF NCLB

NCLB embodies four key principles: stronger accountability for results; greater flexibility for states, school districts, and schools in the use of federal funds; more choices for parents of children from disadvantaged backgrounds; and an emphasis on teaching methods that have been demonstrated to work.

The act also places an increased emphasis on reading, especially for young children; enhancing the quality of our teachers; and ensuring that all children in American schools learn English. In keeping with these principles, NCLB affects virtually every program authorized under the Elementary and Secondary Education Act, ranging from Title I and efforts to improve teacher quality to initiatives for limited-English-proficient (LEP) students and safe and drug-free schools.

ACCOUNTABILITY AND ASSESSMENT

Accountability for school improvement is a central theme of federal and state policies. NCLB sets demanding accountability standards for schools, school districts, and states, including new state testing requirements designed to improve education. For example, the law requires that states develop both content standards in reading and mathematics and tests that are linked to the standards for Grades 3 through 8, with science standards and assessment to follow. States must identify adequate yearly progress (AYP) objectives and disaggregate test results for all students and subgroups of students based on socioeconomic status, race/ethnicity, English language proficiency, and disability. Moreover, the law mandates that 100% of students must score at the proficient level on state tests by 2014. Furthermore, NCLB requires states to participate every other year in the National Assessment of Educational Progress (NAEP) in reading and mathematics.

NCLB requires the state to implement a single accountability system to ensure that all students make adequate yearly progress toward meeting the state's student academic achievement standards. Adequate yearly progress (AYP) must include the following components:

- A timeline for making AYP that ensures that all students in all student groups will meet or exceed the state's proficient level of achievement no later than 2013–2014
- Separate starting points based on 2001–2002 data in reading/language arts and mathematics for measuring the percentage of students meeting or exceeding the state's proficient level of academic achievement
- Intermediate goals that increase in equal increments over the period covered by the timeline, with the first incremental increase to take effect not later than the 2004–2005 school year.
- Annual measurable objectives that identify a minimum percentage of students that must meet or exceed the proficient level of academic achievement

and ensure that all students meet or exceed this level within the established timeline.
- Other academic indicators, one of which must be graduation rate for public high schools and at least one academic indicator for elementary schools and at least one academic indicator for middle schools. These may include, but are not limited to:
  o grade-to-grade retention rates
  o attendance rates
  o percentage of students completing gifted and talented, advanced placement, and college preparatory courses

NCLB requires that economically disadvantaged students, major racial and ethnic groups, students with disabilities, and students with limited English proficiency be included as student groups for determining AYP for schools, school districts, and the state. NCLB requires 95% of each student group participate in the state's academic assessment in order for a school, school district, or the state to make AYP.

Highly Qualified Teachers

NCLB defines "highly qualified" (HQ) differently based upon whether a teacher is a new teacher or an existing teacher, and the criteria also are different for elementary and secondary teachers. The definition of "new" is still undecided in terms of the date when this fully goes into effect. The first step for determining if a teacher is HQ begins with establishing whether the teacher has met all three of the following criteria.

Step I: ALL Teachers

- Bachelor's degree (or higher)
- Full state certification
- Demonstrated competency in assigned teaching field

States must develop a uniform state standard evaluation (USSE)

Step II: Elementary Teachers

New	Existing
Pass the appropriate USSE	Pass the appropriate USSE

New secondary teachers meet the third standard in Step 1 through passing the appropriate USSE or demonstrating competency by having an academic major, graduate degree, or coursework equivalent to an undergraduate major in the subject area taught.

For existing secondary teachers, competency may be demonstrated by passing the appropriate USSE or by having an academic major, a graduate degree, or coursework equivalent to an undergraduate major in the subject area taught.

Step II: Secondary Teachers

New	Existing
Pass the appropriate USSE OR hold an academic major, a graduate degree, or coursework equivalent to an undergraduate major in the courses taught	Pass the appropriate USSE OR hold an academic major, a graduate degree, or coursework equivalent to an undergraduate major in the courses taught

States are in the process of developing a USSE that can be used to assist existing teachers in demonstrating competency. The USDE has guidelines for the development of this evaluation, yet this evaluation does not require approval from the federal government. Currently, a variety of models for USSE are being discussed. One model being considered combines years of experience, professional development hours, coursework in the content area or a related area, and scores on the appraisal system to create a formula that would enable teachers to demonstrate competency (see Figure 1).

This flowchart has been developed to demonstrate the requirements for meeting the provisions of NCLB and the standards to be considered highly qualified.

All teachers must demonstrate competence in every subject area they teach. It is anticipated that once a teacher meets all the standards to be considered HQ, then he or she would not have to again demonstrate competence unless the teaching assignment were to change.

Highly Qualified Paraprofessionals

NCLB requires that paraprofessionals hired after January 8, 2002, and working in a program supported by Title I, Part A funds, must have a high school diploma or a General Educational Development (GED) high school equivalency certificate, and meet one of the following qualifications:

- Completed at least 2 years of study at an institution of higher education
- Obtained an associate's (or higher) degree
- Met a rigorous standard of quality and can demonstrate through a formal state and local academic assessment
  - knowledge of and the ability to assist in instructing reading, writing, and mathematics
  - knowledge of and the ability to assist in instructing reading readiness, writing readiness, and mathematics readiness, as appropriate

Existing paraprofessionals hired before January 8, 2002, and working in a Title I, Part A program, must meet one of the three alternatives listed above for qualifying new paraprofessionals by January 8, 2006 (see Figure 2). This flowchart has been developed to demonstrate the requirements for meeting provisions of NCLB and the standards to be considered highly qualified.

The qualification requirements for new and existing paraprofessionals do not apply to those whose primary responsibility is to serve as a translator or whose duties consist solely of conducting parental involvement activities in Title I, Part A programs. Preliminary guidance from the USDE indicates that these requirements apply on a Title I, Part A schoolwide campus to any paraprofessional who is providing instruction.

There has been some discussion at the state level about creating a statewide assessment that could be used to assist paraprofessionals in meeting the requirements of NCLB. Local school districts may create their own academic assessments to document a paraprofessional's knowledge and ability as described in the statute.

UNSAFE SCHOOL CHOICE OPTIONS

Another key component of NCLB is the unsafe school choice option, "persistently dangerous school." According to NCLB, if a school is identified as "persistently dangerous," the local education agency must (a) notify parents, (b) offer students the opportunity to transfer to another school, and (c) develop a corrective action plan. Schools that do not make progress in making their environments safe for all students will be identified and held to increasingly more rigorous sanctions designed to bring about meaningful changes. Finally, the law mandates the fundamental

Highly Qualified

Bachelor's Degree

All teachers must
be "Highly Qualified"
by the end of School
Year 2005–2006

Full State Certification

Title I, Part A
teachers must be
"Highly Qualified"
when hired

Demonstrates Subject Competency

Elementary

Secondary

New

Existing

New

Existing

Pass
ExCET or TExES

Pass
ExCET or TExES

Pass
ExCET or TExES

Pass
ExCET or TExES

OR

OR

OR

Meet USSE

Meet USSE

For Academic Subject Taught:
• Academic Major, OR
• Graduate Degree, OR
• Coursework Equivalent to
  an undergraduate major

OR

For Academic Subject Taught:
• Academic Major, OR
• Graduate Degree, OR
• Coursework Equivalent to
  an undergraduate major

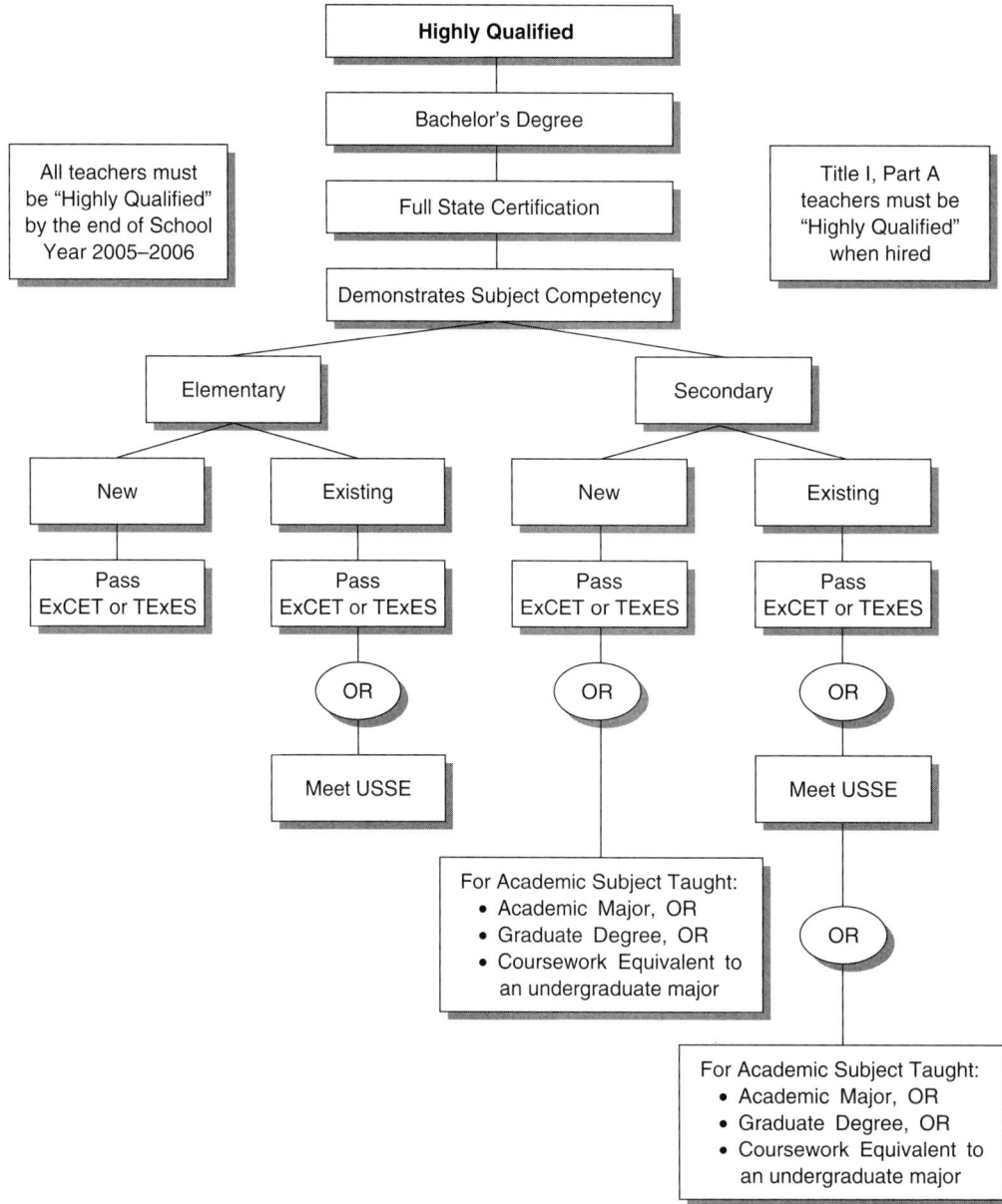

Figure 1   NCLB Highly Qualified Teachers

SOURCE: No Child Left Behind Act of 2001 (www.ed.gov/offices/OESE.esca/).

restructuring of any school that fails to improve its environment over an extended period of time.

—*Fred C. Lunenburg*

See also accountability; at-risk students; behaviorism; Black education; critical race theory; Department of Education; economics, theories of; equality, in schools; equity and adequacy of funding schools; forecasting; governance; Latinos; migrant students; minorities, in schools; National Assessment of Educational Progress; needs assessment; productivity; promotion, social; rational organizational theory; resiliency; school improvement models; standardized testing; state departments of education; systemic reform; time-on-task; underachievers, in schools; value-added indicators; values of organizations and leadership; vulnerability thesis, of superintendents

Further Readings and References

Johnson, R., & Bush, L. (2005). Leading the school through culturally responsive inquiry. In F. English (Ed.), *The*

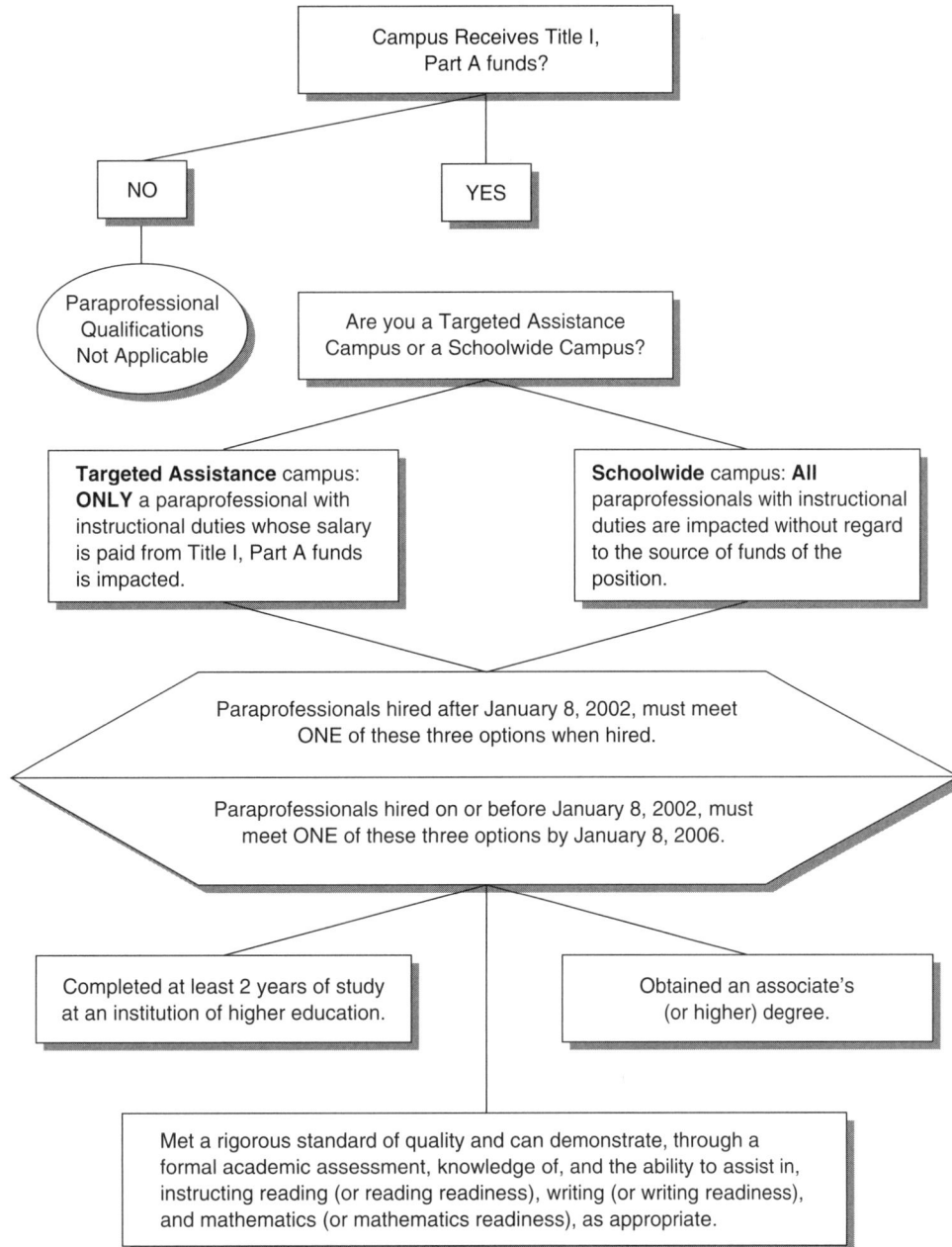

Figure 2　Title I, Part A, Paraprofessionals Who Have Instructional Duties

SOURCE: No Child Left Behind Act of 2001 (www.ed.gov/offices/OESE.esca/).

SAGE handbook of educational leadership (pp. 269–296). Thousand Oaks, CA: Sage.

No Child Left Behind Act of 2001. (n.d.). Retrieved September 6, 2005, from www.ed.gov/offices/OESE.esca/

Ogawa, R. (2005). Leadership as social construct. In F. English (Ed.), *The SAGE handbook of educational leadership* (pp. 89–108). Thousand Oaks, CA: Sage.

🏛 NOMOTHETIC/ IDIOGRAPHIC DIMENSIONS

The school can be viewed as a social system. A social system refers to activities and interactions of group members brought together for a common purpose.

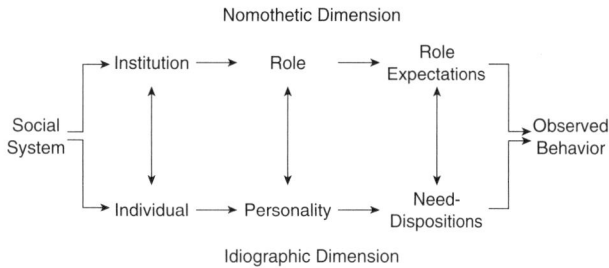

Figure 1   Nomothetic/Idiographic Model

SOURCE: Getzels, J. W., & Guba, E. G. (1957). Social behavior and the administrative process. *School Review, 65,* 423–441. Reprinted with permission.

Thus, a school district, a school, and a classroom can all be viewed as social systems. A useful framework for understanding the administrative process within social systems is the Getzels-Guba nomothetic/idiographic dimensions model (see Figure 1).

As shown in Figure 1, Jacob Getzels and Egon Guba conceive of the social system as involving two dimensions that are independent and interactive. First are institutions with certain roles and expectations that will fulfill the goals of the system. Second are individuals with certain personalities and need dispositions inhabiting the system whose interactions comprise observed behavior. Thus, observed behavior can be understood as a function of these major elements: (a) institution, role, and expectations, which together constitute the *nomothetic,* or normative, dimension of activity in a social system, and (b) individual, personality, and need dispositions, which together constitute the *idiographic,* or personal, dimension of activity in a social system.

Translated into the school setting, this means that an organization is designed to serve one of society's needs to educate. In this organization, there are positions, or roles, such as the roles of the student, teacher, principal, superintendent, and the like. For each individual who occupies a given role, there are role expectations. Role expectations represent not only the duties and actions expected from each role player but also the expectations concerning the quality of performance. The various roles and role expectations constitute the nomothetic dimension of the social system.

The idiographic dimension includes individuals who occupy the roles and their personal needs. Schools as social systems must be "peopled," and all kinds of individuals who have their own idiosyncrasies "people" them. Thus, individuals chosen to occupy

roles are different from one another in action and reaction, and we can analyze these differences in terms of personality. Personality is determined in part by needs, which predispose a person to behave in a certain way in a given situation. In other words, the individual who occupies a given role has needs he or she tries to fulfill. These are personalized needs and may not be associated with the needs of the school system.

Behavior can be stated in the form of the equation:

$$B = f(R \times P)$$

where B is observed behavior, f is function, R is a given institutional role defined by the expectations attached to it, and P is the personality of the role player defined by his or her need dispositions. The proportion of role and personality factors determining behavior varies with the specific role and the specific personality involved.

It is presumed in the military that behavior is influenced more by role than by personality, whereas with the freelance artist, behavior is influenced more by personality than by role. Many other examples can illustrate this variation in the influence exerted by role or personality on behavior. In educational organizations, we could hypothesize that the proportion of role and personality might be balanced somewhere between the two. But different educational systems are characterized by different proportions of role and personality.

EXPANDED MODEL: CULTURAL DIMENSIONS

The developers of this model early recognized its oversimplification. In focusing on the sociological dimension with "role" as the central concept and on the psychological dimension with "personality" as the central concept, other dimensions had been omitted, thus giving the model a closed systems orientation. To overcome the deficiency, the basic model was expanded to describe the classroom as a unique social system. According to these social systems theorists, the sociological aspects of an institution are mediated by cultural factors—the ethos, mores, and values—in which the institution is embedded. The expectations of the roles must, it seems, be somehow related to the ethos or cultural values. Similarly, the individual's personality functions in a biological organism with certain potentialities and abilities, with the need dispositions of the personality mediated in some way by these constitutional conditions.

The model was applied to school administrators. A second cultural dimension was added to interact with the psychological aspects of the individual. The composite model of the school as a social system depicts educational administration as a social process. The bottom line in their model indicates that the culture, ethos, and values held by individuals in schools and school systems explain much social behavior. The model also clearly indicates that any social system (classroom, school, or school district) must operate within a larger environment. The addition of these dimensions gives Getzels's composite model a more open systems orientation.

SOME DERIVATIONS

Getzels's models suggest three sources of potential conflicts: role conflicts, personality conflicts, and role-personality conflicts. *Role conflicts* refer to situations where a role player is required to conform simultaneously to expectations that are contradictory or inconsistent. Adjustment to one set of expectations makes adjustment to the other difficult or impossible. For example, a teacher may attempt to be a devoted mother and simultaneously a successful career woman. A university professor may be expected by her department head to emphasize teaching and service to students and the community, respectively, while the academic dean expects her to emphasize research and publication. Role conflicts represent incongruencies in the nomothetic dimension.

Personality conflicts occur as a result of opposing need dispositions within the personality of the individual role players. For example, a teacher may be expected, as a social norm, to maintain adequate social distance between herself and the students. However, she may feel the need for more extensive interactions. Personality conflicts represent incongruencies in the idiographic dimension of the social systems model.

Role-personality conflicts occur as a result of discrepancies between the institution's role expectations and the individual's need dispositions. For example, suppose an introverted personality type school administrator were placed in the role of superintendent in a small- to medium-sized school district. The board of education makes clear its expectation that the newly appointed administrator maintain high visibility and extensive contact with the community. The superintendent, however, has a high need for privacy and anonymity. The superintendent in this school district would experience a role-personality conflict. Role-personality conflicts represent incongruencies between the nomothetic and the idiographic dimensions of the social systems model. These are symptomatic of administrative failure and lead to a loss in individual and institutional productivity.

Furthermore, the model suggests three leader-followership styles: normative (nomothetic), personal (idiographic), and transactional. The *normative style* emphasizes the fulfillment of institutional role requirements and obligations rather than the personal needs of individuals. Role definition, authority vested in roles, and organizational goal achievement are stressed. The *personal style* emphasizes the personal activities and propensities of individuals. Minimum role definition, a diffusion of authority, and efforts to maximize each individual's meaningful contribution to the organization are stressed. The *transactional style* represents a balance of emphasis on the performance of the role requirements of the organization and the expression of personal needs of individuals. The school administrator moves alternately toward the normative style or the personal style depending on the situation.

GETZELS'S LATEST MODEL: COMMUNITIES DIMENSION

In the late 1970s, Getzels expanded his social systems model still further by including a communities dimension. Here, much more is manifested about the cultural setting of the school as a social system and extends its usefulness as an open systems model. He identifies six communities as groups of people conscious of a collective identity through common cognitive and affective norms, values, and patterns of social relationships. He defines each type of community as follows:

- *Local community* is established in a particular neighborhood or region. Examples include a local neighborhood or school community.
- *Administrative community* is established in a specific, politically determined identity. A country, a city, or a school district are examples.
- *Social community* is established in a particular set of interpersonal relationships not restrained by local or administrative boundaries. An example would be all the people in one's community of friends.

- *Instrumental community* is established through direct or indirect activities and interactions with others who are brought together for a common purpose. Examples include a professional group, such as teachers or professors who make up an educational community, a teacher's union, or a philanthropic community.
- *Ethnic community* is established through affinity with a particular national, racial, or socioeconomic group. Italian, Black, or upper-class communities are examples.
- *Ideological community* is established in a particular historic, conceptual, or sociopolitical community that stretches across the local, administrative, social, instrumental, and ethnic communities. Examples include Christian, scholarly, or communist communities.

The revised and latest models make much more explicit the cultural setting of the school as a social system. The concept of culture, long the mainstay of anthropology since its beginnings, is not new. Recently, the concept or organizational culture has enjoyed tremendous appeal in both the popular and professional management literature.

The Getzels models of the school as a social system are widely treated in introductory textbooks in educational administration, textbooks that deal specifically with the school principalship, textbooks on supervision, and references on organizational behavior and theory in educational administration. In addition, the *Handbook of Research on Educational Administration,* a project of the American Educational Research Association, devotes an entire chapter to Getzels's models in education administration.

—*Fred C. Lunenburg*

See also conceptual systems theory and leadership; feedback; field theory; frame theory; functionalist theory; hierarchy, in organizations; infrastructure, of organizations; management theories; networking and network theory; organizational theories; peer interaction/friendships; quantitative research methods; role ambiguity; role conflict; role theory; social relations, dimensions of; systems theory/thinking; theory movement, in educational administration; values of organizations and leadership

Further Readings and References

Homans, G. C. (1950). *The human group.* New York: Harcourt, Brace, & World.

Getzels, J. W. (1958). Administration as a social process. In A. W. Halphin (Ed.), *Administrative theory in education* (pp. 150–165). New York: Macmillan.

Getzels, J. W. (1978). The communities of education. *Teachers College Record, 79,* 659–682.

Getzels, J. W., & Guba, E. G. (1957). Social behavior and the administrative process. *School Review, 65,* 423–441.

Getzels, J. W., Lipham, J. M., & Campbell, R. F. (1968). *Administration as a social process.* New York: Harper & Row.

Getzels, J. W., & Thelen, H. A. (1960). The classroom as a social system. In N. B. Henry (Ed.), *The dynamics of instructional groups* (pp. 53–83). Chicago: University of Chicago Press.

Lipham, J. M. (1988). Getzels's models in educational administration. In N. J. Boyan (Ed.), *Handbook of research on educational administration* (pp. 171–184). New York: Longman.

NORMAL SCHOOLS

Horace Mann founded the first public normal school in 1839 in Lexington, Massachusetts, and many states quickly followed his example. Normal schools were founded to increase the quality of teaching because an educated citizenry was essential to the new republic. The need for teachers grew rapidly with the common school movement; by 1875, over 100 normal schools enrolled more than 23,000 students, and by 1900 over 300 normal schools enrolled 70,000 students. The majority of students were women. Initially, the normal school education was relatively brief, lasting 1 year, although many students left after a few weeks to take teaching positions. Each region of the country embraced the normal school mission; however, the organization, requirements, curriculum, and administration of normal schools varied by region, state, and school. As normal schools grew in size and stature, they began to focus less on teacher training and more on academic preparation, while lengthening the required course of study. As the schools' curricula diversified and programs became prolonged, they began to evolve into state teachers colleges after 1900. This evolution quickened throughout the 1920s and 1930s, creating the obsolescence of normal schools by 1940.

Three women enrolled in the first normal school in 1839, and women were an overwhelming majority of normal school students throughout the schools' existence, because the majority of teachers were women. By 1900, more than half of all women pursuing post-secondary education did so at normal schools. One reason for the popularity of normal schools was free tuition in many states, sometimes offered in exchange for teaching in common schools after graduation. Women from farm and other working-class families, as well as immigrants, were drawn to normal schools, because they were vehicles of upward mobility and because women were encouraged to teach after finishing common school and before marrying.

Originally, normal schools emphasized basic academic knowledge, pedagogy, management of schools, and practical experience in model schools. Normal schools ran these model schools to give teacher candidates opportunities to apply their skills. Administration of normal schools varied; they were organized, funded, and operated from the state, county, and city level. Faculty and administrators were often university-educated former teachers and principals.

In the eastern normal schools, admission requirements and the program length gradually increased; by 1860, 2-year programs were common, and by 1900, a high school diploma began to be required for admission. Both of these changes encouraged a growing focus on academic preparation at the expense of teacher training. In western states, the focus on teacher training quickly began to shift to academic preparation because of the lack of postsecondary educational institutions and local pressure to expand educational opportunities.

The growing emphasis on academic preparation in normal schools and local desire for more diversified curricular offerings resulted in the evolution of normal schools into state teachers colleges. Following World War I, as the number of college students grew, normal schools declined, replaced by the public 4-year city and state college systems. By 1940, normal schools were obsolete.

—*Mary Beth Walpole*

See also discrimination; gender studies, in educational leadership; Haley, Margaret; schools of education; sexism (glass ceiling); unions, of teachers; women in educational leadership; Young, Ella Flagg

Further Readings and References

Altenbaugh, R. J., & Underwood, K. (1990). The evolution of normal schools. In J. I. Goodlad, R. Soder, & K. A. Sirotnik (Eds.), *Places where teachers are taught.* San Francisco: Jossey-Bass.
Blount, J. M. (2005). *Fit to teach: Same-sex desire, gender, and school work in the twentieth century.* Albany: SUNY Press.
Harper, C. A. (1939). *A century of public teacher education.* Washington, DC: National Education Association of the United States.

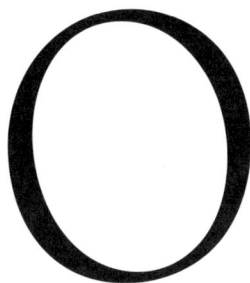

O

⛫ OBJECTIVITY

Objectivity is the idea that there is "out there" a reality apart from the human mind capable of perceiving it. Objectivity thus assumes a real truth, and it also assumes that seekers of that truth must adopt a posture of detachment, not letting their own values intrude in the quest. Being objective is seen as the only way to discover how things *really* are and how things *really* work. Researchers keep their own values and expectations out of the quest both by determining to do so and by adhering to methods of investigation that prevent human contamination of the findings. Objectivity plays out in research in the belief that stating the theory to be tested and gathering evidence to test it must be separate and independent processes. In this view, a subjective theory will be tested against facts that have been gathered and analyzed according to methods that are not subjective.

In school administration, objectivity characterized the "theory movement" or the "behavioral science era" that ran from the mid-1940s to the mid-1980s. In this era, scholars hoped to apply the methods of the social sciences to the study of school administration. They hoped thereby to do away with prescriptions for administration based on folklore and anecdotes from administrators' experiences and replace them with scientific certainty based on studies done by theorists and researchers. Current discussions of best practices for preparing administrators have connotations of objectivity, as do invocations of the need to improve administrator decision making, since these discussions imply that there are decisions that are better than others by some objective standard.

One attack on the notion of objective inquiry comes from those who point out that all observation is theory laden. That is, nobody merely gathers and analyzes facts without bringing theory and perspective to the task. For example, the radiologist attends to different aspects of an X-ray than the layperson whose vision is equally acute, precisely because of being guided by theory. In fact, a radiologist who sees something very unexpected in an X-ray may decide that the X-ray is flawed, so that theory is used to test the validity of evidence instead of evidence being used to test the validity of the theory. Related to this is a second attack from Yvonna S. Lincoln and Egon G. Guba, who wrote in 2000 that even adhering to specific methods of inquiry requires numerous subjective judgment calls and following of values: for example, choice of a problem to study, choice of theoretical framework, choice of how to operationalize variables, choice of data-gathering and analytic methods. A third attack on objectivity particularly as applied to human enterprises like educational administration is that there is no objective organizational reality for human beings, that our view of our organization is largely a matter of our own interpretation: One member's inspiring leader is another's demagogue; one worker's morale-building session is another's manipulative pep rally; a system of rewards that one person finds clarifying and helpful seems stifling to another. Finally, a fourth attack argues that administration is inseparable from valuing, that it is inherently linked to meeting goals and that goals arise from value systems. Thus, removing questions of value from the inquiry is not only fruitless but also inappropriate.

On the other hand, the enterprise of science, a human activity that has been extraordinarily successful at solving problems, presents itself as different from artistic creativity, different from religious faith, and different from political ideology; in fact as somehow attending to evidence more *objectively* than those enterprises. If education in general and educational administration in particular is to benefit from the insights and approaches of science, how should it proceed? There are two approaches: cultivating certain habits of mind in individual researchers and cultivating certain norms in the community. Though these habits and norms are not expected to make the education researcher perfectly objective, the Committee on Scientific Principles in Education Research (CSPER) argued in 2002 that they should yield better knowledge of education. The habit of mind of the individual researcher is to strive for freedom from personal or cultural bias or partiality and to work consciously to report findings independent of the meaning they have for him or her.

Critics of objectivity have raised strong arguments about the extent to which anyone can maintain such a stance, arguing that one cannot step outside oneself. But those who believe that science still has credibility lacking in other approaches to human problem solving offer community norms as an alternative or at least a supplement to habits of mind. Community norms begin with a culture of inquiry, constructive critique, and willingness to engage intellectually with other perspectives. The notion of community norms substitutes intersubjectivity for objectivity, that is, it emphasizes not whether the individual researcher is objective, nor the method by which a study is conducted, but how much merit a community of trained colleagues finds in an interpretation. Thus, the merit of operationalizing variables, for example, is not that this gives researchers an unbiased view of reality but that it opens their research to public scrutiny and debate about the merits of their choices. The CSPER recommended in 2002 six important community norms: (1) investigating claims that are testable or refutable by means of evidence, (2) linking investigations to an overarching theory or conceptual framework, (3) using multiple methods to investigate various aspects of the topic, (4) providing logical reasoning connecting evidence to theory that is coherent, shareable, and persuasive to the skeptical reader, (5) checking and validating findings from individual studies to see if they apply to broader populations and/or settings, and (6) persuading a group of researchers to bring the current state of the art to bear on judging the merits of a study's findings.

—*Gary Ivory*

See also constructivism; empiricism; operational definitions; Popper, Karl; positivism, postpositivism; qualitative research, history, theories, issues; quantitative research methods; research methods; subjectivism, in theory; theory movement, in educational administration; variables

Further Readings and References

Committee on Scientific Principles for Education Research. (2002). *Scientific research in education.* Washington, DC: National Academy Press.

Hoy, W. K. (1996). Science and theory in the practice of educational administration: A pragmatic perspective. *Educational Administration Quarterly, 32,* 366–378.

Lincoln, Y. S., & Guba, E. G. (2000). Paradigmatic controversies, contradictions, and emerging confluences. In N. K. Denzin & Y. S. Lincoln (Eds.), *Handbook of qualitative research* (2nd ed., pp. 163–188). Thousand Oaks, CA: Sage.

Quine, W. V. O. (1995). *From stimulus to science.* Cambridge, MA: Harvard University Press.

OFFICE OF ECONOMIC OPPORTUNITY

Part of President Lyndon Johnson's War on Poverty, the Office of Economic Opportunity (OEO) was created by the Economic Opportunity Act of 1964 (EOA). A controversial umbrella program that administered many antipoverty programs, including education programs, the OEO was abolished in 1974 during the administration of President Gerald Ford; however, many of its programs continue to serve persons with low incomes.

The EOA created and funded community action agencies (CAAs), which administered OEO programs at the local level. CAAs were required to include residents with low incomes in planning and administration of OEO programs. OEO-administered education-related programs included the Job Corps, Head Start, Adult Basic Education, and VISTA (Volunteers in Service to America). Other OEO programs included funding for senior centers, congregate meal sites, family planning, and civil legal aid for persons with low incomes.

The first director of the OEO was Sargent Shriver, who served from 1964 to 1969. The OEO's antipoverty work earned it many enemies, including California Governor Ronald Reagan, who objected to OEO-funded advocacy on behalf of migrant farm workers. The OEO also earned enemies among urban politicians who resented increased federal influence in traditionally local antipoverty programs. The Vietnam War also diverted money and attention from the OEO's work.

During the administration of President Richard Nixon, who promised during the 1968 campaign to limit the OEO's authority, several OEO programs were transferred to other agencies, such as the Department of Health, Education and Welfare. Later in his administration, President Nixon sought to eliminate funding for CAAs and other OEO programs, resulting in litigation forcing the administration to spend money Congress had appropriated.

The Community Services Administration (CSA) replaced the OEO in 1974. In 1981, during the first year of President Reagan's administration, the EOA was repealed, replaced by a system of block grants, and the CSA was dissolved. The OEO's legacy continues, however. CAAs continue to provide assistance and advocacy to persons with low incomes, and many OEO programs, such as Head Start, the Job Corps, and legal aid, are still in existence. Furthermore, many prominent political leaders served in the OEO. Donald Rumsfeld, defense secretary under President George W. Bush, was the first director of the OEO under President Nixon. Other OEO alumni include Vice President Dick Cheney, Bill Bradley, former U.S. senator from New Jersey, Frank Carlucci, defense secretary under President Reagan, Christine Todd Whitman, former governor of New Jersey, and U.S. representative Jim Leach of Iowa.

—*Thomas A. Mayes*

See also achievement gap, of students; affirmative action; at-risk students; Black education; children and families in America; civil rights movement; communities, types, building of; compensatory education; cultural capital; desegregation, of schools; discrimination; diversity; economics, theories of; empowerment; multiculturalism; politics, of education

Further Readings and References

Andrew, J. A. (1998). *Lyndon Johnson and the great society.* Chicago: Ivan R. Dee.

Mann, J. (2003, November). Young Rumsfeld. *Atlantic Monthly*, 89–101.

🏛 OPEN SYSTEMS THEORY

Open systems theory refers to the concept that organizations are strongly influenced by their environment. The environment consists of other organizations that exert various forces of an economic, political, or social nature. The environment also provides key resources that sustain the organization and lead to change and survival. Open systems theory was developed after World War II in reaction to earlier theories of organizations, such as the human relations perspective of Elton Mayo and the administrative theories of Henri Fayol, which treated the organization largely as a self-contained entity.

Virtually all modern theories of organization utilize the open systems perspective. As a result, open systems theories come in many flavors. For example, contingency theorists argue that organizations are organized in ways that best fit the environment in which they are embedded. Institutional theorists see organizations as a means by which the societal values and beliefs are embedded in organizational structure and expressed in organizational change. Resource dependency theorists see the organization as adapting to the environment as dictated by its resource providers. Although there is a great variety in the perspectives provided by open systems theories, they share the perspective that an organization's survival is dependent upon its relationship with the environment.

Open systems theory has profoundly altered how we understand schools as organizations and the demands placed upon educational leaders. Treating schools as if they are independent of their environment would lead to wide misperceptions of the driving factors behind organizational change. Contemporary studies of accountability movements, teacher professionalization, and instructional leadership all benefit from a strongly open systems approach to understanding environmental demands and the resulting adaptation in school policy and its implementation, or lack thereof. Indeed, today scholars are rightfully dubious of work that fails to consider the rich context in which schools develop.

—*Michael N. Bastedo*

See also adaptiveness of organizations; bureaucracy; chaos theory; collaboration theory; conceptual systems theory and leadership; contingency theories; organizational theories; organizations, types of, typologies; rational organizational theory

Further Readings and References

McLaughlin, M. W., & Talbert, J. E. (2001). *Schoolteaching in context.* Chicago: University of Chicago Press.

Pfeffer, J., & Salancik, G. R. (2003). *The external control of organizations: A resource dependence perspective.* Stanford, CA: Stanford University Press. (Original work published 1978)

Scott, W. R. (2002). *Organizations: Rational, natural, and open systems.* Upper Saddle River, NJ: Prentice Hall.

OPEN-DOOR POLICY

An open-door policy permits open access and communication to take place from the bottom of the organization to its top. Communication between supervisor and subordinate receives increased attention. It implies that the supervisors are reachable and that organizational structures and policy have made it possible for each worker to reach them. In hierarchical organizations, access was only to the immediate supervisor, but open-door policy offers a means of access beyond the immediate overseer.

Open-door policies provide structures for regular updates on whether specific tasks are accomplished or neglected, encourage regular staff meetings, and promote trust as management deals with office politics or other difficult problems. Simply listening is not enough; the supervisor should be willing to consider various options, present a climate of mutual support in trying to achieve the ultimate objective, and promote a cooperative work atmosphere. If action is never taken, the policy is perceived as disingenuous and workers will not make an effort.

A study identifying principal behaviors that contribute to a positive school climate found that having an open-door policy was essential. The principal's communication behaviors that teachers described as supportive were active listening, encouragement, clear expectations, and an open-door policy. Teachers appreciated knowing that they could go to the principal with their concerns. Having access to the principal encouraged informal channels of communication and made the principal available to provide individual professional development.

Research on teacher attrition revealed that one of the most frequently mentioned reasons new teachers leave their school or the profession is the quality of support from the principal. A survey of new teachers identified the most prevalent need as emotional support. These teachers indicated that having an open-door policy was one way the principal provided that support. Job satisfaction was positively affected when the principal was accessible, available, and willing to listen.

Some issues associated with implementing an open-door policy may provoke resentment of administrators who are bypassed when a subordinate skips immediate supervisors and approaches higher-level administration. On the other hand, subordinates may be reluctant to approach the supervisor for fear of looking inadequate. An additional problem with open-door policy is that supervisor accessibility may create conditions for constant staff interruptions and unintentional sabotaging of the supervisor's own work. The issue then is providing a little more structure for communication without creating barriers or diminishing access.

Structures for getting valuable contributions from workers require an open-door environment with easy and reliable methods for input, access, and results. Administrators are more available to subordinates when they are out of their offices, observing the operation of the organization, holding regular weekly meetings, and conducting daily "huddles." Huddles are quick stand-up meetings used for questions, information sharing, and follow-up on urgent issues. Furthermore, it is important to meet often with fellow supervisors to make sure that all are sending consistent messages on key issues and policies.

—Bobbie J. Greenlee

See also administration, theories of; chain of command; chief academic officer; communications, theories of, in organizations; consideration, caring; esprit (school climate); ethos, of organizations; feedback; leadership, distributed; leadership, theories of; leadership effectiveness; morale; motivation, theories of; networking and network theory; rational organizational theory

Further Readings and References

Lunenberg, F. C., & Ornstein, A. C. (2000). *Educational administration: Concepts and practices* (3rd ed.). Belmont, CA: Wadsworth/Thomson.

Richards, J. (2004). What new teachers value most in principals. *Principal, 83*(3), 42–44.

Sparks, R. (2003). How well is your "open door" policy working? *Creating Quality, 12*, 10. Retrieved July 21, 2004, from http://www.missouribusiness.net/cq/2003/open_door_policy.asp.

OPERATIONAL DEFINITIONS

An operational definition articulates the operations, processes, or actions of a concept that are necessary to identify examples of it. As a starting point, a construct or variable may be defined with a dictionary-type constitutive definition in which the term is defined in relationship to other concepts. From this, more extensive definitions can be generated, including those of the operational, descriptive, programmatic, and normative types. While the notion of operational definitions emerged from the field of physical science, it became clear that operational definitions could enhance inquiry in all fields.

The goal of an operational definition is to provide a framework for the development and selection of instruments to measure a particular concept or variable. For example, creativity might be defined constitutively as a fluent, vivid imagination, which can be used in accomplishing tasks. An operational definition of creativity might be "as measured by how original a picture and how many elaborations an individual can create on a picture completion task." The operational definition presents a concrete description of the operations of which creativity is comprised, thus providing information for selecting or designing an instrument to measure it.

Alternative ways of constructing operational definitions for different types of concepts have been identified, and include those based on the manipulation, the dynamic properties, or the static properties of a concept. For a definition based on manipulation, it is necessary to identify the operations that the researcher must perform to cause the desired phenomena to occur. An example might be the set of procedures to be implemented for establishing online collaboration among a group of students. These might include the presentation of a problem to be solved by the group, guidelines for roles that individuals in the group should assume, and the required task activities. For an operational definition based on the dynamic properties of a concept, which are typically represented by behaviors, the researcher identifies the observable properties of that concept. An operational definition of collaboration might include group behaviors such as asking questions of each other, providing alternative solutions for a problem, and praising the suggestions made by group members. These behaviors are observable, and a tally of their frequency can be made. An operational definition based on static properties of a concept utilizes self-reports of an internal state. For example, an operational definition of self-efficacy might include an individual's sense of ability to master challenges and achieve goals. An instrument that contained items that

embodied the definitions then could be utilized to determine the presence of the state.

A review of educational research textbooks reveals that most contain a section on the importance of defining concepts and their related variables with operational definitions. Proponents of logical positivism espouse the importance of operational definitions and the associated assumption that complex concepts can be reduced to an operator, an operation, and an observation. Operational definitions may be considered an attempt to establish current understandings of concepts that are acceptable to a particular research community. An operational definition helps to tie down the meaning of a term within the context of a specific system. It is considered successful if the understanding and use of the definition is consistent among a specific set of individuals who may be working with the practical meaning of the term. In this regard, it reduces ambiguity about the concept and enhances its communicability. When a concept is described to include the way it is measured, it allows others to be able to measure the same thing in the same way, thus allowing for replication.

Even so, operational definitions are currently a highly contested notion in social science and educational research. Some argue that operationalism has the disadvantage of producing many different definitions of what is purported to be the same thing. Another concern about operational definitions is that when a concept is defined as the way in which it is measured, a definition that is trite is generated and doesn't account for the richness of the theoretical construct. Also, others have noted that when issues of validity and reliability are considered for the instrument used to measure the construct, a conflation between the meaning of the construct and the instrument may result. Ultimately, one is not interested in the specific operationalisms but in the constructs they represent.

Postmodern relativism and skepticism have contributed to the notion that definitions are neither necessary nor possible to articulate. The difficulties inherent in a community where definitions are not considered a rigorous component of the research process are revealed when the literature in various areas is examined. A review of research on the topics of school improvement and educational leadership reveals a literature that might be considered vast and inconsistent. For example, the variation of definitions of educational leadership and some of the issues related to contextualizing those definitions have been discussed. Several studies producing operational measures of school effectiveness have not enabled educators to implement more effective schools. Researchers are at cross-purposes with one another in that there is either a lack of definitions or the type of definition that is used is not clarified by the researcher. In the education arena, there is a strong press for accountability, making it necessary to assess outcomes. This requires generating clear definitions of constructs so that they can be appropriately assessed. Perhaps an answer is to determine the type of definition that is compatible with the research methodology utilized and that best represents the construct that we seek to assess. A programmatic definition may be utilized for evaluation research, a descriptive or narrative definition for qualitative research, and an operational definition for quantitative research that requires assessment that produces a numerical value. There is little doubt that the debate will continue over the role of definitions and in particular of the place of operational definitions in educational research.

—*S. Kim MacGregor*

See also accountability; bureaucracy; leadership, task-oriented; logic, history and use of in educational leadership; management by objectives; management theories; measurement, theories of; performance evaluation systems; PERT (Performance Evaluation and Review Technique); Planning, Programming, Budgeting System; productivity

Further Readings and References

Bickhard, M. H. (2001). The tragedy of operationalism. *Theory and Psychology, 11*(1), 35–44.

Gall, M., Gall, J., & Borg, W. (2003). *Educational research: An introduction* (7th ed.). Boston: Allyn & Bacon.

Grace, R. C. (2001). The pragmatics of operationism: A reply. *Theory and Psychology, 11*(1), 67–74.

Sager, J. C., & L'Homme, M.-C. (1994). A model for the definition of concepts: Rules for analytical definitions in terminological databases. *Terminology, 1*(2), 351–374.

Thomas, J. Y. (2001). *The public school superintendency in the twenty-first century: The quest to define effective leadership* (Report No. 55). Baltimore, MD: Johns Hopkins University. (ERIC Document Reproduction Service No. ED 460219)

ORGANIZATIONAL DESIGN

Broadly defined, an organization consists of two or more people who cooperate with each other to pursue a shared goal, create a product, or perform a service. At the basic level, organizations exist to perform tasks, produce outputs, and/or generate and disseminate information. Educational institutions (e.g., elementary schools, secondary schools, and postsecondary institutions), which are also organizations, exist to perform a variety of functions such as preparing a knowledgeable cadre of individuals to work in a global economy as well as helping citizens live in a democratic society. The degree to which educational leaders utilize organizational design techniques that incorporate research-based information may help educational leaders to systematically plan and strategically coordinate different levels within the educational institution to produce positive outcomes for all stakeholders involved in the American educational enterprise.

An organizational design can be generally defined as a complex plan and set of approaches, strategies, and techniques used to develop human and technological systems, processes, and structures within an organization that interact and collaborate to produce desired objectives. Jay Galbraith, a leading organizational design theorist, noted that organizational design can be viewed as a series of choices made by management, involving five interrelated policy decisions: (1) *strategy,* which is the organization's statement of goals and objectives for existence, (2) *structure,* which refers to the type and functions of the decision-making system in the organization and the outcomes of various decisions regarding the size and complexity in the organization, (3) *processes,* which relates to the implementation of organizational decisions pertaining to how management and development tasks are achieved, (4) *rewards,* which is the organization's systematic attempt to link appropriate standards of performance to relevant incentives and emoluments for achieving stated goals, and (5) *people,* which refers to the guidelines and procedures that dictate acceptable performance standards and operational rules for the individuals who cooperate to complete organizational goals.

Henry Mintzberg, another leading organizational design theorist, also acknowledged that organizational design decisions result in one of five basic organizational configurations: (1) *simple structure,* which refers to an organization that does not have a specified structure of work processes and procedures to guide the production of work outputs or the delivery of services, (2) *machine bureaucracy,* an organization with a formal and detailed system defining relevant and appropriate organizational communications and organizational behaviors that are needed to produce desired organizational goals, (3) *professional bureaucracy,* which can be characterized by organizations such as schools and universities that are based on a series of separate, yet interrelated, departments, structures, and work processes partitioned in distinct units managed by persons with professional expertise based on similar educational credentials and/or relevant experiences, (4) *divisionalized form,* which is based on the idea that certain units or departments should be managed, grouped, and organized on the basis of a shared output goal, and (5) *adhocracy,* which refers to an organization that can successfully incorporate the ideas, inputs, and inventions of several individuals into an integrated unit designed to solve new problems and create innovations for a variety of processes, products, and procedures.

Utilizing the work of Galbraith and Mintzberg as well as other organizational design scholars, the concept of organizational design can be best understood by focusing on the issues and concerns that all organizations must consider as they design or restructure their organization: (a) mission statement, (b) division of labor, (c) hierarchy of authority, (d) integration, and (e) regulation. The degree to which each of these factors is understood and linked to the other through a purposeful articulation of techniques, individuals, and resources may determine the success or failure of an organization.

An organization's mission statement is the document that specifies the plans, goals, and objectives of the organization. Thus, an organization's mission statement outlines the values of the organization as well as directs the organization's operations while focusing on the purposes of the organization and its intended outcomes. In light of the importance of the mission statement, this document should be examined on a consistent basis to ensure that relevant and intended goals are being pursued and achieved. Also, research should be conducted at the organizational level to provide evidence on the extent to which shared goals are being achieved and processes are performing optimally.

When designing or redesigning an organization, it is also important to consider the most effective way to assign people to various tasks based on their expertise and interests. This organizational design task usually involves separating various job functions among different people within the organization who are trained to perform those functions. If tasks, individuals, and responsibilities are divided into smaller units or departments by level of expertise, organizations are more likely to experience greater levels of effectiveness and

productivity, provided that the division of labor decision stems from and supports the overall mission, values, and goals of the organization. Another design element, which also pertains to the most effective way to divide the labor among individuals within an organization, involves determining how the levels of management will be structured. This set of complex issues requires organizational designers to contemplate and resolve such issues as how many individuals should one person supervise, whether the organization will have a centralized or decentralized decision-making system, and the nature, type, and degree of employee empowerment within the organization. For example, in educational institutions, authority is usually given to a senior-level administrator who has extensive knowledge of the typical issues encountered in the unit or department and is therefore responsible for coordinating the work to be performed by members of a team, committee, or group of faculty members within a department or division. Statutory requirements as well as certification and accreditation requirements by various regulatory agencies also help to inform the management configuration in educational institutions.

Integration involves creating systems and procedures that consist of many levels and conditions to produce a product, perform a service, and/or accomplish the goals of the organization. In educational institutions, this organizational design issue involves creating linkages between units and departments that interact with students, parents, school personnel, and other groups in the external environment to produce a variety of outcomes for students, the educational institution, as well as society. Regulation, another important organizational design concept, involves developing systems to ensure that the entire organization is working toward the purposes, goals, and objectives as stated in the mission statement. Thus, in organizational design terms, it involves the creation of assessment procedures, promotion and reward systems, as well as professional development initiatives that work in concert to support the aims of the organization.

—Lamont A. Flowers

See also accountability; administration, theories of; boundaries of systems; chain of command; conceptual systems theory and leadership; conflict management; decentralization/centralization controversy; frame theory; governance; infrastructure, of organizations; leadership, distributed; management theories; organizational theories; organizations, types of, typologies; role theory; table of organization

Further Readings and References

Clark, P. (1975). Organizational design: A review of key problems. *Administration & Society, 7,* 213–256.

Galbraith, J. R. (1977). *Organization design.* Reading, MA: Addison-Wesley.

Galbraith, J. R. (2002). *Designing organizations: An executive guide to strategy, structure, and process.* San Francisco: Jossey-Bass.

Mintzberg, H. (1983). *Structure in fives: Designing effective organizations.* Englewood Cliffs, NJ: Prentice Hall.

Perrow, C. (1986). *Complex organizations: A critical essay* (3rd ed.). New York: McGraw-Hill.

🏛 ORGANIZATIONAL MEMORY

Despite the fact that memory or remembering remains a core component of organizational learning theory, the understanding of the concept is limited. Organizational memory is generally agreed to consist of both mental (i.e., data, information, and knowledge) and structural artifacts (i.e., roles, architectures, and operating procedures) within an organization. Furthermore, organizational memory is considered important in that it allows organizations to draw upon events from the past to influence present decision-making structures. Focus on the organization's ability to learn and subsequently remember what it has learned suggests the ability for organizations to transcend the fragile limitations of individual knowledge structures.

This conception suggests three constraints in the consideration of organizational memory: the locus of organizational information acquisition, the processes by which information is acquired, stored, and retrieved, and the utility of memory to organizational outcomes and performance.

ACQUISITION

Information about problems encountered, solutions identified, and decisions determined forms the core of any organization's memory. Several types of information are acquired within this process of development. First, a stimulus must be apparent. The identification of the stimulus might be considered a "felt difficulty," a "problem," or an "ecological change." In any episode, the origin of the stimulus is an important aspect of the memory dilemma. Without adequate identification of the stimulus, future efforts to replicate the learning cycle are thwarted as similar issues may well be ignored. Second, the organization's response, including

data collected, information gathered, and knowledge gained, concerning the stimuli must also be identified. Third, the outcomes of the responses must be examined and explored for future use and potential application across the organizational setting.

RETENTION

For memory to be useful to an organization, it must be retained. For the memory to be truly organizational, it must be stored in a variety of locations within the organizational structure. Such knowledge may be stored as "brains or paper"—that is, either within individuals and organizational cultural patterns, values, and beliefs or within the technologies of an organization's written policies, files, and records.

When knowledge is stored within the brains of an organization, it is housed as language based on shared, communal experience. As the belief structures of members shift to include shared norms and values, patterns of retention increase throughout the organization. Conversely, knowledge may be more officially retained as recorded data, policy, or documents. Administrative structures also serve as a mechanism for preserving knowledge as they formalize new practices into organizational commonplaces. As formalization of new knowledge occurs, retention is enhanced through the transformation of prior practice.

RETRIEVAL

When members of an organization seek to use knowledge they have previously stored in its collective archives, several responses are possible. First, retrieval may be automatic; that is, members of the organization may be able to draw effortlessly on knowledge because it has been archived within new policy structures, commonly understood practices, or clearly defined procedural behaviors. Automatic retrieval results from a change in schema toward the problem presented; that is, it no longer appears unique to the collective organization and has become recognizable, given information from past situations. In situations where automatic retrieval functions at high levels, organizations are said to have "learned" or developed the capacity to respond in an "adaptive" manner to ecological change. Memory can be thought of as robust when automatic retrieval occurs.

However, the potential exists for an organization to disregard the need to create lasting structures in which to house the information learned. Knowledge may well have been obtained and applied to a past problem situation, yet members may fail to see the utility of the knowledge for other situations or neglect to develop the necessary organizational structures to draw upon the new learning. The context of the organization's prior history may discourage cultural change, or members may lack skills necessary to create archives adequate to foster changed decision-making processes. In either case, it is difficult to argue that the organizational memory was sufficiently robust to transmit new learning beyond a single case application. In contexts where memory is thin, the potential to draw upon those learnings in future situations is compromised.

—*Sharon D. Kruse*

See also bureaucracy; communications, theories in organizations; compliance theory; conceptual systems theory and leadership; control, managerial; differentiation of stimuli; infrastructure, of organizations; management theories; rational organizational theory; values of organizations and leadership

Further Readings and References

Anand, V., & Manz, C. (1998). An organizational memory approach to information management. *Academy of Management Review, 23*(4) 796–809.

Deal, T., & Peterson. K. (1998). *Shaping school culture.* San Francisco: Jossey-Bass.

Johnson, J., & Paper, D. (1998). An exploration of empowerment and organizational memory. *Journal of Managerial Issues, 10*(4), 503–519.

Markus, M. L. (2001). Toward a theory of knowledge reuse. *Journal of Management Information* Systems, *18*(1) 57–93.

Weick, K. (2000). *Making sense of the organization.* Boston: Blackwell.

🏛 ORGANIZATIONAL THEORIES

There has been a plethora of organizational theories during the past century. Bureaucracy, an organizational theory that emerged in the early twentieth century, has been the basic infrastructure of schools in the industrial world. Bureaucracy is ill suited to the demands of our postindustrial demographically diverse information society. In a period of increasing demands for accountability, demographic changes in school population, and economic crisis, most schools are being forced to examine their fundamental structural assumptions. Bureaucratic characteristics not only are being viewed as less than useful but also are considered to be harmful. Some of these negative features of bureaucracy include the following:

- *Division of labor and specialization.* A high degree of division of labor can reduce staff initiative. As jobs become narrower in scope and well defined by procedures, individuals sacrifice autonomy and independence. Although specialization can lead to increased productivity and efficiency, it can also create conflict between specialized units, to the detriment of the overall goals of the school. For example, specialization may impede communication between units. Moreover, overspecialization may result in boredom and routine for some staff, which can lead to dissatisfaction, absenteeism, and turnover.

- *Reliance on rules and procedures.* Max Weber claimed that use of formal rules and procedures was adopted to help remove the uncertainty in attempting to coordinate a variety of activities in an organization. Reliance on rules can lead to the inability to cope with unique cases that do not conform to normal circumstances. In addition, the emphasis on rules and procedures can produce excessive red tape. The use of rules and procedures is only a limited strategy in trying to achieve coordinated actions. Other strategies may be required. But bureaucracy's approach is to create new rules to cover emerging situations and new contingencies. And once established, it is difficult to remove ineffectual rules or procedures in a bureaucracy.

- *Emphasis on hierarchy of authority.* The functional attributes of a hierarchy are that it maintains an authority relationship, coordinates activities and personnel, and serves as the formal system of communication. In theory, the hierarchy has both a downward and upward communication flow. In practice, it usually has only a downward emphasis. Thus, upward communication is impeded, and there is no formal recognition of horizontal communication. This stifles individual initiative and participation in decision making.

- *Lifelong careers and evaluation.* Weber's bureaucratic model stresses lifelong careers and evaluations based on merit. Because competence can be difficult to measure in bureaucratic jobs and because a high degree of specialization enables most employees to master their jobs quickly, there is a tendency to base promotions and salary increments more on seniority and loyalty than on actual skill and performance. Thus, the idea of having the most competent people in positions within the organization is not fully realized. Loyalty is obtained, but this loyalty is toward the protection of one's position, not to the effectiveness of the organization.

- *Impersonality.* The impersonal nature of bureaucracy is probably its most serious shortcoming. Recent critics of bureaucracy attack it as emphasizing rigid, control-oriented structures over people found to be incompatible with professional learning communities.

The renowned organization theorist Warren Bennis represents one of the extreme critics of bureaucratic structuring in organizations. In 1966, he forecasted the demise of bureaucracy. In a more recent book, *Managing the Dream,* he exposes the hidden obstacles in our organizations—and in society at large—that conspire against good leadership. According to Bennis in 2000, within any organization an entrenched bureaucracy with a commitment to the status quo undermines the unwary leader. This creates an unconscious conspiracy in contemporary society, one that prevents leaders from taking charge and making changes.

In recent years, popular writers have expressed increasing dissatisfaction with bureaucratic structures. This is reflected in the phenomenal appeal of numerous best-selling books such as *In Search of Excellence, The Fifth Discipline, Schools That Learn,* and *Principle-Centered Leadership.* The basic theme permeating these books is that there are viable alternatives to the bureaucratic model. There is a strong implication that warm, nurturing, caring, trusting, challenging organizations produce high productivity in people.

What appears to be emerging to replace bureaucracy is a heterarchical model of organization capable of performing collective activities toward the achievement of school goals. Leadership in these heterarchical organizations will need to be considerably different. In particular, significant changes are envisioned in the leader. Leaders will lead from the center rather than from the top. The major focus of leadership will be in supporting teacher success in the classroom. Change management will be an integral part of the role of the leader. The leader will provide intellectual leadership to support teachers' change efforts. The leader will manage a school culture that supports a professional learning community focused on learning for all. Whatever their title or formal role definition, it is clear that leaders continue to be best positioned to help guide faculty toward new forms of organizational structure. Emergent organizational theories in this tradition include System 4, site-based management, transformational leadership, synergistic leadership theory, and total quality management.

SYSTEM 4

Rensis Likert argued in 1961, 1967, 1979, and 1987 that the bureaucratic approach to leadership fails to consider the human side of organizations. His work focused less on the rational and mechanistic aspects of organizational structure and more on its social and psychological components.

After studying many organizations, including schools, Likert found that there was a significant relationship between organizational structure and effectiveness. Organizations that hewed to the bureaucratic model tended to be less effective, whereas effective organizations emphasized incorporating individuals and groups into the system as an integral part of leading. Likert developed eight dimensions or processes for use in comparing organizations: leadership processes, motivational processes, communication processes, interaction processes, decision processes, goal-setting processes, control processes, and performance goals.

Using these eight dimensions, Likert observed four design approaches that incorporate these dimensions. At one extreme, Likert identified a form of organization he called System 1. In many ways a System 1 design is similar to the ideal bureaucracy. In sharp contrast, he describes a humanistic, interactive, group-oriented design, which he called System 4. Intermediate designs, Systems 2 and 3, are variants of the two extremes, which have received little attention.

A System 4 structure is viewed as the ideal state toward which leaders should try to move their organizations. Trust and confidence in the leader are extremely high among System 4 members. A variety of economic, ego, and social factors are used as incentives in motivating participants. Communication flows freely in all directions—upward, downward, and horizontally. Decision making occurs throughout the organization and involves all members equally. Cooperative teamwork is encouraged in setting goals, and members are expected to engage in self-control and group control. Leaders actively see high-performance goals and are committed to professional development.

SITE-BASED MANAGEMENT

The general public's dissatisfaction with bureaucracy has moved some to support *site-based management*

(SBM) as a solution to the educational quality control problem. Related to this are widespread efforts to decentralize many large school systems, like the Chicago Public Schools, as a possible answer to their perceived administrative failings.

The rationale advanced for both decentralization and SBM is to improve performance by making those closest to the delivery of services—teachers and principals—more responsible for the results of their school's operations. This change involves shifting the initiative from school boards, superintendents, and central office staff to individual school sites. The thinking is that if teachers had the authority to make decisions at the building level, without being subject to the school system's bureaucracy, much better progress could be made. Furthermore, the authority to run schools should be shared with parents in order to establish a coordinated home-school effort.

Site-based management is what management experts refer to when they recommend breaking large businesses into smaller units to improve productivity. And an examination of some programs touted under the SBM banner suggests that the process parallels older models of parent-teacher-administrator collaboration that effective schools and school districts have practiced for years.

TRANSFORMATIONAL LEADERSHIP

Transformational leadership focuses on leaders who have exceptional impact on their organizations. These individuals may be called transformational leaders. This view of leadership is extremely rare. Although the number of leaders involved is minimal, the impact these leaders have on their institutions is significant.

James MacGregor Burns's 1978 prize-winning book, *Leadership*, first drew widespread attention to the concept of transformational leadership. Burns claimed that transformational leadership represents the transcendence of self-interest by both leader and led. Later, in his examination of the concept of transformational leadership, Bernard Bass identified and explored two types of leadership in 1985 and 1997: transactional and transformational. Transactional leaders determine what subordinates need to do to achieve their own and organizational objectives, classify those requirements, help subordinates become confident that they can reach their objectives by expending the necessary efforts, and reward them according to their accomplishments. Transformational

leaders, in contrast, motivate their subordinates to do more than they originally expected to do. They accomplish this in three ways: (1) by raising followers' levels of consciousness about the importance and value of designated outcomes and about ways of reaching them, (2) by getting followers to transcend their own self-interest for the sake of the team, organization, or larger polity, and (3) by raising followers' need levels to the higher-order needs, such as self-actualization, or by expanding their portfolio of needs.

The most fully developed model of transformational leadership in schools was provided by Kenneth Leithwood in 1994—identifying important factors that constitute transformational and transactional leadership: building school vision, establishing school goals, providing intellectual stimulation, offering individualized support, modeling best practices and important organizational values, demonstrating high-performance expectations, creating a productive school culture, and developing structures to foster participation in school decisions.

SYNERGISTIC LEADERSHIP THEORY

Modernist theories of organization were traditionally dominated by masculine incorporation, and lacked feminine presence in development and language. The synergistic leadership theory (SLT) developed by Beverly Irby and colleagues in 2002 seeks to explicate the need for a postmodernist leadership theory by providing an alternative to, and not a replacement for, traditional theories. The SLT includes issues concerning diversity and the inclusion of the female voice in the theory. In a tetrahedron model, the theory uses four factors: (1) attitudes, beliefs, and values, (2) leadership behavior, (3) external forces, and (4) organizational structure to demonstrate aspects not only of leadership but its effects on various institutions and positions.

In short, the synergistic leadership theory provides a framework for describing interactions and dynamic tensions among attitudes, beliefs, and values; leadership behaviors; external forces; and organizational structure. As a result, a leader can analyze and describe particular interactions that may account for tension, conflict, or harmony at specific points in time or over time. If it is discovered that tension exists between even two of the factors, then the effectiveness of the leader or the school itself can be negatively impacted. Not only is the SLT beneficial in determining fit while a leader is employed in a school district, but also it can be of assistance in job selection. Moreover, the SLT can serve to build an understanding of the environment to aid in decisions made by the leader. And SLT fosters a reflective practice approach, as it encourages the leader to engage in self-assessment.

TOTAL QUALITY MANAGEMENT

The Japanese transformed their economy and industry through a visionary management technique called *total quality management* (TQM). School leaders are finding that TQM principles can provide the formula for improving America's schools.

TQM, the latest business concept to reach the schools, is a systematic approach to education reform based on the philosophy of W. Edwards Deming. Deming's work, including *Out of the Crisis* in 1988, is not merely about productivity and quality control; it is a broad vision on the nature of organizations and how organizations should be changed.

Deming's philosophy provides a framework that can integrate many positive developments in education, such as team teaching, site-based management, cooperative learning, and outcomes-based education. Deming's 14 principles are based on the assumptions that people want to do their best and that it is the leader's job to enable them to do so by constantly improving the *system* in which they work. The framework for transforming an organization is outlined in the following fourteen points: create constancy of purpose for improvement of product and service; adopt the new philosophy; cease dependence on inspection to achieve quality; end the practice of awarding business on the basis of price alone; improve constantly and forever every activity in the organization, to improve quality and productivity; institute training on the job, institute leadership; drive out fear; break down barriers among staff areas; eliminate slogans, exhortations, and targets that demand zero defects and new levels of productivity; eliminate numerical quotas for the staff and goals for management; remove barriers that rob people of pride in their work; remove barriers that rob people in leadership of their right to pride in their work; institute a vigorous program of education and retraining for everyone; and put everyone in the organization to work to accomplish the transformation.

—*Fred C. Lunenburg*

See also bureaucracy; Burns, James MacGregor; capacity building, of organizations; communications, theories in organizations;

conceptual systems theory and leadership; contingency theories; decentralization/centralization controversy; Deming, W. Edwards; disequilibrium, theories of; ethos, of organizations; frame theory; hierarchical developmental models; hierarchy, in organizations; infrastructure, of organizations; leadership, distributed; management theories; networking and network theory; open systems theory; organizational memory; organizations, types of, typologies; path-goal leadership theory; productivity; satisficing theory; stewardship; total quality management; Weber, Max

Further Readings and References

Bass, B. M. (1997). *A new paradigm of leadership: An inquiry into transformational leadership.* Mahwah, NJ: Erlbaum.

Bennis, W. G. (2000). *Managing the dream: Reflections on leadership and change.* Cambridge, MA: Perseus.

Burns, J. (1978). *Leadership.* New York: Harper & Row.

Deming, W. E. (1988). *Out of the crisis.* Cambridge: Massachusetts Institute of Technology Press.

Irby, B. J., Brown, G., Duffy, J. A., & Trautman, D. (2002). The synergistic leadership theory. *Journal of Educational Administration, 40,* 304–322.

Leithwood, K. A. (1994). Leadership for school restructuring. *Educational Administration Quarterly, 30*(4), 498–518.

Likert, R. (1987). *New patterns of management.* New York: Garland.

Lunenburg, F. C., & Irby, B. J. (2005). *The principalship: Vision to action.* Belmont, CA: Wadsworth/Thomson.

Lunenburg, F. C., & Ornstein, A. O. (2004). *Educational administration: Concepts and practices* (4th ed.). Belmont, CA: Wadsworth/Thomson.

Weber, M. (1947). *The theory of social and economic organization* (T. Parsons, Trans.). New York: Oxford University Press.

ORGANIZATIONS, TYPES OF, TYPOLOGIES

Formal organizations dominate modern social life. Understanding the types of organizations influencing modern processes can improve researchers' and leaders' understanding of organized group behavior, social and political processes, as well as productivity and group decision making.

First, two types of formal organizations—*political* and *religious*—have existed for thousands of years. Governmental regimes like those of ancient Egypt (dating to around 1800–1300 BC) were highly organized and systematic in running state matters, taxation, justice, defense, and international issues. Long-lasting religious organizations, like the Roman Catholic Church (especially after the fourth century AD) also show the early development of highly organized structures. In fact, both these examples have also been classified as *bureaucratic* organizations, organizations with tightly coupled formal structures, diversified labor (bureaus), and clear lines of authority.

In the late 1800s, increased social diversification linked to the industrial revolution led to an increase in number and type of organizations. This has been called the "Great Transformation" of the West. It brought a decline of institutions based on the family as the central element of social organization. After this period, *economic* and *voluntary* organizations proliferated in size, form, structure, and purpose and therefore in type.

One way of typing the emerging organizations of this time period was to link typing to the shift from Gemeinschaft to Gesellschaft, and the move from mechanical solidarity to organic solidarity, or more simply, a shift from family and homogenous-member organizations structured around member similarities, to organizations based on highly specialized divisions of labor and more complex structures and economically driven goals. With industrialization, the number and types of organizations based on an economic diversified structure increased. For example, transportation improvements—from shipping and canals (before the mid-1800s) to trains (mid- to late 1800s) to trucks and roads (early to middle 1900s)—brought new large-scale national and multinational transportation organizations. Furthermore, public ownership organizations (financial and stock systems) increased the size and types of economic organizations by increasing the flow of cash available for such organizing.

One way to classify this proliferation of organization is by the organization's social *functions*. These organizations may be linked to large-scale social institutions like economics, family services, religious, political, legal, and educational organization, as well as emerging functional sectors like recreational or medical organizations.

In addition to function, organizations can also be typed by *structure*. This can be as simple as large and small, national or multinational, or tightly or loosely coupled. Organizations founded around similar times often have similar structures. As such, as a corollary, organizations can be classified by their *founding periods*. Furthermore, studies of populations of organizations have also shown that often organizations founded at the same period have similar *resources* to create

their organization. Thus, grouping structure, function, resources, and environments, some organizational researchers classify organizations by their *niche*. Such classification refers to organizations operating as *rational*, *natural*, and *open* systems organizations

More recently, organizations have been typed in reference to their *climate* or *cultures*, the populations or *groups* they serve, the underlying *technology* they use, their internal development or *life cycle*, as well as other internal or environmental factors.

As new organizations emerge to provide structured responses to social challenges, issues of meaning and valuation, and to new technological developments and resource issues, new typologies will continue to be developed. As organizational sociologists and psychologists continue to try to understand the rich ways in which organizations influence modern life, new forms of analysis and classification will develop. As this generative field of study continues to inform educational leadership, it will provide innovative, creative, and empirical scholarship that will enrich educational leadership research and practice.

—*Duane M. Covrig*

See also bureaucracy; conceptual systems theory and leadership; frame theory; leadership, distributed; leadership, theories of; management theories; networking and network theory; open systems theory; organizational theories; productivity; rational organizational theory; resource management; satisfaction, in organizations and roles

Further Readings and References

Ashkanasy, N. M., Wilderom, C., & Peterson, M. F. (2000). *Handbook of organizational culture & climate*. Thousand Oaks, CA: Sage.
Bolman, L. G., & Deal, T. E. (2003). *Reframing organizations: Artistry, choice, and leadership* (3rd ed.). San Francisco: Jossey-Bass.
Scott, W. R. (1998). *Organizations: Rational, natural and open systems* (4th ed.). Englewood Cliffs, NJ: Prentice Hall.

OSSORIO, PETER G.

Peter G. Ossorio (1926–) had a major impact on the conceptualization of psychology and its relationship to other disciplines and to tasks in the real world. He found himself profoundly dissatisfied with the ways in which psychology and philosophy described and explained human behavior. During 1963 and 1964, he achieved insights into an alternative formulation that did not succumb to the temptations of reductionism and determinism.

The first presentation of the fundamental concepts of persons and their behavior, language, the real world, and some of the conceptual tools for their rigorous representation was in 1965 with *Persons*. These conceptual distinctions and their elaborations have made it possible for significant advances in organizational analysis and leadership development that are directly relevant to persons engaged in educational leadership. Subsequently, he elaborated on the major components of his conceptualization of psychology and their implications in a 1971 monograph, *"What Actually Happens."* In 1979, the Society for Descriptive Psychology held its first annual meeting in Boulder, Colorado, to further the dissemination of his conceptual, therapeutic, and practical advances. While the core group for the society was clinical psychologists, it attracted computer scientists, linguists, NASA scientists, educational psychologists, management consultants, and theologians. Since 1979, he has developed the insight that it is possible to codify the logic of giving and evaluating descriptions and dynamic explanations of behavior via maxims that derived not from forces, urges, or desires but from the person's position in his or her world, culminating in Ossorio's comprehensive theoretical statement in 2005, *The Behavior of Persons*. For example, one of the most reliable findings of studies of organizational roles is that a person's perspective changes as a function of changes in role, such as that occurring when a teacher becomes a principal or a principal becomes a superintendent. Such changes in one's position in the educational social system provide both new opportunities and new constraints.

Ossorio was born in Los Angeles, California, on May 4, 1926, the youngest of six children. He earned his BA and PhD degrees from UCLA and joined the psychology faculty of the University of Colorado (where he served until his retirement in 1991) and continues an active role as professor emeritus and clinical supervisor. During his tenure at Colorado, he directed more than 50 dissertations because of his theoretical creativity and his willingness to engage students on topics of their choice. He was highly sought out for supervision because he was recognized as a master therapist and diagnostician. A selective listing of his influences include (a) the practice of psychotherapy, (b) multicultural studies, (c) educational practices in the teaching of moral competency, (d) effective programs for educating at-risk students, and (e) creating an alternative technology for computer-assisted information searches. He continues to be active intellectually, and his current work may be described as developing descriptive metaphysics, which he believes will change how we think about and conduct both philosophy and science.

—Keith E. Davis

See also behaviorism; problem solving; psychology, types of; role ambiguity; role model; role theory; self-actualization; systems theory/thinking

Further Readings and References

Ossorio, P. G. (1966). *Persons* (Report No. 3). Boulder, CO: Linguistic Research Institute.

Ossorio, P. G. (1971). *"What actually happens"* (Report No. 17). Boulder, CO: Linguistic Research Institute.

Ossorio, P. G. (2005). *The behavior of persons*. Ann Arbor, MI: Descriptive Psychology Press.

🏛 OUTPUTS, OF SYSTEMS

A system can be defined as a grouping of parts that operate together for a common purpose. Systems may have inputs, processors, and outputs. Outputs can be thought of as a tangible product and as an information source that may inform the system of its operation. The input into a system plus the value added creates the system's output.

A closed system is one characterized by outputs that have little or no influence on the inputs; they give little or no feedback to the system. A closed system is usually not responsive to its own performance. An open system uses results from past actions and outputs as feedback to the processor, which is then used to control future action or modify the system. Figure 1 illustrates these concepts.

GOVERNMENTAL OUTPUTS

Governmental outputs are simply the things that the policy process produces, such as laws, regulations, rules, and the effort that governments expend to address problems. Statute and case law are policy outputs of government. Rules and regulations are also an important output of government.

Open System   **Closed System**

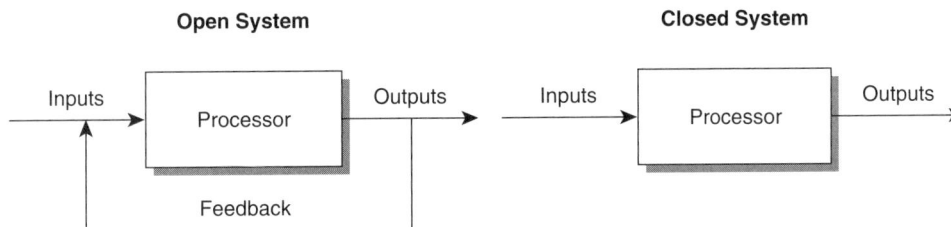

Figure 1   Idealized General System

SOURCE: Author.

EDUCATIONAL OUTPUTS

Educational systems deal with social action, economic concerns, the moral well-being of students, scientific and technological knowledge, aesthetic and political awareness. The outputs that should be produced include students who can perform on specified quality levels, who have gained knowledge, skills, and productive dispositions, and are progressing toward becoming socially competent individuals.

Historically, educational analysts have focused on inputs such as the condition of schools, certification of teachers and administrators, class size, social and economic backgrounds of students, and the most noted of all—standardized testing. Standardized tests continue to be an important output measure of individual schools and school systems. Schools are examined, graded, and even restructured based on the students' yearly standardized testing scores.

With the heavy burden on educational resources and emergence of other effective programs such as home schooling and distance learning programs, a system shift can be seen. These new programs ignore the traditional inputs of education and concentrate on the outputs of learning. Many universities are accepting these alternative approaches to education and basing entrance requirements on the output and achievement of the individual student, without regard to the formal inputs or processors of the traditional educational system.

In higher education, there has also been a shift of emphasis from inputs to outputs. The colleges and universities that offer educational administrator preparation programs have usually accepted any candidate who meets the minimal entrance requirements of the program, with very little regard to whether the intention was to complete the degree to work in that field or for the purpose of merely obtaining a pay increase. Current university programs are now creating databases to track the outputs of students who have completed the program to determine the extent to which the degree helped students to obtain administrative positions.

—*Edward Brown and Janine Brouillette*

See also bureaucracy; capacity building, of organizations; economics, theories of; hierarchical developmental models; management information systems; management theories; measurement, theories of; networking and network theory; organizations, types of, typologies; productivity; resource management; school improvement models; strategic planning; theory movement, in educational administration

Further Readings and References

Banathy, B. H. (1991). *Systems design of education: A journey to create the future.* Englewood Cliffs, NJ: Educational Technology.

Forrester, J. W. (1968). *Principles of systems.* Cambridge: Massachusetts Institute of Technology Press.

Montello, P. A., & Wimberly, C.A. (1975). *Management systems in education: A systems approach to educational decision making.* Lincoln, NE: Professional Educators.

P

🏛 PARADIGM

The term *paradigm,* as used in science and the social sciences, can be traced to a historian of science, Thomas Kuhn, who in 1962 wrote *The Structure of Scientific Revolutions.* Kuhn employed the idea of paradigm change to explain major epochs throughout the progression of science. He reasoned that the history of science could best be interpreted as a succession of scientific revolutions. An interpretation of paradigm shifts or revolutions replaced for Kuhn the commonly held conception of a linear progression toward one explanation or universal truth. The impact of *The Structure of Scientific Revolutions* has affected many disciplines of study and as a result has been applied and examined in many fields. Although the impact has been substantial, the notions of scientific progress espoused by Kuhn have been challenged, and his ideas have not been accepted universally; notable here is philosopher of science Karl Popper and his notion of falsifiability. Popper argued that the process of falsification was the primary impetus behind progression in science rather than paradigm shifts.

Kuhn explained the progression of a particular field. When new challenges or anomalies accumulate to a level that impedes further progress, a crisis emerges. The crisis is diffused when those in the field consensually agree to a new paradigm or world perspective from which to view the field and address previously unexamined issues. A new paradigm, mindset, or perspective is thus adopted to explain more accurately those anomalies that gave rise to a new paradigm. Kuhn fully elaborates on this process in his writing on the definition and explanation of the "transition phase." The notion of paradigms and the theory behind it have been used to explain the progression of many disciplines. More specifically, paradigm shifts have been used to describe major philosophical, theoretical, or practical changes in mindset or general thought patterns. In science, for example, the transitional phase between a heliocentric paradigm and the geocentric paradigm is one application of a paradigm shift. Each new paradigm is said to be incommensurable with the previous, thus making the old no longer applicable to the new sets of questions those within a field seek to answer.

Paradigm shifts have been debated in educational administration, with much of the focus being on whether fundamental assumptions have changed or the manifestations of the assumptions have changed. Kuhn's theory has been misused or misinterpreted within many disciplines as well. One misuse of paradigms and paradigm shifts is associated with claims to relativism. Some claim that since the field of science is subject to paradigm shifts and such shifts can occur with relative frequency, a prior system of belief or a new, emergent system of belief is as good as any other system. Such a view holds that all systems are different but of equal value. However, Kuhn explicitly opposed such a notion of relativism and contended that each emergent paradigm that comes to replace a previous system is inherently better than the one replaced. The new paradigm is not only different but also better, as it (should) adequately explain the anomalies that necessitated the rise of the new system. In terms of educational qualitative or quantitative research, one adopting a relativist stance would argue that both are of equal value, that one is no better than the other, and in this way the field of research has not necessarily progressed.

Another misuse of paradigm shifts comes from those who seek to quickly replace old paradigms or propose a vast number of paradigm shifts within a field or discipline. Such actions within a field, due to the cross-disciplinary influence of Kuhn, have often used the term *paradigm* in order to render scientific standing among other disciplines. Recognition based on scientific relevancy is often characteristic of relatively new fields or subfields of study. Kuhn's original notion of paradigm shifts comes from the concept that the transitional phase of a paradigm shift can take years, often ending only when those who refuse to adopt and accept the new paradigm leave the field. Such a process would not produce a significant number of paradigm changes because a transition in this sense is not a rapid process. Furthermore, Kuhn's theory is based on voluntary consensus within a field; all members within a disciplinary community must accept the new paradigm and acknowledge the passing of the prior belief or thought system. Those who find others' way of thinking incommensurable with their own will assume they are working within a different paradigm but in reality may just be thinking differently within the same paradigm. Paul Feyerabend and Imre Lakatos, critics of Kuhn's idea of scientific change, have applied it to historical cases where a paradigm shift did occur and have found that it is inadequate to account for the change in scientific thinking. Nonetheless, Kuhn's concept of a paradigm as a dominant frame of how things are viewed remains firmly fixed in ideas about how science works, even as notions of how such frames are changed remains contested.

—*Kristina A. Hesbol*

See also critical thinking; dialectical inquiry; knowledge base, of the field; Kuhn, Thomas; management theories; philosophies of education; Popper, Karl; qualitative research, history, theories, issues; quantitative research methods; research methods

Further Readings and References

Feyerabend, P. (1993). *Against method*. London: Verso.

Kuhn, T. (1996). *The structure of scientific revolutions*. Chicago: University of Chicago Press. (Original work published 1962)

Lakatos, I. (1999). *The methodology of scientific research programmes*. Cambridge, UK: Cambridge University Press.

Popper, K. (1979). *Objective knowledge: An evolutionary approach*. Oxford: Clarendon Press.

PARENT TEACHER ASSOCIATION

The National Parent Teacher Association (PTA) is the largest child advocacy organization in the United States, with over 6 million members. There are organizations in all 50 states, the District of Columbia, U.S. Virgin Islands, and in the Department of Defense schools in Europe and the Pacific.

The organization was founded in 1897 in Washington, D.C., as the National Congress of Mothers by Alice McLellan Birney and Phoebe Apperson Hearst. At the time of its founding, women did not have the vote, but these two women felt that there is no stronger bond than that between mother and child. Therefore, the founders believed that it was up to mothers of the United States to eliminate the threats that endangered children. In its initial meetings, more than 2,000 people responded—all with a commitment to children. Problems were identified and strategies devised to resolve them.

The mission of the PTA is to

- Support and speak on behalf of children and youth in the schools, in the community, and before governmental bodies and other organizations that make decisions affecting children
- Assist parents in developing the skills they need to raise and protect their children
- Encourage parent and public involvement in the public schools of the United States

Some of the programs that have evolved from that original group of members include the creation of kindergarten classes, child labor laws, a public health service, hot lunch programs, a juvenile justice system, and mandatory immunization.

By 1922, "A PTA in Every School" became the nationwide goal. Parenting skills were a particular concern and the focus of many local and national conferences. Founder Birney appealed to society as a whole to make education a top priority. But in many states, segregated schools were legally sanctioned. To address those students' special needs, Selena Sloan Butler, with the help of the National PTA, founded the National Congress of Colored Parents and Teachers in 1926. When the two national organizations formally merged in 1970, so did their identical mission to improve the lives of children.

As conditions changed, so did PTA's programs. The age of the automobile brought new concerns about child safety. In the 1930s, National PTA responded with a safety education program for schoolchildren that continues today.

In the 1940s, World War II spearheaded the organization's resolve to find a new and better way to resolve conflicts before they erupted into violence and destruction. National PTA was one of the first organizations to support the fledgling United Nations.

During the 1950s, one of the most high-profile projects in PTA history was the organization's participation in the field testing of the Salk polio vaccine and eventually securing the polio vaccination for all schoolchildren. It was also during this time that the PTA began to recognize America's affinity for prescription and over-the-counter medications, and called for a national conference to address narcotics and drug addiction in youth.

Smoking and drug abuse became increasingly common in American culture during the 1960s, and the PTA called for schools to focus on the risks involved with abuse and also created public service messages to educate parents and the general public about the dangers of addiction. During the 1970s, violence on television spurred the PTA to action regarding the effects of such programming on children. Today, critical viewing skills workshops are held around the country. The alarming rise in sexually transmitted diseases and the advent of AIDS found the PTA advocating comprehensive information about the diseases be made available at school and at home in the 1980s.

In the 1990s, the population of the United States was becoming increasingly diverse. Opportunity abounded for those with the education and training to take advantage of it, but for those with few skills, the gap grew greater than ever. Educational reform became the paramount term in American education, and the National PTA became even more actively engaged in the belief that parents needed to have a say in the education of U.S. children.

In 1994, the PTA's advocacy skills culminated in the Goals 2000 Educate America legislation that, among many reforms, called for local school districts to make parents equal partners on issues affecting their children's education

In 2000, National PTA published the book *Building Successful Partnerships: A Guide to Parent and Family Involvement Programs.* In January of that year, the organization provided field-tested strategies for developing successful parent involvement programs.

Many local schools have determined that they do not want national affiliation with the PTA. Therefore, they opt simply to have a local Parent Teacher Organization (PTO).

—*Carol Engler*

See also Black education; boards of education; children and families in America; community relations; democracy, democratic education and administration; determinism, sociocultural; elections, of school boards, bond issues; Gallup Polls, on public education; governance; Latinos; management theories; minorities, in schools; open-door policy; parental involvement; school improvement models; school safety; school size; schooling effects; site-based management; social capital; social relations, dimensions of; special education; standardized testing; television, impact on students; violence in schools; voucher plans; workplace trends

Further Readings and References

Chadwick, K. (2004). *Improving schools through community engagement.* Thousand Oaks, CA: Corwin Press.

Gaitan, C. (2004). *Involving Latino families in schools.* Thousand Oaks, CA: Corwin Press.

Gold, E., Simon, E., & Brown, C. (2005). A new conception of parent engagement: Community organizing for school reform. In F. English (Ed.), *The SAGE handbook of educational leadership* (pp. 237–268). Thousand Oaks, CA: Sage.

Kochan, F., & Reed, C. (2005). Collaborative leadership, community building, and democracy in public education. In F. English (Ed.) *The SAGE handbook of educational leadership* (pp. 68–84). Thousand Oaks, CA: Sage.

McEwan, E. (2004). *How to deal with parents who are angry, troubled, afraid or just plain crazy.* Thousand Oaks, CA: Corwin Press.

Sexton, R. (2004). *Mobilizing citizens for better schools.* New York: Teachers College Press.

Wasik, B. (2004). *Handbook of family literacy.* Mahwah, NJ: Erlbaum.

🏛 PARENTAL INVOLVEMENT

Parental involvement in K–12 schooling has been linked to the social, emotional, and academic achievement of students. Researchers, policymakers, and district and school site personnel note that these links are particularly important in large urban districts. Research on parental involvement indicates that parental involvement can significantly enhance the school climate and is a critical aspect of effective schooling. The importance of parental involvement is not unique to any one type of school district or any particular race/ethnicity; however, recent literature on parental involvement has primarily focused on urban schools that serve large numbers of minority and low-income children.

The Yale Child Study Center Comer School Development Program (SDP) includes a comprehensive parental involvement component. Developed by James Comer, MD, in 1968, the model has been operationalized in over 700 schools in the United States and abroad, and is a child-centered, data-driven, whole-school change process. The perspective of the home is valued in the Comer Model; school-parent miscommunication and conflict is reduced and parent-child relationships are enhanced. In 1995, Ramirez-Smith & Lofland conducted a study of the Comer model in a Virginia elementary school and found that the principles of the model were instrumental in stopping a cycle of failure at the school. The school had experienced chronic problems with poor student achievement, low teacher morale, and uninvolved parents. Significant increases in student test scores, overall student achievement, and an increase in the number of parents who volunteered at the school and attended school function were realized after implementation of the Comer model. School personnel concentrated on identifying and understanding reasons for low levels of parental involvement rather than concentrating on comparing the levels of parent involvement to other schools. The result was better communication between the home and the school and increases in students' motivation to succeed.

Two other parental involvement initiatives have become prominent in the literature on schools, communities, and families: Joyce Epstein's model for community/school/parental involvement and the 2000 National Education Goals, a national policy initiative on education. Epstein's model consists of six types of parental involvement: parenting, communicating, volunteering, learning at home, decision making, and collaborating with community. In Epstein's model, parental involvement occurs on a continuum ranging from high to low levels, with the level of involvement being dependent on the perceptions of parents and school personnel regarding the importance of involvement. Parental involvement is at the optimum level when the resources of the parents, community, and the school are integrated in a total effort centered on the child. The eighth goal of Goals 2000 specifically targets parents. The specific conceptualization, design, implementation, and evaluation of parental involvement models rests with the individual state departments of

education. Thus, levels of parental involvement may vary from state to state.

Traditional definitions of parental involvement may be insufficient to make any significant impact on policies and practices in urban schools that serve large numbers of poor and minority students. In addition, social and economic changes may leave parents of poor and minority children with limited access to schools compared to middle-class and affluent parents. Schools Reaching Out, a national project of the Institute for Responsive Education, has adopted definitions of parental involvement that (a) broaden the term *parent* to recognize that families may include grandparents, sisters, brothers, aunts, uncles, and legal guardians who are charged with caring for the child and who may act as parents, (b) include community and social service agencies that provide services for children, and particularly those that service urban children and their families, (c) move beyond using the school site as the only meeting place for parent conferences/interaction, (d) consider more innovative methods for communicating with "hard to reach parents," (e) include agendas and priorities of families, and (f) replace deficit theorizing about urban parents and their children with definitions that emphasize family values, cultural differences as strengths, and parents' desires to become active participants in their children's education.

A common theme in microlevel models of parental involvement is an attempt to link parental involvement to school reform. Models such as the Comer model and Epstein's model for school and family connections are similar and have three common themes: (1) providing success for children (all children can achieve academic success regardless of cultural, social, and economic differences), (b) serving the whole child (the emotional, physical, and academic growth of children are linked and are a primary focus at home and at the school site), and (c) sharing responsibility (the responsibility for the social, emotional, physical, and academic development of children is shared among the family, school, and social and community organizations).

Current discussions and research on parental involvement are often situated within the context of school reform. One of the more widely used reform approaches is site-based management—a collaborative governance model that can include parents as members of the school site governing body. Although site-based management remains a popular choice in school reform efforts in many urban school districts, researchers have found that there is limited evidence to suggest that such initiatives actually contribute to increased levels of parental involvement.

—*Linda C. Tillman*

See also achievement tests; Black education; boards of education; children and families in America; collaboration theory; community relations; democracy, democratic education and administration; determinism, sociocultural; elections, of school boards, bond issues; Gallup Polls, on public education; governance; Latinos; management theories; minorities, in schools; open-door policy; Parent Teacher Association; school improvement models; school safety; school size; schooling effects; site-based management; social capital; social relations, dimensions of; special education; standardized testing; television, impact on students; violence in schools; voucher plans; workplace trends

Further Readings and References

Brown, F., & Hunter, R. (1998). School-based management: Involving parents in shared decision making. *Urban Education, 33*(1), 95–122.

Davies, D. (1991). Schools reaching out: Family, school, and community partnerships for student success. *Phi Delta Kappan,* 376–382.

Epstein, J. (1995). School/family/community partnerships: Caring for the children we share. *Phi Delta Kappan,* 701–712.

Fine, M. (1993). [Ap]parent involvement: Reflections on parents, power, and urban public schools. *Teachers College Record, 94*(4).

Haynes, N. (1998). Guest editor's introduction: Overview of the Comer School Development Program. *Journal of Education for Students Placed at Risk, (3)*1, 3–9.

King, S., & Goodwin, A. (2002). *Culturally responsive parental involvement: Concrete understandings and basic strategies.* Washington, DC: American Association of Colleges for Teacher Education.

Lipman, P. (2002). *Chicago school policy and the politics of race: Toward a discourse of equity and justice.* Paper presented at the annual meeting of the American Educational Research Association, New Orleans, LA.

Norwood, P., Atkinson, S., Tellez, K., & Carr Saldaña, D. (1997). Contextualizing parent education in urban schools: The impact on minority parents and students. *Urban Education, 32*(3), 411–432.

Patrikakou, E., & Weissberg, R. (1999). The seven P's of school-family partnerships. *Education Week, 18.*

Ramirez-Smith, C., & Lofland, G. (1995). Stopping the cycle of failure: The Comer Model. *Educational Leadership,* 14–17.

Tillman, L. C. (2003). African American parental involvement in urban school reform: Implications for leadership. In R. Hunter & F. Brown (Eds.), *Challenges of urban education and the efficacy of school reform* (pp. 295–312). Oxford, UK: Elsevier Press.

Tillman, L. (2004). African American parental involvement in a post-*Brown* era: Facilitating the academic achievement of African American students. *Journal of School Public Relations, (25)*2, 161–176.

PARKER, FRANCIS W.

Francis W. Parker (1837–1902) was born in Bedford, New Hampshire, in the fall of 1837. When he was 16, he became a country schoolmaster in New Hampshire. During the Civil War, Parker served with the Union Army and attained the rank of colonel. It was because of his rank that Parker continued to be called Colonel.

After the war, Parker returned to teaching. He became head of a normal school in Dayton, Ohio. During this time Parker began to read the works of Horace Mann and other educational theorists.

Parker inherited a small legacy from his aunt, which allowed him to study abroad, where he became familiar with the work of Johann Pestalozzi and Friedrich Froebel. Parker left the United States to spend two and one half years traveling in Europe. Parker attended lectures at the University of King William in Berlin, through Holland, Switzerland, Italy, France, and Germany. He observed the leading pedagogical innovations of this time. He was especially interested in the work and theories of Johann Herbart. His experiences abroad inspired Parker to encourage similar practices and to reshape American schools. Progressive education in America can be traced to Francis W. Parker. He shared the beliefs of Pestalozzi and Froebel that learning should come from the interests and needs of the child and that the most appropriate curriculum was activity based and one that encouraged children to express themselves freely and creatively.

In 1875, Parker served for 5 years as superintendent of schools in Quincy, Massachusetts. His efforts in the schools drew national attention. He began what came to be known as the Quincy Movement. It emphasized elements of the progressive education such as group activities, informal methods of instruction, science education, and the elimination of rigid discipline. Children began learning simple words and sentences, rather than learning the alphabet by rote. Magazines, newspapers, and teacher-developed materials replaced the texts. Arithmetic was taught inductively with objects instead of rules. Geography was introduced by trips around the local countryside. To improve manual dexterity and individual creativity, drawing was added to the lessons. Teachers stressed observing, describing, and understanding. Parker's program was an immediate success and attracted national attention as the Quincy System. Unfortunately, there were complaints that the fundamentals were being ignored. An inspector from the Massachusetts State Board of Education conducted an independent survey and found that Quincy's students excelled at reading, writing, and spelling and were fourth in their county in arithmetic. Some of the critics believed the survey was biased and unfair.

From 1880 until 1883, Parker was a supervisor of schools in Boston. He extended the progressive education practices he introduced in Quincy. He was principal of the Cook County Normal School in Chicago from 1883 until 1899. In 1883, he published *Talks on Teaching,* and in 1894, *Talks on Pedagogics.* He was founder and principal of the Chicago Institute from 1899 until 1901. It was during this time that Parker formulated his educational theories. His school was a model of progressive education and teacher training. Parker had two goals: move the child to the center of the education process and relate the subjects of the curriculum in such a way as to enhance their meaning for the student. Parker worked to organize schools as democratic communities. The role of the teacher was to start where the students were and gradually lead them into the various fields of knowledge. Art was an important part of the curriculum, as were nature studies, field trips, and social activities. He moved away from teaching discrete subjects. The curriculum attempted to integrate subjects in a way that made it more meaningful to the learner. Parker's pioneering work led to improvements in curricula and teacher training. The Chicago Institute later became part of the school of education of the University of Chicago.

—*Carolyn Sayers Russell*

See also Chicago school reform; communities, types, building of; constructivism; critical theory; democracy, democratic education and administration; Dewey, John; innovation, in education; instructional interventions; philosophies of education; social studies; supervision; Woodson, Carter G.; Young, Ella Flagg

Further Readings and References

Gutek, G. (2001). *Historical and philosophical foundations of education: Selected readings.* Upper Saddle River, NJ: Prentice Hall.
Smith, L., & Smith, J. (1994). *Lives in education: A narrative of people and ideas.* New York: St. Martin's Press.
Webb, L., Metha, A., & Jordan, K. (2003). *Foundations of American education.* (4th ed.). Upper Saddle River, NJ: Prentice Hall.

PARTNERSHIPS, INTERAGENCY

Interagency partnerships refers to formal relationships in which two or more agencies that provide individuals with educational, social, health, or other human services agree to work together to serve their clients. Such partnerships have increased over the past two decades as educational, health, and human service needs have expanded throughout our society and societies around the globe.

HISTORICAL AND SOCIETAL PERSPECTIVES

The familial and societal structures of the twenty-first century are much less cohesive and connected than those of past centuries. Families are separated by space, and in the United States, over 50% end in divorce. Small towns and city neighborhoods in which neighbors were familiar with one another, often attending religious services together, and sometimes even belonging to social groups formed around ethnic and cultural similarities, have been replaced by suburban, sometimes gated communities, and inner cities in which violence and crime keep people inside their homes and apartments. Families that do exist are primarily nuclear, with very little support available from extended family members. Most parents work, meaning that children are either home alone before or after school or in care provided by private providers.

In addition, the expansion of educational accountability mandates focused on student performance on standardized tests has resulted in increased concern about the growing gap between minority and poor children and their more affluent counterparts. Along with this concern has come a growing recognition of the impact of poverty on learning and the need to ensure that all children have the physical, social, and educational support they need to succeed in school.

These factors have resulted in an increased need for educational, mental health, medical, and human services for large percentages of children and their families. The added costs of providing such services have risen steadily over the last few decades, causing local, state, federal, and privately funded agencies to seek new avenues to deliver services in the most economical way possible. Creating interagency partnerships is one strategy that is being used to achieve this goal.

Interagency partnerships involve networking services in simple or comprehensive systems to attempt to ensure that client needs are met in ways that are convenient and cost effective. Although such partnerships have been on the rise in the past two decades, they are grounded in notions developed by such educators as John Dewey and Jane Addams, who stressed making connections with the community and the schools. The current movement was begun in the early 1980s.

CURRENT STATUS

Some partnerships have been mandated by states. Florida was one of the first states to mandate interagency cooperation. Since then, other states such as California and Missouri have instituted similar initiatives. Often state funding is linked to agencies having to work together. In these situations, funds are shared in some manner, and guidelines or regulations for the partnership are usually also mandated.

Other partnerships are voluntary relationships in which two or more agencies freely enter into collaborative arrangement to better serve their clients. Groups involved in these partnerships are varied. In addition to school, health, and human service providers, partners often include those involved in the criminal justice systems, faculty from universities and colleges, members of religious groups, and formal or informal advocacy groups.

Partnerships can be anywhere on a continuum from simple to complex. At the simplest level, agencies may enter into partnerships that are focused on a single task, such as having a health agency unite with a school system to inoculate children against a particular disease. A more complex type of partnership is formed when agencies join together to deliver services to clients on a joint basis, sharing information but not space or personnel. For example, a mental health clinic might join in partnership with a school system to provide free or low-cost services for students, families, or employees using an agreed upon referral system and criteria in which the school refers students to the clinic.

At the furthest end of the continuum, agencies provide integrated services, where they may share space, information, personnel, and/or clients as a unified whole. These partnerships, when operated in conjunction with schools, are often referred to as full-service and/or community schools. These schools often extend the school day to include before- and after-school programs for children and parents. Collaboration is at the heart of service delivery, and the client is the focus of the agency providers. The focus of these integrated services is to provide support that will ultimately enhance student learning and success.

There are also national coalitions and networks that have created partnerships to provide support for student learning. Among the most well known is the Coalition for Community Schools, which includes service learning as a part of its mission. This coalition seeks to connect schools and communities so that not only are student needs met, but students also go out into the community to serve. Community schools are generally found in neighborhoods with high percentages of poverty. They stress prevention, systems change, and networking. They are viewed as avenues for rebuilding a sense of community and ensuring that students and their families have the support they need to succeed.

BARRIERS TO SUCCESS

Forming interagency partnerships is difficult, as these agencies often have conflicting rules and regulations concerning issues such as confidentiality and criteria for providing services. They often have differing governing boards as well. Creating successful partnerships requires extensive planning and a willingness to collaborate to overcome barriers that impede cooperative efforts. They take time to create, as partners must develop mutual trust and confidence in one another.

Another difficulty in building interagency partnership is the negative attitudes that clients and service providers may hold. Often previous failures leave people and agencies feeling hopeless. People involved in interagency partnerships must deal with these attitudes and strive to create a sense of hope and optimism.

Funding is also sometimes a problem, and although some states provide some funding, many schools depend on outside donors to aid them in implementing their models. Thus, when the funding stops, programs sometimes stop as well. However, many of the national models attempt to teach schools and communities to build coalitions of financial support to ensure that funding will be available to sustain their efforts.

Some systems and states have met with resistance from political groups who see such partnerships as infringing on the family and on privacy. Although these groups have sometimes been very vocal, the development of interagency partnerships to meet student and family needs continues to grow, not only in the United States, but in many other countries of the world.

Although there is some resistance to the concept of interagency partnerships, there does seem to be a movement toward ensuring that services to families and students are integrated rather than fragmented. The needs in urban and impoverished schools are great, and interagency partnerships appear to be gaining in acceptance.

—Frances K. Kochan

See also adaptiveness of organizations; Addams, Jane; at-risk students; Black education; boundaries of systems; capacity building, of organizations; Chicago school reform; collaboration, theories of; conceptual systems theory; decentralization/centralization controversy; Dewey, John; diversity; economics, theories of; finance, of public schools; governance; management theories; matrix organization (the "adhocracy"); networking and network theory; organizational theories; politics, of education; systemic reform

Further Readings and References

Chen, J., Horsch, P., DeMoss, K., & Wagner, S. (2003). *Effective partnering for school change.* New York: Teachers College Press.

Corrigan, D. (2000). The changing role of schools and higher education institutions with respect to community-based interagency collaboration and interprofessional partnerships. *Peabody Journal of Education, 75*(3),176–196.

Dryfoos, J. (2002). PARTNERING—Full-service community schools: Creating new institutions. *Phi Delta Kappan, 83*(15), 393–395.

Houck, J., Cohn, K., & Cohn, C. (Eds.). (2004). *Partnering to lead educational renewal.* New York: Teachers College Press.

Quellete, P., Briscoe, R., & Tyson, C. (2004). Parent-school and community partnerships in children's mental health: Networking challenges, dilemmas, and solutions. *Journal of Child & Family Studies, 13*(3), 295–297.

Sailor, W. (Ed.). (2002). *Whole-school success and inclusive education.* New York: Teachers College Press.

🏛 PATH-GOAL LEADERSHIP THEORY

Although first published by Martin G. Evans in 1970, Robert J. House is credited most often for his work on the path-goal theory of leadership. In 1971, Evans published *A Path-Goal Theory of Leader Effectiveness,* which House updated in 1996. Path-goal theory

states that the leadership behaviors of formally appointed superiors directly affect their subordinates and that subordinate performance, motivation, and satisfaction can be increased by subordinates' belief in their own capabilities, by clarifying paths toward attainment, by offering rewards for achieving goals, by removing obstacles, and by increasing opportunities essential for personal satisfaction. The basic premise, then, is that a leader's effectiveness is directly tied to the ability and willingness of that leader to ensure a satisfying work environment that provides rewards for achieving goals that are clearly stated. An ambiguous work environment increases stress, thus decreasing satisfaction and productivity. In 1974, House and R. R. Mitchell refined the idea of subordinate satisfaction by stating that the gratification produced by the work must either be immediate or clearly shown to be crucial to future satisfaction. Tying satisfaction directly to performance and increasing coaching, guidance, and other support can also increase motivation, thereby increasing productivity.

Based in expectancy theory, path-goal theory suggests that leaders who successfully implement appropriate leadership styles can influence the motivation of their employees. Key to path-goal theory is leadership that focuses on elements that are missing from a subordinate's work environment. Four types of leadership behaviors clarify the path-goal journey and enable subordinate satisfaction:

1. *Directive leadership behavior:* sets clear objectives and rules for subordinates; expectations and directions are well defined

2. *Supportive leader behavior:* caters to the needs and desires of subordinates in order to reduce stress and frustration in the work environment

3. *Participative leader behavior:* encourages subordinate participation in decision making by consulting with subordinates as well as sharing information

4. *Achievement-oriented leader behavior:* aimed at individuals with a highly internal locus of control who are motivated by their own personal accomplishments; leaders set challenging goals and encourage high performance while showing confidence in their subordinates' abilities

After many empirical studies had been completed, House realized that path-goal leader behaviors needed to be expanded. In his latest review, he outlines nine leadership behaviors. In addition to supportive leader behavior and achievement-oriented leader behavior, the seven additional categories include the following:

1. Path-goal clarifying behaviors
   a. Clarify performance goals
   b. Clarify the means to achieving the goal
   c. Clarify standards of judging performance
   d. Clarify expectations of others in the organization
   e. Clear rewards for performance

2. *Work facilitation*: clears obstacles for subordinates, allowing them to focus on their work goals

3. *Interaction facilitation:* collaboratively removes obstacles that prevent interaction, including dispute resolution, facilitation of communication, and listening to all voices

4. *Group-oriented decision processes:* focus on decisions that affect group dynamics and production and on increasing acceptance of such decisions.

5. *Representation and networking:* address the need of leaders to network and actively represent the function of the work unit; by effectively networking, a leader establishes the legitimacy of the work unit

6. *Value-based leader behavior:* helps establish extraordinary follower commitment by appealing to values and sentiments held dear by subordinates; such behavior may only be expressed adequately when an ideological goal exists

7. *Shared leadership:* functions best in an interdependent environment, where sharing responsibility for leadership theoretically increases unit cohesiveness and thus performance

In addition to leadership behaviors, path-goal theory acknowledges a subordinate's own characteristics as the key to success. For example, an employee with a great need for affiliation may do best with a supportive leadership style, while employees who gain more satisfaction from figuring things out for themselves might do better with a leader who exhibits achievement-oriented leadership.

Finally, path-goal theory says that subordinate satisfaction, along with leadership behavior, is tied to task characteristics—the work environment. If, for instance, the nature of a task is very clear and repetitive, then directive leadership may not be as effective as it can be viewed as redundant. Or if an environment is team oriented and social interaction is high, a supportive style of leadership may not be effective. The

work environment is important to consider when determining leadership styles.

When examining appropriate leadership styles from a path-goal perspective, a leader must first try and discern the needs of subordinates. In deciding upon a style that will meet these needs, a leader must look at both the characteristics of individual subordinates as well as the task environment. It is the interaction of these factors that shows what is missing from the work environment, and a good leader adds the missing pieces rather than focusing on what employees already have. If all of the necessary motivational factors are addressed, motivation, employee satisfaction, and productivity then can be maximized.

Criticisms of path-goal theory focus primarily on its complexity, incomplete support by research studies, failure to address fully links between leadership and motivation, and the possibility of creating dependent subordinates. Yet this approach to leadership provides leaders with key understandings about work environments, subordinate needs, and potential relations between leadership styles and productivity.

—*Sonia Schaible-Brandon and Rodney Muth*

See also administration, theories of; bureaucracy; goals, goal setting; leadership, complex theory of; leadership, discretionary (and power); leadership, distributed; leadership, participatory; leadership, situational; leadership, task-oriented; management theories; motivation, theories of; workplace trends

Further Readings and References

House, R. (1971). A path-goal theory of leader effectiveness. *Administrative Science Leadership Review, 16,* 321–339.

House, R. (1996). Path-goal theory of leadership: Lessons, legacy, and a reformulated theory. *Leadership Quarterly, 7*(3), 324–352.

House, R., & Mitchell, R. (1974). Path-goal leadership. *Journal of Contemporary Business, 3,* 81–97.

Northouse, P. (2004). *Leadership: Theory and practice* (3rd ed.). Thousand Oaks, CA: Sage.

🏛 PATRI, ANGELO

Angelo Patri (1876–1965) was the first Italian immigrant to become a New York City public school principal. His tenure in inner-city schools stretched from 1908 to 1944—5 years as principal at an elementary school in the Bronx and 31 years as principal at Bronx Junior High School.

At Teachers College, Columbia University, Patri was introduced to the ideas of John Dewey, specifically the essay *Ethical Principles*. From then on, his teaching and leadership reflected the ideals of American progressivism—that is, he fought to release schools from the grip of tradition, rules, records, and endless routine. He combined contemporary ideas on community-parent involvement with a desire to improve schools at the school site level.

In his day, principals and supervisors would inspect, and unless the class was taught in a specific way—according to "the method," the teacher would be criticized. As a principal, Patri opposed the uniformity of instruction: student drawings were all alike, as were their compositions—all with the same topic and the same number of paragraphs. All the subjects—the three Rs—were aligned and sequenced, formalized and logical. The regular, fixed school curriculum never stayed with a beautiful idea long enough to have it become part of the children's lives. Patri sought to vitalize the curriculum by means of firsthand experiences or to push the classroom out into the world.

Patri was aware of the serious problems in the inner-city communities: horrific living conditions inside the tenement buildings, abject poverty of the families and children, lack of jobs, truancy, gang violence in the neighborhood, convoluted feeder patterns and school boundaries, and little parental involvement. He saw the need for both the school and the community to work together, for if only one addressed a problem, it could not be solved.

He created a parent-community association to give parents a stake in their children's school. Perhaps the most significant parent-teacher committee in the association was one that investigated cases of parental neglect, cases of need, and cases of truancy. It was called the Relief Committee, and its mandate ranged from providing parents with information on hygiene, clothes, medicine, groceries, and money (in the form of loans) to looking for jobs. The Relief Committee joined up with a local branch of the settlement house—the emerging social center for schools during the first two decades of the twentieth century.

To many parents throughout the country, Patri was a familiar figure during the first half of the twentieth century. He wrote magazine articles and newspaper advice columns. In his syndicated column, "Our Children," he popularized John Dewey's progressive educational principles on teaching, discipline, and social life. Patri also authored a number of books on raising children and adolescents, including *Your Children in Wartime* (1943) and *How to Help Your Child Grow Up: Suggestions for Guiding Children From Birth Through Adolescence* (1948).

—*Ira Bogotch*

See also children and families in America; Dewey, John; discipline in schools; elementary education; immigration, history and impact in education; principalship

Further Readings and References

Berger, M. (1980). *The settlement, the immigrant and the public school.* New York: Arno Press. (Original work published 1956)

Bogotch, I. (2005). A history of public school leadership: The first century, 1837–1942. In F. English (Ed.), *The SAGE handbook of educational leadership* (pp. 7–33). Thousand Oaks, CA: Sage.

Patri, A. (1917). *A schoolmaster of the great city.* New York: Macmillan.

PEACE EDUCATION

Because the purpose of peace education is to bring an end to violence in the schools, in 1969 Johan Galtung suggested a definition of *peace* as the dearth of violence. Although this appears to be simplistic, in moving toward true peace education he rejects the traditional notion of violence that only considers intentional physical or psychological harm. Instead, Galtung includes circumstances of violence that include when human beings are being influenced physically and psychologically to not be able to realize their potential. Thus, even poverty because of its deprivation is a form of violence.

Peace education has become an especially important topic for schools, because everywhere we look, in the media—newspapers, magazines, television, movies—in our homes and in our schools we are reminded that we live in a violent world. Research indicates that peer violence is stable through development. In fact, children who display violent behaviors in the early grades are more likely to be involved in criminal behavior as they become older. Therefore, it is clearly important for educators to be aware of these direct and indirect kinds of violence that begin in the elementary schools and often escalate into even more severe violence in high schools.

Most of the efforts to create safe schools are focused on peacekeeping, peacemaking and peacebuilding strategies. In fact, it is estimated that 10% of U.S. schools have programs that emphasize peaceful solutions to disputes. Peacekeeping violence prevention efforts attempt to avoid violent behavior from occurring, terminate involvement in violence, and reduce the occurrence of violent behaviors in school. The most common strategy for safety at school is the designing of a school-based violence prevention plan.

Peacemaking approaches to school violence train children to resolve conflicts constructively through the use of conflict resolution programs, teaching mediation, empathy, and alternative dispute resolution methods. Adults who emphasize peacemaking approaches emphasize communication, negotiation, and mediation skills. They work at promoting resiliency in youth.

Peacebuilding approaches to lessening school violence recognize that children must be taught to become more peaceful. As noted by Ian Harris in 2000, there are four components in a peacebuilding approach to preventing school violence:

1. Addressing the sources of violence

2. Filling young people's heads with images of peace to make peace attractive to them

3. Helping young people recover from violence

4. Constructing a peaceable school climate

Peace educators teach cultural diversity, with a goal of creating the conditions of positive peace in children's minds. They draw upon the critical theory and liberation theologies of bell hooks, Paulo Friere, and Henry Giroux.

An example of a peace program is the Peace Education Foundation (PEF), which is a nonprofit organization established in 1980. Its mission is to educate children and adults in the dynamics of conflict and to promote peacemaking skills in homes, schools, and communities throughout the world. PEF provides educational materials, training, and programming that encourages making nonviolent conflict resolution a lifestyle. C. Diekmann wrote in 2004 that significant research themes on which PEF is based include

- Violence prevention
- Multicomponent approach (multimodal, structured social skills training programs)
- Social development (focuses on what can be done to facilitate healthy social development)
- Resiliency (the ability to bounce back from life's stresses)

- Teaching methodology (based on social learning theory as developed by Bandura)
- Process goals and progress feedback
- Developmentally appropriate approach, multilesson and multiyear model (begin young and continue over many years)
- School climate
- Effective schools and student achievement

The PEF model integrates a wide range of social competency concepts that include community building, developmentally appropriate rules, understanding conflict, perception and diversity, anger management and other emotions, and effective communication.

Preventing school violence through a peace approach includes establishing a shared vision among the whole faculty, staff, students, parents, and the larger community. These community representatives should also include local law enforcement and juvenile justice personnel. Training must be provided to all stakeholders in peer mediation, conflict resolution, anger management, or whatever skill the peace program emphasizes. Research suggests that appropriate implementation of peace education programs has a positive impact on the school as a whole.

—*Sandra Harris*

See also at-risk students; bullying; character education; classroom management; conflict management; critical race theory; cultural politics, wars; curriculum, theories of; discipline in schools; diversity; early childhood education; gender studies, in educational leadership; grades, of students; homophobia; mainstreaming and inclusion; multiculturalism; school safety; vandalism in schools; violence in schools

Further Readings and References

Beaudoin, M., & Taylor, M. (2004). *Creating a positive school culture.* Thousand Oaks, CA: Corwin Press.

Diekmann, C. (2004). Research-based effectiveness of the Peace Education Foundation Model. Retrieved August 15, 2004, from http://www.peace-ed.org.

Galtung, J. (1969). Violence, peace, and peace research. *Journal of Peace Research,* 167–191.

Harris, I. (2000). Peace-building responses to school violence. *NASSP Bulletin, 84*(614), 5–24.

Williams, K. (2001, April). *Does increasing awareness of putdowns actually reduce violence? An analysis of two rural elementary schools.* Paper presented at the annual meeting of the American Education Research Association, Seattle, WA.

Williams, K. (2003). *The PEACE approach to violence prevention: A guide for administrators and teachers.* Lanham, MD: Scarecrow Education.

🏛 PEER INTERACTION/FRIENDSHIPS

In an effort to effectively understand children and their development, researchers and psychologists have dedicated tremendous energy toward the study of peer relationships. Friendships are vital to children because they serve as emotional resources for having fun and adapting to stress, expand cognitive resources for problem solving, provide the context for developing social skills, and are the forerunner of all other relationships. During the typical school day, children's peers and friends often become their only sources of companionship, security, and stability. Friends provide one another with recreation, advice, trust, encouragement, support, and other important needs.

Unfortunately, some children have great difficulty developing positive relationships with others. These children lack the social skills that others are developing and fail to have their affective needs fulfilled. This impairs the children's emotional well-being, their self-efficacy, their interrelations with others, and their ability to focus in the classroom. The social and behavioral problems that emerge seem to further the cycle of rejections and make it even more difficult for children to escape from their poor status among peers. In an effort to provide interventions for students who struggle with peer relationships, researchers have developed a method for defining sociometric status among peers. Peer nominations provide a calculated method of determining the degree to which students are "liked" or "disliked" by others in their peer group.

Generally, children are classified according to a sociometric category that their nominations elicit. Popular children are seen as being well liked or "cool," and they are seldom disliked. These children are usually easy to spot within a social setting because they show higher levels of sociability, greater cognitive skills, and low levels of aggression. Generally, popular children attract attention because they are seen as being "fun." Approximately 15% of children are labeled as popular. Controversial children are those who are "liked" by some and "disliked" by others. These students often get attention in the classroom from either acting like a class clown or from bullying behavior. They generally have a crowd of followers that find them entertaining or idolizing, but they also have a number of enemies who see them as absurd or mean. Neglected children are those who go unnoticed within the classroom. They are neither well liked nor disliked. Teachers often see these students as "perfect angels" because they are often shy and polite within the structured classroom. In reality, these students are often at risk for depression or other maladies because they seldom have the opportunity to engage with others.

The category that has received the most attention from educators and researchers are students who are rejected by their peers. These children frequently have a high number of "liked least" nominations and almost no "liked most" nominations. Generally, about 15% of elementary school children are classified as being strongly disliked or rejected by their peers. Research has proven that these students are at the greatest risk for demonstrating disruptive behaviors, loneliness, academic failure, anxiety, and lower self-esteem.

Understanding and identifying peer relationship problems is important because they are often a symptom of and a precursor to a variety of psychological and social difficulties. By learning to identify those children who are rejected by their peers or who struggle socially, educators and other adults will be better able to provide measures that will help them to interact effectively with peers and address the root of the child's peer relationship problems.

—*Lauren M. Likosar and Bonnie C. Fusarelli*

See also adolescence; affective domain; Asian Pacific Americans; at-risk students; Black education; bullying; children and families in America; consideration, caring; critical race theory; cross-cultural studies; democracy, democratic education and administration; desegregation, of schools; discrimination; dropouts; drug education; elementary education; emotional disturbance; esteem needs; grades, of students; Head Start; high schools; homophobia; humanistic education; individual differences, in children; learning, theories of; learning environments; mainstreaming and inclusion; middle schools; motivation, theories of; personality; pregnancy, of students; school safety; schooling effects; sexuality, theories of; social studies; special education; suicide, in schools; underachievers, in schools

Further Readings and References

Connolly, P. (2004). *Boys and schooling in the early years.* New York: Routledge.

Hay, D., Payne, A., & Chadwick, A. (2004). Peer relations in childhood. *Journal of Child Psychology and Psychiatry, 45*(1), 84–108.

Lloyd, G. (Ed.). (2004). *Problem girls.* New York: Routledge.

Milner, M. (2005). *Freaks, geeks and cool kids.* New York: Routledge.

Rasmusson, M. (2005). *Becoming subjects: Sexualities and secondary schooling.* New York: Routledge.

Reifel, S., & Brown, M. (2004). *Social contexts of early education, and reconceptualizing play.* St. Louis, MO: Elsevier.

Smyth, J., & Hattam, R. (2004). *"Dropping out," drifting off, being excluded: Becoming somebody without school.* New York: Peter Lang.

PEIRCE, CYRUS

In 1839, Horace Mann hired Cyrus Peirce to be the first principal of the Lexington Normal School in Lexington, Massachusetts. Mann turned to his long-time supporter and principal of the Nantucket High School after being rebuffed by five other prominent educators—each of whom had religious backgrounds. Peirce agreed to become not only the principal but also the sole lecturer and director of the model school, as well as perform the duties of janitor. His views on teaching and leadership reflected the same values held by Horace Mann with respect to the need for a professional school to train better teachers.

Cyrus Peirce (1790–1860) kept a reflective journal of his first years, 1839 to 1841, at the Lexington Normal School. He also corresponded with prominent educators, including Henry Barnard of Connecticut. His journal entries describe a man willing to fully commit himself to what he called "the Experiment," noting that he would prefer death to the experiment's failure.

In fact, it is clear that both mentally and physically, the work affected his health. Not a sanguine or patient person to begin with, Peirce's journal is an honest and troubled account of the daily demands of school leadership. His workday combined teaching and teacher training, from early morning to late in the afternoon. He rose before dawn to set the fires going in the cast-iron stoves in his little school building, and in winter he arose at intervals all night to keep the stoves going. He sat late over his desk, writing down the events of the day and the progress of the great experiment.

Of the young women (numbering from 7 to 21 during the first 2 years), Peirce noted both their talent and lack of knowledge. He felt that they came to the Normal School to acquire knowledge rather than learn how to teach. The students were neither good readers nor good spellers, nor did they know much arithmetic and grammar. Still, it was Peirce's goal to educate them into becoming better teachers. At the same time, he was keenly aware that knowledge alone did not necessarily make for an excellent teacher.

As a teacher, he too experimented, varying his own classroom approaches. His views were that of an enlightened educator. He came to realize that studying in a few areas for a greater length of time was better than the time spent on too many subjects, and that teaching using fear of corporal punishment was ineffective. And so, in spite his ill health, Peirce continued his work in Lexington until 1842 and then led a second Normal School in West Newton until 1849.

—*Ira Bogotch*

See also administration, theories of; leadership, theories of; normal schools; principalship; schools of education; supervision

Further Readings and References

Bogotch, I. (2005). A history of public school leadership: The first century, 1837–1942. In F. English (Ed.), *The SAGE handbook of educational leadership* (pp. 7–33). Thousand Oaks, CA: Sage.

Cremin, L. (1969). *American education: Its men, ideas and institutions.* New York: Arno Press. (Original title *The first state normal school in America: The journals of Cyrus Peirce and Mary Swift* [1926], Cambridge, MA: Harvard University Press)

Norton, A. (1926). Introduction to *The first state normal school in America: The journals of Cyrus Peirce and Mary Swift.* Cambridge, MA: Harvard University Press.

PERCEPTUAL CONTROL THEORY

Perceptual control theory (PCT) is a systems model for the regulation of actions based on negative feedback loops as used in engineering control theory developed by William T. Powers. The PCT model of behavior is a radical departure from previous theories about why the observed behavior of an individual occurs. The process of perception plays a central role in this theory.

Perceptual processes in PCT can be thought of, in some respects, as being the process that monitors the signals being generated about controlled variables. Most controlled variables reside in the environment, that is, events in the environment that are important to an individual, but some reside within the organism, that is, biological variables such as hunger and cognitive variables such as self-image. One is not aware of all perceptual processes as they take place, nor even most of them. Awareness is usually present only when

↓ 11. Systems Level: Be a responsible person   ← |
↓ 10. Principles Level: Meet commitments   ← |
↓   9. Program Level: Drive to Bill's & return video   ← |
↓   8. Sequence Level: Starting the car   ← |
↓   7. Category Level: Motor skills   ← |
↓   6. Relationship Level: Driving   ← |
↓   5. Events Level: Steering car   ← |
↓   4. Transition Level: Turning wheel to right   ← |
↓   3. Configuration Level: Fingers around wheel   ← |
↓   2. Sensation Level: Gripping   ← |
↓   1. Intensity Level: Muscle tension in fingers   ← |
↓

Effect on Environment
↓

Analysis of Effect
↓

Sensory Feedback ————————————————→|

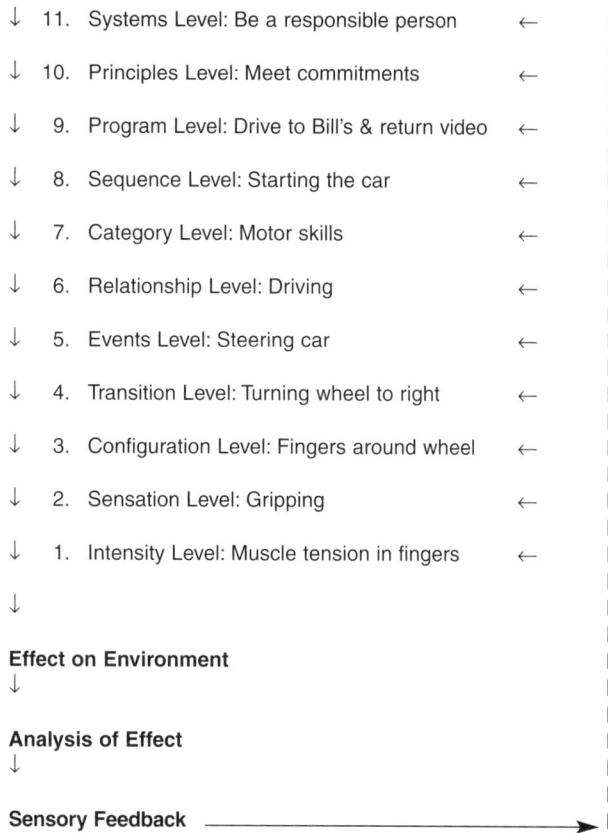

Figure 1   Perceptual Hierarchy and Feedback Loop
Based on the 11-Level PCT Model

SOURCE: Center, D. B. (1999). *Strategies for Social and
Emotional Behavior: A Teacher's Guide.* Norcross, GA: XanEdu,
Inc. Reprinted with permission.

control of a variable is being organized, when there is
a disturbance of a controlled variable that requires a
choice between response programs or after a programmed response fails to produce congruence between
the reference value for a controlled variable and the
perception of that controlled variable. In most cases, a
disturbance of a controlled variable automatically initiates a previously developed and successful programmed response and does not require conscious
awareness. Perception in the PCT model is hierarchical and includes 11 levels of perception (see Figure 1).
Higher levels in the hierarchy set reference values for
lower levels in the hierarchy. With each step up the
hierarchy, the processing time for perceptual input
slows down, so that processing at the highest level in
the hierarchy proceeds at the slowest rate.

The top three levels are of most immediate interest
in this discussion. It is at the systems level that reference

values are set, not to be confused with *personal values*
or standards that come from the principles level.
Reference values can also be thought of as goals or
wants. Reference values may be established in several
ways. Reference values may have a biological basis, as
in the case of physical needs; a social basis, as in the
case of beliefs; and a personal basis, as in personal preferences. At the principles level, *standards* are developed to detect discrepancies between *perceptual
signals* originating from controlled variables and the
reference value or values related to a controlled variable. At the program level there is a repertoire of neu-
rologically programmed actions that are available to
reduce or eliminate any perceived discrepancy (error
signal). Actions, according to PCT, are not responses
caused by environmental stimuli but are caused by an
individual's intent to reduce an error signal and thereby
achieve congruence between a goal or reference value
and the perception of some related controlled variable.
In other words, the actions have a purpose, and the
purpose behind the actions resides not in the environment but within the individual. Purpose in PCT becomes
an important causal variable in human behavior or
actions.

McClelland's PCT conceptualization of social
environments, like schools, suggests that classrooms
are *social designations,* which refer to commonly
shared social environments in our society. Within
these shared social environments, coordinated social
activities like teaching take place that require collective control of the activities. For effective and efficient
collective control of teaching activities, it is necessary
that all individuals sharing the environment accept similar reference values (goals and rules) and standards.
In educational environments, this generally means
that students accept the goals and rules (reference values) and standards of the key players (i.e., administrators, teachers, and support staff) in the educational
environment.

An approach to socializing students based on PCT
is the responsible thinking process (RTP) developed
by Ed Ford. RTP is a program that facilitates collective control of instructional activities through helping
students to accept and adopt the reference values
and standards of school personnel. It is important that
students perceive the school and classroom as having
a positive climate and want to be there. Facilitating a
desire in students to be in school is important, because
the RTP program does not employ any contrived
extrinsic rewards for school attendance or classroom

participation. The reason for this appears to be related to the concept of *cognitive dissonance*. Studies on cognitive dissonance indicate that if people are asked to take a position contrary to their usual attitude about something, there is a greater likelihood that they will identify with the contrary position if they have not received an extrinsic reward for doing so. Thus, when given an extrinsic reward for complying with the goals and standards of a teacher, the effect will only be temporary for most students. When students do not receive an extrinsic reward for compliance, an error signal is generated by the perceived discrepancy between their actions and their goals. One potential outcome of this is to reduce the discrepancy or error signal by adopting the goals and standards of the teacher, that is, incorporating them into one's self identity. In short, PCT and RTP probably view extrinsic reward as a disturbance for a teacher's controlled variable, *student socialization.*

—*David Center*

See also behaviorism; classroom management; cognitive dissonance; critical thinking; discipline in schools; expectations, teacher and student cultures; feedback; group dynamics; learning environments; metacognition; motivation, theories of; perceptual psychology; persuasion; psychology, types of; social context; values education

Further Readings and References

Center, D. (1999). Perceptual control theory: An alternative perspective. In *Strategies for social and emotional behavior: A teacher's guide.* Norcross, GA: XanEdu.
Ford, E. (1997). *Discipline for home and school: Book one* (2nd ed.). Scottsdale, AZ: Brandt.
McClelland, K. (1994). Perceptual control and social power. *Sociological Perspectives, 37*(4), 461–496.
Powers, W. (1973). *Behavior: The control of perception.* New York: Aldine.
Powers, W. (1998). *Making sense of behavior: The meaning of control.* New Canaan, CT: Benchmark.
Taylor, L. (2004). *Introducing cognitive development.* New York: Routledge.

PERCEPTUAL PSYCHOLOGY

Perceptual psychology is the study of the process by which sensations are interpreted through the lens of knowledge and understanding to become meaningful experiences. Perceptual psychology aims to cognize how one attaches and derives meaningful symbols from the simple electrical impulses that provide awareness, for example, of light, dark, and color in our visual systems. From a perceptual viewpoint, behaviors are considered manifestations of underlying beliefs. Perceptual organization is the task performed by the perceptual system to determine what visual and other sensory stimuli are compatible in forming a representation of an object.

Modern perceptual psychology is a conglomeration of three main approaches, computational, constructivist, and ecological, each intended to understand human perception. The computational approach attempts to determine the calculations that machines would necessarily perform while solving perceptual problems. The understanding of these machine computations facilitates the explanation of complex processes within the nervous systems of humans and other animals and how these computations allow the transformation of raw sensory stimulation into a representation of a living world.

On the other hand, the constructivist approach argues that perceptual systems build a representation of reality from fragments of sensory information. Constructivist psychologists are particularly interested in situations where the identical physical stimuli give rise to different perceptions in different people. For example, an optical illusion for one culture may not prove effective in another culture if the two have not had similar lifeworld experience with the objects presented in the illusion. Its emphasis is that perception is strongly influenced by expectations and inferences based on past experience and prior knowledge.

Third and opposite, the ecological approach claims that most perceptual experience is due directly to the wealth of information contained in the array of stimuli presented in an environment. According to this approach, the primary goal of perception is to support actions, such as walking, grabbing, or flying a plane, by focusing on those parts of the environmental stimulus array that are most pertinent to performing those actions. Therefore, psychologists in this field would be little interested in a person's interpretation of a setting but greatly interested in how that person would use visual information gleaned from the environment.

Perceptual organization itself has two basic principles: figure-ground processing and perceptual grouping. In accordance with figure-ground processing, perception is not only an active process but is also a categorizing one. People usually organize sensory stimulation into one perceptual category or another but rarely into two categories or something in between. Perceptual grouping, originated from Gestalt psychology (*Gestalten,* German for *organized wholes),* refers to the human visual ability to extract significant relationships from lower-level primitive image features without any knowledge of the pictorial content and to group them to obtain meaningful higher-level structure. It asserts that people perceive sight and sound as organized wholes, as opposed to just a sum of individual sensations. Perceptual grouping describes how perceptual systems organize a stimulus array of raw sensations into a world of shapes and objects. Certain inherent parts of the stimulus environment lead people to group them together more or less automatically.

—*Eunyoung Kim*

See also brain research and practice; cognition, theories of; cognitive dissonance; cognitive styles; conceptual systems theory and leadership; creativity, theories of; critical thinking; differentiation of stimuli; individual differences, in children; intelligence; learning, theories of; multiculturalism; neuroscience; personality; psychology, types of

Further Readings and References

Lee, S. (2005). *Encyclopedia of school psychology.* Thousand Oaks, CA: Sage.
Smilkstein, R. (2003). *We're born to learn.* Thousand Oaks, CA: Corwin Press.
Sylwester, R. (2004). *How to explain a brain.* Thousand Oaks, CA: Corwin Press.

PERFORMANCE ASSESSMENT

Performance assessment is the formal and informal judgments of how well people complete observable tasks. The two most common uses of the term *performance assessment* in education relate to student achievement and employees, such as teachers, completing the functions of their jobs.

The first use the assessment serves is what has been called the American meritocracy, which is a way of determining who gets America's material rewards. Intelligence tests, and also education itself, can't be counted on to find every form of merit. They don't find wisdom, originality, humor, toughness, empathy, common sense, independence, or determination—let alone moral value. Student performance assessment is not presently able to provide opportunity on the basis

of the various forms of merit that a true meritocracy should have, but it can measure some preestablished academic criteria. One important caution that has been noted by some is that we need to be aware of the impact and limitations of what criteria are used. In this regard, no amount of subsequent manipulation can eliminate all the initial biases that are imposed upon policy and program decisions in the selection of a specific model as a guide to analyze performance.

There have been some improvements in measuring certain identified academic standards, which some argue have a relationship with future potential to succeed within the present university system and at some jobs. This is criterion—rather than norm-referenced—assessment, which measures how well individuals perform in relation to a group of individuals. It should be noted that there is a difference between norms and standards. That is, norms change, standards do not—standards are fixed. Standards promote mixed ability grouping. Norms tend to promote segregation of students by ability.

It is believed that good classroom assessment can improve student achievement. Alan Glatthorn indicated that assessment-driven instruction entirely focused upon performance assessment, from planning to execution. However, he cautioned that performance assessments can have problems. It is important to identify the tasks to be assessed—namely, the standards that are established before teaching begins.

The second use of the term *performance assessment* deals with employee evaluation, most often teachers. Teacher evaluation takes many forms.

The system used to assess teaching performance is important. One confusing aspect of employee performance appraisal is the distinction that is made between formative evaluation and summative evaluation. Formative evaluation occurs when the main purpose is to help an individual improve performance—put another way, it forms a better employee. Summative evaluation, on the other hand, results in a summation or final report as its main purpose and is used to make a personnel decision (such as the nonrenewal of an employee's contract or a promotion).

The distinction is blurred at least in part by the requirement in most states that in order to nonrenew a teacher's contract, the summative evaluation must include at least documentation of formative evaluation. Employees enjoy certain types of legislative protection within the performance appraisal process. These legal issues are one of several reasons that can be offered for paying more attention to the psychometric properties of performance assessments (such as reliability and validity).

Most personnel texts recognize the importance of reliability and validity. While reliability deals with the various types of consistency that may or may not be in a process, the various types of validity deal with how well the performance appraisal process performs relative to the intended purpose of the procedure. The two most salient types of validity are content and construct. Content validity, which is analytically determined, basically examines the process to see whether it evaluates all that it purports to and only that which it purports to evaluate. In other words, content validity evaluates whether there is anything deficient, or is being missed (e.g., if creativity was important, is that part of what is being assessed?), or whether there is anything contaminating the assessment (e.g., if classroom order were one aspect of the process, that should not influence other aspects of the assessment), or whether there is anything extra being assessed that should not be (e.g., if personal appearance was not important to a particular school, then that would not need to be part of the assessment). Construct validity, on the other hand, is more complex and involves multiple approaches attempting to support the process in terms of whether constructs (such as leadership or empathy) are accurately measured.

In conclusion, performance assessment in education has become an issue with very high stakes while the field is struggling with the reliability and validity of both student and employee assessments.

—A. William Place

See also achievement tests; halo effect; job descriptions; management by objectives; merit pay; No Child Left Behind; performance evaluation systems; portfolios; standardized testing; supervision; testing and test theory development; walk-throughs, of classrooms

Further Readings and References

Alexander, P. (2004). Rethinking schooling as academic development. *Mid-Western Educational Researcher, 17*(1), 15–20.

Downey, C., Steffy, B., English, F., Frase, L., & Poston, W. (2005). *The three-minute classroom walk-through: Changing school supervisory practice one teacher at a time.* Thousand Oaks, CA: Corwin Press.

Frase, L. (2005). Refocusing the purposes of teacher supervision. In F. English (Ed.), *The SAGE handbook of educational leadership* (pp. 430–462). Thousand Oaks, CA: Sage.

Glatthorn, A., with Bragaw, D., Dawkins, K., & Parker, J. (1998). *Performance assessment and standards-based curricula: The achievement cycle.* Larchmont, NY: Eye on Education.

McNergney, R., Imig, S., & Pearlman, M. (2003). Teacher evaluation. In J. Guthrie (Ed.), *Encyclopedia of education* (Vol. 7, 2nd ed., pp. 2453–2461). New York: Macmillan.

Young, I., & Castetter, W. (2004). *The human resource function in educational administration* (8th ed.). Upper Saddle River, NJ: Pearson Prentice Hall.

PERFORMANCE EVALUATION SYSTEMS

Performance evaluation systems are managerial tools designed to facilitate an organization in accomplishing certain strategic goals in the human resource area. Within the public school setting, performance appraisal systems encompass and expand traditional employee assessment tasks through a systematic plan of execution design to accomplish specific goals. Underlying the emergence and adoption of performance appraisal systems by public school districts are certain societal events.

Most notably among these societal events is the recent focus on accountability with respect to academic performance of students as measured by state proficiency tests. In the past, formal accountability measures were almost nonexistent relative to student performance. Today, accountability measures of student performance are disaggregated according to school districts, building levels, as well as classroom settings, and this information is reported in the popular press and on the World Wide Web.

Accompanying the accountability movement and influencing the adoptions of performance evaluation systems on the part of school districts is the emergence and saturation of employee unions within the public school setting. Employee appraisal, once an exclusive managerial task, has become a bilateral concern involving unions as well as school administrators. To accommodate the concerns of both parties, performance evaluation systems are more viable than the traditional appraisal process used by most public school districts in the past.

Indeed, in the past, employee appraisals were viewed as an event as opposed to a performance evaluation process. As an event, performance appraisals were conducted on a particular day, based on a single job observation, void of defined goals, and lacked any formal follow-up in most instances. As a result, an employee could fair well or not so well depending on the day chosen for the appraisal.

In contrast to the traditional methods of performance appraisal, performance evaluation systems fill many voids. Structurally, performance evaluation systems impose a formal structure for the employee evaluation process involving input from administrators as well as employees. At minimum, this structure of performance evaluation systems involves a preassessment conference, an on-job observation(s), as well as an assessment of appropriate information, and a postconference debriefing.

Goals of the preassessment conference are to outline organizational expectations relative to purpose, to describe the manner in which the evaluation process will be conducted, to present the employee with appraisal instruments, and to discuss employee concerns. Each of these topics is a necessary part of an effective performance evaluation system, and each deserves further consideration. For example, with respect to the purpose of the appraisal, as fundamental as this may seem, the purpose is often overlooked or unknown by the participants.

The purpose of a performance evaluation system can vary in some important ways, and these ways of variation are often mutually exclusive. Purposes of a performance evaluation system could be to assess if a particular employee should be retained by a school district, to determine among employees those most entitled to awards, merit increases, promotions, or special training, or to identify particular skill enhancement areas for making individuals better employees. Based on these separate purposes that a performance evaluation system can fulfill, different referent standards are utilized by effective performance evaluation systems.

The referent standards appropriate for a performance evaluation system designed to determine if the services of an employee should be retained is a criteria reference system. A criteria reference system is designed to determine if employees achieve a satisfactory performance relative to certain preestablished standards. When employees achieve an acceptable level of performance relative to preestablished standards, they are retained, and when they fail to achieve an acceptable level of performance on preestablished standards, they are released.

In contrast to a criteria referenced system is a norm referenced system. A norm referenced performance evaluation system compares the job performance of an employee to the job performance of all other employees to yield a rank ordering of employees without any reference to an external standard (criteria referenced system). Norm referenced performance evaluation systems provide data necessary for distinguishing among those entitled to awards, merit increases, promotions, or special training.

Still different are self-referenced performance evaluation systems. Self-referenced performance evaluation systems assess the performance of any given employee on all dimensions of job performance performed and provide information about relative levels of performance on each dimension. A measure of relative levels for performance across job dimensions is necessary to identify areas either for remedial work or for work enhancement of employees.

Accompanying each of these referent sources (criteria, norm, or self), varying according to purported purpose, is specific performance assessment techniques that form the foundation of any performance evaluation system. Largely grouped, these techniques are rating procedures, ranking methods, and subjective techniques. Several variations exist for operationalizing performance evaluation systems according to each family of techniques.

Rating procedures used in performance evaluation systems can be differentiated relative to how anchor points are determined for criteria reference scales. Anchor points relative to specific criteria can be numerically determined (e.g., 1–5), verbally determined (e.g., never-always), or behaviorally determined. Behaviorally anchored rating scales (BARS) have produced an entire body of literature and have been found to be by far the most superior rating technique for evaluating employees, because these types of scales exhibit actual levels of job performance for specific levels.

Ranking procedures used to form the foundation for a performance evaluation system range from very simple to very complex. Simple derivations of ranking techniques involve sorting employees in ascending (or descending) order relative to performance, while more complicated derivations involve a paired comparison, where each employee is compared individually to all other employees. The choice between ranking techniques for use in a performance evaluation system depends largely on the number of employees to be evaluated.

Performance evaluation systems relying on self-reference techniques designed to improve the performance of individual employees draw from several subjective techniques. Most common among the traditional techniques for self-referent comparison is management by objectives (MBO), and achieving recent popularity are portfolio assessments. As compared to either rating or ranking techniques, performance evaluation systems using self-referent comparisons afford employees the greatest input within a performance evaluation system.

Finally, performance evaluation systems differ in significant ways when compared to traditional performance appraisal processes. Current performance evaluation systems, as enacted by progressive public school districts, focus specifically on purpose, a referent group, and a defined evaluation technique. By so focusing, those human resource goals are much more likely to be accomplished.

—*I. Phillip Young*

See also accountability; achievement tests; administration, theories of; attitudes toward work; behaviorism; bureaucracy; classroom management; clinical supervision; differentiated staffing; esteem needs; flow theory; halo effect; human resource development; Interstate School Leaders Licensure Consortium; management by objectives; management theories; measurement, theories of; mentoring; merit pay; performance assessment; personnel management; salary and salary models; self-actualization; staffing, concepts of; standardized testing; supervision; work task measurement

Further Readings and References

Alexander, B., Anderson, G., & Gallegos, B. (2004). *Performance theories in education: Power, pedagogy, and the politics of identity.* Mahwah, NJ: Erlbaum.

Conley, S., & Bacharach, S. (1992). Performance appraisal in education: A strategic consideration. In L. Frase (Ed.), *Teacher compensation and motivation* (pp. 261–273). Lancaster, PA: Technomic.

Haas, E., & Poynor, L.(2005). Issues of teaching and learning. In F. English (Ed.), *The SAGE handbook of leadership* (pp. 483–505). Thousand Oaks, CA: Sage.

Heneman, H., & Judge, T. (2002). *Staffing organizations* (4th ed.). Middleton WI: Mendota House.

Peterman, F. (2005). *Designing performance assessment systems for urban teacher preparation.* Mahwah, NJ: Erlbaum.

Young, I. P., & Castetter, W. (2004). *The human resource function in educational administration* (8th ed.). Columbus, OH: Merrill Prentice Hall

PERSONALITY

The psychological construct of personality affects education in a variety of significant ways, including student achievement and performance, faculty performance, and educational leadership styles and capabilities. Understanding the rudiments of personality disorders, and the inventories and profiles used to define them, provides educational leaders with the knowledge to better understand why people behave as they do. From this knowledge, one can better develop and manage successful programs and interventions for students exhibiting a variety of needs and learning preferences.

PERSONALITY

The many existing theories of personality differ in causal explanations, description of behaviors, and perspective (differences vs. commonalities). Despite the number and variety of theories, some commonalities emerge: stages of development, temperament or genetic predisposition, impact and types of learning, motivational effects, impact of emotions on thinking and behavior, and a focus on conscious and unconscious processes. Many theorists describe personality in terms of individual differences. They focus on types and categories of people and behavior, for example, introversion versus extroversion, auditory versus visual learner, self-focus versus altruism. Other theories focus on the commonalities in people. The question is, What do people with this certain type of behavior have in common? These common characteristics may then be used as a basis for developing profiles of individuals suited for certain tasks (e.g., jobs, careers, relationships). Regardless of perspective, personality theorists focus on the psychological structure of the individual and attempt to explain human behavior from that perspective.

The large number of personality theories are typically organized in textbooks into major categories based on similarities in the theories. Common groupings include the following.

Behavioral and Social Learning Theories

Theories in this group tend to explain behavior (personality) in terms of reaction to external stimuli and events. John Watson is credited with beginning this school of thought. He believed that behavior was not related to the mind or human consciousness; rather, behavior was the result of reflexes and conditioning. B. F. Skinner carried Watson's work further and developed the principle of operant conditioning. In addition to responding to their environment, people "operate" on their environment as well as produce certain consequences. Operant conditioning is the situation where when a response is no longer followed by a consequence (it is not reinforced), it will cease to occur. Related to this is the social learning theory developed by Albert Bandura (who also may be categorized as a cognitive social learning theorist). He suggested that memory and feelings operate in conjunction with environmental influences. If one displays an incompatible behavior, the original behavior ceases to be displayed.

Many of the concepts and terminology used in understanding and describing student learning and behavior are derived from behaviorism. Classroom management of students is often described and developed based on behavior principles such as successive approximation (reward successive steps to the final desired behavior), continuous reinforcement (promote new behavior by rewarding every small step toward it), negative reinforcement (to increase a desired behavior, arrange/allow escape from a mild aversive situation by behaving appropriately), modeling (observe a significant person demonstrating the desired positive behavior), and cueing (to remember to act at a specific time in response to an arranged cue, rather than after the fact).

Biological

The biological approach to personality includes investigations of the impact of genetics, evolution, neuropsychology, and other biological functions and processes (e.g., hormones, neurotransmitters) that influence personality. It is not a cohesive approach; rather, it is an amalgam of investigations attempting to relate biological processes to personality. Evolutionary psychologists (sometimes referred to as sociobiologists) think that psychological adaptations are not qualitatively different from physical adaptations in evolution. Examples of some aspects of human psychology that are studied from this perspective include intellectual capacity, language, emotions, and sexual behaviors.

The biological basis of behavior is supported by scientists' ability to reproduce behaviors in successive generations of organisms (e.g., herding behavior of border collies) and to identify species-specific behaviors. A brain injury can produce dramatic changes in one's behavior and personality. Behaviors associated with certain mental illnesses tend to run in families. Some behaviors have an evolutionary history that exists across species. Chimpanzees and humans share traits such as cooperation, altruism, and nurturing.

Researchers in behavioral genetics have made claims for behaviors, including aggression, impulsivity, and nurturing.

Special educators have long acknowledged the biological basis of many learning and behavior differences in students. Students with learning disabilities are sometimes referred to as "hard wired" differently from those without such difficulties. Many children diagnosed as having attention-deficit/hyperactivity disorder (ADHD) respond favorably to stimulant medications (Adderol, Ritalin, Cylert), suggesting a neurochemical basis for the condition. The preliminary returns of the massive Human Genome Project are providing chromosomal maps of components of human personality. Future research in the area of the biological bases of personality will undoubtedly shed more light on the relationship of biology and personality.

Cognitive

Cognitive approaches to personality emphasize the mind and its relationship to behavior. These approaches describe how cognitive processes influence learning, how normal maturation produces increasingly sophisticated thinking, and how people organize things they learn. It also emphasizes that new information is most easily acquired when people can associate it with things they have previously learned and that people control their own learning.

Educators are most familiar with the work of Jean Piaget, who spent a lifetime delving into the basic question of How does knowledge develop and grow? Cognitive development is described in terms of changes in a child's cognitive structures, abilities, and processes. Cognitive performance is directly associated with the cognitive developmental stage they are in. The four major stages are (1) sensorimotor (birth to 2 years)—children "think" with their hands, ears, eyes, nose, mouth; (2) preoperational (2 to 6/7 years)—egocentric thinking and behavior, mental imagery developing, language developing; (3) concrete (6/7 to 11/12 years)—decentering occurs, logical and organized thought processes emerge; and (4) formal (11/12 years to adult)—development of abstract, theoretical thinking. Cognitive change takes place through equilibration encompassing assimilation (transform information to fit existing schemes) and accommodation (adapt schemes to include incoming information).

Educators have used Piaget's work to develop guiding principles of practice. These include the provision of an active, discovery-oriented classroom environment, inclusion of peer teaching and interactional activities, and instructional strategies to make children aware of conflicts and inconsistencies in their thinking (e.g., Socratic dialogue). Specific instructional techniques derived from this theoretical approach include anchored instruction, authentic learning, scaffolding, modeling, and coaching.

Humanistic and Existential

The humanistic and existential theorists focus on the uniqueness of humanity. This school of thought emerged as a backlash to behaviorism, trait, and psychodynamic theories in the 1950s. The free will of people is emphasized. Humanistic theorists focus on the subjective experiences of individuals and their positive drive toward self-fulfillment. Personality is understood and described in the present ("here and now") rather than in the past, with an emphasis on personal responsibility. Hallmarks include a focus on conscious experiences and a belief in the value of phenomenology.

Notable humanistic psychologists include Alfred Adler, Abraham Maslow, and Carl Rogers. Adler, a former student and colleague of Sigmund Freud, developed his theory of individual psychology, with a primary motivating force being the human need to strive for perfection. Secondarily was his idea of social interest, that is, caring for family, society, humanity, and all of life.

Maslow is best known for establishing his theory of the hierarchy of needs. He believed that people are basically trustworthy and capable of self-governance. He categorized basic types of human needs as being physiological, safety, love, and esteem. Satisfying these needs is seen as healthy.

Carl Rogers is often thought of as the founder of humanistic psychology. Humanists view people as basically good or healthy and positive mental health as a normal progression of life. Personality problems are distortions of the human drive to self-actualization. This is very similar to Adler's "striving for perfection" motivator. Rogers developed the concept of positive regard (love, acceptance, affection, attention, nurturance) as a human value. Achieving this positive regard under certain conditions came to be known as conditional positive regard and is seen as the cause of many self-esteem issues in humans.

Educators have seen the influence of humanistic theories of personality in the proliferation of character education programs available in schools. Counseling techniques and practices common in schools have also been developed (e.g., the practice of unconditional acceptance) from a humanistic perspective.

Psychoanalytic

Theories in this group usually focus first on the work of Sigmund Freud. His psychosexual stage development theory highlighted the power of the conscious and unconscious processes that influence emotions and behavior. The goal of therapy is to make the unconscious conscious. The interaction of the three constructs of the id (instincts and wishes), ego (reality mediator), and the superego (conscience) determine one's personality. The id operates on the pleasure principle and the ego on the reality principle. The superego is an internalization of both warnings (conscience) and the ego ideal (positive models).

Other notable theorists in this group include Anna Freud (Sigmund Freud's daughter), Erik Erikson, and Carl Jung. Erikson disagreed with Freud over the influence of instinctual drives: his psychosocial stage theory emphasized the influence of society on the ego and how individuals adapt to different social demands. Jung developed what is described as a transpersonal perspective, focusing on symbolism and the collective unconscious.

Trait

Trait theories emphasize a temporally stable description of one's behavior, rather than a causal explanation. Traits are those cross-situational characteristics of a person that are related to thoughts, feelings, and behaviors, and they tend to fall along a continuum in terms of intensity of expression. For example, a person characterized as an extrovert is likely to be talkative and enjoy the company of others. Several of the major trait theorists include Gordon Allport, Raymond Cattell, Hans Eysenck, Lewis Goldberg, and John Holland.

Allport described three types of traits that vary in degree of expression: cardinal (around which people organize their life—e.g., greed, kindness), central (major characteristics), and secondary (enduring qualities that don't explain general behavior).

Cattell used factor analytic techniques to describe 16 primary personality factors and 5 secondary factors. From this theory, he developed the 16-Personality Factor Questionnaire.

Eysenck developed a hierarchical model of personality that links types, traits, and behaviors. The two primary dimensions include scales labeled introversion-extroversion and neuroticism-stability. He also examined the relationship of human biological processes to behavior and personality.

Goldberg built his work on the theory of Cattell, and developed a five-dimension personality model. The so-called big five are (1) extroversion (assertive vs. shy, quiet, reserved), (2) agreeableness (sympathetic vs. cold, argumentative), (3) conscientiousness (organized, responsible vs. careless, irresponsible), (4) emotional stability (calm, content vs. anxious, temperamental), and (5) intellect (creative, open minded vs. simple, unintelligent).

Holland developed a six-type model often used in career counseling. The types are (1) realistic (physical, hands on), (2) investigative (scientific, technical), (3) artistic (writing, painting), (4) social (supporting, helping), (5) enterprising (organizing, motivating), and (6) conventional (clerical, detail oriented).

PERSONALITY DISORDERS

A personality disorder is a psychological construct characterized by a pervasive pattern of behavior that is abnormal with respect to mood, thought, relationships, and/or impulse control. Individuals with a personality disorder experience tremendous difficulty in interactions with others. They tend to be somewhat inflexible and constricted in their range of adaptable behaviors to normal life situations. In addition, they are typically unaware of the impact their behavior has on others, thinking that their behavior(s) is justified and appropriate.

Personality disorders are often recognizable in adolescence and tend to manifest themselves throughout adulthood. Clinicians often report similar behaviors in children; however, the construct of conduct disorder is used to describe this constellation of behaviors in children. Regardless of one's theoretical orientation to personality, the holy grail of terminology is found in the *Diagnostic and Statistical Manual of Mental Disorders* (4th ed.) *(DSM-IV)*, published by the American Psychiatric Association. Personality disorder is described in the manual as a lasting pattern of behavior that is pervasive and inflexible, remains stable over time, and results in impairment. Ten distinct personality disorders are described in the *DSM-IV*.

The personality disorders and their characteristic features are summarized below:

Antisocial Personality Disorder

These individuals tend to disregard social rules, may be deceitful (lying), impulsive, irritable, or aggressive, demonstrate a disregard for the safety of self or others, are irresponsible at work and/or financially, and/or demonstrate a lack of remorse for having mistreated others.

Avoidant Personality Disorder

These individuals tend to display social inhibition and feelings of inadequacy. They may avoid occupations involving significant personal interactions, demonstrate an inordinate need to be liked, have difficulty forming intimate relationships for fear of being shamed, are preoccupied with fears of rejection in social situations or feelings of inadequacy, view self as inferior to others, and are afraid of appropriate risk-taking due to a fear of being embarrassed.

Borderline Personality Disorder

These individuals have persistent relationship difficulties and marked impulsivity related to efforts to avoid real or imagined abandonment, unstable and intense interpersonal relationships alternating between idealization and devaluation, impulsivity in two or more areas that are considered self-damaging (such as spending, sex, substance abuse, reckless driving), a marked reactivity of mood lasting a few hours or a few days, chronic feelings of "emptiness," difficulty controlling anger, and/or stress-related paranoid ideation or severe dissociative symptoms.

Dependent Personality Disorder

These individuals demonstrate an excessive need to be taken care of that is manifested by submissive and clinging behavior. They often require excessive reassurance from others, have difficulty expressing disagreements, initiating projects, or doing things on their own, feel helpless when alone, and/or immediately seek a relationship when one ends.

Histrionic Personality Disorder

These individuals display excessive emotionality and attention seeking behavior. They may be uncomfortable not being the center of attention, may be inappropriately seductive, display rapidly but shallow emotions, use physical appearance to draw attention to self, are prone to self-dramatization, and/or may consider relationships to be more intimate than they are.

Narcissistic Personality Disorder

These individuals exhibit a pattern of grandiosity, need for admiration, and exhibit a lack of empathy. They may exaggerate achievements and talents, are preoccupied with fantasies of success, power, beauty, and brilliance, believe that they are unique, require excessive admiration, operate with a sense of entitlement, are exploitive of others, demonstrate a lack of empathy, believe that others are envious of them, and/or may demonstrate arrogant behaviors or attitudes.

Obsessive-Compulsive Personality Disorder

These individuals have a preoccupation with orderliness, perfectionism, and interpersonal control at the expense of flexibility, openness, and efficiency. They may be preoccupied with details, rules, lists, order, and organization to the extent that the major focus of the activity is lost, overconscientious and inflexible about matters of morality, ethics, and values, and/or reluctant to delegate tasks or work with others unless things are done exactly their way.

Paranoid Personality Disorder

These individuals demonstrate a pervasive distrust and suspiciousness of others such that their motives are interpreted as malevolent. They may be suspicious that others are exploiting them, doubt the trustworthiness of others, read hidden demeaning meanings into benign remarks or events, bear grudges, are quick to react angrily, and/or may demonstrate recurrent suspicions, without justification, regarding fidelity of their sexual partner.

Schizoid Personality Disorder

These individuals exhibit a detachment from social relationships and a restricted range of expression of emotions in interpersonal settings. They neither desire nor enjoy close relationships, prefer solitary activities, have little interest in sexual experiences with another, take pleasure in few activities, and/or may show emotional coldness, detachment, or flattened affectivity.

Schizotypal Personality Disorder

These individuals experience acute discomfort or reduced capacity for close relationships as well as demonstrate cognitive or perceptual distortions and eccentricities of behavior.

PERSONALITY INVENTORIES AND PROFILES

Personality inventories are standardized instruments that may be administered individually or in a group setting. Many may be computer scored. The scores are compared with norms for each of the categories on the instrument: some measure one factor, such as depression, while others measure a number of personality traits at the same time. There are literally hundreds of inventories and profiles available to clinicians and others trained to interpret the results accurately. The reader is referred to the *Fifteenth Mental Measurements Yearbook* published by the Buros Institute (also available online) for descriptions and reviews of all inventories and profiles.

Some of the more commonly used inventories that educators may encounter include the following.

NEO Personality Inventory Revised (NEO-PI-R)

This inventory is based on the five-factor (neuroticism, extraversion, openness to experience, agreeableness, conscientiousness) model of personality, and provides a general description of personality.

Cattell's 16 Personal Factor Questionnaire (16 PF 5th ed.)

This inventory has been used for over 40 years by clinicians for treatment planning, marriage counseling, and vocational guidance. Global factors addressed are labeled extraversion, anxiety, tough-mindedness, independence, and self-control.

Minnesota Multiphasic Personality Inventory 2nd ed. (MMPI-2)

This inventory was developed in the 1930s for adults but has been used extensively with adolescents. The MMPI-2 does not have adolescent norms; therefore, the user is directed to the MMPI-A normed on an adolescent population. The MMPI-2 contains 10 clinical scales describing the symptoms of a variety of personality-disorder-related behaviors.

California Personality Inventory (CPI)

This inventory was derived from the MMPI. It yields scales on a number of factors, including dominance, self-acceptance, self-control, socialization, and achievement.

Myers Briggs Type Indicator (MBTI)

This inventory is based on the psychological types described by Carl Jung. The essence of the theory is that variation in behavior is orderly and consistent, being due to basic differences in the way individuals prefer to use their perception and judgment. The 16 different personality types result from the interactions among the preferences.

Eysenck Personality Inventory (EPI)

This inventory is based on Eysenck's factor analysis of personality that places people on a pair of independent continua (extraversion-introversion and neuroticism-stability). He believed that personality factors were genetically influenced.

—*George W. Griffin*

See also at-risk students; attitudes; behaviorism; Binet, Alfred; bullying; Burt, Cyril; Cattell, Raymond; cognition, theories of; counseling; cultural capital; dogmatism and scales of Rokeach; dropouts; egocentrism, theories of; emotional disturbance; esteem needs; flow theory; Freud, Sigmund; humanistic education; individual differences, in children; intelligence; Jung, Carl; learning, theories of; Maslow, Abraham; mental illness, in adults and children; multiculturalism; Piaget, Jean; psychology, types of; Rogers, Carl; self-actualization; sexuality, theories of; Skinner, B. F.; Spearman, Charles; standardized testing; subjectivism, in theory; Thorndike, Edward; trait theory; Wolf, Montrose

Further Readings and References

American Psychiatric Association. (1994). *Diagnostic and statistical manual of mental disorders* (4th ed.). Washington, DC: American Psychiatric Association.

Bettis, P., & Adams, N. (2005). *Geographies of girlhood.* Mahwah, NJ: Erlbaum.

Costa, P., & Widiger, T. (Eds.). (2001). *Personality disorders and the five-factor model of personality* (2nd ed.). Washington, DC: American Psychological Association.

Carson, R., Butcher, J., & Mineka, S. (2000). *Abnormal psychology and modern life* (11th ed.). New York: Allyn & Bacon.

Freidman, H., & Schustak, M. (2003). *Personality: Classic theories and modern research* (2nd ed.). Boston: Allyn & Bacon.

Frick, W. (1991). *Personality theories.* New York: Teachers College Press.

Hambleton, R., Merenda, P., & Spielberger, C. (2005). *Adapting educational and psychological tests for cross-cultural assessment.* Mahwah, NJ: Erlbaum.

Kline, T. (2005). *Psychological testing: A practical approach to design and evaluation.* Thousand Oaks, CA: Sage.

Lapsley, D., & Narvaez, D. (2004). *Moral development, self, and identity.* Mahwah, NJ: Erlbaum.

Milton, J. (2002). *The road to Malpsychia: Humanistic psychology and our discontents.* San Francisco: Encounter Books.

Paul, A. (2004). *The cult of personality: How personality tests are leading us to miseducate our children, mismanage our companies, and misunderstand ourselves.* New York: Free Press.

Plake, B., Impara, J., & Spies, R. (Eds.). (2003). *Fifteenth mental measurements yearbook.* Lincoln: University of Nebraska Press.

Wood, J., Nezworski, M., Lilienfeld, S., & Garb, H. (2003). *What's wrong with the Rorschach?* San Francisco: Jossey-Bass.

🏛 PERSONNEL MANAGEMENT

The personnel management process consists of the following steps: (a) recruitment, (b) selection, (c) staff development, and (d) performance appraisal. Figure 1 illustrates these steps. The figure also indicates that all of these various activities are affected by legislative constraints and union demands

RECRUITMENT

Recruitment is the process of attracting a pool of qualified applicants to replenish or expand a school's human resources. To effectively recruit applicants, leaders must (a) have a thorough analysis of job requirements, (b) know the legal constraints that influence recruiting efforts, and (c) cultivate the sources of potential employees. To recruit appropriate

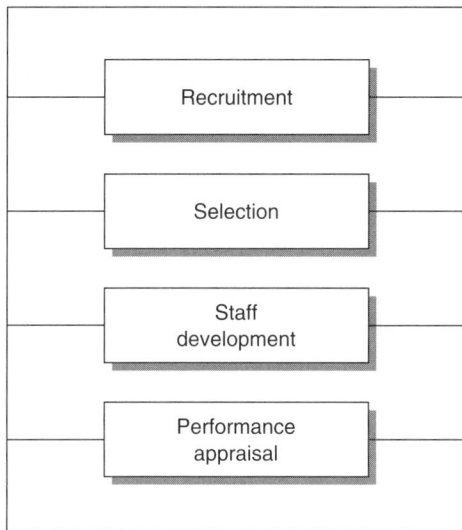

Figure 1 Personnel Management Process

SOURCE: Author.

personnel to fill vacant positions, the leader must know in detail what tasks are to be performed and the personal characteristics necessary to perform the tasks. These determinations are derived through *job analysis.* The information obtained through job analysis is used in most subsequent personnel decisions, such as selection, staff development, and performance appraisal. But its most immediate use is to prepare job descriptions and job specifications.

The *job description* is a written statement of the duties and responsibilities, relationships, and results expected of the job incumbent. It generally includes job title, the person to whom the job incumbent reports, and a statement of the job goal. The *job specification,* also based on job analysis, specifies the minimum acceptable qualification that an incumbent must possess to perform the job successfully. It identifies the degree of education required, the desirable amount of previous experience, and the skills, abilities, and physical requirements needed to do the job effectively.

Every leader is affected to some extent by federal laws governing the recruitment and selection of employees. The laws governing *equal employment opportunity* (EEO) have had an especially long history in the United States; the laws prohibit employment decisions based on race, color, religion, sex, national origin, age, or disability. This legal environment has increased the need for high-caliber leaders who can deal with the complex legal requirements in personnel management.

School districts have a number of sources available for obtaining personnel. The first place that most leaders look when attempting to fill a position is within the school district. Policies for promotion from within are widely used, because they tend to increase employee morale and motivation while reducing recruitment costs.

External sources of potential employees are used when specialized skills, such as those of teachers, counselors, social workers, and computer programmers, are required. Some of the most frequently used external sources include college and university placement offices, state employment services, private employment agencies, newspaper and radio advertisements, professional journals, employee referrals, and professional meetings and conventions.

School districts that are committed to equal employment opportunities and affirmative action programs typically take additional steps to ensure that available positions are provided the broadest possible publicity, for example: (a) advertising in publications designed specifically for minority candidates, (b) contacting colleges and universities that specialize in educating women or minorities, (c) contacting employment agencies that specialize in placing women and minority candidates, and (d) contacting neighborhood groups or national organizations, such as the Urban League or the National Organization for Women, to reach minorities and women. These organizations, and groups like them, have newsletters or other media for contacting minority and female prospects.

SELECTION

Once applicants have been recruited, the next step is *selection*—the process of determining which candidates best meet the job specifications. Steps in a typical selection process include (a) preliminary screening of credentials, (b) preliminary interview, (c) testing, (d) reference checks, (e) in-depth interview, (f) physical examination, and (g) hiring decision.

The actual selection process will vary with school districts and between hierarchical levels in the same school district. For instance, the in-depth interview for classified staff may be quite perfunctory; instead, heavy emphasis may be placed on the preliminary screening interview or on performance tests. In selecting certificated personnel, like teachers, the interview may be extensive—sometimes lasting 1 hour or more—and there may be little or no formal testing. Instead of completing an application blank, the candidate for a certificated position may submit a letter of application and/or a resume. Some school districts omit the physical examination.

STAFF DEVELOPMENT

Schools recruit and select people who match their job specifications as closely as possible, but the match is seldom perfect. Usually staff at all levels—maintenance, service, clerical, and professional—need to be taught how to apply their abilities to the requirements of the specific job. This instruction, which teaches new employees the skills they need, is known as *training*. *Development* usually refers to teaching experienced professionals how to maintain and even improve those skills.

The training and development of faculty and staff is essentially a four-step process: (1) assessing needs, (2) setting objectives, (3) selecting methods, and (4) evaluating the program.

PERFORMANCE APPRAISAL

After employees have been recruited, selected, and trained, the next step in the personnel management process is *performance appraisal*—the process of evaluating the contribution employees have made toward attaining the school's goals. There are several reasons to evaluate employee performance. First, the school needs evidence to justify the selection techniques used in hiring personnel. Second, performance appraisal provides input for determining both individual and organizational staff development needs and later gauges whether these have been effective. Third, it serves as the basis for making decisions about salary and merit increases, promotions, transfers, or terminations. Finally, it is used as a means of communicating to employees how they are performing and suggesting needed changes in behavior, attitudes, skills, or knowledge.

—*Fred C. Lunenburg*

See also affirmative action; American Federation of Teachers; bureaucracy; career stages; chief academic officer; contracts, with teacher unions; differentiated staffing; discrimination; division of labor; evaluation; fringe benefits;

governance; human capital; human resource development; internships; involvement, in organizations; just cause; licensure and certification; line and staff concept; management by objectives; management information systems; management theories; mentoring; merit pay; morale; National Education Association; organizational theories; performance assessment; performance evaluation systems; planning models; politics, of education; principalship; productivity; recruitment, of school administrators; resource management; role ambiguity; role conflict; role theory; satisfaction, in organizations and roles; scalar principle; sexism (glass ceiling); staffing, concepts of; superintendency; supervision; table of organization; total quality management; working conditions, in schools; workplace trends

Further Readings and References

DeMitchell, T. (2005). Unions, collective bargaining, and the challenge of leading. In F. English (Ed.), *The SAGE handbook of educational leadership* (pp. 538–549). Thousand Oaks, CA: Sage.

Fyack, C. (2004). *Hiring sourcebook: A collection of practical samples.* Alexandria, VA: Society for Human Resource Management.

Ivancevich, J. (2003). *Human resource management* (8th ed.). New York: McGraw-Hill.

U.S. Department of Labor, Bureau of Labor Statistics. (2005). *Employment and earnings.* Washington, DC: Government Printing Office.

Walsh, D. (2003). *Employment law for human resource practice.* Mason, OH: Thomson/South-Western West.

Webb, L., & Norton, M. (2003). *Human resources administration: Personnel issues and needs in education* (4th ed.). Upper Saddle River, NJ: Merrill/Prentice Hall.

Young, I. P., & Castetter, W. B. (2004). *The human resource function* (8th ed.). Upper Saddle River, NJ: Merrill/Prentice Hall.

🏛 PERSUASION

Persuasion is a form of social influence that is based on communication. Persuasion occurs when one person intends to and is successful at using communication to affect another person. Persuasive communications can target another's attitudes, beliefs, or behaviors. The focus of persuasion theory and research has been on attitudes: many techniques are actually derived from specific attitude change theories. Attitudes, a central concept in social psychology, are evaluative judgments about an object, person, or issue. Attitudes can be favorable or unfavorable, can vary in strength, and can but do not necessarily include affective, cognitive, and behavioral responses. Current research demonstrates that under certain circumstances, attitudes are predictors of behavior.

Attitudes, though formed by beliefs, are not the same as beliefs. Attitudes are based on judgments; beliefs, be they factual or stereotypical, are information based. Some attitudes are easily changed, while others are more enduring. Attitudes, which are central to human life, help make the social world more predictable, help determine one's behavior, help process information, and even help to define who we are. Knowing what function an attitude serves in any given situation is a key factor in designing persuasive appeals. Attitude change is more likely to occur when the persuasive appeal targets the function served by the existing attitude. The mechanisms behind attitude formation and attitude change are thought to be the same.

Two competing dual-processing theories, the elaboration-likelihood model and the heuristic-systematic model, postulate differing mechanisms for attitude change. One mechanism is based on *effortless* processing of information, and the other is based on *effortful* processing of information.

The effortless processing or "peripheral processing" is a form of persuasion widely used by the media. Peripheral processing is based on associations between the positions being advanced and the objects or people to which a person is attracted. Central-route processing, a more effortful type of processing, involves thinking about or elaborating on significant issues. For central-route processing to result in attitude change, the persuasive arguments must be compelling but not too complex. Factors affecting recipient motivation to process information and the strength of the argument include a match between the persuasive argument and the function that the preexisting attitude serves, the number of arguments contained in the persuasive message, the relevance of the message to the recipient, and the level of recipient need to think about the message.

The effortless processing mechanism is based on heuristics, "simple rules of inference," such as "experts are correct," and occurs whenever the heuristic cue is present. Systematic processing occurs when the heuristic cue is not present or when message recipients do not have enough confidence in their attitudinal judgments. Its mechanisms are thought to be similar to those used in central-route processing.

The dual-processing models account for the fact that people are sometimes responsive to well-organized persuasive appeals, whereas at other times they are influenced by seemingly extraneous factors. Using persuasion to affect attitude formation and effect change can be a complex undertaking, and educational leaders can expect to benefit by becoming skilled in the use of persuasive communication. As a form of influence, persuasion implies that the person being persuaded has some element of freedom. In the absence of freedom, interpersonal transactions may become coercive. As schools move away from autocratic leadership, influence—not control—becomes the basis for leading others.

—*Jami Finn and Rodney Muth*

See also attitudes; attitudes toward work; behaviorism; communications, theories in organizations; conditioning theory; decision making; expert power; heuristics; leadership, theories of; management theories; mentoring; motivation, theories of; tutoring

Further Readings and References

Bohner, G., & Wanke, M. (2002). *Attitudes and attitude change.* New York: Psychology Press.

Devadoss, M., & Muth, R. (1984). Power, involvement, and organizational effectiveness in higher education. *Higher Education, 13,* 379–391.

O'Keeffe, D. (2002). *Persuasion theory and research* (2nd ed.). Thousand Oaks, CA: Sage.

PERT (PERFORMANCE EVALUATION AND REVIEW TECHNIQUE)

PERT (performance evaluation and review technique) is a large project management tool. Developed by the U.S. Navy in 1958 to manage the Polaris Fleet Ballistic Missile Program, PERT provides a visual representation of tasks, both sequential and parallel, that are needed to complete a complex project. For example, educational leaders have found PERT to be very effective at meeting deadlines for curricular implementations and avoiding cost overruns on building projects.

This management tool addresses time, events, costs, and people-power needs in unique projects, although it can be used in twice-run projects. Unlike bar charts, PERT can predict how long completion of tasks will take as well as the entire project. The strength of PERT lies in its visual representation of interdependencies and uncertainties. The resulting diagram allows those involved within the project to see how their work impacts others. Identification of timelines and critical path activities avoids the confusion that can impact completion.

PERT evolves in three stages: planning, establishing time and sequence of events, and diagramming. The first step in a PERT diagram (or network) is the statement of the project objective. The written objective is specific and contains all necessary specifications. A list of needed tasks is the next stage. From these tasks, events evolve. These events are sequenced and time allotments allocated. The next step is the diagram.

The PERT diagram, usually drawn on paper, is constructed of ellipses (bubbles) that march from left to right. Each ellipse is an event, which is a specific instant of time. The event itself does not consume time, but rather marks the start (S) or completion (C) of a physical or mental task. In most networks, the start of one event is the completion of the event before it. An arrow connects events and represents the work required to complete a task. An activity cannot start until the previous event and all events before that have been completed. Ellipses are numbered by 10s so that unforeseen events or forgotten events can be inserted without redrawing the entire network.

A milestone in the PERT network is represented by a triangle. Each milestone symbolizes a key critical event that must be completed on time to avoid project delays.

Timelines on PERT can be done in a variety of different ways. One example is that each event can have three time values: the optimistic time, most likely time, and a pessimistic time. Time is expressed in weeks or fractions of weeks and is written on the arrow lines within the network in this sequence: optimistic time (to), most likely time (mlt), and pessimistic time (tp). To calculate the expected time (te) an activity will take, the three times figures are added together and divided by 3. To know how much time a milestone will take, one adds up the te's on the longest line leading to that event.

Determining the critical path, the longest path in the project, reveals the total calendar time for the project.

The amount of time that a noncritical path activity can be delayed without delaying the project is referred to as slack time. Slack time can be positive or negative. Project crashing accelerates the project by adding required resources to decrease the time for activities in the critical path.

To maintain the logic of the network, dummy activities can be inserted. An example of a dummy activity is an inspector looking at wiring. Although central to the project, the inspection requires no time or work. Time estimates for such dummy activities are represented by 0-0-0 on the activity line.

The most widespread continuing use of PERT in education occurs within the area of school plant management and promoting bond issues to facilitate school construction.

—JoAnn Franklin Klinker

See also economics, theories of; elections, of school boards, bond issues; finance, of public schools; matrix organization (the "adhocracy"); planning models; resource management; strategic planning; time management

Further Readings and References

Evarts, H. (1964). *Introduction to PERT.* Boston: Allyn & Bacon.

Lackney, J. (2005). New approaches to school design. In F. English (Ed.), *The SAGE handbook of educational leadership* (pp. 506–537). Thousand Oaks, CA: Sage.

Latterner, C. (Ed.). (1967). *A programmed introduction to PERT.* New York: John Wiley & Sons.

PHILOSOPHIES OF EDUCATION

Teaching and learning are guided by a variety of beliefs and principles that direct the practice of administrators and faculty responsible for these educational activities. These beliefs and principles make up a philosophy of education that can be used to guide decision making and practice. These philosophies are widely discussed and debated, subsequently giving rise to several schools of thought regarding how institutions of learning should be structured and organized and what teaching and learning look like within these institutions.

Six commonly debated philosophies include essentialism, behaviorism, perennialism, humanism, existentialism, progressivism, and social reconstructionism. This list is neither exhaustive nor agreed upon that all schools of thought should, in fact, be included. Each school of thought does provide a unique perspective on educational practices and will, therefore, be treated as distinctive and legitimate. Depending on the philosophy to which one subscribes, the structure and organization of the instructional environment and the activities that take place within that structure will range from one end of the educational spectrum to the other. An awareness and understanding of the philosophical underpinnings of each are essential to understanding and identifying the structures, organization, and activities that characterize learning environments based on each of the six philosophies. The order in which each is discussed ranges from conservative to liberal perspectives on education.

ESSENTIALISM

Essentialism is the most commonly applied philosophy in the American system of public education. Often referred to as the "back to the basics" approach, essentialism focuses on what some educators consider as the essential elements of academic knowledge and character development. Originating in the late 1800s, essentialism's rise in popularity paralleled America's influx of immigration in the late 1800s and around the turn of the century. Losing favor briefly in the mid-twentieth century with the adoption of more liberal educational philosophies, the essentialist movement was revived in the late 1950s and 1960s with the space race and the launching of Sputnik as a way to address students' needs for stronger math and science skills. This revival was again supported and promoted by the President's Commission on Excellence in Education through their 1983 report, *A Nation at Risk*.

Essentialist philosophy promotes cultural literacy, the traditional moral values, and the knowledge that students need to become productive American citizens. American virtues espoused by the philosophy of essentialism include respect for authority, perseverance, fidelity to duty, consideration for others, and practicality. Essentialism does not view schools as vehicles for societal change. It is important to note that essentialists believe that science and scientific experimentation provide insight into and understanding about the world. Essentialism therefore emphasizes natural sciences rather than nonscientific disciplines such as religion or philosophy. The nonscientific curriculum is often viewed as offering frills and has little, if any, place in the essentialist curriculum.

Building- and district-level administrators subscribing to essentialist thought will often promote and support basic and fundamental academic skills, including math, science, history, foreign language, and literature. A specific body of knowledge and basic techniques and skills are identified as the basis for a schoolwide curriculum that is academically rigorous

and focused on mastery learning. This focus subsequently requires more core course requirements, a longer school day, a longer academic year, and more challenging texts. Instruction that takes place in the classroom is teacher directed and evaluated through the use of standardized test scores. Teachers and administrators work together to identify what is important for students to learn, both intellectually and culturally, and to ensure that students graduate as disciplined, practical, and capable American citizens.

BEHAVIORISM

In the ongoing debate over nature versus nurture, nurture prevails from the perspective of a behaviorist. According to behaviorist philosophy, knowledge and understanding of reality are learned, and therefore the only true reality is that which can be observed and experienced. In addition, learning is the result of our actions and reactions to internal and/or external stimuli. Humans are simply the product of their environment.

The source of behavior results from external factors and variables rather than internal ones. Thus, learning results from stimulation by and observation of external phenomena. Through repetition and experimentation, students learn about the physical world and human nature. A school based on the behaviorist philosophy would typically structure the curriculum in such a way that students would have multiple opportunities to experience and interact with the content to be learned. Teachers and administrators must be aware of the external stimuli and variables inherent in a school that might impact or factor into how and what students are learning in that environment.

PERENNIALISM

Perennialists believe that certain ideas and truths are as relevant today as they were hundreds of years ago when these ideas were first discussed and debated. They believe that these "perennial" or everlasting ideas and truths should be the focus of classroom instruction. Based on the philosophy and teachings of Plato, Aristotle, St. Thomas Aquinas, and later, Robert Hutchins and Mortimer Adler, perennialism addresses these ideas and truths through the study of the humanities and the ongoing development of students' capacity to reason.

Similar to essentialism, perennialism addresses the need for students to develop intellectual powers and moral qualities. Student interests and experiences have little place in the curriculum, since the primary focus of this philosophy is to develop reasoning skills in the context of timeless truths about the universe and the human condition. As such, there is little flexibility in the curriculum, and therefore curricular electives are discouraged. Unlike essentialism, perennialism is universal in its focus and not tied exclusively to American traditions, ideals, and values. Philosophy as a course is an important part of the perennialist curriculum, and serves to help students understand the timeless and universal qualities of certain forms of knowledge. While the perennialist philosophy does recognize the importance of scientific inquiry as a means of developing analytical, flexible, and imaginative reasoning and thinking skills, this school of thought does not emphasize that scientific information or skills that may soon be obsolete have a place in the curriculum. In other words, while it may be of value to study research methodology, it is not as important for students to memorize scientific facts that may change at any given time. Classroom time is to be spent addressing concepts and how these concepts are meaningful to the students' world. Use of textbooks and lectures has minimal importance, while coaching and Socratic seminars comprise a significant amount of class time to engage students in meaningful dialogue to develop a broader and deeper base of understanding.

Adler's Paideia Program, an educational program based on perennialism, promotes a single curriculum for all students, regardless of backgrounds, abilities, or interests, and offers little flexibility in the curriculum because of his belief that vocational or elective courses detract from the focus of developing rational and intellectual powers and critical thinking skills. The core should be truth, knowledge, problem solving, and critical thinking. Goals and expectations are established for all students, followed by supervised practice of the knowledge and skills taught. Without curricular electives, scheduling of courses in a school based upon a perennialist philosophy can be a daunting task. In addition, the inclusion of didactic classes, coaching labs, and seminars, which are common components of a perennialist school, can add to the challenge of scheduling. However, a school that can overcome these minor challenges can provide teachers and administrators a structured environment in which they can assist students in seeing the proverbial trees through the forest.

HUMANISM

Based on the writings of Jean-Jacques Rousseau, humanism is founded on the belief that humans are essentially good and that they possess the capacity for free will. Maslow's hierarchy of needs, addressed in educational psychology courses across the country, emerges out of the humanist philosophy and states that once all the basic human needs are met, one can maximize the use of his or her talents and abilities. With self-actualization as the ultimate goal of the humanist philosophy, students are encouraged to develop as persons and to become self-directed thinkers and learners.

Teachers and administrators who subscribe to a humanistic philosophy do not dwell on specific curricular requirements but are more inclined to focus on the development of close and meaningful relationships with students. While educators might be viewed as experts and "fonts of knowledge" in their respective disciplines, these humanistic educators attempt to create a learning environment where students are less dependent on them and instead develop into independent thinkers and learners. *What* to learn is less important that *how* to learn. These students adopt a positive view of learning and are encouraged to go on to use their own abilities and talents to the fullest extent possible.

EXISTENTIALISM

Based on the writings of Søren Kierkegaard and Jean-Paul Sartre, existentialism focuses on the individual and individualized meaning and action. Existentialist curriculum rejects more traditional schools of thought, notably the essentialist philosophy, in favor of student choice in course selection and an exploration of the students' thoughts, feelings, and actions in their search of their own "essence." Rather than focusing on more objective subject matter, an existentialist curriculum is more self-directed and self-paced, and places a heavier emphasis on creativity and imagination. Students are encouraged and supported in their efforts to find meaning and to develop values on their own and in the context of courses they want to take.

While existentialism is not commonly used as the basis for the structure and organization of most American public schools, certain elements of this philosophy are occasionally integrated into other philosophical approaches. The role of the educator is to create a learning environment where students are exposed to a variety of paths or options from which to choose. Existentialism offers a holistic approach to teaching and learning that gives students a wide variety of choices to help explore and develop their own creativity and self-expression. Most of these options are in the humanities, as it is typically considered less "objective" than the sciences. From these choices, students are encouraged to create meaning as to how the content applies to their own lives.

PROGRESSIVISM

At the very root of progressivism is John Dewey's philosophy of change, reconstruction of experience, and preparation for the future. According to Dewey, textbooks cannot replace the social interactions that lead to learning and the making of meaning. Knowledge is gained through students' application of prior experience to new problems. Progressivism respects individuality, science, and change and connects each of these with American freedom and democracy. Dewey believed that in order to be a nation of democratic, freethinking citizens, Americans must retain their individuality while embracing change. As we alter or change our relationship with our environment, we are changed by the experience.

The progressivist philosophy encouraged schools to broaden the curriculum to make learning more relevant to the needs and interests of students. While this approach was widely accepted in the 1920s, it lost support with the launch of Sputnik in 1957 and the move to a more essentialist approach, which emphasized a more traditional, skills-based curriculum that was less interested in the unique and specific needs and interests of individual students.

A school built upon a progressivist philosophy is child centered. Students' experiences, interests, and abilities are the center of the curriculum. Teachers and administrators create and maintain an environment that students learn by doing and are in constant interaction with one another, with nature, and with society. Cooperation and tolerance of diverse perspectives are promoted, and learning often takes place in the context of interdisciplinary projects and units. Because of the progressivist emphasis on and respect for progress and change, natural and social science comprise an important part of the curriculum. Similar to perennialism, problem solving and critical thinking are promoted and encouraged, and accomplishments by women and other minorities are included. The curriculum is designed to take the whole child into account, providing a choice of opportunities for students to discover truth and gain knowledge through active lessons and activities. Progressivists believe that education is an active, ongoing process and that learning takes place not only in the school but also in the home and workplace. Therefore, learning should be interesting and useful and something that all students should know how to do.

Creating such an engaging and motivating learning environment has significant implications for the building- and district-level administrator. Educators must be aware that promoting and maintaining a progressivist school can be a challenge in a nation that currently embraces a more essentialist philosophy and minimizes the individual interests and experiences of students.

SOCIAL RECONSTRUCTIONISM

Social reconstructionism, also known as pragmatism, focuses on those societal issues that affect students' lives and how students can be active in creating a better world for themselves. The goal of this philosophy is social reform. Students are encouraged to be involved in the identification of solutions to societal problems. Since the school is at the center of the community where these students live, it is the role of the school to be the vehicle for the changes students deem to be necessary. The curriculum is designed to make students aware of their responsibility to self, others, and society and to view education as the vehicle for societal change.

While social reconstructionism focuses on issues and problems students currently face, it can use a more traditional curriculum to analyze and address these issues and problems. History courses can be used to help students understand context; English courses can help to expose students to writing about the problems; and math and science courses can provide tools necessary to scientifically analyze the problems in order to propose a solution. Educators have the responsibility of confronting students with and introducing students to social problems and issues and subsequently organizing the curriculum around these problems and issues. Teachers and administrators should, however, be aware that more empirical methods of evaluation of student achievement in a social reconstructionist school could be difficult to employ, as these methods often do not directly relate to the knowledge and skills being learned in this setting.

SUMMARY

While some of the six schools of thought discussed are in direct opposition to one another, other schools can coexist and even enhance one another. The school to which each educator subscribes may be based on the type of school he or she attended, the influence of a mentor, or the result of personal experience as an educator. Regardless of the philosophy held by any individual, educators must be aware of their own philosophy, the essential elements of those philosophies held by others with whom they may work, and how each of these philosophies can directly and uniquely impact the structure, organization, and activities related to the teaching and learning that he or she is responsible for.

—*Robert L. Sanders*

See also aesthetics, in education; Aristotle; arts education; behaviorism; Catholic education; character education; constructivism; cultural politics, wars; democracy, democratic education and administration; Dewey, John; dialectical inquiry; empiricism; ethics; existentialism; fascism and schools; fundamentalism; idealism, as philosophy in education; knowledge base, of the field; Kuhn, Thomas; Loyola, Ignatius; Marx, Karl; Maslow, Abraham; multiculturalism; objectivity; Piaget, Jean; Plato; positivism, postpositivism; pragmatism and progressivism; postmodernism; research methods; right-wing politics, advocates, impact on education; Skinner, B. F.; Spencer, Herbert; subjectivism, in theory; values pluralism, in schools

Further Readings and References

Adler, M. (1982). *The Paideia proposal: An educational manifesto.* New York: Macmillan.

Dewey, J. (1964). *John Dewey on education: Selected writings.* New York: Modern Library.

Gingell, J., & Winch, C. (2004). *Philosophy of education policy.* New York: Routledge.

Henry, N. B. (Ed.). (1942). *Philosophies of education: The forty-first yearbook of the Society for the Study of Education, Part I.* Bloomington, IL: Public School Publishing.

Martusewicz, R. (2001). *Seeking passage: Post-structuralism, pedagogy, ethics.* New York: Teachers College Press.

Morrow, R., & Alberto Torres, C. (2002). *Reading Freire and Habermas: Critical pedagogy and transformative social change.* New York: Teachers College Press.

Reese, W. (2001). The origins of progressive education. *History of Education Quarterly, 41*(1), 1–24.

Sartre, J. (1957). *Existentialism and human emotions.* New York: Philosophical Library.

Shaw, L. (2004). *Humanistic and social aspects of teaching.* Retrieved July 27, 2004, from http://edweb.sdsu.edu/ LShaw/f95syll/954index.htm.

Turner, R. (2001). *Existentialism.* Retrieved May 3, 2003, from http://www.connect.net/ron/exist.html.

White, D. (2001). Freedom and responsibility: Existentialism, gifted students, and philosophy. *Gifted Child Today, 24*(2), 48–53, 65.

Whittlesey, L. (2004). *Educational philosophies.* Retrieved July 27, 2004, from http://gladstone.uoregon.edu/~lwhittle/Philosophies/.

🏛 PHYSICAL EDUCATION

Physical education covers a broad field of professionals and scholarly areas. The name of physical education is fast disappearing in higher education language and has been replaced by a variety of names underlying the nature of the discipline, that is, the science of human movement. It studies the biological, mechanical, and sociopsychological dimensions of human movement and its enhancement from birth to death. In American schools, physical education is still a well-recognized name, while its content has been changed from the teaching of athletic skills and physical training to teaching of developmentally appropriate movements and sport and recreational activity skills to promote the health and overall well-being of students.

CHANGING PHILOSOPHY OF PHYSICAL EDUCATION

Contrary to the Puritan philosophy, early physical education in colonial America was strongly influenced by muscular Christianity that believed physical fitness and athleticism can facilitate the achievement of moral, religious, and mental growth. It provided confirmation that physical training and competition were desirable activities for boys and young men. During the first half of the twentieth century, physical education revolved around the philosophy of "education through the physical," with a root in progressive education theory. This "new" physical education stressed a child-centered curriculum that encouraged natural play and promoted a body-mind link. Human movement philosophy was introduced to America in the 1950s from England. It was quickly integrated into physical education programs in America since it was believed to be scientifically superior to the "education through the physical" philosophy. Human-movement-based curriculum promotes the development of full potential for movement in humans through body awareness, space awareness, and development of movements and sport skills. Humanistic physical education was the next phase, which was fueled in part by the turmoil in collegiate and professional sports in the 1960s and 1970s. The humanistic approach was characterized by emphasizing cooperation and personal development, promoting enjoyment of sport activities, and criticizing the abuse of athletes. Since the 1950s, America has been a nation is facing a dramatic increase in the prevalence of chronic diseases (i.e., cancers and cardiovascular diseases) that are believed to be caused by an unhealthy lifestyle. As a result, a wellness movement has taken a center role in physical education. It focuses on promoting an active lifestyle for everyone in America, which has shown to prevent diseases and increase longevity. With a lack of physical activity as one of the leading indicators of national health in Healthy People 2010, physical education as a profession and discipline will play a crucial role in the enhancement of the well-being in America for decades to come.

ORIGIN AND FORMATION OF PHYSICAL EDUCATION IN AMERICAN COLLEGES AND UNIVERSITIES

Physical education was introduced to America in the form of "medical gymnastics" from Europe in the late eighteenth century with two dominant systems: Swiss and German. It was a very stringent and vigorous form of physical training for the purpose of restoration of health and/or development of the body. It was different from today's Olympic gymnastics. Two primary goals of early physical education programs were to provide physical training to schoolboys and college-age men and to train "gymnastic teachers." Training of physical education teachers took place in private normal schools in the 1880s and 1890s, mostly through summer programs. The 4-year teacher preparation programs did not start until the turn of the twentieth century. The first five universities were Harvard University, Oberlin College, Stanford University, the University of California, and the University of Nebraska. Teachers College of Columbia University awarded the first master's degree in physical education in 1910 and started the first doctoral program in physical education in 1924. In less than 7 years, the Normal College of the American Gymnastic Union, Wellesley College, the University of Southern California, and the University of Oregon also started

offering graduate coursework in physical education. Today, most states have their own certification program for physical education teachers in public schools. The American Alliance for Health, Physical Education, Recreation and Dance (AAHPERD) is the leading organization of professionals in physical education and other related areas and is responsible for providing leadership in guiding the profession.

CHANGING FOCI OF PHYSICAL EDUCATION PROGRAMS

American physical education has evolved over four periods that shaped the profession and discipline. The first generation (1885–1920) of physical educators, mostly trained in medicine and biological sciences, created a teacher training curriculum with heavy emphasis on the science of physical training (i.e., anatomy, physiology, and physics) and less on sports skill instruction. Physical education was first included as part of the curriculum in elite schools of higher learning such as Harvard.

The second generation (1920–1945) of physical education programs was developed under the new philosophy of "education through the physical" rather than "education of the physical." This was also the period when physical education was widely adopted into the curricula in American schools and universities. The profession of physical education was created as a result. With increasing demands for teachers, physical education departments were created in all major state and private universities. The focus of the curricula was heavily on pedagogy (educational theory of instruction and coaching) and preparation of coaches for athletic sports. This was also the era of gender-separated physical education programs. Most university faculty members were considered generalists who instructed a variety of courses but without expectation for engaging in research. The exception was the faculty with special training in exercise physiology and measurement. The first scholarly journal for physical education professionals, *Research Quarterly,* was published in 1930.

The third generation (1945–1985) of physical education programs was characterized by the striving to establish an academic discipline, like more traditional disciplines such as art, science, and engineering. This was a response to the calling to revamp the profession to meet the expectations of traditional academic disciplines. Through most of this period, the physical education faculty in major universities focused their efforts on identification and organization of a unique "body of knowledge" for the discipline in order to justify the need of its existence. The result was the formation of subdisciplines in physical education based on traditional academic disciplines in the 1960s and 1970s. The first nonteacher preparation specialties were exercise physiology, motor learning and control, pedagogy, sport sociology, and sport psychology at the graduate level and sport science at the undergraduate level. A major milestone in establishing its credential as a scientific discipline came as exercise physiology researchers developed affiliations with researchers in medicine by forming the American College of Sports Medicine in the early 1950s. This period was also accompanied by continued growth of physical education teacher preparation programs at undergraduate and graduate levels that usually reside in colleges or schools of education.

As the discipline of physical education matured, the fourth generation (1985–2005) of physical education programs was born. This was accompanied by increased recognition by peers from traditional academic disciplines. Today, many physical education faculty members serve as college deans or associate deans. Most physical education programs have changed their name from physical education to names reflecting the changing nature of the curricula and research programs of their departments. The most commonly used names are kinesiology, exercise science, human performance, and sport science. Researchers in exercise physiology, biomechanics, motor learning and control, and motor development have become highly competitive and successful in securing external grants to fund their research programs, although physical education teacher preparation programs are still the main resource of revenue generation for physical education departments in most universities. Specializations in undergraduate and graduate programs have created new career opportunities for graduates of physical education programs. Many students study physical education while they prepare their entrance to medical school, nursing programs, and physical or occupational therapy.

CURRENT TRENDS AND ISSUES

The prevalence of overweight American children has tripled over the past 30 years. More recent data show that about one third of American school-age children had body weights that are considered to be unhealthy. Meanwhile, physical education programs in public schools (K–12) are declining. A recent study suggested that such declining rates ranged from 50% in elementary to 50% in Grade 12 when physical education requirements by grade were analyzed. Physical education is only offered daily in 8% of elementary schools in the United States and even less frequently in middle and high schools, although it is a required subject in all states. Physical education is the area with lowest funding and often the first to be cut during a budgetary crisis.

Today, physical education in higher education is not only a profession (teaching) but also a scientific discipline (research). It has moved from its single role as a cradle for preparing physical educators to a more diverse role. This change is well reflected from its program design. Physical education departments in the United States now have both the teacher preparation program and the research-oriented program. Most of them have masters' programs and some have doctoral programs.

Faculties in the departments of physical education have become more and more focused on scholarly study. A group of scientific and scholarly disciplines, such as exercise physiology, biomechanics, and motor learning and control, have been created and further developed in the past four decades. For example, exercise physiologists in physical education have extended their research from the traditional cardiovascular and metabolic exercise physiology to exercise biochemistry to broaden their research scope. Exercise physiology is now the largest subdiscipline of physical education. Similar to exercise physiologists, biomechanists study questions that are also topically diverse. Today, biomechanists continue to apply quantitative and qualitative approaches to seek the optimal movement patterns (e.g., locomotion and throwing movements) that are accompanied with the lowest energy costs, most effective outcome, and minimal injury risks. In addition, they are now also concerned with issues such as maintaining sufficient bone mineral density in space and on earth. Scholars in the field of motor learning and control are traditionally interested in understanding how movement skills are learned and controlled in healthy and young adults. Today, they have extended their research interests to investigating behavioral characteristics and mechanisms associated with aging processes and neurological diseases and injuries such as stroke and Parkinson's disease.

New research indicates that physical activity and exercise are essential components in helping to reduce risk factors related to various diseases, including diabetes, neurological disorders, osteoporosis, and cancer. School physical education is facing the challenge to modify its skill-based instruction to a wellness- and fitness-oriented curriculum that can provide students with lifetime skills to live an active lifestyle. There is no doubt that physical education departments will play an important role in dealing with these critical public health issues in the twenty-first century.

—*Wanxiang Yao and Zenong Yin*

See also adolescence; adult education; ageism; athletics in schools; at-risk students; behaviorism; brain research and practice; children and families in America; curriculum, theories of; elementary education; extracurricular activities; gender studies, in educational leadership; high schools; individual differences, in children; learning environments; mainstreaming and inclusion; mental illness, in adults and children; peace education; resiliency; self-actualization; sexuality, theories of; special education; suicide, in schools

Further Readings and References

Burgenson, C., Wechsler, H., Brener, N., Young, J., and Spain, C. (2001). Physical education and activity: Results from the school health policies and programs study (SHPPS) 2000. *Journal of School Health, 71*(7), 279–293.

Dunn, J. (2001). Honoring the past—Embracing the future. *Quest, 53,* 495–506.

Green, K., & Hardman, K. (2005). *Physical education: Essential issues.* Thousand Oaks, CA: Sage.

Hall, S. (2003). *Basic biomechanics* (4th ed.). New York: McGraw-Hill.

Pangrazi, R. (2003). Physical education K–12: "All for one and one for all." *Quest, 55,* 105–107.

Pellegrini, A. (2005). *Recess: Its role in education and development.* Mahwah, NJ: Erlbaum.

Siedentop, D. (2004). *Introduction to physical education, fitness, and sport.* New York: McGraw-Hill.

PIAGET, JEAN

Jean Piaget (1896–1980), whose work in cognitive and developmental psychology caused many significant changes in elementary education, was one of the most influential psychologists of the twentieth century. He proposed that the cognitive development of children occurred in sequential developmental stages called the sensorimotor, preoperational, concrete operational, and formal operational. Each stage represented a specific type of cognitive functioning that was caused by the individual's level of biological maturation. Piaget believed that all individuals pass through these stages, and within each stage organize the information that they learn into stage-specific structures called schemes. Piaget theorized that as individuals matured and their environment changed, they would adapt to the changes either by assimilating the changes into their current schemes or by accommodating the changes by reorganizing their schemes. The function of assimilation and accommodation is to maintain a balance, through the process of equilibration, between one's scheme and changes within the environment.

Piaget significantly influenced elementary education with the idea that individuals construct their own understanding of reality. His understanding that individuals are active learners who modify and transform information through their engagement with that knowledge provides the foundation for the pervasive constructivist movement in contemporary education. In Piagetian theory, children are not passive recipients of information but active participants in the learning process who construct their own meaning.

Piaget influenced elementary education in a number of ways. First, the children's stage of development limits what they can learn. For instance, children cannot solve an abstract problem until the last stage, formal operational, that begins around the age of 11. Second, what children learn in later stages is affected by what they learned and the cognitive structures that they developed in the earlier stages. Therefore, opportunities must be provided that facilitate the full cognitive development of the child in each stage. Third, the important part of a child's learning is the child's ability to apply or transfer what was already learned to the new information. Fourth, children cannot apply what they learned in a previous stage until they have developed the physical brain structures that will allow the next level of learning to take place. Finally, requiring students to learn information that is beyond their stage of cognitive development is a futile learning experience. For instance, no amount of practice in learning algebra will help middle school students who are not in the formal operational stage.

Research has established the limitations of Piagetian theory. Various researchers have challenged the existence of four separate stages of thinking even though many agree that children do pass through the changes in cognition identified by Piaget. Also, research does not support various aspects of Piagetian theory such as the developmental constraints on learning while in the concrete-operational stage. Also, Piagetian theory does not explain how very young children can perform highly complex tasks in certain areas. However, neo-Piagetian theories have combined Piaget's ideas with new information about cognitive development to better understand how children think and construct knowledge.

—Raymond A. Horn Jr.

See also behaviorism; child development theories; cognition, theories of; creativity, theories of; curriculum, theories of; early childhood education; egocentrism, theories of; giftedness, gifted education; individual differences, in children; intelligence; learning, theories of; Mensa; metacognition; motivation, theories of; personality; philosophies of education; psychology, types of; psychometrics; research methods; sexuality, theories of; special education; subjectivism, in theory

Further Readings and References

Peterson, R., & Felton-Collins, V. (1986). *The Piaget handbook for teachers and parents.* New York: Teachers College Press.

Piaget, J. (1958). *Logic and psychology.* New York: Basic Books.

Piaget, J. (1973). *To understand is to invent: The future of education.* New York: Grossman.

Piaget, J., & Inhelder, B. (1969). *The psychology of the child.* New York: Basic Books.

🏛 PICOTT, J. RUPERT

Executive secretary of the Virginia Teachers Association, vice president of the National Education Association (NEA), president of the American Teachers Association, John Rupert Picott (1910–1989) worked to develop a proficient teacher corps and to correct the educational, social, and political inequities faced by African Americans. Distinguished by his activism in education and politics, Picott was a teacher, principal, and association leader who labored in a state with a wide variation in race relations. In 1941, Picott helped to establish a local chapter of the National Association for the Advancement of Colored People during its salary equalization campaign in Virginia and elsewhere. Dismissed as principal in retaliation for successful litigation for equal salaries for African American teachers, Picott became in 1944 the first full-time executive secretary of the Virginia

Teachers Association (VTA), a Black teacher's association. He shaped its agenda to reflect the legal, political, educational, and social challenges of a segregated society. Picott was editor of the association's publication, wrote a regular column on the Virginia General Assembly, encouraged teacher professional growth and involvement in legislative matters and in voting registration campaigns. At its peak, the VTA had a membership of 10,000. By 1949, Picott was one of the main insurgents to demand equal standing for African American educators in the powerful NEA, in which African Americans had only marginal participation. His remarks and activities in the 1950s and 1960s at NEA conventions helped to promote social justice as NEA policy.

As an NEA delegate, Picott challenged the leadership and membership of the NEA to make equity a reality for African American educators. He also actively sought the NEA's assistance in crises such as the closing of public schools in Prince Edward County in 1959. Picott and VTA members were involved with the placement of dismissed Black teachers, the education of youngsters in "training centers" established by the Prince Edward County Christian Association, and the recruitment of teachers for the Prince Edward County Free Schools. Picott was a skillful communicator who understood the tensions and the perspective of multiple participants in a race conscious society. He developed a network of allies through the National Council of State Teachers Associations (NCOSTA)—an organization he directed until the 1960s—which strengthened the bonds between the Black teacher associations and the American Teachers Association (ATA) and which funneled money to the NAACP to assist teachers unfairly dismissed. He was executive director of the Association for the Study of Negro Life and History (ASNLH), edited the *Negro History Bulletin,* and authored several books on Black education. Picott is credited with making Black History Week a month-long celebration that is widely observed in schools throughout the country. In challenging the Jim Crow laws in Virginia, Picott led a successful campaign to desegregate the Mosque, a Richmond theater, and secured better working conditions for African Americans in the Virginia State Department of Education. Picott regretted the fact that as integration progressed, African American educators did not achieve a full measure of leadership roles in many newly merged teacher associations.

—Carol F. Karpinski

See also American Federation of Teachers; Bethune, Mary McLeod; Black education; civil rights movement; Clark, Septima; desegregation, of schools; discrimination; Du Bois, W. E. B.; leadership, teacher; minorities, in schools; National Educational Association; Sanchez, George; unions, of teachers; Washington, Booker T.; Woodson, Carter G.

Further Readings and References

Kluger, R. (1975). *Simple justice.* New York: Vintage.

Picott, J. (1975). *History of the Virginia Teachers Association.* Washington, DC: National Education Association.

Talbot, A. (1981). *History of the Virginia Teachers Association, 1940–1965* (Doctoral dissertation, College of William and Mary, 1981).

🏛 PLANNING, PROGRAMMING, BUDGETING SYSTEM

Planning, Programming, Budgeting System (PPBS) is an integrated decision-making approach in which scarce resources are allocated based on established objectives and the best alternative methods for achieving those objectives.

PPBS had its beginning in the early 1960s. Economists, first in the RAND Corporation and then in the Department of Defense, did much to develop the basic concepts of PPBS. President Lyndon B. Johnson sent White House Executive Order (Bulletin 66–33) in October of 1965 to heads of federal executive departments and directed that an integrated PPBS be installed in all federal executive departments and establishments. In 1967, Johnson made the concept of PPBS an integral part of his budget message.

With the spotlight on PPBS at the national level, hundreds of articles, papers, and books appeared in the 1960s. PPBS gained attention for use in school budgeting following the interest generated at the federal level. By the early 1970s, PPBS was appearing in the literature related to educational organizations; some version of it had been adopted by many states and began to extend into local school districts.

In 1972, Joseph H. McGivney and Robert E. Hedges identified the essential features of PPBS as need, a goal stated as objective and alternatives and objectives, determining alternative methods, and evaluation.

First, planning is identifying the need, setting goals, determining objectives, and developing alternatives to the goals and objectives. Not all needs are easy to measure, which makes this particular element more challenging than it might seem initially. Next is a goal stated as objective. Third, in PPBS it is important to identify several objectives for each goal. Doing so provides the decision makers with choices of what to pursue.

Element two, programming, is the process of examining various trade-offs, analyzing each alternative method, and making comparisons between and among the alternative methods regarding which is best.

The third element, budgeting, involves the legal and financial means for allocating resources. The school budget is sometimes called the fiscal translation of the educational program. This should not be a short-term endeavor but a multiyear (2 or more) commitment by the organization. Budgeting is a complex process that includes preparation, presentation, adoption, execution, and appraisal, resulting in a budget document.

Finally, though this element, evaluation, does not appear in the title of the PPBS process, it is important for quality implementation. Evaluation goes with all steps in the process and should be done continuously.

Though the label PPBS is not often heard much anymore, the basic elements of it still exist in school budgeting processes. Similar procedures can still be found but may be identified as cost-effective analysis or program evaluation. No matter the name, school districts continue to link the educational objectives of the organization with the resources available, organized in such a way that the objectives are most likely to be achieved for the fewest resources possible, that is, planning, programming, and budgeting.

—Anita Pankake

See also accountability; administration, theories of; budgeting; cost-benefit analysis; decision making; finance, of public schools; management by objectives; management theories; planning models; productivity; resource management; strategic planning; taxes, to support education

Further Readings and References

Knezevich, S. (1973). *Program budgeting (PPBS): A resource allocation decision system for education.* Berkeley, CA: McCutchan.

McGivney, J., & Hedges, R. (1972). *An introduction to PPBS.* Columbus, OH: Charles E. Merrill.

Poston, W. (2005). Finance, planning, and budgeting. In F. English (Ed.), *The SAGE handbook of educational leadership* (pp. 550–570). Thousand Oaks, CA: Sage.

🏛 PLANNING MODELS

Planning is a future-oriented and hierarchical discipline that encompasses various models, each prescribing approaches for actions that will bring about change. By definition, it can be thought of as an attempt to change the future by current and ongoing action. All planning is dedicated to changing some future—either in the very short term or over some longer period, perhaps decades. Its hierarchical structure is composed of several layers of alternative choices as to how to proceed in an attempt to create change. The first of these layers addresses broad questions relative to how one approaches the processes of planning and change. This is essentially a set of philosophies of planning. Within these philosophies there exists a second layer of the hierarchy, the distinct models of planning that have been proposed by various authors as a defined formula or set of activities and approaches—the "how to" of planning. Finally, there are planning tools, dedicated approaches or algorithms for dealing with specific problem types. These tools can cross models and even philosophies. Their popularity enters, fades, and reemerges over time. Planned Program Budgeting, the Program Evaluation and Review Technique, Cohort Analysis, and Delphi methodologies are typical examples.

Unfortunately, the literature has been confounded in the use of the term *models* and has been indiscriminate in describing both the philosophies and the specific approaches to planning as planning models. In addition, authors generally do not distinguish the specific approaches they advocate as being only one of a very large set of approaches to planning, for example, strategic planning is often viewed as the quintessential planning model rather than only one among alternatives.

Planning has been consistently recognized as a key administrative function since Henry Fayol first enumerated those functions in 1916; today it lies at the heart of the school improvement process. As conditions require that an organization change, most have several classic means by which to generate that change, their improvement repertoire (textbook and personnel selection). As Figure 1 illustrates, planning is not the only means by which improvement can occur.

However, planning is an essential process component for most of the large-scale organizational change/improvement that occurs in education, especially when no adequately defined process has been previously created in the organization for managing that change (see item *d.* of Figure 1).

Organizational improvement has been seen to be comprised of three stages, labeled by Kurt Lewin in 1951 as "unfreezing," "moving," and "refreezing" and by David Clark, Linda Lotto, and Terry Astuto later as "adoption," "implementation," and "institutionalization." Planning must address all three phases; many of the criticisms of the effectiveness of educational planning can be traced to a failure to address one or both of the latter stages.

Although many variations exist, the planning philosophies noted above have been classified into four relatively distinct types: (a) the comprehensive-rational philosophy, (b) the bounded (limited) rational philosophy, (c) the incremental philosophy, and (d) the developmental or adaptive philosophy. Figure 2 presents an illustration of these philosophies and mixed scanning, arranged according to the extent that they specify precise goals and the general comprehensiveness used in generating different potential solutions to the planning problem. While theoretical, this arrangement makes clear the relationship of the theories of planning.

Amitai Etzioni also presented a process known as mixed scanning, a combination of bounded rationalism and incrementalism, which was, for a time, considered to be a philosophy but which is now generally thought of as a component of the more specific models. Mixed scanning was an attempt to capitalize on the strengths of both the rational and incremental models while diminishing their individual weaknesses. A mixed scanning model calls for planners to determine key areas where comprehensive rational planning might be warranted or necessary while relegating all other areas to more incremental planning approaches. This offers the advantage of allowing key resources and efforts to be concentrated into a few areas rather than across the full spectrum of organizational goals.

The two rational approaches have now merged to a point where references to rationalism usually pertain to the bounded approach. Comprehensive rationalism is generally traced to military planning during World War II and the writings of Herbert Simon. In models reflecting a rational perspective, goals and alternative means to achieve those goals are clearly defined. A rational, often quantitative, decision-making approach is used to determine the optimum alternative from the set of possible alternatives. An early example within this philosophy was provided by Roger Kaufman in his problem-solving process model.

An Organization's Improvement Repertoire

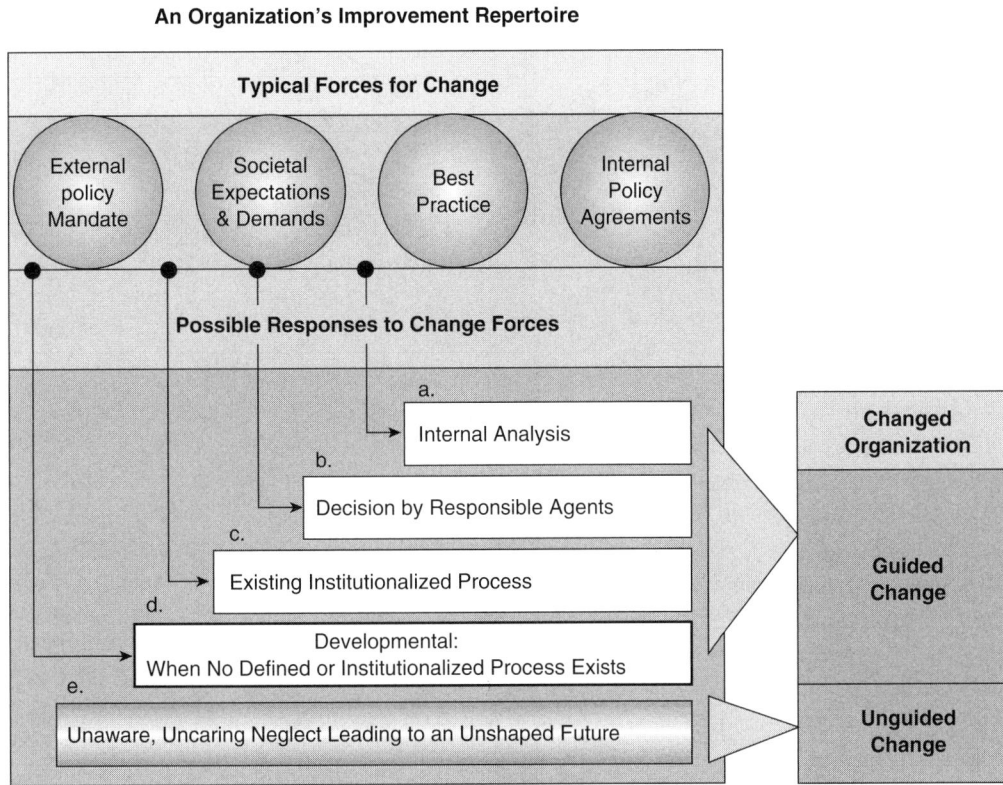

Figure 1   An Organization's Repertoire for Managing the Need for Altered Futures

SOURCE: Modified from Beach, R. H., & McInerney, W. D. Educational planning models and school district practice; originally published in *Planning and Changing, 17*(3), 184. Reprinted with permission of *Planning and Changing*.

Over the past two decades, one particular set of models in the comprehensive-rational philosophy has become predominant in educational planning, the strategic planning models. Although minor variations exist among these models, they generally call for an extensive environmental scan to assess the opportunities and threats arising from such sources as policy, law, public opinion, and financing. Strategic planning models then call for a similarly comprehensive analysis of the organization's strengths and weaknesses vis-à-vis these threats and the organization's mission and goals. Once these have been determined, the school or district devises an extended list of strategies that might enable it to reach its goals and uses a deliberate, rational process to select the most appropriate strategies from this list. Finally, these models call for the development of action and evaluation plans that specify which tasks must be accomplished, the timelines for task initiation and completion, the responsible party or parties, and the process, criteria, and timelines for evaluating the implementation of the plan

and an evaluation of the organization's success in attaining its goals.

Despite its widespread and often mandated use, the comprehensive-rational planning models have frequently been criticized for some of their inherent assumptions. Even its early proponent, Herbert Simon, recognized these concerns, noting that the extensive environmental and organizational scanning, the search for the full range of alternative solutions, and the need for rigorous evaluation of these solutions represent virtually impossible demands on administrators' (and other stakeholders') time. Second, as many of the problems faced by schools are "fuzzy problems," it is often impossible to forecast the consequences of adopting a given alternative or combination of alternatives. Finally, Simon questioned individuals' ability to be as fully "rational" as the model requires, noting that background, psychological factors, problem presentation and interpretation, and social factors all compromise truly rational decisions. This led James March and Herbert Simon to propose what is known as

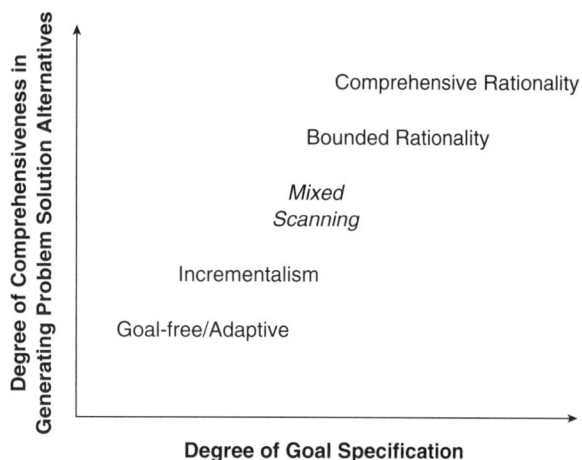

Figure 2   Philosophical Domains of Educational Planning

SOURCE: Adapted from Beach, R., & Lindahl, R. (2004). Identifying the knowledge base for school improvement. *Planning and Changing, 35*(1–2), 1–31.

bounded (limited) rationality, in which these limitations are recognized and "satisficing," or the acceptance of a feasible alternative is deemed workable rather than a search for the "the optimal alternative."

The third planning philosophy, incrementalism, is based on the recognition of these limitations as well. It was used in practice long before Charles Lindblom described this incremental model as *successive limited comparisons.* This model accepts the inherent complexity and difficulties of comprehensive-rational models and circumvents them by limiting planning decisions to a series of successive comparisons that build on past and current achievements to move the organization ahead in small, incremental steps. Because goals are approached slowly and with small advances, they are viewed as relatively flexible, changing over time, perhaps before being accomplished. The planner focuses much more on "the possible" than on "the ideal," more on "next" than on "the ultimate goal." Incremental planning calls for organizations and their members to move only marginally beyond their comfort zone, causing far less resistance to change than most comprehensive-rational planning models. Although relatively simple and not highly demanding of resources (e.g., time, financial, and human), incremental planning is subject to the criticism that it progresses very slowly, may readily become disjointed, and may not be able to maintain a tight focus on the organization's goals, which shift over time.

The fourth planning philosophy is far less goal based and is referred to in a variety of ways, for example,

goal-free planning, adaptive planning, or developmental planning. This is the most recent of the philosophies to be given attention in the professional literature, emerging in the late 1960s; however, several of its themes arose very early as concerns were voiced regarding the other three approaches.

Primary among its themes was the need for widespread, meaningful participation in, and commitment to, the planning process. All three of the other philosophies were originally formulated around the concept of a manager or professional planner doing the majority of data gathering, analysis, and decision making. Unfortunately, this led to low commitment among organizational members and other stakeholders, leading to resistance to change during the implementation and institutionalization phases, often to the downfall of the process. Later versions of strategic planning models recognized this weakness and constructed elaborate mechanisms for wide-scale stakeholder involvement in the process but often in less than meaningful ways.

In a developmental planning model, however, participation occurs in vastly different ways than in the other models. In these models, the administrator/planner works directly with the members and stakeholders of the organization to discern their values and vision for the organization. The administrator/planner then ascertains the common elements of these values and visions; these become the platform for determining the directional, rather than a goal-specific, plan. Obviously, these values and visions are closely linked to the organization's culture in pursuit of the common vision. This gives individuals a great deal of freedom to operate within a common framework, reducing resistance to change.

Naturally, a developmental planning model also invokes a tension between freedom and constraint, for boundaries are relatively nebulous and task and process issues often become enmeshed. One classic purpose of developmental planning is to enhance and guide the professional development of the organization's personnel as they undertake activities that are not only crucial to moving the organization toward its agreed upon direction, but which will also create a greater understanding of the organization, its problem-solving processes, and the employee's role within those processes and within the organization as a whole. This process of "double-loop" learning leads the organization to become what Peter Senge terms "a learning organization," with the goal being not only the successful accomplishment of the organization's current improvement effort but the further capacitation of the organization and its members to engage successfully in future improvement efforts. It is important to recognize that models under this philosophy are not truly goal free; rather, goals are given less prominence and considered after other concerns have been addressed.

Modern planning theory tends to employ an eclectic combination of these four philosophies rather than rely on one specific construct. For example, schools contemplating adoption of a particular established reform model, for example, "Accelerated Learning" or "The Modern Red Schoolhouse," might benefit from use of a mixed-scanning approach that focuses on like alternatives. School districts contemplating the change to a charter or magnet school format might benefit more from the broader scan of opportunities and alternatives available through a comprehensive rational model. Incremental planning serves many school districts well in the annual budgeting process, as it greatly reduces the time and energy required for planning in environments where resources are limited and fairly constant. When properly implemented, a developmental model allows schools to improve on a continuous basis when their external and internal environments are not subjected to a turbulent environment.

Also, because so many variables have been found to have profound effects on the change process, for example, leadership, staff stability, staff development, organizational support for change, institutional history, organizational culture, clarity and agreement on organizational goals, and the demographic characteristics of organizational members, each organization's readiness and capacity for change is unique, and varies across time. Consequently, the selection of the most appropriate planning model varies from organization to organization, task to task, and across time. As with so many aspects of educational leadership and administration, planning is as much art and craft as a science.

—*Robert H. Beach and Ronald A. Lindahl*

See also accountability; chaos theory; conceptual systems theory and leadership; Delphi Technique; economics, theories of; goals, goal setting; governance; group dynamics; human capital; leadership, theories of; management by objectives; management information systems; management theories; measurement, theories of; needs assessment; networking and network theory; open systems theory; organizational theories; paradigm; PERT (Performance Evaluation and Review Technique); Planning, Programming, Budgeting System; research methods; satisficing theory; school improvement models; Simon, Herbert; strategic planning; structural equation modeling; systemic reform; systems theory/thinking; values of organizations and leadership

Further Readings and References

Beach, R., & Lindahl, R. (2004). A critical review of strategic planning: Is it a panacea for public education? *Journal of School Leadership, 14,* 211–234.

Beach, R., & Lindahl, R. (2004). Identifying the knowledge base for school improvement. *Planning and Changing, 35*(1&2), 1–31.

Beach R., & McInerney, W. (1986). Educational planning models and school district practice. *Planning and Changing, 17*(3), 180–191.

Clark, D., Lotto, L., & Astuto, T. (1989). Effective schools and school improvement: A comparative analysis of two lines of inquiry. In J. L. Burdin (Ed.), *School leadership: A contemporary reader* (pp. 159–186). Newbury Park, CA: Sage.

Etzioni, A. (1967). Mixed-scanning: A "third" approach to decision-making. *Public Administration Review, 27,* 418–424.

Faludi, A. (1973). *A reader in planning theory.* Oxford: Pergamon Press.

Fayol, H. (1949). *General and industrial administration.* New York: Pitman [*Administration industrielle et generale* (1916)].

Kaufman, R., Herman, J., & Watters, K. (1996). *Educational planning: Strategic, tactical, operational.* Lancaster, PA: Technomic.

Lewin, K. (1951). *Field theory in social science.* New York: Harper & Row.

Lindblom, C. (1959). The science of "muddling through." *Public Administration Review, 19,* 79–99.

March, J., & Simon, H. (1959). *Organizations.* New York: John Wiley & Sons.

Senge, P. (1990). *The fifth discipline.* New York: Doubleday.

Simon, H. (1955). A behavioral model of rational choice. *Quarterly Journal of Economics, 69,* 99–118.

Simon, H. (1957). *Administrative behavior* (2nd ed.). New York: Free Press.

Simon, H. (1982). *Models of bounded rationality.* Cambridge: Massachusetts Institute of Technology Press.

🏛 PLATO

Plato (427 BC–347 BC) was the second in the line of great philosophers who emerged from the ancient Greek city-state of Athens. He was a student of Socrates and founder of the Academy, which counted Aristotle as a student, among many others. A soldier and aspiring politician in his early life, most of the details of his life have been gleaned from letters attributed to him. These letters have come under fire from several historians as not written by Plato himself. Despite these criticisms, it is clear Plato was not an insulated scholar but a worldly soldier, traveler, and at times diplomat.

Plato fought in the Peloponnesian War from 409 BC to the end in 404 BC. The war pitted Athens against the Greek city-state of Sparta. When Sparta won the war, Plato became involved in the Thirty Tyrants of Athens, a government set up in part by the victorious Spartans. His role in the government is not clear; however, the violence employed by the oligarchy caused Plato to leave its service. When democracy was restored in Athens in 403 BC, Plato once again delved into politics. It was sometime prior to this that Plato became a devoted student of Socrates.

Plato quickly became disgusted with the machinations of Athenian politics, and the execution of his mentor Socrates was the final straw. Plato left politics completely and also left Athens. During his wide travels, he met with many other scholars, including the mathematician Pythagoras. The mathematician apparently had a large influence on Plato, as he embraced mathematics as the most perfect science. The next era of Plato's life is not completely known, but apparently he entered military service again on behalf of Athens in another war. It was during this military service that he started work on his *Dialogues.*

Plato's fame emerges from his Academy he founded in Athens circa 387 BC. The stated goal of the Academy was to prepare young men to be great statesmen. Given the proper values at the Academy, Plato was convinced that these young men would improve Athens. Enlightened political leadership remained Plato's focus for his remaining years.

The philosophy that emerges from Plato's works is not easily stated. Plato wrote 30 dialogues where characters discuss various topics. Unlike many of his contemporaries, Plato chose the dialogue format over treatises. The characters in the dialogues exchange views, but Plato himself never asserts a direct point of view in the works. The characters are historic, and Socrates remains the protagonist throughout most of them. However, Plato's overall philosophical discussions are not systematic in the way of some later philosophers and must be constructed from the dialogues' diverse prose. Plato often criticizes the point he seems to be advocating in the same work, adding to the difficulty of pinning his views down.

Plato's dialogues are most often divided into three periods, early, late, and middle. The early dialogues are thought to accurately represent the views of Socrates, and give the basis of the Socratic method of teaching. Socrates taught by asking constant, probing questions while maintaining no obvious stance and giving no answers. The questioner creates dilemmas that require students to think and rethink their positions until they arrive at the truth. This new kind of sophistry sought not to teach students rhetoric and argument skills to gain victory in debate but to arrive at the truth. The Socratic method is widely advocated in many educational settings today, perhaps most predominately in American law schools.

The middle dialogues contain Plato's masterpiece, *The Republic.* Here a sharp change is manifested in the personality of Plato's Socrates. Socrates is no longer the mere questioner, seemingly unable to provide any positive answers. Instead, Socrates becomes a proactive participant in the debates, defending his theories with zeal. Socrates's conversations were limited to philosophical and ethical debates in the early dialogues, but in the middle dialogues he addresses numerous areas of inquiry. Plato's Socrates evolves from a man who is wisest of all because he admits to having no knowledge in the early dialogues to one who suggests that humans may achieve infallible knowledge.

The theory of forms or ideas that emerges from the middle dialogues is the central, definitive aspect of Platonism. The theory of forms or ideas espouses that one can only see a shadow of any one thing's true form in the material world. The form is the ideal or perfection of the item, while things in the material world are representations of the form. For example, Plato describes the form of a bed in *The Republic,* and anything that has the properties of a bed is truly defined by the form bed. Therefore, for any set of items that shares some property, there is a form that gives a true description of the item. True knowledge comes from recognition of the forms and comparing items in the material realm to those forms.

Throughout the dialogues, Plato progresses through sets of proofs. A proof is a set of agreed facts, often deduced from previously agreed to facts or conclusions. Logical progression from proofs leads in turn to gaining the truth. However, Plato turns from the Socratic method of the earlier dialogues to a more direct or didactic style often labeled the "dialectic" in the middle dialogues.

Plato seems to reconsider his theory of forms in the late dialogues. In *Parmenides* he provides an apparently fatal argument against his theory in an exchange that has become known as the Third Man Argument. This argument states that items in the process of participation, wherein they take on characters of the forms, fall prey to an infinite loop: if certain male things are male by virtue of taking on the form of male, then the form of male and these male things must create a new form (Male 2). However, if the new form (Male 2) is male, then it and all things male must participate in a third form (Male 3), and so on.

There is considerable debate as to whether Plato believed the Third Man Argument refuted his theory of forms. His later works do make it clear that he no longer believed that it was necessary for statesmen and politicians to grasp such abstract concepts for effective governance. In Plato's last, unfinished dialogue, *Laws,* the forms are not present at all. Plato returned to his original questions of practical good governance. No longer was perfection the goal, but practical meaningful knowledge that would increase the happiness of the citizenry.

—Keith Pogue

See also aesthetics, in education; Aristotle; arts education; Catholic education; character education; Christian Coalition; curriculum, theories of; ethics; existentialism; fascism and schools; fundamentalism; idealism, as philosophy in education; knowledge base, of the field; Loyola, Ignatius; philosophies of education; positivism, postpositivism; right-wing politics, advocates, impact on education

Further Readings and References

Biffle, C. (2000). *A guided tour of five works by Plato* (3rd ed.) Mountain View, CA: Mayfield.
Brickhouse, T., & Smith, N. (2000). *The philosophy of Socrates.* Boulder, CO: Westview.
Cooper, J. (Ed.). (1995) *Plato: Complete works.* Indianapolis, IN: Hackett.
Irwin, T. (1995). *Plato's ethics.* New York: Oxford University Press.
Strauss, L. (2001). *On Plato's symposium* (S. Benardete, Ed.) Chicago: University of Chicago Press.

🏛 PLUTARCH

The Greek Maestrius Plutarcus (circa 45–125 AD), known to history as Plutarch, is primarily recognized as the great biographer of antiquity for his seminal work, *Parallel Lives,* a compendium of biographies of famous Greek and Roman military and political figures. A leading thinker in the Roman Empire's golden age, Plutarch was born in the Greek town of Chaeronea, studied philosophy at Athens, traveled to Alexandria and various parts of Italy, and lived for a significant time in Rome. For many years Plutarch served as one of the two priests at the temple of Apollo at Delphi. As a lecturer and teacher of philosophy, he achieved considerable repute. By his writings and lectures, he became a celebrity in the Roman Empire, yet he continued to reside in Greece and actively participated in local affairs, even serving as mayor into the early part of Emperor Hadrian's reign.

In *Parallel Lives* (written between 100 and 125 AD) Plutarch paired equivalent famous Greek and Roman political and military figures in philosophical biographies. Plutarch developed a pattern to the biographies: the subject's family, education, entry into public life, career high points, a change in fortune or attitude, and final years and death. Then a short essay of comparison follows most of the pairs of lives. Among the 48 lives are the pairs Alexander the Great/Julius Caesar and Demosthenes/Cicero, and figures such as Caius Gracchus, Pericles, and Pompey.

Throughout *Parallel Lives,* Plutarch delivers insightful observations on human nature illustrated by his subjects, so it is difficult to classify the *Lives* as history, biography, or philosophy. Plutarch believes history to be a theater of morals, in which great individuals rise and fall by their strengths and weaknesses; thus, he was more concerned with examining the character of great men than with writing a chronicle of great historical events. Because he views history not as a set of vast and mechanistic processes but as a forum within which to study the natures of particularly great men and the influences these natures exerted over events, the chosen lives tend to be anecdotal and to focus on revealing stories. He believed incidents to demonstrate the character of his subjects were far more interesting than their great battles or political struggles.

During Plutarch's life, guests from throughout the empire congregated for serious conversation at his country estate. Many of these dialogues were recorded and published, and the 78 essays and other works that have survived are now known collectively as the *Moralia (Essays on Moral Issues),* which deals with a variety of themes but is strongly centered on virtue, conduct, and ethics, the ruling passion of Plutarch's life.

Readers have appreciated Plutarch for his practical wisdom. C. S. Lewis has stated that Plutarch laid the foundation for the heroic ideal of the Elizabethan Age.

Characters from several of Shakespeare's plays have their foundation from Plutarch's *Lives,* including Marc Antony, Julius Caesar, Brutus, and Coriolanus. Scholars in the field of educational leadership can utilize Plutarch's works as the first theory of leadership: trait theory. From antiquity and Plutarch we have suggested characteristics of the heroic or noble leader. Are the leaders of antiquity comparable to or different from the leaders of modern times? Plutarch provides insight from which to begin the discussion.

—JoAnn Danelo Barbour

See also character education; charisma, of leaders; ethics; great man theory; leadership, theories of; morality, moral leadership; trait theory

Further Readings and References

Lamberton, R. (2001). *Plutarch.* New Haven, CT: Yale University Press.

Plutarch. (1991). *Plutarch's lives* (The Harvard Classics, C. Eliot, Ed.). Danbury, CT: Grolier Enterprises.

Whittemore, R. (1988). *Pure lives: The early biographers.* Baltimore: Johns Hopkins Press.

POLICY ADVOCACY

An area of increasing interest for school-based administrators and educational leadership faculty charged with preparing educational leaders is policy advocacy. Policy advocacy involves actively promoting a stance on an issue and implies there is a shared responsibility among educators, legislators, and other stakeholders to create, implement, and assess outcomes from policies. As educational policies seem to shift from local and state-driven initiatives to federal initiatives, the notion of educators' involvement in policy advocacy has perhaps become more difficult to achieve yet is arguably more essential for the welfare of public education.

Traditionally, personnel in K–12 schools and higher education institutions have not had a voice in policy formation and instead have generally only implemented policies. When stakeholders are not included in policy development, the policies developed are often fragmented and ineffective. Even though legislators and other policymakers may be responsible for creating large-scale educational policies, when educators engage in policy advocacy, their involvement may offer greater sensitivity to educational needs.

Most policies affecting schools are developed using a traditional model of policy creation. The traditional model uses a top-down process in which policies are determined by experts and bureaucrats, generally without the input of those who will implement the policies. Policies are typically formed once a problem has been identified, encouraging a passive approach to policy formation. Although expert opinion is sometimes sought to help determine potential policy solutions, school board members, legislators, and other policymakers, particularly at the local and state level, tend to be understaffed and working under tight deadlines; consequently, little attention is given to prospective policies unless they become highly politicized. Many policies are created at these levels as a reaction to a situation rather than as a proactive approach to addressing areas of concern.

There is controversy over the degree of involvement educators should have in policy advocacy activities. Those arguing against policy advocacy describe the increasingly demanding roles of school administrators and other educators, leaving little time for policy advocacy activities. Others suggest educators may be too focused on their own needs to clearly understand the larger policy issues.

There is some support and legitimacy for the involvement of educators in policy advocacy. Recently adopted educational leadership standards suggest that administrators should be more involved in influencing educational policies. Standards-based expectations for administrators now include collaborating with others, complying with increasingly complex state and national reform legislation, and assuming additional roles while responding to community demands. Although administrators are busy, policy advocacy should be considered an area of priority. Otherwise, educators will continue to have little voice in the policies created for them to implement.

Administrators can become involved in policy advocacy by learning the process of policy making, building relationships with policymakers and other educators, conducting policy research, and sharing the results of this research with policymakers. To be effective policy advocates, educational leaders need to work collaboratively across institutional lines and positions to create a team approach to providing assistance and expertise to policymakers faced with creating policies. Educators play a key role as participants in the policy process by offering potential solutions and providing information to help policymakers and other stakeholders understand the unintended consequences policies may inflict on teachers, students, and communities.

When engaging in policy advocacy, it is important for educators to be mindful of the policymaker's schedule and other competing demands. The development of a strategic plan for maximizing the contact time with the policymaker may be key to the effectiveness of advocacy opportunities. Educators should be cordial, concise, and considerate. After an initial greeting, the policy advocate should begin by stating the reasons for the meeting, express areas of agreement or concern, and provide the policymaker with a well-developed but brief overview of the situation under consideration. A mixture of factual information about the situation as well as anecdotal examples tends to provide the most likelihood for convincing the policymaker to consider the advocate's point of view. It is important to remember that policymakers are not the "enemy" of educators but are either elected by or responsible to many stakeholders. Educators can provide important information to help policymakers better understand educational issues, particularly the unintended consequences of some policy decisions.

Individually, educators generally have the greatest impact as policy advocates at the local level, where it may be easier to form relationships and gain access with decision makers such as school board members, although individuals can also be effective with other policymakers. Elected officials at the state level generally have offices at the local level. Effective policy advocates will take time to meet with these policymakers at their local office as well as at the state capitol. It helps to know the chief aides and office personnel in both the local and state-level offices. These staffers function as gatekeepers for the policymaker and will either help you gain access or prevent you from doing so. It is important to develop relationships with staffers and policymakers prior to your need to ask for support on an issue. These relationships take time to develop but are usually worth the time and energy required because of your increased access to the policymaker.

When policymakers are elected officials, voter reactions and perceptions may influence the policymaker's willingness to take a stand on some issues. However, educators vote too, and it may help to gently remind these policymakers that you will vote based on their actions and statements or lack of action. This approach is especially effective when groups of educators work together advocating for educational policies.

Coalitions of educators such as the National Association of Secondary School Principals (NASSP) and the American Association of School Administrators (AASA) have been successful in gaining access to and providing influential information for policymakers at the state and federal levels. Policy advocacy can be a frustrating and time-consuming process, so joining with other educators to collect and analyze data and prepare it for effective presentation to policymakers can be a more effective use of one's time and energy. In addition, the presence of a coalition or network helps to demonstrate that there is a critical mass of stakeholders involved, often persuading the policymaker of the importance of attention to the issue being addressed.

The process of policy advocacy becomes more complex as policymakers represent greater numbers of people and interests. However, by forming helpful relationships before there is an urgent situation, it may be possible to regularly provide information that will help influence policymakers at all levels. It is important to remember that policymakers are people too. Policymakers want to be treated with respect, be communicated with regularly—not just when there is a problem—and be provided with positive feedback rather than only the negative feedback they are more likely to receive. Educators can be effective policy advocates, but it takes time, energy, and the willingness to become actively engaged in and well informed about issues and prospective policies.

—*Cynthia J. Reed*

See also accountability; authority; Black education; boards of education; bureaucracy; Chicago school reform; consolidation, of school districts; critical race theory; cultural politics, wars; decision making; democracy, democratic education and administration; desegregation, of schools; discrimination; equality, in schools; equity and adequacy of funding schools; ethics; expert power; forecasting; fundamentalism; Gallup Polls, on public education; governance; international education; knowledge base, of the field; law; leadership, theories of; literacy, theories of; minorities, in schools; multiculturalism; persuasion; politics, of education; power; restructuring, of schools; school districts, history and development; state departments of education; Supreme Court, United States, key cases in education law

Further Readings and References

Davies, B., Evans, J., & Fitz, J. (2005). *Education policy and social reproduction.* New York: Routledge.
Heck, R. (2004). *Studying educational and social policy.* Mahwah, NJ: Erlbaum.

Malen, B. (2005). Educational leaders as policy analysts. In F. English (Ed.), *The SAGE handbook of educational leadership* (pp. 191–215). Thousand Oaks, CA: Sage.

Olssen, M., Codd, J., & O'Neill, A. (2004). *Education policy: Globalization, citizenship and democracy.* Thousand Oaks, CA: Sage.

Spring, J. (2005). *Political agendas for education.* Mahwah, NJ: Erlbaum.

Stein, S. (2004). *The culture of education policy.* New York: Teachers College Press.

POLICY MAKING, VALUES OF

Policies, laws, rules, and regulations are pervasive and ubiquitous in public education. Policies frame responsibilities and rights, articulate procedures and process, and state what is important to be pursued by the organization. They seek to impose certainty and uniformity in the behaviors of the organization's actors, and they allocate scarce resources. They endeavor to solve problems the public needs to have resolved. If a problem arises, a policy is devised to solve it. If educators respond differently to similar situations, a policy is developed to bring consistency into the organization. Policies are enacted to achieve certain desired outcomes.

Policies can have profound influence. For example, school leaders need not look far beyond their desk to find policies that define what shall be taught, how it shall be taught, and who shall teach it. A school's curriculum and instruction are currently shaped by high-stakes accountability policies. The federal government through No Child Left Behind legislation defines alternative placements and practices for students in schools that fail to meet Adequate Yearly Progress goals. Special education, bilingual education, English-only instruction, random drug testing of students, and reduced recess time are all examples of policies that impact the public schools and those charged with their management and leadership. The seeming omnipresence of policies, especially those that are done *to* schools, underscores the importance of thoroughly understanding the policy process.

A policy is a set of values issued with authority and expressed in written form or words. It is authoritative when there is sufficient power to induce a shift in behavior toward achieving specified values. In short, policy is the embodiment of a particular value that government deems is in the best interest of the public.

But what values are pursued through the political process of policy making and by whom? Various issue partisans who gather around a particular problem or preferred solution alternative, knowledge brokers with their retinue of researchers, constituencies, and the media all exert pressure on public officials to identify specific problems and propose possible solutions. Likewise, the same groups will react against proposed problems and solutions that run counter to their cherished values. These groups bring their favored values and definitions of those values to the political process, where they often collide or resonate with one another and with the values of the public officials.

For policymakers, the constant dilemma is how to choose among the competing values to ascertain which will be pursued in any given policy. One must ask, What values are fundamental to the policy-making process, or in this case, the educational policy-making process? In 1986, James Guthrie and Rodney Reed identified three deeply held values that are inextricably linked to educational policy—*equality, efficiency,* and *liberty.* Other scholars posit four dominant values in education—*equity, efficiency, choice,* and *quality.* Still others have identified five values that have been historically prominent in policy making in general and in education specifically—*liberty, equality, efficiency, fraternity,* and *economic growth.*

A comparison of these three value sets shows an overlap of values. Choice is just another name for liberty. Equity and equality are similar. Efficiency is the same in both sets. The major differences are quality, fraternity, and economic growth.

Equity, efficiency, and choice are recurring values. Quality subsumes economic growth because an education cannot be a quality education if it does not adequately prepare students to be productive in society. Currently, the term *excellence* is used to describe quality. Fraternity is an important value but it appears to be restricted to curricular issues or it rose in support of other values touted as American or in response to ideas considered un-American.

The following values appear dominant in educational policy making: *equity, efficiency, choice,* and *excellence.* New values may also emerge as new sets of problems are identified. There appears to be evidence that a new fundamental value, security, has been pushed onto the public agenda. Legislatures and Congress have passed laws aimed at making our schools safe by creating rings of protection around the school. School districts have passed regulations regarding gang attire, installed metal detectors, randomly tested students for drug use, and touted the impact that school uniforms have on reducing violence. The courts have shown an increased willingness, especially in the area of search and seizure, to support those actions aimed at providing greater security for the schools.

EQUITY, EFFICIENCY, CHOICE, EXCELLENCE, AND SECURITY

A public policy that values equity means that there are inequities in the distribution of or access to public resources that can be redressed through the redistributive power of government. Policies serving equity issues measure the gap between the expected norms of social life and its actual attainments. It looks to what levels of needs exist that will provide adequate resources. Its precept is fairness, not sameness. A review of a few policies that stress equity will help in defining this value.

Public Law 94-142 and the Individuals with Disabilities Education Act (IDEA), recently reauthorized in 2004, were written to ensure that students with identified disabilities are not denied access to education. Once their access to an important governmental service, education, was assured, these laws looked to the adequacy of the education the students would receive. To receive the exact same education as their nonhandicapped peers would not be fair. In order for handicapped students to enjoy the benefits derived from governmental service, these students may need additional resources, such as specially trained teachers and support services.

Similar to the needs of handicapped students are the needs of the limited and non-English-speaking students. In the seminal court case in this area, the U.S. Supreme Court in *Lau v. Nichols* (1974) stated that Chinese-speaking students were denied a meaningful opportunity at an education in the San Francisco Unified School District, despite receiving the same instruction as their English-speaking counterparts. Equal treatment turned out to be unequal—the Chinese-speaking students needed more instruction.

Other examples of equity issues in education include desegregation, with its drive for equal access for minority students, Head Start programs, and school funding lawsuits in which the plaintiffs claim that a state's method of funding its schools is not equitable because of the great disparity in revenues generated from school district to school district throughout the state.

Efficiency is getting the most out of a given input. It is the greatest benefit for the least cost. Efficiency is an instrumental value; it is a comparative idea that allows for the judging of the merit of doing things in different ways. Efficiency reduces waste and duplication. It husbands resources so that they may be spent on desired items.

Educational policies that are directed at achieving efficiency often involve ratios such as California's law regarding the highest number of administrators to teachers a school district may have without incurring a penalty. Efficiency dominated educational values from the 1920s to around the 1950s. It is still a potent force, as witnessed by Massachusetts Proposition 2-1/2 and California's Proposition 13, which slashed revenue for public schools in both states in a "starve the beast" type of approach to reducing the costs of public education.

Choice as a fundamental value appears to be writ large in the public educational agenda setting stage. Charter schools and vouchers are just two of the most recognizable policy efforts. Both policies embrace the concept of giving choice to parents "to direct the upbringing of the children" by allowing options to attending public schools. Other related policies that embody choice include home schooling, tuition tax credits, and intra- and interdistrict choice programs.

Excellence is the fourth fundamental value. An example of excellence as a value in educational policy making is found in America's response to Sputnik. America was no longer considered the best country technologically and scientifically in the world. Consequently, the nation geared up for a push to increase and strengthen the math and science curricula. The federal government, in pursuit of this goal called "excellence," at that time provided large amounts of money. More recently, the application of this value has been seen in the so-called first wave of reform of the early 1980s prompted by the 1983 report *A Nation at Risk*. This reform effort focused on increasing standards for high school graduation, the institution of minimal standards, and tighter controls on who enters the profession of teaching. The push for high-stakes testing, such as tying graduation to passing a state-mandated test, is the most recent example of a policy that seeks excellence as its core value.

The last and emerging fundamental value is security. Schools long considered safe havens for students have been the target for many policies that seek security. The installation of magnetometers, the resurgence of strip searches for drugs and weapons, zero tolerance policies, and the unprecedented collaboration of the Secret Service and the U.S. Department of Education point to a new fundamental value—security. When New England superintendents were asked if security is a fundamental value on par with other fundamental values, 88.7% agreed or strongly agreed.

Finally, it is worthwhile to note that although these currently represent core educational values, history suggests that all five are not equally pervasive. It is possible to argue that certain values dominated particular time periods. For instance the case could be made that equity was the major value pursued during the civil rights era; indeed, several major education policies (e.g., IDEA) were introduced during or shortly following this time period. The 1980s were witness to a burgeoning standards movement—a time when excellence was on the minds of education policymakers. Soon after, the 1990s brought school choice to the fore—charter schools, voucher initiatives, and tuition tax credit policies were popularly enacted. The present decade has made efficiency a top priority—witness the No Child Left Behind Act and other increased accountability of investments in our schools. And, of course, the Columbine High School massacre and the September 11, 2001, terrorist attacks have heightened sensitivity to security in our schools over the past two decades.

SUMMARY

Educational leaders are policy consumers and policymakers. The more informed they are about the process, the more effective they are at implementing and developing policy. An understanding of the fundamental values that influence and drive policy formation helps provide the leader with a rubric for understanding policy.

—*Casey D. Cobb and Todd A. DeMitchell*

See also accountability; administration, theories of; Asian Pacific Americans; authority; Black education; boards of education; conflict management; critical race theory; cross-cultural studies; cultural politics, wars; decision making; Department of Education; desegregation, of schools; diversity; economics, theories of; equality, in schools; equity and adequacy of funding schools; ethics; finance, of public schools; forecasting; Gallup Polls, on education; governance; international education; knowledge base, of the field; Latinos; management theories; market theory of schooling; minorities, in schools; multiculturalism; No Child Left Behind; organizational theories; parental involvement; philosophies, of education; politics, of education; power; privatization; productivity; right-wing politics, advocates, impact on education; rural education; satisficing

theory; school safety; schooling effects; social capital; Supreme Court, United States, key cases in education law; terrorism; values of organizations and leadership; values pluralism, in schools; violence in schools

Further Readings and References

Cooper, B., Fusarelli, L., & Randall, E. (2004). *Better policies, better schools: Theories and applications.* Boston: Pearson.

Davies, B., Evans, J., & Fitz, J. (2005). *Education policy and social reproduction.* New York: Routledge.

DeMitchell, T., & Cobb, C. (2003). Policy responses to violence in our schools: An exploration of security as a fundamental value. *Brigham Young University Education and Law Journal 2,* 459–484.

Guthrie, J., & Reed, R. (1986). *Educational administration and policy: Effective leadership for American education.* Englewood Cliffs, NJ: Prentice Hall.

Heck, R. (2004). *Studying educational and social policy.* Mahwah, NJ: Erlbaum.

Lau v. Nichols, 414 U.S. 563 (1974).

Sirotnik, K. (Ed.). (2004). *Holding accountability accountable: What ought to matter in public education.* New York: Teachers College Press.

Spring, J. (2005). *Political agendas for education.* Mahwah, NJ: Erlbaum.

POLITICS, OF EDUCATION

As a field of study, politics of education is more appropriately thought of as a subfield of education, rather than of political science. Incorporating frameworks and research methodologies from fields such as sociology, history, law, and public and educational administration, as well as political science, politics of education is multidisciplinary and tends to be more applied and practice-oriented than political science. Politics of education has made substantial contributions to educational administration by providing an alternative lens for viewing the role of the administrator, other than the traditional view of administration as planning, organizing, and managing. The traditional view was that educational administrators acted outside or above the political arena, a view that hampered their effectiveness. By encouraging administrators to view themselves as political leaders, politics of education has given them tools for being more effective in the educational world as it really is. Through studies of educational policy, politics of education has contributed the means for both politicians and educators to anticipate, evaluate, and improve the effects of educational policies. Policy analysis, a subarea that includes program evaluation research, has made contributions to research methodology.

Scholars first took interest in the politics of education in the late 1950s and 1960s when the federal government began playing a larger role in schools via the National Defense Education Act of 1958 and the Elementary and Secondary Education Act of 1965. Conflict and political dissent were beginning to appear more frequently in schools, and school leaders were increasingly less successful in maintaining their politically neutral posture. Interest in the study of the politics of education also coincided with the post–World War II trends in educational administration scholarship, which were built around the theories and methods of the various social sciences. Thomas H. Eliot is frequently credited with being the first to conceptualize a politics of education. The Politics of Education Association was formed in 1969 as a special interest group within the American Educational Research Association (AERA). In 1996, AERA created a division of Educational Policy and Politics.

In 1977, Jay D. Scribner and Richard M. Englert articulated a definition of politics that is widely used in this field—interactions that affect the "authoritative allocation" of principles. They noted that the definition rests on assumptions that in a pluralist society, there are conflicting values and scarce resources. Politics is the means for making decisions that are accepted by all. The processes leading to those decisions involve attempts at influence by competing interests. Scholarship in the field of politics of education investigates questions about political structures, political behavior, policy, social values, international comparisons, and inequality and social justice. Studies often pursue more than one type of question, for example, an international comparison study could investigate questions of political structures and political behavior.

POLITICS OF EDUCATION: KINDS OF QUESTIONS INVESTIGATED

Political Structures

Questions about political structures center on how governance of education is set up at the local, state, and federal levels. Included are legal and organizational analyses of governance structures and procedures; studies of the relationships among the local, state, and federal levels; and research on elections. For example, *federalism* is a term that defines the shared responsibilities of the federal and state governments in the American system. How that federalism works is an area of study. Another area that has received much attention is the local school board: how it should be structured, how it should operate, whether it should be elected or appointed, and whether it should be fiscally dependent on local government or fiscally independent. An example is Michael W. Kirst's work on mayoral takeovers of urban school districts. How schools should coordinate with other community agencies that serve children and families is also a topic in the political structures cluster.

Political Behavior

Power is an organizing concept in studies that examines influence on and control of education decisions. Decentralization and community control of schools are important topics. Studies of community power structures produced community types that predicted who would wield the most influence over decisions about a community's schools. Studies of policy-making processes examine how decisions are made and what policies result from those decisions. Interest groups, bargaining, and voting are examples of political behavior. Paul E. Peterson's study of the politics of the Chicago public schools was an important contribution to the literature on political bargaining in education.

Policy Analysis

Policy analysis involves questions about the formulation, implementation, and effects of educational policies. Some areas of policy for study have been schools of choice, testing and accountability systems, and educational finance.

Catherine Marshall, Douglas Mitchell, and Frederick Wirt studied six states and developed a cultural framework for examining the origins of state education policy. The influential STAR study in Tennessee resulted in published articles about effects of class size on student learning, as well as on the politics of reducing class size in the public schools.

International Comparisons

Comparative and international education is a separate subfield of education; however, many comparative studies analyze political issues. Michael Crossley and Keith Watson have written a history and critique of comparative and international education. Comparative education tends to be more academic, while international education is more oriented toward support of policy decisions. Crossley and Watson criticize the American-European conceptual frameworks that have predominated in the field, the prevalence of statistical comparisons that ignore cultural contexts, the nation-state as the unit of analysis, and the political motivations behind some of the research, which is often done on a consulting basis. Their view is that the strengths of this field include that it is multidisciplinary, it has traditionally recognized the importance of global forces on education, and it has examined the dilemmas of cross-cultural transfer of educational programs and structures. They call for more collaborative work between the researchers with comparative and international orientations, more cultural sensitivity through participatory research with practitioners, and more use of multiple frames of analysis, from global to microethnographic.

Schools and Democratic Values

To what extent do schools behave as democracies in the process of educating children? Some researchers do not attempt to be value neutral. They have a value position and use it to formulate the research questions and to view the data. For example, Jeannie Oakes and her colleagues studied middle school reform in 16 schools, using in-depth qualitative case studies. Their a priori assumption was that good reform advances civic virtue. They viewed the process of reform as key to accomplishing change that serves the common good. They looked for evidence of commitment to student learning, inclusion of diverse learners, development of caring communities, and democratic participation of stakeholders.

Critical Studies

Scholars in politics of education have always been interested in questions of who influences decisions and who benefits from those decisions. For most of these scholars, whether or not education is democratic and expands opportunities for students is a researchable question. But critical theorists assume that schools and government are social institutions that by their nature reproduce the inequities in society. Their research sets out to show how those inequities are institutionalized in schools and what needs to be

changed. For example, Wanda S. Pillow wrote about the education of pregnant and parenting teens from a feminist and race critical point of view.

THEORIES IN POLITICS OF EDUCATION

Systems Theory

David Easton formulated an application of systems theory to political science in the mid-1960s. Frederick M. Wirt and Michael W. Kirst built on Easton's theory when they conceptualized education as a system for the allocation of values. Values are expressed in material things, such as teacher salaries, but also in symbolic things, such as which holidays will be celebrated.

A system exists in an environment. The environment in which schools exist produces demands on the system. For example, a community or state requires an educated workforce. The environment also provides resources, such as tax revenues. Demands and resources are inputs to the system. The system converts some of these inputs into policy. Policies have outcomes, for example, students who have learned mathematics to a certain level. These outcomes produce feedback into the system. For example, the business community or the state legislature may be dissatisfied with the level of student achievement, and put pressure on the school system to improve it. The policy environment also changes. For example, public opinion about federal involvement in school curriculum and student testing has changed enormously in the last 30 years. In systems theory, the continued legitimacy and survival of the political system depends on support, which is the willingness of people to accept the policy decisions made by the system.

Rational Choice Theory

Rational choice theory assumes that all political actors have preferences, and that they make decisions by rationally calculating which choice will maximize their preferences at the lowest cost. Branches of rational choice theory include game theory, bargaining and coalition theory, and the median voter theory. Tyll van Geel outlined some ways that rational choice theories might help school administrators better understand how to produce cooperation and predict election outcomes, for example. Market theory, a branch of rational choice theory, is the basis for advocacy of privatization of schools and school services, as well as for school vouchers and charter schools. The famous pro-voucher argument made by John E. Chubb and Terry M. Moe relies on rational choice theory. Their analysis showed that the competition of the free market would lead to schools that are free of bureaucratic constraints and thus better able to educate students.

Power and Conflict

Frances C. Fowler is an example of an author who bases her view of politics of education on theories of power and conflict. In this view, educational policies are the result of conflict that stems from people having different values with respect to education and different stakes in policy decisions. For example, conservative Christians may have different values than other groups when it comes to the curriculum. Teachers may have a different stake than parents do in the way a school budget is formulated. People also have different amounts of power. School administrators have power over certain decisions, but others in the community may have power over the school administrators. Political actors (either individuals or groups) seek to increase their power so that they may have more influence over policy decisions. Conflict is resolved through negotiation, bargaining, and compromise, or by coercion.

Critical Race Theory

Gloria Ladson-Billings and William F. Tate IV explicated a critical race theory (CRT) of education. Among those who have expanded and used CRT as an analytic tool are Jessica T. DeCuir and Adrienne D. Dixson, who used CRT to analyze the experiences of African American students in an elite White prep school. The elements of CRT they used include (a) counter-story-telling, that is, the stories of racially marginalized students that critique or cast doubt on the dominant discourse; (b) the inevitability and permanence of racism; (c) Whiteness as property, which among other things results in a suppression of Black cultural expression; (d) interest convergence, which means that civil rights gains by minorities occur only to the extent that they also benefit White people; and (e) critique of liberalism, that is, exposing the myth of color blindness.

Theories of the State

What Carlos Alberto Torres called "theories of the state" and James G. Cibulka called "political ideology"

has been used to explain trends in educational policy. This kind of analysis holds that policy reflects the underlying philosophical view of the dominant group of policymakers. The liberal view is based on the value of the individual, equal opportunity, and individual rights. It is an optimistic view of government, holding that government can improve both individual lives and society. The welfare state is a product of the liberal view. The liberal view is compatible with capitalism, but in the welfare state, government acts to regulate the free market in order to make competition fairer and guarantees every citizen a minimum level of health, education, housing, and nutrition. The programs in the United States of the Great Society in the 1960s, such as Head Start and Title I, are examples of the liberal policy trend.

The conservative view is based on different ideas of both government and individuals. The role of government in regulating the free market is minimal, while its major role is to constrain the antisocial and immoral impulses of individual citizens. Government is not effective in changing inequalities in society. What conservatives call traditional values, that is, belief in nation, family, duty, authority, standards, traditionalism, self-interest, competitive individualism, and antistatism, and for many, in God, ground their view of the governmental role in education. Believing strongly in capitalism, conservatives work to reduce the size of government, with more services provided by the profit sector. They oppose both organized labor and governmental bureaucracy. The movement toward school choice is an important example of the influence of the conservative view.

The radical, or neo-Marxist, view is based on the assumption that all of the social institutions of society, including government and education, work to reproduce racial, class, and gender inequalities. In that sense, everything is political. Those in power control knowledge; thus there is no such thing as unbiased expertise. Government is the arena for power struggles based on gender, class, and ethnicity. Capitalism is a cause of societal ills. Michael W. Apple and his colleagues exemplify this view.

An understanding of these theories of the state, or political philosophies, is useful in understanding the origins of policies and policy debates. James Cibulka used this analysis to understand the increasingly partisan nature of educational policy making and the heightened role of ideological interest groups in the United States in the 1990s.

—Carla Edlefson

See also Afrocentric theories; authority; Bell, Ted; boards of education; charter schools; Chicago school reform; choice, of schools; Christian Coalition; civil rights movement; collective bargaining; communities, types, building of; community relations; conceptual systems theory and leadership; consolidation, of school districts; cost-benefit analyses; Council of Chief State School Officers; Council of the Great City Schools; creationism; critical race theory; critical theory; cross-cultural studies; cultural politics, wars; decentralization/centralization controversy; decision making; democracy, democratic education and administration; Department of Education; Education Commission of the States; elections, of school boards, bond issues; equality, in schools; equity and adequacy of funding schools; evaluation; fascism and schools; finance, of public schools; global cultural politics; globalism; governance; Latinos; liberalism; Machiavelli, Niccolò; market theory of schooling; minorities, in schools; multiculturalism; No Child Left Behind; open systems theory; policy advocacy; power; principal-agent theory; reform, of schools; standard setting; system theory/thinking; unions, of teachers; voucher plans; World Bank, influence on education

Further Readings and References

Apple, M., Aasen, P., Cho, M., Gardin, L., Oliver, A., Sung, Y., et al. (2003). *The state and the politics of knowledge.* New York: RoutledgeFalmer.

Chubb, J., & Moe, T. (1990). *Politics, markets, and America's schools.* Washington, DC: Brookings Institution.

Cibulka, J. (1999). Ideological lenses for interpreting political and economic changes affecting schooling. In J. Murphy & K. S. Louis (Eds.), *Handbook of research on educational administration* (2nd ed., pp.163–182). San Francisco: Jossey-Bass.

Crossley, M., & Watson, K. (2003). *Comparative and international research in education: Globalisation, context and difference.* London: RoutledgeFalmer.

DeCuir, J., & Dixson, A. (2004). "So when it comes out, they aren't that surprised that it is there": Using critical race theory as a tool of analysis of race and racism in education. *Educational Researcher, 33*(5), 26–31.

Eliot, T. (1959). Toward an understanding of public school politics. *American Political Science Review, 53,* 1032–1051.

Fowler, F. (2004). *Policy studies for educational leaders: An introduction.* (2nd ed.). Upper Saddle River, NJ: Pearson/Merrill/Prentice Hall.

Kirst, M. (2003). Mayoral influence, new regimes, and public school governance. In W. L. Boyd & D. Miretzky (Eds.), *American educational governance on trial: Change and challenges* (pp. 196–218.) Chicago: University of Chicago Press.

Ladson-Billings, G., & Tate W., IV. (1995). Toward a critical race theory of education. *Teachers College Record, 97,* 47–68.

Marshall, C., Mitchell, D., & Wirt, F. (1989). *Culture and education policy in the American states.* New York: Falmer.

Oakes, J., Hunter Quartz, K., Ryan, S., & Lipton, M. (2000). *Becoming good American schools: The struggle for civic virtue in school reform.* San Francisco: Jossey-Bass.

Peterson, P. (1976). *School politics Chicago style.* Chicago: University of Chicago Press.

Pillow, W. (2004). *Unfit subjects: Educational policy and the teen mother.* New York: RoutledgeFalmer.

Scribner, J., & Englert, R. (1977). The politics of education: An introduction. In J. D. Scribner (Ed.), *The politics of education* (pp. 1–29). Chicago: University of Chicago Press.

Torres, C. (1995). State and education revisited: Why educational researchers should think politically about education. In M. W. Apple (Ed.), *Review of research in education* (pp. 255–331). Washington, DC: American Educational Research Association.

Van Geel, T. (1995). The preparation of educational leaders and rational choice theory. In R. Donmoyer, M. Imber, & J. Scheurich (Eds.), *The knowledge base in educational administration: Multiple perspectives.* Albany: State University of New York.

Wirt, F., & Kirst, M. (2001). *The political dynamics of American education* (2nd ed.). Richmond, CA: McCutchan.

POPPER, KARL

Karl Popper (1902–1994), along with Thomas Kuhn, was one of the most influential philosophers of the twentieth century. Popper was initially trained as a schoolteacher (mathematics and physics) but eventually earned a PhD from the University of Vienna in 1928. Popper left his native Austria in 1937 under the threat of Nazi anti-Semitism and relocated to the University of Canterbury in New Zealand. Eventually, Popper joined the London School of Economics, where he served as professor of the philosophy of science until his retirement. While a positivist, Popper saw himself as a critical rationalist and philosophically tied to the work of Kant. For educators and educational leaders particularly, Popper's work relates to research methodology, empirically based best practices, leadership theory, and the ongoing process of change.

In his work, Popper provided a means of demarcation between those theories that were scientific and those that were unscientific. He felt that creativity and imagination were the foundation of scientific theory development and rejected induction as the basis of theory development. Popper felt that while observational and experimental data could be employed to evaluate theories, they cannot form theoretical foundations.

For Popper, falsification was the ultimate criterion by which any theory could be identified as scientific. His position was that theories could not be verified but simply tentatively refuted via corroboration of data. Those theories that are compatible with data or that have been modified to accommodate the available data are unscientific in nature. Only those that could be falsified were to be considered scientific.

Popper contended that subject matter was irrelevant and argued for the approach of active problem solving in science. He was a serious critic of those who employed the "sociology of knowledge" to further a given ideology. For him, only the problems to be solved and the individual's desire to solve them should be the primary focus of professional activity. His position was that the problem-solving process formed a feedback loop in which the initial problem was addressed by a trial solution. The effect of the trial solution to the problem was then examined via an error elimination process. The resulting situation following the error elimination process became a new problem to address. This process described by Popper forms the basis for Deming's Plan-Do-Study-Adjust Cycle. For Popper, philosophy was active engagement with profound problems rather than a semantic discourse.

Popper's work also addresses change and the change process. In regard to this issue, he adopted an evolutionary view. As with his problem-solving process, Popper felt that change occurred via a process of successive adjustments based upon feedback. He contended that tradition, culture, and history all play a significant role in the change process and that no person is capable of initiating or developing anything independent of the work or influence of others. Popper also felt that the extensive, subtle relationships of each individual influenced his or her personal actions and that no plan was sufficiently encompassing to allow for the actions of each individual within a system. Therefore, the complex issues, institutions, and organizations of our society re-created or re-formed themselves carte blanche but could be gradually changed over time and in stages as knowledge progresses. It is within this framework that Popper argues for creativity and intuition over science to provide the foundation of meaningful, significant change.

Popper considered himself to be pragmatic in his approach to philosophy and practice, and that rational, critical pragmatism was the ultimate means by which one could operate. He opposed conventionalism and relativism in philosophy, science, and society. Popper

supported the concept of an ongoing discourse between individuals rooted in the contention that all persons are infinitely ignorant and that we differ only in the nature of our limited personal knowledge.

—*J. M. Blackbourn, Don Schillinger, and Dennis Rader*

See also Aristotle; critical theory; determinism, sociocultural; hypotheses, in research; idealism, as philosophy in education; Kuhn, Thomas; objectivity; open systems theory; organizational theories; philosophies of education; Plato; pragmatism and progressivism; research methods

Further Readings and References
Popper, K. (1959). *The logic of scientific discovery.* London: Hutchinson.
Popper, K. (1961). *The poverty of historicism.* New York: Harper & Row.
Popper, K. (1965). *Conjectures and refutations: The growth of scientific knowledge.* New York: Harper & Row.
Popper, K. (1979). *Objective knowledge: An evolutionary approach.* Oxford: Clarendon Press.
Popper, K. (1982). *The open universe: An argument for indeterminism.* Totowa, NJ: Rowman & Littlefield.
Popper, K. (1994). *The myth of the framework: In defense of science and rationality.* London: Routledge.

PORTFOLIOS

Portfolio use has become standard practice in many educational institutions, although exact parameters vary widely. Depending on the nature of the portfolio, whether it is for self-assessment, professional assessment, measuring growth, or displaying best accomplishments or even interests, defining what should comprise a portfolio is debatable and often difficult. The use of portfolios in education has become more widespread recently, increasingly used as a means of authentic assessment of students. Technological advances have ushered in e-portfolios, electronic portfolios presented online, enhancing the efficiency and ease of completing and reviewing portfolio products while substantially decreasing the need for hard copies in traditional binders. Maintaining work samples or portfolio artifacts thus has become much simpler, as have revisions to work included. Teachers and students can access a single copy of an artifact in order to exchange feedback easily to enhance student growth. Portfolios even have become a valued tool in the accreditation process for teacher education, for example, with the

National Council for the Accreditation of Teacher Education (NCATE), wherein programs need accurate assessments of student and instructor performance. These factors have played a major role in the increasing popularity of portfolio usage in educational administration.

Two basic categories of portfolios exist, an *all-inclusive portfolio* and a *selection portfolio*. The first includes records containing all of the work that a student has completed in a course or program. Portfolios in this category often are used to document and archive work that a student or professional has accomplished. It serves as a record of events, a history of what the student in a class or program has done.

The second is a more discriminating selection of work used to demonstrate achievement or proficiency. This portfolio represents efforts toward a goal set by the student, the teacher, or both. Artifacts displayed in this type of portfolio normally are carefully selected to address a specific set of criteria. Sometimes the student is solely responsible for choosing the products to be included, and sometimes the instructor decides. Often the decision is made with some level of collaboration between the student and teacher. The main difference between an all-inclusive and a selection portfolio is that the author of the selection portfolio chooses work samples to achieve a particular goal.

Selection portfolios can also be divided into two subcategories: selections that showcase the author's best work and selections used to assess the author's growth and development within a program, often then to facilitate further student learning. Examples of portfolios that could showcase best work include (a) an artist's portfolio in which an artist might want to sell representative pieces or (b) portfolios used by job applicants to demonstrate proficiency in certain job-specific areas. When showcasing work, the goal of the portfolio often is economic advancement.

If the portfolio is used to assesses student performance, several other factors must be considered. The author must know the goal of the portfolio in order to select appropriate material, and self-assessment may require a different selection from teacher assessment. Both of these may differ from a portfolio for which the goal is professional assessment, as in the case of teacher education programs.

By naming the purpose of the portfolio, NCATE is then able to assess whether or not the use of these tools by a program or a college accomplishes the purpose of assessment as NCATE has defined it. In addition, the faculty and programs are enabled to determine appropriate products when preparing portfolios for NCATE review.

Assessment of students using portfolios allows teachers to enhance student learning in a manner not seen with more superficial assessment tools. Students may be asked to use the portfolio process to self-assess or to provide a selection of work that allows an instructor to appraise course or program outcomes. Clearly, portfolios may be used for both.

One method that enhances student learning and assessment is the use of reflections. A reflection allows a student an opportunity, often through reflective writing, to tie together concepts learned in a course or program. Initially, students may have difficulty crafting reflections with any depth. The process requires them to analyze themselves, which can be a difficult task, particularly if they have never been exposed to self-analysis or if the level of their writing skills is wanting. As with other tasks, however, students can become more proficient in these types of analyses, especially when teachers act as coaches or guides through the reflective portfolio journey.

One advantage of the reflection process is that teachers and faculty can achieve a more in-depth understanding of issues involved. They can begin to gauge the extent to which students comprehend materials or competencies to which courses are geared. In addition, by examining groups of portfolios, instructors can begin to examine the comprehension of students related to completing certain expectations, raising issues about program coherence. For example, if many students within a cohort do not display the depth of learning desired by an instructor in a specific area, it may indicate that a particular area or standard needs clarification, restructuring, or greater emphasis. A major benefit of this tool is that, by analysis of learning outcomes, assessment occurs for the teacher as well as the learner.

When using portfolios to enhance student learning, teachers and students begin to work more interactively, in a partnership that focuses on learning. Participants often collaborate on selections placed in the portfolio, along with offering insight on what else might be included to best represent the knowledge acquired by a student throughout a course or program of study. This collaboration can also extend to student peers. Often, more advanced students can offer insights about the construction of portfolios and what they learned during the course of their own journeys. Newer students can offer fresh perspectives and provide reasons for older students sharing and expanding their own knowledge bases. Cohorts of students can grow together and learn with and support one another throughout their course or program. Academic and social integration have been linked not only to increased student productivity but to student retention and success as well.

There are five stages in electronic portfolio development. The first is *developing the context and goals.* Key to this process is defining the purpose of the work and the audience to which it is delivered. If the portfolio is used for student assessment, that needs to be addressed from the beginning. As with any other portfolio process, if this is to be used for student self-assessment where the audience is the author, the layout may be much different than if the instructor is doing the assessment. In any case, accessibility is key to effective presentation.

In the second stage of electronic portfolio development, the *working portfolio,* this is a clearinghouse, a place in which all products are stored as possible artifacts for portfolio insertion. This is a stage of exploration, where a student searches for means to exemplify the standards set in the initial phase. Often at the beginning of the process, a student is not yet able to connect the standards and the products. As a student becomes more comfortable with collecting and organizing products, the ability to be discerning grows.

The third phase of development, the *reflective portfolio,* is key if the portfolio is to add to student learning. One method used for reflection is the What? So what? Now what? philosophy. A written summation of the product is added to the portfolio to show which standard is being exemplified, thus answering What? The learning that leads to the understanding of the standard shows the So what?: when students can begin to define their learning and measure it against the goals of their portfolios, their learning becomes more owned and authentic. By expressing this learning in writing, students can document the extent to which learning has actually occurred. To answer the Now what? question, a student can discuss future implications and what could be added to improve, replace, or correct an artifact. The ability to understand these implications shows depth of understanding critical to authentic learning.

Once completing the reflection phase, in the fourth phase, *connections,* the work is organized and evidenced electronically. Citations and supporting documentation can be linked directly to pertinent portfolio

artifacts. Students can begin to examine the portfolio for continuity and cohesion. Even where the goal of the portfolio is teacher assessment of student growth, during this stage of portfolio development a portfolio developer is encouraged to self-assess and to seek guidance from instructors in constructing the best possible products for presentation.

Finally, the portfolio is ready for the last phase of electronic production, the *presentation portfolio.* This is the student's final compilation of work, artifacts, and evidence to demonstrate the learning that occurred within the course or program. The portfolio is at its most a cohesive stage: it represents the processes as much as the learning and presents a clear and definite picture of a student's learning journey.

In addition to the added value of student learning, working collaboratively also allows instructors to use the information from portfolios to determine where their courses or programs are strong and where they may need some attention. Instructors might even use their own work within the course or program to build a portfolio for use by students as well as themselves. This type of portfolio may ease student fears about producing a large document as well as offer ideas on beginning the portfolio process. Not only can this provide students with an example of expectations, but it allows instructors to begin conversations on any difficulties that students may have with portfolio construction. In addition, the process of constructing a portfolio gives instructors unique perspectives on the work given to students as well as helping faculty gauge the difficulty and time necessary for effective portfolio development.

While compiling a course portfolio is beneficial for instructors and students within a given course, it is beneficial as well for departments and institutions. Portfolios also can be used to display scholarship within a course by providing evidence of how its use can enhance student learning. Also, many accreditation boards and state program evaluators permit portfolio records to meet requirements for compliance with standards for obtaining or maintaining accreditation. In addition, a course portfolio can be useful to an instructor's colleagues who may be interested in starting similar projects. It can offer ideas to other faculty or departments. Even when not following preconceived processes, using course portfolios can provide invaluable insights to fellow teachers. Finally, course portfolios can provide documentation of scholarly work, providing an organized and efficient means to increase publications while supplying building blocks for other professionals. In this way, portfolios become excellent professional development tools.

Student learning is the ultimate benefit of portfolio use. Through more improved courses and instruction, along with individual student assessment, learning is enhanced. Portfolios and the collaborative environment often associated with portfolio-based assessments can provide strong opportunities for teachers to improve their craft while at the same time ensuring that optimal student learning occurs. As with any assessment tool, portfolios are used because of their perceived benefits. In addition to the foregoing, portfolios can benefit instructors in a number of ways. Perhaps the most important benefit for instructors of portfolio programs is the insight and direction gained to improve instruction in a course or program. Improving courses and programs should increase student learning. Also, portfolio use helps identify student weaknesses, facilitating targeted interventions when necessary.

One of the major problems involved in the use of a portfolio program is the lack of planning and definition involved in setting a goal for the portfolio. A good portfolio program involves considerable planning on the front end. Critical to creating a successful portfolio program is that users must define the purpose of the portfolio. Failure to do so often results in a haphazard compilation of student work that can be meaningless.

Another problem with portfolios is the difficulty in scoring. The use of vague rubrics can cause this process to be more subjective than preferred. When requirements for scoring are not specified, validity and reliability of portfolio use are immediately called into question. Vague rubrics are subject to differing interpretations among instructors and students and can undermine expectations. In addition, interrater reliability can become an issue when two or more teachers grade on a rubric that is not well defined.

Recognizing requirements and possible problems with the use of portfolios can help departments and faculties optimize their use of authentic assessment. Properly constructed portfolio guidelines with valid and reliable rubrics offer means to measure student progress and performance to a depth usually not available with traditional assessments such as standardized tests and infrequent field observations. Given the technological advances that now facilitate the development of more efficient portfolios, many educators are turning to portfolios to obtain a more accurate picture of their students' accomplishments, the impact of their courses, and the coherence of their programs.

Targeting issues in instruction and assessment enhances both faculty and student learning, optimizing the process of education and learning.

—*Sonia Schaible-Brandon and Rodney Muth*

See also accountability; accreditation; behaviorism; constructivism; critical thinking; curriculum, theories of; individual differences, in children; instructional interventions; literacy, theories of; measurement, theories of; National Council for the Accreditation of Teacher Education; problem solving; professional development; psychology, types of; psychometrics; student teaching

Further Readings and References

Barrett, H. (2001). *Electronic portfolios.* In *Educational Technology.* Denver, CO: ABC-CLIO. Retrieved April 3, 2004, from http://helenbarrett.com/portfolios/encyclopediaentry.htm.

Campbell, D., Melenyzer, B., Nettles, D., & Wyman, R. (2000). *Portfolio and performance assessment in teacher education.* Boston: Allyn & Bacon.

Cole, D., Ryan, C., Kick, F., & Mathies, B. (2000). *Portfolios across the curriculum and beyond.* Thousand Oaks, CA: Corwin Press.

Huba, M., & Freed, J. (2000). *Learner-centered assessment on college campuses: Shifting the focus from teaching to learning.* Needham Heights, MA: Allyn & Bacon.

Jones, M., & Shelton, M. (2005). *Developing your portfolio: Enhancing your learning and showing your stuff.* New York: Routledge.

Muth, R. (2000). Toward a learning-oriented instructional paradigm: Implications for practice. In P. Jenlink & T. Kowalski (Eds.), *Marching into a new millennium: Challenges to educational leadership* (pp. 82–103). Lanham, MD: Scarecrow Press.

National Council for Accreditation of Teacher Education. (2002). *Professional standards for the accreditation of schools, colleges, and departments of teacher education.* Washington, DC: Author.

Tinto, V. (2000). Linking learning and leaving: Exploring the role of the college classroom in student departure. In J. Braxton (Ed.), *Reworking the student departure puzzle* (pp. 81–94). Nashville, TN: Vanderbilt University.

POSITIVISM, POSTPOSITIVISM

Positivism describes a set of assumptions about knowledge and knowledge acquisition characterized generally as follows: (a) only those phenomena that are observable can be counted as knowledge; (b) facts and values are distinct; scientific investigators must put aside values and inquire objectively; (c) hypotheses

Table 1   Differences of Emphasis Between Positivism and Postpositivism-as-Modified-Positivism

Positivism	*Postpositivism-as-Modified-Positivism*
Empirical knowledge claims are justified when they are shown to be based on the firm foundation of evidence acquired solely through empirical observation.	Empirical observation is neither a strictly necessary nor a sufficient criterion for knowledge claims. The findings of a scientific community are probably true.
Assumes an objective external reality upon which inquiry can converge.	Assumes an objective reality that can be apprehended only imperfectly and probabilistically.
Assumes the investigator can determine "how things really are" and "how things really work."	Assumes it is possible to approximate (but never fully know) reality.
Assumes knowledge is gained through experimental/manipulative methodology to verify hypotheses.	Doubts that theory can be confirmed through verification of hypotheses, but believes theories can be disconfirmed through falsification of hypotheses. Those theories never successfully disconfirmed have credibility.

SOURCE: Adapted from Guba, E., & Lincoln, Y. (1994). Competing paradigms in qualitative research. In N. K. Denzin & Y. S. Lincoln (Eds.), *Handbook of qualitative research.* (pp. 105–117). Thousand Oaks, CA: Sage.

are derived deductively from scientific theories to be tested empirically. Theory and observation are distinct; theory comes out of the investigator's imagination; hypotheses are deduced from the theory and then tested by observation. Justifying a theory means showing that it has more and better observations confirming than disconfirming it; (d) knowledge is developed inductively through generalizing from the accumulation of verified facts; (e) the methods of the natural sciences are appropriate for research on social phenomena; (f) the purpose of natural and social sciences are the same, that is, to offer causal explanations of events; and (g) the higher the level to which a theory can be abstracted (the more context-free it is), the better it is (e.g., a theory of administration in general would be preferable to a theory of just educational administration).

Postpostivism has two meanings: the first describes a modified positivism that expresses skepticism about the strength of positivism's claims while still accepting the notion of an objective reality and/or using scientific knowledge to approach understanding of reality. For example, Karl Popper's argument that fallacies in the logic of induction prohibit us from confirming hypotheses, that instead we can only refute them, has been described as a kind of postpositivism. A second meaning of postpositivism is any position that has rejected positivism, including subjectivism, relativism, interpretivism, criticalism, and postmodernism.

In 1994, Egon G. Guba and Yvonna S. Lincoln described the differences between positivism and

postpositivism-as-modified-positivism. Table 1 is based largely on their explanation.

The theory movement in administration, from about 1945 onward, exemplified aspects of positivism and postpositivism-as-modified-positivism. The theory movement sought the identification and articulation of core theoretical assumptions, the use of operational definitions and value-free methodology, the establishment of correctness of administrative decision making as a matter of fact to be validated by evidence of effectiveness, and the development of context-free, lawlike generalizations. In educational administration, some scholars attempted to describe educational administration as just one subset of administration in general. They then emphasized the discovery of lawlike principles for administration in general that by deduction would apply to educational administration. Preparation programs tended to devalue practitioners' knowledge of administration in favor of knowledge derived from theory and research.

Opponents of such views have criticized positivist approaches to educational administration and leadership on four grounds: (1) for assuming that theory and observation can be separated; critics argue that on the contrary we use theoretical vocabulary to report our observations, and that in fact we trust our observations because of theoretical assumptions we have already made; (2) for overemphasizing the value of operational definitions; critics argue both that the choice to use any particular operational definition is either theory laden or subjective and arbitrary, and that focusing on operational definitions is too narrowing, when what investigators need to concern themselves with in validating any theory is a network of hypotheses; (3) for wanting to overgeneralize from organizations in general to educational organizations; critics argue that the goals of education are so different from the goals of other organizations, and differ so much from one educational organization to another, that it is unhelpful to try to generalize beyond education to administration in general; and, related to criticism 3, (4) for suggesting that researchers exclude values from discussion of educational leadership and administration; critics argue that on the contrary, values inhere in any theory, and education is particularly value laden. The fact that values cannot be validated empirically is not an argument for excluding values from administrative theory but an argument against restricting scholarship to empirical approaches.

On the other hand, defenders of scientific approaches to the study of educational leadership and administration argue that it is a mistake to equate positivism (and even modified versions of it) with science, that we can recognize the flaws of such approaches to knowledge and yet still accept and make the most of science in studying educational administration, just with a broadened view of science. As Colin W. Evers and Gabriele Lakomski described it, this broadened view of science would include naturalism and the extraempirical virtues of a theory. In this view of science, one would prefer a particular theory to others, not merely because it had more observations confirming it (or fewer observations disconfirming it), but because either it was better at helping us solve problems or it had characteristics that scientists in general tend to favor in theories. Among these characteristics are conservatism, modesty, simplicity, generality, and refutability. The broadened view values science for having been extraordinarily successful in solving problems. Even in the social realm, science has produced predictions that have better than chance odds of coming true. This is true of science despite the clear inadequacies of positivism's descriptions of it.

—*Gary Ivory*

See also administration, theories of; authority; critical theory; knowledge base, of the field; Kuhn, Thomas; leadership, theories of; management theories; organizational theories; philosophies of education; Popper, Karl; postmodernism; research methods

Further Readings and References

Chapman, J., Sackney, L., & Aspin, D. (1999). Internationalization in educational administration: Policy and practice, theory and research. In J. Murphy & K. Louis (Eds.), *Handbook of research on educational administration* (2nd ed., pp. 73–98). San Francisco: Jossey-Bass.

Culbertson, J. (1988). A century's quest for a knowledge base. In N. Boyan (Ed.), *Handbook of research on educational administration* (pp. 3–26). New York: Longman.

English, F. (2003). *The postmodern challenge to the theory and practice of educational administration.* Springfield, IL: Charles C Thomas.

Evers, C., & Lakomski, G. (1991). *Knowing educational administration: Contemporary methodological controversies in educational administration research.* New York: Pergamon Press.

Guba, E., & Lincoln, Y. (1994). Competing paradigms in qualitative research. In N. K. Denzin & Y. S. Lincoln (Eds.), *Handbook of qualitative research.* (pp. 105–117). Thousand Oaks, CA: Sage.

Ritchie, J., & Lewis, J. (2003). *Qualitative research practice: A guide for social science students and researchers.* Thousand Oaks, CA: Sage.

Young, M., & Lopez, G. (2005). The nature of inquiry in educational leadership. In F. English (Ed.), *The SAGE handbook of educational leadership* (pp. 337–361). Thousand Oaks, CA: Sage.

POSTMODERNISM

Postmodernism is neither a philosophy nor a unified perspective or doctrine. Rather, it is a loosely assembled collage of voices, ideas, and techniques of criticism that are juxtaposed against the long-established traditions of inquiry, especially in the empirical sciences. However, postmodernism is not antiscientific. Rather, a postmodernist perspective calls into question the privileged position that posits science is the only method of knowing that has value in the world.

Modernity is generally associated with the Age of Enlightenment beginning with the works of René Descartes (1596–1650) and later thinkers such as Immanuel Kant, Georg Wilhelm Friedrich Hegel, and François Voltaire and the assumption that reason could solve most of the world's problems. Postmodernists point out that modernists have not solved the problems of poverty and war. The last century is testimony to the irrationality of the rational mind at work with the devastation of two world wars and the Holocaust.

Postmodernists also question the basic idea of *progress,* that is, the assumption that the future will always be better than the past. Most of all, postmodernism challenges any assertion that there are universal laws, whether they are divine or imposed by the rules of science. Such laws or rules are called metanarratives, meaning that they are proffered as globally valid for all times, places, and people. Philosophies, religions, and political perspectives that serve up all-embracing viewpoints are examples of metanarratives.

Postmodernism relies heavily on knowledge of language and culture, especially the analysis of written texts. Indeed, much of postmodern criticism is literary or textual criticism based on the practice of close reading. A practice such as deconstruction is an examination of texts for antinomies, contradictions, silences, and hidden hierarchies in them.

The implication of postmodernism for educational leadership is that the position taken by postmodernists undermines the very idea of a stable knowledge base upon which a leadership practice can be established. Any knowledge base is an example of a conceit, an assumption that is untenable linguistically and logically. Stability can only be maintained by the exercise of raw political power of the state.

The primary evil for educational leadership is that of certainty, which is offered context free and is based on privileged versions of truth. Postmodernism challenges the "one right way" of thinking about things, especially so-called best practices of anything proffered outside of localism and the primacy of context and culture. The postmodern outlook on such things has been called by some critics a kind of epistemological anarchism. Postmodernism is therefore profoundly antiauthoritarian, whether dogma has been embraced as scientific method or as received truth in any other form. School leaders and those aspiring to become leaders will find preparation practices and outlooks of leading that rest on assumptions of finality or absolute truth in any form vulnerable to postmodern deconstructive criticism, including the scientific method itself.

The advantage of a postmodern outlook for educational administration is that if followed, it can lead to redefining the idea of borders, whether rooted in science or the humanities. It can promote a level playing field in the competition of ideas and perspectives that can free the discipline from the intellectual doldrums in which it has rested since it was established. Confining it to science alone dehumanizes educational leadership. Science has limits. A study of leadership clearly is beyond those limits. The postmodern view is not an argument to abandon science but to recognize science's own borders in the pursuit of greater understanding of educational leadership.

—*Fenwick W. English*

See also authority; chaos theory; cognitive dissonance; critical thinking; deconstruction; Kuhn, Thomas; Popper, Karl; pragmatism and progressivism; problem solving; semiotics

Further Readings and References

English, F. (2002). The point of scientificity, the fall of the epistemological dominos, and the end of the field of educational administration. *Studies in Philosophy and Education, 21,* 2, 109–136.

English, F. (2003). *The postmodern challenge to the theory and practice of educational administration.* Springfield, IL: Charles C Thomas.

Ward, G. (2003). *Postmodernism.* London: Hodder & Stoughton.

POWER

In the social sciences, power is a highly contested and arguably elusive concept. Theorists employ a variety of theoretical frameworks and methodological approaches in defining and refining the concept of power. Common to all views, however, is the notion that power is the ability, often through others, to cause an effect in nature, in other people, or in oneself. It is this "productive" quality of power that generates considerable interest in power as a social science concept.

Many theorists view power as involving an element of coercion. Max Weber believed that power was the probability that one actor within a social relationship would carry out his or her will, even with resistance. Thus when a teacher union strikes for higher pay but then accepts a contract with a decrease in pay, the district is said to have exerted "power over" the union. Asymmetrical relationships, conflict, and constraint are central features of this definition.

Social theorists took various tacks to refining the concept of power. Theorists sought to identify the various sources of power, identifying institutional, economic, military, ideological, and other bases of power. Some compared power to currency, noting how sources of power were exchangeable and not evenly distributed in society. Others identified the forms power could take, such as force (physical or psychological), manipulation, persuasion, or authority, and explored how these forms interacted. Other refinements characterized power by its "extensiveness" (numbers controlled), "comprehensiveness" (variety of controls), "intensiveness" (strength of control), or "authoritativeness" (centralized and conscious as compared to diffused and unconscious).

Behavioral political scientists sought to make power measurable and observable. Robert A. Dahl among others began to define power by means of equations among identifiable actors, measurable intentions, and observable actions. The presence of power then involved knowing the weaker actor's "will" or wishes, the stronger actor's intention, and the results of the interaction. Power existed when the resulting outcomes were against the wishes of the weaker actor and in alignment with the stronger actor's intention. Important features of power, then, included the individual possession and conscious application of power in a dyadic relationship. In taking a positivist's view of measurement and observation, the scope of power, as a concept, was significantly narrowed.

Another set of political scientists, Peter Bachrach and Morton Baratz, emphasized that power could be exerted through nonaction as well as overt, observable action. Their study emphasized the importance of nondecision making and the "mobilization of bias" as the means through which the powerful actor obtains his or her intended result. Called the "hidden face" of power, this view brought to light how power may operate covertly and in ways not directly observable.

The idea of studying power through apparent "nonactions" led to a set of theorists that emphasized how constraint on a weaker actor may function more akin to Karl Marx's notion of "false consciousness." Rather than view power like a boxing match between a stronger and a weaker competitor, Steven Lukes argued that power operated invisibly, setting the desires, and hence behavior, of the weaker actor in line with the objectives of the more powerful actor. This alignment of desires was an exercise of power because it occurred against the objective or real "interests" of the weaker actor. This view of power echoes the work of Antonio Gramsci and the concept of hegemony.

Further emphasizing the social nature of power, other theorists argued that power operates through complex social and organizational structures. Michel Foucault argued that power operated through a "netlike organization," in which weaker actors were both the recipient and "vehicles" for the exercise of power. His term *power/knowledge* emphasized how "disciplinary"

knowledge, through "normalizing" strategies, moves beyond views of power as dyadic (e.g., actor A over actor B), consciously determined (e.g., intentions), and individually held. Another social theorist, Michael Mann, argued that power operates through overlapping and intersecting "sociospatial" networks in which weaker groups are "organizationally outflanked" by strong groups.

A smaller group of theorists emphasized the more positive potential of power. Such theorists view power as the capacity for individuals to shape their environment ("power to") or to work with others to shape their society ("power with"). Erich Fromm, a psychologist, argued that power was the capacity to realize one's potential while acting with others in the world. This view of power emphasizes how the productive nature of power can operate without coercion or domination. Rather than an asymmetrical, zero-sum game, these theorists viewed power as mutual and reciprocal, involving the enhancement of one's own power as well as another's. Some feminist theorists argued further that power could be transformative, as in the case of mothering, in which the mother exerts power over the child in order to enable the child to become her equal. These theorists made an important distinction between the result of power as domination or liberation from the means of power.

—Jennifer Gong

See also authority; bureaucracy; chain of command; chief academic officer; collaboration theories; communications, theories in organizations; critical theory; decision making; division of labor; dogmatism and scales of Rokeach; empowerment; feminism and theories of leadership; goals, goal setting; governance; great man theory; hierarchy, in organizations; ideology, shifts of in educational leadership preparation; infrastructure, of organizations; knowledge base, of the field; law; leadership, system-oriented; leadership, theories of; management theories; morality, moral leadership; organizational theories; politics, of education; principalship; site-based management; span of control; standard setting; superintendency; table of organization; Weber, Max; women in educational leadership

Further Readings and References

Bachrach, P., & Baratz, M. (1962). The two faces of power. *American Political Science Review, 56,* 947–952.
Dahl, R. (1957). The concept of power. *Behavioral Science, 2,* 201–215.
Foucault, M. (1980). *Power/knowledge: Selected interviews and other writing 1972-1977.* New York: Pantheon Books.
Fromm, E. (1947). *Man for himself.* New York: Fawcett.

Gramsci, A. (1972). *Selections from the prison notebooks of Antonio Gramsci* (Q. Hoare & G. Smith, Eds. & Trans.). New York: Irvington Press.

Lukes, S. (1974). *Power: A radical view.* London: Macmillan.

Mann, M. (1986). *The sources of social power: A history of power from the beginning to A.D. 1760* (Vol. 1). Cambridge, UK: Cambridge University Press.

Weber, M. (1968). *Economy and society* (Vol. 1, G. Roth & C. Wittich, Eds. & Trans.). New York: Bedminister Press.

🏛 POWER, REMUNERATIVE

Remunerative power is defined as the act of rewarding job performance with appropriate pay for work completed. The need to improve job performance has been the focus of many theories of motivation in order to maximize the return on global business investments. Under traditional compensation packages, annual wage increases are typically not tied to individual performance, resulting in an entitlement mentality that decreases any real motivation for employees. Because of increasing interest in maintaining their bottom lines in recent years, businesses have begun to reevaluate the effectiveness of their overall operations in order to reduce costs while maintaining the quality of their goods and services to remain competitive. In order to achieve their goals, many companies have begun to seek resources that would explain how to hire, train, and satisfy their workers, who would perform at optimal levels to allow for achievement of their organizational goals. In order to reward excellence more fairly, companies have begun to use variable compensation structures that reward employees for production that exceeds the norms of other employees, allowing for differential wages that are based on actual performance. Remuneration issues in management are primarily based upon the theoretical models of motivation that include Abraham Maslow, Amitai Etzioni, Frederick Herzberg, Eugene Friedman, and Robert Havighurst, who attempted to theorize intrinsic processes, extrinsic factors, internal and external self-concepts, and goal identification in order to determine how to balance pay and productivity. Factors affecting remuneration are based upon an array of issues, including external regulation, power, peer culture, job security, benefits, productivity, and work/life balance, but fairness in compensation for workers is strained when gaps between frontline and executive pay that are enormous lead to resentment, loss of confidence, lack of ownership, and divisiveness, which ultimately lead to an uncommitted workforce. Although the overall employment relationship between workers and ownership is based on the economic assumption that employees are motivated solely by money, psychologists disagree, noting that the employment relationship is more complex than is assumed, and revealed that monetary incentives do not provide the complexity of human behavior that include access to work experience that provides self-actualization as well as other achievements through internal motivation. Newly hired employees also provide their own specialized human capital, a critical resource that each individual worker brings as a value creation to the job, including access, achievement, self-actualization, thereby revealing that remuneration in business and industry is much more complicated than many human resources employees believe. An effective system of motivating employees is necessary to provide the quid pro quo that includes high productivity, goal setting, effectiveness, self-esteem, motivation, intrinsic rewards, satisfaction, personal growth, and relatedness. Current research indicated that both lower-level employees and higher-level employees can be effectively and significantly motivated by higher order needs, indicating that motivational interventions can be highly successful for all employees. Using carefully planned systems to provide more individual attention to workers at all levels, business and industry must ensure fairness to all employees, thereby enhancing organizational effectiveness, making individual decisions regarding compensation, and rewarding strong performance that strengthen the overall economy as a result of fair pay for fair play.

—*Carole Funk*

See also attitudes; attitudes toward work; behaviorism; belonging; capacity building, of organizations; collective bargaining; discrimination, theories of; economics, theories of; finance, of public schools; fringe benefits; governance; Havighurst, Robert; human capital; job descriptions; line and staff concept; management theories; Maslow, Abraham; merit pay; networking and network theory; organizational theories; rational organizational theory; salary and salary models

Further Readings and References

Arnolds, C., & Boshoff, C. (2002). Compensation, esteem valence and job performance: An empirical assessment of Alderfer's ERG's theory. *Human Resources Management, 13*(4), 697–719.

Beer, M., & Cannon, M. (2004). Promise and peril in implementing pay-for-performance. *Human Resources Management, 43*(1), 41–43.

Herzberg, F., Mausner, B., & Synderman, B. (1959). *The motivation to work.* New York: Wiley.

Maslow, A. (1943). A theory of human motivation. *Psychology Review, 50,* 370–396.

PRAGMATISM AND PROGRESSIVISM

Concepts incorporated in theories and philosophies loosely grouped and labeled as pragmatism and progressivism are drawn from a variety of antecedents. However, the basic elements are induction as a way of thinking and problem solving, the importance of experience to human development and action, and the relationship between science and culture.

HISTORICAL BACKGROUND

The roots of pragmatism and progressivism may be found in the thinking of Francis Bacon (1561–1626), who challenged the traditional approach to logic that relied on deduction to establish basic principles of philosophy and problem solving. Deduction begins with certain accepted statements or premises (usually from religious belief or speculation), and other statements or conclusions are deduced logically from them.

Bacon proposed that the old beliefs and generalizations should be subjected to induction based on observation and experimentation (later called the "scientific" method), putting a premium on human experience in everyday life. He advocated limiting the inductive method to material things, but pragmatists extended this approach to include economics, politics, psychology, education, ethics, and all matters of conjecture and concern.

John Locke (1632–1704) used Bacon's inductive methods to study how human beings develop knowledge and ways of living, believing that a human mind begins as a tabula rasa, or blank slate, and develops as a result of the experiences a person goes through. More and varied experiences are, therefore, needed to develop people so they may reach their greatest potential. Consequently, Locke advocated placing children in an environment where they are exposed to the most desirable experiences and influences.

The ideas behind pragmatism and progressivism as related to education may first be found among more modern thinkers in the work and writing of John Amos Comenius (1592–1670). A Moravian bishop and teacher, he believed that education should proceed through a long effort to achieve encyclopedic knowledge. Breaking with tradition emphasizing memorization and recitation, however, he advocated teaching methods that incorporated child development and the study of nature. Exposing children to the world in which they lived, Comenius would let children observe and thereby be led to an understanding of things about them.

Carrying ideas of Comenius a bit further, Jean-Jacques Rousseau (1712–1778), in his book *Emile,* describes how a boy should be educated in a manner that is natural and spontaneous, free from the evil influences of society, so that his real self could emerge. He would live in a world of nature, observing what was around him, not beginning intellectual education through books and more formal teaching until he was 13 years old. Even then, the natural curiosity of the boy would be allowed to guide and mold his educational experiences, with instruction being offered only as it came to be demanded through natural experiences. Not until he reached 15 to 20 years of age was the boy to come into contact with other boys, with the intent then to learn basic principles of religion and good relations with others. Consistent with his times, Rousseau advocated an entirely different kind of education for girls, one that would prepare them to serve men and make them happy.

Rousseau's major contribution to pragmatism was in the educational connection he made between nature and experience. Although some of his views are considered overly romantic and impractical, his connection of nature and experience certainly influenced many later educational theorists who broadened this naturalist approach to include all human experience as the primary force in molding and guiding human development and action.

Greatly influenced by Rousseau, Johann Heinrich Pestalozzi (1746–1827) tried to understand children in order to build teaching techniques consistent with their natural, progressive, and harmonious development. Seeking natural laws of learning, he then developed teaching methods and materials consistent with those laws. These included what he called an "object lesson," in which various kinds of learning and skill development were planned around an object found in nature or the child's normal experiences. He is also credited with developing the first illustrated textbook to make learning more natural and interesting.

Also following Rousseau's ideas, particularly as they could be used with young children, Friedrich Froebel (1782–1852) believed in the natural goodness of the child and the need to allow natural growth and development. Calling his school the "kindergarten," the garden of children, Froebel thought that the teacher should help children to grow just as a gardener would help flowers and plants to grow according to their natural inclinations and in the best natural state for allowing that growth. However, Froebel went further than Rousseau in recognizing that the child is an individual but also a member of a group and a society. Rather than shielding the child from society, Froebel proposed that children should be helped to adjust to society so growth and development could occur in the best interests of the child and the society. Consequently, work in groups and other kinds of social participation were considered necessary to reconcile the sometimes competing interests of the individual and the society. This approach to education later became a foundation stone of pragmatism and progressivism as philosophers and educators tried to balance child-centered ideas with the interests of society and groups within that society.

PRAGMATISM

An American philosophy developed around 1900, pragmatism owes its major concepts and impetus to Auguste Comte (1798–1857), Charles Sanders Peirce (1839–1914), William James (1842–1910), and John Dewey (1859–1952). Darwin's *The Origin of Species* certainly influenced their thinking, along with the utilitarianism of John Stuart Mill, Herbert Spencer, and others.

Pragmatism moved away from earlier attempts by philosophers to identify first causes and universal principles, believing that they were generally beyond the understanding of mortals and without meaning or use. The real value of an idea becomes its practicality—how it can be used and the consequences of its use.

For the pragmatist, knowledge exists only in relation to human experience; it is the product of the interaction between humans and their environment. It exists only in relationship to social experience, and has meaning only as it may be used in life. This knowledge is not permanent or objective, and it continually changes. People develop values and ways of living to fit a particular time and place, and these are subject to constant revision as conditions change. Knowledge and values within traditional philosophies

transcend the experience of men and women, while pragmatism argues their existence only within that experience.

Pragmatism sees human essence as existing within the social being. Men and women are products of experiences resulting from interaction with their environment, including other human beings, and these experiences continually mold each person in unique ways because of their previous experiences and personal attributes. The universe then becomes evolutionary and subjective rather than objective or static as seen by other philosophies.

Pragmatism relies on science and the scientific method as the route to truth. However, truth thus discovered is seen as temporary and related to solving immediate problems, rather than universal, permanent, and objective. It thereby lends itself well to philosophers such as John Dewey who attempt to find a philosophy that is reconcilable with a definition of democracy that resists any kind of authoritarianism brought on by universal, permanent, and objective truth.

Auguste Comte (1798–1857), although not usually categorized as a pragmatist, worked to apply science to society, thus contributing to the later efforts of pragmatists to use science to solve social problems. Discarding theology and metaphysics as a way to understand and guide human behavior, Comte promoted the notion that scientific thinking was the best way to understand humans as well as the physical and material universe. As one of the fathers of modern sociology, he viewed social structures and relationships as subject to systematic study in the scientific mode, thus contributing to elements of social theory that are distinct to pragmatism.

Charles Sanders Peirce (1839–1914) received little attention or recognition during his lifetime, but more recognition is now given to his contributions to the thinking of more well-known contemporaries such as William James. Proposing that true knowledge of anything depends on testing ideas through experience, he seems to have significantly influenced the development of pragmatism as later articulated by James, Dewey, and others.

William James (1842–1910), designated by some as the father of educational psychology, developed ideas and philosophy advocated by Peirce and brought them to the attention of a wide audience. He viewed the truth of an idea in relationship to how it worked in human experience. To identify and understand truth, according to James, we must study human experiences and what they reveal. Experiences thus become a body of knowledge that may be identified as experience and from which truth may be drawn. Concentrating on what he called the "stream" of experience, the sequential, serial course of events, James concluded that there is no Truth, Reality, or Absolute, because the universe is open ended, pluralistic, and in process.

John Dewey (1859–1952) is rightfully known as the most important contributor to the philosophy and theories included in pragmatism and progressivism. James had brought these to the attention of philosophers, educators, and even the general public, but it was Dewey who brought more organization and system to the movement. Dewey accepted James's proposals that there are no immutable absolutes or universals and that the proper basis for solving human problems was experience. He also, like Peirce, advocated the consideration of consequences when approaching solutions to human problems, and he believed that consequences could best be understood through experience rather than conjecture or logic.

Building on James's stream-of-experiences notion, Dewey followed Rousseau's contributions relative to the importance of nature and natural activities to child development and education. Rousseau had proposed three sources of education—nature, human beings, and surrounding material objects. Emphasizing that these did not impact children one by one or separately, Dewey thought that they should be viewed relative to their relationships and interactions. A significant departure from Rousseau was Dewey's insistence that children should be left in a natural social environment as their education progressed through both natural (unplanned) and planned experiences.

Dewey seems to have preferred the terms *experimentalism* and/or *instrumentalism* to designate his approach to problem solving, rather than pragmatism. The term *experimentalism* more accurately reflects his concern with relying on experience rather than absolutes or patent answers in solving human problems. He saw all problem solving as an experiment to "see what works" by observing the consequences of certain actions. He also saw the mind and the scientific method as instruments to be used in carrying out these experiments to arrive at solutions to human problems. Dewey considered something true or false depending on what effects it has on people and society, not on some basic, unchanging philosophy or principle. His Laboratory School at the University of Chicago is an example of this belief that ideas should be tested and refined in real life settings.

PROGRESSIVISM

What is known as the progressive reform movement of the late 1800s and early 1900s was consistent with the basic tenets of pragmatism as it tried to improve the environment in which people lived and were educated. The movement as a whole was concerned with more than education, but ideas from pragmatism, particularly John Dewey's emphasis on method, rather than abstract answers or unchanging principles, as the best way to solve human problems led to the progressive movement in education. Progressivism in education rejected traditional idealistic and realistic notions of education and the imposition of authoritative texts and rules. It was also opposed to an emphasis on the learning of isolated skills and the use of drilling and preestablished educational materials. The final test of truth and how to use it in worthwhile fashion is in the outcome of its application to the needs and problems of human beings, and this may change as the world and its inhabitants change.

John Dewey is considered the prophet of the progressive movement, followed by interpreters of the movement such as William Heard Kilpatrick, John L. Childs, Boyd H. Bode, and those who carried Dewey's ideas in specific directions, such as social reconstructionist George S. Counts. These and others often went to extremes and interpreted Dewey in ways he opposed, but Dewey's ideas and these interpretations did much between 1920 and 1955 to change the face of American education.

The basic principles of progressivism as applied to education are described as follows, as stated by Dewey in 1916:

- Education should be active and related to the interests of the child.
- Learning should take place through problem solving rather than the absorption of subject matter.
- Education of the young should be life itself rather than a preparation for living.
- The teacher's role is not to direct but to advise.
- The school should encourage cooperation rather than competition.
- Education and democracy imply one another; hence, schools should be run democratically.

IMPACT ON EDUCATIONAL LEADERSHIP AND ADMINISTRATION

Pragmatism and the progressive education movement influenced social and educational reform in many ways. Some of these reforms were carried to extremes, with undesirable effects; others simply were not accepted by a traditional and change-resistant society and educational system. Over a period of time, however, with erratic starts and stops, the movement continues to gain momentum and acceptance, albeit often under different names and labels.

One of the major forces limiting the impact of progressivism on education has been the failure of educational leadership and administration to change in similar fashion. Teachers were less likely to change their ways of teaching and classroom organization in democratic and child-centered ways when their leaders not only failed to exhibit similar actions but actually modeled the opposite kinds of behavior. These contradictions are as follows:

- *Education should be active and related to the interests of the child.* Traditional educational leadership stresses order and control, thus limiting opportunities for teachers and students to actively and directly relate teaching and learning to the society and to the interests of the child. The curriculum and teaching methods also tended to reflect interests and preferences of the adults rather than those of the children and youth. More progressive educational leaders have opened the school to the community and encouraged the use of subject matter and teaching methods consistent with active and relevant learning.
- *Learning should take place through problem solving rather than the absorption of subject matter.* More progressive educational leaders avoid extensive control over teachers, leaving them more freedom as they use their own professional skill and initiative to achieve school purposes and to identify and solve the problems of school and classroom. Rather than dictating approved content, classroom management and teaching methods, for instance, they serve as guides and advisers, lending their own expertise to the process as appropriate and invited.
- *Education of the young should be life itself rather than a preparation for living.* Educational leaders demonstrate this aspect of progressivism by emphasizing the practical and problem-solving aspects of teaching and school organization. Parents and the community are brought into daily involvement with the school, its teachers and administrators, as students learn to live by doing rather than by talking and writing.
- *The teacher's role is not to direct but to advise.* Consistent with this principle, the progressive educational leader's role is not to direct but to advise, persuade, and facilitate, particularly in matters closely related to teaching and learning. Teachers and other school staff members become members of a team, with the administrator becoming a "transformational" leader of the team.
- *The school should encourage cooperation rather than competition.* This principle of progressive education again emphasizes the role of the leader as facilitator and adviser, encouraging cooperation and teamwork among the total school staff and the students. It deemphasizes, and many times eliminates, unnecessary and unproductive forms of competition among students and teachers, including things such as honor rolls and valedictorians, achievement tests for other than diagnostic purposes, merit pay, and ranking of students or teachers. Even "teacher of the year" recognitions become suspect, as they may be replaced with recognition for teams that produce good results. Teachers become members of school improvement teams and cooperatively make important decisions about school goals, operations, and management.
- *Education and democracy imply one another; hence, schools should be run democratically.* Application of this principle from progressive education would seem to be relatively obvious. However, major disagreements tend to occur around the meaning of "democracy" and how much authority should be given to teachers, parents, and students. Comparisons to civil government and the business world often lead to inappropriate and even "undemocratic" actions by educational leaders. Perhaps it is in this area of educational leadership that there remains the most to accomplish relative to agreeing to and understanding the purposes and objectives of education and how educational leaders may best facilitate their achievement.

—*Weldon Beckner*

See also administration, theories of; Aristotle; attitudes toward work; authority; behaviorism; bureaucracy; constructivism; creativity, in management; critical theory; democracy, democratic education and administration; Dewey, John; empiricism; empowerment; existentialism; governance; group dynamics; human resource development; humanistic education; individual differences, in children; leadership, theories of; learning, theories of; management theories; motivation, theories of; organizational theories; philosophies of education; Plato

Further Readings and References

Crow, G., & Grogan, M. (2005). The development of leadership thought and practice in the United States. In F. English (Ed.), *The SAGE handbook of educational leadership* (pp. 362–379). Thousand Oaks, CA: Sage.

Dewey, J. (1916). *Democracy and education.* New York: Macmillan.

Dewey, J. (1938). *Experience and education.* New York: Macmillan.

Dumas, W., & Beckner, W. (1968). *Introduction to secondary education: A foundations approach.* Scranton, PA: International Textbook.

English, F. (1994). *Theory in educational administration.* New York: Harper Collins.

Frost, S. (1962). *Basic teaching of the great philosophers* (Rev. ed.). New York: Anchor Books.

James, W. (1907). *Pragmatism: A new name for some old ways of thinking.* London: Longmans, Green.

James, W. (1916). *Talks to teachers on psychology: And to students on some of life's ideas.* New York: Henry Holt.

Kneller, G. (1963). *Foundations of education.* New York: John Wiley & Sons.

Nakosteen, M. (1965). *The history and philosophy of education.* New York: Ronald Press.

Ozman, H. E., & Craver, S. M. (1999). *Philosophical foundations of education* (6th ed.). Upper Saddle River, NJ: Simon & Schuster.

Ravitch, D. (1983). *The troubled crusade: American education 1945–1980.* New York: Basic Books.

🏛 PRAYER IN SCHOOL

There has been volatile controversy over devotionals in public education since the mid-twentieth century. Prior to that time, Protestant observances were common in public schools, especially in the southern Bible Belt. However, in the early 1960s, the Supreme Court relied on the Establishment Clause of the First Amendment to prohibit school-sponsored daily prayer and Bible reading in public education. The Court reasoned that voluntary participation of students in the religious activities was irrelevant; school sponsorship of devotionals abridged the First Amendment. Instead of resolving the school prayer controversy, however, these decisions have generated more than four decades of legislative, administrative, and judicial responses. Moreover, national polls have indicated that about two thirds of Americans support a constitutional amendment to allow public school prayers, although no proposed amendment has yet been adopted.

About one half of the states have laws authorizing a minute at the beginning of the public school day for students to engage in silent meditation or prayer. In 1985, the Supreme Court rendered its only opinion to date on such laws, *Wallace v. Jaffree.* In this case, the Court invalidated a 1981 Alabama silent prayer statute under the Establishment Clause because the law's legislative history exhibited an impermissible intent to encourage students to pray. The Court indicated, however, that provisions calling for silent meditation or prayer in public schools *without* such intent might survive an Establishment Clause challenge. Subsequently, two federal appellate courts upheld state laws calling for a moment for silent reflection or prayer in public school classrooms at the beginning of the school day as being religiously neutral and intended to provide students time for quiet reflection.

More controversial than silent prayer policies have been various attempts to allow spoken devotionals in public schools. Courts have struck down efforts by school staff members to lead devotionals during school or extracurricular activities. In 1992, the Supreme Court in *Lee v. Weisman* invalidated a Rhode Island school district's policy that permitted principals to invite clergy members to deliver invocations and benedictions at middle and high school graduations because of its coercive effect; students felt peer pressure to participate in the devotionals during the school-sponsored ceremony.

Some school districts responded to *Weisman* by designating the graduation ceremony as a forum for student expression, allowing students to select their graduation messages that may include prayers. This practice has been upheld if student speakers are selected based on secular criteria, such as their class rank, and school authorities do not review their speeches. However, if school authorities retain control over the content of the graduation ceremony, they have the right to censor proselytizing messages, and the Establishment Clause may require them to do so.

The most controversial post-*Weisman* strategy to return devotionals to public schools has been to allow students to vote whether to include student-delivered prayers in graduation ceremonies and extracurricular activities. Although the Supreme Court has not directly addressed student-led graduation prayers, in 2000 it struck down a Texas school district's policy authorizing student elections to determine whether to have student-led devotionals before public school football games. The Court in *Santa Fe Independent School District v. Doe* declared that student religious expression at a school event on school property and representing the student body under the supervision of school personnel could not be considered *private* speech and thus violated the Establishment Clause. However, the majority emphasized that the Constitution does not prohibit public school students from voluntarily praying at school if the devotionals are not school sponsored.

Subsequently, the Eleventh Circuit in two cases broadly interpreted constitutionally protected private student speech, declaring that the Establishment Clause does not require and the Free Speech Clause does not permit suppression of *student-initiated* religious expression in public schools. Also, the Eighth Circuit found no Establishment Clause violation in a school board member's unscheduled recitation of the Lord's Prayer in the graduation ceremony, reasoning that the board member's expression was private and thus constitutionally protected, even though it took place at a school-sponsored event.

Federal courts also have recognized students' First Amendment right to hold devotional meetings in public schools during noninstructional time if other student groups are allowed such access. The constitutional right is augmented by the federal Equal Access Act (EAA); if secondary schools receiving federal funds create a forum for noncurriculum student groups during noninstructional time, student groups cannot be barred based on the religious, political, or philosophical content of their meetings. The Supreme Court in *Board of Education v. Mergens* rejected an Establishment Clause challenge to the EAA in 1990. Furthermore, sectarian community groups cannot be denied public school access if other community groups are allowed to use school facilities when classes are not in session, because the First Amendment's Free Speech Clause does not allow viewpoint discrimination against religious speech. In 2002, the Supreme Court upheld the Good News Club's right to meet in the public school after classes ended, even though its devotional meetings targeted young children attending the school.

Recitation of the Pledge of Allegiance in public schools also has generated First Amendment challenges. Although the Supreme Court established in 1943 that students do not have to participate in the pledge in violation of their religious or philosophical beliefs, the current controversy focuses on whether saying the pledge in public schools abridges the Establishment Clause by endorsing a belief in monotheism. Disagreeing with a Seventh Circuit ruling, the Ninth Circuit reasoned that the words *under God* were inserted in 1954 to promote religion rather than to advance the secular goal of encouraging patriotism. The Supreme Court in 2004 reversed the Ninth Circuit's decision but avoided the Establishment Clause issue by ruling that the noncustodial parent did not have standing to challenge the practice.

The No Child Left Behind (NCLB) Act of 2001 directs the U.S. Department of Education to advise school districts regarding permissible religious activities and requires school districts to certify to the state education agency that no school policy prevents participation in constitutionally protected prayer in public elementary and secondary schools. For the first time, such certification is required and tied to school districts' receipt of federal aid. In 2003, the department issued its *Guidance on Constitutionally Protected Prayer in Public Elementary and Secondary Schools.* The *Guidance* covers a number of areas, and for topics without a definitive Supreme Court ruling, the *Guidance* supports an expansive interpretation of permissible religious activities in public schools. As a result, there are discrepancies between the *Guidance* and some judicial decisions, which may generate additional litigation over devotional activities in public schools.

—*Martha McCarthy*

See also Bible, as history; church-state issues; creationism; fundamentalism; law; moral education; politics, of education; religion, in schools; right-wing politics, advocates, impact on education; Supreme Court, United States, key cases in education law

Further Readings and References

Good News Club v. Milford Central Schools, 533 U.S. 98 (2002).
Guidance on constitutionally protected prayer in public elementary and secondary schools, 68 Fed. Reg. 9645 (Feb. 28, 2003).
Lee v. Weisman, 505 U.S. 577 (1992).
Russo, C. (2004). *Reutter's the law of public education.* New York: Foundation Press.
Santa Fe Independent School District v. Doe, 530 U.S. 290 (2000).
Wallace v. Jaffree, 472 U.S. 38 (1985).

PREGNANCY, OF STUDENTS

Despite a 31% decline in teenage pregnancies over the last decade, adolescent pregnancy continues to be a serious public health issue. According to the Centers for Disease Control, 34% of women become pregnant at least once before age 20. According to a 2004 study conducted by the Allen Guttmacher Institute, approximately 1 million American teenage girls aged 15–19 become pregnant each year. The United States continues to have the highest rate of teen pregnancy in the industrialized world. The U.S. rates are double that of Great Britain, 4 times higher than France, and 10 times higher than Japan. Fifty-seven percent of all teenage pregnancies in the United States resulted in births, 28% ended in abortion, and 14% ended in miscarriages.

Teenage pregnancy is replete with challenges for the mother, child, and society. Eighty three percent of teenage mothers are from poor backgrounds and lack the resources to adequately care for and raise their children. One third of teenage mothers receive inadequate prenatal care, resulting in higher rates of low birth weight and childhood health problems. Teenage women are also more likely to be single mothers, drop out of high school, and rely on welfare. Only 1.5% of teens who have a child before age 18 complete a college degree before age 30.

Historically, there has been intense debate over social policies aimed at reducing the teen pregnancies. The gamut of moral, ideological, and social issues surrounding teens and sex have created a sharp divide between conservative and liberal groups as to the most effective and appropriate route to curb teen pregnancy.

In an effort to form a cohesive group committed to reducing teen pregnancy, the National Campaign to Prevent Teen Pregnancy, a bipartisan organization, was founded in 1995. Their goal is to reduce the teen pregnancy rate by one third between 1996 and 2005. In order to bridge the gap between differing perspectives, the organization does not promote one solution to preventing teen pregnancy. Instead, they call on leaders to acknowledge the problem in their communities, take action in a way that best fits their needs, and share their solutions with other struggling communities. While there is no statistical evidence linking the work of the National Campaign with a reduction in teen pregnancy rates, the teenage pregnancy rate declined 7.8% in the organization's first 2 years.

Sex education in public schools has changed dramatically in the United States over the past 25 years. According to a 1981 study by the Alan Guttmacher Institute, 94% of public schools offered comprehensive sex education programs aimed at arming students to make informed decisions regarding their sexual practices. The federal government never directly funded comprehensive sex education, but it did fund organizations, such as the Centers for Disease Control Division of Adolescent and School Health, that supported comprehensive sex education.

Over the past two decades, abstinence education has gained support from public and private organizations

and become a legitimate sex education program. As of 2003, the federal government supported abstinence programs with $100 million annually. Two congressional bills, Title V of the Personal Responsibility and Work Opportunity Reconciliation Act and Special Projects of Regional and National Significance, have also passed over the past 10 years, which support abstinence education.

Abstinence education is currently prevalent in almost all sex education programs, but the abstinence message is inconsistent across groups. Comprehensive sex educators teach teens that abstinence is one option to consider, while other more conservative organizations teach abstinence as the only acceptable option before marriage. A 1999 study by Family Planning stated that 23% of school districts report teaching abstinence as their sole form of sex education; this was up from 2% in 1988. Despite dramatic changes in sex education over the past two decades, there is little data tracking the success of any one approach to sex education. A 2004 study by the Centers for Disease Control explicates the difficulty in pinpointing the catalyst for the declining teen pregnancy rate. Most liberal advocates credit comprehensive sex education starting in earlier grades and creating an open discussion about the risks of sexually transmitted diseases, while more conservative stakeholders argue that abstinence programs are responsible. Others contend that it may be a copycat effect, where younger girls are emulating their older counterparts in waiting to have sex. There are also indications that the welfare system is encouraging women to wait until they are older to start families. It is difficult to isolate many of these variables from one another and create control groups; therefore, it is unclear what approach is responsible for the decline in teen pregnancy.

International teenage pregnancy rates have also dropped significantly over the last 30 years, but many countries continue to face challenges such as those in the United States. England and Wales have the highest rate of teen pregnancy in Western Europe, in part due to the controversial nature of teen pregnancy, which has resulted in decades of inaction. The government is committed to cutting the number of teen pregnancies in half by the year 2010, but they do not have a concrete action plan in place. In contrast, France has taken radical steps since 1999 to reduce its 10,000 teenage pregnancies each year. Schools are required to provide 30 to 40 hours of sex education to eighth- and ninth-grade students, and school nurses are authorized to pass out the morning-after pill to teenagers under extreme circumstances. The government also developed a contraception campaign, informing residents how to protect themselves against unwanted pregnancies through television, radio, and leaflets.

The Netherlands' "Long Live Love" campaign launched in the 1980s has made them an international model for successful sex education. The 2000 data indicated that the Netherlands had one of the lowest teenage pregnancy rates in Europe (12.2 per 1,000 girls between 15 and 19). The media has also created an open dialogue about sexuality to complement the Netherlands' comprehensive sex education programs in primary and secondary schools. The health care system also pledges complete confidentiality, and parents speak with their children candidly about sex. According to the Netherlands Institute of Social and Sexological Research, 85% of sexually active young people use a contraceptive.

—*Sara Suglia*

See also adolescence; at-risk students; belonging; Black education; children and families in America; coeducation; counseling; determinism, sociocultural; dropouts; esteem needs; Federal Privacy Act; gender studies, in educational leadership; high schools; human capital; Latinos; mainstreaming and inclusion; moral education; personality; resiliency; sexuality, theories of; special education; underachievers, in schools

Further Readings and References

Alan Guttmacher Institute. (1999). *Facts in brief: Teen sex and pregnancy.* New York: Author.

Alan Guttmacher Institute. (2004). *U.S. teenage pregnancy statistics: Overall trends, trends by race and ethnicity and state-by-state information.* New York: Author.

Henshaw, S. K. (2004). *U.S. teenage pregnancy statistics with comparative statistics for women aged 20–24.* New York: Alan Guttmacher Institute.

National Campaign to Prevent Teen Pregnancy. (2004). *Factsheet: How is the 34% statistic calculated?* Washington, DC: Author.

National Campaign to Prevent Teen Pregnancy. (2004). *Teen pregnancy—So what?* Washington, DC: Author.

🏛 PRINCIPAL, ASSISTANT

Educators who aspire to enter formal school administration are most likely to enter as an assistant principal. According to the National Center for Education Statistics, there are nearly 17,000 assistant principals in the United States. While there are some career assistant principals, generally, assistant principals are in transition because most are educators who aspire to become principals. A challenge for assistant principals is that they are no longer part of the teaching faculty and they do not yet have full administrative status.

During the 1920s, principals of larger schools often selected teachers (usually male) to assist the school principal as a general supervisor and to help with the facility operations of the school. By the 1940s, this individual generally held the title of assistant principal and was primarily concerned with administrative and managerial details of the school. In the twenty-first century, as the role of the school principal has become increasingly complex, the assistant principal position has begun to include more leadership responsibilities. Assistant principals are most likely to be recruited from the teaching force. Often, these educators are noticed for this entry-level administrative position based on their willingness to volunteer to take on special duties at school that bring them to the attention of their superiors. Other criteria that principals use when deciding which teachers to recommend for the role of assistant principal include individuality; cognitive skills; rapport with students, teachers, administrators, and community; leadership qualities; and professional qualities. Loyalty to the administration is another trait that principals and superintendents consider when considering which faculty members to promote to the assistant principalship.

All states require principals to have some type of an administrative certificate. Requirements for the principal credential vary from state to state but usually include a specified number of years of teaching experience, university coursework, and an advanced degree. More and more states are requiring that a state certification exam be passed in order to earn a principal certificate. Occasionally, assistant principals assume their role prior to actually earning the principal certificate, although in most cases, a temporary credential can be issued that is valid for a certain number of years. Consequently, many assistant principals are working toward completion of state-mandated requirements to obtain the principal credential.

Even though women comprise over 70% of the teaching force, in 1978 only 22% of women were assistant principals. However, by the early 1990s, 48% of assistant principals were women. Assistant principalships are also changing by ethnicity. In 1978, only 5% of assistant principals were minorities, yet by

2000, 10% of assistant principals in New York, for example, were Hispanic, while 19% were Black.

Assistant principals are assigned a variety of job responsibilities that generally focus on assisting the principal as needed; however, the most likely task assigned to assistant principals is discipline. Other typical duties of the job include completing paperwork; attending special education meetings; conferencing with parents, students, and other faculty; coordinating staff development; observing classrooms; evaluating faculty; scheduling; and transportation.

The role of an assistant principal is demanding. At least 70% of elementary, middle school, and high school assistant principals work a minimum of 50 hours per week. In addition, over 26% of high school assistant principals reported that they worked 60 hours or more per week. Assistant principals also report that the job is becoming even more demanding than it was 5 years ago, especially in the areas of paperwork, student discipline, and special education meetings.

Because the role of the assistant principal is often seen as managerial in nature, rather than leadership, it is important for assistant principals to work toward gaining the skills and knowledge needed in a leadership role. A survey of 100 assistant principals found that over 70% of them identified the following skills as essential to being effective: people skills, good communication skills, knowledge of leadership theory, technique for improving curriculum, and ability to work as a team. People skills were emphasized, and these skills included working with others, conducting effective meetings, being flexible, being diplomatic, having patience and empathy, maintaining positive relationships with colleagues, and understanding the school's political environment. Being a peacemaker was also identified as an important aspect.

In 2001, John Daresh suggested several strategies to implement for assistant principals who are interested in becoming principals. These strategies include cultivating leadership skills; cooling your ego; assisting the principal, teachers, and students in whatever ways you can; being discreet; listening; asking to do more; continuing to learn about the role of leadership; and being positive. How well assistant principals use this role to learn more about leadership often determines how soon they will become a principal.

—*Sandra Harris*

See also administration, theories of; career development; career stages; chain of command; discipline in schools; gender studies, in educational leadership; leadership, theories of; management theories; principalship; recruitment of school administrators; school safety; sexism (glass ceiling); violence in schools; women in educational leadership

Further Readings and References

Daresh, J. (2001). Making the most of it. *Principal leadership* (high school ed.), *1*(5), 70–73.

Harris, S., & Lowery, S. (2004). *Standards-based leadership: A case study book for the assistant principal.* Lanham, MD: Scarecrow Press.

Matthews, L., & Crow, G. (2003). *Being and becoming a principal.* Boston: Allyn & Bacon.

National Center for Education Statistics. (2002). *Digest of educational statistics: School staffing survey: 1993–94.* Washington, DC: U.S. Department of Education Center for Educational Statistics.

Weiner, R. (2002). Changing face of assistant principals. *Journal News.* Retrieved May 27, 2003, from www.thejournalnews.com/newdroom/103002/30assistants.html.

PRINCIPAL SUCCESSION

Simply stated, principal succession occurs when an incoming principal replaces a departing principal. Leader succession is not unique to schools; it occurs regularly in all organizations, both large and small, and is usually considered an important event in the life of an organization. In small, hierarchical, and/or interdependent organizations, such as schools, leader replacement can alter the previously predictable rhythm of work flow and social interaction; it can also affect power relationships and decision-making structures.

Early principal succession researchers took cues from those who were interested in the effect of leader succession in business and industry. The interest of the organizational researchers was the impact leader succession on organizational productivity. In both educational and noneducational organizations, researchers anticipated disruption but also overall improvement as a result of changing leaders. However, findings about the effect of a leader succession are inconsistent. Some studies indicate that leader changes resonate throughout the organization; other studies suggest that the core work of the organization continues uninterrupted.

Research on principal succession extends over several decades. In studies of overall school performance, findings indicate that a succession can produce positive effects, deleterious effects, or no effect. One study reports that the prevailing socioeconomic status of the student body mediates the effect of a succession, with larger effects evident where student socioeconomic status is low. Another study suggests that strong teacher leadership attenuates the effect of a new principal on school improvement processes, at least in the short term. Other studies report that teacher response to a succession does not influence classroom practices; thus, the teaching-learning exchange is unaffected, and overall school performance remains unaffected as well. Finally, the effect of a principal succession on school climate is described as difficult to assess.

The contradictory nature of findings suggests that situational characteristics influence research results. The inconsistencies also suggest that inadequate attention is given to the reciprocal nature of the socialization processes that occur with a succession. Not only does a successor principal attempt to socialize those affiliated with the school to new ways of doing things, but also the successor is socialized to the normative behaviors at the school. Whatever the reasons for the contradictions, the widely held expectation that changing principals will bring about increases in student achievement is sufficiently supported to affect practice.

Where researchers tend to agree is that principal succession is a process rather than a single event. The process can span most of an academic year, impact administrators at the district level, affect principals at other schools, and involve prearrival, arrival, and postarrival events and factors. These events and factors do not have precise beginning or ending points and are not independent of one another; nonetheless, the ways in which the succession process unfolds influence teachers' response to it.

One prearrival factor is teachers' feelings toward the incumbent. In some cases, teachers may like the incumbent and anticipate the succession with certain sadness. In other cases, teachers may be eager for a new principal who brings traits not exhibited by the incumbent. Teachers' feelings are also affected by the circumstances leading to the incumbent's exit, such as retirement, transfer, promotion, dismissal, illness, or death.

Other prearrival factors include the process by which the successor was selected. Teachers are not usually involved in making the selection, though they have opinions about it, and may resist the successor when others, such as activist parents, are involved in the selection decision. Resistance also is likely if teachers have a favorite candidate who is not selected and when decision makers are perceived to have violated past practice in making the selection, such as appointing someone from outside the district.

Factors and events surrounding the arrival of the successor are compressed in duration relative to the prearrival and postarrival factors and events. Arrival factors include the successor's behavior toward teachers, especially support of and respect for the faculty, the school, and the academic program. Successors who respect, learn, and behave within the parameters of the normative culture of the school ease the arrival phase. Violation of cherished norms and values can obstruct a smooth transition. The successor principal has no cache of goodwill from the faculty upon arrival. However, a new principal can build teacher trust and confidence by buffering the faculty from perceived vicissitudes of the district office.

The success with which arrival events occur is mediated by the stability of the faculty. When faculty turnover is frequent, the effect of a principal succession is obscured. Not only are teachers who are veteran to the school adapting to new leadership but also to new teaching colleagues as well. Under such circumstances, the effect of a new leader is attenuated.

As the arrival phase evolves to postarrival phase for the successor, expectations of district officials come into effect. When the new principal is expected to be a change agent by district officials, resistance is likely to be encountered from faculty. Faculty resistance can be mitigated to the extent that teachers are genuinely involved in shaping changes. Successors who work to build credibility with the faculty also ease the postarrival adjustment. Teachers expect successor principals to exhibit competence as leaders, be knowledgeable decision makers, and demonstrate commitment to the school. In sum, arrival and postarrival events suggest that a principal succession requires adjustments not only for the school faculty and staff but for the successor and district administrators as well as. Attention to and support for these adjustments help smooth the transition for those involved.

—Dianne L. Taylor

See also administration, theories of; attitudes toward work; bureaucracy; climate, school; collaboration theory; consideration, caring; empowerment; feminism and theories of leadership; governance; leadership, distributed; leadership, teacher; leadership, theories of; loss of position (school principal); management theories; morale; principalship; productivity; site-based management; staffing, concepts of

Further Readings and References

Davidson, B., & Taylor, D. (1999, April). *Examining principal succession and teacher leadership in school restructuring.* Paper presented at the annual meeting of the American Educational Research Association, Montreal, Canada. (ERIC Document Reproduction Service No. ED433618)

Hallinger, P., & Heck, R. (1996). Reassessing the principal's role in school effectiveness: A review of empirical research, 1980–1995. *Educational Administration Quarterly, 32,* 5–44.

Miskel, C., & Cosgrove, D. (1985). Leader succession in school settings. *Review of Educational Research, 55,* 87–105.

Ogawa, R. (1991). Enchantment, disenchantment, and accommodation: How a faculty made sense of the succession of its principal. *Educational Administration Quarterly, 27,* 30–60.

Takahashi, S. (1998, April). *The keeper of the house: Principal succession and the mending of the hearts.* Paper presented at the annual meeting of the American Educational Research Association, Montreal, Canada. (ERIC Document Reproduction Service No. ED421757)

PRINCIPAL-AGENT THEORY

The principal-agent theory explains the relationship between an individual (individuals), called principal, who delegates the authority to an individual (individuals), called agent, to perform certain tasks or behaviors. However, the principal and the agent do not share the same information, and this often creates conflict between them during the process of fulfilling the task, which is called the principal-agent problem.

The principal-agent problem can be observed anywhere, from our daily life to complex organizations. For example, when you take your car to a mechanic, you are involved in the principal-agent problem. Another example would be a group of shareholders choosing a president to run a big corporation or a firm. In both cases, the process can be explained by the principal-agent theory in that you and the shareholders are the principal and the mechanic and the president are the agents in the framework of the theory. Clearly, the objective in the first case is to get the car repaired; however, the mechanic or the agent may engage in other activities to try to take advantage of the ignorance of the owner of the car, such as doing unnecessary work on the car so that more money can be raised for the shop. Similarly, the president of the company may behave in a way that is not compatible with the stockholders' objective of maximizing their profit. For instance, the agent or the president may take long and expensive vacations at the expense of the firm instead of focusing on maximizing the profit, called shirking activities. In either case, the problem arises because the parties, the principal and the agent, do not share the same information, which leads to unwanted actions.

This difference in the information is called asymmetric information, which is the main assumption of the principal-agent theory. The asymmetry of the information is present both before and after the principal and agent are involved in a contract. The existence of the asymmetric information before the contract is called adverse selection, which creates problems when finding the best agent to accomplish the task. On the other hand, the asymmetry of the information after the contract is called moral hazard, which can result in issues when the agent is performing the task. In that respect, the principal-agent problem is more apparent, and it can be thought of as a special case of the moral hazard problem.

The principle-agent theory is extensively used and popularized by economists in explaining the behavior of a profit-maximizing firm. However, it has been extended into other areas because of the uncertainty and asymmetry of the information shared by individuals in organizations. These areas include politics, research, health, and government organizations, and education is no exception. In education, the principal-agent relationship exists in the following situations: school boards and superintendent, superintendent and principals, and principals and teachers and other workers. The superintendent (the agent) is assumed to run the schools, but he or she may have some hidden agenda that the school board (the principal) is not aware of. Likewise, the superintendent (in this case the principal) hires school principals (the agents) to run specific schools, but the school principals can engage in some other activities that are not desired by the superintendent. Finally, teachers and other school workers may have been involved in actions that are in conflict with the objective of teaching students.

—*Orhan Kara, Ibrahim Duyar, W. Keith Christy, and Larry McNeal*

See also accountability; administration, theories of; boards of education; bureaucracy; capacity building, of organizations; chain of command; decision making; economics, theories of; governance; human resource development; leadership, theories of; role conflict; superintendency; working conditions, in schools

Further Readings and References

Braun, D., & Guston, D. (2003). Principal-agent theory and research policy: An introduction. *Science and Public Policy, 30*(5), 302–308.

De Villiers, A. (1999). South African education: A principal-agent problem. *South African Journal of Economics, 67*(3), 381–402.

Ferris, J. (1992). School-based decision making: A principal-agent perspective. *Educational Evaluation and Policy Analysis, 14*(4), 333–346.

Guston, D. (2003). Principal-agent theory and the structure of science policy revisited: "Science in policy" and the U.S. report on carcinogens. *Science and Public Policy, 30*(5), 347–357.

🏛 PRINCIPALSHIP

Principals are midlevel managers responsible for the efficient and effective functioning of the building and the occupants in it. They serve as a vital connecting link between central office/board of education and classrooms and between teachers and parents. As a result, principals face very busy, demanding, unpredictable, stressful workdays filled with conflict, confrontation, and compromise as groups and individuals compete for their attention. It is common knowledge that many principals feel overworked and underappreciated.

The acronym LEA (for leading educational authority) embodies the multidimensional responsibilities and tasks of the principalship. As the LEA in the building, successful principals create a dynamic synergy between themselves and the environment in which they operate. Their knowledge, skills, attributes, and values permeate the system through the decisions they make and their moral behavior/ leadership. Yet a theme of responsiveness to the environment also defines the principalship and has done so throughout the history of the role. That role requires principals to be sensitive to the emergent behavior of the organization and the culture around them, a collective phenomenon that for the individual is a counterintuitive response to the hierarchical demands of the role.

The position at whatever grade level is about decision making related to human and organizational development. Positioned between the superintendent/board and the faculty, the principal enforces school district policy, meets the professional and personal needs of the faculty and staff, leads for change, and remains committed to personal goals. A typical

high school principal makes 150 decisions a day. And decision making is value laden. Such decision making is risky and demanding, for in the world of administration, each interaction demands a response, and that response is a decision through which a principal creates a school.

As a line-management position, the principal is held responsible for crafting an environment in which student learning is optimized. To do that, the principal must tap into the dynamics of student behavior and learning, teacher motivation and beliefs, adult learning theory, community and school board expectations/demands, and his or her own personal motivation and ambition. Principals develop a high tolerance for ambiguity, for within highly complex organizations such as schools, success or failure rarely results from one decision but rather from a series of small decisions that when taken together tip the organization forward or backward. Different theories of leadership, such as the great man theory and transformational leadership versus transactional leadership, attempt to unravel the micro/macro politics of the principalship, but none have fully explained the complexities of the position or the individual who occupies it.

The job description focuses on five functional areas: instructional leadership, student services, curriculum, financial and facility management, and community relations plus any other duties as assigned. This tension between leadership and management duties remains contentious in practice and in preparation, since efficient managers require different skill sets than effective leaders. Toward this dichotomy, higher education programs that prepare principals (a) offer courses in finance, law, organizational theory, public relations, and instructional supervision, (b) explore concepts of power, conflict, systems thinking, and strategic planning, and (c) examine theories of organizations and of leadership in complex systems.

Throughout history the role has attracted individuals with specific dispositions—the ability to make decisions, the ability to deal with conflict and confusion, and the ability to respond to, meet, and anticipate the needs of the people and the organization. Such dispositions are critical to the success of the individual. A glance at the Interstate School Leaders Licensure Consortium (ISLLC) Standards reveals a list of dispositions that 36 states feel a principal should possess:

Standard 1:   The administrator believes in, values, and is committed to

- The educability of all
- A school vision of high standards of learning
- Continuous school improvement
- The inclusion of all members of the school community
- Ensuring that students have the knowledge, skills, and values needed to become successful adults
- A willingness to continuously examine one's own assumptions, beliefs, and practices
- Doing the work required for high levels of personal and organization performance

Standard 2: The administrator believes in, values, and is committed to

- Student learning as the fundamental purpose of schooling
- The proposition that all students can learn
- The variety of ways in which students can learn
- Lifelong learning for self and others
- Professional development as an integral part of school improvement
- The benefits that diversity brings to the school community
- A safe and supportive learning environment
- Preparing students to be contributing members of society

Standard 3: The administrator believes in, values, and is committed to

- Making management decisions to enhance learning and teaching
- Taking risks to improve schools
- Trusting people and their judgments
- Accepting responsibility
- High-quality standards, expectations, and performances
- Involving stakeholders in management processes
- A safe environment

Standard 4: The administrator believes in, values, and is committed to

- Schools operating as an integral part of the larger community
- Collaboration and communication with families
- Involvement of families and other stakeholders in school decision-making processes
- The proposition that diversity enriches the school
- Families as partners in the education of their children
- The proposition that families have the best interests of their children in mind

- Resources of the family and community needing to be brought to bear on the education of students
- An informed public

Standard 5: The administrator believes in, values, and is committed to

- The ideal of the common good
- The principles in the Bill of Rights
- The right of every student to a free, quality education
- Bringing ethical principles to the decision-making process
- Subordinating one's own interest to the good of the school community
- Accepting the consequences for upholding one's principles and actions
- Using the influence of one's office constructively and productively in the service of all students and their families
- Development of a caring school community

Standard 6: The administrator believes in, values, and is committed to

- Education as a key to opportunity and social mobility
- Recognizing a variety of ideas, values, and cultures
- The importance of a continuing dialogue with other decision makers affecting education
- Actively participating in the political and policy-making context in the service of education
- Using legal systems to protect student rights and improve student opportunities

More individuals are in this position than any other leadership position within school systems. Principals can be found at the elementary, middle school, high school, and alternative school levels. Depending on student enrollment, building-level administrative hierarchy may consist of a principal, associate principal(s), and assistant principal(s). Duties for high school assistant principals focus on student discipline, distributing textbooks, cafeteria supervision, locker assignments, and attending student activities, as noted by Ann Hassenpflug in 1991. Associate positions require specialized expertise such as special education or curriculum. Urban schools tend to have this hierarchical structure, while rural schools usually have just one principal per building, a jack-of-all-trades, who may lead the faculty in innovative pedagogical strategies in the morning and lime the playing field for a ballgame that afternoon.

HISTORY

Compulsory education began with the passing of the Massachusetts Law of 1642, but since education took place in the Puritan home, that law did not establish schools. By 1750, with the adoption of the Tenth Amendment to the Constitution, states had assumed responsibility for public education. Schools became places where generations could be socialized to maintain, participate in, and contribute to a democracy.

After the end of the Civil War, cities grew, schools grew, and a need for administrators arose. Never a clearly defined position like teaching, the principalship emerged in response to increased school enrollments, growing numbers of teachers, and school services. The jack-of-all-trades mentality that defines the principalship was present at the beginning. Administrative numbers grew, and the Department of Superintendence, the forerunner of the American Association of School Administrators, became a reality in 1866.

The position of principal (i.e., head) teacher was at first a teaching position with additional duties. Then in several large metropolitan cities, Boston, Chicago, and New York City, these principal teachers were given release time from teaching. That release time brought a professional status to the role of principal as instructional supervisor.

Before 1900, school administration was a profession of high value focus. School leaders were called much like ministers were called by God to the ministry. America was a country chosen by God to fulfill a great destiny, and school and school leaders were responsible for helping the country to achieve that destiny. The industrial revolution brought changes American society enthusiastically embraced. Business and industry took the spotlight from destiny, and school administrators once again reinvented themselves. They became businesspeople. The principal became a middle manager within an educational bureaucracy.

The influx of immigrants at this time revealed another need: the control of large numbers of people, both within schools and without. Three men, Frederick Taylor, Max Weber, and Henri Fayol, had the answers, and they influenced how businesses were run and how schools are now run, for their organizational and economic rationalism holds sway today. Taylor's book *The Principles of Scientific Management,* published in 1911, introduced fundamental principles of scientific management to increase efficiency and maximize production. Weber's contributions included a concept known as chain of command, policy rules and regulations, and impersonal relationships between management and staff, among others. By the 1950s, school administrations had adopted the management concepts of Taylor and Fayol, including Fayol's five key functions of effective managers:

1. Plan and forecast future actions.
2. Organize the structural, material, and human resources of the enterprise.
3. Command and maintain purposeful activity among employees.
4. Coordinate and unify the activities and efforts of employees.
5. Control organizational operations and tasks according to established policies

Between 1946 and 1985, Americans embraced science, which emphasized value-free inquiry and proof. Once again, school leadership reacted quickly to societal forces and reconstructed itself. The science of school administration took hold within preparation programs. Principals struggled to become objective and rational in their decision making. That concept of scientific decision making dominated preparation programs for almost 30 years and overthrew the past wisdom of experience, observation, and reflection that had ruled from the era before 1900.

The scientific concept of value-free decisions emphasized objectivity and scientific realism. As a result, only the beliefs of science could yield reliable insights. A closer look reveals that once again administrators aligned themselves to a higher social order, this time to scientists. As preparation programs focused on science and theory, the study of ethics, morality, values, self-exploration, and reflection lost the spotlight.

During this same general period, the role of school leader as bureaucrat began to emerge. The 1960s were a time of social and political turbulence, and against this tableau, shrewd, politically astute principals protected their authority, respected superiors, and guarded against power takeovers by teachers. By this time, the causal relationship of science had infiltrated evaluation of the principalship. This accountability to so many stakeholders brought, and continues to bring, role conflicts, stress, and opportunities.

Principals in the 1970s were urged to turn their backs on bureaucracy. They were expected to engage in and support emotionally positive relationships within and outside their schools. Three values permeated this era: self-actualization (a Maslowian term), an emotionally supportive school climate, and societal transformation. The 1970s also saw an increase in federal involvement.

If the 1970s were a time for principals to envision this sharing, supportive community, the 1980s brought focus to instructional supervision, being a change agent, and leadership accountability. In the 1990s, principals once again were called upon to be responsive to the environment around them, but this time that environment was exceptionally critical and hostile. Changing demographics, social justice issues, and the retention of the United States as a global powerhouse brought powerful forces of criticism against education.

TODAY'S PRINCIPALS

Today's school principals more than ever embody the jack-of-all-trades mentality that began the profession. Buffeted by the accountability culture, increasing state and federal demands, including No Child Left Behind and state budget cuts, principals are burdened by the demands of the job, frustrated by the lack of resources, and dismayed and angry that the crunching of numbers for student promotion/retention do not take into account the human condition. Moral leadership and democratic leadership are emerging as schools struggle with diversity, injustices, and inequities. For the practitioner, there are not enough hours in the day to accomplish what the job has become.

Today's principals need help to transform schools, and they know it. Generating teacher loyalty and trust are high priorities. The extent to which teachers describe principals as accepting responsibility for their own actions, as nonmanipulative, and as a person first, principal second, determines that leader authenticity.

Proclaiming that strategic planning and large-scale reform have failed to help schools improve, critics now urge school leaders to listen to the voices of professional learning communities within the building. Tapping this sleeping giant has meant retreating from the accepted image of the principal as a charismatic, lone ranger who can transform schools. Nested within the national culture of accountability, jack-of-all-trades mentality, and traditional school hierarchy, this reshaping of power constructs creates moral dilemmas for many principals. A study of the National Association of Secondary School Principals (NASSP) State Principals

of the Year found that when confronted by traditional cultural role obligations, like supervision of personnel, principals knew what to do. When confronted with culturally ambiguous messages, they relied on intuition and gut feelings to do what was right for kids.

CHANGES

After decades of effective schools research and whole school reform, best practices, strategic planning, systems thinking, and other hot topics that promised to change and improve schools, the one-size-fits-all answer to school problems has not been found. The trend now is school improvement research, which is concerned with the *how* of successful schools. Today's principal still gets things done through other people. It is the *how* that has changed. The current climate of standards and high-stakes testing has underscored the importance of teacher performance in the classroom. For learning to occur, students and teachers must be engaged. Constructive criticism remains a tool of instructional supervision, but today's principals recognize that individual teachers are at different levels of development, expertise, and commitment that demand a plethora of constructive interactions. This developmental supervision approach incorporates adult learning theory, particularly the theory of andragogy.

Evidence is emerging that empowering teachers, especially in regard to curriculum, can improve student performance. This sharing of power is a value shift for the principalship. Terms like *shared decision making, empowerment*, and *site-based management* highlight this shift as schools move from coercive organizations to more collegial relationships. The speculation is that this dynamic will change the principalship from an office of coercive, legitimate power to expert power as the most significant element in relationships between teachers and principals.

Expert power will put additional pressures on the principal. Brain research has reconstructed the traditional picture of knowledge transmission within the classroom. For optimal learning, teachers must access students' prior knowledge, build on that knowledge, and then incorporate metacognitive skills to cement the knowledge. Not only do principals have to keep abreast of such new research, but they must also help teachers utilize that research to construct classroom environments that optimize learning. Another profound change taking place within the literature, both educational and public, is the replacement of the word *knowledge* with *lifelong learning.* This indicates a dramatic shift in our culture's perspective on education.

Yet another movement of change is the integration of special needs students into mainstream classrooms. Such restructuring efforts change the lives of the disabled students, their teachers, and nondisabled students. How principals do that in their role as social architect can set the stage for the success or failure of the initiative and of the nation. Historically, schools have not served at-risk or special needs students very well.

To illustrate the complexity of such an initiative, successful leaders in six inclusive elementary schools (a) established a system of communication that allowed for disagreement, (b) involved themselves in the individualized education program (IEP) process, (c) built a philosophy of inclusion with staff, (d) established discipline policies for students with disabilities, (e) followed a personal plan of professional development, (f) used data in decision making, and (g) demonstrated skills in problem solving.

Within preparation programs, a new vision of leadership is emerging. In his book *Centering Educational Administration: Cultivating Meaning, Community, Responsibility,* Robert Starratt presents his theory of what educational administration needs to do in order to be successful. He builds on the 1990s work of three influential educational administration scholars, Kenneth Leithwood, Richard Elmore, and Joseph Murphy, and their contributions to the reorganization of theory and practice. School reform, he contends, must cultivate meaning, cultivate community, and cultivate responsibility, and the work of administrative leadership is intellectual work. That thinking goes against powerful historical and sociological frameworks. For example, most high school principals are expected to supervise athletic competitions. That has little to do with intellectual leadership for a better tomorrow and everything to do with management, a different concept altogether. Transformational leaders set direction, develop people and redesign organizations. Although Starratt acknowledges the value of Leithwood, Doris Jantzi, and Rosanne Steinbach's research, he contends that it is not grounded in *what* schools teach and *what* students learn.

Six conceptions of leadership have emerged in recent times: instructional (teacher behavior affecting student growth), transformational, moral, participative, managerial, and cultural, as discussed by Leithwood and associates. Of the six, only instructional supervision is particular to education.

TRENDS

In the 1960s and 1970s, people thought of education in terms of resources, services, and innovation. Schools, and thus principals, concerned themselves with equity issues, needs of handicapped students, legal battles over means and ends, and the right of teacher organizations to bargain collectively, which gave teachers unprecedented power. With the publication of *A Nation at Risk* in 1983, that emphasis changed, and the American public once again focused on the academic performance of students. In 2003, the Koret Task Force examined the changes wrought by *A Nation at Risk* and concluded that *Risk* had failed to confront essential issues of power and control.

From the recommendations made by the Koret Task Force, a forecast can be made of the educational trends that will confront principals in the coming decade and perhaps beyond. Accountability in the form of high-stakes testing and standards will remain, with increased consequences for students and adults. Choice for parents means competition from charter schools and voucher experiments or through private enterprises sustained through public education funds. Teacher competence (and by association principal competence) will be measured by classroom performance. That implies more reliance on instructional supervision and expert power, requiring both formative and summative evaluations to determine teacher retention or promotion in conjunction with testing results. For many principals, that translates into an old adage: spend more time with people, not with paper.

Behind the number of failing schools published in the newspaper are the faces of children. A grassroots effort is emerging from the schoolhouse, protestor for educational rights of children. Consistent attacks on public schools from state, federal, and private organizations have helped educators to understand that if they do not control their own destiny, that future will be thrust upon them by others. This resistance to the top-down mandates imposed by state and federal governments is centered upon our democracy and the place schools have in sustaining that democracy through the education of students both as individuals and as citizens.

Principals of the future will be called upon to defend and protect the rights of students, educators, parents, and communities. Their charge will be to determine what is in a student's best interests as well as the academic, moral, and societal environment needed to shape individual growth and citizens for tomorrow within a democracy. Support for such democratic supervision has been reinvented in site-based decision making, boundary spanning, and participative leadership.

For principals who have power and influence over others and who are in the business of creating persons, such responsibility implies a duty to be proficient in ethical reasoning and to adhere to ethical codes. Yet current and future principals cannot be absolute. To tie knowledge to absolutes in the arena of ethics creates a puddle of perfection that cannot withstand the droughts brought about by change. In a pluralistic society, change is the only constant.

Mobility is a present trend that will continue into the future. In one southwestern state, the principalship is seen as the highest paid itinerant workforce in the state. Several factors contribute to this mobility rate, including career advances, politics, fit, bureaucracy, disenchantment, and life stage challenges.

—*JoAnn Franklin Klinker*

See also accountability; achievement tests; administration, theories of; at-risk students; attitudes; attitudes toward work; authority; behaviorism; bureaucracy; capacity building, of organizations; career stages; collaboration theory; communities, types, building of; community relations; conflict management; constructivism; decision making; discipline in schools; division of labor; elementary education; empowerment; high schools; human resource development; innovation, in education; Interstate School Leaders Licensure Consortium; junior high schools; leadership, theories of; line and staff; middle schools; National Association of Elementary School Principals; National Organization of Secondary School Principals; organizational theories; school improvement models; site-based management; Taylor, Frederick; Weber, Max; women in educational leadership

Further Readings and References

Blase, J., & Blase, J. (2003). The phenomenology of principal mistreatment: Teachers' perspectives. *Journal of Educational Administration, 41*(4), 367–422.

Brown, K. (2005). Pivotal points: History, development, and promise of the principalship. In F. English (Ed.), *The SAGE handbook of educational leadership* (pp. 89–108). Thousand Oaks, CA: Sage.

Chubb, J. E., Williamson, M. E., Finn, C. E., Hanushek, E. A., Hill, P. T., Hirsch, E. D., et al. (2003). Our schools, our future: Are we still at risk? *Education Next: A Journal of Opinion and Research,* 9–15.

Cooper, B., Fusarelli, L., & Randall, E. (2004). *Better policies, better schools: Theories and applications.* New York: Allyn & Bacon.

Davies, D. (2002). The 10th school revisited: Are school/family/community partnerships on the reform agenda now? *Phi Delta Kappan, 83,* 388–392.

Elmore, R. (2000). *Building a new structure for school leadership.* Washington DC: Albert Shanker Institute.

Glickman, C., Gordon, S., & Ross-Gordon, J. (2004). *SuperVision and instructional leadership: A developmental approach* (6th ed.). New York: Allyn & Bacon.

Grogan, M., & Andrews, R. (2002). Defining preparation and professional development for the future. *Educational Administration Quarterly, 38*(2), 233–256.

Hassenpflug, A. (1991). Commentary: What is the role of the assistant principal? *NASSP Assistant Principal Special Newsletter, 7*(1), 1–7.

Hoy, W., & Miskel, C. (2005). *Educational administration: Theory, research, and practice* (7th ed.). Boston: McGraw-Hill.

Katzenmeyer, M., & Moller, G. (2001). *Awakening the sleeping giant: Helping teachers develop as leaders.* Thousand Oaks, CA: Corwin Press.

Klinker, J., & Hackmann, D. (2004). An analysis of principals' ethical decision making using Rest's four-component model of moral behavior. *Journal of School Leadership, 14,* 434–457.

Leithwood, K., & Duke, D. (1999). A century's quest to understand school leadership. In J. Murphy & K. Seashore Louis (Eds.), *Handbook of research on educational administration* (2nd ed.). San Francisco: Jossey-Bass.

Leithwood, K., Jantzi, D., & Steinbach, R. (1999). *Changing leadership for changing times.* Philadelphia: Open University Press.

Murphy, J., & Forsyth, P. (1999). *A decade of change: An overview.* Thousand Oaks, CA: Corwin Press.

Murphy, J. (1999). *The quest for a center: Notes on the state of the profession of educational leadership.* Columbia, MO: University Council for Educational Administration.

Pounder, J., & Coleman, M. (2002). Women: Better leaders than men? In general and educational management it still "all depends." *Leadership and Organization Development Journal, 23*(3), 122–133.

Schmoker, M. (2004). Tipping point: From feckless reform to substantive instructional improvement. *Phi Delta Kappan, 85*(6), 424–432.

Starratt, R. (2003). *Centering educational administration: Cultivating meaning, community, responsibility.* Mahwah, NJ: Erlbaum.

Webb, L., Metha, A., & Jordan, K. (2003). *Foundations of American education* (4th ed.). Upper Saddle River, NJ: Merrill Prentice Hall.

Williams-Boyd, P. (2002). *Educational leadership: A reference handbook.* Denver, CO: ABC-CLIO.

PRIVATIZATION

Privatization has been the subject of ongoing public policy debates for decades. In a broad sense, privatization involves transferring the production and delivery of a wide range of services from the government to the private sector and/or contracting with private companies to handle public services (e.g., solid waste collection, fire fighting, and the management of jails and prisons). Proponents of privatization favor issues of efficiency and accountability, whereas critics of privatization favor issues of social justice and equity. The theoretical support for privatization is grounded in (a) market theory, (b) public choice theory, and (c) property rights theory. Key tenets of each theory are as follows:

Market theory speaks to the virtues of competition, efficiency, and consumers exercising utility preferences in the private markets and the lack of such market forces in public monopolies. Public choice theory explains that government inefficiency is the result of incentive structures of public agencies that encourage public managers to build empires (e.g., power, budgets, and staffing) out of self-interest over societal interests. Property rights theory states that property will be cared for in proportion to individual gain from tending it; hence, private ownership increases ownership and efficiency, whereas public ownership decreases ownership and increases inefficiency.

BUSINESS SECTOR INFLUENCE

In 1983, the administration of President Ronald Reagan published a document titled *A Nation at Risk: The Imperative for Educational Reform,* which stated that global competitors had replaced the preeminence of the United States in all sectors and that educational foundations had been eroded by mediocrity. Accordingly, the solution lay in educational reform. Business and industrial groups demanded a return to teaching traditional academic subjects, shoring up the quality and quantity of science and math courses, and holding teachers accountable. The accountability movement had begun.

In 2004, Kathy Emery and Susan Ohanian chronicled the vetting process between the Business Roundtable (BRT) and the National Governor's Association over the past 25 years, revealing an undeniable alignment of educational policy with economic development. In the end, the No Child Left Behind Act (NCLB) of 2001 is as much Democratic President Bill Clinton's legacy as Republican President George W. Bush's.

PRIVATIZATION OF K–16 EDUCATION

At the K–12 level, privatization has involved to a lesser extent educational services and to a greater extent noneducational services. With noneducational services, privatization or contracting for transportation, food, and maintenance of facilities has been commonplace. As noted by Katrina Buckley in 2005, a new phenomenon known as educational management organizations (EMOs) have emerged, which offer services (predominately to charter schools) that range from bookkeeping to report writing to managing every aspect of a school's operations.

To a much lesser extent, privatization is associated with charter schools; however, charter schools are nonsectarian public schools that operate independently of many local and state regulations. Charter schools have burgeoned, and their numbers are expected to increase with school districts failing to meet Adequate Yearly Progress (AYP). As of 2005, the Center for Education Reform estimated that there are 37 states with charters (excluding Puerto Rico), 2,695 schools in operation (15% increase from last school year), with nearly 685,000 students enrolled.

The growth of charter schools has surpassed the acceptance of vouchers. Nonetheless, both vouchers and charter schools have long been seen as exemplars of change and founts of improvement to public education by business interests, while opposed by most educators. The proponents of vouchers typically refer to Milton Friedman's inequity arguments. Proponents suggest that vouchers allow parents of underperforming schools a choice, with charter schools serving as an option. Opponents of choice plans and charters argue that diverting public school funding to charter schools is detrimental and their improved student performance unproven.

Privatization in higher education is most visible with technology transfer initiatives. Increasingly, public universities have experienced reduced state appropriations, heightened state regulation, and control, and demand that universities find private sources of funding. According to the National Association of College and University Business officers, in 2003 the University of Virginia became the first public institution to derive a majority of its annual funding from private sources (e.g., $134 million in private funds in fiscal year 2004 compared to $131 million in state support). Many universities have endeavored to commercialize research by becoming entrepreneurial enterprises. Typically, venture capitalists provide resources for the development of labs and facilities and in return acquire positions in market-bearing research. University scientists provide the intellectual labor, and universities often retain a stake in market-bearing research to boot.

APPROPRIATENESS OF PRIVATIZATION OF EDUCATION

Privatization has occurred in the transportation, utilities, and communications industries. However, the success of such privatization appears dubious, considering the solvency issues with the airlines, the California energy crisis, and the corporate malfeasance associated with long-distance phone service providers. For this reason, privatization efforts with education should be viewed with caution.

To be sure, the business sector has successfully guided educational reform policy over the past 25 years to promote economic development. However, is it appropriate to place so much emphasis on the development of human capital? Do the interests of an elite class in corporate America represent the average American?

Most educators would agree that there is room for improvement across the board in the management, structures, personnel, teaching, and assessment of public education. But with that being said, one should not lose sight of one of the greatest problems afflicting public education today: underfunding.

At the K–12 level, privatization of noneducational services seems clear with contracting and EMOs, whereas privatization of educational services seems nebulous with the general association of charters and vouchers with forms of privatization per se. The siphoning of students and funds from public schools that accompanies charter schools and vouchers should be considered. Technology transfer initiatives at the tertiary level, which result in a loss of "autonomy" (e.g., university mission and faculty research) as private, external funding increases, should also be of concern.

Overall, the perils of applying private sector models of efficiency, competition, and utility preferences to public education as reform measures should be heeded and serve as the focus for future scholarship.

—*Paul Melendez*

See also charter schools; competition, forms of, in schools; Friedman, Milton; globalism; human capital; market theory of schooling; *A Nation at Risk;* No Child Left Behind; right-wing politics, advocates, impact on education; voucher plans

Further Readings and References

Buckley, K. (2005). Losing voice? Educational management organizations and charter schools' educational programs. *Education and Urban Society, 37(2),* 204–234.

Emery, K., & Ohanian, S. (2004). *Why is corporate America bashing our public schools?* Portsmouth, NH: Heinemann.

Friedman, M. (1962). *Capitalism and freedom.* Chicago: University of Chicago Press.

Greene, D. J. (2005). *Public administration in the new century: A concise introduction.* Belmont, CA: Wadsworth.

National Association of College and University Business Officers. (2003). *University of Virginia projects more private than public funding for fy04.* Retrieved March 18, 2005, from http://www.nacubo.org/x683.xml?s=x40.

U.S. Charter Schools. (2005). *Basic national statistics.* Retrieved March 18, 2005, from http://www.uscharterschools.org.

PROBLEM SOLVING

Problem solving is a multiple-step process that purposefully analyzes an issue, generates alternatives, evaluates and implements selected choices, and monitors progress. For the purposes of this entry, it will be assumed that a team approach to problem solving will be used. At an early point, the importance of the problem should be evaluated in comparison to the values of a possible solution. The following types of questions need to be addressed: Is this problem important for the school or the district, or what will happen if the problem is unresolved? Is it best that the problem remain unsolved? Some problems can remain unresolved without significant impact on the mission and strategic plan. At a basic level, the steps include the following: identify the problem, generate solutions, evaluate the alternatives, implement the selected alternative, and evaluate progress.

At the first stage, identification and clarification of the problem are essential; describe the problem but avoid potential solutions—solutions will come later. The following types of questions will help the team keep on task: What is the problem, and is the problem relevant to the mission and strategic plan of the organization? What are the symptoms associated with the problem? It must be understood that symptoms, root causes, and the problem are confused but must be kept separate. Do not assume that these differences are understood by the person who presented them or that you totally understand the problem. Collect data that describe the problem and define the impact the problem has had or will have on the organization. In some cases, restating the problem in general terms or providing illustrative examples can clarify the issues.

During the definition of the problem, ambiguous issues should be clarified. To illustrate, "reading scores are too low" is unclear and is an ill-defined statement of a problem. Does this mean all students or selected students? What type of assessment was used to determine reading level? What is an acceptable reading level? When will assessments occur? When will the problem be judged as resolved? The criteria for success should be clearly stated as a part of the definition of the problem; this information is needed at all steps in the problem-solving process.

After the problem is defined and understood, the next step is to generate as many alternative solutions as possible. Because educators are very intent on developing solutions to immediate problems, and complex educational problems have multiple root causes, the team should be encouraged to consider all possible alternatives without judging the value of the alternatives. The generation of multiple possible solutions is time consuming and can produce many false starts, but the process is necessary to identify potential solutions with merit. Often, when complex problems are discussed, assumptions, symptoms, solutions, and subjective data are intermixed and confused.

Teamwork and brainstorming are beneficial skills that can be used to generate alternative approaches to the problem. Alternatives should not be evaluated and assessed; however, avoid blame for the problem, because blame is unproductive and destructive to the process. The goal is to generate a wide variety of solutions: some realistic, some analytical, and some very creative. Traditional rules for brainstorming should guide the brainstorming process. Open discussion that is not personalized encourages communication and supports team building.

Next, the various alternatives must be evaluated and an approach selected to resolve the problem. The possible alternatives should be considered in relationship to the vision, mission, and strategic plan of the organization. Numerous questions should be considered. What are costs, time restraints, and personnel requirements? The strengths and weaknesses of each approach should be considered in relationship to both short-term and long-term impact. In addition, existing policies and procedures should be reviewed in reference to each alternative. During this phase of problem solving, the team should be objective, record data, collect feedback, make pertinent notes, and listen for root causes. The potential results, causes, and impacts of the problem are valuable information.

The bottom line is that an alternative must be selected. The chosen alternative must address the root causes identified, and it must be implemented completely. An action plan should be developed to provide a road map for the implementation process. In schools, most meaningful changes will require a significant adjustment in budget, program adjustments, and staff changes; therefore, the plan will need to address personnel, timelines, facilities, and external issues. Roles and responsibilities related to implementation need to be clarified. Who is responsible for implementation, communication, and evaluation? Each member of the team must commit to making the improvement happen.

At this point, problem solving will become a project management process; the plan must be implemented, managed, and monitored. Formative evaluation of the implementation process can provide feedback on budget, timelines, personnel, and policies. The process of implementation must be monitored to ensure that the plan was implemented. If changes were made during the implementation process, then information must be recorded for consideration during the evaluation component.

Because the criteria for success were identified in early stages, the evaluation of the progress is easier. Evaluation of the success of a selected solution should be a formative process, and many issues related to monitoring progress need to be clarified. Was the plan implemented? Are other measures available as indicators that the problem has been resolved? Do not assume a single problem exists—apply systems thinking. Was the problem resolved, and was the alternative responsible for the improvement? Did the plan result in a systemic change, or is it likely that the problem will reoccur? The evaluation of progress enables the organization to determine the extent of success and level of implementation.

Finally, communication with stakeholders is essential at each step of the problem-solving process. A clear communication plan that openly discusses the alternative will eliminate guessing, develop a broader base of support, and reduce some potential problems if the plan is unsuccessful.

Feedback at each step will support the process of teamwork and group involvement in problem solving. Effective group problem solving requires that a group be creative, systematic, and thorough in its problem-solving approach.

The leader's role helps determine whether group problem solving is effective or not. Although the members also are responsible for the group's ultimate output, the leader can facilitate effective problem solving by making sure that the important problem-solving functions are met. The leader needs to be highly skilled to keep the problem-solving process on track.

—Bill Thornton and George C. Hill

See also accountability; behaviorism; case studies; critical theory; curriculum, theories of; decision making; empiricism; feedback; globalism; Interstate School Leaders Licensure Consortium; knowledge base, of the field; leadership, theories of; management theories; organizational theories; politics, of education; principalship; rational organizational theory; role conflict; school districts, history and development; superintendency; workplace trends

Further Readings and References

Hanson, M. (2003). *Educational administration and organizational behavior* (5th ed.). Boston: Pearson Education.

Lessinger, L., & Salowe, A. (1997). *Game time: The educator's playbook for the new global economy.* Lancaster, PA: Technomic.

Morgan, R., & Smith, J. (1996). *Staffing the new workplace.* Milwaukee, WI: ASQC Press.

Robbins, S. (2001). *Organizational behavior.* Upper Saddle River, NJ: Prentice Hall.

🏛 PROBLEM-BASED LEARNING

Problem-based learning (PBL) is a catchall term for several educational strategies, each of which employs different terminology and instructional purposes. While PBL strategies may be called PBL modules, scenarios, vignettes, critical incident analyses, or teaching cases (not to be confused with case study *methodology*), they share in common that they employ problems in the instructional process. Problem-based learning exercises generally have three distinctive design features: a narrative, responses/activities, and a debriefing.

1. *Narratives* describe a specific, complex predicament that is written as a scenario for exploring critical issues. As used in the preparation, training, and professional development of educational leaders, narratives range from a completely developed case, which includes extensive and detailed qualitative and/or quantitative

information, to narratives that are constructivist in orientation. That is, while PBL strategies may present students with a great deal of data, they may also call for students and instructors to search for or generate additional information to complete the exercise.

2. *Responses/activities* entail analyzing information provided in the narrative and crafting actionable solutions to those problems. It has been suggested that analyses of PBL exercises generally follow the following sequence: (a) recognizing the problems in the narrative, (b) framing the problems in the narrative using a perspective grounded in curricular and/or course content, (c) searching for viable analytic alternatives, (d) developing and implementing a plan of action, and (e) evaluating the processes students used to formulate their solution and the quality and viability of their solutions.

3. *Debriefing,* often the final step of PBL activities, has a twofold purpose. First, debriefing discloses the instructors' evaluation of student work. Second, debriefing provides a chance for the instructor and students to constructively discuss alternative solutions or interpretations (and possibly group processes) they may not have previously considered.

There are many potential benefits to employing PBL educational strategies in the preparation, training, and professional development of educational leaders. Service-oriented fields such as medicine, business, and engineering have employed PBL educational strategies effectively to provide students with opportunities to apply their academic knowledge to the solution of real-life situations as part of preinternship preparation. Increased interest in the use of PBL educational strategies to aid in the development of educational leaders over the latter half of the twentieth and beginning of the twenty-first century has yielded many useful resources, including *The Journal of Cases in Educational Leadership,* a peer-reviewed journal devoted solely to the development and dissemination of high-quality PBL exercises (available in full text online at www.ucea.org). While there are other useful educational strategies available that are designed to help prospective educational leaders understand the complexities of practice, few approaches offer the benefits of PBL strategies. Such benefits have been identified as increasing awareness of where additional knowledge is required within the existing knowledge base and fostering collaboration between professors, practitioners, and students.

—*Jeffrey S. Brooks*

See also academic freedom; accountability; accreditation; behaviorism; case studies; critical theory; curriculum, theories of; decision making; empiricism; feedback; Interstate School Leaders Licensure Consortium; knowledge base, of the field; leadership, theories of; learning, theories of; management theories; organizational theories; politics, of education; principalship; problem solving; rational organizational theory; role conflict; school districts, history and development; superintendency; universities, preparation of educational leaders in

Further Readings and References

Bridges, E., & Hallinger, P. (1997). Problem-based leadership development: Preparing educational leaders for changing times. *Journal of School Leadership, 7*(6), 592–608.

Bridges, E., & Hallinger, P. (1997). Using PBL to prepare educational leaders. *Peabody Journal of Education, 72*(2), 131–146.

Cunningham, W., & Cordeiro, P. (2003). *Educational leadership: A problem-based approach.* Boston: Allyn & Bacon.

Lortie, D. (1998). Teaching educational administration: Reflections on our craft (1994 Mitstifer Lecture). *Journal of Cases in Educational Leadership, 1*(1). Retrieved October 11, 2004, from http://www.ucea.org.

Taylor, L., & Whittaker, C. (2003). *Bridging multiple worlds: Case studies of diverse educational communities.* Boston: Allyn & Bacon.

🏛 PRODUCTIVITY

In its simplest form, productivity can be defined as achieving the maximum output of a process with the use of minimum inputs. Productivity can be applied to education in the same way that economists analyze the relationship between inputs and outputs; however, the difference between the two methods is simply that it is difficult to define and measure the inputs and particularly the outputs of education. The demands for additional funding have been continuously increasing, while the public has been dissatisfied with the outputs of the education system. This development has sparked the American public's desire for increased productivity and accountability in public education.

Traditionally, two concepts of productivity are considered: technical productivity and economic productivity. Technical productivity refers to maximizing the outputs for a given set of inputs and indicates the best input mix through the utilization of production technology. This best mix requires the lowest cost of the output. Schools are criticized for being technically inefficient. The first argument to support this view is that educational organizations do not aim to maximize profits or lower the costs of the teaching and learning. Also, educational decision makers may not understand the production process and therefore may not maximize the outputs for a given set of inputs. A limitation inherent in technical productivity is that this approach assumes that the educational decision makers know and measure all the inputs to the production process. However, skill and ability differences of students and teachers may yield variations in output.

Economic productivity refers to the correct choice of input mix, given the prices of inputs. The question of how resources should be allocated in order to produce different goods and services raises the question of economic efficiency. In economic productivity, the lowest cost is not achieved at the expense of quality of a product. Because of the quality consideration, economic productivity is also called "effectiveness" in the literature. Increasing economic productivity of an educational system can be attained either by educating and training more students without decreasing the quality or by increasing the quality of educational services offered to the same number of students.

Another categorization of productivity calls for internal and external productivity. Both internal and external productivity can be viewed on the quality and quantity dimensions. Internal productivity refers to the relationship between inputs and outputs of a system. In this sense, internal productivity indicates the degree of attainment of the standards or goals of the educational system. These standards may be identified quantitatively such as graduation rate or qualitatively such as behavioral objectives. External productivity refers to the fit between educational system outputs and the needs of society.

Although various models have been developed, the literature recognizes the difficulty and limitations in identifying and measuring inputs, outputs, and quality of education. For instance, education has many different goals to achieve at the same time. Similarly, the same measured inputs may not yield the same outputs because of the skill or quality differences. Therefore, it is sometimes argued that it is impossible to measure the productivity of education. Others, on the other hand, argue that this is equivalent to admitting that schools have no way of judging how successful they are in achieving the goals and standards they set out for themselves.

Being a $450 billion enterprise, productivity in public education is as important for taxpayers as it is for the owners or shareholders of a private organization. Taxpayers want to know where their money is going and whether additional funds are justified. Seemingly minimum or no advancement in student achievement despite the drastic increases in funding over recent decades sparked the American public's desire for increased productivity and accountability in public education. These developments require the close examination of educational productivity in the form of resource allocation and utilization.

Early research in productivity of public education has produced mixed results. Early production function research was inconclusive. This mostly stemmed from the complexity of the schooling process and factors outside the schools' control. It has been difficult to isolate statistically one-to-one correlations between inputs and student learning. The most famous production function study was the U.S. Department of Energy's 1966 *Coleman Report*. This massive survey of 600,000 students in 30,000 schools concluded that socioeconomic background influenced student success more than various school and teacher characteristics. Similarly, in 1989, Eric Hanusek analyzed 187 production function studies in the last 20 years and found no systematic, positive relationship between student achievement and seven schooling inputs.

Recent literature ties the failure to document educational productivity to education production function approach, the approach that has been applied to all studies. Education production is the process of transforming inputs into outputs. There are several reasons why the production function has been relatively unsuccessful in identifying relationships between resource uses and student achievement. First, production function research assumes that all school systems are pursuing the same goals. The fact is that school systems pursue a variety of goals, and in many cases, these goals are not tied to student achievement. Second, it is difficult to identify inputs. Educators and researchers utilize different inputs, and there is no consensus on what exactly constitutes educational inputs. Furthermore, the production function ignores process and its input variables, such as curriculum and instruction. Third, there are difficulties in determining

the functional relationship among variables. Most studies assume a linear relationship among variables, but the relationship may be logarithmic or curvilinear. Finally, most studies use cross-sectional rather than longitudinal data and thus cannot analyze value-added in relating education to student achievement.

Recent research through the advancement and use of sophisticated techniques showed that the increase in average spending or increase in the quality of input and/or process measures would significantly increase student achievement. The research proved that there are factors controllable by the school systems to increase educational productivity despite the existence of uncontrollable factors such as deteriorating socioeconomic background and lack of parental involvement. For instance, in 1994, Larry Hedges and his colleagues found that about 10% or a $500 increase in spending per pupil would significantly increase student achievement. In 1995, Faith Crampton found that expenditures matter when the money is spent for smaller classes. The more experienced and highly trained teachers, in an analysis of inputs, affected the achievement in New York public school students.

Other studies show that investments on selected inputs have paramount effects on educational productivity. There is a consensus in the literature that programmatic expenditures are likely to increase student achievement. There is a widespread agreement that expenditures for programs designed to prevent school failure or enhance student achievement, especially for poor children, increase educational productivity. Similarly, preschool programs for poor children and intervention programs to prevent school dropouts also have relatively high cost-benefit ratios.

In addition, some studies examining factors hindering educational productivity found that poor resource distribution, schools' bureaucratic structure, uneven pay schedules favoring senior teachers, and focus on services and labor-intensive practices increased costs and lowered productivity. Similarly, unstable governance, lack of incentives to leverage productivity improvement, structures favoring continuity over continuous improvement, and inadequate quality controls on innovations were identified as factors reducing educational productivity in a 1995 report of Consortium on Productivity in the Schools.

Challenges of productivity also exist in higher education. At post-K–12 institutions, there is no consistent definition of productivity or agreed upon way to measure it. The traditional measurement of productivity in colleges and universities is the cost per hour of instruction per student. Newer approaches redefine productivity measurement as the cost per unit of learning per student, not the amount of instruction given to them.

—*Ibrahim Duyar, Larry McNeal, Orhan Kara, and Jane McDonald*

See also accountability; administration, theories of; budgeting; cost-benefit analyses; decision making; Deming, W. Edwards; economics, theories of; finance, of public schools; Friedman, Milton; management theories; measurement, theories of; operational definitions; organizations, types of, typologies; resource management; school plant management; taxes, to support education; total quality management; work task measurement

Further Readings and References

Consortium on Productivity in the Schools. (1995). *Using what we have to get the schools we need: A productivity focus for American education.* New York: Author.

Crampton, F. (1995, March). *Is the production function dead? An analysis of the relationship of educational inputs on school outcomes.* Paper presented at the annual conference of the American Education Finance Association.

Duyar, I. (1999). Internal efficiency in education. *Journal of College of Educational Sciences, 11*(2), 223–235.

Hanusek, E. (1987). Educational production functions. In G. Psacharopoulos (Ed.), *Economics of education research and studies.* Elmsford, NY: Pergamon Press.

Hanusek, E. (1989). The impact of differential expenditures on school performance. *Educational Researcher, 18*(4), 45–51.

Hedges, L., Laine, R., & Greenwald, R. (1994). Does money matter? A meta-analysis of the effects of differential school inputs on student outcomes. *Educational Researcher, 23*(3), 5–14.

🏛 PROFESSIONAL DEVELOPMENT

Professional development refers to processes designed to enhance educators' knowledge, skills, and attitudes for the purpose of improving students' learning. Terms that have been used synonymously in the past include *staff development, in-service education, on-the-job training, adult learning,* and *continuing education.* Underlying all of these terms is the premise that, due to an ever-evolving knowledge base pertinent to teaching and learning, educators must continuously expand, renew, and refine their expertise.

Professional development can also be understood as one of several means of school improvement. (Examples of others are curriculum articulation, materials acquisition, community partnerships, special programming, and policy development.) As such, it reflects both instructional and organizational leadership functions for educational administrators.

In practice, principals and superintendents seldom lead particular professional development activities. Nonetheless, they, and other school leaders, are responsible for sharing decision making about professional development content and design, creating supportive contexts for adults' and children's learning, allocating resources, planning, evaluating, and making multiple improvement initiatives cohere.

These leadership responsibilities are complicated by a limited research base and lack of consensus about what characterizes effective professional development practice. Thomas Guskey's analysis indicates that, overall, the professional development knowledge base relies more heavily on theorizing and expert opinion than on conclusive results from empirical study. He also notes that it is understandable that there remain many unknowns and disagreements about processes as context-dependent and complex as leadership and adult learning.

Dennis Sparks points out that current thinking about professional development reflects several differences from the past. For example, consistent with the standards-based reform movement, expert opinion is currently more concerned with potential impact on student learning outcomes than adult participants' satisfaction with their own learning experiences. Contemporary professional development is expected to be an ongoing process integrated into the normal workday rather than intermittent special events occurring a few times a year. Directly related to this job embeddedness, school-based professional development approaches are currently more highly valued than the districtwide experiences of the past.

Moreover, current aspirations for educational improvement are that schools function less like bureaucratic organizations and more like learning communities. The latter shifts professional development goals from exclusive focus on individual growth and development to improved school capacity to solve problems, renew itself, and pursue desired student learning results collectively. This shift also means that the entire school staff, not just teachers and principals, should be continuously learning, so that all parts of the system contribute to children's growth and development.

FIVE COMMON MODELS

In addition to the largely hortatory and normative scholarship summarized above, much of the relevant literature on professional development describes its various forms, formats, or activities. Though scores of particular designs have appeared over time, all correspond fundamentally to one of five models synthesized by Guskey, Sparks, and Susan Loucks-Horsley: individually guided, collaborative problem solving, observation and assessment of teaching, training, or action research.

The essence of the individually guided model is that educators define and direct their own learning, much like when secondary or higher education students exercise options for independent study. As its name suggests, individual choice and self-direction are integral to this type of professional development. In an ideal form of this model, for example, a teacher first determines a goal or learning objective, then decides upon a means of working toward the goal—both completely independently. Often, in practice, either the goal or the planned activities may be required to be approved by an administrator or linked directly to school priorities for student learning. Examples of individually guided activities are self-selected reading, journaling or writing for publication, videotaping and analyzing one's performance, developing a portfolio of work samples and reflections, taking or teaching a college or online course, and attending a professional conference.

In contrast to individually guided professional development, the collaborative problem-solving model involves two or more educators thinking and working together. It is grounded on the premise that, through the collaborative work, worthwhile learning will occur. Constructivist theories suggesting that learning is a social as well as cognitive process provide additional grounding for the kinds of interpersonal and group discussion, dialogue, and reflection that characterize the collaborative problem-solving model.

In contemporary practice, this design also takes a variety of forms, including, for example, (a) school improvement or shared decision-making teams, whose charges can be broad and wide ranging, (b) curriculum development committees, with goals often more narrowly defined by content area, (c) study groups, wherein participants learn together about a topic of mutual interest or concern, (d) assessment teams that create tests or other measures of student learning outcomes, to be used by multiple teachers, (e) mentoring, with a more experienced educator helping and guiding

a novice, (f) critical friends, wherein either pairs or groups challenge and support each other in any number of areas, and (g) student work analysis groups, with participants examining samples of student work to enable improvement of lesson design.

A third model of professional development is observation and assessment. It also is grounded in collaboration, but in this instance primarily by pairs of teachers and focused specifically on observations in each other's classrooms. The goal is to serve as a second set of eyes and ears for one another, for subsequent joint discussion and reflection on the instructor's teaching and the students' learning. Sometimes this model is referred to as peer coaching, cognitive coaching, or collegial supervision. However, the essence of the model is formative, rather than summative, assessment. That is, classroom data and feedback are provided exclusively for the observed teacher's consideration for personal growth and self-improvement. In addition, the observing teacher is expected to benefit from being immersed in a colleague's classroom and seeing first-hand others' approaches to students, the curriculum, and instruction.

Three steps are typically included in this model:

1. *Pre-observation conversation* about what would be most helpful for the observer to focus on

2. *Classroom observation* with some systematic way of recording information about the agreed upon focus

3. *Postobservation dialogue* in which the observer and the observed analyze and discuss the recorded data

A fourth model, called training or skills training, has traditionally dominated professional development in education. The research of Bruce Joyce and Beverly Showers demonstrates that there are five components necessary for training to result in both effective acquisition of skills *and* transfer of those skills to the workplace:

1. *Theory.* Presentation of the theory or rationale that defines the value, importance, and use of the skill. (Often this takes the form of large-group, direct instruction or expert lecturing. It is the "telling" or "describing" portion of training.)

2. *Demonstration* or modeling of the skill, typically by an experienced trainer.

3. *Practice.* Opportunities for learners to practice the skill, both while under the direction of experts and over time in more natural work settings

4. *Feedback.* Timely and constructive feedback on learners' practice, so that they can understand what they are doing well and what needs further refinement

5. *Follow-up or coaching.* Long-term guidance and assistance so that what was practiced in training sessions or other simulations is transferred to the actual work setting

In practice, skills training for educators is often incomplete. That is, it may include one or two of the elements required to be effective, but not all five. Multiple opportunities for practice with feedback, as well as follow-up over time, are frequently neglected or absent. Consequently, the anticipated change in performance on the job does not occur.

The fifth model, action research, also is commonly referred to as inquiry, practitioner research, or reflective action. One way to differentiate this model from the others is to think of it, for example, as teachers conducting miniexperiments, then changing some practice as a result of what is learned from the experiment. The changed practice is what makes this action-oriented research. Its teacher-directed aspects distinguish it from more formal educational research wherein teachers are more likely to be the subjects, rather than the initiators, of empirical studies.

Action research may be an independent, small-group, or whole-school professional development activity. As such, it shares characteristics of the individually guided and collaborative problem-solving models described above. Although action research can take a variety of forms, three steps are common to this model. One or more educators (1) identify a question or area of interest, (2) collect relevant data through active experimentation, and (3) change what they do on the job, based on their interpretation of the data.

RESEARCH ON EFFECTIVE PRACTICES

Despite the emphasis in the professional development literature on varied designs and advocacy for all staff's participation, most of the empirical work on effectiveness has focused on teachers. Recent studies conducted by Beatrice Birman, Laura Desimone, Andrew C. Porter, and Michael Garet suggest that the form or model of professional development is not what matters most to teachers' learning. That is, training in the form of workshops or institutes, as well as multiple variations of any of the other four models summarized

above, all can be effective. Effectiveness derives not from the model but from five other features that cut across design: (1) focus on content knowledge, (2) collective participation, (3) use of active learning strategies, (4) coherence, and (5) duration.

Content Knowledge

First, focusing on content means targeting a staff development activity on a specific subject area or on a subject-specific teaching method, such as increasing teachers' understanding of motion in physics or of the way elementary students solve story problems in mathematics.

This finding is contrary to commonplace practices that focus professional development on generic instructional strategies, such as using cooperative groups, computer technology, or concept maps in the classroom. It is consistent, however, with the increased expectations for student learning reflected in the contemporary curriculum standards of many states and school districts. For example, those standards often expect higher-level thinking of students and abilities to apply, rather than simply recall, information. Accordingly, educators require deeper understanding of particular curriculum content and how students best learn that content. When the latter becomes the focus of professional development, participants' knowledge and skills increase.

Collective Participation

Relatedly, professional development has been found to be more effective when teachers participate in it with grade-level, subject area, or department colleagues from their own school. Such participation contrasts with staff development structures in which teachers from different schools participate individually. Instead, collective participation can beget sharing and problem solving around common concerns, goals, students, curriculum, methods, assessments, and often even supplies and materials.

Active Learning Strategies

In addition to a strong subject matter focus and collective participation, effective professional development is also characterized by opportunities for participants' active learning. This finding is consistent with research on training that demonstrates that hands-on practice is essential for the transfer of new skills to classroom use. Examples of active learning strategies in effective professional development include discussion, application exercises, simulations, planning, reviewing student work, role playing, observing or being observed teaching, and creating presentations, demonstrations, or other written products for authentic audiences.

Coherence

A fourth feature of effective professional development practice is that it is coherent. In this context, synonyms for coherence are *connection, complement,* and *fit.* That is, to be effective, professional development should complement, fit, and be connected to

- Curriculum standards and assessments, because in contemporary schools, both directly influence educators' work and goals
- The substance of previous professional development initiatives, so that learning is experienced as a cumulative and recursive enhancement of prior knowledge

Duration

Last, longer duration contributes to effectiveness, because it increases the frequency of opportunities to incorporate the preceding four features: focus on depth of content, collective participation, active learning strategies, and coherence. The value of longer duration applies to both the professional development activity itself and the time span during which follow-up is supported.

As mentioned earlier, however, consensus on the characteristics of effective professional development remains elusive. Guskey points out that much of the recent research on effective practice has focused on mathematics and science teaching, with no assurances that those findings apply equally well to other subject areas or contexts.

In addition to the five features underscored in Birman and colleagues' work, for example, the National Council for Staff Development's standards for professional development include (a) using disaggregated student data to determine adult learning priorities, (b) linking adult learning closely to student learning goals, (c) organizing adults into learning communities, (d) dedicating sufficient resources to professional development initiatives, (e) attending to equity and quality teaching in professional development content,

(f) creating supportive contexts through skillful leadership, and (g) involving families and other stakeholders in school improvement efforts.

—Marilyn Tallerico

See also adult education; capacity building, of organizations; career stages; collaboration theory; continuing education; human capital; human resource development; learning, theories of; life span development; mentoring; performance assessment; personnel management; portfolios; professional development schools; professional learning communities; school improvement models; schools of education; supervision; working conditions, in schools; workplace trends

Further Readings and References

Birman, B., Desimone, L., Porter, A., & Garet, M. (2000). Designing professional development that works. *Educational Leadership, 57*(8), 28–33.

Gordon, S. (2004). *Professional development for school improvement: Empowering learning communities.* Boston: Allyn & Bacon.

Guskey, T. (2000). *Evaluating professional development.* Thousand Oaks, CA: Corwin Press.

Guskey, T. (2003). What makes professional development effective? *Phi Delta Kappan, 84*(10), 748–750.

Joyce, B., & Showers, B. (2002). *Student achievement through staff development* (3rd ed.). Alexandria, VA: Association for Supervision and Curriculum Development.

National Staff Development Council. (2001). *NSDC Standards for staff development.* Retrieved January 12, 2004, from www.nsdc.org/standards/about.

Sparks, D. (2002). *Designing powerful professional development for teachers and principals.* Oxford, OH: National Staff Development Council.

Sparks, D., & Hirsch, S. (1997). *A new vision for staff development.* Alexandria, VA: Association for Supervision and Curriculum Development & National Staff Development Council.

Sparks, D., & Loucks-Horsley, S. (1990). Models of staff development. In R. Houston (Ed.), *Handbook of research on teacher education* (pp. 234–250). New York: Macmillan.

PROFESSIONAL DEVELOPMENT SCHOOLS

The educational field has been rife with calls for reform over the past several decades. One of these calls for reform has been to create partnerships between K–12 schools and teacher preparation programs in higher education. The Holmes Group, a national coalition of colleges of education in research universities, founded in 1985 and restructured as the Holmes Partnership in 1996, continues to stress the need for developing such relationships. These relationships are typically called professional development schools (PDS).

PDSs are an organizational arrangement pairing K–12 schools with colleges of education or other higher education units preparing teachers or administrators. PDSs are claimed to be a new hybrid educational organization governed by both K–12 school systems and higher education partners. Partners must be accountable to each other as well as to other stakeholders if the PDS is to thrive.

PDSs became popularized in the mid-1980s when the Holmes Group used the term in a report titled *Tomorrow's Teachers.* By definition, a PDS is a collaborative partnership, although there are many structural models, prompting some criticism about what really qualifies as a PDS. Ideally, PDSs are mutually beneficial partnerships between K–12 schools and institutions of higher education responsible for teacher preparation. Other agencies such as teacher unions or human service agencies can be partners. Liberal arts colleges are increasingly being included as partners in PDS arrangements. For these partnerships to flourish, there should be common goals and mutually agreed upon outcomes.

A PDS should have a governance structure drawing from the expertise of group members. This new design for governance suggests that school-based administrators must be willing to share their leadership responsibilities, creating spaces for leaders both within the school and elsewhere. It is essential that the school's higher education and other partners have meaningful input into the running of the school if the PDS is to succeed and become a new type of organization. There must be established, trusting relationships if leaders and others are going to be willing to allow others to share in the leadership responsibilities of their educational worlds.

Teachers tend to play a stronger leadership role in professional development schools as they are called upon to teach and evaluate preservice teachers, work collaboratively with university personnel and other teachers, and engage in research about the effectiveness of teaching and learning practices. This change in role for classroom teachers may encourage a greater sense of efficacy and professionalism, resulting in their ability to be more effective teachers.

All partners must find ways to be accountable to each other. In addition, new evaluation designs must be negotiated so the mutually established goals can be assessed in ways each stakeholder group values.

PROFESSIONAL DEVELOPMENT SCHOOL PURPOSES

The purposes of PDSs generally include the simultaneous renewal of teacher education and public K–12 education, better preparation of teacher candidates, professional development for practicing teachers, better understanding by all parties of the issues and needs facing higher education and K–12 educators, and conducting research to improve teaching and learning. There is supposed to be an increased focus on meeting the needs of diverse learning groups in these settings. There are many claims that the PDS can serve as an important avenue for reform in both K–12 and higher education, prompting deep structural changes in both organizations.

By working collaboratively to prepare future teachers, current teachers and university personnel can learn new practices and ideas from each other. According to the underlying premises about PDSs, the university professors bring insights about educational theory to the practicing teachers. By integrating theory into their daily routines, classroom teachers are supposed to develop deeper understandings about why they do what they do in the classroom and how their efforts to teach young people can be improved. Teachers, in turn, help to inform professors about the daily realities of life in the classroom. This information from teachers is supposed to help professors gain deeper insights about how to better prepare future teachers.

Additional goals for many PDSs include improved student learning at all levels preschool–16, development of new school/university partnerships in regions of intense educational and economic need in order to strengthen both partner institutions and the region, increased capability of schools to solve their problems through collaborative research, expanded relationships between theory and practice, more effective use of scarce educational dollars through sharing of resources and expertise, and creation of a body of research about education to aid others in the creation of effective reform strategies to foster educational improvement at all levels.

Another reason for creating a PDS is to provide ongoing professional development for classroom teachers while creating professional learning communities. Having university professors participate as members of the school community may increase opportunities for whole-school professional development. Job-embedded professional development should occur on a regular basis as teachers and university personnel engage in dialogues about best practices for teaching and learning. Typically, PDS goals emphasize the value of engaging in research to explore what works and what does not. As university and K–12 personnel work collaboratively with future teachers and younger students, each group can gain important insights and information to improve interactions with the other as well as to improve the quality of experiences offered to their students.

PROFESSIONAL DEVELOPMENT SCHOOL STRUCTURES

PDS structures vary, but most include the involvement of classroom teachers, university faculty, graduate students, and school administrators at both the K–12 and higher education level. Ideally, a PDS becomes a unique organization, building upon the strengths of both K–12 and higher education. In this way, a PDS becomes a hybrid organization and theoretically is governed by the most engaged stakeholder groups. Governance in these organizations is not easy work. Relationship building and structural supports cannot be shortchanged if people in a PDS are to work together collaboratively and deep cultural changes are to occur and be sustained.

National groups such as the Holmes Partnership and other coalitions and networks promoting PDS arrangements (e.g., the American Association of Colleges of Teacher Education or John Goodlad's National Network for Educational Renewal) provide support and informational resources to personnel in PDSs, helping to support the difficult work of cultural change.

REPORTED BENEFITS

Many have claimed benefits through PDSs, including an improved quality of teacher education, ongoing professional development for practicing teachers, a deepened understanding of K–12 needs by professors, active and ongoing inquiry into best practices for teaching and learning, and improved student learning due to the increased attention placed on teaching and learning. PDSs are intended to be learner-centered

organizations reflecting the best practices for teaching and learning so educators-in-training can learn effective teaching strategies while providing high-quality educational experiences for K–12 students. All PDS members are viewed as active participants and learners. When it works effectively, a PDS can serve as a site of best professional practices, foster a culture of inquiry where professionals critically examine innovation while seeking to identify best practices, and create empowered communities where all participants share in decision making about the school and the learning process. Ideally, the PDS provides opportunities to engage in practices that refocus the work of schools on adult and student learning.

CONTROVERSIES

Controversies surrounding PDSs include the lack of consistency concerning required participants and objectives, financial and governance issues, accountability to multiple stakeholders, an inadequate supply of human resources to deliver programs, assessment practices, and equity issues. PDSs require at least one higher education partner for each K–12 school or school system, but some areas do not have geographic access to these partners. Lack of access can prohibit some K–12 schools from forming a PDS. There have been legislative and other groups concerned about the inequalities created by having some schools in PDS arrangements and other schools without a partnership, especially when this situation occurs within a single school district.

True PDS relationships require a financial and human resource commitment from all partners. In impoverished schools, these commitments may not be possible due to other financial demands. As many colleges and universities face financial and personnel cutbacks, their ability and willingness to engage in a PDS may be diminished.

Institutional promotion and tenure demands for college professors may inhibit their willingness to participate in a PDS. Professors are expected to chair doctoral and/or master-level committees, teach courses, conduct and publish research, and usually are required to engage in outreach or service activities. The intensive requirements of PDS work can interfere with the more acceptable and rewarded forms of faculty productivity.

It is difficult to evaluate the effectiveness of PDSs due to their hybrid nature as an organization. This difficulty is compounded by the lack of consistency about who should be involved and what objectives should be evaluated. While it is important for local contexts and resources to be considered in the design and implementation of a PDS, the lack of consistency has made it difficult for PDSs to be widely recognized as a potential tool for educational reform.

In addition, there has been substantial debate over assessment practices for students and preservice teachers. Ideally, in a PDS there are opportunities to determine the best practices for assessing student work as well as the work of preservice teachers. In many instances, performance-based assessment and portfolio development have been preferred methods for evaluating learning. With the implementation of the No Child Left Behind legislation in 2001, school systems have been faced with meeting federally mandated standards such as Average Yearly Progress (AYP) that are administered and interpreted by each state. This increased emphasis on high-stakes assessment practices has made it more difficult for PDSs to utilize their collaboratively developed approaches to student assessment. Time is a limited commodity, and there does not appear to be adequate time to meet the demands of both assessment approaches on a regular basis.

Governance struggles, brought on by lack of trust as well as organizational requirements for control on certain issues, have made sustainable collaboration difficult in some PDS settings. Concerns about the financial responsibilities of each stakeholder group may have further complicated the creation and sustainability of new organizations comprising all partners. This has become especially troublesome as state education budgets become leaner.

Increasingly, colleges of education are engaging in partnership relationships with K–12 schools. However, not all K–12/higher education partnerships are true PDSs. There are many PDS relationships in name only as well as other types of partnerships never intended to reform student learning or teacher education. Because of this complexity, it will be important for those interested in PDS work to clearly articulate their structures, goals, and purposes to eliminate confusion with other types of partnerships. PDS work is time consuming and frustrating at times, yet overall it is generally professionally rewarding. A PDS is not a static organization. It takes time, energy, and resources to build and maintain PDS partnerships and create the deep structural changes differentiating a PDS from other K–12/higher education partnerships. PDSs

are a unique arrangement between K–12 schools and teacher preparation programs in institutions of higher education that are focused on the simultaneous renewal of both entities.

—*Cynthia J. Reed*

See also adaptiveness of organizations; collaboration theory; constructivism; decision making; democracy, democratic education and administration; diversity; empowerment; governance; group dynamics; Holmes Group; human resource development; innovation, in education; leadership, theories of; learning environments; life span development; literacy, theories of; management theories; mentoring; motivation, theories of; organizational theories; parental involvement; principalship; rational organizational theory; research methods; school improvement models; schools of education; site-based management; staffing, concepts of; systemic reform

Further Readings and References

Goodlad, J. (1994). *Educational renewal: Better teachers, better schools.* San Francisco: Jossey-Bass.
Holmes Group. (1986). *Tomorrow's teachers: A report of the Holmes Group.* East Lansing, MI: Author.
Holmes Group. (1990). *Tomorrow's schools.* East Lansing, MI: Author.
Holmes Group. (1995). *Tomorrow's schools of education: A report of the Holmes Group.* East Lansing, MI: Author.
Kochan, F., & Kunkel, R. (1998). The learning coalition: Professional development schools in partnership. *Journal of Teacher Education, 49*(5), 325–333.
Levine, M., & Trachtman, R. (Eds.). (1997). *Making professional development schools work.* New York: Teachers College Press.
Reed, C., Kochan, F., Kunkel, R., & Ross, M. (2001). Designing evaluation systems that inform, reform, and transform professional development schools. *Journal of Curriculum and Supervision, 16*(3), 188–205.
Stallings, J., & Kowalski, T. (1990). Research on professional development schools. In W. Robert Houston (Ed.), *Handbook on research on teacher education* (pp. 251–256). New York: Macmillan.

PROFESSIONAL LEARNING COMMUNITIES

The continual search for more effective strategies for school improvement has led to a number of new models of school reform. Some of these rely heavily upon findings in the field of human relations and organizational theory. The professional learning community (PLC) represents an emerging model for school improvement that draws from what we know about human relations and organizational change.

While the literature provides various characteristics that describe the operations of a PLC, extensive research has led Dr. Shirley Hord to propose five attributes or dimensions that characterize professional learning communities:

1. *Supportive and shared leadership:* Collegial and facilitative participation of the principal who shares leadership, power, and authority through involving staff in decision making

2. *Shared values and vision:* Shared vision that is developed from a steadfast commitment on the part of staff to students' learning and one that is consistently articulated and referenced in the staff's work

3. *Collective learning and application of learning:* Collective learning among staff and learning application to solutions for addressing the needs of the students

4. *Supportive conditions:* Physical conditions and human capacities that continually support the operation of a PLC through a collegial atmosphere and collective learning

5. *Shared practice:* Visitation and review of each teacher's classroom behavior by colleagues as feedback and assistance activity to actively support both individual and community improvement

These attributes collapse and comprise the majority of characteristics cited within the literature. Additional descriptors offering a vision of how PLCs function include the incorporation of reflective dialogue, a collective focus on student learning, sharing of norms, family-like atmosphere, connectedness, collaborative teaming, results orientation, always seeking to improve, and possessing a collective resolve. The PLC serves as an infrastructure and provides a new way to organize and arrange staff. This infrastructure becomes critical in seeking and implementing new strategies and methods designed for overall school improvement. Current national and state legislation seeks ongoing improvement, regardless of the current status and/or success of the school, thus establishing a need to incorporate strategies designed to promote continual improvement.

Ongoing research has moved beyond the description of PLCs by investigating how schools become PLCs and how this structure is sustained. This new line of research can provide an infrastructure for schoolwide reform and reculturing while focusing on addressing key phases of change. As this research continues to enhance the knowledge base of PLCs, valuable insights will surface in preparing schools with a structure that focuses on both professional and student learning.

—Dianne Olivier

See also adult education; climate, school; collaboration theory; constructivism; decision making; democracy, democratic education and administration; diversity; empowerment; governance; group dynamics; human resource development; innovation, in education; leadership, theories of; learning environments; life span development; management theories; mentoring; motivation, theories of; organizational theories; principalship; rational organizational theory; research methods; school improvement models; schools of education; site-based management; systemic reform; workplace trends

Further Readings and References

Hord, S. (1997). *Professional learning communities: Communities of continuous inquiry and improvement.* Austin, TX: Southwest Educational Development Laboratory.

Hord, S. (1997). *Professional learning communities: What are they and why are they important?* Austin, TX: Southwest Educational Development Laboratory.

Hord, S. (1998). *Creating a professional learning communities: Cottonwood Creek School.* Austin, TX: Southwest Educational Development Laboratory.

Hord, S. (Ed.). (2004). *Learning together—Leading together.* New York: Teachers College Press.

Olivier, D. (2001). *Teacher personal and school culture characteristics in effective schools: Toward a model of a professional learning community.* Unpublished doctoral dissertation, Louisiana State University.

Olivier, D., Hipp, K., & Huffman, J. (2003). Professional learning. community assessment. In J. Huffman & K. Hipp (Eds.), *Reculturing schools as professional learning communities.* Lanham, MD: Scarecrow Press.

🏛 PROMOTION, SOCIAL

Promotion is the change in grade-level assignment at the end of the school year for a student who meets the criteria for advancement to the next highest grade level. Social promotion is the passing of students who have not mastered the academic requirements to successive grades in order to keep them with their peers. The practice of social promotion is often carried out in the interest of a student's social and psychological well-being, without regard to achievement.

Social promotion evolved as a solution to the serious problems caused by grade retention in the nineteenth century. As graded schools began replacing the one-room schoolhouse, students were promoted on "merit," the mastery of fixed academic requirements for each grade level. Approximately one half of the students were retained during their first eight years of school. Many times, students repeated more than one grade. Attrition of students, especially those from poor and immigrant families, was widespread. With loose compulsory attendance and child-labor laws, children, in the early twentieth century, had alternatives to staying in the education system, and ended up in manual work.

During the 1930s to 1970s, school districts adopted policies of social promotion of students by age rather than by merit, lowering the percentage of students who were overaged for their grade level or who dropped out. A consequence of compulsory attendance laws was the dilemma of what to do with students who do not make progress in schools. Low-performing students could stay with their age grouping or with their academic peers. Educators frequently chose to keep students with their same-age peers and social promoted them.

In 1999, the U.S. Department of Education, acting on the challenge from President Bill Clinton, encouraged educators to end social promotion, while at the same time ensuring that all students have the opportunity and assistance to meet academic standards. Along with the political rhetoric, public opinion strongly favors ending social promotion. Nearly 75% of parents and more than 80% of teachers and employers think it is worse to promote students to the next grade who have not mastered the basics than to retain them. Yet, there are no statistics kept on social promotion, so it is difficult to validate its widespread use. In a survey of 85 urban school districts by the American Federation of Teachers (AFT), including the 40 largest in the United States, there were no districts with a policy endorsing social promotion. There are, however, indicators that it has long been a practice for dealing with low-performing students. A national survey of teachers by the AFT indicated that a majority of them had promoted unprepared students.

The common alternative to social promotion is retention or requiring the student to remain at the same grade level in the subsequent school year. Despite decades of research findings on the negative effects of grade retention, the use of retention has gained momentum. However, most districts have vague criteria for promotion, lack uniform grading policies, and have limitations on retention (e.g., who can be retained and

how often), making the practice of social promotion inevitable.

The negative effects on school budgets resulting from the added costs of increasing the time it takes a student to complete school leads to the abandonment of tough retention policies and renewal of social promotion. As an alternative, retention is expensive, costing an average of $10 billion to $14 billion annually. A phenomenon referred to as "economic" promotion occurs as the added costs of retaining students cause school districts to quietly abandon the counterproductive practice and begin to move children along through the grades. Through the decades, a school reform pendulum swings between the two extremes of retention and social promotion policies that have not worked in the past and lack any evidence they will work in the future.

Critics of social promotion argue that it hurts students by placing them in grades where they cannot do the work, burdens teachers with accommodating the underprepared students, gives parents a false sense of their child's abilities, and does little to address the learning deficits of low-performing students. At the same time, it erodes society's faith in education as colleges and businesses divert millions of dollars to provide remedial instruction to high school graduates who lack skills in reading, writing, and math.

In contrast, if ending social promotion means more retained students, there are additional dilemmas for teachers, children, and parents. Grouping children of varied ages together based only on academic performance is not completely bereft of serious problems. Placing 13-year-olds with 10- and 11-year-olds, or placing 16-year-olds with 12- and 13-year-old students, may not be acceptable alternatives.

Interest in social promotion is clearly tied to standards and accountability. The public believes that students should master higher standards in core subjects as a condition of promotion, while nearly 90% of parents favor policies that require students to pass a test to be promoted. Nationwide, school districts have put in place strict new promotion standards and have abandoned social promotion policies that push students ahead, regardless of their academic performance. Unfortunately, neither social promotion nor retention is effective for improving student achievement. The results of both are unacceptably high dropout rates and diminished life chances.

The social promotion controversy confronts irreconcilable objectives. Differences in social and personal adjustment of children and youth may render varied age groupings based solely on academic performance as undesirable. Moreover, policies requiring only students who achieve at grade level to be promoted does not solve the problem of social promotion. Grade-level promotion standards have not been clearly defined, and regardless of what standard is set for any grade level in any subject, there will be a dispersion of student performance around an average. Discussions about social promotion must address underlying causes for low achievement and seek improvements in schooling and teaching practices to ensure that all children succeed.

—*Bobbie J. Greenlee*

See also achievement tests; Black education; bureaucracy; child development theories; class size; classroom management; cognition, theories of; compensatory education; critical race theory; cultural capital; discrimination; diversity; dropouts; elementary education; expectations, teacher and student cultures; individual differences, in children; intelligence; Latinos; learning environments; literacy, theories of; mainstreaming and inclusion; parental involvement; school improvement models; tracking, of students; underachievers, in schools

Further Readings and References

American Federation of Teachers. (1997). *Passing on failure: District promotion policies and practices.* Washington, DC: Author.

Goodlad, J. (2004). *Romances with schools.* New York: McGraw-Hill

Johnson, J., & Duffett, A. (2003). *Where we are now: 12 things you need to know about public opinion and public schools.* Public Agenda. Retrieved from http://www.publicagenda.org/specials/wherewearenow/wherewearenow.htm.

North Carolina Education Research Council. (1999). *Research on retention and social promotion: Synthesis and implications for policy.* NCERC Policy Brief. Retrieved from http://erc.northcarolina.edu/docs/publications/socialpromo.pdf.

U.S. Department of Education. (1999). *Taking responsibility for ending social promotion: A guide for educators and state and local leaders.* Washington, DC: Government Printing Office.

PROPERTY TAX

The property tax has long been the mainstay of local government finance, including public school finance. In 2000, property tax collections represented 28.6% of total state and local tax collections. Its long-standing role as the primary source of public school revenue was assumed by state governments during the substantial

school finance reforms of the 1970s. Nevertheless, the property tax steadily produces substantial amounts of revenue for local governments, and except for a few local governments that can levy sales and income taxes, it is the only broad-based tax available to local governments, including school districts.

THE PROPERTY TAX PROCESS

The property tax differs from other state and local taxes in at least two important ways. First, both the tax rate and the tax base are determined by government. Unlike an income or sales tax, for which the value of the base (income or sales) is usually established by private economic activity, the property tax base, or *property value,* often must be estimated when market transactions are not available. This is because the property tax is a tax on wealth, a stock variable, rather than an annual economic flow (e.g., income or sales). Therefore, methods and procedures for assessing the value of property for tax purposes must be part of the property tax structure. Second, different government agencies are responsible for establishing the tax base (assessed value), while another sets the tax rate.

Setting the Tax Base

To set the tax base, first, the *assessed value* (taxable value) of each piece of property is computed by an assessor from an estimate of the *market value* of the property made according to a specific set of procedures, usually established by state law. Once the market value is established, the assessed value is set by law or practice as a specific percentage of market value. This percentage is the *assessment ratio.* Tax assessors are generally professional employees of general-purpose local governments such as cities or townships, although in some areas assessors are still locally elected officials. In most states, local assessors are bound by state laws and procedures, and their assessments are subject to county and/or state review. If different types or classes of property (e.g., residential, commercial, industrial, agricultural) are assessed according to different assessment ratio rules so that the *effective tax rate* (i.e., tax paid divided by market value) varies by class, the tax is called a *classified property tax.* Under a classified tax, residential property is usually assessed at a lower ratio than commercial and industrial property. Classification allows government to alter the relative property tax burdens among different types of property. In addition, some types of property may be exempt from property tax. In these cases, the assessed value is implicitly set equal to zero, although in practice exempt properties usually are not assessed.

The property tax base, or net assessed value (NAV), is established at the standard assessment date ("tax day") for the taxing unit (e.g., school district, city, township). As noted above, assessed value is generally a statutorily defined percentage of the value initially appraised by an assessor. The most widely used standard for property appraisal is *market value,* or cash price a property would bring in a competitive market. Since records are kept on home sales, determining the market value of homes is relatively straightforward. For homes that have not sold recently, sale prices for comparable homes are used to set market value. However, while this approach is technically feasible, maintaining updated tax rolls entails political as well as technical challenges. Some feel it is unfair to tax a homeowner on unrealized gains in home value, as happens where tax rolls are updated regularly.

A few states depart from this market value standard. One alternative assessment standard is the acquisition value or assessment-on-sale ("Welcome Stranger") system required in California by Proposition 13 (1978), in Florida by Amendment 10 (1992), and in Michigan by Proposal A (1994). Under this system, assessments are adjusted regularly but rise more slowly than market value until they are sold. At that time, they are revalued at the new transaction price. Such acquisition value assessment creates several problems. First, it distorts the property market, as prospective buyers face a higher property tax than would a prospective seller. Second, it creates a property record substructure of sales without recorded deeds as people seek to avoid reassessment and higher property taxes. Third, this approach creates "horizontal inequities" as owners of homes with equal market value pay widely different property taxes.

The assessment of nonresidential property presents additional issues. For example, commercial enterprises that use land and buildings that are rarely sold cannot be assessed according to market value. Consequently, a process called "capitalizing income" or "capitalizing rents" is often used. By this method, value equals total sales divided by profit expressed as a rate of return. This method of capitalized valuation may not be practical, however, for a business with multiple plants where it is difficult to allocate profits and sales to individual plants. In such cases, value is set as replacement costs less depreciation. Unlike homeowners, businesses are allowed to depreciate plants and factories as an incentive to reinvest and improve properties over time. Thus, true value for a plant or factory would be replacement cost less accumulated depreciation.

Farmland poses another set of issues. Although a market generally exists for farmland, the actual selling price often exceeds the farming value of the land, particularly for farms near growing urban and suburban areas. Furthermore, even if the market value of farmland equaled the capitalized value, a drought or other natural disaster could reduce a farm's earnings to zero in any given year, making it difficult to pay property taxes on a farm that retained some value. Consequently, every state uses some method to limit property taxes on farmland. The traditional approach is to assess the value of farmland in its current use, which may be less than its full market value. For example, farmland on the edge of an urban area might be substantially more valuable if used for residential property. Such *use-value assessment* of farmland serves to prevent increases in property taxes on farmland as these alternative uses become more attractive and may help to curb urban sprawl.

Another variation of use-value assessment is to assess the value of farmland according to current use but impose a deferred tax on the full value for some fixed number of past years if the property is converted to nonfarm use. In this way, the tax advantage conferred by use-value assessment, at least for a number of years, is recaptured by the taxing governments if the tax advantage does not succeed in preventing conversion.

Setting the Tax Rate

To set the tax rate, the revenue from any tax is computed by multiplying the tax base by a tax rate. Most tax rates change only with special legislative action; they are the portion of the fiscal system that changes incrementally while the base is defined in statute and is changed less often. Examples are the state sales tax and state and federal income taxes. Property tax rates, in contrast, are typically set as part of the annual budget process. The rate is generally readopted each year at a level sufficient to balance the government's operating budget and service debt. Thus, the property tax rate (r) may be represented as follows: $r = (E-NPR)/NAV$, where E is total expenditures approved by government, NPR is total estimated revenue from nonproperty tax sources, and NAV is net assessed value in the taxing jurisdiction.

Property tax rates have historically been specified in *mills,* with the rate referred to as the *millage.* One mill is one tenth of 1%, or $1 of tax per each $1,000 of taxable value. In recent years, there has been some tendency to refer to property tax rates in terms of a percentage (similar to other tax rates) or dollars of tax per $100 or $1,000 of taxable value. In every state, the local governments are constrained in setting the property tax rate by state laws limiting the tax rate, property tax revenue, or both. In some cases, a referendum (popular vote) is required to set the property tax rate or revenue.

Property Tax Relief Measures

States use a variety of measures to reduce property taxes for specific groups of taxpayers or classes of property. These measures are generally intended to make the property tax and the overall state and local tax structure more progressive by reducing relative tax burdens for low-income taxpayers. Such methods of tax relief include exemptions of assessed value for homesteads, state government tax credits or rebates for local residential property taxes, and limits on assessed values.

The simplest and most widely used tax relief method for houses is the *homestead exemption.* These exemptions allow homeowners a specified assessed value base before any property taxes are levied. Such exemption programs are politically popular but do create some problems. First, the programs usually have a statewide purpose, but because property taxes generally support local government, the revenue loss is local. Second, the homestead exemption often fails to target relief to low-income households. All people falling into the applicable categories (e.g., all homeowners, seniors, veterans) receive aid regardless of income. Third, if the exemption is sufficiently broad, as in the case of general homestead exemption programs, property tax rates may have to be increased substantially to recover lost revenue. Fourth, individual exemption programs generally exclude renters, many of whom are much less affluent than homeowners.

Another popular property tax relief mechanism is a state-government-financed credit or rebate for property taxes paid to local governments. This type of property tax relief usually takes the form of a rebate paid to the taxpayer or a credit against state income tax. (A refundable credit is paid to a local property taxpayer with little or no state income tax liability.) The relief generally is targeted to specific groups of taxpayers (e.g., seniors, the disabled), and the credit or rebate usually applies to property taxes that exceed a specified percentage of a taxpayer's income. Because of this last feature, these credits are often referred to as "circuit breakers." Just as an electrical circuit breaker will be tripped by a circuit overload, this tax relief

takes effect only when a taxpayer's income is overburdened by property taxes. Property tax credits were devised as a way of preventing senior citizens with high-valued houses relative to their retirement incomes from having to sell their houses because of the property tax. A number of states thus restrict their programs to elderly taxpayers who meet other criteria. Nonelderly low-income homeowners, however, may face similar overloads as well, particularly in the early years of home ownership or when a family income earner becomes unemployed. Some states allow renters to benefit from their circuit breaker programs. This practice is based on the presumption that renters bear a portion of the property tax burden on the units they occupy. (Of course, the ability of landlords to shift all or a portion of the property tax burden onto tenants depends on the market conditions for rental housing.) Renter relief presumes a property tax equivalent as a specified percentage of rent paid.

Circuit breakers employ either *threshold* or *sliding-scale* relief formulas. The former approach defines a threshold percentage of income as the overload level. Property tax payments above that overload level are eligible for partial relief. Relief is computed by a formula of the following sort: $R = t(PT-kI)$, where R is tax relief, t is the percentage of the overload that will be rebated back to the taxpayer, PT is the property tax payment, k is the overload percentage, and I is family income. Some states reduce their cost by increasing the threshold percentage as income increases.

An alternative approach is the sliding-scale relief formula. Here, relief is computed as a percentage of property tax payment, with the percentage falling as family income rises: $R = zPT$, where z is the percentage of property tax relieved for the income class and R and PT are as defined above. Circuit breakers are flexible and easy to administer in conjunction with the state income tax. These formulas can target families in greatest need of relief and are financed from state rather than local revenue. One drawback is that they may encourage higher property tax rates as some costs of local services are shifted to the states. Such concerns, however, are generally outweighed by the circuit breaker's contribution to tax equity.

Finally, in addition to these property tax relief measures adopted by states, property tax payments can be deducted from federal income tax payments. This deductibility reduces the impact of the property tax on homeowners who itemize deductions on their federal income tax and provides some incentive for increased housing consumption.

PROPERTY TAX INCIDENCE

In general, the ultimate payer of a tax can differ from the initial payer. This difference can be most easily seen in the case of business taxation. The initial incidence of a tax on business property is on the business. However, businesses "shift" the final incidence or burden of the tax to others: to the owners of the capital supporting the business, in the form of lower profits; to the vendors supplying the businesses, in the form of lower prices; to the employees of the businesses, in the form of lower wages; or to the customers of the business, in the form of higher prices.

The incidence of the property tax has been the subject of some debate among public finance economists. It has been argued that the property tax is primarily a tax on housing, and therefore regressive. This argument holds that because the tax is essentially a proportional tax on the value of a dwelling unit, and since lower-income families tend to spend a higher proportion of their wealth on housing, property tax liabilities constitute a larger fraction of the incomes of lower-income families. However, the "new view" of the property tax, based upon modern general equilibrium analysis, finds that the average rate of the property tax across all jurisdictions functions essentially as a tax on all capital. That is, because nearly all local communities are taxing local capital, the average rate of the tax essentially becomes a national tax on capital. Because higher income people tend to own more capital, the property tax tends to be progressive. Regarding the tax burden that arises from the differences in property taxes around the national average, a positive correlation among the states between per capita income and effective property tax rates has been reported. Because the effect of these property tax rate differentials across the states is to hurt those with higher rates, these tax burdens appear to be progressive. It is difficult to differentiate empirically between the two models, due to their similar predictions. That is, both theories imply that the benefits and costs of local programs are borne locally and are capitalized into local property values.

STABILITY AND GROWTH

One major criticism of the property tax is that it is not responsive to economic growth. It has been observed that the income elasticity of the property tax is less than one (median estimate was 0.87), meaning that as aggregate income rises, property tax revenues rise more slowly. As a result, governments that depend heavily on property taxes (e.g., most local school districts) must raise their property tax rates to meet the rising service levels demanded by the public, including education.

This low income elasticity of revenue yield is characteristic of a stable revenue source. This attribute is beneficial in times of economic recession because revenue collections will fall more slowly than aggregate income. Thus, the property tax is considered a stable revenue source precisely because it is relatively unresponsive to both economic growth and decline.

—Michael Addonizio

See also accountability; boards of education; budgeting; bureaucracy; class size; collective bargaining; elections, of school boards, bond issues; finance, of public schools; governance; salary and salary models; staffing, concepts of; taxes, to support education; unions, of teachers

Further Readings and References

Aaron, H. (1975). *Who pays the property tax?* Washington, DC: Brookings Institution.

Fisher, R. (1996). *State and local public finance* (2nd ed.). Chicago: Irwin.

Mikesell, J. (1995). *Fiscal administration* (4th ed.). Belmont, CA: Wadsworth.

Monk, D., & Brent, B. (1997). *Raising money for schools: A guide to the property tax.* Thousand Oaks, CA: Corwin Press.

Netzer, D. (1966). *Economics of the property tax.* Washington, DC: Brookings Institution.

Odden, A., & Picus, L. (2004). *School finance: A policy perspective* (3rd ed.). Boston: McGraw-Hill.

Zodrow, G. (2001). Reflections on the new view and the benefit view of the property tax. In W. E. Oates (Ed.), *Property taxation and local government finance.* Cambridge, MA: Lincoln Institute of Land Policy.

PSYCHOLOGY, TYPES OF

Psychology, in its broadest sense, is the study of human behavior. It involves the investigation of learning, motivation, memory, personality, intelligence, and leadership. Psychological theory provides the framework by which causation, prediction, and control of behavior can be systematically addressed. Those types of psychology most closely related to the field of education include

- Behaviorism
- Developmental psychology
- Humanistic psychology
- Descriptive psychology

- Social psychology
- Cognitive psychology
- Psychometry and psychological testing

Behaviorism, or behavioral psychology, is based primarily on the work of Edward Thorndike and B. F. Skinner. It is an attempt to address human behavior from a scientific, functionalist, objectivist perspective. Behaviorism relies on direct observation of measurable behavioral phenomena. The prime focus of behavioral psychology is to determine the effect of consequences on behavior and thereby enhance learning, motivation, and performance. The construct encompassed in Thorndike's law of effect, that behaviors that are followed by positive consequences tend to be repeated and those that are followed by aversive or neutral consequences tend to fall out of use, is the basis for the application of behaviorism in educational settings. By understanding the manner in which consequences are delivered (reinforcement schedules), the nature of past consequences (reinforcement history), and the strength of specific antecedents (discriminative stimuli), environments can be designed to enhance learning and promote positive outcomes.

The work of Donald Baer, Montrose Wolf, Todd Risley, and Vance Hall in the 1970s and 1980s established applied behavior analysis as the preeminent form of behaviorism. At this time, the focus of behaviorism ceased to be on basic research, and the established principles of behaviorism were applied to "real world" problems of social importance (many involving educational settings). During this period, many of those techniques that today are established educational practice were developed and validated (i.e., systematic attention, time-out, token economies, response cost). In addition, behaviors from toilet training to spelling and math proficiency or on-task behavior were targeted for behavior modification. The target of such intervention was usually the specific behaviors of a given individual. Therefore, single subject research designs for applied research were developed. The impact of behaviorism in education has been most directly felt in the areas of special education and classroom management. Leadership and administration have also been impacted by behavioral psychology via Frederick Taylor's scientific management.

Developmental psychology focuses the normal cognitive, affective, and physical processes and how they change as an individual grows. Those developmental psychology theories most pertinent to the profession

of education focus on social development and learning. Such theories are either stage theories (emphasizing movement from one level of functioning to another, more advanced level) or sequence theories (generally age independent and emphasizing a sequential progression through observable behaviors, ways of thinking, or world views).

Stage theories include Erik Erikson's theory of psychosocial development, Jean Piaget's theory of cognitive development, and Robert Havighurst's theory of developmental tasks. All three of these theories have had a significant effect on education and continue to affect the field through applications to curricular and instructional issues. Erikson's theory, emphasizing the successful resolution of problems at a given developmental stage as a predictor of future success, has had a significant effect on K–12 education. Erikson suggests that the stages of his theory are interconnected and possess both important events to be addressed and a developmental crisis to be resolved. In essence, mastering the tasks that make up the significant event and resolution of the developmental crisis at any stage has a long-lasting impact on a person's self-image and view of society. Schools have been influenced by Erikson's theory in curricular, instructional, and social contexts. In addition, compensatory and special education services both have a basis in Erikson's theory. Academic support programs in elementary and middle schools and extracurricular secondary programs (both social and preprofessional) are the direct result of the application of Erikson's theory to educational settings.

Piaget's theory has long held the primary position among those developmental theories employed by educators. The concept of "developmentally appropriate practice" as a catalyst for enhancing student learning and as a precursor for movement to the next stage of development has long been a basic tenet of elementary education. Piaget's principles of activity-based learning and individual construction of knowledge still underpin best practice in elementary education and form the foundation of constructivism.

Havighurst formulated a theory of socially constructed developmental tasks embedded within the schools. He hypothesized that each grade level of the schools is infused with tasks to be mastered that are socially and culturally agreed upon as being important. Havighurst further felt that mastery (or the lack thereof) of these school-related developmental tasks was directly related to future school and life success.

He further hypothesized that the impact of the majority culture on the school curriculum and the associated developmental tasks placed minority students at risk for academic failure. Havighurst's theory formed the foundation for compensatory education and multicultural studies.

While stage theories tend to be more prominent in education, sequence theories have also had significant influence. Sequence theories include Abraham Maslow's hierarchy of needs and Claire Graves's theory of sociobiological development. Maslow's hierarchy of needs, along with behaviorism, has had a primary influence on thought and practice in the field of education. Graves's theory of sociobiological development has long been employed in rehabilitation counseling and business settings but is gaining credence and acceptance in educational leadership.

Graves was a psychologist who developed a sociobiological theory of human development that emphasized an individual's need to solve specific problems or answer specific questions at a given developmental level. Maslow suggested that all behavior is driven by innate needs that range from lower-level needs (physiological, safety, love/belonging) to upper-level needs (self-esteem, self-actualization). The lower-level needs are termed "deficiency needs" or needs that necessarily must be met for a person to function at a minimum level. The upper-level needs he labeled "being needs" or those needs that can never be completely met and lead to growth toward mature psychological functioning. Maslow arranged the needs in a hierarchical pattern and theorized that the needs at a specific level must be adequately addressed before a person could be motivated by higher-level needs.

While self-actualization was seen by Maslow as the ultimate goal of human development, self-actualized individuals are, in a sense, unmotivated. The behavior of self-actualized persons is not directed toward obtaining specific items, objects, or states to satisfy a deficit. They are focused on achieving their potential and knowing and understanding themselves and their world.

Maslow's theory is a theory that bridges the gap between developmental and humanistic psychology. It holds direct application for schools and schooling in programs for gifted and talented children, individual counseling, free and reduced meals, and constructivist learning applications. It further set the stage for the humanistic psychology movement.

Humanistic psychology is rooted in Maslow's work and emphasizes self-determination, self-evaluation, personal perceptions, and individual choice of goals and activities. Humanistic psychology is based on the premise that understanding is individual and personal in nature and that individuals can find the solutions to their own problems via free choice and a supportive environment. Carl Rogers and Art Combs were those humanistic psychologists who have had the most profound influence on education.

Humanistic psychology is a forerunner of postmodernism due to its emphasis on the deconstruction of events and one's individual construction of reality. Both Rogers's client-centered approach and Combs's phenomenology emphasize personal perceptions, attitudes, and feelings.

Rogers's nondirective therapy was built on Maslow's concept of self-actualization, which Rogers termed the *actualizing tendency* present in all individuals. Rogers also developed the concept of *organismic valuing*. This concept states that all persons have the answers to their problems and/or questions within themselves. Rogers's most important contribution to humanistic psychology is likely the concept of unconditional positive regard. This is a positive and accepting feeling toward others and their perceptions or positions. Rogers stated that growth toward more positive psychological states was dependent on the presence of unconditional positive regard.

Arthur Combs was a humanistic psychologist who developed the theory of phenomenology. Phenomenology was a precursor to postmodernism (as was the entire field of humanistic psychology) due to its emphasis on each individual's unique construction of reality. Combs identified "frames of reference" and the associated "phenomenal field" as the means by which individuals interpreted events in the world and selected appropriate courses of action. For Combs, all human behavior was purposeful yet not based on the "facts" as others see them but on the "facts" as that individual sees them. Combs identified the phenomenal field as each person's complete and unique field of awareness at any given moment, and all behavior, without exception, was determined by and pertinent to this field. While each of us sees errors or illusions in the phenomenal field of another, we seldom see the same features in our own perceptual field.

Combs's basic tenet was that we must take individuals as they are and work forward from that point. The reason that students or employees in an educational setting often present problem behaviors is due to the nature of their personal phenomenal field and interpretation of reality. Before behavior can change, the phenomenal field must change.

Combs's work has had a significant impact on both conflict resolution and administrator/teacher perceptions (particularly in relation to the postevaluative conference). His research also forms the foundation for the current "dispositions movement" in teacher education.

Descriptive psychology (DP) is a set of systematically related conceptual distinctions designed to provide formal access to all facts and possible facts about persons, their behavior, and the real world in which persons operate. It grew out of Peter Ossorio's profound dissatisfaction with contemporary psychological theory and practice, which he saw as unnecessarily deterministic and reductionistic in ways that were detrimental both to understanding persons' behavior and to working constructively with persons in educational and therapeutic practices. The relevance of DP to educational theory and leadership can be seen in three examples. How does a person have the ability to create or socially construct his or her own world? Why is the task of providing leadership for schools and school district so challenging? And what principles and concepts are relevant to effective therapy?

Ossorio thought that a person had status in the world as an actor, as an observer, and as a critic. From the actor's perspective, to act is to select among options and to shape one's world by the way one treats those options. In this sense, then, people's behavior is creative rather than merely reflective of their circumstances. Their behavior gives value or meaning to their movements. The observer's role is one of noting what has happened, and the critic's role is that of appraising the success or failure of one's actions and making appropriate corrections if necessary. The actor-observer-critic schema provides the formal distinctions necessary to represent human self-regulation—something that we expect adult humans to be able to do.

In DP, freedom and creativity are built into the notion of a person's behavior. What requires explanation are (a) constraints on a person's freedom and (b) the development of one's ability to create a world. The major constraints lie in (a) human limitations vis-à-vis the physical world, (b) one's embodiment (its age, health, damage due to accidents or illness, and strength of one's physical body), and (c) one's eligibilities due to membership in various communities. With respect to (a), I will not be able to wave my arms and then take off flying like Peter Pan. With respect to (b), diseases may strike that lead to long-term limitations in what I can do for myself. With respect to (c), each community that I am a member of provides me with some positions, but not others, from which to play the game of life. One's ability to create one's own world gets enhanced by empirical discoveries or inventions that alter how we can treat the physical world. With the variety of aircraft that we have invented, persons can fly—although not just like Peter Pan. The state of one's body can be altered through exercise, diet, and physical therapy. One's position in one's communities can be changed by education, training, and other preparation for new roles. Relationships can be changed via changes in one's own behavior. Treating another as someone to be trusted invites reciprocation; whether the other reciprocates or not is informative about the relationship. DP provides a framework within which both the freedom to construct one's world and the constraints on successful constructions can be understood.

In DP, significance is a formal parameter of behavior, and the classic assessment question is, What is the person doing by doing that? Following one's answers to the question that are consistent with the facts of the case will typically permit the development of a coherent explanation of behavior. Actions are things that one can choose to engage in or not, whereas happenings are beyond one's control. The critic's function is for the benefit of the actor. When functioning in the critic's position, one has tremendous power to define what is acceptable versus not and to hand down judgments. For many clients, opportunities to learn forgiveness and compassion are central to being in a new behavioral world. Rather than Rogers's single status of "unconditional acceptance," DP identifies nine statuses that offer a positive place but not a total positive regard that is naïve and unrealistic. Among these are "one who makes sense," "one whose interests come first," and "one who is an agent."

Many DP advances in organizational psychology have been directed toward the conflicts within organizations between different functions and toward systematic procedure to enhance productivity. Two crucial features of organizations have been identified. The first is that an organization is a community with a distinctive mission and that this feature of organizations provides a rationale both for a manager and for his or her moral authority in the stewardship of resources. Resources and activities not directed toward the accomplishment of the organizational mission are, at the least, wasteful and, in the extreme, criminal. The

DP approach allows for a form of systems theory that distinguishes the multiple perspectives from which any single organization may be viewed. The crucial feature of this analysis is the notion that every organization, to be well managed, requires the manager to view it from multiple perspectives. Typically, these perspectives will take the form of financial, people and production perspectives, and any organizational policy or principle that does not allow success from all three perspectives will ultimately produce problems and organizational failure. Of particular interest to descriptive psychologists are the "on-behalf-of" organizations as opposed to the classic command-and-control or market-driven organizations. Such organizations (i.e., schools) provide services to a group of people (students and parents) who may have little say about the nature of services provided and that are paid for by yet another group (taxpayers). When a school system attempts to introduce a new instructional curriculum for the benefit of students, parents may not see the curriculum as the best method of teaching the subject, because it differs from the way they were taught, and school board members may wonder whether the proposal constitutes the best use of funds provided by the taxpayers. Differences can arise in this type of situation because each group has a different customer in mind and thus a different perspective on what constitutes a success.

What is required to work out such differences is leadership—not merely management. Leadership, from a DP perspective (in contrast to management), is a behavioral notion, whereas management implies that one has a certain formal position, for example, chairman of the board or principal of a school. Leaders work through any of a number of practices such as motivational, helping to develop relevant perspectives that are missing, providing training in skills required to solve organizational dilemmas, or providing the coordination required for successful action. In the special case of "on-behalf-of" organizations, the leader has the special task of helping members to recognize their different perspectives and to create an atmosphere in which these perspectives and values can each be honored. Because each group's best solution in the educational example above will often not be a best solution for the others, the task is to keep members looking at the issues from all viewpoints to look for good, rather than "perfect," solutions for each. When and if everyone can see a good solution, then the dilemma has been resolved. Such a process

serves to keep each group committed to the final product and willing to work for it.

Social psychology emphasizes human social behavior and how that behavior influences us. Social psychologists apply scientific methodology to human behavior in an attempt to understand that it is influenced by the actual, imagined, or implied presence of other persons. Kurt Lewin's field theory and Albert Bandura's social learning theory are among the most influential social psychology theories in the field of education.

Lewin is considered to be the founder of the field of social psychology. He developed field theory on the perspective that both internal and external factors influenced behavior. He felt that internal, goal-directed forces came into conflict with external, restraining forces to influence individual behavior. Individuals' "cognitive field" allowed them to interpret environmental events and determine courses of action. Lewin's research has influenced the educational areas of management, organizational behavior, and group dynamics.

Bandura's social learning theory incorporates the principles of behaviorism with those of social psychology. Bandura felt that while behavior was indeed influenced by antecedents and consequences, it also was influenced (primarily) by observing the relationship between behavior and consequences in others. He stated that the relationship between reinforcement and antecedents was mediated by internal structures and that most reinforcement was naturalistic (naturally existing in the environment) and vicarious in nature. Special education practices such as attending to a student producing desirable behaviors (e.g., in seat, on task) while ignoring those producing less desirable behaviors are rooted in Bandura's research. The importance of positive role models, mentoring, field-based practica, and shadowing programs in schools and schooling also find support in Bandura's work.

Cognitive psychology is an area of psychology that emphasizes internal cognitive processes such as language, problem solving, and memory. It first emerged in the 1950s and became formalized during the 1970s. Cognitive psychology includes the emerging field of cognitive neuroscience, which focuses on the molecular and chemical basis of cognition and consciousness and metacognitive approaches to problem solving.

While cognitive psychology developed from and was influenced by a wide variety of theoretical perspectives, the individual primarily responsible for the initial influences of cognitive psychology on education was Donald Hebb. Hebb developed the notion of synaptic firing as the basis for learning and memory. In essence, repeated firing of a synapse during a learning activity strengthened the neurons and caused metabolic changes at the synapse, which increased its future efficiency. When groups of these neurons became associated or consolidated into a cell assembly during learning, memory was strengthened. Many groups of neurons can become so interconnected that once a behavior begins, it persists long after the original stimulus has disappeared. This "consolidation theory" is currently the most widely accepted explanation of neural learning. Hebb also suggested that the connections of neurons into phase cycles or phase sequences in complex ways was the basis for thinking and reasoning. This theory influenced and continues to influence the field of education in the drill, repetition, and guided practice methodologies in classroom instruction. The additional practice provided by homework also has support in Hebb's theory.

The work of cognitive psychologist David Ausubel has also had a significant impact on the field of education. Ausubel felt that the most important factor that influenced individuals' learning was what they already knew. In essence, he felt that individuals built links between old knowledge and new knowledge to construct meaningful knowledge. The concept that individuals perceive patterns in objects, information, and events based on previous experience is the foundation of Ausubel's position. For Ausubel, learning was an interactive process in which prior knowledge, personal experience, previous instruction, sensory awareness, and direct observation play a critical role. A major problem in learning and instruction, according to Ausubel, was the presence of misconceptions on the part of the student that resulted in "buggy algorithms" or flawed procedures in relation to thinking and application. Ausubel's work (along with that of Piaget) forms the foundation of constructivist philosophy and practice in our schools.

A final area of cognitive psychology that has been important to the field of education is that of metacognitive research. The leading individuals in this area are Ann Brown, Judith Flavel, Gordon Alley, and Don Deshler. These individuals have focused their work on how we organize information, know when, what, and how to remember, and monitor our cognitive activity. In essence, their research has involved understanding the deliberate conscious control of our individual cognitive actions. Flavel and Brown conducted much of the initial basic research in metacognition, seeking to build a theoretical and philosophical basis for the phenomenon. Alley and Deshler built on the work of Brown and Flavel to develop the learning strategies approach to instruction and provide teachers with the instructional means to help students understand and apply content flexibly in a variety of situations. This area of cognitive psychology is currently impacting the education of students with learning disabilities and students at risk for academic failure in significant ways.

Psychometry and psychological testing are those areas of psychology, aptitude, ability, and the probability that a given individual can benefit from a specific curriculum, program, or placement. The measurement of intelligence, academic achievement, specific abilities, and attitudes is of prime importance. Given this fact, psychometry and psychological testing have a direct impact on both social and educational policy. Important individuals in the field of psychometry and psychological testing include Alfred Binet, Louis Terman, Louis Thurstone, Robert Thorndike, David Wechsler, Jerome Sattler, Raymond Cattell, Charles Spearman, and Alfred Jensen.

Psychological testing and psychometry involve the development, refinement, and validation of instruments to measure human attributes, achievement, and abilities. In its purest sense, this area of psychology is focused on determining the soundness of assessment instruments. At the heart of psychometry and psychological testing is the notion that all measurement is imperfect. That is, all test scores contain some degree of error, whether systematic, nonsystematic, or both. This error compromises the integrity of scores and reduces the precision with which absolute or relative judgments concerning the scores can be rendered. In essence, the primary goal of psychologists operating in this field is to minimize error so that more accurate judgments can be made. Improving the internal consistency of instruments (reliability) and the soundness of the instruments' procedures/items (validity) allows for greater relevance, predictive accuracy, precision of measurement, and degree of response element interface.

Accurate measurement of academic progress has become the holy grail of public education. Both state and federal government agencies have focused a significant amount of attention and resources on student progress and the accurate measurement thereof. In addition, the use of such measurement has been extended beyond the realm of student progress into the efficacy of teaching, administration/leadership, and school district culture.

While academic achievement has been a major feature of psychological testing and psychometry, the most controversial feature has been the measurement of intelligence. This is due to the social implications of intelligence and intelligence testing to policy, cultural, and racial issues. Concepts such as general intelligence, fluid and crystalline intelligence, and multiple intelligences have all been proposed to explain and delineate the variation in human intellectual abilities. Furthermore, the ongoing nature/nurture debate among psychologists and its relationship to the genetic (and racial) basis of intelligence has impacted psychometry and psychological testing in relation to schools and schooling.

The various areas and disciplines of psychology have provided a plethora of philosophies, policies, procedures, and practices to those involved in educational settings.

Virtually all aspects of the field of education have been affected by psychology and psychological research. The study of the physical, affective, and cognitive aspects of our behavior will continue to have direct application to continued work in the schools.

—J. M. Blackbourn, William Barrios,
Keith E. Davis, and Jennifer Fillingim

See also achievement tests; at-risk students; Baer, Donald; behaviorism; Binet, Alfred; brain research and practice; Burt, Cyril; Cattell, Raymond; child development theories; cognition, theories of; Csikszentmihalyi, Mihalyi; discipline in schools; flow theory; Freud, Sigmund; Graves, Claire; Havighurst, Robert; Jung, Carl; life span development; Maslow, Abraham; metacognition; neuroscience; Ossorio, Peter G.; perceptual psychology; Piaget, Jean; psychometrics; Rogers, Carl, self-actualization; social psychology; Spearman, Charles; testing and test theory development; Thorndike, Edward; Wolf, Montrose

Further Readings and References

Alley, G., & Deshler, D. (1979). *Teaching the learning disabled adolescent: Strategies and methods.* Denver, CO: Love.
Ausubel, D. (1968). *Educational psychology: A cognitive view.* New York: Holt, Rinehart, & Winston.
Baer, D., Wolf, M., & Risley, T. (1968). Some current dimensions of applied behavior analysis. *Journal of Applied Behavior Analysis, 1,* 91–97.
Baer, D., Wolf, M., & Risley, T. (1987). Some still current dimensions of applied behavior analysis. *Journal of Applied Behavior Analysis, 20,* 313–337.
Bandura, A. (1977). *Social learning theory.* Englewood Cliffs, NJ: Prentice Hall.
Binet, A., & Simon, T. (1905). Methodes nouvelles pour le diagnostic du niveau intellectuel des anormaux. *L'Annes Psychologique, 11,* 191–244.

Blackbourn, J., & Fillingim, J. (2004). Leadership and human development. *The Record in Educational Leadership, 18*(1), 28–33.
Brown, A. (1975). The development of memory: Knowing, knowing about knowing, and knowing how to know. In W. Reese (Ed.), *Advances in child behavior.* New York: Academic Press.
Flavel, J. (1973). Metacognitive aspects of problem solving. In L. B. Resnick (Ed.), *The nature of intelligence.* Hillsdale, NJ: Erlbaum.
Graves, C. (1970). Levels of existence: An open system of values. *Journal of Humanistic Psychology, 10,* 131–155.
Graves, C. (1974). Human nature prepares for a momentous leap forward. *The Futurist, 8,* 72–87.
Lee, S. (2005). *The encyclopedia of school psychology.* Thousand Oaks, CA: Sage.
Lewin, K. (1935). *A dynamic theory of personality.* New York: McGraw-Hill.
Ossorio, P. (1995). *Persons.* Ann Arbor, MI: Descriptive Psychology Press. (Original work published 1966)
Ossorio, P. (1998). *Place.* Ann Arbor, MI: Descriptive Psychology Press.
Sattler, J. (2002). *Assessment of children: Behavioral and clinical applications* (4th ed.). La Mesa, CA: Jerome M. Sattler.
Spearman, C. (1923). *The nature of intelligence and the principles of cognition.* London: Macmillan.
Terman, L. (1916). *The measurement of intelligence.* Boston: Houghton Mifflin.
Thorndike, R. (1971). The concept of culture-fairness. *Journal of Educational Measurement, 8,* 63–70.
Wolf, M. (1978). Social validity: The case for subjective measurement, or how behavior analysis is finding its heart. *Journal of Applied Behavior Analysis, 11,* 203–204.

PSYCHOMETRICS

Psychometrics is the science of mental measurements. The focus of this discipline is on theories and techniques for quantifying psychological attributes. Psychometrics provides the scientific foundations and the standards that guide the development and use of mental measurements common in education and the social sciences. It is essential for educational administrators to be familiar with the basic concepts of psychometrics such as reliability and validity.

ORIGINS

The origins of psychometrics can be traced to the work of experimental psychologists in the nineteenth century who sought to bring the rigor of "scientific methods" to the measurement of mental attributes. Following the traditions of physicists and other natural scientists, German psychologists sought to quantify the relationship between the intensity of a mental sensation and the magnitude of the stimulus needed to invoke the sensation. Similar efforts to quantify psychological attributes were also being developed in England in the mid-nineteenth century. Influenced by the work of Charles Darwin, his cousin, Francis Galton, sought to develop scientific measures and procedures for studying the relationship between intelligence and other characteristics of individuals. Because of his development of mental tests, use of the normal distribution and work on the statistical techniques of correlation and regression, he is considered by many to be a key figure in the development of modern psychometrics. However, it is Charles Spearman who is credited with development of the classical model of mental test scores, introducing the term *reliability coefficient*, and creating factor analysis and the two-factor theory of intelligence during the first decade of the twentieth century.

Psychometrics is a relatively young science but one that has seen tremendous advances in the past 100 years. When Spearman introduced the concept of the reliability of a measure, his intent was to show how measurement errors adversely affected the measurement of an attribute and the resulting correlation of that attribute with any other. His definition relied on the possibility of measuring a single trait with two similar measures. Since his initial work, the concept of reliability has changed tremendously. Researchers have expanded the concept from a focus on two measures to many and shown that as the number of similar measures increases, reliability increases. The traditional view or model of reliability did not permit researchers to differentiate sources of measurement errors. The emergence of generalizability theory not only permitted researchers to isolate the source of measurement errors, but equally important, it made it possible to plan a measurement process so as to minimize specific sources of error. Recent developments in reliability have emphasized the fact that reliability coefficients reflect the influence of measurement error on test scores and can vary from one group to another.

There have also been significant developments in mathematical models of test scores. The simple classical model guided test development and use for most of the early part of the twentieth century. However, in the 1950s, Fred Lord introduced a series of models that made strong assumptions about the relationship between observed test performance and the underlying trait measured by the test but yielded many advantages over the classical model. The so-called item response theory models explicitly modeled the probability that an examinee would respond correctly to an item as a function of his or her ability. The shift in focus permitted test developers to develop tests that did not rely for their properties on the specific group of examinees on which they were field tested or normed and the measurement of an examinee's ability independent of the specific group of items which he or she happened to take. This latter result facilitated the development of computerized adaptive tests that measure examinees with considerable accuracy in less time by targeting their ability level based on their response patterns to selected items. Item response theory models have become the dominant theory behind most large-scale testing programs. They have developed significantly over the past 50 years. They now include multivariate models, models that permit ordinal or nominal test items, and even models that generate ability estimates for multiple aggregates such as classes or schools.

The concept of the validity of a measure has also undergone significant developments over the past century. In particular, the focus has changed from different types of validity, seen as distinct, to a unified concept in which the test developer collects data to support the validity of a test for a particular purpose. This conceptual shift has also been accompanied by many technical developments, principally the use of factor analysis models for investigating the latent structure of a test. Since Spearman's early work, factor analysis has evolved from exploratory techniques to structural equation models that explicitly permit the researcher to model the relationship between unobserved latent variables and observed indicators and the relationships among latent constructs.

RECENT DEVELOPMENTS

For most of their early years, mental measurement was used largely to sort and compare individuals. This was especially true of large-scale testing programs such as the Scholastic Aptitude Test (SAT), which were designed to select examinees for admission into colleges. More recently, in response to changes in the ways in which learning is thought to happen, achievement testing has changed to more of a focus on open-ended items and items that present more cognitively complex tasks. Much of the technical characteristics of these newer types of assessments are only now being developed. The focus on performance-based assessments in recent years, for example, has created new problems regarding the validity and reliability of measurements, as well as test development and use.

Psychometricians, for example, have been challenged to develop and investigate measurement techniques that provide more information than simply a score about an individual and that have greater instructional utility than traditional measures. A final arena that has seen many developments is the use of computers and technology in mental measurements. Computers greatly expand the types of assessments that can occur from those that parallel paper-and-pencil measures to those that are adapted to the individual taking the test to those that appear to learn and diagnose the strengths and weaknesses of an individual tester and proscribe instructional next steps. Because of their flexibility, computers present significant challenges for measurement specialists.

—*Eugene Kennedy*

See also accountability; achievement gap, of students; achievement tests; at-risk students; Baer, Donald; behaviorism; Binet, Alfred; Black education; brain research and practice; Burt, Cyril; Cattell, Raymond; child development theories; cognition, theories of; cultural capital; Graves, Claire; Havighurst, Robert; intelligence; item response theory; J-curve theory; Latinos; metacognition; neuroscience; Ossorio, Peter G.; perceptual psychology; Piaget, Jean; Rogers, Carl; S-curve theory; self-actualization; social psychology; Spearman, Charles; testing and test theory development; Thorndike, Edward

Further Readings and References

American Educational Research Association, American Psychological Association, & National Council on Measurement in Education. (1999). *Standards for educational and psychological testing.* Washington, DC: American Educational Research Association.

Haertel, E., & Herman, J. (2005). *The uses and misuses of data in accountability testing.* Malden, MA: Blackwell.

Kane, M. (2001). Current concerns in validity theory. *Journal of Educational Measurement, 38*(4), 319–342.

Kilne, T. (2005). *Psychological testing. A practical approach to design and evaluation.* Thousand Oaks, CA: Sage.

Wood, J., Nezworski, M., Lilienfeld, S., & Garb, H. (2003). *What's wrong with the Rorschach?* San Francisco: Jossey-Bass.

🏛 PYGMALION EFFECT

The possibility of increasing student achievement through modifications in teacher behavior has produced research and controversy for more than half a century.

The first major experiment to address the issue was conducted by Robert Rosenthal and Lenore Jacobson in the mid-1960s with the results being published in their book *Pygmalion in the Classroom.* Their "experiment" used false information about students to influence teacher expectations, which resulted in a reported significant increase in student scores on a general intelligence test, even though the teachers were unaware that their behavior toward the students had changed. Influencing teachers to subconsciously raise expectations for student achievement has become known as the Pygmalion effect. The study and subsequent book came under sustained attack from the research community, which accused the researchers of overgeneralizing from their data and resorting to using tables with false zero lines and elastic scales. The study was also scored for design and sampling problems as well as for the selection of a measuring instrument that had not been normed on young children, especially those from low-income brackets. The Janet Elashoff and Richard Snow critique of the so-called Pygmalion effect was that it failed to be demonstrated in the Rosenthal and Jacobson study.

Several subsequent studies of teacher expectations for student performance used different treatments that produced mixed results, but they helped to broaden understanding of the conditions through which teachers may influence student achievement. Researchers also have been interested in discovering if the Pygmalion effect could apply to leadership activities in other leader-follower relationships not related to teaching. Studies such as those by Dov Eden, whose work focused on military leadership, have provided significant information about the strengths and limitations of the Pygmalion effect.

In a work environment, the Pygmalion effect shows more prominently when the group is new and the leaders and followers do not know each other well. The effect has not been observed in groups that have been established for a significant length of time and where the members are well acquainted with the leaders and with each other.

Sex differences also influence the Pygmalion effect. Men seem to be better at developing increased performance than women. Males do well leading groups of men or women. Females are not as effective in creating higher levels of performance when they are leading either male or female groups.

—*Max S. Skidmore*

See also at-risk students; behaviorism; child development theories; climate, school; cognition, theories of; compensatory education;

expectations, teacher and student cultures; gender studies, in educational leadership; grades, of students; halo effect; Hawthorne Studies, The; individual differences, in children; intelligence; learning, theories of; motivation, theories of; research methods; resiliency; validity and reliability

Further Readings and References

Eden, D. (1984). Self-fulfilling prophecy as a management tool: Harnessing Pygmalion. *Academy of Management Review, 9*(1), 64–73.

Eden, D. (1988). Pygmalion, goal setting, and expectancy: Compatible ways to boost productivity. *Academy of Management Review, 13*(4), 639–652.

Elashoff, J., & Snow, R. (1971). *Pygmalion reconsidered.* Worthington, OH: Charles A. Jones.

Rosenthal, R., & Jacobson, L. (1992). *Pygmalion in the classroom.* Williston, VT: Crown House. (Original work published 1968)

White, S., & Locke, E. (2000). Problems with the Pygmalion effect and some proposed solutions. *Leadership Quarterly, 11*(3), 389–416.

Q

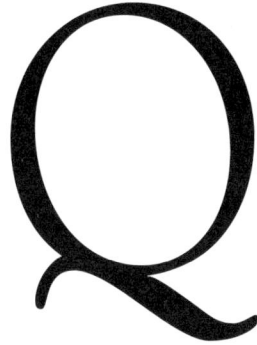

⛪ QUALITATIVE RESEARCH, HISTORY, THEORIES, ISSUES

The term *qualitative research* was first used in the social sciences in the 1970s to refer to a broad array of research traditions, assumptions, and methods. Many theoretical paradigms and disciplines employ qualitative methods. Widespread use in social sciences, humanities, and professional fields makes it difficult to concisely define qualitative research. However, qualitative research has common characteristics across paradigms and disciplines. Naturalistic qualitative research is conducted in the field where events occur. The researcher collects data through observation, interviewing, and document analysis. The researcher seeks to understand the context of research participants and sites. Concerned with process and meaning, the researcher tries to discover how participants interpret their situations. Data are descriptive. Research findings emerge from the data through inductive analysis. Multiple interpretations of data are possible, depending on the theoretical framework, yet all interpretations are grounded in the data.

Qualitative methods were first used in social science research in the late 1800s and early 1900s. Qualitative research originated in ethnography, anthropology, and sociology as researchers collected data in the field. Anthropologists Franz Boas and Bronislaw Malinowski established fieldwork as a legitimate method. Fieldwork is still associated with anthropology. Ethnographers of the 1800s studied the evolution of culture and civilization. In the late 1800s, they shifted their attention to racial and cultural groups inhabiting urban areas. They conducted social surveys to understand

people's lives. Well-known social surveys include Frederick LePlay's study of working-class families and Charles Booth's descriptive surveys of the London poor. In the eastern United States, churches sponsored social surveys to aid in the social adjustment and moral development of diverse ghetto populations. W. E. B. Du Bois's 1899 *The Philadelphia Negro,* the first qualitative community study, grew out of this movement. The Robert and Helen Lynd 1929 study of *Middletown* used anthropological methods to collect data about a typical American community. Church and corporate surveys dominated social research until the 1920s.

The University of Chicago Sociology Department made a major contribution to qualitative research from approximately 1910 to 1940. Robert Park and other Chicago School sociologists directed a number of ethnographic case studies that examined urban groups outside the middle class. For three decades, studies of minority communities described the Jewish ghetto, Little Italy, Chinatown, and other marginalized, deviant, and immigrant groups from the context of the subjects' lives. Other students of Park studied the "folk society" of rural, homogeneous small towns. August Hollingshead's study of Elmtown's youth represents this group of studies. E. Franklin Frazier's ethnographic work on the exclusion of Blacks drew on the life histories of his subjects and himself, stressing the importance of personal experience in ethnographic description and interpretation. William Foote Whyte's *Street Corner Society,* a study of Italian slums, labeled participant observation as a formal research technique and remains a model for participant observation.

Changes taking place in the United States beginning in the 1940s had a profound impact on the evolution of qualitative research. Despite declining interest in qualitative methods in the 1940s and 1950s, they were still used to study people in the context of their lives. During the Depression, the Works Progress Administration sent out unemployed writers and photographers to record oral biographies and to shoot documentary photographs of dispossessed people.

Educational researchers became interested in qualitative research in the 1960s. The civil rights movement made it obvious that there was little understanding of children's experience in schools. Federal monies funded ethnographies of children's unsuccessful school experiences, integration, new teachers in urban schools, and racism in schools. The emphasis in these studies on studying the powerless fit well with the democratic focus of the times. Qualitative research grew in other fields as anthropologists began to study American urban culture and sociologists began using ethnomethodology. A number of methods books were published, among them the idea of grounded theory in 1967.

Qualitative research gained widespread acceptance in the 1970s and most of the 1980s. Interdisciplinary and professional fields, including education, women's studies, social work, nursing, and human services, contributed to the field. Feminist researchers made gender a central topic in studies employing qualitative methods, giving unprecedented attention to the importance of relationships between researchers and their subjects. The first book devoted to qualitative research in education was published by Robert Bogdan and Sari Biklen, in 1982.

In the late 1980s and 1990s, qualitative research was accepted in a broad range of paradigms and disciplines that focus on race, class, and gender. With widespread acceptance, however, traditional qualitative methods became the center of debate. Postmodernists criticized inductive reasoning and focused on the qualitative researcher as interpreter. They supported interpretive theories in place of traditional grounded theories, blurring the distinction between fieldwork and writing. Critical theorists challenged traditional approaches in research as insufficient to benefit the marginalized, whom they believe are made powerless by an unjust society. The wide variety of approaches in the 1980s and 1990s led to an extensive discussion of methodology in the literature. A number of scholarly journals began publishing qualitative research, including the *International Journal of Qualitative Studies in Education, Anthropology and Education Quarterly,* and *Qualitative Inquiry.*

In the 1990s and 2000s, participatory and advocacy practices have been the center of discussion about qualitative research. Action and activist research are conducted and reported in narrative form. Research is seen not as a neutral process, but as a collaborative process shaped by class, gender, and race. In the 2000s, multiple, often conflicting, paradigms and methods for reporting qualitative research are available.

The qualitative researcher's theoretical perspective determines what is studied, how the study is conducted, and how the data are interpreted. Theory development in qualitative research emphasizes the inductive development of theory instead of deductive theory development based on a priori assumptions. There is a strong connection between how a theory is developed and how data are collected. How the study is conducted determines what is learned from the study.

Most qualitative researchers in the social sciences use some form of phenomenology as a theoretical perspective. Phenomenology, rooted in philosophy and sociology, is interpretivist. The researcher's goal is to understand social phenomena or experiences from the participant's own point of view. Phenomenologists strive to understand the motives and beliefs behind people's actions. The development of phenomenology began with the work of German philosopher Edmund Husserl. The work of Alfred Schutz extended and established phenomenology as a philosophical and social science perspective. Husserl's work was based on the assumption that people can know only what they experience. They interpret what they experience to the point that descriptions and interpretations of experience are intertwined. There is no objective reality for people. Subjective experience incorporates the objective experience and the individual's interpretation.

Methodologically, the phenomenological perspective may mean one of two things. It may mean that the researcher focuses on people's experiences and interpretations of those experiences, or it may mean that the researcher actually experiences the phenomena being studied. In both cases, the researcher examines how the participant experiences his or her world. In the first case, the researcher may rely on interviews to collect data. In the second case, the researcher must be a participant observer to experience the phenomena. In both instances, the researcher defines *reality* as people perceive it to be. The phenomenological perspective assumes, however, that there are shared essences to experiences and that it is possible to analyze and compare them. Phenomenologists search for commonalities in experiences. They can report their findings as plausible given that the data are grounded empirically in their participants' experiences. Results can be compared and integrated with results of other phenomenological studies of the same phenomena.

Symbolic interactionism is a major theoretical perspective within the phenomenological tradition. Symbolic interactionism emphasizes the importance of social meanings that people attach to their experiences. People create shared meanings through interactions and act according to how they see their world, not according to external rules or norms. Shared meanings become reality. Symbolic interactionists look for common sets of symbols and understandings that give meaning to interactions. The importance of symbols and the interpretive process distinguish symbolic interactionism.

Symbolic interactionism originated in the work of John Dewey, Herbert Blumer, Margaret Mead, Robert Park, and others. Students of Mead's work at the Chicago School, including Howard Becker, Blanche Geer, and Everett Hughes, were influential in the development of symbolic interactionism. Mead's 1934 book, *Mind, Self, and Society,* was the most influential discussion of this perspective.

Given that interpretation of human experience is central to symbolic interactionism, the researcher must be a part of the defining and interpretation process. Close contact and direct interaction are important for the researcher through participant observation. Blumer is credited with being one of the first researchers to use group discussions and interviews to grasp understanding of their interpretive process.

Ethnomethodology is a theoretical perspective that fits within phenomenology. Ethnomethodology has influenced phenomenology and has been particularly important in sociology. Ethnomethodologists study how people create and understand daily life. They focus on the ordinary, routine details of everyday life. Ethnomethodologists are interested in a group's tacit knowledge. Harold Garfinkel, who invented the term, explains the perspective in his 1967 book, *Studies in Ethnomethodology.* Ethnomethodology was popular in the 1960s and 1970s, but its popularity waned in the 1980s. Ethnomethodologists made criticisms of empiricism that have been raised more recently by postmodernists. For example, ethnomethodologists urge researchers to suspend their assumptions and worldviews instead of taking them for granted. More recently, postmodernists raise the same concern.

Ethnomethodologists study the methods by which people make sense of their worlds. They are interested in the norms and assumptions that people take for granted because they are deeply ingrained in their lives. They believe that people do not think about why they do the things that they do, making meanings behind actions complex and ambiguous. Unlike other phenomenologists, ethnomethodologists conduct intrusive research. They violate cultural norms in ethnographic experiments to see how people react. For example, they might stand too close to another person in casual conversation. Other methodological techniques include depth interviews and participant observation. Ethnomethodologists study transition points in people's lives to see how they adapt and develop routine responses to daily events. Ethnomethodologists deal with specific elements of conversations and vocabulary and have contributed to the development of conversational analysis.

Ethnography, another theoretical perspective, has as its framework the concept of culture. Intensive fieldwork through participant observation by anthropologists has been traditionally associated with ethnography. Today, other researchers conduct ethnographies with expanded definitions of culture. Ethnographies describe cultures or aspects of culture. Classic ethnographies by anthropologists studied primitive cultures. Modern ethnographies focus on contemporary societies, social problems, organizations, organizational development, and education. Ethnographies are used in program evaluation and applied educational research. Today, many educational researchers use the term *ethnography* synonymously with *qualitative studies.*

The theoretical framework of ethnography assumes that any group of people together over a period of time will develop a culture. As researchers in various fields have conducted ethnographies, several definitions of culture have evolved. Most simply, culture includes a group's beliefs, knowledge, and behavior patterns. Clifford Geertz's concept of "thick description" describes what ethnographers do. The researcher describes the meanings of behaviors in a specific culture and interprets them to outsiders. Some ethnographies are semiotic or study signs in language. These studies are interested in the interaction of culture and the meanings that people attribute to events. Ethnographers interpret shared cultural meanings known to participants but unknown to outsiders. What distinguishes ethnographies is the interpretation of findings from a cultural perspective.

Theoretical perspectives under the phenomenological umbrella are traditional qualitative frameworks. Phenomenologists believe that the researcher can be objective and report empirical findings from participation with research subjects. The newer theoretical perspectives challenge the traditional view. Most of the newer theoretical perspectives are postmodern. Philosophically, they come after modernism and challenge the scientific objectivity of the modern era. These interpretive theories, maintaining that the researcher is not an objective, all-knowing outside observer, focus on how the researcher's background influences the research setting and report. Of particular interest are the researcher's race, gender, class, and social position. The primary purpose of the postmodernists is to change social structures and processes. Another newer perspective, feminist research, focuses on women but is conducted in a number of disciplines. Feminists have emphasized the importance of relationships in research. Critical theorists examine social organizations that privilege some people while marginalizing others. Their goal is to empower the marginalized and remedy social injustice. Among other newer perspectives are action/participatory action research, critical ethnography, narrative analysis, and poststructuralism.

Qualitative research is used extensively in evaluation studies. Qualitative methods have been used in problem solving, decision making, policy analysis, organizational/community development studies, and educational policy/program evaluations. Process studies and evaluations study the internal dynamics of program or organizational operations. In programs that emphasize individualized outcomes for clients, individual case studies of clients may be used to construct an overview of patterns of client outcomes. Case studies, a mainstay of educational research and evaluation, may be used to study unusual outcomes of programs. A number of case studies may be used to synthesize larger conclusions about overall processes of programs. Qualitative methods may be used to evaluate the inputs, activities, processes, and structures of program implementation. Studies of quality use qualitative methods to describe program meaning and quality for participants. Qualitative methods may be used in other applications; among them are legislative monitoring and documentation of program development over time.

Widespread acceptance has been accompanied by debate among qualitative researchers over basic principles guiding the field. The absence of a single definition of qualitative research prohibits unity across paradigms,

theoretical perspectives, and disciplines. The result is the absence of a common set of standards by which to conduct and evaluate qualitative research. Instead, each discipline has its own language and strategies. The languages of theoretical perspectives and disciplines can be obscure to the point that different disciplines are unable to communicate with each other.

Postmodernism's rejection of traditional qualitative perspectives and methods has challenged long-standing beliefs about the role of the researcher in the research process. Challenging the objective stance of traditional qualitative researchers, postmodernists think that it is impossible for the researcher to remain detached from the research setting and participants. Rather than providing what were once considered scientific, objective research reports, postmodernists believe that the researcher should provide an interpretivist discussion of his or her role in the research. Traditional qualitative researchers believe it is still possible to maintain a certain level of objectivity and report empirical conclusions. This shift from objective to an interpretivist position leaves traditional methods in disfavor. Yet both traditional and interpretivist approaches are subscribed to and practiced by researchers with different disciplinary and theoretical perspectives. This debate leaves researchers faced with many choices, while the field is pulled in contradictory directions.

—*Carolyn L. Wanat*

See also constructivism; constructivism, social; contextual knowledge; cross-cultural studies; ethnography; feminism and theories of leadership; gender studies, in educational leadership; interpretive studies; postmodernism; quantitative research methods; research methods

Further Readings and References

Becker, H., & Geer, B.(1960). Participant observation: The analysis of qualitative field data. In R. Adams & J. Preiss (Eds.), *Human organization research.* Homewood, IL: Dorsey Press.

Blumer, H. (1969). *Symbolic interactionism: Perspective and method.* Englewood Cliffs, NJ: Prentice Hall.

Bogdan, R. C., & Biklen, S. K. (2003). *Qualitative research for education* (4th ed.). Boston: Allyn & Bacon.

Du Bois, W. E. B. (1967). *The Philadelphia negro: A social study.* New York: Benjamin Bloom. (Original work published 1899)

Garfinkel, H. (1967). *Studies in ethnomethodology.* Englewood Cliffs, NJ: Prentice Hall.

Geertz, C. (1973). Thick description: Toward an interpretive theory of culture. In *The interpretation of cultures.* New York: Basic Books.

Glaser, B., & Strauss, A. L. (1967). *The discovery of grounded theory: Strategies for qualitative research.* Chicago: Aldine.

Hollingshead, A. B. (1961). *Elmtown's youth: The impact of social classes on adolescents.* New York: Science Editions. (Original work published 1949)

Hughes, E. (1971). *The sociological eye.* Chicago: Aldine.

Lynd, R. S., & Lynd, H. M. (1937). *Middletown in transition: A study in cultural conflicts.* New York: Harcourt, Brace.

Mead, M. (1934). *Mind, self, and society.* Chicago: University of Chicago Press.

Whyte, W. F. (1955). *Street corner society: The social structure of an Italian slum* (2nd ed.). Chicago: University of Chicago Press.

🏛 QUALITY CONTROL

Quality control is a process of continual connection between a work standard or objective, work assessment, and work activity directed toward attaining desired work outcomes or standards. For an organization to attain quality control, people in the organization must connect these three elements together in an operational environment. There should be ongoing and purposeful interaction between these three elements. It is assumed as these elements are adjusted that the work itself reaches more of its intended objectives as revealed by the measure or measures of the work, and these data become the basis for tighter connections between work activity, work assessment, and the attainment of the desired work objectives. This is the idea behind the concept of *data-driven decision making.* It is also the idea undergirding the concept of total quality management, or TQM, as advanced by W. Edwards Deming.

When quality control is applied in educational settings, the designation of the work standard is often contained in state curricular standards or objectives (state frameworks), state high-stakes testing, and the configuration of teaching activities (the work) toward attaining tighter connections between all three on a day-to-day basis. The results are assumed to be improved test scores on whatever else has become the measurement of the work activity. The practice of tightly connecting teaching objectives and teaching activities lies behind the idea of *curriculum alignment,* which has demonstrated empirically that test scores do improve when this occurs.

Quality control can be divided into two basic parts. The first part involves *curriculum design.* Design issues involve needs assessment, curricular format, and the specification or specificity and the type of

"fit" to the schooling environment. This latter idea refers to the extent to which the curriculum (as work specification) is compatible with the basic organizational structure. The second part is *curriculum delivery,* and it involves the matter of the skills of the teacher, the fidelity of the implementation (classroom learning environment), monitoring to ascertain if there is a fit between the curricular objectives and the teaching objectives, the use of feedback (test or other assessment data), and the overall aspect of utilization/application in an ongoing process of tightening the linkage between all elements to attain improved test or assessment scores.

The use of quality control is predicated on schools and classrooms being orderly places. By that is meant that there is a measure of stability present in the schooling environment. For internal school activities to be directed toward accomplishing measurable objectives that are aligned with the measurement instruments does require some stability upon which improvement rests. Another assumption is that there is a conscious awareness on the part of administrators and teachers about the connections between work objectives as exemplified in a reliable and usable curricular format (sometimes called "guides") and the actual work teachers do in the classrooms. Another activity is the deliberate use of test or assessment data as feedback by which the school faculty judges its progress. Schools have been used to functioning despite such information. Newer forms of accountability require a change in this regard. Historically, schools have not been tightly connected to precise work specifications. Teachers have historically enjoyed great latitude in working within loose curricular frameworks. When schools are to be judged as adequate or inadequate in state and/or federal accountability schemes, this ambiguity becomes a major problem in securing improved performance. Teacher resistance to such schemes is often a sign that many view the intrusion of testing and attendant requirements for the use of test data in the classroom as intrusions in the sanctity of their workplace. Other criticisms center on the use of industrial concepts in educational settings as inappropriate, examples of a penchant for cost reduction strategies, and a reinforcer for social inequality.

—*Fenwick W. English*

See also accountability; achievement tests; alignment, of curriculum; curriculum, theories of; Deming, W. Edwards; Department of Education; economics, theories of; Educational

Testing Service; goals, goal setting; J-curve theory; learning environments; management theories; measurement, theories of; operational definitions; outputs, of systems; performance assessment; planning models; productivity; rational organizational theory; school improvement models; standard setting; standardized testing; state departments of education; systemic reform; testing and test theory development; total quality management; unions, of teachers

Further Readings and References

English, F. (1978). *Quality control in curriculum development.* Arlington, VA: American Association of School Administrators.

English, F., & Hill, J. (1994). *Total quality education: Transforming schools into learning places.* Thousand Oaks, CA: Corwin Press.

Juran, J. M. (1979). *Quality control handbook.* New York: McGraw-Hill.

🏛 QUANTITATIVE RESEARCH METHODS

DATA, VARIABLES, AND MEASUREMENT

Quantitative research begins with the idea that to measure something, particularly in numerical form, is to understand it better. The information that is collected is referred to collectively as *data.* The things that are measured are variables, meaning simply something that varies in value in repeated observations. Observational units can be individual students or teachers, school districts, states, or any other entity for which data are collected.

Variables come in two primary forms: qualitative and quantitative. Qualitative, or nominal, variables are simply names for categories. An example is sex, categorized as male or female. Although sex is a qualitative variable, it can be expressed, or coded, in numeric terms; for example, we could code sex as male = 0 and female = 1. Quantitative variables differ in that they have a clear direction, with values representing more or less of the variable. The simplest form of quantitative variable is measured at the ordinal level, which means that it consists of categories that are ordered from smallest to largest values of the variable. An example of an ordinal variable is educational attainment, measured as:

1 = less than high school education

2 = high school diploma

3 = some higher education, but no degree

4 = associate's degree

5 = bachelor's degree

6 = some graduate education, but no graduate degree

7 = Master's degree

8 = MD, PhD, or other terminal professional degree

The next-highest level of sophistication in measurement is an interval variable, for which there is a constant increment between successive values of the variable, but no fixed and meaningful zero point. An example is Stanford-Binet intelligence quotient (IQ) scores, which are calibrated to have mean 100 and standard deviation 16. A student with IQ of 150 has a score that is 75 points higher than another student who scores 75, but the higher-scoring student is not twice as intelligent as the lower-scoring student. The ratio of 150/75 does not translate as a meaningful multiple because IQ scores do not have a meaningful zero; that is, zero IQ does not mean that a person has no intelligence and probably would not be a meaningful value in any event.

For some quantitative variables, however, it is possible to form a ratio of values that is meaningful. An example of these ratio-level variables is family income. A family earning $100,000 a year has 4 times as much income as another family earning $25,000 a year. In practical quantitative applications, the distinction between ratio and interval levels of measurement is not very important, and these variables are treated as though they were measured at the same level.

Variables also can be distinguished as to whether they are composed of discrete or continuous measurements. Discrete variables are measured in units that cannot be divided into smaller quantities. An example is the number of buildings in a school district (you can't have a fraction of a building). Continuous variables in principle can be divided into an infinite number of fractional values, although it is common to round such variables to an arbitrary number of decimal places. An example of a continuous variable is an annual school district budget, which can be divided down to the nearest penny (or even fraction of a cent).

SAMPLING AND STATISTICAL INFERENCE

Most quantitative analyses involve samples of larger populations, either because the entire population isn't available or because it would be too costly to collect that much data. Samples are selected from populations that can be either finite or infinite. A finite population is countable, although it may have a large number of observations, like the total K–12 enrollment in the United States. An infinite population is uncountable, which may mean either that it literally is infinitely large or that it can't be determined because the number is increasing over time and therefore does not constitute a fixed amount (for example, the number of textbooks that have ever been used or will be used in public school classrooms).

Samples are essential for understanding statistical inference, which has to do with making informed guesstimates about the unknown characteristics of the population from which the sample was drawn. According to the Central Limit Theorem, the information from a single sample of sufficient size is needed to establish desirable properties for the sampling distribution of the parameter that is being estimated—usually the population mean, proportion, or variance. The larger the sample, the better the estimate will be. If the sample is more than about 5% of the population size, it is necessary to adjust the estimated standard error of the parameter estimate by the finite population correction factor, to take into consideration the changing odds of selecting successive observations without replacement from the population to place into the sample. Generally, to simplify the process of estimation, it is assumed that the sample has been selected at random from an infinite (or at least very large) population, which avoids such complications.

DESCRIPTIVE STATISTICS

Before statistical inference can be undertaken, it is important to have valid and meaningful measures of the characteristics of the sample. This can be accomplished both visually and numerically.

Visual representations of the sample can be obtained through pie charts, bar charts (for categorical variables), or histograms (for continuous variables), stem and leaf displays, radar/spider charts, box plots, maps, trend lines, scatter plots for two or more variables, multidimensional rotations (using XGobi and other advanced software), dot charts, and a large number of other designs.

Numerical descriptive statistics measure central tendency and dispersion. Central tendency can be measured, for example, by the most commonly occurring value or range of values (the mode), the value at

the 50th percentile (the median), the values at each quartile, or the arithmetic average (the mean). Dispersion is measured, among other ways, by the difference between the largest and smallest values (the range), the difference between the 50th and 25th percentile values (the interquartile range), the average distance any observation is from the mean (the mean absolute deviation), the sum of squared deviations around the mean divided by the sample size minus one (the variance), the square root of the variance (the standard deviation, which measures how far any observation is from the mean), and the ratio of the standard deviation to the mean multiplied by 100 (the coefficient of variation).

SIMPLE LINEAR CORRELATION AND REGRESSION

Bivariate correlation and regression evaluate the degree of relationship between two continuous variables, such as the size of school districts (measured by certified enrollment) and the number of dollars expended in their annual budgets. Bivariate correlation measures the association between two variables without assuming that one variable depends on the other. In contrast, bivariate regression predicts values of the dependent variable from values of the independent variable. For example, we could use district size to predict district expenditures, under the assumption that larger districts have bigger budgets.

MULTIPLE LINEAR CORRELATION AND REGRESSION

Multiple correlation assesses the degree to which one continuous dependent variable is related to two or more other variables that are usually continuous. Its value is the result of correlating the actual values of the dependent variable with the predicted values of the dependent variable. For example, we could correlate district budgetary expenditures with the combination of district size, student/teacher ratio, and total assessed property value in the district.

Multiple regression is used to predict the value of the dependent variable (say, annual district budget) from the combination of size, student/teacher ratio, and assessed property value. The predictive ability of a multiple regression can be measured either for the entire set of predictor variables simultaneously or sequentially, in order of importance determined by the researcher.

Automated forms of sequential multiple regression come in several different forms: (a) forward selection, which enters the most important predictor variables one at a time; (b) backward elimination, which starts with all of the predictors and deletes the least important predictor at each step; (c) stepwise, which combines forward and backward approaches by permitting a variable previously deleted to be added back in if doing so improves the model; (d) maximum R-square, which produces the best model for any given number of predictor variables; and (e) minimum R-square, which starts with the worst combination of different numbers of predictor variables and improves each until the best possible combination is attained.

CANONICAL CORRELATION AND MULTIVARIATE REGRESSION

It is also possible to correlate one set of continuous variables with another set of continuous variables, which results in a canonical correlation. For example, we could correlate several measures of district expenditures (such as capital budget, teacher salaries, and supplies) with district size, student/teacher ratio, and assessed property value. If we predict one set of variables (the expenditure measures, as three dependent variables) from the other set of variables (district size, student/teacher ratio, and assessed property value, treated as three independent variables), the result is known as a multivariate regression.

FREQUENCY TABLES AND LOGIT MODELS

Two-way frequency tables are used to assess the relationship between discrete variables, particularly those measured at a nominal or ordinal level with a relatively small number of categories. A large family of nonparametric measures of general association and correlation coefficients are used to measure the relationships between these cross-classified variables. These analyses can be extended to include three or more categorical variables, although doing so requires a large data set because the analysis divides the total number of observations into "cells" at the intersection of all of the variables' categories. An example of a three-way frequency table would examine the relationship between whether students participated in a special reading curriculum and their ethnicity, controlling for the students' sex.

A logit analysis, commonly expressed in the form of a log-linear model, is conducted when one of the

cross-tabulated variables is treated as a dependent variable and the others as independent variables. Such models involve the logarithms of the odds ratios of the likelihood of one outcome of the dependent variable for different combinations of the categories of the independent variables.

ANALYSIS OF VARIANCE (ANOVA) AND RELATED METHODS

A number of different forms of analysis of variance are appropriate when the goal is to compare mean levels of a continuous dependent variable across the levels of a categorical "main effect" (which consists of a series of dummy variables indicating whether any given observation is in a given category or not).

One-way ANOVA is basically the same as a *t* test to compare means between two groups. For example, we might want to compare mean district budgetary expenditures between urban districts and rural districts. An extension to comparing means across more than two categories requires the use of ANOVA methods, which compare variation across the group means with variation within the groups. A comparison of mean district expenditures across four geographical regions of the country (Northeast, Southeast, Midwest, and West) would be conducted using one-way ANOVA.

If one or more continuous predictor variables are added to a one-way ANOVA, the result is a one-way analysis of covariance (ANCOVA). For example, we could add district size and assessed property value to the one-way ANOVA comparison of mean district expenditures across geographical regions. This analysis permits the comparison of adjusted mean expenditures across regions, after adjusting for differences across the regions in mean district size and mean assessed property value.

Factorial ANOVA involves the use of more than one categorical main effect. For example, we could predict district expenditures from both region and whether the district is in an urban or suburban location. The distinctive aspect of factorial models is that they also make it possible to measure the effect of the two-way interaction between the main effects—for example, to see whether there is a difference in mean district expenditures between rural districts in the Southeast and urban districts in the West. Factorial models can include several categorical main effects, resulting in complex multiway interactions and high degrees of multicolinearity that often produce nonsignificant model parameters. Factorial ANCOVA models also can be estimated by adding continuous predictor variables (e.g., district size) to the factorial structure.

If the F test results in rejecting the null hypothesis that the means are equal for all categories of a main effect, multiple comparison procedures can be used to compare across selected categories of the main effect variables. We could compare, for example, all six possible pairs of regions, to see which specific regional differences in mean district expenditures are significant, using a wide array of different post hoc multiple comparison methods. There are many such multiple comparison methods, because which approach is optimal depends on whether there are equal variances within each group, whether each group has an equal number of observations, and how many groups are being compared at one time. In addition, a priori, or preplanned, multiple comparisons can be constructed to test for mean differences across compound combinations of groups—for example, whether mean district expenditures in the Southeast and Northeast combined are significantly different from mean district expenditures in the West and Midwest combined.

MULTIVARIATE ANALYSIS OF VARIANCE (MANOVA) AND COVARIANCE (MANCOVA)

Multivariate forms of ANOVA and ANCOVA are appropriate when there are two or more continuous dependent variables and one or more categorical main effects, taking into account correlations among the dependent variables (MANOVA), and adjusting for continuous covariates (MANCOVA). Factorial MANOVA and factorial MANCOVA models also can be estimated. Multiple comparisons and preplanned comparisons may be used with any of these multivariate ANOVA and MANCOVA methods.

Repeated measures is a special type of MANOVA in which we either measure the same thing at different times or have multiple measures of the same trait. The classic pretest-posttest comparison, of, for example, student knowledge scores before and after taking a course is the simplest form of repeated measures. More elaborate repeated measures models can be estimated for a larger number of time periods, as we might measure the motor ability of children every 6 months from birth to entry into kindergarten. We also would use repeated-measures ANOVA in comparing scores of students on several different subscales of

intelligence, to ascertain whether the various instruments all measure the same underlying trait. These models are all examples of within-subjects designs, which do not require categorical main effects or continuous covariates to predict outcomes. However, main effects and covariates may be added to produce between-subjects repeated-measures MANOVA or MANCOVA models. An important condition that must be satisfied for repeated measures results to be satisfied, at least without appropriate adjustments, is sphericity, or constant correlations among values of the same variable measured repeatedly over time or among different measures of the same trait.

DISCRIMINANT ANALYSIS

If the goal is to correctly predict the membership of an observation on a categorical outcome variable and all the independent variables are continuous and normally distributed, then discriminant analysis is the appropriate procedure to use. This is the opposite of the measurement characteristics of a MANOVA model. For example, discriminant analysis would use district size, assessed property value, and enrollment to predict (that is, to discriminate between) whether a given district has a budget that is in balance or in deficit. The goal is to see if there are differences in these continuous traits between the two sets of districts. The utility of a discriminant analysis is determined by how well it predicts the correct classification overall, and for each of the outcome categories separately. Sequential forms of discriminant analysis are available, comparable to those employed in sequential regression.

LOGISTIC REGRESSION

Similar to discriminant analysis, logistic regression is used to produce models that correctly classify outcomes for a categorical dependent variable. However, logistic regression is a more flexible procedure for two reasons: It is more appropriate when there is a combination of continuous (district size, assessed property value, and enrollment) and categorical (e.g., urban or rural) predictor variables, and it is a better procedure when the dependent variable consists of an ordinal set of categorical outcomes (for instance, district budgets with large deficits, small deficits, precisely balanced budgets, small surpluses, and large surpluses).

FACTOR ANALYSIS

Factor analysis consists of a complex combination of procedures that are appropriate when the goal is to establish construct validity, which involves determining the number of composite variables (factors) underlying a usually large number of continuous variables. For this reason, factor analysis often is referred to as a method of data reduction. Using correlations among a set of items, factor analysis involves a two-step procedure: (a) extract an appropriate number of factors, or latent variables, that do a good job of summarizing the correlations among those items and (b) rotate the resulting factors to improve the fit of each item on a factor. The ideal outcome is "simple structure," in which any one item has a strong correlation ("loading") with only one factor and each item is attached to a factor. For example, in a complex survey of teachers' perceptions of school administration, 30 separate questions might be reduced to only five factors, each of which represents a dimension of teacher/administrator interaction (e.g., curriculum, governance, relations with parents, student achievement, and policy priorities).

STRUCTURAL EQUATION MODELING (SEM)

Structural equation models combine aspects of factor analysis, canonical correlation, and multiple regression to estimate complex relationships among variables by estimating several equations simultaneously. SEM is most appropriate when a dependent variable in one equation is an independent variable in another equation. In its simplest form, called path analysis, SEM uses observed variables (as opposed to composite factors) to estimate continuous dependent variables. SEM results are sensitive to problems with lack of normality, particularly kurtosis, in the dependent variables. The validity of SEM is assessed largely by the extent to which the simplified model accurately reproduces the sample covariances among the model variables. SEM is particularly important for its ability to estimate both direct relationships among variables, which can be done in other linear models (regression and ANOVA, and their offshoots), and indirect effects, in which other variables intervene between a predictor variable and a dependent variable, which cannot be estimated by other linear models methods. For example, SEM could be used to estimate the relationship between college undergraduate students' ACT scores and their first-year cumulative grade point averages, mediated by their high school grade point averages.

HIERARCHICAL LINEAR MODELS (HLM)

Hierarchical linear models are used when variables in a model are measured on two or more types of observational units. National Assessment of Educational Progress (NAEP) data are structured this way, with student-level information such as their scores on, say, five mathematics strands, together with their gender and race, combined in a two-level model with teacher-level variables such as training in or acceptance of National Council of Teachers of Mathematics classroom reform practices, as well as teacher gender, race, and years of experience. Student-level data vary for the students in the same teacher's classroom, but the teacher-level variables are constant for those same students, which requires a nested, or mixed-model, HML analysis.

TIME-SERIES ANALYSIS

If a variable is measured repeatedly over long stretches of time, preferably at regular intervals, then time-series analysis is an appropriate method. Particularly when there are 50 or more such repeated observations, it is possible to develop forecasting models to predict future values of outcomes such as certified enrollment. This can be done as a univariate model, based on determining the patterns that exist over time among successive repeated values of the variable (such as certified enrollment), or as a multivariate input-output model for one or more continuous predictor variables measured repeatedly over the same time interval (e.g., size of the school-aged population) or a transfer function model with categorical input variables that measure the onset of an intervention and the extent of its intensity and duration (e.g., annexation of a new subdivision or consolidation with another district).

FORMAL MATHEMATICAL MODELS

Other forms of quantitative models also are used in education research. These include:

- Survival/failure (life testing, or event history) models to estimate the time it takes for something to happen, such as achieving metropolitan status with a population of at least 50,000 (survival) or a district going into bankruptcy (failure).

- Proportional hazards models, which model the rate of occurrence of an event, rather than the length of time until an event occurs, that could be used, for example, to estimate the number of times per year (i.e., the rate) that students will be expelled or suspended for behavior reasons.
- Stochastic process models, of which Markov chains are the simplest example, can be used to measure the transition probabilities, for example, by which educational achievement increases or decreases across generations.
- Bayesian methods cover a large number of different applications, but are particularly relevant to the use of simulations (such as Markov chain Monte Carlo methods) to estimate parameters for models when little or no data exist, and when the assumptions of classical statistical methods are inappropriate.

—*Mack C. Shelley*

See also accountability; achievement tests; hierarchical developmental models; measurement, theories of; questionnaires; standardized testing; surveys and survey results; research methods

Further Readings and References

Agresti, A., & Finlay, B. (1997). *Statistical methods for the social sciences* (3rd ed.). Upper Saddle River, NJ: Prentice Hall.

Hinkle, D. E., Wiersma, W., & Jurs, S. G. (2003). *Applied statistics for the behavioral sciences* (5th ed.). Boston: Houghton Mifflin.

Howell, D. C. (2002). *Statistical methods for psychology* (5th ed.). Pacific Grove, CA: Duxbury.

Tabachnick, B. G., & Fidell, L. S. (2001). *Using multivariate statistics* (4th ed.). Boston: Allyn & Bacon.

QUEER THEORY

An epistemological perspective that emerged in the 1990s as a poststructural constructivist critique of identity and sexual subjectivities, queer theory represents a philosophical framework that aids in the analysis of the modes in which power and desire are hegemonically enacted in social spaces in such a way that sexuality is normalized and differences are repressed. Queer theory has as one of its principal aims to disrupt both terms of the homo/hetero binary and to destabilize each of these categories and the

relationships between them; that is to say, queer theory argues for the possibility that neither *homosexual* nor *heterosexual* are reliable and valid descriptors of identity. Queer theory's fundamental challenge to the notion of a foundational homosexual subject is based in part on the objection that an essentialized homosexual identity replicates the hetero/homo binarism that perpetuates the heteronormativity of society.

To define *queer* remains an elusive task given its multiple and elastic significations. Once a derogatory term to denote homosexuality, *queer* has been reappropriated by some to represent an expression of empowerment. At times, the word queer equates to lesbian, gay, or bisexual and is used by some authors as a convenient shorthand for the unwieldy laundry list of identity categories. Yet queer theorists argue that this facile association of queer with identity-based analyses ignores the oppositional stance of queer theory toward the foundational categories of lesbian, gay, bisexual, and transgender. Queer, then, represents a paradoxical tension between an identity category that seeks ever to remain unstable and fluid and a theoretical critique of the notion of identity itself.

Because queer destabilizes the concept of sexual and other identities, it offers the political advantage of allowing new coalitions to emerge amongst individuals who would otherwise be separated by the essentializing categorization mechanism that prevails in a social system of compulsory heterosexuality. Thus, the rigid classification scheme that sorts everyone into straight, lesbian, gay, bisexual, transgender, and other identity categories—which allows identity-based political movements to flourish—collapses as identity is subjected to interrogation. It must be noted, however, that queer can never escape the social realities of a heteronormative milieu that (re)produce the social inequalities and material effects of the categorization it seeks to transcend. Individuals in the heteronormative system experience these material effects with very real consequences, indeed, as a result of the social meanings and relationships that accrue from the process of categorization. Thus, race, gender, class, age, ability, and sexual orientation (amongst others) continue to generate inequitable distributions of power, even as queer theorists attempt to subvert the theoretical implications of identity.

Attempts to circumscribe the definitional parameters of queer theory have often met with resistance. As a theoretical posture that is permeated with a frustration with the tyranny of normalizing processes, queer theory defies a stance of positivity, always maintaining, instead, an antithetical relation to the process of normalization. This precise resistance to be delimitated has resulted in many affirmative declarations concerning the (highly valued) indeterminacy and flexibility of the theory.

Queer theory allows researchers to interrogate commonsense practices by exposing and examining the links between knowledge and ignorance from a perspective situated at the margins of normality. One of the most influential and controversial texts that deals with the relationship between sexuality and knowledge/ignorance is E. K. Sedgwick's 1990 *Epistemology of the Closet,* a thoroughly argued discussion the pervasive effect that sexuality has had on twentieth-century Western systems of thought. Queer theory, then, seeks to deconstruct—in a Derridean sense—the binary oppositions that regulate the formation of identities and to expose the inequitable power structures that underlie the construction of subjectivities.

Building on the seminal works of literary critics, sociologists, anthropologists, and philosophers, queer theorists in education have explored the implications of a queer perspective on curriculum, pedagogy, gender relations, reading practices, and the tensions between knowledge and ignorance. Others have used queer theory to examine the social, legal, economic, and professional relationships amongst the stakeholders in the public education system. Common to all these studies is an insistence on queering the taken-for-granted assumptions that underlie the current hegemonic practices of public education. Such assumptions include, for example, the assignment of proper roles for male and female subjects, the notion that "family" is monolithically and naturally defined rather than socially constructed, and the idea that the privileging of some sexual identities at the expense of others is both normal and justified.

Critiques of queer theory abound amongst scholars and activists who argue that queer analyses privilege the fragmentation of identity and the deconstruction of the community over the acknowledgment of oppressive structural forces within society. Some educational scholars have responded, however, by uniting the theoretical postulates of queer theory with a sense of practical activism imbued with a mission of social justice. Whether or not these efforts contain an element of theoretical inconsistency, they are faithful to the paradoxical concerns of a theory that defines itself both as against the oppressive processes of normalization and for social change, even as the theory itself might

have no way of knowing for certain beforehand the direction of such change.

Ironically, the strength of queer theory as an analytical tool derives from its effort to point toward possibilities that it cannot define in advance. Queer is ever engaged in the process of becoming rather than seeking the realization of a preestablished goal. The very oppositional and negative stance that characterizes queer is precisely what allows queer theorists to uncover the power dynamics of an inequitable society and to resist the formidable forces of normalization. A perspective that dares to *know the unknowable,* to *speak the unspeakable,* and to *unhide the hidden,* queer theory disrupts everything we take for granted in education.

Queer theory may find application amongst educational leaders by providing a way to decenter and disrupt the heterosexist normalization processes that surround, constrain, and essentialize administrators, teachers, parents, children, and community members. It can incite educational leaders to examine and think differently about curriculum and pedagogy—and the way these are used to construct knowledge and perpetuate inequitable power systems—in order to intervene in the hegemonic discourses that stifle diversity. Finally, through its ontological interrogation of identity formation, queer theory can help educational leaders to discover new ways of building coalitions amongst individuals and groups in order to promote more democratic relationships in the public schools.

—*James W. Koschoreck*

See also discrimination; gender studies, in educational leadership; homophobia; lesbian/gay/bisexual/transgender issues in education; sexuality, theories of

Further Readings and References

Blount, J. M. (2005). *Fit to teach: Same-sex desire, gender, and school work in the twentieth century.* Albany: SUNY Press.

Kumashiro, K. (2002). *Troubling education: Queer activism and antioppressive pedagogy.* New York: RoutledgeFalmer.

Lugg, C. A., & Koschoreck, J. W. (Eds.). (2003). The final closet [Special Issue]. *Journal of School Leadership, 13*(1).

Sedgwick, E. K. (1990). *Epistemology of the closet.* Berkeley and Los Angeles: University of California Press.

QUESTIONNAIRES

Probably the most common method for collecting survey data is the questionnaire, which can be administered in a number of ways. Questionnaires can be sent through the mail, filled out on the Web, attached to an e-mail and returned via e-mail to its sender, filled out by an interviewer who is present in person with the respondent, completed on laptop computers just about anywhere on the planet, delivered over the telephone with data possibly entered instantly by the interviewer using computer-assisted telephone interviewing (CATI) software, and dropped off on the seats of an audience attending a class or some other public event. Interactive voice response can be solicited to prerecorded telephone messages. Whether the survey is self-administered or administered by a trained interviewer makes a big difference in response rate and cost. Responses can be handwritten, entered directly on a computer file or Web page, entered on a telephone keypad, scanned from "bubble sheets," or imaged. Some modes of delivery decay in their utility with time and societal changes. Telephone questionnaires have become more difficult owing to "no call" national legislation designed to avoid an annoying blizzard of phone call solicitations particularly around meal times, the rapid proliferation of unlisted cell phone numbers and the corresponding disappearance of land lines, and a shift in attitudes toward the intense personal use of portable phones that most people do not want used for anything other than contact with family or friends.

Generally, response rates are higher for questionnaires that are filled out during a personal interview, probably because of the eye contact and other personal connections established that make it difficult for a respondent to say no, lower for telephone or Web surveys, and lower still for mailed questionnaires. If you have a captive audience, such as a class full of students, however, it is relatively easy to get a high response rate. The cost of getting useable data from questionnaires is highest for personal interviews because of the expert personnel time and travel costs required to produce high response rates, lowest for Web surveys, and somewhere in between for questionnaires delivered on the telephone or through the mail. This combination of cost and response rate considerations has led to contemporary use of mixed-mode surveys, with a mixture of face-to-face interviews, phone or mail contacts, and Web or e-mail contacts.

Donald Dillman, who developed the tailored design survey method, provided expert guidance in 2000 about how to get the best response rate and most valid data from questionnaires, based on social exchange theory, which places a premium on establishing trust, increasing rewards for participation, and reducing social costs associated with completing the questionnaire. For establishing trust, provide a token of appreciation in advance, make it clear that the questionnaire is sponsored by legitimate authority (for example, a building principal, a district superintendent, or a university provost or college dean), make the task of filling out the questionnaire seem to be important, and invoke other exchange relationships (such as helping a student complete her dissertation research or offering to share a summary of the results with the respondent). Increasing rewards can be accomplished by showing the prospective respondent due respect, politely asking the respondent for help and thanking the respondent once the questionnaire is completed, asking the respondent for advice, supporting group values, providing tangible rewards such as by enclosing a small financial contribution, making the content and purpose of the questionnaire interesting, providing social validation, and communicating to the respondent the need to respond because of the scarcity of response opportunities from others. Social costs can be reduced by avoiding language that might make the respondent feel subordinate to the questionnaire writer, avoiding language that might be embarrassing, avoiding anything in the questionnaire that might be inconvenient to the prospective respondent, making the questionnaire brief and easy to fill out, minimizing requests on the survey instrument for personal information, and emphasizing that the requested questionnaire is similar to other requests for information.

Questions, of course, are at the heart of a questionnaire survey instrument. Broadly speaking, there are two kinds of survey questions: fixed format (or multiple choice) and open-ended. Fixed-format questions can come in many forms. One type of fixed-format item is the simple dichotomy; for example, students might be asked:

Have you ever studied in small groups? ☐ Yes ☐ No

A more complex, and more informative, fixed-format question provides an ordinal range of alternatives on the same topic:

In the last month, how many times have you studied in small groups?

☐ None   ☐ 1   ☐ 2–5   ☐ 6–10   ☐ More than 10

Other fixed-format questionnaire items provide a set of categories that are not necessarily ordered. For example, teachers might be asked:

Which of the following do you think is the best description of your feelings about building a new middle school?

☐ It's a good idea, but the district can't afford it now.

☐ It's a good idea, but a vote at the next election isn't going to succeed.

☐ I'd rather wait until next year, after the school board elections.

☐ We ought to work harder to build public support before pushing for a new building.

☐ Other (please specify) _____

Actually, the "Other (please specify)" choice is followed by room for the teacher to write in a brief open-ended explanation of what he or she wants to convey that isn't covered in the other available choices. This is probably the simplest possible example of open-ended questions. A more elaborate form of open-ended item is common particularly in Web-delivered surveys, in which the respondent might be asked:

If you had advice for the school board, what would you tell them about the best strategy for building a new middle school?

_____
_____
_____
_____
_____
_____
_____
_____

Producing survey items that are valid, that is, do the best possible job of measuring what they are intended to measure, is an art form. There are a few basic guidelines and matters of common sense to follow.

It is better to use simple words that are easily understood, rather than more complex words that might sound fancy but can produce misleading results, and fewer words rather than more. In questionnaires that are meant to be sent to the public, a general guideline is to write items that can be read at a sixth-grade level. More generally, the wording of questions should be consistent with the level of knowledge or expertise of the intended audience.

It is common in longer surveys to use a series of fixed-response items and to try to create scales from the entire set of items or from a subset of them. In such cases, it is a good idea to have as much as possible an equal number of items that have positive and negative "valence," or direction. After reverse coding, say, the negative-valence set of items, a meaningful summated rating scale can be established that validly measures a full range, from least to most favorable.

Leading questions should be avoided because they will produce biased results. For example, a biased question about public school prayer might read:

How do you feel about public schools that take God out of the classroom?

whereas more valid responses would be obtained from this unbiased question on the same subject:

There is a lot of discussion these days about whether students in public schools should be allowed time for silent reflection prayer when they are at school. How do you feel about this issue?

Response choice categories should be mutually exclusive and collectively exhaustive. That is, there should be no overlap in the choice between two alternatives, and the choices should cover all possible responses. For example, a poorly designed questionnaire item on the frequency with which students watch television is:

How often do you watch TV during an average week?

☐ I don't ever watch TV

☐ Just a couple of hours a day

☐ 3–5 hours a day

☐ about 10 hours a week

☐ Just about every day

A much better version of this question would be:

On average about how many hours a week do you watch TV:

☐ 0

☐ 1–5

☐ 6–10

☐ 11–15

☐ 15–20

☐ 21–25

☐ more than 25

It also is good practice to avoid double-barreled items, which contain more than one question. For example, in a recent telephone survey, the author (who is a faculty member) was asked the following question:

Do you think that faculty and administrators at the Regents universities are overpaid?

The obvious problem is that a faculty member probably would want to answer "no" to faculty salaries and might want to say "yes" to administrators' salaries. Incidentally, when the faculty author asked the survey interviewer about this option, he was told to answer the question as posed, although "no opinion" was offered as an alternative. In such cases, it is usually best to ask two different questions:

Do you think that faculty salaries are too high at the Regents universities?

Do you think that administrator salaries are too high at the Regents universities?

Other complications and other options abound regarding how best to structure survey questions to obtain valid data from respondents. Including a "don't know" response option will reduce the useable sample size of the survey data because such responses probably will need to be treated as missing data. Occasionally, it will be ambiguous whether a "don't know" response means the same thing as "I really don't have any opinion on this subject" (what Philip Converse and other survey researchers have called "nonattitudes") or "I have an opinion all right, but you haven't given me the right set of options."

On Likert-type ordered response items, another consideration is whether an even or odd number of categories should be used. An odd number of categories usually means that there will be a middle "neutral" category that permits respondents to avoid having to lean in one direction or the other. For the question, "Do you agree or disagree with the school board's policy banning political statements on T-shirts?" an odd number of categories would be:

☐ Strongly agree

☐ Agree

☐ Both agree and disagree

☐ Disagree

☐ Strongly disagree

An even number of categories makes it more difficult to evade a directional answer and for that reason probably would be preferable in most circumstances. For this example:

☐ Strongly agree

☐ Agree

☐ Disagree

☐ Strongly disagree

There are a number of design and style issues that should be considered in constructing questionnaires. For one thing, the order in which questions are asked can have a powerful, and often unintended, impact on the validity of the responses obtained. One particular manifestation of the effect of question order is the *halo effect,* or carryover effect, in which responses to a general question carry over to other, more specific items. If a survey of citizen satisfaction with the governor's education policy leads off with "How good a job do you think the governor is doing?" then attitudes about any later questions about specifics (such as the state budget for special education, initiatives for new bonding, or efforts to consolidate smaller districts) are likely to be influenced by the general attitude evoked by the stimulus of the initial question about the governor's overall performance. Consequently, respondents who agree with the governor in general may be more likely to say they agree with specifics of her education policy, to avoid cognitive dissonance, and their actual attitudes may not be measured.

In addition, it is essential to think through the implications of questionnaire design and style for response rate, validity of the responses you get, and how the data will be analyzed after they have been collected and cleaned. Issues such as the following need to be considered:

- For printed questionnaires, a booklet format generally is better received by respondents.
- Make sure the first question applies to all potential respondents, is easy to answer, and holds their interest.
- Every respondent should be guided through the survey with effective visual and verbal instructional stimuli, so they see and understand everything in the questionnaire in the same sequence.
- Minimize the use of complex answer formats, such as matrices in which more than one answer is required for each item (for example, how important are various aspects of the school board's policy decisions, and how well is the school board doing each of them now?).

- Make good use of white space, shading, and brightness.
- Make the instrument as attractive as possible for the respondent, paying attention in particular to the aesthetics of the first and last pages (or screens for an online questionnaire).
- Be prepared to go through a number of revisions until the instrument is as effective as it can be.
- Use a pilot study (i.e., a pretest) to make sure the questionnaire items are answerable by the target audience, that the survey is not too long, and that there are no unforeseen problems with wording, question order, or layout.

Recently, particular attention has been directed to enhancing the value of questionnaire pretests. Although pretesting is the only way to evaluate in advance whether a questionnaire may cause problems either for the respondents or for the interviewers (if the questionnaire involves face-to-face or voice contact), most applications of pretesting have taken the form of being only a dress rehearsal for the actual application of the questionnaire, with little scientific basis for concluding whether the instrument is valid and reliable. The need for more carefully conducted pretests arises from (a) the increased need to improve data quality for the sake of attaining the objectives of the questionnaire; (b) the application of new methods for testing questionnaire validity and reliability, such as cognitive interviews, behavior coding, response latency, vignette analysis, formal respondent debriefings, experiments, and statistical modeling; (c) the emergence of new modes of administration, including self-administered questionnaires, computer-assisted questionnaires, and Web questionnaires; (d) questionnaires designed for increasingly specialized populations, including children, special education students, the disabled or infirm elderly, establishments, and multilingual or non-English-speaking respondent groups; and (e) the emergence of multimodal survey methods using a mixture of questionnaire types. Improved questionnaires depend on correctly diagnosing the problem to reduce measurement error, controlling survey costs, repairing the flaws in questionnaires by applying the best of basic research and theory, and developing a database to facilitate the accumulation of knowledge about optimal questionnaire design and implementation.

Future applications of questionnaires in educational administration will need to be responsive to newly evolving subject areas and to new technologies and methods that can produce valid and reliable data for data-driven decision making.

—Mack C. Shelley

See also attitudes; evaluation; measurement, theories of; quantitative research; research methods; surveys and survey results; validity and reliability

Further Readings and References

Dillman, D. A. (2000). *Mail and Internet surveys: The tailored design method* (2nd ed.). New York: Wiley.

Presser, S., Rothgeb, J. M., Couper, M. P., Lessler, J. T., Martin, E., Martin, J., & Singer, E. (Eds.). (2004). *Methods for testing and evaluating survey questionnaires*. Hoboken, NJ: Wiley.

Schuman, H., & Presser, S. (1996). *Questions & answers in attitude surveys: Experiments on question form, wording, and context*. Thousand Oaks, CA: Sage.

R

RATIONAL ORGANIZATIONAL THEORY

Theories have histories, and rational theories of organizations are no exception. Rational views of organizations dominated the early world of organizational development and leadership (mid-1800s to World War II) as well as the early study of organizational sociologists in Germany and America (pre-1950s). During these periods, organizations were largely viewed as "pure" forms of bureaucratic structure, complete with hierarchical authority, driven by goal specificity and rational understandings and formalization. Rationality refers not to the selection of goals but to their implementation as well as their technical and functional rationality that structures work activity with emphasis upon information, efficiency, optimization, implementation, and design.

Scientific management research became the main vehicle by which rational theories of organizations were applied to organizations. Its focus was to improve specific technical and skill actions of workers, time and space management, task analysis, and factory efficiency. Scientific management influenced education in similar ways, including grading and grouping processes, structuring of classrooms and administrative functions, and even curricular content and teaching.

Nevertheless, even as early as the 1930s, rational or closed views of organizations were being challenged, at first by those emphasizing social aspects of organizing such as Mary Parker Follett, and then later by those researching the influence of environments on organizing.

Subsequent thought and study over a four-decade period, starting with the human relations theory (in the late 1930s), through Herbert Simon's concept of *satisficing* (with strongest influence in the 1950s), and research on the nonrationality of internal processes and the influence of environments on organizational planning and function from the 1960s and on, did much to unravel the tight hold efficiency and closed systems played in rational theory.

Three challenges did the most to moderate the "rationality" in rational theory. First, the emerging field of industrial and organizational psychology, specifically the work of Karl Weick, worked to nuance rationality as sense making. Organizational design, communication, planning, and administrative decision making was not so linear but informed by creativity, improvisation, and enactment. Sense making was constructed and bootstrapped within organizations. Second, institutional theorists argued and then showed that rationality itself was framed by both broad and local (a) regulatory, (b) normative, and (c) mimetic processes. Finally, contingency and environmental organizational researchers documented the heavy influence of external pressures, resources, and forces on organizational process.

Contingency theory championed the view that the best way to organize is dependent on the context of the environment in which it must function. As that environment changes, organizations must adapt and alter their strategic plans to respond to those external constraints. This view challenged naive views of formal and closed systems. It dismissed the notion that organizational structure can be explained without reference to external constraints. "Contingencies" can be sporadic, intermittent, and unpredictable, and continue to challenge linear and systematic rationality.

However, noting the constraints or limits of rationality in organization did not itself replace rational explanations. Organizations still must attend to structuring their work in effective and efficient ways, and many of the early findings of rational theorists, even scientific management researchers, provide useful ways of doing so.

—*Duane M. Covrig*

See also administration, theories of; bureaucracy; goals, goal setting; governance; knowledge base, of the field; leadership, situational; leadership, system-oriented; leadership, task-oriented; management by objectives; management information systems; management theories; organizational theories; organizations, types of, typologies; productivity; resources management; school improvement models; strategic planning; systemic reform; work task measurement

Further Readings and References

Follett, M. P. (1942). *Dynamic administration.* New York: Harper.
Simon, H. A. (1997). *Administrative behavior: A study of decision-making processes in administrative organization* (4th ed.). New York: Free Press.
Taylor, F. W. (1911). *The principles of scientific management.* New York: Harper & Brothers.
Weick, K. E. (1995). *Sensemaking in organizations.* Thousand Oaks, CA: Sage.
Weick, K. E. (2001). *Making sense of the organization.* Malden, MA: Blackwell.

🏛 READING, HISTORY OF, USE IN SCHOOLS

Reading may be defined as an activity characterized by the understanding of the written word through the translation of symbols, or letters, into words and sentences that have meaning to the individual. The reader also brings knowledge and understanding to the written word to be able to make sense of it. The history of reading gives a clearer perspective on current practices in the field of reading. In any school, it is not uncommon to find different teachers whose procedures exemplify the outstanding characteristics of several of the movements in reading. It is advantageous that teachers analyze their own techniques and materials of instruction from the standpoint of the historical periods from which they evolved.

The history of reading to convey meaning dates back to 4000 BC, where the first writings of Sumerian logographs portray pictures of objects and activities.

The first writings were probably invented in early Mesopotamia for commercial reasons with the advantage that tablets could store an insurmountable amount of information compared to relying on one's memory. In approximately 2000 BC, Phoenicians developed the first method to represent spoken language consisting of an alphabet of four consonants, and in 1000 BC, the Greeks added vowels to the alphabet, creating essentially the same alphabet we use today. In 200 BC, punctuation appeared in Alexandrian manuscripts. Before then, written words were strung together in one continuous line. Medieval scribes invented the lowercase characters around 700 AD and the insertion of spaces between words in 900 AD. The invention of spaces made it possible for the vast majority of readers to be able to read silently, when previously most readers had to read out loud in order to be able to determine appropriate pauses and stopping points.

THE PRIMER

Early in the history of religious instruction, priests believed that certain religious selections were so fundamental that they should be memorized by all adults and children. In the year 813 in the 44th Canon of the Council of Mainz, children were to receive the universal instruction of religious selections, which created the first books to be taught to children. In the Middle Ages, this book generally contained the Creed, the Lord's Prayer, the Ten Commandments, and a few psalms. It was called a "primer" because it was primary in containing the minimum essentials deemed necessary for one's spiritual existence. Gradually, the alphabet and lists of syllables and words were added to this simple religious manual, and it became the standard book for instruction in reading. *The New England Primer,* probably printed in England in late 1600s, became the first reading textbook printed in America, and it was the standard textbook of reading instruction throughout the colonial period.

THE PERIOD OF RELIGIOUS EMPHASIS, 1607–1776

In this period, the Church of England changed from Catholicism to Protestantism, and the Church maintained the right to control the schools. Each individual was to be directly responsible to God for his or her own salvation and was directed to read the word of God directly and draw his or her own conclusions. This new religion fostered reading instruction and provided school training that gave the children a thorough grounding in their reading ability so that they could read the word of God for themselves. In the 1600s, methods of teaching reading including learning the ABC book (a manual of church services) by rote forward and backward and pointing out letters first in the alphabet then in any other place. Another method included mastery of the alphabet, followed by syllabarium, which initiated the child into those few syllables that consist of one vowel after a consonant such as *ba, be, bi, bo,* and *bu.*

The Lord's Prayer, the Creed, and the Ten Commandments were to be memorized by the child in many cases. After finishing the primer, the child was permitted to read from the Bible, and used spelling as the only technique for solving new words. Toward the end of the 1700s, learning the alphabet, spelling syllables and words, memorizing sections of content, and reading orally were prevalent methods of reading instruction. Oral reading was very important, as illiteracy was highly prevalent, and it was customary for the uneducated members of the family to gather to listen to the oral readings of the scriptures.

THE PERIOD OF NATIONALISTIC-MORALISTIC EMPHASIS, 1776–1840

The establishment of America as an independent nation precipitated reading content that was expected to purify the American language, to develop loyalty to the new nation's traditions, institutions, occupations, and resources, and to inculcate the high ideals of virtue and moral behavior that were considered a necessary part of the general program of building good citizenship. Materials for reading instruction in this period had exercises and rules for pronunciation and enunciation designed to overcome the diversity of dialects and to promote greater unity in the American language. They contained patriotic selections and selections by American authors designed to promote an appreciation of the talent within America, historical selections to acquaint children with the history of America and Europe, informational selections to better enlighten children about their own country, and oratorical selections.

Prominent authors such as Noah Webster, Caleb Bingham, Lyman Cobb, George Hillard, and Lindley Murray created the idea of a set of readers during this period. Learning the alphabet was the most important first step of reading instruction. Emphasis on articulation and pronunciation brought about the practice of teaching the sounds of letters as well as their names. Methods were included in each series for committing a lengthy set of rules to memory.

THE QUEST FOR INTELLIGENT CITIZENSHIP, 1840–1880

Educators came to realize that the success of the new democracy depended on developing the intelligence of the people who would choose its leaders and determine the policies of a new nation. Horace Mann was one of the most influential leaders of this period as he brought Prussian influence reflecting Pestalozzian principles to American reading instruction. Reading texts of this period included information on the subjects of science, nature study, geography, history, and general informational content, as well as emphasis upon teaching the sounds of letters and the arrangement of subject matter proceeding from the simple to the complex. Primers and first readers contained realistic materials, and pictures in these readers became more plentiful and representative of objects familiar to children and their lives.

Methods of this period discontinued syllabarium as a means of inducting children into reading and introduced the concept of proceeding from the simple to the complex along with introducing a small number of new words through repetition. Teaching the alphabet remained prevalent, along with a strong tendency to teach the sounds of the letters with the letter names or instead of the letter names. Hence, the alphabet-phonetic method was born. Spelling and reading were closely tied together during this period, coupled with writing as children were required to copy the letters and phonetic combinations as well as script sentences that appeared in the primer. Attention to meaning in the upper grades became apparent through questions about the content and definitions of words. Elocution continued to be stressed with the upper readers.

The graded school evolved during this period, resulting from reports concerning German Pestalozzian schools in which the children were divided according to age and attainments. The McGuffey series was the most widely used reader of this period and must be given credit for being the first series produced to clearly define one reader for each grade in the elementary school.

THE NEW MOVEMENT, 1880–1900

The nation was in a status of tranquility and security and now had the leisure and peace of mind to turn to cultural pursuits in music, art, and literature. Aims, methods, and materials were directed toward the goal of developing permanent interest in literature, gaining thought from the author from the written or printed page, and giving oral expression to these thoughts. Professional books in reading came into prominence during this period with Scudder's *Literature in the Schools* published in 1888 and Sarah Louise Arnold's *Reading: How to Teach It* published in 1899. Edmund Burke Huey produced the first scientific contribution to reading instruction, *The Psychology and Pedagogy of Reading*. Beginnings in reading research and reading disability were noted in this period.

As an outgrowth of the word method, elaborate phonetic methods appeared, such as the Pollard method, which taught sounds within the context of a story. The sentence or story method also appeared, which had students memorize a story or rhyme and then read and analyze the separate words and phrases. Supplemental materials in the form of classic literature also appeared during this period.

THE SCIENTIFIC MOVEMENT, 1910–1924

During World War I (1917–1918), it was discovered that thousands of American soldiers could not read well enough to follow printed instructions. This initiated the improvement of reading instruction and also made teacher improvement a growing concern. The term *functional literacy* was born with standardized tests used frequently to determine students' reading levels. The advent of instruments of measurement, which made it possible to obtain scientific information about the effectiveness of reading methods and materials in the classroom, occurred.

Major innovations of this period include the switch from oral to silent reading, rapid expansion of reading research, and the development of remedial reading techniques. Teachers' manuals were emphasized during this period as every author of new reading textbooks furnished generous instructions for the use of their materials. Experience charts were initiated in which teachers invited discussion of some experience, and students dictated sentences about that experience, which were written on the chalkboard and then read by the children.

From 1925 to 1935, reading philosophies were divided between teaching students using sequential skills using basal readers or having students learn by permitting children to carry out their own purposes through the needs and experience of their own activities (the Activity Program). The Activity Program was actuated by the principles of Rousseau, Froebel, Pestalozzi, Dewey, and Kilpatrick. Other developments

in this period were expansion and application of reading research, establishment of the readiness concept, and extended development in diagnosis. A general tendency to teach reading in connection with various activities and interests throughout the school day and not to confine it to periods devoted solely to reading instruction was a new method of this period. Phonics was being taught much more moderately and was subordinate to other phases of reading instruction. Phonics were taught only to those who needed it, and the teacher began grouping to individual needs. The beginning readers used in most schools after the 1920s were usually based on the word or look-say method, with "Dick," Jane," and "Spot" becoming household names. Although these books were supposed to be based on meaning, they showed a remarkable lack of substance.

NATIONAL AND INTERNATIONAL UNREST, 1935–1960s

Reduction in teaching personnel due to World War II produced crowded classrooms and low-quality teaching. It was rediscovered that thousands of young men in the military could not read well enough to follow simple printed instructions. Therefore, renewed emphasis was placed on systematic reading instruction developing from one stage to another. New emphasis was placed on integrating reading into other subject areas and teaching reading in other curricular areas. The use of context clues and structural analysis appeared for the first time as techniques that should be taught to children. Long, organized skill charts were provided that indicated the many different reading skills to be developed with more attention to comprehension using "critical reading." Educators feared that listening to the radio, looking at comics, and viewing movies would reduce the interest in reading and decrease the amount of reading done.

In response to the high adult illiteracy of the 1960s, new methods were instituted in reading instruction. They included rewriting books using a limited graded vocabulary, teaching words and letters simultaneously, and the most common, teaching phonics directly. Most publishers of school texts put out developmental readers and supplementary texts such as DISTAR (Direct Instructional System for Teaching and Remediation). Improving skills in speed and comprehension became popular using devices to train eye movements. Special courses were introduced into teacher training for reading specialists, and learning theorists contributed "taxonomies" so that levels and types of achievement could be tested.

THE GREAT DEBATE: PHONICS VERSUS WHOLE WORD INSTRUCTION, 1960s–1980s

The "great debate" erupted in the 1960s because of the predominance of two methods for teaching reading: phonics and whole word. Phonics instruction guided children to learn the relationship between sounds and letters using an explicit set of phonics rules (code emphasis), while the whole word method used carefully prepared texts that would enable children to discover the relationship of word families (meaning emphasis). The great debate encompassed the dispute between these rival approaches to reading instruction. The phonics method incorporating intense, systematic phonics instruction with constant teacher-student interaction prevailed during the 1960/1970s. But it did not last.

WHOLE LANGUAGE, 1980–1990

In the 1980s, the amazing results of Marie Clay's Reading Recovery program in New Zealand transpired to the whole-language philosophy in America. This method of teaching reading focused on students actually reading real books using context clues, pictures, and known words to understand the text. The learning was child centered, not teacher directed, and was suggested as a revival of the look-and-say method. Kenneth Goodman and Frank Smith are cited as the leaders of the whole-language movement in the United States. They had found that readers rely on context to determine an upcoming word rather then using the spelling of the word. Some evidence supported the effectiveness of whole language, and many schools and teacher training institutions embraced it. However, the explosion of learning disabilities resulted in schools having to hire costly psychologists, special education teachers, and reading specialists. Also, many parents become frustrated by what they perceived as inadequate development of language skills by their children and bought into using commercial phonics programs. The "back to basics" movement had begun as a reaction to the whole-language movement. In the late 1990s, some states even decreed that phonics must be taught, which precipitated the idea of a balanced approach in the teaching of reading using both components of phonics and whole language.

THE CURRENT SITUATION

Currently, the emphasis on reading instruction centers on the proper mix of each approach in a comprehensive reading program. Many federal and state policies require that explicit skills instruction be part of a reading curriculum. In 2000, the National Reading Panel (NRP) released an extensive review of reading research that defined five elements that yielded positive results in reading achievement. Those five elements are phonics, phonemic awareness, fluency, vocabulary, and comprehension. The NRP report helped to shape the requirement of the Reading First initiative authorized under the No Child Left Behind Act of 2001. Reading First requires that states spend federal money to use only those components of reading instruction and materials with sound evidence that work. Subsequently, many reading programs are being restructured to incorporate those elements from the NFP's review, and many school systems are adopting new materials and providing specific teacher training to align with those five elements. Reading instruction has become politicized, and it continues to be hotly debated in curricular corners as well as in mainstream politics.

—Kimberley Martinez

See also accountability; at-risk students; brain research and practice; compensatory education; critical theory; cultural capital; cultural politics, wars; Department of Education; diversity; individual differences, in children; language theories and processes; Latinos; metacognition; resiliency; right-wing politics, advocates, impact on education; underachievers, in schools; writing, teaching of

Further Readings and References

Allington, R. (2002). *Big brother and the national reading curriculum: How ideology trumped evidence*. Portsmouth, NH: Heinemann.

Borman, G., & Hewes, G. (2002). The long-term effects and cost-effectiveness of success for all. *Educational Evaluation and Policy Analysis, 24*(4). 243–266.

Coles, G. (2003). *Reading the naked truth: Literacy, legislation, and lies*. Portsmouth, NH: Heinemann.

D'Agostino, J., & Murphy, J. (2004). A meta-analysis of reading recovery in United States schools. *Educational Evaluation and Policy Analysis, 26*(1), 23–38.

Goodman, Y. (1989). Roots of the whole-language movement. *Elementary School Journal, 90*(2), 113–128.

McLeod, S., D'Amico, J. J., & Protheroe, N. (2003). *K–12 principals' guide to No Child Left Behind*. Arlington, VA: Educational Research Service.

Miskel, C., & Song, M. (2004). Passing reading first: Prominence and processes in an elite policy network. *Educational Evaluation and Policy Analysis, 26*(2), 89–110.

Pearson, P. (2004). The reading wars. *Educational Policy, 18*(1), 1–37.

Staresina, L. N. (2004). Reading. *Education Week on the Web.* Retrieved May 13, 2004, from http://www.edweek.org/context/topics/issuespage.cfm?id=101.

Svobodny, D. (Ed.). (1985). *Early American textbooks, 1775–1900.* Washington, DC: Government Printing Office.

Wilson, R. M. (2000). *Teaching reading: A history.* Retrieved May 13, 2004, from http://www.socsci.kun.nl/ped/whp/histeduc/wilson10.html.

Whitehurst, G., & Lonigan, C. (2001). Emergent literacy: Development from prereaders to readers. In S. Neuman & D. Dickinson (Eds.), *Handbook of early literacy research.* New York: Guilford Press.

RECOGNITION THEORY/IDENTITY POLITICS

The etymology of the word *recognition* (the Latin *recognoscere*, "to know again") intimates this insistence on knowability, and current uses of the word rely on such a meaning. The concept of recognition offers a robust picture of people who are imbricated instead of isolated. People live and flourish with "circuits of recognition." Recognition theory acknowledges that individuals need a positive reflection by others of their group affiliation. Humans need more than to be left alone.

Recognition, as identity shaping, is situated in social-cultural contexts and is concerned with public space, such as a school. Within this public space, one's particularity, one's very identity, is itself vulnerable, malleable, and even multiple in public spaces such as the school. The recognitive process that an individual experiences within social-cultural contexts is replete with multiple encounters that shape identity, one's own and the identity of others. Such encounters begin with the assumption that neither knowledge nor acknowledgment is ever just ours to decide, that recognition always takes place within a larger horizon of socially imbued discourses, and that those discourses are circumscribed by social power, institutional constraints, and hegemonic norming. Both knowing *about* a person and *confirming* a person need to be considered within the context of the largely unspoken cultural assumptions that inform them.

Such cultural assumptions are all the more prevalent, and all the more enforced, in the "ideological state apparatus" of the school. Recognition, as sociocultural process, must consider both the constructive nature it has in relation to identity shaping as well as the cultural politics of the recognitive process, that is, how the dominant ideologies of different cultures work to shape one's identity through the recognitive process. Any analysis of recognition must consider the ability of both mirroring and confirmation as acts of acknowledgment.

One way to describe the event of public recognition in sociocultural contexts, such as schools, is to speak in terms of mirrors. That is to say, when individuals enter the public sphere, they need someone, or some thing, that will mirror back to them an affirming sense of who they are. Charles Taylor explained that our identity is partially shaped by recognition or its absence, often by misrecognition of others, and so our identity is damaged or distorted if people or society mirror back to us a confining or demeaning or contemptible picture of ourselves.

These social mirrors not only "reflect" us, they constitute us. Mirrors, in relation to recognition theory, afford a double mode of reflection and constitution during the public encounter, which is why the recognitive interchange is both promising and uncertain. Mirroring brings on a new sense of self at the same time that it solidifies the old sense. The encounter is reflective and reflexive, as it both portrays the self and works on the self. Confirmation, as Martin Buber explained, has to do with what one does in relation to the "other" and what "can become" by means of a recognitive reaction that cannot be prepared beforehand. In order to foster recognition in the public space of school, these aspects must be fostered within relationships of presence. A major aspect of recognition is presence with the other. Experiencing the other authentically is as important as knowledge of the other, and that interpersonal confirmation is fundamental to recognition in the classroom. Confirmation is achieved only with face-to-face experience between self and other. As Charles Bingham wrote in 2001, the classroom should be a public space of confirmation between self and other. However, the classroom must also be a place, with respect to shaping identity, that students and teachers are cognizant of the effect that ideologically embedded discourse, curriculum, and instruction present. Within the context of classroom teaching, this is especially significant, since curriculum and pedagogy are too often thought of as somehow distinct from the identity of the one who does the teaching.

Recognition as identity shaping is concerned with identification, within social, cultural, and political contexts. Two lessons can be learned in relation to identity. Identities and the acts attributed to them are always forming and re-forming in relation to historically specific contexts, and these contexts are political in nature, that is, defined by issues of diversity such as race, ethnicity, language, sexual orientation, gender, and economics.

Relatedly, identities and their cultural resources are responses to, develop in, and so include the dilemmas by the struggles, personal crises, and social recruitment under which they form. Recognition, or the absence of recognition, or ideologically charged recognition, gives way to a politics of identity. Identity politics, the tendency to base one's politics on a sense of personal identity, assumes that the most radical, activist politics develop when one comes to understand the dynamics of how one is oppressed and how one oppresses others in one's daily life.

Recognition, as identity shaping, is often framed by difference, understood not as fact but as perspective. "What is not" defines the boundaries of "what is." Who is the same as I am, who is other, and according to what criteria? How are racial differences essential or constructed, and what do they mean in our lives?

The second lesson is that identity forms in and across intimate and social contexts, over long periods of time. The historical timing of identity formation cannot simply be dictated by discourse. The identities posited by any particular discourse become important and a part of everyday life, based on the intersection of social histories and social actors. Most important, the social-cultural use of identities leads to another way of conceptualizing histories, personhoods, cultures, and their distributions over social and political groups.

—Patrick M. Jenlink

See also anti-Semitism; Asian Pacific Americans; Black education; bullying; civil rights movement; competition, forms of, in schools; critical race theory; critical theory; cross-cultural studies; cultural capital; determinism, sociocultural; diversity; Du Bois, W. E. B.; equality, in schools; esteem needs; ethnicity; ethnocentrism; expectations, teacher and student cultures; Fascism and schools; homophobia; immigration, history and impact in education; Latinos; lesbian/gay/transgender issues in education; minorities, in schools; moral education; multiculturalism; peer interaction/friendships; personality; queer theory; resiliency; sexism (glass ceiling); social context; social relations, dimensions of; underachievers, in schools

Further Readings and References

Bingham, C. (2001). *Schools of recognition: Identity politics and classroom practices*. New York: Rowman & Littlefield.

Buber, M. (1965). *Between man and man*. New York: Collier Books.

Holland, D. (1998). *Identity and agency in cultural worlds*. Cambridge, MA: Harvard University Press.

Kerr, D. (1997). Toward a democratic rhetoric of schooling. In J. I. Goodlad & T. J. McMannon (Eds.), *The public purpose of education and schooling* (pp. 73–83). San Francisco: Jossey-Bass.

Nieto, S. (2000). *Affirming diversity: The sociopolitical context of multicultural education* (3rd ed). New York: Addison Wesley Longman.

Taylor, C. (1991). *Sources of self*. Cambridge, MA: Harvard University Press.

Taylor, C. (1994). The politics of recognition. In Amy Gutman (Ed.), *Multiculturalism: Examining the politics of recognition* (pp. 25–73). Princeton, NJ: Princeton University Press.

RECRUITMENT, OF SCHOOL ADMINISTRATORS

Recruitment refers to both formal and informal processes aimed at eliciting applicants for administrative position vacancies. The goal of recruitment is to replace or enhance the supply of administrators. Common recruitment activities include alerting prospective applicants to current or upcoming job openings, identifying individuals believed to have the potential to succeed in a particular leadership role, sharing information about employment opportunities, and encouraging the completion of certification, licensure, and application requirements.

Formal recruitment processes can entail personnel officials: advertising administrative vacancies in public media internal or external to schools, establishing structured relationships with the placement offices of colleges and universities that prepare educational leaders, accessing the resume databases of administrators' professional organizations, participating in job fairs and conference sessions attended by administrative aspirants, offering training programs for career change into administration for teachers, and hiring search consultants or firms that specialize in administrator placement. (The latter have been more frequently relied upon for superintendencies than for other administrative roles.)

Informal recruitment can involve more exclusive and less publicly visible processes such as incumbent administrators; networking with others who share common interests, affiliations, or backgrounds; seeking personal referrals from experienced leaders or others in positions of power and influence in education; selectively communicating job opportunity information to friends, acquaintances, and other preferred prospects; mentoring, sponsoring, or promoting protégés for position vacancies; and grooming favored successors by providing special counsel, coaching, or opportunities to enhance leadership skills.

The history of K–12 schooling in the United States includes deep-seated traditions of informal recruitment leading to administrative hiring. That is, employment in the field has not relied exclusively on unsolicited applications submitted in response to publicly announced job openings. Instead, college professors and veteran administrators have always played active, influential roles in targeting, supporting, and paving the way for selected associates' career advancement.

Because of these traditions, recruitment practices have been criticized for being more closed than open and for contributing to the demographic homogeneity that has characterized educational administration historically. In the vernacular, such practices are sometimes referred to as a self-perpetuating "good old boys'" system at work, since most incumbent administrators, college professors, and search consultants are White males.

Affirmative action and the enforcement of equal opportunity employment laws are often cited as means of making recruitment and selection practices more inclusive. Advocates for greater diversity in educational leadership underscore the importance of recruitment practices that include and support people of color, women, persons with disabilities, and other populations historically underrepresented in educational administration.

—*Marilyn Tallerico*

See also affirmative action; Black education; career stages; diversity; human resource development; licensure and certification; mentoring; minorities, in schools; networking and network theory; personnel management; principal succession; sexism (glass ceiling); staffing, concepts of; teacher recruitment and retention; women in educational leadership; workplace trends

Further Readings and References

Brown, K., & Wynn, S. (2004). Why leadership-skilled women teachers are saying "no" to the principal's role: A matter of individual choice or institutional constraint? *Journal of School Leadership, 14*(6), 686–712.

Jones, B. (2001). *Supply and demand for school principals: A nationwide study.* Columbia, MO: Consortium for the Study of Educational Policy.

Kowalski, T., & Brunner, C. (2005). The school superintendent: Roles, challenges, and issues. In F. English (Ed.), *The SAGE handbook of educational leadership.* Thousand Oaks, CA: Sage.

Lunenburg, F., & Ornstein, A. (2004). *Educational administration: Concepts and practices* (4th ed.). Belmont, CA: Wadsworth/Thomson Learning.

Pounder, D., & Merrill, R. (2001). Job desirability of the high school principalship: A job choice theory perspective. *Educational Administration Quarterly, 37*(1), 5–26.

REDUCTION IN FORCE

Most states have statutes directly dealing with the abolition of teaching or other positions without fault on the part of individual employees, commonly referred to as reduction in force (RIF). The grounds for RIF, the order in which employees are released, can "bump" others, and call-back rights are matters of state law subject to modifications by board policies and collective bargaining contracts.

RIFs are most commonly permitted for declines in student enrollment, financial exigencies, elimination of positions or programs, and board discretion. While courts usually defer to board discretion on the good faith needed for RIFs, if challenged, administrators must prove that they carried out justifiable RIFs in accord with state law and their own policies and/or bargaining contracts. In addition, courts expect policies to include descriptions of the criteria that board officials rely on and how they are weighed in implementing RIFs.

Once boards find that RIFs are necessary, they must determine the order of release. Although RIFs are ordinarily based on seniority, seniority rights must be based on statutes or collective bargaining contracts. Even though boards typically bear the burden of proving that a job is no longer necessary, they are not ordinarily required to interchange large numbers of courses between and among existing positions to create positions for teachers who were subjected to RIFs.

In evaluating seniority, absent modifications based on board policy or bargaining contracts, the first criterion is full-time service. Beyond that, board methods must be reasonable and not prohibited by statute. Furthermore, where tenured teachers lose their jobs as part of RIFs, nontenured faculty members typically cannot remain in similar positions, nor may board policies grant them the status of tenured faculty. In other words, incumbents of eliminated positions are entitled to retain jobs for which they are certificated even if jobs are occupied by colleagues with less seniority.

Individuals who lose their jobs in RIFs are responsible to assure board officials that their certifications for other positions are valid when it is time for bumping. *Bumping* is a term of art that permits employees with more seniority, and the same credentials, to preserve their jobs at the expense of more junior colleagues.

Subject to board policy and collective bargaining contracts, RIF statutes typically provide that the positions of certificated employees who have been released cannot be filled until they have first been offered their jobs back. State law may even specify how many years of seniority they retain on preferred eligibility lists for positions. Under preferred eligibility provisions, employees are usually called back in the order of seniority such that the first to be let go is the first to be called back.

—*Charles J. Russo*

See also collective bargaining; contracts, with teacher unions; job security; management theories; satisfaction, in organizations and roles; working conditions, in schools

Further Readings and References

DeMitchell, T. (2005). Unions, collective bargaining, and the challenges of leading. In F. English (Ed.), *The SAGE handbook of educational leadership* (pp. 538–549). Thousand Oaks, CA: Sage.
Hartmeister, F., & Russo, C. J. (1999). "Taxing" the system when selecting teachers for reduction-in-force. *Education Law Reporter, 130*(3), 989–1008.
Lieberman, M. (1997). *The teacher unions.* New York: Free Press.

REDUCTIONISM/PARSIMONY

Reductionism is a deliberate outcome of traditional theory making, while parsimony is regarded as one of the premier virtues that qualifies theory as commendable. Reductionism is based in the assumption that the appearance of complexity can be accurately and usefully abridged by creating a concise schematic representation or theoretical picture of underlying, more fundamental, factors, which are often regarded as existing in a causal relationship to observed phenomena. A ready example is the Marxist reduction of the epiphenomena of social institutions, practices, and

individual fates to their purportedly economic origins. In educational administration, such a neo-Marxist reduction is characteristic of critical theory, which depicts the school and its administrative arrangements as the visible consequences of the unequal distribution of wealth or capital among definable social classes.

The Marxist and neo-Marxist would claim that the reduction of experience to economy produces "true consciousness," or a more accurate and objective picture of what is, in fact, the case. Similarly, most reductivist theories suggest that their particular reduction contributes substantially to a true or, more modestly, to a more useful picture of reality than that yielded by raw observation. Theories are typically tested for truth or utility—their theoretical adequacy—by measuring the extent to which the principles and assertions that result from reductivist operations facilitate the explanation, prediction, and the control of circumstance.

A theory's truth or usefulness, then, is verified by the predictive power of the more fundamental principles disclosed through reduction. This verification may come through the prediction of future occurrences or in the design of interventions that accomplish predicted effects. In sum, empirical adequacy is determined by a theory's ability to make what previously appeared as mysterious and intractable (e.g., fate, fortune, or chance) available for understanding and mastery. To refer to critical theory once again, the neo-Marxist reduction of schools and their administration to more fundamental matters of economy should permit an enhanced understanding of school life made evident in the prediction of observable realities and in the design of measures that result in desired improvements.

Parsimony or economy of explanation has traditionally been considered to be a cardinal virtue in theory making and a robust principle to be applied in the adjudication of competing theoretical schemas. As the reductivist purpose of theory is to represent complexity in simplified form, parsimony is a self-evident measure of a theory's success, providing that the theory proves its empirical adequacy. Said with appropriate shortness, brevity is taken to be a powerful measure of a theory's potential worth. The familiar "KISS principle," which can be politely summarized in the admonition "keep it simple," both abides by the principle of parsimony and conveys its content accurately.

The most historically esteemed expression of the principle of parsimony is Ockham's Razor, so named because it is found in the writings of William (1285–1349), a Franciscan friar and philosopher with a logician's sensibilities who lived in the English village of Ockham. Echoing Aristotle's assertion that nature itself operates in the most economic way possible, William's avowal that the logic of parsimony calls for the cutting away of extraneous aspects of theory would be repeated by many philosophers and scientists, including Gottfried Leibniz, Isaac Newton, and Albert Einstein.

When multiple theories that meet the test of empirical adequacy contest for predominance, parsimony dictates that the theory of greatest simplicity is to be preferred. There is an aesthetically pleasing as well as an epistemologically satisfying quality that characterizes theories that effect the reduction of extreme complexities to the barest formulations. The extent to which Einstein's $E = mc^2$ has become a cultural icon is reflective of the cachet attached to parsimonious reductions of what may at first glance appear impenetrably complex. In educational administration, a similar value attaches, for example, to the Getzels-Guba diagrammatic reduction of the seemingly endless complexities of organizational life to the interaction of "nomothetic" (collective) and "idiographic" (individualistic) elements, values, and practices.

Reductionism and parsimony, however, have not been without their critics, particularly in educational administration. T. B. Greenfield's idea that notions of organizations must be as complex as the reality we are trying to understand would counterbalance the hazards of oversimplification that can result from the indiscriminate application of the reductionism and parsimony favored in the positivistic sciences. Greenfield's caution is amplified by Christopher Hodgkinson's observation that reduction and parsimony are necessarily held in check by the irreducible and sometimes ineffable human realities that are the subject matter of educational administration.

Because of its concern with such protean "raw material," theory in educational administration is necessarily pluralistic, diverse, and changing. Given the likelihood that many of the truths associated with the thoroughly human enterprise of education will inevitably be multiplex, local, and unstable, the value of reductionism and the virtue of parsimony may benefit from qualification in both research and practice.

—*Martin Barlosky*

See also chaos theory; critical theory; deconstruction; empiricism; hypotheses, in research; knowledge base, of the field; organizational theories; postmodernism; quantitative research methods; research methods

Further Readings and References

Barlosky, M. (1996). Knowledge, certainty and openness in educational administration. In C. Evers & G. Lakomski (Eds.), *Exploring educational administration: Coherentist applications and critical debates* (pp. 247–261). Oxford: Pergamon/Elsevier Science.

Barlosky, M. (1996). A rejoinder to Evers and Lakomski. In C. Evers & G. Lakomski (Eds.), *Exploring educational administration: Coherentist applications and critical debates* (pp. 271–278). Oxford: Pergamon/Elsevier Science.

Barlosky, M. (2001). Leadership study and administrative practice: Shall the twain ever meet? In K.-C. Wong & C. W. Evers (Eds.), *Leadership for quality schooling: International perspectives* (pp. 67–89). London: Routledge.

English, F. (2003). *The postmodern challenge to the theory and practice of educational administration.* Springfield, IL: Charles C Thomas.

Greenfield, T. B., & Ribbins, P. (1993). *Greenfield on educational administration: Towards a humane science.* London: Routledge.

Hodgkinson, C. (1991). *Educational leadership: The moral art.* Albany: State University of New York Press.

Young, M., & Lopez, R. (2005). The nature of inquiry in educational leadership. In F. English (Ed.), *The SAGE handbook of educational leadership* (pp. 337–361). Thousand Oaks, CA: Sage.

REFORM, OF SCHOOLS

The call to reform K–12 public schools has been an enduring movement in the United States since the 1850s, when Horace Mann helped establish common schools in Massachusetts. School reform is characterized by cycles of what educational historians have termed *progress and regress.* One day schools are the best vehicle for the nation's overall progress toward a well-educated citizenry. In the next period, their failure is predicating the downfall of the nation's future. Reform tends to occur when the public is convinced that schools are regressing and something must be done to fix them, but at the heart of such pessimism is an inherent progressive ideal that schools can be fixed and that fixing them will indeed lead to a better nation.

HISTORY OF PROGRESS AND REGRESS

Progressivism

After the 1850s, many states passed compulsory schooling laws not only to educate native-born American citizens but also to "Americanize" growing numbers of immigrant children. In addition to language instruction, schools included vocational training and social services such as vaccinations and school meals. Some of these efforts in schooling were rooted in the Progressivism Movement from about 1890 to 1920, which aimed to reform society's ills, from poverty to unfair labor laws. Public schools, with their captive population of children, became one more institution (in addition to religious bodies and legislatures) that social progressives could use to create programs and practices that would improve society.

While the progressives were reforming society through social programs in schools, some progressives also sought to reform pedagogy and curriculum by making it more child centered. John Dewey's work at the University of Chicago lab school led the way for schools to build upon children's experiences to make education meaningful to them. Dewey also espoused Mann's desire for schools to foster a democratic society, claiming that schools allow the opportunity for knowledge to be built through shared experiences and interests.

Progressivism in education also included the "administrative progressives" who sought to make schools more efficient by means of standardized testing and curriculum differentiated for different abilities, whether vocational or college preparation.

This emphasis on differentiated curriculum for efficiency's sake led progressive education in the 1940s and 1950s to the life adjustment movement. Undergirding life adjustment was the theory of vocational educator Charles Prosser that only 20% of students would be ready for college and 20% for vocational work, so that schools should prepare the remaining 60% of students for everyday life by teaching skills such as parenting and health. In the 1950s, critics of the life adjustment movement claimed that schools had become too child centered, were "dumbing down" their curriculum, and needed to return to extensive academic preparation. Thus was born a "back to the basics" movement, which continues today. The preference for basics over life skills was reinforced by a national event that started yet another push for extensive school reform: Sputnik.

Post-Sputnik Reform

In 1957, the Soviet Union launched the satellite Sputnik I, thus winning the first heat of a space race between the Soviet Union and the United States. Because of Cold War-era tension, Americans were immediately concerned about falling behind in space, viewing it as a threat to national security and attributing the failure to poor public schools. In 1958, President Eisenhower signed the National Defense Education Act, which dedicated federal funds to improving public education. Schools became much more focused on rigorous curriculum to teach math, science, and foreign languages. The National Science Foundation sponsored science fairs and provided training for teachers as well as led less successful initiatives such as New Math and an elementary school anthropology curriculum called Man: A Course of Study. While the focus on science, math, and languages continued, the concern over the United States's place in the space race was assuaged somewhat by the successful Apollo 11 landing on the moon in 1969. However, Sputnik established what has become a recurring theme of concern about how America's schoolchildren compete compared to the rest of the world's.

Civil Rights, Brown, Desegregation, and Access

In addition to post-Sputnik concerns about what schools should be teaching and how, the civil rights movement of the 1950s and 1960s led schools to reform access. The 1954 *Brown v. Board of Education* decision outlawed racial segregation and "separate but equal" schools. In some places, desegregation occurred grudgingly but peacefully; in others, violently. Resistance by Whites to the enrollment of Black students in Central High School in Little Rock, Arkansas, led President Eisenhower to call out the National Guard. In 1974, Boston erupted under a forced-busing policy of integration.

In 1965, the Elementary and Secondary Education Act allocated federal funds for schools as part of President Johnson's war on poverty. Since it followed the 1964 Civil Rights Act, which prohibits federal funds going to programs or activities that discriminate on the grounds of race, color, or national origin, states that wanted to receive the federal funds had to comply with desegregation orders. Schools also eventually integrated Latinos, Asian Americans, and Native Americans.

In the years since *Brown*, courts and schools have tried to determine how to decide whether they are desegregated enough and whether they have demonstrated a good faith commitment to desegregation. Parents and educators have echoed Justice Clarence Thomas's caution in *Missouri v. Jenkins* that it should not be assumed that Black schools are inherently inferior to White schools, and some have called for strengthening Black schools instead of integrating them with White schools.

Desegregation has certainly not been accomplished; researchers at the Harvard Civil Rights Project indicate that, in fact, desegregation is reversing to segregation, and that while the minority population grows across the United States, White students are more likely to attend school with other Whites.

Elementary and Secondary Education Act

Besides its effect of forcing schools to desegregate or risk losing federal money, the Elementary and Secondary Education Act (ESEA) of 1965 reformed schools most notably by means of its Title I funding, which provided a billion dollars a year to high-poverty schools and disadvantaged children. The ESEA directed funds toward programs for children with disabilities, bilingual education, and Head Start. From a reform perspective, the ESEA was one of the first instances of the federal government taking a larger role in schooling and tying that role to funding. The ESEA was reauthorized in 1994 under the Improving America's Schools Act and most recently in 2001 under the No Child Left Behind Act.

A Nation at Risk, *Standards, and Goals 2000*

In 1983, the National Commission on Excellence in Education, created by Secretary of Education Terrel H. Bell, issued an "open letter to the American people" reporting in rhetorically powerful language that schools were failing. The commission found that schools were inadequate in their content, expectations, use of time, and teaching. Their recommendations included strengthening graduation requirements, adopting rigorous and measurable standards, lengthening the school day or year, and improving teacher quality.

States responded to *A Nation at Risk* by increasing graduation requirements, setting content standards, and adding tests. The nation's governors convened and set national goals, formalized by Congress in 1994 under President Clinton as the Goals 2000: Educate America Act. Goals 2000 provided participating states with grants in return for initiating reforms aimed at improving student achievement, such as standards, teacher quality, and technology. In a 1999

review of progress toward the goals, journalist David Hoff noted that although student achievement was not markedly improved as the year 2000 approached, the goals did serve to heighten public concern and focus state reform efforts, which by itself is some progress. Goals 2000 has since been supplemented by a much more extensive reform: the reauthorization of the ESEA, or the No Child Left Behind Act.

No Child Left Behind

The No Child Left Behind Act (NCLB) of 2001 once again increased the federal role in school reform by tying federal Title I funding to states' cooperation. NCLB introduced extensive annual testing through Grade 8 and the goal of proficiency for every student by 2014, including students in four subgroups: low socioeconomic status, students with disabilities, students with limited English proficiency, and major racial and ethnic groups. Individual schools must make "adequate yearly progress" toward their state's proficiency goal for each subgroup. Schools that do not make adequate yearly progress for 2 consecutive years must notify parents, provide students with the option to attend school elsewhere in the district, provide supplemental services such as tutoring, and receive technical assistance from the state. NCLB also requires teachers hired with Title I funds to be "highly qualified," meaning degreed and certified in their subject area.

NCLB has been controversial. Some hail it as much-needed accountability and for its seeking to reduce inequities in achievement by identifying student subgroups' test results. Others criticize it for the weight it places on testing as a measure of school success and for what they see as an impossible goal of universal proficiency by 2014. There is also little agreement about whether or not the law has been adequately funded. Some states, such as Utah, see NCLB as an infringement on their own role in education or, because of its strict state reporting requirements, as a drain on resources. Since its enactment, the U.S. Department of Education has clarified some of NCLB's requirements, such as how districts can use Title I funds for professional development, and it is likely that such clarification and modification will continue.

ISSUES AND TRENDS

There are several factors that continue to surface in the cycle of educational reform: who is in charge, what should be taught and how, how students can have equal opportunity to learn, how to measure progress toward learning, and how to prepare students to compete in a global economy.

Governance and Accountability

School reform tends to be not only a history of progress and regress but of response to shifting current events and political pressures. Schools are expected simultaneously to shape the future of society and respond to its needs. One issue that naturally arises, then, is one of governance, or of who should be in control of schools. Related to that issue is accountability, meaning how responsive schools are to reform efforts.

As publicly funded institutions usually administered by professional educators who report to locally elected or appointed school boards or officials, it is not clear what roles local, state, and federal governments play. The state of Iowa, for example, maintains local control so strongly that it remains the only state without statewide content standards, thus earning an F every year on the standards and accountability section of the "Quality Counts" reports compiled by *Education Week*. According to popular reform initiatives, Iowa's students should therefore be low achieving. Yet about 75% of Iowa's fourth graders are proficient on statewide tests, it ranks in the top 10 or so of states on national tests, and it has the second highest graduation rate in the nation. While some of this success is attributable to the state's relatively homogeneous and stable student population, such good results belie the statewide standards and accountability that other states have worked so hard to implement and allow Iowa to continue to rely on local rather than state control.

Another issue of governance has been that of professional versus nonprofessional interests. The culture of efficiency established by administrative progressives valued professionalism, specialization, hierarchy, and credentials, all of which have led educators to be somewhat resistant when noneducators want to critique and reform schools. This resistance was enacted in the 1960s during the civil rights movement and continues in response to NCLB. While NCLB demands more accountability from educators than ever before, the research on accountability tells us that external demands such as NCLB are always mediated by the internal structures a school has in place. It takes time for schools to develop such complex internal structures. Thus one can expect that whatever reform is enacted—be it desegregation or NCLB—it will take time to implement.

Instructional Leadership

From the early days of progressive education, an ongoing issue in school reform has been curriculum and pedagogy: what should be taught and how. Goals 2000 and the standards movement helped nearly all states establish content standards—what students should know—as well as performance standards—how well students should be able to do what they know. NCLB also provides some standards for teacher quality in terms of credentialing. Some reform initiatives are aimed at how teachers should teach, such as the National Board for Professional Teaching Standards and the Coalition for Essential Schools' Critical Friends Groups. Some design pedagogical scripts, like Success for All and Direct Instruction. But for the most part the educational community does not address what good pedagogy looks like. This lack of discussion means that administrators, who are supposed to be instructional leaders, have less guidance about what teachers should be doing, let alone be able to build an instructional community based on distributed leadership.

Equity

A motivating concern in school reform has continued to be equity, or the opportunity for all children to learn. As noted earlier, NCLB has been hailed for its efforts to acknowledge and reduce the achievement gap between subgroups of students. Reforms such as reducing class size, inclusion of students with disabilities, and the plan in Cambridge, Massachusetts, of desegregating schools by socioeconomic status are all promising.

Testing

The extensive testing required by NCLB has historical roots in the world of differentiated instruction and progressive education, as noted earlier, as well as in eugenics. Students then were to be tested to discover the occupation to which they were best suited. Students now are to be tested to make sure they are proficient. Several states have also adopted high-stakes tests that students must pass in order to graduate from high school. The American Educational Research Association has cautioned against using tests as a single measure of student progress, and other scholars have noted adverse effects, such as dropping out, of high-stakes testing on minority students. However, the American public currently favors testing of students.

Competing Globally and Providing Alternative Schooling Models

Since Sputnik and *A Nation at Risk*, both of which were concerned with how United States students measured up to their counterparts across the globe, a continuing rationale for schooling has been preparing students to compete in a global economy. This rationale is rooted in America's capitalist structure, and one of the ensuing trends in school reform has thus been to model schools after business. Some school systems have privatized, offering school operations to for-profit companies such as the Edison Schools. Other systems have created alternative schools from which parents can choose. Advocates of school choice suggest that providing a market in which schools compete for students will improve schooling quality overall. Thus, several states have enacted charter school laws so that new schools, freer of bureaucratic strictures and open to new ideas, can be created by innovative leaders. Some communities, notably Milwaukee and Cleveland, have also enacted voucher systems where parents can send their children to private schools, including private religious schools, using public funds.

All of these efforts are true to the experimental spirit of progressivism while continuing the cycle of regressive reaction to school reform.

—*Joanne M. Marshall*

See also accountability; achievement tests; Black education; charter schools; choice, of schools; civil rights movement; class size; desegregation, of schools; Dewey, John; equality, in schools; governance; immigration, history and impact in education; innovation, in education; Kentucky Education Reform Act; Latinos; Mann, Horace; *A Nation at Risk*; No Child Left Behind; politics, of education, privatization; restructuring, of schools; school improvement models; standard setting; standardized testing; state departments of education; systemic reform; tracking, of students; voucher plans

Further Readings and References

American Educational Research Association. (2000). *AERA position statement: High-stakes testing in Pre-K–12 education.* Retrieved from http://aera.net/policyandprograms/?id=378.

Dewey, J. (1916). *Democracy in education: An introduction to the philosophy of education.* New York: Macmillan.

Report card: Iowa. Quality Counts 2005: No small change: Targeting money toward student performance. (2005, January 6). *Education Week, 24,* 118.

Frankenberg, E., Lee, C., & Orfield, G. (2003). *A multiracial society with segregated schools: Are we losing the dream?* Cambridge, MA: Civil Rights Project, Harvard University.

Fuhrman, S. (2003). *Redesigning accountability systems for education* (CPRE Research Report Series No. RB-38). Philadelphia: Consortium for Policy Research in Education.

Fullan, M. (2000). The three stories of education reform. *Phi Delta Kappan, 81*(8), 581–584.

Greene, J. P., & Winters, M. A. (2005). *Public high school graduation and college-readiness rates: 1991-2002.* New York: Center for Civic Innovation at the Manhattan Institute.

Madaus, G., & Marguerite, C. (2001). The adverse impact of high stakes testing on minority students: Evidence from 100 years of test data. In G. Orfield & M. L. Kornhaber (Eds.), *Raising standards or raising barriers? Inequality and high-stakes testing in public education* (pp. 85–106). New York: Century Foundation Press.

McNeil, L., & Valenzuela, A. (2001). The harmful impact of the TAAS system of testing in Texas: Beneath the accountability rhetoric. In G. Orfield & M. L. Kornhaber (Eds.), *Raising standards or raising barriers? Inequality and high-stakes testing in public education* (pp. 127–150). New York: Century Foundation Press.

Missouri v. Jenkins, 515 US 70 (1995).

National Association of Secondary School Principals. (2004). *Breaking ranks II: Strategies for leading high school reform.* Reston, VA: Author.

O'Day, J. A. (2002). Complexity, accountability, and school improvement. *Harvard Educational Review, 72*(3), 293–329.

Spillane, J. P., Halverson, R., & Diamond, J. B. (2001). Investigating school leadership practice: A distributed perspective. *Educational Researcher, 30*(3), 23–28.

U.S. Department of Education. (1996). *Goals 2000: Increasing student achievement through state and local initiatives: Introduction.* Washington, DC: Author.

🏛 REHABILITATION ACT OF 1973

The Rehabilitation Act of 1973, as amended, is a federal statute providing funding for occupational rehabilitation services to people with disabilities. Commonly referred to as the Rehab Act, it replaced federal vocational rehabilitation statutes and amendments passed in 1920 and 1943. The act also contains important provisions protecting persons with disabilities from discrimination and is designed to provide the federal government with a leadership role in improving the lives of persons with disabilities.

THE ACT'S DEFINITIONS OF INDIVIDUALS WITH DISABILITIES

The act provides two definitions of individuals with disabilities. As a general rule, it defines an individual with a disability as someone (a) with a physical or mental impairment that constitutes or results in a substantial impediment to employment and (b) who may benefit from vocational rehabilitation. For nondiscrimination and advocacy provisions (most notably Section 504), however, an individual with a disability is defined as someone (a) with a physical or mental impairment that substantially limits one or more major life activities, (b) with a record of such an impairment, or (c) who is regarded as having such an impairment. This second definition is similar to the definition used in the Americans With Disabilities Act (ADA). The Rehab Act excludes several persons from these definitions, depending on which part of the act is implicated, such as illegal drug use, individuals with infectious diseases, certain sexual minorities, and individuals with certain mental illnesses.

For purposes of vocational rehabilitation, the act defines an individual with a significant disability. One has a significant disability when one (a) has a severe physical or mental impairment that seriously limits one or more functional capacities (which impairment is listed in the definition or is of a comparable severity) and (b) will need vocational rehabilitation over a lengthy period. Individuals with significant disabilities may be entitled to priority in states with wait-lists for vocational rehabilitation services.

THE REHABILITATION SERVICES ADMINISTRATION

The act established the Rehabilitation Services Administration (RSA). Housed in the Department of Education, the RSA approves and monitors each state's vocational rehabilitation plan. The RSA provides grants to states and nonprofit organizations to train rehabilitation services personnel. The RSA also may make grants for pilot projects and demonstration programs related to vocational rehabilitation, grants to provide vocational rehabilitation to migrant farm laborers, and grants for recreation programs that assist in maximizing the independence and integration of persons with disabilities. One percent of the funds appropriated to the RSA are to be spent on projects serving traditionally underserved populations, such as the African American and Hispanic communities and American Indian tribes.

VOCATIONAL REHABILITATION SERVICES

An example of cooperative federalism, the act's provisions for vocational rehabilitation are similar to the provisions for special education under the Individuals With Disabilities Education Act (the IDEA). The RSA will approve grants to states for the provision of vocational rehabilitation, so long as each state submits a plan conforming to the act's requirements. To receive a grant, each state must submit a plan containing 24 required elements. Each state's plan must designate a responsible state agency (or agencies, in case the state elects to separately provide vocational rehabilitation services to individuals who are blind). The plan must ensure that the whole state is served. To ensure an adequate supply of persons trained in vocational rehabilitation, the plan must set forth a comprehensive system of personnel development and necessary interagency agreements to guarantee that the state complies with the act's requirements. The plan must ensure that each individual eligible for vocational rehabilitation is provided with services under an individualized plan for employment, unless the plan provides for a wait-list in case of insufficient resources. The plan must provide for public comment, frequent review, and citizen involvement. Each state must report annually to the RSA regarding its compliance with its plan. If the RSA rejects a state's plan, the state is entitled to an impartial hearing. Each state may spend some of its grant to train employers about the employment requirements of the ADA.

The responsible state agency must have a procedure to determine eligibility for vocational rehabilitation. One must benefit from vocational rehabilitation services, yet all are presumed to benefit, and the state agency must rebut that presumption before denying services due to inability to benefit. Individuals who receive disability benefits under the Social Security Act, including SSI, are presumptively eligible. The agency has 60 days to determine eligibility.

Each state must provide an individualized plan for employment to all who receive vocational rehabilitation services. The plan must be a written document, must contain the individual's procedural rights, must focus on the individual's strengths, must be developed with the individual's input and with regard for the individual's choice of a vocational outcome, must contain measurable goals and objectives, and must state how and where specific vocational rehabilitation services are to be provided, and by whom. Services are to be provided in the most integrated setting possible. If an individual is dissatisfied with any aspect of the plan, including an adverse eligibility determination, that individual may seek mediation, an impartial hearing, and, ultimately, review in state or federal court. Each state is required to offer a client assistance program to provide advice, information, advocacy, and problem-solving assistance to people receiving assistance from a vocational rehabilitation program. The client assistance program may not be housed in the agency responsible for vocational rehabilitation services.

Vocational rehabilitation services include, but are not limited to, assessment, counseling and guidance, job search and retention assistance, vocational training, funding not otherwise available (such as tuition assistance or health care assistance), transportation, interpretation services, start-up costs, licensing fees, assistive technology, referrals, and supported employment. These services may be provided to individuals with disabilities or to groups of persons with disabilities.

Vocational rehabilitation services are often an important part of any postsecondary transition plan required under the IDEA.

INDIVIDUAL RIGHTS AND ADVOCACY

The Rehab Act contains several provisions requiring affirmative action in employment and prohibiting discrimination against individuals with disabilities by federal agencies, by recipients of federal contracts of over $10,000, and, under Section 504, by recipients of federal financial assistance. The act imports the ADA's employment discrimination standards by cross-reference. Remedies for violating the act's nondiscrimination provisions are set forth and include damages, equitable relief, and attorneys' fees for prevailing parties.

Section 508 of the Rehab Act requires that federal departments maintain electronic and information technology that is accessible to individuals with disabilities. The act also creates the Access Board, which is to promulgate standards for barrier-free accessible buildings and transportation. The act provides technical and financial assistance to certain groups seeking

to remove architectural, transportation, or communication barriers.

The act also provides appropriations for protection and advocacy services to individuals with disabilities.

MORE ABOUT SECTION 504

As noted above, Section 504 prohibits employers who receive federal financial assistance from discriminating against workers with disabilities. This provision, however, does so much more. It protects any individual with a disability, who is otherwise qualified, from being excluded from participating in *any* program or activity receiving federal financial assistance. To maintain a cause of action under Section 504, plaintiffs must show four things: (1) they are individuals with a disability, (2) they were otherwise qualified, and (3) they were discriminated against solely because of their disability (4) by a program or activity receiving federal financial assistance.

Regarding the first element, an individual with minor or correctable impairments is not an individual with a disability. Certain individuals are excluded by the act's definitions. For example, an employee with an infectious or communicable disease may not be an individual with a disability if that disease is a direct threat to others or prevents the employee from performing job duties. In nearly all cases, the direct threat posed by an employee must be assessed in light of each employee's unique facts and based on reasonable medical judgment.

Regarding the second element, individuals are "otherwise qualified" if they may participate in the program or activity with or without reasonable accommodation. Failure to accommodate may violate Section 504; however, major alterations in the program or activity are not required.

Regarding the third element, discrimination may include failure to interview, hire, promote, or retain an employee with a disability, failure to make a program or activity accessible to people with disabilities, failure to make reasonable accommodations for individuals with disabilities, and retaliation against individuals who assert rights under Section 504. Certain small providers need not make significant structural changes to comply with Section 504.

Regarding the fourth element, "program or activity receiving federal financial assistance" is broadly defined. The phrase includes cash and in-kind assistance. In nearly all cases, a recipient is covered if any of its units or divisions receives qualifying assistance.

Nearly all state and local governments are covered (including school systems at all levels), as well as most private schools, colleges, universities, and medical institutions.

While the ADA contains many identical protections, Section 504 remains a critically important antidiscrimination statute. First, Section 504 applies to all recipients of federal money and aid; in contrast, certain of the ADA's employment provisions, for example, apply only to employers that have a certain threshold number of employees. Second, many actions in federal court under the ADA against state government have been barred by the U.S. Constitution's Eleventh Amendment; however, most federal court actions against states under Section 504 have not been barred by the Eleventh Amendment.

SECTION 504 IN EDUCATION

As noted above, Section 504 covers nearly all education institutions, and the act reaches nearly all aspects of education. The following nonexhaustive list of examples illustrates Section 504's reach:

- The act requires school leaders to reasonably accommodate employees with disabilities. It requires schools to provide special education or related services to children with disabilities, who may or may not be covered by the IDEA.
- It may require accommodations to policies or practices, such as waivers of eligibility rules for extracurricular activities.
- It may require structural alterations to make the school facility accessible to persons with disabilities.
- Finally, it may require school leaders to intervene and prevent harassment and bullying based on disability.

OTHER PROVISIONS

The act has several other important features. It created the National Institute on Disability and Rehabilitation Research, which conducts and funds research on rehabilitation services and disseminates results. It created the National Council on Disability (NCD), an independent agency composed primarily of individuals with disabilities, which is empowered to promote equal opportunity for persons with disabilities in all aspects of society. The NCD advises the president of the United States, executive agency heads, the commissioner of the RSA, and the director of the National

Institute on Disability and Rehabilitation Research, as well as annually submitting a report on disability policy to the president and Congress. The act also provides support for independent living centers and services for individuals with significant disabilities and individuals who are blind and are age 55 and older. Finally, the act provides for cooperative efforts with industry to encourage employment of persons with disabilities including supported employment.

—*Thomas A. Mayes*

See also accountability; adaptiveness of organizations; affirmative action; architecture of schools; bureaucracy; cost-benefit analyses; Department of Education; Federal Privacy Act; individual differences, in children; law; learning environments; negligence; politics, of education; school safety; working conditions, in schools

Further Readings and References

Americans With Disabilities Act, 20 U.S.C.A. §§ 12101-213 (West 1998 & Supp. 2004).

Bender, W. (2002). *Differentiating instruction for students with learning disabilities.* Thousand Oaks, CA: Corwin Press.

Imber, M., & van Geel, T. (2005). *Education law.* Mahwah, NJ: Erlbaum.

Karten, T. (2004). *Inclusion strategies that work.* Thousand Oaks, CA: Corwin Press.

Longmore, P. (2003). *Why I burned my book and other essays on disability.* Philadelphia: Temple University Press.

Mayes, T. A., & Zirkel, P. A. (2000). State educational agencies and special education: Obligations and liabilities. *Boston University Public Interest Law Journal, 10,* 62–90.

McLaughlin, M., & Nolet, V. (2004). *What every principal needs to know about special education.* Thousand Oaks, CA: Corwin Press.

Michalko, R. (2002). *The difference that disability makes.* Philadelphia: Temple University Press.

Obiakor, F., & Ford, B. (2002). *Creating successful learning environments for African American learners with exceptionalities.* Thousand Oaks, CA: Corwin Press.

Osborne, A., & Russo, C. (2003). *Special education and the law: A guide for practitioners.* Thousand Oaks, CA: Corwin Press.

Rehabilitation Act of 1973, as amended, 20 U.S.C.A. §§ 701-796*l* (West 1998 & Supp. 2004).

School Board of Nassau County v. Arline, 480 U.S. 237 (1987).

Southeastern Community College v. Davis, 442 U.S. 397 (1979).

Thompson, S., Quenemoen, R., Thurlow, M., & Ysseldyke, J. (2001). *Alternate assessments for students with disabilities.* Thousand Oaks, CA: Corwin Press.

🏛 RELIGION, IN SCHOOLS

In the United States, religion and its place within the public school walls has been a source of ongoing controversy for well over 150 years. Under the rubric of secularism, the early common schools of the nineteenth century generally favored a loosely Protestant ethos, and the textbooks and daily practices tended to reflect this. Textbooks generally carried an overt Protestant orientation and could be fiercely anti-Catholic, with some even warning against the evils of "popery." Many public schools began their days with collective prayers and readings out of the King James Version of the Bible. Such vaguely Protestant practices were viewed by the courts as secular, and consequently, unproblematic. These daily practices would remain the norm in many public schools—but not all—until the mid-twentieth century.

The most important change regarding religion and public schooling occurred during the early 1960s, when the U.S. Supreme Court more narrowly defined secularism. In a series of Supreme Court decisions, state-sponsored prayer was invalidated and then a year later, compulsory Bible readings. In each instance, the court ruled that nonspecific, nondenominational religious exercises were still state-sponsored religious, not secular, exercises and, as such, were banned under the establishment clause of the U.S. Constitution. Subsequent court decisions invalidated (a) bans on the teaching of evolution in public schools and (b) state requirements to teach creationism if evolution were taught in public schools, as well as legislated "moment of silence" mandates. Since the 1960s, secularism has meant that public schools could neither favor nor disfavor religion. Public schools were and are free to teach *about* various religions and religious history, but they cannot teach religion as "truth" or as history or science.

While there was strong support for the Supreme Court's redefinition of secularism, some Protestants strenuously objected to the elimination of collective school prayer and Bible readings. By the late 1970s, as part of a larger movement, Protestant conservatives mobilized in hopes of gaining a large enough political majority to roll back these recent court decisions. One part of their agenda was to return more overt religious practices and displays to the public school while eliminating those aspects that were considered a threat to faith, under the rubric of fostering a common morality for an increasingly diverse America. As a consequence, movement activists employed a multifaceted strategy focused on (a) running like-minded adherents for the local school board or securing their appointment to the state board of education and (b) litigation, particularly in the areas of curriculum, student, and faculty religious expression, and providing public monies for parents who send their children to private religious schools.

However, beginning in the 1960s, the religious and political culture was moving in simultaneous and contradictory directions. While many Americans were increasingly public regarding their Protestant devotion, there was an explosion of religious innovation and exploration, with over half of the current 2,000 religious organizations forming after 1960. Such heterodoxy has been a hallmark of American religious culture, which has also been remarkably individualistic, entrepreneurial, and idiosyncratic since the colonial era.

For public schools, this heightened and polyglot of religiosity and faith is playing out in interesting ways. First, while a vague Protestantism once permeated most schools, this is much less the case since the 1960s. In addition, not only are U.S. students increasingly diverse across Christian denominations, but they are incredibly diverse across religious faiths, as well as those students who follow no theological tradition. One result of the religious diversity is that students are free to pursue their religious beliefs during the school day so long as this pursuit does not interfere with the maintenance of an orderly school environment.

Furthermore, it is clear that public schools are free to teach students about various religious heritages so long as they do not endorse or demean religion itself. Academic study of religion is constitutional in public schools. Public schools can also cover material, such as sexuality education and evolution, that some religious parents might find morally objectionable. The federal courts have been clear that mere exposure to possibly religiously objectionable material does not burden a student's free exercise rights.

Finally, the politics surrounding public education and religion might be as intense as at any point in U.S. history, given the sheer religious diversity interacting with a highly mobilized religious political constituency. These long-standing issues have only become more complex over time. It is clear that issues of religion, religious faith, belief, nonbelief, and secularism will continue to shape U.S. public education.

—Catherine A. Lugg

See also Bible, as history; Christian Coalition; creationism; dogmatism and scales of Rokeach; fundamentalism; right-wing politics, advocates, impact on education

Further Readings and References

Armstrong, K. (2000). *The battle for God*. New York: Knopf.

Detwiler, F. (2000). *Standing on the premises of God: The Christian Right's fight to redefine America's public schools*. New York: New York University Press.

French, R. (2003). Shopping for religion: The change in everyday religious practice and the importance to the law. *Buffalo Law Review, 51*, 127–199.

Lugg, C. A. (2001). The Christian Right: A cultivate collective of interest groups. *Educational Policy, 15*(1), 41–57.

Lugg, C. A. (2004). One nation under God? Religion and the politics of education in a post-9/11 America. *Educational Policy, 18*(1), 169–187.

🏛 RESEARCH METHODS

Educational research and its associated methodologies comprise a vast array of investigative methods, all of which are intended to improve the quality and delivery of educational services today. Traditionally, scientific studies have been thought of as either basic or applied. Whereas the purpose of the former has been simply to advance knowledge, the purpose of the latter has been to solve immediate, practical, or pressing problems. However, not all studies fit this simple dichotomy, particularly those in the social and biobehavioral sciences. Recently, a third term has been put forth by the scientific community to include those studies that are neither exclusively basic nor exclusively applied and that serves as a bridge between the two. These studies are referred to as *translational research* and have the express purpose of linking new developments in the laboratory with improvements in clinical practice and care. In the applied social sciences, like education, investigators tend to further classify their methods based on the nature of their data rather than simply the type of outcome. In this regard, educational researchers tend to describe their methods as either quantitative or qualitative. The following discussion of educational research methods is organized this way as well.

SCIENTIFIC METHOD

Within any scientifically justifiable form of research resides a scientific method. Although the sequence of

events may vary based on the type of research practiced, investigators of all disciplines recognize the importance of a sound and verifiable methodology. For example, investigators using quantitative methods tend to follow a linear sequence of events in the execution of their studies:

Observe → Define → Hypothesize → Test → Conclude

Investigators using qualitative methods tend to follow a different, more circular path to knowledge generation. The qualitative approach requires that the investigator repeatedly cycle through the first three steps of the sequence, at increasingly greater depths, before ending with a hypothetical statement. Both approaches are scientifically valid and philosophically justifiable, but neither one alone is capable of capturing the breadth and depth of investigative educational research methodologies today, despite the recent attempt to reinforce the primacy of some methods by the National Research Council's 2002 book *Scientific Research in Education*.

QUANTITATIVE METHODS

Quantitative research methods are those in which statistical techniques are applied to data gathered as a part of well-defined, carefully executed study. Very often these studies involve experimental methods using numerical data or, more formally, a numerical explanation of some aspect of reality. Quantitative methods assume that the characteristics of events can be accurately represented with numbers, and that if we can understand how the numbers fluctuate or covary with other factors, we will be closer to understanding the events and the problems that give rise to them well enough to intervene. The philosophical basis for this line of thinking is considered to be *positivism*, the premise of which assumes that true knowledge can come only from the natural sciences and is derived from verifiable observations of actual events. A hallmark of most quantitative studies is that of deductive reasoning, which is interpreted to mean that all scientific problems can actually be subdivided into smaller problems based on prior verifiable truths that are now amenable to more focused investigation. Listed below are several of the more prominent quantitative research methods and a brief explanation of their defining criteria:

- Experimental: experiments with active manipulation of a condition in which individuals are the units of analysis

- Quasiexperimental: experiments with active manipulation of a condition in which naturally occurring groups are the units of analysis
- Survey: oral or written questionnaires in which the thoughts, beliefs, or opinions of respondents are solicited
- Validity: attributes of an instrument, theory, or measure are studied and compared with the attributes of another instrument, theory, or measure
- Descriptive: computation of frequency counts and/or measures of central tendency, variability, or association, exclusively

Most quantitative studies are hypothesis driven and have a twofold purpose: (1) to describe attributes of a group (or groups) of participants on one or more variables of interest and (2) to compare the group's performance with an established population value (one-sample test) or with the performance of another appropriately comparable group (two-sample test). In either case, it is usually the group means that are compared and usually within the context of some measure of variability such as the variance or standard deviation. In some cases, when only very few subjects are available for analysis, or the data deviate substantially from normality, the medians and ranges are compared in lieu of the means and variances. The former is referred to as a nonparametric test, while the latter is considered a parametric test.

Educators have a wide range of designs available to them when studying the performance of groups. In the case of two groups, it is imperative that one group serve as the control (no treatment) or at least the standard of treatment to which the new approach is being compared. Without some type of control group, it is impossible to estimate how much of the change in performance is attributable to the new treatment and how much is due to chance fluctuation. Where possible, investigators should strive to collect information on the variables of interest immediately prior to the experimental period (baseline observations) as well as immediately after the experimental period (follow-up observations). There are two major benefits to the pretest-posttest approach to experimentation: (1) it increases the sensitivity of the design by adjusting the follow-up scores for the baseline scores and (2) it enhances the potential experimental validity of the study by minimizing the number of alternative explanations for the change. More sophisticated designs for longitudinal studies actually allow for multiple pretest and multiple posttest evaluation periods to get a better sense of change over smaller intervals as

well as to offset some of the potential threats to experimental validity.

These sources are also referred to as sources of invalidity and include factors that relate to internal validity (or factors that confound the effect of the experimental condition) and internal validity (the representativeness of the research results). Internal variance or invalidity can be due to

- History: specific events other than the experimental condition that occur between the first and second measurement
- Maturation: processes such as growing older, hungrier, and so on that operate within the subjects as a function of the passage of time
- Testing: the impact or effect of an initial test or measurement on a following test or measurement
- Instrumentation: changes in obtained measurements due to changes in observers or changes in the calibration of the instrument employed
- Statistical regression: a naturally occurring phenomenon related to selection of subjects based on their extreme scores
- Selection: differential, nonrandom selection of subjects due to bias
- Experimental mortality: loss of respondents over the course of the research project
- Selection-maturation interaction: effects related to how the subjects were selected and interacted with the processes encountered

External sources of variance or invalidity include

- Reactive/interactive effects of testing: the effect of a pretest or initial measurement on the subject's sensitivity to the implementation of the experimental condition
- Interactive effects of selection and the experimental condition: effects related to bias in the selection of subjects and their responsiveness to the experimental condition
- Reactive effects of experimental arrangements: effects related to possible exposure to the experimental condition in nonexperimental settings
- Multiple treatment interference: the effect of previous treatments on future performance when more than one experimental condition is employed

QUALITATIVE METHODS

Qualitative research methods are those in which interpretive frameworks are applied to subjectively obtained themes observed in narrative data. Most often the interpretive frameworks are based on the feelings, beliefs, or subjective experiences of the investigator. Field notes, written records of interviews, and physical artifacts typically constitute the units of analysis in these studies. For the qualitative investigator, the key to understanding a given problem lies in seeing it through the eyes of others, complete with the conditions and contexts that accompany individual evaluations. In this regard there is little in the way of universal truths, numerical or otherwise, on which to base conclusions. Hence, qualitative studies tend to embrace inductive thinking and, as a result, derive interpretive themes from a collection of actual events but always within a given context. The philosophical roots of qualitative research run deeply and multifariously throughout history; however, most seem to credit postpositivism and its more applied offshoot, constructivism, as providing the intellectual basis for the methodology. For many qualitativists, it is not simply movement from specific cases to a general one that advances science but rather the pursuit of multiple realities (as opposed to a single truth). Listed below are several of the more prominent qualitative methods and a brief explanation of their defining criteria:

- Case study: organized, in-depth investigation of a specific person, place, or set of events
- Historiography: formal analysis of past events to understand some aspect of contemporary behavior
- Ethnography: systematic descriptions of cultural phenomena using specifically defined segments of society
- Grounded theory: iterative, data-driven account of general trends and/or themes present in observations capable of producing a theoretical description of some aspect of reality
- Phenomenology: in-depth account of individually held evaluations of life experiences

Qualitative research is focused on contextual understanding and/or contextual factors. Qualitative research often focuses on naturally existing conditions and forgoes the introduction of experimental interventions. Induction and inductive logic/reasoning form the foundation of qualitative research. Unanticipated or serendipitous results are of prime interest to those working in the area of qualitative research. A precondition of such inferencing is that of the validity of the descriptive findings; that is, the ability of an investigative team to validate that the test has different implications for the ethnographic and phenomenological types of studies.

Whereas quantitative researchers tend to emphasize the context-independent nature of their findings, qualitative researchers strive to interpret their findings within a particular context. It is precisely the conditions under which the events of interest occur and the values placed on these events by specific groups of people that help explain the meaningfulness and the richness of events. As such, qualitative research is usually but not always descriptive in nature.

Qualitative studies have a number of defining criteria. First and foremost is that hypotheses generally derive from a study's findings rather than serve as the basis for one. Whether one is analyzing transcripts, field notes, or a completed ethnographic record, it is only after the recorded information has been thoroughly analyzed that hypothetical statements can actually be obtained from the information at hand. Second, the subjective nature of the evaluation necessitates that the investigator state any preconceived notions, beliefs, or biases about the project a priori so that reviewers are able to evaluate the findings in light of the investigator's predisposing positions in a given area. Third, although the scientifically justifiable methods are used in both quantitative and qualitative studies, the pathway to science in the qualitative studies is much more circular than linear, and necessitates revisiting elements of a study at increasingly more sophisticated levels of specification as the study progresses.

MIXED METHODS RESEARCH

Published research today tends to exist in distinct methodological forms; that is, either exclusively quantitative or exclusively qualitative. Because of the very different philosophical orientations of each and the limitations inherent in both paradigms, incorporating elements of both types of methods into a single, well-integrated study remains a difficult task even for the most experienced investigator. Nonetheless, investigators are trying to incorporate elements of both methodologies into their studies with increasing frequency. *Mixed methods studies* is the term given to such studies. Integration of the different approaches can occur in many different forms throughout a given study, either by using single applications (quantitative or qualitative method) within alternating phases of the study or by using multiple applications (quantitative as well as qualitative) with a single phase of a study—either to confirm findings, extend findings, or to provide complementary information that may not be available with either method alone. As with other forms of research methods, the designs themselves can get complex. There are a number of fairly straightforward types of mixed methods designs for investigators wishing to experiment with such applications.

A further demarcation that exists in research methodology is the delineation between group research and single-subject research. Group research and designs involve the comparison of specific groups of individuals related to a feature of interest. Often it is the effect of a particular experimental condition on the identified feature that is of interest to the investigator. Group designs can encompass both survey and experimental research. Group research yields an average or overall effect of a particular experimental condition on the group as a whole, and the results of any research using a group design are compared to the likelihood that those results could have occurred by chance.

Group designs involve the examination of an experimental condition's effect on a group of individuals. Generally, the effect of the condition on the members of an experimental group is compared to the effect on a similar or equivalent group whose members did not receive the condition (i.e., a control group). The vast majority of educational research involves the use of group designs, and much of what is established as best practice in the field is based on data derived from such research. However, the great shortfall of group design is that the results obtained from such research may result in outcomes that may not naturally exist (as they are averages of the individual performance of each group member). Group designs can be either experimental or quasiexperimental in nature. Examples of group designs include

- The pretest-posttest control group design
- The posttest only control group design
- The Solomon four-group design
- The nonequivalent control group design
- The separate sample pretest-posttest design
- The separate sample pretest-posttest control group design

The pretest-posttest control group design is arguably the most commonly employed design for educational research. The design involves randomly selecting two groups of participants and measuring a behavior of interest among the members of each group. One group (the experimental group) then is exposed to an intervention or condition that might affect the behavior of interest, while the other group (control group) is excluded from this exposure. The

measurement procedures are then repeated with both groups, and the posttest scores are then compared with each other and significant differences are noted and analyzed. Any significant differences in postintervention functioning by the experimental group is attributed to the effect of the intervening condition. Pretest scores are used in this design as a comparison to posttest functioning and as a covariate in statistical analysis.

The posttest only control group design is an experimental design in which two randomly selected groups of participants are selected with one (the experimental group) exposed to an intervening condition while the second (control group) is not. No pretests are conducted in this design, and the equivalence of the two groups is assumed based upon the nature of the random selection process. A pretest is not necessary within the confidence limits of any selected measures of significance, given the lack of bias inherent in randomization. For psychological reasons, many educators possess a distrust of this design based upon a need to know the nature of both groups' performance prior to the application of the experimental condition. The design does address any invalidity that could be due to the interactive effect of testing and the experimental condition.

The Solomon four-group design is an extended modification of the pretest-posttest control group design in which four randomly selected groups of participants are employed. In structure, this design is a combination of the two previous designs. Initially, the design is identical to the pretest-posttest control group design, but two additional groups (one that receives both the experimental condition and a posttest and one that is posttested only but is not exposed to the experimental condition) are included as extensions of the experimental and control groups. While this design parallels the pretest-posttest control group design, it can provide greater support for the generalizability of any experimental condition and greater understanding of the interactive effects of intervention.

The nonequivalent control group design is one of the most common designs employed in real-world school settings. It is similar to the pretest-posttest control group design in that two groups are identified as either the experimental or control group and pretested. The experimental group then receives the prescribed intervention while the control group does not. Posttests are then conducted on both groups, and the data are compared and analyzed. The primary difference in this design and the pretest-posttest control group design is that the two groups are not randomly selected but rather are drawn from naturally assembled collections (i.e., classrooms). The assignment of the experimental intervention is randomly applied to one group, or the other is assumed to be random.

Another quasiexperimental design is the separate sample pretest-posttest design. This design involves the use of two samples, one of which is pretested and may or may not receive the prescribed intervention and a second group to which the experimental condition is applied and then posttested. These samples can consist of a variety of subgroups that cannot be randomly selected and segregated to receive the prescribed intervention. Those conducting the research can, however, exercise control over when the measurements will take place and who will be assessed. The various groups are assembled into the two samples based upon whether or not they were exposed to the experimental conditions, and the resulting data are compared and analyzed.

The separate sample pretest-posttest control group design is an extension of the previous design and is identical to the separate sample pretest-posttest design except for the addition of two samples that are not exposed to the experimental condition. This design allows for the inclusion of large subgroups in each sample (as does the previous design) yet also provides a control group sample (one group that receives only the pretest and another group that receives only the posttest) to be used for comparison.

Single-subject research and designs evolved as a reaction to the focus of group designs on the mean or average performance of the various groups. It was felt that this average could (and often did) result in a measured level of performance that did not naturally exist. Single-subject research involves the effect of manipulating a specific experimental condition on the observable and measurable behavior of a single individual. Formal single-subject research designs were developed in the 1960s by behavior analysts as a means of validating certain behavior modification practices/procedures. Single-subject research designs include

- The reversal design
- The multiple baseline design

The reversal design involves measuring a behavior of interest over time to obtain a picture of its operant level and stability. The experimental condition is then

applied, and the behavior continues to be measured to determine if the experimental condition produces an observable change. If this is the case, the experimental condition is then discontinued (or altered) to determine if the behavior change is indeed related to the presence of the experimental condition. If the behavior change seems to be dependent on the experimental condition, then the expectation is that the behavior of interest would return to preexperimental levels. Should this be the case, the experimental condition is then applied again to recover the behavior change. In essence, the efficacy of the experimental condition is demonstrated by the predictable behavior change when that condition is systematically applied and removed.

Special cases of the reversal design are the alternating treatments and multielement designs. The alternating treatments design is employed to examine the relative efficacy of two or more experimental conditions. The design is identical to the reversal design except that during the experimental conditions, several techniques are applied sequentially. The impact of each condition on behavior is then compared both to baseline conditions and to each other. The multielement design is a modification of the reversal design in which different experimental conditions are applied individually and sequentially to determine their relative efficacy. The impact of each experimental condition is compared to the baseline level of the target behavior and to each other to identify which had the most positive effect.

The multiple baseline technique is an additional single-subject design that may be employed as an alternative to the reversal technique. This approach is appropriate when a behavior is irreversible (such as reading) or when reversing a behavior is not ethically or practically desirable (such as physical aggression). In this design, several different behaviors are measured over time to establish a baseline of their stability and level. An experimental condition is then applied to one of the behaviors to produce an observable and measurable change. Both the change produced in that particular behavior and any lack of change in the other observed behaviors is noted. If this is indeed the case, the experimental condition is then applied to a second (unchanged) behavior. If the experimental condition results in a similar change in the second behavior, and no change is noted in the other unchanged behaviors, it is then applied to those unchanged behaviors in a systematic manner over time. Continued similar changes in the various behaviors under study over time upon the application of the experimental condition provides evidence that the observed changes are due to the condition and not to coincidence.

The changing criterion design and the intensified treatments design are special types of multiple baseline techniques. In the changing criterion design, a baseline level of the target behavior is determined and a series of stepwise changes in a criterion or performance level necessary for reinforcement are established. Changes in behavior to meet the preset criterion are noted and compared to previous performance. In the intensified treatments design, the delivery of reinforcement or punishment itself is intensified across sequential experimental phases. In essence, the experimenter looks for behavior changes consistent with increasing intensity or higher criterion levels.

A combination of the multielement or alternating treatments and multiple baseline designs can also be employed to compare the effect of different experimental conditions over time and with different individuals. In these designs, a baseline level of the target behavior is established for three or more individuals, and a sequence of discrete experimental conditions are applied to the behavior in the different individuals. As with the multiple baseline design, the experimental conditions are initiated at different points in time and the experimenter looks for similar changes in subject behavior across the different conditions and baselines. The only difference for the alternating treatments, multiple baseline design is that two experimental conditions are alternated during the intervention phase and are again both initiated across each individual situation at differing points in time.

Regardless of whether a group or single-subject approach to research is employed, errors in the interpretation of experimental results are inevitable. Some errors are due to experimenter bias and some are naturally occurring side effects of the research itself. Of those errors due to the design of research, both paradigms are subject to Type 1 and Type 2 errors.

Type 1 errors occur when one affirms that an experimental condition is functional, when in fact it is not. Type 1 errors occur in group designs at a rate determined by the level of statistical probability set for a given experiment. For example, if a 0.05 level of significance is set for a particular study, a 1 in 20 chance exists for the experimenter to make a Type 1 error. As single-subject research has no preset confidence level, but rather depends on visual inspection related to an experimental condition's functionality, the chances of making a Type 1 error are infinitesimal by comparison.

Type 2 errors occur when an experimental condition is functional yet is identified as being ineffective. Group designs have statistically predictable rates for the occurrence of Type 2 errors that are moderately high and directly related to their preset significance levels. Single-subject designs, due to their extraordinarily low rates of Type 1 errors, are inherently subject to extremely high rates of Type 2 errors.

In essence, the lower the chance of committing a Type 1 error in any experiment, the higher the chance of committing a Type 2 error and vice versa. Group research has moderately low levels of potential Type 1 errors and correspondingly moderately high rates of Type 2 errors. Single-subject research operates at very low levels of Type 1 errors and correspondingly higher rates of Type 2 errors in relation to group research.

When designing experiments, those conducting research must decide whether it is more desirable to reject potentially effective practices (Type 2 errors) at a higher rate in order to ensure that only the most effective, robust interventions are validated by using single-subject designs or to accept the moderate levels of Type 1 and Type 2 errors in group research and thereby ensure the validation of both many ineffective practices and the rejection of a similar number of effective ones.

Research errors stem, in large part, from bias on the part of the experimenter. Bias can affect the selection of subjects, the evaluation of data, and the interpretation of results. Bias can influence data via variables whose effects cannot be separated from the effect of the experimental condition. Control of selection though randomization and control of confounding variables through their identification and elimination are the experimenter's only options to reduce existing bias. The use of nonrandom (nonprobability) sampling makes generalization of the study's results to other populations and settings invalid, as the sample use is distorted and not representative of the overall population.

While all research is subject to influences of individual interpretation, concern exists among professionals in relation to the identification and measurement of subjective factors. Social validity, or the concept that any research effort should address issues of social importance, may be the most critical feature of any research project. However, the very concept of social validity has subjective connotations. Further contextual factors such as unique environmental conditions or the personal perceptions of subjects, research observers, or the public in general have been a focus of the concern related to research subjectivity. Indeed, understanding those unique contextual factors related to the success of any experimental intervention is often critical to validating the efficacy of that intervention.

The concern over subjective contextual factors has led many to question the certitude of empirical data. The perspective that each individual constructs personal meaning from data has also given rise to concerns over the meaningfulness of research findings. These positions have brought the postmodern perspective to the forefront and placed it in direct opposition to the traditional approaches to conducting, analyzing, and reporting research findings.

The postmodern perspective has arisen in reaction to the traditional approaches and the position that modern scientific research methods are the singular foundation of determining the definition and nature of "truth." Postmodernism attempts to take an atheoretical approach to understanding data and constructing meaning. Postmodernism, in relation to educational research, attempts to provide possible alternative explanations or interpretations of experimental data by expanding the parameters used to define and support these explanations and/or interpretations. The inclusivity of the postmodern approach allows for the consideration of all interpretations or explanations except for the modernistic perspective of exclusivity that would subordinate these alternatives.

—*J. M. Blackbourn, Richard Ittenbach, and Jennifer Fillingim*

See also action research; Baer, Donald; behaviorism; effect size; empiricism; item response theory; Kuhn, Thomas; mixed methods, in research; postmodernism; qualitative research, history, theories, issues; quantitative research methods; questionnaires; surveys and survey results

Further Readings and References

Blackbourn, J. M., & Fillingim, J. G. (2004). *The multi-element multiple baseline design.* Proceedings of the Southeastern Association on Mental Retardation Conference, Philadelphia, MS: AAMR.
Burke, J. (2001). Toward a new classification of nonexperimental quantitative research. *Educational Researcher, 30*(2), 3–14.
Creswell, J. W. (2003). *Research design: Qualitative, quantitative, and mixed methods approaches.* Thousand Oaks, CA: Sage.
Creswell, J. W., Plano Clark, V. L., Gutmann, M. L., & Hanson, W. E. (2003). Advanced mixed methods research designs. In A. Tashakkori & C. Teddlie (Eds.), *Handbook of mixed methods in social and behavioral research* (pp. 209–240). Thousand Oaks, CA: Sage.
Eisner, E. (1997). The promise and perils of alternative forms of data representation. *Educational Researcher, 26*(6), 4–9.
Goodall, H. (2000). *Writing the new ethnography.* Walnut Creek, CA: Altamira.
Janesick, V. J. (2001). The choreography of qualitative research design: Minuets, improvisations, and crystallization. In N. K. Denzin & Y. S. Lincoln (Eds.), *Handbook of qualitative research* (2nd ed., pp. 379–399). Thousand Oaks, CA: Sage.
Johnson, R., & Onwuegbuzie, A. (2004). Mixed methods research: A research paradigm whose time has come. *Educational Researcher, 33*(7), 14–26.
King, G., Keohane, R. O., & Verba, S. (2001). *Designing social inquiry: Scientific inference in qualitative research.* Princeton, NJ: Princeton University Press.
Morse, J. M. (2003). Principles of mixed methods and multimethod research designs. In A. Tashakkori & C. Teddlie (Eds.), *Handbook of mixed methods in social and behavioral research* (pp. 189–208). Thousand Oaks, CA: Sage.
Towne, L., & Shavelson, R. (Eds.). (2002). *Scientific research in education.* Washington, DC: National Academies Press.
Van Houten, R., & Hall, R. V. (2001). *The measurement of behavior: Behavior modification.* Austin, TX: Pro-Ed.
Wersma, W., & Jurs, S. G. (2004). *Research methods in education: An introduction.* Boston: Allyn & Bacon.

RESILIENCY

Resiliency or resilience is the ability to "bounce back" from a stressful or traumatic experience. Resiliency has been an issue in psychology and counseling for years. More recently, it has become a topic of increasing interest to educators generally. Discovering what makes an individual resilient and learning how to develop conditions in schools to help students and staff become more resilient are current interests of administrators. In addition, administrators themselves are assessing their own resiliency and trying to find ways to increase their resiliency as the roles of school and district leaders become more and more complex and stressful.

The ability to adapt or adjust becomes of particular importance as the research accumulates indicating that those people who are resilient will be more likely to overcome adversity and cope with and/or adapt to change. A major factor in resilient adaptation is good relationships. Investigators have consistently pointed to the critical importance of strong connections with at least one supportive adult: in many instances a primary caregiver, who is among the earliest, most proximal, and most enduring of socializing influences. Sound interpersonal relationship in the early years can foster the growth of effective coping skills that, in turn, can help children in managing assorted adversities subsequently encountered in life.

Of particular interest to educators is the consistent finding that relationships with individuals outside the family can positively influence the development of resiliency. Neighborhood networks and/or home-visit interventions can be invaluable in helping parents cope with their own stressors and consequently avoiding the transfer of personal stress to their own children. Teachers and informal mentors in the community can be just as valuable as support systems as family members. If such relationships reach a critical point, these connections can compensate greatly for difficult family situations.

DEVELOPMENT OF RESILIENCE

Rather consistently, studies on resilience point to a common set of findings regarding what influences the development of resilience. There appear to be three major categories of protective factors: *individual attributes*, such as good intellectual skills, positive temperament, and positive views of the self; *family qualities,* such as high warmth, cohesion, expectations, and involvement; and *supportive systems outside the family*, such as strong social networks or good schools.

A list of attributes of individuals and their contexts often associated with resilience have been developed. They include cognitive abilities (IQ scores, attention skills, executive functioning skills), self-perceptions of competence, worth, confidence (self-efficacy, self-esteem), temperament and personality (adaptability, sociability), self-regulation skills (impulse control, affect and arousal regulation), and a positive outlook on life (hopefulness, beliefs that life has meaning, faith) as examples in the individual differences perspective. In the area of relationships, some examples include parenting quality (including warmth, structure and monitoring, expectations), close relationships with competent adults (parents, relatives, mentors), and connections to prosocial and rule-abiding peers (among older children). As for community resources and opportunities, good schools, connections to prosocial organizations (such as clubs or religious groups), neighborhood quality (public safety, collective supervision, libraries, recreation centers), and quality of social services and health care are offered.

While Jerry Patterson's 2001 work addresses school administrators rather than children and adolescents, his point that resilience is not a short-term characteristic that changes daily but a capacity individuals have to move ahead under adversity is important, regardless of developmental stage. Like those who have researched resiliency in children, Patterson declares that there is no single, magic checklist for strengthening resilience. He does, however, identify two central points that can be used as guides. First, keep in mind that it is not so much what you do, it is how you think about what you do that makes all the difference. Second, keep in mind that people don't choose to be nonresilient. They simply choose not to do what it takes to become resilient.

—Anita Pankake and Sylvia Mendez-Morse

See also at-risk students; Black education; child development theories; esteem needs; immigration, history and impact in education; individual differences, in children; Latinos; leadership effectiveness; mentoring; networking and network theory; personality; psychology, types of; social capital

Further Readings and References

Cortina, R., & Gendreau, M. (2003). *Immigrants and schooling: Mexicans in New York.* New York: Center for Migration Studies.

Luthar, S. S., & Zelazo, L. B. (2003). Research on resilience: An integrative review. In S. S. Luthar (Ed.), *Resilience and vulnerability: Adaptation in the context of childhood adversities* (pp. 510–549). Cambridge, UK: Cambridge University Press.

Masten, A. S., & Powell, J. L. (2003). A resilience framework for research, policy, and practice. In S. S. Luthar (Ed.), *Resilience and vulnerability: Adaptation in the context of childhood adversities* (pp. 1–15). Cambridge, UK: Cambridge University Press.

Patterson, J. (2001). Resilience in the face of adversity. *The School Administrator, 6*(58), 18–21.

Yates, T. M., Egeland, B., & Stroufe, A. (2003). Rethinking resilience: A developmental perspective. In S. S. Luthar (Ed.), *Resilience and vulnerability: Adaptation in the context of childhood adversities* (pp. 243–266). Cambridge, UK: Cambridge University Press.

RESOURCE MANAGEMENT

Resource management is the facilitation and coordination of fiscal, human, and physical resources in alignment with the mission and strategic plan of the organization. In public schools, resource management involves planning, development, and control of restricted and unrestricted resources available to the organization or division. Resource management focuses on efficient direction and control of staff, facilities, equipment, budget, and resource development to accomplish organizational goals. The key question is, How does the school allocate resources to most effectively support the strategic plan?

Because personnel-related costs represent 80% to 90% of a public school budget, staffing patterns, recruiting, retaining, and development are major components of resource management. Most school districts have central office functions that direct and control employee benefits and compensation, employee records, and personnel policies. In addition, the staffing patterns of most schools are established by district policies.

Resource management involves an ongoing process of developing systems, policies, and procedures that are designed to improve productivity in relationship to fiscal, personnel, and facilities. Cost-effective analysis, feasibility studies, and the evaluation of fiscal data are integral elements of resource management. Data analysis and systems thinking are necessary skills for effective resource management. Education leaders need to be able to use financial information data as readily as they use other forms of data.

Since state and federal laws can affect both current and future funding, resource management requires ongoing reviews of legislation, proposed funding, and new laws. It also requires research, program evaluation, and recommendations for more cost-effective procedures.

Cash flow is an ongoing issue for districts; potential negative cash flow is the primary problem. Most school districts have centralized policies and procedures that ensure that expenditures and revenues are in balance. As a result, most operating expenses and personnel costs are controlled by the district's central office. Principals are provided guidelines and procedures for expenditures of funds.

Resource management requires that leadership establish basic functions and evaluate between competing alternatives. The relationships between school district goals, scope of services, costs, and performance benchmarks are complex. District leadership needs to seek input and feedback from stakeholders and balance proposed improvements with existing services. For example, most districts have centralized purchasing, transportation, and capital construction to promote efficiency. However, leaders are continuously faced with evaluating centralized efficiency compared to advantages of site-based decision making.

Overriding issues for resource management include the efficient use of resources and the elimination of waste. Resource management is complex; education leaders must coordinate, integrate, and formalize resource utilization and develop revenue projections, expenditures, and baseline data. Organizational efforts to ensure that all stakeholders actively work to eliminate waste are ongoing and never ending.

Many believe that principals and other stakeholders must be empowered in meaningful ways if resource management is to be effective within schools. The General Accounting Office (GAO) identified three large school districts (Prince William County, Virginia, Dade County, Florida, and Edmonton, Alberta) that have successfully delegated substantial authority for budget, personnel, and instruction to school site-based decisions. If districts hope to develop meaningful site-based resource management, they need to establish proactive systems that empower stakeholders. Because most of budget and human resource management have become centralized routines, districts must engage stakeholders in special efforts to redesign the systems, to counteract the centralized bureaucracy, and to meet the needs of the students served.

—Bill Thornton and George C. Hill

See also accountability; administration, theories of; budgeting; capacity building, of organizations; Chicago school reform; cost-benefit analyses; decentralization/centralization controversy; finance, of public schools; governance; innovation, in education; principalship; reform, of schools; restructuring, of schools; salary and salary models; school improvement models; site-based management; staffing, concepts of; systemic reform; work task measurement; working conditions, in schools; workplace trends

Further Readings and References

Catterall, J. S. (1998). A cost-effectiveness model for the assessment of educational productivity. *New Directions for Higher Education, 103,* 61–84.

Hummel-Rossi, B., & Ashdown, J. (2002). The state of cost-benefit and cost effectiveness analyses in education. *Review of Educational Research 72*(1), 1–30.

Monk, D. H., Pijanowski, J. C., & Hussain, S. (1997). How and where the education dollar is spent. *Financing Schools 7*(3), 51–62. Retrieved from http://www.packard.org/.

Morgan, R. B., & Smith, J. E. (1996). *Staffing the new workplace.* Milwaukee, WI: ASQC Press.

Ward, R. (2004). *Improving achievement in low performing schools.* Thousand Oaks, CA: Corwin Press.

🏛 RESTRUCTURING, OF SCHOOLS

Since the mid-1950s, the United States has legislated billions of dollars to improve education and secure America's competitive edge in the modern world. The publication of *A Nation at Risk* in 1983 provided evidence that earlier attempts at school reform had not succeeded. In a renewed effort to correct what was wrong with American education, *restructuring* became the new buzzword for educators interested in boosting student performance that would link 1980s research findings with policy and practice. The focus of restructuring was to place the student at the center of the learning environment by addressing individual needs within the school organization. Innovative efforts included site-based management, interdisciplinary team teaching, flexible scheduling, and portfolio assessment.

Historically, a bureaucratic model has provided the frame for the development of the nation's school system. Under this model, large comprehensive schools, especially at the secondary level, were built to offer students variety in course choice and activities. Principals and administrative staffs typically manage the schools in a top-down manner through formalized goals and procedures. Subjects and teachers are divided into departments and students are often placed according to ability and career objectives. The concept of restructuring has provided opportunities to look beyond the bureaucratic model in search of new possibilities.

In an effort to provide stakeholders with a greater voice and meet the rising needs of the increased accountability that accompanied the 1990s, states began instituting site-based decision making while districts experimented with a wide variety of comprehensive reform models that included *best practices*. At about the same time, a new movement began that encouraged large inner-city high schools to make significant departures from conventional school organizations and practices to a new model that viewed teaching and learning as processes that cannot be controlled through standardized practices. This model was a call for increased collaboration among teachers to examine and solve the challenges they and their students were facing. In essence, it called for restructuring the way schools met the needs of its stakeholders. Key to any restructuring effort was the attention given to size—the size of the classes and the size of the school.

Findings resulting from efforts to change the way schools are led and organized documented that school restructuring can improve student learning, but for it to be most effective it should focus on four key factors: student learning, authentic pedagogy, school organizational capacity, and external support. By the mid-1990s, efforts to study the long-term effects of restructuring began when agencies such as the Center on Organization and Restructuring of Schools gathered data from public schools involved in the process. It soon became obvious that major departures from conventional practice were taking place in student experiences; the professional life of teachers; leadership, management and governance; and the coordination of community services.

Supported by the U.S. Department of Education and collected by the Center on Organization and Restructuring Schools, the initial conclusions concerning restructuring were derived from four national studies: *School Restructuring Study* (1994), in which data were drawn from 24 significantly restructured urban public schools, evenly divided among K–12 and located in 16 states; *National Educational Longitudinal Study of 1988* (1992), in which data were drawn from a nationally representative sample of over 10,000 students that began in 1988 and followed participants from Grade 8 through Grade 12 in 800 high schools; *Study of Chicago School Reform* (1994), which included survey data from 8,000 teachers and principals in 400 elementary and 40 high schools; and the *Longitudinal Study of School Restructuring* (1994), which included 4-year case studies of eight schools that had embarked on different forms of restructuring in four different communities.

Data from the studies found that in successful schools (a) a vision for the school's mission was seen as essential to the planning, implementation, and evaluation of restructuring changes, (b) the communication of clear goals was essential for all stakeholders and included in-depth understanding of core subjects as well as the ability of students to solve problems that have real world meaning, and (c) the building of internal capacity as schools promoted not only improved achievement for all students but also higher expectations for the staff to work collaboratively as a single unit.

Research also showed that in restructured high schools, teachers were assuming the role of coaches and encouraging students to become self-directed learners. Students were being given more hands-on experiences and encouraged to go beyond their textbooks. The expectation for student learning offered the potential of moving from knowledge, comprehension, and application to analysis, synthesis, and evaluation. The results had a positive impact on school climate as well as student achievement. Classrooms began to change their appearance. No longer controlled by lecture, recitation, and teacher-assigned work, students were encouraged to participate in open discussion and to focus on more complex self-directed learning, often in collaborative groupings.

By 1999, the U.S. Department of Education began to offer comprehensive school reform demonstration grants as a way to assist public schools in their restructuring efforts. Researchers began looking for additional innovative ways to improve student achievement, and public and private educational institutions began to design reform models to assist schools with best practices and building capacity. With so much interest in restructuring as a way to increase student achievement and close the existing gaps among students at risk of academic failure, it was not long before a growing body of research confirmed that smaller is better if one is trying to improve a school's instruction and achievement, student behavior, climate, and community relationships. Smaller learning communities as an important piece of restructuring, especially for high schools, gained momentum.

The obvious reason for focusing on smaller learning communities as a viable way to increase achievement is that in a smaller environment, teachers and students come to know each other better, there is greater collaboration among the staff, and parents feel they have a stronger voice in their child's learning. In addition, the increase in student violence led many educational reformers to call for the creation of a better system to meet the needs of the whole child. Creating smaller learning environments has since become synonymous with restructuring, especially at the high school level, because it is more apt to personalize the educational experience.

With most American high school students attending schools enrolling more than 1,000 students, the debate surrounding how to meet individual student needs had generally centered on class size—the number of students a teacher can effectively teach during a class period. In the last few years, however, the debate has shifted to school size and the consequences for students and teachers if large metropolitan schools are divided into what has come to be known as smaller learning communities, house plans and families, or schools within a school.

Students in schools that were restructured into smaller learning communities by dividing a large high school population into groups of approximately 400 students developed sustained relationships with their teachers and other participating adults. Teachers improved their working relationships with each other and increased the time they were able to devote to meeting individual student needs. Student achievement improved as students were given greater opportunities to work productively with one another in mixed-ability groups using cooperative learning approaches. Parental participation in school activities increased, with greater numbers acting as volunteers and becoming actively involved in their child's progress.

The research efforts of Mary Anne Raywid, Kathleen Cotton, Neal McClusky, and the Bank Street College of Education in the late 1990s and early 2000 provided strong evidence to the U.S. Department of Education that restructuring schools into smaller communal families improved student learning. Downsizing within a large high school, researchers argued, provided the same environment that naturally small schools achieved and could be seen in improved achievement, effective governance, stronger internal supports, improved staff effectiveness and satisfaction, better advisement, and enhanced curricula. Equally important, Craig Howley and Robert Bickel in 2000 found the larger the school, the greater the negative effect of poverty on student achievement.

Armed with compelling evidence, a movement began that suggested that smaller learning communities could be a partial answer to correcting much that is wrong with American education. Implementing a variety of structures and strategies, each attempts to promote academic achievement and prepare all students for graduation with the knowledge and skills necessary to make the successful transition to college and careers (see Tables 1 and 2).

The belief in the benefits of restructuring large schools, particularly inner-city high schools into smaller learning communities, is broad based and includes not only the U.S. Department of Education but private interests such as the Bill and Melinda Gates Foundation, Carnegie Foundation of New York, and the Annenberg Institute. Together, these groups have made millions of dollars available to schools willing to pursue the concept of smaller learning communities as a way of improving education. In addition

Table 1   Smaller Learning Community Structures

Name	Description	Observation
Academies	Subgroups within schools are organized around particular themes such as a career. They combine principles of the school-to-career movement with academic and vocational instruction.	Often providing work-based learning opportunities as well as mentors and work internships, the emphasis is on building relationships with teachers and employers.
House Plans	Students within a large school are divided into groups of several hundred, either across grade levels or by grade levels. All houses within the larger school share the same curriculum and instruction with only minimal changes.	Students take some or all courses with their house members and from their house teachers. House plans personalize the high school experience by having its own discipline plan, student government, and cocurricular and extracurricular activities.
A School-Within-a-School	A small, autonomous program housed within a larger school building. Generally responsible to the district rather than to the host school's principal; each has its own culture, program, budget, and school space.	Like academies, schools-within-a-school support constructive relationships between students and staff by taking core courses with the same group of teachers.
Magnet Schools	Programs use a specialty core focus such as math, science, and creative arts to attract students from the entire school district. They may be located within an existing school or have their own building.	With acceptance based either on competitive admission or an open enrollment, students stay together for their core classes. They may take other courses with nonmagnet students depending on the logistics of their location.

SOURCE: Adapted from U.S. Department of Education. (n.d.). *Smaller Learning Communities.* Retrieved August 11, 2004, from http://www.ed.gov/programs/slcp/strategies.html.

to improving student achievement, the hope exists that smaller learning communities will also have a positive impact on teachers and parents by making effective communication easier, offering opportunities for collaboration, and encouraging meaningful relationships between students and adults.

To assist schools interested in restructuring with the formation of smaller learning communities, the U.S. Department of Education has since 2000 offered discretionary and competitive funding in the form of 12-month planning grants and 36-month implementation grants. Awards range from $25,000 to $250,000 for planning grants and $250,000 to $550,000 for implementation grants. With the signing of the No Child Left Behind Act of 2001, the important purpose of smaller learning communities was clearly outlined. It ensured that the funding for smaller learning communities will continue to assist large public high schools that are defined as schools that include Grades 11 and 12 and enroll at least 1,000 students in Grades 9 and above. Recipients of the grants are authorized to use

their funds to (a) study the feasibility of creating smaller learning communities, (b) research, develop, and implement strategies for creating smaller learning communities, (c) provide professional development for school staff in the teaching methods that would be used in smaller learning communities, and (d) develop and implement strategies to include parents, business representatives, community-based organizations, and other community members in the activities of the smaller learning community.

Current trends in restructuring continue to represent an interest in fundamentally changing the way schools meet the needs of their students and staff. Because it enables practitioners to identify and resolve their own problems, restructuring remains a dynamic force in educational reform.

—*Shirley Jackson*

See also accountability; achievement gap, of students; Black education; expectations, teacher and student cultures; innovation, in education; Latinos; learning, theories of; learning environments;

Table 2   Smaller Learning Community Strategies

Name	Description	Observation
Freshman Transition Activities	First-year high school students are placed in their own setting, sometimes in a separate wing or building.	Placement helps ease the difficulties students often encounter as they move from middle school to high school.
Multi-year Groups	Several teachers stay with a group of students over a period of 2 or more years, fostering trust and intimacy.	Similar to "looping," this is a strategy often used in elementary and middle schools but is found to be equally effective in high school.
Alternative Scheduling	It allows teachers to develop lessons that are more compatible with learning objectives and often include work-based learning opportunities. The length of the class period, the school day, and even the school year can be changed to support academic achievement.	Most easily done in smaller schools, it is often referred to as "block scheduling," and provides extended class periods for in-depth and experimental learning opportunities. Facilitating tutorial opportunities as well as enrichment, lagging students can catch up while advanced students can delve more deeply into self-directed learning opportunities.
Adult Advocate Systems	They ensure that at least one adult knows each student well. By meeting with 15–20 students, individually or in small groups, on a regular basis over several years, adult advocates can provide rapport, academic, and personal guidance while fulfilling the role of the caring adult.	One quarter of the nation's students report being concerned that they and their friends lack an adult who talks with them about problems and decisions. For the program to be successful, training for adult advocates and administrative support for the advocate system are critical to its success.
Teacher Advisory Systems	Similar to adult advocate systems, they organize adults to personalize the high school experience and support academic achievement, working with small groups of students.	Meeting times vary and are formal or informal as well as one-on-one or in small groups. Their purpose is to develop personal learning plans, and introduce students to career clusters, advising with course selection, and postsecondary plans.
Academic Teaming	It organizes groups of teachers across departments so that the teachers share the same students rather than the same subject. Teaming links teachers, who teach different subjects, in a team that shares responsibility for the curriculum, instruction, evaluation, and sometimes scheduling and discipline of a group of 100–150 students.	Teams share the same planning period and sometimes share a specific area of the school building. Formerly found primarily in middle schools, academic teaming is being used effectively in high schools because it is another way to personalize the learning environment and enables a group of teachers to focus on the whole student.

SOURCE: Adapted from U.S. Department of Education. (n.d.). *Smaller Learning Communities.* Retrieved August 11, 2004, from http://www.ed.gov/programs/slcp/strategies.html.

No Child Left Behind; problem-based learning; reform, of schools; satisfaction, in organizations and roles; school improvement models; school size; site-based management

Further Readings and References

Bank Street College of Education. (2001). *Executive summary: Small schools: Great strides.* Retrieved from Technical Questions, webmaster@bankstreet.edu.

Cotton, K. (2001). *New small learning communities: Findings from recent literature.* Portland, OR: Northwest Regional Educational Laboratory.

Criteria for school restructuring. (n.d.). Retrieved August 11, 2004, from http://www.wcer.wisc.edu/achives/completed/cors/issues_in_restructuring_schools/issues.

Evans, P. M. (2003). A principal's dilemmas: Theory and reality of school redesign. *Phi Delta Kappan, 84*(6), 425–437.

Frymier, J., & Joekel, R. (2004). *Changing the school learning environment*. Lanham, MD: Scarecrow.

Gates Foundation. (2004). *Research & Evaluation: Bill & Melinda Gates Foundation*. Retrieved July 15, 2004, from http://gatesfoundation.org/education/researchandevaluation/default.htm.

Goldenberg, C. (2004). *Successful school change*. New York: Teachers College Press.

Howley, C., & Bickel, R. (2000). *When it comes to schooling small works: School size, poverty, and student achievement*. Randolph, VT: Rural School and Community Trust Policy Program.

Langer, J. (2004). *Getting to excellent: How to create better schools*. New York: Teachers College Press.

McClusky, N. (2002). *Sizing up what matters: The importance of small schools*. Center for Education Reform. Retrieved September 11, 2002, from http://www.edreform.com/pubs.

National Center for Restructuring Education, Schools, and Teaching. (n.d.). Retrieved August 11, 2004, from http://www.tc.columbia.edu/~ncrest/home.htm.

Odden, A., & Archibald, S. (2001). *Reallocating resources*. Thousand Oaks, CA: Corwin Press.

Raywid, M. A. (1999). *Current literature on small schools*. Charleston, WV: ERIC Clearinghouse on Rural Education and Small Schools.

U.S. Department of Education. (n.d.). *Smaller learning communities*. Retrieved August 11, 2004, from http://www.ed.gov/programs/slcp/strategies.html.

U.S. Department of Education. (2001). *An overview of smaller learning communities in high schools*. Retrieved June 19, 2002, from http://www.ed.Gov/offices/OESE/SLCP/overview.html.

U.S. Department of Education. (2004). *Smaller learning communities (SLC) program: Discretionary grant application packages*. Retrieved August 11, 2004, from http://www.ed.gov/searchResults.jhtml.

RICE, JOSEPH MAYER

Joseph Mayer Rice (1857–1934) was born May 20, 1857, in Philadelphia, Pennsylvania. He earned a degree in medicine from the College of Physicians and Surgeons at Columbia University in 1881. From 1887 until his death, he was an advocate for empirically set goals and scientific measurement in education. His concern for the health of children led him to abandon his medical practice and travel to the Universities of Leipzig and Jena in Europe to study psychology and education. While there, he witnessed early efforts at empirical research and Herbartism, an early system of educational psychology.

After his return to America, Rice shared his experiences in interviews published in *Epoch*, a weekly newspaper, and *Forum*, a monthly magazine. At the suggestion of his brother Isaac Leopold Rice, owner of the *Forum*, Joseph conducted a survey of schools in the United States and shared his findings with the *Forum*. The period in which Rice lived and worked was one of intense muckraking activity and competition among publishers. Education was uncharted territory for investigative reporting, and its close connection to local politics made it an attractive choice. Rice visited schools in 36 cities and spoke with teachers, school officials, parents, and school board members. Starting in October 1892, the *Forum* published a series of nine articles that galvanized public attention to the condition of American public schools. Rice described the schools as mechanistic, the current teaching methods as inefficient and stultifying, and the treatment of the students in the classrooms as bordering on barbaric.

Rice's main contribution was his groundbreaking use of empirical testing to determine if the current methods of spelling, mathematics, and English were successful. He suggested changing the curriculum to make learning more efficient. By integrating instruction in the social sciences, science, grammar, composition, and penmanship, students would be challenged and stimulated to learn better. While the *Forum* articles were still in publication, Rice completed a second tour to identify the best schools and teaching practices. Masses of information were compiled over the next several years and provided the grist for several books. They included *The Public School System of the United States* in 1893, *The Rational Spelling Book* in 1898, *Scientific Management in Education* in 1913, and *The People's Government* in 1915. In 1897, Rice became the editor of the *Forum* until he left the magazine in 1907.

Rice was associated with the efficiency movement, but his efforts were directed toward the efficiency to be gained in the classroom rather than in the administration. His main concern was always the children who had to endure the enervating drill and practice found in most schools. His suggestions were directed at ways to energize the learning process, abolish wasted time, and make learning productive if not fun again.

—*Christopher J. Fontenot*

See also accountability; achievement tests; bureaucracy; elementary education; individual differences, in children; measurement, theories of; performance assessment; research methods; scientific management; surveys and survey results; testing and test theory development

Further Readings and References

Kliebard, H. M. (1995). *The struggle for the American curriculum: 1893–1958* (2nd ed.). New York: Routledge.

Rice, J. M. (1915). *The people's government.* Philadelphia: John C. Winston.

Rice, J. M. (1969). *The public school system of the United States.* New York: Arno Press.

Rice, J. M. (1969). *Scientific management in education.* New York: Arno Press.

🏛 RIGHT-WING POLITICS, ADVOCATES, IMPACT ON EDUCATION

Advocates promoting right-wing or conservative education policies and practices include think tanks, interest groups, business associations, news organizations, foundations, and politicians. Right-wing, conservative advocates are well organized, well funded, and often well coordinated, making them very influential in education policy formation. The rightward swing of education policy since the Reagan administration is credited in large part to right-wing advocates. Their influence is generally considered to have greatly polarized education policy making, such that it is less research based and more values based, less driven by a cooperative distribution toward an accepted public good and more by competing, narrow agendas.

Advocates for right-wing education policies are linked together in a web of supporting networks. By coordinating their efforts, right-wing advocates make their policies appear to come from a variety of independent actors, thereby magnifying their impact. The Heritage Foundation is a prominent example of a right-wing organization that advocates for conservative education policies. It is a think tank that began promoting conservative education policies and practices through its booklet *A New Agenda for Education* in 1985. The foundation promotes its education agenda through a multidimensional strategy that creates a need for education reform by broadcasting alleged failures of public education while also distributing conservative policy solutions. The foundation delivers its message simultaneously through studies, opinion pieces, newsletters, policy briefs, and its Web site. These messages are sent to all who might be interested in their education positions, including the news media, politicians, government agencies, businesses, and the general public. The foundation has been using and perfecting this public relations system since the early 1970s.

The Heritage Foundation was a founding member of the State Policy Network, a national coalition of 100 conservative advocacy organizations operating in 42 states. Members of the network use the foundation's model of extensive, simultaneous public relations to influence state and local public policy, including education policy. The network creates a national conservative influence on education policy through coordinated state and local effects.

The Heritage Foundation and the State Policy Network are funded by conservative foundations that use them to promote the privatization of public education and the inclusion of conservative curricula such as abstinence-only sex education and school prayer. These include the Olin Foundation, the Bradley Foundation, and the Coors family foundations. The entire conservative network is estimated to have spent $1 billion in advocacy-related activities since the 1970s.

The Heritage Foundation, as well as other right-wing organizations, also support and promote the careers of individual conservative politicians and bureaucrats. These right-wing organizations act as a lucrative waiting room, preparing up-and-coming conservatives for a career in politics and allowing defeated conservatives to continue to influence policy until their appointment in the next Republican administration. Nina Shokraii Rees, a former chief education analyst at the Heritage Foundation, became an assistant secretary of education in the George W. Bush administration. Former Secretary of Education William J. Bennett became a distinguished fellow at the Heritage Foundation. Former House Speaker Newt Gingrich became a fellow at the American Enterprise Institute, where Lynne Cheney was an education scholar while Second Lady of the United States.

In general, right-wing advocates argue for the privatization of public schools, fundamentalist Christian values in schools, the preparation of students as workers, and high-stakes standardized testing based on a banking model of teaching and learning. A privatized school system is built on the capitalist business principle that competition between schools will provide the most effective education for students. Privatization program ideas include vouchers, charter schools, tuition tax credits for private schools, and home-schooling. As the means of administering education is based in business, so is the outcome. More emphasis is placed on education productivity, preparing able workers for a limited job market in a globally competitive marketplace, than on other possible outcomes like social justice, personal development, and critical thinking. To the extent that nonbusiness values are emphasized, they are fundamental Christian viewpoints found in activities such as abstinence-only sex education and school prayer, organized patriotism (i.e., mandating the pledge of allegiance), and a curriculum focused on American exceptionalism in the form of White, male, Western content that emphasizes U.S. achievements with little or no acknowledgment of U.S. failures. These school activities are based in the largely discredited ideas that intelligence is innate and unalterable, that individual learning is accurately measured by standardized tests, and that knowledge is something that is uncovered in its pure form by experts and then poured by the teacher into the minds of the students.

Right-wing organizations have successfully pursued a populist divide-and-conquer strategy to make education policy more conservative. As American society has become more diverse, right-wing advocates have often rallied supporters around a few controversial issues, arguing that assistance to historically oppressed groups is not only unnecessary but deprives the majority White, Protestant population of its deserved share of resources or its values. If poor students deserve Head Start, then wealthy parents deserve more gifted programs. If humanists teach evolution, then fundamentalist Christians can demand intelligent design. Under the influence of right-wing successes, education policy formation has become a marketplace of competing interests, where justice is the same assistance to all groups regardless of their different needs and where one seeks to win at all costs over one's opponents. In the end, right-wing advocates have been leaders in forming the current winner-takes-all marketplace of education policy formation in which conflict has become the norm, self-interest has become a noble ideal, and the notion of developing an inclusive, research-based public good across race, class, and need has been lost.

—Eric Haas

See also Bible, as history; charter schools; choice, of schools; Christian Coalition; corporal punishment; creationism; ethnocentrism; fundamentalism; history, in curriculum; homophobia; intelligence; *Lemon* test; market theory of schooling; moral education; morality, moral leadership; politics, of education; prayer in school; privatization; religion, in schools; standardized testing; values education; values pluralism, in schools; voucher plans

Further Readings and References

Anderson, G., & Pini, M. (2005). Educational leadership and the new economy: Keeping the "public" in public schools. In F. English (Ed.), *The SAGE handbook of educational leadership* (pp. 216–236). Thousand Oaks, CA: Sage.

Emery, K., & Ohanian, S. (2004). *Why is corporate America bashing our public schools?* Portsmouth, NH: Heinemann.

Evans, R. (2004). *The social studies wars: What should we teach the children?* New York: Teachers College Press.

Poyner, L., & Wolfe, P. (Eds.). (2005). *Marketing fear in America's public schools: The real war on literacy.* Mahwah, NJ: Erlbaum.

Ravitch, D. (2003). *The language police: How pressure groups restrict what students learn.* New York: Vintage Books.

RISK TAKERS, IN EDUCATIONAL ADMINISTRATION

Decision-making theory regarding risk indicates that there are risk takers and risk averters. Risk taking in administration involves leaders' willingness to openly share and be true to their values, ideas, and philosophy. Risk taking is key to personal, professional, and organizational growth. Risk taking involves the leaders' openness to trial and error—to being developed, stretched, and challenged.

Research has validated a clear relationship between risk-taking behavior and school success. Researchers have noted that when principals, teachers, and other staff members possessed strong inclinations for risk, they were more likely to experience positive growth. Leaders understand that risk-taking behaviors often have a positive impact on others. The best leaders take risks because they realize the affirming effect that risk-taking behavior has on others. Compared to bureaucrats who avoid taking risks, a point beyond which a risk averter will not even engage a problem, leaders encourage risk taking. Taking risks also signals that there are elements of trust present in working situations. Leaders are more willing to delegate tasks to others when trust levels are high.

A balance of risk taking and trust establishes an environment conducive to learning. With the contention that schools exist to promote high levels of learning, the conditions that give rise to risk taking within working contexts in which trust is high are also important to promote learning.

—Jean M. Haar

See also accountability; administration, theories of; climate; creativity, in management; decision making; Halpin, Andrew William; human resource development; management theories; morale; motivation, theories of; productivity; satisfaction, in organizations and roles; Theory X, Theory Y; work task measurement

Further Readings and References

Barth, R. (2001). *Learning by heart.* San Francisco: Jossey-Bass.
Goens, G. (2000). Leadership and illusion. *School Administrator, 57*(8), 30–32.
Pellicer, L. (2003). *Caring enough to lead.* Thousand Oaks, CA: Corwin Press.

RISLEY, TODD R.

Todd R. Risley (1937–) was among the behavioral scientists responsible for the development and refinement of applied behavior analysis. He was a faculty member in the Department of Human Development and Family Life at the University of Kansas during the mid-1960s to the mid-1980s. Along with Donald Baer, Montrose Wolf, and R. Vance Hall, he studied those environmental variables that affected the lives of children, adults, and families within the ongoing context of their daily lives. Risley's work influenced the field of education via (a) his work on the impact of early experiences in the home environment on academic performance, vocational success, and the nature of life outcomes, (b) his work in the areas of single-subject research design and the development of research methods allowed for the study of behavior in the context of their natural setting, and (c) his work related to positive behavioral support. For educational leaders, Risley's work is important in its melding of direct, systematic observation with contextual understanding of human behavior, allowing for a greater depth of understanding of the environmental influences on individual behavior.

Risley's work in the area of positive behavioral support involved an emphasis on addressing challenges in the natural ecological context of their occurrence. Pragmatically, the environment in which the challenging behavior developed and was maintained was the only place that sustainable solutions could be identified and implemented. Risley also identified three levels of behavioral interventions for positive behavioral supports: (1) the behavior analytic level—in essence the level at which the relationships between antecedents,

behaviors, and consequences were analyzed and arranged to bring about desirable outcomes, (2) the contingency management level—in which consequences were structured to enhance the regular occurrence of target behaviors, and (3) the life arrangements level—involving the emphasis on lifestyle and focusing on quality of life as both an intervention and outcome.

In the area of research, Risley coauthored the seminal article on the dimensions of applied behavior analysis with Wolf and Baer, as well as a partner article with them 20 years later. This work defined the direction and initial parameters of the field. However, Risley's most significant contribution to the area of educational research was the development of the action research model. He pioneered a field-based model in which research was conducted within the context of the lives of families. Research problems involved real persons, in real situations, with real problems. School-based action research has its foundation in Risley's ongoing professional work.

Risley's most notable work involved the effect of early experiences on life outcomes, particularly that of the impact of early experiences on language acquisition and proficiency. Years of research in this area led to a seminal work on the development of language in young children and those variables embedded in the environmental structure, which directly influenced the nature of an individual's functional language ability. Risley's results indicated that almost all the variance in the measured intelligence and academic performance of children was due to the amount of talking parents did in the presence of their children. This research, in book form, was later nominated for a Pulitzer Prize.

Risley's work has had and continues to have widespread influence on the field of education. The contextual focus and research methods he initiated allow educators to examine and consider the wider expanse of those environments and variables that affect those served by the schools.

—*J. M. Blackbourn*

See also Baer, Donald; behaviorism; conditioning theory; Hall, R. Vance; learning, theories of; life span development; psychology, types of; research methods; Wolf, Montrose

Further Readings and References

Hart, B. M., & Risley, T. R. (1995). *Meaningful differences in the everyday experience of young American children.* Baltimore: Brookes.

Risley, T. R. (2001). Do good, take data. In W. T. O'Donohue, D. A. Henderson, S. C. Hayes, J. E. Fisher, & L. J. Hayes (Eds.), *A history of the behavioral therapies: Founders' personal histories* (pp. 223–242). Reno, NV: Context Press.

ROGERS, CARL

The major contribution if Carl Rogers (1902–1987) to the field of education was his perspective on psychological development as a process on individual growth through personal understanding. His precepts related to (a) warm, positive interactions between people, (b) motivation to learn as an internal process, and (c) personal readiness as the foundation of all learning have greatly influenced the profession. Rogers was born in 1902 in Oak Park, Illinois. He originally was an agriculture major at the University of Wisconsin, but graduated with a BA in religion. He earned his doctorate in clinical psychology from Columbia University in 1931. Rogers served on the faculties of Ohio State University (1940–1945), the University of Chicago (1945–1957), and the University of Wisconsin (1957–1964).

Rogers developed the theory of nondirective counseling. This theory is built on the "actualizing tendency," which is the motivation present in every life form to develop its potentials to the fullest extent possible. Within this principle is the concept of organismic valuing, or the fact that all organisms know what is good for them. Therefore, persons have the answers to all their problems and questions within themselves. The job of the counselor or therapist is to empathically reflect the client's feelings, beliefs, and attitudes in order to identify problem solutions for themselves.

Rogers hypothesized that personal growth is facilitated when counselors are open in the relationship with their client, that is, the counselor is genuine and without "front" or "façade." Rogers used the term *congruence* to describe this condition. By this he meant that the feelings counselors are experiencing are available to them, available to their awareness, that they are able to live these feelings, be them in the counseling relationship, and able to communicate them if appropriate.

The second essential condition in the relationship, according to Rogers, is that counselors are experiencing an accurate empathic understanding of their clients' private worlds and are able to communicate some of the significant fragments of that understanding. To sense the clients' inner world of private personal meanings as

if it were one's own, but without ever losing the "as if" quality—this is empathy, and this seems essential to a growth-promoting relationship.

The third condition hypothesized by Rogers is that growth and change are more likely to occur the more that the counselor is experiencing a warm, positive, acceptant attitude toward what is in the client. This condition is labeled unconditional positive regard.

Rogers advanced the hypothesis that the relationship was more effective if this condition existed. He believed that when this condition was present in the encounter between counselor and client, constructive changes in the client are more likely to occur.

Rogers further hypothesized that actual changes in behavior occurred only when the individual provided the initiative to change. He felt that you could not teach a person anything until that person was emotionally and psychologically ready to accept instruction, direction, or guidance.

Rogers's nondirective theory is an "if-then" theory. It involves no intervening variables. Although there are speculations as to the way the relationships between the conditions and the events that follow them occur, the "why" is not a part of the theory.

For educational leaders, Rogers's theory provides a foundation for the mentoring process, whether those mentored are faculty or subordinate administrators. From Rogers's perspective, leaders can easily solve problems themselves by issuing instructions or dealing with them directly. However, for persons to grow, it is often necessary for leaders to be "strategically absent." In such cases it can be difficult to watch those one supervises struggle with a problem, but in Rogers's theory, this is how real growth and learning occur. Such instances create opportunities for both success and failure and allow those being mentored to engage in personal examination to find the necessary solutions.

—*J. M. Blackbourn*

See also counseling; esteem needs; flow theory; humanistic education; Maslow, Abraham; motivation, theories of; psychology, types of; self-actualization

Further Readings and References

Milton, J. (2002). *The road to Malpsychia: Humanistic psychology and our discontents*. San Francisco: Encounter Books.
Rogers, C. R. (1951). *Client centered therapy*. Boston: Houghton Mifflin.

Rogers, C. R. (1961). *On becoming a person.* Boston: Houghton Mifflin.

Suhd, M. (Ed.). (1998). *Positive regard: Carl Rogers and other notables he influenced.* Palo Alto, CA: Science & Behavior Books.

⌐ ROLE AMBIGUITY

Role ambiguity occurs when people are unclear or uncertain about their expectations within a certain role, typically their role in the job or workplace. Role ambiguity arises when the definition of the person's job is vague or ill defined. Workers may be unclear regarding the goals, expectations, or responsibilities associated with the performance of their positions. Unclear roles may involve expectations for behavior or performance levels. In order to be proficient in their role, people should be made aware of the responsibilities and obligations of that role, the actions necessary to fulfill the role, and the effects that the role has on various constituents, including the workers themselves, their coworkers, and the organization itself. If employees are unaware of the expectations surrounding their responsibilities or performance, then they may not be working on the things necessary to accomplish what is expected of them.

Role ambiguity has been studied in four dimensions: (1) goal/expectation/responsibility ambiguity, (2) process ambiguity, (3) priority ambiguity, and (4) behavior ambiguity. With goal/expectation/responsibility ambiguity, people are unsure of what they should actually be doing within a particular role; they are unclear as to what expectations are included for fulfilling the position's requirements. Process ambiguity involves a lack of clarity regarding how a job or task should be accomplished or how certain organizational objectives can be met. Priority ambiguity implies that a person does not know when tasks should be completed or which tasks are more important than others. Behavior ambiguity occurs when people are unaware of how they should act in specific situations or what behaviors are required in order to achieve personal or organizational outcomes. Each dimension focuses on the lack of clarity or understanding people experience regarding their ability to be successful in a given role.

Persistent or ongoing role ambiguity can result in a number of problems for an employee. For example, role ambiguity has been associated with issues that include job tension, anxiety, frustration, and burnout.

Low levels of job satisfaction have also been associated with role ambiguity. In fact, job satisfaction and job performance have both been found to have an inverse relationship with role ambiguity, meaning that as ambiguity increases, job satisfaction and performance actually decrease.

Role ambiguity can be reduced or avoided in many instances by a clear articulation of the expected behaviors and outcomes associated with a particular role. With its negative relationships to job satisfaction and job performance, role ambiguity should be avoided whenever possible. Interventions to alleviate role ambiguity are often effective, more so than with other role stresses, which indicates that the identification of role ambiguity and its causes in the workplace at an early stage is critical to the development of a healthy organization and a productive worker.

—*Stacey Edmonson*

See also accountability; administration, theories of; attitudes toward work; behaviorism; bureaucracy; chain of command; division of labor; locus of control; management theories; matrix organization (the "adhocracy"); organizational theories; productivity; rational organization theory; resource management

Further Readings and References

Hart, A. (1994). Creating teacher leadership roles. *Educational Administration Quarterly, 30*(4), 472–497.

Lunenburg, F. C., & Ornstein, A. C. (2004). *Educational administration: Concepts and practices* (4th ed.). Belmont, CA: Wadsworth.

Sawyer, J. E. (1992). Goal and process clarity: Specification of multiple constructs of role ambiguity and a structural equation model of their antecedents and consequences. *Journal of Applied Psychology, 77*, 130–142.

⌐ ROLE CONFLICT

Role conflict occurs when a person must adhere at the same time to two or more conflicting or contradictory sets of expectations. Fulfilling the expectations for one role interferes with or prohibits fulfilling the expectations for the other role(s). Thus, the two roles are incompatible and make it difficult, if not impossible, for the person to be successful in both settings. For example, role conflict frequently occurs in persons who juggle career and family. The roles associated with a successful career may interfere with the roles associated with a quality family life. Long hours at the office result in fewer hours available for family activities, just as staying home with a sick child results in missed meetings or less productivity at the office.

When people are faced with expectations for more than one role, they must choose which expectations to fulfill; thus, one set of expectations is necessarily left unfulfilled, and people often feel stress or anxiety that one of their roles is not being adequately carried out. Or the person may choose to partially fulfill both roles, which yields problems in that neither role is implemented successfully or completely.

Role conflict is typically bidirectional, meaning that both roles interfere with one another. In using the previous example, a successful career can impede family concerns, or family issues can impede the needs of a successful career.

Role conflict can appear in the form of time-based conflict, strain-based conflict, or behavior-based conflict. Time-based conflict takes place when two or more roles compete simultaneously for an individual's time. The family versus work issue mentioned previously demonstrates this type of conflict: a parent who needs to pick up a child from school may be expected to attend a meeting at that same time; the two roles to which the person is obligated require incompatible time constraints. Strain-based conflict is a more relationship-based type of role conflict in which a person's professional role conflicts with the personal role he or she has with others, that is, a person who is elevated to a supervisory position over coworkers who are his or her friends. The roles of supervisor and friend are often incompatible, thereby causing the person to experience role conflict. Behavior-based conflict describes a situation in which the behaviors a person must exhibit in one role are contradictory to the behaviors associated with another role. For example, if a person who is a supervisor at work must be reserved and uncompromising in the job place, these same behaviors in the home environment might cause conflicts with family members.

Role conflict may negatively impact the effectiveness and productivity of workers in a variety of career settings. It also has the potential to be detrimental to a person's home or family life. Because of these serious consequences, reducing role conflict whenever possible or developing coping mechanisms for dealing with role conflict are important considerations for leaders in any field.

—*Stacey Edmonson*

See also accountability; behaviorism; bureaucracy; chain of command; compliance theory; contingency theory; critical theory; empowerment; hierarchy, in organizations; involvement, in organizations; line and staff concept; locus of control; role ambiguity; scalar principle

Further Readings and References

Boyan, N. (1988). Describing and explaining administrative behavior. In N. Boyan (Ed.), *Handbook of research on educational administration* (pp. 77–97). New York: Longman.

Hammer, L., & Thompson, C. (2004). Work-family role conflict. Retrieved August 11, 2004, from http://www.bc.edu/bc_org/avp/wfnetwork/rft/wfpedia/wfpWFRCent.

Marks, S. R. (1977). Multiple roles and role strain: Some notes on human energy, time, and commitment. *American Sociological Review, 42,* 921–936.

ROLE MODEL

Role models may be defined as individuals who are worthy of imitation in some area of life. In educational circles, a role model is at times used as a synonym with the terms *mentor* or *hero* and at other times as a way to describe a relationship that falls somewhere in between the two terms. There is evidence that interacting with individuals defined as role models has an effect on children's perceptions and behavior.

ADULTS AS ROLE MODELS

Children view adults—such as parents, teachers, principals, and ministers—as the most important role models in their lives. Adults, then, serve as a visible, influential model for children. In connection to education, modeling and teaching life skills can serve as the foundation for building academic achievers.

One important responsibility of an educator is to model active learning—by making his or her learning visible, students come to see their own learning as serious. Because of the influence of the position, the responsibility of role modeling for principals is essential; teachers, staff, parents, students, and community members look to them as role models

STUDENTS AS ROLE MODELS

The value of students as role models has been identified as an influential resource for educating other students. Models and programs have been developed that allow students to learn from each other. For instance, the Peer Group Connection is a program that trains seniors to serve as mentors to freshmen. The seniors and their advisers are trained in human relations and facilitation skills. Research completed on the program suggests that freshman grades, attendance, and behavior improve. In turn, senior peer leaders acquire expanded interpersonal skills.

Another example of a student role model program is the Program for Women in Science and Engineering (PWSE). The program identifies college science and engineering female students to present hands-on activities at schools and career conferences and to encourage women and underrepresented populations to pursue careers within traditionally male-dominated fields, like science, technological, engineering, or mathematical fields of study.

—Jean M. Haar

See also adult education; collaboration theory; empowerment; esteem needs; expectations, teacher and student cultures; leadership, theories of; mentoring; professional development; role conflict; role theory; supervision; tutoring; working conditions, in schools

Further Readings and References

Fiore, D. (2004). *Introduction to educational administration: Standards, theories, and practice.* Larchmont, NY: Eye on Education.

Nazzal, A. (2002). Peer tutoring and at-risk students: An exploratory study. *Action in Teacher Education, 24*(1), 68–80.

Program for Women in Science and Engineering. Retrieved from www.pwse.iastate.edu/oncampus/ugrolemodels.html.

Somers, C., & Piliawsky, M. (2004). Drop-out prevention among urban, African American adolescents: Program evaluation and practical implications. *Preventing School Failure, 48*(3), 17–22.

Tournaki, N., & Criscitiello, E. (2003). Using peer tutoring as a successful part of behavior management. *Teaching Exceptional Children, 36*(2), 22–29.

ROLE THEORY

For at least a generation of scholars and practitioners of educational leadership, *role theory* stood as a fundamental component of social systems theory. Social systems theory provided a structural-functionalist view of the interactions and relationships between people, their work, the organization, and its purposes for their work. Role conflict studies focused on the ways that people negotiated their own needs against the requirements of their jobs or the expectations of others, those in their role set, including complementary role holders.

Although through the ensuing decades educational leadership studies based on role theory seem to have waned considerably, role theory expanded in other social science disciplines. *Social role theory* as developed in the disciplines of sociology and industrial psychology explains gendered actions and relationships between men and women, the ways they approach work as well as differences in their managerial styles. Continued works in these disciplines demonstrate how role models derive from social networks and group dynamics. The influence of role on individuals depends on role saliency. Role saliency represents the strength of a role within the organization and provides a structural-functional lever to organizations in rewarding specific role enactments and role models.

The ways that people interpret their place within a group and organization depend on the dynamics of the group interacting with personalities and personal experiences. People inhabit roles in life from their behavior within their families to their socialization through school days, community groups and agencies, and their work groups. Educational leaders face students, teachers, parents, and community members whose interactions depend on their personal interpretations about the roles they hold socially, informally, and in formal, titled positions. School leaders must understand the ways that people's expectations and behaviors derive from their socialization into social, group, and work roles.

Despite the relevance of role theory to the group and individual dynamics that shapes school leaders' work, recent educational research lacks mention of role theory. Role theory suffers the taint of its association with the much-maligned social systems theory. Social systems theory suffered repeated attacks over the past two decades for failing to provide a nuanced insight into the dynamics of schools. Nevertheless, as each person holds multiple social, personal, informal, and formal roles in the complex communities within and surrounding schools, role theory can provide insights into the ways that socialization works to shore up as well as erode social support for education.

—Jane Clark Lindle

See also accountability; administration, theories of; attitudes toward work; behaviorism; bureaucracy; chain of command; compliance theory; contingency theories; frame theory; governance; hierarchy, in organizations; leadership, distributed; line and staff concept; management theories; organizational theories; personnel management; role ambiguity; role conflict; span of control; staffing, concepts of

Further Readings and References

Eagly, A. H., & Johannesen-Schmidt, M. C. (2001). The leadership styles of women and men. *Journal of Social Issues, 57*(4), 781–797.

Heck, R. H., & Hallinger, P. (1999). Next generation methods for the study of leadership and school improvement. In J. F. Murphy & K. S. Louis (Eds.), *Handbook of research on educational administration* (2nd ed., pp. 141–162). San Francisco: Jossey-Bass.

Lieberman, A. (2004). Confusion regarding school counselor functions: School leadership impacts role clarity. *Education, 124*(3), 552–558.

Shivers-Blackwell, S. L. (2004). Using role theory to examine determinants of transformational and transactional leader behavior. *Journal of Leadership & Organizational Studies, 10*(3), 41–49.

RURAL EDUCATION

Rural education has been defined by a number of different criteria over the last half century. The National Rural and Small Schools Consortium considers a district rural if inhabitants number fewer than 150 per square mile or if the district is located in a county where 60% or more of the population lives in communities of 5,000 or fewer. Other organizations and government entities have applied either a 25,000 resident criteria to classify communities as rural, or some have applied a more restrictive 2,500 resident restriction. Five terms were used by the U.S. Department of Education's Center for Education Statistics in 1987 to define or imply rurality: rural, nonmetropolitan, small town, small place, and school size. Rural and nonmetropolitan were identified as subsets for metropolitan status, as were suburban and urban.

The National Center for Education Statistics (NCES) reported that approximately 90,000 public schools operate within the United States, of which 38,000 were located in rural areas or small towns in 1999–2000. Schools in rural areas or small towns account for about 42% of all schools in the nation, and 30% of all students. Characteristics unique to rural areas include geographic isolation, small populations, and declining enrollments.

According to an open-ended survey of 50 small rural school superintendents, the most critical issues facing their districts were funding inequities, meeting the No Child Left Behind (NCLB) requirements, attracting and retaining highly qualified teachers, declining enrollments, along with implementation of technology and distance learning. Most crucial were funding issues, meeting the Adequate Yearly Progress standard of NCLB and recruitment/retention of highly qualified teachers. In the other pressing issues category were problems associated with declining enrollments and the need to provide vital learning resources to students effectively through distance learning

FUNDING

Three decades of litigation and a considerable number of studies document the inequities in educational funding for property-poor rural schools. Persistent dependence on local property tax revenues has perpetuated funding disparities among urban, suburban, and rural districts. School districts with high-priced residential or commercial property have substantially greater resources available to support education. In the midst of this wealth of knowledge, state legislatures continue to rely on the property tax as a primary tax base source for public schools, which ultimately results in disproportionate funding for poorer rural schools and specifically rural students.

The overwhelming majority of states have been unwilling thus far to abandon the property tax, though more progressive states such as Michigan and Wisconsin have met the challenge and overcome political fears to fund education with a more progressive approach. As a result of continued taxpayer discontent with local property taxes, the Michigan legislature abolished local school property taxes in 1993. A referendum was initiated to construct a system that would replace the abolished system of school revenue generation. Michigan's new finance approach approved in 1994 obtains revenue for funding education from a variety of other sources. First, the state sales tax was increased from 4% to 6%, and a statewide property tax was enacted. Next, additional real estate transfer fees were imposed and sin taxes were instituted or increased. Finally, a new system of assessing property and a state foundation grant formula for distributing funds were formulated and enacted.

Waves of litigation have been funneled through the court systems in an attempt to provide a more effective system of providing adequate and equitable funding to public schools. Approximately one half of the litigation has resulted in rulings for the property-poor plaintiff; however, little to no funding equity has found its way to these districts. School law firms and the courts are now relying on the "adequacy" standard rather than "equity" to reflect a more progressive focus of funding all schools and all children in a fair, adequate, and accountable manner. State legislatures are sure to be confronted with problems associated with funding schools in the future as long as there is a continued reliance on the property tax as a primary source of funding public schools.

NO CHILD LEFT BEHIND

Superintendents of rural schools identify the requirements of NCLB as a major source of concern in the schools and communities. Specifically, the Adequate Yearly Progress (AYP) requirement of NCLB specifies that states must develop objectives for improved achievement of all students and for specific student subgroups that include English language learners (ELL), special needs students, economically disadvantaged, and ethnic minorities. Assessment of AYP objectives must be established at the school level and reported for each subgroup of students. Rural and small schools are in greater jeopardy of receiving the designation of "in need of improvement" than are large schools, due to the volatile nature of school-level reporting from year to year. In schools where small numbers of students are assessed in a grade level, averages are subject to significant variation from one test administration to another and from year to year for reasons unrelated to overall school performance. Robert Linn indicates that test score volatility arises from two sources. First, variation in the groups of students being tested each year can cause fluctuations. Contributing factors may include the attitudes and abilities of students in each cohort, student mobility, or an influx of immigrants. Second, one-time factors such as teacher turnover, a flu epidemic, or construction noise on the day of testing can also affect scores. In districts with small student populations, these differences can cause dramatic fluctuations in annual average test scores. One solution or remedy to test score volatility allowable under NCLB is to average test scores over several years. A study by David Figlio in 2002 indicates that the stabilizing benefit of a 3-year rolling average is greatest among smaller schools.

HIGHLY QUALIFIED TEACHERS

A February 2005 personal interview study of small rural school superintendents targeted the "highly qualified" teacher requirement of NCLB as one of the most noteworthy concerns in their districts. The highly qualified teacher requirement, though highly relevant, has the propensity of intensifying the already existing problem of attracting and retaining certified teachers in rural communities. High-needs-area teachers fully certified or with proper teaching credentials in special education, science, math, foreign language, as well as bilingual/ESL, are already scarce commodities in many rural schools. Greater demand for these high-needs-area teachers is resulting in high-stakes competition among schools. Salary levels may reach a cost-prohibitive status for schools with scarce financial resources, yielding a competitive disadvantage for the smaller property-poor rural schools. Recently, the difference between average rural teacher salaries and other teacher salaries varied by state from around $250 to as much as $10,400. Small rural schools that lack the financial resources to compete with larger, more often richer, urban and suburban districts will likely have an inability to meet the NCLB requirements of highly qualified teachers and staff, resulting in lower ratings and possible loss of vital funding.

Teacher compensation in rural schools is significantly less than their nonrural counterparts. Nationally, beginning teachers earn 11.3% less in rural schools than entry-level teachers in nonrural districts. In addition, overall average teacher salaries are 13.4% higher in the suburban and urban districts, and experienced teachers in the nonrural areas (those with master's degrees plus 20 years) can expect in excess of 17.2% more than their rural counterparts. Thus, rural districts must compete for the highly qualified teachers with more innovative approaches that may include advertising and recruiting blitzes concentrating on lower costs of living, cheaper housing, along with resourceful community support programs. Showcasing benefits along with the perks of rural life, such as higher quality learning environments and superior school climates, are essential to regaining a competitive edge for the NCLB compliant teacher.

DECLINING ENROLLMENT

Rural school superintendents identify decreasing enrollment as one of the key issues in their districts. In almost half of the 50 states, more than 50% of the rural schools lost students between 1994 and 1997. Global shifts in environmental, economic, and social trends have initiated radical changes in business, industrial, and agricultural organizations, leaving many rural communities in a sedentary state. Once thriving communities with robustly profitable industrial and agricultural constituents are now left with high unemployment and devalued economic resources. In the age of information and the emerging biotechnical age, the competitive edge to attract business and industry will continually bypass rural areas for the more robust suburban and urban districts. All these changes in corporate America leave rural schools with an exodus of residents, students, teachers, and administrators. As a result of continuing paradigm shifts, major initiatives are needed to revitalize America's rural communities and their innate resources.

Research continues to support the educational superiority of small-school over large-school systems. Though they are not a panacea, small schools continue to exhibit higher achievement levels among students with significantly fewer problems in the areas of discipline and school safety. Students in smaller schools have a sense of belonging in the community and graduate at higher rates than their larger-school peers. Small schools and communities will need to emphasize their strengths in strong campaigns to attract residents with school-age children in the future. Coalitions of highly active business/industry development councils should be formed to attract investment in rural America to revitalize and sustain a strong rural base in an effort to continue the legacy of high-quality rural education.

DISTANCE LEARNING

Advancements in technology and digital communications have led to innovations plus unprecedented change in instructional delivery for many rural schools. Distance learning has evolved as a new strategy for diminishing or lessening problems associated with isolation or remoteness of rural schools. Professional development of teachers and administrators, vital training of ancillary staff, and the delivery of comprehensive curriculum can now be delivered via digital communications in a cost-effective environment.

Distance learning research studies in rural schools have resulted in mixed reviews and inconclusive evidence in assessing overall effectiveness. Inequalities and differentiation in technological resources, hardware, software, and professional development of teachers as well as ancillary staff provide extensive data, suggesting that rural schools are inconsistent in the application of advanced video conferencing and Web-based technologies in the delivery of classroom instruction. According to Phil Westfall, president of the U.S. Distance Learning Association, the primary goal of any distance learning program should be to maximize both student achievement and student satisfaction. While there are certainly scenarios under which virtually all distance learning technologies may be appropriate, two-way interactive television or video conference technology provides the best technology foundation for small and rural K–12 schools to meet their needs to enhance curriculum offerings, stem the effect of teacher shortages, provide for ongoing teacher professional development, and meet the requirements of No Child Left Behind.

Distance learning provides rural schools with an opportunity to provide students with a more inclusive and comprehensive curriculum, along with advanced academic courses, while maintaining the benefits of small community educational environments. Critical teacher shortages in the key areas of math, science, and foreign languages can be reduced through school district collaborations, consortia, and connectivity. Nevertheless, it is imperative to consider the benefits, limitations, and variable effectiveness encompassed within the emerging world of telecommunications and distance learning.

SUMMARY

Extensive research findings indicate that small schools and districts graduate a higher percentage of students, resulting in lower dropout rates. Rural schools have continually exhibited a safer environment with fewer incidents of violence and vandalism, higher levels of parental involvement, and superior attendance rates. Research and literature provide a basis for concentration of attention on school size that is particularly important in turning around low performance and giving poor and minority students the extra boost that a community of caring, competence, and high expectations offers. Finally, a more human scale is a potent antidote to student alienation. While impersonal bigness may actually provoke disruptive behavior, small schools conducive to trust and respect tend to defuse violence.

In light of the fact that all small schools may not be the pinnacle of educational excellence and may not emanate solutions to all problems, they may possess some catalytic ingredients for a comprehensive approach to improvement of student success. Specifically, in the case of high schools, which have exhibited an impervious nature to change, reduction of school size has progressively emerged as a relentless reform effort. Though rural schools may be in command of many issues plaguing larger schools, they continue to face unique challenges such as inequitable funding, recruiting and retaining highly qualified teachers, declining enrollments, and meeting the requirements of No Child Left Behind. In the final analysis, the importance of rural schools to their communities is significant, and the educational value of retaining small, community-based schools is undeniable.

—Robert L. Marshall and William A. Kritsonis

See also accountability; boards of education; capacity building, of organizations; cultural politics, wars; economics, theories of; elementary education; enrollment projections; ethnocentrism; finance, of public schools; high schools; No Child Left Behind; productivity; school safety

Further Readings and References

Courant, P., Gramlich, E., & Loeb, S. (1995). Michigan's recent school finance reforms: A preliminary report. *American Economic Review, 85*(2), 372–377.

Declining enrollments: Silent killer of rural communities. (2000). Retrieved March 26, 2005, from http://www.aasa .org/issues_and_insights/prof_dev/rural_small/decline_ 6-16-00.htm.

Enliten Management Group. (2003). An interview with Philip J. Westfall, PhD, president of the U.S. Distance Learning Association: Thoughts & perspective on distance learning. Retrieved March 26, 2005, from http://www.enliten.net/ useus/Enlitenment/Enlitenment_Jan.pdf.

Figlio, D. (2002). Aggregation and accountability in No Child Left Behind: What will it take? Paper presented at conference sponsored by Thomas B. Fordham Foundation, Washington, DC.

The Finance Project. (1997). *Money matters: A guide to financing quality education and other children's services.* Washington, DC: Author.

Hobbs, V. (2004). The promise and the power of distance learning in rural education. Retrieved March 26, 2005, from http://www.ruraledu.org/docs/distancelearning.pdf.

Jimmerson, L. (2003). *The competitive disadvantage: Teacher compensation in rural America.* Washington, DC: Rural School and Community Trust.

Kane, T., Staiger, D., & Geppert, J. (2002). Randomly accountable. *Education Next, 2*(1). Retrieved March 26, 2005, from http://www.educationext.org/20021/56.html.

Linn, R. L., Baker, E. L., & Betebenner, D. W. (2002). Accountability systems: Implications of requirements of the No Child Left Behind Act of 2001. *Educational Researcher, 31*(6), 3–16.

Marshall, R. (2005). Critical issues in small rural schools: Superintendents' perspectives. Retrieved March 26, 2005, from http://www.pvamu.edu/edir/rmarshall/pubs/ruralis sues.pdf.

McRobbie, J. (2001). Are small schools better? School size considerations for safety and learning. Retrieved March 26, 2005, from http://www.wested.org/online_pubs/po-01-03.pdf.

National Rural and Small Schools Consortium. (1986). *Definitions of rural, small, and remote schools.* Bellingham: Western Washington University.

Reeves, C. (2003). *Implementing the No Child Left Behind Act: Implications for rural schools and districts.* Naperville, IL: North Central Regional Educational Laboratory. Retrieved March 12, 2005, from http:// www.ncrel.org/policy/pubs/html/implicate/.

Rural School and Community Trust. (2003). School size: Research-based conclusions. Retrieved March 26, 2005, from http://www.ruraledu.org/docs/arkansas/schoolsize.doc.

Russell, T. (1999). *The no significant difference phenomenon.* Montgomery, AL: International Distance Education Certification Center. Retrieved March 26, 2005, from http:// www.nosignificantdifference.org/nosignificantdifference/.

U.S. Department of Education. (1987). *The condition of education: A statistical report* (1986 ed.). Washington, DC: Center for Educational Statistics.

U.S. Department of Education. (2001). *Overview of public elementary and secondary schools and districts: School year 1999-2000* (NCES Statistical Analysis Report). Retrieved March 4, 2005, from http://nces.ed.gov/pubs2001/ overview/ table08.asp.

RUSSELL, BERTRAND

Philosopher, educator, writer, and political activist, Bertrand Russell (1872–1970) is best known for his work in mathematical and symbolic logic and in philosophy. His philosophy of education included strong convictions on the need to teach critical thinking skills to children. Russell was born in Wales into a politically liberal and educated family; however, his parents died when he was of preschool age. Raised by his grandmother, Russell was educated privately and attended Trinity College in Cambridge, England, where he received degrees in mathematics and the moral sciences (philosophy).

Russell wrote over 90 books and hundreds of articles during his lifetime. He wrote his first book, *German Social Democracy*, in 1896, and his first book on mathematical logic and philosophy, *The Principles of Mathematics*, in 1903. From 1907 to 1910, he worked tirelessly with Alfred North Whitehead, culminating with the publication of the first volume of *Principia Mathematica* in 1910. During this time, Russell also began to express his radical and decidedly liberal political views, and he ran unsuccessfully as a suffragist candidate for parliament in 1907 (and in 1922, 1923). In 1916, he was convicted and fined for his antiwar activities and was dismissed from his position at Trinity College. In 1918, he was convicted again and spent 6 months in prison where he wrote *Political Ideals: Roads to Freedom* and the widely acclaimed *Introduction to Mathematical Philosophy* in 1919.

Seven years later, Russell published *On Education*, in which he called for an education that would liberate children from unthinking obedience to parental and religious authority. With his second wife (he married four times) and former student Dora Black, he established in 1927 the experimental Beacon Hill School in West Sussex, England. The school highlighted Russell's belief that students should not be required to follow a strictly academic curriculum. He believed that students needed opportunities to develop what today are commonly referred to as critical thinking skills. He championed a belief that students needed to be trained to form opinions, find solutions to problems, and to be able to identify and question assumptions. The experimental school operated for 5 years and resulted in a 1932 book titled *Education and Social Order*.

After that, Russell made a living as a writer, journalist, and lecturer. He created quite a stir in 1932 with the publication of *Marriage and Morals*, a book espousing his views on free love. He taught at several American universities from 1938 to 1944. One appointment at City College, New York, was rescinded following public protests and a judicial decision stating that he was morally unfit to teach at the college.

Russell ceased to be a pacifist during the 1930s with the rise of Hitler in Germany. As a result, his fellowship at Cambridge was eventually restored. In 1950, he was awarded the Nobel Prize for literature. In his later years, he was quite vocal and active in his opposition to nuclear weapons. Russell became an inspirational figure to many youth in the late 1950s and 1960s as a result of his continued antiwar and antinuclear protests. In 1961, at the age of 88, he was imprisoned for a week in connection with an antinuclear protest. Until his death at the age of 97, Russell remained a visible and vibrant public figure.

—*George W. Griffin*

See also Aristotle; critical theory; empiricism; existentialism; liberalism; philosophies of education; Plato; research methods

Further Readings and References

Monk, R. (1999). *Russell.* London: Orion.

Russell, B. (1946). *History of Western philosophy.* London: George Allen & Unwin.

Russell, B. (1957). *Why I am not a Christian.* New York: Simon & Schuster.

Russell, B. (1960). *On education.* London: Unwin.

Russell, B. (1988). *The problems of philosophy.* New York: Prometheus Books.

Russell, B. (1998). *The autobiography of Bertrand Russell.* London: Routledge.

S

S-CURVE THEORY

The S-curve is a graphic of a frequency distribution that visualizes growth and change. The growth of most organisms follows an S-curve. Growth processes do not simply reach a limit and then stop. Instead, they often follow one of two configurations with respect to limits. The first is a pattern of exponential (even superexponential) growth up to a turning point and then a pattern of slowing growth. The pattern exhibits a slow-slow-quick-quick-slow progression: an S-curve. When a young tree is very small, it tends to grow only a few inches each year, but as time passes, it accelerates in both height and girth, until it reaches its natural limit, declines, and dies.

The second growth pattern also resembles an S-curve, but it extends the upward growth by tracing another S-curve back down. The overall pattern becomes a bell-shaped curve and may indicate the phenomenon of overshoot and decline. An example might be population growth in many historic empires. The failing empires outgrow their capacity to provide food or energy and subsequently break down.

These generic patterns of growth were adopted in social science research to frame the diffusion of innovation theory. The French sociologist, Gabriel Tarde, carried out the original diffusion research in 1903 and plotted the S-shaped curve. Modern diffusion research is traceable to the 1943 study by two sociologists, Bruce Ryan and Neal Gross, of the diffusion of hybrid corn among Iowa farmers. Everett M. Rogers, more than any other individual, has been responsible for synthesizing the theories and findings of diffusion research and formulating a unified theory. Rogers discusses four prominent theories of diffusion. His rate of adoption theory concerns us here. This theory visualizes the pattern of the adoption of an innovation as an S-shaped curve, with potential for stabilization and/or ultimate decline.

Figure 1 displays a typical S-curve for the adoption of an innovation. The simple S-curve, however, is an incomplete view of the process. It is more helpful to think of the "S" in terms of Hughes's second growth pattern as the front half of a "bell-shaped" curve. The "S" outlines the developmental stages of the change, but the process can easily revert at the "turning point" when operational or ideological doubt sets in. An educational change process would start with innovators, often aided by formal change agents, and progress through a period of acceleration and rapid growth when the early and late majorities join the process, to a period of saturation—stabilization or exhaustion—when only the laggards remain to be converted. At this point, if a school staff is able to reenergize the process—deal with the increasing complexity and reinforce existing commitments—the innovation will likely succeed. If not, the process will shrink to safe levels or finally collapse.

—*James W. Keefe*

See also at-risk students; chaos theory; ethos, of organizations; instructional interventions; leadership, theories of; leadership styles; learning, theories of; learning environments; problem solving; psychology, types of; psychometrics; research methods; standardized testing; testing and test theory development; underachievers, in schools; validity and reliability; variables

Further Readings and References

Goerner, S. (2002). *Rethinking education in light of great change.* Retrieved September 7, 2005, from New Horizons

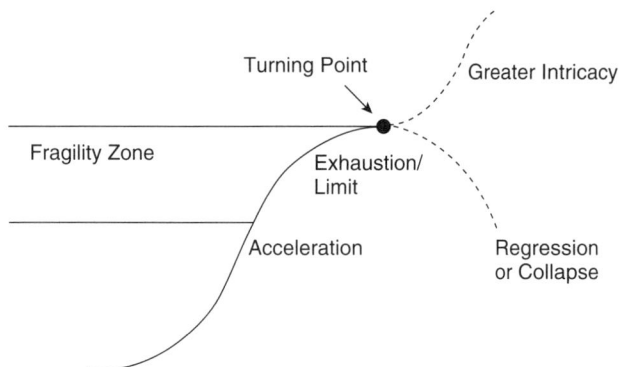

Figure 1   Innovation Adoption Curve

SOURCE: Adapted with permission from Goerner, S. (2002). *Rethinking education in light of great change.* New Horizons for Learning Web site, available from http://www.newhorizons.org/trans/goerner.htm.

for Learning Web site, http://www.newhorizons.org/trans/goerner.htm

Hughes, B. (1999). *International futures: Choices in the face of uncertainty.* Boulder, CO: Westview Press.

Rogers, E. (1976). New product adoption and diffusion. *Journal of Consumer Research, 2,* 290–301.

Rogers, E. (1995). *Diffusion of innovations* (4th ed.). New York: Free Press.

🏛 SALARY AND SALARY MODELS

Salary is the monetary compensation workers receive in return for their services (salary is also called wage earnings or pecuniary rewards). Workers often receive additional benefits, such as medical coverage and/or contributions to pension funds, but salary is the most visible and tangible aspect of employee compensation. Salaries paid for jobs both across and within occupations are readily amenable to comparison; therefore, salary is often used to assess the relative attractiveness of different positions.

Salary models represent alternative approaches to the distribution of monetary compensation. Salary models are usually based upon traditional economic assumptions about worker behavior. Specifically, it is assumed that a positive relationship exists between income and effort and that employees will work harder if they can earn more money. Examining the criteria used by salary models to distribute employee wages can help to explain what is of value to an organization.

THE EVOLUTION OF SALARY MODELS IN EDUCATION

Salary models in education have evolved from so-called boarding round approaches in the 1800s, which provided teachers room and board as a major component of their compensation, to *grade-based models* in the late 1800s and early 1900s. Grade-based schedules differentiated salary primarily on the basis of level of instruction (paying higher salaries to secondary than to elementary teachers) but were often used to discriminate on the basis of gender and race as well (with higher salaries paid to men than women and to White teachers than Black).

The inequities of grade-based models were addressed in the 1920s to 1940s with the widespread adoption of the *single or uniform salary schedule,* which distributes additional wage increments among teachers solely on the bases of longevity and advanced training. Two characteristics distinguish one single salary schedule from another:

1. The slope or steepness of the pay gradient (i.e., how quickly wages increase from the entry level to the top step on the schedule)

2. The magnitude of the increments paid for different levels of advanced training (i.e., how much a system is willing to expend to encourage teachers to engage in formal professional development)

ADVANTAGES AND DISADVANTAGES OF THE SINGLE SALARY SCHEDULE

Using experience and advanced training as the primary criteria for wage differentials is considered relatively objective and easy to quantify without direct supervision, thus the cost of administering a single salary schedule is relatively low. Furthermore, paying higher salaries to teachers with more experience and training creates incentives for individuals to remain within a school system, which should promote stability, and to continue to develop professionally, which should promote better instruction and higher student achievement. As a result of these perceived advantages, the single salary schedule remains the most commonly used salary model in the education.

Nevertheless, the utility of paying teachers based on criteria not directly related to performance or the achievement of students has been challenged repeatedly, most notably in 1983 with the publication of *A Nation at Risk,* which advocated the adoption of merit pay salary models, which explicitly link teacher performance to student performance, usually as measured by standardized achievement tests.

Another concern about teacher salaries is that entry wages in education typically lag behind those in other professions requiring equivalent levels of educational preparation (e.g., accounting or engineering). It is often argued that starting salaries in teaching need to be increased if the profession is to become more competitive in attracting "the best and the brightest."

ALTERNATIVE SALARY MODELS

Alternatives to the single salary model include:

- *Career ladders.* Unlike the single salary schedule, which makes no differentiation regarding teacher work at different points of a career, the career ladder creates a staged profession that allows a teacher's responsibility, status, and salary to change markedly over the course of a career. For example, as teachers proceed through the steps of the career ladder in the Cincinnati Public School, they can move from Apprentice to Novice to Career to Advanced to Accomplished teacher. Each step up the ladder requires sustained high performance, which is accompanied by a higher salary and more responsibilities.
- *Merit- or performance-related pay.* The use of merit pay has a long but erratic history in American public education.
- *Skill and competency based pay.* Group performance incentives.

OTHER SALARY MODEL ADJUSTMENTS

The following adjustments, paid as either annual bonuses added but not built in to the salary base or as salary increments, can be made to any of the salary models listed above:

- *Scarcity bonuses* can be used to attract high-quality teachers to low-performing schools or to attract teachers with high-need subject expertise, such as mathematics or science.
- *Attendance incentives* are used to induce teachers to improve their attendance by offering bonuses for perfect or near-perfect attendance.
- *Deferred salary leave plans* (DSLPs) allow teachers to voluntarily defer a part of their annual salaries for a given number of years in order to self-fund a leave of absence. For example, a participating teacher would spread 4 years of salary over 5 years, working the first 4 years at 80% of salary and then using the accumulated deferred payments to self-fund a paid leave during the fifth year. DSLPs have been used widely in Canada since the late 1970s, but rarely in the United States.

—*Stephen Jacobson*

See also career stages; classification of education; differentiated staffing; economics, theories of; merit pay; performance evaluation systems; personnel management; staffing, concepts of; unions, of teachers

Further Readings and References

Chamberlin, R., Haynes, G., Wragg, E., & Wragg, C. (2004). *Performance pay for teachers.* London: Routledge.

English, F. (1984). Merit pay: Reflections on education's lemon tree. *Educational Leadership, 41*(4), 72–79.

English, F. (1992). History and critical issues of educational compensation systems. In L. Frase (Ed.), *Teacher compensation and motivation* (pp. 3–24). Lancaster, PA: Technomic.

Frase, L. (1992). The effects of financial and nonfinancial rewards: Program description and research results. In L. Frase (Ed.), *Teacher compensation and motivation* (pp. 217–238). Lancaster, PA: Technomic.

Gratz, D. (2005). Lessons from Denver: The pay for performance pilot. *Phi Delta Kappan, 86,* 569–581.

SALES TAX

The most common tax levied on goods or services is the sales tax applied at the retail level of transaction. Used primarily by the states, its popularity is relatively recent. As of 1931, no state levied a retail sales tax (RST). Until that time, states had relied mostly on property taxes, business taxes, excise taxes, and, in a few states, income taxes. By the 1930s, however, state revenue was under pressure, because of both the Depression and a movement to transfer the property tax to local governments. In 1932, Mississippi adopted a 2% retail sales tax as a replacement for a business tax. Seventy years later, sales and use taxes (taxes on use when a customer buys out of state for delivery in the state) now account for about 32% of state government tax collections nationwide, trailing only the individual income tax as a source of revenue. They are imposed by 45 states and the District of Columbia, as well as over 7,500 local jurisdictions.

While retail sales taxes are the most common tax levied on goods and services, such taxation may take a variety of forms. A *general sales tax* applies to all transactions at a specified level of economic activity, except for enumerated exemptions (e.g., a sales tax may apply to all sales at retail except food or medicine). A *selective sales tax* (commonly called an excise tax) applies only to enumerated transactions (e.g., retail sales of tobacco products or liquor). A *specific tax* applies only to the number of physical units bought or sold (e.g., a motor fuel tax may be 30¢ per gallon). An *ad valorem tax* applies to the value of the good or service purchased (e.g., a hotel tax may be 10% of the hotel bill). A tax may apply every time a transaction occurs (multistage tax) or only at one stage in the production and distribution process (single-stage tax).

The RST is an example of a single-stage tax and is the preferred form of goods and services taxation for several reasons. First, the tax paid by the consumer will likely be the amount received by the government. Multistage and preretail taxes, in contrast, tend to pyramid. Second, multistage taxes impact each market transaction, thereby favoring integrated firms (e.g., those that manufacture, wholesale, and retail) with a lower tax. Third, the RST applies to the full value of the product.

EQUITY

It is often held that the RST imposes a regressive burden because on average in any given year, those with lower income spend a higher percentage of their income than do higher-income households. However, a growing research literature suggests that a single-year snapshot of income and consumption overestimates this regressivity. That is, over a lifetime, all income is spent. By this reasoning, the burden of a uniform (i.e., no exceptions) consumption tax is comparable to the burden of a flat-rate tax on labor income. The analysis will change, of course, if particular goods are exempted from the tax. For example, the exemption of food would make the tax more progressive.

EFFICIENCY

The efficiency of the RST concerns its cost to the economy. That is, does the RST raise revenue with a lower cost to the economy than an alternative tax, such as the income tax? A pure, uniform RST does not tax capital income and therefore does not distort individuals' and firms' decisions about saving and investment. An income tax, in contrast, does tax capital and thus does distort these decisions. This comparison is complicated, however, because the RST often involves capital taxation by taxing business-to-business sales.

The efficiency analysis of the RST is further complicated by the fact that its base is virtually never comprehensive, taxing few services and exempting various goods on distributional and administrative grounds. In light of the administrative and political realities of the RST, observers generally assert that a broader tax base taxed at a lower rate is more efficient than a more narrowly defined base taxed at a higher rate.

STABILITY

Government functions continue during recessions and may increase during such periods due to increasing social problems (e.g., rising unemployment, crime). Revenue stability is particularly important for state and local governments because they lack the borrowing capacity and money-creating powers of the federal government. Some researchers have found that general sales taxes are somewhat less stable than individual income taxes, probably because business equipment purchases comprise a substantial share of the general sales tax base.

EXPORTING AND FEDERAL DEDUCTIBILITY

A state may "export" a fraction of its RST burden to nonresidents (usually tourists) if they buy products when visiting. However, a more likely form of exporting occurs via the deductibility of state taxes against federal taxable income. The Tax Reform Act of 1986 eliminated the deductibility of state sales tax, leading many observers to predict a shift away from sales tax. Interestingly, this has not happened. A study done by Citizens for Tax Justice in 1991 noted that between 1986 and 1991, 26 states increased their sales tax, and only 2 reduced it. During the same period, 11 states increased their personal income tax, while 28 reduced it.

—*Michael Addonizio*

See **also** budgeting; economics, theories of; equality, in schools; equity and adequacy of funding schools; finance, of public schools; lottery systems; property tax

Further Readings and References

Casperson, E., & Metcalf, G. (1994). Is a value-added tax progressive? Annual versus lifetime incidence measures. *National Tax Journal, 47,* 731–746.

Due, J. F., & Mikesell, J. L. (1994). *Sales taxation: state and local structure and administration* (2nd ed.). Washington, DC: Urban Institute Press.

Lyon, A. B., & Schwab, R. M. (1995). Consumption taxes in a life-cycle framework: Are sin taxes regressive? *Review of Economics and Statistics, 37,* 389–406.

Mikesell, J. L. (1995). *Fiscal administration* (4th ed.). Belmont, CA: Wadsworth.

Slemrod, J. (2003). Michigan's sales and use taxes: Portrait and analysis. In C. L. Ballard et al. (Eds.), *Michigan at the millennium.* East Lansing: Michigan State University Press.

⌂ SANCHEZ, GEORGE

A pioneering educator who worked tirelessly on behalf of improving education for Mexican American children, George I. Sanchez (1906–1972) first attended school in Jerome, Arizona. Moving to Albuquerque, New Mexico, he completed high school there in 1923. Becoming a school teacher in Yrisarri, New Mexico, he often had to travel by horseback to get to work.

As a recipient from several eastern foundations, Sanchez received his M.S. in educational psychology and Spanish from the University of Texas in 1931. His thesis was concerned with issues of validity on language IQ tests in English for Spanish speaking children. Sanchez went on to complete his PhD at the University of California at Berkeley. He returned to New Mexico, where he worked in the New Mexico State Department of Education and became president of the New Mexico Educational Association. Battling for improved tax support for schools, he began to acquire an understanding of how to improve funding for public schools.

Continuing his foundation work, he surveyed rural schools in Mexico and African American schools in the southern United States. He became the Minister of Education in Venezuela for 1 year and returned to become a nontenure-track faculty member at the University of New Mexico from 1938 to 1940. During that time, he wrote *Forgotten People: A Study of New Mexicans.* In 1940, he was elected president of LULAC (League of United Latin American Citizens) and became the first professor of Latin American studies in the United States. However, he came up against vested interests as a result of his advocacy of improved funding in New Mexico, and he was not going to obtain a full professor position at the University of New Mexico.

During this time, the University of Texas offered him a full-professor position. In Texas, he worked with LULAC, the Alianza Hispano-Americana, and other organizations in pushing lawsuits for improved funding and for equal rights for Mexican Americans. He worked to utilize the courts to establish better funding and to fight segregation of Mexican American students in the public schools. In the landmark case *Delgado v. Gracy et al.* (1948), he helped strike down segregated schools for Mexican American students. He was instrumental in fighting for and winning several other critical cases in the courts. He was honored by the University of California at Berkeley Law School for his work in improving education for Mexican American students. A special location in the U.S. Department of Education is named after him.

—Fenwick W. English

See also Chavez, Cesar Estrada; immigration, history and impact in education; Latinos; League of United Latin American Citizens; literacy, theories of; Mendez, Felicitas

Further Readings and References

Calderon, M., & Minaya-Rowe, L. (2003). *Designing and implementing two-way bilingual programs.* Thousand Oaks, CA: Corwin Press.

Gaitan, C. (2004). *Involving Latino families in schools.* Thousand Oaks, CA: Corwin Press.

Garcia, E. (2005). *Teaching and learning in two languages: Bilingualism and schooling in the United States.* New York: Teachers College Press.

Gibson, M., Gandara, P., & Koyama, J. (2004). *School connections: U.S. Mexican youth, peers, and school achievement.* New York: Teachers College Press.

Pedraza, P., & Rivera, M. (2005). *Latino education.* Mahwah, NJ: Lawrence Erlbaum.

Ybarra, R., & Lopez, N. (2004). *Creating alternative discourses in the education of Latinos and Latinas.* New York: Peter Lang.

⌂ SATISFACTION, IN ORGANIZATIONS AND ROLES

In organizations and roles, satisfaction can be defined as the degree of an individual's affective orientation toward his or her role in an organization or simply as the degree to which an individual likes his or her role in an organization. Satisfaction is important because it affects a variety of individual and organizational outcomes.

An individual's satisfaction with his or her role in an organization affects that person's physical and mental well-being, overall quality of life, and satisfaction in roles outside the organization. Individuals who are satisfied with their roles in organizations are generally physically and mentally healthier, experience a higher quality of life, and are more satisfied with their roles outside their organizations than individuals who are not satisfied with their roles in organizations. Research has found in some occupations, low work satisfaction is associated with alcohol abuse.

Satisfaction also affects commitment, motivation, productivity or performance, absenteeism, and turnover. Individuals who are satisfied with their roles in organizations are generally more committed to their organizations, more motivated, and more productive within their organizations than individuals who are not satisfied with their roles in organizations. For example, research indicates the job satisfaction of teachers is positively associated with student achievement. All things considered, the students of teachers with high job satisfaction do better on standardized assessments than do students of teachers with low job satisfaction. Individuals who are satisfied with their roles in organizations are also less likely to fail to show up or voluntarily leave their organizations than individuals who are not satisfied with their roles in organizations. Absenteeism and turnover are costly and disruptive to work organizations, as hiring, acclimating, and training new employees require time and energy that could otherwise be spent providing support to employees and clients.

Researchers have studied satisfaction within organizations since the early 1900s, especially with respect to turnover. Many characteristics of roles in organizations have been identified as affecting the degree to which individuals are satisfied with their roles, although the relevancy and relative strength of characteristics' effects on satisfaction can vary greatly by occupation, education, personality, age, tenure, union membership, marital status, sex, and other factors. The following paragraphs describe some—but certainly not all—of the characteristics that affect satisfaction within organizations.

Routinization is the degree to which a role is repetitive, and it negatively affects satisfaction. The more a person's role is repetitive, the less satisfied that person is likely to be with that role. Research also indicates, in occupations like teaching, year-to-year routinization can affect satisfaction in the same manner that daily or hourly routinization does. In other words, teaching the same subject the same way year after year can negatively affect satisfaction among teachers the same way that doing the same task hour after hour can negatively affect satisfaction.

Participation is the degree to which individuals exercise control within their organizations, and it positively affects satisfaction. The more a person exercises control within his or her organization, the more satisfied that person is likely to be with his or her role in the organization. Instrumental communication is the degree to which information about an organization is transmitted by an organization to its members, and it positively affects satisfaction.

Distributive justice is the degree to which rewards and punishments are consistent with an individual's input into an organization, and it positively affects satisfaction. Not to be mistaken for pay (which, when applicable, also positively affects satisfaction), distributive justice refers to the full set of rewards and punishments that organizational members experience and perceive. Distributive justice is the degree to which individuals feel they are treated fairly in general, given their effort.

Support is the degree of assistance or consideration given or expressed by others, and researchers have consistently found support to have strong positive effects on satisfaction. For example, many studies indicate administrative support is the most important determinant of job satisfaction among K–12 teachers. The satisfaction of individuals in organizational roles is also affected by the support individuals receive from family members and friends outside organizations.

Satisfaction in organizations is also affected by the degree to which organizational members are afforded the opportunity to develop skills and knowledge and the degree to which members are afforded the opportunity to be promoted within an organization. Increases in opportunities to develop skills and knowledge and to be promoted within organizations lead to increases in satisfaction among members.

The degree to which an individual's role in an organization matches his or her preconceived ideas about organizational life is positively associated with satisfaction. Individuals whose organizational roles do not match the preconceived ideas they had about organizational life are generally less satisfied in their roles than individuals whose roles match the preconceived ideas they had. Of course, it is possible to be pleasantly surprised by a role that is better than previously imagined. However, both human nature and many aspects of organizational life that are unnoticed or unconsidered by outsiders (including some of the characteristics mentioned in the previous paragraphs) cause most mismatches between preconceived ideas and actual organizational life to lead to decreases in satisfaction.

—Eric J. Reed

See also behaviorism; capacity building, of organizations; class size; collaboration, theory; climate, school; communities, types, building of; conflict management; creativity, in management; empowerment; esprit (school climate); esteem needs; ethos, of organizations; flow theory; group dynamics; Halpin, Andrew William; human resource development; involvement, in organizations; job security; leadership effectiveness; management theories; Maslow, Abraham; mentoring; morale; motivation, theories of; performance evaluation systems; personality; politics, of education; productivity; rational organizational theory; role conflict; satisficing theory; stress, in school administration

Further Readings and References

Barth, R. (2003). *Lessons learned.* Thousand Oaks, CA: Corwin Press.

Frase, L. (2005). Refocusing the purposes of teacher supervision. In F. English (Ed.), *The SAGE handbook of educational leadership* (pp. 430–462). Thousand Oaks, CA: Sage.

Giancola, J., & Hutchison, J. (2005). *Transforming the culture of school leadership: Humanizing our practice.* Thousand Oaks, CA: Corwin Press.

Pellicer, L. (2003). *Caring enough to lead.* Thousand Oaks, CA: Corwin Press.

Sergiovanni, T. (2000). *The lifeworld of leadership.* San Francisco, CA: Jossey-Bass.

Starratt, R. (2003). *Centering educational administration.* Mahwah, NJ: Lawrence Erlbaum.

🏛 SATISFICING THEORY

Classical decision-making theory presumes decision makers to be rational actors who seek optimal or maximum solutions. This model, also known as rational choice, suggests that decision makers follow a linear sequence to arrive at a solution:

1. Identify desired outcome(s) in light of the organization's goals and objectives.

2. Consider all possible alternatives.

3. Consider the consequences of each alternative.

4. Select the alternative that will most likely result in the desired outcome.

Inherent in this model is the assumption that a decision maker is capable of knowing all possible solutions as well as all consequences and will consider each equally. Herbert A. Simon, the originator of satisficing theory, asserts that the classical decision-making model is an ideal rather than practical strategy. He suggests that inherent limitations within organizations and decision makers themselves preclude the use of the pure rationality required by the classical model. Rather, decision makers employ bounded rationality. That is, they act rationally within the constraints of external and internal limitations.

These external limitations include, for example, the multifaceted structure of organizations. This structural complexity limits the information to which any one person within the organization has access. Thus, with only limited access to information, a decision maker is precluded from considering all possible alternatives or knowing all possible consequences of any alternative. Similarly, organizations tend to have multiple and, oftentimes, conflicting goals. Multiple or conflicting goals may prevent any one solution from being "best" in that a particular solution may maximize one goal while inhibiting another. Moreover, and perhaps more important, because decision makers are human, they have internal limitations that prevent them from employing pure rationality. For instance, all humans have unconscious biases that cause them to accept some data while rejecting others. In addition, humans have a limited cognitive capacity to manage complexity. As a result, humans attempt to simplify highly complex situations. Again, this causes a decision maker to ignore some data in favor of others.

Therefore, because decision makers are constrained by this bounded rationality, they are incapable of identifying the optimal solution. Rather, they search for the first alternative that is at least minimally satisfactory. That is, they seek to satisfice.

—Sarah W. Nelson

See also administration, theories of; Barnard, Chester I.; behaviorism; boundaries of systems; bureaucracy; cognition, theories of; compliance theory; conceptual systems theory and leadership; consideration, caring; contingency theories; decision making; organizational theories; problem solving; Simon, Herbert

Further Readings and References

Simon, H. (1957). *Administrative behavior: A study of decision-making processes in administrative organization.* New York: Macmillan.

Simon, H. (1967). *Organizational decision making.* Englewood Cliffs, NJ: Prentice Hall.

Tarter, C., & Hoy, W. (1998). Toward a contingency theory of decision making. *Journal of Educational Administration, 36*(3), 212–228.

SCALAR PRINCIPLE

The scalar principle or scalar chain is based on a precept of management, which reasons that the authority and responsibility of leadership flows downward from top management in an unbroken line, which includes every worker in the organization. It coexists with the concept of chain of command, which is the line of authority that flows from the top of an organization down to rank-and-file members working within the organization. The concept of authority is associated with the right to direct others, which is aligned with a formal appointment to a particular supervisory job or title. According to some experts, the terms *scalar chain, line of authority,* and *chain of command* are used synonymously.

The development of the scalar principle derives from the classical principles of management theory developed when Henri Fayol's work was introduced into the United States in the 1940s. Fayol, a French manager, derived 14 principles of management. Fayol's approach to organizing included concepts such as lines of authority, centralization, delegation, departmentalization, division of work, span of control, specialization of jobs, unity of command, and unity of direction. Fayol's work was compatible with the work of Frederick W. Taylor, a pioneer in the field of scientific management principles who linked organizational management theory to the scientific principles of research. Fayol's precepts broadened Taylor's principles in their focus on the structured organizational process of management. Even though the scientific management and classical theorists applied their theoretical constructs to business organizations, their hierarchical principles were also adopted and applied to schools.

A classical organizational theorist would maintain that when the scalar principle is applied properly, there is a clear reporting structure and embedded within it, supervisory relationships, and a distinct communication process. With a clear reporting procedure in place, each person in the organization knows who to report to for direction in regard to work activities. The advantage in adopting the scalar principle would be improved efficiency and coordination through faster decision making and direction, which, in turn, would lead to effective performance within the organization. When the scalar principle is applied to a school district, the supervisory line of authority would begin with the school superintendent or chief administrator and then flow downward accordingly, to the assistant superintendents, principals, assistant principals, departmental chairpersons, teachers, and staff personnel. This arrangement would be laid out visibly in an organizational chart, which would indicate supervision in the various schools, divisions, and departments within the school system.

The scalar principle could be applied within each school unit or building starting with the chief administrator of that building and proceed downward to every person or staff member assigned regardless of the job or job description. It would be the responsibility of the chief administrator assigned to the unit or building to coordinate work activities and establish the lines of communication with the workers assigned to these activities. If there are problems regarding performance, coordination, or unity, then responsibility for those problem situations could also be traced upward, along the chain of command, and back to the chief administrator in authority over that division.

The channel of communication is organized into structured and delineated levels of communication, which are imposed up and down the chain of command. With a clear reporting structure in place, communication would be established only with individuals above or below the indicated reporting level. A disadvantage of such a system would be that communication becomes restricted as each level communicates only with a level in descending or ascending order. Currently, with widened avenues of communication available through electronic means as well as an increased prevalence in the formation of teams across departments and divisions in business organizations and across disciplines and grade levels in schools, communication processes have become less restrictive and more open. As a result, the scalar principle may have to be revised as technology and teaming impact functional management processes and procedures.

—Patricia Ann Marcellino

See also authority; bureaucracy; chain of command; communications, theories in organizations; division of labor; functionalist theory; goals, goal setting; hierarchy, in organizations; organizational theories; rational organizational theory; scientific management; span of control; staffing, concepts of; working conditions, in schools; workplace trends

Further Readings and References

Fayol, H. (1949). *General and industrial management* (C. Storrs, Trans.). London: Sir Isaac Pitman.

Mintzberg, H. (1979). *The structuring of organizations.* Englewood Cliffs, NJ: Prentice Hall.

Taylor, F. (1947). *The principles of management.* New York: Harper & Row. (Original work published 1911)

SCHEDULING, TYPES OF IN SCHOOLS

The school schedule is the administrative mechanism by which the instructional day is divided into manageable timeframes so that school personnel can deliver the curriculum. An effective scheduling model maximizes available instructional time for learning activities, empowers teachers with decision-making authority to group learners for skills instruction, and provides teachers with the flexibility and creativity to design and deliver instructional methods that fully engage students in the process of learning. Mastery of curriculum content for all learners is the goal of an efficacious scheduling model.

The number of minutes allocated for instruction within a discipline is a critical variable when considering curriculum mastery. Educators, therefore, must consider issues related to curriculum breadth, depth, and balance when designing the school schedule because mastery of curriculum standards is closely correlated with the time spent on learning activities. For example, requiring the curriculum to include a variety of disciplines will expose the student to an array of subjects (thereby ensuring curriculum breadth) yet may provide insufficient time within the school day for the in-depth instruction that is necessary for the student to master any discipline. Conversely, limiting the curriculum to a few core disciplines may ensure that ample time is available for content mastery of these core subjects, but the student may then not receive a well-rounded education through instruction in disciplines such as the arts and humanities.

Curriculum balance also must be carefully considered because instructional minutes will not be equally allocated for every subject. Greater time must be allocated for the core disciplines than for elective or other subjects, so that students can master the basic state and local curriculum standards.

Another consideration when designing the school schedule is developmental appropriateness for the learner at each grade level. Special attention and consideration should be given to easing transitions for the student—from the home environment into the kindergarten setting, through each subsequent grade, and when moving from one building level to another. For example, kindergarten students would find an assignment with numerous teachers and classrooms to be overwhelming; at the other end of the spectrum, high school seniors may consider being scheduled with only one teacher for the entire instructional day as too confining and boring. Because the developmental and instructional needs differ for students at the elementary, middle, and high school levels, the remainder of this entry will address effective scheduling arrangements at each building level.

ELEMENTARY

At the elementary level, the one-teacher, self-contained classroom generally is considered the preferred scheduling approach. Young children, particularly in the early primary grades, have the opportunity to form a close personal bond with one teacher, who is responsible for delivery of the core curriculum standards. The elementary teacher is provided with large, unencumbered blocks of time for heterogeneous whole-group classroom instruction, with the flexibility for homogeneous grouping and regrouping of learners for skills instruction in curricular areas such as reading and mathematics. The classroom teacher also is empowered to reach decisions related to the amount of allocated time that is necessary for curriculum mastery, dependent upon the subject area and the learning needs of each individual student.

Parallel scheduling often is used in elementary schools, making large blocks of planning time available so that the regular classroom teachers can be released from their instructional responsibilities for either individual planning or to meet as members of grade-level planning teams. Specialists in areas such as music, art, physical education, computers, and library/media rotate through the classroom groupings during these periods, providing instruction to the students in these subjects.

MIDDLE LEVEL

The middle-level schedule should be responsive to the developmental needs of the emerging adolescent, providing a personalized learning environment that promotes supportive relationships among teachers and learners. Interdisciplinary teaming is considered to be the hallmark of effective middle-level schools, in which small learning teams of teachers and students are created. Through the utilization of common planning periods, teaching teams design and deliver instruction in the core disciplines in an interdisciplinary fashion so that students can make connections across the curriculum. Advisory time also is provided within the schedule, ensuring that teachers and students can form close personal relationships and providing an opportunity to address issues related to the emerging adolescents' physical, cognitive, social, and emotional development.

An effective middle-level schedule empowers the teaching teams to collaboratively reach decisions related to how instructional time is configured each day, and the flexible interdisciplinary schedule is considered to be the basic organizational framework of the exemplary middle-level school. With this approach, teams may choose to dedicate more time to selected subjects, providing instruction to core classes each day, on an alternating-day basis, or as needed. Teams may contain as few as two teachers or as many as six or more, although four- or five-person teams are the most commonly utilized. Typically, the core subjects (language arts, reading, social studies, mathematics, science) are contained within the team block, and the remaining subjects (the elective or "exploratory" subjects) are scheduled with teacher specialists, either in exploratory blocks or in daily 40- to 45-minute timeframes.

Junior highs and middle schools that do not utilize interdisciplinary teaming commonly utilize a disciplinary or departmentalized approach, employing scheduling models typically mimicking high school schedules.

HIGH SCHOOL

Scheduling models at the high school level commonly fall into three varieties: daily-period models, block-scheduling formats, and combination or hybrid models. Although a small number of high schools have been experimenting with the use of interdisciplinary teaming in the lower high school grades, the vast majority of high schools tend to maintain a discipline-based approach to teaching and learning.

Daily-period models typically divide the instructional day into uniform "periods" of approximately 45 to 55 minutes in length, and a school may choose to schedule students into six, seven, eight, or more classes each day. Daily-period schedules usually do not permit cross-disciplinary teaching approaches, and each subject area retains its distinct place within the instructional day. Although daily-period models were the dominant high school format for much of the twentieth century, this approach has been increasingly criticized in the past 20 years. Critics assert that daily-period models contribute to the fragmentation of the school day, continue rigid reliance on the Carnegie unit, create an impersonal learning environment, contribute to teachers' overreliance on the lecture method, discourage the use of constructivist learning strategies, and restrict efforts to deliver interdisciplinary instruction.

Block-of-time models, or block scheduling, have rapidly grown in popularity since the late 1980s. These formats often employ 80- to 95-minute timeframes or "blocks" for each course, and the two most frequently used block models are the 4 × 4 semester plan and the eight-block, alternating-day model. If teachers use the instructional time effectively, proponents state that these approaches permit a more supportive learning climate, encourage the incorporation of constructivist teaching strategies, and promote enhanced teacher-student interactions. With the 4 × 4 semester plan, classes are scheduled into four instructional blocks of 80 to 90 minutes, which meet for only one half of the academic year. The student enrolls in four daily courses the first semester (half) of the year and an additional four courses the second semester. The eight-block, alternating-day schedule permits the student to complete eight classes on a 2-day cycle: Blocks 1 through 4 and 5 through 8 rotate every other day throughout the school year.

Combination or hybrid models attempt to incorporate features of both daily-period and block schedules, often because school faculties may decide that some disciplines may more appropriately be delivered in a standard timeframe or to provide increased variety and flexibility to the instructional day. For example, an alternating-day model could include daily periods 3 days weekly and blocks the remaining 2 days. Another hybrid approach might incorporate blocks for morning classes (either an alternating-day or semester plan format), with daily-period classes in the afternoons.

Regardless of the scheduling model that is developed, school faculties should understand that any division of time is arbitrary. The schedule should empower teachers with the flexibility to maximize their instructional time and provide opportunities for active student engagement in learning. The schedule permits the development of a personalized learning environment that promotes improved student achievement.

—Donald Gene Hackmann

See also accountability; administration, theories of; classroom management; class size research; curriculum guides; discipline in schools; grades, of students; high schools; infrastructure, of organizations; individual differences, in children; instruction, survey of; junior high schools; learning, theories of; learning environments; middle schools; organizational theories; site-based management

Further Readings and References

Canady, R. L., & Rettig, M. D. (1995). *Block scheduling: A catalyst for change in high schools.* Princeton, NJ: Eye on Education.

Hackmann, D. G., & Valentine, J. W. (1998). Designing an effective middle level schedule. *Middle School Journal, 29*(5), 3–13.

Queen, A. (2002). *The block scheduling handbook.* Thousand Oaks, CA: Corwin Press.

Robbins, P., Gregory, G., & Herndon, L. (2000). *Thinking inside the block schedule.* Thousand Oaks, CA: Corwin Press.

Williamson, R. D. (1998). *Scheduling middle level schools: Tools for improved student achievement.* Reston, VA: National Association of Secondary School Principals.

🏛 SCHOLASTIC APTITUDE TEST

The College Board SAT Program consists of the "SAT Reasoning Test" and "SAT Subject Tests." The SAT Reasoning Test is a 3-hour, 45-minute multiple-choice test that includes the Critical Reading section, the Math section, and the Writing section. Each section is scored on a scale of 200 to 800; thus, the perfect score for the test is 2,400. The SAT Subject Tests are 1-hour, multiple-choice tests in specific subjects. These tests are achievement tests that measure knowledge of particular subjects and the ability to apply that knowledge. Many colleges require or recommend one or more of these tests for admission or placement purposes. The Subject Tests include Literature, U.S. History, World History, Mathematics Level 1, Mathematics Level 2, Biology E/M (Ecological or Molecular), Chemistry, Physics, French, French With Listening, German, German With Listening, Spanish, Spanish With Listening, Modern Hebrew, Italian, Latin, Japanese With Listening, Korean With Listening, and Chinese With Listening. Each individual test is worth 800 points. Some colleges require certain Subject Tests for admission or placement; others allow students to take tests of their choosing.

HISTORY

The SAT test was originally used by the College Board to measure the level achieved by students for admission purposes. The test first took root in the United States during the early part of the twentieth century. At that time, applicants for elite northeastern universities had to sit for entrance examination at each of the institutions. In an effort to simplify the application process, the 12 top northeastern universities founded a new organization, the College Entrance Examination Board. Later, the board developed a new exam that contained mostly multiple-choice questions: the Scholastic Achievement Test (SAT). In 1941, after considerable development, the test was renamed Scholastic Aptitude Test.

In 1947, the Educational Testing Service (ETS) was founded in Princeton, New Jersey. Since then, the SAT test has been developed and administered by ETS for the College Board, which is the owner of the test. After that time, the SAT test was widely used by universities and colleges around the country for admission purposes.

With success of SAT came the success of SAT coaching schools, for example, Kaplan and Princeton Review. Under the pressure that a test that can be coached cannot really measure innate aptitude, College Board changed the name in 1990 to Scholastic

Assessment Test. In 1994, the College Board further announced that SAT was not an acronym any more, but the actual name of the test.

CHANGES TO THE SAT

In March 2005, ETS first administered the SAT Reasoning Test. The previous test (known as the "SAT I: Reasoning Test") was criticized for not being aligned enough with the high school curriculum. As a result, the test was redesigned to enhance its relation with current high school curriculum and to emphasize skills necessary for success in college, including reading, writing, and math.

Changes included renaming the "Verbal Reasoning Section" of the test the "Critical Reading Section." Analogies questions were replaced by more questions on short and long reading passages.

In the Math Section, items from more advanced math courses such as second-year Algebra were added to the test, while quantitative comparison items were eliminated.

To highlight writing skills, the Writing Section, including an essay, was added to the test. Also, multiple-choice questions on grammar appeared in the redesigned version. Because of all these changes, the length of the SAT Reasoning Test increased to 3 hours and 45 minutes, and the perfect score became 2,400 instead of the previous 1,600.

SAT ISSUES: ACHIEVEMENT OR APTITUDE?

The aptitude test measures a person's natural ability, while the achievement test measures knowledge learned by the person. The SAT originated from the intelligence test popular in the early twentieth century. The designer of SAT assumed that intelligence was an inherited attribute that would remain unchanged over one's lifetime and that it could be measured. Also, individuals could be ranked by their intelligence and assigned their places in society accordingly. Anti-testers often ask the question: Assuming we can measure aptitude, do we want an educational system that prizes hard work or a system that rewards inherited genes? They claim that achievement tests, such as SAT Subject Tests, are better admission tests because they measure what the students have accomplished rather than what they start with. Comprehensive studies by the University of California system also suggested

that SAT Subject Tests are better predictors of freshmen grade point average than the SAT Reasoning Test.

RACIAL DIFFERENCES IN SAT

Another argument charges that the SAT test is inherently biased against Blacks and Latinos, who score worse on average than Whites. People against the SAT claim that the racial gap emerged because most test writers are Whites and culture biases are introduced into SAT. The College Board fights back by saying that most SAT items are reviewed by a large sample of experts and test takers, so that any biased items will be eliminated.

The racial gap may also be explained by the socioeconomic status of the students. Although the College Board says that coaching on average adds less than 40 points to the scores, there is an emerging consensus that effective coaching can improve student SAT scores. Test prep itself had become a $400 million business by 1999. The racial gap may be attributed to different family backgrounds, or, in other words, Whites score higher on average on SAT than Blacks and Latinos because they are in better school districts and can afford coaching classes.

—*Xiaogeng Sun*

See also achievement tests; Asian Pacific Americans; Black education; critical race theory; cross-cultural education; cultural capital; cultural politics, wars; determinism, sociocultural; diversity; grades, of students; high schools; individual differences, in children; intelligence; Latinos; learning, theories of; measurement, theories of; minorities, in schools; multiculturalism; motivation, theories of; resiliency; social capital; testing, testing and test theory development; validity and reliability

Further Readings and References

Geiser, S., & Studley, R. (2004). UC and the SAT: Predictive validity and differential impact of the SAT I and SAT II at the University of California, In R. Zwick (Ed.), *Rethinking the SAT: The future of standardized testing in university admissions* (pp. 125–153). New York: RoutledgeFalmer.
Kronholz, J. (2004, September 1). SAT scores show little improvement. *Wall Street Journal*, pp. D1, D2.
Young, J. (2003). Researchers charge racial bias on the SAT. *The Chronicle of Higher Education, 50*(7), 34–35.
Zwick, R. (Ed.). (2004). *Rethinking the SAT: The future of standardized testing in university admissions.* New York: RoutledgeFalmer.

🏛 SCHOOL DISTRICTS, HISTORY AND DEVELOPMENT

The American public school district is a unit of local government with authority over education in a community or other geographic area. A district derives its power from a statutory delegation of the state legislature, and it is responsible for developing, implementing, and evaluating all aspects of the local educational program. As such, school districts can be seen as an arm of state government established to ensure the rights and privileges of a free education to its people. According to U.S. Department of Education statistics from 2001, there are almost 15,000 local school districts in the nation—ranging in number from a single school district in Hawaii to nearly 1,200 districts in Texas.

Under the U.S. Constitution and pursuant to its reserved-powers clause, education is a responsibility left to the states primarily. Because they are political entities of the state, created for the express purpose of helping the state discharge this responsibility, each state legislature has the authority to create, modify, or abolish local school districts unless otherwise restrained by its state constitution. State control over each local district is exercised through a policy-making agency (usually known as the state board or state department of education), while federal influence is experienced both through direct grants for specific purposes (e.g., No Child Left Behind) and through the Supreme Court's interpretations of various local school district practices and effects. State legislators are hesitant to change existing district boundaries and structures without voter approval in the governmental unit, but local school districts often find themselves caught in a legal and political crossfire between federal court orders and local community desires not in sympathy with such orders.

The local school district is a descendant of the "common" (public elementary) school movement that dominated the nineteenth century. Whether viewed as charity schools that developed in the cities of the industrial northeast, the ad hoc town schools of colonial New England, one-room schoolhouses of the agricultural Midwest, or the southern schools run initially by the parish vestry and church wardens, each prototype of the common school contributed in some way to the modern notion of the local school district.

Through various acts in the colonial states—such as those enacted in Connecticut in 1776 and Massachusetts in 1789—granting the right to elect school trustees, levy taxes, and select a teacher, a district system of education came to be established. Common school reformers later moved to force the consolidation of small school units into larger standardized town systems, hoping to lessen sectarian religious practices in the schools. (In some states during this "city unification" period in the 1840s and 1850s, legislation to encourage consolidation would pass, then be repealed as the dominant political party changed, then passed again over a period of years.) In the southern states, where the county was traditionally viewed as the local unit of government, it was likewise adopted as the unit of school control. In the more sparsely populated Midwest and West, district organization was suited to the geographic needs of the region: When some number of families lived near enough together to make organization possible, they were permitted by early state laws in those regions to come together and form a school district—no matter how irregular the boundaries.

While the common school movement put education fully in the arena of public policy, state system centralizers and progressive urban reformers seized upon this opportunity. A system composed of local school districts provided an acceptable level of local control that was politically necessary, while using their own oversight and supervisory responsibilities to encourage values they saw as more important, namely free access to education, a modest equalization of resources, the assimilation of a diverse population, and a more comprehensive system of education for the developing economy.

Because the district system worked well initially in the New England colonial states and conditions that supported the system were present in other parts of the growing nation, the idea of the local school district moved westward along with the migrating population. So while the responsibility for and control of education has been centralized at the state level in law and in practice for over 200 years, the political subdivision of the school district has been critical for states in making the fulfillment of their responsibilities for education manageable.

There are three broad areas of responsibility that local school districts must meet: implementing state laws, rules, and regulations; establishing policy in areas not covered by the state; and employing a superintendent to serve as chief executive officer. Specific duties assigned to districts within state statutes can include erecting school buildings, levying and expending public funds, hiring staff, and providing pupil transportation and food service. However, school districts typically have broad discretion in their actions as exercised by the local board of education—the governing body responsible within the provisions of state law for operating a school district. The board members are usually elected by popular vote (or appointed in some large cities) and are responsible directly to the people of the separate school districts.

Because they provide the most extreme example of community control in government, school districts can be seen as both the most common and most diverse agencies of local government. The base of authority that gives them discretion in the exercise of power, their "closeness" to the community, and their centrality as a social institution all contribute to the local school district's continuing importance as an instrument of school governance.

This importance has been somewhat lessened over the past decade as states and cities, in response to calls for increased accountability, have permitted takeovers of a school district—usually by the state education agency or the mayor. Most of the recent district takeover laws across the states focus on cases of fiscal mismanagement or breaches of academic accountability. Other reformers emphasize the need for city-suburban or metropolitan relationships as a means of improving urban school districts (e.g., to address desegregation or special education), though such arrangements may be viewed as diluting the power and authority of the local system.

Despite these trends, the typical school district remains a largely independent entity and a uniquely American contribution in extending state power to a local governmental unit.

—*Randy J. Dunn*

See also boards of education; Chicago school reform; collective bargaining; consolidation, of school systems; Council of the Great City Schools; decentralization/centralization controversy; finance; governance; Kentucky Education Reform Act; planning models; politics, of education; productivity; rational organizational theory; restructuring, of schools; scalar principle; state departments of education; superintendency; systems theory/thinking; taxes, to support education

Further Readings and References

Bogotch, I. (2005). A history of public school leadership: The first century, 1837–1942. In F. English (Ed.), *SAGE handbook of educational leadership* (pp. 7–33). Thousand Oaks, CA: Sage.

Carter, G., & Cunningham, W. (1997). *The American school superintendent.* San Francisco: Jossey-Bass.

Hess, G. (1991). *School restructuring, Chicago style.* Thousand Oaks, CA: Corwin Press.

Kowalski, T. J. (1999). *The school superintendent: Theories, practice, and cases.* Upper Saddle River, NJ: Merrill.

Steffy, B., & English, F. (1995). Radical legislated school reform in the United States: An examination of Chicago and Kentucky. In D. Carter & M. H. O'Neill (Eds.), *Case studies in educational change: An international perspective* (pp. 28–42). London: Falmer Press.

U.S. Department of Education. (2002). *Digest of education statistics.* Retrieved August 30, 2004, from nces.ed.gov/programs/digest/d02/list_tables2.asp#c2_4

Wong, K. K., & Shen, F. X. (2003). Big city mayors and school governance reform: The case for school district takeover. *Peabody Journal of Education, 78*(1), 5–32.

SCHOOL IMPROVEMENT MODELS

A *school improvement model* is a specific design or framework for school reform that can be adopted by schools. The interchangeable term *school reform models* also appears in the literature. A variety of school improvement models exist, including externally developed models—created by organizations outside local schools—and internally developed models—designed by people within school organizations. These models vary by purpose, featured design elements, degree of specificity regarding the implementation of design elements, and extent of research that has been conducted on the model's effects specific to school conditions and student achievement.

HISTORY

While the history of education in the United States displays a series of attempts at reform, the contemporary era has seen a degree of political intensity brought to bear upon the reform agenda. The beginning of this period was marked by the rebuke to the educational system delivered in the 1983 report *A Nation at Risk: The Imperative for Educational Reform,* and it continued with the National Governor's Summit in 1988 and with federal educational initiatives under the Bush and Clinton administrations. The amplified federal interest in primary and secondary schooling coincided with a growing private sector involvement in education, resulting in a host of school reform models that were developed independent of specific schools and adopted by a limited number of schools.

The beginning of the twenty-first century has seen a particular increase in the number of schools engaged in improvement efforts, through both externally and internally developed reform models, in response to the enactment of No Child Left Behind Act (NCLB), in January of 2002. Specifically, NCLB has increased schools' accountability for results, focusing considerable attention on student achievement by establishing the expectation that schools demonstrate yearly progress with all students and disaggregated subgroups of students. These expectations are linked to logistical, financial, and public relational consequences that intensify the need for school improvement. Increases in the use of externally developed improvement models may in part be linked to the availability of federal funding for the purchase and operation of comprehensive, research-based reform models. Such an inducement can be seen in the Comprehensive School Reform Program.

DESCRIPTION

Most external school improvement models are comprehensive in nature, connect the school to external support structures, and require substantial financial commitments by the local schools for the purchase of the improvement design, materials, and assistance. Comprehensive designs offer a coherent improvement approach by changing a constellation of factors related to student learning, such as curriculum, instruction, assessment practices, leadership and governance, resource allocation, student grouping and scheduling, and professional development. While specific design elements vary by model, the use of design teams to provide ongoing external assistance is a relatively consistent practice across models. Over time, reform models may become increasingly reliant on local expertise and funding.

Numerous issues have been associated with the implementation of external reform models and their effectiveness. Faculty resistance related to reform implementation is well documented in the literature and points to teacher participation in the selection and approval of reform models as a critical factor for success. Implementing multiple facets of comprehensive reform models simultaneously has also proven a challenge in many schools. Local adaptation of models

can impact the coherence of the original design, lessening its effectiveness. Overall, a synthesis of extant research studies offers a mixed conclusion as to the success of external reform models.

Given the complexity of implementation, local political and economic factors have discouraged widespread adoption of external reform models. Instead, many schools continue to adopt a patchwork of reforms. A growing body of literature calls for coherent locally designed reform models, grounded in evidence-based practices. Such reforms are guided by a variety of school and student assessment mechanisms to pinpoint necessary reform areas.

At the time of publication, the Northwest Regional Educational Laboratory (NWREL) lists 26 whole-school improvement models. Several of these models are described in Table 1.

—*Shelby Cosner*

See also accountability; adaptiveness of organizations; alignment, of curriculum; at-risk students; behaviorism; Black education; charter schools; Chicago school reform; choice, of schools; decentralization/centralization controversy; innovation, in education; instruction, survey of; Kentucky Education Reform Act; leadership, teacher; learning environments; management theories; parental involvement; principalship; productivity; professional learning communities; school size; site-based management; tracking, of students; underachievers, in schools

Further Readings and References

Beaudoin, M., & Taylor, M. (2004). *Creating a positive school culture.* Thousand Oaks, CA: Corwin Press.
Chadwick, K. (2004). *Improving schools through community engagement.* Thousand Oaks, CA: Corwin Press.
Gaiton, C. (2004). *Involving Latino families in schools.* Thousand Oaks, CA: Corwin Press.
Goldenberg, C. (2004). *Successful school change.* New York: Teachers College Press.
Goodman, J., Baron, D., & Myers, C. (2005). Constructing a democratic foundation for school-based reform: The local politics of school autonomy and internal governance. In F. English (Ed.), *SAGE handbook of educational leadership* (pp. 297–332). Thousand Oaks, CA: SAGE.
Holland, H. (2005). *Whatever it takes: Transforming American schools.* New York: Teachers College Press.
Johnson, R., & Bush, L. (2005). Leading the school through culturally responsive inquiry. In F. English (Ed.), *SAGE handbook of educational leadership* (pp. 269–296). Thousand Oaks, CA: Sage.
Langer, J. (2004). *Getting to excellent: How to create better schools.* New York: Teachers College Press.

Table 1   Examples of Externally Developed Comprehensive School Improvement Models

Model	Primary Goal and Approaches	Level	Developer
Accelerated Schools	Improve achievement with all students at grade level by the end of elementary; focus on instruction that was often reserved for gifted and talented.	K–8	Henry Levin, Stanford University
America's Choice	Improve achievement in core areas; focus on identifying and supporting students behind grade level in reading, writing, and math.	K–12	Pat Harvey, National Center on Education and the Economy
Atlas Communities	Improve achievement by creating a pathway that connects elementary, middle, and high school; to support student learning; focus on 5 core strategies.	PK–12	Harvard Project Zero and others
Coalition of Essential Schools	Improve achievement by developing essential skills in core content areas; focus on total restructuring through 10 principles designed to enhance learning.	K–12	Ted Sizer, Brown University
Comer School Development Program	Improve achievement by meeting the needs of the whole child; focus on total restructuring.	K–12	James Comer, Yale University
Core Knowledge	Improve achievement by having all students gain access to core knowledge; focus on specified curriculum.	K–8	E. D. Hirsh, Jr., University of Virginia
Modern Red School House	Improve achievement by raising expectations and individual ; education for all students; focus on 6 principles.	K–12	Hudson Institute
Success for All/Roots and Wings	Improve achievement by helping all students to read; focus on prevention and intervention.	K–6	Robert Slavin and Nancy Madden, Johns Hopkins

SOURCE: Adapted from Northwest Regional Educational Laboratory. (2005). *Catalog of school reform models.* Portland, OR: Author. Available at http://www.nwrel.org/scpd/catalog/index.shtml

McNeil, F., & Sammons, P. (Eds.). (2004). *Improving schools: The future of school improvement and effectiveness.* New York: Routledge.

Northwest Regional Educational Laboratory. (2005). *Catalog of school reform models.* Portland, OR: Author. Retrieved September 8, 2005, from http://www.nwrel.org/scpd/catalog/index.shtml

Ward, R., & Burke, M. (Eds.). (2004). *Improving achievement in low-performing schools.* Thousand Oaks, CA: Corwin Press.

🏛 SCHOOL PLANT MANAGEMENT

For centuries, education was envisioned primarily as the process through which human beings interact and improve their potential. Today, the importance of school plants, where this interaction takes place, is widely recognized. Education plants are no longer the shelters for education; rather, they are significant educational inputs capable of enriching or impeding educational outcomes. Recent studies showed that when a school's condition improved from one category to the next, for example, from poor to fair, students' standardized achievement test scores rose an average of 5.45 percentage points, as noted by Maureen Edwards in 1991. Today's educational plants are no longer one-classroom spaces. Parallel to the progress in educational programs and processes, school plants have become complex settings acquiring substantial resources. Managing these plants effectively is an important function of educational leadership. However, school plant management has been one of the most neglected areas in educational leadership.

Historically, funding school plants has been considered the responsibility of local school districts.

While contribution by federal government and states has been minimal, school districts have spent a steadily decreasing proportion of their budgets on constructing new buildings and maintaining and repairing increasingly deteriorating school facilities. In fact, maintenance and operations expenditures have become first to be cut during the financial austerity, as noted by Linda Frazier. Consequently, maintenance and operations spending for school plants have fallen 14% in 1920 to 9.6% in 1960, to 6.7% in 1982, to an 9.09% in 1999, and to all-time low of 7.4% in 2003.

The consequences of deferred maintenance of school plants resulted in premature building deterioration, inadequate ventilation, insufficient access for disabled students, poor heating and air-conditioning, insufficient security, crumbling roofs, nonfunctioning toilets, increased repair and replacement costs, and reduced operating efficiency of equipment, as noted by the Center for Educational Statistics in 1999 and Linda Frazier in 2001. Recent studies show that 50% of the school buildings in the United States were constructed before 1960. While there are great variations within each state, 25% of schools were built before 1950, and 20% before 1940. The average age of the school building is approaching 50 years, according to the American School and University in 1999. An Association of School Business Officials (ASBO) International study in 1999 indicated that 33% of all school buildings in the United States are unsatisfactory. Twenty-five million students attend schools with at least one unsatisfactory condition, such as leaky roofs, asbestos, plumbing problems or lack of space. The General Accounting Office (GAO) conducted an audit on the state of the public school facilities and determined that the nation's schools needed $112 billion in repairs in 1995. National Center for Education Statistics (NCES) found a need for $127 billion to put school facilities into good condition in 1999. A National Education Association (NEA) study in 2000 documented that about $322 billion dollars is needed for the unmet renovation, maintenance, repairs, and technology needs of American public schools.

Policymakers and educators have realized that the construction, maintenance, and operations of school plants involve substantial public funds. Therefore, effective management of school plants has become an important factor in maximizing the utilization of scarce resources. Planning is the first and crucial step in effective school plant management. As stated in a 2003 report by National Forum on Education Statistics (NFES), planning integrates a wide range of facilities management components, including facilities, staff, users, work orders, scheduling, and compliance and regulatory issues. Planning of school plant management enables administrators to identify the needs, prioritize projects, and maximize the utilization of available resources. In other words, planning of school plant management prevents school leaders from falling victim to inefficiencies and missteps. The *Planning Guide for Maintaining School Facilities,* compiled by NFES and ASBO in 2003, offered a step-by-step planning guide of school plant management to school leaders.

An American Schools and Universities (ASU) study in 2002 showed that 70% of school plant managers use a manual system for the management of their school plants. They often do not have data systems that support the complex and demanding responsibilities of decision making, planning, management, and funding of school plants. Even when school plant data are maintained and available at the building and district level, these data are not uniform and mostly not available to state education agencies, as noted by the NFES in 2003. As noted by Joe Agron in 2004 and Mike Kennedy in 2003 and 2004, the need for a standard school plant data system utilizing computer technology is heavily recognized by the authorities and the government agencies in the field. Computerized school plant management systems let schools tap the potential of technology to operate their systems and equipment more efficiently, reduce energy consumption, manage inventory more accurately, keep track of supplies and maintenance schedules, and save money. These systems can bring about greater efficiencies, as written by Kennedy in 2003.

Kennedy noted in 2004 that in addition to taking advantage of technology, literature offers valuable strategies for effective school plant management, including (a) having a school plant database help school leaders update the data on the status of school plant and help their financial readiness for renovations, maintenance, and operations; (b) focusing preventive maintenance is another strategy that not only prevents sudden and unexpected equipment failure but also reduces the overall life cycle cost of the building; (c) schools can cut utility costs by installing more efficient equipment, such as low-flow toilets, showerheads, and faucets or, where allowed, urinals that do not use water. Capturing rainwater for reuse and using drought-resistant plants for landscaping will reduce a school's water needs. Similarly, maintenance workers who are vigilant about detecting and repairing leaks can save significant amounts of water; (d) energy conservation and management is another strategy to increase the efficiency of school plant management. In this regard, the new lighting systems and heating and air-conditioning units use less energy; modern windows are more efficient at keeping unwanted heat out of a building in the summer and preventing cold from penetrating the building in the winter. Motion sensors and timers allow schools to turn off lights automatically in areas not in use. Design strategies that enhance the use of natural light allow schools to lessen the need for artificial lights to illuminate classrooms and other spaces; (e) joint use of school facilities and opening school buildings to community use is another strategy to effectively manage school plants. Education buildings are the second-least-utilized facilities in the United States—only churches are used less frequently. More and more people feel that schools should be more available to serve the community beyond the limits of the traditional school day, as noted by ASU in 2002; (f) outsourcing especially noninstructional services may be another way to increase the efficiency of school management systems. Seventy-seven percent of the school districts outsourced at least one service in 1999, as noted by Agron in 2001; (g) finally, schools planning to build or renovate facilities can benefit by opening up the planning process to include all those affected: students, staff members, business leaders, and neighbors. By involving people early in the process, planners can avoid design flaws that those who actually will use the building can identify, as written by Kennedy in 2004.

In ASU's 2002 study, school plant managers stated that they could improve their school plant management with a system that accurately measures, monitors, and bills the actual cost of facilities use; reduces the time that staff spends on scheduling facilities; improves efficiency through better coordination with various departments regarding after-hours facility usage; and improves community relationships while increasing cost recovery.

—Ibrahim Duyar

See also cost-benefit analyses; economics, theories of; enrollment projections; finance, of public schools; planning models; resource management; school safety; school size; state departments of education; strategic planning; taxes, to support education; workplace trends; year-round education

Further Readings and References

Agron, J. (2001). Keeping it close to home: Privatization study. *American School and University.* Retrieved September 8, 2005, from http://asumag.com/mag/university_privatization_study_keeping/index.html

Agron, J. (2004). Small change. *American School and University.* Retrieved July 2, 2004, from http://asumag.com/Maintenance/university_small_change

American Schools and Universities. (2002). *Know-how: Facilities management.* Retrieved December 1, 2004, from http://asumag.com/mag/university_facilities_management/index.html

Edwards, M. M. (1991). *Building conditions, parental involvement, and student achievement in the D.C. public school system.* Unpublished master's thesis, Georgetown University.

Frazier, L. (1993). *Deteriorating school facilities and student learning.* (ERIC Digest No. 82, ED356564)

Kennedy, M. (2003). Machines that manage. *American School and University.* Retrieved May 1, 2004, from http://asumag.com/Maintenance/university_machines_manage

Kennedy, M. (2004). Getting more for less. *American School and University.* Retrieved September 8, 2005, http://asumag.com/mag/university_getting_less/index.html

Kennedy, M. (2004). Know-how: Facilities management. *American School and University.* Retrieved May 1, 2004, from http://asumag.com/mag/university_facilities_management_2/index.html

U.S. Department of Education, National Center for Education Statistics. (2000). *Condition of America's public school facilities: 1999* (NCES 2000-032). Washington, DC: Author.

U.S. Department of Education, National Forum on Education Statistics. (2003). *Facilities information management: A Guide for state and local education agencies.* Washington, DC: Author. Retrieved September 8, 2005, http://nces.ed.gov/pubs2003/2003400.pdf

U.S. Department of Education, National Forum on Education Statistics and the Association of School Business Officials International. (2003). *Planning guide for maintaining school facilities.* Washington, DC: Author. Retrieved September 8, 2005, http://www.ed.gov/pubs/edpubs.html

U.S. General Accounting Office. (1995). *School facilities: Conditions of America's schools.* Washington, DC: Author.

U.S. General Accounting Office. (2001). *School facilities: Construction expenditures have grown significantly in recent years.* Washington, DC: Author.

SCHOOL SAFETY

Although many opinions surround schooling's purposes, the public shares a fundamental assumption that U.S. students and teachers work in safe schools.

Despite persisting government reports stating students experience more crimes en route to and from school and also that teaching remains a safer public service career than similar occupations, sensational acts of school violence in the 1990s increased public concern over school safety. School safety issues include the following: (a) physical plant and security accommodations, (b) schoolwide discipline and classroom management plans, and (c) curricular interventions. Most schools and systems adopted all three measures.

PHYSICAL PLANT AND SECURITY

The retrofitting of school plants to increase security provided an immediate response to mass school shootings in the 1990s. Schools made major investments in security technology, from video cameras to weapons detectors. Law enforcement and security officials reevaluated school grounds and erected fences. Today, most schools restrict visitors to a single entrance, and all other doors have refitted hardware to prevent access but allow emergency egress.

School security studies reveal that school staff's visibility provides the largest deterrent to crime. With large school plants, schools hire their own security personnel or form partnerships with local law enforcement. Even with these measures, research shows that the status of teachers' relationships with students forms the primary predictor of school safety.

DISCIPLINE AND CLASSROOM MANAGEMENT

Teachers' ability to create positive relationships with students provides the cornerstone for all other student-adult relationships and strongly influences student-to-student interactions in schools. Large class sizes and high student-teacher ratios challenge teachers' ability to ascertain and address every pupil's expressed and unexpressed needs. In addition, novice teachers report a limited repertoire in dealing with diverse student populations' instructional and behavioral issues. Inappropriate student behavior further erodes limited instructional time. Some teachers refuse to address student behavioral problems because they view teaching as restricted to dissemination of content knowledge and separated from development of students' social skills.

As a result, teacher organizations have negotiated for and won exemptions from student supervision in hallways, restrooms, playgrounds, and lunchrooms, leaving such venues to oversight by paraprofessionals or volunteers. Some research shows that students interpret such division of labor as a hierarchy of power, and, in turn, show differential responses to the interventions of certified educators and noncertified school support personnel.

From the 1970s on, education entrepreneurs have developed a variety of programs and packages for teachers to adopt in maintaining classroom deportment. Many of these programs depend on the tenets of behaviorism providing tangible rewards and sanctions for individual student or group deportment. Most of these programs do not adequately address diversity among pupils; that is, a classroom system may work for the majority of students, but rewards may not be adequately desirable for every student, and conversely, sanctions may not be substantial deterrents for all students. Often, the small number of students who resist these behavioral programs may be among those who are most disruptive. Their failure to conform to behavioral programs may aggravate teacher-student and student-student rifts. Most teachers refer such problems to the school disciplinarian, typically the principal, or to special programs. Too often removing the particular student allows the instructional environment to flourish for the teacher and remaining students, but that student's educational and social needs may be exacerbated rather than remedied.

Students' disciplinary referrals place them under a schoolwide code of conduct. Some school systems establish these codes, and others are school based. Typically, the codes provide a range of punitive measures, usually administered by the school principal or an assistant principal. Usually, disruptive students serve penance for breaking school infractions through in-school or after-school detentions and out-of-school suspensions; and for drugs or weapons possession and assaults, school boards can expel students from the school system.

Most of the schoolwide codes tolerate disruptive class behavior and verbal disrespect by assigning time to detention. School codes show little to no tolerance for fighting, vandalism, drugs, and weapons infractions. Recent studies suggest students who feel victimized by other students and their teachers may account for most incidents of fighting, vandalism, drugs, and weapons infractions. Further studies on victims and bullies show that individual students may play both roles at school, in the community, and at home.

In some jurisdictions, criminal and civil laws require school officials to file police reports or complaints for severe infractions involving assaults, drugs, or weapons. Such legal requirements place school personnel as well as students in untenable positions, as educational law concerning confidentiality for students can be more stringent than civil and criminal protections for juveniles. As illustrated in several sensational 1990s cases, school officials' actions in upholding zero-tolerance laws demonstrated the conundrum of how to educate individuals while protecting all students. Generally, discipline reports show that all students fare poorly under punitive schoolwide codes.

CURRICULAR INTERVENTIONS

Because teachers' abilities to develop and maintain good relationships with and among their students is the key to school safety, many schools turn to direct curricular and instructional interventions. For many children, schools represent their first experiences with large groups of people. Teachers need to mediate new experiences and teach students to cope with school. The purpose of curricula and instruction focused on student behavior is to help students develop appropriate prosocial skills and self-awareness.

Such curricula evolved from the values education movement of the 1970s to the character education movement of the 1990s. Both kinds of curricula created controversy in some communities, as some groups viewed the goals and objectives as subjective, at least, and tied to specific religious doctrine, at worst.

Conflict resolution curriculum and activities form another curricular approach. Teachers or counselors help students develop a variety of responses to verbal or physical conflict. For older students, some curricula develop their skills in monitoring and resolving each other's disputes. Students form mock courts and boards to air both sides of a dispute and mediate a resolution. Arguably, students' abilities to regulate themselves and each other represents a desirable outcome for public education.

—Jane Clark Lindle

See also accountability; at-risk students; bullying; conflict management; curriculum, theories of; discipline in schools; dropouts; drug education; emotional disturbance; law; mainstreaming and inclusion; mental illness, in adults and children; special education; terrorism; vandalism in schools; violence in schools

Further Readings and References

Beaudoin, M., & Taylor, M. (2004). *Breaking the culture of bullying and disrespect, Grades K–8.* Thousand Oaks, CA: Corwin Press.

Duke, D. L. (2002). *Creating safe schools for all children.* Boston: Allyn & Bacon.

Fishbaugh, M., Berkeley, T., & Schroth, G. (2003). *Ensuring safe school environments.* Mahwah, NJ: Lawrence Erlbaum.

Fontaine, N. S. (2003, May). Threats to the quality of school safety data. *Research in Education, 69,* 16–26.

Garcia, C. A. (2003). School safety technology in America: Current use and perceived effectiveness. *Criminal Justice Policy Review, 14*(1), 30–54.

Glasser, W. (1990). *The quality school: Managing students without coercion.* Scranton, PA: Harper & Row.

Lee, C. (2004). *Preventing bullying in schools.* Thousand Oaks, CA: Corwin Press.

Petersen, G. (2005). Student misbehavior and violence: A reexamination of the enemy within. In F. English (Ed.), *SAGE handbook of educational leadership* (pp. 463–482). Thousand Oaks, CA: Sage.

Schreck, C. J., Miller, J. M., & Gibson, C.L. (2003). Trouble in the school yard: A study of the risk factors of victimization at school. *Crime & Delinquency, 49,* 460–484.

Shoop, R. (2004). *Sexual exploitation in schools: How to spot it and stop it.* Thousand Oaks, CA: Corwin Press.

SCHOOL SIZE

School size as a factor influencing student experience and educational success has been discussed by educational researchers for over 40 years. The primary focus of the impact of school size has been at the secondary level, especially in regard to American high schools. Initially, Roger Barker and Paul Gump explored the topic of school size in their 1964 book, *Big School, Small School,* to understand its impact on students' participation in school-related activities. More recently, school size is a subject of considerable attention by researchers and school reform advocates interested in the effect of smaller, personalized school environments on students' academic success. While reformers recommend moderate school sizes for new secondary schools, data from the U.S. Department of Education indicate that among American high schools, 44% of central city schools tend to house upward of 900 students.

In their study of the influence of school size on student participation in a variety of school-related activities, Barker and Gump were careful to distinguish their research as not focusing specifically on academic achievement. In fact, the range of activities they did study would be better described as "extracurricular," yet their work carried implications for the broader experiences students had in large versus small schools. They found that in smaller schools, students experienced more access to and a wider variability of the different school-related activities investigated. This finding was somewhat counterintuitive, given that larger high schools were in a better position to offer a wider range of activities. However, the organizational nature of large schools lent themselves more to what is referred to as "specialization" or participation in a relatively narrow set of activities with a particular subset of students. Thus, while large schools had more offerings of activities, Barker and Gump found that small schools enabled more students to participate in a greater variety of activities. They also spoke to the question of optimality by recommending that no school be so large that students become "redundant" or so numerous that their school-related needs would go unaddressed.

The breadth-versus-depth trade-offs inherent in school size considerations were revealed in a number of ways in the research that succeeded the Barker and Gump study. For example, researchers such as James Conant and Theodore Sizer were interested in investigating the benefits of large high schools, particularly given the diversity of students attending such schools. It is in their work that more direct attention was paid to the influence that school size might have on academic engagement and outcomes. They focused their work on the "comprehensive" high school, which was initially defined as a school that provided enough of a variety of offerings to educate all of the students attending the school. In reexamining this early work by Conant, it is clear that the support for comprehensive high schools was premised on the assumption that regardless of the educational path a student might take, every student would have access to vocational and academic offerings that would be of comparably high quality.

Personalization in large schools is a challenge, yet it is a factor positively associated with student engagement and academic success. Given that many American high schools remain large in their design and structure, current efforts are under way to incorporate the positive aspects of a more personalized learning environment into existing large school structures. Through his studies of the American high school,

Theodore Sizer provided some of the earliest analyses of secondary schooling that influenced the development of more personalized educational settings, focused on teaching and learning that engaged students' and teachers' minds. While his critique of secondary schooling did not indicate an optimal size for schools to ensure positive teaching and learning environments, Sizer's conceptualization of the problems of secondary schooling influenced others to look more deeply at the relationships among students and teachers that were implied by his emerging framework of "essential schools."

Deborah Meier continued to build upon Sizer's work in the creation of schools that embodied the principles he developed; however, her work did begin to articulate the need for schools to remain small enough to foster the types of working relationships and structures implied by contemporary research on secondary schools. Meier's involvement in the development of such schools is the subject of her book, *The Power of Their Ideas*. Likewise, Linda Darling-Hammond contributed to the understanding of the role of teacher-teacher and teacher-student relationships through her research on smaller secondary schools and, in turn, has continued to contribute to contemporary thinking on the impact of school size on students' academic performance.

School size as an equity issue emerged when the realization was made that the students experiencing the greatest challenges in their persistence and success in school attended large schools, many within large urban school systems. Indeed, the current policy and reform environment now includes significant attention on the impact of small schools' development in increasing the opportunities for academic success among students of color, low-income students, and other students previously underserved by large, impersonal schools. This movement has been further supported by the work of researchers such as Valerie Lee, who has documented the impact of school size on student outcomes over the past decade. While small school size alone is by no means suggested to be the panacea for reversing the negative trends seen in large, urban school systems, the work of William Ayers, Nancy Mohr, Evans Clinchy, and Meier suggests that small schools offer students and teachers the opportunity to create teaching and learning environments that are more likely to produce positive educational outcomes. Of course, as Mohr pointed out in her discussions of the pitfalls of small schools, an important consideration is to distinguish small schools not as smaller versions of large schools, but as alternative structures that carry with them unique challenges that require serious investments in staff development, complex roles, and responsibilities distributed among all staff and interdependent professional relationships. In addition, Darling-Hammond recently outlined in her book *10 Features of Good Small Schools—Redesigning Schools: What Matters and What Works* a discussion of the key elements that promote the best that small schools can offer, as well as the enabling conditions that are required to ensure their success. As noted by these researchers, the use of small schools to better serve the equity needs of particularly urban school communities requires a reconceptualization of the organizational, policy, and school-community contexts to realize their full potential. Several urban communities throughout the country are currently involved in creating such new systems that seek to optimize the positive impact of small schools to better serve their student populations.

Many school systems are failing to keep pace with educational facility needs because securing the funding and land requirements for new schools is a difficult undertaking. In addition, the call for multiple small schools is countered by arguments for the economies of scale associated with the construction of large schools that can house greater numbers of students. Perhaps because of this challenge, the advocacy for smaller schools has included the transformation of large existing high school structures into interconnected schools within schools or multiple autonomous small school units situated within one campus. It is unclear whether states are incorporating small-school considerations into their facilities planning efforts. Indeed, 2003 data from the U.S. Department of Education indicate that among rural communities, 51% of the high schools had enrollments of less than 300 students and 29% had enrollments of between 300 and 600 students. This compares to central city high schools with 32% housing 900 or more students.

—*Gloria M. Rodriguez*

See also charter schools; class size; consideration, caring; curriculum, theories of; discipline in schools; elementary education; high schools; learning environments; middle schools; politics, of education; reform, of schools; resiliency; restructuring, of schools; school improvement models; school plant management

Further Readings and References

Ayers, W., Klonsky, M., & Lyon, G. H. (2000). *A simple justice: The challenge of small schools.* (Teaching for Social Justice Series). New York: Teachers College Press.

Barker, R., & Gump, P. (1964). *Big schools, small schools: High school size and student behavior.* Stanford, CA: Stanford University Press.

Clinchy, E. (Ed.). (2000). *Creating new schools: How small schools are changing American education.* New York: Teachers College Press.

Conant, J. (1967). *The comprehensive high school.* New York: McGraw-Hill.

Darling-Hammond, L. (2002). *10 features of good small schools—Redesigning schools: What matters and what works.* Stanford, CA: School Redesign Network at Stanford University.

Lee, V., & Smith, J. (1994). *Effects of high school restructuring and size on gains in achievement and engagement for early secondary school students.* Madison, WI: Center on the Organization and Restructuring of Schools.

Lee, V., Smith, J., & Croninger, R. (1997). How high school organization influences the equitable distribution of learning in mathematics and science. *Sociology of Education, 70*(2) 128–150.

Meier, D. (1995). *The power of their ideas: Lessons for America from a small school in Harlem.* Boston: Beacon Press.

Mohr, N. (2000). Small schools are not miniature large schools: Potential pitfalls and implications for leadership. In W. Ayers, M. Klonsky, & G. H. Lyon (Eds.), *A simple justice: The challenge of small schools* (pp. 139–158). (Teaching for Social Justice Series). New York: Teachers College Press.

Sizer, T. R. (1984). *Horace's compromise: The dilemma of the American high school.* Boston: Houghton Mifflin.

U.S. Department of Education, National Center for Education Statistics. (2003). Indicator 30: Size of high schools. *The condition of education 2003.* Washington, DC: U.S. Government Printing Office.

🏛 SCHOOL-BUSINESS PARTNERSHIPS

School-business partnerships are intended to encourage a cooperative relationship between a school and a business or organization. An effective partnership is ongoing and mutually beneficial to the school and the business. In the early 1980s, businesses and schools combined forces to address problems facing school administrators, teachers, and students. The effort grew through the 1990s. Seventy percent of all school districts now engage in some form of business partnership, and 76% of schools that partner collaborate with small businesses. Schools and business are linked more tightly in light of budget shortfalls and efforts to meet high academic standards. Businesses engage in arrangements with public schools including direct donations, contributions toward instructional programs and activities, and volunteer projects and mentoring. Partnerships contribute an estimated annual $2.4 billion and 109 million volunteer hours to schools.

One area of emphasis in school business partnerships is effective school-to-work programs based on strong partnerships between local schools and businesses. Businesses work directly with students and provide career talks, job shadowing, mentoring, and apprentice programs. The School-to-Work Opportunities Act of 1994 supported collaboration and partnerships between schools and businesses. The act made funds available for local partnerships to undertake the development of systems involving school-based learning activities and work-based learning activities as well as connecting activities.

Partnerships have developed as long-term, sustainable programs through a collaborative process between the business and education partners and in cooperation with the National Association of Secondary School Principals. NASSP recommends that schools (a) choose companies that promote academics and learning, (b) assess the school's needs, (c) determine the corporate motives, (d) do not make decisions in a vacuum, (e) consider the political climate, and (f) research the concepts being applied.

Recent research indicated that schools benefited through (a) increased school-to-career opportunities, (b) increased funds for schools, (c) parent involvement, (d) student scholarships, and (e) increased teacher preparation. Businesses and communities benefited through (a) increased collaboration, (b) increased publicity, (c) improved recruitment for businesses, (d) better-prepared work force, (e) employee commitment, and (f) improved product development. Schools and businesses see benefits in four general areas: (a) human capital development, (b) community development, (c) student achievement, and (d) financial impact. Mutual benefit is also provided in three areas: (a) philanthropy, (b) commerce, and (c) partnerships.

Scholars have stressed four guiding principles that define the "ideal partnership":

1. Foundation—build on shared values, mutual goals

2. Implementation—integrate activities into both cultures, have a clear management process, and produce measurable outcomes

3. Continuity—provide support at highest level of each organization, devise detailed internal and external communication plans

4. Evaluation—determine strengths, weaknesses, and future directions

Some in both the education and business communities have concerns about school-business partnerships. Educators fear that businesses will influence education to focus on labor force training and stress only occupational skills that may not be useful for career advancement of the students. Business partners cite high expectations, unequal levels of partnership, and the political environment as elements that may discourage business involvement.

—*Barbara Y. LaCost*

See also budgeting; business education; capacity building, of organizations; collaboration theory; communities, types, building of; competition, forms of, in schools; cost-benefit analyses; economics, theories of; finance, of public schools; human capital; human resource development; internships; management theories; market theory of schooling; site-based management; social capital

Further Readings and References

Anderson, G., & Pini, M. (2005). Educational leadership and the new economy: Keeping the "public" in public schools. In F. English (Ed.), *SAGE handbook of educational leadership* (pp. 216–236). Thousand Oaks, CA: Sage.

Emery, K., & Ohanian, S. (2004). *Why is corporate America bashing our public schools?* Portsmouth, NH: Heinemann.

National Association of Secondary School Principals. (2002) *Guiding principles for school and business partnerships* Retrieved August 30, 2004, from http://www.corpschool-partners.com/pdf/guiding_principles.pdf

Paris, K. (1997). *Critical issue: Working in partnership with business, labor, and the community.* Retrieved August 30, 2004, from http://www.ncrel.org/sdrs/areas/issues/envrn-mnt/stw/sw600.html

Saltman, K. (2000). *Collateral damage: Corporatizing public schools–A threat to democracy.* Lanham, MD: Rowman & Littlefield.

🏛 SCHOOLING EFFECTS

Research on the schooling effects has developed along two broad lines. The first draws upon the theory of economic growth to assess the contribution of education to economic development of nations. The second has employed analytic methods based on microeconomic theories to examine the effects of investments in education on the size and distribution of individual incomes. At the national level, education is seen as a means to develop essential skills that are prerequisite for reducing poverty, sustaining development, and empowering people through democracy. This understanding has led all nations to devote considerable resources to education from their budgets and gross national products. Education has been high on the political agenda of every country at all developmental levels. At the individual level, people rank education of their children highly when they are asked about their priorities in life. Individuals invest in education because they expect high personal earnings due to schooling. In this sense, schooling has both social and private benefits. Nations invest in schooling for social benefits, and individuals invest in schooling for private benefits of education.

References to establishing an economic value for both nations and individuals based on increased productivity reflects several centuries of thought. This line of thinking, however, began to be systematically formulated in the theory of human capital. The theory of human capital in the early 1960s presented a rationale that investment in human capital (e.g., education and health) increases human productivity and thus yields economic and social returns in just the same way as investment in physical capital.

Early macro- and micro-cost-benefit analyses of schooling showed that not only is it profitable, but the rate of return to schooling is as high as or even higher than to physical capital. Furthermore, these studies found that the private rate of return is consistently higher than the social rate of return to schooling. It should be noted that early studies of human capital theory treated education as a purely economic activity. Cost-benefit analysis tended to look at benefits that can be evaluated in monetary terms. Schooling is not a purely economic activity, but has many other objectives, and its cost-benefit analysis can never provide a complete understanding of its effects or benefits. In fact, although early human capital studies showed economic benefits of schooling, it has now proven difficult to document many of the indirect effects of schooling as well as effects of schooling relative to other factors. Conceptual and methodological problems are noted for the studies attempting to measure all effects of schooling.

The screening hypothesis theory and segmented markets theory have offered different views on effects of schooling. These two approaches have developed as a reaction to the human capital theory. The screening hypothesis, sometimes called "filtering hypothesis," asserts that schooling does not improve productivity by developing necessary knowledge and skills. It merely identifies students with particular attributes, acquired either at birth or by virtue of family background. Schooling alone does not itself produce or in any way improve those attributes. Schooling acts merely as a filter to separate individuals who have those particular attributes. Employers select individuals with higher schooling credentials because they know that there is a concordance between the attributes required at various levels of schooling and educational attainment. In this sense, educational credentials function as a proxy for qualities that employers regard as important. Employers use schooling credentials to predict a certain level of job performance without, however, making any direct contribution to those demanded attributes. The argument about employers using educational credentials in selecting employees has been widely supported by the economics of education literature. However, the argument regarding schooling not having any effect on graduates' productivity has been refuted by the literature. The screening hypothesis has helped to refine human capital theory. Human capital theory has now increasingly recognized that schooling affects attitudes, motivation, and other personal characteristics, as well as providing knowledge and skills.

The theory of segmented markets asserts that labor markets are fragmented into two self-contained submarkets or segments. In the primary segment, wages are high, and working conditions are good. The secondary market, on the other hand, contains jobs involving low wages, low status, poor working conditions, and no opportunity for advancement. The segmented-labor theory hypothesizes that good jobs are not randomly assigned to workers whatever their personal characteristics. This hypothesis has been generally corroborated by the literature. Second, and more important, segmented-labor market theory asserts that there will be very little mobility over time between these well-defined job clusters. According to this hypothesis, schooling develops sets of attitudes and personality characteristics satisfying the segmented-labor markets and reinforces class differences between workers. This hypothesis has been refuted in the literature.

Both the screening hypothesis and segmented-labor markets theories resulted in refined human capital and effects of schooling. It is now recognized that in addition to the cognitive effect, which was once recognized by the early human capital studies as the only schooling effect, schooling also has affective, psychological, and behavioral effects for individuals. Similarly, schooling has many social effects, also called externalities, to society. The effects of schooling upon society are exerted through the change it produces in its graduates, who eventually become members of the society. The social schooling effects may occur in a variety of areas, including creativity, family planning and child care, appreciation of arts, culture and learning, health service, political participation, understanding of social issues, acceptance of social change, and a sense of common culture and social solidarity. Their presence may influence the prevailing patterns of interests, values, and behavior.

The public's displeasure concerning the outcome of schools, along with the maturation of the schooling effects literature, has shifted researchers' attention to the quality of the educational inputs and the education process at school level. Some studies have used *school effects* and *schooling effects* interchangeably. In this sense, researchers have studied effects of various school characteristics on the educational performances and educational development of children. Although school effects gained momentum with effective schools research, a literature review illustrates the lack of consensus about both theory and methodology. School effects and schooling effects still differ in their scope despite some overlapping areas.

—Ibrahim Duyar, W. Keith Christy, and Orhan Kara

See also accountability; budgeting; economics, theories of; feedback; human capital; organizational theories; outputs, of systems; planning models; productivity; quality control; rational organizational theory; resource management; schooling inputs and outputs

Further Readings and References

Heyneman, S. P. (1995). Economics of education: Disappointments and potential. *Prospects, 25,* 559–583. (UNESCO, International Bureau of Education, Paris)

Jones, I., Gullo, D. F., Burton-Maxwell, C., & Stobier, K. (1998). Social and academic effects of varying types of early schooling experiences, *Early Child Development and Care, 146,* 1–11.

Kroch, E. A., & Sjoblom, K. (1994). Schooling as human capital or a signal: Some evidence. *Journal of Human Resources, 29*(1), 156–180.

Wilson, K. (2002). The effects of school quality on income, *Economics of Education Review, 21*(6), 579–588.

World Bank. (1999). *Education sector strategy: The human development network.* Washington, DC: Author.

🏛 SCHOOLS OF EDUCATION

The history of schools of education for the preparation of educators in the United States has been influenced by a number of factors, especially the continuous need for professionally educated teachers to meet the growing demands of the public schools in a self-governing nation. Early on, the founding fathers realized that the success of this country was dependent on an educated citizenry and this education was to be provided by a cadre of trained teachers. In addition, the Industrial Revolution, mass transportation and communication, educational methodology, and the rise of science all contributed to the establishment of a public system of education and exerted even greater pressure on the need for formalized teacher training. Thus, the movement to prepare professional educators resulted in the establishment of formal schools of education to better prepare the nation's educators.

TEACHERS' INSTITUTES

One of the earliest formal forms of teacher preparation is credited to Henry Barnard for the establishment of the first teacher institute, held in Hartford, Connecticut, in 1839. Other states followed suit with support from both commissioners of education and those who authorized such teacher-training institutes. Typically held during the summer months, the emphasis was on methodology, while considerable emphasis continued to focus on subject matter. In some ways, these institutes served to provide training for the vastly growing numbers of teachers that surpassed the growing number of normal schools. Historians also point out that the nature of these institutes created a forum for teachers to come together to address issue, topics and areas of concerns of their evolving profession which, in some ways, served as forerunners of teachers' organizations and the growing emphasis on in-service teacher education. However, these training institutes served mostly the basic content needs of teachers for elementary schools. A seminary for the preparation of teachers was established in Concord, Vermont, in 1823, by Reverend Samuel R. Hall.

NORMAL SCHOOLS

The evolving state-supported system of public education placed great demands on the need for qualified teachers and insisted on individuals trained in more than content knowledge but also in the so-called science of teaching. In the early 1800s, both private and publicly supported normal schools began to appear in a number of states. The movement toward this type of teacher training was influenced by the writings of American travelers who had written extensively and convincingly about European normal schools. Whereas prior to this development, private seminaries, high schools, academies, and teacher institutes served as places where potential teachers could receive specialized training, in many ways, they were giving over their functions and served as the forerunners for the evolving normal schools.

The first normal school was founded in Lexington, Massachusetts, in 1839, due to the efforts of Horace Mann and support from the state legislature. To better meet the growing demand for qualified teachers, some cities sponsored their own local training schools for teachers, with county normal schools also being established in some states as well. By 1898, the National Education Association (NEA) reported 166 state and 165 private normal schools in operation. During the period between the establishment of state systems of public education and recovery from the Civil War, normal schools were recognized all across the nation as the place to train teachers, in particular for positions in elementary schools. Teachers for high schools were expected to get their training at the liberal arts institutions. However, the public-supported normal schools for the preparation of teachers continued to grow, and most private normal schools had disappeared by 1920. Eventually, these public institutions carried the designation "state normal school."

The normal school curriculum focused on the practical "nature of school keeping" and what were defined as the "common branches of learning," such as reading, spelling, writing, or arithmetic. Some advanced studies such as algebra, philosophy, and natural history; child development; and the science and art of teaching were eventually added. Most normal schools also required practice teaching. The period of study was typically 2 years and initially admitted students who had only an elementary education. However, with the growth of public high schools, a high school diploma for admission became a more common practice in most normal schools, which was further supported by a 1908 resolution drafted by the Department of Normal Schools in the NEA, calling for high school graduation as a prerequisite for admission. Along with the tremendous growth in public 4-year high schools and the growing body of knowledge about the science of teaching, by 1930, most normal schools had adapted a 4-year curriculum, and the term *normal school* was slowly giving way to *teachers' college.* In 1920, there were 137 normal schools and 46 teachers' colleges. By 1933, the number of state teachers' colleges had risen to 146, with only 50 normal schools. However, the state teachers' colleges were soon to become multipurpose state colleges or state universities, granting both liberal arts degrees and degrees in education, and these colleges continued to be a major source of supply of teachers for the nation's schools.

TRANSITION TO SCHOOLS OF EDUCATION

Although there is no sharp demarcation between the development of normal schools and schools of education, as stated above, after 1900, state normal schools began to transform themselves into teachers' colleges or colleges of education. One of the first such schools was established in 1889, when New York College for the Training of Teachers was chartered; it eventually became known as Teacher College in 1892. By 1930, most normal schools had become teachers' colleges, with the century-old term normal school disappearing by 1940. Within the first 20 years of the twentieth century, teachers' colleges began to convert into multipurpose state colleges, many dropping the term *teachers* from their names, and began to grant liberal arts degrees as well as undergraduate and graduate degrees in education. This change marked the shift from 2- or 3-year programs to 4-year teacher training colleges and the requirement of an earned bachelor's degree to teach.

Teachers' colleges brought about changes in curriculum as well with the liberal arts playing an increasingly important role in teacher preparation. In some teachers' colleges, preparation for elementary teaching required a longer stay than 2 years, with a bachelor's degree becoming the basic requirement for secondary teaching. Although the professional practice aspect of becoming a teacher was strongly emphasized in these new institutions, there was increased recognition of teaching as a profession and the need to lay down an adequate base in the theoretical foundations of teaching as well as the liberal and general education components of study. Another change was related to the diversity of function and the need to prepare educators for a variety of roles in public schools, such as counselors, superintendents, and principals.

In the late 1800s, teachers' colleges were not the sole institutions involved in the preparation of teachers. A number of liberal arts colleges and universities made provisions for the professional preparation of teachers, especially at the secondary level, by offering teacher education courses and establishing chairs of pedagogy and departments of education In 1890, it was reported that 114 colleges and universities, out of 400, enrolled students in teacher preparation courses. The pressures for colleges and universities to expand efforts to prepare teachers found support in the fact that the need to address an adequate supply of trained teachers for the growing number of secondary schools had accelerated. This force contributed to the expanding number of departments or schools of education within universities. As teacher preparation became more closely associated with all individuals who worked in the field of education, resulting in the development of a number of fields of specialization, diversification of preparation programs and various patterns of organization within schools of education evolved. These programs could be found in institutions such as junior colleges, 4-year state colleges, liberal arts colleges and departments or colleges within universities. Compounded with growing needs for teachers, especially at the secondary level, new functions within the schools, and the vexing social problems education was forced to address, programs and departments to reflect this growing diversification proliferated, adding to the complexity of schools of education.

UNIVERSITY SCHOOLS OF EDUCATION

Although some colleges and universities had offered professional courses for teachers during the 1800s, actual schools or colleges of education within universities did not become firmly established until the first half of the twentieth century. At the turn of the century, normal schools and teachers' colleges enrolled approximately 75% of prospective teacher candidates, with the colleges and universities accounting for about 8%. However, between 1879 and 1910, schools of education had appeared in such institutions as the State University of Iowa, the University of Chicago, Stanford, Harvard, Berkeley, Ohio University, and Yale. By 1915, of the 600 colleges and universities in the United States, over 300 offered courses in education, with the university department, school, or college of education becoming the model type toward which other institutions were moving. A survey of college or university departments of education in 1915 revealed that 40 state universities, 22 non-state universities, a number of women's colleges, and agricultural and technical colleges had been established. Many started with the appointment of a university chair in pedagogy, with the State University of Iowa credited with founding the first professorship in education in 1873. These "pedagogy departments" emerged into departments and/or schools of education, thus attaining an organizational separation from other departments within the institution.

The curricular and organizational changes of these departments of pedagogy and schools of education within universities emphasized a greater focus on the theoretical and philosophical aspects of teaching as well as sociological and psychological foundations. A logical sequence became the mission of serving both undergraduate and graduate education. In addition to their role in preparing elementary and secondary teachers, the preparation of other education personnel—administrators, specialists, and college teachers—was considered an essential function of the university schools. They developed advanced degrees and certificate programs to address the emerging areas of specialization. As the demands of the public schools increased, with the increased need for leadership and other academic services such as counseling, recreation, vocational education, and health education, schools of education were adding courses and professors to represent these areas. Along with this market demand came the recognition of the importance of graduate education and the perceived prestige of their schools of education. A number of institutions established PhD and EdD programs in education as well as vast and comprehensive bureaus or centers of research. The first PhD was earned at Berkeley in 1897, with Ohio State University recognized as having established the first bureau for furthering educational research. By 1930, education schools produced some of the highest numbers of doctorates awarded in the country, and many schools of education had developed research units within their structures. At the same time, state departments of education looked more and more to the universities to prepare the needed educators and administrators for their schools and to begin to address the vexing problems that emerged from unprecedented growth. By midcentury and since, schools of education, in their various forms, had earned the needed place in their universities.

HISTORICAL ISSUES CONFRONTING SCHOOLS OF EDUCATION

Given that schools of education are located within the university structures of higher education, a conflict began between the traditions of liberal education and the growing traditions of professional education for teachers. As schools of education expanded to meet the changes of midcentury, how to meet the demands for professionally trained teachers and for teachers who have adequate liberal education and the scholarly discipline and knowledge in their subject matter resulted in controversies that find voice in current day literature. Professors from the liberal arts and professors of education gained the impression that their academic critics were opposed to a major occupation with either professional training or with academic knowledge of subject matter. The controversy resided in two cultures within the institution of higher education fulfilling the mission of professional education and the orientation of the research and inquiry culture of the university. The participation of academic scholars in teacher preparation continues as a problem for schools of education.

Another set of issues that impacts schools of education is teacher certification and teacher examination. During the early years of public education, the selection of teachers and the authority for their qualifications rested in the hands of selectmen and school committees. Competency was limited to basic core skills in reading, writing, arithmetic grammar, and geography. School committees from different communities gave oral examinations, none of which were standardized and all of which reflected the local culture and traditions. With the growth of county and state superintendents, these functions were eventually handed over, leading to more formal state examining boards being given the responsibility for examination and certification. Eventually, this function became the sole responsibility of the state as the certifying authority for teacher certification, the responsibility being completely vested by legislative authority in the state

departments set up for teacher licensure. However, given the changing supply of qualified teachers, state departments often modify their requirements to respond to state needs. However, by the early part of the twentieth century, certification was exercised by the state by setting up state licensing agencies that certified teachers based on a set of standards set through legislation or other authority of the state. As a result, schools of education were required to establish programs that would lead to certification. The issue remained as to who had the greatest influence on setting standards—teacher-represented groups or policy groups.

Accreditation of institutional programs remains another issue facing schools of education. Although often voluntary at the national level, it is often compulsory at the state level. Prior to 1930, there were no standards for accreditation of teacher education. Regional accreditation of schools of education developed during the early part of the century, governed by the American Association of Teacher Colleges (AACTE), founded in 1918. In 1954, AACTE turned its accreditation function over to the newly formed National Council for Accreditation of Teacher Education (NCATE). In 1997, a rival organization to NCATE was formed, Teacher Education Accreditation Council (TEAC). While both groups profess to be focused on outcomes, there are differences between the two based on the extent to which prescriptions for specificity pertain. The quality of teacher preparation remains a key national issue.

—*Judith Aiken*

See also American Association of Colleges for Teacher Education; Holmes Group; leadership, teacher; licensure and certification; Mann, Horace; normal schools; professional development; professional learning communities

Further Readings and References

Anderson, A. W. (1962). The teaching profession: An example of diversity in training function. In N. Henry (Ed.), *Education for the Professions* (pp. 140–167). Sixty-First Yearbook of the National Society for the Study of Education, Part II. Chicago: University of Chicago Press.

Clifford, G., & Guthrie, J. (1988). *Ed school: A brief for professional education.* Chicago: University of Chicago Press.

Darling-Hammond, L., Berry, B., & Thoreson, A. (2001, Spring). Does teacher matter? Evaluating the evidence. *Educational Evaluation and Policy Analysis, 23,* 57–78.

Elsbree, W. S. (1939). *The American teacher: Evolution of a profession in a democracy.* New York: American Book Company.

Giroux, H. (1988). *Teachers as intellectuals: Toward a critical pedagogy of learning.* New York: Bergin & Garvey.

Goodlad, J. I. (1990). *Teachers for our nation's schools.* San Francisco: Jossey-Bass.

Goodlad, J. I., Soder, R., & Sirotnik, K. A. (Eds.). (1990). *Places where teachers are taught.* San Francisco: Jossey-Bass.

Olson, L. (2005). Education schools use performance standards to improve graduates. *Education Week, 24*(36), 1, 20–21.

Richey, H. G. (1957). *Growth of the modern conception of in-service education* (pp. 35–66). Fifty-Sixth Yearbook of the National Society for the Study of Education, Part I. Chicago: University of Chicago Press.

Shen, J. (1999). *The school of education: Its mission, faculty, and reward structure.* New York: Peter Lang.

Woodring, P. (1975). The development of teacher education. In K. J. Rehage (Ed.), *Teacher education* (pp. 1–24). Seventy-fourth Yearbook of the National Society for the Study of Education, Part II. Chicago: University of Chicago Press.

🏛 SCIENCE, IN CURRICULUM

Science is paradoxical. It is both process and product. It also defies brief yet comprehensive definition. As process, it involves particular ways of knowing that value reason, logic, observation, imagination, experimentation, and validation. As product, science is a resultant body of knowledge about nature derived by its practitioners and theorists using such consensual ways of knowing. Science's integration with mathematics and technology comprises what historians call *the scientific endeavor,* a human project to understand the natural world and the universe.

In the school curriculum, science is one of the four core academic subjects taught in Grades K–12, along with English, mathematics, and social studies. Its importance as a core subject was once again validated in the 2001 No Child Left Behind Act, the current major federal law for K–12 education. In many ways, the spirit of this law reflects changes in science educational thought and subsequent curricular revision across the past two decades.

In 1985, the American Association for the Advancement of Science (AAAS) launched its long-term K–12 science education reform campaign named "Project 2061." Because 1985 was also the year that the ever-popular Halley's Comet was visible from Earth, the intent of using the year 2061 in the project's title was future oriented. That distant year, 2061, was to serve as a numerical reminder that the children starting school in 1985 were likely to be alive to see the predicted return of Halley's Comet in 2061. In contrast to the many shortsighted, short-term science education reform efforts of the past, Project 2061 was to be both anticipatory and sustained, ever mindful that today's science curriculum would shape the quality of these youngsters' lives as they developed and then matured during the twenty-first century—a period of even more rapid scientific and technological change. Thus, science teachers' and students' requisite knowledge and skill bases (i.e., the science curriculum) needed to evolve in synchrony with accelerating societal and knowledge evolution.

In contrast to the past, the focus of the AAAS reform effort was not on creating new scientists or keeping the economic engines of technology humming or racing another country into space, but to populate the nation with scientifically literate citizens. It was to be science for all—not just for the chosen few who excelled. AAAS defined *science literacy* broadly, emphasizing the connections among carefully chosen key ideas in the natural and social sciences, mathematics, and technology. Project 2061's primer on the subject was *Science for All Americans.* This book set forth national consensus-based recommendations for what all students should know and be able to do in science and technology by the time they graduated from high school. It is accurate to say that almost all K–12 science curricula in U.S. schools today have their roots in this landmark document. A countervailing book, *The Myth of Scientific Literacy,* written by physicist Morris H. Shamos, who contended that striving for universal science literacy was a futile educational goal, failed to negate its influence, and the scientific and science education communities rallied around the themes of *science for all* and *science literacy.* They also endorsed the idea of setting national science standards in such an egalitarian context.

The second most influential publication of AAAS was the book *Benchmarks for Science Literacy,* published in 1993, which translated the science literacy goals in *Science for All Americans* into learning goals (or *benchmarks*), demarcated within grade ranges (or *grade bands*), for Grades K–12. AAAS drew upon and cited exemplary science education research as justification for its decisions. The majority of today's state science curriculum framework documents have drawn their content from the AAAS *Benchmarks,* as well as from the National Research Council's derivative yet more expansive consensus document, the *National Science Education Standards.*

It is important to note that the *National Science Education Standards* do not require a specific science curriculum. A curriculum is a design for how content is to be organized and taught in the classroom. The content identified in the *Standards* can be organized and presented with varied emphases, and from multiple perspectives via many different curricula. However, state departments of education now require that all science classroom materials and experiences be aligned with state and national standards—both in content and process—and must reflect an appropriate developmental level and level of depth of the standard for a given science grade level. Some states are even developing more explicit documents called *grade-level expectations* (GLEs), statements that define what all science students should know and be able to do at the end of a stated grade level, adding further definition and specificity to the state/national content standards and benchmarks.

Paralleling the influence of the inclusive science literacy and science standards movements are science education research advances (for example, the thousands of research studies worldwide on students' scientific thinking and their misconceptions about important science concepts, principles, and theories) that have led science curriculum evaluators to ask questions such as these:

- *Constructivist learning theory:* Do the curriculum materials and experiences offer adequate opportunities for students to construct a sound procedural and conceptual understanding of the standards-based science content and to apply their new understanding in both authentic and novel situations?
- *Sociocultural learning theory:* Is the science student an integral part of a social group or ensemble engaged in collaborative learning activities, and may that social group change throughout the activity? Is this science learning activity informed by the individuals who comprise the social group; yet does the activity reciprocally inform the individuals within the group? Is this social learning activity mediated by appropriate tools, language, people, symbols, signs, and actions?
- *Inquiry-based instruction:* Is the development of scientific inquiry abilities an explicit student learning goal? Are these to be learned directly, via student investigations? Will students' investigations lead to deeper understanding and greater transfer of knowledge? Can teachers select specific inquiry abilities on which to focus and develop strategies to achieve those outcomes?

To end on a cautionary note, despite all the progress that has been made in reenvisioning K–12 science education, Paul Adams and Gerald Krockover's research indicated that contrary to their reformed preservice teaching experiences, beginning science teachers often implement traditional "survival strategies" instead of the innovative instructional moves advocated by the *National Science Education Standards.* James Ellis wisely distinguishes between the *intended curriculum,* the *enacted curriculum,* and the *assessed curriculum.* Like a food product that moves from farm to processor to distributor to consumer, each stage along the way can impact quality negatively. Even if the intended science curriculum meets criteria of excellence, the enacted science curriculum and/or the assessed science curriculum may misguide and misrepresent students' science learning. The challenge for educational leadership is even greater than that needed to protect the food chain: All three stages of the science curriculum must be monitored for quality— yet be continuously updated and upgraded, and remain in sync.

—*James H. Wandersee and Renee M. Clary*

See also achievement gap, of students; achievement tests; cognition, theories of; curriculum, theories of; international education; literacy, theories of; math education; multiculturalism; National Council for the Accreditation of Teacher Education; No Child Left Behind; validity and reliability

Further Readings and References

Adams, P., & Krockover, G. (1999). Stimulating constructivist teaching styles through use of an observation rubric. *Journal of Research in Science Teaching 36,* 955–971.

American Association for the Advancement of Science. (1989). *Science for all Americans.* Washington, DC: Author.

American Association for the Advancement of Science. (1993). *Benchmarks for science literacy.* New York: Oxford University Press.

American Association for the Advancement of Science. (1997). *Project 2061: Science literacy for a changing future: Update 1997.* Washington, DC: Author.

Atkin, J., & Black, P. (2003). *Inside science education reform: A history of curricular and policy change.* New York: Teachers College Press.

Carin, A., Bass, J., & Contant, T. (2005). *Teaching science as inquiry.* Columbus, OH: Charles E. Merrill.

Mintzes, J., Wandersee, J., & Novak, J. (Eds.). (2000). *Assessing science understanding: A human constructivist approach.* Orlando, FL: Academic Press.

National Research Council. (1996). *National science education standards.* Washington, DC: National Academies Press.

Wandersee, J., Mintzes, J., & Novak, J. (1994). Alternative conceptions [misconceptions] in science. In D. Gabel (Ed.), *Handbook of research on science teaching and learning* (pp. 177–210). New York: Macmillan.

🏛 SCIENTIFIC MANAGEMENT

Scientific management refers to an organizational management style developed in the early 1900s following so-called scientific concepts and emphasizing a logical, standardized, and deterministic way to perform a task or carry out a work responsibility. It is still today a strong tradition and dominant force in organizational development and leadership style.

Before 1900, the study of organizational behavior and effective management focused on the structuring and design of work and organizations, with the basic organizational models being the military and the Catholic Church. But with development of the factory system came demands for new theories of management. This led to what came to be called scientific management, followed by ideas embodied in what is known as classical organizational theory and then to the tenets identified as bureaucratic. School systems as we know them today did not exist, so there was little need for organizational models to use in education, but this changed as larger and more complex school systems began to develop.

Throughout their history, theories of management and leadership in education have been strongly influenced by those developed to serve business and industry. This has had both positive and negative results, with those more negative in nature resulting from a failure to recognize the unique purposes of public education and the need for an educated and professional work force. To gain an understanding of this situation requires some attention to the development of management and leadership theories outside the domain of education.

So-called scientific management emerged as a field of study in the early twentieth century with the theorizing of Frederick W. Taylor, a foreman at the Bethlehem Steel Works in Pennsylvania. His observations about industrial efficiency and management focused on manufacturing organizations and prescribed effective structure of organizations and design of management activities. Management was described as a science, with managers and employees having clearly specified yet different responsibilities.

Taylor saw human problems as the major deterrent to productivity and proposed the scientific selection and development of the worker to overcome this obstacle. He developed a system to use a stopwatch to time the physical movements that went into a type of work, such as pig iron handling, in order to identify the most efficient movements to accomplish a particular task. Taylor's main premise was that the old traditional (that is, *nonscientific*) working methods had to be replaced with a scientifically verified, objectively determined set of duties, rules, and standards. Workers and managers had to be scientifically trained, since "natural work" was patently uneconomical and wasteful. His principles had the greatest impact when applied to increasing productivity on a relatively simple task.

Taylor viewed the goal of management as efficiency, and standardization was the major means to achieve it. He was concerned with how to analyze tasks and work methods, standardize them, and then control the workers so that these methods would be used consistently. Detailed objective analysis facilitated development of standardized tools and methods.

Scientific management theory sees work in organizations as similar to a machine or unthinking organism. This implies systems that are predictable, rational, and deterministic. People are seen as cogs in the machinery, and the leader is an all-knowing machine operator. A good organization is, therefore, one that is efficient, hierarchical, highly centralized, planning oriented, highly regulated, highly organized, and tightly controlled. Productivity is the most vital measure of success and effectiveness. It relies on deterministic principles exemplified by the development of simple schedules or plans or on larger, more encompassing strategic plans.

Taylor's work in the area of scientific management evolved into five principles of work design: (a) shift work responsibility to management (managers plan and design work, while workers implement); (b) use scientific analysis to devise precise worker actions; (c) select the best workers for a given job; (d) train workers effectively; and (e) monitor work and worker performance.

Machine-like organizations move slowly and deliberately. They are highly rational, creating consistency and maintaining stable environments. They are mass production oriented. Differentiation of function and specialization of task are primal, and communication is straightforward and usually top-down. Communication

tends to be slow, as levels of hierarchy need to be traversed for decision making and problem solving to occur.

The machine organization positions the human component at two very different extremes. Management controls and subordinates are controlled. Conflict between management and labor, including a mutual mistrust, is almost inevitable. In addition, political conflict between those involved in different functions often results, with power being sought to control resources.

Taylor's approach was followed by those of Henri Fayol and others of the classical school of organizational management as they listed duties of a manager and specified principles of management. Further developments by Max Weber led to the bureaucratic type of theory, emphasizing order, system, rationality, uniformity, and consistency.

Early management theorists, following various kinds of evolution from Taylor's basic principles, contributed to many of today's management and organizational problems in education, as well as in most other kinds of organizational activity. Focusing on organizations from a rational or technical point of view tends to seriously reduce attention to human components. In addition, because of organizational size and complexity and various political and human relations factors, the constant and intimate cooperation between worker and management called for by Taylor himself are often lost or at least seriously depleted.

The need for substantial rationality, allowing for more reflection and self-organizing is largely missing in the Taylor model. This is discouraged or even negated by the careerism focus in the machine organization as individuals compete within a closed system. The emphasis on efficiency by Taylor and other organizational theorists of the early twentieth century strongly influenced early educational administration. These men relied on engineering principles, giving little attention to human relations and the interactions of social systems. Scientific management focused on finding the one best way to accomplish a task and then selecting and training the workers to follow this one best way. The one best way could be found only by experts studying the process "scientifically" (behavioristically and objectively). This created much resentment among factory workers, even though they tended to have little education. Is it any wonder that attempts in school systems to establish teacher rating and merit pay, for instance, have met with strong resistance? Such efforts have generally led to unproductive conflict and impaired or destroyed the leadership

potential of the school executives responsible for inaugurating such policies. The current widespread demand for "accountability," management by objectives, strategic planning, and student testing would appear to be a revival of Taylorism.

Scientific management is certainly still in evidence. Managements, especially educational managers, are still firm proponents of Frederick Taylor's basic premises. Behaviorism and its offshoots dominate school administration, from the behavioral objectives, to the experimental models that are supported by the concept of verification, to the statistical models that give it all an appearance of "objectivity." For instance, Taylorism seems to have been reincarnated in the form of Deming's TQM (total quality management).

Criticism of this current tendency to follow versions of Taylorism in school organization and administration is common, sometimes couched in the philosophical language of modernism and postmodernism. Modernism refers to a broad acceptance of the tenets of reason and logic as the paramount virtues based on assumptions that reality is as it is perceived, that human language is a clear window through which we observe the world, that context is not important, that the purpose of science is to engage in a search for general laws that are exclusive of specific contexts, that logic should guide a search for truth, that truth is discerned by its "correspondence" to the world we see, and that what is true controls and predicts what happens in this world (which is a measure of its worth and its "truth-telling" capability).

Many recent educational reform efforts seem to have strong connections to the above tenets of modernism. Reports like *A Nation at Risk* (1983) stressed accountability in a setting that reaffirmed standardization, hierarchy, testing, centralization, and formalized procedures aimed at management for efficiency and productivity. New versions of scientific management for American schools have included state-mandated, uniform approaches to teacher evaluation, supposedly to produce increased scores on student tests, curriculum alignment to ensure that what will be tested will be taught, the concept of "best practice," and various other "scientifically proven" programs and practices.

Challenges (often termed postmodern) to the modernistic approach to developing ideas and practices in education and educational administration suggest that administrators must conceptualize and put into effect a multitheoretical, broad-based array of research programs that are not dependent on notions of "right science" or "right methods" for their legitimization or sustenance, in short, to abandon the 100-year agenda of modernistic science. This will require that both researchers and practitioners accept the notion that there are various ways to discover truth and that it is ever changing and subject to context, interpretation, culture, and ambiguity. Many theories about learning, organization, and educational administration are worth considering and investigating in various ways. As they show promise for constructive practice in schools, administrators must be ready and willing to go well beyond scientific management, beyond simply trying to improve the status quo and create new theories to ground new forms of practice, regardless of tradition, current pressures, and unavoidable uncertainties. Otherwise, little significant progress is likely to be made in overcoming the many problems and weaknesses of current educational theory and administrative practice.

—Weldon Beckner

See also accountability; administration, theories of; authority; bureaucracy; division of labor; economics, theories of; elementary education; hierarchy, in organizations; knowledge base, of the field; leadership, theories of; management theories; planning models; principalship; superintendency; Taylor, Frederick; total quality management

Further Readings and References

Crow, G., & Grogan, M. (2005). The development of leadership thought and practice in the United States. In F. English (Ed.), *SAGE handbook of educational leadership* (pp. 362–379). Thousand Oaks, CA: Sage.

English, F. (2003). *The postmodern challenge to the theory and practice of educational administration.* Springfield, IL: Charles C Thomas.

Kanigel, R. (1997). *The one best way: Frederick Winslow Taylor and the enigma of efficiency.* New York: Viking.

Leithwood, K., & Duke, D. (1999). A century's quest to understand school leadership. In J. Murphy & K. Louis (Eds.), *Handbook of research on educational administration* (2nd ed., pp. 45–72). San Francisco: Jossey-Bass.

Razik, T., & Swanson, A. (2001). *Fundamental concepts of educational leadership* (2nd ed.). Upper Saddle River, NJ: Merrill Prentice Hall.

Taylor, F. (1911). *The principles of scientific management.* New York: Harper.

🏛 SELF-ACTUALIZATION

Abraham Maslow (1908–1970) originated the concept of self-actualization from his study of humanistic psychology. This element of psychology focuses on the well-being of people and purports that humans are intrinsically good and have unrealized potential. When humans meet this unrealized potential, self-actualization occurs.

In 1943, while a professor at Brooklyn College, Maslow developed a keen interest in two mentors: anthropologist Ruth Benedict and psychologist Max Wertheimer. He viewed them as being highly fulfilled people and began extensive studies on understanding their characteristics, habits, personalities, and abilities as well as those of other adults who were similarly exceptional. From those early studies, his theory of the self-actualization arose.

In "A Theory of Human Motivation," Maslow characterized self-actualization as a motivational state that comes forth when the more basic needs have been satisfied. He contended that all people are born with a set of basic needs that they seek to fulfill. Once the lower needs have been gratified, then the next set of higher needs emerge and fulfillment of them is sought. Maslow described the five basic needs in his "Hierarchy of Human Needs." The first set of needs, physiological, include food, water, shelter, sex, and sleep. Second are the safety needs, which include feelings of security, stability, dependency, protection, and freedom from fear. Third are the belongingness and love needs. Love, friendship, and affectionate relationships with others in a family or group are characteristics at this level. The fourth category of needs, the esteem needs, is classified into two categories: self-esteem and esteem from others. Satisfaction of self-esteem needs leads to feelings of self-confidence. Esteem from others leads to feelings of recognition, attention, importance, dignity, or appreciation. The need for self-actualization is the final stage in the hierarchy of human needs. Those who have reached this stage are no longer motivated to gratify the needs for safety, belongingness, love, status, and self-respect. Therefore, the individual is free to advance toward the highest potential.

Maslow believed that gratification of one need leads to only a temporary happiness that is followed by another higher level of discontent that involves the individual being consumed with the desire for gratification at the next level of needs. When the individual is dominated by obtaining gratification of a set of needs, his or her motivation increases, and unmet needs on the hierarchy cease to exist. Maslow felt that people function best when they are striving for something lacking, when wishing for something they are not in possession of, and when they are putting forth energies to gratify that wish.

Maslow described 18 characteristics of self-actualizing (SA) people in *Motivation and Personality*:

1. *Realistic.* Self-actualizing (SA) people have a more efficient perception of reality and are comfortable with it. They are able to distinguish the concrete from the abstract, are able to see what is there rather than their own wishes, and are logical and efficient.

2. *Acceptance.* They accept themselves, others, and the natural world the way they are. They see human nature as it is, do not experience guilt or shame, enjoy life without regret or apology, and are without any unnecessary inhibitions.

3. *Spontaneity, simplicity, naturalness.* SA people are spontaneous in their inner lives, thoughts, and impulses. They are not deterred by convention and do not allow it to inhibit them from doing anything that they consider to be important.

4. *Problem centering.* SA people focus on problems outside themselves. They are problem centered rather than ego centered. They have a mission in life requiring energy because it is the sole reason for their existence.

5. *Detachment: The need for privacy.* They are alone but are not lonely. They find it easy to be aloof, reserved, calm, and almost serene. They are unflappable and retain dignity amid confusion.

6. *Autonomy: Independent of culture and environment.* SA people are not dependent on the external world for their fulfillment. Rather, they rely on the inner self for satisfaction. They are independent of others' love and opinions.

7. *Continued freshness of appreciation.* They have a fresh appreciation of people and things. They appreciate and are inspired by the basic good in life and view moment-to-moment living as thrilling.

8. *Mystic (peak) experiences.* SA people experience episodes of feeling ecstasy, wonder, and awe. These moments cause them to lose placement in time and space while feeling that something extremely important and valuable has happened. These experiences allow them to become transformed and strengthened in their daily lives.

9. *Gemeinschaftsgefuhl (feeling of community, brotherhood).* SA people have sympathy and affection for all mankind and have a genuine desire to help the human race.

10. *Interpersonal relations.* SA people prefer a few profound friendships to many superficial ones. They are capable of greater love than others consider possible

11. *Democratic values and attitudes.* They are able to learn from anyone and are humble and friendly with all regardless of class, education, political belief, race, or color.

12. *Discrimination: Means and ends, good and evil.* SA people do not confuse means and ends. They enjoy the present and the process of achieving a goal, not just the result. They transform the most tedious task into an enjoyable game. They are strongly ethical and have their own inner moral standards.

13. *Philosophical, unhostile sense of humor.* They view jokes as teaching metaphors, intrinsic to the situation and spontaneous. They can laugh at themselves and never engage in jokes that are hostile, superior, or authoritative in nature.

14. *Creativity.* SA people have a special creativeness or originality that carries over into everything they do. They are inventive and uninhibited.

15. *Resistance to enculturation: Transcendence of any particular culture.* SA people have an inner detachment from culture. They are not driven by the rules of society. They observe folklores but are not controlled by them.

16. *Imperfections.* SA people show many of the lesser human failings (stubbornness, vanity, ruthlessness, etc.).

17. *Values.* SA people have a strong value system because of a philosophical acceptance of self, human nature, social life, physical reality, and nature.

18. *Resolution of dichotomies.* For SA people, polar opposites merge into a third, higher phenomenon, as if the two have united. For example, work becomes play, desires are in accord with reason, and they retain childlike qualities while remaining wise.

Maslow felt that self-actualization is a characteristic only in people who are approximately 60 years of age or more and that everyone else is in the process of working toward this goal; they are moving toward maturity and the discovery of the true self. Examples of those, in Maslow's judgment, who achieved self-actualization include Abraham Lincoln, Thomas Jefferson, Albert Einstein, Eleanor Roosevelt, and Jane Addams, among others. He also identified several potential or possible cases of those who were, at the time, developing in the direction of self-actualization. Those included G. W. Carver, Ralph Waldo Emerson, Frederick Douglass, George Washington, Harriet Tubman, Pierre Renoir, Walt Whitman, and Benjamin Franklin.

Maslow contended that not all highly successful, productive, and talented people reach self-actualization. He maintained that all people at birth have the potential for self-actualization, but a majority are eliminated as a result of childhood experiences prior to being given the opportunity to develop it. Early deprivation of any basic need, such as safety, love, esteem, or belongingness, inevitably damages or emotionally cripples an individual in later adult life, which makes it more difficult for self-actualization to occur. Maslow emphasized that self-actualization is rare because most adults are still seeking to satisfy those lower, unmet needs. The healthy person, on the other hand, is motivated by the need to develop and self-actualize to his fullest potential. Those who have reached self-actualization, as established by Maslow, are a fraction of the total population (less than 1%). They are the best possible of all humans. They are different from the average person and are understood by few. Maslow's work continues to be influential in educational leadership, though it has recently come under criticism related to the notion that there is not necessarily a one-to-one correlation between high self-esteem and job success.

—*Marie Byrd-Blake and Larry McNeal*

See also behaviorism; cognition, theories of; egocentrism, theories of; esteem needs; flow theory; hierarchical developmental models; Maslow, Abraham; metacognition; motivation, theories of; personality

Further Readings and References

Hoffman, E. (1988). *The right to be human: A biography of Abraham Maslow.* Los Angeles: Jeremy P. Tarcher.

Maslow, A. H. (1943). A theory of human motivation. *Psychological Review, 50,* 370–396.

Maslow, A. H. (1954). *Motivation and personality.* New York: Harper & Row.

Maslow, A. H. (1962). *Toward a psychology of being.* New York: Van Nostrand.

Maslow, A. H. (1970). *Motivation and personality* (2nd ed.). New York: Harper & Row.

Milton, J. (2002). *The road to malpsychia: Humanistic psychology and our discontents.* San Francisco: Encounter Books.

Tribe, C. (1982). *Profile of three theories: Erikson, Maslow, Piaget.* Dubuque, Iowa: Kendall/Hunt.

SEMIOTICS

Semiotics (from the Greek *semeioun,* meaning "signs"), also called *semiology,* is generally defined as the systematic study of signs. The founding figures of semiotics are the Swiss linguist Ferdinand Saussure (1857–1913) and the American philosopher Charles Sanders Peirce (1839–1914). Working independently and on different continents, Saussure and Peirce contemporaneously arrived at models of meaning that subsequent writers drew upon to develop semiotic theories and practices. Of the two, Saussure's work has been more influential, serving as the basis for the founding and development of structuralism ("structural semiotics"). Saussure's work provided writers from many disciplines—for example, Levi-Strauss in anthropology, Frye in literature, Lacan in psychoanalysis, Foucault in history, and Metz in cinema—with a method of analysis and a rich store of insights, terms, and concepts that could be used to analyze a wide range of cultural texts and practices.

It is well beyond the scope here to identify and define the proliferation of terms and concepts derived from the work of Saussure and Peirce: langue and parole, paradigm and syntagm, connotation and denotation, chains of meaning, codes, encoding and decoding, modes of address, articulation, intertextuality, and so on. However, a brief explanation of their basic models of meaning is necessary. As a linguist, Saussure's main interest was in words as signs. In his model, the sign consists of a signifier (a word either spoken or written) and a signified (the mental image or concept that the word refers to). Most important in this model is the arbitrariness of the sign, which is to say that there is no inherent or necessary relation between the signifier and the signified. For example, the word *cat* could just as well have been *tree, sky, boat,* or any other word. Another aspect of the Saussurian model is that it analytically focuses only on the relation of signs with other signs and methodologically brackets off the importance of the relation of the sign with extralinguistic reality (i.e., the social world). By contrast, Peirce's emphasis on the social context is embedded in his definition of a sign as "something which stands to somebody for something in some respect or capacity." This emphasis on the social context is also apparent in Peirce's conception of three different kinds of signs: iconic (a sign that resembles in some way what it stands for, such as a photograph); the indexical (a sign that is associated somehow with what it is a sign of, like smoke with fire); and the symbolic (signs that are arbitrarily or conventionally connected to their referents, which mirrors Saussure's conception of all signs). Of these two models, Saussure's was to become the dominant one for decades after the posthumous publication of his book *Course in General Linguistics* (1916/1974).

Terry Eagleton analyzed the work of the main figures of the Prague school of linguistics (founded in 1926)—the Russian Formalist Roman Jakobson and the Czech linguist Jan Mukarovsky—as he traced Saussure's influence in the development of modern linguistics and the founding of structuralism. Eagleton explained that Jakobson and Mukarovsky developed an analytic framework based on Saussurian linguistics: Poems were to be viewed as functional structures in which signifiers and signifieds are governed by a complex set of relations. These signs must be studied in their own right, not as reflections of an external reality. Saussure's stress on the arbitrary relation between sign and referent word and thing helped detach the text from its surroundings and make of it an autonomous object. As a result, there came about a gradual merging of the terms structuralism and semiotics with the work of the Prague school. The word *structuralism* itself indicates a method of inquiry, which can be applied to a whole range of objects, while the term semiotics denotes rather a particular field of study, that of systems that would in an ordinary sense be regarded as signs, such as poems, bird calls, traffic lights, or medical symptoms.

This overlapping of structuralism and semiotics is exemplified in key works by Roland Barthes, among the most well-known contemporary semioticians. For example, Barthes's book *Mythologies* comprises 28 articles, written in the mid-1950s, that are exemplary semiotic analyses of a variety of cultural texts, objects, and practices. John Fiske explained that what Barthes called a "myth" was simply a story by which a culture explains or understands some aspect of reality or nature and that a myth was a chain of related concepts that worked together to create meanings that made the myth seem natural and commonsensical rather than socially constructed. For example, Barthes treated phenomena such as a wrestling match, a restaurant menu, children's toys, a haircut, a magazine advertisement, a film, and photographs as "texts" or "messages" to be "read" for the "myths" (ideologies) they attempted to naturalize. Works by John Fiske also serve as examples of semiotic analyses of a wide range of phenomena (the shopping mall, the beach,

Madonna, quiz shows, architecture, blue jeans, and more). Fiske engaged in semiotic readings that attempted to explicate how ideology is at work in cultural texts, figures, and practices. Some have called this ideological approach "social semiotics" to distinguish it from what they refer to as the "traditional" and "mainstream" (also "structural") semiotics. Traditional semiotics likes to assume that the relevant meanings are frozen and fixed in the text itself, to be extracted and decoded by the analyst by reference to a coding system that is impersonal and neutral, and universal for users of the code. In contrast, social semiotics cannot assume that texts produce exactly the meanings and effects that their authors hope for. It is precisely the struggles and their uncertain outcomes that must be studied at the level of social action and their effects in the production of meaning.

—*James Trier*

See also classification of education; cognition, theories of; communication, theories in organizations; conceptual systems theory and leadership; constructivism, social; critical theory; curriculum, theories of; frame theory; functionalist theory; heuristics; hypotheses, in research; interpretive studies; knowledge base, of the field; language theories and processes; literacy, theories of; paradigm; postmodernism

Further Readings and References

Barthes, R. (1972). *Mythologies.* New York: Noonday Press.
Fiske, J. (1989). *Reading the popular.* Boston: Unwin Hyman.
Fiske, J. (1989). *Understanding popular culture.* New York: Routledge.
Foucault, M. (1972). *The archeology of knowledge.* London: Tavistock.
Frye, N. (1957). *Anatomy of criticism.* Princeton, NJ: Princeton University Press.
Lacan, J. (1968). *The language of the self: The function of language in psychoanalysis.* Baltimore: Johns Hopkins University Press.
Saussure, F. (1974). *Course in general linguistics* (W. Baskin, Trans.). London: Fontana/Collins.

🏛 SENIORITY, RULE OF

Under the rule of seniority, employees are granted benefits and privileges based on length of service. The rule of seniority is derived from many sources, most significantly collective-bargaining agreements and state statutes.

In the field of public education, the most important benefit provided to senior employees is employment protection during periods of layoff or reduction in force. During times of layoff, an employee who has less seniority will be released before an employee with more seniority: in the common phrase, "Last hired, first fired." Furthermore, laid-off teachers are often called back to work or rehired in order of their seniority.

In addition to increased protection from layoffs, senior employees typically receive higher salaries and greater benefits, such as increased vacation time. Other benefits associated with seniority include but are not limited to preference in assignments to particular buildings; assignments to particular class sections, such as honors sections; assignments to particular classrooms, such as larger classrooms or those with better lighting or temperature control; preferences in scheduling, such as preferred preparatory periods; and preferences in assignments to extracurricular activities. Often senior employees are given the responsibility of mentoring or supervising their junior colleagues.

Seniority-based systems reward longevity and loyalty, and this provides many benefits to both employers and employees. Employees who have attained the benefits of seniority are likely to remain with their employers, providing those employers with an experienced workforce and decreasing the costs associated with filling vacancies and training new employees. Junior employees, who aspire to attain the rewards offered by seniority, may choose to remain with their current employers. Seniority systems do have drawbacks, however. Most notably, many senior teachers exercise their seniority rights to avoid assignments to particularly difficult classrooms or schools, where their skills are most needed. In addition, some have argued rules of seniority may serve as a barrier to diversity in the workforce.

Sometimes, employees who change employers may be given credit for some (or all) seniority or time in service accumulated in their former employment. In addition, the rule of seniority often poses difficulties during mergers of organizations, such as consolidations of school districts. Organizational mergers present difficulties when employees lose seniority rights to their new coworkers.

Rules of seniority have been subject to two recent legal challenges. In the first, the U.S. Supreme Court considered the relationship between rules of seniority in collective-bargaining agreements and rights to

reasonable accommodation under the Americans with Disabilities Act (ADA). In *U.S. Airways, Inc., v. Barnett* (2002), the Court stated seniority systems may not, with rare exceptions, be modified or ignored to provide an accommodation to an employee with a disability. Second, the No Child Left Behind Act, according to many administrators, requires abandoning or modifying seniority rules, especially in schools or districts that do not meet performance standards.

—*Thomas A. Mayes*

See also American Federation of Teachers; collective bargaining; contracts, with teacher unions; governance; job security; National Education Association; reduction in force; unions, of teachers

Further Readings and References

DeMitchell, T. (2005). Unions, collective bargaining, and the challenges of leading. In F. English (Eds.), *SAGE handbook of educational leadership* (pp. 538–549). Thousand Oaks, CA: Sage.

Gewertz, C. (2004, September 8). Collective bargaining bumping up against No Child Left Behind law. *Education Week.*

Lieberman, M. (1997). *The teacher unions.* New York: Free Press.

U.S. Airways, Inc., v. Barnett, 535 U.S. 392 (2002).

SEXISM (GLASS CEILING)

Most societies privilege men over women. That is, men are seen as inherently more valuable or worthy than women. This assumption of women as "less than" men results in discriminatory treatment of women. For instance, whereas males are traditionally granted positions of power and authority, females are expected to assume lesser, more limited societal roles. Moreover, women are frequently denied basic liberties such as property rights and access to education. In more extreme cases, women are viewed as not only less than men, but less than human, and as such, women are the property of men who may subject them to demeaning and abusive treatment.

Until recent decades, the privileging of men over women was seen as natural and, therefore, correct. Although early feminists, such as Elizabeth Cady Stanton, attempted to raise awareness of women's rights issues in the United States as early as the 1840s, the cause did not gain widespread support until the civil rights movement of the 1960s. Through this movement, the unjust treatment of people of color and women was exposed. And, just as the term *racism* rose from this movement to describe the systematic oppression of non-Whites, *sexism* emerged as a way to describe institutionalized discrimination against women.

With the naming of sexism came greater social awareness of women's issues and the opportunity to change society's assumptions about the roles of women. This led to advancements for women in many arenas, including education, employment, and family planning. For example, women did not attend institutions of higher education in significant numbers until the 1960s and even then were only half as likely as men to graduate. Nonetheless, women currently earn the majority of bachelor and master's degrees in the United States. Moreover, whereas women were once expected to work only out of economic necessity, and then only in a limited number of fields, today almost an equal percentage of women as men are employed outside the home. Moreover, women are employed in a wide variety of fields, including those that historically were open only to men.

Much of the credit for the advances of women is given to the availability of reliable birth control. Prior to the development of convenient and dependable methods of contraception, women had little control over their fertility. As a result, untimely pregnancy often caused women to abandon their pursuit of education or employment. Today, generally widespread access to contraception allows women to delay both marriage and motherhood. In turn, women have greater opportunity to access education and employment.

Despite recent advances for women, sexism and gender discrimination continue, as evidenced in outcomes of all measures. For example, throughout the world, women have less access to basic resources such as adequate shelter, health care, and nutrition. Moreover, even in the economic sphere, an area often thought of as one of great gains for women, gender inequity remains. For instance, although women earn the majority of bachelor and master's degrees, men earn more PhD and first-professional degrees. Similarly, while women are almost as likely as men to be employed, they earn only three fourths of what men do. Moreover, women are more likely to be employed in gender-segregated jobs with fewer benefits and opportunities for advancement.

Even when women enter fields with considerable opportunity for promotion, they face gender discrimination in the form of an unseen yet real barrier to advancement. While women may be able to overcome the effects of gender discrimination to reach lower- or midlevel positions, as they move up the organizational structure, they face increasing resistance to their advancement. Eventually, women reach a point beyond which they are not allowed to advance. The point, "the glass ceiling," is an invisible and unacknowledged limit, which cannot be explained by differences in job-related qualifications between men and women. Furthermore, the glass ceiling results in women rarely having access to the uppermost levels of corporate and government structures. Evidence of the glass ceiling effect is found in demographic data for the largest U.S. business organizations. Ninety-five percent of senior-level managers of *Fortune* 1,000 industrial and *Fortune* 500 service companies are men. Moreover, in 2004, only eight *Fortune* 500 companies were headed by women, and only 10.6% of those on the boards of directors of these same companies were women. Within institutes of higher education, which typically have policies aimed at ensuring institutional equity, men dominate the administrative and upper-professorate ranks. Even in PK–12 schools, where the vast majority of professionals are women, men continue to hold most of the administrative positions. Given that the glass ceiling exists even when job-related characteristics such as education, experience, abilities, and motivation are held constant, this phenomenon is best explained by organizational beliefs and practices rather than by differences in the credentials of men and women.

—*Sarah W. Nelson*

See also Addams, Jane; Bethune, Mary McLeod; Clark, Septima; coeducation; discrimination; division of labor; Dorsey, Susan Miller; equality, in schools; feminism and theories of leadership; Follett, Mary Parker; gender studies, in educational leadership; lesbian/gay/bisexual/transgender issues in education; Haley, Margaret; Lawrence-Lightfoot, Sara; Meier, Deborah; role theory; women in educational leadership; Young, Ella Flagg

Further Readings and References

American Association of University Women. (2001). *Beyond the "gender wars": A conversation about girls, boys, and education.* Washington, DC: Author.

Blount, J. (2005). *Fit to teach: Same-sex desire, gender, and school work in the twentieth century.* Albany: SUNY Press.

Brown, K. (2005). Pivotal points: History, development, and promise of the principalship. In F. English (Ed.), *SAGE handbook of educational leadership* (pp. 109–141). Thousand Oaks, CA: Sage.

Federal Glass Ceiling Commission. (1995). *A solid invest-ment: Making full use of the nation's human capital.* Washington, DC: U.S. Government Printing Office.

Kowalski, T., & Brunner, C. (2005). The school superinten-dent: Roles, challenges, and issues. In F. English (Ed.), *SAGE handbook of educational leadership* (pp. 142–167). Thousand Oaks, CA: Sage.

Shakeshaft, C. (1999). The struggle to create a more gender-inclusive profession. In J. Murphy & K. Louis (Eds.), *The handbook of research on educational administration* (2nd ed., pp. 99–118). San Francisco: Jossey-Bass.

SEXUALITY, THEORIES OF

Scholarship on sexuality quite frequently begins with a set of definitions. This is a wise move in a field that is rapidly expanding in the academy yet comparatively underdeveloped in education. Given that the terminol-ogy is complex and much of it refers to concepts that are not fixed, definitions are imperative. *Gender,* the socially constructed roles, behaviors, and expectations regarding what it means to be male and female, shifts over time and between cultures and varies from person to person. *Sex* is defined biologically, although this concept cannot be reduced to a simple pairing of chromosomes; common variations exist between XX (female) and XY (male), and millions of intersexed people are born with or develop physical ambiguities that preclude sex classification on the basis of visual inspection. Some people are transgendered; their gen-der identity does not correspond to their biological sex.

Sexual orientation is a state of being; it has to do with whom one is drawn to, emotionally and sexually. Heterosexual people are attracted to people of the opposite sex, gay men and lesbians are attracted to people of the same sex, and bisexual people are attracted to people of the opposite sex and the same sex. All people have a basic sexual orientation, whether or not they engage in sexual behavior. People who are uncomfortable claiming a sexual orientation identity are referred to as *questioning.* Many people have reclaimed the word *queer* as a term of empower-ment. Some use it primarily as an inclusive term for all people who have a homosexual or bisexual orien-tation and for those who are intersexed or transgen-dered. Others use it to emphasize the complexity and fluid nature of human sexuality and gender, to decon-struct the dominant belief in a heterosexual/homosexual binary.

The question of what determines one's sexual orien-tation is as much (if not more) about politics and culture as it is about science. Before the sexologists of the late nineteenth century suggested that one's sexual desires were tied to an inherent characteristic, sexual behavior was explained as an act of free choice. The dominant culture classified homosexual behavior as a moral trans-gression generally, but an act of free choice nonetheless. Later, when sexologists such as Havelock Ellis theo-rized about women's sexual desires for other women, their science attributed "sexual inversion" to genetics even as concerns about the influence of feminism inter-polated their writings. Throughout the twentieth cen-tury, scientists offered an array of psychological and biological theories to explain sexual orientation, and claims for tipping the scale toward "nature" or "nurture" headline newsmagazines still today. It is generally accepted among scholars, however, that a multifactor model is most accurate; sexual orientation is quite likely the product of biological disposition and environmental factors and, some would add, free choice.

Although same-sex desire is known to have existed across centuries and cultures, the notion of homosex-uality dates to the late nineteenth century. Throughout the 1980s, historians debated whether or not same-sex identity has existed across time. Essentialists argued that people who loved people of their own sex have always incorporated this aspect of their lives into their sense of self and that they were conscious that their sexual orientation set them apart from others. Social constructionists countered that social forces shape human identities; that is, certain social conditions were necessary before one could conceive of an identity based on sexual orientation. To be sure, they argued, people are aware of particular human differences such as sexual orientation or skin color, but these are not always the basis for constructing one's sense of self. Although some activists still call up the essentialist argument for political purposes, in recent years, this debate has subsided among historians. In the give-and-take of scholarly discourse, writers have clarified their perspectives, moved from the extremes of the theoreti-cal poles, and acknowledged some critical observations in both theories. The social constructionist approach, fitting so well with the historian's disciplinary practice of setting events in their political-economic context, now provides the major theoretical framework for scholarship in gay and lesbian history.

Most of the lesbian/gay/bisexual/transgendered/ queer (LGBTQ) scholarship and activism in the field of education generated since 1990 is anchored in liberal theories that focus on the role of the public school in sustaining a democratic, civil society. Scholars and educators have done important work in arguing on behalf of students' fundamental right to a safe, nurturing learning environment and, less successfully, for a workplace free of discrimination for teachers and administrators. In *Nabozny v. Podlesny* (1996), the first case of its kind to advance to trial, a U.S. federal court examined the record of school-sanctioned violence in the Ashland, Wisconsin, school district and found the district guilty of gender and sexual orientation discrimination. Given the severity of antigay harassment in schools across the nation as documented by the research of groups such as the Gay, Lesbian and Straight Education Network (GLSEN), it is clear that liberal standards for tolerance and equity have yet to be met. But advances are being made on this front, as indicated by students' well-founded application of the Equal Access Act to the proliferation and defense of gay-straight student alliances. Legal protections for LGBTQ educators have lagged behind those just beginning to surface for students; however, the 2003 *Lawrence v. Texas* decision may prove a critical lever in wrenching educational employment practices free of discrimination based on sexual orientation.

In addition to trying to secure the basic rights to learn and to work in a safe and equitable school environment, liberal and critical theorists recognize the importance of one's right to know and thus argue for the inclusion of issues of sexuality in the K–12 curriculum. Pragmatism underscores the liberal argument. If schools are to prepare students for life in a democracy, the learning should include information about all citizens. Children and adolescents already encounter information (and misinformation) about sexuality in American culture, and they are curious about the topic; it is the school's responsibility to present accurate information about human sexuality. Educators from a range of theoretical perspectives recognize that an intellectually honest curriculum must include LGBTQ issues. Human sexuality is a part of life and, therefore, a part of history, literature, arts, and sciences. Critical theorists emphasize the connections between knowledge and power. They argue that acknowledging issues of sexuality in the curriculum and school structure will not only benefit LGBTQ students and those who have LGBTQ family members in the short term but also may lead to significant social transformation. For instance, homophobia is closely tied to gender restrictions. As long as schools reinforce limited notions of gender and heterosexist assumptions, they shut off educational opportunities for all students.

Among critical theory scholars, queer theorists have the most to say about the problems inherent in analyses that focus nearly exclusively on victimization and oppression of LGBTQ people. They consciously reject the essentializing tendency to see the school-student relationship as a fixed, oppressor-oppressed relation and claim agency for both LGBTQ students and educational institutions. Queer legal theory, in particular, offers a framework worthy of consideration by those seeking to go beyond the most basic principles of protection. It is akin to feminist legal theory, critical race theory, and gay and lesbian legal theory, but its multidimensionality curbs propensities of the other theories toward gender essentialism, heteronormativity, or racist and classist assumptions. Queer legal theory challenges legal and social structures that require LGBTQ people to hide or distort their identities in exchange for full access to these systems.

—Karen Graves

See also discrimination; feminism and theories of leadership; gender studies, in educational leadership; Hay, Henry (Harry); homophobia; lesbian/gay/bisexual/transgender issues in education; multiculturalism; queer theory

Further Readings and References

Barnard, I. (2005). *Queer race.* New York: Peter Lang.

Halperin, D. (2002). *How to do the history of homosexuality.* Chicago: University of Chicago Press.

Jordan, M. (2005). *Blessing same-sex unions: The perils of queer romance and their confusions of Christian marriage.* Chicago: University of Chicago Press.

Lawrence et al. v. Texas, 41 S.W. 3d 349 (2003).

Nabozny v. Podlesny, 92 F.3d 446 (7th Cir.) (1996).

Renold, E. (2005). *Girls, boys and junior sexualities.* New York: Routledge.

Robinson, P. (2005). *Queer wars: The new gay right and its critics.* Chicago: University of Chicago Press.

Shoho, A., Merchant, B., & Lugg, C. (2005). Social justice: Seeking a common language. In F. English (Ed.), *SAGE handbook of educational leadership* (pp. 47–67). Thousand Oaks, CA: Sage.

SIMON, HERBERT

American polymath, intellectual virtuoso, and Renaissance man are among the terms used to describe

Herbert A. Simon (1916–2001), whose pioneering contributions to problem-solving and decision-making processes of individuals and organizations won him worldwide recognition. A professor of computer science and psychology at Carnegie Mellon University from 1949 until his death in 2001, Simon described himself as a mathematical, social, and behavioral scientist when he received the Nobel Prize for economics in 1978. Yet his interests and accomplishments spanned several fields, including political science, organizational theory, game theory, economics, public administration, cognitive psychology, and artificial intelligence. Simon, though, stayed focused on the philosophy of physics and the use of computers for simulating human cognition throughout his career.

Simon was influenced strongly by his excellent public school education in Milwaukee and ably supported at home by an electrical engineer father and pianist mother. His interest in the social sciences was stimulated by the psychology and economics books of his uncle, Harold Merkel. Recognizing inherent internal cognitive limitations (including knowledge, experience, self-interest, and power drives) and external social constraints of individuals, he advocated the notion of *satisficing,* which describes the "good enough" choices and decisions that people make. These limited rational choice-making abilities of individuals Simon called "bounded rationality," indicating that people are incapable of objectively processing the overwhelming information and decision alternatives available to them.

A second concept that Simon used to characterize bounded rationality was *selective search,* which decision makers use to explore alternatives. Both concepts, satisficing and searching, were founded on the psychological theories of dynamic goal setting and levels of individual aspiration, outlined by Kurt Lewin. Simon's explorations of human choice and decision making in administration, which also incorporate his scientific inquiry into expertise and budgeting, provide the central theme in *Administrative Behavior.*

Simon's passion for understanding how people think and process information led him to write *The Sciences of the Artificial.* Here, he made a compelling case for teaching pattern recognition to all learners to help them develop problem-solving strategies and purposeful self-directed learning. With an abundance of information available from people, print, media, and the Internet, Simon redefined *knowledge* as the ability to find and use information and learning as changes that allow systems to adapt and perform better with repeated attempts.

Simon's autobiography, *Models of My Life,* provides a vivid description of his extraordinary life. His departmental Web pages, maintained at Carnegie Mellon University, link to articles on how he enriched the life of his colleagues; his research in psychology, economics, philosophy of science, and computer science; and his publications from 1930 to 2001. The prolific Simon authored over 25 books and 1,000 articles. His legacy will continue to engage and challenge researchers in a broad range of disciplines.

—Nathan Balasubramanian and Rodney Muth

See also administration, theories of; behaviorism; cognition, theories of; decision making; economics, theories of; feedback; human capital; organizational theories; problem solving; productivity; psychology, types of; satisficing, theory of

Further Readings and References

English, F. (1994). *Theory in educational administration.* New York: HarperCollins.

Simon, H. (1996). *The sciences of the artificial* (3rd ed.). Cambridge: MIT Press.

Simon, H. (1997). *Administrative behavior: A study of decision-making processes in administrative organizations* (4th ed.). New York: Macmillan.

Willower, D., & Forsyth, P. (1999). A brief history of scholarship on educational administration. In J. Murphy & K. Louis (Eds.), *Handbook of research on educational administration* (2nd ed., pp. 1–14). San Francisco: Jossey-Bass.

SITE-BASED MANAGEMENT

Site-based management in schools was promoted in the early 1980s as a way to decentralize and democratize educational policy making and to involve those closest to the child and classroom in decisions. Site-based approaches to management usually involve a council, committee, or team made up of building administrators, teachers, and parents at each school. Ironically, the effective schools research of roughly the same period called for "strong" leadership in schools in the form of a principal capable of "turning a school around." However, trends in the field of business administration called for devolving greater decision making to workers through teams or "quality circles."

While this devolution of decision making in business was limited to relatively trivial decisions and was largely viewed as a way to increase production rather than to empower workers, it has become confused in the minds of many with democratic management that links shop floor democracy with broad forms of empowerment that involve the right to organize unions.

Research on site-based management has shown that bringing diverse stakeholders to the table is no guarantee that power will be devolved or that students will learn more.

Betty Malen and Rod Ogawa studied shared governance arrangements in schools in Salt Lake City that were set up with near-ideal conditions. All relevant stakeholders were included and given broad jurisdiction, policy-making authority, parity protections, and training provisions. Existing literature suggests that such conditions should enable teachers and parents to wield significant influence on significant issues. However, Malen and Ogawa found that although the site councils were authorized policymakers, they functioned as ancillary advisors and pro forma endorsers. Second, while teachers and parents were granted parity, principals and professionals controlled the partnerships. Third, although teachers and parents had access to decision-making arenas, their inclusion maintained, not altered, the decision-making relationships typically and traditionally found in schools.

According to Malen and Ogawa's findings, the lack of parent and teacher influence was due to the fact that principals ultimately controlled knowledge and resources in the school, defended administrative "turf," and viewed the councils as channels for dispensing information, moderating criticisms, and garnering support. They were not viewed as arenas for redefining roles, sharing power, or making policy. Teachers did not challenge administrative authority because they feared social and professional sanction, or else, as was the case for many issues, they shared a common professional perspective with administration. Parents tended to lack "insider" information and familiarity and were unclear on the parameters of their power. They also shared many characteristics, and thus interests, with the teachers and principals (i.e., middle class, Caucasian, and well educated). Furthermore, council agendas were generally controlled by principals (even though the councils were chaired by parents) and confined to safe issues. Institutional norms of propriety and civility kept principals, teachers, and parents on traditional turf and cast disagreements as personal affronts, thus restricting discussion, suppressing conflict, and confining discussions to noncontroversial matters. Finally, because district oversight of site council regulations and procedures was minimal, they were often disregarded. Thus, the micropolitics of participation are such that even when participation is carefully orchestrated, most often, power and influence remain in the same hands.

More current versions or shared governance, often referred to as "distributed leadership" promote more teacher-centered approaches to professional development, instructional leadership, and evaluation, such as peer assistance and review (PAR). Distributed leadership also aims at "involving" parents and building "partnerships" with local communities, businesses, and social service agencies. These are all attempts at expanding leadership more widely and deepening the conversations that can take place when schools move from bureaucratic designs toward learning communities. However, while teachers have acquired greater involvement through distributed leadership, much of this autonomy has been curbed by current accountability measures and in many cases mandated scripted instructional packages.

Furthermore, current versions of site-based management have still failed to provide significant community involvement. Emerging approaches to community involvement in low-income communities include using organized community groups to leverage influence and build alliances with schools in order to pursue common interests Greater community involvement encourages stronger forms of democracy that view participation as a basic right at all levels of the system.

Gary Anderson developed a conceptual frame that might aid in determining the degree of authenticity of participatory practices in site-based management. This framework consists of five central questions: (a) Participation toward what end? (b) Who participates? (c) What are relevant spheres of participation? (d) What conditions and processes must be present locally to make participation authentic? (e) What conditions and processes must be present at broader institutional and societal levels to make participation authentic? Addressing issues of authenticity promises to bring greater clarity to why schools engage in site-based management. Ideally, more democratic management can be both a means to more humane and productive organizations as well as an end in itself.

—*Gary L. Anderson*

See also accountability; administration, theories of; bureaucracy; Chicago school reform; decentralization/centralization controversy; decision making; division of labor; Kentucky Education Reform Act; leadership, distributed; leadership, participatory; leadership effectiveness; management theories; principalship; school districts, history and development

Further Readings and References

Anderson, G. L. (1999). Toward authentic participation: Deconstructing the discourse of participatory reforms. *American Educational Research Journal, 35,* 571–606.

Brown, K. (2005). Pivotal points: History, development, and promise of the principalship. In F. English (Ed.), *SAGE handbook of educational leadership* (pp. 109–141). Thousand Oaks, CA: Sage.

Burrello, L., Hoffman, L., & Murray, L. (2004). *School leaders building capacity from within.* Thousand Oaks, CA: Corwin Press.

Goodman, J., Baron, D., & Myers, C. (2005). Constructing a democratic foundation for school-based reform: The local politics of school autonomy and internal governance. In F. English (Ed.), *SAGE handbook of educational leadership* (pp. 297–332). Thousand Oaks, CA: Sage.

Malen, B., & Ogawa, R. (1988). Professional-patron influence on site-based governance councils: A confounding case study. *Educational Evaluation and Policy Analysis, 10,* 251–270.

🏛 SIZEMORE, BARBARA A.

Called by her contemporaries "the complete educator," Barbara Ann Sizemore (1927–2004) spent 57 years in education, from classroom teacher, high school principal, and professor to college dean. She was an activist, a practitioner, and an outspoken realist, challenging both Whites and Blacks with her passion and pursuit of what she believed to be the truth.

Dr. Sizemore was born in 1927 in Chicago, Illinois, and spent her early years in Terre Haute, Indiana. At 16, she graduated from high school and went to Northwestern University, where she studied Latin, graduating with a BA in classical languages in 1947 and an MA in elementary education in 1954. She worked in the Chicago Public Schools from 1947 through 1972 as a classroom teacher and high school principal. She earned her PhD in educational administration from the University of Chicago in 1979. When she was appointed to the superintendency of the Washington, D.C., public schools, she was the first African American woman to become the leader of that troubled school district. Her leadership there was tumultuous and lasted only from 1973 to 1975. Many believe that Dr. Sizemore's vision was far ahead of the times. As always, she displayed a commitment to community involvement and the establishment of high standards.

After leaving the nation's capitol, Dr. Sizemore became a professor at the University of Pittsburgh from 1977 to 1992, even serving as chair of her department. She specialized in performing research on high-achieving schools serving mostly African American students, and she wrote about how they had accomplished their tasks when so many other schools were failing. In 1992, Dr. Sizemore became the inaugural dean of the School of Education at DePaul University, in Chicago. She continued her role as activist-scholar and assisting low-performing schools to become high performing. She was a keen observer of sociopolitical trends, and her final book, *Walking in Circles: The Black Struggle for School Reform,* documents how African Americans were turning back to some of the same remedies they had earlier abandoned. She has been portrayed as having a "take no prisoners voice" and exemplified "the power of the lived agenda." Her idea that the change agent had to have a platform of power to confront power was based on her insight into social systems change, closely paralleling those of the great Chicago community activist Saul Alinsky.

—Fenwick W. English

See also Bethune, Mary McLeod; Black education; civil rights movement; Coppin, Fanny Jackson; critical race theory; critical theory; cultural politics, wars; curriculum, theories of; diversity; Du Bois, W. E. B.; equality, in schools; intelligence; minorities, in schools; multiculturalism; parental involvement; underachievers, in schools; Washington, Booker T.; women in educational leadership; Woodson, Carter G.

Further Readings and References

Lee, C. (2004, November). In memoriam: Remembering Barbara Ann Sizemore (1927–2004). *Educational Researcher, 33*(8), 37.

Sizemore, B. (2005). *Walking in circles: The Black struggle for school reform.* Chicago: Third World Press.

🏛 SKINNER, B. F.

B. F. Skinner (1904–1990) was one of the most important influences in education. His work with reinforcement schedules provides a foundation for effective instruction. His work on the development, elimination, and control of behavior is reflected in both instructional and administrative procedures. In addition, his analytical approach to the understanding of behavior underpins practices in all areas of education.

Skinner was born in 1904 in Susquehanna, Pennsylvania. As an undergraduate, he attended Hamilton College and majored in English. Skinner later attended Harvard, receiving his PhD in psychology in 1931. Following graduation, he spent 5 years in a postdoctoral position with Crogier Laboratory and 3 as a junior fellow (Harvard's most prestigious position for a young scholar). From 1945 to 1948, Skinner was chairman of the Psychology Department at Indiana University. In 1948, he returned to Harvard, where he remained until his retirement. He is one of only three behavioral scientists to have received the President's Medal of Science. He has been referred to as the "most-well-known psychologist since Freud." Skinner has become more closely identified with "behaviorism" or "behavioral psychology" than any other individual.

In his studies of reinforcement schedules, Skinner provided findings that had a regularity and specificity that rivaled those of any physical scientist. Skinner demonstrated that particular schedules of reinforcement generated characteristic and replicable learning-response curves. In essence, he found that steady rates of learning (a desirable condition) could be established and maintained via intermittent schedules in which the delivery of reinforcement varied according to an average rate and therefore was unpredictable to the subject. Fixed schedules, defined by reinforcement delivery according to a specific time interval or number of responses, resulted in rates of learning exemplified by pauses in the learning curve.

Skinner also studied the effect of reinforcement on "shaping" up or developing new behaviors in his subjects. His concept of continuously reinforcing successive approximations of a target behavior was employed in a variety of studies involving developing novel behaviors in animals.

Skinner's assumption that all behavior is purposeful and subject to the laws of behaviorism implies the possibility of behavioral control. Skinner preferred the term *control,* as the development and management of behavior involved control of either (or both) antecedent and consequent events. He consistently argued that the study of behavior was based on the consideration of how it (the behavior) was related to antecedents and consequences. For educational leaders, Skinner's work is relevant in that both conditions are often amenable to manipulation. Therefore, the control of others' behavior (e.g., students, teachers, parents) becomes more easily achieved and predictable.

In the study of behavior, Skinner held that a functional analysis was the most appropriate approach. By this, he meant an analysis of observable and measurable behavior based upon the antecedent-behavior-consequence relationship. His work and writing in this area became the foundation of applied behavior analysis.

Skinner's perspective and focus on observable behavior under conscious control, learning, behavior change, and the development of new behaviors is of particular interest to educators. His theory is particularly relevant to special education, child development, and classroom management.

—J. M. Blackbourn

See also behaviorism; child development theories; classroom management; differentiation of stimuli; discipline in schools; feedback; knowledge base, of the field; learning, theories of; measurement, theories of; rational organizational theory; scientific management; schooling effects; special education; supervision; theory movement, in educational administration; variables

Further Readings and References

Cyert, R., & March, J. (1963). *A behavioral theory of the firm.* Englewood Cliffs, NJ: Prentice Hall.

Fielding, M. (2005). *Quality behaviour management in schools.* New York: Routledge.

Owen, R. (1987). *Organizational behavior in education.* Englewood Cliffs, NJ: Prentice Hall.

Skinner, B. F. (1953). *Science and human behavior.* New York: Macmillan.

Skinner, B. F. (1964). Behaviorism at fifty. In T. W. Wann (Ed), *Behaviorism and phenomenology: Contrasting bases for modern psychology* (pp. 79–97). Chicago: University of Chicago Press.

SOCIAL CAPITAL

Like other forms of capital, such as financial capital, social capital refers to the available resources upon which an individual or a community can draw. In the case of social capital, the resources are formed by people's networks and relationships. The two main theorists of social capital as applied to education are

James Coleman and Robert Putnam. Coleman's work stems from his 1966 report, which indicated that family background accounts for student achievement more than variations in schools do. His subsequent work comparing the greater success of private school students to that of public school students expanded the role of family background to include all the social resources available to a student. The greater success of students in religious private schools was attributable to the overlapping, cross-generational social networks provided by the partnerships among families, church, and school. Coleman defined these partnerships as *social capital,* which pertained to the norms, the social networks, and the relationships between adults and children that were of value for the child's growing up. Social capital existed within the family but also outside the family, in the community. Within the family, social capital depended upon the strength of parents' relationships with their children. Coleman found, for example, that even when controlling for parents' socioeconomic status, dropout rates for high school students were lowest when there were two parents, only one sibling to share parental attention, and mothers who expected their children to attend college. Thus, a family's social capital increases children's socioeconomic success, or the children's human capital. Outside of the family, social capital depends upon people's sense of obligation and reciprocity, like quid pro quo, within a community.

Putnam's work in 2000 concentrated on the social capital sustained by communities, arguing that social capital helped people resolve collective problems, created trust which made transactions less costly, and fostered positive character traits such as tolerance and empathy. Based on measures such as the number of per capita social organizations and turnout in presidential elections, he developed a social capital index for each state. He then correlated that index with the Annie E. Casey Foundation's Kids Count index, which included measures such as the teen birthrate and percentage of children in poverty. States ranked as high in social capital were also high on the Kids Count Index and had higher scores on standardized tests. He argued that greater social capital indicated that parents and communities were more involved with their schools. Again, this involvement was independent of socioeconomic status.

Additional research on social capital has indicated that it is positively related to student success. As an example at the family level, in 1995, F. F. Furstenberg

and M. E. Hughes measured social capital with "within family" constructs, such as involvement with an extended family, and "family links to community," such as quality of school. They found that both of these constructs were positively related to students' socioeconomic success, even when controlling for family socioeconomic status.

In 2001, Glenn Israel, Lionel Beaulieu, and Glen Hartless reported that social capital in both the family and the community were associated with educational achievement, and they argued that states should work to strengthen the capacity of families as well as schools, perhaps by means of parental education programs.

Anthony Bryk, Valerie Lee, and Peter Holland complemented Coleman's work with religious schools by finding that Catholic school students were more successful partly because of the relationships between school, family, and church. Public schools can also foster social capital. Mary Driscoll and Charles Kerchner asserted that school leaders should be aware of how to create social capital within their schools. They suggested that administrators create programs to involve parents and include parents in site-based management programs. School leaders can change structures and scheduling to foster social capital by means of small schools, schools within schools, teaming, and looping. A number of school reforms (e.g., the Coalition for Essential Schools and the Small Schools movement) have attempted to formalize these kinds of structures.

Administrators can also encourage positive teacher and student interactions. In 2001, R.G. Croninger and V. E. Lee investigated the role that teachers played in providing students with social capital, based on teachers' reports about whether they'd talked with students about school or other items and on students' reported beliefs about how much their teachers support their school success. Powerfully, they noted that if these two forms of social capital provided by teachers were present, the probability of students' dropping out decreased by half and that these effects were most powerful for at-risk students.

At least one educational effort has attempted to institutionalize social capital by building its capacity from the beginning. An evaluation of the first 4 1/2 years of a Chicago foundation's creation of a neighborhood learning network focused on one of the foundation's goals, to establish social trust between school principals, neighborhood leaders, and the foundation. While this effort was successful, the partners' attempts to build trust by being flexible led to less clarity about goals, norms, and priorities, which led to lack of focus and accountability. The researchers suggested that structures that promote elements of social capital, such as trust, may exclude structures that promote a coherent vision and accountability.

Research on social capital thus provides support for strong relationships between schools and the families and communities they serve, as well as for strong relationships between students and staff within schools.

—Joanne M. Marshall

See also at-risk students; class, social; community relations; cultural capital; dropout; human capital; parental involvement; social context; underachievers, in schools

Further Readings and References

Bryk, A. S., Lee, V. E., & Holland, P. B. (1993). *Catholic schools and the common good.* Cambridge, MA: Harvard University Press.

Coleman, J. S. (1966). *Equality of educational opportunity.* Washington, DC: U.S. Department of Health, Education, and Welfare.

Croninger, R. G., & Lee, V. E. (2001). Social capital and dropping out of high school: Benefits to at-risk students of teachers' support and guidance. *Teachers College Record, 103,* 548–581.

Driscoll, M. E., & Kerchner, C. T. (1999). The implications of social capital for schools, communities, and cities: Educational administration as if a sense of place mattered. In J. Murphy & K. S. Louis (Eds.), *Handbook of research on educational administration: A project of the American educational research association.* San Francisco: Jossey-Bass.

Furstenberg, F. F., & Hughes, M. E. (1995). Social capital and successful development among at-risk youth. *Journal of Marriage and the Family, 57,* 580–592.

Israel, G. D., Beaulieu, L. J., & Hartless, G. (2001). The influence of family and community social capital on educational achievement. *Rural Sociology, 66*(1), 43–68.

Putnam, R. D. (2000). *Bowling alone: The collapse and revival of American community.* New York: Simon & Schuster.

🏛 SOCIAL CONTEXT

Social context is the broad framework for understanding that learning occurs in a specific constellation of personal interactions and effects. There are two aspects of social context in schools: literacy is the key to unlocking a world of interaction, while at the same time interaction within school is the key to unlocking the world of literacy.

There are several social purposes for schools in terms of preparing students for civic life and to transmit a knowledge base (cultural literacy), but in terms of social learning theory, school simply provides a context for a student to make meaning of the experience. Schools try to establish effective learning environments within classrooms in order to increase achievement and therefore opportunities for students to change themselves and their contexts. Educational leaders are therefore interested in analyzing and improving the social context within schools, while understanding the students' contexts outside of school and the school's context. In addition, as seen in state and national standards, all educators are expected to understand the diversity of student background and how to structure an optimal learning environment that includes positive rapport. The goal is to control negative and distracting student behavior that would intimidate other students from participating in the discussions necessary to develop ideas.

Social context is a key factor in current ideologies of teaching and learning. Behaviorist models of learning identify social context as external influences on motivation and perception in an effort to codify predictable human behavior using the scientific method. Classroom management is often equated with discipline policies for controlling bad behavior with consequences and incentives, based on behavior modification principles. William Glasser considered this approach coercive and recommended a quality-schools approach that included metacognition. In contrast, there are several critical theories, in that they assume the context will continuously change and that human response is therefore not completely predictable. Few educators embrace the most radical constructivism that argues that all knowledge is socially constructed, that is, exists only in as much as society agrees on it.

The more practical ideology of sociopsychological constructivism considers social context not only influential but also essential for learning because knowledge is constructed by the individual who is compelled to find personal meaning in experience. The developmental theories of Jean Piaget and Lev Vygotsky emphasized the importance of interacting with objects and people. John Dewey maintained that school is not a preparation for life, but it is life. This emphasis on the relevance of study to the student's real world was a major component of the Progressive movement, based on his philosophy, which began with child study.

Another branch of constructivism, reconstructionism, regards schools as the vehicle for improving the social order. An early example was William James, who not only popularized the new field of psychology but also worked tirelessly for peace, and George Counts, who dared schools to attempt social reform. This legacy may be seen in a current concept of the ideal social context in school: a community of learners wherein all members—students, faculty, staff, families—are deliberately and continuously expected to change for the better as individuals and as a culture. In the last half of the twentieth century, greater scrutiny of social context for students traditionally marginalized due to minority status resulted in legislation, such as Public Law 94-142 and Title IX of the Elementary and Secondary Education Act (ESEA), and court cases, such as *Brown v. Board of Education* (1954), to address equity of access. Schools are therefore the child as well as the change agent of social context.

Despite the ideals behind the federal mandates and incentives, there remain strong local cultures that resist adjusting the social context. There is a strong and vocal segment of American society that seeks to limit the school's role in defining the social context by narrowing the focus to acquisition of essential knowledge and skills, which clearly favors students of advantaged backgrounds. The recent reenactment of ESEA, also known as the No Child Left Behind Act, emphasized the achievement of "adequate yearly progress" in academic objectives and the use of research-based methods to achieve them. In the high-stakes aftermath, many educators report a trend away from community involvement and holistic projects that are associated with social context goals.

Technology is another important factor in current social context. Students with cell phones are able to instant message (IM) their friends in every possible context, thus extending their private networks and limiting the scope of a teacher to develop a cohesive community of learners within the classroom. By the same token, instant and mass communication make it possible to monitor and analyze student performance to an astonishing degree that, ideally, can inform instructional decisions to meet the needs of individual differences. At the same time, mass communication has created a more cohesive culture with shared entertainment experiences that include models of society. There is an active strand of educational inquiry regarding the optimal means to foster an online learning community that replicates or improves on the face-to-face interaction possible on campus; a similar conversation concerns the advantage of interactive instructional methods even in large lecture classes, using handheld devices to signal opinion or comprehension for immediate assessment of the class's learning. Finally, the publication of assessment data has created a national social context in response to reforms such as the No Child Left Behind Act, which eliminates the autonomy and isolation that has obscured the differences in social context among school environments.

Narrative studies, such as Dan Lortie's *Schoolteachers,* and theoretical works, such as C. S. Lewis's *Abolition of Man,* have inspired thoughtful analysis of school context. A related concept is the hidden curriculum, which includes not only what students are failing to learn as a result of the school environment but also what unintended life lessons are being constructed by the students' efforts to find meaning in their everyday lives. For example, it is highly ironic for students to learn about democratic principles in an environment governed authoritatively; it is similarly paradoxical for teachers to promote collaboration among their students if the faculty, as a result of policies and proximity, are marginalized from decisions and isolated in their experiences. The sad conclusion of John Gatto, an award-winning teacher, is that no matter how good the teachers or how progressive the texts, it is the structure of the school system that is the dominant factor in a child's education, teaching them to obey without question, give the answer that is expected, do only what is demanded, and conform at all costs. He has since left public schools and now champions homeschooling, a practice widely criticized for its limited social context.

John Goodlad's body of work combined qualitative and quantitative data to establish an authoritative voice in the area of school effects research. The effort to identify effective teaching practice is confounded by external validity limitations, that is, the difficulty in generalizing findings to new contexts. The great variety of interacting social context factors were a challenge to the neat experimental designs considered most valid; the simplest demographic data (i.e., age, gender, ethnicity) became routine in order to establish similarity in samples. Kurt Lewin's field theory provided a framework for considering social context; his other contribution was action research, widely embraced by schools to evaluate an educational innovation in the local context. Systems theories, including Bowen's family systems and Urie Bronfenbrenner's ecological model, consider microsystems, mesosystems, and macrosystems to understand a dynamic interaction. The emerging field of ecopsychology focuses on stressors to systems.

With more sophisticated statistical procedures, it is now possible to consider multiple factors simultaneously, and a more nuanced portrait may be described. In its landmark 1997 report, the National Center for Education Statistics found the social context (i.e., language, socioeconomic status, and family structure) was significantly correlated with school success and, incidentally, minority status. High-poverty schools reported less parent involvement, more disruptive and aggressive behavior, and greater absenteeism, creating a less effective learning environment. The physical context, such as the building, materials, and equipment, are actually indicators of social context, for they are highly correlated with economic resources and the education level of the community. Poverty is therefore a more complex construct than a student qualifying for free or reduced lunch, the most common measure of socioeconomic status. Much more difficult to measure is the composite of factors creating the learning environment.

Ultimately, social context figures in the nature versus nurture debate. The early field of psychology developed into social psychology and sociology with an assortment of theories addressing the nature of people. Alfred Adler departed from Freud's drive-dependent psychoanalytic approach to suggest the influence of teaching and also the importance of a social interest; his student, Carl Rogers, proposed client-centered therapy, which encouraged a learner-centered pedagogy. These theories have greatly influenced schools, ranging from models of comprehensive counseling (school-based interagency collaborations) to cooperative learning groups. In fact, there is no educational innovation with a broader and more authoritative research base than *cooperative learning;* in sum, personal and cognitive adjustment as well as learning environment tend to be positively influenced by its use. One component of cooperative learning is the direct instruction of social skills needed for successful cooperation. There are many programs designed for schoolwide intervention to foster a healthy climate and incidentally manage behavior. Information is provided not only about social contexts but also in social skills to successfully navigate them. This is sometimes categorized as *guidance curriculum,* but is lately appearing in state academic standards in areas such as communication, social studies, and health. Failure to engage in the social fabric of the school was given in explanation of the Columbine High School massacre, in which two boys opened fire at a Colorado high school, prompting efforts nationwide to prevent isolation and malaise that could result in violence.

Social context is important not only in how students learn but also in the scope and sequence of the curriculum. Hilda Taba's expanding horizons model organized investigations of the world, beginning with the child's family, then proceeding to ever-larger circles of influence. The social context of the school therefore includes controlling negative and distracting student behavior that would intimidate other students from participating in the discussions necessary to develop ideas, and deliberate efforts to coordinate the students' life experiences in and out of school.

—Naomi Jeffery Petersen

See also behaviorism; character education; classification of education; classroom management; cognition, theories of; egocentrism, theories of; esteem needs; ethnocentrism; hierarchical developmental models; intelligence; learning environments; literacy, theories of; mental illness, in adults and children; metacognition; motivation, theories of; psychology, types of; schooling effects; self-actualization; social psychology

Further Readings and References

Bandura, A. (1997). *Self-efficacy: The exercise of control.* New York: Freeman.

Bronfenbrenner, U. (1977). Toward an experimental ecology of human development. *American Psychologist, 32,* 513–531.

Dewey, J. (1907). *The school and society.* Chicago: University of Chicago Press.

Dewey, J. (1922). *Human nature and conduct: An introduction to social psychology.* New York: Modern Library.

Gatto, J. (1991). *Dumbing us down: The hidden curriculum of compulsory schooling.* New Society.

Glasser, W. (1992). *The quality school: Managing students without coercion.* New York: Harper & Row.

Goodlad, J. (1983). *A place called school.* New York: McGraw-Hill.

Lee, V. (2000). Using hierarchical linear modeling to study social contexts: The case of school effects. *Educational Psychologist, 35,* 125–142.

Lewis, C. S. (1947). *The abolition of man: Or, reflections on education with special reference to the teaching of English in the upper forms of schools.* New York: Macmillan.

Lortie, D. (1975). *Schoolteachers: A sociological study.* Chicago: University of Chicago Press.

Ornstein, J. (2002). *Teaching and schooling in America: Pre- and Post-September 11.* Boston: Allyn & Bacon.

Wertsch, J. (1985). *Vygotsky and the social formation of mind.* Boston: Harvard University Press.

🏛 SOCIAL PSYCHOLOGY

Social psychology is a branch of psychology concerned with the social behavior of human beings, how humans influence and are influenced by each other, and how personal beliefs affect perception and create a subjective reality. It is a field that applies scientific methodology to explain and understand how human behavior is influenced by the actual, imagined, or implied presence of other persons.

Unlike behaviorism, which is rooted in the micro-objectivist, functionalist paradigm, social psychology finds its foundation in the interpretivist, subjectivist model. Group dynamics, conflict resolution, causal attributions, cognitive dissonance, interpersonal relationships, nonconformity, organizational environments, attitudes, stereotypes, and prejudice are all of concern and interest to social psychologists. Social psychologists attempt to understand how the relationships between the above concepts impact human functioning.

Kurt Lewin is generally considered the founder of the discipline of social psychology. He developed field theory based on the position that human behavior was purposeful and a function of internal (individual) and external (environmental) forces. Lewin employed the process of force field analysis to better understand the goal-directed and restraining forces that influence individual behavior. This process was adopted as a means for understanding and explaining organizational behavior by Dr. W. Edwards Deming and is still employed as a continuous improvement, managerial, and leadership tool. Lewin's work formed the basis for much of what is considered "best practices" related to group dynamics and organizational behavior.

Other noted social psychologists were Gordon Allport, who studied stereotypes, prejudices, and attributions, and Art Combs, who focused on individual perception and phenomenology. Allport's work had a significant impact on conflict resolution and interpersonal relationship development. Combs's research has recently come to the forefront and forms the foundation for the "dispositions" movement in teacher education. His work has long influenced research in the area of teacher/administrator perceptions.

Albert Bandura, through his social learning theory, attempted to bridge the gap between social learning theory and behaviorism. His position was that while behavior change was affected by antecedents and consequences, observation of the behavior of others and the consequences associated with that behavior was the primary means by which human learning occurred. In addition, reinforcement in such social learning situations was primarily vicarious rather than direct. The process of modeling and imitation with associated natural communities of reinforcement (naturally occurring reinforcers) was seen as the basis for human development. Bandura also felt that internal cognitive processes, rooted in both the social structure and mind, were employed to mediate between and connect antecedents, behaviors, and associated consequences. Educational practices such as the emphasis on effective role models, mentoring, field-based practica/internships, and "shadowing" have their foundation in Bandura's social learning theory.

Social psychology has had a significant impact on education, particularly educational leadership and administration. Teacher perceptions of specific instructional practices, the nature of the postevaluative conference, and leadership effectiveness all have their foundation in social psychology research. Administrator methods for managing personnel, resolving organizational conflict, selecting new faculty, and designing school organizations are also tied to this research.

Social psychology has allowed professional educators to extend their study and understanding beyond observable and measurable behaviors into the subjective areas of feelings, perceptions, values, and attitudes. In essence, social psychology has allowed educators to examine and address those salient features of schools and schooling that relate to persons as both individuals and group members. Social psychology currently seems to be evolving in a macrosubjectivist, humanistic direction. Basically, contemporary social psychology focuses on the connections that make up our interrelated social fabric. It is becoming a blend between psychology and sociology in which the impact of events, institutions, culture, community, social class, race, and gender on thought, perception, and behavior is the primary focus. This position supports a developing perspective among social psychologists that human behavior is significantly rooted in individual factors and less deterministic than previously thought.

Social psychology has long been an integral part of the field of education. Its new direction is more in line with emerging postmodern and humanistic trends in educational leadership and administration. Given this feature, the field of social psychology is likely to exert a greater influence on schools and schooling in the coming century.

—*J. M. Blackbourn, J. Larry Tyler, and Conn Thomas*

See also action research; administration, theories of; attitudes; behaviorism; cognitive dissonance; group dynamics; Hawthorne Studies, The; human resource development; learning, theories of; mentoring; networking and network theory; peer interaction/friendships; personnel management; psychology, types of; satisfaction, in organizations and roles; satisficing theory; social relations, dimensions of; supervision

Further Readings and References

Allport, G. (1958). *The nature of prejudice*. New York: Doubleday.

Bandura, A. (1977). *Social learning theory*. Englewood Cliffs, NJ: Prentice Hall.

Bush, T., & Middlewood, D. (2005). *Leading and managing people in education*. Thousand Oaks, CA: Sage.

Lewin, K. (1935). *A dynamic theory of personality*. New York: McGraw-Hill.

Ogawa, R. (2005). Leadership as social construct: The expression of human agency within organizational constraint. In F. English (Ed.), *SAGE handbook of educational leadership* (pp. 89–106). Thousand Oaks, CA: Sage.

🏛 SOCIAL RELATIONS, DIMENSIONS OF

Education has seen substantive change over the past century. A school community consists of students, teachers, administrators, building personnel, parents, community agencies, businesses, district personnel, legislators, and governmental agencies. Despite their complexity, effective social relations are grounded in strong relations. Successful partnerships are a two-way street, where all comprehend they have something to learn. There are at least five sources that schools must contend with: parents and community, technology, corporate connections, government-related policy, and the wider teaching profession. The challenge for schools is to figure out how to make their relationships with them productive.

Parents are important stakeholders; communication is vital if the relationship is to be a powerful bridge between home and school. When families are actively involved in schools, teachers learn more about the students and are better able to provide educational services for them. Schools that are able to reach out and become partners with families, teachers, and parents can create common ground that bridges differences and creates mutually supportive practices in the home and school. The relationships among a school's faculty, students, and parents are crucial. Schools can also connect with the community through educational programs for adults, collaborations with community-based recreation and youth service organizations, and partnerships with health care and social service agencies.

Schools need to make choices about how they will use their time with computers. The biggest weaknesses in the use of new technologies are pedagogical and strategic, however; supporters of partnerships between education and the working world need for schools to develop skill sets more suited for the demands of the information age.

The business world can be a valuable community partner. If schools are to benefit, they must know what they are doing. Those who work in internally collaborative schools are less vulnerable and so more open to forming outside relationships. When businesses see families involved in local activities, they may be more likely to give back to the community themselves.

Government policy has also become increasingly demanding. As a result of the sweeping changes enacted by legislation like No Child Left Behind, the move to standards-based teaching and learning is alive; consequently, schools must pool resources from governmental agencies so that services are effectively provided to students and their families.

Educators must find ways to step out into wider learning networks, for schools and universities to form partnerships in which teacher education and school improvement are pursued in tandem, and for government and union leaders to go beyond the dance of despair that often ends up demoralizing the best of our teachers.

Social relations will always be threads that interlay within our schools. The critical component is how leaders respond and in some contexts embrace the factors in an effort to continue in the quest to educate all children well. Trust holds together any coalition built among schools, businesses, government, and the community.

—*Curtis Cain*

See also adult education; collaboration theory; communities, types, building of; computers, use and impact of; continuing education; cultural capital; cultural politics, wars; global cultural politics; governance; group dynamics; human capital; involvement, in organizations; life span development; multiculturalism; networking and network theory; organizational theories; parental involvement; partnerships, interagency; social capital

Further Readings and References

Beveridge, S. (2004). *Children, families, and schools: Developing partnerships for inclusive education.* New York: Routledge.

Chrispeels, J. (2004). *Learning to lead together: The promise and challenge of sharing leadership.* Thousand Oaks, CA: Sage.

Maurrasse, D. (Ed.). (2004). *A future for everyone: Innovative social responsibility and community partnerships.* New York: Routledge.

Pflaum, W. D. (2004). *The technology fix: The promised reality of computers in our schools.* Alexandria, VA: Association for Supervision and Curriculum Development.

Stephen, W., & Vogt, W. (2004). *Education programs for improving intergroup relations: Theory, research, and practice.* New York: Teachers College Press.

Tileston, D. W. (2004). *What every teacher should know about the profession and the politics of teaching.* Thousand Oaks, CA: Corwin Press.

SOCIAL STUDIES

In 1992, the National Council for the Social Studies (NCSS) defined *social studies* as an integrated study of social sciences and humanities to promote civic competence of citizens of a culturally diverse and democratic society in an interdependent world. More broadly defined, it is the preparation of students in the knowledge, skills, and values that will lead to active participation in their society. This understanding of social studies as a multidisciplinary activity that integrates a diversity of content and skills to promote democratic participation is only one position in the ideological debate over the teaching of the social sciences.

Differing positions are typically summarized as the social studies versus the single-discipline approach. The latter subject-centered view ranges in focus from the study of social science in the form of history and geography as separate disciplines, to the inclusion of other disciplines, such as anthropology, psychology, economics, political science, and sociology. The commonality of this view is that each discipline is taught separately from the others, and students will benefit from the rigor and methods of each discipline.

Social studies can be civics centered in its primary concern with the development of an individual and social understanding of interrelated content and values that lead to citizenship development. Or it can be issues centered in that students critically explore specific issues that can relate to their own personal development and the resolution of social problems. Single-discipline proponents argue that without concentrated study of the disciplines, students fail to learn the important facts that promote traditional understandings of the American culture and society. Social studies proponents demur and insist that to understand the complexity of human activity and to develop active democratic participation, students need to study all aspects of past and current human activity in a multidisciplinary manner that is authentic and relevant to their lives.

The study of social science has been and continues to be a thorny political football. In the 1890s, through the study of social science, populists sought to create individuals who would participate in mass movements that challenged the power of organized wealth. On the other hand, corporate interests sought to promote citizens who would be loyal to the existing social order in which their wealth and position were embedded.

In the early twentieth century, faced with the increasing national diversity due to immigration, various national committees and commissions, such as the Committee of Ten and the National Education Association's Committee of 1916, promoted the organization of social studies into separate disciplines by grade level to facilitate immigrant assimilation into the dominant American culture.

Progressive educators, such as John Dewey, argued against this curriculum in favor of student-centered curriculum that would require students to become active researchers in a multidisciplinary context. In 1958, the single-discipline approach was formally promoted by the federal government in the New Social Studies, which eventually failed due to the inability of teachers to implement this expert-driven, top-down curriculum approach. In the liberalism of the 1960s, social studies was promoted as multidisciplinary inquiry with students as researchers; however, this movement also failed to gain general acceptance.

With the conservative restoration of the 1980s, the content, skills, and values promoted in social studies became centralized through the standards and accountability movement. In response to the call for standards, professional organizations, such as the NCSS, developed issue-centered, multidisciplinary standards. When they were issued in 1994, various conservative groups and proponents of the single-discipline approach quickly attacked them. Opposition ranged from their focus on multiculturalism and globalism to their use of critical thinking skills that could contest what were deemed traditional American values and historical interpretations. This debate highlighted the different views on what constituted citizenship. On one hand, some individuals defined citizenship development as the transmission of established culture and values through the teaching of traditional interpretations of American history and culture. Others defined citizenship as the development of critically reflective individuals, who, informed by multidisciplinary study and critical thinking skills, would take informed social action. In this view, students would study the nature of race, gender, and social class oppression in American society. Of course, central to this ongoing debate is the purpose of social studies education, which can focus on the reproduction of traditional societal and cultural knowledge and values or focus on the development of critically informed, responsible, and politically active citizens.

How social studies is taught reflects this ongoing tension between the two views. If citizenship transmission is the focus, then social studies pedagogy is designed to provide students with the correct knowledge, skills, and values and subsequently test them to determine if they acquired the correct information. Conversely, if the focus is on developing reflective inquiry, personal development, and social criticism, then students are required to critically inquire through their own research into social phenomena. In this case, assessment is multiple, authentic, and formative. The pervasive use of textbooks also tends to transmit standardized curricula. Some individuals argue that since textbooks in many states are adopted as statewide textbooks and are scrutinized by interest groups for content and values, publishers tend to promote content and values that maintain traditional, dominant culture. In line with their desire to develop critically conscious student researchers, social studies proponents promote the use of locally developed curriculum and instructional materials.

Both of these pedagogical positions have significant implications for the role of the social studies teacher. In a top-down transmissional curriculum, teachers may be required to use "teacher-proof" materials that minimize their influence over the social studies

curriculum. In a critical social studies curriculum, teachers actively implement locally developed curriculum, promote student critique of commercial materials, and act as skilled facilitators of student research. In this approach, teachers are aligned with a Deweyian perspective on pedagogy and act as social researchers who facilitate their students' production of knowledge and their critique of social values. In critical social studies pedagogy, teachers focus on the goals of a democratic society, promote these values through curriculum and instruction, integrate student experiences into the curriculum, facilitate student critique of how power operates within the contemporary social context, and require students to understand the historical context of contemporary social issues.

—*Raymond A. Horn Jr.*

See also civics, civic education; critical theory; cross-cultural studies; cultural politics, wars; curriculum, theories of; democracy, democratic education and administration; dialectical inquiry; diversity; global cultural politics; immigration, history and impact in education; liberalism; minorities, in schools; multiculturalism

Further Readings and References

Evans, R. (2004). *The social studies wars.* New York: Teachers College Press.
Parker, W. (2002). *Teaching democracy.* New York: Teachers College Press.
Ross, E. (2001). *The social studies curriculum: Purposes, problems, and possibilities.* New York: SUNY Press.
Shapiro, H., & Purpel, D. (2005). *Critical social issues in American education.* Mahwah, NJ: Lawrence Erlbaum.
Shaver, P. (Ed.). (2001). *Handbook of research on social studies teaching and learning.* New York: Macmillan.
Steiner-Khamsi, G., Torney-Purta, J., & Schwille, J. (2002). *New paradigms and recurring paradoxes in education for citizenship.* New York: Peter Lang.

SPAN OF CONTROL

Span of control is a concept that refers to the number of people that a manager supervises. In the private sector, the typical span of control ranges from 1:5 to 1:25. The current trend is to increase the span of control to increase efficiency, levels of worker involvement, and, in many cases, productivity. For example, from 1992 to 1994, Chrysler Corporation changed from an average of one supervisor for every 25 hourly workers to one supervisor for every 45 hourly workers. If the total number of employees in an organization is held constant, then the span of control relates to the number of hierarchical levels of supervision within the organization. If the span of control is large, then the number of levels will be less and a flat organization will result. High spans of control tend to decrease cost of supervision, increase employee empowerment, reduce bureaucracy, and promote efficient decision making. Flat organizations have better lines of communications but have fewer opportunities for advancement.

On the other hand, if the span of control is small, then the number of levels will increase and a tall organization will develop. Low spans of control are associated with control of employees and top-down management. A tall organization is appropriate if close supervision is required, mistakes are costly, or new employees are a constant occurrence. Small spans of control allow supervisors to invest time in high-leverage activities (e.g., strategic planning, organizational change, and problem solving). However, tall organizations can be highly bureaucratic and discourage initiative. In the private sector, management actively seeks to establish a balance between level of supervision needed, productivity, and efficiency.

Because building-level leadership is very complex and demanding, a principal should strive to maintain an appropriate span of control. However, schools have high spans of control and flatter structures; in part, these characteristics exist because of legislatively funding formulas. In public education, the span of control is driven by school finance laws and the corresponding funding equations. In most state funding equations, the key component is the number of students enrolled in the district. Most states provide money to fund a ratio of teachers to students and administrators to teachers; thus, the basic span of control is determined by the states and not the leadership team of the schools.

Given the financial restrictions common in public schools, principals must seek to develop alternatives to low spans of control. A capable, experienced staff needs much less direct supervision than new teachers do. Effective programs include teacher teams, teacher empowerment, and effective staff development. Teacher teams have been used to increase teacher autonomy and decision making. Developing procedures to share the power within a building can be very empowering for teachers, and this sharing can improve the role of both teachers and principals.

—*Bill Thornton*

See also administration, theories of; bureaucracy; chain of command; efficacy theory; governance; hierarchy, in organizations; leadership, theories of; loss of position (school principal); management theories; matrix organization (the "adhocracy"); organizational theories; rational organization theory; role conflict; role theory; scalar principle; table of organization; working conditions, in schools

Further Readings and References

Meier, K., & Bothe, J. (2003). Span of control and public organizations: Implementing Luther Gulick's research design. *Public Administration Review, 63*(1), 61–70.

Robbins, S. P. (2001). *Organizational behavior.* Upper Saddle River, NJ: Prentice Hall.

🏛 SPEARMAN, CHARLES

Charles Spearman (1863–1945) is the originator of the two-factor intelligence theory, the father of factor analysis, and a pioneer of the classical test theory. Spearman was born to a well-known family in London. After he graduated from Learmington College, he joined the British army and became a much-decorated officer in Burma and India. While in the army, he developed his interest first in philosophy and later in psychology. He earned his PhD with Wilhelm Wundt from the University of Leipzig, in Germany, in 1906. From 1907 to 1931, he worked at University College, London, first as a reader in experimental psychology and then as a professor of mind and logic. He conducted psychological research for the army during the First World War. After his retirement as an emeritus professor from University College, he traveled and taught in the United States, India, and Egypt. He received several honors in Britain, Germany, and the United States.

In 1904, Spearman published "The Proof and Measurement of Association Between Two Things," in the *American Journal of Psychology*. In this article, Spearman proposed that the correlation between two variables could be weakened by errors of measurement. To restore the true relationship between variables p and q, Spearman invented the *attenuation correction formula:*

$$r_{pq} = r_{p'q'} / \sqrt{(r_{p'p'} * r_{q'q'})},$$

meaning that the true correlation coefficient between p and q equals the observed correlation coefficient divided by the square root of the product of the reliability coefficients of variables *p* and *q*. Using this formula, Spearman calculated the correlations between various measures of mental abilities obtained at the time and identified an overall mental ability or general intelligence. This concept of general intelligence, or "g," became the focus of his second article, "General Intelligence Objectively Determined and Measured," which was published in the same year. In this landmark article, Spearman proposed that the "g" factor underlies all human abilities. In addition to this "g," there is a second level of specific factors, or "s," that account for the differences among various specific abilities. Any act of human intellect is a function of both the "g" and "s" factors. In his development of the two-factor intelligence theory, Spearman became the pioneer of a new statistical procedure, namely factor analysis. His concepts about true score and measurement errors became the basis of the classical test theory. His interest in statistics also led him to develop the Spearman rho, a correlation coefficient to be used when a sample size is small and data are in rank order. He is also accredited with the Spearman-Brown prophecy formula, which predicts test reliability based on the size of a test. Spearman's influence in the fields of psychology and education can still be felt today, especially through his two-factor intelligence theory. Other works published by Spearman include "The Nature of Intelligence and the Principles of Cognition" (1923), "The Abilities of Man: Their Nature and Measurement" (1927), "Creative Mind" (1930), and "Psychology Down the Ages" (1937).

—*Yuankun Yao*

See also achievement tests; behaviorism; cognition, theories of; intelligence; measurement, theories of; psychology, types of; testing and test theory development; validity and reliability; variables

Further Readings and References

Lee, S. (2005). *The encyclopedia of school psychology.* Thousand Oaks, CA: Sage.

Spearman, C. (1904). General intelligence objectively determined and measured. *The American Journal of Psychology, 2,* 201–293.

Williams, R., Zimmerman, D., Zumbo, B., & Ross, D. (2003). Charles Spearman: British behavioral scientist. *Human Nature Review, 3,* 114–118. Retrieved September 10, 2005, from http://human-nature.com/nibbs/03/spearman.pdf

🏛 SPECIAL EDUCATION

Special education is an integral component of the public education system. It includes the collective means by which children and youth with disabilities are provided an appropriate public education. Though special education as a professional practice has existed over a century, only in the past 30 to 40 years has it assumed a position of prominence and relevance in our schools.

The history of service to persons with disabilities extends back to the eighteenth century. Early attempts at humane treatment were initiated by Philippe Pinel and his student Jean Itard in their work with the mentally ill. Their methods of treatment were widely known, accepted, and employed in both Europe and North America.

Dr. Benjamin Rush, the father of modern psychiatry, applied and extended the work of Pinel and Itard in the United States after the Revolutionary War. Rush developed the concept of *moral therapy* (based on Pinel's philosophy of "moral treatment") and public education and support of children and youth with behavior problems. This was the initial suggestion that individuals with disabilities were due the same educational rights and privileges as other children.

Samuel Gridley Howe and Edward Seguin continued the growth and expansion of intervention programs for persons with disabilities in the nineteenth century. In 1832, Howe established Perkins School for the Blind in Boston and worked for the establishment by Massachusetts of the first state-supported school for persons with mental retardation in 1859. Upon the initiation of these two programs, the state of Massachusetts became the pioneer and leader in serving persons with disabilities. However, public school intervention programs became a reality only after the first compulsory attendance laws were passed in the late nineteenth century.

Seguin immigrated to the United States in 1850 to work with Howe at the Perkins School. He later worked as an administrator in state schools for the mentally retarded. Seguin's belief that persons with mental retardation were capable of meaningful learning led him to develop the first special education programs to focus on the development of self-help skills and vocational abilities.

While much of the history of special education has focused on the contributions of individual professionals, since 1950 (the date of the founding of the Association for Retarded Citizens), the field's history has revolved around legislation and litigation. In 1963, President John F. Kennedy signed the first federal legislation to solely address the needs of persons with disabilities: PL 88-164: The Mental Retardation Facilities and Community Mental Health Centers Construction Act. This law:

- Provided for the construction of community mental health centers
- Provided for the construction of research centers and facilities relating to mental and developmental disorders
- Provided for the training of teachers and other professionals to work with persons with disabilities
- Provided for research and demonstration projects related to the education of persons with disabilities

The prime result of this legislation was the establishment of University Affiliated Programs (UAP) at major research institutions across the nation. These UAPs conducted research and trained the professionals that significantly enhanced services to persons with disabilities.

A second legislative act that had a lasting impact on special education in the public schools was PL 93-112 (Section 504): The Civil Rights Provision of the Vocational Rehabilitation Amendments of 1973. Basically, Section 504 declares that no individual can be denied access solely on the basis of a disability to any program or activity that receives federal funds. Section 504 opened the doors of vocational and trade schools for students with disabilities as well as setting the stage for mainstreaming and inclusion.

The most significant legislation related to special education. PL 94-142: The Education for all Handicapped Children Act, was passed in 1975. PL 94-142 was designed to:

- Ensure that all persons with disabilities were provided with a free, appropriate public education in the least-restrictive environment
- Ensure that the rights of persons with disabilities and their families were protected through due process
- Ensure the effectiveness of educational efforts concerning persons with disabilities

All the policies and procedures of PL 94-142 must be adhered to by local education agencies and monitored by state education agencies under the supervision of the U.S. Office of Education. PL 94-142 includes seven mandates:

1. Free Appropriate Public Education (FAPE): This means that all education and related services must be provided to a student with a disability at public expense and that these services must be appropriate to the student's individual needs.

2. Age Requirements: This mandates that schools must serve all persons with disabilities between the ages of 3 and 21.

3. Due Process: These are the procedural safeguards that are guaranteed to persons with disabilities and their parents with regard to identification, evaluation, and educational placement.

4. Least-Restrictive Environment (LRE): This means that persons with disabilities are to be educated in the environment that affords them the opportunity to develop at the optimum level and most closely approximates a normalized learning environment.

5. Individual Education Program (IEP): This is mandated as a document that must be developed annually and reviewed periodically to ensure that each individual's needs are being met.

6. Nondiscriminatory Evaluation: This means that a person with disabilities must be given diagnostic and evaluation instruments that do not discriminate along racial or gender lines, in a manner that follows equitable procedures (the referral to placement process).

7. Zero Reject: This means that local education agencies cannot refuse to serve any person with disabilities within their jurisdiction.

PL 94-142 also outlined the various disabilities that were eligible to be served under the legislation. The reauthorization of PL 94-142 as PL 101-476: The Individuals With Disabilities Education Act (IDEA) included a revision and expansion of the disability categories. These categories include:

- Autism: "a developmental disability significantly affecting verbal and nonverbal communication and social interaction, generally evident before age 3, that adversely affects a child's educational performance."
- Deaf-blindness: a condition where students exhibit "concomitant hearing and visual impairments, the combination of which causes such severe communication and other developmental and educational needs that they cannot be accommodated in special education programs solely for children with deafness or children with blindness."
- Deafness: a hearing impairment that is so severe that the child is impaired in processing linguistic information through hearing, with or without

amplification, that adversely affects a child's educational performance.

- Emotional disturbance: a constellation of characteristics involving inappropriate interpersonal relationships, feelings, behaviors, unhappiness, or depression over a long period of time and to a marked degree that are not due to intellectual, sensory, or health factors.

- Hearing impairment: an impairment in hearing, whether permanent or fluctuating, that adversely affects a child's educational performance but that is not included under the definition of deafness.

- Mental retardation: significantly subaverage general intellectual functioning, existing concurrently with deficits in adaptive behavior and manifested during the developmental period, that adversely affects a child's educational performance.

- Multiple disabilities: when a child exhibits more than one major type of disability that results in a need for special education services that cannot be delivered in one of the impairment areas alone (e.g., a child who is mentally retarded and blind).

- Orthopedic impairment: students who exhibit congenital anomalies or some type of physical disability, such as clubfoot, missing limbs, poliomyelitis, cerebral palsy, and fractures.

- Other health impairment: limited strength, vitality, or alertness due to chronic or acute health problems. These difficulties are severe enough to impact educational performance.

- Specific learning disability: difficulties in learning (often reading or math) that cannot be accounted for by any other disability.

- Speech or language impairment: a communication disorder, such as stuttering, impaired articulation, a language impairment, or a voice impairment, that adversely affects a child's educational performance.

- Traumatic brain injury (TBI): students who have acquired a brain injury due to "physical force, resulting in total or partial functional disability or psychosocial impairment" that stems from closed or open head trauma and is not due to congenital issues or injuries induced by birth trauma.

- Visual impairment: an impairment in vision that even with correction adversely affects a child's educational performance. The term includes both partial sight and blindness.

With this revision, language was changed to reflect a "people first" orientation, autism and traumatic brain injury were added as disability categories, rehabilitation counseling and social work were added as related services, and transition services were added as a direct service intervention for those covered by the

act. IDEA was amended in 1997 and went through a second reauthorization in 2004.

Litigation also has had a significant effect on the operation of special education programs in the public schools. Among those court cases involving persons with disabilities and having the greatest impact on schools and schooling are:

- *Honig v. Doe* (1988): The U.S. Supreme Court affirmed the "stay put" provision of PL 94-142 and held that schools were limited to 10 days of suspension in relation to students with disabilities and that exceeding this limit denied such students their right to a free, appropriate public education. The court further rejected the "dangerousness" concept as an exemption to the "stay put" provision.

- *Board of Education v. Rowley* (1982): In this case, the U.S. Supreme Court defined the term "appropriate education" contained in PL 94-142. The court held that the state satisfies this requirement via personalized instruction and adequate support services.

- *Irving ISD v. Tatro* (1984): In this case, the U.S. Supreme Court held that certain medical services were covered by PL 94-142 as related services if they allowed students with disabilities to be placed in less restrictive educational environments and that failure to provide such services violated the equal access provision of Section 504 in the Rehabilitation Amendments of 1973.

- *Timothy W. v. Rochester School District* (1989): In this case, the U.S. First District Court held that under PL 94-142, all children with disabilities must be provided with a free, appropriate public education that meets their individual, unique needs and that the ability to benefit from such services was irrelevant.

- *Daniel R. R. v. Texas State Board of Education* (1989): The Fifth Circuit Court of Appeals ruled in this case that schools need not mainstream all students with disabilities without regard for whether the regular education setting provides the least-restrictive educational environment or meets the condition of "appropriateness" as defined in the *Rowley* case. In essence, the court held that placement decisions must be made on a case-by-case basis grounded in each student's unique individual needs.

- *Oberti v. Clementon Board of Education* (1993): In this case, the First District Court of the United States held that school districts must make a "reasonable effort" to include students with disabilities in the regular classroom environment and to ensure that to as great an extent as possible, such environments are of educational benefit to these students.

- *Florence County School District 4 v. Carter* (1993): The Supreme Court of the United States found that parents who unilaterally withdraw their children from a school district that provides an inappropriate education (as defined by PL 94-142 and the *Rowley* case) and place that child in an alternative program that meets the child's unique, individual needs are entitled to the reimbursement of their costs by the original school.

One of the most important aspects of special education in the public schools stems from the requirement in PL 94-142 that students with disabilities be provided with a "continuum of alternative educational placement options." This requirement is based upon the premise that the nature of the least-restrictive educational environment differs on an individual basis and that a range of possible place options is necessary to increase the chances that an appropriate environment can be identified for each student. Educational professionals have proposed and implemented a cascade model of educational services in which the levels interface.

In this model, students are placed in the program that seems to best meet their unique educational needs. In many instances, the placement option selected serves as an environment in which those skills critical to moving to a less restrictive educational environment are taught and refined. Once the student has mastered those requisite skills for a less restrictive environment, he or she is moved to that environment and the instructional process begins anew with a new target environment. In some cases, students with disabilities fail to succeed in settings that are believed to be their least-restrictive educational environment. In such cases, students are moved to a more restrictive environment to better address their individual needs and to teach the skills necessary to return to their initial placement.

Instructional methodology and practice in the field of special education focuses on addressing four areas of student learning. These are:

1. Acquisition: the initial learning of the information, process, or procedures that is the target of instruction

2. Proficiency: the mastery of the information, process, or procedure that is the target of instruction

3. Maintenance: the ongoing functional use of the information, process, or procedure that was previously taught

4. Generalization: the ability to use the information, process, or procedure in novel ways or situations

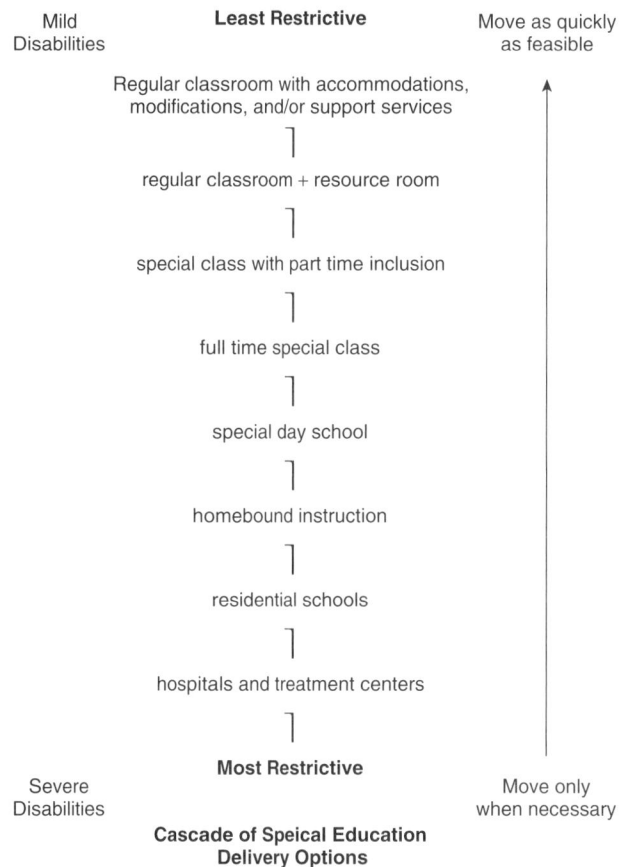

Mild Disabilities — **Least Restrictive** — Move as quickly as feasible

Regular classroom with accommodations, modifications, and/or support services

regular classroom + resource room

special class with part time inclusion

full time special class

special day school

homebound instruction

residential schools

hospitals and treatment centers

Most Restrictive

Severe Disabilities — Move only when necessary

Cascade of Speical Education Delivery Options

All areas of instruction must be planned for and included in the IEP. The ultimate goal of all special education is to allow the student to live a life that is as independent of supports as possible. Therefore, the development and mastery of specific skills and the generalization of those skills to the "real world" are of prime importance.

Special education, like all areas of professional endeavor, has been marked by specific milestones that have moved professional practice forward and fundamentally changed the manner in which persons with disabilities are served. Those milestones for special education include:

- Applied behavior analysis
- Normalization
- Learning strategies
- Vocational transition and career education
- Early childhood intervention

Each of these perspectives has had a significant, positive impact on the philosophy and practice in the field of special education.

Applied behavior analysis, or the application of the principles of behaviorism to "real-world" problems of social importance, has been a mainstay of effective intervention programs for persons with disabilities for over 40 years. From the development of academic skills, to classroom management techniques, to facilitating community/vocational integration, applied behavior analysis has been instrumental in improving the lives of persons with disabilities. Techniques such as task analysis have allowed teachers to break down complex skills to their constituent parts. Combining the task-analytic process with the techniques of chaining and positive reinforcement have facilitated the development of self-help skills (feeding, toileting, dressing, tying shoes, selecting appropriate clothing, etc.); vocational skills (making change, taking orders for food, cleaning tables, etc.); and community skills (buying a drink from a vending machine, shaking hands with people one meets, riding a bus to work or home, ordering and eating in a restaurant, etc.) in persons with the most severe mental disabilities. Through the behavior analysis of those contingencies that exist naturally in "real-world" environments and programming these contingencies into instruction, teachers have been able to ensure that these skills are maintained in settings outside of the schools and are generalized to new settings.

Normalization is a concept that has had one of the most positive impacts on persons with disabilities over the past 30 years. Developed by Wolf Wolfensberger, normalization is essentially using culturally normative means to create or maintain culturally normative behaviors and characteristics. The application of the principle of normalization to the education of persons with disabilities had a significant, positive impact on their quality of life. The use of community-based group homes for persons with disabilities reduced the population of residential institutions by 80% between 1975 and 2000. The application of the principle of normalization resulted in training programs for persons with disabilities that emphasized vocational and community adjustment skills. This resulted in an increase in the number of individuals with disabilities who were contributing to the good of society. Normalization, with its emphasis on integrating individuals with disabilities into society to as great an extent as possible, was the foundation for today's inclusion (mainstreaming) movement in the public schools.

Learning strategies, content enhancement, and the strategic instruction model are among of the most notable innovations in the field of special education. These approaches were pioneered and refined by Gordon Alley and Don Deshler from 1972 to the present. Based on the research of Ann Brown and Judith Flavel on metacognition, learning strategies refers to an instructional approach in which the academic content serves as the vehicle to teach persons with disabilities how to decode, store, retrieve, and use the information included in textbooks and instructional activities. Learning strategies are basically techniques in which the student is taught how to identify pertinent information in a text or a lecture, communicate an interest in classroom activities nonverbally to teachers and peers, and effectively address test questions to demonstrate their knowledge. The philosophical foundation of the learning strategies approach is to help the student become an independent learner. The Kansas University Center for Research on Learning has validated 32 different learning strategies to address student behaviors, ranging from test-taking skills, to note-taking skills, to listening skills, to organizational skills for class materials. The learning strategies approach has been extended to address the needs of persons without disabilities yet at risk for academic failure.

Another notable innovation in special education was the development and implementation of vocational transition/career education programs for persons with disabilities. Initially developed by Oliver Kolstoe and refined by D. E. Brolin and Gary Clark, these programs addressed the life span needs of persons with mild to moderate disabilities. These programs targeted secondary students with disabilities and provided them with information concerning social, academic and physical job requirements, working conditions, and job stability. This program led to progressively longer internship job placements during the student's high school career, so that those skills taught could be practiced in the work setting, and was combined with individual vocational adjustment counseling. For this reason, these programs were often described as "work-study" programs. The goal of the vocational transition/career education programs was to ensure that all students in the program had a viable employment option upon graduation.

Early childhood intervention for persons with disabilities emerged from the work of Harold Skeels, Samuel Kirk, Benjamin Bloom, Joseph Hunt, and B. M. Caldwell. Based on the premise that the impact of disabilities could be minimized via intensive early intervention and experiences, early childhood special education has become a critical component in the delivery of appropriate services to individuals with disabilities and their families. Research has indicated that structured, positive early experiences and stimulation can reduce or minimize the physical, affective, and cognitive impact of disabilities. A lack of such stimulation or training can result in a cumulative deficit that is difficult to remediate during the school years and often persists over the life span.

Early intervention programs are designed to address the needs of both children with obvious disabilities and those who are simply "at risk" for developing a disability in the future. Early intervention programs also established innovations such as direct involvement of parents via training and consulting and the integration of children with and without disabilities in educational settings. In the first instance, the training of parents in those skills critical to optimum child development essentially addressed the need to ensure that a child's "natural, first teacher" is one of good quality. Parents who understand their child's needs and how to meet those needs can provide continuous, appropriate intervention for their child in the home environment. In terms of the integration of children with and without disabilities in the same early childhood classroom, the focus was on providing models of age-appropriate, normal behaviors to those children with disabilities. Drawing from Wolfensberger's concept of "normalization" and Bandura's social learning theory, these "normal models" were essentially utilized as standards for children with disabilities to copy. The teacher could then reward any attempts of these children to imitate age-appropriate developmental skills.

The philosophy and practice of special education is currently undergoing an upheaval due to the influence of the work of W. Edwards Deming, Thomas M. Skrtic, and, increasingly, the perspective of postmodernism. Each of these influences has caused special education professionals to think, reflect, and consider the nature of the assumptions and beliefs upon which their field is founded.

Deming's influence has been most profound in his focus on quality and emphasis on systems and systems thinking. For Deming, educational organizations are systems that must be understood before reform efforts can be successful. These systems are designed to produce a given product. In his "Experiment With the Red Beads," Deming demonstrated that inflexible systems in which change was superficial produced a consistent

rate of defective products (much like the persistent dropout rate in our schools). These defective products must either be discarded or repaired. From Deming's perspective, special education is a subsystem in the schools where "repair work" is done. However, Deming warns about the nature of repair work in that:

- Repair work is twice as costly as doing something right the first time.
- The proposed repairs are seldom accomplished.

This perspective and its associated problems well describe the nature of many special education programs and the outcomes for students with disabilities in our schools. Students with disabilities experience more academic and disciplinary problems than those without disabilities, they are more likely to be excluded from traditional educational programs and placements, and they are more likely to experience a wide range of social problems over the life span.

Skrtic has examined the nature of special education practice and philosophy within the context of school culture and organization via the framework of critical pragmatism. Skrtic holds that the critique of modern knowledge requires a reconsideration of the basic assumptions of the field of special education. Specifically, he questions whether special education itself is a rational system and is critical of the proposition that disabilities are usefully understood as pathological conditions. Skrtic further holds that the historical traditions that underpin the knowledge base in special education differ significantly from those that underpin elementary and secondary education. Rather than being an alternative program model for persons who possess disabilities, Skrtic holds that special education emerged primarily to contain and conceal the failures of conventional elementary and secondary education practice. In addition, should educational systems attempt to become more inclusive and democratic, an adhocracy or learning organization must necessarily develop. Professional culture and practice in special and general education would mirror the adhocracy's focus on innovation, personalization, and inclusion through collective problem solving. The adhocracy configuration is the inverse of the bureaucratic organizational structure of public schools, which focuses on the standardization of practice. Skrtic proposes the nonfoundational approach of critical pragmatism for dealing with the paradox of special education and establishing true personalization and innovation of practice in our education systems.

Much of Skrtic's work involves the contradiction between the contextual nature of disability and conventional special education practice and how the field's inclusive ideal is stymied by its own theory of knowledge and the manner in which schools are structured. A related perspective influencing special education, postmodernism, also relies on contextual understanding and how the social construction of knowledge influences professional philosophy and practice. The conflict in the profession of special education revolves around the challenge that postmodernism presents to its modern tenets. Many special education professionals fear that the postmodern perspective involves a rejection of those practices that have been validated as effective and that it represents a retreat from the scientific, empirical approach to disability studies. The postmodernists counter that this objectivist, functionalist approach is neither objective nor effective and that an alternative perspective that examines professional biases and conventional practices is necessary for the field to advance. This debate will inevitably continue and influence philosophy and practice in the field.

Currently, the field of special education is a prominent component of the public education system. The majority of the federal monies that are provided to the public schools are targeted for special education. As schools become more inclusive in nature, it is anticipated that the field will grow concurrently and that philosophy and practice will change to meet the new demands of educating all children in a unified system.

—*J. M. Blackbourn, James S. Payne,*
J. Larry Tyler, James Mann, and G. Franklin Elrod

See also behaviorism; child development theories; deaf education; Deming, W. Edwards; disabilities, of students; discipline in schools; discrimination; early childhood education; emotional disturbance; giftedness, gifted education; individual differences, in children; intelligence; learning, theories of; learning environments; mainstreaming and inclusion; mental illness, in adults and children; psychology, types of; parental involvement; performance assessment; psychometrics; resiliency; schooling effects; staffing, concepts of; state departments of education; tutoring; underachievers, in schools

Further Readings and References

Alley, G. R., & Deshler, D. (1979). *Teaching the learning disabled adolescent: Strategies and methods.* Denver, CO: Love.

Bartlett, L., Weisenstein, G., & Estcheidt, S. (2002). *Successful inclusion for educational leaders.* Upper Saddle River, NJ: Pearson.

Blackbourn, J., Patton, J., & Trainor, A. (2004). *Exceptional individuals in focus.* Columbus, OH: Merrill.

Blackbourn, J., Tyler, L., Vinson, T., Thomas, C., & Elrod, G. (1999). Social studies for students at risk for academic failure. *Journal of At-Risk Issues, 6*(1), 20–23.

Bloom, B. (1964). *Stability and change in human characteristics.* New York: Wiley.

Caldwell, B. (1970). The rationale for early intervention. *Exceptional Children, 36,* 717–726.

Deming, W. (1993). *The new economics for industry, government, and education.* Cambridge: MIT Center for Advanced Engineering Study.

Hunt, J. (1966). *Intelligence and experience.* New York: Ronald Press.

Skeels, H. (1942). A study of the effect of differential stimulation on mentally retarded children: A follow-up report. *American Journal of Mental Deficiency, 46,* 340–350.

Skeels, H. (1966). Adult status of children with contrasting early life experiences: A follow-up study. *Monographs of the Society for Research on Child Development, 31*(3, Serial No. 105).

Skeels, H., & Dye, H. (1939). A study of the effects of differential stimulation on mentally retarded children. *Proceedings and Addresses of the American Association on Mental Deficiency, 44*(1), 114–136.

Sitlington, P. L., Clark, G., & Kolstoe, O. (2000). *Transition education and services for adolescents with disabilities* (3rd ed.). Boston: Allyn & Bacon.

Skrtic, T. (1991). *Behind special education: A critical analysis of professional culture and school organization.* Denver, CO: Love.

Skrtic, T. (1991). The special education paradox: Equity as the way to excellence. *Harvard Educational Review, 61*(2), 148–207.

Skrtic, T. (1995). *Disability and democracy: Reconstructing (special) education for postmodernity.* New York: Teachers College Press.

U.S. Department of Health, Education, and Welfare. (1969). *The six-hour retarded child.* Washington, DC: U.S. Government Printing Office.

Wolfensberger, W. (1972). *The principle of normalization in human services.* Toronto, Canada: National Institute on Mental Retardation.

SPENCER, HERBERT

A pioneering English sociologist and popularizer in the United States of Social Darwinism, Herbert Spencer's principal contribution to education came in his influential 1860 book, *Education: Intellectual,*

Moral, and Physical, in which he coined the curriculum question, "What knowledge is of most worth?" and proposed categories of life activity that comprised the sources of educational objectives. Born in Derby, England, Spencer (1820–1903) received his elementary education at home and at day school. His secondary education involved study mostly of scientific, mathematical, and political subjects with little attention to foreign languages or the classics. Spencer received no university education. Upon completing his formal education, Spencer became a civil engineer for the railway, a position he held until 1846. After a disillusioning stint in radical politics, Spencer tried his hand at inventing and at journalism, the latter including work on the staff of *The Economist,* before becoming a freelance writer. His major works include *Social Statics* (1851) and *Synthetic Philosophy* (9 volumes, 1862–1896). After 1860, book sales provided him financial independence. Despite his prolific intellectual work, Spencer had no university affiliation.

Well-known tenets of Spencer's educational thought include a critique of academic formalism or "ornamentation"; an emphasis on education as practical preparation for life; the five categories of life activity (personal health, making a living, child rearing, citizenship, leisure); the importance of science, as both knowledge and method, in the curriculum; and the now famous curriculum question, "What knowledge is of most worth?" Spencer's educational thought, however, is best understood in the context of his Social Darwinism. Spencer argued, for example, that because the development of mind follows the inexorably slow evolutionary process, education can only help humans adapt to existing circumstances and that, therefore, formal education can never significantly impact human progress. In addition, Spencer adamantly opposed state-supported schooling on the grounds that it fostered conformity, encouraged unquestioning acceptance of authority, smacked of totalitarianism, unjustifiably separated taxpayers from their property, and, by supporting those who cannot afford formal education on their own, undermined natural selection. Instead, Spencer supported private education.

What influence did Spencer's educational thought have in the United States? Some American educators derived ideas from Spencer in ways consistent with his original work. William Graham Sumner, for example, favored electives and science as components of the curriculum, doubted the possibility of social progress through education, and opposed public secondary and higher education. Similarly, David Snedden conceived of education as a matter of fitting students into extant social and economic circumstances. Other American educators departed significantly from Spencer's social and educational theory. Both Lester Ward and John Dewey held that unlike the rest of the natural world, humans benefited from the ability to control the environment through the exercise of intelligence and that therefore education, especially publicly supported schools, should function as a vehicle of human progress and social improvement. Policy proposals, as well, both derived and departed from Spencer's theory. The 1893 Committee of Ten report restricted secondary education to a select few adolescents and accorded science parity with literary subjects, but embraced subject matter for its disciplinary, not its practical, value. The 1918 report of the Commission on the Reorganization of Secondary Education favored a practical preparation for life and categorized educational aims into areas of life activity much like those proposed by Spencer but, unlike Spencer, endorsed universal state-supported secondary education as a means of individual and social growth.

—William G. Wraga

See also curriculum, theories of; philosophies of education

Further Readings and References

Cremin, L. (1962). *The transformation of the school: Progressivism in American education, 1876–1957.* New York: Knopf.

Egan, K. (2002). *Getting it wrong from the beginning: Our progressivist inheritance from Herbert Spencer, John Dewey and Jean Piaget.* New Haven, CT: Yale University Press.

Peel, J. (1978). *The social and political thought of Herbert Spencer.* Oxford: Oxford University Press.

STAFFING, CONCEPTS OF

Arguably the most important administrative task accorded to educational leaders and administrators is staffing schools and school districts with the qualified teachers, administrators, and support staff required to deliver a quality educational program. Stated another way, staffing is the process whereby organizations acquire the human talent needed to accomplish the organization's goals and mission. Staffing includes two subprocesses that overlap to a considerable degree: recruitment and selection. Recruitment encompasses all activities conducted by the organization to generate initial pools of qualified applicants for position vacancies. Selection includes those activities used by the organization to reduce a pool of applicants down to a group of highly qualified finalists and, ultimately, the preferred job candidate who will receive a formal job offer.

Although staffing potentially impacts virtually every aspect of school and school district operations—from instruction in the classroom to leadership at the school and school district levels—many individuals charged with carrying out the staffing function operate under two false assumptions. The first false assumption is that qualified applicants for position vacancies will always be available in sufficient numbers. With respect to the supply of qualified educational personnel, the United States entered the twenty-first century with a well-documented shortage of classroom teachers and a less-well-understood emerging shortage of qualified applicants for administrator positions, especially the position of school principal. Retirements among the post–World War II baby boom generation are resulting in large numbers of position vacancies of all types, and this trend will continue for the foreseeable future. With respect to the supply of teachers, researchers such as Richard Ingersoll note that a teacher retention problem also exists as a long-term staffing trend and is exacerbating the already-critical teacher shortage. Teachers in very large numbers exit the profession within their first 5 years on the job, thus contributing to a shortage of qualified classroom instructors. The shortage is especially acute in certain locations (e.g., inner city schools and small rural school districts) and in certain academic disciplines such as mathematics, science, foreign languages, and special education. Other researchers, such as Diana Pounder, note there may also be a shortage of qualified applicants for principal vacancies with the vast majority of individuals who are principal certified but not yet in the job, failing to apply for vacant positions, possibly because the job is too demanding and stressful in today's environment of high-stakes accountability and school reform. These trends suggest the supply of teachers and administrators is not ensured for decades to come and educational administrators will have to make a concerted effort to generate adequate pools of qualified applicants for position vacancies or lose in the competition to hire qualified educational personnel.

The second false assumption is that employees of the hiring organization are the sole decision makers in the staffing process. To the contrary, it is important for hiring organizations to realize staffing is a dual decision-making process, with both representatives of the hiring organization and job applicants making decisions regarding whether or not the staffing process will continue to a successful conclusion. People doing the hiring make the decisions to retain individuals in the applicant pool after initial screening, invite applicants to interview for the job, and make a job offer to the preferred job candidate.

However, simultaneous with the above organizational decision making, job applicants make decisions critical to successful staffing, such as the decisions to apply for the job, accept an interview for the position vacancy, and accept the job if offered. All organizational decisions and applicant decisions must be affirmative or the staffing process will fail. Educational personnel specialists are well-advised to adopt the above dual decision-making perspective, focused on applicant as well as organizational needs. Maurer and his associates articulated the perspective best in their formulation of recruitment-as-job-marketing theory. This theory posits staffing as being analogous to consumer product marketing. According to recruitment-as-job-marketing theory, the hiring organization (vendor) operates in a competitive labor market (product market) and offers jobs (products) to potential job applicants (customers) with the hope the finalist for a position vacancy will accept a job offer (purchase the product). The proponents of recruitment-as-job-marketing theory advise personnel administrators to embed the above perspective in staffing operations or risk the best job candidates opting out of the hiring process because the hiring organization's staffing practices are less attractive than those of other similar organizations competing for the services of the same labor pool.

In addition to the staffing philosophy schools and school districts adopt, there are other staffing factors—external and internal to the organization—to consider. As Herbert Heneman and his associates noted, external factors (e.g., economic conditions, labor markets, unions, employment law) impact staffing. Internal to the organization, educational administrators should manage staffing as an integral component of both long-term and short-term planning and strategy formulation. Technically, staffing involves analyzing the knowledge, skills, and abilities (KSAs) required for each educational position and specifying the identified

KSAs and associated job duties in formal job descriptions that will serve as the basis for subsequent hiring procedures. Further operational steps in the staffing process include establishing a manpower plan with measurable hiring objectives and creating the recruitment and selection programs and practices needed to accomplish the objectives specified.

Administrators performing staffing at the school and school district levels are most likely to succeed if they recognize, as noted earlier, staffing is a dual decision-making process, and develop recruitment practices (e.g., job postings, position advertisements, recruitment Web sites, recruitment brochures, recruitment videos, job fair interviews, central office interviews, school site interviews) that are attractive to potential job applicants and, therefore, maximally effective in generating adequate pools of qualified applicants. Only when an adequate applicant pool exists can the hiring organization implement subsequent selection practices (e.g., applicant file screening, selection interviews, job candidate site visits, formal job offers) that meet established staffing objectives.

—Paul Winter

See also administration, theories of; class size; collective bargaining; contracts, with teacher unions; enrollment projections; human resource development; job descriptions; leadership, teacher; loss of position (school principal); management theories; personnel management; principal succession; reduction in force; unions, of teachers

Further Readings and References

Heneman, H., Judge, T., & Heneman, R. (2000). *Staffing organizations* (3rd ed.). New York: Irwin McGraw-Hill.
Ingersoll, R. (2001). Teacher turnover and teacher shortages: An organizational analysis. *American Educational Research Journal, 37,* 499–534.
Maurer, S., Howe, V., & Lee, T. (1992). Organizational recruiting as marketing management: An interdisciplinary study of engineering graduates. *Personnel Psychology, 45,* 807–833.
Pounder, D., & Merrill, R. (2001). Job desirability of the high school principalship: A job choice theory perspective. *Educational Administration Quarterly, 37,* 27–57.
Pounder, D., & Young, I. (1996). Recruitment and selection of educational administrators: Priorities for today's schools. In K. Leithwood (Ed.) & A. W. Hart (Section Ed.), *The international handbook of educational leadership* (pp. 279–308). Netherlands: Kluwer.
Winter, P. (1996). Recruiting experienced educators: A model and a test. *Journal of Research and Development in Education, 29,* 163–171.
Winter, P. (1997). Educational recruitment and selection: A review of recent studies and recommendations for best practice. In L. Wildman (Ed.), *Fifth NCPEA yearbook* (pp. 133–140). Lancaster, PA: Technomic.
Young, I., & Castetter, W. (2004). *The human Resource function in educational administration* (8th ed.). Upper Saddle River, NJ: Merrill.

STANDARD SETTING

The quest to set educational standards has become ubiquitous in North America and abroad. In many jurisdictions, ambitious standards have been set for student achievement, school effectiveness, teacher professionalism, and administrator competence. In jurisdictions where such standards are not yet in place, the standard-setting agenda is being moved forward expeditiously, often in order to comply with legislated requirements. As the movement to set educational standards gains traction and momentum, a spirited and an increasingly partisan debate has grown in both scholarly and practitioner journals as well as in the popular press. The participants in this debate include those who would make existing standards still more encompassing and consequential, researchers who seek to understand the many and sometimes unintended effects that standards have had, and those who aggressively dispute both the content of and the benefits claimed for educational standards.

Despite this debate, the movement to set and enforce standards appears entrenched in the mood of the times. The arguable but seemingly widely held view that the educational enterprise is both lacking in accountability and facing a crisis in quality has heightened the hope that standard setting will restore responsibility and purpose to the public schools. A brief review of the origin and development of concerns with educational accountability and quality permits a fuller appreciation of how each has contributed to the current appetite for standard setting.

A primary source of the perception that education is not sufficiently accountable to its many and diverse publics is the distance that citizens feel separates them from the once familiar institution of the school. With the industrialization, urbanization, and globalization emblematic of the twentieth century, the locally governed and consensually administered community schoolhouse has been replaced by multifaceted, organizationally unwieldy, and, to an increasingly wary lay public, remote institutions made both inscrutable and impenetrable by the adoption of bureaucratic structures and practices. In the opinion of many, public education has steadily become less public and more the domain of professional insiders, putative experts, and self-serving interests. As the educational enterprise becomes vaster, costly, and complex, an intensifying sense of estrangement threatens the trust, transparency, and respect traditionally associated with the neighborhood school. Such an environment makes understandable the broadly shared desire for a renewal of educational accountability to be achieved through the setting of clear and objective standards.

The wish to make schooling a more publicly comprehensible venture is given added urgency by the perception that educational quality has eroded significantly and that this erosion has had a deleterious effect upon national security and prosperity. When international events and economic worries have called national confidence into question, the adequacy of existing educational institutions and practices has routinely been challenged. The emblematic historical event that cemented the relationship between national security and educational practices was the October 1957 launch of the satellite Sputnik by the Union of Soviet Socialist Republics.

The successful launching of Sputnik propelled modern western nations, most consequentially the United States, into a period of existential uncertainty and educational doubt. The national security threat posed by a technologically superior and inimical superpower was widely interpreted as both a critique of and a challenge to American education. Accordingly, a prominent aspect of President Eisenhower's response to Sputnik was educational. The National Defense Education Act, which would direct more than a billion federal dollars into support for higher education, was signed into law, and additional federal monies were provided for the revamping of mathematics, science, and language programs in America's schools.

A similar shock to national well-being and hence to educational sufficiency would be delivered by the emergence of once economically dependent nations as full-fledged, robust, and innovative global economic competitors. The transformation of Germany and Japan from nations vanquished in World War II into industrial powerhouses capable of challenging the economic hegemony of the United States inaugurated a period of prolonged national consternation. This malaise continues as still other nations previously

regarded as marginal test America's economic mettle with increasing success. The suspected linkage between a worsening economic situation and a decline in academic quality has been buttressed in the popular imagination by equally troubling educational news.

In the United States and Canada, challenges to both national complacency and economic prosperity have been sharpened by seemingly unremitting comparisons of educational achievement in which North American students fare less well than many of their international counterparts. But unflattering international rankings—especially in math and science test comparisons—were not the only source of unsettling news concerning educational achievement. In the United States, a precipitous drop in scores on the Scholastic Aptitude Test over three decades, beginning in the 1960s, raised new doubts concerning the caliber of the best and the brightest who were destined for higher education. The National Assessment of Education Progress test funded by the federal government indicated not only that these declines were real but also that they extended downward in the K–12 system.

The cumulative sense that schools had fallen out of touch with public sentiment and that they had failed to adequately fuel national ambitions, and the growing suspicion that they were performing poorly led to widespread calls for educational accountability. Perhaps the most notable, visible, and galvanizing of these calls was contained in *A Nation At Risk: The Imperative for Educational Reform,* the 1983 report of the National Commission on Excellence in Education—a commission appointed by President Ronald Reagan's Secretary of Education, T. H. Bell. Created because of Bell's sensitivity to the widespread public perception that something was remiss in the nation's educational system, the commission would among its many recommendations call for a national system of standardized student achievement tests, more rigorous college and university admissions standards, and academic and aptitudinal competency standards for those who would teach in the nation's schools. Key recommendations of the commissioners thus underscored the practical utility of translating a growing sense of apprehension about educational accountability and quality into a call for setting educational standards.

Perhaps ironically, the educational community's time-honored penchant for self-criticism would fortify the push for standard setting. The literature of deschooling, which unabashedly argued and continues to argue that schooling practices inevitably retard the development of the educated person, became surprisingly popular among those most suspicious of educational institutions and the interests that control them. Another impassioned, if arguably misguided, critique of education came in the form of Alan Bloom's book *The Closing of the American Mind,* published in 1987. The fact that Bloom's book would be republished in a mass market paperback edition within a year, bearing the subtitle *How Higher Education Has Failed Democracy and Impoverished the Souls of Today's Students,* is an index of how widespread and dour public disillusionment with education had become.

Also published in 1987, E. D. Hirsch's book *Cultural Literacy: What Every American Needs to Know* became a beacon, particularly for parents who felt that the educational system had replaced curricular specificity with obscurantist rhetoric. In addition to enumerating specifically what the culturally literate citizen should know, Hirsch linked possession of this knowledge to a larger agenda that included social equity, community building, and raising the quality of national life. Sharply critical of what he regarded as the laissez-faire attitude progressivists had taken toward content learning, Hirsch concluded his book with an abundant and unambiguous list of items that constituted the core knowledge with which culturally literate Americans should be conversant. Hirsch had not only advocated educational standards; many felt that he had also provided a convincing demonstration of how standards could be sensibly and expeditiously set.

The movement to make standards the preferred medium through which educational accountability could be realized and educational quality ensured gained political momentum in the United States through the work of the National Governors Association. The association's 1986 calls for accountability would be moved forward into the 1990s by the administration of President George H. W. Bush, which called upon states to voluntarily set standards and measures for educational achievement. President Clinton, who as governor of Arkansas had been a key advocate for setting measurable educational goals, extended the Bush initiative by signing 1994 legislation that compelled states to set standards and to create the means through which progress toward their accomplishment could be monitored. Although compliance was uneven, the agenda to achieve educational accountability and quality through standard setting evoked public support and, therefore, had become politically advantageous.

Figuring prominently in the 2000 presidential elections, the growing public desire to achieve educational accountability and quality led President George W. Bush to champion the No Child Left Behind Act (NCLB), which received bipartisan support. Under Bush's signature and with Democratic support rallied by Edward Kennedy, the self-identified liberal senior senator from Massachusetts, NCLB would become law in January 2002, less than 4 months after the nationally unnerving terrorist attacks of September 11, 2001. Once again, in a time of national crisis, attention would be focused on America's schools.

Incorporating the argument set out by Hirsch that standards can be effective tools for achieving equity and social justice, the NCLB legislation challenged the nation's schools to deliver a comprehensive education to all students. The quality of this delivery would be monitored by a regimen of annual standardized tests beginning in Grade 3. Aggregated test results would be translated into a public ranking of individual schools, and those students who found they were attending a poorly performing school would have the right to transfer to a school that was either meeting or exceeding standards for student achievement. Schools that perform poorly over a 5-year period are subject to district determined restructuring. By transforming tests of individual student achievement into measures of school effectiveness, NCLB had made schools rather than students the primary focus of standard setting and assessment.

Although how standards are to be set and enforced remain points of contention, there is a still larger and arguably more significant set of questions concerning how standards will be used and the purposes standards will serve. Regardless of whether the standards that would advance educational accountability and quality are to be applied to people or to institutions, the question of how standards are to be used remains largely unanswered and vexing. But when standards are used exclusively to identify and discipline poorly performing students, teachers, and schools, they may not only do little to advance improvement, they may also speed decline and inequity, not to mention iniquity.

Like all criteria and measures, standards and the assessments they engender are thoroughly human and hence fallible conventions that have significant individual and institutional impact. If standards are to be an aid to authentic educational improvement, their ultimate uses as well as their content, immediate applications, and actual effects demand continuous, careful, and pragmatic documentation and analysis.

The considerable energies that are being devoted to the many ongoing arguments about the crafting and application of standards for academic achievement leave largely unaddressed thornier questions concerning broader issues of educational purpose. The assumption that students, teachers, and schools are to be measured solely by intellectual accomplishment disregards the fact that schools simultaneously serve multiple and not infrequently contradictory purposes. In 1986, Charles Perrow provided a pointed reminder that confusion of purpose, whether intentional or inadvertent, can stymie the setting of standards that are genuinely useful: because to establish standards one had to know the *real* goals of the organization. The struggle to articulate the goals of real schools that exist in specific places and are peopled by diverse and self-directed individuals is an inexorably messy, conflicted, and interminable process. It is understandable, then, that the promise of standard setting to bring final and definitive resolution to what is necessarily a complex, incessant, and exacting struggle concerning educational purpose is as tempting as it may be misleading.

Finally, the standard setting movement invites the criticism that education is once again making the mistake of turning too much to industry for models and ideologies of practice and administration. With some updating, Raymond Callahan's classic and unrelenting critique of the educational administrators who in the early years of the twentieth century looked to business practices, particularly to Frederick Winslow Taylor's scientific management, speaks critically to the contemporary project to set educational standards. Perhaps Callahan would not be surprised that a number of American schools have sought and received certification as ISO 9000 organizations—organizations that prize quality achieved through uniformity of product and define accountability as customer satisfaction secured through managerial control of process—by the industrially focused International Organization for Standardization. Education, as Christopher Hodgkinson argues, may ultimately and appropriately share very little with its industrial neighbors who possess unambiguous technologies and who exercise tight control over inputs, outputs, and employees.

To see mystery embodied in thoroughly human beings as a virtue that distinguishes the school from other organizational types is not to dismiss the quest for accountability and quality. It is, on the contrary, to see this quest as inflected by the particular characteristics and values of the school that give unique context and existential significance to the current debate on standard setting. The press to develop standards through which experience and outcomes would be rationalized and regulated may ultimately matter less than the opportunity presented by the current debate about standard setting to reconsider what citizens can reasonably expect of their educational institutions and what these institutions can reasonably expect of citizens. If the attempt to set comprehensive educational standards does nothing more than to motivate an informed and often deferred conversation about educational purpose and collective social aspirations, it will be an issue that has nudged education forward.

—*Martin Barlosky*

See also accountability; achievement tests; curriculum, theories of; educational equity; expectations, teacher and student cultures; goals, goal setting; learning environments; measurement, theories of; *A Nation at Risk;* National Assessment of Educational Progress; No Child Left Behind; performance assessment; philosophies of education; psychometrics; Scholastic Aptitude Test; standardized testing; testing and test theory development

Further Readings and References

Barlosky, M. (2003). In search of leadership standards: Quest or quagmire? Some philosophical and practical reflections. *Leadership and Policy in Schools, 2*(1), 47–64.

Barth, R.(2001). *Learning by heart.* San Francisco: Jossey-Bass.

Bloom, A. (1988). *The closing of the American mind: How higher education has failed democracy and impoverished the souls of today's students.* New York: Simon & Schuster.

Callahan, R. (1962). *Education and the cult of efficiency.* Chicago: University of Chicago Press.

English, F. (2003). Cookie-cutter leaders for cookie-cutter schools: The teleology of standardization and the de-legitimization of the university in educational leadership programs. *Leadership and policy in schools, 2*(1), 27–46.

Hirsch, E. (1988). *Cultural literacy: what every American needs to know.* New York: Vintage.

Hirsch, E. (1996). *The schools we need and why we don't have them.* New York: Doubleday.

Horne, R. (2004). *Standards primer.* New York: Peter Lang.

International Organization for Standardization. (2004). *Introduction.* Retrieved August 1, 2004, from http://www.iso.org/iso/en/aboutiso/introduction/index.html

National Commission on Excellence in Education. (1983). *A nation at risk: The imperative for educational reform.* Washington, DC: U.S. Department of Education. Retrieved August 1, 2004, from http://www.ed.gov/pubs/NatAtRisk/intro.html

National Defense Education Act. (2001). *Columbia Encyclopedia* (6th ed.). New York: Columbia University

Press. Retrieved July 1, 2004, from http://www.bartleby
.com/65/na/NatlDefe.html

Perrow, C. (1986). *Complex organizations: A critical essay.* New York: Random House.

Popham, J. (2005). *America's "failing" schools.* New York: Routledge.

Schrag, P. (2003). *Final test: The battle for adequacy in America's schools.* New York: New Press.

Stein, S. (2004). *The culture of education policy.* New York: Teachers College Press.

U.S. Department of Education. (2002). *No Child Left Behind Act of 2001.* Retrieved June 1, 2004, from http://www.ed
.gov/policy/elsec/leg/esea02/index.html

STANDARDIZED TESTING

A standardized test uses certain procedures to reduce errors of measurement. It is usually developed by a group of content experts and psychometricians. The former's responsibility is to ensure that the test items adequately sample important content areas of the subject tested. The latter's work is to select items with the appropriate difficulty and discrimination levels. The experts and psychometricians also work together to avoid item bias or test bias. A standardized test also uses standardization to reduce errors during the test administration and scoring processes. Standardization of test administration includes the use of uniform testing time, procedures, and testing environment. People responsible for test administration usually go through special training to ensure the uniformity of the administration process, a prerequisite for the fair comparison of test scores. Standardized tests also use machines for scoring objective items such as multiple-choice questions. For subjective items such as essay questions, special training is used to ensure an adequate degree of agreement between different raters rating the same items. The training also helps a scorer to apply the scoring rubrics in a consistent way during the scoring period.

TYPES OF STANDARDIZED TESTS

A standardized test is often norm referenced. In other words, the purpose of a standardized test is to compare student test performance to that of a representative student group, or the norm. Students in the norm group are selected based on their demographic background and academic status. Every few years, the norm group is updated so that the results of the representative group are kept current and meaningful. Comparison of student test results against the norm is usually accomplished through the use of standardized test scores. One norm-referenced test score is the percentile rank, which stands for the percentage of students a student outperforms in the norm group. Standardization is considered imperative when there is a need to make comparison of student performance against the norm. The counterpart of a norm-referenced test is a criterion-referenced test. Instead of comparing student performance against other students, a criterion-referenced test uses external criteria or standards as the point of reference, usually local or national performance standards. A more recent term for this type of test is *standards-based assessment.* To facilitate the understanding of test scores, different performance levels are designed that correspond to different ranges of scale scores. For instance, students who answer most of the items on a subject test correctly will receive very high scale scores; they also receive an "Excellent" score in terms of their performance level. On the other hand, students who answer a minimal yet an acceptable number of items may receive a barely passing scale score, hence a "Basic" score in terms of performance level. It is possible for a test to be both norm referenced and criterion referenced. For instance, most statewide tests that are being used serve both the purpose of comparing students against each other and comparing their performance against state performance standards.

Standardized tests may also be divided into achievement tests and aptitude tests. The former is an assessment of what students have learned or achieved over a period of time, while the latter is a measure of students' potential for future success in academic achievement. It is possible, however, for an achievement test to be used as a measure to predict student future performance. For instance, the subject tests of the Scholastic Achievement Tests (SAT) measure what students have learned in a number of key subject areas. The tests are used to predict if students will succeed in future studies in those areas. On the other hand, the SAT Reasoning Test is an aptitude test that is used to measure student future success in college. Related to aptitude test is the intelligence test, a test used in and outside of education to measure a person's mental ability in general as well as specific areas. One example is the Wechsler Intelligence Scale for Children (WISC).

HISTORY

The history of standardized testing may be traced back to the Chinese civil service testing that started more than 2,000 years ago, when certain standardization procedures were regularly used in test administration and scoring. The pioneering work of modern testing occurred in the late 1800s, when the emergence of laboratory or experimental psychology opened a new venue to measurement. Interest in human intelligence was on the rise at the time, due to the need to differentiate an increasing number of students in terms of their academic potential and the need to differentiate people for clinical or employment purposes. The first formal testing was made possible by the publication in 1905 of the Binet-Simon scales of mental ability, a joint effort of Alfred Binet and Théophile Simon. In 1916, the test was revised by Lewis Terman of Stanford University to become the first American intelligence test, the Stanford-Binet Intelligence Scale, whose fourth edition is widely used today. Around the same time, Charles Spearman made significant contributions to the field of measurement by his theory of measurement error and reliability and the theory of general intelligence. World War I brought a period of significant advancement in measurement in the United States, where a number of psychologists worked in the army to develop measurements for military purposes. This period saw the first large-scale testing instruments, such as the Army Alpha, used for the measurement of a person's verbal ability. During and after the war, the instruments that were developed measured aspects of human behavior such as verbal and nonverbal ability, personality, attitudes, and values. The early 1920s saw the birth of the first major instrument to measure academic achievement, the Stanford Achievement Test. The Wechsler-Bellevue Intelligence Scale, another major intelligence test, came into being in the 1930s. Around the same time, Louis L. Thurston refined factor analysis, a statistical procedure originally developed by Charles Spearman, and developed the theory of multiple intelligences. Thurston's work helped to bring about the emergence of a large number of instruments during World War II for the measurement of distinct mental abilities related to military services. The cognitive taxonomy developed by Bloom and his colleagues in the 1950s furthered the efforts at measuring a variety of human ability and personality. This was a time when assessment in psychology and education became widespread and testing became a big business. It was also a time when people became aware of potential inappropriate use of tests and the impact of such uses on the society. The late 1960s and early 1970s saw the birth of the National Assessment of Educational Progress (NAEP), a federal attempt at measuring student achievement and progress across the nation. The release of the report *A Nation at Risk* in the 1980s spurred a nationwide effort to increase accountability in the nation's education system. A direct result of the public expectation for educational accountability was the movement toward more challenging academic standards and the development of standardized tests to measure outcomes against those standards. The 1990s saw a spread of state developed high-stakes assessments across the nation. Around the same period, developments in computer technology and modern measurement methods, such as item response theory, made possible computer adaptive testing (CAT), which adapts a test to the examinee's specific performance level. Along with CAT, alternative forms of assessment that used few objective items came into existence, including performance assessment and portfolio assessment. Another development in the 1990s is the increasing use of alternative assessment format for students with disabilities. The No Child Left Behind Act (NCLB) represented a recent commitment at the federal level in educational accountability. It is expected that standardized testing at both the national and state levels will continue to grow in scope.

USE

Standardized tests are used widely in education. As mandated by NCLB, every state has a testing program in place to measure student achievement and progress in important content areas. Student test results often form the basis for government agencies and the public to determine the effectiveness of a school system. NCLB has set up very specific criteria in terms of achievement and progress a school needs to make within a given period. Schools that fail to perform adequately or make sufficient progress within a period may be required to go through restructuring. Teachers and principals are often evaluated by the results of state-mandated tests. Poor test results may cause teachers or principals to lose their jobs. For the students, state test results become the primary basis for decisions in program placement, grade promotion, or graduation from high school. The NAEP is used both at the national level and more recently at the state level to monitor student achievement and progress. What is unique about the program is that results are reported for individual students. As a result, neither students nor teachers are held directly accountable for unfavorable test results. Aside from being used for accountability purposes, a standardized test such as a statewide test may be used by teachers for instructional improvement purposes. Some of the well-known commercial tests may be used by a school district specifically for this kind of purpose. The results of such tests enable teachers to compare their students' achievement to that of the nation. At the same time, the tests yield specific diagnostic information in terms of the strengths and weaknesses of the students in different content strands of a subject area. There are also standardized tests particularly designed for determining the eligibility of a student for more advanced studies. The American College Test (ACT) and the Scholastic Aptitude Test (SAT), for example, are both used as college entrance exams that assess the potential of high school graduates to succeed in college. Standardized tests may also be used as a basis for awarding diploma or licensure. For instance, many states have currently in place a high school exit exam, the result of which is used as the sole basis for awarding the high school diploma to a senior. The General Educational Development (GED) testing program is a standardized test used to provide adults with an opportunity to receive an alternative high school diploma. In the teaching profession, the Praxis series are used to determine if a student is eligible to enter a teacher education program or the teaching profession.

While most tests are administered to groups of students, there are also individually administered standardized tests that are used for a variety of purposes. For instance, the Wechsler Individual Achievement Test is a standardized achievement test that is administered individually to students. The Wechsler Intelligence Scale, on the other hand, is an individually administered intelligence test. These tests are particularly useful when there is a need to test only a few students in a school, especially to identify a small number of students who have difficulty in their learning or students who may be eligible for placement in gifted/talented programs.

Despite the wide use of standardized tests, there are various kinds of criticisms toward such tests. One criticism often directed at national standardized tests is the irrelevance of the standards to the local schools.

Because of the diversity across the nation in terms of content standards, it is a real challenge for a national standardized test to use items that cover every state or district's standards. A second criticism is about the inappropriate use of statewide test results. Some of the decisions that are made based on test results are, according to the critics, not justified. Should teachers be responsible for the failure of their students to meet certain achievement goals? There are more factors involved that affect student achievement than just teaching. Another criticism directed at standardized tests is their overuse of multiple-choice questions that often test lower levels of cognitive learning. Such use also encourages teachers to teach to the test rather than helping them focus on the important instructional objectives. Although attempts are being made to include more performance-based items, it seems more effort is needed in this area so that the test can reflect a student's real academic performance.

—*Yuankun Yao*

See also accountability; at-risk students; Binet, Alfred; Cattell, Raymond; diversity; Education Testing Service; individual differences, in children; intelligence; item response theory; literacy, theories of; minorities, in schools; multiculturalism; National Assessment of Educational Progress; No Child Left Behind; performance assessment; productivity; psychology, types of; psychometrics; quantitative research methods; Spearman, Charles; testing and test theory development; underachievers, in schools

Further Readings and References

Cohen, R. J., & Swerdlik, M. E. (2002). *Psychological testing and assessment: An introduction to tests and measurement.* Monterey, CA: CTB/McGraw-Hill.

Haladyna, T. (2002). *Essentials of standardized achievement testing.* Boston: Allyn & Bacon.

Jones, L. V., & Olkin, I. (2004). *The nation's report card: Evolution and perspectives.* Bloomington, IN: Phi Delta Kappa Education Foundation.

Linn, R. (2000, March). Assessments and accountability. *Educational Researcher, 29*(2), 4–16.

Phelps, R. (Ed.). (2005). *Defending standardized testing.* Mahwah, NJ: Lawrence Erlbaum.

Popham, W. J. (2002). *Classroom assessment: What teachers need to know.* Boston: Allyn & Bacon.

Spearman, C. E. (1904). General intelligence objectively determined and measured. *The American Journal of Psychology, 2,* 201–293.

Yeh, S. (2001). Tests worth teaching to: Constructing state-mandated tests that emphasize critical thinking. *Educational Researcher, 30*(9), 2–11.

⚏ STATE DEPARTMENTS OF EDUCATION

The state department of education is the major state agency responsible for the overall planning, delivery, and evaluation of educational programs and services. It typically operates under the direction of either the governor or a state board of education, which, in turn, appoints a chief state school officer to administer the agency. In 14 states, the chief state school officer is elected directly by the population.

The large majority of the states' departments of education use that same nomenclature to designate the agency, but some state departments may also be referred to by any number of related titles: state board of education (e.g., Illinois), department of public instruction (e.g., North Carolina, Wisconsin), or some other name (e.g., Utah State Office of Education, Minnesota Department of Children, Families, and Learning). Certain states (e.g., Missouri, Tennessee) draw a special distinction between the state department of education as the *agency* that administers education policy and the state board of education as the *governmental body* that oversees that agency.

The traditional function of the early state departments of education was fairly innocuous, limited to the collection and dissemination of education statistics. More recently, however, state departments have had to grow in scope and function to include such responsibilities as accrediting schools, certifying teachers, allocating funds, monitoring compliance with state and federal laws, and conducting research. By reason of this expansion of their duties, the aggregate number of employees of the 50 state education departments has risen over the past years, with some agencies employing in the thousands.

In their history of modern school reform, the influence of the state education agency has declined over the past 50 years. In the post-Sputnik era from the late 1950s through the early 1970s, the state agency and the chief school officer played a dominant role in shaping public education policy. However, starting in the 1980s and continuing through to the present, other groups—including governors, business leaders, the media, and federal policy makers—have staked their own claims in driving the educational reform movement.

Still, the role of the state department of education remains an important one in the American system of public school governance. While their prominence in providing direction for the reform movement may have waned over the past two decades, their leadership for reform implementation is crucial. That education remains primarily a state function under the reserved-powers clause of the U.S. Constitution (the varied interests driving reform efforts have tended to coalesce at the state level) and federal involvement in education—indeed, from the 1981 Education Consolidation and Improvement Act up through the No Child Left Behind Act passed in 2002—are all factors that present states with a broad number of options in determining how to spend education funds. For these reasons and others, state departments of education will continue as key players in educational governance and reform.

State departments of education in particular and state systems of education in general have evolved in incremental fashion as the result of a variety of constitutional and legislative provisions in each of the states. The constitutions of the newly formed states from the first half of the nineteenth century were reflective of a changing philosophy of the citizenry toward education. There was a growing recognition of the need for public schooling, and the nascent state constitutions served to push that endeavor from a private or religious matter toward a state system of education. State school codes then developed progressively in the state legislatures, leading to variation across state systems, differences often due to economic and population differences between the states and the regions.

The first superintendency in the United States was at the state level in New York in 1812. A similar process followed in other states—albeit with some interruptions in the continuity of the office for about half of the states—to the point that nearly all states had some state department in place by 1880. State boards came into prominence on the heels of the early state superintendents—Massachusetts being the first in 1837—and neither were given any significant power. (According to Harry Gehman Good, Americans in those days still recalled the memory of the tyranny of George III and disdained all executive power, whether wielded by the governor or the lowly school superintendent of the state.)

In these early superintendencies, the modern state department of education had its origins. But from those distant beginnings, the historical tradition of the state agency having relatively little political power or influence has remained. In their six-state study of educational policy elites, Catherine Marshall, Douglas Mitchell, and Frederick Wirt ranked 18 policy influencers, finding surprising consistency in the composite ranking of the states. They displayed their findings as concentric circles of influence, with the following labels: Insiders, Near Circle, Far Circle, and Forgotten Players.

The Insiders shared constitutional authority in making laws, while the Near Circle consisted largely of school professional organizations. The Far Circle group was viewed as having some influence on certain topics or issues but was not seen as vital to educational policy making in the states. Of the four actors in the Far Circle, the state board/state department of education was most prominent. Others have observed that they are only marginal policy actors in the educational arena. This regularity in the low standing of the policy impact of the state agency speaks to the residual effect of their founding and history.

Today, every state has a department of education, and any differences in power and focus among the agencies themselves have moderated significantly from their early days, in part due to the common challenges that all states have been required to address. While some state departments exercised strict and explicit control over local schools early on, others (notably in the plains and across the South) allowed the locality to exercise broad discretion in providing education to its children. Though vestiges of those differences remain, the fact that all states must now deal with policy problems such as desegregation, special education, financial distress, and the like have made their departments of education more alike than different.

In that sense, certain fundamental problems are shared by state departments of education as they go about the business of implementing state education policy goals and programs. Shifting expectations exist for state departments of education as continuing demands for reform, especially in the form of heightened academic standards and erasing the achievement gap, place burdens on them that their traditional operating style has difficulty addressing. This circumstance has led to calls for a reframed leadership from the state education agency and recommendations for improvement in policy implementation and program delivery.

Reform measures centered within or emanating from the state department of education will not likely be viewed as meaningful at the school district level unless they are responsive to local needs and within the capacity of the local school district to successfully carry out. Ignoring local school district context is not an effective strategy for state departments of education to utilize in implementing systemic reform initiatives. Rather than employing a unitary response pattern, local school districts make sense of state education department-initiated change in vastly different ways.

James Spillane's study of local educational practice and state instructional policy illustrates that local policy-making initiatives can actually undermine a state's systemic reform strategy. As more robust and coherent policies and practices are established at the state level in support of ambitious reform outcomes, more occasions are therein provided for school district policy making, especially in states where there is a strong history of local control. Because local policy making is inherently more responsive to local district context, capacity for reform at the district level often surpasses that of the state education agency.

To counter these difficulties, it is increasingly recognized that state departments of education need to revise their missions and structures if they are to have any relevance for school reform and improvement. An examination of the organizational charts of many of the state education agencies shows they have frequently been organized around the administration of discrete programs and the disbursement of their funding; likewise, the department's mission was primarily to ensure that program budget amounts were expended and services were delivered. In the view of Wirt and Michael Kirst, the fundamental problem of state departments of education is that they have been organized around their many categorical grant programs but that new educational quality standards will require a "cross-cutting" integration that links teaching, learning, management, funding, and assessment.

Overall, the organizational structure of the state departments has been focused around budgets, audits, and program compliance. The modern evolution of state departments of education around program grants has created agencies characterized by organization "silos" and a concomitant system of processes and procedures that support a narrow view of each of the program areas.

The evolutionary development of state departments of education will need to encourage cross-program and cross-organizational analysis and response. This may force a reconsideration of the mission and goals of the state agencies in ways that will increase a department's flexibility in accommodating local school district needs and state policymakers' demands in meaningful ways. The current structure of the typical state department, which is presently customized tightly around its various program areas, will likely require the development of new service delivery models that can meet the needs of the particular accountability mandates within a state.

Toward this end over the past decade, about 30 state departments of education have looked at some sort of restructuring to foster innovation and better address large policy goals (e.g., reducing the achievement gap) as opposed to individual program outcomes (e.g., Title I reading scores). The actions of a number of state departments of education in particular are illustrative of this transition to a new way of doing business for these agencies.

The Kentucky Department of Education was abolished and reconstituted as part of the Kentucky Education Reform Act. Texas repealed a third of its state education code and restructured its state department around six broad functions. Minnesota abolished its department of education in favor of a new department of children, families, and learning—with the goal of coordinating the full range of social and educational services available to children and their families. The Ohio Department of Education reinvented the state education agency around a collection of five broadly conceived, cross-functional service delivery centers (e.g., Center for Students, Families and Communities; Center for the Teaching Profession). North Carolina has been battling to decentralize its state board of education for the entire span of the last 10 years.

Educational historians remind us the development of state departments of education (as well as the office of the state superintendent) was crucial to the hierarchical structure adopted by educational organizations in general. They are outgrowths of the common school movement, the purpose of which was to secure a uniform system of common schools.

The mandates and demands for accountability emerging from the modern era of school reform are more complex and require a wider range of policy responses and program innovations than could have been imagined during the common school era. More important, local school districts expect some variation in treatment by the state agency to better match the unique characteristics and needs of their communities. Thus, the roles, structures, and functions of state departments of education will continue to evolve to support a refined notion of shared responsibility between the local district and the state agency for school change and improvement.

—*Randy J. Dunn*

See also accountability; administration, theories of; bureaucracy; consolidation, of school districts; Council of Chief State School Officers; curriculum, theories of; Department of Education; Education Commission of the States; elections, of school boards, bond issues; governance; innovation, in education; Interstate School Leaders Licensure Consortium; Kentucky Education Reform Act; management theories; Mann, Horace; No Child Left Behind; organizational theories; politics, of education; restructuring, of schools; rural education; school districts, history and development; school improvement models; standardized testing

Further Readings and References

Apple, M. (2003). *The state and the politics of knowledge.* New York: Routledge.
Books, S. (2004). *Poverty and schooling in the U.S.* Mahwah, NJ: Lawrence Erlbaum.
Good, H. (1962). *A history of American education.* New York: Macmillan.
Lunenburg, F., & Ornstein, A. (2004). *Educational administration: Concepts and practices* (4th ed.). Belmont, CA: Wadsworth.
Marshall, C., Mitchell, D., & Wirt, F. (1989). *Culture and education policy in the American state.* London: Falmer.
Spillane, J. (1996). School districts matter: Local educational authorities and state instructional policy. *Educational Policy, 10*(1), 63–87.
Spring, J. (2001). *The American school: 1642–2000.* Boston: McGraw-Hill.
Steffy, B., & English, F. (1994). Wild card educational reform in Kentucky. In C. Finn & H. Walberg (Eds.), *Radical education reforms* (pp. 51–74).
Wirt, F. M., & Kirst, M. W. (1997). *The political dynamics of American education.* Berkeley, CA: McCutchan.

STEWARDSHIP

Stewardship involves the use of one's own time, energy, and resources. A person's stewardship goes beyond physical and into cognitive, aesthetic, and personal matters. Resources vary in type and quantity, but each individual is ultimately responsible to make profitable use of what he or she has been given. Stewardship directly affects people. Thomas Sergiovanni said that stewardship taps into people's emotions, appeals to their values, and responds to their connections with others.

STEWARDSHIP AND LEADERSHIP

Stewardship responsibilities are at the heart of the administrator's role. Stewardship represents an act of trust. People and institutions entrust a leader with specific obligations and duties with the expectation that the leader will fulfill and perform the obligations and duties on their behalf. Stewardship also involves the leader's personal responsibility to manage his or her life and affairs with consideration for the rights of other people and for the common welfare.

Stewardship also involves placing oneself in service to the organization's ideas and ideals and to others who are committed to their fulfillment. Stewardship acknowledges and accepts all members of the school as community and all those who are served by the community. Parents, teachers, and administrators share stewardship responsibility for students. Students also are involved in stewardship responsibility for the school as a learning community.

STEWARDSHIP AND SERVANT LEADERSHIP

Robert Greenleaf, recognized for developing the concept of "servant-leadership," contends that true leadership evolved from those whose main motivation was to help others. Stewardship and servant leadership assume a commitment to serving the needs of others. Other common characteristics include (a) use of openness and persuasion rather than control, (b) commitment to the growth of people, (c) appreciation for the fact that people have an intrinsic value beyond their visible contributions, (d) a commitment to listening to others in order to identify the will of the group, (e) an understanding and empathy of others, (f) commitment to "healing" relationships—recognizing and helping others maintain a positive spirit, (g) establishing group and self-awareness, (h) reliance on persuasion rather than a position of authority, (i) ability to maintain day-to-day tasks while nurturing the larger view of possibilities, and (j) ability to foresee the likely outcome of a situation. Stewardship and servant leadership are based on the responsibility of nurturing the personal, professional, and spiritual growth of others.

There are a number of areas where the principles of servant leadership are being applied: (a) servant-leadership as an institutional philosophy and model with the focus on the group-oriented approach to analysis and decision making as a way to improve the institutions and society, (b) servant-leadership as a pivotal role in the theoretical and ethical framework of boards of directors and trustees as a way to reanalyze their approach to their roles focusing more on asking "Whom do we serve?" and "For what purpose?" (c) servant-leadership and its role with community leadership

organizations as a way to build a true sense of community, (d) servant-leadership and experiential education as a way to strengthen service learning, (e) servant-leadership and its use in formal and informal training programs as part of a conceptual framework for leadership and management models, and (f) servant-leadership and its use in programs that address personal growth and transformation as a way to encourage individuals to take advantage of opportunities to serve and lead others.

—*Jean Haar*

See also administration, theories of; attitudes toward work; capacity building, of organizations; collaboration theory; consideration, caring; diversity; great man theory; human resource development; leadership effectiveness; leadership styles; management theories; mentoring; morality, moral leadership; organizational theories; satisfaction, in organizations and roles; self-actualization; supervision; women in educational leadership

Further Readings and References

Greenleaf, F. (1977). *Servant leadership.* New York: Paulist Press.
Sergiovanni, T. (1992). *Moral leadership: Getting to the heart of school improvement.* San Francisco: Jossey-Bass.
Sergiovanni, T. (2000). Leadership as stewardship. In *The Jossey-Bass reader on educational leadership.* San Francisco: Jossey-Bass.
Todd, S. (1994, July/August). Stewardship: Helping the gifted help themselves. *Gifted Child Today,* pp. 32–35, 42.

🏛 STRATEGIC PLANNING

The pace of change in organizations is accelerating. Consequently, high-performing organizations or units within them attempt to engage in planning, designing, and managing their own desired future rather than simply reacting and responding to changes imposed on them by the environment. Strategic planning is believed to be an important aspect of organizational health, and processes outlined to complete this task are thought to be unifying for the organization.

Strategic planning may be defined as a disciplined effort to produce fundamental decisions about possible actions that will frame what an organization is, what it does, and why it does it. Whether an organization chooses to select a process developed by a consultant or they opt to design their own process, it should be compatible with the culture of the organization. While there is no standardized method for engaging in strategic planning, there is some consensus about what constitute key tasks of the process. The leader of the unit involved in strategic planning should appoint a coordinator(s) for the process, and together they should select a representative steering committee. The steering committee members will serve as leaders of the small groups, who will facilitate the selected and/or designed process. The unit leader can write a charge to the steering committee that outlines the ultimate expectation of what is to be accomplished and the time frame for completion of the strategic-planning document.

A broadly participative process should be selected or designed that will allow stakeholders or constituents in multiple locations to be involved. Teleconferencing and videoconferencing, in addition to small groups, should be utilized as tools to facilitate broad participation in the planning process. Broad participation and having input into the planning process elevates commitment (or buy-in) to the outcome and the eventual, long-range plans that emerge for the planning unit. A 3- to 5-year plan for the future defines the life of the plan.

Reviewing, revising, or writing the mission statement of the planning unit should be a precursor activity for strategic planning, because unless an organization honestly knows who it is, whom it serves, and why it exists, the strategic-planning process may outline great plans that do not meet the needs of the stakeholders.

The planning coordinator(s) and the steering committee can work together to design or select a process that will meet the needs of the organization. At least two approaches exist to identify themes that will provide the organizational direction in planning for the future: a strengths, weaknesses, opportunities, and threats (SWOT) analysis or a strategic-issues focus. The SWOT analysis can involve people both inside and outside the organization, while a strategic issues approach involves interviewing the people within the organization to determine what the themes are for the unit. Either approach has its positives and negatives, but both will generate information the organization should consider in creating its strategic plan.

Before the first meeting with unit constituents, the planning coordinator(s) and the steering committee should agree on the definition of terms they will use in small group meetings. This will ensure the internal cohesiveness of the final document. Focusing on the outline of the final document will be time well

invested, prior to beginning small-group work. At a minimum, the outline of the final document should include: goals or themes (what we want to do), action plans (what will be done), steps for implementation (how it will be done), an accountability assignment (who will do it), date for completion (when it will be done), and the project budget (what it will cost) for implementing the action plan to achieve the goal or theme for the planning unit. Establishing a timeline for completing each phase of the planning process will prescribe the beginning and end of deliberations.

Adding an evaluation date subsequent to implementation to review the effectiveness of the goal or action plan also signals the critical importance of the planning process to the nature of the educational unit. Setting an evaluation point in the future represents a proactive expectation that strategic planning is an ongoing process that seldom ends, once begun. Revising and updating become a continuous cycle.

If the steering committee communicates frequently and substantively with all members of the organization (including clerical and custodial staff), even those who are unable to fully participate in a small discussion group will be apprised of the progress and direction resulting from the planning process. Involving classified staff in appropriate planning groups will encourage their assistance in implementation and also garner their ideas to improve the organization.

When the final strategic-planning document is compiled, the members of the unit should have an opportunity to discuss the contents, including providing a written reaction form. This form allows even a reticent person in the organization with an avenue to affect the outcome of the planning process, and it offers the steering committee specific alternative suggestions for the final document.

In addition to developing and conducting the planning process, the unit leader and the steering committee need to identify the appropriate route for approval of the final document. Once approval of the strategic plan is secured, a monitor (individual or small group) for implementation may be appointed. To assure the fulfillment of the desired future, the monitor can be instructed to report progress on achieving the goals, themes, or action plans that are outlined in the document.

A planning unit that has undertaken a continuous quality improvement journey can adjust the strategic-planning document to meet this objective by making one slight change to the process. Because benchmarking and data-driven decision making are intimate partners within organizations engaged in quality processes, if key performance indicators (KPIs) are added to the goals or action plans in the document, this provides a means through which data can be examined and documented for change. KPIs are essential for tracking qualitative progress over time and establishing improvement trends.

The final strategic-planning document should always be considered a dynamic and changing plan, akin to building a bridge while it is being walked on.

Critics of strategic planning indicate that strategic change is mostly ad hoc and irregular and can't be accurately predicted. Much of what passes for "strategic" is simply financial forecasting in disguise and therefore works against the organization being flexible when changes are required. Finally, the legacy of strategic planning is scientific management and represents an unusual effort to control things when such control is also illusory. Strategic planning results in a perpetuation of the status quo because only that is actually known.

—*Mary Drushal*

See also adaptiveness of organizations; collaboration theory; communications, theories in organizations; democracy, democratic education and administration; finance, of public schools; leadership, participatory; management information systems; organizational theories; performance evaluation systems; planning models; problem solving; quality control; rational organization theory; scientific management

Further Readings and References

Alvino, K. (Ed.). (1995). *Strategic planning: A human resource tool for higher education.* Washington, DC: College and University Personnel Association.

Bryson, J. (1995). *Strategic planning for public and nonprofit organizations: A guide to strengthening and sustaining organizational achievement.* San Francisco: Jossey-Bass.

Carnoy, M. (1999). *Globalization and educational reform: What planners need to know.* Paris: UNESCO.

Dolence, M., Rowley, D., & Lujan, H. (1997). *Working toward strategic change: A step-by-step guide to the planning process.* San Francisco: Jossey-Bass.

French, W., Bell, C., & Zawacki, R. (2004). *Organization development and transformation: Managing effective change.* Boston: McGraw-Hill.

Kaufman, R., Herman, J., & Watters, K. (1996). *Educational planning: Strategic, tactical, operational.* Lancaster, PA. Technomic.

Mintzberg, H. (1994). *The rise and fall of strategic planning.* New York: Free Press.

🏛 STRATIFICATION, IN ORGANIZATIONS

Stratification in organizations generally refers to the difference in status between higher and lower levels in an organization's hierarchy, which are also connected to and represented by differences in salary, prestige, privileges, and mobility among position occupants

SOCIAL SYSTEMS: THE BASIC BUILDING BLOCKS OF ORGANIZATIONS

Stratification occurs as organizations increase in size (the one-room school had only two levels: teacher and students). The underlying mechanism is that as people interact in organizations, they inevitably develop subgroups called *social systems,* that is, any two or more people interacting meaningfully. As a matter of fact, a small group of five people generates 22 different social systems. Social systems comprise the basic building blocks of organizations. Obviously, then, as organizations increase in size, so do the number of their social systems. In 1938, Chester I. Barnard was an early observer who noted that the informal systems, that is, the social systems, have considerable impact on governance and on the processes that organizations must develop to function.

With the increase of social systems comes increased stratification, since humans have limited spans of control; that is, being able to handle a number of subordinates reporting directly to a supervisor. At lower levels, spans can be larger than at higher levels. The implication of this is that with increased complexity and size comes greater hierarchical structure, greater stratification.

MINTZBERG'S PULLS

Henry Mintzberg's logo (see Figure 1) provides intriguing insights into the impact of stratification on the functioning of organizations. In 1979, Mintzberg identified five basic structural configurations in complex organizations. The Strategic Apex comprises those running the operation (top management), while middle management (principals and assistant principals) is considered the Middle Line. The Operating Core in school organizations would be teachers, while computer experts, budgetary, and other analysts compose the Technostructure. Last, Support Staff consists of secretaries, custodians, aides, and similar personnel.

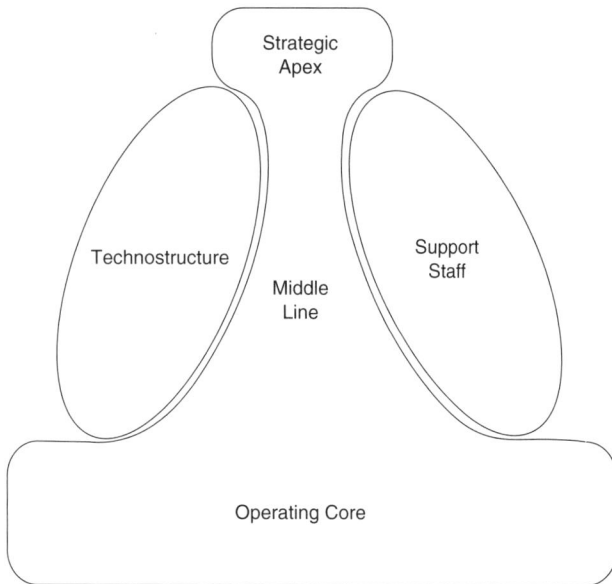

Figure 1   The Five Basic Parts of Organizations

SOURCE: Mintzberg, H. (1979). *The Structuring of Organizations*. Englewood Cliffs, NJ: Prentice-Hall. Reprinted with permission.

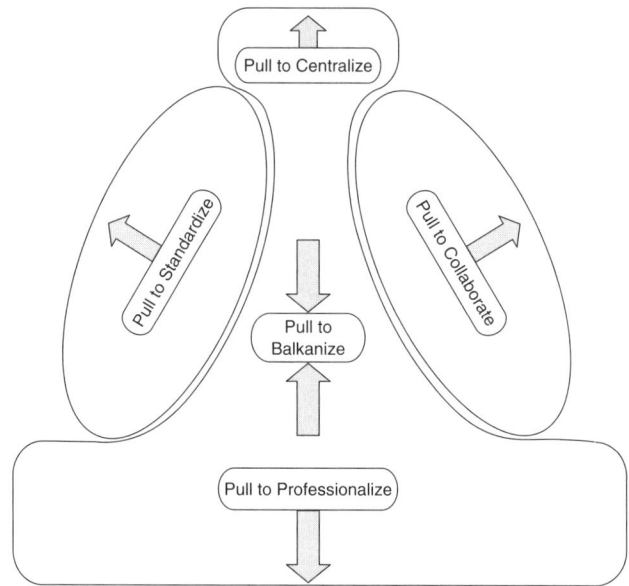

Figure 2   Five Pulls on the Organization

SOURCE: Mintzberg, H. (1979). *The Structuring of Organizations*, 1st edition (p. 20). Reprinted with the permission of Pearson Education, Inc., Saddle River, NJ.

Figure 2, depicting Mintzberg's five organizational "pulls," provides insights into the dynamics of complex organizations, certainly borne out by empirical evidence. All five basic social systems work to maximize their power, control, influence, and autonomy. The Strategic Apex clearly is interested in controlling, with their efforts focusing on pulling to *centralize* decision making. Middle Line managers generally try to maximize their autonomy in decision making, thus striving to *Balkanize*. The Operating Core struggles to control its own destiny by pulling to *professionalize,* as is evident in the decades-long efforts of both teachers and nurses to professionalize. (Recently, we have seen the National Board for Teacher Certification established for teachers as evidence of high levels of professional accomplishment.)

As for the Technostructure, this social system pulls to *standardize* work processes, which can be seen by computer experts insisting on using the same models of computers everywhere, or in standardizing high school scheduling in districts with several high schools. Last, to gain influence and control, Support Staff press to *collaborate.*

By using Mintzberg's insights into organizational structure and pulls, we can describe, analyze, and predict a considerable range of behavior, thereby flushing out hitherto hidden and puzzling agendas relating to stratification and other organizational phenomena.

STRUCTURALISM AND BUREAUCRACY

While we are indebted to Frederick Taylor for the construct of scientific management, the construct of structuralism entered into the United States when translations of Max Weber's works became available. Weber's work provided the concept of bureaucracy, and for him, the distinctive characteristics of bureaucracy included the following: (a) a clear-cut division of labor to permit specialization, (b) positions organized into a hierarchical authority structure, (c) a formally established system of rules and regulations, (d) an impersonal orientation on the part of officials, and (e) career employment in the organization. Clearly, bureaucratic organization is the main model supporting a structuralistic approach to organizations, and its components of division of labor and a hierarchical authority structure are the twin supports for organizational stratification.

COUNTERING APPROACHES: DECENTRALIZATION

While centralizing and decentralizing comprise two ends of a continuum, decentralizing approaches to organizations flatten out the hierarchy, thus reducing hierarchical levels and, therefore, stratification. Some critics have claimed that hierarchical bureaucracy was paralyzing American education. Others promoted the individual school as the unit to focus on for school improvement efforts. Site-based management, the small-schools movement, and the Small Learning Communities movement, the latter particularly supported by the National Association of Secondary Schools, have begun to press for and to develop professional support for decentralizing efforts.

—Arthur Shapiro and Steve Permuth

See also accountability; administration, theories of; Barnard, Chester I.; bureaucracy; chain of command; Chicago school reform; differentiated staffing; hierarchy, in organizations; line and staff concept; management theories; matrix organization (the "adhocracy"); span of control; power; organizational theories; systemic reform

Further Readings and References

Barnard, C. I. (1938). *The functions of the executive.* Cambridge, MA: Harvard University Press.

Gerth, H., & Mills, C. (Eds.). (1946). *From Max Weber: Essays in sociology.* New York: Oxford University Press.

Lunenberg, F. C., & Ornstein, A. C. (2000). *Educational administration: Concepts and practices* (3rd ed.). Belmont, CA: Wadsworth.

Mintzberg, H. (1979). *The structuring of organizations.* Englewood Cliffs, NJ: Prentice Hall.

National Association of Secondary School Principals. (2004). *Breaking ranks II: Strategies for leading high school reform.* Reston, VA: National Association of Secondary School Principals; Providence, RI: Education Alliance, Brown University.

Razik, T., & Swanson, A. (2001). *Fundamental concepts of educational leadership* (2nd ed.). Upper Saddle River, NJ: Merrill Prentice Hall.

Taylor, F. (1911). *The principles of scientific management.* New York: Harper & Row.

Vecchio. R. P. (1994). *Organizational behavior* (3rd ed.). Orlando, FL: Dryden Press.

🏛 STRAYER, GEORGE D.

A leading figure in school administration at Teachers College, Columbia University, George D. Strayer, along with Robert M. Haig, is best known as the originator of the Stayer-Haig plan, which has served as the basic formula for states to make general grants of aid to school districts on an equalized basis.

Strayer (1876–1962) started his long career in education with an interest in classroom teaching, specifically in the area of mathematics, and he coauthored a popular arithmetic textbook series of the time. However, he came to be regarded as a founding light in the new field of educational administration. An alumnus of Columbia, he studied at Teachers College at a time when it was the heralded breeding ground and center of a new, empirically based, progressive educational philosophy. As head of the division of field studies at Teachers College for over 20 years (1921–1942), Strayer also served as director of the Division of Organization and Administration of Education at Teachers College from 1937 to 1942. His national reputation led to service with numerous respected organizations, among these the presidency of the National Education Association.

Along with Columbia professors Paul Mort and N. L. Engelhardt, Strayer was influential in the creation of the school survey movement. Their studies of school systems across America, conducted through Strayer's field studies unit, provided the groundwork for many of the recommendations that helped shape administrative practice in the first half of the twentieth century. From this basis, then, Strayer came to be seen as a national authority on school administration and finance.

Professor Strayer, though, probably gained his greatest renown for work that literally established the field of school finance. Richard King, Austin Swanson, and Scott Sweetland noted that Strayer, partnering with Robert Haig, first devised a plan to share educational costs between states and localities through the use of what is still known today as the *foundation formula*. According to their model, Strayer and Haig envisioned that each school district would levy a uniform local property tax rate sufficient to meet education costs only in the most property-wealthy school system; the state would then make up the difference between this foundation level and what could be raised locally in each of the other districts.

Under a strict Strayer-Haig formula, as utilized presently, the state specifies a dollar amount per student that all school districts must receive to guarantee a minimally adequate education. The state then guarantees the difference between the amount raised locally using some qualifying tax rate and the guaranteed expenditure level.

As part of this groundbreaking work in 1923, Strayer and Haig were first to address the need to equalize resources across school systems within a state to provide an education program for every student that at least met some minimal standard. Previously, general state aid to schools had been solely in the form of flat grants without regard to district fiscal capacity—the Strayer-Haig formula remedied this primary defect of the dominant flat grant system for funding schools.

—*Randy J. Dunn*

See also budgeting; cost-benefit analyses; efficacy theory; equity and adequacy of funding schools; finance, of public schools; management theories; National Education Association; organizational theories; taxes, to support education

Further Readings and References

King, R., Swanson, A., & Sweetland, S. (2003). *School finance: Achieving high standards with equity and efficiency* (3rd ed.). Boston: Allyn & Bacon.

Kowalski, T., & Brunner, C. (2005). The school superintendent: Roles, challenges, and issues. In F. English (Ed.), *SAGE handbook of educational leadership* (pp. 142–167). Thousand Oaks, CA: Sage.

Strayer, G., & Haig, R. (1923). *The financing of education in the state of New York: Report of the educational finance inquiry commission* (Vol. 1). New York: Macmillan.

🏛 STRESS, IN SCHOOL ADMINISTRATION

Stress intrigues and plagues the practitioner and researcher alike. Popular writers and academic researchers have added extensive literature in the past decades to the study of occupational stress. Internationally, over 100,000 books, journals, and articles have dedicated their attention to the phenomenon of stress. While the early writings tended to be anecdotal in nature with little substantive connect to empirical evidence, the past three decades have seen refined interest from researchers.

Researchers from the disciplines of medicine, psychiatry, clinical psychology, and behavioral sciences have undertaken studies to understand the phenomena of stress and coping. The research on stress in schools has examined several levels of stress, including the nature of stress, types and sources of stress, responses to stress, and the consequences of stress.

THEORETICAL FRAMEWORK

In 1976, Joseph McGrath first explained stress as a four-stage, closed-loop process, beginning with situations in the environment perceived by the individual, to which the individual selects the response, resulting in consequences for both the individual and situations, which closes the loop. Each of the four stages is connected by linking process of cognition appraisal: decision, performance, and outcome.

Other models or conceptual frameworks represent hybrids, elaborations, or extensions of the McGrath model. The four stages postulated by McGrath have served as sound building blocks over the past three decades for research on administrator stress. The administrative stress cycle, built on McGrath's foundation, has four stages. The first stage is a set of demands, or stressors, placed on administrators. In 1984, Walter Gmelch and Boyd Swent studied 1855 principals and superintendents and discovered four factors of administrative stress. Over 45 research studies have replicated this study and have found similar types of stress. The first source, *role-based stress,* is perceived from administrators' role-set interactions and beliefs or attitudes about their roles in schools. The second source, *task based stress,* arises from the performance of day-to-day administrative activities, from telephone and staff interruptions, meetings, writing memos and reports, to participating in school activities outside of the normal working hours. The third source, *boundary-spanning stress,* emanates from external conditions, such as negotiations and gaining public support for school budgets. Boundary-spanning stress appears to be unique to the field of school administration. *Conflict-mediating stress* is the fourth source. This type of stress arises from the administrator handling conflicts within the school such as trying to resolve differences between and among students, resolving parent and school conflicts, and handing student discipline problems.

The second state consists of perceptions or interpretation of the stressors by administrators. Those who perceive demands as harmful or demanding will create stress within their lives and approach their work with intensity. Certain personality types, such as Type A behavior, accentuate the stress and create conditions impacting the health of administrators.

The third stage of the cycle presents choices to the administrators. If they perceive the stressors to be harmful, threatening, or demanding, they will respond to them physiologically or psychologically. Most data-based studies have investigated sources of stress (Stage 1), while fewer have addressed how educators cope with their job pressures. However, the general literature on coping is significant in volume and diverse in attention and addresses popular and academic concerns as well as conceptual, theoretical, and empirical investigations.

The fourth stage of stress cycle, consequences, takes into account the long-range effects of stress. The consequences can lead to headaches, ulcers, illnesses, or disability. There appear to be three dimensions of burnout: emotional exhaustion, depersonalization, and feelings of low personal accomplishments. All three factors of burnout are significantly associated with the factors of stress, for all levels of school administration, particularly between emotional exhaustion and task-based stress.

In conclusion, within the leadership ranks, the superintendent is often popularly identified as the administrator most susceptible to stress and disease. This exclusive assumption, however, remains open to question. Principals suffer more severe stress from conflict and time pressures than superintendents do. On the other hand, superintendents experience excessive stress from trying to negotiate with multiple clients in the school system.

—*Walter H. Gmelch*

See also administration, theories of; attitudes toward work; conflict management; consideration, caring; creativity, in management; flow theory; human resource development; leadership effectiveness; mentoring; politics, of education; principalship; role conflict; satisfaction, in organizations and roles; self-actualization; superintendency; working conditions, in schools; workplace trends

Further Readings and References

Brock, B., & Grady, M. (2002). *Avoiding burnout.* Thousand Oaks, CA: Corwin Press.

Gmelch, W. (1982). *Beyond stress to effective management.* New York: Wiley.

Gmelch, W., & Chan, W. (1994). *Thriving on stress for success.* Thousand Oaks, CA: Corwin Press.

Gmelch, W. H., & Swent, B. (1984). Management team stressors and their impact on administrators' health. *Journal of Educational Administration, 2,* 293–205.

McGrath, J. (1976). *Stress and behavior in organizations.* Chicago: Rand McNally.

Torelli, J., & Gmelch, W. (1993). Occupational stress and burnout in educational administration. *People and Education, 1,* 363–381.

🏛 STRUCTURAL EQUATION MODELING

The complex analysis of quantitative data in much contemporary education research and evaluation is conducted using structural equation models (SEM), also referred to as covariance structure analysis, covariance structure modeling, or analysis of covariance structures, which permit the simultaneous prediction of several outcome variables. Generally, this form of data analysis is undertaken using specialized statistical software, including the Statistical Analysis System (SAS, particularly PROC CALIS), EQS, M-PLUS, LISREL, and AMOS. SEM is appropriate when causal interpretations are desired, measuring the effects of exogenous variables (e.g., student demographic characteristics or parental socioeconomic status) on endogenous (dependent, or outcome) variables, such as student achievement, and the effects of endogenous variables on other endogenous variables. SEM analyses can be conducted for a single group (for example, all eighth-grade students in a district) or for subgroups to be able to make comparisons in model characteristics across groups (for example, comparing model results for male and female eighth graders).

In SEM, one equation is estimated for each dependent (endogenous) variable using predictors that can be exogenous (independent) or endogenous in another equation. The model estimates both the direct effects of independent variables on the endogenous variables and the indirect effects of independent variables mediated through other endogenous variables. Variables may be either observed, that is, already present in the data set, or latent, in which case the variable is constructed as a linear combination of observed variables through a process of confirmatory factor analysis. This combination of traits separates SEM from other linear models methods—simple and multiple regression and correlation, analysis of variance, analysis of covariance, and multivariate analysis of variance and covariance—and from other methods of simultaneous equation estimation used commonly in econometrics and related disciplines. SEM frequently is referred to as *causal modeling,* because it is used to rule out alternative explanations through complex combinations of variable paths. However, like other linear models methods, SEM results are sensitive to problems associated with lack of normality (particularly kurtosis), missing data, and outliers. Furthermore, it is highly debatable whether causation in the experimental science sense is achieved.

The most fundamental form of SEM is path analysis, in which all variables are observed and none are latent. An example from research on undergraduates at a research-extensive large Midwestern land grant institution is shown in Figure 1, where "ACT/HSR" denotes the average of standardized values for ACT

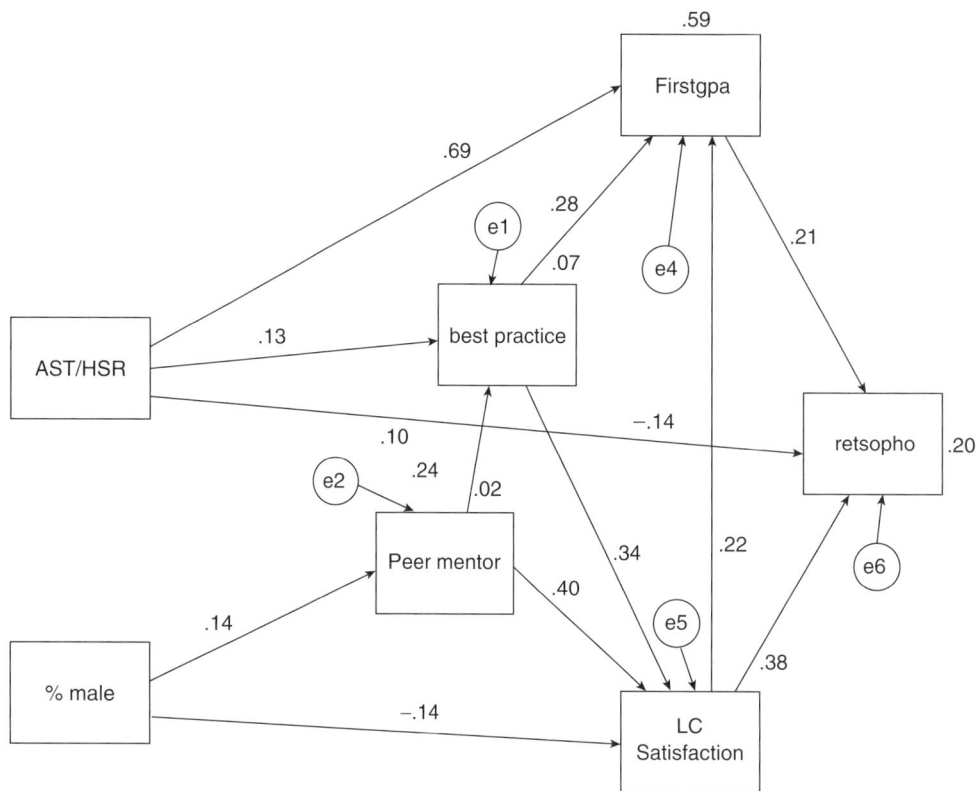

Figure 1   Effects of Learning Team Characteristics on First-Year Undergraduate Retention: Evidence From Structural Equation Models

SOURCE: Shelley, M., Huba, M., Epperson, D., Cook, M. Zhang, B., & Hoekstra, P. "Effects of Learning Team Characteristics on First-Year Undergraduate Retention: Evidence From Structural Equation Models." Presented at the Annual Meeting of the American Educational Research Association, April 11–15, 2005, Montréal, Canada. Reprinted with permission.

composite score and high school rank, "%male" is the percentage of a learning team who are male, "best practice" denotes the mean factor score for student perceptions of the extent to which the learning team experienced best practices, "peer mentor" represents the mean factor score for student and learning community coordinator evaluation of team peer mentors, "firstgpa" is mean first-year cumulative grade point average for the team, "LC satisfaction" is mean learning team student satisfaction with their learning community experience, and "retsopho" measures the percentage of students in each learning team persisting to the second fall semester.

This is a reduced version of the "saturated" model in which all possible paths are estimated. The reduced model has the important properties that all of the reported paths are statistically significant and that even with some paths deleted due to their nonsignificance, the reduced model does an excellent job of reproducing

the sample covariances among the variables. The model fits exceptionally well ($\chi^2 = 1.393$, $df = 9$, $p = .998$, $n = 390$). Of the five dependent variables in the model, the best fit, measured by squared multiple correlations, is for first-term GPA (R2 = .585), and the worst fit is for peer mentor evaluation (R2 = .020). Other dependent variables had intermediate squared multiple correlations (R2 = .377 for learning community satisfaction, .195 for retention to the sophomore year, and .071 for experience of best practices). A wide array of other fit statistics is available.

In this model, direct effects were significant from %male to evaluation of peer mentors ($\beta = .142$, CR = 2.303) and learning community satisfaction ($\beta = .145$, CR = 2.913). β is the standardized regression weight and CR is the critical ratio, defined as the unstandardized parameter estimate divided by the standard error of the unstandardized parameter estimate. A larger value of β and a higher CR value indicate a stronger model component. There also are significant direct effects from ACT/HSR to experience of best practice ($\beta = .126$, CR = 2.043), first-term GPA ($\beta = .693$, CR = 20.085), and retention to the sophomore year ($\beta = .193$, CR = 2.902). Significant direct effects also are found from experience of best practice to first-term GPA ($\beta = .282$, CR = 6.146) and to learning community satisfaction ($\beta = .339$, CR = 6.265), from evaluation of peer mentors to experience of best practices ($\beta = .235$, CR = 3.646) and learning community satisfaction ($\beta = .398$, CR = 7.626), from first-term GPA to retention to the sophomore year ($\beta = .213$, CR = 3.188), and from learning community satisfaction to first-term GPA ($\beta = -0.144$, CR = -3.219) and retention to the sophomore year ($\beta = .221$, CR = 4.060).

Total effects in the model can be decomposed into direct and indirect components, with some effects entirely direct, others entirely indirect, and others a mixture of direct and indirect. For example, in the path model, the effects of male on best practices experience, ACT/HSR on Item 58, evaluation of peer mentors on firstgpa, %male on retention, evaluation of peer mentors on retention, and best practices experience on retention, are entirely indirect. Most other effects are entirely or largely direct.

One major complication with SEM is that it works best with large samples, which are not always available. SEM requires the simultaneous estimation of a substantially larger number of parameters than is needed for most applications of other linear models methods, and it is recommended to have 5 to 10 observations per estimated parameter. A SEM model with only a few variables can have complex path coefficients that add up to a surprisingly large number of estimated parameters and hence require large data sets.

—*Mack C. Shelley*

See also empiricism; factor analysis; frame theory; hierarchical developmental models; item response theory; networking and network theory; quantitative research methods; research methods

Further Readings and References

Bollen, K., & Long, J. (Eds.). (1993). *Testing structural equation models.* Newbury Park, CA: Sage.

Jöreskog, K., & Sörbom, D. (1996). *LISREL 8: Structural equation modeling with the SIMPLIS command language.* Chicago: Scientific Software International.

Jöreskog, K., & Sörbom, D. (1996). *LISREL 8: User's reference guide.* Chicago: Scientific Software International.

Schumacker, R., & Lomax, R. (2004). *A beginner's guide to structural equation modeling.* Mahwah, NJ: Lawrence Erlbaum.

Shelley, M., Huba, M., Epperson, D., Cook, M., Zhang, B., & Hoekstra, P. (2005, April 11–15). *Effects of learning team characteristics on first-year undergraduate retention: Evidence from structural equation models.* Paper presented at the Annual Meeting of the American Educational Research Association, Montréal, Canada.

STUDENT TEACHING

Student teaching is the capstone experience of a preservice teacher's preparation program. Student teaching is intended to provide preservice teachers with supervised, extended experiences in real classroom settings and the opportunity to be assessed in relation to their strengths and weaknesses as prospective teachers. While student teaching has traditionally been viewed as a capstone experience, it is increasingly seen as an initial rather than a terminal learning opportunity with schools, districts, and state departments of education looking at the role of induction and mentoring as a much-needed, job-embedded extension of the student teaching experience.

The nature of the student teaching experience varies greatly among teacher education programs. The length of a student teaching placement can vary from 5 weeks to 2 semesters. Typically, a student teacher is assigned a cooperating or supervising teacher at a school site, and a university supervisor makes periodic visits to observe the student teacher in practice. The typical student teaching assignment requires the student teacher to spend about half of the student teaching placement teaching, with the remaining time spent observing and participating in classroom or school-level activities with experienced teachers.

Typically, the student teacher's responsibility in the classroom increases during the course of the student's placement in the school. The student teacher sometimes has the opportunity to participate in all aspects of a teacher's work in a school (e.g., parent conferences, supervisory duties, committee or grade-level teamwork) and to meet and confer with other school personnel that support the teacher in the classroom (e.g., counselors, administrators, academic area curriculum and instructional specialists, special education teachers).

Traditionally, preservice teachers had little real experience with schools until the student teaching experience in their senior year. In the late 1980s and early 1990s, some universities experimented with the concept of a professional development school where the research knowledge of the university was integrated with the practical knowledge of K–12 classroom teachers to enhance the preservice teacher's preparation for the real world of the classroom. In some cases, student teaching was increased from one semester to two and included intensive supervision and guided reflection by public school teachers or clinical faculty rather than faculty from the university. The student teaching experience sometimes involved working with two different cooperating teachers at two different grade levels.

The role of the cooperating teacher cannot be underestimated in the development of the preservice teacher. The ability of the cooperating teacher to observe instruction, communicate with preservice teachers about strengths and weaknesses observed, and guide the novice teacher in selecting teaching, learning, management, and assessment approaches to address problems that may surface is key to the preservice teacher's progress. For this reason, some universities have required cooperating teachers to take training in clinical supervision to strengthen their ability to observe instruction, communicate their observations, and help the preservice teacher explore and reflect on experiences using appropriate adult learning principles.

To better prepare preservice teachers for the student teaching experience, teacher education programs are requiring field experiences in school sites early and throughout preservice teachers' preparation programs. Disparities between preservice teacher preparation and the reality of the requirements of the actual job of teaching are key contributors to novice teachers' leaving the profession. Early field experiences that increase preservice teachers' responsibilities in the classroom are seen as possible ways to reduce the effects of these disparities. Early in the preservice teacher's introduction to real classrooms, the preservice teacher may take the role of observer or paraprofessional. Then the preservice teacher may work as a tutor or classroom monitor. Next, the preservice teacher may work as a teaching assistant. Such early and sustained field experiences aid preservice teachers in making a final decision about entering the teaching field and increase the likelihood of their successful transition to the student teaching experience.

An important component of student teaching is the development of the preservice teacher's ability to reflect critically on teaching practice and experiences in the classroom. Journal writing and the reflective teaching log are common means of promoting reflection during the student teaching experience. Journal writing helps student teachers begin the process of critiquing and guiding their own professional practice. Reflective teaching logs provide opportunities for the preservice teacher to describe the daily sequence of classroom events, select a single classroom episode to explore, analyze the reason for selecting the episode and what was learned from it, and consider the possible future implications of what was learned.

Several states have developed performance-based standards for what preservice teachers should know and be able to do when they exit a preservice teacher preparation program. The basic assumption underlying the movement toward performance-based standards is that performances require preservice teachers to demonstrate learning in authentic settings and reflect the complexity of the teacher's real life role in today's school classrooms. Standards established by the National Council for the Accreditation of Teacher Education (NCATE) and the Interstate New Teacher Assessment and Support Consortium (INTASC) reflect this trend.

—*Judith A. Ponticell*

See also clinical supervision; mentoring; National Council for the Accreditation of Teacher Education; normal schools; schools of education; teacher recruitment and retention

Further Readings and References

Heller, D. A. (2004). *Teachers wanted: Attracting and retaining good teachers.* Alexandria, VA: Association for Supervision and Curriculum Development.

Parkay, F. W., & Stanford, B. H. (2004). *Becoming a teacher* (6th ed.). Boston: Allyn & Bacon.

Wentz, P. J. (2001). *The student teaching experience: Cases from the classroom.* Upper Saddle River, NJ: Merrill Prentice Hall.

SUBJECTIVISM, IN THEORY

Subjectivism is the philosophical notion that knowledge is mediated through individual human bias. It is an epistemological perspective that questions the possibility of absolute truth and a knowable world. This perspective implies that theory and research inquiry are shaped by subjective knowledge. This epistemological stance emerged in the twentieth century due to philosophical doubts about the ideal of an objective, knowable world. For example, literary theory suggests that language is an abstract concept in the sense that the signs (words and symbols) used to represent objects and ideas are independent of their referents. Thus, language and discourse do not come out of the interplay between subject and object, but are imposed on the object by the subject. The object or idea, then, makes no contribution to the creation of meaning making, and meaning does not come through an interaction with the object and is not bound by any correlation with an absolute.

Subjectivism stands in contrast to the two other primary epistemological perspectives: objectivism and constructionism. Modernist theory rests on objectivist (positivist and postpositivist) epistemological assumptions that suggest that there are generalizable, universal and static truths about reality that are waiting to be discovered through scientific inquiry. Sociology of knowledge perspectives rest on constructionist epistemological assumptions that assume that all knowledge is socially constructed, thus, knowledge is created through the social interaction between humans and the evolving social world they construct over time. Subjectivism offers a sharp divergence from objectivist and constructionist views of knowledge, since it evolved out of structuralist, poststructuralist, and postmodern thought. These perspectives view truth as ambiguous, relative, fragmented, particular, and discontinuous. Subjectivist epistemological assumptions are central to understanding structural, poststructural, and postmodern thought and challenge the possibility of objective knowledge contained in objectivism and constructionist assumptions that a shared truth can be created through social interaction.

Subjectivist epistemology has implications for how knowledge is viewed and how research is conceived. In an era when standards and scientifically based research are heralded as the key to improving education, subjectivism suggests that research is value laden and raises questions about the possibility of objective research. Rather than understanding reality in any true sense, subjectivism suggests that research knowledge is always partial, biased, and particular. In its purest form, this perspective further posits that subjective assumptions are always embedded in the theories used to shape research questions and inquiry. Thus, seemingly "objective" research questions are shaped by subjectivity, so claims of "truth" are really subjective interpretations mediated by the personal bias of researchers.

—Cynthia Gerstl-Pepin

See also aesthetics, in education; affective domain; arts education; character education; constructivism; creativity, theories of; cultural politics, wars; deconstruction; egocentrism, theories of; esteem needs; ethnocentrism; flow theory; humanistic education; objectivity; paradigm; philosophies of education; semiotics

Further Readings and References

Achinstein, P. (2002). Subjective views of Kuhn. *Perspectives on Science, 9,* 423–432.
Crotty, M. (1998). *The foundations of social research: Meaning and perspective in the research process.* Thousand Oaks, CA: Sage.
Papastephanou, M. (2005). Can subjectivity be salvaged? *Common Knowledge, 11*(1), 136–159.

SUICIDE, IN SCHOOLS

Student suicide refers to self-inflicted termination of one's life. Student suicide may also be categorized as accidental deaths. Student suicide in the United States has increased from 3% per 100,000 in 1960 to approximately 9% per 100,000 persons from the age of 5 to 24 in 1992. For the age group between the ages of 15 to 24 years old, suicides have gone from 5% to 13% per 100,000 persons. Next to homicides and accidents, suicides represent the third leading cause of death for youth in the United States. Homicides have gone from 5.9% per 100,000 in 1960 in the age group of 5 to 24 years of age to 22% in 1992. According to the National Center for Educational Statistics, deaths by accident, suicide, or homicide are collectively identified as violent deaths. They are considered measures indicating that youth bear a burden of problems that compete with schools for their attention. They represent the most extreme responses to larger and deeper social problems among a state's or a nation's youth.

CHARACTERISTICS OF SUICIDE VICTIMS

Suicide is categorized as a health and safety issue along with poor diet, reckless sexual activity, lack of exercise, drug and alcohol abuse, eating disorders, school violence, physically or sexually abused children, and peer-to-peer sexual harassment. While suicide is an issue that affects students from wealthy, middle-class, and poor communities, certain groups are more prone than others; however, characteristics change over time. Prior to 1980, African Americans were less likely than Whites to commit suicide; however, between 1980 and 1996, the suicide rate among African Americans doubled. Nationally, the suicide rate for White males has nearly tripled since 1950. American Indians, because of alcoholism, rural isolation, and fewer services, are more likely to take their own lives. Also at heightened risk are gay and lesbian youth and students with learning disabilities. Gender and suicide methods for adolescents nationally are similar. Boys tend to commit suicide at a higher rate than girls do. They also tend to use guns more than girls do. Girls tend to seek intervention to reduce suicidal impulses. According to the National Center for Educational Statistics, 47% of suicides are committed in the home with a parent-owned gun, 10% in another residence, and 10% on a public road.

ADMINISTRATOR RESPONSIBILITIES

Suicides present unique challenges to school administrators. The alarming increase in completed suicides means that assistant principals who are responsible for student discipline will come in touch with completed or attempted suicides. For every completed suicide, an estimated 7 to 10 others are attempted.

One suicide in a school may lead to other suicides. Suicide clustering may be a copycat act or response to news reporting. Clustering is a by-product of youth suicide and a challenge for school administrators and counselors. School administrators play an important role in suicide prevention through early detection of risk factors, warning signs of depression, and student programs. Depression, anger, anxiety, drug abuse, hopelessness, reduced academic performance, learning problems, or interactions among factors are predictors of suicidal behavior. Schools can address issues of depression, coping, problem solving, and stress management. While administrators must be proactive, they must also use good judgment in selecting preventions to assure that prevention programs do not induce suicide in a delicate teen. Boys who commit suicide may not exhibit these factors in the same way as do girls and may be misdiagnosed. There are some typical circumstances, attributes, and behaviors that are useful for administrators, teachers, social

service providers, counselors, physicians, and other adults in contact with adolescents.

—Augustina Reyes

See also adolescence; at-risk students; bullying; child development theories; climate, school; cognition, theories of; discipline in schools; discrimination; diversity; emotional disturbance; esprit (school climate); expulsion, of students; learning environments; lesbian/gay/bisexual/transgender issues in education; mental illness, in adults and children; motivation, theories of; parental involvement; personality; queer theory; resiliency; sexuality, theories of; underachievers, in schools; violence in schools

Further Readings and References

American Foundation for Suicide Prevention. (2005). Available online at http://www.afsp.org/

Centers for Disease Control. (1996). *Youth suicide prevention programs: A resource guide.* Washington, DC: U.S. Department of Health and Human Services, National Center for Injury Prevention and Control.

Centers for Disease Control. (2005). *Program in suicide prevention.* National Center for Injury Prevention and Control. Available online at http://www.cdc.gov/ncipc/dvp/suifacts .htm#2

Francis, B., & Skelton, C. (2005). *Reassessing gender and achievement.* New York: Routledge.

Renold, E. (2005). *Girls, boys, and junior sexualities.* New York: Routledge.

Reyes, A. (1999). How school leaders help students be healthier and safer in the new millennium. *Texas Study of Secondary Education, 9*(1), 16–21.

SUPERINTENDENCY

Over the past one-and-a-half centuries, superintendents have been the persons vested with the greatest individual responsibility for the welfare of local, intermediate, and state school systems. Their jobs have required managing the political complexities of tax-supported institutions, facilitating intensely bureaucratic processes, possessing keen wisdom and understanding of intertwined social subcultures that comprise school communities, providing leadership for the persons who work and study in schools, and demonstrating expertise in curricular and instructional matters. In short, the demands of the job have been staggeringly complex. That complexity likely will increase into the future.

Not only have the demands of the work shifted, but the path to the superintendency has changed sharply since the first superintendents assumed their duties in the mid-1800s. During these early years, schoolmasters with little professional experience or preparation could be tapped for the work, particularly in small, rural districts. In contrast, the persons who become superintendents now have served as teachers for an average of 6 or 7 years before moving into their first administrative positions, typically principalships or assistant principalships. Those who work in large districts usually move into central office positions before finally assuming the superintendency. In smaller districts, individuals tend to leap directly from principalships/assistant principalships to superintendencies. Before assuming superintendencies today, administrative aspirants typically engage in extensive graduate study to obtain advanced administrative credentials. Another important change in the path to the superintendency is that the promotional path used to wind through the aspirant's home district. Currently, however, over two thirds of superintendents have been hired from outside their current districts.

Despite changes such as these, the demographic characteristics of superintendents as a group have remained remarkably stable over time. Men have held between 87% and 97% of all superintendencies during the twentieth century. Nearly all male superintendents have been married. Though accurate historical data describing the number of persons of color holding superintendencies does not exist, persons of color probably have accounted for no more than 1% of all superintendents at any given time. And most superintendents have been middle-aged. Some of this demographic data has been collected on a semiregular basis first by the Department of Superintendence of the National Education Association (NEA), then later by the American Association of School Administrators (AASA). It is worth noting that the demographic homogeneity of superintendents today stands in stark contrast with the ever-growing diversity of school communities.

The matter of who serves as superintendent may be shifting subtly during the early years of the twenty-first century, however. For example, the proportions of women and persons of color in the position are growing in some regions such as the Northeast and South. The range of acceptable leadership styles may be expanding as well. The nature of the work itself has changed along with technologies facilitating internal communication, curriculum and instruction, information management, testing and measurement, and public relations. Future directions for the superintendency no doubt will be grounded both in how the position has evolved as well as emerging social conditions.

School superintendents and supervisors first served in urban areas when women began teaching in large numbers during the mid-1800s. Because men were chosen for these administrative positions, some observers conclude that sex segregation was part of the design of schoolwork. School board members believed that male administrators assured female teachers' safety, especially from the threat supposedly posed by adolescent male students. The presence of male administrators in schools and districts also preserved a gender symmetry that typically existed in White, middle-class homes with male heads of household who represented family interests to the community and women minding domestic affairs while submitting to male authority. The substantially higher salaries required for newly created district administrative positions were funded through savings achieved by hiring relatively less expensive women teachers.

Other needs factored into the initial decision to hire school superintendents or supervisors. During the early- to mid-1800s, school board members, particularly in rural districts, each managed particular aspects of creating and maintaining schools. Some hired teachers. Others built or maintained the physical facility. School board members built desks, bought instructional materials, and inspected the quality of teaching. As districts grew, however, the task of managing schools quickly exceeded what lay board members could undertake without compromising their primary wage-earning activities. Consequently, they hired superintendents to act on their behalf.

Counties and states also added superintendencies to their structures. State superintendencies were created to serve two primary functions. First, states, such as those in the Northeast, initially established state school offices so that all school-related matters could receive some central oversight. Horace Mann (secretary of the Massachusetts Board of Education, 1837–1848) and Henry Barnard (secretary of the Board of Commissioners of Common Schools in Connecticut, 1838–1842, later serving as the first federal commissioner of education) each effected reforms, largely through the collection and dissemination of information about schools. They chose this route to service because otherwise they were empowered with little funding or real authority for managing schools. Persuasion remained their most formidable means of shaping policy and practice. Second, some states and territories, particularly those in the Midwestern and Western regions, required state school officers to manage land set aside by law for schools. School land that was sold generated revenue to be distributed for educational purposes. State superintendents managed this business, ensuring that intermediate districts received their proportional share.

Intermediate (or county) superintendencies were established mainly during the mid- to late-1800s. Persons holding these positions received funds and resources from offices of state superintendents. Intermediate superintendents subsequently distributed such resources to local districts. They also adjudicated boundary disputes that arose all too frequently among adjoining local districts. In addition to these responsibilities, intermediate superintendents assumed a wide variety of other duties, depending on the state. Some intermediate superintendents performed roles remarkably similar to those of local superintendents, traveling between schoolhouses, inspecting instruction, organizing professional development activities for teachers, and overseeing the use of resources. Others worked primarily in their county offices, mainly handling bureaucratic matters. Because intermediate superintendents managed the distribution of public funds, they tended to be elected, rather than appointed, officials. Women teachers began to campaign for and win county superintendencies as the women's suffrage movement gathered strength during the late nineteenth and early twentieth century. By 1930, women accounted for as many as 27% of all intermediate (county) superintendents.

Local superintendents initially did not manage the financial affairs of their districts directly. Elected school board members customarily provided direct oversight of school funds. However, as schools and districts grew in size and complexity during the late 1800s, boards eventually ceded fiscal authority to school superintendents. School board size also decreased over this time, shrinking from as many as several hundred board members in some urban school districts to as few as a handful. Obviously, as board size decreased, board members relinquished much of the direct oversight they previously had provided for routine school administrative functions. In the end, superintendents assumed substantially greater authority for managing schools as board members simultaneously relinquished it. The increase in the authority

of the superintendency made it more desirable for educators seeking executive pay, duties, and status.

As the superintendency evolved, a number of talented individuals attained the position and provided remarkable organizational skill, capacity for institution building, and broad intellectual leadership. Men such as William Torrey Harris (superintendent of St. Louis Schools and later commissioner of education of the U.S.), a Transcendentalist and leading exponent of Hegelian philosophy, pursued educational leadership as a means of enacting educational reform. These early superintendents established curricula grounded both in practical skills and broad liberal knowledge. They systematized the hiring and training of large numbers of teachers and other school workers, often establishing institutions to prepare teachers such as normal schools or institutes. They led campaigns for the initial construction of school buildings. They wielded significant influence in shaping local political and bureaucratic mechanisms for daily management of schools, processes eventually reified as those recognizable today. Some urban superintendents created districts where there had been none and in the process enabled the public education of vast numbers of children

Despite clear successes, however, the growing field of school administration also attracted public criticism. Newspapers hastened to point out inefficiency or corruption in school practices. Even one well-regarded public champion of educational leadership, Charles Francis Adams Jr., sternly cautioned members attending the NEA annual meeting in 1880 that superintendents must become more professional and less pseudointellectual or mindlessly bureaucratic in their focus, or otherwise risk irrelevance. Within two decades of what later was regarded as a seminal address to the field, one that demanded the professionalization of the superintendency, higher-education institutions such as Stanford, the University of Chicago, and Teachers College of Columbia University had created graduate programs specifically to prepare high-quality candidates for school executive positions. Stanford's Ellwood Cubberley not only created a remarkably successful graduate program but also wrote numerous texts that, in time, became essential scholarship of the rapidly emerging field. During the early decades of the twentieth century, these and a few other elite educational administration preparation programs had become centrally important in producing superintendents for the most desirable school districts around the country.

Then, in the years following the 1920 enactment of national women's suffrage, the increasingly powerful members of the NEA Department of Superintendence endeavored to upgrade the status of the profession once again, this time by deemphasizing the political nature of the work and instead stressing the need for experts prepared in rigorous, reputable programs. These reform efforts were interrupted by the social and financial turbulence of the Depression, followed shortly afterward by the upheaval of World War II. The years following World War II, though, saw unprecedented activity aimed at improving the status of school administration, particularly the superintendency. Hundreds of colleges and universities hastened to establish or improve their educational administration preparation programs. Thousands of veterans with G.I. Bill benefits in hand enrolled in these programs.

Several new organizations formed during these early cold war years to address the quality of the educational administration profession. 1947 saw the establishment of the National Conference of Professors of Educational Administration, an organization tasked with assessing the theory and practice of the field. The Cooperative Program in Educational Administration was founded to improve the quality of educational administration preparation programs and collaboration with practitioners. This venture, generously supported by the Kellogg Foundation and joined by the AASA, the National Council of Chief State School Officers, and a number of other organizations, sought to establish rigorous requirements for credentialing programs. In 1956, the Kellogg Foundation supported the formation of yet another group, the University Council for Educational Administration (UCEA). This organization endeavored, in addition to improving administrative practice, to stimulate quality research and its dissemination. To this end, the UCEA produced *Educational Administration Quarterly* and *Educational Administration Abstracts,* journals that continue to influence the field.

Although the years following World War II brought impressive agreement on ways to improve professional practice and ensure that educational administrators were prepared in quality programs, the resulting reforms produced some unintended consequences as well. School superintendents as a group reached a peak of demographic homogeneity. AASA's 10-year studies of the superintendency indicate that exceedingly few persons of color served as superintendent during these years. Men accounted for the vast majority of superintendents, married ones at that. As

the civil rights movement gained strength in the 1950s and 1960s, then as the Women's Liberation movement launched in the 1970s, the matter of who held the most important local school offices around the country became hotly contested. These rights movements and the rapid increase in the nation's diversity stood as tests for a field that seemingly had resisted racial, ethnic, and gender diversity in its own ranks. In the face of this stubborn demographic discrepancy between the highest-ranked school officials and the school communities they served, persons of color and women initiated a variety of legal challenges from the 1950s through the 1980s, demanding that systematic discrimination against students and all school workers—including administrative aspirants—on account of race, ethnicity, and sex be eliminated. School boards responded to pleas for more diverse administrators by including women and persons of color in applicant pools but typically not hiring them in appreciable numbers. Needless to say, the selection of chief school officers who demographically resemble the communities they serve remains an important concern for districts around the country. Not only would this represent improved fairness in access to the superintendency, but it also would increase the likelihood that the primary decision makers in schools understand well the students and families they serve.

The 1990s and early years of the twenty-first century have brought a host of new challenges to the already gargantuan task of superintending school districts. The role of the federal government in regulating schools has shifted substantially with No Child Left Behind, which requires strict forms of accountability in return for federal funding. Many states have implemented increasingly strict standards for students, teachers, schools, and districts, which often are assessed through high-stakes testing. At the same time, state and local governments have suffered serious budget shortfalls, in many cases allocating lower levels of funding to schools. Stretching resources even further, many districts have experienced rapid student enrollment growth.

Despite these significant challenges, survey results published in *The 2000 Study of the American School Superintendency* indicate that two thirds of all superintendents would choose their current profession again. Over half report "considerable" fulfillment in their work. Of superintendents completing the survey, 69% stated that their boards had given them "excellent" evaluations. Though national media reported in the early years of the twenty-first century that a dire shortage of qualified superintendent candidates loomed on the horizon, an ever more diverse pool of credentialed and experienced school leaders appears ready for a turn at the helm of the nation's school districts. Whether these leaders are to be prepared in schools of education through accredited programs is being increasingly contested by right-wing think tanks and business-sponsored forums that are seeking to create alternative routes to the superintendency.

—*Jackie M. Blount*

See also administration, theories of; American Association of School Administrators; boards of education; bureaucracy; Council of Chief State School Officers; Council of the Great City Schools; Cubberley, Ellwood; elections, of school boards, bond issues; feminism and theories of leadership; governance; Harris, William Torrey; hierarchy, in organizations; Interstate School Leaders Licensure Consortium; leader effectiveness; leadership styles; licensure and certification; management theories; morality, moral leadership; No Child Left Behind; organizational theories; politics, of education; power; resource management; school districts, history and development; Sizemore, Barbara A.; systems theory/thinking; University Council for Educational Administration; values of organizations and leadership; women in educational leadership; workplace trends; Young, Ella Flagg

Further Readings and References

American Association of School Administrators (1952). *The American school superintendency*. Washington, D.C: Author.

Blount, J. (1998). *Destined to rule the schools: Women and the superintendency, 1873–1995*. Albany: SUNY Press.

Broad and Thomas B. Fordham Foundation. (2004). *Better leaders for America's schools*. Washington, DC: Author.

Brunner, C., Grogan, M., & Bjork, L. (2002). Shifts in the discourse defining the superintendency: Historical and current foundations of the position. In J. Murphy (Ed.), *The educational leadership challenge: Redefining leadership for the 21st century* (pp. 211–238). Chicago: University of Chicago Press.

Cambron-McCabe, N., Cunningham, L., Harvey, J., & Koff, R. (2004). *The superintendent's fieldbook: A guide for leaders of learning*. Thousand Oaks, CA: Corwin Press.

English, F. (2004). Learning "manifestospeak": A metadiscursive analysis of the Fordham Institute's and Broad foundation's manifesto for better leaders for America's schools. In T. Lasley (Ed.), *Better leaders for America's schools: Perspectives on the manifesto* (pp. 52–91). Columbia, MO: UCEA.

Glass, T., Bjork, L., & Brunner, C. (2000). *The study of the American schools' superintendency, 2000*. Arlington, VA: American Association of School Administrators.

Hoyle, J., Bjork, L., Collier, V., & Glass, T. (2004). *The superintendent as CEO*. Thousand Oaks, CA: Corwin Press.

Kowalski, T. (2004). The ongoing war for the soul of school administration. In T. Lasley (Ed.), *Better leaders for America's schools: Perspectives on the manifesto* (pp. 92–114). Columbia, MO: UCEA.

Kowalski, T., & Brunner, C. (2005). The school superintendent: Roles, challenges, and issues. In F. English (Ed.), *SAGE handbook of educational leadership* (pp. 142–167). Thousand Oaks, CA: Sage.

Tallerico, M. (2000). Gaining access to the superintendency: Headhunting, gender, and color. *Educational Administration Quarterly, 36,* 18–43.

SUPERVISION

Supervision can be traced throughout the evolution of education in the United States from the enactment of the 1642 "ye olde deluder Satan Act" to the present reauthorization of the Elementary and Secondary Education Act of 1965, known as the No Child Left Behind Act of 2001.

The earliest forms of educational supervision were tied to religious control and then to secular interests, traced to the provisions in the Massachusetts Act of 1642, which required New Hampshire parents and masters to teach children reading, citizenship, and religion as a way to promote religious freedom, capital laws, as well as social harmony. Supervision was defined largely by religious leaders, with laymen ensuring that teachers were religiously orthodox, loyal to the civil government, and morally responsible.

From approximately 1642 to 1875, schools began to take form, and supervision was characterized by observance of the school plant, pupil discipline, and teaching process by laymen and professionals in mostly rural schools. Common schools emerged as a way to increase efficiency while accommodating swelling school enrollments, with free secondary schools surfacing in the 1820s and 1830s, in which supervision was a periodic visit made by the superintendent of schools.

Following the end of the American Revolution (1783) and the Civil War (1865), with supervision removed from religious control, board members with titles such as "acting visitor," "school clerk," and "superintendent of schools" conducted supervision. Referred to as a "surrogate circuit rider," the superintendent enlisted assistants when geographical distance and the number of schools exceeded the ability to inspect, and the focus of supervision was not on instruction and its improvement, but rather on dismissal of incompetent teachers given their lack of preparation.

Schools flourished in the nineteenth century at an unprecedented rate, and superintendents could not adequately supervise. Supervision by others, namely the "principal teacher" and then later by curriculum specialists, evolved due to the emergence of graded schools, new subject areas introduced to the curriculum (science, music, art, physical education), and compulsory education laws. Principals were the main supervisors and were expected to train teachers with new materials and techniques that had been adopted.

Paralleling the American Industrial Revolution, supervision became bureaucratic. In this setting, supervision was concerned with (a) exacting implementation of rules and regulations, (b) emphasis on centralized control, and (c) harsh conformance to hierarchical notions of school management. Teachers were considered factory workers and had little role in making independent judgments about their work. The supervisor served as a surrogate factory foreman. The model employed was distinctly inspection oriented.

The efficiency movement paralleled progressivism in which John Dewey believed schools needed to promote the development of democratic principles, experience should serve as the basis for education, and as a field, supervision struggled to define itself due to the complexities of the process being undemocratic and coercive. From the late 1880s to approximately the late 1940s, two related trends in supervision emerged: democratic supervision and human relations supervision.

This period has been characterized as one in which supervision emerged as a function of a democratic setting in which the human factor was finally recognized as something to be considered while striving for efficient, productive instruction.

In the 1930s and 1940s, shifts in supervision began with an increased emphasis on teachers' participation and shared responsibility for instructional improvement. The human relations movement and the work of Elton Mayo proffered that the productivity of workers could be increased by meeting their social needs at work, providing them with opportunities to interact with each other, treating them decently, and involving them in the decision-making process. In this setting, teachers were viewed as whole persons in their own right rather than as packages of needed energy, skills, and aptitudes to be used by administrators and supervisors.

Changes occurred in supervision in that inspection gave way to cooperative conference, discussion, and mutual planning by teachers and supervisors as they faced the learning problems of students and sought better materials, methods, and goals for the teaching process. However, the human relations trend in the field of supervision did not endure, because inadequate attention was given to independent human reasoning.

The decades spanning from 1950 to approximately 1970 included supervisory focus on human resource development and organizational change. Most notably before the launching of Sputnik in 1957, the teaching workforce of the 1950s was underprepared, with as many as half of the elementary teachers not holding college education. Supervision in this era was more concerned with inspection, poorly planned, and imposed on teachers, whereas modern supervision was cooperative, included others beside supervisors, and focused more on teacher needs. Methods such as the clinical supervision model emerged primarily through the work of Morris Cogan and Keith Goldhammer.

In the 1960s and 1970s, the supervisor was envisioned as an "organizational change agent" who drew on social system theory and the business management literature. The field of supervision was influenced by the human resource development movement in business and industry. Supervision emphasized creating the conditions of successful work as a means of increasing a person's satisfaction and self-esteem. Supervision was influenced, for example, by Douglas McGregor's Theory X and Y model. Supervisors who exhibited Theory Y behaviors were more concerned with promoting individual worth and dignity and worked under the assumption that organizational goals could be met through the mutual work of teachers and supervisors and that supervisors could build trust and authentic human relations if there was a shared vision for the work needed to deliver the instructional program. The work of others such as Frederick Herzberg promoted job enrichment, empowerment, and self-direction.

During the 1960s until the early 1980s, supervisors relied primarily on the clinical supervision model that consisted of a preobservation conference, a classroom observation, and a postobservation conference. This trend signaled a shift away from single classroom observations made as inspection to a multiprocess system in which supervisors could work with teachers in cycles throughout an extended period. Supervisory practices began to shift in the 1980s with trends such as developmental supervision, differentiated supervision, and peer coaching. This shift was important in that differentiated and developmental models of supervision moved the processes away from inspectional practices that regarded all teachers as identical to practices that promoted teacher responsibility for growth and development.

Carl Glickman altered the model of clinical supervision by adding a developmental element in which the type of supervision used by a school leader with teachers would be based on the experience levels and needs of the individual teacher. Glickman's conception of instructional supervision was that supervisors needed to work with teachers to determine their conceptual levels and to match supervisory interactions (nondirective, collaborative, and directive) within these levels of development. Glickman believed that a supervisor might better serve his or her staff by responding to individual needs instead of using a single, uniform approach and that supervision should focus on function and process rather than on role or position. The crux of developmental supervision is that a supervisor's responsibility is to select the model or technique that had the greatest growth potential for the person.

In the 1980s, Alan Glatthorn developed another stream of supervisory thought: differentiated supervision. As an approach, differentiated supervision provides teachers with options about the kinds of supervision and evaluative services they receive, because not all teachers need the same degree of assistance or direct assistance from an administrator. Supervision continues to be differentiated through methods as such peer coaching, action research, and the portfolio. Differentiated and developmental supervision acknowledged and relied on teacher involvement, giving rise to teacher voice while supporting reflection, open dialogue, and self-directed learning— all prerequisites of effective adult learning strategies.

Concurrently in the 1980s, the report *A Nation Prepared* signaled a heightened sense of accountability that continues with federal legislation such as the No Child Left Behind Act of 2001. The field of supervision from the 1990s to present has encountered entanglements with accountability and teacher professionalism that indicate that a new era, neoscientific management, has evolved, in which supervisors revert to impersonal means such as checking daily lesson plans or visiting classes daily to inspect teaching, controlling what they do.

The intents and purposes of supervision throughout its earliest inception have created conflicts (e.g.,

supervision vs. evaluation, supervision vs. inspection), and several authors have argued that the field of supervision has continued to exist in a state of uncertainty. Some have called for supervision to be abolished or referred to as something else. Others, however, have indicated that supervision plays a pivotal role in school improvement and that the professionalization of teachers can be enhanced through supervisory efforts.

—Sally J. Zepeda

See also accountability; achievement tests; capacity building, of organizations; career development; career stages; clinical education; conflict management; consideration, caring; creativity, in management; curriculum, theories of; division of labor; human capital; human resource development; innovation, in education; involvement, in organizations; leader effectiveness; leadership styles; management theories; McGregor, Douglas; motivation, theories of; networking and network theory; organizational theories; personnel management; politics, of education; principalship; supervision; Theory X, Theory Y

Further Readings and References

Burton, W., & Brueckner, L. (1955). *Supervision* (3rd ed.). New York: Appleton-Century Crofts.

Butts, R., & Cremin, L. (1953). *A history of education in American culture.* New York: Henry Holt.

Cogan, M. (1973). *Clinical supervision.* Boston: Houghton Mifflin.

Dewey, J. (1889). *The school and society.* Chicago: University of Chicago Press.

Glanz, J. (1998). Histories, antecedents, and legacies of school supervision. In G. Firth & E. Pajak (Eds.), *Handbook of research on school supervision* (pp. 39–79). New York: Macmillan.

Glatthorn, A. (1984). *Differentiated supervision.* Alexandria, VA: Association for Supervision and Curriculum Development.

Glickman, C. (1981). *Developmental supervision: Alternative practices for helping teachers improve instruction.* Alexandria, VA: Association for Supervision and Curriculum Development.

Glickman, C., Gordon, S., & Ross-Gordon, J. (1998). *Supervision of instruction: A developmental approach* (4th ed.). Boston: Allyn & Bacon.

Goldhammer, R. (1969). *Clinical supervision: Special methods for the supervision of teachers.* New York: Holt, Rinehart & Winston.

Herzberg, F. (1964). The motivation-hygiene concept and problems of manpower. *Personnel Administration, 27*(12), 3–7.

McGregor, D. (1960). *The human side of enterprise.* New York: McGraw-Hill.

Pajak, E., & Arrington, A. (2004). Empowering a profession: Rethinking the roles of administrative evaluation and instructional supervision in improving teacher quality. In M. A. Smylie & D. Miretzky (Eds.), *Developing the teacher workforce* (pp. 228–252). 103rd Yearbook of the National Society for the Study of Education. Chicago: University of Chicago Press.

Zepeda, S. (2002). Linking portfolio development to clinical supervision: A case study. *Journal of Curriculum and Supervision, 18*(1), 83–102.

🏛 SUPREME COURT, UNITED STATES, KEY CASES IN EDUCATION LAW

The key U.S. Supreme Court cases are classified by area, highlighting the role that the Court has played in shaping American education and policy. Overall, the Court has left few aspects of public education untouched.

EQUAL EDUCATIONAL OPPORTUNITIES

Race, Ethnicity, Funding

Brown v. Board of Education of Topeka, Kansas (Brown I) (1954) not only addressed race but also opened the door for developments in civil rights and equal educational opportunities culminating for all. In *Brown I,* the Court ruled that de jure segregation in public schools on the basis of race deprived minority children of equal educational opportunities in violation of the Equal Protection Clause of the Fourteenth Amendment. A year later, in *Brown v. Board of Education of Topeka, Kansas (Brown II)* (1955), the Court began dismantling segregated school systems as part of a 50-year battle and more than 30 cases in this important area.

On the related matter of ethnicity, in *Plyler v. Doe* (1982), the Court held that under the Equal Protection Clause, Texas could not deny a free public school education to undocumented school-aged children whose parents were from Mexico. A year later, in *Martinez v. Bynum* (1983), the Court rejected a challenge to constitutionality of a residency requirement that denied tuition-free admission to public schools to minors who lived apart from their parents if they were in districts primarily to obtain free education. The Court declared that "A bona fide residence requirement, appropriately defined and uniformly applied, furthers the substantial state interest in assuring that services provided for its residents are enjoyed only by residents."

In *San Antonio Independent School District v. Rodriguez* (1973), parents challenged a state's system of funding, based on the value of taxable property in local school districts, as unconstitutional in that it violated the Equal Protection Clause since it resulted in disparities in per pupil expenditures based on wealth. Ruling in favor of the state, the Court held that the system neither discriminated against a definable class of poor people on the basis of wealth nor impermissibly interfered with a fundamental right or liberty. In rejecting the equal protection claim, the Court unambiguously declared that education is not afforded Constitutional protection.

Special Education

Board of Education of the Hendrick Hudson Central School District v. Rowley (Rowley) (1982) was the first Supreme Court case involving special education. In *Rowley,* the Court interpreted the Education for All Handicapped Children Act, now the Individuals With Disabilities Education Act (IDEA), as providing a floor of opportunities rather than being a vehicle to maximize a child's potential. The Court ruled that an appropriate education met the IDEA's procedures and did produce educational benefits for a child. Insofar as the Court was convinced that the child received "some educational benefit" without a sign language interpreter, the Court maintained that she was not entitled to one even though she might have achieved at a higher level had officials provided her with such assistance.

In *Honig v. Doe* (1988), a dispute over disciplining students with disabilities, the Court refused to write in a "dangerousness" exception into the IDEA. The Court thus affirmed that the IDEA's stay-put provisions prohibit educators from unilaterally excluding students with disabilities from school for dangerous or disruptive conduct that was a manifestation of their disabilities while review proceedings took place. The Court added that officials could impose normal, non-placement-changing procedures, including temporary suspensions for up to 10 school days for students who posed immediate threats to the safety of others.

Most recently, in *Cedar Rapids Community School District v. Garrett F.* (1999), the Court held that the IDEA required the school board to provide and pay for, regardless of cost, a full-time nurse while a quadriplegic student was in school, since his medical condition needed constant monitoring. This decision expanded in *Irving Independent School District v. Tatro* (1984), wherein the Court decided that a procedure such as catheterization that can be performed by a school nurse or trained layperson is a required related service under the IDEA.

Gender

Franklin v. Gwinnett County Public Schools (1992) was the first Supreme Court case to address sexual harassment in a school setting. In *Franklin,* the Court ruled in favor of a former high school student who sued her school board for monetary damages under Title IX of the Education Amendments of 1972 because officials failed to take proper action when she informed them that one of her male teachers coerced her into engaging in sexual relations.

In *Gebser v. Lago Vista Independent School District* (1998), the Court rejected a claim filed by a student in Texas against her school board after she had a sexual relationship with a teacher. In light of the board's promptly taking corrective actions in firing the teacher and acting to have his teaching license revoked, the Court held that it was not liable under Title IX unless administrators in positions of authority were notified of the situation but failed to act.

Davis v. Monroe County Board of Education (1999), a case from Georgia, set the standards for peer-to-peer sexual harassment. The Court ruled that a school board can be liable for peer-to-peer sexual harassment only if educators, who have substantial control over the students and the context within which the harassment occurred, are deliberately indifferent to harassment of which they have actual knowledge that is so severe, pervasive, and objectively offensive that it deprives the victim of access to the educational opportunities or benefits.

STUDENT RIGHTS

Student Speech and Expression

Tinker v. Des Moines Independent Community School District (Tinker) (1969) arose when junior and senior high school students challenged their being suspended for refusing to remove the black armbands they wore to protest American involvement in Vietnam. The Court ruled in favor of the students, noting that

wearing armbands as a form of passive, nondisruptive protest was the type of symbolic act that was protected by the First Amendment. The Court reasoned that since school officials lack absolute power and that pupils do not surrender freedom of speech rights when then enter the school building, limits can be placed on the extent to which educators may regulate student speech. The Court ruled that absent a reasonable expectation of disruption of normal school activities, educators could not infringe upon students' constitutional right to freedom of expression.

In *Bethel School District No. 403 v. Fraser* (1986), the Court restricted *Tinker* in holding that school officials in Washington state could discipline a student for violating school rules by delivering a lewd speech at a school assembly. The Court distinguished the speech from *Tinker,* where the armbands were a passive, nondisruptive expression of a political position rather than a lewd and obscene speech, totally lacking in any political viewpoint, at a student election that was delivered to an unsuspecting captive audience.

Hazelwood School District v. Kuhlmeier (Hazelwood) (1988) arose when a principal in Missouri deleted two articles, one on teenage pregnancy, the other about divorce, from a newspaper that was written and edited by members of a journalism class that was part of school's curriculum. The Court reasoned that educators may exercise editorial control over student speech in school activities as long as the control of the overall educational process is at stake.

Discipline/Due Process

Goss v. Lopez (Goss) (1975) is the leading case on the due process rights of students in public schools who face short-term disciplinary suspensions. *Goss* was filed on behalf of high school students in Ohio who challenged their being suspended without hearings for a variety of infractions. Ruling in favor of the students, the Court explained since a short-term suspension was not a minimal deprivation of their right to an education, they could not be excluded from school for up to 10 days unless they received at least notice of the charges against them and had an opportunity to respond. Furthermore, aware of educators' need to maintain a safe and orderly learning environment, the Court asserted that there was no reason to delay the time between giving notice and students' responses. The Court also noted that students who pose a continuing danger or who are disruptive can be removed immediately but must be provided with due process as soon as is practicable.

Fourth Amendment

In *New Jersey v. T. L. O.* (1985), after a 14-year-old student, identified as "T. L. O.", and a friend were accused of violating school rules by smoking cigarettes in a lavatory of their high school, they were questioned by a teacher. When questioned by the assistant principal, he opened T. L. O.'s purse, discovered that she had cigarettes, removed them, and accused her of lying. In a second search, he found cigarette rolling papers, some marijuana, a pipe, plastic bags, a substantial quantity of $1 bills, an index card that appeared to be a list of students who owed T. L. O. money, and two letters implicating her in dealing marijuana. After a trial court adjudicated T. L .O. delinquent, the state Supreme Court reversed in her favor.

On further review, the Supreme Court reversed in favor of the state. Finding that the Fourth Amendment's prohibition against unreasonable searches and seizures applies to public school officials, the Court devised a two-part test to evaluate the legality of a search: Was the action justified, and was the search limited to the scope of the original interference? According to the Court, a search is ordinarily justified at its inception when school officials have reasonable grounds to suspect that a search of a student will uncover evidence that the pupil has violated or is violating either school rules or the law. As to scope, the Court held that a search is permissible if its goals are reasonably related to its objectives and is not excessively intrusive in light of the age and sex of a student and the nature of an infraction.

Ten years after *T. L. O.,* the Supreme Court revisited the Fourth Amendment in a dispute over drug testing of student athletes in Oregon in *Vernonia School District 47J v. Acton* (1995). In *Acton,* the Court applied a three-part balancing test in upholding the policy. First, conceding that students have a lesser expectation of privacy than ordinary citizens, the Court reasoned that student athletes experience diminished privacy since they are subject to physical examinations before becoming eligible to play and dress in open areas of locker rooms. Second, the Court pointed out that urinalysis was minimally intrusive since it was coupled with safeguards that allowed little encroachment on students' privacy. Third, given the perception of increased drug use, the Court agreed that there was a significant need for a policy to eliminate drug use and that the one in place was an effective means for doing so. Seven years later, in *Board of Education of Independent School District No. 92 of Pottawatomie v. Earls* (2002), the Court applied *Acton* in upholding a board policy that required all middle and high school students to consent to urinalysis testing for drugs before participating in extracurricular activities.

EMPLOYEE RIGHTS

Free Speech

In *Pickering v. Board of Education of Township High School District (Pickering)* (1968), a teacher in Illinois challenged his being fired for sending a letter to a local newspaper containing an erroneous critique of a board's allocation of funds for educational and athletic programs and proposals to raise revenue for these items. The Court held that the First Amendment protects the free speech rights of public employees who address matters of public concern, adding that absent proof that they knowingly or recklessly make false statements on such matters, their speech is protected by the First Amendment.

The Court subsequently refined the *Pickering* balancing test into a three-step process (*Mt. Healthy City School District Board of Education v. Doyle,* 1977; *Connick v. Myers,* 1983). First, public employees must show that their speech was protected. Second, employees must prove that the protected speech was a substantial or motivating factor in the adverse employment decision. Third, employees must demonstrate that employers would have taken the adverse employment action even if they had not engaged in the protected activity.

Due Process

In *Cleveland Board of Education v. Loudermill* (1985), the Court clarified the minimum requirements of constitutional due process that must be afforded before boards can dismiss tenured teachers who have property interests in their jobs. Specifying that teachers are entitled to some kind of hearing prior to being discharged, the Court noted that such informal pretermination hearings need not be elaborate, since teachers could present their cases at posttermination hearings.

—Charles J. Russo

Further Readings and References

Bethel Sch. Dist. No. 403 v. Fraser, 478 U.S. 675 (1986).

Board of Educ. of the Hendrick Hudson Cent. Sch. Dist. v. Rowley, 458 U.S. 176 (1982).

Board of Educ. of Indep. Sch. Dist. No. 92 of Pottawatomie v. Earls, 536 U.S. 822 (2002).

Brown v. Board of Educ., I, 347 U.S. 483 (1954).

Brown v. Board of Educ., II, 349 U.S. 294 (1955).

Cedar Rapids Community Sch. Dist. v. Garrett F., 526 U.S. 66 (1999).

Cleveland Bd. of Educ. v. Loudermill, 470 U.S. 532 (1985).

Connick v. Myers, 461 U.S. 138 (1983).

Davis v. Monroe County Bd. of Educ., 526 U.S. 629 (1999).

Franklin v. Gwinnett County Pub. Schs., 503 U.S. 60 (1992).

Gebser v. Lago Vista Indep. Sch. Dist., 524 U.S. 274 (1998).

Goss v. Lopez, 419 U.S. 565 (1975).

Hazelwood Sch. Dist. v. Kuhlmeier, 484 U.S. 260 (1988).

Honig v. Doe, 484 U.S. 305 (1988).

Irving Indep. Sch. Dist. v. Tatro, 468 U.S. 883 (1984).

Martinez v. Bynum, 461 U.S. 321 (1983).

Mt. Healthy City Sch. Dist. Bd. of Educ. v. Doyle, 429 U.S. 274 (1977).

New Jersey v. T.L.O., 469 U.S. 325 (1985).

Pickering v. Board of Educ. of Township High Sch. Dist., 205 391 U.S. 563 (1968).

Plyler v. Doe, 457 U.S. 202 (1982).

San Antonio Indep. Sch. Dist. v. Rodriguez, 411 U.S. 1 (1973).

Tinker v. Des Moines Indep. Community Sch. Dist., 393 U.S. 503 (1969).

Vernonia Sch. Dist. 47J v. Acton, 515 U.S. 646 (1995).

🏛 SURVEYS AND SURVEY RESULTS

Surveys provide school personnel and educational researchers an avenue through which a large number of people can be accessed for feedback or information. For example, often school personnel conduct needs assessments to plan effective student, teacher, or parent educational programs. In this situation, every member of the population of interest can be given the opportunity to provide input through the dissemination of surveys. Educational researchers also frequently employ surveys to learn about how specific variables, such as leadership belief systems, are applied in the "real world." This knowledge of the practical application of theory informs both educational policy and instruction in higher education, which may influence practice at the public school level. Because decisions about policy and practice are made from survey results, consideration must be given to the representativeness of both the survey content in relation to the topic addressed and the sample in relation to the population.

One disadvantage of using surveys is the lack of control over who does or does not respond. Due to this lack of control, the survey responses may not represent those of the whole group for whom the survey was intended. Suppose, for instance, that a survey was used to gather information about teachers' professional development needs. If only 5% of the teachers return the survey, the professional development activities offered based on the survey results could easily represent the needs of a select group of teachers rather than most or all teachers.

Alternatively, the response rate may be very high, but items on the survey presented a narrow range of professional development possibilities, which is a content coverage or representativeness issue. Potentially, the activities offered as a result of the survey responses would be minimally useful to teachers in their efforts to increase educational effectiveness. Issues related to content and sample representativeness make it essential to develop or use surveys and design survey research to maximize return rates and ensure that items contain all facets of the topic of interest necessary to make valid inferences from the scores or information obtained.

When developing or evaluating existing surveys, particular attention must be given to the content representativeness issues to be sure that they provide the needed information. The survey content is often derived from goals and objectives or relevant theory. If the goal is to find out about teachers' professional development needs in teaching reading, a search of the literature is needed to identify "best practices" in teaching reading, and the content of the survey should represent these best practices. Assuming a good response rate, the professional development activities offered as a result of the survey should validly reflect the skill development needs teachers feel they have in relation to teaching reading and will also reflect teaching practices that show real promise, as evidenced by the research, for improving students' reading ability.

In research, surveys are often used to gather information about beliefs, attitudes, values, or knowledge. For example, a researcher may gather information from school administrators about their beliefs related to effective teaching practices. The survey developer must consult the research and theoretical literature in order to identify effective teaching practices to ensure that survey items appropriately reflect these practices. If the content of items does not represent all facets of effective teaching (content underrepresentation) or if items are written that are not representative of teaching practices (content irrelevance), inferences made from the scores may not be valid.

Experts can help evaluate the content of surveys. For example, reading teachers might be employed to assess the content of a survey designed to gather information about best practices in reading. In addition, experts can assess clarity of items. Clarity is an important consideration because even if the content is appropriate, poorly written items can yield inaccurate results, in which case inaccurate inferences are made. Items must be easily understood, simply written, and written in a language and at a reading level that is suitable for the respondent. In addition to experts, statistical procedures are used to help the survey user or developer assess the validity and reliability of inferences made from the instrument's scores. The reader is referred to articles in this volume on validity and reliability in tests and factor analysis for more information about these statistical procedures.

Sample representativeness is also an important issue to consider. Unless the administrator or researcher has access to the whole population of interest, drawing a sample that accurately represents the population must be undertaken. A sample of convenience may well accurately represent the population. However, sample demographics (gender, socioeconomic status, ethnic background) should be assessed to ascertain the demographic match between the sample and population. If it is found that the convenience sample does not well represent the population, the administrator or researcher may want to use a stratified sampling method in which the sample is chosen based on the demographics of the population. For example, if twice as many females as males are needed, the sample chosen should contain this proportion of females to males.

Dissemination to a sample representative of a population does not guarantee that the respondents who return the survey will represent the population well. Every effort should be made to maximize the return rate in order to increase the likelihood that the sample will be a representative one. A cover letter that captures the interest of the respondent and multiple contacts to encourage completion of the survey are suggested. In addition, return rates are likely to be higher if the survey is attractive, professional in appearance, and not too long.

In addition to content and sample representativeness, the researcher must consider the logistics related to distribution of the survey. Though an advantage of survey methods is that a large number of people can be accessed, the printing, formatting, and dissemination of a survey can be costly and/or time consuming. Interviews may be conducted face-to-face or by telephone. Phone interviews, of course, can be expensive, and face-to-face and telephone interviews both take much time. Assuming addresses are readily available, mailing surveys is less time-consuming but may still be costly. If a budget does not allow for the cost of mailings on top of the printing and formatting costs, administrators may want to pursue dissemination options. Electronic dissemination is economical if confidentiality is not an issue and if the electronic format allows for a representative sample. Also, researchers and administrators might take advantage of scheduled meetings such as conventions or professional conferences.

When using or designing surveys, the researcher or administrator must be cognizant of issues that can affect the validity of inferences made from results. If the information is important enough to gather in the first place, then it logically follows that it is important that the information be accurate. Due to limited space, many survey research design topics were not addressed (e.g., item writing, response formats, analysis and interpretation, and reporting results), and topics presented were not detailed enough to act as a guide to those utilizing survey methods. The reader who plans to gather information via surveys is encouraged to make use of resources that provide detailed information about survey research methods.

—Margaret E. Ross

See also attitudes; behaviorism; Delphi technique; effect size; empiricism; factor analysis; feedback; halo effect; measurement, theories of; quantitative research methods; questionnaires; research methods; validity and reliability; variables

Further Readings and References

Biemer, P. Groves, R., Lyberg, L., Mathiowetz, N., & Sudman, S. (Eds.). (2004). *Measurement errors in surveys.* San Francisco: Jossey-Bass.

Chambers, R., & Skinner, C. (1999). *Analysis of survey data.* San Francisco: Jossey-Bass.

Creswell, J. (2003). *Research design.* Thousand Oaks, CA: Sage.

Dillman, D. (2000). *Mail and Internet surveys: The tailored design method* (2nd ed.). New York: Wiley.

Fink, A (Ed.). (2003). *The survey kit* (2nd ed.). Thousand Oaks: Sage.

Groves, R., Biemer, P., Lyberg, L., Massey, J., Nicholls, W., & Wakesberg, J. (Eds.). (2001). *Telephone survey methodology.* San Francisco: Jossey-Bass.

🏛 SYSTEMIC REFORM

A system is a group of parts that operate together and influence the operation of the whole. The characteristics of a system are properties of the whole and not of the parts. Human bodies, schools, factories, buildings, airplanes, and automobiles are examples of familiar systems. School reform is like that. Many schools are not unified systems, but collections of parts (programs) that have been brought together at different times for differing reasons. They were never designed to work together. They just happened that way because of periodic accretions or unchallenged tradition. Schools, like all systems, operate according to the first principle of systems thinking: *Structure influences behavior.* A system functions in a certain way because of its structure. In a very real sense, a system causes its own behavior. The systemic structure of a school is the pattern of relationships among the key components of its organization. Most schools function in traditional ways because their structures make it difficult to operate in any other way. Systemic renewal requires that the system be changed at all levels (school, district, state).

Many models have been proposed for school renewal and reform, each with its own assumptions about change and related set of strategies, each with its own strengths and weaknesses. Marshall Sashkin and John Egermeier describe four broad strategies for change that have flourished in varying degrees over the past 50 years. These strategies are as follows:

1. *Fix the parts by transferring innovations:* Help principals be better leaders and teachers better instructors and school curricula more effective by developing and transferring specific innovations to schools (like the "county agent" model in agriculture).

2. *Fix the people by training and developing professionals:* Provide preservice and in-service training programs for principals and teachers.

3. *Fix the school by developing the organization's capacity to solve problems:* Focus on changing the organization's culture by collecting data to identify and solve problems and evaluate which solutions really work.

4. *Fix the system by comprehensive restructuring:* Move beyond approaches to adopt/adapt the best of innovative programs, staff development, and organizational strategies to redesign the structure of the total school in a comprehensive and interconnected way. This fourth approach to change and renewal is often called *systemic reform* because it is concerned with deliberately designing and linking all the various structures within the school and connecting externally with state, district, and community agencies.

Renewal efforts by the Coalition of Essential Schools provide an excellent example of the systemic reform strategy. David Conley also has proposed a framework of restructuring in 12 dimensions and 3 subsets that meets many of the demands of systemic reform. James Keefe and Eugene Howard have developed a comprehensive school improvement process for the National Association of Secondary School Principals and the Learning Environments Consortium International that offers a comprehensive model of systemic reform planning. The process begins with the formation of a school management/design team that is charged with conducting awareness, commitment, and development activities, working to create a school learning organization and leading the staff in collecting school data and conducting a literature search on current educational trends. The school staff then defines the basic components of the school design—mission and vision statements, culture and climate statements, and student goals and outcomes—and the key systemic components of the design: curriculum specifications; instructional strategies; school structure and organization; leadership, management, and budgeting procedures; staffing and staff development provisions; communication and political structures; school resources, physical plant and equipment specifications; and the evaluation plan. The process culminates in an action plan, task force formation and coordinated activity, and ongoing review and evaluation.

—*James W. Keefe*

See also budgeting; curriculum audit; Chicago school reform; culture, school; ethos, of organizations; evaluation; Fullan, Michael; goals, goal setting; innovation, in education; J-curve theory; Kentucky Education Reform Act; management information systems; needs assessment; organizational theories; paradigm; partnerships, interagency; planning models; problem solving; resource management; restructuring, of schools; S-curve theory; school districts, history and development; school improvement models; school plant management; systems theory/thinking

Further Readings and References

Bartunek, J. (2003). *Organizational and educational change.* Mahwah, NJ: Lawrence Erlbaum.

Conley, D. (1993). *Roadmap to restructuring: Policies, practices, and the emerging visions of schooling.* Eugene, OR: ERIC Clearinghouse on Educational Management.

Day, D., Zaccaro, S., & Halpin, S. (2004). *Leader development for transforming organizations.* Mahwah, NJ: Lawrence Erlbaum.

Fullan, M. (2001). *The new meaning of educational change.* New York: Teachers College Press.

Gaynor, A. (1998). *Analyzing problems in schools and school systems.* Mahwah, NJ: Lawrence Erlbaum.

Keefe, J., & Howard, E. (1997). *Redesigning schools for the new century: A systems approach.* Reston, VA: National Association of Secondary School Principals.

Keefe, J., & Jenkins, J. (2000). *Personalized instruction: Changing classroom practice.* Larchmont, NY: Eye on Education.

Sashkin, M., & Egermeier, J. (1993). *School change models and processes: A review and synthesis of research and practice.* Washington, DC: U.S. Department of Education, U.S. Government Printing Office.

Thurston, P., & Ward, J. (1997). *Improving educational performance: Local and systemic reforms.* St. Louis, MO: Elsevier.

Wardman, K. (1994). From mechanistic to social systems thinking (A digest of a talk by Russell L. Ackoff). *The Systems Thinker, 5*(1), 1–4.

🏛 SYSTEMS THEORY/THINKING

Systems thinking is a thought process that considers the interconnections and reactive relationships among the parts of a system. It considers that component parts of a complex system are interacting and are interdependent; therefore, small actions at one level are evaluated to determine potential significant impacts at various levels across the whole organization. Systems thinking seeks to understand all meaningful effects on the whole organization, rather than the effects on a division, a department, or a school.

As an example, systems thinking would seek to understand the impact of a decision to delay starting times by 1 hour and the effects on all parts of the district; the process would look beyond a subset of school that might potentially benefit. The systems discipline considers organizational change theory, decision making, and human behavior to study changes in complex systems within an organization.

The use of systems thinking will enable educators to design and implement solutions that address the reality of the complex environments of schools. Systems thinking requires that leaders address long-term solutions. How will proposed program changes affect student achievement at the end of 3 to 5 academic years? What are the unintended consequences of creating learning teams? Systems thinking uses basic principles and management tools to help leaders detect holistic changes and evaluate potential impact.

A system is a group of interacting and interdependent components that make up a whole. Schools have many systems: the transportation department, the personnel department, teacher evaluation process, and many others. When all systems are considered in relationship to each other, a holistic view of a school district develops. A school district is parallel to a living organism because it is constantly changing, any adjustment to any subsystem affects the whole, and all subsystems must function properly for a healthy district. For example, teachers, books, students, and buildings are all necessary parts of the educational system. When any one of these components is changed, all others are affected and the impact exceeds those obviously expected.

A basic assumption of systems theory is that systems will change based on feedback. Effective feedback can be at many levels and take many forms. For example, feedback about student achievement can be qualitative and quantitative data and can provide information at many levels: students, teachers, administrators, and so on. The feedback must have utility, be economical to collect, and be meaningful. For example, mean achievement scores for all fourth-grade students is simplistic feedback for a fourth-grade teacher, but disaggregated achievement scores by student by content by construct is meaningful feedback for teachers. This type of feedback can be used to plan improvements; the feedback must be available within the system and at appropriate levels.

Systems thinking and feedback help educators identify patterns as different from events. For example, assume that data indicate that a group of fourth graders cannot perform long division. If the school teaches those fourth graders the necessary math skills, then it has reacted to the feedback. This action will not enable future fourth graders to perform long division. However, systems thinking would require the organization to consider the curriculum, assessment procedures, teacher characteristics, and student characteristics to identify the root causes of failure. What patterns exist? Have all students failed to master the skill? What systems changes can be made to influence the scores of future fourth grade students? A common example of systems thinking is that alignment of curriculum, instruction, and assessment can positively affect achievement scores. Systems thinking promotes a holistic view of the school and district and allows leaders to improve the school.

Systems thinking expects circular patterns of feedback that can be used for continuous systems improvement. In the above example, if the school strives for alignment of important components with the vision and mission, then curriculum drives instruction, instruction drives assessment, and assessment leads to evaluation and adjustment of the curriculum. A traditional view would consider a linear relationship between key components: standards drive the curriculum, the curriculum drives instruction, and instruction drives assessment, and so on. Traditional approaches lack feedback loops and are likely to repeat the same errors year after year. Finally, the students move to the next grade, a different group replaces them, and the process repeats without feedback; linear cause-effect models fail to consider the impact of end components on initial components.

Unfortunately, many education leaders fail to use systems thinking to address problems; to a great extent, education thinking is highly linear, traditional, and fragmented. Many educators are highly skilled at problem solving at the individual issue level and have been reinforced for sequential and hierarchical solutions. Traditional approaches are not productive because schools are no longer isolated systems that can operate independent of the larger community. Systems thinking will become a more important management tool because many current problems within education are systematic in nature.

—*Bill Thornton*

See also accountability; boards of education; boundaries of systems; chaos theory; Chicago school reform; communities, types, building of; conceptual systems theory and leadership; consolidation, of school districts; innovation, in education; Kentucky Education Reform Act; leadership, system-oriented; management theories; networking and network theory; open systems theory; organizational theories; philosophies of education; planning models; policy making, values of; rational organizational theory; restructuring, of schools; school improvement models; strategic planning; systemic reform

Further Readings and References

Cooper, B., Fusarelli, L., & Randal, E. (2004). *Better policies, better schools: Theories and applications.* Boston: Pearson Education

Goldenberg, C. (2004). *Successful school change.* New York: Teachers College Press.

Morrison, K. (2002). *School leadership and complexity theory.* New York: Routledge.

Sarason, S. (2002). *Educational reform.* New York: Teachers College Press.

Wallace, M., & Pocklington, K. (2002). *Managing complex educational change.* New York: Routledge.

T

TABLE OF ORGANIZATION

The social organization of institutions for most of the nineteenth century was marked by individualism and casual cooperation. With the emergence of an urban industrial society, organizing people for work or public service required more deliberate and formalized models. German sociologist Max Weber wrote extensively about the importance of rationalization for organizing people for optimal problem solving. *Bureaucracy* was Weber's optimal rationalization model. The table of organization, or organizational chart, is a graphic representation of an organization's structure—the division of labor, roles, and hierarchy of authority that characterize the formal structure of the organization.

A division of labor breaks the work of the organization into separate jobs, each with a specific set of tasks clearly differentiated from other tasks. The division of labor assumes that the responsibilities of one job are well-defined and can be clearly delineated from the responsibilities of other jobs. Differentiation is aimed at reducing redundancy and interpersonal conflict and increasing efficiency.

Organizations most commonly differentiate their structures vertically and horizontally. Vertical differentiation refers to the number of authority levels in an organization. Authority and power in a bureaucracy are largely centralized at the higher levels of the organization. An organization's vertical coordination involves people at higher levels of the organization coordinating and controlling the actions of people at lower levels of the organization through positional authority and rules. Offices within the hierarchy have clearly defined authority over lower-level offices and are, in turn, supervised by clearly specified higher-level offices. With responsibilities and authority clearly defined, the system can be coordinated top-down from level to level, with rules and procedures rather than through personal supervision.

Horizontal differentiation is the degree of differentiation among workers at the same level of authority or the number of subtasks required to process raw material or produce a product. Horizontal differentiation breaks tasks into manageable pieces. Lateral coordination of tasks occurs through communication among individuals who work at the same level of authority or engage in the same tasks or subtasks in the organization.

The problem with organizational charts or any graphic representation of organizational structure is that they often fail to represent actual work groups and dynamics. While it is true that organizations may have clearly visible, formal structures, they also have often invisible, informal structures, norms, groups, relationships, and dynamics that are less tangible but highly influential.

—Judith A. Ponticell

See also bureaucracy; chain of command; conflict management; division of labor; governance; hierarchy, in organizations; infrastructure, of organizations; management theories; organizational theories; rational organizational theory; role conflict; role theory; span of control; systems theory/thinking; Weber, Max

Further Readings and References

Cunningham, W. G., & Cordeiro, P. A. (2003). *Educational leadership: A problem-based approach* (2nd ed.). Boston: Allyn & Bacon.

Hall, R. H. (1991). *Organizations: Structures, processes, and outcomes* (5th ed.). Englewood, NJ: Prentice Hall.

Weber, M. (1947). *The theory of social and economic organization* (A. H. Henderson & T. Parsons, Trans.). Glencoe, IL: Free Press.

TAXES, TO SUPPORT EDUCATION

Societal agencies must decide who should pay for the resources (e.g., teachers, buildings, equipment, materials) required for schooling. One criterion for payment is benefits received. Who benefits from education? Certainly, the students benefit because education provides them with skills and knowledge that will improve their intellectual facility and cultural appreciation and by increasing their human capital and, thus, their social status, earnings, and access to opportunities. To that extent, students or their families should bear some of the costs of education.

At the same time, however, schooling has considerable benefits for society as a whole. Education can be a powerful force for socialization. Education provides society with a common language and set of values. Educated citizens better understand and more readily accept their governments, thereby enhancing political stability. In our democratic republic, education prepares citizens to be more effective participants in self-government.

In most societies, the majority view holds that elementary and most secondary education provides social benefits of such magnitude as to justify public financing and provision. The question then arises as to what type of tax system is best to support public elementary and secondary schools. The design of a tax system generally rests upon three principles: *taxpayer equity, revenue stability, and economic efficiency.*

In general, there are two concepts of taxpayer equity that might be considered: benefits received and ability to pay. Because of the considerable social benefits of education, the benefits received approach provides little guidance for designing a tax system to support elementary and secondary education.

The ability-to-pay principle holds that individuals with greater ability to pay taxes, generally those with greater income and wealth, should pay more tax than those with less ability. This rule rests upon two related assumptions: first, that the generation of any given level of tax revenue should entail the minimum sacrifice of social welfare and, second, that this sacrifice is minimized when the rich pay more taxes than the poor. Thus, the ability-to-pay principle requires that the economic burden, or incidence, of a tax rises with income. By this principle, a tax is characterized as *progressive, proportional, or regressive.* These concepts are best defined in terms of the average tax rate, or ratio of taxes paid to income. If the average tax rate increases with income, the tax is progressive. If it falls, the tax is regressive. If it remains constant regardless of income, the tax is proportional.

Efficiency in taxation refers to the effects of the tax system on the economy and the costs of collection and compliance associated with raising any given level of revenue. If one believes that the workings of a free-market economy result in the most efficient allocation of resources, then the imposition of a tax should alter resource allocation decisions as little as possible. For firms, such decisions would concern what to produce and what resources to employ. For consumers, these decisions would include what to buy and how much to work. To the extent a tax does distort economic decisions, it creates an *excess burden;* that is, a loss of welfare over and above the revenue collected. Excess burden is sometimes referred to as "welfare cost" or "deadweight loss." The only tax that does not entail an excess burden is a lump sum tax, a certain amount that must be paid regardless of the taxpayer's behavior (e.g., decisions regarding work, consumption). There is nothing a taxpayer can do to avoid a lump sum tax. Such a tax is efficient but inequitable and rarely invoked. With this exception, taxes generally impose some measure of excess burden.

Efficiency in collection and compliance refers to minimizing the costs of gathering a given level of tax revenue. These costs involve not only the resources required by the government to collect the revenues but also the resources and effort of the taxpayers in complying with the tax law. The latter may include expenditures on accountants and tax lawyers, as well as the value of taxpayers' time in keeping records and filling out tax forms. These costs vary across tax systems. For example, the government's costs in collecting the U.S. personal income tax are relatively low, while the taxpayers' costs of compliance are high. In contrast, collection costs for the property tax are relatively high, while compliance costs are low.

Because taxes are raised by governments to finance public services deemed essential by the electorate, it is desirable that tax systems exhibit two additional characteristics: stability and growth. Stability refers to the revenue yield of a tax from year to year as levels of economic activity and incomes vary over the same period. Stable tax revenues decrease proportionately less than aggregate income during economic downturns but also increase proportionately less during periods of economic expansion. An example of a stable tax is the property tax. Sales and income taxes, on the other hand, tend to rise and fall proportionately more than aggregate income over the economic cycle. Such taxes are termed *income elastic,* while stable taxes are *income inelastic.*

To the extent that school enrollments grow over time and societies seek to improve school quality (e.g., with more and better teachers, better physical plants, improved technology), growth is another desirable characteristic for a tax system. Some tax bases have greater growth potential than others. For example, as the U.S. economy has moved toward having a greater service sector, a sales tax that includes services in its base will likely exhibit more growth than a sales tax that is limited to tangible personal property. The argument most frequently made against the expansion of the sales tax to include services is that such a change would significantly increase collection and compliance costs. Any tax should be evaluated in terms of its potential to raise revenue that will keep pace with the rising demand for the public services that it is intended to finance.

Although responsibility for public elementary and secondary education rests almost entirely with our nation's nearly 15,000 local school districts, about half the money spent on public K–12 education is provided by the states, while local districts provide about 42% and the federal government about 7%. The state share has risen substantially since 1970 for several reasons. First, in response to lawsuits in the majority of states, state legislatures have increased school aid to offset differences in the ability of local districts to support schools through the local property tax. Second, states have sought to ease local property tax burdens. Finally, the school accountability movement has prompted an increased state role in assisting local schools.

Local districts have traditionally financed nearly their entire share of public school revenue through the property tax. States generally depend on income and sales taxes, traditionally less stable than the property tax. Indeed, state revenues have become increasingly sensitive to economic cycles in recent years. Therefore, as states continue to expand their share of public school revenue and the relative importance of local property taxes continues to decline, public school finance becomes more sensitive to economic cycles.

—*Michael F. Addonizio*

See also accountability; economics, theories of; equality in schools; equity and adequacy of funding schools; finance, of public schools; *Kalamazoo* case; lottery systems; productivity; property tax; sales tax

Further Readings and References

Blumenthal, M., & Slemrod, J. (1992). The compliance cost of the U.S. individual income tax system: A second look after tax reform. *National Tax Journal, 45,* 185–202.
Bowen, H. R. (1977). *Investment in learning: The individual and social value of American higher education.* San Francisco: Jossey-Bass.
Levin, H. M. (1987). School finance. In G. Psacharopoulos (Ed.), *Economics of education: Research and studies* (pp. 426–436). Oxford, UK: Pergamon Press.
Odden, A. R., & Picus, L. O. (2004). *School finance: A policy perspective* (3rd ed.). Boston: McGraw-Hill.
Rosen, H. S. (1995). *Public finance* (4th ed.). Chicago: Irwin.
Weisbrod, B. A. (1964). *External benefits of public education: An economic analysis* (Research report No. 105). Princeton, NJ: Princeton University, Department of Economics, Industrial Relations Section.

TAYLOR, FREDERICK

Frederick Winslow Taylor (1856–1915), "father" of scientific management, formalized the principles of scientific management and rational efficiency during an era of industrial growth at the height of the Progressive era. Though Taylor is best known for his experiments designed to make labor more productive and his work on tool steel, the impact of scientific management on organizations, including schools, was enduring. He viewed workers as rational people who were motivated by money, and from an organizational perspective, this meant the provision of incentive schemes, clear delineation of authority, task specialization, and division of labor.

Born to a well-to-do Quaker family in Germantown, Pennsylvania, Taylor traveled extensively in Europe and attended Phillips Exeter Academy as a young man. Due to headaches probably attributable to poor eyesight (he was diagnosed with astigmatism later in life), Taylor left Exeter to apprentice at a small machine shop, which served to solidify his interest in an engineering career.

After his apprenticeship, Taylor took a position at Midvale Steel in Philadelphia. While employed full-time, he also enrolled at the Stevens Institute of Technology, in New Jersey, but never attended classes. Despite this fact, he earned an engineering degree. He spent 12 years at Midvale Steel, advancing rapidly from a laborer to a foreman and ultimately to chief engineer. At Midvale, he developed and implemented the fundamental essentials of what later became known as *scientific management,* including the dissection of work tasks into discrete actions and the timing of each action based on repeated stopwatch studies. The time studies led to the implementation of a differential rate, which meant that workers earned an amount that depended on the output for the whole day. Consumed with finding the most efficient way to perform tasks, Taylor realized that productivity meant standardizing work, tools, and maintenance techniques.

Taylor left Midvale and moved to Maine to run a pulp mill, a largely unsuccessful and unprofitable move for him. His next move was to Pennsylvania in 1898 to take a position at Bethlehem Steel, where he was hired to introduce a piecework system in the machine shop. However, Taylor was initially more interested in improving machine tools and machine shop processes, an interest that led to the development of a new "high-speed" tool steel, a material that allowed machine tools to cut metal at 3 to 4 times the previous speeds, as well as a special slide rule for calculating machine speed and feed. Both were innovative engineering breakthroughs.

Bethlehem was also the site of one of Taylor's most famous industrial time-and-motion experiments. Common laborers were hired to load pig iron from the yard pile into railcars for shipment. With an immigrant worker he named Schmidt, Taylor conducted a series of tests on the effect of pace, rest periods, method of handling the load, and compensation. Taylor demonstrated that an efficient worker could earn higher wages with an increase in total output. In Schmidt's case, he earned $1.85 a day rather than $1.15, earning a 60% higher wage for loading 380% more pig iron.

Bethlehem would be Taylor's last permanent job. After leaving Bethlehem Steel, he worked primarily as a consultant and lecturer, preaching the gospel of scientific management. In 1910, his most well-known essay, "The Principles of Scientific Management," was published. Labor leaders and other critics denounced "Taylorism" as oppressive and antidemocratic. A strike at a government arsenal over the introduction of scientific management prompted a congressional investigation of the Taylor system, though little was accomplished other than a general denouncement of Taylorism. Wounded by the conflict, Taylor withdrew from public life, letting his growing number of followers carry the battle for "the one best way," a catchword of the movement he introduced. After his death in 1915, his followers continued his efforts.

Taylor's development of a science of management had a profound impact on American industry. Under Taylor, standardization and managerial control, professionalism, and scientific method were championed as never before. To Taylor's critics, however, Taylorism was the quintessence of the mechanistic, alienating character of modern industrialism. Factory workers gradually lost control of their tools, the process of production, even the way they moved their bodies as they worked. This de-skilling of the workforce served to control knowledge and centralize decision making.

Scientific management, with its focus on efficiency, impacted many facets of American life, including education. According to Taylor, application of scientific management could be generalized into every arena of national life, even to the pulpit, and certainly to schools. Administration of the schools was largely in the hands of large, politicized school boards. With the professed goal being to take the schools out of politics, there was impetus to centralize school boards and take power away from local ward bosses. The vision of a liberal education for all students was replaced with an education that prepared students to take their appropriate role as workers. Schools increasingly focused on centralization, expert knowledge, and accountability as the route to school reform. Efficiency experts advocated school reform based on a manufacturing analogy, comparing schools to factories, referring to students as the "raw material," and renaming school officials as administrators. The factory model of schooling was evident in the efforts to standardize the schools with the emergence of supervision standardization, standardized testing, standardized curriculum, and standardized clusters of children.

Taylor's scientific management also had a lasting effect on the field of educational administration, making educational administration a "science," which gave the field status and prestige similar to that claimed by medicine and law. Educational study became more technical during this time with the development of large school bureaucracies. School administrators were taught that accountability was one of the major goals of educational administration. Taking their cue from the ideology of scientific management, new educational administrators demanded autonomy, authority, and discretion to perform their duties. This new educational profession, along with the many structural and organizational changes schools underwent during this era, is attributable in part to Taylor and his view of industrial organization as a great machine.

—*Susan R. Wynn*

See also accountability; administration, theories of; bureaucracy; chain of command; cost-benefit analyses; division of labor; line and staff concept; management theories; organizational theories; outputs, of systems; performance evaluation systems; productivity; scientific management; table of organization; work task measurement

Further Readings and References

Gabor, A. (2000). *The capitalist philosophers: the geniuses of modern business—their lives, times, and ideas.* New York: Random House.

Kanigel, R. (1997). *The one best way: Frederick Winslow Taylor and the enigma of efficiency.* New York: Viking Penguin.

Nelson, D. (1980). *Frederick W. Taylor and the rise of scientific management.* Madison: University of Wisconsin Press.

Taylor, F. (1911). *The principles of scientific management.* Retrieved June 8, 2004, from http://melbecon.unimelb.edu .au/het/taylor/sciman.htm

🏛 TEACHER RECRUITMENT AND RETENTION

Research in recent years has made it apparent that excellence in education is dependent upon having a well-qualified teaching force. A highly competent teacher appears to be the most important element in student academic success. However, the ability to recruit and retain highly qualified teachers in U.S. public schools appears problematic. If teacher/pupil ratios remain constant or increase, more than 2 million new teacher hires will be required by the 2008–2009 academic year. Although many teachers enter the field each year, the average age of the teaching force is higher than in past decades, and retirements will be increasing at a rapid rate over the next 10 years.

PROBLEMS RELATED TO TEACHER RECRUITMENT AND RETENTION

Problems with teacher shortages and retention exist everywhere, but they are more pronounced and severe in some content areas and school systems than in others. The greatest teacher shortages exist and are expected to escalate in urban and rural districts enrolling low-income, low-performing, and primarily minority students. Schools in the West and South are also facing teacher shortages, particularly in communities where enrollment is increasing due to an influx of new industry. Due to present shortages and teacher transfer and turnover rates, a child in public school has a 1 in 14 chance of beginning the school year without a permanent teacher who is certified and qualified to teach the grade level or subject area the child is studying. The odds of having uncertified teachers are considerably higher in urban and rural schools than in suburban ones. Schools with high percentages of minority and low-income students, low standardized test scores, and very limited financial resources tend to have more severe teacher shortages.

Greater shortages exist and are expected to expand more rapidly in some specialty subject areas than in others. The biggest problem areas are foreign language, English as a second language, and special education, with somewhat smaller shortages for science, mathematics, and vocational education teachers. In some school systems, English and social studies teachers are also becoming scarce.

Another problematic issue related to the recruitment and retention of teachers is the anticipated shift in the demographics of the public school population. The U.S. population is expected to change dramatically in the next decade and beyond so that 50% or more of the population will be classified as being from minority groups. Many of them may speak languages other than English. Yet most of the teachers in these schools will likely be White and English speaking unless drastic changes are made in the recruitment processes for potential teachers.

Ethnic and language minority teachers presently comprise only about 5% of the teaching population. Although teachers from minority groups tend to remain in the teaching profession in greater numbers than nonminorities, the shortage of minority teachers, who may have a better understanding of the cultures and languages of minority students, is another issue to be addressed as schools seek to recruit and retain high-quality teachers. Many teachers are not adequately prepared to meet the needs of urban youth, nor are they prepared for dealing effectively with culturally diverse populations.

The solution to the teacher shortage is not simply preparing a diverse group of individuals to teach. The teacher shortage is exacerbated because many individuals who are certified to teach choose not to do so or leave school systems or schools with the most limited resources and with children who have the greatest needs in order to teach in more affluent, less stressful, and better-resourced school systems. Each year, 40% of those who are trained to teach choose not to do so. The annual teacher turnover rate has been estimated at 16% a year. In high-poverty schools, the turnover rate reaches 20%. Thirty-three percent of new hires leave teaching in their first 3 years, and 46% are gone before 5 years. The turnover rates among individuals under 30 appear to be the highest of all age groups. Teachers with midlevel grade point averages in college are more likely to remain in teaching than high and low performers, suggesting that most teachers remaining in the field are average performers academically.

Those teachers holding regular certification, masters, and specialist degrees tend to stay in the field longer than others. The reasons for these findings are unknown. There is some evidence their decision to remain in the field may be related to an increased level of competence or a greater commitment to the field. Higher salaries may be paid to these teachers due to advanced degrees held, perhaps helping them to see themselves as professionals more so than lower-paid colleagues.

Although some teachers leave the field because of family circumstances, such as having a spouse change jobs or wanting to stay home to raise a family, this is not the primary reason they leave. There are many factors related to teachers' working conditions affecting their decisions to leave teaching, including poor student discipline, lack of administrative support, lack of involvement in decision making in areas directly related to teaching and learning, and a public perception that teachers are not doing their jobs adequately. There are also identified reasons why people do not enter the field, such as low pay and a lack of respect for the profession. A first step in developing solutions to teacher shortages is to examine the issue more fully.

EXPLORING REASONS FOR TEACHER SHORTAGES

Although teacher recruitment and retention may seem to be separate issues, they are closely related. Factors keeping individuals from entering the profession often cause those in it to leave. Teachers are not entering the profession for reasons such as low pay, a negative public perception of teachers and public education, and a lack of mentorship and knowledge. Most leave because of dissatisfaction with their jobs. This dissatisfaction is related to many factors, such as lack of status, increasing societal demands for public education, inadequate resources and financial support, lack of administrative support, immediate immersion into teaching without adequate mentoring, and poor working conditions in general.

Changes in society have caused changes in the perception of teaching and teachers and a change in the relationships between schools, teachers, and communities, often with negative consequences. The social structure has changed, causing schools and teachers to take on many roles previously assumed by families and communities, adding to the complexity of the job. Factors related to working conditions of teachers sometimes make it difficult for even those most committed to the students and the profession to remain in the field. Organizational and structural constraints hinder recruitment and retention efforts. Each of these issues is described in the following sections.

CHANGES IN THE TEACHING PROFESSION

Over the last few decades, the context of teaching has changed as our society in the United States has become more complex and disconnected. This has led to a change in the way teachers are perceived by the public and the context within which schooling occurs.

During the first half of the nineteenth century, schools generally had widespread public support. Although salaries and working conditions were often dismal, teaching was a highly regarded profession, and schools were viewed as a major asset for communities. Teachers had a great deal of autonomy within the school and community support for education, although many personal sacrifices were required from teachers. For example, female teachers were not allowed to marry. As schools became consolidated, growing larger in size, they began to become disassociated from the communities and families they served.

The professionalization of teaching and administration, which excluded parents from the teaching/learning process, increases in costs associated with schools and education, and rapid changes in society prompting people to become more separated from the social institutions that serve them have all added to a growing disconnect between schools and their communities. This sense of disconnect often causes teachers to feel isolated from the communities they serve and unappreciated for the job they perform.

Although some research suggests many parents believe the schools their children attend are good, the general perception of public education is that it is failing. The disconnect between schools and society has led to dwindling levels of respect for teachers, teaching, and schools. This perception has, in turn, led to and been further promoted by the imposition of external mandates at the state and national levels with no acknowledgment of the increasingly complex context of the teaching setting or the increasing needs of the students involved. The mandates, largely developed without input from educators, have placed teachers and administrators in the untenable position of being held publicly accountable for meeting all of their students' needs in an environment of dwindling resources, high-stakes testing, and little community support.

These factors often combine to create a sense of powerlessness, leading to discontent with the job. Teachers tend to leave the profession when they no longer believe they can make a difference for students. Instead, they choose professions bringing more esteem, more freedom, and less pressure, leaving classrooms without qualified teachers and students without the guidance and support they need.

THE CHANGING STRUCTURE OF SOCIETY

During the later quarter of the twentieth century through today, societies have been enmeshed in rapid changes accelerated by technological advances and the rise of the global marketplace. There has been a breakdown in traditional family structures, with new and different family arrangements emerging. Increasing levels of poverty, crime, and violence have become pervasive realities in much of the country, particularly in urban areas. Consequently, many students now come from homes unable to provide the financial or emotional support they need.

School personnel are being called upon not only to teach the basic skills and subjects; they are also expected to take on issues previously addressed by families, such as character education and sex education, while providing for students' health and psychological care. Some schools have even taken on the responsibility for providing sleeping accommodations for children from homeless families. In addition to teaching students, schools are being held responsible for many social agency services.

These societal expectations, coupled with external mandates imposing rigid standards for all students and schools, without consideration of the resources or context, place a heavy burden on teachers. As a result, some decide to leave teaching, and others decide against even considering the profession.

WORKING CONDITIONS OF TEACHERS

In addition to the problems related to the context of teaching and the expectations society has placed on schools, the conditions of daily work under which teachers operate serve as an obstacle in teacher recruitment and retention. One of the primary reasons teachers leave the profession, in addition to feeling they do not receive adequate parent and community support, is that they are also faced with inadequate support from administrators and school colleagues. This lack of support is transmitted in many ways: Limited demonstrated means of appreciation, a lack of professional community within the school, and inadequate resources, reflecting the low priority placed on public education.

Administrators can play a key role in whether or not teachers remain in a school. When teachers feel supported and encouraged, they are more likely to feel satisfied with their situation. A lack of empowerment, coupled with mandated curriculum and teaching practices, can cause teachers to feel deprofessionalized. Intelligent and creative teachers will quickly become frustrated in those types of situations. However, when provided with opportunities for meaningful decision making, teachers tend to feel more fulfilled, have a stronger sense of identity as a teacher, and are satisfied with their working conditions.

It is common for new teachers to be given the most difficult classes or schools without someone assigned to guide or support them as they face difficulties in these situations. Although many states have mentoring systems for new teachers, these are often underfunded mandates having little effect on new teachers' professional lives. Without someone to help new teachers learn about complex local contexts, it is difficult for these educators to master and survive the formal and informal organizational and political cultures in their schools and school systems.

Principals and other teachers often take a hands-off approach to other teachers' classrooms and expect teachers to solve their own problems. Student disciplinary problems may become problematic, particularly for inexperienced teachers. With no one to turn to, they may find the task just too difficult. The National Center for Policy Analysis claims about one quarter of teachers leaving teaching because of dissatisfaction cite student disciplinary problems as their primary factor for leaving.

Another reason teachers leave the classroom is that they become frustrated with the lack of resources available to support teaching and learning. Low salaries are one of the reasons individuals leave early in their careers or do not choose teaching as a profession. In general, this factor holds more importance for males than for females. Low teaching salaries make it more difficult to hire and retain teachers in high-demand fields such as foreign language, science, mathematics, and vocational education, as professionals can earn higher salaries working in their fields of practice where their skills are in high demand. Another factor hindering teacher retention is a lack of adequate teaching materials and supplies. This situation often results in teachers having to use their own money to support their classrooms and students. This lack of resources combined with low salaries lessens the likelihood of top achievers entering or remaining in the teaching profession.

A related issue closely connected to financial resources is class size. In some settings, teachers are asked to teach 30 or more students of diverse abilities, making the job extremely difficult, particularly in the lower grades. Large class sizes, limited classroom space and other resources, and increasing levels of public accountability can raise teachers' levels of frustration, causing them to leave the field. Knowledge about these problems can likewise cause potential teachers to select other career fields.

Inadequate resources are generally reflected in poor facilities. Although this might seem an unlikely reason for teachers to leave teaching or to not consider it as a profession, unattractive or unsafe facilities, inadequate heating and cooling systems in buildings, and insufficient classroom space represent a lack of support and can cause people to feel unappreciated. When considered in combination with other issues, poor facilities have been found to affect teacher dropout rates.

ORGANIZATIONAL AND STRUCTURAL CONSTRAINTS

Another reason for the teacher shortage is organizational and structural constraints that discourage people from entering or staying in the teaching profession. Some of these constraints hinder people from teaching in high poverty schools, where the greatest need for highly qualified personnel exists. These organizational and structural factors are hiring practices and policies, certification requirements, teacher assessment systems, and policies related to teacher salaries.

Hiring Practices and Policies

Hiring practices, particularly in large urban schools, where needs are great, are sometimes culprits in perpetuating teacher shortages. These systems often have outdated procedures for posting and filing positions, making it difficult for people to know what jobs are available. Such systems may have personnel staff shortages, causing late hiring and outdated, inflexible rules. In addition, when staff members are overworked, resultant attitudes within personnel offices may not be "people-friendly." In such settings, new teachers may be hired at the last minute, sometimes even after school starts, causing even those committed to teaching in low-income schools to take other jobs.

Transfer policies, which sometimes impact hiring practices, impact teacher shortages and particularly teacher dropout rates. In most school district settings, teachers are permitted to transfer to a new school based on seniority. Thus, teachers who are new to a system are often placed in the most difficult schools as teachers who are already in the system transfer out of these schools. Schools where student performance is chronically low, discipline problems are high, or resources are limited often have the highest turnover rate among teachers. This can result in a disproportionately high percentage of new teachers or teachers with alternative certification, who may not be able to support or mentor one another effectively, being left to fend for themselves in these difficult situations.

State Certification Policies

State teacher certification policies may help to cause teacher shortages. Debates around certification requirements have become a very politically charged area. Those who support stringent certification requirements requiring a degree in an education field believe accepting people who have not gone through traditional educational channels to acquire their training will reduce the quality of teachers and teaching. These proponents of traditional certification approaches suggest alternative approaches will further exacerbate the problems in low-performing and underfunded schools, the places where alternatively trained and uncertified teachers are most often hired.

Those proposing more flexible certification requirements or the elimination of certification requirements state there is insufficient data to support the case for certification solely through acquiring college degrees in education. They suggest those who prepare educators and support traditional models of certification are only concerned about keeping control over the profession.

PERFORMANCE ASSESSMENT OF TEACHERS

Issues related to teacher assessment and evaluation are sometimes a consideration when teachers leave the field. Assessment systems are often haphazard or ineffective, allowing little differentiation between good and poor teachers in terms of feedback or rewards. This lack of meaningful feedback can affect morale of stronger teachers and the reputation of the profession. There has been much dissension about this issue, with concerns expressed about the fairness and integrity of any evaluation system. The creation of more accurate performance assessment measures has often required cooperative efforts between teacher unions and state or local school boards.

Closely related to the lack of rewards for good teaching are the standard salary scales used in most systems. In these pay scales, teachers receive salary increases based on the level of increased educational degree and years of service. Although most systems increase salaries for teachers who receive National Board Certification, there are few systems tying salaries to student performance, teacher competence, or to subject areas based on shortages, need, and the marketplace. Thus, outstanding teachers may believe their efforts are not recognized, and teachers in fields where there are higher salaries in other jobs, such as science and mathematics, may leave the field or simply fail to select teaching as a viable vocation. Like assessment systems and alternative certification, differentiated salary scales have strong proponents on both sides of the issue.

RECRUITMENT STRATEGIES TO OVERCOME TEACHER SHORTAGES

It is imperative to understand the intertwined nature of issues pertaining to teacher recruitment and retention and to deal with these two issues as parts of a whole. Although some strategies may impact retention, they may be primarily focused on recruitment and vice versa. Typically there has been more attention given to recruitment efforts than to retention strategies. Among the approaches used to recruit teachers are recruiting from selected audiences or groups, using alternative methods for preparing teachers, changing hiring practices and policies, and enhancing financial rewards.

Recruiting From Selected Audiences or Groups

It has become a common practice among more affluent or larger school districts to recruit potential teachers from selected audiences or groups. Several types of targeted recruitment are described below.

Recruiting Teaching Professionals

One of the most prominent strategies for recruiting new teachers is focusing upon selected audiences or groups as the primary source for prospective teachers. A common approach involving selected audiences or groups is to recruit teachers from other schools or states who are already teaching and lure them with better working conditions, salaries, or other financial incentives. While this might aid the school system hiring these teachers, it does little to solve the overall teacher shortage. Another approach involving selected audiences is hosting hiring days on college campuses known to produce the quality, race, or subject matter of teachers needed by a school district.

In some situations, particularly in large cities, systems recruit international teacher groups with a particular emphasis on filling positions in mathematics, science, foreign language, and bilingual education. For example, Palm Beach County, Florida has been recruiting in the Philippines and Spain for a number of years and appears to be satisfied with the quality of the teachers they have employed because they are continuing this hiring practice.

Foreign teachers are being employed throughout the country, particularly in urban areas. Although the numbers of these teachers are minimal overall because of a limitation on visas, most U.S. school systems report the use of foreign teachers has been quite successful. These teachers bring new dimensions and perspectives to the school. Often, however, they are put into difficult schools in which the differences in language and culture can sometimes cause problems for them. The primary difficulty these teachers appear to have is in the area of classroom management. Thus, as with all new teachers, it is essential that support networks are incorporated into the system to ensure their success.

Many school systems that recruit foreign teachers do so through external companies that specialize in this area. They appear to be pleased with the results, as hiring from abroad is a rather complicated issue, particularly after increased security demands emanating from the September 11, 2001, terrorist attacks.

Recruiting Minority Faculty

One of the most difficult issues to resolve in teacher recruitment is ensuring adequate numbers of minority teachers enter and stay in the profession. Whatever the specific program strategies used, ensuring an adequate number of minority and bilingual teachers to serve our schools requires extensive planning and implementation.

Some school systems have developed programs to reach out to minority groups, particularly African Americans and Hispanics, to encourage them to enter teaching and to support them once they have entered the field. Jefferson Country, Kentucky, has developed what might be considered a model program for addressing this need. A staff person responsible for minority recruitment utilizes scholarships, loans, and work-study programs to entice promising teacher candidates. The system also provides staff positions for minority individuals, allowing them to work while studying to become teachers. The district works in conjunction with the local university and the community to identify potential educators and support them throughout their preparation process.

The Fontana Unified School District, in San Bernardino County, California, has developed a program with six components to recruit and retain bilingual teachers. These include (a) policies to ensure students' needs are met, (b) a career ladder for bilingual teacher aides, (c) assistance in the credentialing process, (d) a recruitment plan, (e) staff development activities, and (f) working relationships with the community.

Some universities have become engaged in efforts to recruit minorities into the teaching field. For example,

Clemson University, in partnership with three historically Black colleges, initiated the "Call Me Mister" program, which recruits young Black males into the teaching field. Students receive tuition, room and board, and a stipend. In exchange, these students agree to teach in South Carolina schools for 4 years when they graduate.

The DeWitt Wallace-Reader's Digest Fund was instrumental in developing the Pathways to Teaching Careers Program, focused primarily on recruiting African Americans into the teaching profession. While implementing this program, the developers discovered Peace Corps volunteers were a prime group for recruitment as were paraprofessionals already working in schools.

Professional Outreach

Some school systems and states have established networks and advertising campaigns to recruit people with degrees in education who have left the field or never entered it. This recruitment approach is often enhanced with scholarships, loan forgiveness, or alternative certification routes for these potential teachers.

Another recruiting approach is to reach out to those in other professions who have the skills and knowledge in a particular area of need or who have proven themselves as highly qualified professionals. Individuals in careers such as engineering, who may not be happy in their jobs or are retired from their careers and are seeking fulfillment in another arena, are prime candidates.

Outreach efforts such as "Troops to Teachers" encourage retired or other military personnel who have at least a baccalaureate degree to select a career in teaching. This is sometimes combined with alternative certification programs. Participants can receive tuition assistance while getting certified by making a commitment to teach in a low-income school. Retention rates and satisfaction levels for the teaching performance of this group are high among principals.

Research indicates teachers often like to teach in communities near their homes and in situations both culturally and economically familiar to them. Retention levels are high for teachers in schools near their homes. Thus, many schools and states are focusing on "growing their own" approaches to teacher recruitment. This involves strategies such as recruiting individuals in the local community colleges, encouraging teaching assistants and paraprofessionals to consider getting education degrees or participating in alternative certification programs, or implementing extensive career awareness programs for students in middle or high schools. The recruitment of teaching assistants into the profession is expected to increase due to requirements in the No Child Left Behind legislation requiring they have at least 2-year degrees.

Some schools have instituted "Future Teacher Clubs" and "Investigating Teaching" classes in their schools, taking a long-term approach to recruiting teachers into the field. Some combine this effort with recruiting future teachers at local community colleges.

Sometimes community members become involved in encouraging other community members to enter the teaching profession. For example, in Detroit, a local philanthropist working with Michigan State University (MSU) has provided funds to encourage people to teach in Detroit Public Schools. Within this program, high school students may attend summer sessions to learn about teaching, get funds providing loan forgiveness clauses for teaching in Detroit, and obtain summer fellowships for professional development. The local union has joined in the effort by connecting a mentoring program for new teachers to this effort. This combination of support addresses recruitment and retention in meaningful ways.

IMPLEMENTING ALTERNATIVE CURRICULAR AND CERTIFICATION PRACTICES

One of the most controversial approaches to expanding the pool of teachers is the use of alternative curricular models or varied routes to obtaining a degree in education. These approaches fall into three categories: adapting college preparatory programs, changing the venue of teacher preparation, and waiving or changing teacher certification requirements.

Adapting College of Education Programs

To expand the teaching pool, some colleges of education have adopted a fifth-year program model in which students who have degrees in fields other than education acquire a master's degree in education enabling them to become a certified teacher. Sometimes these programs are combined with outreach efforts to those who may have had careers outside of education and include scholarships or loan forgiveness programs.

A more recent addition to changing teacher preparation programs is using distance education as a means of making the pursuit of a degree or certification more flexible. Such programs permit students the opportunity to work on their degree on their own schedule and in distances far away from the college in which the program is offered. There is some controversy regarding the quality of such programs. Research indicates the best of these generally involve both "high-tech and high-touch," meaning the technology is of high quality but the human element is also considered and dealt with.

A final change in curriculum that is meant to make the field more enticing is the development of school/university partnerships in which both parties take responsibility for teacher preparation. Formally called "professional development schools," these partnerships may have a beneficial effect on teacher retention, as teachers in the field are usually engaged in professional development activities as a part of the partnership. Such partnerships tend to raise the status of teachers, because they are recognized as a vital part of the teacher preparation process.

There is some evidence preservice teachers working in professional development schools are better prepared to teach than those who go through a regular internship program. It is purported they will stay in the field longer because they are better prepared. However, there is not presently a solid body of literature to substantiate this claim.

Changing the Venue for Teacher Preparation

One approach to expanding the teaching pool is to move the location of teacher preparation from colleges of education to other venues. In some states, community colleges are instituting teacher education programs. In other states, community colleges are working in conjunction with 4-year colleges to provide the first 2 years of teacher preparation. Nearly half of all minorities in higher education are enrolled in community colleges, so this makes an excellent location for recruitment of minorities. These joint programs, often called "2 + 2," differ from traditional articulation agreements because students are enrolled at both institutions, and thus they provide more student support and an easier transition from the community college to the university.

Another change in venue is offering teacher preparation programs through private enterprise, often using distance education programs. The use of online programs, offered by groups such as Sylvan Learning Centers, is expanding. Although online courses increase accessibility and scheduling flexibility, issues of quality are not fully resolved.

*Changing or Waiving
Certification Requirements*

A "quick fix" approach to recruiting teachers is changing or waiving certification requirements. Those supporting such changes suggest we need to open up teaching to a broader range of people. Those who oppose such actions believe it negates the presence of a knowledge base of teaching, deprofessionalizes teaching, and will result in higher teacher drop rates, as teachers who do not have an in-depth preparation experience will find themselves unprepared for the rigors of the classroom.

Currently, 41 states and the District of Columbia have instituted alternative certification programs. Some states, such as Texas and Delaware, have eliminated or lessened teacher certification requirements. Others have instituted "quick" routes into teaching. "Teach for America" recruits college graduates who do not have teaching degrees into inner cities and rural schools to teach for 2 years. They receive intense training in a summer program prior to beginning their teaching careers. Some also receive loan forgiveness for each year they teach.

Alternative certification programs have not been in place long enough to definitively determine whether teachers who are certified through them or who do not have to meet any certification standards are as qualified to teach or as successful or whether they stay in the field as long as or longer than teachers who have obtained their degrees and certification through a traditional route. Data in Delaware indicate these teachers are staying in the field, but findings from other studies are not as clearly supportive of alternative certification programs.

Factors appearing to enhance teaching success for alternatively certified teachers are a rigorous screening process, a strong well-developed mentor program, field-based experiences, recruiting people who hold at least a bachelor's degree and an interest in teaching, and having high performance standards.

ADJUSTING HIRING PRACTICES AND POLICIES

A third approach to teacher recruitment that can affect retention rates is adjusting hiring practices and policies. The first element deals with how personnel are hired. The second focuses on financial issues.

Improving Hiring Practices

If school systems want to hire teachers, they need to make the process as easy as possible. As noted previously, often the poorest districts have the most archaic hiring systems. The rise of technology is aiding systems to improve their procedures. Using technology allows potential employees to gain information about employment possibilities and apply on a 24-hour basis and helps make the process more accessible. Providing an e-mail address where questions can be answered is another strategy boosting teacher recruitment.

Minimizing paperwork and ensuring a positive attitude among employees are all factors in the recruitment and successful hiring of new teachers. Staff in personnel offices must be well trained to be "customer-friendly" and to understand they are competing in a marketplace where making applicants feel welcome is essential.

Financial Rewards

One of the more recent innovations in teacher recruitment, which can also be a factor in retention, is the use of financial incentives and rewards. Some school systems give cash, signing bonuses to teachers who will accept contracts to teach in hard-to-fill positions. Some states give scholarships or loans to students with a caveat they must teach in particular types of schools or teach in specific subject areas for a certain period. These strategies appear to be effective methods for recruiting teachers into the field and for keeping them in a school system. However, they are less effective in recruiting and retaining teachers than recruiting teachers from professions outside of the teaching field.

A small percentage of school systems are paying moving expenses and/or giving low interest loans for housing or other personal needs. Some systems are experimenting with the concept of differentiated salaries, paying people in some subject areas more than others, which can aid in hiring teachers for high-need subject areas. Some are providing new faculty credit for work experience and thus starting them higher on the salary scale when they enter the profession. Other systems retrain present staff, such as middle school teachers, assisting them to gain certification in a hard-to-fill area such as mathematics or English as a second language. These types of incentives are new, and there is not yet a body of research about their effectiveness.

TEACHER RETENTION STRATEGIES

There appears to be more attention given to teacher recruitment than retention. This may be true because it is somewhat easier to develop and implement recruitment strategies than to develop systems for retaining teachers. Retention strategies often require creating new structures, engaging in innovative practices, and overcoming longstanding policies and procedures. These changes require time and money, which are often in short supply in most school systems. They also are tied to political realities and need community support.

However, some retention strategies are being implemented or have been recognized as possibilities for keeping teachers in the profession. These strategies include enhancing professional status and restructuring working conditions through the creation of internal and external support systems. Teachers value working in a collegial atmosphere led by a principal with a strong instructional emphasis. They want to see evidence that the work they do each day is important and makes a positive difference in the lives of children.

Enhancing Professional Status

While salaries and benefits are not a primary reason why teachers leave teaching, improving pay may raise the status of the profession, and if implemented in ways tied to professional competence, it may enhance retention rates. A financial reward system that appears to be used fairly commonly is paying people for proven skill development such as completing a specific number of college credits or obtaining an advanced degree, successfully completing some specified professional development activities, or demonstrating skills through avenues such as portfolio development or obtaining National Board Certification. There is some evidence this encourages people to stay in the field.

National Board Certification is a standards-based approach to fostering self-reflection and analysis of one's own teaching practice. By engaging in the dual process of creating a portfolio and participating in assessments on content expertise and knowledge about how children learn at various developmental stages, teachers demonstrate, and receive recognition for, their expertise as effective teachers. According to literature produced by the National Board Certification, this process helps teachers become more focused,

reflective, and confident and provides an important professional development experience for each participating teacher. Once a teacher has earned National Board Certification, there is usually a salary increase for achieving this designation.

There is much discussion about moving beyond standard methods for improving salaries. Some school systems and states are changing retirement rules to allow retired teachers to come back into the field without losing retirement benefits. This approach enhances the finances of those teaching and also keeps some of the most experienced teachers available. Some systems use them to mentor younger teachers or to serve as lead teachers.

Another approach being considered is to develop mechanisms connecting student performance to teacher pay. In some states, such as Florida, schools receive bonuses for student improvement. These bonuses are used to enhance school resources or to give bonuses to teachers in the schools.

Attempts are also being made to isolate factors affecting student success and develop assessment and evaluation systems that reward excellence in teaching and weed out poor teachers. While such an approach will raise the prestige and credibility of teachers, it will require cooperation between unions and school boards and a body of research supporting what is assessed and measured. While there appears to be a desire on the part of the field and the general public to identify strategies impacting student learning, a strong enough body of knowledge to create an acceptable system is lacking. There are other constraints as well, including collective-bargaining agreements and the organizational culture of schools, that tend to minimize individual contributions and rewards and instead focus upon the profession as a whole. However, it appears there will be much pressure to develop some type of assessment system tying teaching to learning, along with a system of financial rewards for those teachers who improve student learning.

Restructuring Work Environments

One of the most common reasons for teachers to leave the profession is the isolation of teaching and the lack of opportunities for collaboration within the teaching environment. There are strategies being used in many situations that seek to change that environment. Some involve internal systems of support, and others depend on external support systems.

Internal Support Systems

Traditionally, schools have been organized in cell-like structures, with teachers operating somewhat independently under the headship of a principal who has been seen as the "leader" of the school. This model has led to a sense of isolation and is a factor in teachers leaving the profession. Some of the most promising retention strategies involve changing this model by developing a sense of team and teacher support systems and ensuring administrative support for collaboration and empowerment.

High-quality leaders who empower teachers through meaningful involvement in decision making about teaching and learning issues and help create and support learning communities also help improve the retention rates for teachers. Teachers appreciate principals who support them when it is needed, make efforts to address teacher concerns, and communicate effectively. Having a shared vision and high yet realistic expectations for teaching and learning also affect a teacher's perception about the working conditions at the school. Strong leaders are essential for improving the working conditions of teachers.

A 2001 study by North Central Regional Educational Laboratory in seven states indicates attrition can be reduced by half or more by providing support systems for new teachers. Many schools have implemented new-teacher mentoring programs to guide them through their first year and in some instances, their second year of teaching. Because so many new teachers become disillusioned within their first few years, it is essential to have strong support systems in place to assist new teachers as they learn the social and political realities of their schools and school systems.

Some schools have developed school improvement teams in which teachers and parents and sometimes students engage in dialogue about school needs, goals, and actions. Often these teams develop into learning communities in which people are encouraged to support and work collaboratively with one another. Methods for improving teacher working conditions can be built into school improvement plans, ensuring that the multiple stakeholders representing a school community understand and value the connection between teachers engaged in ongoing learning and effective learning for students.

Some schools have developed common planning times or a common lunch hour to ensure that people have opportunities to think, learn, and share with one another. Some research on teacher working conditions has identified lack of time to plan, discuss educational issues, and teach as a major issue for teachers. It is not unusual for teachers to work nights and weekends to plan, assess student work, and collaborate with others. When these obligations conflict with family needs, it presents concerned teachers with a dilemma—meet student needs or meet family needs? If a teacher does not feel valued by a community or school system, the frustration of this situation may cause him or her to leave the teaching profession.

Many teachers believe they cannot meet the educational needs of all students with their large class sizes and heavy student loads. This too is a frustrating situation for teachers who want to make a positive difference in the lives of children. Structures such as common planning times and school improvement teams help alleviate difficulties, particularly in problem schools, and aid in making teaching a more rewarding experience.

Having meaningful opportunities to participate in the decision-making process appears to positively influence retention. When teachers, administrators, and parents work together for the common good of the school and students, faculty develop a stronger loyalty to and bond with the school and tend to remain in it. The relationships with the community also tend to improve. The more teachers feel valued and efficacious, the more likely they are to remain in the teaching profession.

An important part of supporting all teachers is having strong professional development programs meeting their individual needs. Although new teachers have special training needs, the nature of teaching and learning requires all teachers to update their skills and to engage in continuous learning. Providing funds and time to allow teachers to grow professionally is an important element in teacher retention. Sometimes these programs are developed in conjunction with universities and bring in the most recent researchers to ensure that teachers are familiar with innovative information. Having such partnerships tends to strengthen the collaborative efforts of the school.

Restructuring schools to make them smaller appears to be one of the most successful strategies in teacher retention. It reduces isolation and makes problems appear to be more solvable. Some schools have developed schools within a school to enhance communications and interactions, ensuring stronger relationships between and among students, teachers, and parents.

Reforms, policies, and organizational patterns can help improve teacher working conditions by attending to issues mattering most to teachers. For example, many teachers believe an important area for improvement is to increase their time available for teaching and their ability to participate in decisions directly affecting teaching and learning. Class size reductions, reduced teaching loads (especially for new teachers), adequate time for planning and collaborative work, and high-quality professional development focused on individual needs may improve teachers' perceptions about their working conditions. School districts create some of the policies contributing to school working conditions. This is especially true in the areas of facilities, resource allocation, and professional development. Therefore, it is important to identify policies in districts that act as catalysts or barriers for improving working conditions.

External Support Systems

Other methods for restructuring schools so teachers are supported and are more professionally engaged involve making connections with individuals, groups, or organizations external to the school. Among the most prominent are school assistance teams, local, regional, or national educational networks, professional development schools, the involvement of external stakeholders or intermediary organizations, and state or federal policies.

School Assistance Teams

In 2002, the federal government identified over 8,000 schools as low performing, based on state definitions under the No Child Left Behind (NCLB) legislation. The number of low-performing schools is expected to increase in the next few years due to the NCLB standards for student adequate yearly progress (AYP).

Morale among students and faculty within low-performing schools is often low, making it difficult to hire and retain qualified teachers. School assistance teams, composed of experts who work with troubled schools under the direction of state departments of education, are being created across the nation. Implementation methods and strategies vary. Many states, such as North Carolina, Texas, and Alabama, report impressive school improvement gains resulting from the efforts of the school assistance team models.

School assistance teams can facilitate an increased focus on student learning needs, promote collaboration, and mandate that adequate time be earmarked for professional development and inquiry into best practices for teaching and learning. Although it is not primarily a strategy for teacher retention, improving troubled schools has the potential for retaining teachers and is a promising strategy requiring further research.

Professional Education Networks

Many researchers have emphasized the importance of professional education networks as an avenue for enhancing schools and teacher professionalism. For example, teacher leadership networks help mature teachers prepare for new leadership roles within their schools and school systems. As teacher leaders, they are able to serve as a resource for new teachers, facilitate active engagement by multiple stakeholders in collaborative decision making, serve as critical friends for other teachers, and assist with learning-focused leadership activities within the school.

Professional Development Schools

Professional development schools and networks connecting them with others emphasize the need for mutually beneficial partnerships between and among colleges of education or other higher-education entities and pre-K–12 schools and systems. As with the professional education networks described above, an underlying purpose for professional development schools is to improve the quality of education for today's students and teachers as well as for teachers of tomorrow. By interacting with a variety of stakeholders, all focused on the improvement of teaching and learning, classroom teachers are able to become engaged in meaningful and ongoing professional development that enriches their own practice.

External Constituents and Intermediary Organizations

Opportunities to understand and participate in activities strengthening the intersection among educational improvement and community and economic development can help teachers develop new skills and understandings. Schools and their communities have become disconnected, according to some research. As such, educational, community leadership, and economic development tasks are viewed in isolation rather than as interdependent parts of a whole. When teachers can interact with external constituents in ways that embrace the interdependent nature of communities, rather than having to defend their practice from undue criticism, there can be opportunities for all members of the community to gain a deeper appreciation and respect for each other.

Intermediary organizations, groups actively promoting a reform effort in a school or school system, can serve an important role in improving teacher working conditions by focusing regular attention on issues or situations. The role of intermediary organizations often is to ask provoking questions, conduct research on practices, and evaluate the results of initiatives. The Annenberg Challenge is one example of educational reform efforts benefiting from the involvement of intermediary organizations.

State and Federal Policies

States help ensure teaching quality, set standards for the preparation of new and current teachers, and develop licensing requirements. States can provide assistance to schools and districts by offering incentives for retaining strong teachers, especially in hard-to-staff and low-performing schools. Additional funding or incentives for improved school facilities and other working condition issues can go a long way to help retain quality teachers. Federal policies such as No Child Left Behind or Title II allocations should include adequate funding to support the recruitment and retention of qualified teachers in all school districts. The unintended consequences of state and federal policies must be taken into consideration by policymakers, particularly as they affect the morale of teachers and the public perception of the teaching profession and public education if the teacher retention issue is to be resolved.

—Cynthia J. Reed and Frances K. Kochan

See also attitudes toward work; career stages; class size; differentiated staffing; leadership, teacher; morale; National Council for the Accreditation of Teacher Education; professional development schools; satisfaction, in organizations and roles; schools of education; student teaching; team teaching

Further Readings and References

Allen, R. (2002). *Teacher education at the community college: partnership and collaboration.* (ERIC Clearinghouse for Community Colleges, EDO-JC-02-05). Retrieved September 7, 2005, from http://www.gseis.ucla.edu/ccs/digests/dig01205.htm

Boyd, D., Lankford, H., Loeb, S., & Wyckoff, J. (2003). *The draw of home: How teachers' preferences for proximity disadvantage urban schools.* National Bureau of Economic Research. Retrieved September 7, 2005, from http://nber.org

Dzvimbo, K. P. (2003). *The international migration of skilled human capital from developing countries.* Washington, DC: World Bank, HDNED.

Edwards, V. B. (Ed.). (2000). Quality counts 2000: Who should teach? [Special issue]. *Education Week, 19*(18).

Evelyn, J. (2002, March 8). States give community colleges a role in educating teachers. *The Chronicle of Higher Education.* Retrieved September 7, 2005, from http://chroniclecom/

Hanushek, E. A., Kain, J. F., & Rivkin, S. G. (2004). The revolving door. *Education Next, 4*(1), 76–82.

Hare, D., & Hare, J. (2001). *Effective teacher recruitment and retention strategies in the Midwest: Who is making use of them?* Naperville: IL: North Central Regional Educational Laboratory.

Harrington, P. E. (2001). Attracting new teachers requires changing old rules. *The College Board Review, 192*, 6–11.

Hussar, W. J. (2002). *Projections of education statistics to 2011.* Washington, DC: U.S. Department of Education, National Center for Education Statistics.

Kochan, F. K., & Reed, C. J. (2005). Collaborative leadership, community building, and democracy in public education. In F. English (Ed.), *The SAGE handbook of educational leadership* (pp. 68–84.) Thousand Oaks, CA: Sage.

Koop, W. (2000). Ten years of Teach for America. *Education Week, 19*(41), 48–53.

Legler, R. (2002). *Alternative certification: A review of theory and research.* North Central Regional Educational Laboratory. Retrieved September 7, 2005, www.ncrel.org/policy/pubs/html/alcert/index.html

Mantle-Bromley, C., Gould, L. M., McWhorter, B. E., & Whaley, D. C. (2000). The effect of program structure on new teachers, employment, and program satisfaction patterns. *Action in Teacher Education, 22*(1), 1–14.

Mathews, D. (2003). *Is there a public for public schools?* Dayton, OH: Kettering Foundation.

Milanowski, A. (2003). The varieties of knowledge and skill-based pay design: A comparison of seven new pay systems for K–12 teachers. *Education Policy Analysis Archives, 11*(4). Retrieved January 30, 2003, from http://www.epaa.asu.edu/epaa/v11n4

Moir, E. (2003). *Launching the next generation of teachers through quality induction.* New York: National Commission on Teaching & America's Future.

Murphy, P. J., & DeArmond, M. M. (2003). *From the headlines to the frontlines: The teacher shortage and its implications for recruitment policy.* Seattle: University of Washington Center on Reinventing Public Education, Daniel J. Evans School of Public Affairs.

Nieto, S. (2003). *What keeps teachers going?* New York: Teachers College Press

Odden, A. (2000). New and better forms of teacher compensation are possible. *Phi Delta Kappan, 81,* 361–366.

Schneider, M. (2003). *Linking school facility conditions to teacher satisfaction and success.* Washington, DC: National Clearinghouse for Educational Facilities.

Theobald, N. D., & Michael, R. S. (2001). *Turnover in the Midwest: Who stays, leaves, and moves?* Naperville: IL: North Central Regional Educational Laboratory.

U.S. General Accounting Office. (2001) *Troops to teachers program helped address teacher shortages: Report to Congress 2001.* Washington, DC: Author.

Useem, E. (2003, March 1). *The retention and qualifications of new teachers in Philadelphia's high-poverty middle schools: A three-year cohort study.* Philadelphia Education Fund. Paper presented at the annual conference of the Eastern Sociological Society, Philadelphia, PA.

TEAM TEACHING

Team teaching, conceptualized and developed at Harvard University in the mid-1950s, calls for teachers to work together to plan, teach, and evaluate a common group of students. Initiated in 1957, a team project sponsored by Harvard University and Lexington, Massachusetts, Public Schools, attracted worldwide attention and influenced the design of school buildings. A great many schools were designed to accommodate team teaching and featured large, open classrooms or spaces with collapsible partitions. Many of these school buildings, however, were poorly utilized, and some of these facilities were reconverted into self-contained classrooms with hard walls. Many early team-teaching efforts were abandoned or modified because of the presumed failures of the open-space architecture. Team teaching seemed unsuccessful because teachers were poorly prepared to take advantage of teaming, and support from administrators was lacking.

Functional divisions of curriculum and student tracking have characterized the bureaucratic organizational structure of schools. This structure promoted teacher isolation and detachment, forcing them to work both physically and intellectually separate from their colleagues with limited professional sharing. Influenced by organizational theory literature from the corporate sector, authentic teamwork, collegial interaction,

and collaborative decision making are associated with successful school improvement and have become prominent in the literature on school reform. Team teaching has become a major element of school organizational and curricular reform.

The team-teaching approach is being promoted partly because of increased expectations that all students meet standards of learning performance through inclusive practices. At the same time, professional standards adopted by the National Board for Professional Teaching Standards, the Interstate New Teacher Assessment and Support Consortium, and the National Staff Development Council endorse working collaboratively, fostering relationships with school colleagues, and creating time for teachers to work together.

The middle school movement of the 1980s promoted school restructuring from individualized teaching in junior highs to middle schools organized around team teaching. The influential report, *Turning Points,* released by the Carnegie Council on Adolescent Development, urged school restructuring around organizational cultures that are characterized by collaborative inquiry, teacher teaming, and collegial sharing. In 2000, 79% of middle school principals reported that they had teams, up from 57% in 1992.

The restructuring of high schools to smaller learning communities includes interdisciplinary teaching teams and planning periods designed for teacher collaboration. Teacher teaming in high school can ease student transition from middle school and ensure that instruction for English language learners and special education students includes high-level concepts in content area studies.

In elementary schools, the team-teaching approach is being advanced because of special education mandates for inclusion classrooms and as a way to provide developmentally appropriate educational experiences and individualized instruction that will benefit all students. Teacher teams with multiage groups of students, looping, and coteaching distinguish staffing models that are changing the elementary school norm of the self-contained classroom-based teacher.

In essence, teachers in teams seek to accomplish collaboratively what self-contained teachers seek to accomplish independently. It shifts the role of instruction from the individual to a team. Team teaching must include basic elements: (a) long- and short-range curriculum planning by all team members, (b) coteaching, (c) team assessment of instructional sequences and entire instructional program, (d) students regularly connecting with all team members, (e) team responsibility for evaluating student progress, and (f) unselfish sharing of classroom materials and space.

Proponents of team teaching maintain that it reduces teacher isolation, provides avenues for professional growth, promotes greater instructional interaction to examine classroom challenges, and improves student achievement. Researchers contend that teamed teachers are more likely to collaborate and share their knowledge, as well as create stronger relationships among themselves and students. Teachers benefit from opportunities to focus collaboratively on improving curriculum and teaching practices, activities that may affect student achievement.

Teaming is associated with implementation of more effective classroom practices and greater teacher capacity for change. A number of researchers report that teachers who work collaboratively in teams increase curriculum coordination, authentic instruction, interdisciplinary practices, and authentic assessment. In addition, studies show schools that have implemented teaming report a more positive school climate, higher teacher job satisfaction, and more frequent contact with parents.

School arrangements critical to the success of teaming are common planning time, lower student numbers, and team longevity. Studies provide evidence that restructuring school schedules to offer sufficient common planning time enables teachers to learn and problem solve together. Research also suggests that successful team activities, particularly curriculum coordination and coordination of student assignments, are more likely to occur when teams of teachers work with fewer students. Furthermore, teachers who have teamed together 3 or more years implement more effective classroom practices and team activities.

Teachers value the benefits of teaming and prefer to work in teams rather than work individually. However, in some studies, creating and maintaining habits of collaborative work patterns in schools continues to be an elusive objective. Common obstacles to effective teaming practices are the lack of time for professional collaboration, increasing work demands, and a lack of commitment by teachers. Teacher conflict within teams also affects collaborative work. Furthermore, team continuity and constantly changing team membership is a challenge in schools with high teacher turnover and affects the team's impact on student outcomes. Perhaps the most debilitating barrier is the lack of administrator resolve to promote and sustain collaborative practice. This kind of endeavor requires

leadership that is prepared and committed to confront and deal with the challenges of reforming schools.

—Bobbie J. Greenlee

See also career stages; instructional interventions; leadership, distributed; learning environments; mentoring; restructuring, of schools; teacher recruitment and retention

Further Readings and References

Cotton, K. (2001). *New small learning communities: Findings from recent literature.* Portland, OR: Northwest Regional Educational Laboratory.

Erb, T. O. (2001). Transforming organizations for youth and adult learning. In T. S. Dickinson (Ed.), *Reinventing the middle school* (pp. 176–200). New York: RoutledgeFalmer.

Flowers, N., Mertens, S. B., & Mulhall, P. F. (2000). How teaming influences classroom practices. *Middle School Journal, 32*(2), 52–59.

Jackson, A. W., & Davis, G. A. (2000). *Turning points 2000: Educating adolescents in the 21st century.* New York: Teachers College Press.

Leonard, L., & Leonard, P. (2003). The continuing trouble with collaboration: Teachers talk. *Current Issues in Education, 6*(15). Retrieved September 7, 2005, from http://cie.ed.asu.edu/volume6/number15/

Valentine, J. W., Clark, D. C., Hackman, D. G., & Petzko, V. N. (2002). *A national study of leadership in middle level schools: Vol 1. A national study of middle level leaders and school programs.* Reston, VA: National Association of Secondary School Principals.

TECHNOLOGY AND THE LAW

How we communicate has changed because of the explosive growth of the Internet, which has prompted the development of many new technologies (e.g., digital cameras, wireless computers).

The Internet and the World Wide Web (WWW) are often confused, and the terms are used interchangeably. The Internet is a networking infrastructure. It is a network of networks that is capable of connecting computers around the world utilizing a variety of protocols. The WWW is the medium by which one accesses information over the Internet using a browser that connects the end user to Web documents or pages that contain video, graphics, text, and sound. The Internet is available in over 200 countries, millions of people use it daily, and there are over 100 million Web pages of information. The Internet is a teaching and learning tool that has tremendous potential for the user; therefore, students must have free access to the Internet to learn how to analyze, locate, evaluate, and communicate information and ideas.

The Internet coupled with the need to provide access to information has become the challenge for twenty-first century schools. However, this access to information comes with the potential for abuse. Most discussion concerning the abuses of technology centers around access to inappropriate material on the Internet.

State and federal governmental officials often find themselves being reactive rather than proactive when it comes to technology abuses. In an effort to protect children from pornography and predatory behavior, the U.S. Congress passed several pieces of legislation in the last decade. First, the Communications Decency Act (CDA) was enacted as part of the Telecommunications Act of 1996. The act made it law that any individual who transmitted obscene or indecent material to a minor under 18 years old was criminally liable. It was challenged in *Reno v. American Civil Liberties Union* in 1997, and the Supreme Court struck down the statute because it was "facially overboard" and a constitutional violation that abridged free speech.

Second, the Congress, in 1998, passed the Child Online Protection Act (COPA) before the ink was dry on *Reno*. In an attempt to address issues raised by the Court in *Reno,* they wrote COPA so that it applied only to information displayed on the Internet, restricts only the material that is harmful to minors, and applied to communication made for commercial purposes. The legislation was challenged by Internet providers who believed that the statute violated the First Amendment free speech rights of adults by banning constitutionally protected speech. The Supreme Court based their decision on the fact that by using community standards to identify harmful material, the statute was overboard, and they remanded the case to the lower court.

Finally, the Congress passed the Children's Internet Protection Act (CIPA) in 2001. This statute requires that public schools and libraries implement Internet safety policies and install Internet filters on computers to prevent users from accessing pornography, obscene material, and other material that is harmful to minors. CIPA applies to schools and libraries that receive federal discounts for purchasing Internet access under the federal E-rate program and those who receive funds to purchase computers or Internet access under Title III of the Elementary and Secondary Education Act of 1965. CIPA was challenged by the American Library Association and others on the grounds that it violated the constitutional rights of adults and children using libraries. The Supreme Court upheld CIPA. It is important to note that the American Library Association case applied only to public libraries. Public schools did not participate in the case, and they have been meeting CIPA's requirements since October 2002.

Filtering is Internet commercial-blocking software that denies access to inappropriate materials or activities. Nancy Willard noted in 2002 that commercial filtering software used in schools may be legally challenged for the following reasons:

- Blocking decisions are not being made by professional educators or librarians.
- Category definitions and categorization decisions of the companies are made without reference to local community or school standards.
- Lists of block sites, as well as the specific methods that filtering software companies use to compile and categorize lists, are considered proprietary information.
- There is no vehicle to ensure public accountability on the part of the commercial filtering software companies. They are not subject to freedom of information/access to public records laws. Their board of directors cannot be held accountable to the citizens of a community through an election process.
- Several filtering companies have extensive marketing relationships with conservative religious organizations. The primary target markets for many filtering companies are employers in government and business. It is unknown how the existence of other markets may be impacting the blocking decision making of these companies.

To further protect students, most schools require students and their parents to sign an "Acceptable Use Policy" agreement. This document outlines specific guidelines for Internet use at school. The typical policy informs the user that the Internet is not to be used for private, commercial, business, religious, or political reasons. It also informs them that materials on the Internet and the content of e-mail messages are not confidential; they are expected to respect the rights and property of others; and they may not improperly access, misappropriate, or misuse the files, data or information of another. Those who fail to follow the policy guidelines will have their privileges to use the Internet suspended or revoked.

Student-created Web pages are another area of concern. Many school districts do not allow students to create personal Web pages during school time. This does not mean that student cannot create his or her own personal Web page. If students create Web pages away from school and do not disrupt school activities, they are within their rights and should not be disciplined. When issues of this nature arise, administrators must realize that students retain their right to free expression. Finally, school-sponsored Web pages are typically maintained by the school's technology specialist and are used to display school-related business or activities. Students should not be permitted to link their personal Web pages to the school Web page. However, student work may be exhibited on the school page with prior permission from the student.

—*John S. Gooden*

See also computers, use and impact of; digital divide; instructional interventions; instructional technology; law, trends in; learning, online; Web-based teaching and learning

Further Readings and References

Child Online Protection Act, 47 U.S.C. 231 (1998).

Communications Decency Act, 47 U.S.C. 223 (1996).

Coppola, E. (2004). *Powering up: Learning to teach well with technology.* New York: Teachers College Press.

Fabos, B. (2004). *Wrong turn on the information superhighway.* New York: Teachers College Press.

Reno v. American Civil Liberties Union, 117 S.Ct. 2329 (1997).

Supreme Court rules on Child Online Protection Act. (2002, July). *The Computer & Internet Lawyer, 19,* p. 30.

Tenenbaum, L. (2000). Disciplining student for off-campus Web sites. *New York Law Journal, 31*(2), 110–115.

Tinker v. Des Moines Independent Community School District, 393 U.S. 503 (1969).

United States v. American Library Association, Inc., 539 U.S. 194 (2003).

Wenglinsky, H. (2005). *Using technology wisely.* New York: Teachers College Press.

Willard, N. (2002). *The constitutionality and advisability of the use of commercial filtering software in U.S. public schools.* Eugene, OR: Center for Advanced Technology in Education.

🏛 TELEVISION, IMPACT ON STUDENTS

Television is a telecommunication system that transmits images of objects (stationary or moving) between distant points and most often comes into schools via cable or satellite transmission. Television programs have positive effects on teaching and learning, especially when teachers use television programs that are produced and used explicitly for instructional purposes. Even greater benefits are noted when teachers are involved in the selection, utilization, and integration of television programming into the curriculum. Through the use of television programs, teachers are able to focus on the latest news and current events along with exposing their students to world events and cultures other than their own. Students are able to see beyond their teachers' own perspectives and can explore truth without sensationalism or condescension. Dramatic television (fictional stories) with educational messages can engage and motivate students, model healthy behaviors, stimulate students' minds, and engage children's emotions. Interactive cable televising can even link classrooms and teach advanced high school courses that could be prohibitively expensive for any one system to offer alone.

A number of companies and services are available to school systems to provide televised educational programming. The Stars Schools Consortium, Cox Communications, Galaxy Classroom, Sunburst Technology, Direct TV, and the JASON Project provide a multitude of telecourses, live broadcasts, and educational materials to thousands of students nationwide. CNN's Student Newsroom delivers a daily 10-minute news segment produced by students, while Channel One produces a daily 12-minute news summary, containing 2 minutes of advertisements, that is fed directly into classrooms.

Although the widespread public belief is that television has detrimental effects on student achievement, the sum of the research on television viewing does not support that belief. For example, National Assessment of Educational Progress (NAEP) surveys from 1980 to 1984 reveal that viewing 1 to 2 hours of TV a day actually correlates positively with students' reading achievement. However, achievement falls with longer daily viewing periods. Also, the evidence is insufficient to suggest that television viewing displaces academic activities or has a negative impact on school achievement. The viewing of television by very young children does not lead to significant learning gains. Students may be very attentive while they watch TV and still have a very small understanding of what is happening in the program. There are a few negative aspects of TV viewing that are supported by research.

Viewing violence on television is moderately correlated with aggression in children and adolescents. Also, television viewing is correlated with child obesity and a decline in the overall physical fitness of American children.

Despite the positive effects of using TV in the classroom, teachers use TV less then 30 minutes a week in school. It is likely that prevailing negative public beliefs about television viewing will continue to limit the use of appropriate and enriching educational programs in schools.

—Kimberly Martinez

See also computers, use and impact of; discipline in schools; instructional technology; literacy, theories of; National Assessment of Educational Progress; violence in schools

Further Readings and References

Bray, M., Brown, A., & Green, T. (2004). *Technology and the diverse learner.* Thousand Oaks, CA: Corwin Press.

DeRoche, T. (2003, October 22). Classroom TV. *Education Week.* Retrieved September 7, 2005, from bpn.net/pdfs/Education_Week_GALAXY.PDF

Lehr, F. (2000). *Television viewing and reading.* Urbana, IL: ERIC Clearinghouse on Reading and Communication Skills. (ERIC Document Reproduction Services No. ED272855)

Wenglinsky, H. (2005). *Using technology wisely.* New York: Teachers College Press.

Winn, M. (2002). *The plug-in drug. Television, computers, and family life.* New York: Penguin Books.

🏛 TERRORISM

Terrorist attacks and impact on schools has necessitated a new role for leaders at local and district, as well as at university and policy-making, levels. *Terrorism* means the use of terror to repress or domineer by means of panic and fear, and *bioterrorism* is the intentional use of infectious biological agents, or germs, to cause illness. While learning how to deal with terrorism has become central to U.S. foreign policy, transference has only just begun for educational institutions. Principals and superintendents have been called upon to guide action for preventing catastrophe and simultaneously promote the health of school populations.

Governmental agencies claim that schools increasingly constitute *soft* targets for attracting terrorist attacks, mainly because they draw overwhelming media attention and house society's most innocent citizens. Schools as national icons may be in preeminent danger, not unlike renowned buildings, as demonstrated by the terrorist attacks on America on September 11, 2001. The President of National School Safety and Security Services warns that Al-Qaeda has already threatened America's children and victimized school buses abroad. Moreover, the American Red Cross has alerted citizens to prepare for the unthinkable. "Code Orange" (high security) dictates that school leaders report suspicious activity, review emergency plans, and address children's fears. Specialized curricula address racial issues and powerful feelings, especially involving wrongful attribution as a result of terrorism.

The K–12 school system's mandate is to demonstrate the necessary problem solving for developing emergency response systems consistent with the expectations for homeland security. As one major change, comprehensive partnerships with agencies, communities, and universities must be forged. Systematically integrated schools can effectively exploit the expertise of public health organizations, security agencies, disease and poison control centers, and more. However, legislative mandates involving safety and liability issues for schools have sprung forth marketers in the form of consulting firms that target crisis preparedness training. Such coalescing realities make it difficult to ascertain how much emergency school responsiveness is "rational" and "authentic" apart from corporate America's own motives. Terrorism cannot escape scrutiny, then, as a marketing and media concept that strategically garners material for both profit and headlines.

Although efforts to counter escalated violence can create safer schools, goals of democracy must not be sacrificed in the process. *Diversity awareness* in the context of terrorism reflects social justice missions to build inclusive communities and eliminate "systemic racism." Racial profiling denies particular groups the right to equal treatment in all public spheres, including schools. Similarly, as security tightens, *rationalized racism* escalates in the form of scapegoating, leading some scholars and policy analysts to describe a "dangerous" "security regime" emerging in the United States. Since the September 11, 2001, terrorist attacks and the passage of the USA Patriot Act in 2001, the FBI's vigilant activity has reportedly increased at college campuses, in effect suspending the civil rights of those for whom terrorist connections have been alleged.

New scholarship stresses that emergency procedures should not be enforced independent of a school's diversity conduct, an action that may counter the national climate or racist agendas. Racial targeting is seen as inextricably linked to terrorism—one area profoundly affecting the other. The protection of schools through emergency preparation therefore demands vigilance. Personal stories of racially motivated acts have abounded since the terrorist attacks of September 11, 2001. For example, a Middle Eastern university student was handcuffed and detained after registering, as required, by the U.S. Immigration and Naturalization Service. He had aroused suspicion, "guilty" only of carrying a part-time course load that semester, even with his advisor's approval. Once triggered, incidents involving racially motivated assaults in the guise of security, protection, and patriotism can produce a domino effect.

A new leadership attitude toward safety as inseparable from tolerance, diversity, and inclusion is necessary. Professors who prepare administrative leaders are similarly challenged. The Educational Leadership Constituent Council (ELCC) (2002) standards have one safety benchmark: "Develop and administer policies that provide a safe school environment and promote student health and welfare." In contrast with this picture, the momentous forces school leaders must face are grave, revolving around the powerful missions of antiviolence crisis preparedness and human rights protection. Innovative programming that addresses links between crisis intervention and terrorism awareness offers a solution, as in the case of the Texas School Safety Center, where administrators learn how to create more secure environments. A deeper goal is to simultaneously carry out diversity awareness building to reinforce their interrelatedness.

In addition, few living accounts exist of emergency preparedness within the context of democratic citizenship. In one principal's school in Israel, safety issues required a nontraditional communal deliberative process in response to ongoing violent turbulences. Action research by leadership aspirants in the United States may be comparatively less developed where focus is on crisis planning for virtually every type of catastrophe imaginable: Concern has shifted to how administrators would respond in the event of a bioterrorist attack, especially involving airborne gases. But terrorism preparedness is not foreign to Florida's schools, for example, where bomb threats and evacuations are regularly rehearsed. Prospective administrators asked penetrating questions during the 2003 U.S.

coalition war with Iraq, when the media suddenly announced ways to prepare for a terrorism attack: This Code Orange raised everyone's consciousness level about the possibility and realities of terrorism. Are school leaders adequately trained to deal with an emergency of this magnitude? Such perplexing questions hint at the profound change on the horizon for American schools and society.

—Carol A. Mullen

See also adaptiveness of organizations; capacity building, of organizations; culture, school; diversity; global cultural politics; international education; mentoring; partnerships, interagency; right-wing politics, advocates, impact on education; role model; school improvement models; school safety; violence in schools

Further Readings and References

American Red Cross. (2003, February). *Homeland Security Advisory System recommendations.* Retrieved September 7, 2005, from http://www.tallytown.com/redcross/hsas

Arnone, M. (2003). Watchful eyes: The FBI steps up its work on campuses, spurring fear and anger among many academics (Special report). *Chronicle of Higher Education, 49*(31), A14.

Dorn, M. S. (2002). Terrorism and schools. *School Planning and Management, 40*(11), 19–35.

Educational Leadership Constituent Council. (2002). *Educational Leadership Constituent Standards.* Arlington, VA: National Policy Board for Educational Administration. Retrieved April 16, 2003, from http://www.npbea.org

Hoover, E. (2003). Closing the gates: A student under suspicion (Special report). *Chronicle of Higher Education, 49*(31), A12.

Jolly, E. J., Malloy, S. M., & Felt, M. C. (2001). *Beyond blame: Reacting to the terrorist attack. A curriculum for middle and high school students.* Newton, MA: Education Development Center. Retrieved June 8, 2003, from http://www.edc.org/spotlight/schools/beyondblame

Mullen, C. A. (2004). *Climbing the Himalayas of school leadership: The socialization of early career administrators.* Lanham, MA: Scarecrow Press/Rowman & Littlefield.

National School Safety and Security Services. (2001). *Terrorism & school safety,* 1–8. (Full report available at Web site). Retrieved July 15, 2003, from http://www.schoolsecurity.org/resources/nasro_survey_2002

Rizvi, F. (2003). Democracy and education after September 11. *Globalisation, Societies, and Education, 1*(1), 25–40.

Schechter, C. (2002). Marching in the land of uncertainty: Transforming school culture through communal deliberative process. *International Journal of Leadership in Education, 5*(2), 105–128.

Trump, K. S. (2002). The impact of terrorism on school safety planning. *School Planning & Management, 41*(7), 22–26.

⬛ TESTING AND TEST THEORY DEVELOPMENT

In education, a test is a tool or technique intended to measure students' knowledge, intelligence, or ability. It usually consists of a series of questions, problems, or physical responses. A standardized test is a written test whose score is interpreted by reference to the scores of a norm group. An aptitude test ostensibly measures a person's "natural ability," while the achievement test measures knowledge learned by the person. There are generally two types of questions in a test. First, there is the multiple-choice question. For a multiple-choice question, the test taker will check one or more of the choices in a list. Second is the free-response question. The free-response question requires the test taker to state an opinion or to write an essay or short answer. This latter type of question usually requires a deeper level of analytical thinking.

There are two branches to testing theory—classical test theory and the item response theory (IRT). The British psychologist Charles Spearman laid the foundation for the classical test theory, also called the true score model. The key concepts of classical test theory are reliability and validity. Reliability is the accuracy of the scores of a measure. A test is considered reliable if it allows for stable estimates of student ability. In other words, it achieves similar results for students who have similar ability and knowledge levels. On the other hand, a valid measure is one that is measuring what it is supposed to measure. Validity implies reliability (accuracy). A valid measure must be reliable, but a reliable measure need not be valid.

The essence of classical test theory is that any observed test score is the composite of two hypothetical components: a true score and a random error component.

$$X = T + E$$

Where X is the observed score, T is the true score, and E is the error score.

In classical test theory, reliability is defined mathematically as the ratio of the variation of the true score and the variation of the observed score, which means how much of the variation in the observed score is explained by the variation of the true score. Or equivalently, reliability is defined as 1 minus the ratio of the variation of the error score and the variation of the observed score:

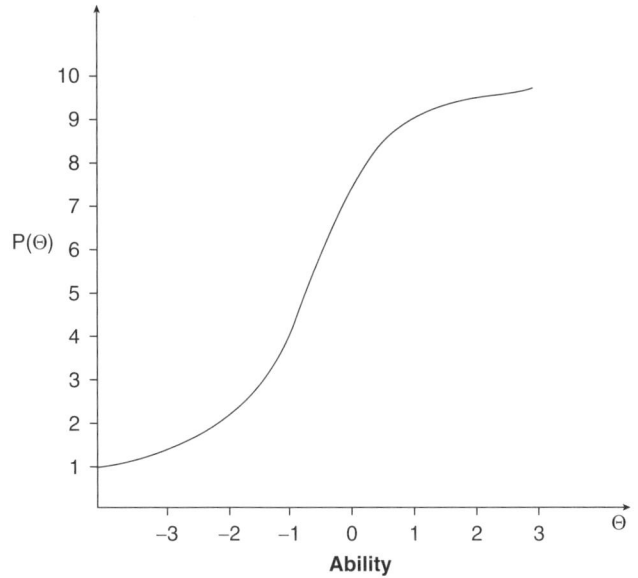

Figure 1   Item Characteristic Curve

SOURCE: Author.

$$\rho_{XX'} = \frac{\sigma_T^2}{\sigma_X^2} = \frac{\sigma_{T'}^2}{\sigma_{X'}^2} = 1 - \frac{\sigma_E^2}{\sigma_X^2} = \rho_X^2 T.$$

where $\rho_{XX'}$ is the symbol for the reliability of the observed score X, and σ_X^2, σ_T^2, σ_E^2 are the variances of the observed, true, and error scores, respectively. We can see that the reliability coefficient can be mathematically defined as the ratio of true score variance to observed score variance.

IRT, also called latent trait theory, is a modern test theory. IRT requires stronger assumptions than classical test theory. First, a single common factor accounts for all item covariance. This common factor is the latent trait of interest, and there is a single latent trait. Second, relations between the latent trait and observed response have a specific form. The line relating the trait and response is called the *item characteristic curve* (ICC, see Figure 1).

In IRT, the latent trait is usually represented as theta (Θ), as represented by the vertical axis in Figure 1. The vertical axis is the probability of getting the correct response. The ICC curve is usually represented by the logistic ICC.

The standard mathematical model for the item characteristic curve is the cumulative form of the logistic function. The equation for the two-parameter logistic model is shown as:

$$P(\Theta) = \frac{1}{1 + e^{-L}} = \frac{1}{1 + e^{-a(\Theta - b)}}$$

where Θ is the ability level and $P(\Theta)$ is the test subject's standing on the underlying trait. Item parameters, a and b, indicate the individual's standing in the latent trait. This logistic model relates the level of the latent trait and item parameter to the probability of answering the question correctly.

The difficulty parameter, b, is the point on the ability scale where $p(\Theta) = 0.5$; that is, a person whose ability is b has a .50 chance of answering the question correctly. The discrimination parameter, a, is the steepness of the ICC curve at its steepest point. It indicates the degrees to which the item distinguishes individuals with trait levels above and below the slope of the ICC.

The most general form of the logistic curve is called the three-parameter logistic model:

$$P(\Theta) = c + (1 - c)\frac{1}{1 + e^{-a(\Theta - b)}}$$

where c is the guessing parameter, and a and b are the discrimination parameter and difficulty parameter, respectively.

Some of the test takers will get the correct response by guessing. Therefore, the most general form of the logistic curve adds a component, c, which denotes the probability of getting the item correct by guessing alone.

In the classical test theory, there is only one reliability estimate, whereas in IRT, each item contributes some information about the test taker's latent trait. The amount of information relies on the steepness of the ICC (a parameter), and the location of the information depends on the difficulty parameter (b parameter).

—*Xiaogeng Sun*

See also accountability; item response theory; J-curve theory; school improvement models; quantitative research methods; standardized testing; validity and reliability

Further Readings and References

Goldberg, M. (2005). Test Mess 2: Are we doing better a year later? *Phi Delta Kappan, 86*, 389–395.
Linn, R. (2000, March). Assessments and accountability. *Educational Researcher, 29*(2), 4–16.
Madaus, G., & Kellaghan, T. (1992). Curriculum evaluation and assessment. In P. Jackson (Ed.), *Handbook of research on curriculum* (pp. 119–154). New York: Macmillan.
National Commission on Testing and Public Policy. (1990). *Reframing assessment: From gatekeepers to gateway to education.* Chestnut Hill, MA: Boston College.
Phelps, R. (Ed.). (2005). *Defending standardized testing.* Mahwah, NJ: Lawrence Erlbaum.
Sacks, P. (1997, March/April). Standardized testing: Meritocracy's crooked yardstick. *Change,* pp. 25–28.

TEXTBOOKS

Textbooks have been an important part of American education almost from the beginning of efforts to provide universal public education. A common text from which to teach and learn was viewed as essential for teaching groups of students. In addition to being a tool for teaching, the textbook was considered useful for instilling desirable values in children and establishing American traditions. As schools progressed and changed during the nineteenth century and twentieth century into the twenty-first century, textbooks have remained an integral part of schools. As such, textbooks have been a focus in attempts to improve schools, an element of efforts to influence the minds of children and thereby the character of the nation, and the target of criticisms of schools.

THE ROLE OF TEXTBOOKS IN AMERICA'S CLASSROOMS

It is widely recognized, though not always viewed favorably, that the teacher is at the center of the classroom and the textbook the teacher's most frequently used tool. Textbooks are the primary resource for teachers for several practical reasons. In early American education, students were instructed individually using a variety of books brought from home. Innovators, including Horace Mann, viewed this practice as impractical and proposed the use of common textbooks as a means of facilitating group instruction. Through the years, the use of common textbooks has provided the organization and structure necessary to instruct groups of students. Textbooks are also viewed as a source of accurate subject matter content and helpful instructional strategies, especially for teachers who may not be strong in a particular subject area.

In addition to being used for instructional purposes, schoolbooks have served to both form and defend America's image of itself. Schools in America have always been viewed in part as a means of presenting to children moral, political, cultural, social, and economic concepts. The provision of free public education and free textbooks provided a means of presenting those concepts deemed desirable by textbook authors and the public. The textbook as both an instructional tool and a way of influencing the values of children has changed through the years.

HISTORY

The first American textbooks were similar to their English counterparts and were compilations of selections from diverse sources. The "primers," as all elementary books for children were called, were united by the teaching of religion and reading. The selections were chosen to represent the best literature, but they were ill-suited for students to acquire a taste for reading or to learn about the world.

From the late eighteenth century and to the middle of the nineteenth century, textbooks began to take into account the interests and needs of children and to appeal to the middle class. Around 1790, Noah Webster published a reader that contained familiar stories in common language. Webster also published a speller that helped to standardize spelling, helped to reform the language, and took a leading place among spellers for decades. In the 1830s, books began to be written to reflect better teaching strategies. The *McGuffey Eclectic Reader,* which appeared in 1836, and Warren Colburn's *Intellectual Arithmetic,* published in 1821, contributed to improved instruction in their fields.

Through the latter part of the nineteenth century and into the twentieth century, textbooks showed a reduced emphasis on religion and became more professional. Teachers and professional educators replaced clerics and Latin professors as authors of textbooks. Textbooks reflected advances in educational methods. Print and illustrations were improved.

The role of textbooks expanded throughout the twentieth century. Textbooks are now available for practically all subjects taught in schools. The amount of subject matter content included in textbooks has increased in attempts to appeal to various users. A variety of ancillary materials such as workbooks, test banks, remedial and enrichment activities, plans for teaching, and critical thinking exercises are often available to teachers as a part of textbook packages. In general, textbook publishers have attempted to provide complete sets of material to meet teacher needs.

AMERICAN CULTURE AS PRESENTED IN TEXTBOOKS

Through the years, textbooks have reflected not only advances in instructional methods but also changes in American values and culture. The provision of free public education made the decisions regarding schools, including the selection and use of textbooks, a part of the public and political domain. As such, the role of textbooks in presenting America's ideology has reflected political struggles and changing public values.

The ideology presented in nineteenth century textbooks was both simple and unrealistic. America was considered a nation blessed by God. Its heroes were presented without flaws, its opponents as villains. America was the land of liberty and the home of the brave. Honesty, thrift, love of God, love of country and hard work were all valued. America was presented as superior to other nations. Ownership of private property was highly valued, and stealing was immoral. Textbooks divided people into races that supposedly possessed inherent and unchangeable qualities. The ideal person was male, White, of Northern European background, Protestant, and self-made. Indians were considered to be savages, but with primitive purity. Jews were presented as crafty, greedy, and sly. Blacks, then referred to as Negroes, were regarded as the most inferior of races and incapable of improvement. Blacks were considered lazy, shiftless, lacking in intellectual ability, and irresponsible. Social standing in nineteenth-century textbooks was important, but it was to be achieved through one's own efforts rather than through rank or privilege of the Old World. Everyone, even the poor, was considered worthy of the opportunity to get ahead. Women were valued, worthy of respect, and equal to man before God. However, women were not extended economic or social equality. A woman's interest was to be in her husband and children.

Textbook authors presented to nineteenth-century schoolchildren the image of America they deemed worthy of preservation. Successive generations challenged the generalizations and assumptions present in this image. Issues of religion, nation, and race were prominent among the issues addressed.

Textbooks at the turn of the twentieth century reflected a societal increase in religious diversity and secular values. As a result, religious passages in textbooks decreased, and morals were presented in ways acceptable to various religions. In the 1920s and continuing into the second half of the twentieth century, those concerned that evolution conflicted with religion challenged the teaching of evolution in schools through legal channels, blacklists, and appeals to school boards. In 1968, the Supreme Court in *Epperson v. Arkansas* ruled against state bans on teaching evolution. Textbook publishers attempted to avoid the issue. In some books, the word *evolution* was replaced with *adaptation* or other terminology. Others omitted chapters on evolution altogether. At the end of the twentieth century, religious leaders again took issue with textbooks, charging that publishers attempted to take God out of the schools by reflecting a humanistic philosophy in textbooks. Local district selection of textbooks served to mediate among those who sought to ban or censor what they considered religiously unacceptable textbooks, educators, and publishers. In general, publishers have attempted to avoid controversial religious issues that adversely affect the market for their texts.

Nationalistic concerns relative to textbooks have involved a variety of issues related to the American way of life. Various groups have objected to textbooks that questioned the events leading to the American Revolution and the motives of early American patriots, contained perceived anticapitalist sentiments, reflected positively on communism or socialism, or in other ways questioned the traditional way of life in America. Even though some individuals and groups have reacted negatively and aggressively to nationalistic concerns, the overall impact has been minimal—the results being some revisions and a few books to be removed from adoption lists.

The most consistent and successful efforts to revise the culture of America as portrayed in textbooks concerns the portrayal, or lack thereof, of the role of African Americans and other ethnic groups. For some ethnic groups, the struggle was only to obtain recognition of their contributions. African Americans also had to overcome inaccurate representations of their capacity, character, and history. From the 1930s through the 1960s, African Americans succeeded in removing offensive texts, being portrayed in texts in professional roles, and being credited with their contributions to America.

In the 1970s, interest turned to eliminating gender bias in textbooks. Protests were made that women were consistently depicted in domestic roles or traditionally female occupations. Those involved in textbook selection and textbook publishers, in turn, have successfully reduced gender bias.

CRITICISMS OF TEXTBOOKS AND PUBLISHERS' PERSPECTIVES

As the primary instructional resource in American schools, both the content and quality of textbooks have been the target of criticism. According to critics, the desire by publishers to produce commercially successful material has resulted in lower-quality textbooks. The desire to satisfy the content requirements of various school districts often results in superficial coverage of topics and in central concepts being obscured. Attempts to include features such as real-world applications, critical thinking, technology connections, and cooperative learning in the textbook narrative have resulted in visual confusion and poor readability. Nationally marketed textbooks cannot reflect local needs or concerns. The end products have been widely viewed as pedagogically unsound.

The most far-reaching concern of educators is that publishers, through textbooks, provide a de facto national curriculum. Textbook publishers have assumed the role of curriculum developers in the absence of governmental action in this area. At the federal level, there is minimal direct influence over education, as evidenced by the lack of a national education curriculum and the absence of a national testing program that would influence the curricula of schools. Federal efforts at curricular reform, even well-funded federal curriculum projects of the 1960s and 1970s, have been unsuccessful at making widespread and lasting impact. State support in terms of curriculum development, where it exists, is commonly in the form of curriculum frameworks or structures, rather than specific, detailed curricula. Many in the local schools have been content letting textbooks define the curricula. The lack of federal, state, or local governmental control of the curricula of schools coupled with the almost universally acknowledged teacher reliance on textbooks has placed textbook publishers as the primary determiners of the curricula in America's schools.

Publishers contend that even though their primary goal is to produce books that will sell, they attempt to produce books that will help students and teachers. The books they produce are a reflection of what schools say they need and want. State curriculum frameworks and other guides are used to determine the content and teaching needs. The needs of teachers are determined through surveys, focus groups, and through direct contact by sales representatives. Further feedback is obtained from consultants consisting of teachers, researchers, and others considered experts in the field. The various sources of information are used to help determine the content, teaching strategies, and format that will be useful to teachers and acceptable to those selecting textbooks.

The reaction by publishers to the perceived needs of practitioners and researchers can be misapplied as they are incorporated in textbooks. As an example, publishers responded quickly to research indicating that textbooks were too difficult to read and that certain characteristics of text in books influenced comprehension. Readability formulas were developed to evaluate textbooks relative to the favorable characteristics. Subsequently, many textbooks were written to readability formulas, which, in turn, invalidated the readability tests. Other textbooks were oversimplified, diminishing their usefulness to students and teachers. Publisher response to the call for the inclusion of special features or topics such as real-life applications in mathematics textbooks has often been superficial, satisfying reviewers' checklists without contributing to the instructional quality. In general, the struggle to satisfy legitimate marketing concerns is often misapplied, overgeneralized, or superficially addressed.

Publisher reaction to school needs is in part due to the nature of a profit-making industry that is unregulated and national in scope. The economics of textbook publishing dictates a large number of prints, and therefore texts appeal to a large number of school districts. Adoption cycles of 5 to 7 years and copyright limitations that do not protect the underlying ideas or approaches used in textbooks also increase the need to publish a textbook that sells. Risk taking is minimized, and textbooks by different publishers become more alike.

Publishers receive confirmation that they are meeting the needs of teachers and students based on the selection and use of their products. Publishers produce products based on the perceived needs of schools, schools select and purchase from among available textbooks, and publishers make a profit. This cycle will change only when teachers and schools select and buy different books.

TEXTBOOK SELECTION

Selection of textbooks generally occurs in two different ways. In approximately half the states, statewide textbook committees select a number of textbooks that then comprise a list of books approved for selection by the local school districts. These states are referred to as "adoption" states. Other states, referred to as "open states," allow local school districts to select textbooks with few restrictions. In both adoption states and open states, final selection is usually by local school district committees consisting of classroom teachers with administrators in advisory roles.

Selection of textbooks at the local level is hindered by a variety of factors. Local school districts often have informal methods of selecting textbooks that consist of little more than checklists or superficial rating methods. These methods place equal importance on minor issues as on more important issues. Teachers typically receive little or no training in the selection process and are not given adequate time to review texts. The selection process is complicated by the logistics involving the arrival of textbooks at the schools and their distribution to textbook committee members. Textbooks selection committees can be distracted during the selection process by the offer of free inducements and presentations by sales representatives. Combinations of these factors often relegate selection of textbooks to a less significant position than warranted by their prominent and central use in classrooms.

SUMMARY

The difficulty with the selection of textbooks, as with the various criticisms and controversies, has not diminished their use. Textbooks are acknowledged as both an important and imperfect guide for American teachers. Imperfections sometimes result from a profit-making industry taking the lead role in curriculum development. Teachers can misuse textbooks or overuse them to the exclusion of other resources. The content and teaching strategies of textbooks can be inadequate. However, as schools have changed and evolved through the centuries of American existence, textbooks have remained ubiquitous. As the American society has battled to establish values, guard traditions, and define the culture of America, textbooks continue to be used widely in schools. Textbooks are present in all regions of the country, are used in schools of varying quality, and are the primary teaching tool of the vast majority of the teachers in America. They are widely considered by both teachers and the public as essential to quality instruction and important to forming public opinion. Even with technological gains and advances in teaching methods, textbooks remain the central tool in America's classrooms.

—Gregory D. Freeman and Lisa B. Lucius

See also Asian Pacific Americans; Black education; civics, history in schools; civil rights movement; creationism; cultural politics, wars; curriculum, theories of; discrimination; diversity; ethnicity; ethnocentrism; feminism and theories of leadership; gender studies, in educational leadership; history, in curriculum; ideology, shifts of in educational leadership preparation; Latinos; literacy, theories of; Mann, Horace; minorities, in schools; religion, in schools; sexism (glass ceiling); social studies

Further Readings and References

Altbach, P., Kelly, G., Petrie, H., & Weis, L. (1991). *Textbooks in American society: Politics, policy, and pedagogy.* Albany: SUNY Press.

Brophy, J., & VanSledright, B. (1997). *Teaching and learning history in elementary schools.* New York: Teachers College Press.

DelFattore, J. (1992). *What Johnny shouldn't read: Textbook censorship in America.* New Haven CT: Yale University Press.

Elliot, D. L., & Woodward, A. (Eds.). (1990). *Textbooks and schooling in the United States.* Eighty-Ninth Yearbook of the National Society for the Study of Education (Part 1). Chicago: National Society for the Study of Education.

Evans, R. (2004). *The social studies wars.* New York: Teachers College Press.

Giordano, G. (2003) *Twentieth-century textbook wars: A history of advocacy and opposition.* New York: Peter Lang.

Ravitch, D. (2003). *The language police. How pressure groups restrict what students learn.* New York: Vintage.

Zimmerman, J. (2002). *Whose America? Culture wars in the public school system.* Cambridge, MA: Harvard University.

🏛 THEORIES, USE OF

A theory is essentially a set of assumptions from which a set of empirical laws (or principles) may be derived. What makes a theory a theory? For a proposal to be a theory, it must be descriptive, analytical, and predictive. To be descriptive, it must point to the phenomenon being described, such as a series of behaviors being described by a leadership theory. Next, it must analyze relevant phenomena. For example, some leadership behavior may be classified as structuring tasks, while others as concern for subordinates' well-being. Last, the predictive criterion requires the theory to predict that certain leadership behaviors to be perceived as effective will focus on achieving tasks, while other behavior will be directed at meeting subordinates' emotional needs.

These criteria for theory separate it from models (the Getzels-Guba model) and taxonomies; the former is more descriptive, while the latter is both descriptive and analytic. Models function as metaphors, while taxonomies function as classification devices. Both lack the capacity to predict.

While most Americans separate theory and practice, most scientists perceive their connection. John Dewey's deliberate use of the singular notes his perception of the unity of theory and practice. Further uses of theory include its *objectivity*, although Thomas Kuhn noted that scientists and the public subscribe to a paradigm until some divergent theory comes along to challenge accepted conventional wisdom. Theory ought to be *comprehensive*, covering a considerable range of phenomena under its rubric, such as the leadership behavior of a large number of individuals. A theory also should be a *guide to new knowledge*. Any theory in the behavioral sciences should be a *guide to action*, as well as a guide to collecting relevant data, such as what the impact on morale will be of the superintendent reducing principals' degree of freedom.

Last, issues of validity and reliability arise. Validity concerns whether we actually are investigating what we think we are investigating. Reliability refers to the issue of whether we can replicate the processes and results achieved in our first attempts. Qualitative studies, many of which deal with cases, focus more on descriptive validity, moving away from dealing with reliability.

—Arthur Shapiro

See also critical theory; deconstruction; empiricism; hypotheses, in research; philosophies of education; quantitative research methods; research methods; validity and reliability

Further Readings and References

Crow, G., & Grogan, M. (2005). The development of leadership thought and practice in the United States. In F. English (Ed.), *The SAGE handbook of educational leadership* (pp. 362–379). Thousand Oaks, CA: Sage.

Dewey, J. (1938). *Experience and education.* New York: Macmillan.

Kuhn, T. (1970). *The structure of scientific revolutions.* Chicago: University of Chicago Press.

🏛 THEORY MOVEMENT, IN EDUCATIONAL ADMINISTRATION

The theory movement in educational administration began shortly after World War II, with the emergence of educational administration as an established academic discipline. The creation of the National Conference of Professors of Educational Administration (NCPEA) in 1947 and the University Council for Educational Administration (UCEA) in 1956, led by Daniel Griffiths, Jack Culbertson, and Paula Silver, spurred the emergence of the theory movement in educational administration. The theory movement reflected the belief that educational administration consisted of more than a loose collection of individual, anecdotal experiences—more than a mere collection of "war stories" told and retold by retired school administrators. Beginning in the 1950s, superintendents and other school leaders were being trained to be applied social scientists. Coursework in educational administration was thoroughly infused with theories and concepts borrowed from the social and behavioral sciences, reflecting the belief that the practice of administration was more than the execution of technical tasks. Through the lens of the theory movement, scholars began to view schools as complex sociopolitical systems and sought a way to explain and predict behavior in those systems.

The theory movement was founded on an intellectual paradigm borrowed from social psychology, management, and the behavioral sciences and emphasized empiricism, predictability, and scientific certainty. The movement reflected a determined effort to bring the social science disciplines (particularly psychology, sociology, and social psychology) to bear upon administrator preparation in education. Theories and conceptual tools borrowed from political science and economics were also used, allowing educational leaders to become schooled in the principles of resource allocation, motivation, individual and group interaction, and the nature and functioning of public bureaucracies.

Because of the theory movement, the focus of educational administration shifted from "how to do it" to an orientation based on inquiry, with the field itself a legitimate area of study. This shift is readily identifiable in texts on educational administration. The study of theory was necessary to deal effectively with the wide array of social issues facing school administrators.

As the theory movement became dominant, the field of educational administration emerged as a legitimate academic discipline, on par with business management and public administration. As the field matured, the study and practice of administration, which had historically faced inward upon relations within the school system, necessarily turned its focus outward to relations of the school system with other systems with which it was inextricably bound: political, legal, and economic systems, among others. School administrators were encouraged to adopt a holistic approach and to see how education fit within the larger social system—how education was related to the larger political, social, economic, and legal order—and, conversely, how other institutions and organizations impacted the educational system.

The rise of the theory movement in educational administration has not been without problems. As an applied, professional discipline, much like business or public administration, tension has always existed between the role and integration of theory into programs designed to prepare educational leaders. University-based administrator preparation programs have been criticized as being too theoretical and divorced from the actual practice of school administration. The knowledge base in educational administration has been questioned, and sharp disagreements have arisen over whether education schools are the best place to train and prepare school leaders. Because of this fundamental tension, efforts are being made to more effectively integrate the theory movement into the actual practice of educational administration.

—*Lance D. Fusarelli*

See also behaviorism; bureaucracy; contingency theories; empiricism; Greenfield, Thomas Barr; Halpin, Andrew William; hypotheses, in research; National Council of Professors of Educational Administration; quantitative research methods; research methods; University Council for Educational Administration

Further Readings and References

Culbertson, J. A. (1981). Antecedents of the theory movement. *Educational Administration Quarterly, 17,* 25–47.

Culbertson, J. A. (1995). *Building bridges.* University Park, PA: UCEA.

Greenfield, T., & Ribbons, P. (1993). *Greenfield on educational administration.* London: Routledge.

Griffiths, D. (1988). Administrative theory. In N. Boyan (Ed.), *Handbook of research on educational administration* (pp. 27–52). New York: Longman.

THEORY X, THEORY Y

Theories X and Y were developed by Douglas McGregor to indicate the two major belief systems managers held about the basic nature of workers under their supervision. Descriptions of the two differing concepts of supervisor attitudes and discussion of the positive effects of adopting the human approach to management of Theory Y were discussed in his classic work, *The Human Side of Enterprise.*

McGregor's definitions of the two theories came from the analysis of manager behavior in many business organizations during the 1950s. McGregor concluded that manager beliefs about employees' attitudes toward their jobs affected the productivity of those workers. Supervisors who believed their employees were lazy, uncommitted, and needed coercion to force them to perform their duties were defined as Theory X managers. Productivity was not optimal in those groups. Other supervisors who believed their employees were interested in work, sought responsibility, and were committed to helping the organization succeed were identified as Theory Y managers. Productivity of these groups was usually maximized.

McGregor characterized the Theory X supervisor as one who believed in traditional authoritarian scientific management principles: (a) The average person has an inherent dislike of work and will avoid it if possible; (b) because they dislike work, people must be coerced, controlled, directed, and threatened with punishment to get them to put forth effort necessary to accomplish the organizational objectives; (c) the average person prefers to be directed, wishes to avoid responsibility, has relatively little ambition, and desires security above all else.

Supervisors who established meaningful and productive relationships with their workers McGregor labeled Theory Y managers. Their beliefs about employees were: (a) The expenditure of mental and physical effort in work is as natural as play or rest; (b) if committed, employees will exercise self-direction and self-control to achieve objectives for the organization; (c) worker commitment to accomplishing objectives is connected with the rewards associated with achievement, two of which are ego satisfaction and self-actualization; (d) the average person not only learns to accept responsibility, but actually seeks it; (e) the capacity to engage in creative acts using imagination and ingenuity is distributed widely throughout the population and not just among a few special people; and (f) present organizations are designed to tap into only a small percentage of potential available in the population.

McGregor wanted to demonstrate that the principles of scientific management were ineffective, but even more, he wanted to advance new understandings of management concerns such as motivation, an internal force not dependent on external factors of authority or coercion; employee evaluation procedures; and the structure of employee compensation plans. Theory Y included a fourth element, integration, the concept that the needs of the organization could be met as well as the needs of the individual. Integration was a most important consideration for changing the behavior of both supervisors and workers because the human approach to supervision significantly increases worker levels of commitment to the organization and their productivity. This idea was not considered possible or important by the practitioners of scientific management. McGregor defined the concepts as theories to encourage additional study, analysis, and development of his ideas, and in this endeavor, he was highly successful. Not only did his work receive wide recognition for its significance in understanding principles of successful management, his models provided a large portion of the theoretical underpinning for the field of organizational development and the emphasis on human resource management practiced in most organizations for 30 years prior to release of his ideas. As awareness of the significance of these theories grew, managers reduced their adherence to the concepts of scientific management that had been promoted by Frederick Taylor a generation earlier.

Studies comparing supervisor beliefs with supervisory behavior have shown that people usually espouse the values of Theory Y but often take actions that are based on Theory X. This finding supported the belief of McGregor and others that an orientation to Theory Y management required education programs to change manager beliefs about the factors that affected worker productivity. Theories X and Y have been studied, debated, and even criticized, but they are widely recognized for their originality and the important contributions to better understanding the world of organizational management and productivity in industrial, service, and educational organizations.

Educational administration scholars often recommend that school leaders use Theory Y concepts in their approach to management of educational organizations. To do so, they argue, reinforces recognition of the professionalism of educators and results in better learning environments for students. Success in this endeavor often has been modest, however, because the detailed mandates and expectations for immediate results of federal and state legislative and policy groups and the clients of educational organizations usually pressure educational leaders to adopt more coercive and directive behaviors in the belief that quick direction and pressure produces quality results.

The Theory Y concept has been criticized by a few scholars as being in part an unrealistic statement of human nature. McGregor assumed that if workers were given freedom, flexibility, and opportunity for commitment without coercion, they would become serious and highly productive workers. He did not acknowledge that workers with the freedom to become committed and serious workers also have the freedom to not become serious about their work or their commitment to the organization. Without recognition that individuals have the freedom to choose either way, the theory may become a kind of personal determinism that guarantees certain worker responses to specific supervisory behaviors. This very real option to choose noncommitment may explain research results that have documented supervisors quickly retreating from a Theory Y attitude to a more Theory X operational approach when their followers do not become dedicated and productive within a short time.

—*Max S. Skidmore*

See also adaptiveness of organizations; attitudes toward work; belonging; collaboration theory; human resource development; leadership styles; management theories; mentoring; motivation, theories of; personnel management; satisfaction, in organizations and roles; self-actualization

Further Readings and References

Heil, G., Bennis, W., & Stephen, D. (2000). *Douglas McGregor Revisited: Managing the human side of the enterprise.* New York: Wiley.

McGregor, D. (1960). *The human side of enterprise.* New York: McGraw-Hill.
McGregor, D. (1967). *The professional manager* (W. Bennis & C. McGregor, Eds.). New York: McGraw-Hill.
Weisbord, M. (2004). *Productive workplaces revisited: Dignity, meaning, and community in the 21st century.* San Francisco: Jossey-Bass.

THORNDIKE, EDWARD

Edward Thorndike's (1874–1949) work was among the initial attempts to examine and explain memory and learning. His work, along with that of John B. Watson, is relevant to educators, as it has had a direct impact on academic instruction, classroom management, and administrative practices.

Thorndike was born August 31, 1874, in Williamsburg, Massachusetts. He took a BA in 1895 at Wesleyan University and an MA at Harvard in 1897. He received his PhD in 1898 from Columbia University.

In 1927, while working on a grant from the Carnegie Corporation, he launched a series of investigations on learning that led to Thorndike's *law of effect.* This law that had its origin in early tests and experiments by Watson related to the impact of positive and negative consequences on behavior and was ultimately substantially supportive of these experiments in human learning. Through this early work, Thorndike concluded that repetition and reward were critical factors in learning. In 1932, he reported on a series of six experiments with chicks, concluding that rewarding a connection strengthens it; punishing consequences weakened it a little or not at all.

The basis of learning accepted by Thorndike in his earliest writings was association between sense impressions and impulses to action. Such associations became known as "bonds" or "connections." Because the bonds or connections were thought to become strengthened or weakened in establishing and breaking habits, Thorndike's system has sometimes been called a "bond" psychology or simply "connectionism." Thorndike's work formed the foundation for later work by John B. Watson and B. F. Skinner and underpins the theory of behaviorism.

Thorndike developed three basic laws to underpin his theory. The first of these, the *law of readiness,* is an accessory principle that describes a physiological substratum for the law of effect. It describes the following conditions under which a learner tends to be satisfied or annoyed: (a) When a conduction unit is ready to conduct, conduction is satisfying; (b) for a conduction unit ready to conduct, not to conduct is annoying; this condition provokes any response related to the annoyance; (c) when a conduction unit is not ready for conduction and is forced to conduct, conduction is annoying.

The second of Thorndike's laws, the *law of exercise,* refers to the strengthening of connections with practice (law of use) and to weakening of connections or forgetting when practice is discontinued (law of disuse). Strengthening is defined by the increase in probability that the response will be made when the situation recurs.

Thorndike's third important law, the *law of effect,* refers to the strengthening or weakening of a connection as a result of its consequences. When a response or behavior is accompanied by or followed by a satisfying consequence, the strength of the connection is increased; if the connection is made and followed by an annoying consequence, the strength is decreased.

Thorndike's theory, grounded in these laws, was an initial attempt to study "how we learn, remember, and forget." It is significant for educators in that it underpins philosophy and practice in the schools and forms a foundation for the field of educational psychology. For educational leaders, Thorndike's law of effect is relevant to understanding how to motivate others. In addition, the impact of repetition or practice encompassed by his law of exercise provides a foundation for ensuring that specific behaviors tend to appear in the desired situations.

—*J. M. Blackbourn*

See also achievement tests; behaviorism; empiricism; intelligence; learning environments; psychology, types of; psychometrics; quantitative research methods; testing and test theory development; validity and reliability

Further Readings and References

Thorndike, E. L. (1913). *Educational psychology.* New York: Columbia University Teachers College Press.

Thorndike, E. L. (1927). *The measurement of intelligence.* New York: Columbia University Teachers College Press.

Thorndike, E. (1963). *The concepts of over- and under-achievement.* New York: Teachers College Press.

Travers, R. (1996). Apprentice to Thorndike. In C. Kridel, R. Bullough, & P. Shaker (Eds.), *Teachers and mentors: Profiles of distinguished twentieth-century professors of education* (pp. 95–100). New York: Garland.

THREE-FACTOR MODEL, FIVE-FACTOR MODEL

Personality has been called by Abram Kardiner an essential adaptive organization of biological and behavioral functions that is of paramount importance to social life. Psychologists have generated a plethora of personality theories and measures of personality during this century.

However, the major contenders at this time appear to be the three-factor model (TFM) and the more recent five-factor model (FFM). The TFM employs these traits: Extroversion, Neuroticism (or Emotional Instability) and Psychoticism. The five traits represented in the FFM are Extroversion, Emotional Instability, Agreeableness, Conscientiousness, and Openness.

The Eysenck model (TFM) is generally preferred for three reasons. First, this theory of personality is strongly supported by a very long and continuous history of research and development. Eysenck's dedication to research on personality has made him the most frequently cited psychologist in the world. Eysenck points out that nearly all large-scale studies of personality find the equivalent of the three traits he proposes, that the traits are found worldwide, that an individual's status relative to the traits is consistent across time and that research on the genetics of personality support the three traits. Second, the development of the theory and related research has focused on measurement. The instrument associated with the model includes both adult and child versions, which makes comparisons between teachers and students possible and extends the possible areas for research. Third, it is a rich explanatory theory that suggests many potential research hypotheses, in contrast to the FFM, which is largely a descriptive model.

The three Eysenckian traits can be briefly characterized as follows. The Extroversion ("E") trait is a bipolar scale that is anchored at the high end by sociability and stimulation seeking and at the other end by social reticence and stimulation avoidance. This trait is tied to basal levels of arousal in the neocortex. The Neuroticism trait is anchored at the high end by emotional instability and spontaneity and by reflection and deliberateness at the other end. This trait's name is based on the susceptibility to anxiety-based problems of individuals high on the "N" trait. This trait is related to one's degree of reactivity to emotional stimuli. The Psychoticism trait is anchored at the high end by aggressiveness and divergent thinking and at the low end by caution and empathy. The label for this trait is based on the susceptibility to psychotic disorders of a significant subgroup of individuals high on the "P" trait. This trait is polygenic in nature and may, to some degree, be a reflection of the amygdala's sensitivity to androgen. None of the traits are intended as indicators of psychopathology. The scales based on these traits are measures of temperament source traits that in interaction with experience produce personality.

Eysenck's theory and the research it has generated suggest linkage to a variety of developmental problems such as overactivity, shyness, antisocial behavior, and anxiety disorders, as well as other characteristics, such as creativity. Center and Kemp have discussed how the theory and research might be applied to dealing with children and youth with antisocial behavior. James Wakefield has described the implications of the TFM theory for educational settings and learning. In his discussion of Eysenck's personality traits (PEN), he covers each relative to behavior, central nervous system arousal, learning, discipline, and achievement. The details of that discussion are too involved to cover here but are well worth reading. Furthermore, Wakefield has worked out 12 of the possible combination scores that a student might get on the Eysenck instruments (see Table 1).

Wakefield also offers descriptions of and suggestions for working with students having these personality (temperament) patterns (see Table 2). The EB3

theory has a great deal of heuristic potential for education on a variety of fronts and should receive more attention than it has in the past.

—David Center

See also affective domain; child development theories; counseling; creativity, theories of; emotional disturbance; individual differences, in children; learning environments; mental illness, in adults and children; personality; psychology, types of

Further Readings and References

Center, D., & Kemp, D. (2002). Antisocial behavior in children and Eysenck's theory of personality: An evaluation. *International Journal of Disability, Development, and Education, 49,* 353–366.
Center, D., & Kemp, D. (2003). Temperament and personality as potential factors in the development and treatment of conduct disorders. *Education and Treatment of Children,* 26(1), 75–78.
Eysenck, H. (1991). Dimensions of personality: The biosocial approach to personality. In J. Strelau & A. Angleitner (Eds.), *Explorations in temperament: International perspectives on theory and measurement* (pp. 87–103). London: Plenum.
Eysenck, H. (1991). Dimensions of personality: 16, 5, or 3: Criteria for a taxonomic paradigm. *Personality and Individual Differences, 12,* 773–790.
Wakefield, J. (1979). *Using personality to individualize instruction.* San Diego, CA: Educational and Industrial Testing Service.

Table 1   PEN Combinations and Labels

PEN Combinations	*Descriptive Labels*
1. Low or Avg P, Avg E, Low or Avg N	Typical, the majority of children
2. Low or Avg P, High E, Low or Avg N	Sociable and Uninhibited
3. Low or Avg P, Low E, Low or Avg N	Shy and Inhibited
4. Low or Avg P, Avg E, High N	Emotionally Overreactive
5. Low or Avg P, High E, High N	Hyperactive
6. Low or Avg P, Low E, High N	Anxious
7. High P, Avg E, Low or Avg N	Disruptive and Aggressive
8. High P, High E, Low or Avg N	Extremely Impulsive
9. High P, Low E, Low or Avg N	Withdrawn and Hostile
10. High P, Avg E, High N	Frequently Agitated
11. High P, High E, High N	Very Disruptive and Aggressive
12. High P, Low E, High N	Very Anxious and Agitated

SOURCE: Reprinted with permission from Center, D. B. (1999). *Strategies for Social and Emotional Behavior: A Teacher's Guide.* Norcross, GA: XanEdu, Inc.; adapted from Wakefield, J. (1979). *Using personality to individualize instruction.* San Diego, CA: Educational and Industrial Testing Service.

Table 2   Descriptions of and Suggestions for Working With Students Having PEN Personality Patterns

	Behavior	*Arousal*	*Learning*	*Discipline*
High E	Works quickly. Careless. Easily distracted. Easily bored.	Works well under stress from external stimulation.	Focus on major points. Needs continuous reinforcement. Good short-term recall. Does best in elementary school.	Most responsive to rewards and prompts, but also responsive to punishment and admonitions.
Low E	Works slowly. Careful. Attentive. Motivated.	Works poorly under stress from external stimulation.	Intermittent reinforcement is sufficient. Good long-term recall. Does best in high school.	Most responsive to punishment and admonitions, but also responsive to rewards and prompts.
High N	Overreacts to emotional stimuli. Slow to calm down. Avoids emotional situations.	Easy arousal interferes with performance, especially on difficult tasks. Susceptible to test anxiety.	Compulsive approach to learning. Can study for long periods. Does best in high school.	Similar to low E but high N in combination with low E requires a more subdued approach.
Low N	Underreacts to emotional stimuli. Quick recovery from emotional arousal.	Hard to motivate and tends to underachieve. Needs high arousal to sustain effort on easy tasks.	Exploratory learner. Short study periods are best. Does best in elementary school.	Similar to high E. However, both reward and punishment need to be more intense.
High P	Solitary. Disregard for danger. Defiant and aggressive.	Seeks stimulation for an arousal high. Confrontation and punishment may stimulate.	Slow to learn from experience. Responds impulsively. Creative, if bright.	Stimulated by punishment and threats. Responds best to highly structured settings.
Low P	Sociable. Friendly. Empathetic.	Not a sensation seeker. Can be too "laid back."	Teachable. Convergent thinker. Does well in school.	Responsive to both reward and punishment.

SOURCE: Reprinted with permission from Center, D. B. (1999). *Strategies for Social and Emotional Behavior: A Teacher's Guide.* Norcross, GA: XanEdu, Inc.; adapted from Wakefield, J. (1979). *Using personality to individualize instruction.* San Diego, CA: Educational and Industrial Testing Service.

🏛 TIME MANAGEMENT

Time management is not only a technique but also an approach to managing one's energies and the demands of a role or job. The concept of time management stems from Frederick Taylor's early analysis of work and how persons spend their time doing specific tasks. Taylor's aim was to reduce unproductive work tasks and hence reduce the amount of time allocated to waste. Becoming more efficient was the goal of the original time-and-motion studies. It remains the objective with time management.

School leaders are beset with expanding role expectations. The costs for not taking charge of one's time, for losing control over what is done and how it is done, and for complaining and being cynical about the demands of the job are far too great for a school leader to not develop a personal time management plan.

Effective time management requires several components:

- Setting priorities to meet complex and multiple challenges
- Developing specific techniques to cope with difficult and time-consuming tasks
- Deciding on the most productive ways to spend limited amounts of time
- Delegating responsibility effectively
- Handling routine tasks efficiently
- Structuring the day in order to see what needs to be done and what has actually been accomplished by the end of the day
- Making the environment work for the school leader
- Maximizing output through minimizing time spent on administrivia, such as needless meetings and extemporaneous paperwork

There are four key steps to help a school leader study the time structure of the workday. First, become familiar with time management techniques. Second, analyze present time management practices. Third, decide what needs to be changed to help being effective rather than just being busy. Fourth, design, then implement strategies that will lead to accomplishing the identified time management changes.

Time is the single resource available to a school leader that does not come out of the budget, can't be spent in advance, can't be banked for future use, can't be taken back once it is used, and is used completely at the discretion of the owner. The key is how the time that is available, with all its limitations, is used.

Principals and other school leaders should be able to fulfill their responsibilities within a reasonable workweek of 40 to 50 hours. Everyone has available 60 seconds every minute, 60 minutes every hour, 8 hours every workday, 5 workdays every workweek, and 4 or 5 workweeks every work month.

No one can control the moving of time, but everyone is able to decide how to use the time that is available. One approach is to differentiate among the different "kinds" of time, such as:

- Work time
- Worry time
- Leisure time
- Free time
- Peak time
- Busy time
- Sleep time

Work time is the set hours on the job each day. The key to effective use of this time is how much of it is actually devoted to accomplishing the major goals of the organization. Worry time is wasted time and should be converted to one of the productive time modes. Leisure time must be built in to the workday to ensure productive output. Free time is not synonymous with leisure time. There is no reason to have every day tightly scheduled. Free time can be used throughout the workday to accomplish unanticipated tasks or simply to do something that has previously been put on a back burner, even if it is just for fun.

Peak time should be identified by the school leader and used to focus on the highest priority from the priority or to-do list. Busy time is, indeed, synonymous with phony time. School leaders must be cautious about falling into the trap of showing others how busy one is.

Sleep time is crucial. It is clear that insufficient rest causes errors, irritability, inefficiency, and ineffectiveness. So it is permissible to take a 10-minute power nap or to take a walk or to find another way to get some rest and relaxation when tired. This is a credible use of time that may result in increasing effectiveness.

Time management as an approach to improving school leadership skills can be enhanced by frequently and on a regularly scheduled basis reviewing the following characteristics of successful leaders. An effective school leader has:

- The ability to set goals and priorities
- The ability to project into the future (vision)
- The ability to place activities and issues in order of priority
- The ability to identify key staff and delegate to them key tasks
- The courage to refuse to waste time on needless tasks
- The ability to *do it now*
- The ability to take time to support, encourage, and show concern for all people
- The ability to recognize that time is passing
- The ability to know when is the best time to use a specific skill.

Each school leader is different in style and will be in a different setting with different goals. Only in a specific situation can it be decided which mix of time management skills will work for a particular place and those goals. Each situation will require adjustments, rearrangements, and flexibility.

—*Neil J. Shipman*

See also accountability; administration, theories of; behaviorism; division of labor; economics, theories of; efficacy theory; leadership effectiveness; management by objectives; management theories; productivity; quantitative research methods; resource management; time-on-task

Further Readings and References

Kanigel, R. (1997). *The one best way: Frederick Winslow Taylor and the enigma of efficiency.* New York: Viking.

Shaver, H. (2004). *Organize, communicate, empower! How principals can make time for leadership.* Thousand Oaks, CA: Corwin Press.

Shipman, N., Martin, J., McKay, B., & Anastasi, R. (1983). *Effective time management techniques for school administrators.* Englewood Cliffs, NJ: Prentice Hall.

Simon, R., & Newman, J. (2004). *Making time to lead.* Thousand Oaks, CA: Corwin Press.

TIME-ON-TASK

For students in PK–12 schools, the school day is segmented to allocate time for instruction and time for noninstructional activities, such as lunch, recess, and moving from one classroom to another. During instructional time, students have opportunities to engage in learning. When students take advantage of these opportunities during instruction, they are considered to be "on-task." Researchers measure on-task behavior and call it "time-on-task."

On-task time is differentiated from total time spent in the classroom or other learning venues, because students do not spend all the time they are in a classroom engaged in learning. Time is also consumed as students enter and leave the room, when materials are collected, and when student misbehavior is corrected. In addition, though the teacher may provide instruction, students do not always concentrate on learning activities that take place. Students daydream, converse with classmates, doodle, complete assignments for other teachers, and sometimes sleep.

Time for learning is affected by events within and also beyond the control of the teacher. Time-on-task is interrupted by events such as unplanned announcements over the public address system, students and other teachers entering the room to procure materials or share information, unannounced visits from guest artists or speakers visiting the school, and the late or early arrival of teachers of special programs, such as art, music, keyboarding, and drug awareness. In short, time allocated for learning is not synonymous with time used for learning.

Numerous studies conducted over nearly 40 years support a positive relationship between time-on-task and achievement, especially for low-performing students. Though the research is consistent, one criticism of these studies is that data gathering relies on the observation of the researcher, and therefore, results may overestimate the amount of time that students are actually on-task. That is, a student may appear to be on-task while actually daydreaming or may perfunctorily perform a rote task without attempting to learn from the task.

The amount of time students attend to learning varies (a) by subject matter—more time is spent on-task during mathematics lessons than during English, reading, or social studies lessons; (b) by achievement level—higher-achieving students attend more during instruction than lower-achieving students; (c) by instructional strategy—students' time-on-task is higher during laboratory and group work than during lecture; (d) by age—older students spend more time off-task than younger students; (e) by task relevance and challenge—students are more likely to engage in content they deem relevant and challenging; and (f) by ethnicity—Asian and White students report more time-on-task than do African American and Hispanic students. Ethnic differences in attention to task begin to disappear when lesson quality and instructional quality are high, however.

Time-on-task also appears to increase when class size is lower. Some research suggests that lowering class size for primary-aged youngsters increases the time teachers are able to devote to individual students, thereby increasing the students' attention to the task. Similarly, as teachers spend more time assisting individual and small groups of students with learning tasks, the students also spend more time-on-task.

Researchers argue whether overall time-on-task is better increased by lengthening the school day and year or by limiting lecture in favor of other methods found in the research to engage students in learning. Resolution of this argument has implications for both policy and practice.

—*Dianne L. Taylor*

See also accountability; achievement tests; Asian Pacific Americans; Black education; class size; compensatory education; discipline in schools; giftedness, gifted education; individual differences, in children; instructional interventions; Latinos; motivation, theories of; productivity; resiliency; scheduling, types of in schools; site-based management; time management; underachievers, in schools

Further Readings and References

Alexander, K., Entwisle, D., & Olson, L. (2001, Summer). Schools, achievement, and inequality: A seasonal perspective. *Educational Evaluation and Policy Analysis, 23,* 171–191.

Cohen, D., Raudenbush, S., & Ball, D. (2003). Resources, instruction, and research. *Educational Evaluation and Policy Analysis, 25,* 119–142.

Smith, B. A. (2000). Quantity matters: Annual instructional time in an urban school system. *Educational Administration Quarterly, 36,* 652–682.

Yair, G. (2000). Not just about time: Instructional practices and productive time in school. *Educational Administration Quarterly, 36,* 485–512.

🏛 TOTAL QUALITY MANAGEMENT

Total quality management (TQM) is a philosophy and practice where organizational members strive to meet the needs of customers and where the structure and functioning of the organization is designed to allow them to do so. Organizationally, TQM is about developing and continuously improving quality systemic processes. TQM is based on W. Edwards Deming's Fourteen Points of Quality Management. Joseph Juran and Philip B. Crosby are also associated with the early development of TQM.

A quality systemic process is one that is predictable and repeatable, including achieving intended performance results, conforming to or exceeding specifications and standards set by the needs and requirements of customers (i.e., students) and stakeholders (e.g., parents, community, state), continuously improving, and well deployed to all appropriate organizational units. A process is well deployed when it can be identified in everyday practice of organizational members. It is important to remember when TQM is applied to education, the product, better described as a service, is the education of the student.

Ongoing school improvement efforts to address equity (e.g., standards-based reform) have frustrated many educators because traditionally, schools are not designed for change. The industrial model, on which twentieth-century schools were based, was designed for uniformity of product, not process improvement. Continuous improvement requires a dynamic, open, self-examining, interactive system. TQM can provide a framework for the development of the type of system that can support continual change and improvement in schools.

A school either has a quality program or it does not based on systemic processes. For example, a quality teaching and learning process could start with developing curriculum based on state, national, and local learning standards (i.e., needs and requirements) and identifying key measures (i.e., state and local assessments) for monitoring successful implementation.

Educators are trained on using the curriculum and assessments. Teachers deliver the curriculum (i.e., educational service) to students and use assessments to monitor in-process quality, as well as end-process performance results. Feedback from monitoring and end-process results is used by administrators and teachers to make changes to the curriculum, educator training, method(s) of delivery, or monitoring and data collection.

Changes to teaching and learning processes are undertaken to improve the predictability, reliability, and deployment of processes, including achieving, or demonstrating positive trends toward intended performance results. From the above example, if one fourth-grade teacher emphasizes instruction in English, because that is what he feels is important, and another fourth-grade teacher emphasizes instruction in Math, because that is what she feels is important, then the process is not reliable.

The fifth-grade teachers may predict which student had which teacher by their academic strengths but must now spend time addressing academic deficiencies because the curriculum was not followed and students don't reliably come to them with the needed academic skills to be successful in fifth grade. The fifth-grade teachers are internal customers of the fourth-grade teachers; they rely on the services of the fourth-grade teachers to be successful in teaching fifth grade.

Furthermore, both fourth-grade teachers could reliably follow the curriculum but make changes in delivery so that from year to year, the incoming fifth-grade students' academic skills are not predictable. Regarding deployment, a school district may have a well-planned curriculum that is aligned to state, national, and local standards, but if teachers do not follow it to guide instruction, then the curriculum is not being used in everyday practice and is not well deployed, even though students may have predictably high test scores.

When test scores are reliably and predictably high for most students, even though the teaching and learning process is not well deployed, then a quality process does not exist. It is not possible to identify if, or how, teaching contributes to learning, and high test scores may be the result of other factors, such as the student's home life (e.g., high socioeconomic status, well-educated parents), as much as the teaching and learning process.

The above example follows the core component of TQM that makes continuous quality improvement possible: the *Plan-Do-Check-Act* (PDCA) cycle. To *Plan* is best identified as strategic planning on a large scale (i.e., district, school) or action planning on a smaller scale (i.e., program, curriculum). To *Do* is implementing the plan; development of trust and shared norms helps ensure what was planned is implemented. A normative environment in schools, a characteristic of tight coupling, is necessary for classroom practice to reflect the rhetoric of reform.

To *Check* is to collect and analyze formative (in-process) and summative (end-process) data on key measures of successful implementation. Key measures should be multiple, rather than rely on one measure of program success. To *Act* is to make changes to program implementation, if needed, based on data analysis of key measures. Effective action can be taken in-process or end-process.

As TQM moved from a lesser-known organizational improvement model to literally becoming a fad in the 1990s, the definition of TQM grew increasingly broad as technical dimensions of TQM were replaced with institutional dimensions. This replacement process reflects how TQM is practiced within specific organizations over time and may not reflect the technical dimensions that initially resulted in successful practice.

To ensure successful implementation of TQM, it is important to determine the extent of implementation efforts. A review of 99 papers on TQM from 1989 to 1993 in academic and practitioner journals found only 4% assessed the degree to which TQM was actually in place. Studies that examine Baldrige Award organizations are the exception, since the award process ensures that award winners have TQM fully implemented. State award programs that mirror the Baldrige National Quality Award can provide a similar service to organizations (e.g., schools) in identifying the extent of TQM implementation.

—*George R. Stanhope*

See also accountability; achievement tests; behaviorism; cost-benefit analyses; empiricism; expert power; globalism; human resource development; Interstate School Leaders Licensure Consortium; motivation, theories of; performance assessment; personnel management; problem solving; productivity; research methods; resource management; school improvement models; scientific management; Taylor, Frederick

Further Readings and References

Deming, W. E. (1986). *Out of the crisis.* Cambridge: MIT, Center for Advanced Engineering Study.

Deming, W. E. (1993). *The new economics.* Cambridge: MIT Press.

Elmore, R. E. (2000). *Building a new structure for school leadership.* Albert Shanker Institute.

English, F., & Hill, J. (1995). *Calidad total en la educacion.* Mexico: EDAMEX.

Sallis, E. (2002). *Total quality management in education* (3rd ed.). Sterling, VA: Stylus.

Weller, L. D., & McElwee, G. (1997). Strategic management of quality: An American and British perspective. *Journal of Research and Development in Education* 30(4), 201–213.

Zbaracki, M. J. (1998). The rhetoric and reality of quality management. *Administrative Science Quarterly, 43,* 602–636.

TRACKING, OF STUDENTS

Two different definitions of *tracking* have been used in textbooks over the past several decades. Historically, tracking began with curriculum grouping, or selecting students based on their educational and occupational plans. This type of tracking differentiates instruction according to students' interests, desires, and ambitions. A more recent definition of tracking, seen pervasively in public schools, is ability grouping, or grouping that tailors curriculum and instruction to each student's unique intellectual abilities. Hence, tracking is a term that can be used to refer to either of the different grouping arrangements, curriculum grouping or ability grouping.

In 1985, Jeannie Oakes defined tracking as the practice of dividing students into separate classes according to their achievement level (high, medium, or low). It involves different curriculum paths for students who are college bound and for those who are headed directly for the workplace. Other measures for tracking are the categorizing of students according to particular measures of intelligence for purposes of teaching and learning. In this scenario, students are provided with curriculum and instruction that school officials deem best suited to their abilities and that match spoken or unspoken assessments of each student's future. In most senior high schools, students are assigned to a particular curriculum track that provides sequences of courses for college-preparatory, vocational, or general-track students.

Marked increases in high school attendance after the turn of the twentieth century led to increases in the diversity of secondary student populations, as well as to an increase in the practice of testing students for career interests. Tracking became widely practiced then to deliver specific skills to different student groups. No longer were high schools exclusively serving a population of college-bound individuals due to compulsory education laws being strictly enforced around 1900.

In 1954, the Supreme Court struck down the "separate but equal" clause of the constitution with the landmark court case *Brown v. Board of Education.* Separation of students by race, ethnicity, and gender was considered unconstitutional, and education was to be made available to all on equal terms. Since it was against the law to segregate students into different schools, within school separation became a common practice in schools. Because of this, there is a double-jeopardy effect for Hispanic and African American students, who are less likely to have access to high-track courses, and they are more likely than their White peers to be placed in low-track classes

Between 1965 and 1975, most American secondary schools dismantled their tracking practices that assigned students to predetermined programs of study. Track labels were no longer assigned to programs, but were instead applied to specific coursework in which students enrolled.

Two landmark cases have found that tracking by ability groups results in a disproportionate number of minority students in lower tracks. In *Hobson v. Hansen* (1967, 1969), courts ruled against ability grouping because it resulted in unequal resources and no educational benefits. In *Marshall v. Georgia* (1984, 1985), the courts ruled in favor of ability grouping; however, the practice was found to be equitable for all students. Therefore, in *Hobson,* the practice of tracking was found to be inequitable and discriminatory, and in *Marshall,* the practice was found to be equitable.

Tracking has not historically worked well for students in the low- and middle-ability groups, who experience clear and consistent learning disadvantages. Many studies have shown that highly capable students do as well in mixed-ability classes as they do in high-track homogeneous groups.

Tracking and ability grouping also characterize the organization of classrooms for middle and elementary students. Some evidence suggests that the ways elementary schools define ability may help to solidify students' perceptions of their own achievement abilities and may eventually exaggerate initial performance differences among them. In a recent survey, approximately two thirds of middle-level principals reported the use of whole-class grouping by ability in at least some academic subjects. Whole-class ability grouping also increased as students moved from fifth through ninth grade. These findings mirror others who discerned that eighth graders are almost always grouped homogeneously for at least part of their school day, with 89% of the classrooms using some form of ability grouping.

Students rarely move up from noncollege tracks to college tracks; however, 7 times as many students move down from college tracks to noncollege tracks. Despite these claims, several studies have found that tracking has little, if any, direct impact on student achievement. On the contrary, Jeannie Oakes found in 1990 that assessments of academic ability, placement in different tracks or ability-grouped classes, and the reduced educational opportunities often parallel race and social class difference. Once tracked into the lower-ability group, students are almost always restricted in their access to quality mathematics programs and courses, qualified mathematics teachers, resources, and learning opportunities. Hence, many lower-tracked classes are forever subjected to inexperienced or unqualified teachers, once again perpetuating the prevailing power structure that favors White, middle- and upper-class males. Research indicates that students in lower-track classes receive a different education from other students both in terms of material covered and quality of instruction.

As a result of the growing criticism of tracking, schools are increasingly eliminating it. In a 1993 survey conducted by the National Center for Education Statistics, more than half the schools reported that they had begun to modify their approaches to ability grouping, and only 15% reported using traditional tracking mechanisms.

—*Karen Watt*

See also achievement tests; Black education; child development theories; class, social; compensatory education; critical race theory; critical theory; cross-cultural studies; curriculum, theories of; discrimination; diversity; early childhood education; equality, in schools; ethnicity; eugenics; expectations, teacher and student cultures; giftedness, gifted education; grades, of students; Head Start; individual differences, in children; intelligence; learning, theories of; measurement, theories of; metacognition; minorities, in schools; *A Nation at Risk;* No Child Left Behind; performance assessment; productivity; reform, of schools; schooling effects; special education; standardized testing; underachievers, in schools

Further Readings and References

Carey, N., Farris, E., & Carpenter, J. (1994). *Curricular differentiation in public high schools.* Rockville, MD: Westat.
Grossen, B. (1996). *How should we group to achieve excellence with equity?* Eugene, OR: National Center to Improve the Tools of Educators.

Lucas, S. R. (1999). *Tracking inequality: Stratification and mobility in America high schools.* New York: Teachers College Press.

Oakes, J. (1985). *Keeping track: How schools structure inequality.* New Haven, CT: Yale University Press.

Oakes, J. (1990). *Multiplying inequalities: The effects of race, social class, and tracking on opportunities to learn mathematics and sciences.* Santa Monica, CA: RAND.

Oakes, J., Ormseth, T., Bell, R., & Camp, P. (1990). *Multiplying inequalities: The effects of race, social class, and tracking on opportunities to learn mathematics and science* (Report to the RAND Corporation). Santa Monica, CA: RAND.

🏛 TRAIT THEORY

Trait theory represents researchers' earliest attempts to investigate leadership. Around the turn of the twentieth century, researchers sought to identify traits that effective leaders possessed by examining leaders who had achieved a level of greatness. These preliminary attempts to identify traits of leaders focused on well-known historical figures who were men, which is why this theory is often called the "great man" approach.

Early proponents of the classic trait perspective suggested that certain individuals have special innate characteristics or qualities that make them leaders and it is these qualities that differentiate them from non-leaders. Fundamental to this theory was the idea that some people are born with traits that make them natural leaders. Influenced by the interest in mental testing and the functionalism that characterized the time, psychologists began to correlate specific individual differences, in particular intelligence and mental ability, with performance in leadership positions.

An ambiguous term, trait theory has been used to refer to personality, temperaments, dispositions, and abilities, as well as to physical and demographic attributes. One of the first systematic attempts to review trait leadership research was conducted by Ralph Stogdill. This seminal research study analyzed over one hundred trait studies that took place over a period of four decades. His results showed that a person who holds a position of leadership surpasses the average member of the group in several ways, including intelligence, scholarship, dependability, and sociability. Though Stogdill determined that there was indeed a high consistency in the relationship between intelligence and being a leader, he concluded that it is

difficult to isolate a set of traits that are characteristic of leadership without factoring situational effects into the equation. A leader in some situations might not be a leader in other situations. Several researchers during this era substantiated this point.

Based on numerous research studies conducted between 1940 and 1960, trait theory lost its appeal as a premise for understanding leaders. One problem highlighted by the studies was the lack of consensus on the definitive traits that set great leaders apart from each other. The only point on which theorists agreed was that great leaders were special; they had qualities that were born within them. Another criticism of trait theory was the fact that it overlooked the importance of situations and the relationship to leadership.

Despite these criticisms, interest in trait theory resurged in the 1980s. Numerous meta-analytic reviews of earlier leader-trait research were conducted. Based on a reexamination of the original data, several researchers concluded that traits are indeed associated with leadership. Another line of research related to trait theory is the study of charismatic leadership. These researchers postulate that specific leader qualities are linked to charismatic leaders who act in special ways to influence and inspire their followers. Recent studies on leader attributes focus on five categories of traits or qualities: cognitive abilities, personality, motivation, social appraisal, and leader expertise. Still another aspect of the examination of the traits of leaders regards their gender roles and the manner in which the public perception of gender has had an enormous impact on who is selected to become and remain an educational leader. The impact of trait theory is evident in its continued influence on leadership theories and research.

—Susan R. Wynn

See also charisma, of leaders; discrimination; feminism and theories of leadership; gender studies, in educational leadership; great man theory; homophobia; intelligence; leadership, theories of; leadership effectiveness; personality; role theory; sexism (glass ceiling); superintendency; Theory X, Theory Y; three-factor model, five-factor model

Further Readings and References

Blount, J. (2003). Homosexuality and school superintendents: A brief history. *Journal of School Leadership, 13,* 7–26.

Lugg, C. (2003). Sissies, faggots, lezzies, and dykes: Gender, sexual orientation, and a new politics of education? *Educational Administration Quarterly, 39,* 95–134.

McEwan, E. (2003). *Ten traits of highly effective principals.* Thousand Oaks, CA: Corwin Press.

Zaccaro, S., Kemp, C., & Bader, P. (2004). Leader traits and attributes. In J. Antonakis, A. Cianciolo, & R. Sternberg (Eds.), *The nature of leadership* (pp. 101–124). Thousand Oaks, CA: Sage.

🏛 TRANSACTIONAL ANALYSIS

Eric Berne developed transactional analysis for use in psychotherapy. It was further popularized in the best-selling books *Games People Play* and *I'm OK—You're OK*. More recently, managers have used transactional analysis as an organizational change technique.

Transactional analysis is concerned with three areas of analysis: *structural analysis* (the analysis of individual personality); *time structuring* (the analysis of the way people structure their time); and *life scripts* (the analysis of the roles that people learn to play in life). The focus in organizational change has been on structural analysis and time structuring.

STRUCTURAL ANALYSIS

The personality of each person is made up of ego states. Berne defines an *ego state* as a consistent pattern of feeling and experience directly related to a corresponding consistent pattern of behavior. Although school administrators cannot direct ego states, they can observe behavior and from this infer which of the three ego states is operating at any given time. This should help them better understand others in the workplace and the reasons for their behavior.

The three ego states—the Parent, the Adult, and the Child—are common to all people, but the content of each is unique to each individual, based on his or her background and experiences.

- *The Parent ego state* derives from one's parents or other powerful figures in one's childhood. It is expressed toward others as nurturing, critical, or standard-setting behavior. A school administrator exhibiting a Parent ego state tends to talk down to subordinates and to treat them like children.

- *The Adult ego state* reflects maturity, objectivity, problem analysis, logic, and rationality. It is oriented toward objective information gathering, careful analysis, generating alternatives, and making logical choices. A school administrator who behaves fairly and objectively in dealing with subordinates is exhibiting an Adult ego state.

- *The Child ego state* derives from one's experiences as a child. This ego state can range from being submissive and conforming to being insubordinate, rebellious, emotional, or perhaps inadequate.

TIME STRUCTURING

Another focus of transactional analysis is the way in which people structure their time. There are six basic ways to structure time: withdrawal, rituals, pastimes, activities, games, and authenticity:

1. *Withdrawal* can be either physical or psychological. Examples include walking away from an argument (physical), withdrawing to avoid pain and punishment (physical), withdrawing to think through a problem and examine alternatives (psychological), or daydreaming (psychological).

2. *Rituals* are stylized transactions, such as "Good morning, how are you?" Such a rhetorical question suggests the response, "Fine, how are you?" Such interchanges have little meaning except to recognize the other person. Should the receiver of the message actually respond to the question, the sender would be distressed because no answer is expected.

3. *Pastimes* are nonstylized transactions that have a repetitive quality. Discussing the weather or politics during social occasions are examples.

4. *Activities* consist of transactions centered on getting work done. Work fulfills various needs in people, such as recognition and accomplishment. We all know of cases where people die shortly after retirement. Explanations for this phenomenon include people's loss of a constructive way of structuring time and feeling worthwhile and important to society.

5. *Games* are sets of ulterior transactions, repetitive in nature, with well-defined psychological payoff. People use games to avoid authenticity or intimacy. Other books provide several descriptions of games. Therefore, we describe only a few of the more well-known games used in organizations. Superior and subordinate frequently play "Blemish." For example, a principal brings a report to the superintendent, and he quickly skims it. Regardless of how good the report is, the superintendent finds one or more "blemishes" in it and points these out to the principal. In this way, the superintendent maintains his power position. This game can be played at any level along the hierarchy (principal-department head, department head-teacher, teacher-student). Another game in which the superior maintains a power position is called, "Yes,

but. . . ." For example, the superintendent asks her principals for input in solving a problem. Each suggestion from the principals is followed with a "Yes, but . . ." response from the superintendent. Finally, there is the game of NIGYYSOB (Now I've Got You, You SOB). In this game, one employee lures another into a work situation (for example, a superintendent and principal) in which the victim, the subordinate, is programmed for failure. When the mistake occurs, the superintendent pounces on the principal, which results in embarrassment, a reprimand, or even dismissal.

6. *Authenticity* refers to transactions that are devoid of game playing and exploitation of people.

Andrew Halpin and Don Croft are two early researchers who recognized the significance of authenticity in organizational behavior. The chief consequence of their research on organizational climate was identifying the pivotal importance of authenticity in schools. Later, James Henderson and Wayne Hoy, after an extensive review of the literature, identified three basic aspects of leader authenticity in schools: accountability, nonmanipulation, and salience of self over role.

Accountability is the aspect of authenticity that describes the leader as accepting responsibility and admitting errors. The authentic leader accepts responsibility for his or her own actions as well as those of subordinates and admits mistakes when they are made. On the other hand, inauthentic leaders are unwilling to accept responsibility and admit mistakes; they blame others and circumstances for their shortcomings and failures.

Nonmanipulation of subordinates reflects the perception of subordinates that their leader avoids exploiting them. Authentic leaders are seen as those who avoid manipulating others as if they were objects, whereas inauthentic leaders are perceived as dealing with subordinates as if they were things.

Salience of self over role refers to the ability to break through the barriers of role stereotyping and behave in congruence with personal and situational needs. Authentic leader behavior is relatively unconstrained by traditional role requirements. Inauthentic leaders, in contrast, adhere to the narrow behavior of their job descriptions, never allowing self to override the routinized behavior of the office. In a follow-up study, authenticity was related to commanding trust and loyalty from teachers. An atmosphere of trust facilitates organizational change in schools.

How does transactional analysis relate to organizational change? People are trained in seminars to identify dysfunctional aspects enumerated by transactional analysis in its three areas: time structuring, analysis of transactions, and structural analysis. The assumption is that this knowledge will make school administrators more effective in their relationships with faculty and in collegial relationships among the faculty. Increased effectiveness in interpersonal relations in schools should help to reduce resistance to change efforts proposed by school administrators.

—*Fred C. Lunenburg*

See also behaviorism; collaboration theory; decision making; egocentrism, theories of; human resource development; Maslow, Abraham; mentoring; motivation, theories of; organizational theories; personality; psychology, types of; Theory X, Theory Y; transformational leadership

Further Readings and References

Berne, E. (1986). *Transactional analysis in psychotherapy.* New York: Ballantine.
Berne, E. (1996). *Games people play* (Rev. ed.). New York: Ballantine.
Halpin, A. W. (1966). *Theory and research in administration.* New York: Macmillan.
Halpin, A. W., & Croft, D. B. (1963). *The organizational climate of schools.* Chicago: University of Chicago Press.
Harris, T. A. (1993). *I'm OK—you're OK.* New York: Avon.
Henderson, J. E., & Hoy, W. K. (1983). Leader authenticity: The development and test of an operational measure. *Educational and Psychological Measurement, 3,* 63–75.
Hoy, W. K., & Kupersmith, W. (1984). Principal authenticity and faculty trust: Key elements in organizational behavior. *Planning and Changing, 15,* 80–88.

TRANSFORMATIONAL LEADERSHIP

Transformational leadership is composed of multiple forms, originally concerning administration of educational organizations. Developed by James MacGregor Burns in 1978, it was later extended by Bernard Bass, noting its occurrence when leaders expand and promote employee interests. This involved the encouragement of employees beyond their self-interests, generating benefits for the organization and highlighting the mission and goals of the organization to maintain awareness and acceptance among its members.

Transformational leadership recognizes and exploits existing needs or demands of followers by looking for their potential motives, seeks to satisfy these higher needs, and engages the abilities of the followers. The strengths of this form of leadership lie in its collective vision and effective communication with all employees.

Transformational leadership consists of four components: *charisma* or *idealized influence, inspirational motivation, intellectual stimulation,* and *individualized consideration.* Furthermore, transformational leaders pursue three fundamental goals: to assist staff in developing and maintaining a collaborative, professional organizational culture; to foster development of professional growth; and to help staff members solve problems more effectively by engaging them in new activities and requiring from them an appurtenant effort.

There are two fundamental goals of transformational leadership. The first goal is to assist staff development and maintain a collaborative, professional school culture by means of communicating, observing, critiquing, and planning in collaboration. Norms of collective responsibility and continuous improvement encourage staff to exchange teaching techniques. Transformational leaders involve staff in collaborative goal setting, reduce teacher isolation, use somewhat bureaucratic mechanisms to support cultural changes, share leadership by delegating power, and actively communicate a school's norms and beliefs. The second goal is to foster teacher development; teachers' motivation for development is enhanced when they internalize goals for professional growth. This process is facilitated when they are strongly committed to a school's mission.

Ultimately, the third goal of transformational leadership is to assist teachers to solve problems more effectively, which is of value because it stimulates teachers to engage in new activities and put forth an appurtenant effort. These leaders share a genuine belief that their staff, as a group, could develop better solutions than the principal alone. However, critics argue that transformational leadership is unethical and contend that it lacks the checks and balances of democratic discourse and power distribution. They also contend that it manipulates followers into ignoring their own best interests.

Proponents of transformational leadership claim it increases the organization's productivity and customer satisfaction, generating higher commitment to the organization from employees and increasing

employee trust in management and organizational citizenship behavior (i.e., discretionary extra-role work-related behavior, such as conscientiousness, altruism, and sportsmanship, all of which are not related to the formal reward system of the organization). This also enhances employee satisfaction with both their jobs and leaders, reduces employee stress, and increases well-being. Evidence of the effects of transformational leadership is deemed positive. This is because its practices have a sizable influence on teacher collaboration and because significant relationships exist between aspects of transformational leadership and educators' own reports of changes in both attitudes toward school improvement and altered instructional behavior.

Transformational leadership begins with the development of a vision, a view of the future that will excite and convert potential followers. This vision may be developed by the leader or the senior team or may emerge from a series of general discussions, requiring energy and commitment, as few people immediately buy into a radical vision, and some much more slowly than others. Transformational leaders thus seize opportunity and employ tools at their disposal to gain numbers and create a following. However, transformational leaders have to exercise caution with matters of trust, as personal integrity is a critical element of the package that they are promoting. In effect, they are selling themselves as well as the common vision. They motivate followers by appealing to strong emotion regardless of the ultimate effects on the followers, not necessarily always tending to positive ethical values. Transformational leaders are often charismatic but may not be as self-absorbed as this description would suggest. In this way, they succeed through esoteric, rather than exoteric, motivation.

Transformational leadership exists in a continuum with transactional leadership, and therefore, a leader may exhibit traits of both leadership styles. It recognizes the need for organizational practices such as performance appraisals, job descriptions, management by objectives, performance-based pay, position grading, and organizational process analysis and clarification. It also recognizes and uses praise, recognition, and the delegation of responsibility and work when both leaders and followers are in agreement as to which tasks hold importance. The transactional leader works through creating clearly structured frameworks whereby it is unambiguous to subordinates what is required and what rewards are received for obedience. Reprimand is not always explicit but well understood, and formal systems of discipline are usually administrable. The transactional leader is responsible and fully accountable for allocating work to subordinates, irrespective of whether the latter have resource or capability to perform the assigned tasks. In the event of mishap, the subordinate is considered to be personally at fault and penalized for failure. Alternatively, in contrast to transactional leaders, transformational leaders motivate by appealing to followers' self-interests.

One of the drawbacks of transformational leadership is that passion and confidence can easily be mistaken for truth and reality. While it is true that great strides have been taken through enthusiastic leadership, it is also true that many passionate people have led the charge into extirpation. Transformational leaders often have tremendous amounts of enthusiasm, which, if applied relentlessly, can exhaust followers. They tend to see the big picture, but not detail. If they do not have delegated personnel to monitor finer levels of specification, they face failure. Transformational leaders, by definition, seek to transform all elements. When the organization does not need transformation and members are content, then such a leader will become frustrated. Given the appropriate situation, however, they can develop their own momentum and have been known to change entire organizations.

—Eunyoung Kim

See also administration, theories of; charisma, of leaders; Follett, Mary Parker; leadership, complex; leadership, distributed; leadership, participatory; leadership effectiveness; leadership styles, management theories; Maslow, Abraham; Theory X, Theory Y; transactional analysis

Further Readings and References

Bass, B. M. (1985). How to succeed in business according to business students and manager. *Journal of Applied Psychology, 52,* 254–262.

Bass, B. M. (1985). *Leadership and performance beyond expectation.* New York: Free Press.

Bass, B. M. (1990). *Bass and Stodgill's handbook of leadership.* New York: Free Press.

Bass, B. M. (1990, Winter). From transactional to transformational leadership: Learning to share the vision. *Organizational Dynamics,* pp. 19–31.

Burns, J. M. (1978). *Leadership.* New York: HarperCollins.

Joyner, E., Ben-Avie, M., & Comer, J. (2004). *Transforming school leadership and management to support student learning and development.* Thousand Oaks, CA: Corwin Press.

Northouse, P. (2003). *Leadership.* Thousand Oaks, CA: Sage.

Starratt, R. (2003). *Centering educational administration.* Mahwah, NJ: Lawrence Erlbaum.

TRENDS INTERNATIONAL MATHEMATICS AND SCIENCE STUDY

The Trends International Mathematics and Science Study (TIMSS, originally titled Third International Mathematics and Science Study) is a multicountry, multilevel study of math and science instruction and achievement in 1995, 1999, and 2003. Hosted by the International Association for the Evaluation of Educational Achievement (IEA), the study is administered by Boston College's TIMSS International Study Center to provide important information for policy development, to foster public accountability, to allow areas of progress or decline in achievement to be identified and monitored, and to address concerns for equity. TIMSS data are rich for education research, resulting in hundreds of articles, including empirical analyses and comparisons, conference papers, commentaries and the like on individual country achievement, instructional policies and practice in math and science, as well as international comparisons.

TIMSS operates on a 4-year cycle, with 2007 slated for the fourth round of testing. Each of first three rounds included different types of data collection, which led to a number of technical reports, data analyses, and international databases.

In 1995, three grades were assessed in 42 countries, the fourth, eighth, and final year of secondary school. This initial year also included several other portions, including benchmark, video, curriculum, and case studies, which required teacher and principal participation. In 1999, only eighth graders were assessed in 38 countries. A benchmark and video study were included. Twenty-six of the 38 nations had also participated in the 1995 study, which allowed for a variety of comparative analyses. Study information included school and home environments as well as curriculum and instruction. In 2003, only the paper-and-pencil assessment was used for fourth and eighth graders in 46 countries.

TIMSS student tests are developed with the aid of math, science, and assessment experts guided by grade-level assessment frameworks. Frameworks

Trenholm, Harper Councill 1033

reflect math and science curriculum and were revised in 2003 to include assessment objectives for fourth- and eighth-grade students and added problem solving and inquiry (PSI) tasks. Tests include field-tested, multiple-choice, and written-response items. Student answers are scored using specific grading criteria. After each TIMSS cycle, some test items are publicly released. Students, teachers and building administrators fill out questionnaires to provide additional data on a variety of instructional practices, students' own learning expectations and their family characteristics, teacher quality and development, community and school culture, local policy, and the like.

Science assessment areas include earth, life, and environmental sciences, and physics and chemistry, while math areas include numbers, algebra, geometry, data, and measurement.

The 1995 TIMSS included a curricular study. Researchers gleaned information on math and science instruction from textbooks, curriculum guides, and other materials. Through 1996 and 1997, the results of the cross-country curricular study were available through a number of reports.

The TIMSS benchmarking studies compare states' and districts' science and mathematics programs and subsequent achievement to international practice and results. In 1995, 5 states and 1 school district consortium participated, and in 1999, 13 states and 14 district consortia participated. The assessments were administered to representative samples of eighth-grade students.

The 1995 and 1999, TIMSS video studies captured eighth-grade students in several countries in order to examine classroom instructional practices. The 1999 study was expanded to include seven of the top-performing countries in the 1995 assessment.

The 1995 TIMSS case study of Japan, Germany, and the United States included data gathering on teacher training and work environments, educational standards, and how schools handle differing student abilities.

In the United States, a variety of partnerships collect and analyze TIMSS data, including the National Science Foundation (NSF), which both funds the project and uses the subsequent data for advocating improvement in math and science instruction. The U.S. National Center for Education Statistics also analyzes data and releases various reports, published on its TIMSS Web site. The U.S. Department of Education's then Office of Educational Research and Improvement (now Institute of Educational Sciences)

also sponsored a number of reports, using several elements of the TIMSS data.

Books and peer-reviewed articles emerged from the study as well, comparing student achievement across countries, as well as cultural, school and family influences, instructional practices, tracking policies, and the like. Articles also reported on achievement and practice in individual countries. Some articles questioned the rigor and usefulness of TIMSS cross-country comparisons.

—Angela M. Hull

See also accountability; achievement tests; curriculum guides; evaluation; math education; performance assessment; questionnaires; science, in curriculum; standardized testing

Further Readings and References

Baker, D., Akiba, M., LeTendre, G., & Wiseman, A. (2001). Worldwide shadow education: Outside-school learning, institutional quality of schooling, and cross-national mathematics achievement. *Educational Evaluation and Policy Analysis, 23,* 1–18.

Kuiper, W., & Plomp, T. (1999). TIMSS in a Western European context. *Educational Research and Evaluation (An International Journal on Theory and Practice), 5*(2), 78–246.

Stigler, J. W., Gonzales, P., Kawanaka, T., Knoll, S., & Serrano, A. (1999). The TIMSS videotape classroom study: Methods and findings from an exploratory research project on eighth-grade mathematics instruction in Germany, Japan, and the United States. *Education Statistics Quarterly, 1*(2), 109–112.

Wang, J. (2001). TIMSS primary and middle school data: Some technical concerns. *Educational Researcher, 30*(6), 17–21.

🏛 TRENHOLM, HARPER COUNCILL

President of Alabama State College and Executive Secretary of the American Teachers Association, Harper Councill Trenholm (1900–1963) promoted education equity, the professional growth of teachers, and the inclusion of African Americans in the National Education Association (NEA) on equal footing. Using a professional perspective to counter the legal, economic, and social boundaries imposed by race, Trenholm valued cooperation between Black and White educators and placed a high premium on developing pride in Black history, heritage, and professional status. Assuming the presidency of the State Normal School, later Alabama State, he worked for the accreditation of Black schools using the same standards as for White schools. He strengthened the Alabama State Teachers Association, which became the largest Black teacher organization in the South. In addition, he nurtured the American Teachers Association (ATA), formerly the National Association of Teachers in Colored Schools (NATCS), which enhanced the professional development of African American educators, elevated their professional status, and secured their place in the expanding Black middle class. His life work stressed the agency displayed by African Americans in securing equity in multiple arenas and the value of education in the African American community.

Trenholm had significant influence on the ATA-NEA Joint Committee's agenda, which included the dissemination of information on Black schools, the support of textbook revision to incorporate African American history, and the expanded use of the media to accomplish these ends. Trenholm's work underscored self-determinism and pride in Black history and culture. Denied membership in White educational associations in the South and only marginal participation in the NEA, African American educators organized and sustained their own educational associations, such as the Alabama State Teachers Association (ASTA), which was the backbone of the American Teachers Association (ATA). Trenholm saw inclusion in the White associations as an ultimate goal. In 1950, he formulated a "transitional interpretation" of the NEA's bylaws that allowed affiliation of the Black state associations if members were forbidden because of race from joining the White affiliate. This interpretation of the bylaws, in effect in 1951, facilitated the participation of African Americans in the NEA and brought their interests directly to the association's membership.

During Trenholm's tenure as college head, institutional power remained in the hands of the president, and Trenholm labored to retain state aid to Alabama State College for Negroes (ASCN) as it experienced phenomenal growth. As the civil rights movement progressed, ASCN teachers and students were active in the Montgomery bus boycott and in lunch counter sit-ins. These acts of civil disobedience pitted Trenholm, an employee of the state, against the opponents of desegregation, but he did not acquiesce to demands to release files of ASCN professors and students, many of whom were supporters of Martin Luther King Jr. In 1961, the NEA took a decisive step toward the merger of the ATA and NEA—a goal he had long labored for and which was finally realized in 1966, 3 years after his death. The NEA recognizes educators who have contributed to human and civil rights with an award named in Trenholm's honor.

—*Carol F. Karpinski*

See also affirmative action; Afrocentric theories; American Federation of Teachers; Bethune, Mary McLeod; Black education; civil rights movement; Coppin, Fanny Jackson; desegregation, of schools; discrimination; diversity; Du Bois, W. E. B.; law, trends in; National Educational Association; Supreme Court, United States, key cases in education law; Washington, Booker T.

Further Readings and References

Gray, J. A., Reed, J. L., & Walton, N. W. (1987). *History of the Alabama State Teachers Association.* Washington, DC: National Education Association.
Perry, T. D. (1975). *History of the American Teachers Association.* Washington, DC: National Education Association.

TUTORING

Tutoring is providing individual, guided instruction on specific subject matter, concepts, or skills for a particular purpose. Studies have consistently found that tutoring is a valuable instructional tool. Tutoring has been shown to improve academic performance and attitudes toward school of students tutored. There appears to be an initially high rate of success in achievement gains in a relatively short time. Benjamin Bloom wrote in 1984 that tutoring yielded achievement 2 standard deviations above the level of conventional classroom group instruction and that the average tutored student ranked above 98% of the students in the control group classes.

Tutoring can be conducted by students, volunteers, or trained tutors. Bloom's study was conducted using trained tutors, and research shows that children, youth, and adult volunteers can and should be trained in fundamental tutoring skills. Training should be systematic, providing specific instruction in effective tutoring strategies and providing for practice with other tutors before pairing tutors with the students they will help.

Cross-age tutoring involves older students (e.g., sixth grade) tutoring younger students (e.g., second grade), generally in basic academic skills (e.g., reading). Students selected to be cross-age tutors should not only be older but also more psychologically mature than the students they will be tutoring. Peer tutoring involves students being tutored by other students in the same class or same grade.

Some studies have shown that tutoring appears to produce good effects on the tutors as well as the students they help. Other studies indicate that positive effects have consistently been found in achievement and self-esteem. Student tutors improve their own level of achievement, and some have shown higher rates of maturity, conceptual complexity, leadership, and empathy to peers. With appropriate orientation and training, cross-age tutoring has shown benefits for both the tutor and the learner.

—*Judith A. Ponticell*

See also collaboration theory; instructional interventions; learning, theories of; mastery learning; mentoring; parental involvement; peer interaction/friendships

Further Readings and References

Allen, D., & LeBlanc, A. (2004). *Collaborative peer coaching that improves instruction.* Thousand Oaks, CA: Corwin Press.
Bloom, B. S. (1984). The 2 sigma problem: The search for methods as effective as one-to-one tutoring. *Educational Researcher, 13*(6), 4–16.

TYLER, RALPH WINIFRED

Ralph Winifred Tyler (1902–1994) made significant contributions in the areas of curriculum design, testing, and evaluation. Some consider him "the father of behavioral objectives." Tyler was among the first to advocate student testing, not to produce a normal curve distribution, but to provide information for improvement of curriculum and determine if students had reached the aims intended. His book, *Basic Principles of Curriculum and Instruction,* written in 1949, has been in continuous print and has been translated into many languages. This document is a syllabus for a curriculum class that Tyler taught during his time at the University of Chicago. Within the document are four questions that may have influenced

curriculum development, perhaps more than any other document. The perspective offered by the questions in this work has come to be known as the "Tyler Rationale." He directed the famous *Eight-Year Study* and was instrumental in the creation of the National Assessment of Educational Progress (NAEP), which is still administered today as a measure of educational attainment for children across the nation.

Tyler was born April 22, 1902, in Chicago, Illinois. Shortly after his birth, Tyler's family moved to Nebraska, where he spent his childhood. Tyler attended Doane College in Crete, Nebraska, where he earned an AB degree at the age of 19 and began teaching high school science in Pierre, South Dakota, in 1921. His MA degree was earned from the University of Nebraska in 1923 and in 1927, he earned a PhD from the University of Chicago. His work in higher education began as assistant supervisor of sciences at the University of Nebraska-Lincoln. He was there from 1922 to 1927, and during this time completed his MA and PhD. He served as an associate professor at the University of North Carolina; in 1929, he moved to Ohio State University, where he achieved the rank of full professor. At Ohio State, Tyler began his work as director of the now classic *Eight-Year Study,* involving 30 high schools and some 300 colleges and universities. The secondary schools served as educational laboratories pursuing innovative programs and creating their own forms for evaluating student performance. In *Recording and Appraising Student Progress,* coauthored with E. R. Smith, many of today's advocated "authentic assessment" practices can be seen (criterion testing, performances, student projects, etc.).

In 1938, Tyler moved to the University of Chicago as the chairman of the Department of Education and later the Dean of Social Sciences and the University Examiner. He continued his work on *The Eight-Year Study* through 1941. Tyler became the first director of the Center for Advanced Study in the Behavioral Sciences, based at Stanford University, in California. He remained in this position from 1953 until his retirement. While Tyler officially retired in 1967, he remained active in education for another 25 years through teaching, lecturing, consulting, writing, and serving on a variety of committees, commissions, and foundations. In his 70-plus years as an educator, he authored or coauthored hundreds of articles and books.

—*Anita Pankake*

See also accountability; achievement tests; curriculum, theories of; curriculum guides; evaluation; National Assessment of Educational Progress; performance assessment; standardized testing; testing and test theory development

Further Readings and References

Brandt, R., & Tyler, R. (1983). Goals and objectives. In F. English (Ed.), *Fundamental curriculum decision* (pp. 40–52). Alexandria, VA: ASCD.

Eisner, E. W. (2001). Ralph Winifred Tyler, 1902–94. In J. A. Palmer (Ed.), *Fifty modern thinkers on education: From Piaget to the present* (pp. 54–58). London: Routledge.

Encyclopedia of World Biography. (1998). Ralph W. Tyler (2nd ed. Vol. 15, pp. 370–371). Farmington Hills, MI: Thomson Gale Research Group.

U

⌂ UNDERACHIEVERS, IN SCHOOLS

Little consensus exists in the educational literature about the definition of *underachievement,* particularly concerning how it is measured or to whom it applies. Yet the term is used often by academics, practitioners, journalists, and politicians somewhat indiscriminately in describing poor academic performance in school without any clarity about to what the underachievement relates. At times underachievement refers to the relationship between an individual's perceived innate ability to learn and actual learning performance, while at other times it refers to comparisons between an individual's performance with that of a larger group. The lack of a universally accepted definition of underachievement in the literature requires the presentation of an operational definition in this context. Hence, underachievement is defined here as a discrepancy between expected and actual academic achievement by an individual, particularly among those students who possess the cognitive ability to achieve at high levels.

The term *underachievement* appears to have been used initially within the literature about students identified as academically gifted (i.e., those perceived to have high learning potential) whose performance in school (usually measured by grade point averages, sometimes measured by behaviors) falls below anticipated achievement. Despite evidence of the existence of underachieving students among those identified as having high learning potential, prior to 1980 there existed almost no substantive research on the topic of gifted underachievement. Reasons cited in the literature tended to focus primarily on the individual

student and issues unrelated to school: (a) poor family relationships, particularly between father and son, (b) low self-image or self-concept, often generating feelings of nonacceptance by peers and social isolation, and (c) asocial personality traits and blaming others for poor performance. Male students generally were perceived more likely to become underachievers than female students. These notions of underachievers in schools tended to place the burden of responsibility on the students or families or on academic performance and behaviors associated with one gender.

Through her school-based case studies of gifted students, Joanne Whitmore, in 1980, was the first to identify school-based influences contributing to underachievement: (a) students' perception of a lack of genuine respect by teachers, (b) competitive social climate among students, (c) inflexibility and rigidity of curriculum and instruction, (d) emphasis on evaluation by others, (e) negative comments by teachers about students failing to achieve or conform, (f) constant teacher control over classroom activities, and (g) students' perception of unrewarding curriculum based almost solely on textbook learning. She also found that teachers rarely considered the roles that curriculum, instruction, assessment, and their own behaviors as influencing conditions that can lead to student underachievement.

Initial indicators of underachievement are often manifested in late elementary grades by student behaviors and attitudes such as unfinished work, disorganization, excuses for forgotten assignments and homework, uninterest in most academic subjects, and descriptions of school as boring or useless. Children who are hyperactive, rebellious against authority, highly critical of others, physically undercoordinated, and socially isolated by peers suffer from low self-esteem and chronic inattention. Over time these behaviors and attitudes lead to poor study habits, lack of perseverance, procrastination, and use of external escapes (e.g., video games, social life, drugs) that support a student's energies toward learning avoidance. Prolonged illness, emotional stress caused by family changes, perceived academic inabilities based upon race or language, and learning difficulties requiring differentiated services also contribute toward fostering underachievement.

Underachievers often display poor academic self-concepts, hold low values in learning attainment, and have limited skills in using effective learning strategies. Loss of motivation for learning often stems from a vicious cycle of low self-confidence and poor self-concept by the students and unrealistic or too high expectations for academic performance by parents and teachers. Unless addressed appropriately through early intervention in elementary school, underachievement becomes a more stable pattern in middle and junior high and well entrenched by high school. Underachievement among secondary students is manifested by poor school attendance, underdeveloped study habits resulting in low grades, family and school behavior problems, and even dropping out of school. Chronic underachievement can also lead to criminal behavior.

Enriched curriculum that includes topics interesting to students, differentiated instruction that is student centered and student engaging, and opportunities to complete alternative assessments are ways to mitigate the development of underachieving characteristics. Despite implementation of such efforts, some students still fail to work at their full academic potential. Prior to taking action toward helping underachievers, teachers, administrators, counselors, and parents need to understand that underachievers are psychologically at risk of long-term failure based upon three interacting reasons. First, underachievement is a learned set of behaviors, which can be changed through appropriate interventions. Second, underachievement is content and situation specific, rarely evident across all academic disciplines. Third, underachievement is a self-concept developed by expectations imposed by others: academic performance judged poor by others may well be acceptable performance by the student. Three types of intervention are often cited: (1) supportive strategies that affirm the student's work and convey promise of further success and greater potential, (2) intrinsic strategies

that serve as unique motivating factors for that student, and (3) remedial strategies that help the student develop appropriate learning skills and behaviors. Diminishing a student's underachieving behaviors requires significant time, attention, effort, and patience.

Identification of gifted students varies greatly because the field lacks a universally accepted definition for giftedness. Students from special populations (e.g., those with limited English proficiency, from low socioeconomic backgrounds or minority groups) often are not included among those identified by traditional academic measures (i.e., high scores on IQ tests, high GPA) or nominated by teachers or parents. In addition, students possessing intrapersonal and interpersonal skills or artistic talents are also often underidentified. The actual number of truly gifted students in American schools is unknown, and thus the breadth of underachievement among students with high potential who are unidentified, underutilizing their gifts in schools, or are at risk of school failure are unknown. Estimates of underachievement among identified gifted students range from 15% to 40% of gifted students, while approximately 20% are school dropouts. The problem of underachievement in our schools remains one of the greatest social wastes of our time.

—*Tricia Browne-Ferrigno*

See also at-risk students; cultural capital; dropouts; individual differences, in children; instructional interventions; intelligence; learning environments; metacognition; productivity; promotion, social; resiliency; schooling effects; tracking, of students

Further Readings and References

Peterson, J. S. (2003). Underachievers: Students who don't perform. In J. F. Smutny (Ed.), *Underserved gifted populations: Responding to their needs and abilities* (pp. 307–332). Cresskill, NJ: Hampton Press.

Rayneri, L. J., Gerber, B. L., & Wiley, L. P. (2003). Gifted achievers and gifted underachievers: The impact of learning style preferences in the classroom. *Journal of Secondary Gifted Education, 14*(4), 197–204.

Rimm, S. (2003). Underachievement: A continuing dilemma. In J. F. Smutny (Ed.), *Underserved gifted populations: Responding to their needs and abilities* (pp. 333–344). Cresskill, NJ: Hampton Press.

Smith, E. (2003). Understanding underachievement: An investigation into the differential attainment of secondary school pupils. *Journal of Sociology of Education, 24*(5), 575–586.

Vlahovic-Stetic, V., Vidovic, V., & Arambasic, L. (1999). Motivational characteristics in mathematical achievement:

A study of gifted high-achieving, gifted underachieving and non-gifted pupils. *High Ability Studies, 10*, 37–49.

Whitmore, J. R. (1980). *Giftedness, conflict, and underachievement.* Needham Heights, MA: Allyn & Bacon.

Whitmore, J. R. (1986). Understanding a lack of motivation to excel. *Gifted Child Quarterly, 30*, 66–69.

🏛 UNIONS, OF TEACHERS

The lineage of teacher unions can be traced directly to industrialization and to the industrial-model school organizations that resulted. Just as trade union structures mirrored their industry counterparts, teacher unions often established structures that mirrored those of school districts.

Before the industrial age, workers organized themselves largely around their work. Guilds were created to control entrance into a work group and restrict the availability of certain types of work. Trade unions regulated apprentice practices and established hiring halls. Craft unions contributed money that was used to pay members who were sick or unemployed and regulated standards in their craft by creating sanctions when members violated rules that were created by the association. However, as the hierarchical structures of factories became the norm, the organizational structures of unions changed to match the workplace. Industrial unionism took hold during the turn of the century, waned during hard economic times, and was revived again during the industrial prosperity of the late 1940s. Although, like many workers, teachers had been organizing for a long time, they did not formally associate with unions in the beginning of their organizational efforts. The formal association of teachers with unions began with the formation of the National Education Association (NEA).

DEVELOPMENT OF THE NATIONAL EDUCATION ASSOCIATION

Just as industrial workers were organizing, so were educational workers. Although not considered a union at the time, the NEA was founded in 1857. During its first 30 years, the NEA functioned more like a debating society and then later merged with the National Association of School Superintendents. By the turn of the century, college presidents controlled the organization and classroom teachers had little to do with its activities for

several decades. By the1890s, 50% of active members were administrators and 11% were teachers.

Industrial practices and the growing labor movement influenced the development of teachers' unions as well as policies aimed at preventing them. Although NEA was not formally affiliated with organized labor, in 1915 the Chicago Board of Education adopted a "yellow-dog" contract, which stipulated that teachers who belonged to unions would not be rehired. In spite of these scare tactics, some teachers were dissatisfied with how the NEA dealt with teachers, and started to work to create a new national organization of teachers. These teachers wanted an organization focused on the needs of teachers, and they were interested in affiliating with organized labor. The result was the creation of a second national teacher organization—the American Federation of Teachers (AFT).

DEVELOPMENT OF THE AMERICAN FEDERATION OF TEACHERS

The AFT was founded in 1916 partly at the urging of Samuel Gompers, the president of the American Federation of Labor. Although the NEA had been in existence for quite some time, the formulation of a teachers' organization that was associated with organized labor signified a shift in attitude. The new national organization, the AFT, created locals affiliated with the labor movement and was not dominated by administrators. The NEA traditionally felt that unionism lowered the ideals of teaching and that unionization led to teachers losing their image of being public servants. Defining and promoting teacher professionalism is a recurring theme in the development of teacher unionism and in the union's role in education reform.

EVOLUTION OF THE NATIONAL EDUCATION ASSOCIATION AND THE AMERICAN FEDERATION OF TEACHERS

For more than three decades, the NEA, unlike the AFT, included everyone in public education—teachers, principals, and superintendents—and was the primary voice that defined teaching. In the late 1950s, the AFT began a push for collective bargaining and started to win elections against the NEA. In response, the NEA agreed to start collective bargaining for teachers, and control of the organization began to switch from administrators to teachers. On April 11, 1962, the United Federation of Teachers (UFT) went on strike for one day, an event that brought forth a permanent change in the relationship between organized teachers and their schools. The strike in New York also signified the start of intense competition between the NEA and AFT for the representation of large cities. Because of the events in New York City, teacher unionism and collective bargaining experienced rapid growth in the1960s.

Collective bargaining began to define the relationship between teachers and school boards, a transition that some viewed as significant and positive.

COLLECTIVE BARGAINING

Collective bargaining has played a significant role in the industrialization of business and the subsequent industrial model of public schooling. Although teacher unionists have long seen the pursuit of formal collective bargaining relationships with districts as a vehicle for teacher professionalization, negotiating contracts has not traditionally been viewed as a tool for educational reform and in fact is often misunderstood and misrepresented.

Negotiating about educational policy does not negate the need to negotiate about traditional bread-and-butter issues, nor are these two mutually exclusive. Negotiating around standard settings is an activity around which unions and management can create common ground. While these are not the traditional bread-and-butter issues of unionism, and such activities cannot substitute for negotiation around wages, benefits, and job protections, they can supplement and complement bargaining.

PROFESSIONAL TEACHER UNIONISM

Some teacher unions are changing to embrace reform through what is sometimes called "new" or "professional" unionism. *Professional unionism* is a term used to describe a changing role for unions. In this new role, unions use the collective bargaining process to include negotiating about educational policy, with a focus on professional issues, as well as negotiating about traditional bread-and-butter issues. Negotiating for peer review, evaluation systems, professional development, mentor and induction programs, and new compensation systems are used as examples of how negotiating about policy can shape the work of teachers and transform industrial-style teacher unions into professional unions.

Professional unionism is a way to transform the union's bargaining strategy by focusing on the professional theme. This strategy is important in order to restore the public's confidence in organized teachers. Professional unionism allows for proactive engagement in school improvement and will alter certain features of traditional unionism. Professional unionists hope to supplement the traditional concerns for teacher rights, wages, and benefits with broader concerns for educational improvement. By creating both the appearance and the reality of direct teacher engagement, of professional accountability and education improvement, unions hope to enhance teachers' cultural authority as well as their economic status. Professional unionism is a hybrid of sorts. Unions engaged in reform bargaining do not forsake bread-and-butter concerns for reform ideas but instead combine the two into one.

Professional unionism is called upon to balance teachers' legitimate self-interests with the larger interests of teaching as an occupation and education as an institution. Most professional teacher unionists would agree that a new relationship between the union and the district is essential for the transition from industrial-style unionism to professional unionism to occur. Many of those engaged in professional unionism and collaborative relationships with school district leaders are members of a national network of union locals known as the Teacher Union Reform Network (TURN).

The Teacher Union Reform Network

TURN is a group of union leaders who are dedicated to the concept of new or professional unionism. Started in 1995 by Adam Urbanski and Helen Bernstein, both local union leaders, TURN's stated purpose is to challenge teacher union leaders to advance teachers as professionals, construct a broad-based unionism, and link professionalism and new unionism to ways for enhancing student achievement. TURN's mission statement includes

- Improving continuously the quality of teaching
- Promoting in public education and in the union democratic dynamics, fairness, and due process for all
- Seeking to expand the scope of collective bargaining to include instructional and professional issues
- Improving on an ongoing basis the terms and conditions under which both adults and children work and learn

The union leaders who belong to TURN are at the forefront of creating professional unionism and are among the most notable examples of unions working in collaboration with management and using these relationships to negotiate successful mentor and induction programs, peer appraisal and review programs, and new compensation systems.

REFORMING TEACHER UNIONS

Teacher unions have been structured to mirror industrial unions. The organizational structures inherited from these industrialized roots are just as entrenched and difficult to reform in our unions as they are in our schools and school districts, because teacher unions modeled themselves after the structure they once organized against. Unions became organized by a central authority, and they bargained with a central authority, the school board.

As a precursor to the more collaborative relationship with management necessary for professional unionism to thrive, it is essential for teachers' unions to focus first on their own internal organizational structures. Without internal transformation, it is less likely that a progressive professional union will be able to create a working relationship with the school district and to sustain the changes necessary to influence educational reforms. These structures can be characterized using the following categories typically found in most teacher unions: governance, human resources, site leadership, partnerships, communication and committees, and task forces.

—*Ellen J. Bernstein and Judith A. Ponticell*

See also American Federation of Teachers; collective bargaining; conflict management; contracts, with teacher unions; division of labor; National Education Association

Further Readings and References

Bernstein, E. (2003). *A journey toward professional unionism: The struggle for a transformation of a local teacher's union.* Unpublished doctoral dissertation, University of New Mexico, Albuquerque.
Boyd, W., Plank, D., & Sykes, G. (2000). Teacher unions in hard times. In T. Loveless (Ed.), *Conflicting missions? Teachers unions and educational reform* (pp. 174–210). Washington, DC: Brookings Institution.
Cresswell, A., Murphy, M., & Kerchner, C. (1980). *Teachers, unions, and collective bargaining in public education.* Berkeley, CA: McCutchan.
Kerchner, C., & Koppich, J. (1993). *A union of professionals: Labor relations and educational reform.* New York: Teachers College Press.
Kerchner, C., Koppich, J., & Weeres, J. (1997). *United mind workers: Unions and teaching and the knowledge society.* San Francisco: Jossey-Bass.
Litzcke, K. (2001). *Teacher unions as players in education reform: A Canadian look at an American trend.* Kelowna, BC: Society for the Advancement of Excellence in Education.
Murphy, M. (1990). *Blackboard unions: The AFT and the NEA, 1900–1980.* Ithaca, NY: Cornell University Press.
Perez Castillo, X. (2000). *A TURN-ing point for teacher union locals: A case study of Los Angeles, Minneapolis, and Rochester.* Unpublished doctoral dissertation, University of California, Los Angeles.

UNIVERSITIES, PREPARATION OF EDUCATIONAL LEADERS IN

The preparation of educational leaders has been an accepted activity of colleges of education, especially of comprehensive universities in the United States, for the past 80 to 100 years. As teaching and administration developed into two separate vocations around the turn of the twentieth century and the role of the school principal became more specialized and complex, university training became more of the requirement and K–12 educational administration became a foremost area of graduate study in education. The scientific management movement, coupled with state policies in certifying principals, stimulated the growth of such university preparation programs. Initially, novices learned from highly experienced, retired administrators who tended to stress the technical, mechanical, and rational aspects of control, authority, and management rather than the curricular and instructional aspects of leadership.

This trend lasted until after World War II, when the social sciences came into their own and the theoretical literature in educational administration began to grow. Throughout the theory movement, hopes were high that a solid knowledge base was to be generated and that verified standards of practice would be established. A spirit of inquiry permeated the field, and several milestones in the preparation of principals occurred, including the establishment of the Committee for the Advancement of School Administration (CASA) and the University Council for Educational

Administration (UCEA) in the mid-1950s. As a result, graduate programs in educational administration were to be improved through the stimulation and coordination of research and training activities, the publication and distribution of literature, and the exchange of ideas. By this time, approximately 125 universities were offering graduate programs in K–12 educational leadership and administration, and nearly all states required some form of administrative certificate for superintendents and principals. University faculty were selected on the basis of their academic preparation rather than their experience as administrators, and the subject matter became more rigorous. The field shifted from a practical orientation to a more theoretical one, from the use of one discipline to the use of several disciplines, and from a technical orientation to a more general one.

As the educational reform movement of the early 1980s began to mature, school administration, the role of educational leadership in school improvement, and the preparation of educational leaders were pushed to the center of the educational reform stage. By this time, leadership preparation was further removed from hands-on learning and experiential applications, and those receiving the training became skeptical of its utility. A chasm between theory and practice developed, and pressures for change in the preparation of educational administrators increased significantly. The theory movement failed to deliver on its promises, outcomes of the quest for a science of administration were considerably less robust than had been anticipated, and the knowledge base employed in preparation programs had not been especially useful in solving real problems in the field (i.e., a behavioral science knowledge base had little effect). Absent a conceptual unity, content tended to focus on the managerial and institutional dimensions of administration compared to teaching and the psychology of learning. In 1987, the education administration profession self-identified several key trouble spots in *Leaders for America's Schools,* prepared by UCEA. These concerns included (a) the lack of definition of good leadership, (b) an absence of collaboration between school districts and colleges and universities, (c) the low number of minorities and females in the field, (d) a lack of systemic professional development, (e) the poor quality of candidates for preparation programs, (f) the irrelevance of preparation programs; programs devoid of sequence, modern content, and clinical experiences, (g) the need for licensure systems that

promote excellence, and (h) an absence of a national sense of cooperation in preparing school leaders. This report was followed by the National Policy Board for Educational Administration's (NPBEA) highly visible 1989 publication *Improving the Preparation of School Administrators: The Reform Agenda,* recommending that a common core of knowledge and skills in preservice programs be defined to include the following: (a) societal and cultural influences on schooling, (b) teaching and learning processes and school improvement, (c) organizational theory, (d) methodologies of organizational studies and policy analysis, (e) leadership and management processes and functions, (f) policy studies and politics of education, and (g) moral and ethical dimensions of schooling. The content of these areas was to be grounded in the "problems of practice" and supported by an increased emphasis on clinical experiences.

Reforms of the 1990s brought new standards for school leaders, new and restructured programs, shifts in content and instructional strategies, and new licensure exams. A reconceptualization of the administrator role as one focused on leadership for student learning led 24 states and the District of Columbia to unite and form the Interstate School Leaders Licensure Consortium (ISLLC). In conjunction with the Council of Chief State School Officers (CCSSO), ISLLC generated a set of national standards that help link leadership more directly to productive schools and enhanced educational outcomes. The primary objective of this initiative was to strengthen the professional development of school leaders. The standards serve two main purposes: (1) provide a model for university preparation programs to assist in assessing their curriculum, instruction, and assessment and (2) provide the basis of the School Leaders Licensure Assessment (SLLA), a national test used by states as a licensing tool for initial principal certification. The ISLLC Standards and their corresponding indicators in the areas of knowledge, dispositions, and performance reflect what the two organizations feel are basic operating norms that successful principals employ.

Although many institutions of higher learning have used the ISLLC Standards to revise preparation programs for prospective school leaders, implementing the No Child Left Behind Act (NCLB) of 2001 forced them to confront the weaknesses of contemporary school leadership and made it impossible to ignore the escalating need for higher quality principals—individuals who have been prepared to provide the instructional leadership necessary to improve student achievement. In 2002, the National Council for the Accreditation of Teacher Education (NCATE) aligned its accreditation standards for educational leadership training programs with the ISLLC Standards. This merger provided a unified set of standards, the Educational Leadership Constituent Council (ELCC) standards, for review and accreditation of administrator preparation programs. Candidates who complete the program are educational leaders who have the knowledge and ability to promote the success of all students by

Standard 1: facilitating the development, articulation, implementation, and stewardship of a school or district vision of learning supported by the school community

Standard 2: promoting a positive school culture, providing an effective instructional program, applying best practice to student learning, and designing comprehensive professional growth plans for staff

Standard 3: managing the organization, operations, and resources in a way that promotes a safe, efficient, and effective learning environment

Standard 4: collaborating with families and other community members, responding to diverse community interests and needs, and mobilizing community resources

Standard 5: acting with integrity, fairness, and in an ethical manner

Standard 6: understanding, responding to, and influencing the larger political, social, economic, legal, and cultural context

Standard 7: the internship: provides significant opportunities for candidates to synthesize and apply the knowledge and practices and develop the skills identified in ELCC Standards 1–6 through substantial, sustained, standards-based work in real settings, planned and guided cooperatively by the institution and school district personnel for graduate credit.

While each state establishes licensing, certification and recertification requirements for school leaders and, in most places, approves the college and university programs that prepare school leaders, research findings reveal that changes in the nature of principal preparation programs have been slow to follow the change in the conceptualization of the work of the principals (i.e., the shift in perspective highlighting principals' role in the improvement of instruction and their greater impact on student performance and

achievement). Frequently cited role changes in the literature are connected to increased time and stress associated with accountability issues, management tasks, staff development, curriculum design, shared decision making, site-based management, budgetary constraints, students' changing demographics, special education issues, complex discipline and safety issues, and issues associated with school choice. In keeping pace with today's diverse society and ever-changing social, political, and technological issues, educational leaders are expected to be experts on current education law and policy, standards-based reform, student learning, instructional programs, curricular issues, models of assessment, social services, public relations, and fundraisers. Because of this, efforts to rethink, redefine, and restructure the preparation of school leaders require advocates who understand that school leadership is a multifaceted issue that includes political and managerial as well as instructional and educational components.

Effective educational leadership programs ensure that their students gain the knowledge, skills, and attributes of an instructional leader and the capacity to galvanize the internal and external school communities in support of increased student achievement and learning by creating opportunities for students to work collegially as part of their graduate experience. To do this, leadership preparation programs engage in proactive and collaborative plans to identify, recruit, prepare, and retain diverse cohorts of highly qualified candidates. They have active, involved faculty who are connected to the field and are willing and able to create and implement activities and environments that enable adult students to challenge their assumptions, clarify and strengthen their values, and work on aligning their behaviors and practice with these beliefs, attitudes, and philosophies. Because school leaders in the twenty-first century are much more heavily invested in purpose-defining activities, in reflective analysis, and in active intervention as opposed to simply managing existing arrangements (i.e., maintaining the status quo), curricular and instructional practices in preparation programs need to address issues of power and privilege, issues of social justice and equity, and issues of excellence and equality. The fabric of educational leadership curriculum, pedagogy, programs, and policies must shift from faculty-centered to student-centered approaches that actively involve students in the learning process, eliminate student anonymity, and personalize instruction. Courses must be fashioned and infused with critically reflective curricula and methodologies that stimulate students to think beyond current behavioral and conceptual boundaries in order to study, research, and implement leadership practices that will fundamentally and holistically change schools in ways and in manners that are consistent with an equitable, inclusive vision.

These recommendations are consistent with others who are encouraging the use of inductive, problem-based strategies that are grounded in adult learning theory and the integration of practical lessons of academic coursework with the day-to-day realities of schools. Promising approaches and practices include extensive, field-based, mentored internships in a variety of settings that connect knowledge and interpretive frameworks with practical experiences and ideological commitments. Many innovative and exceptional programs use cohorts, case study methods, administrative simulations, inquiry-based praxis, and action research. They tend to be more demanding, more selective, more coherent with a focus on sequencing and scheduling and strong collaborations with area districts. Strong leadership is the heart of all effective organizations. Given new roles, multiple perspectives and values, changing school demographics, limited resources, and heightened expectations, strong school leadership is needed. Principals need emotional muscle for interpersonal dynamics and preparation and programs need to foster it.

—Kathleen M. Brown

See also human resource development; Interstate School Leaders Licensure Consortium; standard setting; state departments of education; theory movement, in educational administration; University Council for Educational Administration

Further Readings and References

Andrews, R., & Grogan, M. (2001). *Defining preparation and professional development for the future.* A paper commissioned for the first meeting of the National Commission for the Advancement of Educational Leadership Preparation, Racine, WI.

Hale, E. L., & Moorman, H. N. (2003). *Preparing school principals: A national perspective on policy and program innovations.* Washington, DC: Institute for Educational Leadership.

Jackson, B. (2001). *Exceptional and innovative programs in educational leadership.* A paper commissioned for the first meeting of the National Commission for the Advancement of Educational Leadership Preparation, Racine, WI.

McCarthy, M. (1999). The evolution of educational leadership preparation programs. In J. Murphy & K. Seashore Louis (Eds.), *Handbook of research on educational administration.* (pp. 119–139). San Francisco: Jossey-Bass.

Sirotnik, K. A., & Kimball, K. (1996). Preparing educators for leadership: In praise of experience. *Journal of School Leadership, 6,* 180–201.

UNIVERSITY COUNCIL FOR EDUCATIONAL ADMINISTRATION

The University Council for Educational Administration is a consortium of major research universities with doctoral programs in educational leadership and policy. The dual mission of UCEA is to improve the preparation of educational leaders and promote the development of professional knowledge in school improvement and administration. UCEA's origins date to 1954 when members of the Cooperative Program in Educational Administration (Middle Atlantic Region) proposed an organization that would be devoted to improving the professional preparation of educational administrators. To help establish such an organization, a central office with part-time staff was established on the campus of Columbia University, financed by a grant from the W. K. Kellogg Foundation to Teachers College of Columbia.

Between 1956 and 1959, UCEA's constitution and by-laws were formulated, the organization's purposes were defined, and additional financial support was obtained in the form of a 5-year grant from the Kellogg Foundation. The organization was officially founded in 1959, and the UCEA central office moved to Ohio State University when a small, full-time staff was hired. Since that period, UCEA has been housed at Arizona State University, Pennsylvania State University, and the University of Missouri-Columbia.

UCEA has been a major contributor to

- Broadening the content of preparation programs for educational administrators
- Extending the use of more effective methods of inquiry in educational administration
- Shifting educational administration from an anecdotal orientation to a more scientific one, leading to generalizations about organization and leadership
- Developing new instructional materials for administrator programs

- Fostering exchanges in research and in program development between professors and administrative leaders in the United States and their counterparts in other countries
- Continuing efforts toward standards of excellence in research and in preparation programs for administration.

With the expiration in 1969 of a second 5-year grant from the Kellogg Foundation, UCEA has been supported through a combination of membership dues, donations of resources, facilities, equipment and staff time from member institutions, sales of publications and instructional materials, and investment income. The council's governance is vested in two official bodies, the executive committee and the plenum. The executive committee is composed of nine individuals elected from member institutions. The executive committee makes decisions about appointments and compensation of personnel, develops plans for and makes recommendations to the plenum, and, when necessary, makes interim program decisions. The plenum, comprised of one representative from each member university, elects the executive committee, helps make governance, finance, and membership decisions, provides linkages with member university faculty and students, and promotes programmatic involvement with UCEA. Day-to-day operations of UCEA are the responsibility of the executive director. In its history, UCEA has had seven executive directors (including two interim executive directors). Two of these executive directors, Jack Culbertson and Patrick Forsyth, guided the organization for 37 years of its 51-year history.

The founding of UCEA in 1956, led by Daniel Griffiths, Jack Culbertson, Daniel Davies, and Paula Silver, coupled with the creation of the National Conference of Professors of Educational Administration (NCPEA) in 1947, has been instrumental in the emergence of the theory movement in educational administration, which represents an attempt to define the knowledge based in the fledgling field of educational administration. The activities of professional organizations such as UCEA and NCPEA reflect the belief that educational administration is more than a loose collection of individual, anecdotal experiences—a collection of war stories told and retold by retired school administrators. Accordingly, UCEA has been a major player in shaping (and reshaping) the knowledge base in educational administration.

To further this mission, UCEA has created eight program centers that facilitate work in a target area of interest over a substantial period of time through identifying and coalescing the interests and resources of UCEA-member and nonmember institutions, school districts, and governmental agencies. UCEA program centers address the following key areas: patterns of professional administrator preparation, academic leadership, educational finance, field practices, special educational leadership and policy, ethics, urban education, school site leadership, and the superintendency. In the near future, another program center will address school technology leadership. The centers contribute greatly to UCEA's mission through their involvement of faculty in timely and significant work in focused areas of inquiry, and have made substantial contributions to knowledge production and exchange of ideas in the field of educational leadership and the varied organizations served by educational leaders and administrators.

Recently, UCEA has expanded its scope and focused considerable attention on strengthening relationships among institutions that prepare administrators for service and the school districts and other agencies in which administrators serve. Although initially composed of a select number of elite universities, in recent years UCEA has become much more inclusive, welcoming in a diverse array of member universities.

—*Lance Fusarelli*

See also standard setting; systems theory/thinking; theory movement, in educational administration

Further Readings and References

Culbertson, J. A. (1981). Antecedents of the theory movement. *Educational Administration Quarterly, 17*(1), 25–47.

Donmoyer, R., Imber, M., & Scheurich, J. J. (Eds.). (1995). *The knowledge base in educational administration: Multiple perspectives.* Albany: State University of New York Press.

University Council for Educational Administration. Retrieved from http://www.ucea.org.

V

🏛 VALIDITY AND RELIABILITY

Reliability and validity are two basic concepts in test theory. *Reliability* refers to the consistency of measures. One type is the test-retest reliability. In this approach, a test is administered to the same group of people twice, with a certain interval between the two administrations. If most examinees get similar test results across the two occasions, evidence is established for high reliability. This type of reliability is also called temporal stability. There are a number of factors that may affect this type of reliability. One factor is the memory effect. If a test is given twice within a short period of time, the examinees will most likely remember their answers to the exam the second time they take the exam. This may result in unusually high correlations between two sets of test scores, hence high reliability. On the other hand, if there is too long a period between two test administrations, students may not remember what they have learned previously. This may lead to lower test scores at the second administration.

The second type of reliability is the alternate-form, or equivalent-form, reliability. It refers to the comparability of test scores one obtains if given two equivalent forms of the same test. Factors affecting this type of reliability include the extent to which the two forms are equivalent and the extent to which the conditions of two administrations are comparable.

The third type of reliability is internal consistency. It refers to the extent to which items on the same test instrument are homogenous with each other. It is distinguished from the previous two types of reliability in that it requires only one test administration. There are a number of formulas used for estimating internal consistency, such as the Cronbach's coefficient alpha and, for dichotomously scored items, the Kuder-Richardson formulas (KR-20 and KR-21). A simpler approach to estimate internal consistency is the split-half method, which divides a test into two halves and correlates the scores on the two to obtain the reliability coefficient.

The fourth type of reliability is the interrater reliability, which refers to the agreement between different raters in their scoring of subjective items for the same examinee. A further type of reliability is intrarater reliability, which refers to the consistency with which a rater applies the same scoring rubrics to score different examinees.

One index for reliability is the reliability coefficient, which is obtained by correlating scores from the same test for a group of examinees. Another index is the standard error of measurement, which is the average difference between the true score and observed scores for an individual. The various types of reliability reflect different sources of error. The generalizability theory uses a single index to take all sources of error into consideration.

Validity refers to the extent to which a test measures what it is supposed to measure and the legitimacy or appropriateness of inferences one makes based on test scores. Traditionally, validity is broken down into content, criterion-related, and construct validity. Content validity refers to the extent to which a test adequately samples the content domain that it tries to measure. The content validity of a fifth-grade math test, for example, may be established if it is determined that what the test covers adequately represents the important mathematical concepts and skills students learned in that grade. A useful tool is the test blueprint, which is often used during test development to link specific items to important instructional objectives. Expert panel review is often used for standardized tests to ensure content validity.

Criterion-related validity refers to the use of an external measure in judging the validity of a test. One subcategory is the so-called concurrent validity, which uses a concurrent measure of a variable as criterion for validation. For instance, in order to judge the validity of a newly developed intelligence test, one may use an existent intelligence test and administer both the newly developed instrument and the concurrent test to the same group of students. A comparison of results on the two tests would provide evidence for concurrent validity. The second subcategory of criterion-related validity is predictive validity, which uses a future measure as the criterion. It is often used with aptitude tests. For instance, the SAT (Scholastic Aptitude Test) is used to predict student academic performance in college. A comparison of student performance on the SAT and his or her subsequent college grade point averages would establish predictive validity for the test.

Construct validity refers to the extent a test measures the intended construct. Its validation comes from the confirmation of a theory-based relationship through a number of approaches. For example, discriminant analysis is used to correlate the results of a construct measure with a variable that is theoretically unrelated. Convergent analysis, on the other hand, is used to correlate the results with a theoretically related variable. A test is considered to have high construct validity if the correlation through the first approach is very low or if the correlation through the second approach is very high. Construct validity may also be established through factor analysis, which examines the structure of the construct itself by looking at the relationships between its internal components.

Another type of validity that is sometimes mentioned is face validity. It refers to the extent to which a test appears to measure what it is supposed to measure. Although some people tend to dismiss face validity as too trivial a concept, face validity can have significant impact on the potential use of a test.

The traditional separation of content, criterion-related, and construct validity received some challenges in the 1980s and 1990s. For instance, one critic suggested validating a test in terms of its value implications and social consequences of test use. Construct validity is treated as a unifying concept. The process of construct validation is considered never ending.

Reliability and validity are closely related to each other. Reliability of a test is considered a necessary condition for validity, while validity is considered a sufficient condition for reliability.

—*Yuankun Yao*

See also attitudes; measurement, theories of; research methods; Scholastic Aptitude Test; testing and test theory development; variables

Further Readings and References

Anastasi, A., & Urbina, S. (1997). *Psychological testing.* Upper Saddle River, NJ: Prentice Hall.

Crocker, L., & Algina, J. (1986). *Introduction to classical and modern test theory.* Orlando, FL: Holt, Rinehart & Winston.

Messick, S. (1995). Validity of psychological assessment: Validation of inferences from persons' responses and performance as scientific inquiry into scoring meaning. *American Psychologist, 9,* 741–749.

Wainer, H., & Braun, H. I. (Eds.). (1988). *Test validity.* Hillsdale, NJ: Lawrence Erlbaum.

VALUE-ADDED INDICATORS

The concept of value-added indicators of educational performance rests on the assumption that schools add value to the achievement of their pupils. Value-added indicators would measure or approximate the contribution of a school to its students' learning and achievement. Though the concept originated in the field of economics, it has been widely used in the school effectiveness literature in educational research.

STATISTICAL DERIVATION

Value-added indicators of school effectiveness evaluate growth or progress with a given group of students on cognitive outcomes, usually reading or mathematics, during a specified time period. Therefore, panel or longitudinal data on individual students are used in their statistical derivation.

Unlike average student test scores, which often cannot reveal whether a given school is serving its students effectively, value-added indicators capture the difference between a school's actual and expected performance or growth on specific outcome measures. The indicators attempt to measure school performance or the effect of school policies and inputs using a statistical regression that includes, to the extent possible, all the factors that contribute to a growth in student achievement, in particular prior achievement and student, family, and neighborhood characteristics. In statistical terms, a value-added indicator is a residual: the deviation from the predicted value of dependent variables or outcomes for each school. It is the residuals from the regression equation that would allow a policymaker to tell whether a school is falling short of or exceeding its predicted performance goals.

An important feature of being able to measure a school's contribution to learning involves statistical control for influences *beyond the contribution of the school.* There are many possible variables for obtaining an expected level of growth: students' previous attendance, gender, ethnicity, socioeconomic status, and prior achievement levels.

UTILIZATION IN UNITED STATES EDUCATION

Value-added indicators of effectiveness are not used extensively in the U.S. system of elementary and secondary education. The Tennessee Value-Added Assessment System (TVAAS), developed by William Sanders, is the most developed accountability program employing value-added indicators. TVAAS tracks individual students' progress on state tests and attempts to approximate schools' and classroom teachers' effects on performance. The state aggregates data from a given teacher's students over a 3-year period and then compares the gains to a national sample of students, as well as state and district gains. North Carolina and Mississippi also use value-added measures of school performance in their accountability systems. As of 2002, districts in Ohio, Colorado, and Pennsylvania were participating in a pilot program of value-added indicators. The federal No Child Left Behind Act of 2001 requires states to test all students annually in Grades 3 through 8. Thus, federal policy has created the conditions for states to develop accountability systems based on value-added indicators, as they will have the longitudinal data on student performance that would enable them to measure growth from year to year.

USE IN ACCOUNTABILITY SYSTEMS: IMPLICATIONS

Proponents of using value-added indicators for school accountability argue that these indicators help to determine how schools are performing, discourage harmful instructional practices, particularly for disadvantaged students, and reward teachers and administrators for factors that are under their control. The claims of advantages for equity are based on the idea that value-added indicators are superior to yearly average test scores as measures of student performance.

The primary advantage of using value-added indicators for accountability is that they allow policymakers to determine how effectively schools are educating the students they serve. Schools that serve economically advantaged students may be contributing very little to the education of their students, and above-average test scores could contribute to complacency in those communities; on the other hand, students might abandon good neighborhood schools simply because the students served were proportionately disadvantaged.

When policymakers can discern which schools are performing well and which poorly with the resources they have, there is another equity advantage: It can aid them in learning about what is making schools ineffective. In the policy context of performance-based accountability systems, the designers of the reform assume that schools' performance will improve continuously. Schools start from very different places and need information to improve their performance. Average test scores that states and district policymakers gather do not enable them to understand how schools are effective and why.

A second major argument in favor of using value-added indicators for accountability is that they would discourage educationally disadvantageous instructional practices, referred to by educators as "creaming." Such practices might encourage schools and districts to reject prospective students, particularly disadvantaged students. Likely, these practices are subtler: preventing students from participation in statewide assessments, tracking them into special education, or neglecting their needs by offering courses geared toward academically advantaged students.

A third potential advantage of a value-added system is fairness to teachers and administrators. This is possible because the model enables a state or district to measure the performance of schools based on students in all grades and the students who are in the school for a large part of the year. Recent attempts to demonstrate fairness by researchers has called this potential advantage into question by showing that teachers in districts with higher numbers of nondisadvantaged students would look better on state tests than teachers who taught large numbers of disadvantaged students. The failure of the TVAAS proponents to fully share their data and statistical procedures with the wider educational community has raised great suspicion about the claims of the advantages of the system.

From an equity perspective, there are at least three major objections to the use of value-added indicators. The first potential disadvantage of the use of the indicators is that controlling for student background characteristics might institutionalize lower performance expectations for disadvantaged students. Policymakers might send the undesirable message that the state or district has lower expectations for some groups of students than others.

A second concern for policymakers with the use of these indicators is whether they are clear to teachers and administrators. For instance, in Dallas in the 1990s, district officials linked school rewards to an elaborate value-added model that controlled for race. Some researchers found that school personnel found it difficult to make the connection between behavior they can directly observe or affect and the types of performance needed to win an award.

Finally, there is the argument against the use of the indicators for accountability purposes because of an important assumption in the model that is violated in practice. There is a built-in assumption of adequate resources that account for the mix of students served and schools' autonomy to obtain these resources. When these indicators are used in an accountability system, policymakers are assigning causality to schools' performance. The state or district assigns rewards and sanctions for schools as though they had autonomy to do whatever they needed to optimize their performance. Yet in making this causal attribution, policymakers assume that the schools are free to choose their resources: that they have the autonomy to hire and fire employees, for instance, and to obtain other instructional resources that they would need to serve the students they have. Such an assumption is problematic in most American public school districts, where schools do not have wide latitude to determine the resources that they will use.

—*Elizabeth H. DeBray*

See also accountability; Black education; contracts, with teacher unions; economics, theories of; factor analysis; functionalist theory; hierarchical developmental models; individual differences, in children; instructional interventions; Latinos; management information systems; No Child Left Behind; performance assessment; productivity; psychometrics; school improvement models; schooling effects; standardized testing; state departments of education; tracking, of students; validity and reliability

Further Readings and References

Clotfelter, C., & Ladd, H. (1996). Recognizing and rewarding success in public schools. In H. Ladd (Ed.), *Holding schools accountable.* Washington, DC: Brookings Institution.

Goertz, M. (2003). *Implementing the No Child Left Behind Act: the potential for a "perfect storm."* Paper presented at the annual meeting of the American Educational Research Association, Chicago, Illinois.

Hanushek, E. (1997). Assessing the results of school resources on student performance: An update. *Educational Evaluation and Policy Analysis, 19,* 141–164.

Kupermintz, H. (2003). Teacher effects and teacher effectiveness: A validity investigation of the Tennessee value added assessment system. *Educational Evaluation and Policy Analysis, 25,* 287–298.

Ladd, H., Roselius, B., & Walsh, R. (1997, November 8). *Using test scores to measure the effectiveness of schools.* Paper presented at the Nineteenth Annual Research Conference of the Association for Public Policy Analysis and Management, Washington, D.C.

Meyer, R. (1997). Value-added indicators of school performance: A primer. *Economics of Education Review, 16,* 283–301.

Mullens, J. E., Murnane, R. J., & Willett, J. B. (1996). The contribution of training and subject matter knowledge to teaching effectiveness: A multilevel analysis of longitudinal evidence from Belize. *Comparative Education Review, 40,* 139–157.

Raudenbush, S. W., & Willms, J. D. (1995). The estimation of school effects, *Journal of Educational and Behavioral Statistics, 20,* 307–335.

Sanders, W. L., & Horn, S. P. (1995). The Tennessee value-added assessment system (TVAAS): Mixed model methodology in educational assessment. In A. J. Shinkinfred & D. L. Stufflebeam (Eds.), *Teacher evaluation: Guide to effective practice.* Boston: Kluwer.

🏛 VALUES EDUCATION

Fully functioning people have beliefs, values, and convictions. People without values, convictions, and beliefs lack the inner strength needed in a society whose survival relies on responsible, participating, and trustworthy people. Self-actualizing people have a strong and clear set of values. They have convictions and beliefs, and their values are part of their daily lives. They are able to see themselves clearly and frankly.

According to some theorists, we need a usable and validated system of values in which we can believe and to which we can be devoted because the values are true. Fully functioning people have sincere beliefs and values with a high degree of clarity. They also have the courage of their convictions. Their beliefs are deep and consistent convictions that affect their actions. Fully functioning people operate within their value systems and have the courage to be themselves and to be imperfect. They see mistakes as opportunities for learning.

Some proponents of values education posit value education in the public schools should be restricted to that which the school has the right and mandate to develop. This would include an awareness of justice or of the rights of others in our constitutional system. The teaching of religious beliefs and specific value systems would be prohibited by the Bill of Rights. They also note that the Bill of Rights does not prohibit the teaching of the principles of justice and the awareness of rights that are fundamental to the Constitution itself.

One approach to values education is values clarification. Many people have difficulty making decisions because the process seems too complex, pressures are too varied, and change seems too upsetting. Therefore, some people feel confused or apathetic. They are unable to decide on their values or on a satisfying life style. The theory of values clarification offers help for people who feel confused or whose behavior is inconsistent. It encourages people to give more thought to value-related ideas.

Schools are filled with values whether they are taught or not. It is not necessary to adopt a values education program because values are always being taught. Those who are opposed to values education generally mean that they do not want values that are different from their own to be taught. This position leads to the dilemma of determining which values should be taught. Many maintain that there are some basic values that students need to have and that these values should be taught in schools. Unfortunately, there are those who have concerns about the most basic values. The discussions of some of the basic values might include: fairness, honesty, diligence, obedience, patriotism, respect, self-control, citizenship, responsibility, compassion, punctuality, perseverance, cooperation, loyalty, and work ethics. One example of such a discussion might include the value of teaching students to complete assignments when they do not want to do the work. The argument develops around the problem of teaching children to do what they are told to do

without questioning the value of what they have been told to do. When children do whatever they are told to do, that activity becomes right and the children become obedient, diligent, cooperative, responsible, and good workers because they followed orders. They did what they were told to do by a teacher or adult. Studies reveal that American soldiers who could be brainwashed while imprisoned by enemies were primarily people without convictions and firm beliefs. People who do not stand for something within themselves will be the easiest to brainwash.

The leaders of the Central Park East Secondary School, in New York, suggested that educators focus on teaching skepticism and empathy. By teaching empathy, students would learn to consider circumstances from another's point of view. By teaching skepticism, students would learn to consider the validity and worth of what they encounter. There is a difference between a school that promotes skepticism and empathy and the school that teaches students to be loyal, patriotic, and obedient, and other similar values. Schools should address the need for schools to help students learn autonomy and self-determination. When students feel that they can be "origins" rather than "pawns," they can develop the power of self-determination. Schools offer students very little power, except, for example, as a hall monitor. Schools cannot promote the learning of autonomy in the intellectual realm while it is suppressed in the moral and social realms.

Values education may succeed on a temporary basis. Children may perform a specific behavior, but they are not likely to develop a commitment to that behavior. Educators can produce students who will say the right words or do the right thing in a particular setting. Unfortunately, students will probably not continue that behavior or transfer the desired behavior to other situations. Values must be integrated into the child's own value system if they are to be transferred to other settings. John Dewey recognized the problem when he explained that beliefs cannot be plastered on or hammered in.

Educators may want to determine which values are currently taught or cultivated in our schools. Schools are and have been promoters of traditional values, but we may not notice this because these values are the same as our own or because we simply take them for granted. The process of learning values requires that children be provided with opportunities to ponder, contemplate, and make sense of such concepts as fairness and courage. Children must be encouraged to reflect on complex issues, to compare them to their own experiences, to determine for themselves and with others what kind of person one should be. Students need to examine traditions and determine which should be kept. Children need to examine and consider how to proceed when two basic values seem to be in conflict.

—Carolyn Sayers Russell

See also Binet, Alfred; character education; civics, history in schools; coeducation; democracy, democratic education and administration; Dewey, John; dogmatism and scales of Rokeach; elementary education; esteem needs; ethics; fundamentalism; Maslow, Abraham; moral education; philosophies of education; politics, of education; psychology, types of; self-actualization; television, impact on students; values of organizations and leadership

Further Readings and References

Anastasi, A. (1968). *Psychological testing* (3rd ed.). Toronto, Canada: Macmillan.

Pollack, B. (1995). *The experimental psychology of Alfred Binet, selected papers.* New York: Springer.

Pulliam, J. D. (1976). *History of education in America* (2nd ed.). Columbus, OH: Merrill.

Raths, L. E., Harmin, M., & Simon, S. B. (1978). *Values and teaching* (2nd ed.). Columbus, OH:. Merrill.

Rogers, T. B. (1995). The *psychological testing enterprise, an introduction.* Pacific Grove, CA: Brooks/Cole.

Webb, L. D., Metha, A., & Jordan, K. F. (2003). *Foundations of American education* (4th ed.) Upper Saddle River, NJ: Merrill Prentice Hall.

VALUES OF ORGANIZATIONS AND LEADERSHIP

Values are defined as beliefs and attitudes held by individual persons or collectivities. Values are also viewed as the principles that guide behavior. The values held within a group or an organization are the values shared by the group's members, which go beyond individual values.

An organization's or group's beliefs, desires, behavior, accountability, initiatives, innovation, integrity, and flexibility reveal its core values, which influence organizational perceptions and decisions. Core values are timeless, guiding principles that require no external justification. Such principles have intrinsic value and importance to those inside the organization. An organization's culture is made up of core values that unify the social dimensions of organizations. Core values become the foundation and conscience of the organization, which distinguish successful organizations from the unsuccessful.

Within enduring organizations, values became the organizations' essential and enduring tenets. Values cannot be instilled into people; people must already have a predisposition to holding them. However, it is acknowledged that a clear and well-articulated ideology will attract people to the enterprise whose personal values are compatible with the organization's core values, and conversely, may repel those whose personal values are not similar. The task for executives is to find and retain people who have a disposition to share the organization's core values.

Values inform leadership practices. Prominent leadership researchers recognize the significant correlation among attitudes, values, beliefs, leadership, and organizations. In their 2002 Synergistic Leadership Theory (SLT), Beverly Irby and Genevieve Brown stressed the interconnectedness of four particular factors: (a) beliefs and values, and attitudes; (b) leadership behavior; (c) external factors; and (d) organizational structure. The SLT theory proposes that an alignment between the leader's attitudes, values, and beliefs and those of the organization are important to the success of the leader and the organization. Without this alignment, those who do not share the similar attitudes, values, and beliefs may counter changes necessary for reform with resistance.

Sometimes value conflict occurs within organizations when the interest of one group indicates one course of action, while the other group's welfare demands another. Many scholars and researchers on value conflict resolution stress the "person-situation fit" in organizational settings, which is generally defined as the congruence between norms and values of organizations and the values of persons. Thus, leaders have two responsibilities: (a) to articulate, model, and emphasize the core values of the organization so that all members work together toward meeting organizational goals and (b) to make the effort to incorporate employees' values so that there is a congruity between an organization's values and the values of its members.

—Beverly Irby, Genevieve Brown, and Ling Ling Yang

See also administration, theories of; capacity building, of organizations; career development; collaboration theory; conflict management; consideration, caring; constructivism; empowerment; esteem needs; ethos, of organizations;

group dynamics; human resource development; leadership, participatory; management theories; morality, moral leadership; open-door policy; personnel management; transactional analysis; values pluralism, in schools

Further Readings and References

Irby, B. J., Brown, G., Duffy, J. A., & Trautman, D. (2002). The synergistic leadership theory. *Journal of Educational Administration, 40,* 304–322.

Scott, W. A. (1965). *Values and organizations.* Chicago: Rand McNally.

VALUES PLURALISM, IN SCHOOLS

The definition of pluralism has changed over time as a result of a greater focus on diversity and inequities in opportunities and resources for groups not considered part of the dominant culture. In the early 1900s, philosophers and writers, including Horace Kallen, began to challenge prevailing theories of assimilation that posited the potential for various racial and ethnic groups to blend together in a melting pot designed to create a homogeneous citizenry in the United States. Kallen proposed an alternative view known as *cultural pluralism,* which valued the distinct contributions that each minority culture made to American society. Subsequent definitions of pluralism vary somewhat. In the 1960s, Milton Myron Gordon advocated for a degree of separation among groups that would guarantee each group's ethnic identity and traditions while promoting cooperation among groups in the areas of political action, economic life, and civic responsibility. More recent notions of pluralism have been influenced by the concept of multiculturalism, which views diversity as part of the normal human experience and advocates for the acquisition and demonstration of dispositions and behaviors that promote understanding and interactions with more than one culture. Contemporary definitions of pluralism recognize diversity as a resource yet acknowledge that inequities in political, economic, and educational opportunities exist for members of historically oppressed groups. To some, pluralism has taken on a more political dimension in which the recognition of differences must be accompanied by action for the purpose of reducing or erasing inequity among groups.

Numerous issues arise for educational leaders who value a contemporary view of pluralism in schools. Critics have argued that leaders must allow every culture within a school fair and adequate time and resources for the reproduction of its distinctive values and definition of citizenry. This approach requires a focus on multicultural education for the purpose of ensuring that all members of a school community appreciate, understand, and learn about each other's cultures. In addition, school leaders who value pluralism and a commitment to social justice need to understand and address how members of various cultural and ethnic groups have been denied economic, educational, and political opportunities in schools as well as in the community at large. Leaders can contribute by promoting policies and instructional practices that assert the need for high expectations for all students and attempt to eliminate differential educational outcomes on the basis of race, ethnicity, gender, disability, or economic and other differences. Literacy for all students is considered to be essential to positive educational outcomes, while the inclusion of family and community perspectives promotes the values associated with a pluralistic educational environment. At issue for educational leaders is the identification of processes that promote rich dialogue and subsequent action needed to realize the goals of a pluralistic educational environment.

—*Katharine Shepherd Furney and Susan Brody Hasazi*

See also Afrocentric theories; Black education; civil rights movement; creativity, in management; cross-cultural education; cultural capital; diversity; equality, in schools; ethnocentrism; fundamentalism; humanistic education; Latinos; minorities, in schools; multiculturalism; philosophies of education; right-wing politics, advocates, impact on education; semiotics; values of organizations and leadership

Further Readings and References

Gordon, M. M. (1964). *Assimilation in American life: The role of race, religion, and national origins.* New York: Oxford University Press.

Nash, R. J. (2001). *Religious pluralism in the academy: Opening the dialogue.* New York: Peter Lang.

VANDALISM IN SCHOOLS

Vandalism is a willful degradation of the environment with no apparent motivation of profit or gain, the results of which are considered as damage by the perpetrators as well as by the victim in relation to the social norms that are applicable in any particular situation. Vandalism is associated with monetary costs as well as social costs. Monetary costs are obvious as schools spend millions of dollars each year to repair or replace the willful damage that school vandals cause. Social cost is more complex and has an impact on education program, has psychological impact on students, and disruptive impact on intergroup relations. Clearly, vandalism is a very important topic and is a cause for concern for school leaders at a time when dollars for education are scarce.

Some acts of vandalism are intentional and malicious. Other acts that result in property damage or property disfigurement are not intentional, but rather may be a consequence of thoughtlessness and carelessness.

The two major categories of vandalism are school defacement and property damage. Examples of defacement are writing, painting, and drawing or graffiti on school buildings or property. Examples of property damage include breaking windows, equipment, and plumbing.

There is no single factor that fully explains school vandalism. Sociologists have found that there are many reasons other than dissatisfaction with school or education that cause vandalism. The causes are complex and at times interrelated. Society, the individual vandal, the school, and family are among the causal factors of school vandalism. The Safe Schools Study (1987), in examining the nature of vandalism, sociopsychological characteristics of vandals, and the school-home environment, revealed that the amount of school damage and vandalistic behavior were related to low-socioeconomic community status, low level of personal identification with the schools, inadequate administration, and poor relations among teachers, administrators, and students.

It is mostly middle school or junior high students that commit acts of school vandalism. However, the "typical" school vandal does not exist. There are six types of vandals: (a) *the vindictive,* who carry a grudge against a particular teacher or other staff member; (b) *the malicious,* who commit vandalism out of sheer deviltry; (c) *the ideological,* who wish to dramatize some particular stance or cause; (d) *the acquisitive,* who combine destruction with theft; (e) *the bored,* who have few constructive outlets for their energy; and (f) *the frustrated,* who for one reason or another see the neighborhood school as a symbol of a society that is callously indifferent to their needs and aspirations.

There are many theories and recommendations on reducing school vandalism. Most deal with physical environment analysis of school sites prone to frequent vandalism, promotion of positive school climate and training in conflict resolution of school staff and students, and involvement of the community.

—*Sandra Harris*

See also at-risk students; belonging; community relations; competition, forms of, in schools; compulsory education; consideration, caring; determinism, sociocultural; dropouts; esteem needs; school safety; self-actualization; underachievers, in schools; violence in schools

Further Readings and References

U.S. Department of Health, Education, and Welfare. (1978). *Violent schools-safe schools: The safe school study report to Congress.* Washington, DC: U.S. Government Printing Office.

VARIABLES

A *variable* may be defined as a concept or a characteristic that involves variations. Researchers use variable rather than concept or characteristic because most of what is studied varies, that is, involves variation that can be described numerically or categorically.

Variables are composed of attributes or levels. An attribute is the value or category that makes up the variation. Thus, for example, the variable *gender* would have as attributes *female* and *male*. These categories may also be referred to as levels.

A precise definition of each variable communicates clearly the researcher's intent and enhances the usefulness of the results. Two types of definition of variables are commonly used in research: conceptual and operational.

A conceptual definition uses other words and concepts to describe the variable, as in a dictionary. Conceptual definition is important in communicating what is being investigated but may not indicate precisely what the variable means.

An operational definition indicates how the concept is measured or manipulated, that is, what operations are performed to measure or manipulate the variable.

There are several types of variables in educational research. The most important are *independent* and *dependent, extraneous* and *confounding,* and *continuous* and *categorical.*

In research, one variable precedes another, either logically or in time. The variable that comes first and influences or predicts is called the independent variable. The second variable, the one that is affected or predicted by the independent variable, is the dependent variable. In an experiment, at least one independent variable is the presumed cause of differences between groups on the dependent variable. The independent variable is the antecedent, and the dependent variable is the consequence. In nonexperimental research, the independent variable cannot be manipulated or controlled by the investigator. Such variables may still be considered independent if they clearly precede the dependent variable or if they are used to create categories for comparison.

EXTRANEOUS AND CONFOUNDING VARIABLES

An extraneous variable affects the dependent variable but is unknown or not controlled by the researcher. These variables change the result and disrupt the study. In designing research, investigators try to control or account for whatever extraneous variables may be present.

A confounding variable is one that varies systematically with the independent variable.

CONTINUOUS AND CATEGORICAL VARIABLES

A continuous variable can theoretically take on an infinite number of values within a given range of scores. In other words, the value of a continuous variable could be any point on a continuum. The values are rank ordered, from small to large or low to high, to indicate some properties or characteristics. Common continuous variables in education research are achievement and aptitude test scores.

A categorical variable is used to assign an object or person to a group that is defined to have specific characteristics. The simplest type of category has two groups (dichotomous), such as male/female. Other categorical variables can have three or more groups, for example, grade level and nationality. It is also common to use continuous variables to create categories. For instance, an aptitude test score is generally treated as a continuous variable, but the scores can be grouped into categories such as high, middle, and low categories. Thus, depending on how the researcher uses the variable, it can be either continuous or categorical.

—Xiaogeng Sun

See also achievement tests; case studies; fieldwork, in qualitative research; functionalist theory; hierarchical developmental models; instrumentation; item response theory; objectivity; operational definitions; research methods; standardized testing; structural equation modeling

Further Readings and References

Center, D., & Kemp, D. (2002). Antisocial behavior in children and Eysenck's theory of personality: An evaluation. *International Journal of Disability, Development, and Education, 49,* 353–366.
Center, D., & Kemp, D. (2003). Temperament and personality as potential factors in the development and treatment of conduct disorders. *Education and Treatment of Children, 26,* 75–78.
Eysenck, H. J. (1991). Dimensions of personality: the biosocial approach to personality. In J. Strelau & A. Angleitner (Eds.), *Explorations in temperament: International perspectives on theory and measurement* (pp. 87–103). London: Plenum.
Wakefield, J. (1979). *Using personality to individualize instruction.* San Diego, CA: Educational and Industrial Testing Service.

VIENNA CIRCLE

The Vienna Circle, or *Wiener Kreis,* was a group of intellectuals actively engaged in philosophical discussion from the early 1920s until Nazism dispersed its members. The group included Austrian, Czech, and German professors with a cross-disciplinary interest in ways to establish meaning. Although its members each developed singular ideas of analytic philosophy, as a group, they are known for *logical positivism,* an insistence on scientific reasoning based on real experience.

The premise behind logical positivism is *realism;* that is, all understanding emerges from sensory experience, and only things that can be experienced are real. This was related to *phenomenology,* a nineteenth-century philosophy that focused on the individual's understanding of phenomena, or description of events that have occurred within memory. In 1835, Auguste

Compte defined *positivism* and its goal of discovering "unchangeable aspects of the universal Order." By comparison, logical positivism does not presume a perennial truth, but rather a perennial search for truth by using scientific reason.

Members Hans Hahn, Otto Neuwarth, and Philipp Frank had begun interdisciplinary conversations connecting science and *epistemology,* or the study of knowledge and how it is gained, as early as 1907, but Moritz Schlick helped organize the group around discussion of the work of Ernst Mach (known for Mach numbers of sonic speed) in 1922. The philosophical aspect of his work rested on the issue of *empiricism,* specifically on measurement in seeking experimental proof.

The Vienna Circle popularized the scientific methods of *critical rationalism,* meaning that any statement will always be open to challenge, and rational, meaning that agreed rules of logic must be used to arrive at a decisive conclusion. This assumed a *dialectical* approach, meaning that the understanding can always be better informed with subsequent study because humans automatically use the *Hegelian triad:* An idea *(thesis)* and its contrast *(antithesis)* are reconciled *(synthesis),* becoming a new thesis to challenge.

One goal of the Vienna Circle was the unity of science: Through logic, all phenomena can be reduced to some basic concepts such as those in physics. This required unity of language with which to express it; this led to artificial languages that were eventually discarded for exhibiting the same difficulties as regular language. However, *linguistic analysis* remains necessary for valid collection of data used to verify or falsify a thesis, because logic rests on the understanding of the terms used to make the argument of meaning. Some Vienna Circle members limited their interest to the role of language itself as a source of defining personal truth. In this way, they are compatible with *existential* philosophy and *radical constructivism,* which deny any existence outside of one's personally socially constructed experience.

The American philosophy of *pragmatism,* that is, scientific thinking for practical application, also relied on logical analysis. Whereas pragmatism uses logic to solve problems, logical positivism studies the method of logic itself and the nature of the problems. Charles S. Peirce's influence as the founder of pragmatism cannot be underestimated, for he was a mentor to William James, who, in turn, influenced Bertrand Russell and Alfred North Whitehead, and they influenced Wittgenstein, who stimulated the Vienna Circle. Russell's *logical atomism*

regarded individuals' thoughts as the building blocks, or atoms, for constructing an understanding of the world. Pragmatism and the subsequent logical positivism contrasted the prevailing transcendental and romantic philosophy of the mid-nineteenth century as well traditional Cartesian certainty.

Another strong influence was *phenomenology,* which added a metacognitive, or self-aware, element to philosophical inquiry. Not only must all information be gathered through sensory experience, it can be understood using only conscious processes. The result was strictly scientific, in that all conclusions must be verifiable, but *pluralistic,* that is, open to more than one perspective. Although reality may be constant, our understanding of it is not, and therefore "truth" is always subject to change.

According to Herbert Feigl, the Vienna Circle member who coined the term *logical positivism,* the circle was collegial and very self-aware of its own intentionality to seek understanding together and tolerantly. In addition, individual members contributed greatly varying related concepts. Hans Hahn is known for his work in *set theory,* a mathematical model that eventually influenced "new math" and the infusion of algebraic logic. The complete thought of the equation correlates to the complete thought of a statement, both requiring logic. Franz Clemens Brentano responded to Moritz Schlick's willingness to apply the phenomenological methods of describing experience to questions of ethics by emphasizing *intentionality* as part of the logical process. Friedrich Waismann focused language conventions and their influence on logic. Rudolf Carnap's syntactic perspective distinguished between timeless truth and temporary confirmation, influencing Noam Chomsky and Richard Rorty.

Alfred Jules (A. J.) Ayers studied under members of the Vienna Circle. He brought logical positivism to a wider English-speaking audience with his 1936 book, *Language, Truth, and Logic.* Karl Popper never met with them but helped spread the concepts. Edgar Zilsel, another close contact, combined their ideas more closely with Marxism. Kurt Gödel, an occasional visitor, concluded that eventually, all mathematical proof must rest on something that cannot be proven. This undermined logical positivism, for it established that the logic could not be consistent.

The Vienna Circle perceived personal and intellectual threat in the rise of Hitler. They began to leave Austria for safer, democratic environments tolerant of Marxist views and Jewish heritage and became an exiled network that continued to influence philosophical thought, primarily through the *Journal of Unified Science* and the publication of the *International Encyclopedia of Unified Science.* Schlick, around whom the circle had coalesced, did not leave Vienna and was ultimately killed in 1936 by a Nazi sympathizer.

The Society for the Advancement of the Scientific World View, organized in 1991, documents the Vienna Circle's many contributions, among them the democratization of knowledge.

—*Naomi Jeffery Petersen*

See also axiomatic theory; constructivism; dialectical inquiry; functionalist theory; Harris, William Torrey; ideology, shifts of in educational leadership preparation; knowledge base, of the field; knowledge, practical; Marx, Karl; objectivity; philosophies of education; positivism, postpositivism; pragmatism and progressivism; reductionism/parsimony; semiotics; theory movement, in educational administration

Further Readings and References

Ayer, A. J. (1936). *Language, truth, and logic.* Oxford University.

English, F. (1994). *Theory in educational administration.* New York: HarperCollins.

English, F. (1998). The postmodern turn in educational administration: Apostrophic or catastrophic development? *Journal of School Leadership, 8,* 426–447.

🏛 VIOLENCE IN SCHOOLS

There is no agreed-on definition among educators for *violence in schools.* Definitions vary from that of the American Psychological Association, which defines violence as "purposefully hurting someone," to a definition provided by the Centers for Disease Control (CDC), which includes "deprivation." The CDC definition of violence is a threat of use of force, with a high probability of inflicting pain or damage, or power against a person or group. Yet there is clear agreement that a safe, nonviolent learning environment is necessary for student learning.

The most complete report on school crime and safety is the *Indicators of School Crime and Safety: 2003 Report,* which is a joint effort by the Bureau of Justice Statistics and National Center for Education Statistics. This report looks at crime at school from the perspectives of students, teachers, principals, and the general population. It also provides information regarding crime occurring in school, as well as on the way to and from school. Indicators of school violence specifically addressed in this report are victimization, fights, bullying, disorder, teacher injury, weapons, student perceptions of school safety, and others.

The most recent report found that students aged 12 to 18 were victims of nearly 1.2 million crimes of theft and 764,000 nonfatal crimes of violence or theft at school in 2001. However, between 1992 and 2001, overall school violence declined from 48 violent victimizations per 1,000 students to 28. Since 1995, the percentage of students who reported being a victim of violent crime or theft at school decreased from 10% to 6%.

Other findings from this report indicate that some behaviors have neither increased nor decreased, such as percentages of suicides of school-aged youth, students being threatened or injured with a weapon on school property, teachers being physically attacked by a student, hate-related graffiti, and measures of marijuana use, alcohol use, and drug distribution. However, the prevalence of bullying has increased from 5% in 1999 to 8% in 2001, with students reporting that they had been bullied at school in the last 6 months.

Although the report suggests that in general, violence at school is lessening, still, 48 people died in school-related violence in the 2003/2004 school year, the highest number in any year in the past decade. This has caused advocates of school safety to have an additional concern, since a 40% drop in spending for juvenile crime prevention was proposed in the 2005 federal budget.

—*Sandra Harris*

See also bullying; discipline in schools; esprit (school climate); learning environments; peace education; school safety; underachievers, in schools; vandalism in schools

Further Readings and References

American Psychological Association. (1999). *Warning signs: Recognizing signs of violence in others.* Retrieved August 1, 2004, from http://helping.apa.org/warningsigns/recognizing.html

Centers for Disease Control. (2001). *Unintentional injuries, violence, and the health of young people.* School Health Program Fact Sheet. National Center for Chronic Disease Prevention and Health Promotion Adolescent and School Health. Retrieved August 1, 2004, from http://www.cdc.gov/nccdphp/dash/guidelines/injury_facts.htm.

DeVoe, J. F., Peter, K., Kaufman, P., Ruddy, S. A., Miller, A. K., Planty, M., Snyder, T. D., & Rand, M. R. (2003).

Indicators of school crime and safety, 2003 (NCES 2004-004/NCJ-201257). Washington, DC: U.S. Bureau of Justice Statistics and National Center for Education Statistics.

Toppo, G. (2004, June 28). 48 school deaths highest in years. *USA Today,* p. 1A.

🏛 VOUCHER PLANS

Under a basic voucher proposal, as proposed by Milton Friedman in the mid-twentieth century, the per-pupil amount of state aid for public school students would be made available for parents to use to send their child to a private or public school of their choice. Families could supplement the voucher for their children to attend a private school that charges more for tuition than the voucher amount. A number of variations on the basic plan are possible, such as restricting participation in the voucher program to those private schools that agree to limit the copay amount charged to parents. Also, the vouchers can be made available only to specific student populations, such as children with disabilities, economically disadvantaged students, or those attending public schools rated as deficient on various criteria.

Voucher systems have been discussed in the educational literature for several decades, and there was a brief, federally supported voucher experiment in the 1970s, but the Alum Rock School District, in California, was the only demonstration site. Several New England states, however, have had de facto voucher systems for years, because they authorize school districts that cannot support high schools to provide a stipend for resident high school students to attend neighboring public high schools or nonreligious private schools. Other than such tuition reimbursement plans, no significant voucher experiments were implemented in the United States until the 1990s. In 1999, Florida was the first state to adopt a statewide voucher system, and this program targeted only students attending public schools rated as deficient. Publicly funded voucher programs for disadvantaged youth also are operating in Cleveland, Milwaukee, and Washington, D.C.

Vouchers are getting renewed attention as a strategy to give families more educational choices. Indeed, one of the central themes of the federal No Child Left Behind Act of 2001 is to increase educational options for students attending public schools that are not making adequate yearly progress toward student performance objectives.

In a significant 2002 ruling, the U.S. Supreme Court in *Zelman v. Simmons-Harris* held that voucher programs including sectarian schools do not violate the Establishment Clause of the First Amendment. With the First Amendment barrier eliminated, the legality of voucher plans will be decided on the basis of state law. In 2004, the Supreme Court ruled in *Locke v. Davey* that although the Establishment Clause *permits* states to fund certain services in sectarian institutions, state law might prohibit the use of public funds for religious purposes. The Supreme Court rejected the argument that the First Amendment's Free Exercise Clause demands that religious and secular purposes be treated the same in distributing government benefits (e.g., college scholarships) and allowed states to require greater separation of church and state than mandated by the Establishment Clause.

Thirty-six states have constitutional provisions that prohibit public support of sectarian schools, and voucher plans seem destined to generate litigation based on these state provisions. A Florida court found that state funds could not be used to support a voucher plan that allowed students to attend religious schools. Florida also has enacted a tuition tax credit program allowing a state tax break for donations to support private school tuition, and the Arizona Supreme Court has upheld the constitutionality of a similar Arizona program. However, the U.S. Supreme Court ruled in 2004 that the federal Tax Injunction Act does not bar a federal suit claiming that the Arizona program abridges the Establishment Clause, so the constitutionality of this tax benefit for private school tuition remains unresolved.

Maine's tuition reimbursement program for children attending high school outside their home districts has generated several rulings in which state and federal courts have rejected challenges to the program's exclusion of religious schools. Also, the Vermont Supreme Court ruled that the state's constitutional prohibition on using public funds for religious worship precluded school districts from using tuition reimbursement funds in parochial schools. The Colorado Supreme Court in 2004 avoided the issue of public support for religious schools by striking down a voucher plan for low-income students as violating the state constitutional provision requiring local school districts to retain control over instruction. The court reasoned that the voucher program would unconstitutionally require districts to give part of their locally raised funds to nonpublic schools whose instruction they do not control.

About half of the states currently are considering some type of voucher program to provide educational options for specific groups of students. However, it appears unlikely that a state will convert its entire school funding system to vouchers in the near future, in part because of the fiscal implications. If all students were eligible for vouchers, the students currently supported by parents in private schools or home education programs could receive state support (about 12% of the students nationally). This would carry a high price tag for financially strapped state and local governments, so it is not surprising that voters have rejected statewide voucher proposals in several states, including California, Colorado, Michigan, and Washington.

Nonetheless, voucher plans targeting economically disadvantaged students or those attending "failing" public schools are likely to increase during the next decade. Such limited voucher plans are viewed as less costly than some other reform strategies (e.g., reducing class size in public schools). Also, proponents contend that such programs can give poor children options that only the wealthy have traditionally enjoyed. But critics are concerned that voucher programs will have a negative impact on the democratizing function of public schools and will increase economic and racial segregation.

Some voucher programs that allow students to attend religious schools are privately funded, so they avoid the legal issues confronting publicly funded voucher plans. For example, after Indiana's legislature rejected a state-funded voucher proposal in 1990, the Golden Rule Insurance Company in Indianapolis established the Charitable Choice Program to provide partial tuition scholarships for disadvantaged students to attend private schools of their choice. The Children's Scholarship Fund and the Children's Educational Opportunity Foundation of America also have offered partial scholarships for students in New York City, Washington D.C., and more than 30 other cities across the nation.

Too few voucher programs are operating to make sound judgments about their merits, and the studies of voucher programs in Milwaukee and Cleveland have been inconclusive regarding student achievement. Also, the public support of vouchers has been mixed. According to the Annual Phi Delta Kappa/Gallup Polls, slightly more than half of the respondents favored publicly funded vouchers from 2000 through 2002, but the percentage dropped to 42% in 2003. Voucher proposals raise a number of questions that have not yet been resolved. If students at private schools are funded with public dollars, should those schools be required to accept all students, including disabled students? Should the requirements of state standards and accountability systems accompany the payment of public dollars for students enrolled in private schools?

There is some sentiment that charter schools, adopted now by four fifths of the states, represent a backdoor approach to vouchers. Charter schools remain public schools but are exempt from many state regulations based on a charter with state or local education agencies or with universities. They are politically more popular than vouchers as a strategy to increase parental choice in education.

—*Martha McCarthy*

See also accountability; charter schools; choice, of schools; economics, theories of; Gallup Polls, on public education; law; market theory of schooling; productivity; schooling effects; underachievers, in schools

Further Readings and References

Friedman, M. (1962). *Capitalism and freedom.* Chicago: University of Chicago Press.
Hibbs v. Winn, 124 S. Ct. 2276 (2004).
Locke v. Davey, 124 S. Ct. 1307 (2004).
Witte, J. (1998). The Milwaukee voucher experiment. *Educational Evaluation and Policy Analysis, 20,* 229–251.
Zelman v. Simmons-Harris, 536 U.S. 639 (2002).

🏛 VULNERABILITY THESIS, OF SUPERINTENDENTS

The vulnerability thesis was developed by Raymond Callahan in his enduring 1962 historical work, *Education and the Cult of Efficiency: A Study of the Forces That Have Shaped the Administration of Public Schools.* Callahan's work engaged in an intensive investigation of educational history covering the period 1910 to 1929 and intended to explore the predominance of the business model and practices in educational administration. The outcome of his study included what he described as the predominance of the business ideology and influence upon the American education system juxtaposed, unexpectedly, with the extreme vulnerability of superintendents. Thus came about the vulnerability thesis.

Callahan discussed the uniquely American pattern of local control and financial support as a backdrop that exacerbates the vulnerability of superintendents in schools. The vulnerability thesis suggests that public pressure and criticism of the local school is applied most often to the superintendent, who, being in a position of vulnerability, often lacking tenure or contractual protections, will naturally be pressed to respond to the public or fiscal pressures by appeasing the critics. This prevents school administrators from making decisions based upon what is professionally or academically advantageous to the school system and moves them to proffer a response focused on job retention or at least justifications to reduce vulnerability.

The contribution of Callahan's *Education and the Cult of Efficiency,* with his vulnerability thesis, has been credited as an ongoing explanatory theory for past, present, and future superintendent decision making and behavior and for having a national as well as a local dimension in its description of school politics. Many theorists credit the vulnerability thesis with breaking the traditional Cubberlerian paradigm characterized as the "great schoolmen notion" or "boosterism." In other words, the vulnerability thesis redefined governance of schools, which had been thought of as politically neutral institutions of progress and equality, as leadership of institutions by persons who were regularly influenced by political and financial pressures and power wielding.

The vulnerability thesis has been applied most appropriately to governance structures and political processes within the local school district, which some believe directly led to the inception of present-day policy studies in educational administration. School policy researchers have applied the vulnerability thesis in a variety of ways, both theoretical and practical. They have posited:

- The superintendent's vulnerability led to the struggle for power between school boards and their executives, role confusion of board members, and the embracing of the specialist-versus-generalist leadership role by superintendents;
- Superintendents' vulnerability led to their proclivity to apply scientific management and quantitative research as a way of defending themselves from public criticism, an observed trend both in the 1930s and now in the No Child Left Behind Act of 2001 reform era.

- Superintendents have maintained their jobs based mostly upon their mental agility in convincing boards and the general public of their awareness of issues and work toward shaping public response, while couching their comments in the rhetoric of national educational politics. This speaks more toward the superintendent as politician rather than educational leader.
- Successful superintendents have recognized the importance of knowing how to predict and control political conflict and thus have not only valued the inclusion of more practical coursework in traditional administrator preparation programs, like management, finance, law, and politics, but are also turning in greater numbers to practitioner-led alternative licensure programs focused on political survival skills.

The vulnerability thesis has also led to the inception of several organizational governance theories, perhaps most closely tied to the inception of Laurence Iannaccone and Frank Lutz's dissatisfaction theory of American Democracy. Dissatisfaction theorists suggest that their theory empirically tests the real definition of the vulnerability thesis, that is, whether political pressure can force superintendent turnover.

Far from being merely a theory meant to encourage the formulation of strategies for job security in the superintendency, the vulnerability thesis is a major paradigm shift that turns our eye toward political structures and governance mechanisms in local school districts. Some have suggested that with federally mandated reform and decentralization of fiscal and policy decision making, the ensuing lessening of superintendent vulnerability may lead to districts unresponsive to the citizenry. Raymond Callahan, conversely, called for reform that would lessen superintendent vulnerability leading to high turnover and possible instability in a school district. As this dichotomy of thought surrounding the application of the thesis exemplifies, the vulnerability theory stands as a seminal treatise that ushered in a new paradigm and redefined the field of educational governance and policy studies.

—*Thomas L. Alsbury*

See also accountability; boards of education; governance; leadership, distributed; leadership, theories of; leadership effectiveness; management theories; power; productivity; risk takers, in educational administration; role ambiguity; role conflict; superintendency

Further Readings and References

Callahan, R. E. (1962). *Education and the cult of efficiency: A study of the social forces that have shaped the administration of the public schools.* Chicago: University of Chicago Press.

Iannaccone, L. (1996). Callahan's vulnerability thesis and "dissatisfaction theory." *Peabody Journal of Education, 71*(2), 110–119.

Iannaccone, L., & Lutz, F. W. (1970). *Politics, power, and policy: The governing of local school districts.* Columbus, OH: Merrill.

Lutz, F. W., & Iannaccone, L. (Eds.). (1978). *Public participation in local school districts.* Lexington, MA: Heath.

Provenzo, E. F. Jr. (1990). "The emperor's new clothes": Raymond Callahan's *Education and the cult of efficiency.* In W. E. Eaton (Ed.), *Shaping the superintendency: A reexamination of Callahan and the cult of efficiency* (pp. 1–10). New York: Teachers College Press.

W

🏛 WALK-THROUGHS, OF CLASSROOMS

A walk-through or "walk-about" of a classroom has come to be considered a brief, structured visitation to a classroom while it is in use, in which the observer is comparing what is seen to a preestablished perspective or norm. Walk-throughs are not open-ended "blank-slate" visitations. While walk-throughs can be announced or unannounced, a preference is usually made for the unannounced visitation. Walk-through approaches vary in the following areas: use of a prestructured format or checklist type of feedback to the teacher, the extent to which the hierarchy of relationships is reinforced or changed, and the extent to which the approach aims at conformity to preestablished norms of practice or encourages professional growth from such norms.

Classroom supervision is a part of a school or school system's discursive practice. Such a practice creates the social identities of the participants, frames the communication between them, and positions the participants within the patterns of communication. This interlocking context is part and parcel of the "institutional gaze" or organizational disciplinary/normative practices in any organization. In schools, the normative gaze has been historically performed by the school principal. The teacher is universally perceived as a subordinate partner in this relationship. Traditional evaluation practices preserve this superior/subordinate relationship, providing the principal with the institutional means to discipline teachers in the performance of their duties. Classroom observations have then been correctly perceived by teachers as an exercise in organizational discipline and as such are generally feared. Since they are part and parcel of maintaining normative control, classroom visitations are rarely perceived by teachers as a vehicle to engage in a true collegial and professional dialogue with the principal or anyone else performing the observational function.

Some approaches to classroom walk-throughs freeze the current practices of evaluation in schools. The emphasis of these approaches is to find a more time-effective means of performing the traditional evaluative function by reducing its scope, finding means of recording observations by routinizing and standardizing the classroom visitation so that it can be recorded more easily mechanically. This may be done by use of a palm pilot or similar device. This approach is an emphasis on technique, as opposed to changing the professional culture of a school. And the outcome is still a piece of paper such as composite checklists or other such evaluative forms.

One different approach to classroom walk-throughs was developed in 2004 by Carolyn Downey and is based on a contrary idea of the exchange between principals and teachers as a fulcrum for creating a *reflective teaching practice.* A true reflective teaching practice is centered on creating adult-to-adult relationships in a collaborative dyad in which the emphasis is not on institutional compliance to preordained norms, but on pushing the borders of the teacher's expertise via self-analysis. The teacher should be stimulated to engage in a search for improved concepts, skills, and understandings within a relationship of support and inquiry. This approach is very different from installing newer techniques of supervision in which conformity is the expected outcome. Such a process in the Downey model is near paperless and is not aimed at supplying the data for traditional evaluation forms.

Most walk-throughs or walk-abouts gather information about the activities of the teacher, the students, the curriculum, and the context in which the teaching/learning process is occurring. The walk-through is concerned about the curricular decision-making points within a classroom, though they vary greatly in how such decisions are generated and how they are judged, recorded, and discussed. Key differences among the models emerge in response to the following questions:

- Is the emphasis within the walk-through approach on doing more evaluations within the current structure of evaluation as opposed to changing it?
- Is the emphasis on the walk-through model on technique and efficiency as opposed to engaging in a reflective conversation with the teacher about his or her practice?
- Is the emphasis on filling out forms and checklists to gather data to support traditional evaluative activities?
- Is the emphasis of the approach aimed at maintaining a superior-subordinate relationship between the principal and teachers, or does it see an adult-to-adult relationship?
- Does the approach always insist that there is a "correct" or "right answer" to matters of professional practice?

A person considering using a walk-through or walk-about model in his or her school or school system should consider each of these possibilities before adopting one and select the model that is compatible with the aims and objectives of the institution.

—*Fenwick W. English*

See also accountability; alignment, of curriculum; curriculum, theories of; decision making; empowerment; leadership, teacher; performance evaluation systems; principalship; professional development; rational organizational theory

Further Readings and References

Annunziata, J. (1997). Linking teacher evaluation and professional development. In J. Stronge (Ed.), *Evaluating teaching: A guide to current thinking and best practice* (pp. 288–301). Thousand Oaks, CA: Corwin Press.

Downey, C., Steffy, B., English, F., Frase, L., & Poston, W. (2004). *The three-minute classroom walk-through: Changing school supervisory practice one teacher at a time.* Thousand Oaks, CA: Corwin Press.

Mezirow, J. (1991). *Transformative dimensions of adult learning.* San Francisco: Jossey-Bass.

WASHINGTON, BOOKER T.

Booker Taliaferro Washington (1856–1915) was born a slave in Franklin County, Virginia in 1856. His duties included taking water to slaves working in the fields. Later, he worked in the salt and coal mines of West Virginia, but at the age of 16, Washington entered the Hampton Normal and Industrial Institute in Virginia. He was noted for his abilities by former brigadier general in the Union Army, Samuel Chapman Armstrong, the principal, who then mentored and trained him in the Hampton model of Negro education. The Hampton Institute prepared teachers for training Black workers across the South, a systematic approach to mitigating the disenfranchisement and economic subordination of African American people. Armstrong was committed to economically and politically stabilizing the South and advocated a belief that Black people were most suited for manual labor and the vocational trades. Despite persistent protest emanating from the Black press and Black leaders interested in higher and professional education, the 1880s saw industrial programming surge with the course of studies offered in Black colleges and secondary schools. Booker T. Washington was chosen to lead a new school in Tuskegee, Alabama.

On July 4, 1881, Washington formally opened Tuskegee Institute. The school not only launched its teacher training and industrial trades curriculum, it offered extension courses for the community surrounding the school and annual conferences for farmers, and developed popular night classes for laborers. Tuskegee grew rapidly, from its first student body of 30. With an emphasis on skilled trades and an all-Black faculty, Tuskegee became, 25 years later, one of the largest and best-supported educational institutions in the United States. It seeded an extensive network of other industrial schools by preparing educators who migrated throughout the country and spread many of the same beliefs as Washington and the Tuskegee Institute.

Washington's 1895 speech at the Cotton States and International Exposition, in Atlanta, moved U.S. President Grover Cleveland to write a letter of commendation for the Black speaker. Washington's message was clear: being patient with existing conditions, while staying rooted in the South. Blacks should eschew civil rights, political power, and attempts for racial equity. The future for Black development, according to Washington, was in the security of industrial training, starting businesses, acquiring land, and developing the necessary skills of good conduct, thriftiness, and cleanliness. Wielding more political power than any other Black American of the era, Washington offered answers to the postslavery problems of poverty and lack of education for African Americans, the problem of the relationship between the Black and White races, the "Negro Question."

Downgrading civil and political rights in the list of Black priorities, Washington's leadership supported an agenda of solidarity and institution building, small-business development and industrial education. Opposition to this accommodationist view was expressed by many, including the president of Atlanta University, John Hope; William Trotter, founder of the *Boston Guardian;* W. E. B. Du Bois and members of the Niagara movement, an activist group of professionals and college-educated African Americans that promoted an end to racial discrimination in education and public life. But Washington's voice often dominated the public discourses, especially in the South.

Washington gradually built a national constituency, later called the "Tuskegee Machine," composed of artisans, farmers, fraternal orders, educators, small-business owners, and newspaper editors. This machine influenced not only educational decisions but also larger political decisions made through favors and political clout.

Washington, as the most influential Black educator of the time, was able to garner enormous financial resources for Tuskegee and other Black institutions. White philanthropists George Eastman and John D. Rockefeller supported his efforts by providing for libraries and dormitories. Andrew Carnegie gave buildings to 29 Black schools because of Washington's influence. He also served as a conduit and gatekeeper for federal appointees serving the Black community.

In 1900, Washington founded the National Negro Business League, promoting entrepreneurship, and in 1901, he published *Up From Slavery,* his autobiography. Until his death in 1915, Booker T. Washington was a prominent, powerful leader, not only influencing Black education but also shaping national social policies for many years to come.

—*Khaula Murtadha*

See also Bethune, Mary McLeod; Black education; Cooper, Anna Julia; Coppin, Fanny Jackson; critical race theory; cross-cultural education; cultural politics, wars; Du Bois, W. E. B.; higher education; minorities, in schools; multiculturalism; politics, of education; Woodson, Carter G.

Further Readings and References

Franklin, V., & Anderson, J. (1978). *New perspectives on Black educational history.* Boston: G. K. Hall.

Harlan, L. (1972). *Booker T. Washington, the making of a Black leader, 1865–1901.* New York: Oxford University Press.

Marable, M. (1998). *Black leadership: Four great American leaders and the struggle for civil rights.* New York: Columbia University Press.

White, J. (1985). *Black leadership in America: 1895–1968.* New York: Longman.

WEB-BASED TEACHING AND LEARNING

Web-based teaching and learning (WBTL) has experienced a dramatic change in delivery technologies over the past few years. Computer-aided teaching and learning and the World Wide Web allow significantly faster interactions between student and faculty and among students during the teaching and learning process. WBTL is a system that has features and capabilities such as synchronous or asynchronous discussions and chat rooms, e-mail, Web-based conferencing, hypermedia capabilities, and development options, such as Web-CT, that permit students or instructors to complete tasks such as giving presentation, responding through threaded discussion, and conducting discussions through chat rooms.

As Web-based teaching and learning systems become more commonplace, it is vital that the knowledge base for understanding how to design and deliver Web-based instruction becomes understood and implemented because of the dramatic change in course and program delivery systems. As an example, research has looked at how student-driven learning (constructivist) and cognitive models of learning on the Web are defined. The knowledge base of the student model takes both domain and pedagogical knowledge into account. Numerous models are available online, and the options are endless as one searches for sites on almost any topic in education; however, there are advantages and disadvantages of online programs.

One of the advantages of online teaching and learning is the ability to access the program or course anytime and anywhere in the world where there is Web access. In discussing the issue of getting to "know" students, instructors find it very easy to communicate with students, in addition to tracking their progress on a daily basis. Another positive can be the cost per pupil; however, class size obviously is the determiner.

Limitations or disadvantages include the problems encountered by students and instructors with network connections and the data feed. Kevin Kruse wrote that low bandwidth, which will be solved in the coming years, can make the operations perform very slowly. In addition, the lack of multimedia in many programs detracts from the potential of compelling programs.

As an example, a University of California-Berkeley site lists a four-tier model for managing course Web sites. Tier 1 is what is described as an "enterprise-level integrated course Web site management system." Tier 2 includes "in-depth course Web sites." Tier 3 includes the "standard course Web page template for faculty." A faculty member or graduate students generally create these pages. Tier 4 is designated as a "minimal administrative course Web page." Generally, minimal course Web pages would be generated by the departmental administrative staff, and support the other tiers' sites.

Typical teaching and learning online systems feature student and faculty tools. Instructor tools may include online grade books, grade reporting, quiz or survey options, student access tracking, e-mail (individual and group), and a complete course system, including syllabus, projects, references, instructions, and support systems information. Student tools might include real-time chat rooms, grade reporting, cooperative work areas, self-evaluation options, and e-mail capabilities to the instructor, to individual students, or to all students.

If administrators, faculty, or students are interested in comparing the various teaching and learning systems on the market, there are a number of sites that are available online to do so. For example, Online Educational Delivery Applications contain comparative data on a large number of teaching-learning systems. There is a Web site that compares WebCT and CourseInfo, which lists the functions of each, such as a bulletin board and online quizzes. There are many pitfalls in attempting to find and implement the best choice in hardware and software.

Some of the problems linked to finding and testing software and hardware include the following. The choice of the management system is the biggest hurdle to overcome. It is often difficult for faculty and administrators to agree on the platform best suited to online operations. In addition to the wide range of systems available, new or enhanced products flood the market constantly. Program and course developers need to be cognizant of the product development cycle. Generally, it is a full-time job just to keep up with the best choices.

—*C. Daniel Raisch*

See also computers, use and impact of; digital divide; instructional technology; learning, online

Further Readings and References

Berge, Z. L. (Ed.). (1999, January-February). Interaction in post-secondary Web-based learning. *Educational Technology.* Retrieved September 18, 2005, from http://www.saskschools.ca/~parkland/interaction.htm

Beshears, F. M. (2000, November). *Web-based learning management systems.* Presentation at the Web-based Learning Management System Training Workshop. Retrieved March 1, 2005, from http://socrates.berkeley.edu/~fmb/articles/web_based_lms.html

Brown, P., & Schwarz, G. (Eds.). (2005). *Media literacy: Transforming curriculum and teaching.* Chicago: National Society for the Study of Education/Blackwell.

EduTools. (n.d.). Available at http://www.edutools.info/course/compare

Kruse, K. (n.d.). *Using the Web for learning: Advantages and disadvantages.* Retrieved February 15, 2005, from http://e-learningguru.com/articles/art1_9.htm

🏛 WEBER, MAX

Max Weber (1864–1920), a prominent German economics scholar, was a founding theorist in the field of sociology. His *Verstehen* doctrine, controversial and widely debated, presupposed that to understand a particular economic or social phenomenon, a person must be capable of interpreting actions and not be satisfied to merely describe a situation based on actions. As part of the "interpreting" process, he specified four behavioral "Ideal Types": rational means to rational ends, rational means to irrational ends, guided by emotion, and guided by custom or habit. Weber's other economic research included studies of capitalism in the context of idealism and materialism, *Economy and Society,* and his best-known writing, *The Protestant Ethic and the Spirit of Capitalism,* where he posited that seeds of capitalism are germinated in the Protestant work ethic and that advanced capitalism creates a new middle class whose livelihood is based on human capital rather than labor.

Weber, one of the first to observe and write on bureaucracies, posited that bureaucracies function according to six principles: Jurisdictional areas are ordered by rules (administrative regulations and laws); lower offices are supervised by higher offices; official documents (files) are the basis for management; officials must be trained and educated to do the job; management requires a full-time official, and management follows rules. While compared to today's theories of leadership, these six principles seem rudimentary, Weber posited these concepts in an era when existing management practices dated back to the Middle Ages and management precepts were based on loyalty to kings and to the church. As a part of distinguishing between charismatic, traditional, and legal forms of authority, Weber encouraged economists and sociologists to evaluate (people and situations) based on facts rather than values.

Born in Erfurt, Prussia (Germany), Weber was raised in a home where the Calvinist beliefs of his mother and the political aspirations of his father frequently conflicted. In 1882, Weber enrolled in the University of Heidelberg. Two years later, he left the university to fulfill his military obligation. During his military service, Weber strengthened bonds with Hermann and Ida Baumgarten (his maternal aunt and uncle), whose influence on Weber's intellectual development was substantial. At the conclusion of his military service and at the behest of his father, Weber returned to his father's home, where he lived until 1893, when he married. During the time he resided with his father, Weber completed his studies at the University of Berlin, served as a legal apprentice, and also served as a university assistant.

After his father's death in 1897, Weber began experiencing increased nervousness, and in 1898, he suffered a nervous breakdown. During the next 5 years of his illness, Weber suffered sudden relapses and was institutionalized intermittently. By 1903, Weber was able to work as a private scholar but did not return to university teaching until after World War I. In the 17 years from the onset of his mental illness until his death, Weber studied the relationship between Calvinist morality and compulsive processes. Weber's work remains significant in educational leadership as the cornerstone of examining bureaucracy and its many facets, which remain controversial today. He was the first sociologist to understand that the universe has no true meaning. In this sense, he was postmodern before postmodernism.

—*Brenda R. Kallio*

See also bureaucracy; chain of command; charisma, of leaders; class, social; division of labor; hierarchy, in organizations;

infrastructure, of organizations; job descriptions; line and staff concept; management theories; organizational theories; organizations, types of, typologies; postmodernism; principalship; rational organizational theory; restructuring, of schools; role ambiguity; role conflict; salary and salary models; school improvement models; site-based management; social psychology; superintendency

Further Readings and References

Collins, R. (1986). *Max Weber: A skeleton key.* Thousand Oaks, CA: Sage.
Diggins, J. (1996). *Max Weber: Politics and the spirit of tragedy.* New York: Basic Books.
Eisenstadt, S. N. (1968). *Max Weber: On charisma and institution building.* Chicago: University of Chicago Press.
Samir, E. (2005). Toward a Weberian public administration: The infinite web of history, values, and authority in administrative mentalities. *Halduskultuur* (An Interdisciplinary Public Administration Journal), *6,* 6–59.
Schroeder, R. (1992). *Max Weber and the sociology of culture.* Thousand Oaks, CA: Sage.

WOLF, MONTROSE

The work of Montrose Wolf (1935–2004) had a significant impact on educational practice. His pioneering efforts in applied behavior analysis formed the foundation of current classroom management procedures, educational research design, and intervention methods for persons with antisocial behaviors, emotional disorders, and mental retardation.

Wolf was born on May 29, 1935, in Houston, Texas. He earned his doctorate in 1962 from Arizona State University. In that same year, he accepted a postdoctoral fellowship at the University of Washington Institute for Child Development, where he remained until 1965. In 1965, Dr. Wolf joined the Department of Human Development and Family Life at the University of Kansas, a position he held until his retirement in 2000. In 1996, he received the Father Flannigan Award for Service to Youth, joining such notable former awardees as Mother Teresa and Dr. Jonas Salk.

Wolf was one of the "founding fathers" (many professionals consider him *the* founder) of applied behavior analysis and the founding editor of the *Journal of Applied Behavior Analysis.* His work, along with that of Don Baer, Todd Risley, and Vance Hall, brought behaviorism out of the laboratory and into a focus on solving significant human problems in applied settings. This focus was drawn from a foundation of

(a) theories of learning that should guide research and practice, (b) the nature and types of data to be gathered, (c) the types of designs to be employed in structuring research activities, and (d) facilitation of the generalization of functional skills and behaviors to new environments and situations.

Wolf developed many intervention techniques still employed in educational settings today. These include "time out," the "token economy," and the "Good Behavior Game." Wolf also developed and articulated the concept of *social validity* in research. In essence, social validity is a position that any research activity should address issues or problems of social importance. That is, it should address "real problems of real people." Wolf felt that social validity constituted the foundation or "heart" of all meaningful research. In addition, Wolf was instrumental in the development of two of the major single-subject research designs. The reversal design and the multiple baseline design were both presented and explained by Wolf and his colleagues in 1968.

Wolf's work is significant in that it addresses both educational research and practice. Much of special education methodology is rooted in his research. In addition, classroom management in both regular and special education draw much of their practice from Wolf's research. His work provided the model for much of what is current practice in these fields.

—*J. M. Blackbourn*

See also behaviorism; child development theories; classroom management; cognition, theories of; conditioning theory; constructivism, social; curriculum, theories of; feedback; learning, theories of; psychology, types of; social psychology; special education

Further Readings and References

Risley, T. R. (1997). Montrose M. Wolf: The origin of the dimensions of applied behavior analysis. *Journal of Applied Behavior Analysis, 30,* 377–381.
Wolf, M. M. (1978). Social validity: The case for subjective measurement or how applied behavior analysis is finding its heart. *Journal of Applied Behavior Analysis, 11,* 203–214.

🏛 WOMEN IN EDUCATIONAL LEADERSHIP

Women have provided significant leadership since they began entering school work in appreciable numbers during the mid-1800s. Much of this leadership, however, has been informal, with men holding the overwhelming majority of formal leadership positions. Essentially, school work largely has been polarized and stratified by sex, with large numbers of women teaching and relatively few men serving in administrative positions. Despite this strong tendency, there have been two periods during which the proportion of women school leaders increased notably. The first occurred during the turn-of-the-twentieth-century women's suffrage movement, as women attained elected county and state superintendencies, appointed principalships, and other administrative positions in precedent-setting numbers.

After a precipitous decline during the cold war years, once again women appear to be moving into school administrative and other leadership positions at an impressive rate. In 2000, women held 13% of all school superintendencies, up from a mere 3% during 1970. Women hold about one third of principalships nationwide, many at the elementary level. Women currently account for 39% of school board memberships as well. They also serve in a variety of other important district, state, and federal positions. Finally, the professional preparation of educational leaders in postsecondary institutions is undertaken by a professorate increasingly composed of women.

Despite these real and important gains, however, women still do not serve in formal school leadership positions in proportions comparable to their representation in teaching. Although men held only 21% of all teaching positions in 2000, they accounted for 87% of superintendent positions. The reasons for this long-standing imbalance, a critically important component of women's experience in educational leadership, must be understood in historical context.

HISTORICAL CONTEXT

School supervisors and superintendents appeared in schools around the United States when large numbers of women began teaching during the mid-1800s. School board members, all of whom were men, unfailingly chose men for these administrative duties, which included keeping an eye on teachers and performing routine school chores that school board members no longer wanted to handle themselves. As board proxies, early supervisors and superintendents traveled between far-flung schoolhouses to inspect the work of teachers, repair buildings, ensure availability of instructional materials, and assure board members that school resources were used well.

Women rarely held these early administrative positions for several reasons. First, by tradition, women did not hold positions of authority over men. This practice was informally but powerfully enforced throughout the country. Second, women did not have legal status to vote. Until the late 1800s, women generally were barred from public office if they also could not vote, though there were a few exceptions. Third, many states and territories did not accord women the right to own property or participate in civic affairs on their own behalf. Instead, male family members automatically received these rights. If women legally could not represent themselves, they were even less likely to be permitted to represent schools.

Even with these and other early restrictions on women's potential administrative service, though, a pressing shortage of qualified male educators after the Civil War compelled some midwestern school districts to experiment with hiring women superintendents. Julia Addington, chosen to lead her county district in Iowa in 1869, may have been the first female superintendent. Her opponent immediately challenged her victory, however, because as a woman, she technically was not a citizen. A few years later, Iowa changed its law to permit women to hold any public school office. Illinois law first permitted women to hold school offices in 1873. That same year, 10 women sought and won elected county superintendencies.

As women began attaining county superintendencies in midwestern and western states and territories, word quickly spread that they provided outstanding—and relatively inexpensive—service. Also, growing numbers of states and territories lifted their legal restrictions on women's public service. Suffrage activists, who long had championed the cause of women superintendents, publicly lauded the emerging successes of these pioneering school leaders, holding such educators out as examples of the fine service women could provide if simply allowed. Ella Flagg Young, who was chosen to serve as superintendent of the Chicago Schools in 1909, symbolized to suffragists the high-minded public service that women might offer if only given the chance.

In large part because of steady suffrage-related victories, the number of women holding elected county superintendencies rose dramatically around the turn of the century. Women held 228 of these positions in 1896. By 1913, the figure had risen to 495. Several women even won election to state superintendencies. A full decade after passage of national women's suffrage, women held 862 county superintendencies, or an astonishing 27% of all such positions. Local superintendencies did not yield to women's campaigns as easily, however. Local superintendents typically were appointed by their school boards rather than popularly elected. School boards rarely appointed women to local superintendencies, doing so only when acceptable male candidates were unavailable or if such a choice did not place women in authority over men.

As suffrage-inspired women attained expanding numbers of elected county superintendencies and even a few state superintendencies, a powerful campaign to take the superintendency "out of politics" emerged around the country. After Colorado granted women suffrage, women ran for and won surprising numbers of county superintendencies. Male school leaders immediately organized the Colorado Schoolmasters' Club, which worked to "remove the schools from politics" by converting elected superintendencies to appointed ones. The pattern of women's suffrage victories followed by campaigns to eliminate elected school offices repeated itself around the country. Then, after enactment of national women's suffrage, leaders of the National Education Association (NEA) and other prominent groups lobbied against elected superintendencies, arguing instead for the selection of educational experts prepared in the leading graduate programs of the time, programs that admitted few, if any, women. In the end, the political backlash against women's suffrage era gains in educational leadership succeeded impressively. By the mid-twentieth century, most elected superintendencies had become appointed ones, and women held exceedingly few of these.

A number of other changes occurred after WWII that further contributed to women's declining presence in school leadership positions of all kinds. In a sharp postwar gender repolarization of men's and women's roles, individuals who crossed gender-specific boundaries encountered bracing social resistance. Laws penalized persons who wore gender-nonconforming clothing in public settings. Informal though powerfully enforced practices kept women out of jobs deemed as fitting for men and vice versa. Men who wished to teach young children and women who aspired to school leadership positions were discouraged. During an era consumed with fear of homosexuals, school boards also increasingly sought married rather than single persons for high school principalships and superintendencies. Because a sizable number of the women who had attained school administration positions were unmarried, their prospects for continuing in the work dimmed.

As millions of male veterans returned from combat seeking civilian employment, school boards actively recruited them to serve as teachers with the promise of rapid promotion. Many received coaching offers, which included desirable salary supplements unavailable to women. Veterans who taught often pursued graduate preparation in educational administration with the full support of G.I. Bill benefits. These shifts together contributed to an increase in the number of men who chose to teach following World War II. Many of these men then rose quickly into principalships. In the case of elementary principalships, they tended to displace women. One report indicated that women had held the majority of elementary principalships as late as 1950 but that their numbers had declined to an astonishing 4% by 1960. Women lost superintendencies as well. In 1950, women held 9% of all superintendencies, including local, intermediate, and state positions. By 1970, however, their representation in that position had dropped to a mere 3%. This change is partly attributable to a postwar consolidation movement that saw the elimination of many of the intermediate or county districts that had supported women superintendents.

Aspiring women school leaders lost further ground as national school administrator organizations initiated a wave of reforms intended to upgrade the profession. In the past, women who had attained school administrative positions tended to rise through the ranks, demonstrating their skill in the classroom before assuming ever-greater responsibilities. By midcentury, the practice of promoting school administrators from within a district largely had been replaced by efforts to attract and hire trained experts from the outside. At the same time, professional preparation programs in educational administration had expanded considerably in size and number after the war. Faculty in these programs sought to increase the stature of the still relatively new academic field by employing scientific methods in emerging scholarship. Many educational administration preparation programs also limited the number of women who could be admitted. Not surprisingly, few women could be found among the faculties of these institutions. A University Council for Educational Administration (UCEA) study reported in 1971 that women accounted for only 2% of all faculty members in educational administration preparation programs.

CURRENT CONTEXTS

These declining conditions for women reversed during the 1970s and then slowly began improving to facilitate an increase in the number of women holding formal school leadership positions. Women's liberation activists issued calls for more women school leaders. Betty Friedan, President of the National Organization for Women, cowrote an article published in a 1971 issue of the *American School Board Journal*, telling school leaders that they would be on the front lines of the battle to end sex discrimination, both by changing the demographics of school leadership and by altering school climate. As feminist organizations gained strength, they appealed to courts to enforce Title VII of the Civil Rights Act of 1964, which enabled women to sue on account of sex discrimination in employment. The enactment of Title IX of the Educational Amendments of 1972 provided another avenue for pursuing redress of grievances. This legislation stipulated that educational programs could lose federal funds if they discriminated on the basis of sex. The threat of financial loss compelled educational institutions to respond to charges of systematic sex discrimination more vigorously than they had in the past. One important consequence of this legislation was that educational administration preparation programs dropped their severely restrictive quotas on the number of women who could be admitted. In 1972, the year that Title IX passed, women accounted for only 11% of all doctoral degree recipients in educational administration. A decade later, however, the percentage reached around 40%, a figure that has increased steadily since.

After women gained full access to educational administration preparation programs in the wake of Title IX, the androcentric scholarship of the field faced feminist opposition. In 1986, Charol Shakeshaft and Marjorie Hanson challenged the editors and readers of the influential *Educational Administration Quarterly* to publish work by and about females in schools. Shakeshaft's seminal work, *Women in Educational Administration*, followed a year later. Since then, a burgeoning body of research that places gender at the center of analysis has been written by scholars such as Catherine Marshall, Margaret Grogan, Marilyn Tallerico, Flora Ida Ortiz, Susan Chase, Colleen Capper, Xenia Montenegro, Sandra Gupton, Michelle Young, Cryss Brunner, Linda Skrla, and many others. Essentially, this work has broadened the discourse of the field to include an array of different underlying philosophical beliefs, new understandings about leading, expanded ways of building relationships with school communities, and innovative approaches to developing and implementing curricula.

Along with the expansion of the scholarship of the field, women's representation in school superintendencies increased from 5% in 1990 to 13% in 2000. Though this increase occurred relatively quickly, the percentage of women superintendents still pales in comparison with the 79% of teachers who are women. Furthermore, women, who now account for the majority of degree recipients in educational administration preparation programs, are not moving into school leadership positions at comparable rates.

Contemporary researchers have posited a number of factors that continue to affect women's access to formal school leadership positions. School board members and executive headhunters employ recruiting and screening processes that privilege nonminority men. The leadership styles expected by school boards and districts often do not align well with those valued by many women. Both subtle and overt discrimination still greet women as they navigate higher in school bureaucracies. A number of women, who still bear a disproportionately large share of family maintenance responsibilities, simply choose not to enter administrative work because of its additional heavy demands. And even as newspaper headlines at the turn of the millennium announced impending dire shortages of qualified school administrators, school boards were urged to recruit in the corporate and military sectors rather than among the administratively credentialed women still serving in the classroom.

Despite these problems, women are expanding rapidly into school leadership positions in some parts of the country. In places where administrator salaries have not kept pace with inflation with those of comparable fields, men, who typically enjoy greater employment choices and higher salary options than women, have been leaving the field or retiring. Even in areas where administrator salaries have remained competitive, the demands of the job, always heavy, have increased substantially in recent years. Those privileged with choice tend to move on. Ultimately, however, the women and men who choose to become school leaders in these conditions are bringing new styles of leadership, fresh notions for improving school quality, and extensive classroom experience to their service. The decades ahead will reveal if this current broadening of the demography of school leadership, which greatly resembles that of a century ago,

will continue until there is full equity, will level off, or will cycle back downward, as happened in the mid-twentieth century. The coming years also will show the degree to which the intellectual underpinnings and practice of educational leadership will expand to reflect those of the field's newest members.

—*Jackie M. Blount*

See also Addams, Jane; boards of education; Cooper, Anna Julia; Coppin, Fanny Jackson; cultural politics, wars; discrimination; feminism and theories of leadership; gender studies, in educational leadership; leadership, theories of; leadership styles; Mendez, Felicitas; minorities, in school; Montessori, Maria; politics, of education; power; principalship; recruitment, of school administrators; sexism (glass ceiling); Sizemore, Barbara A.; superintendency; Supreme Court, United States, key cases in education law; universities, preparation of educational leaders in; University Council for Educational Administration; Young, Ella Flagg

Further Readings and References

Blount, J. (1998). *Destined to rule the schools: Women and the superintendency, 1873–1995*. Albany: SUNY Press.

Brown, K., & Wynn, S. (2004). Why leadership-skilled women teachers are saying "No" to the principal's role: A matter of individual choice or institutional constraint? *Journal of School Leadership, 14,* 686–712.

Glass, T., Bjork, L., & Brunner, C. (2000). *The study of the American school superintendency, 2000.* Arlington, VA: American Association of School Administrators.

Hess, F. (2002). School boards at the dawn of the 21st century. Report prepared for the *National School Board Journal.* Retrieved January 1, 2005, from <http://www.nsba.org/site/docs/1200/1143.pdf>

Iowa teachers. (1894, January 18). *Journal of Education, 39,* p. 44.

McCarthy, M., & Kuh, G. (1998). A new breed of educational leadership faculty members. *Journal of School Leadership, 8,* 360–372.

National Education Association. (2003). *Status of the American public school teacher, 2000–2001.* Washington, DC: Author.

Shakeshaft, C. (1987, 1989). *Women in educational administration.* Newbury Park, CA: Sage.

Tallerico, M. (2000). Gaining access to the superintendency: Headhunting, gender, and color. *Educational Administration Quarterly, 36,* 18–43.

WOODSON, CARTER G.

In 1926, Carter G. Woodson (1875–1950) organized the first Negro History week celebration in the second week of February. The week was later expanded to

Black History Month. Often referred to as the "Father of Black history," Woodson wrote the classic text *The Miseducation of the Negro* in 1933. Educator and noted historian of African American history, Woodson was born to former-slave parents, December 19, 1875, in New Canton, Virginia. His father, James Henry Woodson, and his mother, Anne Eliza Riddle Woodson, raised nine children. Woodson worked in the coal mines of West Virginia, having little formal education before the age of 20. After completing high school, Woodson entered Berea College, in Kentucky, known at the time for its coeducation of the races.

Woodson began teaching in West Virginia in 1898 and subsequently held numerous teaching and educational leadership roles, including serving as an instructor at Miner Normal College (later to become the D.C. Teacher's College). From 1900 to 1903, he served as principal of Douglass High School, and from 1909 to 1918, Woodson taught French, Spanish, English, and History at the M Street School in Washington, D.C.

In 1912, Woodson was awarded the doctorate of philosophy in history from Harvard University, the second African American to have obtained this distinction. Woodson cofounded the Association for the Study of Negro Life and History in 1915 and served as the founding editor of the association's *Journal of Negro History,* launched in 1916.

Between 1921 and 1925, Woodson published four books, including *Early Negro Education in West Virginia, The History of the Negro Church, The Negro in Our History,* and *Black Orators and their Orations.* Other texts by Dr. Woodson include *The Education of the Negro Prior to 1861: A History of the Education of the Colored People of the United States From the Beginning of Slavery to the Civil War,* and *African Myths Together With Proverbs,* a supplementary reader composed of folk tales from various parts of Africa that was adapted for the use of children in the public schools. His journal publications include numerous articles in the *Journal of Negro History, Howard University Record, Crisis, American Historical Review,* and *Negro History Bulletin.* He also published widely about educational reform in the press, including articles in the *Chicago Defender,* engaging topics such as "Is the Educated Negro a Liability?"; "Service Rather Than Leadership"; and "More Teachers, Texts, Needed for Growth of Race History." Awarded the Spingarn Medal for his leadership and historical scholarship, Woodson died in 1950, in Washington, D.C.

—*Khaula Murtadha*

See also Afrocentric theories; Bethune, Mary McLeod; Black education; Coppin, Fanny Jackson; cross-cultural education; desegregation, of schools; discrimination; diversity; Du Bois, W. E. B.; elementary education; equality, in schools; equity and adequacy of funding schools; governance; history, in curriculum; individual differences, in children; law; minorities, in schools; multiculturalism; Washington, Booker T.

Further Readings and References

The Carter G. Woodson collection of Negro papers and related documents, 1803–1936. Archival manuscript material, Washington, D.C., Library of Congress.

Conyers, J. L. (2000). *Carter G. Woodson: A historical reader.* New York: Garland.

Bennett, L. (1988). *Before the Mayflower: A history of Black America.* Chicago: Johnson.

WORK TASK MEASUREMENT

The topic of work task measurement may be approached from several different perspectives. Typically, one thinks of task measurement as a component of assessment that addresses objective criteria, while the concept of assessment includes both objective and subjective information. Measurement refers to the process by which something is differentiated and described in precise and generally quantitative terms. More specifically, measurement is the process of quantifying objective criteria to express the relative nature or the presence or absence of some characteristic, such as individual attributes, performance, behaviors, or cognition. In a business and industry environment, one views work measurement as the time it takes to complete a given task when it is performed by a qualified worker. Predetermined times for completion of a task are set based on time-and-motion studies of qualified workers performing the tasks. Task performance may be assessed by direct observation. An experienced evaluator may use a rating scale and a stopwatch to determine the proficiency with which one completes a given unit of work based on predetermined times and/or standards.

In an educational context, measurement is the process of using students' responses to some stimuli in order to make judgments about students' knowledge, skills, or dispositions. In one sense, measurement may be thought of as a data collection activity that requires that numbers be assigned in a systematic way to represent some characteristics of individuals. However, measurement in the social and behavioral sciences goes beyond such objective data collection instruments to describe some phenomenon by observation. In many of these situations, some variables cannot be measured directly with finely tuned instruments because some behaviors cannot be observed directly. For example, job requirements of workers in the service sector focus on nonstandardized tasks to be accomplished rather than specific number of hours worked or procedural steps to be performed. In addition, the increase in flexible working hours makes measurement more challenging. Consequently, the measurement must be inferred from a sample of indicators of the behaviors. The paradox is that using indicators of behaviors makes true measurement more difficult and introduces a greater degree of measurement error than when using variables that can be assessed directly. Common measuring devices such as those used to assess objective quantities, such as height, weight, and age, are not easily discernable. For example, one's mathematical abilities, perceptions of work, and value of others cannot be assessed with the same precision as blood pressure and growth rate.

Work task measurement may be described in relation to data, people, and things. Each of these elements is involved to some extent in every work task. Clearly, there are differences in work task measurement due to measurement restrictions in many areas and in the qualitative and quantitative differences in task performance. For example, tasks that include complex human variables such as working effectively as a team player are obviously more difficult to measure than are simple laboratory experiments. Although realistic work situations may be simulated, the nature of the task itself varies from one situation to another in the course of normal work. Consequently, task performance and measurement have to be modeled on more than one level, using more than one technique.

A variety of methods for measuring work tasks have been developed. One of the most common methods is to base the measurement on predetermined objectives. The first step is to conduct an analysis of the work such that the work to be done is portioned into logical and discrete components or elements. In other words, one would be hard-pressed to measure any task without prior knowledge of the task or its associated indicators. Three common methods for measuring work tasks are based on analyses of procedures, hierarchical tasks, and concept mapping. These methods are grounded in taxonomies for identifying learning domains (cognitive or intellectual, psychomotor

or physical, and affective or dispositions), such as those in Bloom's taxonomy of educational objectives and Gagné's levels of learning.

The basic idea of procedural analysis is to divide the task into mental and/or physical steps necessary to complete the task. Procedures to be analyzed may be simple, requiring an individual to follow some basic steps in a sequential order, or they may be complex, requiring decision points along the way to completing the task. The person performing the analysis will arrange the steps in a logical order and present them in a readable format, such as a flowchart showing decision points along the way or in outline form. The completed procedure itself or associated steps may then be used as the basis for work task measurement.

An analysis of hierarchical tasks requires that a given task be analyzed and divided into enabling skills (subordinate skills) or elements of the task. The elements are arranged in a sequence that shows the hierarchical relationship among the tasks in terms of what an individual must know or be able to do to perform the task. Work task measurement may take place at any point in the hierarchical arrangement. The important point is that the subordinate skills are arranged from most basic to complex, with the idea that an individual who can perform at the higher levels will also be able to perform at the lower levels.

Work task measurement may be based on a conceptual graph, which is similar to concept mapping with the exception that elements of the graph may include specific goals or events. Predetermined questions may be used to elaborate the information included on the graph.

Measurement theory is a branch of applied statistics designed to describe, categorize, and evaluate measuring instruments in an attempt to improve their usefulness, accuracy, and meaningfulness in real-life situations. The mental and/or physical steps that one must go through to complete a task are the major concerns. One should always keep in mind the purpose to be served by the measurement and the degree of accuracy needed to accommodate that purpose. Only then can an appropriate measurement instrument be selected or designed. One should consider the following criteria when selecting a measurement technique: (a) purpose of the measurement and decisions to be made, (b) level of accuracy required, (c) level of detail required in the measurement, (d) time constraints, (e) resources (i.e., special laboratories or materials required), and (f) cost of the measurement. Furthermore, in all cases, measurements should reference the objectives (work or task) to be measured. Also, the circumstances or conditions under which the work is to be performed or demonstrated, along with appropriate time requirements, should be defined. In addition, the acceptable level of performance or a predetermined level of proficiency should be identified. Any qualifiers related to the work to be measured should be included. Work hours, responsibilities, and job tenure are becoming increasingly varied. Such variability demands that more appropriately designed and detailed measuring instruments and methods be developed to measure work tasks more systematically and accurately.

—*Marie Kraska*

See also accountability; bureaucracy; division of labor; economics, theories of; goals, goal setting; hierarchy, in organizations; job descriptions; leadership, task-oriented; management theories; operational definitions; performance evaluation systems; personnel management; power; productivity; quantitative research methods; rational organizational theory; resource management; role ambiguity; role conflict; role theory; span of control; table of organization

Further Readings and References

Aft, L. S. (2000). *Work measurement and methods improvement.* Hoboken, NJ: Wiley-Interscience.
Bond, T. G., & Fox, C. M. (2001). *Applying the Rasch model: Fundamental measurement in the human sciences.* Chicago: Institute for Objective Measurement.
Booher, H. R. (2003). *Handbook of human systems integration.* Wright-Patterson AFB, OH: Human Systems Information Analysis Center.
Niebel, B. W., & Freivalds, A. (2003). *Methods, standards, and work design* (11th ed.). New York: McGraw-Hill.

WORKING CONDITIONS, IN SCHOOLS

The mandate to improve the nation's schools has focused attention on school reform, curriculum, testing, accountability, teacher quality, and a host of related issues. With the improvement of educational performance high on the nation's agenda, attracting and retaining quality teachers has become a high priority. Little attention, however, has been paid to the relationship between working conditions, teacher retention, and teaching outcomes.

The term *school working conditions* includes both the physical and emotional aspects of "life" within a school, including adequacy of the building, facilities, teaching resources, cleanliness, air quality, noise control, thermal conditions, administrative leadership and organization, student discipline, safety, teacher autonomy, and teacher support.

Working conditions tend to mirror the socioeconomics of the school's attendance area, varying in accordance with school location, age, size, and the percentage of low-income students in the school. According to a 2000 report from the National Educational Association, most of the nation's public schools are on average 40 years old with one third of them in need of repair. A large proportion of older schools are located in large urban centers and remote rural areas that serve a high proportion of poor children. Some of these older schools have crumbling infrastructures that contain environmental hazards, such as asbestos, mold, lead, dust, inadequate lighting, ventilation, and thermal conditions. Inadequacy and scarcity of teaching materials and equipment often contribute to inferior working conditions.

Schools in higher-socioeconomic areas are usually new, well maintained, climate controlled, and filled with abundant teaching materials. However, overcrowded conditions of some suburban and urban schools have necessitated the addition of portable classrooms and the attendant problems associated with isolation from the main school, poor ventilation, high noise levels, and concerns about hazardous chemicals emitted from the building materials.

Numerous studies demonstrate links between school conditions and student achievement. After controlling for socioeconomic status, test scores of students attending older schools are consistently lower than students in newer buildings. In addition to the factor of building functionality, attendance at an old, ill-equipped school may convey a message to students that they are less valued than their counterparts in more affluent areas.

Not surprisingly, schools with good working conditions are more likely to attract and retain experienced teachers and administrators, while schools with inferior conditions experience continual turnover and usually employ the least-experienced personnel. Beginning teachers hired to work in schools with unfavorable conditions usually migrate to different schools or leave the profession. Valuable time, attention, and resources are wasted recruiting, hiring, and inducting new personnel.

Although research on the linkage between school working conditions, teachers' retention, and student outcomes is available, policymakers have given little attention to the findings. Recent research chronicles those relationships.

In the late 1980s, The U.S. Department of Education's National Center for Educational Statistics conducted the Schools and Staffing Survey (SASS) and its supplement, the Teacher Follow-Up Survey (TFS). Findings of the study revealed that teachers worked longer than a 40-hour work week; received salaries lower than many other professionals; felt they had little control over curriculum, textbooks, and student discipline; and were concerned about school safety. Teachers' perceptions of working conditions varied considerably depending on school size, location, and percentage of low-income students in the school. Results of the study focused attention on the issue of working conditions and paved the way for additional research.

Subsequent research included that of Ingersol and Smith, whose 2003 study revealed that teacher dissatisfaction and turnover were fueled by inadequate administrative support, lack of faculty influence, intrusions into teaching, and no opportunities for advancement. A 2003 survey of teachers in North Carolina by the North Carolina Professional Teaching Standards Commission supported many of those findings. Teachers wanted involvement in decisions, protection from intrusion into teaching duties, clerical assistance, time for curriculum work, and for new teachers, time to work with mentors. Analysis further revealed that satisfaction levels varied according to school characteristics. Teachers in schools with higher accountability scores, higher graduation rates, and more fully licensed personnel were more satisfied with their working conditions. Teachers serving in schools with a higher proportion of poor students reported that schools were in need of physical repairs. They expressed a need to work with administrators who empowered them to select teaching strategies that matched student needs and learning styles.

Schneider's 2003 study of teachers' working conditions in Chicago and Washington, D.C., public schools revealed working conditions that adversely affected academic outcomes and teachers' health. Teachers surveyed reported dissatisfaction with indoor air quality, thermal comfort, poor lighting, dirty and inoperable windows, dirty restrooms, and high noise levels. They also reported that schools were too large and classrooms for science and the arts were inadequate.

A survey of 900 teachers in Texas regarding high-stakes testing revealed that although teachers reported stressing more of the tested curriculum, they also reported that such tests did not motivate students to learn more, nor were the tests accurate measures of student learning or school effectiveness. Teachers in England actually boycotted the national test.

These recent studies clearly document the relationship between school conditions, teacher retention, and teaching outcomes. Inferior working conditions make it difficult for teachers to perform well, difficult for students to learn, and increase the likelihood that teachers will leave the school or profession. In some schools, health and safety of teachers and students are adversely affected as well. If national school reform is based on the premise that quality teachers and teaching are the keys to student learning, then the working conditions of the nation's teachers need to become part of reform initiatives.

—*Barbara L. Brock*

See also class, social; climate, school; differentiated staffing; equity and adequacy of funding schools; esprit (school climate); expectations, teacher and student cultures; flow theory; hazards, environmental, in schools; merit pay; productivity; reform, of schools; satisfaction, in organization and roles; school plant management; school safety; stress, in school administration; student teaching; values of organizations and leadership; violence in schools; workplace trends

Further Readings and References

Environmental Protection Agency's Indoor Air Quality (IAQ) Tools for Schools Kit. (n.d.). Retrieved June 16, 2004, from http://www.epa.giv/iaq/schoolstoolkit.html

Ingersol, R. M., & Smith, T. M. (2003). The wrong solution to the teacher shortage. *Educational Leadership, 60*(8), 30–33.

National Center for Education Statistics. (1996). *An overview of the schools and staffing survey (SASS).* Washington, DC: U.S. Department of Education, Office of Educational Research and Improvement.

Robertson, S. (1996). Teachers' work, restructuring, and postfordism: Constructing the new "professionalism." In I. Goodson & A. Hargreaves (Eds.), *Teachers' professional lives* (pp. 28–55). London: Falmer Press.

Schneider, M. (2003, August). Linking school working conditions to teacher satisfaction and success. *National Clearinghouse for Educational Facilities.* Retrieved April 18, 2004, from http://www.edfacilities

Southeast Center for Teaching Quality. (2003). Creating working conditions so teachers can help all students achieve: Teaching in the Southeast. *Best Practices & Policies, 3*(2),

1–2. Retrieved April 18, 2004, from http://www.teaching quality.org

North Carolina Professional Teaching Standards Commission. (2004). *Governor Mike Easley's Teacher Working Conditions Initiative.* Retrieved April 18, 2004, from http://twc.learnnc.org/gov/twc.nsf

WORKPLACE TRENDS

Workplace trends refers to aspects of the work environment such as structural arrangements, roles, relationships, procedures, policies, or employment conditions that appear to be undergoing transformation but are not yet fully integrated into the workplace as a whole. The trends may become permanent elements of most workplaces in which the profession or industry operates, may become adopted by a minority of these workplaces, or may be tried in a few of them and then dropped.

Workplace trends generally mirror what is occurring within a professional field, industry, or society. In educational settings, these trends are directly related to the social, political, economic, and educational contexts in which they operate. Among the primary influences on the workplace today are the accountability environment; family, societal, and workplace transformations; teacher and administrative shortages; and the technological revolution.

ACCOUNTABILITY ENVIRONMENT

In the last few decades, accountability demands on schools have increased, culminating with the national No Child Left Behind Act of 2001 legislation. This law has imposed requirements upon schools and students, based primarily on student performance on standardized tests. These expanded accountability requirements have subjected educational institutions to increased public scrutiny. The effect on the workplace has been mixed, with two different management models unfolding. It is too soon to determine which of these trends will become more prominent or whether they will continue to coexist.

In some situations, there has been an increase in control over teacher autonomy, resulting in teaching models such as direct instruction, in which teachers must follow explicit steps and sometimes even scripts in their teaching. The use of standardized tests to measure performance has also resulted in many systems adopting more rigid curriculum standards, with directions

that all children must use the same textbooks, giving teachers little freedom to vary their instruction or curricular approach. Thus, the workplace has become more controlled and the role of the teacher more constricted.

In other settings, schools and systems have decided to restructure the workplace to make it more collaborative. Shared leadership that includes teachers, staff, parents, and sometimes students has emerged, making the workplace a center of teamwork and joint decision making. In some situations, new organizational structures that include team teaching are also being formed. In such settings, there is often an increase in partnerships with parents, schools, universities, businesses, and communities focused upon the problems facing schools and enhancing educational resources and student success.

FAMILY, SOCIETAL, AND WORKPLACE TRANSFORMATIONS

Today's families are much more mobile and much less cohesive than in the past. Most children come from single-parent homes or from homes in which both parents are working and lack the support that came from extended families in the past. Poverty is on the rise, and many children are in need of social and health services that parents cannot always provide. In many instances, family problems and needs fall on the shoulders of the schools. Seeking to meet these needs, many schools are changing the workplace to include interagency partnerships with human service providers. Such partnerships have resulted in hiring and/or placing additional personnel in some schools, including nurses, social workers, and family counselors. Preschool and after-school programs have also been added to many school settings, thus extending the workday of the school and changing the responsibilities of the school and school personnel in caring for students.

Some work policies are also being implemented to assist those who work in the school to meet their own family needs. Job sharing and providing child care services on campus are two examples of the types of efforts being initiated to address employee family needs.

The Americans with Disabilities Act and PL 94-142 and the changes in the demographics of our country are adding more diversity to the student body and are causing schools to reach out to diversify faculty as well. This diversity in the workplace brings with it new models for sharing, more professional development focused on the need to ensure that people understand and work well with each another, and increases in language and cultural diversity in the workplace environment. This diversity sometimes brings a questioning about values in the workplace. In educational settings, issues such as whose values count, what activities and holidays will be celebrated and recognized, and what types of clothing or accessories will be considered acceptable are topics and concerns affecting the workplace and increasing the daily dilemmas people must face.

Increases in violent crime and a rise in terrorism around the globe have also changed the workplace and the role of schools in ensuring a safe environment. Most schools must now have safety and security plans. School personnel are adopting new roles, and new personnel, such as security guards, are being added to the school setting. Increased screening and more stringent hiring practices are being added. These changes have resulted in increased struggles to find a balance between security and privacy in the workplace.

All of these issues have added stress to the workplace, making it necessary to add additional psychological and other support services. Some schools now offer exercise and other health-related services, such as yoga, to aid employees in dealing with stress and maintaining a healthy lifestyle. Some systems have added such benefits to their health plans.

TEACHER AND ADMINISTRATOR SHORTAGES

Retirements and large percentages of people leaving the field are causing a shortage of teachers and administrators in public education. This shortage is expected to worsen in the next decade. In some settings and subject areas, shortages already exist. New workplace structures are being implemented to meet this demand. Whether these will be integrated into educational environments or be dropped, should there be fewer shortages in the future, is unknown.

Among the personnel changes resulting from shortages of educational professionals is the entry into the educational workplace of older individuals who have retired or who are changing careers. Some are beginning to teach and serve as administrators without holding formal education degrees. There is also more involvement of school systems, private enterprise, and others in the teacher and administrator preparation and certification process.

These differences in the types of individuals entering the profession and greater diversity in where and how they are educated and certified have numerous effects on the working environment. For example, the types of professional development experiences that need to occur have had to be broadened. There is also an expanded need for mentoring and induction programs to ensure a smooth transition for those not familiar with the educational setting who are entering the teaching or administrative ranks. Although not highlighted in the literature, it appears likely that schools will need to develop strategies to bring about open dialogue between people who are entering the field from nontraditional backgrounds with nontraditional preparation and those who come from more traditional backgrounds.

THE TECHNOLOGICAL REVOLUTION

The technological revolution has caused some workplace trends that will probably expand in the next decade. Some work, particularly that done by staff, is being completed from home. Distance education is also impacting the workplace, adding virtual schools with students doing work online, sometimes from home. The type of skills employees of all types need to adapt to technological change is becoming increasingly complex, making professional development and online learning an integral part of the workplace.

Technology has also created a workplace trend that connects the home and the school and changes the role of the teacher. The teacher is much more accessible, and communication between home and school is expanding through numerous technological means. The expanded access to information has also changed the context of teaching and learning, making the workplace more global for both students and teachers.

WORKPLACE TRENDS AND THE FUTURE

The accountability environment, our rapidly changing society, and the increasing use of technology has and will continue to alter roles, responsibilities, and educational environments. The only known element in this environment is that change will be continuous and require flexibility and adaptability in the workplace.

—*Frances K. Kochan*

See also achievement gap, of students; achievement tests; at-risk students; behavior, student; diversity; drug education;

empowerment; fundamentalism; globalism; governance; individual differences, in children; innovation, in education; leadership, participatory; locus of control; market theory of schooling; No Child Left Behind; parental involvement; planning models; politics, of education; privatization; productivity; professional learning communities; right-wing politics, advocates, impact on education; school improvement models; school safety; standard setting; state departments of education; stress, in school administration; systemic reform; underachievers, in schools; voucher plans

Further Readings and References

Anderson, G. (2005). Educational leadership and the new economy: Keeping the "public" in public schools. In F. English (Ed.), *The SAGE handbook of educational leadership* (pp. 216–236). Thousand Oaks, CA: Sage.

Gold, E., Simon, E., & Brown, C. (2005). A new conception of parent engagement: Community organizing for school reform. In F. English (Ed.), *The SAGE handbook of educational leadership* (pp. 237–268). Thousand Oaks, CA: Sage.

Goldring, E., & Sims, P. (2005). Modeling creative and courageous school leadership through district-community-university partnerships. *Educational Policy, 19,* 223.

Jaksec, C. (2004). *The difficult parent.* Thousand Oaks, CA: Corwin Press.

Jukes, I., Dosaj, A., & Macdonald, B. (2000). *Net saavy.* Thousand Oaks, CA: Corwin Press.

Lawrence, C., & Vachon, M. (2003). *How to handle staff misconduct.* Thousand Oaks, CA: Corwin Press.

Queen, J., & Queen, P. (2004). *The frazzled principal's wellness plan.* Thousand Oaks, CA: Corwin Press.

WORLD BANK, INFLUENCE ON EDUCATION

The World Bank was founded in 1944. With the end of World War II more than a year away, delegates from 44 of the nations pledged to form the United Nations met at Bretton Woods, New Hampshire, in July 1944 to discuss pressing international economic problems. From this conference emerged two prominent organizations: the International monetary Fund (IMF) and the International Bank for Reconstruction and Development (IBRD), now known as the World Bank.

As the name reflects, the IBRD was primarily created to assist and provide loans for rebuilding the war-torn areas of World War II, especially in Europe. Currently, the World Bank consists of five institutions: the IBRD, the International Development Association (IDA), the International Finance Corporation (IFC), the Multilateral Investment Guarantee Agency (MIGA), and the International Centre for Settlement of Investment Disputes (ICSID). Also, its focus has changed. Since 1950, it has provided loans for projects and programs in less developed countries. Only developing nations can now borrow from the World Bank.

The mission of the World Bank is to reduce poverty and improve the living standards of people in developing countries. Education is seen as the most important key to achieving this mission. As the largest financier of education in the world, the World Bank has provided $42 billion for education loans and credits and currently supports 157 education projects in 83 countries. The World Bank first started lending in education in 1963 (to Tunisia for vocational training), and its lending has averaged $1 billion a year since then. In addition to its loans for education, it offers nonlending services for education in policy and strategy formulation, mobilizing resources, creating national consensus for education reforms, and creating capacity to design and implement programs. The World Bank pursues its education objectives with a range of expert staff, 40% of which is based in country offices outside its headquarters in Washington, D.C.

The World Bank's influence in education is best understood by examining its several published comprehensive reports on education. These reports summarize its implemented educational programs and provide information on its objectives in education, its policies, and its priorities in lending. In the early 1960s, the funds were directed to vocational and technical education, the expansion of general secondary education, and the construction and equipment for schools. By the 1970s, the program and loan objectives were extended to primary, secondary, and higher education. They also included the education of teachers, technicians, staff, and general support personnel. Later, the focus shifted to topics such as skill development, mass participation in education, equity, and efficiency and to improvement of educational planning and management. In the 1980s, the World Bank focused on basic primary education for all children and educational opportunities for everyone. The new focus includes increasing the quantity and quality of education. It encompasses education that relates to work and environment, to increasing the skills and knowledge for performing economics and social functions, and to developing and maintaining institutional capacities to design, analyze, manage, and evaluate educational programs to achieve its objectives.

Because of the influence of the World Bank, access to schooling improved markedly. In the 1960s, only half of the primary school-aged children were enrolled in primary education. In the 1990s, the ratio exceeded three fourths. However, the 1990s brought new challenges. The end of the cold war era and the breakup of the old Soviet nations led to an increase in market economies, the spread of democratization, globalization, increasing technological innovation, and changes in public and private roles. In response to these changes, the World Bank adopted new strategies and objectives for its educational programs in the 1990s.

First, the World Bank increased its educational funds to developing countries, which averaged $6 billion a year in the first half of the 1990s. Second, it adopted new programs and involved other institutions in its joint programs, such as "Education for All (EFA)." The EFA commitment was made in 1990 by over 150 countries, and reaffirmed in 2000. The EFA program aims at accomplishing the following objectives, which are included in the "Millennium Development Goals":

- Universal primary education for all children by 2015
- Elimination of gender disparities in primary and secondary education
- Improvement of early childhood education
- Ensuring equitable access to "life skills" programs
- Achieving a 50% increase in adult literacy by 2015
- Improving the quality in education

Education is seen as the key to attaining the "2015 Millennium Development Goals," adopted by 189 countries. These goals require that the following objectives are met by 2015:

- Elimination of poverty and hunger
- Universal primary education
- Gender equality
- Reduction in child mortality
- Improvement of maternal health
- Combating diseases such as HIV/AIDS and malaria
- Environmental stability
- Global partnership

The direction of the World Bank education policies is toward achieving a good education through three pillars of education: access, equity, and quality. The World Bank is seeking access to education at all levels by all people. It also wants to make sure that people in the poor areas of the world and girls in all areas will have adequate education, at least at the basic level. Furthermore, the World Bank is focusing on early interventions such as early child development and school health programs. Innovative delivery systems are integrated in the education programs with an emphasis on distance education, open learning, and the use of new technologies to reach more people in the developing countries. Quality of education is also improved by an approach called *systemic reform,* which requires standards in achievement, assessment, and curriculum, as well as decentralization of education, and finding providers and financiers outside the government. In this process, the World Bank not only works with governments in developing nations as its clients but also enters partnership with other organizations, such as UNESCO, the United Nations, and the IMF, to reach its goals in education. The influence in education of the World Bank, with its more than 600 projects, is extensive, though not without criticism. Martin Carnoy has observed that the main strategy of the World Bank has been the efficiency of resource use. Its main focus has been on "finance-driven reform," which has at its heart the reduction of public spending on education. One thrust of this effort is the privatization of secondary and higher education and the reduction of per-pupil costs at the elementary level by increasing class size.

—Orhan Kara and Ibrahim Duyar

See also accountability; administration, theories of; capacity building, of organizations; choice, of schools; competition, forms of, in schools; cost-benefit analyses; cultural politics, wars; economics, theories of; global cultural politics; globalism; innovation, in education; leadership, task-oriented; life span development; management theories; market theory of schooling; multiculturalism; performance assessment; privatization; productivity; rational organizational theory; restructuring, of schools; school improvement models; school safety; social capital; systemic reform; systems theory/thinking; values of organizations and leadership

Further Readings and References

Carnoy, M. (1999). *Globalization and educational reform: What planners need to know.* Paris: UNESCO.

Grindle, M., & Thomas, J. (1991). *Public choices and policy change: The political economy of reform in developing countries.* London: Johns Hopkins University Press.

Henig, R. (1994). *Rethinking school choice: Limits of the market metaphor.* Princeton, NJ: Princeton University Press.

Jones, P. W. (1997). On World Bank education financing. *Comparative Education, 33*(1), 117–129.

Jones, P. W. (1997). The World Bank and the literacy question: Orthodoxy, heresy, and ideology. *International Review of Education, 43*, 367–375.

World Bank. (2004). *Opening doors: Education and the World Bank.* Washington, DC: Author.

🏛 WRITING, TEACHING OF

Writing, specifically the teaching of writing, has been exposed to a variety of subjective questions, including ways to teach writing, what constitutes good writing, and ways to keep up with trends in the field. Historically, writing has also been included in the early curriculum, although the need for writing has never been questioned.

Approaching writing from a utilitarian point of view would consider sentence-level reinforcement, extended prose, and vocabulary as basic elements of writing. In some programs, there is more emphasis on contextual meaning.

The teaching of writing is also connected closely with reading. Practice in using cohesive devised and discourse markers; in relating rhetorical determinants such as audience, topic, and purpose; in organizing texts into various rhetorical structures; and in deciding how much information should be made explicit and how much should be inferred, all contribute to the process of comprehension.

Communication with other people in the social world is the third reason for the teaching of writing. Although the communicative approach has a strong oral bias, directing meaningful discourse to a particular audience for a specific purpose is as relevant in writing as in oral expression. Personal or occupation-related correspondence is a genuine need for many students. Collaborative means of producing and monitoring writing of various types and genres also stimulates authentic communication between student writers.

Overall, research suggests that the teaching of writing is an effective means of eliciting the use of vocabulary and grammatical structure, of practicing reading comprehension, and encouraging communication. Writing instruction at the discourse level ("the rhetorical approach") basically consists of the paralleling of formulaic patterns. Rhetorical modes (narration, description, exposition, and argumentation) are demonstrated as consisting of component paragraphs (introduction, body, conclusion), which are composed according to "rules" governing the organization of sentence elements (topic sentences, support sentences, transitions, conclusion, etc.).

The patterning method is based upon analysis of texts composed by others. On the other hand, the communicative approach acknowledges the social function of text, meaning the dynamic effect exerted by the relationship between the author's purpose in writing and the audience. Textbooks feature functional tasks (inviting, explaining, addressed to specific audiences) in various forms (messages, reports, advertisements, different types of letter writing) and combine these with rhetorical-syntactic patterns listed above. The experiential approach draws upon the need for communication and is based upon students' personal knowledge and affect. Descriptive writing is encouraged by means of group discussions of the individual's personal memories, sensory experiences, and observations. Dialogues and monologues lead to reasoned arguments.

Writing is a complex, recursive process that is subject to false starts, trial and error, and constant revision. Drafting and revising, self- and peer editing, and review are valuable means of improving text. Writing is no longer regarded as a tiered skill, moving from smaller to larger pieces. Research suggests that information contained in a higher processing stage can influence the production of a lower stage, as well as vice versa.

With regard to current curriculum design, it is doubtful that one "best" method exists. Prescriptive product methodologies have been criticized for being too simplistic. For example, rather than developing from thesis statement to support, Standard English text is varied in structure. Instructional approaches that prompt students to focus on a single aspect of their writing, such as syntactic errors, may have the disadvantage of directing learners' attention away from considerations of the complexity of their composing. However, expectations as to the qualities of "good" writing exist, and it is the instructor's responsibility to convey this to the student.

Trends in the teaching of writing are varied. Some of the more common trends include collaborative writing, writing for a profession, and the impact of technology on writing. Although collaborative theories have not gained the popularity needed to teach at the undergraduate level, research has demonstrated many benefits of teaching collaboration in a writing course. Some of the benefits of collaboration are that it promotes a heuristic for discovery both of ideas and of organizing principles, focuses on writing as problem writing; gives writers a sense of audience early in the process, allows writers to learn that finding a voice depends on understanding the social milieu in which they write, allows for editing intervention early in the process, and parallels the way writing is done in the professional world.

Another trend in the teaching of writing involves writing for special genres. Research shows that college-aged students often do not recognize key characteristics in writing for a specific field. Often students will design drafts that "look like" a form by imitating section headings, the number of pages, and so on. Instructors can promote effective writing in a particular form by offering the following steps: provide samples of the form and help students identify and analyze key characteristics, create a "form guide" that students can use to assist them in composing, and offer students several opportunities to write in the form. Instructors should offer several opportunities to develop proficiency.

The advent of the computer and the Internet have had a dramatic impact on the research and writing process. An Internet environment that fosters research writing can encourage the student to become an active, reflective learner by prompting written responses of various kinds. Computers and word processors contain a variety of tools that help with layout and construction of all types of texts. In using technology, authors can look at the text they have just written and rewrite, reorganize, and redraft with very little effort. Redrafting is a valuable way to clarify the writer's developing purpose and understanding. In a sense, a word processor allows the writer to "think on the screen" in partnership with technology. In doing so, writers can develop their own knowledge in a lasting way. Researchers note, however, that to realize the long-term cognitive effects of such a partnership, it needs to take place within appropriate surroundings that foster learning. These include the technology, activity, goal setting, teacher's role, and the classroom culture—each of which can dramatically influence the type of learning within a student.

—*Carolyn N. Stevenson*

See also computers, use and impact of; cultural capital; curriculum, theories of; early childhood education; elementary education; learning, theories of; literacy, theories of; measurement, theories of; motivation, theories of; performance assessment; philosophies of education; reading, history of, use in schools

Further Readings and References

Applebee, A. (1984). *Contexts for learning to write: Studies of secondary school instruction.* Norwood, NJ: Ablex.

Dougiamas, M. (1999). *Reading and writing for Internet teaching.* Retrieved September 18, 2005, from http://www.dougiamas.com/writing/readwrite.html

Greenberg, K., Wiener, H., & Donovan, R. (1986). *Writing assessment: Issues and strategies.* New York: Longman.

Spandel, V., & Stiggins, R. (1990). *Creating writers: Linking assessment and writing instruction.* New York: Longman.

White, E. (1994). *Teaching and assessing writing: Recent advances in understanding, evaluating and improving student performance.* San Francisco: Jossey-Bass.

Woolever, K. (1991). Reassessing the role of collaborative learning and teaching writing. In B. W. McClelland & T. R. Donovan (Eds.), *Perspectives on research and scholarship in composition.* New York: Modern Language Association of America.

Y

🏛 YEAR-ROUND EDUCATION

Year-round education (YRE) is a reorganization of the traditional school calendar into shorter attendance sessions with more frequent vacations. There is generally no increase in the number of attendance days, merely a rearrangement. Various scheduling options are available within the two design types of single and multi-track systems. Configurations are selected based on need, purpose, budget, or some combination of these.

The current 9-month school calendar emerged when 85% of Americans were involved in agriculture. Today, only about 3% of American livelihoods are tied to the agricultural cycle, and air-conditioning makes it possible for schools to provide comfortable learning environments year-round. Even rural America is no longer made up of individuals and families whose lives revolve around growing crops or tending livestock. With these drastic economic and technological changes, many find it puzzling that the school calendar remains agrarian based with the extended summer vacation.

Educators and parents often voice concerns about the possible negative impact of summer vacation on student learning. Harris Cooper wrote in 2003 that the long summer break disrupts continuous instruction and can lead to students forgetting the learned material, requiring significant review when the next school year begins. This can be even more detrimental for students with special needs.

Research is clear that extended vacation with the traditional calendar may result in loss of learned academic material, especially in math-related areas. Therefore, it seems reasonable to theorize that more frequent and shorter vacations would help reduce this loss. To that end, many have proposed changes in the school calendar that would do away with the long summer break and allow shorter and more frequent breaks throughout the year, that is, year-round or balanced calendar.

The first recorded opening of a year-round school was in Bluffton, Indiana, in 1904; the first multitrack school was in St. Charles, Missouri, in 1969; and the first year-round district was established in 1971 in the Valley View School District, Romeoville, Illinois. Currently, over 2 million students in the United States are enrolled in some form of year-round education; there are almost 3,000 schools in 41 states that operate on a year-round education schedule.

There are two types of YRE programs—single track and multitrack. Single-track programs have the entire staff and student body attending and vacationing on the same schedule. For multitrack programs, students and teachers are divided into groups, and each group is assigned to a track; the attendance and vacation schedules for each track are different and staggered. Multitrack is frequently selected to reduce facilities overcrowding.

C. C. Kneese in 2000 and Louis Wildman and others in 1999 wrote that within these two types of YRE, several scheduling models are available. The following are among the most common:

- 60–20/60–15. In 60–20, the year is divided into three 60-day sessions with three 20-day vacation periods between these sessions. The 60–15 model has the 60-day attendance sessions with vacation periods of 15 days. The additional 3–4 weeks of common vacation are added to the schedule.

- 45–15/45–10. In the 45–15 schedule, there is a cycle of 45 days of instruction and 15 days of vacation. The 45–10 schedule follows the same pattern, with the vacation sessions being 10 rather than 15 days. The additional 4 weeks in the 45–10 schedule are used for common vacation time. The 45–15 and 45–10 plans account for the largest portion of all year-round school calendars.
- Concept 6. The Concept 6 calendar is divided into six terms of approximately 43 days each. Students and teachers attend two consecutive sessions of 43 days each and then have one session off; this cycle is repeated, totaling 175 instructional days per student.

Though research has been done regarding positive and negative impacts of YRE, results are mixed. Advantages of YRE are labeled "perceived."

Among the "perceived disadvantages" of YRE are (a) increased administrator burnout, (b) difficulties in scheduling professional development, (c) increased operations costs, and (d) scheduling conflicts between family vacations and school/community activities. In addition, as written by Elisabeth A. Palmer and Amy E. Bemis in 1999, with a multitrack program, there is often a lack of sufficient time for facilities maintenance, teachers may need to change rooms multiple times during the year, sometimes it creates difficulties communicating with parents and staff, and students often miss school events when they are off track.

Perceived advantages include increased student achievement and attendance, decreased teacher absenteeism, and increased positive attitudes for student and teachers. Results from research on student achievement is mixed, with some studies showing significant differences and others not. According to Palmer and Bemis, teacher absenteeism studies show some differences, but few are statistically significant. Attitudes of students, teachers, and parents become more positive about YRE the more experience they have with the system.

Much has been written about year-round education; however, some of the research to date has been either incomplete or poorly designed and therefore not particularly conclusive. Students in year-round schools are likely to perform as well as if not better than their peers in traditional 9-month programs, especially in upper elementary schools. However, mixed results on the effects for different demographic groups have been generated and need additional investigation.

Before any policy making occurs, additional research is needed. However, even without additional research, student achievement, budgets, overcrowding, and discipline problems are among the reasons schools and districts choose year-round education.

—*Anita Pankake*

See also enrollment projections; infrastructure, of organizations; instructional interventions; learning environments; reform, of schools; scheduling, types of in schools

Further Readings and References

Cooper, H. (2003). Summer learning loss: The problem and some solutions. Retrieved from http://ericeece.org/pubs/digests2003/cooper03.pdf.
Kneese, C. C. (2000). The impact of year-round education on student learning: A study of six elementary schools. *ERS Spectrum, 18*(1) 20–26.
McGlynn, A. (2002). Districts that school year-round. *School Administrator 59*(3), 34–39.
Palmer, E. A., & Bemis, A. E. (1999). *Just in time research: Children, youth & families—Year-round education.* University of Minnesota Extension Service, BU-07286. Retrieved from http://www.extension.umn.edu/distribution/familydevelopment/components/7286-09.html.
Wildman, L., Arambula, S., Bryson, D., Bryson, T., Campbell, K., Dominguez, T., et al. (1999). The effect of year-round schooling on administrators. *Education, 119*(3), 465–474.

YOUNG, ELLA FLAGG

Ella Flagg Young (1845–1918), who served as superintendent of the Chicago Schools from 1909 to 1915, arguably was one of the greatest public school educators in U.S. history. From 1862, when she began teaching, until 1915, when she retired at the age of 70, Young amassed formidable public education experience. She became the first woman to lead a major school district in the United States when she assumed the Chicago superintendency. During her years in office, the school system faced severe city budget shortfalls, political corruption, rapid enrollment growth, a range of social problems, and a new teacher union movement. She addressed these withering challenges with a series of innovative programs that district employees enthusiastically adopted and educators around the country emulated. A year into her superintendency, she also became the first woman elected to the presidency of the powerful National Education Association, a role that placed her squarely in the national spotlight. For two decades, she served as well on the Illinois State Board of Education, where she influenced the direction of tax-supported schooling in the state.

After earning her PhD under the direction of John Dewey, Young briefly served as an immensely popular professor at the University of Chicago. She authored five volumes describing her educational theories, including perhaps her most important work, *Isolation in the School,* in 1901. In this volume, she described how industrialism typically filtered into schools, resulting in rigid compartmentalization that alienated students and school workers alike. This segmentation accompanied an overall mechanization of schooling, which included clear differentiation among categories of students and divisions of responsibilities among workers, clock-driven scheduling, and vertically increasing hierarchies. She argued that this mechanization robbed persons of their humanity, creativity, and intelligence because it made no room for it. Instead, such qualities were reserved for those better placed within the hierarchy. An unfortunate and necessary consequence of this system, she argued, was that those vested with power also were those most removed from the situations over which their judgment was directed, thereby minimizing the possibility of responsible decision making. Ultimately, this system thrived on isolation or division between people as well as between thinking and doing.

Young's views expressed in *Isolation* ran contrary to those of most school administrators of the time, who instead valued adopting industrial practices to improve efficiency in schools. While many administrators argued that they needed more power to run schools, Young contended that power needed to be distributed among all members of school communities, especially school workers and students. Such individuals only develop skillful decision making when they are required to make meaningful decisions. Her belief that teachers needed more power was controversial among administrators at a time when teachers had begun organizing in Chicago. However, she held that if teachers were imbued with the authority to create and implement their own ideas, then the profession would attract a highly talented pool of candidates while simultaneously discouraging those more disposed toward dry, rote, and punishment-driven pedagogies. Young also strongly believed that teachers needed time within the school day and space for engaging in the intellectual, legislative, and logistical functions of running their schools. Essentially, Young

articulated in *Isolation* the general principles by which schools truly could function as democratic institutions in an increasingly industrialized, segmented, and alienated society.

Although John Dewey served as Young's doctoral adviser while she wrote *Isolation,* Young heavily influenced Dewey's ideas about democracy and education. Indeed, he regarded her as the "wisest educator" he had ever encountered. Dewey, in 1951, wrote that Young showed him how democracy in education might be implemented and what its ramifications might be. Young also strongly influenced Dewey to focus his efforts on teachers, an important component of his work that he generally ceased when he moved to New York.

Young instituted a range of important innovations during her career. She nurtured professional study groups that met in teachers' and administrators' homes. These Ella Flagg Young Clubs fostered enhanced professionalism, pride, and esprit de corps among teachers *and* administrators. When social problems emerged in schools, Young advocated careful scientific analysis combined with a search for practical yet ethical solutions. For instance, she implemented the first public school sex education program in the nation, created student social spaces in school buildings, required school desegregation, provided penny lunches for students—in a manner that eliminated any possible humiliation for those who were impoverished (as she had been in childhood)—and launched groundbreaking programs to address the unique needs of girls. As the leader of several innovative teacher preparation programs throughout her career, she was known as a tough but fair instructor and mentor. Previous superintendents and school board members commended her as having contributed dramatically to the overall improved quality of teaching in the city.

Finally, Young's career successes epitomized the dreams held by suffragists and other women's activists. To them, she stood as a towering symbol of the public good that women might accomplish if given the opportunity. Her well-documented leadership as well as her administrative and instructional gifts reflected well on all women. Because of her extraordinary visibility, Young's work was scrutinized closely by friends and critics alike as evidence of women's possibilities in high-level civic work. Chicago teachers and administrators, many of them women, helped propel her into leadership positions. They engaged in extensive public support activities when Young encountered opposition. In turn, she supported school workers and women's progressive causes generally. She endeavored to lead in ways that were consistent with her stated beliefs. For example, she frequently called on school workers to participate in making critically important decisions. She made sure that time and space were provided for school workers to exert meaningful leadership. Though these strategies were neither easy nor fast, they engendered deep commitment among Chicago school workers and quality work. Similarly, her relationships with organized women and the general public were intense, mutual, and ongoing. Indeed, the strong support she gave and in turn received were necessary for her to conceive and carry out the multiple, complex, and daring progressive reforms that mark her career.

—Jackie M. Blount

See also democracy, democratic education and administration; Dewey, John; feminism and theories of leadership; superintendency; women in educational leadership

Further Readings and References

Dewey, J. (1951). Biography of John Dewey. In *The philosophy of John Dewey* (Paul A. Schlipp, Ed.). New York: Tudor.

Donatelli, R. (1971). *The contributions of Ella Flagg Young to the educational enterprise.* Unpublished doctoral dissertation, University of Chicago.

McManis, J. (1916). *Ella Flagg Young and a half-century of the Chicago Public Schools.* Chicago: A. C. McClurg.

Smith, J. (1979). *Ella Flagg Young: Portrait of a leader.* Ames, IA: Educational Studies Press.

Young, E. (1901). *Isolation in the school.* Chicago: University of Chicago Press.

Index

children, 60. *See also* **Children and families in America**
education of, 668
feminist analysis of, 217
labor union work for, 45
textbook presentation of, 1014
underrepresentation as principals, 79–80
African American educators. *See* **Bethune, Mary McLeod**
African American students, 775
Afrocentric theories, 39–40
Age Discrimination Act (ADEA), 4, 41
Ageism, 40–41
age discrimination, 41
reducing, 41
Agostini v. Felton, 134–135
Agron, Joe, 907
Aguilar v. Felton, 135
AHERA (Asbestos Hazard Emergency Response Act), 51, 450
Air quality, in schools, 450
AL. *See* **Action learning**
Alabama State College for Negroes, 1034
Alabama State Teachers Association, 1034
Alan Guttmacher Institute, 791–792
Albrecht, Karl, 529
Alexander, William, 536
Alexander the Great, 767
Alienation perspective, on student behavior, 69
Alignment, of curriculum, 41–42, 254
backload method of, 42
deep curriculum, 42
frontload method of, 42
guides for, 259–260
quality control in, 835
Alley, Gordon, 826, 948
All-inclusive portfolio, 778
Allport, Gordon, 745, 939
Alpha grading (5-point scale), 435
Al-Qaeda, 1009
Alternate-form/equivalent-form reliability, 1047
Alternate hypothesis, 486
Alternating treatments design, 869
Alternative scheduling, 877 (table)
Alternative secondary schools, 461
Altruism, 123
Alum Rock School District, 1058
Ambach, Gordon M., 222
Amendment 10, 819
American Alliance for Health, Physical Education, Recreation and Dance (AAHPERD), 757
American Association for Counseling and Development (AACD), 227
American Association for the Advancement of Science (AAAS), 919
American Association of Adult and Continuing Education (AAACE), 208
American Association of College Professors, 466
American Association of Colleges for Teacher Education (AACTE), 42–43, 569
American Association of Colleges of Teacher Education, 814

American Association of School Administrators (AASA), 27, **43–44,** 158, 381–382, 568–569, 615, 769, 975
American Association of Teacher Colleges (AATC), 42–43, 918
American Association of University Women (AAUW), 418
American Board for Certification of Teacher Excellence (ABCTE), 8
American College of Sports Medicine, 758
American College Test, 959
American Counseling Association (ACA), 227
American Educational Research Association (AERA), 568, 706, 773, 860
American Federation of Labor, 44, 1039
American Federation of Teachers (AFT), 44–46, 408, 693, 817, 1039. *See also* **Collective bargaining**
American Indians, 60
Americanization, 499–500
American Journal of Psychology, 943
American literature. *See* **Bryant, William Cullen**
American Mathematical Society, 648
American Normal School Association, 692
American Personnel and Guidance Association (APGA), 227
American Psychological Association, 67, 94
American School Counselors Association (ASCA), 103, 226
American School for the Deaf, 265
American Schools and Universities (ASU), 907
American Sign Language, 265
American Society for Training and Development (ASTD), 480
Americans with Disabilities Act, 4, 861, 1076
American Teacher, The, 45
American Teachers Association (ATA), 693, 760, 1033–1034
America's Choice, 906 (table)
Amicus briefs, 657
Analysis
convergent, 1048
discriminant, 1048
factor, 377–378, 840, 1048
force field, 442
forecasting, 403–405
hierarchical task, 1073
linguistic, 1056
needs assessment, 694–695
procedural, 1073
time-series, 840
Analysis of covariance, 838
Analysis of variance (ANOVA), 838–839
Analytical psychology, 534
Analytic phonics, 618
Anderson, Gary, 932
Anderson, James D., 78
Anderson, John, 160
Anderson, Paul, 479
Andragogy vs. pedagogy, 30
Anglo-conformity, of school systems, 56
Anima/animus, 534
Annie E. Casey Foundation, 59–60, 935
Annual Reports, 640
Anorexia nervosa, 70
Anthropology, qualitative research in, 831
Antibullying campaigns, 90

Due process
    description of, 186, 219, 537
    U.S. Supreme Court cases regarding, 982–983
Duhring, Karl, 46
Duncan, Arne, 120
Duran, Richard, 558
Durkheim, Émile, 411
Dynamic complexity, 384
Dynamic systems approach, 383–384
Dynamic traits, 110
Dyson, Michael Eric, 309

Eagleton, Terry, 926
Early childhood education, 311–315
Early Childhood Longitudinal Study Kindergarten
    Cohort (ECLS-K; USDE), 144
Earthman, Glen I., 47
Eason-Watkins, Barbara, 120
Eastman, George, 1065
Easton, David, 473, 774
Ebonics, 506
Ecological approach, to perceptual psychology, 739
Econometric modeling, 396
Economic growth, theory of, 913–914
Economic Opportunity Act (EOA), 451, 710
Economic organizations, 721
Economic productivity, 807
Economics, theories of, 315–318
Economy of explanation, 855
E-DEL-I technique, 274–275
Edelman, Gerald, 85
Edelman, Marian Wright, 59
Eden, Dov, 829
Edgewood Independent School District v. Kirby, 393
Edison, Thomas, 512
Education
    benefits of, 641
    equity issues in, 771
    external effects of, 641
    funding of, 667–668
    intergroup, 678–679
    middle level, 536, 665
    moral, 672–673
    multicultural, 677–681
    museum, 681–682
    peace, 734–735
    personality effects on, 743
    philosophies of, 752–756
    politics of, 772–776
    private, 641
    privatization of, 803–804
    productivity applied to, 807
    public perception of, 995
    salary models in, 892
    schools of, 915–919
    Section 504 in, 863
    social psychology effects on, 939
*Education: Intellectual, Moral, and
    Physical,* 950–951

Educational administration. *See also* **Cocking, Walter**
    description of, 491
    under neoconservative ideology, 492–493
    politics of education effects on, 772
    positivist approaches to, 781
    postmodernist view of, 783
    privatization of, 493
    World War II effects on, 624
Educational Administration Directory, 691
Educational Administration Quarterly, 524
Educational administrators. *See also* **Admissions; American
    Association of School Administrators; National Council
    of Professors of Educational Administration**
    community function of, 623
    Latinos as, 555, 556 (table)
    licensure of, 615
    logic use by, 624–625
    in policy advocacy, 768
    recruitment of, 853–854
    as scientific manager, 623
    shortage of, 1077
    skills needed by, 27
    suicide preventions by, 974
Educational Consolidation and Improvement Act, 182
Educational equity, 319–322
Educational governance, 507
Educational inputs, 723
Educational leaders
    instructional interventions developed by, 510
    instruction innovations evaluated by, 509–510
Educational leadership. *See also* **Gender studies,
    in educational leadership**
    certainty and, 783
    logic in, 623–625
    pragmatism effects on, 788–789
    progressivism effects on, 788–789
Educational Leadership Constituent Council (ELCC),
    12, 493, 521, 570, 1010
Educational management organizations, 803
Educational organizations, 651
Educational outputs, 723
Educational performance audit (EPA), 256
Educational reform movement, 1042
Educational Resources Information Center (ERIC), 208
Educational service agencies, 322–324
Educational technology, 512
Educational Testing Service (ETS), 324–325, 685, 901
Education and Social Order, 890
Education and the Cult of Efficiency (Callahan), 1059–1060
Education Commission of the States, 215, 318–319
Education Consolidation and Improvement Act, 960
Education for All (EFA), 1079
Education for All Handicapped Children Act, 599, 630, 945
Education law. *See* **Law**
Education Leadership Review, 691
Education markets, 641
Education production, 808
Education Rate Program (E-rate), 187
Education Reform Act, 269

Multicultural education, 432
  approaches to, 677
  assumptions of, 677
  Civil Rights Movement effects on, 679
  content integration, 679
  equity pedagogy dimension of, 680
  as field of study, 677
  history of, 678–679
  influences, 680
  issues in, 680–681
  knowledge construction process, 679–680
  measurement of institutional commitment to, 677–678
  prejudice reduction dimension of, 680
  research of, 679–680
  school culture empowerment and, 680
  trends in, 680–681
Multiculturalism, 468, **676–681.**
  See also **Afrocentric theories**
  definition of, 676–677
  as field of study, 677
  implications of, 677
  pluralism and, 1053
  principles of, 677
Multielement design, 869
Multilateral Investment Guarantee Agency (MIGA), 1078
Multiple baseline design, 869–870
Multiple-choice questions
  inception of, 16
  for knowledge assessment, 15
Multiple disabilities, 946
Multiple intelligence, 200
Multiple intelligences theory, 85–86
Multiple linear correlation, 837–838
Multiple linear regression, 837–838
Multiple regression, 838
Multitrack school calendar, 1083
Multivariate analysis of covariance (MANCOVA), 839
Multivariate regression, 838
Murphy, Joseph, 801
Murray, Charles, 14
Murray, Frank B., 471
Murray, Lindley, 849
Murray v. Curlett, 134–135
Museum education, 681–682
Musical intelligence, 505, 515
Musical intelligence/music smart, 417
Mussolini, Benito, 380
Myers Briggs Type Indicator (MBTI), 748
Myth of Scientific Literacy, The, 919
Mythologies, 926

NAACP. *See* National Association for the Advancement of Colored People
Nabozny v. Podlesny, 930
NAEP. *See* **National Assessment of Educational Progress**
NAESP. *See* **National Association of Elementary School Principals**
NAESP Leadership Academy (NLA), 688
Nantucket High School, 737

Narcissistic personality disorder, 747
Narrative/descriptive grading, 436
Narratives, 806
Nash, Samuel, 171
NASSP. *See* **National Association of Secondary School Principals**
National Alliance, 696
National Alliance of Business, 215
National Arts Education Association, 50
National Assessment Governing Board, 648
National Assessment of Educational Progress (NAEP), 17, 205, 541, 647–648, **685–686,** 700, 840, 958, 1008
National Association for the Advancement of Colored People (NAACP), 23, 79, 139, 141, 542, 632, 642, **686–688**
  antilynching campaign, 687
  education and, 687
  G. W. Bush, 687–688
  Picott's work with, 760
National Association of College and University Business, 803
National Association of Colleges and Departments of Education, 42–43
National Association of Corporation Schools, 480
National Association of Elementary School Principals (NAESP), 156, 615, **688–689**
  professional development, 688
  programs/services, 688–689
National Association of School Superintendents, 43, 692, 1059
National Association of Secondary School Principals (NASSP), 20, 536, 567, 569, 615, **689–690,** 693, 769, 800, 913
National Association of Teacher Education Institutions in Metropolitan Districts, 42–43
National Association of Teachers in Colored Schools, 1034
National Association of Teachers of Mathematics, 258
National Association of Wage Earners, 93
National Board Certification, 1001
National Board for Professional Teaching Standards (NBPTS), 223, 614, 859
National Bureau of Economic Research, 408
National Campaign to Prevent Teen Pregnancy, 792
National Center for Educational Statistics (NCES), 17, 187, 474, 685, 793, 886, 1075
  school consolidation report, 193–194
National Center for Education Statistics, 907, 938
National Center for Health Statistics (NCHS), 128
National Commission on Excellence in Education (NCEE), 59. *See also* **Bell, Ted**
National Commission on Teacher Education and Professional Standards (NEA), 693
National Conference of Professors of Educational Administration (NCPEA), 158, 446, 521, 544, 568, 977, 1017
National Conference of State Legislatures, 215
National Conference on Large-Scale Assessment, 223
National Council for Negro Women (NCNW), 75, 142
National Council for Staff Development, 812
National Council for the Accreditation of Colleges of Teacher Education (NCATE), 223, 569